STATE PROFILES

State
Profiles

The Population and Economy of Each U.S. State

Ninth Edition
2017

Edited by Hannah Anderson Krog

Bernan Press

Lanham, Maryland

Published in the United States of America
by Bernan Press, a wholly owned subsidiary of
The Rowman & Littlefield Publishing Group, Inc.
4501 Forbes Boulevard, Suite 200
Lanham, Maryland 20706

Bernan Press
800-865-3457
www.rowman.com/bernanpress

Copyright © 2018 by Bernan Press

ISBN 13: 978-1-59888-941-3
E-ISBN: 978-1-59888-942-0

∞™ The paper used in this publication meets the minimum requirements of
American National Standard for Information Sciences—Permanence of
Paper for Printed Library Materials, ANSI/NISO Z39.48-1992.
Manufactured in the United States of America.

CONTENTS

LIST OF TABLES

The following tables are included for each state and the District of Columbia:

Bernan Press is pleased to present the ninth edition of *State Profiles*, a publication that provides a state-by-state view of the United States. Topics covered include population composition by age, sex, race, and ethnicity; marital status; migration, origin, and language; households and housing; income and poverty; health insurance; employment; educational indicators; voting; crime; and other important aspects of the economy.

The publication's primary focus is on the 50 states and the District of Columbia, each of which possesses considerable differences in economic structure and demographics and has experienced various changes over time. Changes at the national level, including the diminished importance of agriculture and manufacturing and the growing influence of global trade, have resulted in today's information-based, service-providing economy. While national trends have laid the broad framework for change, each state has been affected differently. Cyclical fluctuations have also affected states in various ways during the nationwide recessions and the subsequent recovery periods. Recessions and recoveries spread unevenly among regions and states. Migration patterns have also reflected these changes, as states have experienced different influxes of workers from within the country and new residents from abroad.

Beyond the market forces, local and national government policies and expenditures on items such as education, health care, energy production and conservation, national defense, and homeland security have influenced economic circumstances.

The information provided in *State Profiles* aims to illuminate these trends. As such, the analysis and statistics are of interest not only to researchers and policy analysts but also to businesses seeking a broad basis for investments and expansion or relocation plans. The volume also profiles recent voting patterns, which will be of interest to political scientists.

DATA SELECTION

This edition of *State Profiles* generally continues the broad selection of information from previous editions. Most, but not all, of the data items have been updated through 2014, 2015, and even 2016, as demographic estimates from the U.S. Census Bureau became available.

As in the past, space constraints have influenced the amount of data presented for each state. The most meaningful and relevant data have thus been selected, analyzed, and highlighted. This edition expands upon the available information to include more detailed data on the demographics of each state, especially in regard to diversity of spoken languages and the foreign-born population. For most of the subjects addressed in this edition, further data are generally available from the source government agencies. Locations of sources of information are listed in notes and definitions at the end of the volume.

Although the editor has taken care to present accurate data, all statistical data are subject to a degree of error, resulting from sampling variability, erroneous reporting, and other causes. Many of the data are subject to subsequent revision.

The data in this book meet the publication standards of the federal agencies from which they were obtained. The responsibilities of the editor and publisher of this volume are limited to reasonable care in the reproduction and presentation of the data from the established sources.

Hannah Anderson Krog has edited the past three editions of *State Profiles*. She previously worked as an assistant editor for Bernan Press and is now a freelance writer and editor for several reference titles. She has a B.A. in journalism from the University of Maryland.

USING THIS BOOK: ORGANIZATION AND CONTENTS

STATE PROFILES 2017 PROVIDES:

- Rankings of states for key demographic and economic indicators
- A chapter for each state, complete with tables and figures that summarize and illustrate demographic and economic characteristics
- Notes and definitions to assist with interpreting the information contained in this volume

THE U.S. OVERVIEW. This short introduction to the demographics of the United States provides commentary on overall trends within the country.

THE STATE RANKINGS. The ranking tables that follow the national overview give state rankings by more than 30 characteristics, including population, demographic and age composition, income, per capita gross domestic product, homeownership, poverty, health indicators, education, and federal aid. These rankings provide the user with a quick analysis of the performance of each state in relation to the other states.

THE STATE CHAPTERS. The state chapters are the focus of this book. Each chapter follows a standard format and contains text highlighting the key features shown in the tables and figures. Some of these tables and figures contain references to the U.S. averages for the same characteristics.

Each of the state chapters is organized as follows:

Population: This table provides data on the state's total population and average annual population growth in comparison with the national average. It also shows the major population groups by sex, age, race, and ethnicity.

Marital status: The table shows the marital status for all men and women age 15 years and over.

Housing: This table showcases data pertaining to housing, such as number of households, types of households, housing characteristics, and median gross rent, mortgage, and monthly owner cost amounts.

Origin, migration, and language: This table provides statistics on residence one year ago, year of entry, place of origin, language spoken at home, and the native-born and foreign-born populations.

Income and poverty: Median household and family income and poverty rates by sex and age are contained in this table.

Health insurance coverage: This table provides information on health insurance, by type and coverage.

Employment: These tables illustrate each state's particular economic configuration. Employment status by detailed demographic group, labor force, participation rates, employment, unemployment, average wages and salaries by industry, and employment by family type.

Education: This section provides the user with details on educational attainment, elementary and secondary school enrollment, student/teacher ratios, per student expenditures, and higher education enrollments.

Voter participation: Information is given on voter registration and voter participation in the 2016 election, categorized by sex and race and ethnicity.

Crime: This table includes the number and rates of violent and property crime.

Government finance: These tables provide data on revenues and expenditures by source. In addition, tax information is included.

NOTES AND DEFINITIONS. Each chapter relies on the same standard set of federal data sources. Since the basic data sources are common to all chapters, the main body of the volume contains few footnotes. Basic data and corresponding definitions and sources are identified in the notes and definition section at the end of the volume. It provides brief descriptions, methodologies, data availability, information on calculations made by the editors, and references to additional sources of information.

Introduction

During the early 2000s, the United States experienced several economic fluctuations that had a great impact on the strength, size, and performance of its economy. The recession that began in March 2001 was concluded in a few months; however, the longer-lasting recession that began in December 2007 left a more serious impact on the country. The data in this book track the impact of that recession and subsequent recovery on the United States' economy over the past decade.

This edition of *State Profiles: The Population and Economy of Each U.S. State* creates a snapshot of the people and economy in each state and the District of Columbia. Each chapter (one per state/district) includes information on topics such as population, health, marital status, crime, government finance, housing, education, and language.

Summary

The U.S. population grew 4.7 percent between 2010 and 2016. The District of Columbia experienced the largest population growth in the nation at 13.2 percent. The states with the largest population growth included the North Dakota (12.7 percent), Texas (10.8 percent), Utah (10.4 percent), Colorado (10.2 percent), Florida (9.6 percent), Nevada (8.9 percent), Arizona (8.4 percent), Washington (8.4 percent), Idaho (7.4 percent), South Carolina (7.3 percent), Oregon (6.8 percent), and Georgia (6.4 percent). Three states' populations declined during that time period: Vermont (-0.2 percent), Illinois (-0.2 percent), and West Virginia (-1.2 percent).

Maine had the highest percentage of White alone residents in 2016, at 94.8 percent, followed by Vermont at 94.6 percent. Hawaii had the smallest percent of White alone residents, at 25.8 percent. The District of Columbia had the highest percentage of Black or African American alone residents at 47.7 percent, followed by Mississippi at 37.7 percent. At 0.6 percent, Montana had the lowest percentage of Black or African American alone residents. New Mexico had the highest percent of Hispanic or Latino residents (48.5 percent), and West Virginia had the lowest percentage at 1.5 percent. Those classified as Hispanic or Latino may be of any race.

In 2015, the median household income in the United States was $55,775. Maryland had the highest median household income at $75,847, followed by the District of Columbia ($75,628), Hawaii ($73,486), Alaska ($73,355), and New Jersey ($72,222). The states with the lowest median household incomes were Mississippi ($40,593), Arkansas ($41,995), West Virginia ($42,019), Alabama ($44,765), and Kentucky ($45,215). Some correlation to the percentage of residents with a bachelor's degree or more can be inferred, as Maryland, and the District of Columbia rank in the top five states in this category. Mississippi, Arkansas, and West Virginia rank as the bottom three states in this category, with Alabama ranking 45th and Kentucky ranking 47th. The unemployment rate for the United States was 4.9 percent in 2016, which was down from 5.3 percent in 2015. New Mexico had the highest percentage of unemployed residents in 2016 (6.7 percent), followed by Alaska (6.6 percent) and Louisiana (6.1 percent). South Dakota (2.8 percent) had the lowest percentage of unemployed residents.

In the United States in 2015, 14.7 percent of the population lived below the poverty level. Mississippi, which had the lowest median household income, also had the highest poverty rate, with 22.0 percent of its residents below the poverty level. New Hampshire had the lowest poverty rate, at 8.2 percent. Mississippi also had the highest rate of persons under 18 years of age below the poverty level (31.3 percent), followed by New Mexico (28.6 percent), Louisiana (28.4 percent), Arkansas (27.2 percent), and Alabama (26.6 percent). The states with the fewest residents under 18 years of age below the poverty level included New Hampshire (10.7 percent), North Dakota (12.1 percent), Utah (12.9 percent), Minnesota (13.1 percent), and Wyoming (13.2 percent).

UNITED STATES RANKINGS

Population, 2016

Rank	State	Population
	United States......................	323,127,513
1	California............................	39,250,017
2	Texas.................................	27,862,596
3	Florida...............................	20,612,439
4	New York............................	19,745,289
5	Illinois...............................	12,801,539
6	Pennsylvania.......................	12,784,227
7	Ohio..................................	11,614,373
8	Georgia..............................	10,310,371
9	North Carolina.....................	10,146,788
10	Michigan............................	9,928,300
11	New Jersey	8,944,469
12	Virginia..............................	8,411,808
13	Washington.........................	7,288,000
14	Arizona..............................	6,931,071
15	Massachusetts	6,811,779
16	Tennessee	6,651,194
17	Indiana..............................	6,633,053
18	Missouri.............................	6,093,000
19	Maryland............................	6,016,447
20	Wisconsin...........................	5,778,708
21	Colorado	5,540,545
22	Minnesota...........................	5,519,952
23	South Carolina	4,961,119
24	Alabama.............................	4,863,300
25	Louisiana	4,681,666
26	Kentucky............................	4,436,974
27	Oregon...............................	4,093,465
28	Oklahoma...........................	3,923,561
29	Connecticut.........................	3,576,452
30	Iowa..................................	3,134,693
31	Utah..................................	3,051,217
32	Mississippi..........................	2,988,726
33	Arkansas............................	2,988,248
34	Nevada..............................	2,940,058
35	Kansas	2,907,289
36	New Mexico	2,081,015
37	Nebraska............................	1,907,116
38	West Virginia.......................	1,831,102
39	Idaho.................................	1,683,140
40	Hawaii...............................	1,428,557
41	New Hampshire....................	1,334,795
42	Maine................................	1,331,479
43	Rhode Island.......................	1,056,426
44	Montana.............................	1,042,520
45	Delaware............................	952,065
46	South Dakota	865,454
47	North Dakota.......................	757,952
48	Alaska...............................	741,894
49	District of Columbia	681,170
50	Vermont.............................	624,594
51	Wyoming	585,501

Population, Percent Change, 2010–2016

Rank	State	Percent
	United States.....................	4.7
1	District of Columbia	13.2
2	North Dakota......................	12.7
3	Texas.................................	10.8
4	Utah..................................	10.4
5	Colorado	10.2
6	Florida...............................	9.6
7	Nevada..............................	8.9
8	Arizona..............................	8.4
8	Washington.........................	8.4
10	Idaho.................................	7.4
11	South Carolina	7.3
12	Oregon...............................	6.8
13	Georgia..............................	6.4
13	North Carolina.....................	6.4
15	South Dakota	6.3
16	Delaware............................	6.0
17	Montana.............................	5.4
17	California............................	5.4
19	Virginia..............................	5.1
20	Hawaii...............................	5.0
21	Tennessee	4.8
22	Oklahoma...........................	4.6
23	Alaska...............................	4.5
24	Nebraska............................	4.4
25	Maryland............................	4.2
26	Minnesota...........................	4.1
27	Massachusetts	4.0
28	Wyoming	3.9
29	Louisiana	3.3
30	Iowa..................................	2.9
31	Arkansas............................	2.5
32	Indiana..............................	2.3
33	Kentucky............................	2.2
34	Kansas	1.9
34	New York............................	1.9
36	Alabama.............................	1.7
36	Missouri.............................	1.7
36	New Jersey	1.7
39	Wisconsin...........................	1.6
40	New Hampshire....................	1.4
41	New Mexico	1.1
42	Mississippi..........................	0.7
42	Ohio..................................	0.7
44	Pennsylvania.......................	0.6
45	Michigan............................	0.5
46	Rhode Island.......................	0.4
47	Maine................................	0.2
48	Connecticut.........................	0.1
49	Vermont.............................	-0.2
49	Illinois...............................	-0.2
51	West Virginia.......................	-1.2

Percent Population Under 18 Years Old, 2016

Rank	State	Percent
	United States......................	22.8
1	Utah..................................	30.2
2	Texas.................................	26.2
3	Idaho.................................	26.0
4	Alaska...............................	25.2
5	Nebraska............................	24.8
6	South Dakota	24.6
6	Kansas	24.6
8	Oklahoma...........................	24.5
9	Georgia..............................	24.4
10	Mississippi..........................	24.1
11	Louisiana	23.8
11	Indiana..............................	23.8
13	Wyoming	23.7
14	Arkansas............................	23.6
14	New Mexico	23.6
16	Arizona..............................	23.5
17	Minnesota...........................	23.3
17	Iowa..................................	23.3
17	North Dakota.......................	23.3
20	California............................	23.2
21	Nevada..............................	23.0
22	Illinois...............................	22.9
23	Kentucky............................	22.8
23	Colorado	22.8
23	Missouri.............................	22.8
26	North Carolina.....................	22.7
27	Tennessee	22.6
27	Alabama.............................	22.6
29	Ohio..................................	22.5
30	Maryland............................	22.4
30	Washington.........................	22.4
32	Wisconsin...........................	22.3
33	Virginia..............................	22.2
33	New Jersey	22.2
35	South Carolina	22.1
35	Michigan............................	22.1
37	Montana.............................	21.8
38	Hawaii...............................	21.6
39	Delaware............................	21.5
40	Oregon...............................	21.2
40	New York............................	21.2
42	Connecticut.........................	21.1
43	Pennsylvania.......................	20.9
44	West Virginia.......................	20.5
45	Massachusetts	20.2
46	Florida...............................	20.1
47	Rhode Island.......................	19.7
48	New Hampshire....................	19.5
49	Maine................................	19.1
50	Vermont.............................	19.0
51	District of Columbia	17.7

Percent Population 65 Years and Over, 2016

Rank	State	Percent
	United States......................	15.2
1	Florida..............................	19.9
2	Maine..............................	19.4
3	West Virginia....................	18.8
4	Vermont...........................	18.1
5	Montana...........................	17.7
6	Delaware..........................	17.5
7	Pennsylvania....................	17.4
8	Hawaii.............................	17.1
9	New Hampshire.................	17.0
10	Arizona............................	16.9
11	Oregon............................	16.8
12	South Carolina..................	16.7
13	Rhode Island....................	16.5
13	New Mexico......................	16.5
15	Iowa................................	16.4
16	Arkansas..........................	16.3
17	Ohio................................	16.2
17	Michigan..........................	16.2
19	Connecticut......................	16.1
19	Alabama...........................	16.1
19	Wisconsin.........................	16.1
19	Missouri...........................	16.1
23	South Dakota....................	16.0
24	Massachusetts...................	15.8
25	Tennessee........................	15.7
26	Kentucky..........................	15.6
27	North Carolina..................	15.5
28	New York..........................	15.4
29	New Jersey.......................	15.3
30	Idaho..............................	15.1
30	Mississippi.......................	15.1
30	Minnesota........................	15.1
33	Oklahoma.........................	15.0
33	Nebraska..........................	15.0
33	Kansas............................	15.0
33	Nevada............................	15.0
33	Wyoming..........................	15.0
38	Indiana............................	14.9
39	Washington.......................	14.8
40	Illinois.............................	14.6
40	Virginia............................	14.6
40	Maryland..........................	14.6
43	North Dakota....................	14.5
44	Louisiana.........................	14.4
45	California..........................	13.6
46	Colorado..........................	13.4
47	Georgia............................	13.1
48	Texas..............................	12.0
49	District of Columbia...........	11.6
50	Utah................................	10.5
51	Alaska.............................	10.4

Percent White Alone, 2016

Rank	State	Percent
	United States......................	76.9
1	Maine..............................	94.8
2	Vermont...........................	94.6
3	New Hampshire.................	93.8
4	West Virginia....................	93.6
5	Idaho..............................	93.3
6	Wyoming..........................	92.8
7	Iowa................................	91.4
8	Utah................................	91.1
9	Montana...........................	89.2
10	Nebraska..........................	88.9
11	Kentucky..........................	88.0
12	North Dakota....................	87.9
13	Wisconsin.........................	87.5
13	Colorado..........................	87.5
15	Oregon............................	87.4
16	Kansas............................	86.6
17	Indiana............................	85.6
18	South Dakota....................	85.2
19	Minnesota........................	85.0
20	Rhode Island....................	84.4
21	Arizona............................	83.3
22	Missouri...........................	83.2
23	New Mexico......................	82.6
24	Ohio................................	82.5
25	Pennsylvania....................	82.4
26	Massachusetts...................	81.8
27	Connecticut......................	80.6
28	Washington.......................	80.0
29	Michigan..........................	79.6
30	Texas..............................	79.4
30	Arkansas..........................	79.4
32	Tennessee........................	78.7
33	Florida.............................	77.6
34	Illinois.............................	77.2
35	Nevada............................	75.1
36	Oklahoma.........................	74.6
37	California..........................	72.7
38	New Jersey.......................	72.4
39	North Carolina..................	71.0
40	Delaware..........................	70.1
41	Virginia............................	70.0
42	New York..........................	69.9
43	Alabama...........................	69.3
44	South Carolina..................	68.5
45	Alaska.............................	66.1
46	Louisiana.........................	63.2
47	Georgia............................	61.2
48	Mississippi.......................	59.3
48	Maryland..........................	59.3
50	District of Columbia...........	44.6
51	Hawaii.............................	25.8

Percent Black or African American Alone, 2016

Rank	State	Percent
	United States......................	13.3
1	District of Columbia...........	47.7
2	Mississippi.......................	37.7
3	Louisiana.........................	32.6
4	Georgia............................	32.0
5	Maryland..........................	30.7
6	South Carolina..................	27.5
7	Alabama...........................	26.8
8	Delaware..........................	22.6
9	North Carolina..................	22.2
10	Virginia............................	19.8
11	New York..........................	17.7
12	Tennessee........................	17.1
13	Florida.............................	16.8
14	Arkansas..........................	15.7
15	New Jersey.......................	15.0
16	Illinois.............................	14.7
17	Michigan..........................	14.2
18	Ohio................................	12.8
19	Texas..............................	12.6
20	Missouri...........................	11.8
20	Pennsylvania....................	11.8
20	Connecticut......................	11.8
23	Indiana............................	9.7
24	Nevada............................	9.6
25	Massachusetts...................	8.6
26	Kentucky..........................	8.3
27	Rhode Island....................	8.1
28	Oklahoma.........................	7.8
29	Wisconsin.........................	6.6
30	California..........................	6.5
31	Minnesota........................	6.2
31	Kansas............................	6.2
33	Nebraska..........................	5.0
34	Arizona............................	4.9
35	Colorado..........................	4.5
36	Washington.......................	4.1
37	Alaska.............................	3.8
38	Iowa................................	3.7
39	West Virginia....................	3.6
40	North Dakota....................	2.9
41	New Mexico......................	2.5
42	Hawaii.............................	2.2
43	Oregon............................	2.1
44	South Dakota....................	2.0
45	New Hampshire.................	1.5
45	Maine..............................	1.5
47	Utah................................	1.4
48	Wyoming..........................	1.3
48	Vermont...........................	1.3
50	Idaho..............................	0.8
51	Montana...........................	0.6

Percent American Indian and Alaska Native Alone, 2016

Rank	State	Percent
	United States....................	1.3
1	Alaska	15.2
2	New Mexico	10.6
3	Oklahoma..........................	9.2
4	South Dakota	9.0
5	Montana	6.6
6	North Dakota.....................	5.5
7	Arizona.............................	5.4
8	Wyoming	2.7
9	Washington	1.9
10	Oregon	1.8
10	Idaho................................	1.8
12	California..........................	1.7
13	Nevada	1.6
13	Colorado	1.6
13	North Carolina...................	1.6
13	Utah	1.6
17	Nebraska	1.4
18	Minnesota	1.3
19	Kansas	1.2
20	Wisconsin	1.1
21	Texas	1.0
21	Rhode Island.....................	1.0
21	Arkansas	1.0
21	New York...........................	1.0
25	Louisiana	0.8
26	Michigan	0.7
26	Maine	0.7
26	Alabama............................	0.7
29	Delaware	0.6
29	District of Columbia	0.6
29	New Jersey	0.6
29	Mississippi........................	0.6
29	Illinois..............................	0.6
29	Maryland...........................	0.6
29	Missouri............................	0.6
36	South Carolina	0.5
36	Virginia.............................	0.5
36	Connecticut.......................	0.5
36	Iowa	0.5
36	Georgia	0.5
36	Florida..............................	0.5
36	Massachusetts	0.5
43	Tennessee	0.4
43	Indiana.............................	0.4
43	Hawaii	0.4
43	Vermont	0.4
43	Pennsylvania......................	0.4
48	Kentucky	0.3
48	New Hampshire..................	0.3
48	Ohio	0.3
51	West Virginia.....................	0.2

Percent Asian Alone, 2016

Rank	State	Percent
	United States....................	5.7
1	Hawaii	37.7
2	California..........................	14.8
3	New Jersey	9.8
4	New York...........................	8.9
5	Nevada	8.7
6	Washington........................	8.6
7	Massachusetts	6.7
8	Virginia.............................	6.6
8	Maryland...........................	6.6
10	Alaska	6.3
11	Illinois..............................	5.5
12	Minnesota	4.9
13	Texas	4.8
14	Connecticut.......................	4.7
15	Oregon	4.5
16	District of Columbia	4.1
16	Georgia	4.1
18	Delaware	4.0
19	Rhode Island......................	3.6
20	Pennsylvania......................	3.5
21	Arizona.............................	3.4
22	Colorado	3.3
23	Michigan	3.1
24	Kansas	3.0
25	North Carolina...................	2.9
25	Florida..............................	2.9
27	Wisconsin	2.8
28	New Hampshire..................	2.7
29	Utah	2.5
29	Iowa	2.5
29	Nebraska	2.5
32	Indiana.............................	2.2
32	Oklahoma..........................	2.2
32	Ohio	2.2
35	Missouri............................	2.0
36	Louisiana	1.8
36	Tennessee	1.8
36	Vermont	1.8
39	New Mexico	1.7
40	South Carolina	1.6
40	Arkansas	1.6
42	North Dakota.....................	1.5
42	Kentucky	1.5
42	South Dakota	1.5
42	Idaho................................	1.5
46	Alabama............................	1.4
47	Maine	1.2
48	Mississippi........................	1.1
49	Wyoming	1.0
50	West Virginia.....................	0.8
50	Montana	0.8

Percent Native Hawaiian and Other Pacific Islander Alone, 2016

Rank	State	Percent
	United States....................	0.2
1	Hawaii	10.2
2	Alaska	1.3
3	Utah	1.0
4	Nevada	0.8
4	Washington	0.8
6	California..........................	0.5
7	Oregon	0.4
8	Arkansas	0.3
8	Arizona.............................	0.3
10	Idaho................................	0.2
10	Colorado	0.2
10	Rhode Island......................	0.2
10	Oklahoma..........................	0.2
10	New Mexico	0.2
10	District of Columbia	0.2
16	Missouri............................	0.1
16	Texas	0.1
16	New York...........................	0.1
16	Nebraska	0.1
16	North Carolina...................	0.1
16	Georgia	0.1
16	Wyoming	0.1
16	Iowa	0.1
16	Florida..............................	0.1
16	Virginia.............................	0.1
16	Kansas	0.1
16	Maryland...........................	0.1
16	Connecticut.......................	0.1
16	Alabama............................	0.1
16	New Jersey	0.1
16	Massachusetts	0.1
16	Tennessee	0.1
16	Delaware	0.1
16	South Carolina	0.1
16	Montana	0.1
16	Kentucky	0.1
16	South Dakota	0.1
16	North Dakota.....................	0.1
16	Pennsylvania......................	0.1
16	Minnesota	0.1
16	Louisiana	0.1
16	Illinois..............................	0.1
16	Indiana.............................	0.1
16	Mississippi........................	0.1
16	Ohio	0.1
16	Wisconsin	0.1
16	New Hampshire..................	0.1
48	Vermont	Z
49	Michigan	Z
50	Maine	Z
51	West Virginia.....................	Z

Z = Value greater than zero but less than half of the unit shown.

Percent Two or More Races, 2016

Rank	State	Percent
	United States......................	2.6
1	Hawaii	23.7
2	Alaska	7.3
3	Oklahoma............................	6.1
4	Washington..........................	4.6
5	Nevada	4.2
6	California.............................	3.8
6	Oregon	3.8
8	Colorado	3.0
9	Virginia................................	2.9
9	Kansas	2.9
11	Arizona................................	2.8
11	Maryland..............................	2.8
13	District of Columbia	2.7
13	Rhode Island........................	2.7
13	Montana..............................	2.7
16	Delaware	2.6
17	New Mexico	2.5
17	New York	2.5
17	Utah....................................	2.5
20	Minnesota	2.4
20	Michigan	2.4
20	Idaho..................................	2.4
23	Massachusetts	2.3
23	Connecticut.........................	2.3
23	South Dakota	2.3
26	Missouri...............................	2.2
26	Ohio....................................	2.2
26	North Carolina......................	2.2
26	New Jersey	2.2
30	Nebraska.............................	2.1
30	North Dakota........................	2.1
30	Florida.................................	2.1
30	Georgia	2.1
30	Wyoming	2.1
35	Arkansas	2.0
35	Indiana................................	2.0
37	Pennsylvania	1.9
37	Texas..................................	1.9
37	Illinois.................................	1.9
37	Vermont...............................	1.9
37	Kentucky	1.9
37	Wisconsin	1.9
37	Tennessee	1.9
44	South Carolina	1.8
44	Iowa....................................	1.8
46	Maine..................................	1.7
46	West Virginia........................	1.7
46	New Hampshire.....................	1.7
49	Louisiana	1.6
49	Alabama..............................	1.6
51	Mississippi..........................	1.2

Percent Hispanic or Latino,[1] 2016

Rank	State	Percent
	United States......................	17.8
1	New Mexico	48.5
2	Texas..................................	39.1
3	California.............................	38.9
4	Arizona................................	30.9
5	Nevada	28.5
6	Florida.................................	24.9
7	Colorado	21.3
8	New Jersey	20.0
9	New York	19.0
10	Illinois.................................	17.0
11	Connecticut.........................	15.7
12	Rhode Island........................	14.9
13	Utah....................................	13.8
14	Oregon	12.8
15	Washington..........................	12.4
16	Idaho..................................	12.3
17	Kansas	11.6
18	Massachusetts	11.5
19	District of Columbia	10.9
20	Nebraska.............................	10.7
21	Hawaii	10.4
22	Oklahoma............................	10.3
23	Wyoming	10.0
24	Maryland..............................	9.8
25	Georgia	9.4
26	North Carolina......................	9.2
26	Delaware	9.2
28	Virginia................................	9.1
29	Arkansas	7.3
30	Pennsylvania	7.0
30	Alaska	7.0
32	Indiana................................	6.8
33	Wisconsin	6.7
34	Iowa....................................	5.8
35	South Carolina	5.5
36	Minnesota	5.2
36	Tennessee	5.2
38	Louisiana	5.0
38	Michigan	5.0
40	Alabama..............................	4.2
41	Missouri...............................	4.1
42	South Dakota	3.7
42	Ohio....................................	3.7
44	North Dakota........................	3.6
44	Montana..............................	3.6
46	New Hampshire.....................	3.5
46	Kentucky	3.5
48	Mississippi..........................	3.1
49	Vermont...............................	1.9
50	Maine..................................	1.6
51	West Virginia........................	1.5

[1] May be of any race.

Percent White Alone, Not Hispanic or Latino, 2016

Rank	State	Percent
	United States......................	61.3
1	Maine..................................	93.5
2	Vermont...............................	93.1
3	West Virginia........................	92.3
4	New Hampshire.....................	90.8
5	Montana..............................	86.5
6	Iowa....................................	86.2
7	North Dakota........................	85.0
7	Kentucky	85.0
9	Wyoming	84.1
10	South Dakota	82.5
11	Idaho..................................	82.4
12	Wisconsin	81.7
13	Minnesota	80.6
14	Missouri...............................	79.7
15	Indiana................................	79.6
15	Nebraska.............................	79.6
17	Ohio....................................	79.5
18	Utah....................................	78.8
19	Pennsylvania	77.0
20	Oregon	76.4
21	Kansas	76.3
22	Michigan	75.4
23	Tennessee	74.2
24	Rhode Island........................	73.3
25	Massachusetts	73.0
26	Arkansas	72.9
27	Washington..........................	69.5
28	Colorado	68.6
29	Connecticut.........................	67.7
30	Oklahoma............................	66.2
31	Alabama..............................	65.8
32	South Carolina	63.9
33	North Carolina......................	63.5
34	Delaware	62.9
35	Virginia................................	62.4
36	Illinois.................................	61.7
37	Alaska	61.2
38	Louisiana	59.0
39	Mississippi..........................	56.9
40	New Jersey	55.8
40	New York	55.8
42	Arizona................................	55.5
43	Florida.................................	54.9
44	Georgia	53.4
45	Maryland..............................	51.5
46	Nevada	49.9
47	Texas..................................	42.6
48	New Mexico	38.1
49	California.............................	37.7
50	District of Columbia	36.4
51	Hawaii	22.1

Birth Rate, 2015

Rank	State	Rate per 1,000 population
	United States......................	12.4
1	Utah	17.0
2	Alaska	15.3
3	North Dakota	15.0
4	Texas..........................	14.7
5	South Dakota	14.4
6	District of Columbia	14.3
7	Nebraska	14.1
8	Louisiana	13.9
9	Idaho..........................	13.8
10	Oklahoma	13.6
11	Kansas	13.5
12	Wyoming	13.3
13	Arkansas	13.1
14	Hawaii	12.9
14	Georgia	12.9
16	Mississippi..........................	12.8
17	Minnesota	12.7
17	Indiana	12.7
17	Kentucky	12.7
20	Iowa	12.6
20	California..........................	12.6
20	Nevada	12.6
23	Arizona..........................	12.5
24	Washington	12.4
24	New Mexico	12.4
24	Tennessee	12.4
27	Missouri..........................	12.3
27	Virginia..........................	12.3
27	Illinois	12.3
27	Alabama	12.3
27	Maryland	12.3
32	Colorado	12.2
32	Montana..........................	12.2
34	North Carolina..........................	12.0
34	New York..........................	12.0
34	Ohio	12.0
37	South Carolina	11.9
38	Delaware	11.8
39	Wisconsin	11.6
40	New Jersey	11.5
41	Michigan	11.4
42	Oregon	11.3
43	Florida	11.1
44	Pennsylvania..........................	11.0
45	West Virginia..........................	10.7
46	Massachusetts	10.5
47	Rhode Island..........................	10.4
48	Connecticut..........................	10.0
49	Maine	9.5
50	Vermont	9.4
51	New Hampshire..........................	9.3

Drug Overdose Death Rate, 2015

Rank	State	Age-adjusted rate per 100,000 population
	United States......................	16.1
1	West Virginia......................	41.5
2	New Hampshire..................	34.3
3	Kentucky	29.9
3	Ohio	29.9
5	Rhode Island..........................	28.2
6	Pennsylvania..........................	26.3
7	Massachusetts	25.7
8	New Mexico	25.3
9	Utah	23.4
10	Tennessee	22.2
11	Connecticut..........................	22.1
12	Delaware	22.0
13	Maine	21.2
14	Maryland	20.9
14	Michigan	20.4
15	Nevada	20.4
17	Indiana	19.5
18	Arizona..........................	19.0
18	Louisiana	19.0
18	Oklahoma	19.0
21	District of Columbia	18.6
22	Missouri..........................	17.9
23	Vermont	16.7
24	Wyoming	16.4
25	New Jersey	16.3
26	Florida..........................	16.2
27	Alaska	16.0
28	North Carolina..........................	15.8
29	Alabama	15.7
29	South Carolina	15.7
31	Wisconsin	15.5
32	Colorado	15.4
33	Washington	14.7
34	Idaho..........................	14.2
35	Illinois	14.1
36	Arkansas	13.8
36	Montana..........................	13.8
38	New York..........................	13.6
39	Georgia	12.7
40	Virginia..........................	12.4
41	Mississippi..........................	12.3
42	Oregon	12.0
43	Kansas	11.8
44	California..........................	11.3
44	Hawaii	11.3
46	Minnesota	10.6
47	Iowa	10.3
48	Texas..........................	9.4
49	North Dakota	8.6
50	South Dakota	8.4
51	Nebraska	6.9

Voting Population, 2016

Rank	State	Percent voted, total population
	United States......................	56.0
1	Maine	71.3
2	District of Columbia	68.7
2	Wisconsin	68.7
4	New Hampshire..................	66.9
5	Mississippi..........................	66.7
6	Minnesota	65.3
7	Montana..........................	65.2
8	Colorado	63.8
9	Wyoming	63.5
10	Nebraska	63.4
11	Missouri..........................	62.8
12	Virginia..........................	62.6
13	North Dakota	62.1
14	Michigan	61.8
15	Massachusetts	61.7
16	North Carolina..........................	61.6
17	Ohio	61.4
18	Vermont	61.0
18	Oregon	61.0
20	Iowa..........................	60.7
21	Washington	60.5
22	Pennsylvania..........................	60.2
23	South Carolina	59.8
24	Louisiana	59.7
25	Alaska	59.4
26	Maryland	59.2
27	Utah	58.9
28	Illinois	58.8
29	Idaho..........................	58.3
30	Kansas	58.0
31	Connecticut..........................	57.5
32	South Dakota	57.3
33	Delaware	57.2
34	Alabama	56.4
35	Indiana	56.0
35	Arkansas	56.0
37	Georgia	55.7
38	Rhode Island..........................	55.5
39	Kentucky	55.3
40	Nevada	53.5
41	New Jersey	53.4
42	Arizona..........................	53.3
43	Oklahoma	53.2
44	Florida..........................	52.9
45	Tennessee	52.0
46	New York..........................	50.7
47	West Virginia..........................	50.4
48	New Mexico	49.4
49	California..........................	48.2
50	Texas..........................	47.7
51	Hawaii	43.3

Percent of Persons 25 Years and Over with a Bachelor's Degree or More, 2015

Rank	State	Percent
	United States......................	30.6
1	District of Columbia	56.7
2	Massachusetts.....................	41.5
3	Colorado	39.2
4	Maryland..............................	38.8
5	Connecticut..........................	38.3
6	New Jersey	37.6
7	Virginia................................	37.0
8	Vermont...............................	36.9
9	New Hampshire....................	35.7
10	New York..............................	35.0
11	Minnesota............................	34.7
12	Washington..........................	34.2
13	Illinois.................................	32.9
14	Rhode Island........................	32.7
15	California..............................	32.3
16	Oregon.................................	32.2
17	Utah	31.8
18	Kansas	31.7
19	Hawaii	31.4
20	Delaware..............................	30.9
21	Montana...............................	30.6
22	Nebraska..............................	30.2
23	Maine...................................	30.1
24	Georgia................................	29.9
25	Alaska	29.7
25	Pennsylvania.......................	29.7
27	North Carolina......................	29.4
28	North Dakota........................	29.1
29	Florida.................................	28.4
29	Texas...................................	28.4
29	Wisconsin	28.4
32	Michigan...............................	27.8
32	Missouri...............................	27.8
34	Arizona................................	27.7
35	South Dakota	27.5
36	Iowa....................................	26.8
36	Ohio.....................................	26.8
36	South Carolina	26.8
39	New Mexico	26.5
40	Wyoming..............................	26.2
41	Idaho...................................	26.0
42	Tennessee	25.7
43	Indiana................................	24.9
44	Oklahoma.............................	24.6
45	Alabama...............................	24.2
46	Nevada................................	23.6
47	Kentucky..............................	23.3
48	Louisiana	23.2
49	Arkansas..............................	21.8
50	Mississippi...........................	20.8
51	West Virginia........................	19.6

Violent Crime, 2015

Rank	State	Rate per 100,000 population
	United States......................	383.2
1	District of Columbia	1269.1
2	Alaska	730.2
3	Nevada................................	695.9
4	New Mexico	656.1
5	Tennessee	612.1
6	Louisiana	539.7
7	Arkansas..............................	521.3
8	South Carolina	504.5
9	Delaware..............................	499.0
10	Missouri...............................	497.4
11	Alabama...............................	472.4
12	Florida.................................	461.9
13	Maryland..............................	457.2
14	California..............................	426.3
15	Oklahoma.............................	422.0
16	Michigan...............................	415.5
17	Texas...................................	412.2
18	Arizona................................	410.2
19	Massachusetts.....................	390.9
20	Kansas	389.9
21	Indiana................................	387.5
22	Illinois.................................	383.8
23	South Dakota	383.1
24	New York..............................	379.7
25	Georgia................................	378.3
26	Montana...............................	349.6
27	North Carolina......................	347.0
28	West Virginia........................	337.9
29	Colorado	321.0
30	Pennsylvania.......................	315.1
31	Wisconsin	305.8
32	Hawaii	293.4
33	Ohio.....................................	291.9
34	Iowa....................................	286.1
35	Washington..........................	284.4
36	Mississippi...........................	275.8
37	Nebraska..............................	274.9
38	Oregon.................................	259.8
39	New Jersey	255.4
40	Minnesota............................	242.6
41	Rhode Island........................	242.5
42	North Dakota........................	239.4
43	Utah	236.0
44	Wyoming..............................	222.1
45	Kentucky..............................	218.7
46	Connecticut..........................	218.5
47	Idaho...................................	215.6
48	New Hampshire....................	199.3
49	Virginia................................	195.6
50	Maine...................................	130.1
51	Vermont...............................	118.0

[1] Includes offenses reported by the Zoological Police and the Metro Transit Police.

Property Crime, 2015

Rank	State	Rate per 100,000 population
	United States......................	2,487.0
1	District of Columbia	4,676.2
2	Hawaii	3,796.2
3	New Mexico	3,697.4
4	Washington..........................	3,463.8
5	Louisiana	3,353.4
6	South Carolina	3,293.3
7	Arkansas..............................	3,251.5
8	Arizona................................	3,033.2
9	Georgia................................	3,022.3
10	Utah	2,980.0
11	Alabama...............................	2,978.9
12	Oregon.................................	2,946.6
13	Tennessee	2,936.2
14	Oklahoma.............................	2,885.9
15	Missouri...............................	2,854.2
16	Mississippi...........................	2,833.6
17	Texas...................................	2,831.3
18	Alaska	2,817.6
19	Florida.................................	2,813.2
20	North Carolina......................	2,750.1
21	Kansas	2,720.1
22	Delaware..............................	2,691.0
23	Nevada................................	2,668.3
24	Colorado	2,641.5
25	Montana...............................	2,623.6
26	California..............................	2,618.3
27	Indiana................................	2,596.0
28	Ohio.....................................	2,587.7
29	Maryland..............................	2,315.0
30	Nebraska..............................	2,241.1
31	Minnesota............................	2,222.1
32	Kentucky..............................	2,177.6
33	North Dakota........................	2,116.5
34	Iowa....................................	2,047.3
35	West Virginia........................	2,020.0
36	Illinois.................................	1,988.6
37	Wisconsin	1,974.0
38	South Dakota	1,943.0
39	Wyoming..............................	1,902.6
40	Rhode Island........................	1,897.5
41	Michigan...............................	1,885.6
42	Virginia................................	1,866.5
43	Maine...................................	1,830.0
44	Pennsylvania.......................	1,812.8
45	Connecticut..........................	1,812.0
46	New Hampshire....................	1,745.7
47	Idaho...................................	1,743.8
48	Massachusetts.....................	1,690.7
49	New Jersey	1,626.5
50	New York..............................	1,604.0
51	Vermont...............................	1,406.6

X = Not applicable.

State Government Employment, 2015
(Full-time equivalent employees)

Rank	State	State employees per 1,000 residents
	United States......................	13.4
1	Hawaii	40.9
2	Alaska	35.3
3	Delaware	27.5
4	North Dakota......................	25.5
5	Vermont	23.3
6	Wyoming	23.0
7	New Mexico	22.1
8	West Virginia	21.9
9	Arkansas	21.2
10	Montana	20.0
11	Kentucky	19.3
12	Mississippi..........................	19.0
13	Alabama	18.4
14	Utah	18.1
15	Connecticut	17.8
16	Oklahoma............................	17.6
17	Rhode Island	17.4
18	Kansas	17.3
19	Nebraska	16.8
19	Washington..........................	16.8
21	South Dakota	16.7
22	Oregon	16.3
23	South Carolina	16.2
24	Iowa	16.0
25	Louisiana	15.8
25	Maine	15.8
25	New Jersey	15.8
28	Virginia................................	15.1
29	Massachusetts	15.0
30	Minnesota	14.9
31	Maryland	14.6
31	Colorado	14.6
33	Missouri	14.4
34	Michigan	14.3
35	New Hampshire	14.2
36	Idaho	13.9
37	North Carolina.....................	13.8
38	Indiana	13.3
39	Wisconsin	12.9
40	Pennsylvania.......................	12.8
41	Georgia	12.4
42	New York..............................	12.3
43	Ohio	11.9
44	Tennessee	11.8
45	Arizona................................	11.4
46	Texas	10.9
47	California.............................	10.3
48	Illinois	9.7
48	Nevada	9.7
50	Florida	8.7
	District of Columbia	X

X = Not applicable.

Unemployment Rate, 2016

Rank	State	Unemployment rate
	United States......................	4.9
1	New Mexico	6.7
2	Alaska	6.6
3	Louisiana	6.1
4	Alabama	6.0
4	District of Columbia	6.0
4	West Virginia	6.0
7	Illinois	5.9
8	Mississippi..........................	5.8
9	Nevada	5.7
10	California.............................	5.4
10	Georgia	5.4
10	Pennsylvania.......................	5.4
10	Washington..........................	5.4
14	Arizona................................	5.3
14	Rhode Island	5.3
14	Wyoming	5.3
17	Connecticut	5.1
17	North Carolina.....................	5.1
19	Kentucky	5.0
19	New Jersey	5.0
21	Florida	4.9
21	Michigan	4.9
21	Ohio	4.9
21	Oklahoma............................	4.9
21	Oregon	4.9
26	New York..............................	4.8
26	South Carolina	4.8
26	Tennessee	4.8
29	Texas	4.6
30	Missouri	4.5
31	Delaware	4.4
31	Indiana	4.4
33	Maryland	4.3
34	Kansas	4.2
35	Montana	4.1
35	Wisconsin	4.1
37	Arkansas	4.0
37	Virginia................................	4.0
39	Maine	3.9
39	Minnesota	3.9
41	Idaho	3.8
42	Iowa	3.7
42	Massachusetts	3.7
44	Utah	3.4
45	Colorado	3.3
45	Vermont	3.3
47	Nebraska	3.2
47	North Dakota......................	3.2
49	Hawaii	3.0
50	New Hampshire	2.8
50	South Dakota	2.8

Employees on Nonfarm Payrolls, Percent Change, 2015–2016

Rank	State	Percent
	United States......................	1.7
1	Utah	3.6
2	Idaho	3.5
3	Florida	3.4
4	Nevada	3.3
5	Washington..........................	3.1
6	Oregon	2.9
7	Georgia	2.7
8	California.............................	2.6
8	Arizona................................	2.6
10	Tennessee	2.5
11	South Carolina	2.4
12	North Carolina.....................	2.3
13	Colorado	2.2
14	Michigan	1.9
14	New Hampshire	1.9
16	Massachusetts	1.7
16	District of Columbia	1.7
18	Missouri	1.6
19	Indiana	1.5
19	Virginia................................	1.5
19	Arkansas	1.5
19	Kentucky	1.5
19	New Jersey	1.5
19	New York..............................	1.5
25	Hawaii	1.4
25	Minnesota	1.4
25	Alabama	1.4
28	Texas	1.3
28	Montana	1.3
28	Maryland	1.3
31	Wisconsin	1.1
31	Maine	1.1
31	Ohio	1.1
34	South Dakota	1.0
34	Delaware	1.0
34	Rhode Island	1.0
34	Mississippi..........................	1.0
38	Nebraska	0.8
38	Pennsylvania.......................	0.8
40	Illinois	0.7
41	Iowa	0.6
42	Kansas	0.5
43	Vermont	0.3
43	New Mexico	0.3
43	Connecticut	0.3
46	Oklahoma............................	-1.0
47	Louisiana	-1.2
47	West Virginia	-1.2
49	Alaska	-1.9
50	Wyoming	-3.9
51	North Dakota......................	-4.1

Per Capita Personal Income, 2015 (2015 Dollars)

Rank	State	Dollars
	United States...........	48,190
1	District of Columbia	73,505
2	Connecticut....................	68,822
3	Massachusetts................	62,697
4	New Jersey	60,101
5	New York....................	58,814
6	Alaska.......................	56,202
7	Maryland....................	56,078
8	Wyoming....................	56,038
9	North Dakota................	55,956
10	New Hampshire...........	55,926
11	California....................	53,949
12	Virginia.....................	52,148
13	Washington.................	51,971
14	Colorado....................	50,971
15	Minnesota...................	50,938
16	Illinois......................	50,377
17	Rhode Island................	50,050
18	Pennsylvania................	49,786
19	Nebraska....................	48,606
20	Vermont.....................	48,584
21	Hawaii......................	48,506
22	South Dakota	47,912
23	Delaware....................	47,727
24	Kansas......................	47,241
25	Texas.......................	47,015
26	Wisconsin...................	45,942
27	Iowa........................	45,930
28	Oklahoma...................	45,619
29	Florida......................	44,487
30	Oregon......................	43,830
31	Ohio........................	43,597
32	Louisiana	42,963
33	Michigan....................	42,833
34	Maine.......................	42,795
35	Missouri.....................	42,352
36	Tennessee...................	42,127
37	Nevada......................	41,992
38	Indiana......................	41,984
39	Montana.....................	41,845
40	North Carolina...............	40,790
41	Georgia.....................	40,367
42	Utah........................	39,378
43	Arizona.....................	39,217
44	Kentucky....................	38,592
45	Idaho.......................	38,440
46	South Carolina	38,312
47	Arkansas....................	38,257
48	Alabama.....................	38,070
49	New Mexico	38,025
50	West Virginia................	36,820
51	Mississippi..................	34,805

Real Gross Domestic Product in Chained (2009) Dollars, 2015

Rank	State	Dollars (millions)
	United States..................	16,094,516
1	California....................	2,235,433
2	Texas.......................	1,492,761
3	New York....................	1,265,637
4	Florida......................	791,435
5	Illinois......................	686,010
6	Pennsylvania................	644,947
7	Ohio........................	543,421
8	New Jersey	504,605
9	Georgia.....................	447,887
10	North Carolina...............	442,515
11	Massachusetts................	437,633
12	Virginia.....................	432,742
13	Michigan....................	422,800
14	Washington.................	399,401
15	Maryland....................	329,090
16	Indiana......................	296,235
17	Minnesota...................	292,655
18	Colorado....................	286,728
19	Tennessee...................	282,251
20	Wisconsin...................	270,277
21	Arizona.....................	261,891
22	Missouri.....................	260,933
23	Connecticut..................	228,517
24	Louisiana	206,802
25	Oregon......................	200,394
26	South Carolina	180,111
27	Oklahoma...................	179,210
28	Alabama.....................	178,893
29	Kentucky....................	170,803
30	Iowa........................	156,369
31	Kansas......................	136,296
32	Utah........................	132,199
33	Nevada......................	125,874
34	Arkansas....................	107,786
35	District of Columbia	106,742
36	Nebraska....................	100,139
37	Mississippi..................	94,564
38	New Mexico	86,495
39	Hawaii......................	71,714
40	New Hampshire..............	67,112
41	West Virginia................	67,111
42	Delaware....................	60,458
43	Idaho.......................	58,621
44	Maine.......................	51,118
45	North Dakota................	50,939
46	Alaska......................	49,947
47	Rhode Island................	49,738
48	Montana.....................	40,958
49	South Dakota	40,928
50	Wyoming....................	35,726
51	Vermont.....................	27,232

Real Gross Domestic Product in Chained (2009) Dollars, Percent Change, 2014–2015

Rank	State	Percent
	United States..................	2.6
1	Oregon......................	4.5
1	Texas.......................	4.5
3	California....................	4.4
4	Utah........................	4.3
5	Massachusetts................	3.7
6	Florida......................	3.6
7	Nevada......................	3.5
8	Tennessee...................	3.1
9	Colorado....................	3.0
10	Washington.................	2.9
11	South Carolina	2.8
12	Michigan....................	2.7
12	North Carolina...............	2.7
12	Oklahoma...................	2.7
15	Pennsylvania................	2.6
15	South Dakota	2.6
17	Georgia.....................	2.5
18	Virginia.....................	2.4
19	Hawaii......................	2.3
20	Connecticut..................	2.2
20	Delaware....................	2.2
20	Idaho.......................	2.2
20	Iowa........................	2.2
20	Kansas......................	2.2
25	Maryland....................	2.1
25	Montana.....................	2.1
25	New Hampshire..............	2.1
28	New Mexico	1.7
29	District of Columbia	1.6
29	New Jersey	1.6
31	Arizona.....................	1.4
31	Missouri.....................	1.4
33	Minnesota...................	1.3
33	Wisconsin...................	1.3
35	New York....................	1.2
36	Alabama.....................	1.1
36	Kentucky....................	1.1
36	Maine.......................	1.1
36	Rhode Island................	1.1
40	Illinois......................	1.0
40	Ohio........................	1.0
42	Vermont.....................	0.9
43	Indiana......................	0.8
44	Alaska......................	0.6
45	Louisiana	0.5
46	West Virginia................	0.4
47	Mississippi..................	0.3
47	Nebraska....................	0.3
49	Arkansas....................	0.2
50	Wyoming....................	-0.3
51	North Dakota................	-3.1

Median Household Income, 2015

Rank	State	Dollars
	United States......................	55,775
1	Maryland............................	75,847
2	District of Columbia	75,628
3	Hawaii	73,486
4	Alaska	73,355
5	New Jersey	72,222
6	Connecticut........................	71,346
7	Massachusetts....................	70,628
8	New Hampshire...................	70,303
9	Virginia	66,262
10	California............................	64,500
11	Washington.........................	64,129
12	Colorado	63,909
13	Minnesota...........................	63,488
14	Utah	62,912
15	Delaware	61,255
16	New York............................	60,850
17	North Dakota.......................	60,557
18	Wyoming	60,214
19	Illinois	59,588
20	Rhode Island.......................	58,073
21	Vermont	56,990
22	Pennsylvania......................	55,702
23	Texas	55,653
24	Wisconsin	55,638
25	Nebraska............................	54,996
26	Iowa	54,736
27	Oregon	54,148
28	Kansas	53,906
29	South Dakota	53,017
30	Nevada	52,431
31	Maine	51,494
32	Arizona	51,492
33	Georgia	51,244
34	Michigan	51,084
35	Ohio	51,075
36	Indiana	50,532
37	Missouri	50,238
38	Montana..............................	49,509
39	Florida	49,426
40	Oklahoma...........................	48,568
41	Idaho	48,275
42	North Carolina.....................	47,830
43	Tennessee	47,275
44	South Carolina	47,238
45	Louisiana	45,727
46	New Mexico	45,382
47	Kentucky	45,215
48	Alabama.............................	44,765
49	West Virginia.......................	42,019
50	Arkansas	41,995
51	Mississippi	40,593

Median Family Income, 2015

Rank	State	Dollars
	United States......................	68,260
1	District of Columbia	94,846
2	Maryland............................	91,567
3	Connecticut........................	91,388
4	Massachusetts....................	90,590
5	New Jersey	90,245
6	Alaska	86,376
7	New Hampshire...................	85,873
8	Hawaii	83,823
9	Virginia	80,403
10	Minnesota...........................	79,893
11	North Dakota.......................	79,642
12	Colorado	78,384
13	Washington.........................	76,954
14	Rhode Island.......................	76,623
15	Vermont	75,595
16	Wyoming	75,540
17	Delaware	74,931
18	Illinois	73,884
19	New York............................	73,854
20	California............................	73,581
21	Utah	71,594
22	Nebraska............................	71,039
23	Wisconsin	70,870
24	Pennsylvania......................	70,194
25	Kansas	69,401
26	Iowa	69,382
27	South Dakota	67,643
28	Oregon	66,287
29	Texas	65,316
30	Ohio	65,176
31	Maine	64,651
32	Montana..............................	64,061
33	Michigan	63,893
34	Nevada	63,206
35	Indiana	63,165
36	Missouri	62,989
37	Georgia	61,250
38	Arizona	61,042
39	Oklahoma...........................	60,215
40	Idaho	60,081
41	North Carolina.....................	60,074
42	Florida	59,339
43	South Carolina	59,282
44	Louisiana	58,964
45	Tennessee	57,830
46	Alabama.............................	57,160
47	New Mexico	56,207
48	Kentucky	56,187
49	West Virginia.......................	53,463
50	Arkansas	52,449
51	Mississippi	50,069

Persons Below Poverty Level, 2015

Rank	State	Percent
	United States......................	14.7
1	Mississippi	22.0
2	New Mexico	20.4
3	Louisiana	19.6
4	Arkansas	19.1
5	Alabama.............................	18.5
5	Kentucky	18.5
7	West Virginia.......................	17.9
8	Arizona	17.4
9	District of Columbia	17.3
10	Georgia	17.0
11	Tennessee	16.7
12	South Carolina	16.6
13	North Carolina.....................	16.4
14	Oklahoma...........................	16.1
15	Texas	15.9
16	Michigan	15.8
17	Florida	15.7
18	New York............................	15.4
18	Oregon	15.4
20	California............................	15.3
21	Idaho	15.1
22	Missouri	14.8
22	Ohio	14.8
24	Nevada	14.7
25	Montana..............................	14.6
26	Indiana	14.5
27	Rhode Island.......................	13.9
28	South Dakota	13.7
29	Illinois	13.6
30	Maine	13.4
31	Pennsylvania......................	13.2
32	Kansas	13.0
33	Nebraska............................	12.6
34	Delaware	12.4
35	Iowa	12.2
35	Washington.........................	12.2
37	Wisconsin	12.1
38	Colorado	11.5
38	Massachusetts....................	11.5
40	Utah	11.3
41	Virginia	11.2
42	Wyoming	11.1
43	North Dakota.......................	11.0
44	New Jersey	10.8
45	Hawaii	10.6
46	Connecticut........................	10.5
47	Alaska	10.3
48	Minnesota...........................	10.2
48	Vermont	10.2
50	Maryland............................	9.7
51	New Hampshire...................	8.2

Persons Under 18 Years Old Below Poverty Level, 2015

Rank	State	Percent
	United States	20.7
1	Mississippi	31.3
2	New Mexico	28.6
3	Louisiana	28.4
4	Arkansas	27.2
5	Alabama	26.6
6	Kentucky	25.9
7	District of Columbia	25.6
8	West Virginia	25.2
9	Arizona	24.7
10	Georgia	24.5
11	Tennessee	24.2
12	South Carolina	24.0
13	North Carolina	23.5
14	Florida	23.1
15	Texas	23.0
16	Michigan	22.4
17	Oklahoma	22.2
18	New York	22.0
19	Ohio	21.3
20	California	21.2
21	Indiana	20.9
21	Nevada	20.9
23	Oregon	20.3
24	Missouri	20.2
25	Delaware	19.4
25	Montana	19.4
25	Pennsylvania	19.4
25	Rhode Island	19.4
29	Illinois	19.1
30	South Dakota	18.1
31	Idaho	17.8
32	Maine	17.4
33	Kansas	17.2
34	Nebraska	16.8
35	Wisconsin	16.4
36	New Jersey	15.6
37	Washington	15.5
38	Alaska	15.2
39	Iowa	14.8
39	Massachusetts	14.8
39	Virginia	14.8
42	Colorado	14.7
43	Connecticut	14.5
44	Hawaii	14.2
45	Vermont	13.3
46	Maryland	13.2
46	Wyoming	13.2
48	Minnesota	13.1
49	Utah	12.9
50	North Dakota	12.1
51	New Hampshire	10.7

Energy Consumption Per Capita, 2015

Rank	State	Million Btu
	United States	303.1
1	Louisiana	912.2
2	Wyoming	892.9
3	Alaska	840.3
4	North Dakota	802.8
5	Iowa	478.8
6	Texas	470.2
7	Nebraska	450.5
8	South Dakota	447.0
9	Indiana	430.4
10	West Virginia	420.9
11	Oklahoma	417.4
12	Alabama	393.4
13	Kentucky	390.0
14	Montana	379.3
15	Mississippi	378.9
16	Kansas	372.5
17	Arkansas	354.5
18	South Carolina	336.8
19	Tennessee	328.6
20	New Mexico	324.7
21	Minnesota	322.8
22	Ohio	322.3
23	Idaho	317.3
24	Wisconsin	307.9
25	Illinois	307.1
26	Maine	305.1
27	Pennsylvania	303.4
28	Missouri	300.6
29	Delaware	294.5
30	Virginia	283.0
31	Georgia	279.5
32	Michigan	279.0
33	Washington	277.7
34	Colorado	271.7
35	District of Columbia	266.7
36	Utah	264.5
37	New Jersey	256.0
38	North Carolina	251.5
39	Oregon	237.7
40	Maryland	233.4
41	New Hampshire	229.5
42	Nevada	225.2
43	Massachusetts	213.0
44	Arizona	211.2
45	Vermont	210.8
46	Connecticut	209.7
47	Florida	209.5
48	Hawaii	198.2
49	California	196.9
50	Rhode Island	192.0
51	New York	188.6

Homeownership Rate, 2016

Rank	State	Percent
	United States	63.4
1	West Virginia	74.8
2	Delaware	73.0
3	Michigan	72.8
4	Maine	72.6
5	Minnesota	72.4
6	New Hampshire	71.8
7	Utah	71.3
7	Vermont	71.3
9	Indiana	70.9
10	Idaho	70.5
11	Wyoming	70.2
12	Iowa	70.0
13	Alabama	69.7
13	Mississippi	69.7
15	South Dakota	69.4
16	South Carolina	68.9
17	Pennsylvania	68.5
18	Nebraska	68.0
19	Kentucky	67.9
20	Wisconsin	67.7
21	Arkansas	67.6
22	New Mexico	67.4
23	Kansas	67.1
23	Montana	67.1
25	Oklahoma	66.8
26	Missouri	66.7
27	Maryland	66.5
28	Tennessee	66.4
29	Virginia	66.3
30	Ohio	66.1
31	North Carolina	65.7
32	Illinois	65.3
33	Alaska	65.2
34	Florida	64.3
35	Connecticut	64.2
35	Louisiana	64.2
37	Oregon	62.6
38	Colorado	62.4
39	Georgia	62.3
40	New Jersey	62.2
41	Arizona	61.9
42	Washington	61.6
43	Texas	61.5
44	North Dakota	61.4
45	Massachusetts	59.7
46	Hawaii	57.7
47	Rhode Island	56.3
48	Nevada	54.5
49	California	53.8
50	New York	51.5
51	District of Columbia	40.8

One-Unit Detached or Attached Housing Units, Percent of Total Housing Units, 2015

Rank	State	Percent
	United States	68.4
1	Kansas	78.2
2	Iowa	77.8
3	Idaho	77.5
3	Indiana	77.5
3	Nebraska	77.5
6	Michigan	77.1
7	Pennsylvania	76.7
8	Oklahoma	76.5
9	Missouri	75.8
9	Utah	75.8
11	Delaware	75.6
12	Ohio	74.7
13	Minnesota	74.5
14	West Virginia	74.3
15	Maryland	73.6
16	Virginia	73.1
17	Tennessee	73.0
18	South Dakota	72.8
19	Alabama	72.4
19	Arkansas	72.4
21	Mississippi	72.1
21	Montana	72.1
23	Wyoming	71.3
24	Georgia	71.1
25	Colorado	70.9
25	Wisconsin	70.9
27	Kentucky	70.7
28	Arizona	70.1
29	Maine	69.9
30	Louisiana	69.6
30	North Carolina	69.6
32	Texas	69.0
33	Vermont	68.9
34	New Mexico	68.6
35	New Hampshire	68.4
35	South Carolina	68.4
37	Alaska	68.1
38	Oregon	67.9
39	Washington	67.7
40	Nevada	66.6
41	Illinois	66.0
42	Hawaii	65.6
43	Connecticut	65.4
44	California	65.0
45	North Dakota	64.4
46	Florida	64.0
47	New Jersey	63.1
48	Rhode Island	58.7
49	Massachusetts	57.3
50	New York	46.5
51	District of Columbia	38.2

Percent of Population Not Covered by Private or Public Insurance, 2015

Rank	State	Percent
	United States	9.4
1	Texas	17.1
2	Alaska	14.9
3	Georgia	13.9
3	Oklahoma	13.9
5	Florida	13.3
6	Mississippi	12.7
7	Nevada	12.3
8	Louisiana	11.9
9	Montana	11.6
10	Wyoming	11.5
11	North Carolina	11.2
12	Idaho	11.0
13	New Mexico	10.9
13	South Carolina	10.9
15	Arizona	10.8
16	Utah	10.5
17	Tennessee	10.3
18	South Dakota	10.2
19	Alabama	10.1
20	Missouri	9.8
21	Indiana	9.6
22	Arkansas	9.5
23	Kansas	9.1
23	Virginia	9.1
25	New Jersey	8.7
26	California	8.6
27	Maine	8.4
28	Nebraska	8.2
29	Colorado	8.1
30	North Dakota	7.8
31	Illinois	7.1
31	New York	7.1
33	Oregon	7.0
34	Maryland	6.6
34	Washington	6.6
36	Ohio	6.5
37	Pennsylvania	6.4
38	New Hampshire	6.3
39	Michigan	6.1
40	Connecticut	6.0
40	Kentucky	6.0
40	West Virginia	6.0
43	Delaware	5.9
44	Rhode Island	5.7
44	Wisconsin	5.7
46	Iowa	5.0
47	Minnesota	4.5
48	Hawaii	4.0
49	District of Columbia	3.8
49	Vermont	3.8
51	Massachusetts	2.8

Traffic Fatalities Per 100 Million Vehicle Miles, 2015

Rank	State	Percent
	United States	1.13
1	South Carolina	1.89
2	Montana	1.81
3	Mississippi	1.70
4	Kentucky	1.56
5	Arkansas	1.52
6	Louisiana	1.51
6	Wyoming	1.51
8	South Dakota	1.43
9	Florida	1.42
10	Arizona	1.37
11	Texas	1.36
12	Oklahoma	1.35
12	West Virginia	1.35
14	North Dakota	1.31
15	Idaho	1.30
16	Alaska	1.29
17	Delaware	1.27
18	Alabama	1.26
19	Nevada	1.25
19	Tennessee	1.25
21	Oregon	1.24
22	North Carolina	1.23
23	Nebraska	1.22
24	Georgia	1.21
24	Missouri	1.21
26	Pennsylvania	1.19
27	Kansas	1.13
28	New Mexico	1.09
29	Colorado	1.08
30	Maine	1.07
31	Indiana	1.04
32	Michigan	0.98
32	Ohio	0.98
34	Iowa	0.96
35	California	0.95
35	Illinois	0.95
35	Washington	0.95
38	Utah	0.93
39	Hawaii	0.91
39	Virginia	0.91
39	Wisconsin	0.91
42	Maryland	0.89
43	New York	0.88
44	New Hampshire	0.87
45	Connecticut	0.84
46	Vermont	0.78
47	New Jersey	0.75
48	Minnesota	0.72
49	District of Columbia	0.65
50	Rhode Island	0.57
51	Massachusetts	0.52

ALABAMA

Facts and Figures

Location: Southeastern United States; bordered on the N by Tennessee, on the E by Georgia, on the S by Florida and the Gulf of Mexico, and on the W by Mississippi

Area: 52,420 sq. mi. (135,765 sq. km.); rank—30th

Population: 4,863,300 (2016 est.); rank—24th

Principal Cities: capital—Montgomery; largest—Birmingham

Statehood: December 14, 1819; 22nd state

U.S. Congress: 2 senators, 7 representatives

State Motto: *Audemus jura nostra defendere* ("We dare defend our rights")

State Song: "Alabama"

State Nicknames: The Yellowhammer State; The Heart of Dixie; The Cotton State

Abbreviations: AL; Ala.

State Symbols: flower—camellia; tree—Southern longleaf pine; bird—yellowhammer

At a Glance

- With an increase in population of 1.7 percent, Alabama ranked 36th among the states in growth from 2010 to 2016.

- Alabama's per capita personal income in 2015 was $38,070, ranking 48th in the nation.

- Ranking 34th in the nation, 56.4 percent of Alabama's population voted in the November 2016 election.

- In 2015, 18.5 percent of Alabama residents lived below the poverty level, a percentage that ranked 5th in the nation.

- Alabama's violent crime rate in 2015 was 472.4 per 100,000 residents, compared to 383.2 for the entire nation.

- Alabama's median household income of $44,765 ranked 48th in the nation in 2015.

Table AL-1. Population by Age, Sex, Race, and Hispanic Origin

(Number, percent, except where noted.)

Sex, age, race, and Hispanic origin	2000	2010	2016 [1]	Average annual percent change, 2010–2016
Total Population..	4,447,100	4,779,736	4,863,300	0.1
Percent of total U.S. population	1.6	1.5	1.5	X
Sex				
Male..	2,146,504	2,320,188	2,355,586	0.1
Female	2,300,596	2,459,548	2,507,714	0.1
Age				
Under 5 years..	295,992	304,957	292,565	-0.3
5 to 19 years...	960,177	971,355	930,544	-0.3
20 to 64 years...	2,611,133	2,845,632	2,855,640	0.0
65 years and over..	579,798	657,792	784,551	1.2
Median age (years)...	35.8	37.9	38.9	0.2
Race and Hispanic Origin				
One race...				
White...	3,162,808	3,362,877	3,372,524	-
Black..	1,155,930	1,259,224	1,303,516	0.2
American Indian and Alaska Native	22,430	32,903	33,932	0.2
Asian..	31,346	55,240	68,864	1.5
Native Hawaiian or Other Pacific Islander	1,409	5,208	5,068	-0.2
Two or more races..	44,179	64,284	79,396	1.5
Hispanic (of any race)...	75,830	192,498	203,845	0.4

X = Not applicable.
[1] Population figures for 2016 are July 1 estimates. The 2010 estimates are taken from the 2010 Census.
- = Zero or rounds to zero.

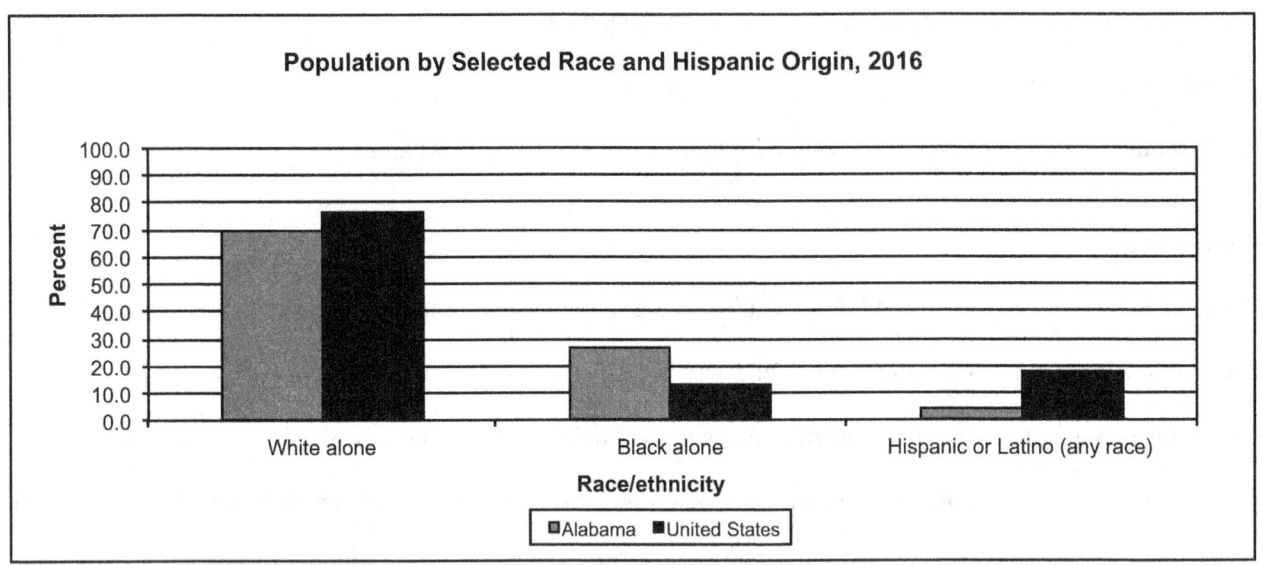

Population by Selected Race and Hispanic Origin, 2016

Table AL-2. Marital Status

(Number, percent distribution.)

Sex, age, and marital status	2000	2010	2015
Males, 15 Years and Over	1,666,798	1,844,661	1,885,840
Never married	26.7	32.5	34.1
Now married, except separated................................	59.0	50.6	49.0
Separated...	1.8	2.5	2.1
Widowed..	2.8	3.0	3.0
Divorced..	9.8	11.4	11.8
Females, 15 Years and Over	1,847,401	2,004,450	2,061,364
Never married	21.4	26.1	28.5
Now married, except separated................................	52.5	45.9	44.4
Separated...	2.5	3.1	2.9
Widowed..	12.4	11.2	10.8
Divorced..	11.2	13.6	13.4

Table AL-3. Households and Housing Characteristics

(Number, percent, dollars.)

Item	2000	2010	2015	Average annual percent change, 2000–2015
Total Households...	1,737,080	1,815,152	1,846,390	0.4
Family households..	1,215,968	1,227,884	1,213,540	-
Married-couple family..	906,916	868,946	863,674	-0.3
Other family..	309,052	358,938	349,866	0.9
Male householder, no wife present......................	62,586	79,308	78,239	1.7
Female householder, no husband present.............	246,466	279,630	271,627	0.7
Nonfamily households...	521,112	587,268	632,850	1.4
Householder living alone.....................................	453,898	511,708	552,672	1.5
Householder not living alone...............................	67,214	75,560	80,178	1.3
Housing Characteristics				
Total housing units...	1,963,711	2,174,428	2,218,391	0.9
Occupied housing units	1,737,080	1,815,152	1,846,390	0.4
Owner occupied..	1,258,705	1,272,846	1,253,595	-
Renter occupied...	478,375	542,306	592,795	1.6
Average household size...	2.49	2.57	2.57	0.2
Financial Characteristics				
Median gross rent of renter-occupied housing	447	667	729	4.2
Median monthly owner costs for housing units with a mortgage	816	1,130	1,124	2.5
Median value of owner-occupied housing units	85,100	123,900	134,100	3.8

- = Zero or rounds to zero.

Table AL-4. Migration, Origin, and Language

(Number, percent.)

Characteristic	State			U.S.		
	2014	2015	Percent change	2014	2015	Percent change
Residence 1 Year Ago						
Population 1 year and over	4,791,931	4,801,599	0.2	315,095,393	317,635,720	0.8
Same house	85.2	85.7	X	85.1	85.3	X
Different house in the U.S.	14.5	14.1	X	14.3	14.1	X
Same county	9.0	8.5	X	8.7	8.5	X
Different county	5.5	5.5	X	5.6	5.6	X
Same state	3.2	3.1	X	3.3	3.2	X
Different state	2.3	2.4	X	2.3	2.4	X
Abroad	0.3	0.2	X	0.6	0.7	X
Place of Birth						
Native born	4,692,021	4,689,007	-0.1	276,465,262	278,128,449	0.6
Male	48.4	48.3	X	49.3	49.3	X
Female	51.6	51.7	X	50.7	50.7	X
Foreign born	157,356	169,972	8.0	42,391,794	43,290,372	2.1
Male	50.0	52.1	X	48.7	48.6	X
Female	50.0	47.9	X	51.3	51.4	X
Foreign born; naturalized U.S. citizen........................	54,716	61,631	12.6	19,984,738	20,697,103	3.6
Male	42.6	47.1	X	45.9	45.9	X
Female	57.4	52.9	X	54.1	54.1	X
Foreign born; not a U.S. citizen.................................	102,640	108,341	5.6	22,407,056	22,593,269	0.8
Male	54	54.9	X	51.2	51.1	X
Female	46	45.1	X	48.8	48.9	X
Entered 2010 or later	14.3	20.7	X	12.3	15.6	X
Entered 2000 to 2009	38.6	34.6	X	28.6	27.9	X
Entered before 2000...	47.2	44.7	X	59.1	56.5	X
World Region of Birth, Foreign						
Foreign-born population, excluding population born at sea	157,356	169,972	8.0	42,390,705	43,289,646	2.1
Europe	11.0	12.2	X	11.2	11.1	X
Asia	30.7	28.1	X	30.1	30.6	X
Africa	4.5	5.7	X	4.6	4.8	X
Oceania	0.5	0.6	X	0.6	0.6	X
Latin America...	50.7	51.8	X	51.6	51.1	X
North America	2.6	1.6	X	1.9	1.9	X
Language Spoken at Home and Ability to Speak English						
Population 5 years and over..	4,558,217	4,573,857	0.3	299,084,046	301,625,014	0.8
English only	95.1	94.9	X	78.9	78.5	X
Language other than English.....................................	4.9	5.1	X	21.1	21.5	X
Speaks English less than "very well".........................	2.0	2.2	X	8.6	8.6	X

NA = Not available.
X = Not applicable.
- = Zero or rounds to zero.

Table AL-5. Median Income and Poverty Status, 2015

(Number, percent, except as noted.)

Characteristic	State		U.S.	
	Number	Percent	Number	Percent
Median Income				
Households (dollars)....................	44,765	X	55,775	X
Families (dollars)	57,160	X	68,260	X
Below Poverty Level (All People)	876,016	18.5	46,153,077	14.7
Sex				
Male	381,195	16.7	20,599,407	13.4
Female	494,821	20.2	25,553,670	16.0
Age				
Under 18 years....................	290,825	26.6	15,000,273	20.7
Related children under 18 years....................	288,007	26.4	14,693,239	20.4
18 to 64 years	511,611	17.6	26,960,369	13.9
65 years and over	73,580	9.9	4,192,435	9.0

X = Not applicable.

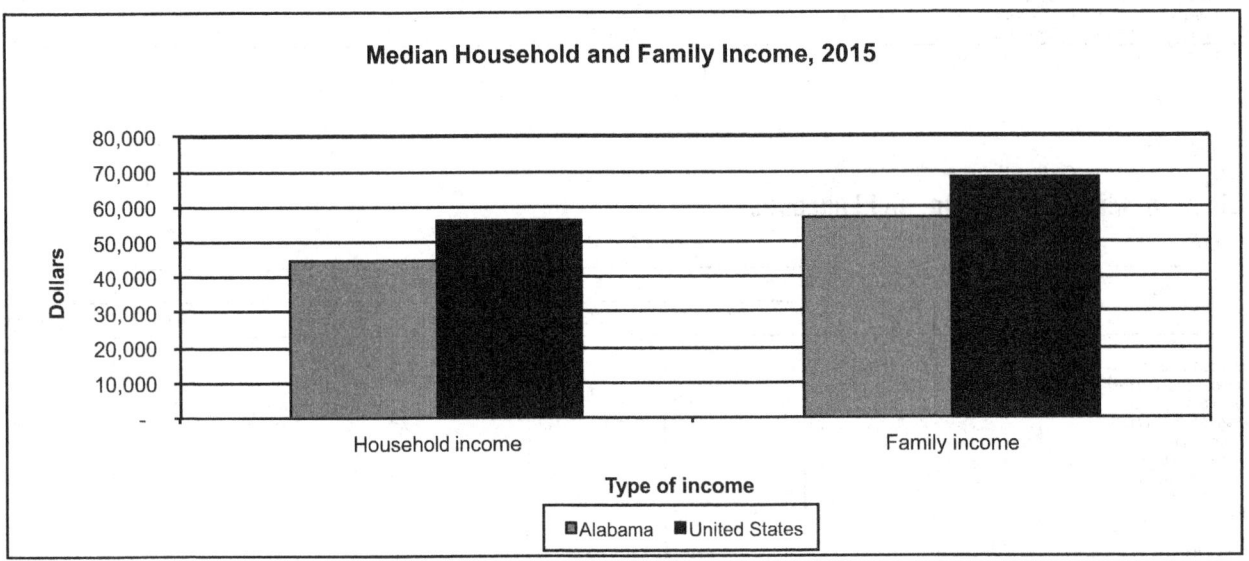

Median Household and Family Income, 2015

Table AL-6. Health Insurance Coverage Status for the Civilian Noninstitutionalized Population and Children Under 18 Years of Age

(Numbers in thousands, percent.)

Item	2007	2008	2009	2010	2011	2012	2013	2014	2015
Civilian Noninstitutionalized Population	4,570	4,574	4,616	4,703	4,720	4,742	4,755	4,767	4,781
Covered by Private or Public Insurance									
Number....................	4,021	4,023	3,979	4,016	4,046	4,109	4,110	4,118	4,297
Percent....................	88.0	88.0	86.2	85.4	85.7	86.7	86.4	87.9	89.9
Not Covered									
Number....................	549	551	637	687	674	632	645	579	484
Percent....................	12.0	12.0	13.8	14.6	14.3	13.3	13.6	12.1	10.1
Percent in the U.S. not covered................	15.3	15.1	15.1	15.5	15.1	14.8	14.5	11.7	9.4
Children Under 18 Years of Age	1,083	1,120	1,124	1,134	1,122	1,123	1,108	1,107	1,107
Covered by Private or Public Insurance									
Number....................	1,041	1,030	1,057	1,067	1,063	1,077	1,060	1,064	1,073
Percent....................	92.7	92.0	94.1	94.1	94.7	95.9	95.7	96.2	96.9
Not Covered									
Number....................	82	90	67	67	59	46	48	42	34
Percent....................	7.3	8.0	5.9	5.9	5.3	4.1	4.3	3.8	3.1
Percent in the U.S. not covered................	11.0	9.7	8.6	8.0	7.5	7.2	7.1	6.0	4.8

Table AL-7. Employment Status by Demographic Group, 2016

(Numbers in thousands, percent.)

Characteristic	Civilian noninstitutional population	Civilian labor force		Employed		Unemployed	
		Number	Percent of population	Number	Percent of population	Number	Percent of population
Total...	3,824	2,172	56.8	2,041	53.4	131	6.0
Sex							
Male..	1,809	1,148	63.5	1,072	59.3	76	6.6
Female	2,016	1,024	50.8	968	48.0	56	5.4
Race, Sex, and Hispanic Origin							
White	2,695	1,509	56.0	1,440	53.4	69	4.6
Male	1,298	842	64.8	797	61.4	45	5.3
Female	1,397	667	47.8	643	46.0	24	3.7
Black or African American..........................	986	580	58.9	521	52.9	59	10.1
Male	437	260	59.5	231	52.7	29	11.3
Female	548	320	58.4	291	53.0	29	9.2
Hispanic or Latino ethnicity[1]	127	88	69.6	84	66.0	5	5.2
Male	65	54	84.3	51	78.6	4	6.8
Female	NA	NA	NA	NA	NA	NA	NA
Age							
16 to 19 years...	245	81	33.0	65	26.6	16	19.3
20 to 24 years...	357	246	68.9	221	62.0	25	10.0
25 to 34 years...	596	473	79.4	434	72.8	39	8.3
35 to 44 years...	581	444	76.4	425	73.1	19	4.3
45 to 54 years...	654	479	73.2	463	70.8	16	3.3
55 to 64 years...	649	338	52.0	324	49.9	13	3.9
65 years and over	743	112	15.0	109	14.6	3	2.8

NOTE: Data in Table 7 are from the Current Population Survey (CPS) and do not match the estimates in Table 8. See notes and definitions for further information.
[1] May be of any race.
NA = Not available.

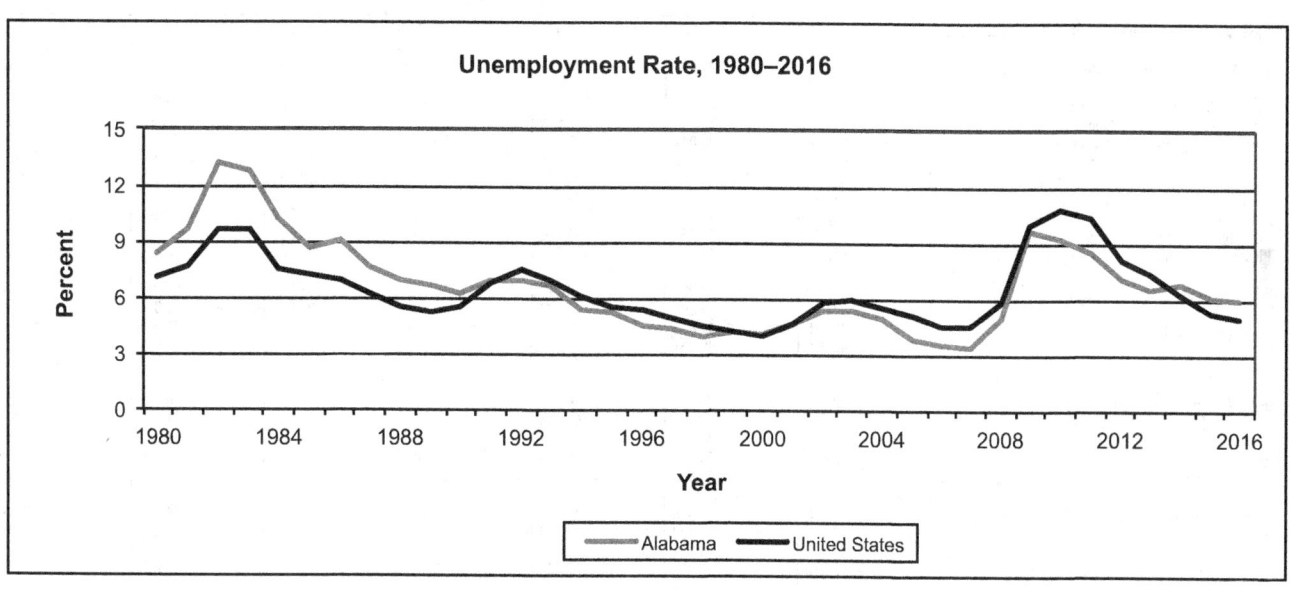

Unemployment Rate, 1980–2016

Table AL-8. Employment Status of the Civilian Noninstitutional Population Age 16 Years and Over

(Number, percent.)

Year	Civilian labor force	Civilian participation rate	Employed	Unemployed	Unemployment rate
2008...	2,176,489	60.6	2,053,477	123,012	5.7
2009...	2,162,999	59.7	1,924,747	238,252	11.0
2010...	2,196,042	59.5	1,964,559	231,483	10.5
2011...	2,202,670	59.1	1,990,413	212,257	9.6
2012...	2,174,972	58.1	2,001,849	173,123	8.0
2013...	2,167,238	57.6	2,010,431	156,807	7.2
2014...	2,161,313	57.1	2,014,284	147,029	6.8
2015...	2,146,157	56.4	2,015,189	130,968	6.1
2016...	2,168,608	56.8	2,038,775	129,833	6.0

Table AL-9. Employment and Average Wages by Industry

(Estimates through 2010 are based on the 2007 *North American Industry Classification System* [NAICS]. Estimates from 2011 onward are based on the 2012 NAICS.)

Industry	2009	2010	2011	2012	2013	2014	2015
				Number of Jobs			
Wage and Salary Employment by Industry..................	1,975,962	1,951,485	1,951,695	1,965,084	1,980,147	1,997,256	2,024,641
Farm Wage and Salary Employment.........................	9,440	7,826	8,188	7,348	7,724	5,317	7,452
Nonfarm Wage and Salary Employment....................	1,966,522	1,943,659	1,943,507	1,957,736	1,972,423	1,991,939	2,017,189
Private wage and salary employment......................	1,554,940	1,530,423	1,535,438	1,554,240	1,571,512	1,591,548	1,618,368
Forestry, fishing, and related activities......................	8,681	8,751	8,512	8,581	8,806	8,893	8,874
Mining...................	7,723	7,765	8,287	8,593	7,990	7,548	6,836
Utilities................	13,867	14,089	14,262	14,246	14,382	14,293	14,438
Construction	95,969	90,243	83,447	82,010	81,853	82,096	83,729
Manufacturing.........	246,574	236,759	237,850	243,929	249,470	253,170	258,185
Durable goods manufacturing..........	152,573	146,518	148,059	154,435	159,675	165,098	169,251
Nondurable goods manufacturing..........	94,001	90,241	89,791	89,494	89,795	88,072	88,934
Wholesale trade	75,210	72,084	72,331	72,915	73,383	73,221	73,925
Retail trade............	228,377	225,250	226,833	225,986	226,212	229,291	232,630
Transportation and warehousing...........	53,443	52,615	53,889	55,519	57,164	58,978	59,631
Information	25,324	23,973	23,134	22,696	22,590	21,952	21,505
Finance and insurance	71,646	70,108	71,785	72,133	73,213	74,330	74,690
Real estate and rental and leasing..................	24,054	22,294	21,624	21,751	22,268	22,195	22,364
Professional, scientific, and technical services	97,920	95,256	94,483	95,043	95,300	95,337	96,750
Management of companies and enterprises..................	15,193	15,503	15,986	16,882	15,935	15,132	15,425
Administrative and waste services..................	94,477	99,964	104,326	107,967	109,121	113,746	117,814
Educational services	27,034	28,218	28,615	28,789	29,455	29,519	29,561
Health care and social assistance.................	195,160	197,726	198,675	201,010	204,147	205,388	209,653
Arts, entertainment, and recreation.................	18,086	16,625	16,050	15,774	16,004	16,274	16,906
Accommodation and food services.................	153,926	152,075	154,265	158,987	163,867	168,533	174,048
Other services, except public administration................	102,276	101,125	101,084	101,429	100,352	101,652	101,404
Government and government enterprises..................	411,582	413,236	408,069	403,496	400,911	400,391	398,821
				Dollars			
Average Wages and Salaries by Industry	38,628	39,635	40,485	41,317	41,592	42,644	43,622
Average Farm Wages and Salaries	18,427	22,863	18,821	27,739	19,497	23,998	26,452
Average Nonfarm Wages and Salaries	38,725	39,703	40,577	41,368	41,678	42,694	43,686
Average private wages and salaries...................	37,752	38,838	39,699	40,704	41,060	42,064	43,116
Forestry, fishing, and related activities................	28,958	32,048	32,595	33,458	33,957	35,373	36,448
Mining.................	68,410	74,445	77,634	76,348	78,022	80,858	80,462
Utilities................	80,492	78,776	85,829	88,196	88,367	88,433	95,521
Construction	41,226	43,392	43,501	45,271	45,536	47,815	48,737
Manufacturing.........	45,754	48,307	49,091	50,345	50,898	52,863	53,485
Durable goods manufacturing..........	48,015	51,067	51,712	52,908	53,255	55,079	55,710
Nondurable goods manufacturing..........	42,084	43,827	44,768	45,921	46,707	48,709	49,251
Wholesale trade	53,130	54,926	56,118	56,936	57,881	59,941	62,108
Retail trade............	24,013	24,509	24,732	25,299	25,618	25,876	26,493
Transportation and warehousing...........	40,145	41,823	42,913	44,147	44,152	45,960	46,790
Information	47,908	48,351	50,865	51,279	51,608	53,961	55,865
Finance and insurance	58,267	58,221	62,067	64,327	65,035	67,920	71,712
Real estate and rental and leasing..................	32,572	35,290	36,639	38,782	38,487	40,046	41,564
Professional, scientific, and technical services	64,835	66,031	68,145	69,703	70,637	71,513	73,288
Management of companies and enterprises..................	69,178	74,562	78,601	80,751	83,524	85,363	87,561
Administrative and waste services..................	25,044	26,198	26,109	26,721	26,705	27,120	27,388
Educational services	24,026	24,088	24,538	25,214	25,225	26,045	26,516
Health care and social assistance.................	41,132	41,578	42,263	43,284	43,381	44,159	45,494
Arts, entertainment, and recreation.................	18,904	18,832	18,850	19,878	20,329	20,478	21,418
Accommodation and food services.................	14,669	15,206	15,578	16,051	16,281	16,587	17,201
Other services, except public administration................	26,679	27,863	28,435	28,975	29,785	30,815	32,136
Government and government enterprises..................	42,403	42,907	43,879	43,927	44,101	45,200	45,995

Table AL-10. Employment Characteristics by Family Type

(Number, percent.)

Family type and labor force status	2013 Total	2013 Families with own children under 18 years	2014 Total	2014 Families with own children under 18 years	2015 Total	2015 Families with own children under 18 years
All Families..	1,222,568	492,554	1,229,579	485,990	1,213,540	486,977
FAMILY TYPE AND LABOR FORCE STATUS						
Married-Couple Families.........................	857,865	305,444	867,090	305,881	863,674	306,591
Both husband and wife in labor force................	46.7	63.6	46.3	63.6	45.6	64.0
Husband in labor force, wife not in labor force	23.4	28.8	23.7	29.0	23.7	28.5
Wife in labor force, husband not in labor force	8.7	5.1	8.5	4.8	8.0	4.2
Both husband and wife not in labor force..............	20.9	2.3	21.5	2.5	22.2	3.0
Other Families	364,703	187,110	362,489	180,109	349,866	180,386
Female householder, no husband present................	77.9	81.4	78.6	82.7	77.6	80.8
In labor force....................................	49.5	64.4	48.8	64.5	49.1	63.7
Not in labor force	28.5	16.9	29.8	18.2	28.5	17.1
Male householder, no wife present...................	22.1	18.6	21.4	17.3	22.4	19.2
In labor force....................................	16.1	16.7	14.4	14.7	15.5	16.3
Not in labor force	6	2.0	7.0	2.6	6.8	2.9

Table AL-11. School Enrollment and Educational Attainment, 2015

(Number, percent.)

Item	State	U.S.
Enrollment		
Total population 3 years and over, enrolled in school	1,191,243	81,618,288
Enrolled in nursery school or preschool (percent)...............	5.5	6.0
Enrolled in kindergarten (percent).............................	5.5	5.0
Enrolled in elementary school, grades 1-8 (percent).............	41.7	40.3
Enrolled in high school, grades 9-12 (percent).................	21.9	20.9
Enrolled in college or graduate school (percent)...............	25.4	27.7
Attainment		
Total population 25 years and over	3,282,252	216,447,163
Less than ninth grade (percent)...............................	4.8	5.5
9th to 12th grade, no diploma (percent).......................	10.3	7.3
High school graduate, including equivalency (percent)...........	31.0	27.6
Some college, no degree (percent).............................	21.6	20.7
Associate's degree (percent)..................................	8.1	8.2
Bachelor's degree (percent)...................................	15.4	19.0
Graduate or professional degree (percent)......................	8.8	11.6
High school graduate or higher (percent)	84.9	87.1
Bachelor's degree or higher (percent).........................	24.2	30.6

Table AL-12. Public School Characteristics and Educational Indicators

(Number, percent; data derived from National Center of Education Statistics.)

Item	State	U.S.
Public Schools, 2014–2015 (except where noted)		
Number of school districts...................................	179	18,260
Number of schools...	1,519	98,373
Number of students..	744,164	50,312,581
Number of teachers..	42,737	3,132,351
Student-teacher ratio..	17.4	16.1
Expenditures per student (dollars), FY 2014....................	9,036	11,066
Four-year adjusted cohort graduation rate (ACGR)[1,2]	89.3	83.2
Students eligible for free or reduced-price lunch (percent).....	51.8	51.8
English language learners (percent)..........................	2.4	9.4
Students age 3 to 21 served under IDEA, part B (percent)........	11.1	13.0

Public Schools by Type	Number	Percent of state public schools
Total number of schools....................................	1,519	100.0
Regular	1,333	87.8
Special education...	35	2.3
Vocational education..	67	4.4
Alternative education.......................................	84	5.5

NOTE: Every school is assigned only one school type based on its instructional emphasis.
[1] ACGR data represents a new method of calculating high-school completion rates and may not be comparable to previous years' data for Averaged Freshmen Graduation Rates (AFGR).
[2] The United States 4-year ACGRs were estimated using both the reported 4-year ACGR data from 49 states and the District of Columbia and using imputed data for Idaho. The estimate for American Indian/Alaska Native students also includes imputed data for Virginia.

Table AL-13. Reported Voting and Registration of the Voting-Age Population, November 2016

(Numbers in thousands, percent.)

Item	Total population	Total citizen population	Registered			Voted		
			Total registered	Percent registered (total population)	Percent registered (total citizen population)	Total voted	Percent voted (total population)	Percent voted (total citizen population)
U.S. Total	245,502	224,059	157,596	64.2	70.3	137,537	56.0	61.4
State Total.....................	3,717	3,651	2,526	68.0	69.2	2,095	56.4	57.4
Sex								
Male	1,761	1,718	1,155	65.6	67.2	944	53.6	54.9
Female	1,955	1,933	1,371	70.1	70.9	1,151	58.9	59.6
Race								
White alone....................	2,633	2,604	1,772	67.3	68.0	1,465	55.6	56.2
White, non-Hispanic alone	2,532	2,526	1,742	68.8	69.0	1,441	56.9	57.0
Black alone....................	962	953	694	72.2	72.8	579	60.2	60.8
Asian alone....................	27	10	3	(B)	(B)	3	(B)	(B)
Hispanic (of any race)	117	83	32	(B)	(B)	27	(B)	(B)
White alone or in combination	2,673	2,644	1,801	67.4	68.1	1,489	55.7	56.3
Black alone or in combination..........	985	976	704	71.5	72.1	587	59.6	60.2
Asian alone or in combination..........	36	19	6	(B)	(B)	6	(B)	(B)
Age								
18 to 24 years....................	513	497	283	55.2	57.0	212	41.4	42.7
25 to 34 years....................	583	568	393	67.5	69.2	310	53.1	54.5
35 to 44 years....................	566	548	363	64.1	66.3	306	54.0	55.8
45 to 64 years....................	1,293	1,280	881	68.1	68.8	761	58.8	59.4
65 years and over	761	758	606	79.5	79.9	507	66.5	66.9

- = Zero or rounds to zero.
B = Base is less than 75,000 and therefore too small to show the derived measure.

Table AL-14. Crime

(Number, rate per 100,000. Data are derived from the FBI Uniform Crime Reports.)

Item	State [1]			U.S. [1,2,3,4]		
	2014	2015	Percent change	2014	2015	Percent change
TOTAL POPULATION[5]	4,846,411	4,858,979	0.3	318,907,401	321,418,820	0.8
VIOLENT CRIME						
Number....................	20,727	22,952	10.7	1,186,185	1,231,566	3.8
Rate	427.7	472.4	10.4	372.0	383.2	3.0
Murder and Nonnegligent Manslaughter						
Number....................	276	348	26.1	14,164	15,696	10.8
Rate	5.7	7.2	25.8	4.4	4.9	10.0
Rape[6]						
Number....................	2,005	2,039	1.7	118,027	124,047	5.1
Rate	41.4	42.0	1.4	37.0	38.6	4.3
Robbery						
Number....................	4,702	4,611	-1.9	322,905	327,374	1.4
Rate	97.0	94.9	-2.2	101.3	101.9	0.6
Aggravated Assault						
Number....................	13,744	15,954	16.1	731,089	764,449	4.6
Rate	283.6	328.3	15.8	229.2	237.8	3.7
PROPERTY CRIME						
Number....................	154,087	144,746	-6.1	8,209,010	7,993,631	-2.6
Rate	3,179.4	2,978.9	-6.3	2,574.1	2,487.0	-3.4
Burglary						
Number....................	39,723	35,255	-11.2	1,713,153	1,579,527	-7.8
Rate	819.6	725.6	-11.5	537.2	491.4	-8.5
Larceny-Theft						
Number....................	104,223	99,156	-4.9	5,809,054	5,706,346	-1.8
Rate	2,150.5	2,040.7	-5.1	1,821.5	1,775.4	-2.5
Motor Vehicle Theft						
Number....................	10,141	10,335	1.9	686,803	707,758	3.1
Rate	209.2	212.7	1.6	215.4	220.2	2.2

NOTE: Although arson data are included in the trend and clearance tables, sufficient data are not available to estimate totals for this offense. Therefore, no arson data are published in this table.
X = Not applicable.
- = Zero or rounds to zero.
[1] Because of changes in the state's reporting practices, figures are not comparable to previous years' data.
[2] The crime figures have been adjusted.
[3] The data collection methodology for the offense of forcible rape used by the Minnesota state Uniform Crime Reporting (UCR) Program (with the exception of Minneapolis and St. Paul, Minnesota) does not comply with national UCR Program guidelines. Consequently, its figures for forcible rape and violent crime (of which forcible rape is a part) are not published in this table.
[4] Includes offenses reported by the Zoological Police and the Metro Transit Police.
[5] Populations are U.S. Census Bureau provisional estimates as of July 1 of each year.
[6] The figures shown for the 2013 offense of rape were estimated using the revised Uniform Crime Reporting (UCR) definition of rape. Figures are not comparable to data from previous years.

Table AL-15. State Government Finances, 2015

(Dollar amounts in thousands, percent distribution.)

Item	Dollars	Percent distribution
Total Revenue	26,896,290	100.0
General revenue	24,624,640	91.6
Intergovernmental revenue	8,838,667	32.9
Taxes	9,755,439	36.3
General sales	2,463,912	9.2
Selective sales	2,472,137	9.2
License taxes	493,883	1.8
Individual income tax	3,336,587	12.4
Corporate income tax	533,586	2.0
Other taxes	455,334	1.7
Current charges	4,600,676	17.1
Miscellaneous general revenue	1,429,858	5.3
Utility revenue	0	-
Liquor stores revenue	308,180	1.1
Insurance trust revenue[1]	1,963,470	7.3
Total Expenditure	29,377,161	100.0
Intergovernmental expenditure	6,612,535	22.5
Direct expenditure	22,764,626	77.5
Current operation	15,965,471	54.3
Capital outlay	2,082,490	7.1
Insurance benefits and repayments	3,651,229	12.4
Assistance and subsidies	699,293	2.4
Interest on debt	366,143	1.2
Exhibit: Salaries and wages	4,638,869	15.8
Total Expenditure	29,377,161	100.0
General expenditure	25,436,524	86.6
Intergovernmental expenditure	6,612,535	22.5
Direct expenditure	18,823,989	64.1
General expenditure, by function:		
Education	10,786,908	36.7
Public welfare	6,872,757	23.4
Hospitals	2,353,941	8.0
Health	526,982	1.8
Highways	1,810,319	6.2
Police protection	185,170	0.6
Correction	562,859	1.9
Natural resources	281,706	1.0
Parks and recreation	19,647	0.1
Governmental administration	608,951	2.1
Interest on general debt	366,143	1.2
Other and unallocable	1,061,141	3.6
Utility expenditure	0	-
Liquor stores expenditure	289,408	1.0
Insurance trust expenditure	3,651,229	12.4
Debt at End of Fiscal Year	8,969,350	X
Cash and Security Holdings	44,861,358	X

X = Not applicable.
- = Zero or rounds to zero.
[1] Within insurance trust revenue, net earnings of state retirement systems is a calculated statistic (the item code in the data file is X08), and thus can be positive or negative. Net earnings is the sum of earnings on investments plus gains on investments minus losses on investments. The change made in 2002 for asset valuation from book to market value in accordance with Statement 34 of the Governmental Accounting Standards Board is reflected in the calculated statistics.

Table AL-16. State Government Tax Collections, 2016

(Dollars in thousands, percent.)

Item	Dollars	Percent distribution
Total Taxes	9,919,794	100.0
Property taxes	346,277	3.5
Sales and gross receipts	5,106,102	51.5
General sales and gross receipts	2,596,223	26.2
Selective sales and gross receipts	2,509,879	25.3
Alcoholic beverages	210,535	2.1
Amusements	6	-
Insurance premiums	317,657	3.2
Motor fuels	526,763	5.3
Pari-mutuels	1,401	0.0
Public utilities	695,626	7.0
Tobacco products	180,301	1.8
Other selective sales	577,590	5.8
Licenses	507,479	5.1
Alcoholic beverages	4,224	-
Amusements	0	-
Corporations in general	162,117	1.6
Hunting and fishing	22,931	0.2
Motor vehicle	213,550	2.2
Motor vehicle operators	33,964	0.3
Public utilities	14,443	0.1
Occupation and business, NEC	56,250	0.6
Other licenses	0	-
Income taxes	3,869,584	39.0
Individual income	3,492,904	35.2
Corporation net income	376,680	3.8
Other taxes	90,352	0.9
Death and gift	0	-
Documentary and stock transfer	43,730	0.4
Severance	46,622	0.5
Taxes, NEC	0	-

- = Zero or rounds to zero.

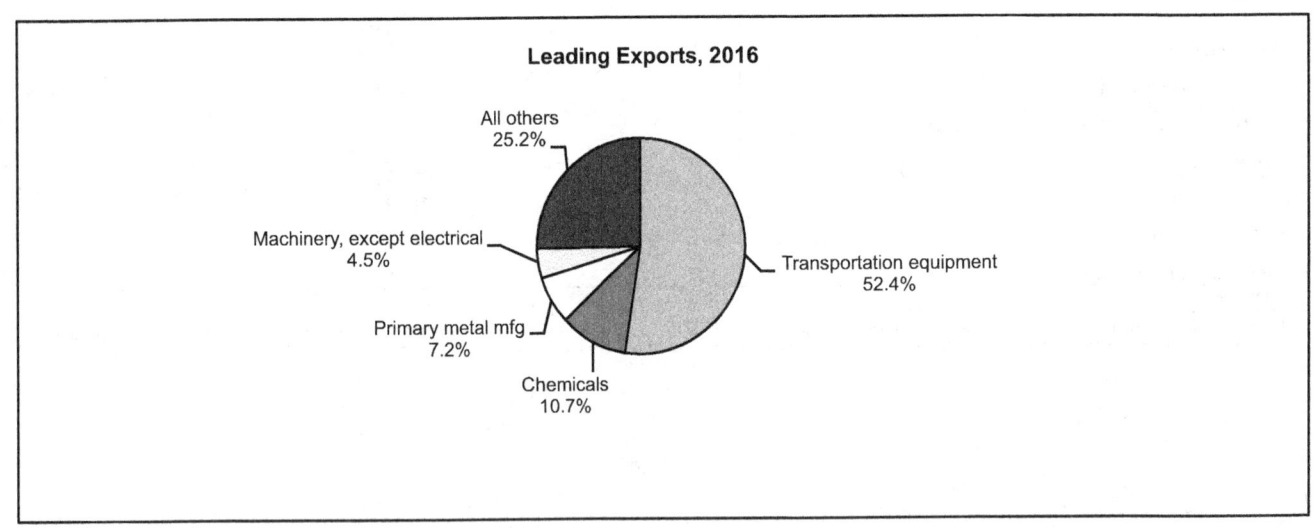

Leading Exports, 2016

All others 25.2%

Machinery, except electrical 4.5%

Primary metal mfg 7.2%

Chemicals 10.7%

Transportation equipment 52.4%

ALASKA

Facts and Figures

Location: Northwestern North America; bordered on the N by the Arctic Ocean, on the E by Canada, on the S by the Pacific Ocean and the Gulf of Alaska, and on the W by the Bering Sea

Area: 665,384 sq. mi. (1,717,854 sq. sq. km.); rank—1st

Population: 741,894 (2016 est.); rank—48th

Principal Cities: capital—Juneau; largest—Anchorage

Statehood: January 3, 1959; 49th state

U.S. Congress: 2 senators, 1 representative

State Motto: North to the Future

State Song: "Alaska's Flag"

State Nicknames: The Last Frontier; The Land of the Midnight Sun

Abbreviations: AK

State Symbols: flower—forget-me-not; tree—Sitka spruce; bird—willow ptarmigan

At a Glance

- With an increase in population of 4.5 percent, Alaska ranked 23rd among the states for growth from 2010 to 2016.

- Alaska's 2015 violent crime rate ranked 2nd in the nation at 730.2 per 100,000 population, and the property crime rate (2,817.6 per 100,000 population) ranked 18th.

- Alaska was the state with the second highest birth rate in 2015, at 15.3 births per 1,000 population.

- In 2015, 10.3 percent of Alaskans lived below the poverty level, the 5th lowest percent in the nation.

- Of all the states, Alaska had the 4th highest percentage of residents under 18 years old (25.2 percent) and the lowest percentage of residents age 65 and over (10.4 percent) in 2016.

Table AK-1. Population by Age, Sex, Race, and Hispanic Origin

(Number, percent, except where noted.)

Sex, age, race, and Hispanic origin	2000	2010	2016 [1]	Average annual percent change, 2010–2016
Total Population....................................	626,932	710,231	741,894	0.3
Percent of total U.S. population	0.2	0.2	0.2	X
Sex				
Male...	324,112	369,628	388,132	0.3
Female	302,820	340,603	353,762	0.2
Age				
Under 5 years..	47,591	53,996	54,115	-
5 to 19 years..	160,526	153,844	151,122	-0.1
20 to 64 years...	383,116	447,453	459,451	0.2
65 years and over......................................	35,699	54,938	77,206	2.5
Median age (years)	32.4	33.8	33.9	-
Race and Hispanic Origin				
One race..				
White..	434,534	483,873	490,389	0.1
Black..	21,787	24,441	27,898	0.9
American Indian and Alaska Native	98,043	106,268	112,404	0.4
Asian..	25,116	38,882	46,912	1.3
Native Hawaiian or Other Pacific Islander	3,309	7,622	9,870	1.8
Two or more races	34,146	49,105	54,421	0.7
Hispanic (of any race)	25,852	44,490	51,599	1.0

X = Not applicable.
[1] Population figures for 2016 are July 1 estimates. The 2010 estimates are taken from the 2010 Census.
- = Zero or rounds to zero.

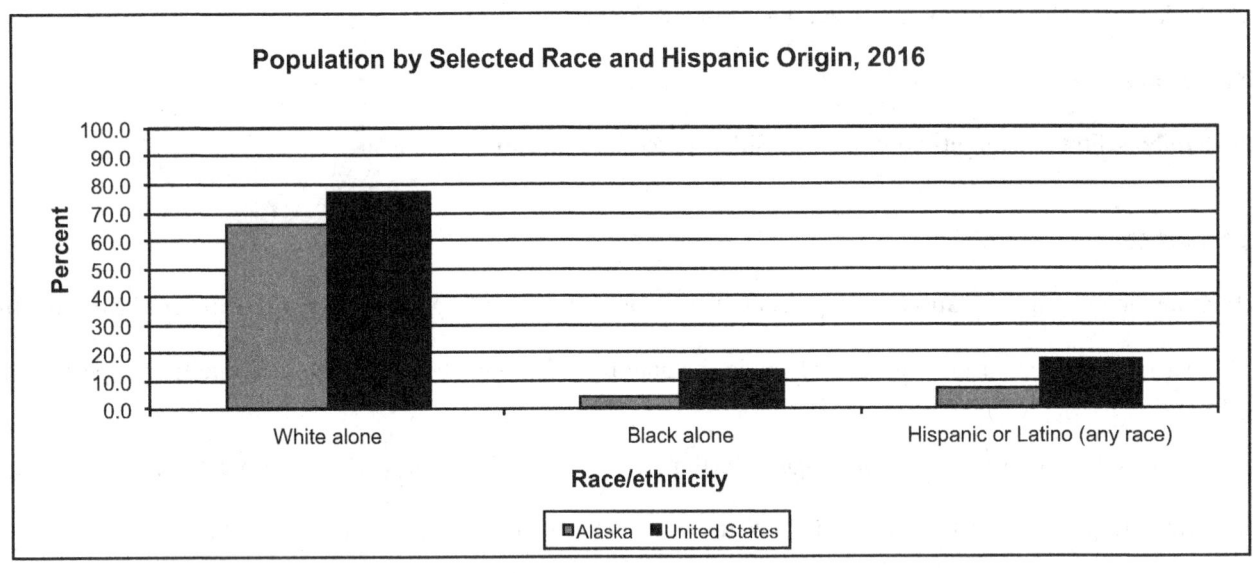

Population by Selected Race and Hispanic Origin, 2016

Legend: ■ Alaska   ■ United States

(X-axis: Race/ethnicity — White alone, Black alone, Hispanic or Latino (any race); Y-axis: Percent)

Table AK-2. Marital Status

(Number, percent distribution.)

Sex, age, and marital status	2000	2010	2015
Males, 15 Years and Over	243,024	290,598	308,121
Never married	32.5	35.5	40.4
Now married, except separated...........................	53.6	49.7	46.2
Separated..	1.7	1.7	1.7
Widowed..	1.4	1.8	1.8
Divorced...	10.8	11.4	10.0
Females, 15 Years and Over	225,837	267,563	274,498
Never married	24.1	27.3	30.5
Now married, except separated...........................	55.6	50.2	48.2
Separated..	2.3	2.6	2.3
Widowed..	5.6	6.1	5.7
Divorced...	12.5	13.7	13.3

Table AK-3. Households and Housing Characteristics

(Number, percent, dollars.)

Item	2000	2010	2015	Average annual percent change, 2000–2015
Total Households...	221,600	254,610	250,185	0.9
Family households...	152,337	170,859	163,800	0.5
Married-couple family................................	116,318	127,969	120,348	0.2
Other family...	36,019	42,890	43,452	1.4
Male householder, no wife present............	12,082	14,211	15,109	1.7
Female householder, no husband present....	23,937	28,679	28,343	1.2
Nonfamily households.....................................	69,263	83,751	86,385	1.6
Householder living alone.............................	52,060	63,698	66,763	1.9
Householder not living alone.......................	17,203	20,053	19,622	0.9
Housing Characteristics				
Total housing units..	260,978	307,065	309,453	1.2
Occupied housing units	221,600	254,610	250,185	0.9
Owner occupied...	138,509	162,785	159,922	1.0
Renter occupied..	83,091	91,825	90,263	0.6
Average household size...................................	2.74	2.70	2.84	0.2
Financial Characteristics				
Median gross rent of renter-occupied housing	720	981	1,163	4.1
Median monthly owner costs for housing units with a mortgage	1,315	1,772	1,817	2.5
Median value of owner-occupied housing units	144,200	241,400	259,600	5.3

Table AK-4. Migration, Origin, and Language

(Number, percent.)

Characteristic	State			U.S.		
	2014	2015	Percent change	2014	2015	Percent change
Residence 1 Year Ago						
Population 1 year and over	725,206	727,862	0.4	315,095,393	317,635,720	0.8
Same house	80.8	80.1	X	85.1	85.3	X
Different house in the U.S.	18.6	19.3	X	14.3	14.1	X
Same county	10.9	11.9	X	8.7	8.5	X
Different county	7.7	7.4	X	5.6	5.6	X
Same state	2.5	2.7	X	3.3	3.2	X
Different state	5.2	4.8	X	2.3	2.4	X
Abroad	0.6	0.6	X	0.6	0.7	X
Place of Birth						
Native born	682,060	679,888	-0.3	276,465,262	278,128,449	0.6
Male	52.5	53.3	X	49.3	49.3	X
Female	47.5	46.7	X	50.7	50.7	X
Foreign born	54,672	58,544	7.1	42,391,794	43,290,372	2.1
Male	49.9	44.8	X	48.7	48.6	X
Female	50.1	55.2	X	51.3	51.4	X
Foreign born; naturalized U.S. citizen................	30,598	32,367	5.8	19,984,738	20,697,103	3.6
Male	49.0	45.7	X	45.9	45.9	X
Female	51.0	54.3	X	54.1	54.1	X
Foreign born; not a U.S. citizen.....................	24,074	26,177	8.7	22,407,056	22,593,269	0.8
Male	51.0	43.6	X	51.2	51.1	X
Female	49.0	56.4	X	48.8	48.9	X
Entered 2010 or later	10.7	17.8	X	12.3	15.6	X
Entered 2000 to 2009	32.5	29.6	X	28.6	27.9	X
Entered before 2000....................................	56.8	52.7	X	59.1	56.5	X
World Region of Birth, Foreign						
Foreign-born population, excluding population born at sea	54,672	58,544	7.1	42,390,705	43,289,646	2.1
Europe	17.1	15.4	X	11.2	11.1	X
Asia	53.7	55.9	X	30.1	30.6	X
Africa	4.0	4.3	X	4.6	4.8	X
Oceania	2.2	1.9	X	0.6	0.6	X
Latin America...	17.6	18	X	51.6	51.1	X
North America	5.4	4.4	X	1.9	1.9	X
Language Spoken at Home and Ability to Speak English						
Population 5 years and over............................	683,324	683,671	0.1	299,084,046	301,625,014	0.8
English only	83.4	83.8	X	78.9	78.5	X
Language other than English........................	16.6	16.2	X	21.1	21.5	X
Speaks English less than "very well"............	5.1	5.1	X	8.6	8.6	X

NA = Not available.
X = Not applicable.
- = Zero or rounds to zero.

Table AK-5. Median Income and Poverty Status, 2015

(Number, percent, except as noted.)

Characteristic	State		U.S.	
	Number	Percent	Number	Percent
Median Income				
Households (dollars)..	73,355	X	55,775	X
Families (dollars)	86,376	X	68,260	X
Below Poverty Level (All People)	74,532	10.3	46,153,077	14.7
Sex				
Male	35,945	9.6	20,599,407	13.4
Female	38,587	11.2	25,553,670	16.0
Age				
Under 18 years..	27,849	15.2	15,000,273	20.7
Related children under 18 years..........................	26,659	14.6	14,693,239	20.4
18 to 64 years	43,545	9.3	26,960,369	13.9
65 years and over	3,138	4.5	4,192,435	9.0

X = Not applicable.

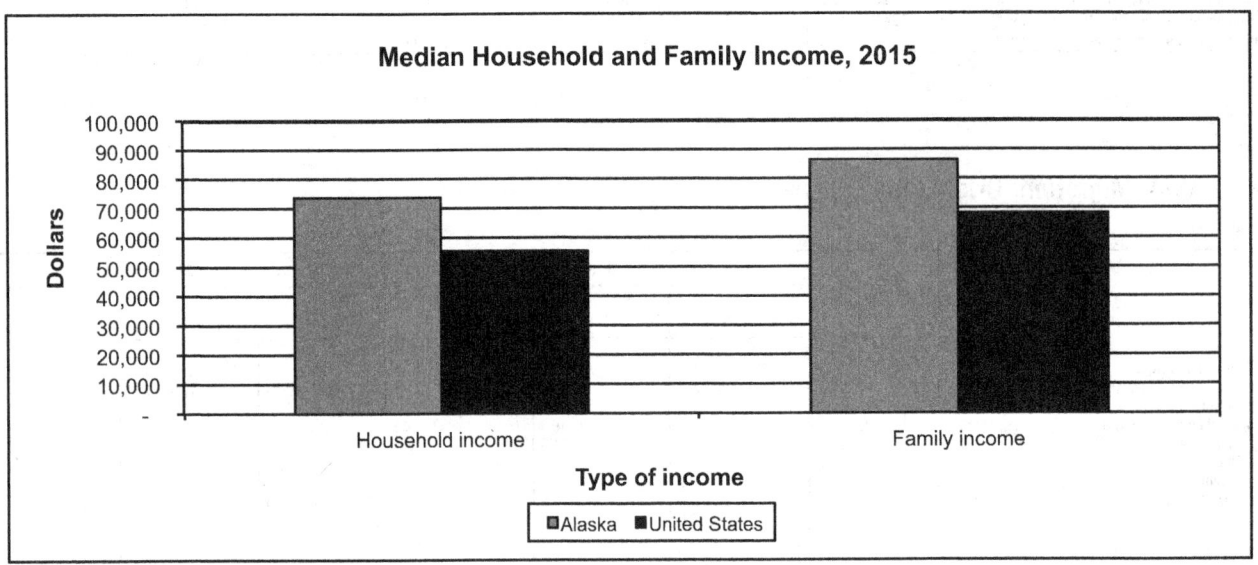

Median Household and Family Income, 2015

Table AK-6. Health Insurance Coverage Status for the Civilian Noninstitutionalized Population and Children Under 18 Years of Age

(Numbers in thousands, percent.)

Item	2007	2008	2009	2010	2011	2012	2013	2014	2015
Civilian Noninstitutionalized Population	675	659	678	689	699	709	712	712	713
Covered by Private or Public Insurance									
Number...	552	635	535	552	559	564	580	589	607
Percent..	81.8	96.4	78.9	80.1	79.9	79.5	81.5	82.8	85.1
Not Covered									
Number...	123	24	143	137	141	145	132	122	106
Percent..	18.2	3.6	21.1	19.9	20.1	20.5	18.5	17.2	14.9
Percent in the U.S. not covered...............................	15.3	15.1	15.1	15.5	15.1	14.8	14.5	11.7	9.4
Children Under 18 Years of Age	185	180	183	188	188	187	188	186	186
Covered by Private or Public Insurance									
Number...	164	156	158	165	166	161	166	165	166
Percent..	88.6	86.7	86.4	87.8	88.2	86.1	88.4	88.6	89.4
Not Covered									
Number...	21	24	25	23	22	26	22	21	20
Percent..	11.4	13.3	13.6	12.2	11.8	13.9	11.6	11.4	10.6
Percent in the U.S. not covered...............................	11.0	9.7	8.6	8.0	7.5	7.2	7.1	6.0	4.8

Table AK-7. Employment Status by Demographic Group, 2016

(Numbers in thousands, percent.)

Characteristic	Civilian noninstitutional population	Civilian labor force		Employed		Unemployed	
		Number	Percent of population	Number	Percent of population	Number	Percent of population
Total	543	357	65.8	334	61.5	24	6.6
Sex							
Male..	279	192	68.9	178	63.9	14	7.2
Female...	264	165	62.6	155	58.9	10	6.0
Race, Sex, and Hispanic Origin							
White...	361	242	67.0	230	63.7	12	5.0
Male...	188	132	70.1	124	66.1	8	5.7
Female......................................	173	110	63.7	106	61.0	5	4.2
Black or African American.................	19	15	79.4	14	74.6	1	6.1
Male...	NA	NA	NA	NA	NA	NA	NA
Female......................................	NA	NA	NA	NA	NA	NA	NA
Hispanic or Latino ethnicity[1].............	33	25	75.5	24	72.4	1	4.4
Male...	17	13	80.4	13	76.0	1	5.0
Female......................................	16	11	70.4	11	67.5	...	3.7
Age							
16 to 19 years...............................	38	13	35.1	11	28.1	3	19.7
20 to 24 years...............................	53	38	71.5	34	64.7	4	9.2
25 to 34 years...............................	108	86	79.3	80	73.8	6	7.0
35 to 44 years...............................	86	71	82.9	67	78.1	4	5.9
45 to 54 years...............................	91	74	81.1	70	77.2	3	4.6
55 to 64 years...............................	88	56	63.9	54	60.7	3	5.0
65 years and over...........................	79	19	24.4	18	22.9	1	6.8

NOTE: Data in Table 7 are from the Current Population Survey (CPS) and do not match the estimates in Table 8. See notes and definitions for further information.
[1] May be of any race.
NA = Not available.
... = Fewer than 500 persons.

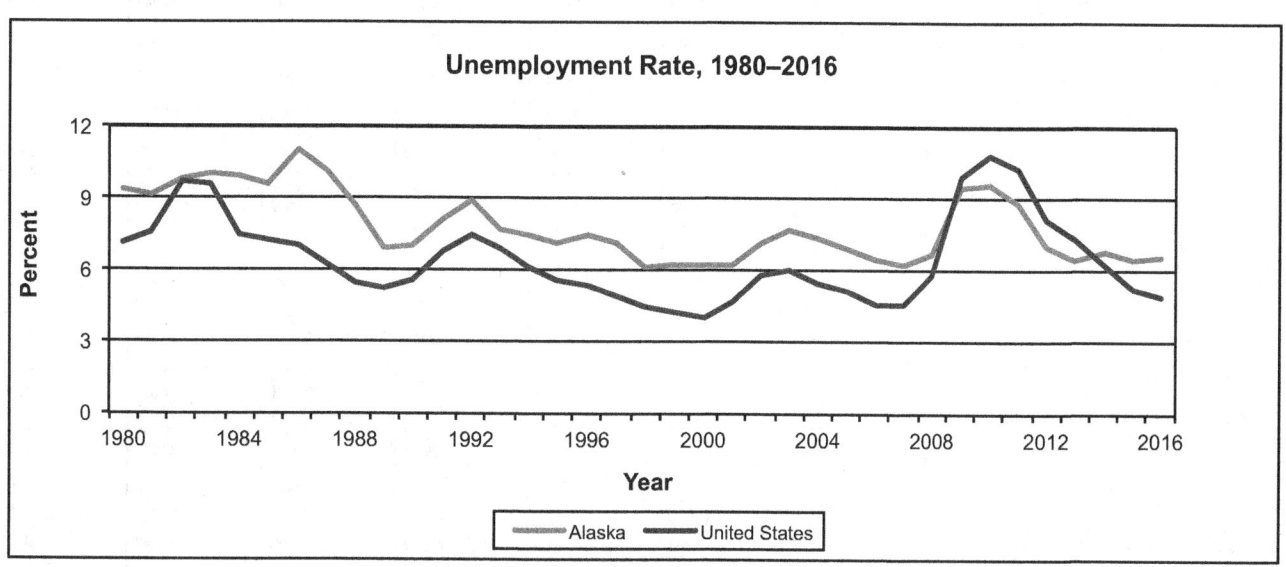

Table AK-8. Employment Status of the Civilian Noninstitutional Population Age 16 Years and Over

(Number, percent.)

Year	Civilian labor force	Civilian participation rate	Employed	Unemployed	Unemployment rate
2008..	356,109	71.0	332,285	23,824	6.7
2009..	359,647	70.3	331,792	27,855	7.7
2010..	361,913	69.8	333,416	28,497	7.9
2011..	365,913	69.2	338,161	27,752	7.6
2012..	365,674	68.3	339,608	26,066	7.1
2013..	365,216	67.8	339,957	25,259	6.9
2014..	365,890	67.7	340,804	25,086	6.9
2015..	363,822	67.1	340,227	23,595	6.5
2016..	360,426	66.1	336,620	23,806	6.6

Table AK-9. Employment and Average Wages by Industry

(Estimates through 2010 are based on the 2007 *North American Industry Classification System* [NAICS]. Estimates from 2011 onward are based on the 2012 NAICS.)

Industry	2009	2010	2011	2012	2013	2014	2015
	Number of Jobs						
Wage and Salary Employment by Industry..................	351,916	352,718	358,857	365,191	365,944	366,208	367,355
Farm Wage and Salary Employment.........................	496	522	602	421	427	510	465
Nonfarm Wage and Salary Employment.....................	351,420	352,196	358,255	364,770	365,517	365,698	366,890
Private wage and salary employment.......................	243,512	244,008	249,399	255,836	258,465	260,634	262,320
Forestry, fishing, and related activities.....................	505	657	896	656	660	693	702
Mining...	14,879	15,020	15,592	16,611	16,997	17,586	17,062
Utilities...	1,982	2,141	2,106	2,117	2,135	2,112	2,139
Construction...	17,053	16,607	16,324	16,721	16,882	17,597	18,137
Manufacturing...	12,878	12,758	13,705	14,109	14,462	14,436	14,067
Durable goods manufacturing..............................	2,042	1,888	1,862	2,203	2,253	2,073	2,143
Nondurable goods manufacturing.........................	10,836	10,870	11,843	11,906	12,209	12,363	11,924
Wholesale trade	6,379	6,310	6,354	6,309	6,647	6,541	6,572
Retail trade..	36,223	35,845	36,123	36,195	36,201	37,094	37,727
Transportation and warehousing............................	19,577	18,995	19,383	19,900	19,633	19,536	19,786
Information..	6,607	6,449	6,327	6,210	6,156	6,248	6,303
Finance and insurance	7,299	7,303	7,386	7,393	7,412	7,325	7,354
Real estate and rental and leasing........................	5,049	5,129	5,039	4,956	4,966	4,961	4,926
Professional, scientific, and technical services...........	13,837	13,980	14,560	15,010	15,214	14,919	14,766
Management of companies and enterprises.................	2,697	2,724	2,773	3,008	3,058	3,003	3,140
Administrative and waste services	11,570	11,389	11,614	12,123	12,166	12,298	12,300
Educational services	3,022	3,143	3,212	3,207	3,295	3,298	3,385
Health care and social assistance.........................	38,701	40,538	41,911	43,874	44,652	44,256	44,681
Arts, entertainment, and recreation........................	4,574	4,472	4,801	4,902	4,912	4,861	4,845
Accommodation and food services	26,912	27,226	27,921	28,593	29,015	29,544	30,337
Other services, except public administration.................	13,768	13,322	13,372	13,942	14,002	14,326	14,091
Government and government enterprises.........................	107,908	108,188	108,856	108,934	107,052	105,064	104,570
	Dollars						
Average Wages and Salaries by Industry	49,842	51,070	52,365	53,658	54,545	56,348	57,740
Average Farm Wages and Salaries	33,111	29,933	24,882	39,606	39,466	33,643	38,966
Average Nonfarm Wages and Salaries	49,866	51,101	52,411	53,674	54,563	56,380	57,764
Average private wages and salaries........................	48,489	49,575	50,861	52,290	53,460	55,541	57,093
Forestry, fishing, and related activities.....................	43,497	48,457	51,664	58,331	63,388	61,359	60,128
Mining...	119,750	121,745	124,558	128,007	130,797	137,532	141,148
Utilities...	76,026	75,420	81,402	85,969	88,148	88,473	93,159
Construction...	70,203	72,663	72,537	74,449	77,220	81,759	83,914
Manufacturing...	39,482	41,145	41,325	43,338	45,126	45,425	50,817
Durable goods manufacturing..............................	51,699	51,287	51,402	55,714	58,459	59,753	63,015
Nondurable goods manufacturing.........................	37,180	39,383	39,740	41,048	42,666	43,023	48,624
Wholesale trade	54,227	54,317	55,474	56,158	56,190	57,655	60,027
Retail trade..	29,532	30,026	30,580	31,394	31,630	32,448	32,951
Transportation and warehousing............................	59,621	60,853	62,591	63,158	64,324	66,085	66,515
Information..	58,388	57,703	61,579	62,060	63,544	65,843	68,255
Finance and insurance	57,280	58,382	60,060	62,606	63,364	65,800	68,410
Real estate and rental and leasing........................	38,691	40,481	40,715	41,833	42,492	44,021	45,352
Professional, scientific, and technical services...............	65,994	67,780	70,873	72,401	74,276	77,030	77,656
Management of companies and enterprises...................	79,013	83,852	85,027	84,446	81,416	87,302	87,662
Administrative and waste services	42,892	43,681	43,607	44,461	44,421	46,346	47,820
Educational services	28,839	28,712	28,378	29,406	29,646	29,049	29,069
Health care and social assistance............................	44,173	44,870	46,811	47,687	48,882	50,398	52,897
Arts, entertainment, and recreation........................	19,594	20,823	21,858	22,490	23,463	24,326	25,102
Accommodation and food services	22,700	23,129	23,934	24,694	25,312	26,739	27,742
Other services, except public administration.................	32,379	34,280	34,795	35,092	36,093	37,282	38,645
Government and government enterprises.........................	52,973	54,542	55,962	56,923	57,225	58,460	59,445

Table AK-10. Employment Characteristics by Family Type

(Number, percent.)

Family type and labor force status	2013 Total	2013 Families with own children under 18 years	2014 Total	2014 Families with own children under 18 years	2015 Total	2015 Families with own children under 18 years
All Families..	165,431	76,918	164,518	81,338	163,800	77,964
FAMILY TYPE AND LABOR FORCE STATUS						
Married-Couple Families.....................................	126,502	54,850	123,531	56,246	120,348	50,683
Both husband and wife in labor force....................	58.1	64.2	55.9	61.4	56.4	64.3
Husband in labor force, wife not in labor force	22	28.5	23.2	30.0	24.2	30.4
Wife in labor force, husband not in labor force	8.8	5.2	8.2	5.3	6.5	3.5
Both husband and wife not in labor force................	10.9	2	12.8	3.3	12.4	1.5
Other Families	38,929	22,068	40,987	25,092	43,452	27,281
Female householder, no husband present.....................	63.8	64.4	64.2	65.7	65.2	66.7
In labor force....................................	47.6	54.6	47.6	54.1	50.0	58.8
Not in labor force	16.2	9.8	16.6	11.5	15.2	7.9
Male householder, no wife present........................	36.2	35.6	35.8	34.3	34.8	33.3
In labor force....................................	30.5	32.4	28.5	30.5	27.9	28.4
Not in labor force	5.7	3.2	7.3	3.9	6.9	4.9

Table AK-11. School Enrollment and Educational Attainment, 2015

(Number, percent.)

Item	State	U.S.
Enrollment		
Total population 3 years and over, enrolled in school	189,880	81,618,288
Enrolled in nursery school or preschool (percent)................................	5.7	6.0
Enrolled in kindergarten (percent)................................	5.4	5.0
Enrolled in elementary school, grades 1-8 (percent)................................	39.8	40.3
Enrolled in high school, grades 9-12 (percent)	22.0	20.9
Enrolled in college or graduate school (percent)................................	27.0	27.7
Attainment		
Total population 25 years and over	469,523	216,447,163
Less than ninth grade (percent)................................	2.6	5.5
9th to 12th grade, no diploma (percent)	4.8	7.3
High school graduate, including equivalency (percent)................................	27.3	27.6
Some college, no degree (percent)................................	27.5	20.7
Associate's degree (percent)................................	8.1	8.2
Bachelor's degree (percent)	18.7	19.0
Graduate or professional degree (percent)................................	11.0	11.6
High school graduate or higher (percent)	92.6	87.1
Bachelor's degree or higher (percent)................................	29.7	30.6

Table AK-12. Public School Characteristics and Educational Indicators

(Number, percent; data derived from National Center of Education Statistics.)

Item	State	U.S.
Public Schools, 2014–2015 (except where noted)		
Number of school districts................................	54	18,260
Number of schools................................	507	98,373
Number of students	131,176	50,312,581
Number of teachers	7,759	3,132,351
Student-teacher ratio	16.9	16.1
Expenditures per student (dollars), FY 2014................................	18,466	11,066
Four-year adjusted cohort graduation rate (ACGR)[1,2]	75.6	83.2
Students eligible for free or reduced-price lunch (percent)	43.1	51.8
English language learners (percent)................................	11.5	9.4
Students age 3 to 21 served under IDEA, part B (percent)................................	13.7	13.0

Public Schools by Type	Number	Percent of state public schools
Total number of schools................................	507	100.0
Regular	461	90.9
Special education................................	3	0.6
Vocational education................................	3	0.6
Alternative education................................	40	7.9

NOTE: Every school is assigned only one school type based on its instructional emphasis.
[1] ACGR data represents a new method of calculating high-school completion rates and may not be comparable to previous years' data for Averaged Freshmen Graduation Rates (AFGR).
[2] The United States 4-year ACGRs were estimated using both the reported 4-year ACGR data from 49 states and the District of Columbia and using imputed data for Idaho. The estimate for American Indian/Alaska Native students also includes imputed data for Virginia.

Table AK-13. Reported Voting and Registration of the Voting-Age Population, November 2016

(Numbers in thousands, percent.)

Item	Total population	Total citizen population	Registered				Voted		
			Total registered	Percent registered (total population)	Percent registered (total citizen population)		Total voted	Percent voted (total population)	Percent voted (total citizen population)
U.S. Total	245,502	224,059	157,596	64.2	70.3		137,537	56.0	61.4
State Total.............................	518	502	358	69.1	71.3		308	59.4	61.3
Sex									
Male	267	258	181	67.9	70.1		152	57.0	58.8
Female	251	243	177	70.3	72.6		156	62.0	64.0
Race									
White alone................................	346	340	261	75.5	76.8		234	67.7	68.9
White, non-Hispanic alone	334	329	252	75.5	76.7		226	67.7	68.7
Black alone................................	17	17	10	(B)	(B)		8	(B)	(B)
Asian alone	27	19	9	(B)	(B)		8	(B)	(B)
Hispanic (of any race).....................	24	23	17	(B)	(B)		17	(B)	(B)
White alone or in combination	369	363	279	75.8	77.0		250	67.9	69.0
Black alone or in combination..........	26	26	14	(B)	(B)		12	(B)	(B)
Asian alone or in combination..........	32	24	13	(B)	(B)		12	(B)	(B)
Age									
18 to 24 years.................................	65	65	32	(B)	(B)		26	(B)	(B)
25 to 34 years.................................	113	109	71	62.6	64.8		58	51.0	52.7
35 to 44 years.................................	83	79	58	(B)	(B)		48	(B)	(B)
45 to 64 years.................................	180	174	138	77.0	79.6		122	67.9	70.2
65 years and over	77	75	59	(B)	(B)		54	(B)	(B)

B = Base is less than 75,000 and therefore too small to show the derived measure.

Table AK-14. Crime

(Number, rate per 100,000. Data are derived from the FBI Uniform Crime Reports.)

Item	State			U.S. [1,2,3,4]		
	2014	2015	Percent change	2014	2015	Percent change
TOTAL POPULATION[5]	737,046	738,432	0.2	318,907,401	321,418,820	0.8
VIOLENT CRIME						
Number...	4,684	5,392	15.1	1,186,185	1,231,566	3.8
Rate	635.5	730.2	14.9	372.0	383.2	3.0
Murder and Nonnegligent Manslaughter						
Number...	41	59	43.9	14,164	15,696	10.8
Rate	5.6	8.0	43.6	4.4	4.9	10.0
Rape[6]						
Number...	771	901	16.9	118,027	124,047	5.1
Rate	104.6	122.0	16.6	37.0	38.6	4.3
Robbery						
Number...	629	761	21.0	322,905	327,374	1.4
Rate	85.3	103.1	20.8	101.3	101.9	0.6
Aggravated Assault						
Number...	3,243	3,671	13.2	731,089	764,449	4.6
Rate	440.0	497.1	13.0	229.2	237.8	3.7
PROPERTY CRIME						
Number...	20,334	20,806	2.3	8,209,010	7,993,631	-2.6
Rate	2,758.9	2,817.6	2.1	2,574.1	2,487.0	-3.4
Burglary						
Number...	3,150	3,511	11.5	1,713,153	1,579,527	-7.8
Rate	427.4	475.5	11.3	537.2	491.4	-8.5
Larceny-Theft						
Number...	15,445	15,249	-1.3	5,809,054	5,706,346	-1.8
Rate	2,095.5	2,065.1	-1.5	1,821.5	1,775.4	-2.5
Motor Vehicle Theft						
Number...	1,739	2,046	17.7	686,803	707,758	3.1
Rate	235.9	277.1	17.4	215.4	220.2	2.2

NOTE: Although arson data are included in the trend and clearance tables, sufficient data are not available to estimate totals for this offense. Therefore, no arson data are published in this table.

X = Not applicable.

- = Zero or rounds to zero.

[1] Because of changes in the state's reporting practices, figures are not comparable to previous years' data.

[2] The crime figures have been adjusted.

[3] The data collection methodology for the offense of forcible rape used by the Minnesota state Uniform Crime Reporting (UCR) Program (with the exception of Minneapolis and St. Paul, Minnesota) does not comply with national UCR Program guidelines. Consequently, its figures for forcible rape and violent crime (of which forcible rape is a part) are not published in this table.

[4] Includes offenses reported by the Zoological Police and the Metro Transit Police.

[5] Populations are U.S. Census Bureau provisional estimates as of July 1 of each year.

[6] The figures shown for the offense of rape were estimated using the revised Uniform Crime Reporting (UCR) definition of rape.

Table AK-15. State Government Finances, 2015

(Dollar amounts in thousands, percent distribution.)

Item	Dollars	Percent distribution
Total Revenue	8,419,335	100.0
General revenue	7,693,036	91.4
Intergovernmental revenue	2,642,995	31.4
Taxes	1,394,310	16.6
General sales	0	-
Selective sales	255,971	3.0
License taxes	146,846	1.7
Individual income tax	0	-
Corporate income tax	227,852	2.7
Other taxes	763,641	9.1
Current charges	655,667	7.8
Miscellaneous general revenue	3,000,064	35.6
Utility revenue	16,828	0.2
Liquor stores revenue	0	-
Insurance trust revenue[1]	709,471	8.4
Total Expenditure	13,039,766	100.0
Intergovernmental expenditure	2,036,112	15.6
Direct expenditure	11,003,654	84.4
Current operation	7,747,540	59.4
Capital outlay	1,510,970	11.6
Insurance benefits and repayments	1,294,550	9.9
Assistance and subsidies	196,622	1.5
Interest on debt	253,972	1.9
Exhibit: Salaries and wages	1,740,153	13.3
Total Expenditure	13,039,766	100.0
General expenditure	11,581,076	88.8
Intergovernmental expenditure	2,036,112	15.6
Direct expenditure	9,544,964	73.2
General expenditure, by function:		
Education	2,703,433	20.7
Public welfare	2,113,211	16.2
Hospitals	68,984	0.5
Health	299,156	2.3
Highways	1,271,514	9.8
Police protection	161,965	1.2
Correction	340,726	2.6
Natural resources	375,310	2.9
Parks and recreation	23,949	0.2
Governmental administration	752,588	5.8
Interest on general debt	250,304	1.9
Other and unallocable	3,219,936	24.7
Utility expenditure	164,140	1.3
Liquor stores expenditure	0	-
Insurance trust expenditure	1,294,550	9.9
Debt at End of Fiscal Year	5,727,891	X
Cash and Security Holdings	81,306,779	X

X = Not applicable.
- = Zero or rounds to zero.
[1] Within insurance trust revenue, net earnings of state retirement systems is a calculated statistic (the item code in the data file is X08), and thus can be positive or negative. Net earnings is the sum of earnings on investments plus gains on investments minus losses on investments. The change made in 2002 for asset valuation from book to market value in accordance with Statement 34 of the Governmental Accounting Standards Board is reflected in the calculated statistics.

Table AK-16. State Government Tax Collections, 2016

(Dollars in thousands, percent.)

Item	Dollars	Percent distribution
Total Taxes	1,042,164	100.0
Property taxes..	111,736	10.7
Sales and gross receipts	260,846	25.0
General sales and gross receipts	0	-
Selective sales and gross receipts	260,846	25.0
Alcoholic beverages...............................	42,430	4.1
Amusements..	10,306	1.0
Insurance premiums..............................	64,400	6.2
Motor fuels..	48,773	4.7
Pari-mutuels......................................	0	-
Public utilities	4,027	0.4
Tobacco products................................	67,918	6.5
Other selective sales	22,992	2.2
Licenses..	120,529	11.6
Alcoholic beverages..............................	1,919	0.2
Amusements.......................................	0	-
Corporations in general..........................	0	-
Hunting and fishing..............................	29,500	2.8
Motor vehicle.....................................	38,000	3.6
Motor vehicle operators.........................	0	-
Public utilities	838	0.1
Occupation and business, NEC	46,957	4.5
Other licenses	3,315	0.3
Income taxes..	212,252	20.4
Individual income.................................	0	-
Corporation net income	212,252	20.4
Other taxes..	336,801	32.3
Death and gift.....................................	0	-
Documentary and stock transfer	0	-
Severance	336,801	32.3
Taxes, NEC	0	-

X = Not applicable.
- = Zero or rounds to zero.

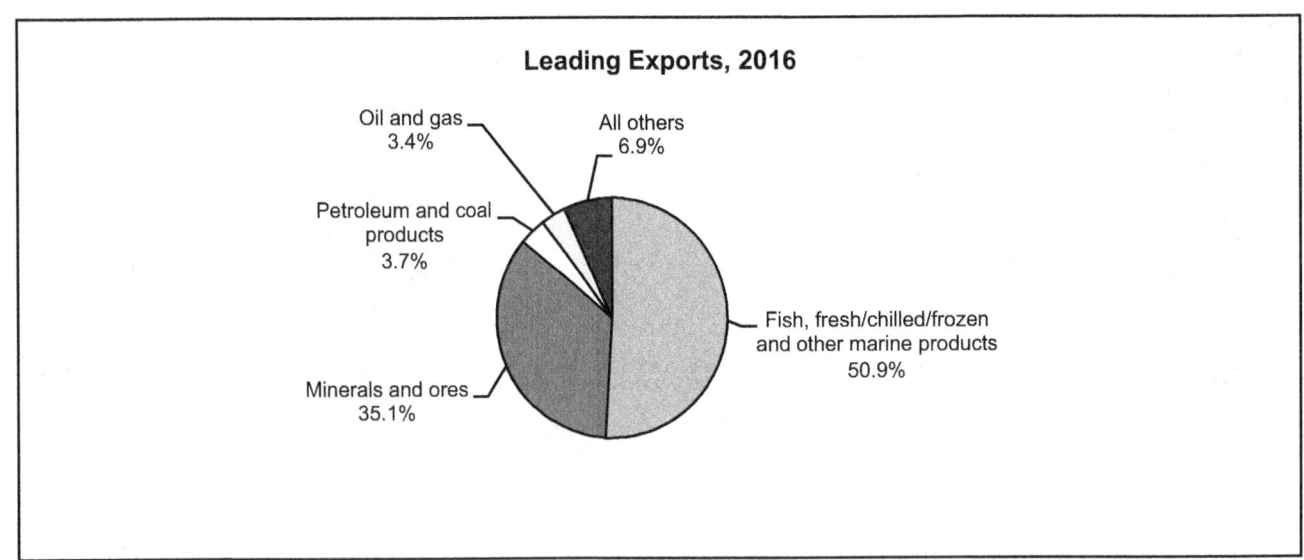

Leading Exports, 2016

Oil and gas 3.4%

All others 6.9%

Petroleum and coal products 3.7%

Fish, fresh/chilled/frozen and other marine products 50.9%

Minerals and ores 35.1%

ARIZONA

Facts and Figures

Location: Southwestern United States; bordered on the North by Utah, on the East by New Mexico, on the South by Mexico, and on the West by Nevada and California; Arizona is one of the Four Corner states—at its NE corner it touches Colorado, New Mexico, and Utah

Area: 113,990 sq. mi. (295,254 sq. km.); rank—6th

Population: 6,931,071 (2016 est.); rank—14th

Principal Cities: capital—Phoenix; largest—Phoenix

Statehood: February 14, 1912; 48th state

U.S. Congress: 2 senators, 9 representatives

State Motto: *Ditat Deus* ("God enriches")

State Song: "Arizona"

State Nickname: The Grand Canyon State

Abbreviations: AZ; Ariz.

State Symbols: flower—saguaro cactus blossom; tree—paloverde; bird—cactus wren

At a Glance

- With an increase in population of 8.4 percent, Arizona ranked 8th among the states in growth from 2010 to 2016.

- In 2016, 16.9 percent of Arizonans were age 65 and older, the 10th highest percent in the nation.

- Arizona's median household income in 2015 was $51,492, compared to the national median household income of $55,775.

- In 2015, 17.4 percent of Arizonans lived below the poverty level, a percentage that ranked 8th in the country.

- Arizona's violent crime rate in 2015 was 410.2 per 100,000 population, ranking 18th in the nation.

Table AZ-1. Population by Age, Sex, Race, and Hispanic Origin

(Number, percent, except where noted.)

Sex, age, race, and Hispanic origin	2000	2010	2016 [1]	Average annual percent change, 2010–2016
Total Population...	5,130,632	6,392,017	6,931,071	0.5
Percent of total U.S. population	1.8	2.1	2.1	X
Sex				
Male..	2,561,057	3,175,823	3,442,895	0.5
Female..	2,569,575	3,216,814	3,488,176	0.5
Age				
Under 5 years..	382,386	455,715	439,319	-0.2
5 to 19 years..	1,135,802	1,363,926	1,379,685	0.1
20 to 64 years..	2,944,605	3,690,545	3,941,143	0.4
65 years and over...	667,839	881,831	1,170,924	2.0
Median age (years)	34.2	35.9	37.6	0.3
Race and Hispanic Origin				
One race...				
White	3,873,611	5,418,483	5,772,667	0.4
Black..	158,873	280,905	339,472	1.3
American Indian and Alaska Native	255,879	335,278	371,605	0.7
Asian..	92,236	188,456	236,628	1.6
Native Hawaiian or Other Pacific Islander	6,733	16,112	18,423	0.9
Two or more races..	146,526	152,783	192,276	1.6
Hispanic (of any race)..	1,295,617	1,943,466	2,144,775	0.6

X = Not applicable.
[1] Population figures for 2016 are July 1 estimates. The 2010 estimates are taken from the 2010 Census.

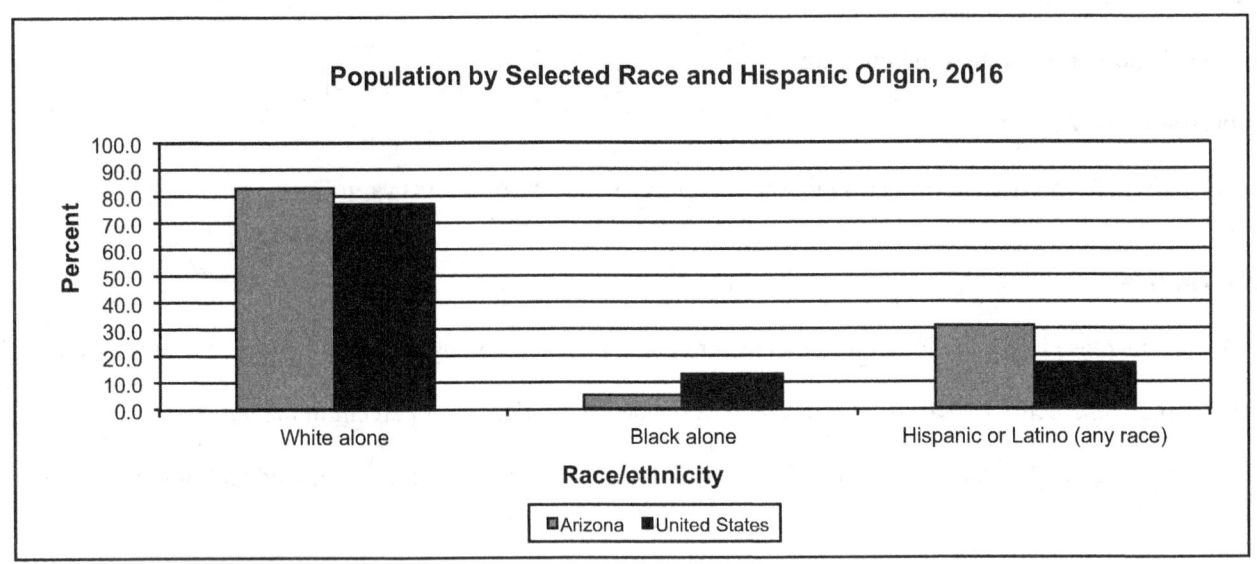

Population by Selected Race and Hispanic Origin, 2016

Table AZ-2. Marital Status

(Number, percent distribution.)

Sex, age, race, and Hispanic origin	2000	2010	2015
Males, 15 Years and Over	1,966,032	2,492,590	2,701,575
Never married	29.6	35.3	37.4
Now married, except separated...............................	56.4	50.1	47.3
Separated...	1.6	1.4	1.4
Widowed..	2.6	2.5	2.6
Divorced..	9.8	10.7	11.4
Females, 15 Years and Over	2,013,304	2,559,409	2,780,421
Never married	22.5	28.0	29.8
Now married, except separated...............................	53.6	48.0	45.4
Separated...	2.1	2.2	2.0
Widowed..	9.4	8.3	8.6
Divorced..	12.3	13.5	14.2

Table AZ-3. Households and Housing Characteristics

(Number, percent, dollars.)

Item	2000	2010	2015	Average annual percent change, 2000–2015
Total Households..	1,901,327	2,334,050	2,463,008	2.0
Family households...	1,287,367	1,548,428	1,598,414	1.6
Married-couple family...	986,303	1,134,229	1,153,542	1.1
Other family..	310,064	414,199	444,872	2.9
Male householder, no wife present..........................	90,283	123,772	137,228	3.5
Female householder, no husband present.................	210,781	290,427	307,644	3.1
Nonfamily households...	613,960	785,622	864,594	2.7
Householder living alone...	472,006	621,291	679,338	2.9
Householder not living alone.....................................	141,954	164,331	185,256	2.0
Housing Characteristics				
Total housing units...	2,189,189	2,846,738	2,929,173	2.3
Occupied housing units	1,901,327	2,334,050	2,463,008	2.0
Owner occupied	1,293,556	1,522,938	1,524,828	1.2
Renter occupied...	607,771	811,112	938,180	3.6
Average household size...	2.64	2.69	2.71	0.2
Financial Characteristics				
Median gross rent of renter-occupied housing	619	844	933	3.4
Median monthly owner costs for housing units with a mortgage	1,039	1,442	1,319	1.8
Median value of owner-occupied housing units............	121,300	168,800	194,300	4.0

Table AZ-4. Migration, Origin, and Language

(Number, percent.)

Characteristic	State 2014	State 2015	State Percent change	U.S. 2014	U.S. 2015	U.S. Percent change
Residence 1 Year Ago						
Population 1 year and over	6,651,964	6,747,595	1.4	315,095,393	317,635,720	0.8
Same house	81.6	82.0	X	85.1	85.3	X
Different house in the U.S.	17.6	17.3	X	14.3	14.1	X
Same county	12.1	11.8	X	8.7	8.5	X
Different county	5.5	5.4	X	5.6	5.6	X
Same state	1.8	1.7	X	3.3	3.2	X
Different state	3.8	3.8	X	2.3	2.4	X
Abroad	0.7	0.7	X	0.6	0.7	X
Place of Birth						
Native born	5,811,925	5,913,665	1.8	276,465,262	278,128,449	0.6
Male	49.9	49.9	X	49.3	49.3	X
Female	50.1	50.1	X	50.7	50.7	X
Foreign born	919,559	914,400	-0.6	42,391,794	43,290,372	2.1
Male	48.4	47.7	X	48.7	48.6	X
Female	51.6	52.3	X	51.3	51.4	X
Foreign born; naturalized U.S. citizen.........................	358,978	380,187	5.9	19,984,738	20,697,103	3.6
Male	45.3	45.0	X	45.9	45.9	X
Female	54.7	55.0	X	54.1	54.1	X
Foreign born; not a U.S. citizen	560,581	534,213	-4.7	22,407,056	22,593,269	0.8
Male	50.4	49.6	X	51.2	51.1	X
Female	49.6	50.4	X	48.8	48.9	X
Entered 2010 or later	11.7	14.6	X	12.3	15.6	X
Entered 2000 to 2009	27.1	25.1	X	28.6	27.9	X
Entered before 2000..	61.2	60.3	X	59.1	56.5	X
World Region of Birth, Foreign						
Foreign-born population, excluding population born at sea	919,559	914,400	-0.6	42,390,705	43,289,646	2.1
Europe	8.9	9.0	X	11.2	11.1	X
Asia	19.5	20.2	X	30.1	30.6	X
Africa	2.6	3.0	X	4.6	4.8	X
Oceania	0.6	0.5	X	0.6	0.6	X
Latin America	63.5	62.9	X	51.6	51.1	X
North America	4.8	4.3	X	1.9	1.9	X
Language Spoken at Home and Ability to Speak English						
Population 5 years and over..	6,298,821	6,398,205	1.6	299,084,046	301,625,014	0.8
English only	73.0	72.9	X	78.9	78.5	X
Language other than English..	27.0	27.1	X	21.1	21.5	X
Speaks English less than "very well"........................	9.3	8.9	X	8.6	8.6	X

NA = Not available.
X = Not applicable.
- = Zero or rounds to zero.

Table AZ-5. Median Income and Poverty Status, 2015

(Number, percent, except as noted.)

Characteristic	State		U.S.	
	Number	Percent	Number	Percent
Median Income				
Households (dollars)	51,492	X	55,775	X
Families (dollars)	61,042	X	68,260	X
Below Poverty Level (All People)	1,159,043	17.4	46,153,077	14.7
Sex				
Male	531,785	16.2	20,599,407	13.4
Female	627,258	18.5	25,553,670	16.0
Age				
Under 18 years	393,858	24.7	15,000,273	20.7
Related children under 18 years	387,037	24.4	14,693,239	20.4
18 to 64 years	665,969	16.8	26,960,369	13.9
65 years and over	99,216	9.0	4,192,435	9.0

X = Not applicable.

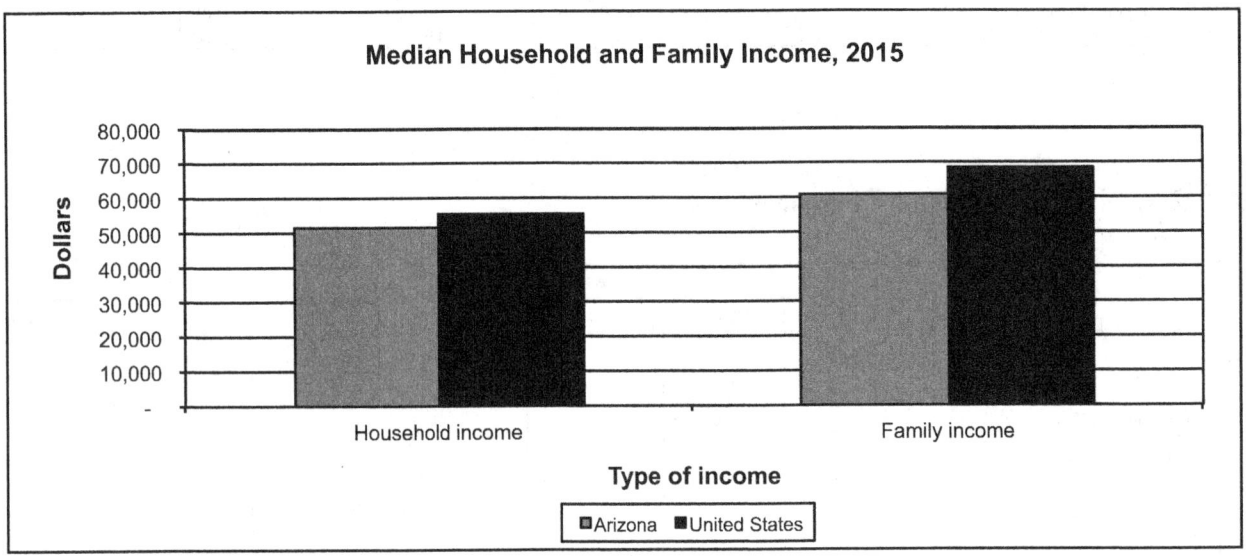

Median Household and Family Income, 2015

Table AZ-6. Health Insurance Coverage Status for the Civilian Noninstitutionalized Population and Children Under 18 Years of Age

(Numbers in thousands, percent.)

Item	2007	2008	2009	2010	2011	2012	2013	2014	2015
Civilian Noninstitutionalized Population	6,368	6,403	6,502	6,310	6,378	6,444	6,521	6,623	6,719
Covered by Private or Public Insurance									
Number	5,204	5,207	5,375	5,245	5,283	5,313	5,403	5,720	5,991
Percent	81.7	81.3	82.7	83.1	82.8	82.4	82.9	86.4	89.2
Not Covered									
Number	1,164	1,196	1,127	1,065	1,095	1,131	1,118	903	728
Percent	18.3	18.7	17.3	16.9	17.2	17.6	17.1	13.6	10.8
Percent in the U.S. not covered	15.3	15.1	15.1	15.5	15.1	14.8	14.5	11.7	9.4
Children Under 18 Years of Age	1,697	1,706	1,730	1,630	1,622	1,617	1,614	1,621	1,619
Covered by Private or Public Insurance									
Number	1,463	1,430	1,522	1,422	1,622	1,403	1,422	1,459	1,485
Percent	86.2	83.8	88.0	87.2	87.1	86.8	88.1	90.0	91.7
Not Covered									
Number	234	276	208	208	208	214	192	162	134
Percent	13.8	16.2	12.0	12.8	12.9	13.2	11.9	10.0	8.3
Percent in the U.S. not covered	11.0	9.7	8.6	8.0	7.5	7.2	7.1	6.0	4.8

Table AZ-7. Employment Status by Demographic Group, 2016

(Numbers in thousands, percent.)

Characteristic	Civilian noninstitutional population	Civilian labor force		Employed		Unemployed	
		Number	Percent of population	Number	Percent of population	Number	Percent of population
Total...	5,361	3,236	60.4	3,068	57.2	167	5.2
Sex							
Male...	2,608	1,762	67.6	1,672	64.1	90	5.1
Female..	2,753	1,473	53.5	1,396	50.7	77	5.2
Race, Sex, and Hispanic Origin							
White	4,636	2,793	60.2	2,652	57.2	141	5.1
Male...	2,254	1,529	67.8	1,453	64.5	76	5.0
Female..	2,382	1,264	53.0	1,198	50.3	65	5.2
Black or African American.................................	251	170	67.9	159	63.3	12	6.8
Male...	127	92	72.4	87	68.7	5	5.2
Female..	123	78	63.3	71	57.9	7	8.6
Hispanic or Latino ethnicity[1]	1,689	1,094	64.7	1,017	60.2	77	7.1
Male...	848	632	74.6	590	69.6	42	6.7
Female..	842	462	54.9	427	50.7	35	7.6
Age							
16 to 19 years..	374	138	36.8	118	31.7	19	14.0
20 to 24 years..	481	343	71.3	309	64.2	34	9.9
25 to 34 years..	846	679	80.3	649	76.8	30	4.4
35 to 44 years..	851	680	79.9	656	77.0	25	3.6
45 to 54 years..	935	729	78.0	698	74.7	31	4.3
55 to 64 years..	816	496	60.8	476	58.3	20	4.0
65 years and over	1,059	171	16.2	163	15.4	8	4.8

NOTE: Data in Table 7 are from the Current Population Survey (CPS) and do not match the estimates in Table 8. See notes and definitions for further information.
[1] May be of any race.
NA = Not available.

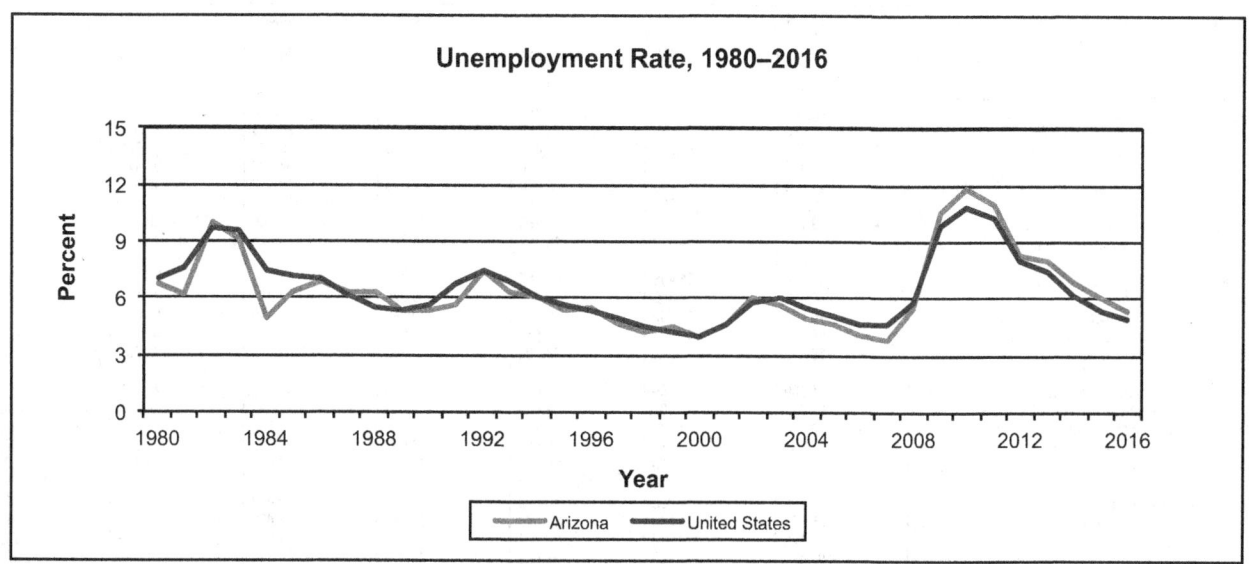

Unemployment Rate, 1980–2016

Table AZ-8. Employment Status of the Civilian Noninstitutional Population Age 16 Years and Over

(Number, percent.)

Year	Civilian labor force	Civilian participation rate	Employed	Unemployed	Unemployment rate
2008..	3,104,863	63.8	2,913,903	190,960	6.2
2009..	3,128,110	63.2	2,817,577	310,533	9.9
2010..	3,089,705	63.1	2,769,454	320,251	10.4
2011..	3,037,017	61.7	2,748,470	288,547	9.5
2012..	3,031,199	60.6	2,778,425	252,774	8.3
2013..	3,039,865	59.8	2,804,338	235,527	7.7
2014..	3,097,112	59.8	2,886,412	210,700	6.8
2015..	3,152,708	59.8	2,959,518	193,190	6.1
2016..	3,237,864	60.3	3,066,264	171,600	5.3

Table AZ-9. Employment and Average Wages by Industry

(Estimates through 2010 are based on the 2007 *North American Industry Classification System* [NAICS]. Estimates from 2011 onward are based on the 2012 NAICS.)

Industry	2009	2010	2011	2012	2013	2014	2015
				Number of Jobs			
Wage and Salary Employment by Industry..................	2,526,934	2,476,001	2,503,192	2,560,624	2,619,199	2,671,930	2,743,361
Farm Wage and Salary Employment.........................	12,134	11,417	11,523	12,626	13,966	12,360	13,584
Nonfarm Wage and Salary Employment....................	2,514,800	2,464,584	2,491,669	2,547,998	2,605,233	2,659,570	2,729,777
Private wage and salary employment......................	2,061,998	2,015,596	2,049,819	2,104,857	2,160,867	2,214,415	2,285,701
Forestry, fishing, and related activities.........................	11,885	12,364	12,464	12,114	12,000	12,143	12,166
Mining..	10,559	10,285	10,918	11,925	12,615	.12,303	11,740
Utilities...	12,437	12,076	11,971	12,290	11,934	11,952	12,089
Construction..	134,737	115,305	114,556	119,652	127,236	128,519	130,904
Manufacturing...	151,961	146,607	148,223	153,571	153,973	155,052	156,565
Durable goods manufacturing...........................	121,389	116,467	117,570	121,639	121,323	121,562	121,133
Nondurable goods manufacturing......................	30,572	30,140	30,653	31,932	32,650	33,490	35,432
Wholesale trade	102,528	98,420	98,233	98,901	99,415	95,697	95,547
Retail trade..	302,595	295,500	297,748	300,258	301,971	315,447	324,639
Transportation and warehousing...........................	70,119	66,901	70,603	72,849	73,490	75,765	79,866
Information	38,182	36,660	36,764	38,239	41,815	43,400	45,142
Finance and insurance	122,875	121,252	124,943	129,249	135,852	140,639	149,790
Real estate and rental and leasing............................	49,183	46,260	45,935	47,027	48,170	48,850	49,215
Professional, scientific, and technical services...........	125,308	122,700	125,139	124,986	128,549	131,778	134,606
Management of companies and enterprises..................	26,585	25,435	25,216	26,607	28,756	29,704	31,362
Administrative and waste services........................	199,382	196,580	200,401	208,356	220,794	226,119	235,043
Educational services	47,294	52,022	54,240	57,053	55,988	57,492	59,002
Health care and social assistance...........................	285,782	296,149	303,221	312,356	319,633	326,240	340,732
Arts, entertainment, and recreation.......................	33,500	33,480	33,345	34,905	35,690	38,215	40,176
Accommodation and food services........................	225,304	221,955	227,441	233,464	241,618	249,775	260,758
Other services, except public administration..................	111,782	105,645	108,458	111,055	111,368	115,325	116,359
Government and government enterprises.........................	452,802	448,988	441,850	443,141	444,366	445,155	444,076
				Dollars			
Average Wages and Salaries by Industry	43,424	44,140	45,407	46,489	46,839	47,842	48,854
Average Farm Wages and Salaries	36,462	34,082	34,114	35,557	36,287	39,505	34,127
Average Nonfarm Wages and Salaries	43,458	44,186	45,459	46,543	46,896	47,881	48,928
Average private wages and salaries...........................	42,969	43,931	45,282	46,536	46,906	47,953	48,960
Forestry, fishing, and related activities.........................	21,678	22,508	23,244	23,708	24,088	25,945	27,459
Mining..	68,460	71,527	78,684	80,883	79,002	79,256	81,527
Utilities...	91,019	92,220	95,406	95,578	97,520	102,471	101,084
Construction..	44,326	45,048	45,979	47,923	48,410	49,558	50,250
Manufacturing...	63,433	66,962	70,152	70,717	70,917	72,604	73,931
Durable goods manufacturing...........................	69,117	73,536	77,288	77,914	78,209	80,159	82,036
Nondurable goods manufacturing......................	40,861	41,560	42,782	43,300	43,821	45,183	46,220
Wholesale trade	62,246	64,449	67,052	71,450	68,757	72,257	74,860
Retail trade..	28,499	29,359	30,909	30,879	30,350	31,171	31,946
Transportation and warehousing...........................	46,457	48,736	49,680	50,441	50,619	51,002	52,726
Information	57,447	57,968	59,857	61,681	63,189	66,702	67,836
Finance and insurance	58,876	61,074	63,794	67,151	69,575	70,991	73,041
Real estate and rental and leasing............................	41,569	42,689	44,645	46,793	46,633	48,599	50,255
Professional, scientific, and technical services...............	65,848	67,432	69,939	73,473	74,383	74,824	76,593
Management of companies and enterprises..................	75,076	74,633	77,280	82,733	85,738	92,231	89,840
Administrative and waste services........................	33,090	33,338	33,594	33,997	34,832	35,957	37,113
Educational services	39,004	39,255	39,910	40,687	40,912	41,221	40,846
Health care and social assistance...........................	48,156	48,035	48,735	49,210	49,488	50,264	51,173
Arts, entertainment, and recreation.......................	36,036	36,740	36,934	38,221	38,427	39,536	39,062
Accommodation and food services........................	19,576	19,903	20,337	20,993	21,309	21,959	22,802
Other services, except public administration..................	27,494	28,230	28,689	29,575	30,718	31,984	32,819
Government and government enterprises.........................	45,682	45,332	46,283	46,579	46,849	47,520	48,761

Table AZ-10. Employment Characteristics by Family Type

(Number, percent.)

Family type and labor force status	2013		2014		2015	
	Total	Families with own children under 18 years	Total	Families with own children under 18 years	Total	Families with own children under 18 years
All Families..................................	1,572,310	671,500	1,573,546	657,330	1,598,414	665,587
FAMILY TYPE AND LABOR FORCE STATUS						
Married-Couple Families......................	1,136,593	429,785	1,135,360	428,399	1,153,542	426,411
Both husband and wife in labor force...........	43.3	57.6	43.9	58.9	42.7	59.1
Husband in labor force, wife not in labor force......	23.8	35.3	23.9	34.4	23.4	34.2
Wife in labor force, husband not in labor force........	7.8	4.4	7.7	3.9	8.0	4.5
Both husband and wife not in labor force...........	24.7	2.5	24.5	2.7	25.2	2.0
Other Families	435,717	241,715	438,186	228,931	444,872	239,176
Female householder, no husband present..............	70.3	73.2	69.4	71.8	69.2	71.5
In labor force............................	49.9	59.6	48.3	58.0	48.5	59.3
Not in labor force.......................	20.3	13.6	21.1	13.8	20.6	12.3
Male householder, no wife present................	29.7	26.8	30.6	28.2	30.8	28.5
In labor force...........................	23.1	24.0	24.3	25.6	24.5	25.4
Not in labor force........................	6.6	2.7	6.3	2.6	6.4	3.1

Table AZ-11. School Enrollment and Educational Attainment, 2015

(Number, percent.)

Item	State	U.S.
Enrollment		
Total population 3 years and over, enrolled in school	1,739,821	81,618,288
Enrolled in nursery school or preschool (percent)................................	4.6	6.0
Enrolled in kindergarten (percent)................................	4.9	5.0
Enrolled in elementary school, grades 1-8 (percent)................................	42.3	40.3
Enrolled in high school, grades 9-12 (percent)................................	21.3	20.9
Enrolled in college or graduate school (percent)................................	26.8	27.7
Attainment		
Total population 25 years and over	4,536,954	216,447,163
Less than ninth grade (percent)................................	6.0	5.5
9th to 12th grade, no diploma (percent)................................	7.9	7.3
High school graduate, including equivalency (percent)................................	24.5	27.6
Some college, no degree (percent)................................	25.5	20.7
Associate's degree (percent)................................	8.4	8.2
Bachelor's degree (percent)................................	17.4	19.0
Graduate or professional degree (percent)................................	10.3	11.6
High school graduate or higher (percent)................................	86.1	87.1
Bachelor's degree or higher (percent)................................	27.7	30.6

Table AZ-12. Public School Characteristics and Educational Indicators

(Number, percent; data derived from National Center of Education Statistics.)

Item	State	U.S.
Public Schools, 2014–2015 (except where noted)		
Number of school districts................................	692	18,260
Number of schools................................	2,281	98,373
Number of students	1,111,695	50,312,581
Number of teachers	48,124	3,132,351
Student-teacher ratio................................	23.1	16.1
Expenditures per student (dollars), FY 2014................................	7,457	11,066
Four-year adjusted cohort graduation rate (ACGR)[1,2]	77.4	83.2
Students eligible for free or reduced-price lunch (percent)................................	43.0	51.8
English language learners (percent)................................	6.4	9.4
Students age 3 to 21 served under IDEA, part B (percent)................................	11.8	13.0

Public Schools by Type	Number	Percent of state public schools
Total number of schools................................	2,281	100.0
Regular	1,971	86.4
Special education................................	20	0.9
Vocational education................................	229	10.0
Alternative education................................	61	2.7

NOTE: Every school is assigned only one school type based on its instructional emphasis.
[1] ACGR data represents a new method of calculating high-school completion rates and may not be comparable to previous years' data for Averaged Freshmen Graduation Rates (AFGR).
[2] The United States 4-year ACGRs were estimated using both the reported 4-year ACGR data from 49 states and the District of Columbia and using imputed data for Idaho. The estimate for American Indian/Alaska Native students also includes imputed data for Virginia.

Table AZ-13. Reported Voting and Registration of the Voting-Age Population, November 2016

(Numbers in thousands, percent.)

Item	Total population	Total citizen population	Registered			Voted		
			Total registered	Percent registered (total population)	Percent registered (total citizen population)	Total voted	Percent voted (total population)	Percent voted (total citizen population)
U.S. Total	245,502	224,059	157,596	64.2	70.3	137,537	56.0	61.4
State Total..........................	5,196	4,585	3,145	60.5	68.6	2,769	53.3	60.4
Sex								
Male	2,525	2,256	1,485	58.8	65.8	1,273	50.4	56.5
Female	2,671	2,329	1,660	62.2	71.3	1,496	56.0	64.2
Race								
White alone............................	4,471	3,950	2,773	62.0	70.2	2,480	55.5	62.8
White, non-Hispanic alone	2,940	2,875	2,145	73.0	74.6	1,963	66.8	68.3
Black alone...........................	252	237	165	65.6	69.8	121	47.9	50.9
Asian alone	169	108	69	40.6	63.3	56	33.1	51.6
Hispanic (of any race)	1,613	1,145	654	40.5	57.1	543	33.7	47.4
White alone or in combination	4,571	4,048	2,815	61.6	69.5	2,518	55.1	62.2
Black alone or in combination..........	296	281	183	61.7	65.0	138	46.6	49.1
Asian alone or in combination..........	180	117	78	43.0	66.1	56	31.0	47.7
Age								
18 to 24 years	735	654	346	47.1	52.8	263	35.8	40.2
25 to 34 years	854	729	460	53.9	63.1	377	44.1	51.7
35 to 44 years	776	663	423	54.5	63.7	349	45.0	52.6
45 to 64 years	1,736	1,510	1,143	65.9	75.7	1,038	59.8	68.7
65 years and over	1,096	1,028	774	70.6	75.3	743	67.8	72.2

Table AZ-14. Crime

(Number, rate per 100,000. Data are derived from the FBI Uniform Crime Reports.)

Item	State			U.S. [1,2,3,4]		
	2014	2015	Percent change	2014	2015	Percent change
TOTAL POPULATION[5]	6,728,783	6,828,065	1.5	318,907,401	321,418,820	0.8
VIOLENT CRIME						
Number..............................	26,422	28,012	6.0	1,186,185	1,231,566	3.8
Rate	392.7	410.2	4.5	372.0	383.2	3.0
Murder and Nonnegligent Manslaughter						
Number..............................	311	309	-0.6	14,164	15,696	10.8
Rate	4.6	4.5	-2.1	4.4	4.9	10.0
Rape[6]						
Number..............................	3,272	3,108	-5.0	118,027	124,047	5.1
Rate	48.6	45.5	-6.4	37.0	38.6	4.3
Robbery						
Number..............................	6,225	6,360	2.2	322,905	327,374	1.4
Rate	92.5	93.1	0.7	101.3	101.9	0.6
Aggravated Assault						
Number..............................	16,614	18,235	9.8	731,089	764,449	4.6
Rate	246.9	267.1	8.2	229.2	237.8	3.7
PROPERTY CRIME						
Number..............................	213,406	207,107	-3.0	8,209,010	7,993,631	-2.6
Rate	3,171.5	3,033.2	-4.4	2,574.1	2,487.0	-3.4
Burglary						
Number..............................	43,412	37,957	-12.6	1,713,153	1,579,527	-7.8
Rate	645.2	555.9	-13.8	537.2	491.4	-8.5
Larceny-Theft						
Number..............................	152,683	152,365	-0.2	5,809,054	5,706,346	-1.8
Rate	2,269.1	2,231.5	-1.7	1,821.5	1,775.4	-2.5
Motor Vehicle Theft						
Number..............................	17,311	16,785	-3.0	686,803	707,758	3.1
Rate	257.3	245.8	-4.4	215.4	220.2	2.2

NOTE: Although arson data are included in the trend and clearance tables, sufficient data are not available to estimate totals for this offense. Therefore, no arson data are published in this table.
X = Not applicable.
- = Zero or rounds to zero.
[1] Because of changes in the state's reporting practices, figures are not comparable to previous years' data.
[2] The data collection methodology for the offense of forcible rape used by the Minnesota state Uniform Crime Reporting (UCR) Program (with the exception of Minneapolis and St. Paul, Minnesota) does not comply with national UCR Program guidelines. Consequently, its figures for forcible rape and violent crime (of which forcible rape is a part) are not published in this table.
[3] Includes offenses reported by the Zoological Police and the Metro Transit Police.
[4] The crime figures have been adjusted.
[5] Populations are U.S. Census Bureau provisional estimates as of July 1 of each year.
[6] The figures shown for the offense of rape were estimated using the revised Uniform Crime Reporting (UCR) definition of rape.

Table AZ-15. State Government Finances, 2015

(Dollar amounts in thousands, percent distribution.)

Item	Dollars	Percent distribution
Total Revenue	35,346,766	100.0
General revenue	31,212,866	88.3
Intergovernmental revenue	12,752,207	36.1
Taxes	14,082,100	39.8
General sales	6,466,167	18.3
Selective sales	1,780,226	5.0
License taxes	458,737	1.3
Individual income tax	3,760,883	10.6
Corporate income tax	690,960	2.0
Other taxes	925,127	2.6
Current charges	2,650,381	7.5
Miscellaneous general revenue	1,728,178	4.9
Utility revenue	27,589	0.1
Liquor stores revenue	0	-
Insurance trust revenue[1]	4,106,311	11.6
Total Expenditure	35,687,278	100.0
Intergovernmental expenditure	7,832,147	21.9
Direct expenditure	27,855,131	78.1
Current operation	19,524,316	54.7
Capital outlay	1,548,304	4.3
Insurance benefits and repayments	4,485,569	12.6
Assistance and subsidies	1,893,638	5.3
Interest on debt	403,304	1.1
Exhibit: Salaries and wages	4,317,125	12.1
Total Expenditure	35,687,278	100.0
General expenditure	31,172,671	87.3
Intergovernmental expenditure	7,832,147	21.9
Direct expenditure	23,340,524	65.4
General expenditure, by function:		
Education	10,458,097	29.3
Public welfare	10,440,648	29.3
Hospitals	61,510	0.2
Health	2,439,944	6.8
Highways	1,957,688	5.5
Police protection	248,909	0.7
Correction	1,115,675	3.1
Natural resources	279,188	0.8
Parks and recreation	63,044	0.2
Governmental administration	751,641	2.1
Interest on general debt	401,481	1.1
Other and unallocable	2,954,846	8.3
Utility expenditure	29,038	0.1
Liquor stores expenditure	0	-
Insurance trust expenditure	4,485,569	12.6
Debt at End of Fiscal Year	14,243,659	X
Cash and Security Holdings	58,944,872	X

X = Not applicable.
- = Zero or rounds to zero.
[1] Within insurance trust revenue, net earnings of state retirement systems is a calculated statistic (the item code in the data file is X08), and thus can be positive or negative. Net earnings is the sum of earnings on investments plus gains on investments minus losses on investments. The change made in 2002 for asset valuation from book to market value in accordance with Statement 34 of the Governmental Accounting Standards Board is reflected in the calculated statistics.

Table AZ-16. State Government Tax Collections, 2016

(Dollars in thousands, percent.)

Item	Dollars	Percent distribution
Total Taxes	14,676,375	100.0
Property taxes..	943,008	6.4
Sales and gross receipts	8,680,009	59.1
General sales and gross receipts	6,660,817	45.4
Selective sales and gross receipts	2,019,192	13.8
Alcoholic beverages....................................	72,281	0.5
Amusements..	3,830	-
Insurance premiums....................................	545,124	3.7
Motor fuels..	898,234	6.1
Pari-mutuels..	160	-
Public utilities..	22,337	0.2
Tobacco products..	317,331	2.2
Other selective sales	159,895	1.1
Licenses..	482,362	3.3
Alcoholic beverages....................................	7,416	0.1
Amusements..	0	-
Corporations in general................................	18,342	0.1
Hunting and fishing......................................	35,059	0.2
Motor vehicle..	228,970	1.6
Motor vehicle operators...............................	31,373	0.2
Public utilities..	0	-
Occupation and business, NEC	159,454	1.1
Other licenses	1,748	0.0
Income taxes..	4,538,472	30.9
Individual income..	3,967,924	27.0
Corporation net income	570,548	3.9
Other taxes..	32,524	0.2
Death and gift..	0	-
Documentary and stock transfer...................	17,328	0.1
Severance..	15,196	0.1
Taxes, NEC..	0	-

- = Zero or rounds to zero.

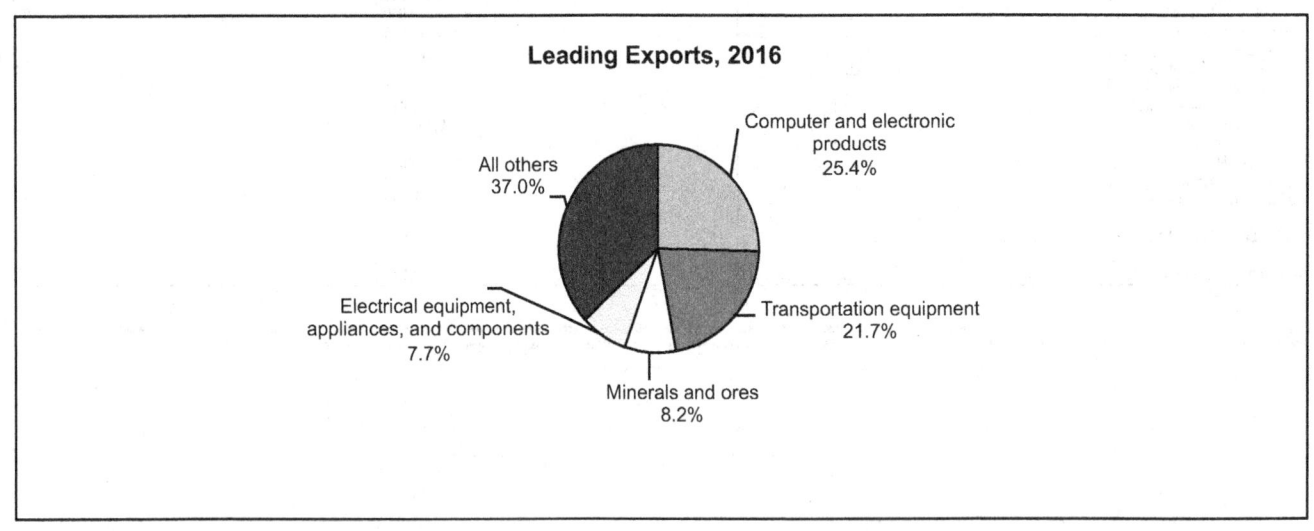

Leading Exports, 2016

Computer and electronic products 25.4%

All others 37.0%

Electrical equipment, appliances, and components 7.7%

Minerals and ores 8.2%

Transportation equipment 21.7%

ARKANSAS

Facts and Figures

Location: South central United States; bordered on the N by Missouri, on the E by Tennessee and Mississippi, on the S by Louisiana, and on the W by Oklahoma and Texas

Area: 53,178 sq. mi. (137,733 sq. km.); rank—29th

Population: 2,988,248 (2016 est.); rank—33rd

Principal Cities: capital—Little Rock; largest—Little Rock

Statehood: June 15, 1836; 25th state

U.S. Congress: 2 senators, 4 representatives

State Motto: *Regnat populus* ("The people rule")

State Song: "Arkansas"

State Nicknames: The Natural State; The Land of Opportunity

Abbreviations: AR; Ark.

State Symbols: flower—apple blossom; tree—pine; bird—mockingbird

At a Glance

- With an increase in population of 2.5 percent, Arkansas ranked 31st among the states in growth from 2010 to 2016.

- In 2015, 21.8 percent of Arkansas residents had a bachelor's degree or higher, the third lowest percent in the nation.

- Arkansas's median household income in 2015 was $41,995, and 19.1 percent of the population lived below the poverty level.

- In 2015, 9.5 percent of Arkansans did not have health insurance, which was down from 11.8 percent the previous year.

- Arkansas's property crime rate in 2015 was 3,251.5 per 100,000 population, which ranked 7th in the nation.

Table AR-1. Population by Age, Sex, Race, and Hispanic Origin

(Number, percent, except where noted.)

Sex, age, race, and Hispanic origin	2000	2010	2016 [1]	Average annual percent change, 2010–2016
Total Population..	2,673,400	2,915,918	2,988,248	0.2
Percent of total U.S. population	0.9	0.9	0.9	X
Sex				
Male..	1,304,693	1,431,637	1,467,873	0.2
Female	1,368,707	1,484,281	1,520,375	0.2
Age				
Under 5 years...	181,585	197,689	190,277	-0.2
5 to 19 years..	578,924	598,241	593,174	-0.1
20 to 64 years..	1,538,872	1,700,007	1,718,063	0.1
65 years and over	374,019	419,981	486,734	1.0
Median age (years)	36.0	37.4	38.0	0.1
Race and Hispanic Origin				
One race..				
White	2,138,598	2,342,403	2,373,726	0.1
Black..	418,950	454,021	468,502	0.2
American Indian and Alaska Native	17,808	26,134	29,049	0.7
Asian..	20,220	37,537	47,326	1.6
Native Hawaiian or Other Pacific Islander	1,668	6,685	9,000	2.2
Two or more races	35,744	49,138	60,645	1.5
Hispanic (of any race)	86,866	191,535	218,561	0.9

X = Not applicable.
[1] Population figures for 2016 are July 1 estimates. The 2010 estimates are taken from the 2010 Census.

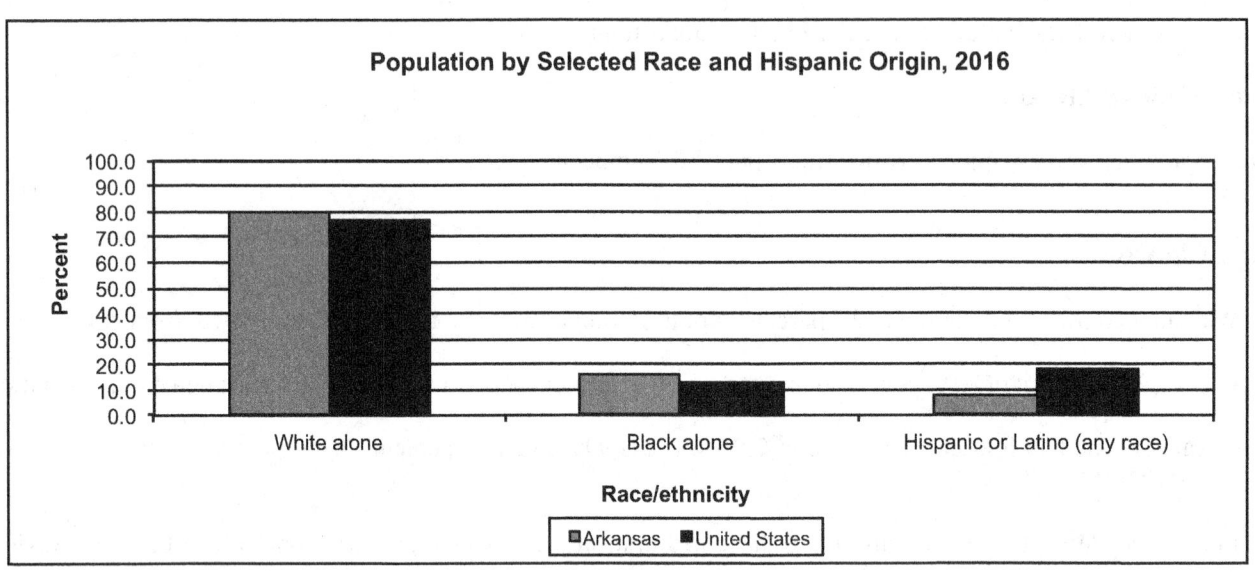

Population by Selected Race and Hispanic Origin, 2016

□ Arkansas   ■ United States

Table AR-2. Marital Status

(Number, percent distribution.)

Sex, age, race, and Hispanic origin	2000	2010	2015
Males, 15 Years and Over..	1,015,594	1,128,804	1,162,989
Never married	24.2	29.5	30.7
Now married, except separated...	61.0	53.3	52.0
Separated..	1.6	2.2	1.9
Widowed..	2.7	3.1	3.1
Divorced..	10.4	12.0	12.3
Females, 15 Years and Over..	1,096,069	1,200,974	1,227,992
Never married	18.4	23.5	24.3
Now married, except separated...	55.7	48.8	48.4
Separated..	2.2	2.9	2.3
Widowed..	12.2	11.2	11.0
Divorced..	11.6	13.6	14.0

Table AR-3. Households and Housing Characteristics

(Number, percent, dollars.)

Item	2000	2010	2015	Average annual percent change, 2000–2015
Total Households..	1,042,696	1,114,902	1,144,663	0.7
Family households..	732,261	761,361	761,494	0.3
Married-couple family..............................	566,401	554,946	561,297	-0.1
Other family..	165,860	206,415	200,197	1.4
Male householder, no wife present............	39,299	51,620	50,124	1.8
Female householder, no husband present....	126,561	154,795	150,073	1.2
Nonfamily households....................................	310,435	353,541	383,169	1.6
Householder living alone..........................	266,585	302,127	324,908	1.5
Householder not living alone.....................	43,850	51,414	58,261	2.2
Housing Characteristics				
Total housing units......................................	1,173,043	1,317,818	1,347,598	1.0
Occupied housing units	1,042,696	1,114,902	1,144,663	0.7
Owner occupied.......................................	723,535	751,568	746,000	0.2
Renter occupied......................................	319,161	363,334	398,663	1.7
Average household size................................	2.49	2.55	2.53	0.1
Financial Characteristics				
Median gross rent of renter-occupied housing	453	638	695	3.6
Median monthly owner costs for housing units with a mortgage	737	987	1029	2.6
Median value of owner-occupied housing units......................	72,800	106,300	120,700	4.4

Table AR-4. Migration, Origin, and Language

(Number, percent.)

Characteristic	State 2014	State 2015	State Percent change	U.S. 2014	U.S. 2015	U.S. Percent change
Residence 1 Year Ago						
Population 1 year and over	2,931,123	2,938,341	0.2	315,095,393	317,635,720	0.8
Same house	84.1	83.1	X	85.1	85.3	X
Different house in the U.S.	15.6	16.6	X	14.3	14.1	X
Same county	9.5	9.9	X	8.7	8.5	X
Different county	6.2	6.7	X	5.6	5.6	X
Same state	3.6	3.9	X	3.3	3.2	X
Different state	2.5	2.8	X	2.3	2.4	X
Abroad	0.3	0.3	X	0.6	0.7	X
Place of Birth						
Native born	2,826,372	2,835,363	0.3	276,465,262	278,128,449	0.6
Male	49.0	49.0	X	49.3	49.3	X
Female	51.0	51.0	X	50.7	50.7	X
Foreign born	139,997	142,841	2.0	42,391,794	43,290,372	2.1
Male	50.9	51.2	X	48.7	48.6	X
Female	49.1	48.8	X	51.3	51.4	X
Foreign born; naturalized U.S. citizen.............	42,221	47,232	11.9	19,984,738	20,697,103	3.6
Male	43.9	47.5	X	45.9	45.9	X
Female	56.1	52.5	X	54.1	54.1	X
Foreign born; not a U.S. citizen	97,776	95,609	-2.2	22,407,056	22,593,269	0.8
Male	53.9	53.1	X	51.2	51.1	X
Female	46.1	46.9	X	48.8	48.9	X
Entered 2010 or later	13.6	16.3	X	12.3	15.6	X
Entered 2000 to 2009	36.0	37.4	X	28.6	27.9	X
Entered before 2000......................................	50.5	46.2	X	59.1	56.5	X
World Region of Birth, Foreign						
Foreign-born population, excluding population born at sea	139,997	142,841	2.0	42,390,705	43,289,646	2.1
Europe	7.6	6.9	X	11.2	11.1	X
Asia	21.0	24.3	X	30.1	30.6	X
Africa	1.2	2.4	X	4.6	4.8	X
Oceania	3.1	3.2	X	0.6	0.6	X
Latin America	65.7	61.3	X	51.6	51.1	X
North America	1.4	1.9	X	1.9	1.9	X
Language Spoken at Home and Ability to Speak English						
Population 5 years and over.............................	2,775,973	2,789,500	0.5	299,084,046	301,625,014	0.8
English only	93.1	92.7	X	78.9	78.5	X
Language other than English..........................	6.9	7.3	X	21.1	21.5	X
Speaks English less than "very well"..........	3.3	3.3	X	8.6	8.6	X

NA = Not available.
X = Not applicable.
- = Zero or rounds to zero.

Table AR-5. Median Income and Poverty Status, 2015

(Number, percent, except as noted.)

Characteristic	State		U.S.	
	Number	Percent	Number	Percent
Median Income				
Households (dollars)....................	41,995	X	55,775	X
Families (dollars)	52,449	X	68,260	X
Below Poverty Level (All People)	550,508	19.1	46,153,077	14.7
Sex				
Male	248,564	17.7	20,599,407	13.4
Female	301,944	20.4	25,553,670	16.0
Age				
Under 18 years..................	187,693	27.2	15,000,273	20.7
Related children under 18 years..................	183,332	26.8	14,693,239	20.4
18 to 64 years..................	315,532	18.2	26,960,369	13.9
65 years and over	47,283	10.3	4,192,435	9.0

X = Not applicable.

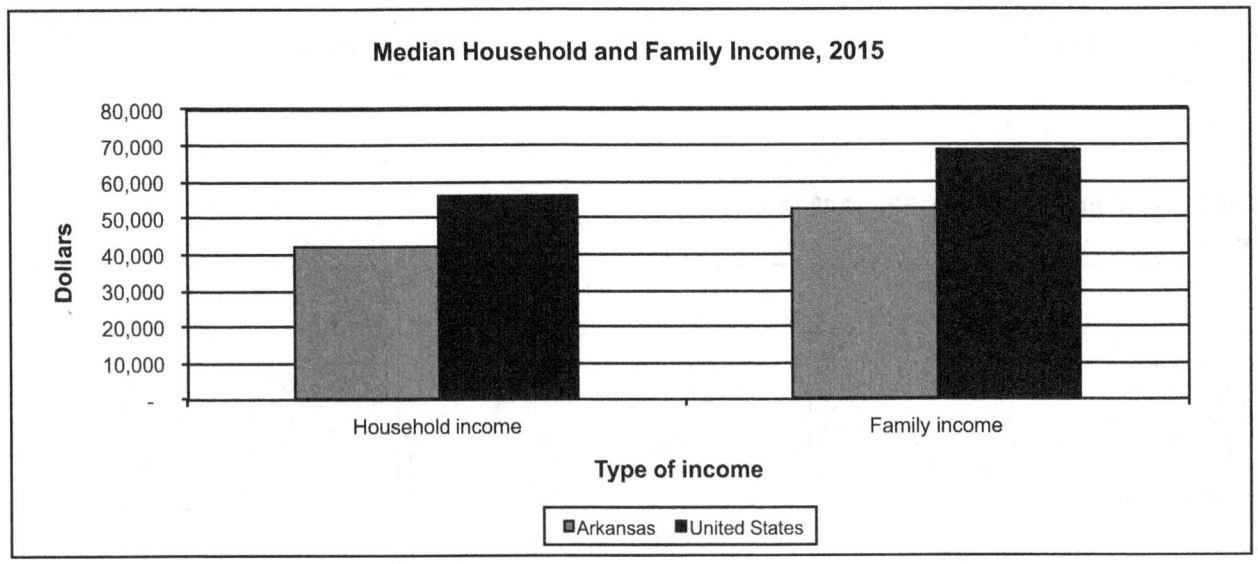

Median Household and Family Income, 2015

Table AR-6. Health Insurance Coverage Status for the Civilian Noninstitutionalized Population and Children Under 18 Years of Age

(Numbers in thousands, percent.)

Item	2007	2008	2009	2010	2011	2012	2013	2014	2015
Civilian Noninstitutionalized Population	2,805	2,802	2,833	2,868	2,885	2,896	2,907	2,914	2,924
Covered by Private or Public Insurance									
Number.........................	2,354	2,296	2,351	2,367	2,393	2,420	2,442	2,571	2,647
Percent.........................	83.9	81.9	83.0	82.5	82.9	83.6	84.0	88.2	90.5
Not Covered									
Number.........................	451	506	483	501	492	476	465	343	278
Percent.........................	16.1	18.1	17.0	17.5	17.1	16.4	16.0	11.8	9.5
Percent in the U.S. not covered.........................	15.3	15.1	15.1	15.5	15.1	14.8	14.5	11.7	9.4
Children Under 18 Years of Age	720	701	707	709	709	709	709	704	704
Covered by Private or Public Insurance									
Number.........................	679	640	663	663	669	667	670	670	669
Percent.........................	93.8	91.3	93.8	93.4	94.4	94.1	94.5	95.2	95.1
Not Covered									
Number.........................	44	61	44	46	40	42	39	34	35
Percent.........................	6.2	8.7	6.2	6.6	5.6	5.9	5.5	4.8	4.9
Percent in the U.S. not covered.........................	11.0	9.7	8.6	8.0	7.5	7.2	7.1	6.0	4.8

Table AR-7. Employment Status by Demographic Group, 2016

(Numbers in thousands, percent.)

Characteristic	Civilian noninstitutional population	Civilian labor force		Employed		Unemployed	
		Number	Percent of population	Number	Percent of population	Number	Percent of population
Total..	2,316	1,351	58.4	1,299	56.1	53	3.9
Sex							
Male...	1,115	717	64.3	691	62.0	26	3.6
Female	1,201	634	52.8	608	50.6	27	4.2
Race, Sex, and Hispanic Origin							
White...	1,881	1,093	58.1	1,058	56.3	35	3.2
Male..	914	588	64.3	570	62.3	18	3.1
Female..	966	505	52.2	489	50.5	17	3.3
Black or African American....................	339	201	59.3	186	54.7	16	7.7
Male..	153	94	61.8	88	57.5	7	6.9
Female..	186	107	57.3	98	52.5	9	8.4
Hispanic or Latino ethnicity[1]	134	98	73.2	94	70.6	4	3.6
Male..	73	62	85.4	60	82.6	2	3.2
Female..	61	35	58.4	34	56.0	2	4.2
Age							
16 to 19 years......................................	152	52	33.8	44	29.2	7	13.6
20 to 24 years......................................	176	128	72.6	119	67.5	9	7.0
25 to 34 years......................................	401	320	79.8	305	76.2	14	4.4
35 to 44 years......................................	363	289	79.7	280	77.2	9	3.1
45 to 54 years......................................	380	288	75.7	280	73.7	8	2.6
55 to 64 years......................................	377	203	53.8	198	52.5	5	2.3
65 years and over	466	73	15.6	71	15.3	1	1.7

NOTE: Data in Table 7 are from the Current Population Survey (CPS) and do not match the estimates in Table 8. See notes and definitions for further information.
[1] May be of any race.

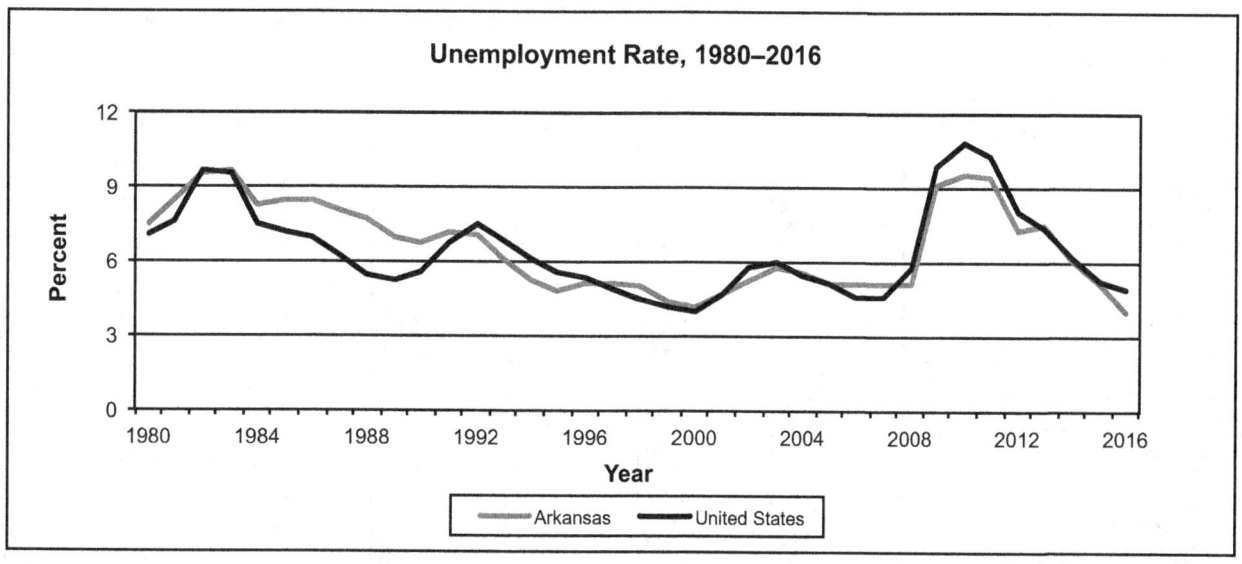

Table AR-8. Employment Status of the Civilian Noninstitutional Population Age 16 Years and Over

(Number, percent.)

Year	Civilian labor force	Civilian participation rate	Employed	Unemployed	Unemployment rate
2008..	1,375,257	62.9	1,300,017	75,240	5.5
2009..	1,358,911	61.7	1,252,399	106,512	7.8
2010..	1,353,338	60.6	1,242,496	110,842	8.2
2011..	1,362,682	60.5	1,249,514	113,168	8.3
2012..	1,342,327	59.3	1,240,646	101,681	7.6
2013..	1,307,986	57.5	1,212,009	95,977	7.3
2014..	1,304,141	57.0	1,224,398	79,743	6.1
2015..	1,330,099	57.9	1,260,615	69,484	5.2
2016..	1,342,691	58.1	1,288,994	53,697	4.0

Table AR-9. Employment and Average Wages by Industry

(Estimates through 2010 are based on the 2007 North American Industry Classification System [NAICS]. Estimates from 2011 onward are based on the 2012 NAICS.)

Industry	2009	2010	2011	2012	2013	2014	2015
	Number of Jobs						
Wage and Salary Employment by Industry..................	1,226,505	1,221,252	1,225,681	1,230,546	1,232,187	1,244,466	1,264,657
Farm Wage and Salary Employment.........................	12,371	12,869	12,021	9,006	11,182	11,319	12,578
Nonfarm Wage and Salary Employment....................	1,214,134	1,208,383	1,213,660	1,221,540	1,221,005	1,233,147	1,252,079
Private wage and salary employment........................	977,956	971,515	979,016	985,988	987,105	1,000,809	1,021,901
Forestry, fishing, and related activities......................	8,025	8,258	7,967	8,101	8,115	8,157	8,046
Mining..	8,388	8,523	8,985	8,657	7,530	6,708	5,873
Utilities...	7,029	7,313	7,169	7,705	8,089	7,903	7,951
Construction	54,400	50,544	48,838	48,847	46,791	47,407	50,485
Manufacturing..	161,967	158,433	157,440	154,607	152,129	153,251	155,058
Durable goods manufacturing..............................	79,406	77,131	77,746	76,820	75,356	76,252	75,989
Nondurable goods manufacturing.........................	82,561	81,302	79,694	77,787	76,773	76,999	79,069
Wholesale trade	47,345	46,626	46,850	47,441	46,495	46,754	47,426
Retail trade..	131,360	130,519	132,451	133,585	134,090	137,217	141,488
Transportation and warehousing...............................	53,350	52,146	53,934	54,596	54,171	55,061	56,828
Information	17,436	16,515	16,108	15,592	15,365	14,843	13,319
Finance and insurance	36,441	36,372	37,239	36,780	37,092	37,069	37,430
Real estate and rental and leasing............................	14,343	13,789	13,547	13,510	13,460	13,227	13,360
Professional, scientific, and technical services	38,345	38,900	39,528	39,151	40,225	40,964	41,677
Management of companies and enterprises..................	27,107	26,738	26,907	30,913	31,441	32,437	33,438
Administrative and waste services.............................	49,898	53,009	55,576	54,558	57,999	61,233	64,365
Educational services	14,449	15,129	15,655	15,678	16,390	16,584	16,870
Health care and social assistance.............................	153,213	156,054	156,453	159,899	160,153	160,680	163,557
Arts, entertainment, and recreation...........................	9,957	9,883	9,731	9,788	10,121	10,572	10,772
Accommodation and food services.............................	91,001	89,699	91,063	93,593	95,424	97,765	101,566
Other services, except public administration..................	53,902	53,065	53,575	52,987	52,025	52,977	52,392
Government and government enterprises..........................	236,178	236,868	234,644	235,552	233,900	232,338	230,178
	Dollars						
Average Wages and Salaries by Industry	35,915	36,691	37,817	38,937	39,629	40,543	41,486
Average Farm Wages and Salaries	18,221	18,934	17,819	29,729	26,322	22,053	25,880
Average Nonfarm Wages and Salaries	36,096	36,880	38,015	39,005	39,751	40,712	41,642
Average private wages and salaries..........................	35,775	36,679	37,880	39,082	39,854	40,899	41,839
Forestry, fishing, and related activities......................	28,789	30,742	31,572	32,519	33,099	34,505	36,005
Mining..	62,630	64,511	67,673	67,717	69,194	71,794	70,910
Utilities...	72,615	71,615	74,945	76,779	79,103	82,609	83,802
Construction	39,797	40,231	40,819	42,242	41,654	43,215	44,960
Manufacturing..	38,748	40,887	42,273	43,532	44,371	45,840	46,351
Durable goods manufacturing..............................	40,446	42,775	44,395	45,634	46,752	48,169	48,428
Nondurable goods manufacturing.........................	37,115	39,095	40,202	41,456	42,034	43,534	44,355
Wholesale trade	54,164	56,406	58,129	59,853	62,363	63,910	66,669
Retail trade..	23,230	23,930	24,346	24,925	25,296	25,762	26,274
Transportation and warehousing...............................	40,069	41,535	44,119	45,360	46,259	47,697	48,217
Information	65,581	48,326	50,153	49,648	51,185	53,445	55,801
Finance and insurance	51,106	52,581	54,870	57,766	57,838	59,827	61,952
Real estate and rental and leasing............................	30,131	31,484	32,897	34,298	34,671	35,918	37,125
Professional, scientific, and technical services	51,263	53,109	56,451	55,002	57,066	58,223	59,886
Management of companies and enterprises..................	79,901	88,420	89,560	95,986	103,321	105,614	107,717
Administrative and waste services.............................	25,143	25,905	26,984	27,163	26,922	27,590	28,080
Educational services	25,893	26,038	26,731	26,725	27,338	27,793	27,842
Health care and social assistance.............................	36,030	36,313	37,536	38,496	39,139	40,283	41,617
Arts, entertainment, and recreation...........................	19,609	19,233	20,402	20,771	21,039	21,418	22,336
Accommodation and food services.............................	14,084	14,573	15,048	15,616	15,831	16,287	16,931
Other services, except public administration..................	24,674	25,831	26,395	27,368	28,254	29,334	30,670
Government and government enterprises..........................	37,423	37,705	38,582	38,680	39,318	39,909	40,769

Table AR-10. Employment Characteristics by Family Type

(Number, percent.)

Family type and labor force status	2013		2014		2015	
	Total	Families with own children under 18 years	Total	Families with own children under 18 years	Total	Families with own children under 18 years
All Families..............................	751,124	313,438	749,751	310,218	761,494	311,436
FAMILY TYPE AND LABOR FORCE STATUS						
Married-Couple Families............................	548,537	204,825	544,067	197,290	561,297	205,898
Both husband and wife in labor force..............................	46.4	63.5	46.9	64.9	47.0	62.4
Husband in labor force, wife not in labor force	22.9	28.7	22.5	27.5	21.7	29.2
Wife in labor force, husband not in labor force	9.3	5.2	9.1	5.0	9.0	5.0
Both husband and wife not in labor force...............	21.2	2.6	21.5	2.6	21.8	3.1
Other Families	202,587	108,613	205,684	112,928	200,197	105,538
Female householder, no husband present..............................	74.1	75.7	74.0	75.6	75.0	74.9
In labor force..................................	48.5	59.8	48.3	59.8	48.0	59.3
Not in labor force	25.6	15.8	25.6	15.8	26.9	15.5
Male householder, no wife present...............	25.9	24.3	26.0	24.4	25.0	25.1
In labor force..................................	18.3	19.9	19.5	21.5	18.3	21.5
Not in labor force	7.6	4.4	6.6	3.0	6.8	3.6

Table AR-11. School Enrollment and Educational Attainment, 2015

(Number, percent.)

Item	State	U.S.
Enrollment		
Total population 3 years and over, enrolled in school	742,104	81,618,288
Enrolled in nursery school or preschool (percent)	6.4	6.0
Enrolled in kindergarten (percent)	5.5	5.0
Enrolled in elementary school, grades 1-8 (percent)................................	42.4	40.3
Enrolled in high school, grades 9-12 (percent)................................	20.5	20.9
Enrolled in college or graduate school (percent)................................	25.1	27.7
Attainment		
Total population 25 years and over	1,987,819	216,447,163
Less than ninth grade (percent)	5.3	5.5
9th to 12th grade, no diploma (percent)	9.3	7.3
High school graduate, including equivalency (percent)................................	34.1	27.6
Some college, no degree (percent)	22.7	20.7
Associate's degree (percent)	6.8	8.2
Bachelor's degree (percent)	14.0	19.0
Graduate or professional degree (percent)................................	7.8	11.6
High school graduate or higher (percent)	85.4	87.1
Bachelor's degree or higher (percent)	21.8	30.6

Table AR-12. Public School Characteristics and Educational Indicators

(Number, percent; data derived from National Center of Education Statistics.)..

Item	State	U.S.
Public Schools, 2014–2015 (except where noted)		
Number of school districts................................	287	18,260
Number of schools................................	1,100	98,373
Number of students	490,917	50,312,581
Number of teachers	35,430	3,132,351
Student-teacher ratio	13.9	16.1
Expenditures per student (dollars), FY 2014................................	9,752	11,066
Four-year adjusted cohort graduation rate (ACGR)[1,2]	84.9	83.2
Students eligible for free or reduced-price lunch (percent)................................	62.3	51.8
English language learners (percent)................................	7.8	9.4
Students age 3 to 21 served under IDEA, part B (percent)................................	13.6	13.0

Public Schools by Type	Number	Percent of state public schools
Total number of schools................................	1,100	100.0
Regular	1,064	96.7
Special education................................	4	0.4
Vocational education................................	26	2.4
Alternative education................................	6	0.5

NOTE: Every school is assigned only one school type based on its instructional emphasis.
[1] ACGR data represents a new method of calculating high-school completion rates and may not be comparable to previous years' data for Averaged Freshmen Graduation Rates (AFGR).
[2] The United States 4-year ACGRs were estimated using both the reported 4-year ACGR data from 49 states and the District of Columbia and using imputed data for Idaho. The estimate for American Indian/Alaska Native students also includes imputed data for Virginia.

Table AR-13. Reported Voting and Registration of the Voting-Age Population, November 2016

(Numbers in thousands, percent.)

Item	Total population	Total citizen population	Registered			Voted		
			Total registered	Percent registered (total population)	Percent registered (total citizen population)	Total voted	Percent voted (total population)	Percent voted (total citizen population)
U.S. Total	245,502	224,059	157,596	64.2	70.3	137,537	56.0	61.4
State Total............................	2,216	2,116	1,456	65.7	68.8	1,241	56.0	58.7
Sex								
Male	1,055	1,001	679	64.4	67.8	574	54.4	57.4
Female	1,161	1,115	777	66.9	69.7	667	57.4	59.8
Race								
White alone.................	1,822	1,749	1,196	65.6	68.4	1,032	56.7	59.0
White, non-Hispanic alone	1,689	1,674	1,166	69.1	69.7	1,008	59.7	60.2
Black alone...........	321	316	231	71.9	73.0	186	57.9	58.8
Asian alone	36	16	6	(B)	(B)	6	(B)	(B)
Hispanic (of any race)......................	135	77	29	(B)	(B)	24	(B)	(B)
White alone or in combination	1,848	1,775	1,213	65.6	68.3	1,043	56.5	58.8
Black alone or in combination.......	325	320	235	72.2	73.3	190	58.4	59.3
Asian alone or in combination.......	36	16	6	(B)	(B)	6	(B)	(B)
Age								
18 to 24 years...........	187	180	92	49.1	51.2	62	33.1	34.5
25 to 34 years...............	409	367	224	54.8	61.1	173	42.3	47.1
35 to 44 years...............	387	362	244	63.1	67.5	211	54.5	58.3
45 to 64 years...............	716	697	503	70.2	72.2	452	63.1	64.8
65 years and over	516	510	392	76.0	76.9	343	66.6	67.3

B = Base is less than 75,000 and therefore too small to show the derived measure.

Table AR-14. Crime

(Number, rate per 100,000. Data are derived from the FBI Uniform Crime Reports.)

Item	State			U.S. 1,2,3,4		
	2014	2015	Percent change	2014	2015	Percent change
TOTAL POPULATION[5]	2,966,835	2,978,204	0.4	318,907,401	321,418,820	0.8
VIOLENT CRIME						
Number........................	14,248	15,526	9.0	1,186,185	1,231,566	3.8
Rate	480.2	521.3	8.6	372.0	383.2	3.0
Murder and Nonnegligent Manslaughter						
Number........................	175	181	3.4	14,164	15,696	10.8
Rate	5.9	6.1	3.0	4.4	4.9	10.0
Rape[6]						
Number........................	1,816	1,931	6.3	118,027	124,047	5.1
Rate	61.2	64.8	5.9	37.0	38.6	4.3
Robbery						
Number........................	2,037	2,098	3.0	322,905	327,374	1.4
Rate	68.7	70.4	2.6	101.3	101.9	0.6
Aggravated Assault						
Number........................	10,220	11,316	10.7	731,089	764,449	4.6
Rate	344.5	380.0	10.3	229.2	237.8	3.7
PROPERTY CRIME						
Number........................	99,452	96,836	-2.6	8,209,010	7,993,631	-2.6
Rate	3,352.1	3,251.5	-3.0	2,574.1	2,487.0	-3.4
Burglary						
Number........................	24,816	22,640	-8.8	1,713,153	1,579,527	-7.8
Rate	836.4	760.2	-9.1	537.2	491.4	-8.5
Larceny-Theft						
Number........................	69,001	68,424	-0.8	5,809,054	5,706,346	-1.8
Rate	2,325.7	2,297.5	-1.2	1,821.5	1,775.4	-2.5
Motor Vehicle Theft						
Number........................	5,635	5,772	2.4	686,803	707,758	3.1
Rate	189.9	193.8	2.0	215.4	220.2	2.2

NOTE: Although arson data are included in the trend and clearance tables, sufficient data are not available to estimate totals for this offense. Therefore, no arson data are published in this table.

X = Not applicable.

- = Zero or rounds to zero.

[1] The crime figures have been adjusted.

[2] The data collection methodology for the offense of forcible rape used by the Minnesota state Uniform Crime Reporting (UCR) Program (with the exception of Minneapolis and St. Paul, Minnesota) does not comply with national UCR Program guidelines. Consequently, its figures for forcible rape and violent crime (of which forcible rape is a part) are not published in this table.

[3] Includes offenses reported by the Zoological Police and the Metro Transit Police.

[4] Because of changes in the state's reporting practices, figures are not comparable to previous years' data.

[5] Populations are U.S. Census Bureau provisional estimates as of July 1 of each year.

[6] The figures shown for the offense of rape were estimated using the revised Uniform Crime Reporting (UCR) definition of rape.

Table AR-15. State Government Finances, 2015

(Dollar amounts in thousands, percent distribution.)

Item	Dollars	Percent distribution
Total Revenue	21,665,918	100.0
General revenue	19,379,762	89.4
Intergovernmental revenue	7,002,577	32.3
Taxes	9,190,212	42.4
General sales	3,182,211	14.7
Selective sales	1,228,129	5.7
License taxes	384,306	1.8
Individual income tax	2,664,153	12.3
Corporate income tax	476,553	2.2
Other taxes	1,254,860	5.8
Current charges	2,204,297	10.2
Miscellaneous general revenue	982,676	4.5
Utility revenue	0	-
Liquor stores revenue	0	-
Insurance trust revenue[1]	2,286,156	10.6
Total Expenditure	21,352,833	100.0
Intergovernmental expenditure	5,214,039	24.4
Direct expenditure	16,138,794	75.6
Current operation	12,462,381	58.4
Capital outlay	1,180,020	5.5
Insurance benefits and repayments	1,882,832	8.8
Assistance and subsidies	478,053	2.2
Interest on debt	135,508	0.6
Exhibit: Salaries and wages	2,962,086	13.9
Total Expenditure	21,352,833	100.0
General expenditure	19,470,001	91.2
Intergovernmental expenditure	5,214,039	24.4
Direct expenditure	14,255,962	66.8
General expenditure, by function:		
Education	7,638,610	35.8
Public welfare	6,642,465	31.1
Hospitals	953,576	4.5
Health	288,644	1.4
Highways	1,443,062	6.8
Police protection	118,080	0.6
Correction	404,172	1.9
Natural resources	246,045	1.2
Parks and recreation	63,732	0.3
Governmental administration	604,315	2.8
Interest on general debt	135,508	0.6
Other and unallocable	931,792	4.4
Utility expenditure	0	-
Liquor stores expenditure	0	-
Insurance trust expenditure	1,882,832	8.8
Debt at End of Fiscal Year	4,985,140	X
Cash and Security Holdings	33,603,128	X

X = Not applicable.

- = Zero or rounds to zero.

[1] Within insurance trust revenue, net earnings of state retirement systems is a calculated statistic (the item code in the data file is X08), and thus can be positive or negative. Net earnings is the sum of earnings on investments plus gains on investments minus losses on investments. The change made in 2002 for asset valuation from book to market value in accordance with Statement 34 of the Governmental Accounting Standards Board is reflected in the calculated statistics.

Table AR-16. State Government Tax Collections, 2016

(Dollars in thousands, percent.)

Item	Dollars	Percent distribution
Total Taxes	9,452,883	100.0
Property taxes............................	1,119,958	11.8
Sales and gross receipts	4,590,072	48.6
General sales and gross receipts	3,314,363	35.1
Selective sales and gross receipts	1,275,709	13.5
Alcoholic beverages	55,164	0.6
Amusements	56,031	0.6
Insurance premiums	192,020	2.0
Motor fuels	479,879	5.1
Pari-mutuels	2,616	-
Public utilities	0	-
Tobacco products............................	230,527	2.4
Other selective sales	259,472	2.7
Licenses............................	396,891	4.2
Alcoholic beverages	4,624	-
Amusements	473	-
Corporations in general............................	26,703	0.3
Hunting and fishing............................	26,579	0.3
Motor vehicle	163,023	1.7
Motor vehicle operators	21,825	0.2
Public utilities	8,351	0.1
Occupation and business, NEC	143,422	1.5
Other licenses	1,891	-
Income taxes............................	3,231,617	34.2
Individual income............................	2,781,458	29.4
Corporation net income	450,159	4.8
Other taxes............................	114,345	1.2
Death and gift............................	3	-
Documentary and stock transfer	38,844	0.4
Severance	48,340	0.5
Taxes, NEC	27,158	0.3

- = Zero or rounds to zero.

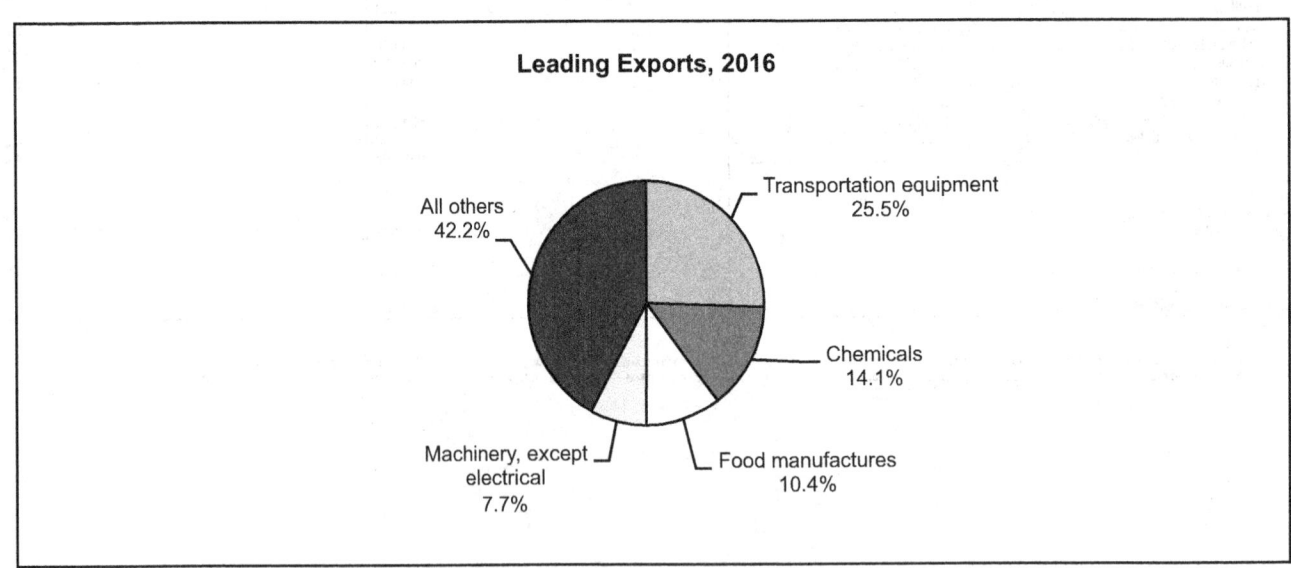

Leading Exports, 2016

- All others 42.2%
- Transportation equipment 25.5%
- Chemicals 14.1%
- Food manufactures 10.4%
- Machinery, except electrical 7.7%

CALIFORNIA

Facts and Figures

Location: Western United States; bordered on the N by Oregon, on the E by Nevada and Arizona, on the S by Mexico, and on the W by the Pacific Ocean

Area: 163,694 sq. mi. (423,970 sq. km.); rank—3rd

Population: 39,250,017 (2016 est.); rank—1st

Principal Cities: capital—Sacramento; largest—Los Angeles

Statehood: September 9, 1850; 31st state

U.S. Congress: 2 senators, 53 representatives

State Motto: *Eureka* ("I have found it")

State Song: "I Love You, California"

State Nickname: The Golden State

Abbreviations: CA; Calif.

State Symbols: flower—California poppy; tree—redwood; bird—California valley quail

At a Glance

- With an increase in population of 5.4 percent, California ranked 17th among the states in growth from 2010 to 2016.

- In 2015, California's median household income was $64,500, and 15.3 percent of the population lived below the poverty level.

- California's violent crime rate in 2015 was 426.3 per 100,000 population, compared to 383.2 for the entire nation.

- In 2016, California's unemployment rate of 5.4 percent ranked 10th in the nation.

- Approximately 14.8 percent of Californians self-identified their race as "Asian Alone" in 2016, which was the second highest percent in the country.

Table CA-1. Population by Age, Sex, Race, and Hispanic Origin

(Number, percent, except where noted.)

Sex, age, race, and Hispanic origin	2000	2010	2016 [1]	Average annual percent change, 2010–2016
Total population	33,871,648	37,253,956	39,250,017	0.3
Percent of total U.S. population	12.0	12.1	12.1	X
Sex				
Male	16,874,892	18,517,830	19,493,361	0.3
Female	16,996,756	18,736,126	19,756,656	0.3
Age				
Under 5 years...	2,486,981	2,531,333	2,487,372	-0.1
5 to 19 years..	7,747,590	7,920,709	7,642,087	-0.2
20 to 64 years..	20,041,419	22,555,400	23,773,923	0.3
65 years and over...	3,595,658	4,246,514	5,346,635	1.6
Median age (years)	33.3	35.2	36.4	0.2
Race and Hispanic origin				
One race...				
White	20,170,059	27,636,403	28,539,253	0.2
Black	2,263,882	2,486,549	2,547,480	0.2
American Indian and Alaska Native	333,346	622,107	648,055	0.3
Asian...	3,697,513	5,038,123	5,817,509	1.0
Native Hawaiian or Other Pacific Islander	116,961	181,431	196,944	0.5
Two or more races	1,607,646	1,289,343	1,500,776	1.0
Hispanic (of any race)	10,966,556	14,440,187	15,280,773	0.4

X = Not applicable.
[1] Population figures for 2016 are July 1 estimates. The 2010 estimates are taken from the 2010 Census.

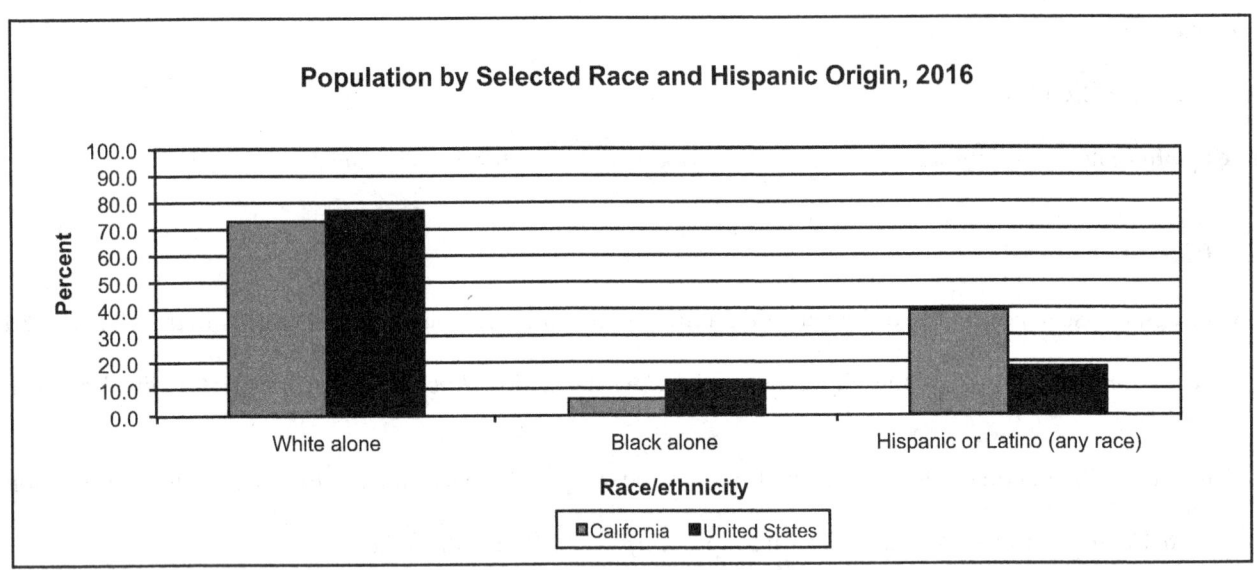

Population by Selected Race and Hispanic Origin, 2016

Table CA-2. Marital Status

(Number, percent distribution.)

Sex, age, race, and Hispanic origin	2000	2010	2015
Males, 15 Years and Over	12,844,669	14,662,335	15,576,921
Never married	33.8	39.8	40.6
Now married, except separated....................................	54.1	48.2	47.5
Separated...	2.0	1.9	1.8
Widowed..	2.2	2.1	2.1
Divorced..	7.9	8.0	8.0
Females, 15 Years and Over	13,231,494	15,043,190	15,999,819
Never married	26.5	32.3	33.6
Now married, except separated....................................	50.7	45.7	45.0
Separated...	2.9	2.7	2.6
Widowed..	8.9	8.1	7.8
Divorced..	11.0	11.2	11.0

Table CA-3. Households and Housing Characteristics

(Number, percent, dollars.)

Item	2000	2010	2015	Average annual percent change, 2000–2015
Total Households..	11,502,870	12,406,475	12,896,357	0.8
Family households..	7,920,049	8,507,856	8,835,906	0.8
Married-couple family...	5,877,084	6,082,566	6,342,293	0.5
Other family..	2,042,965	2,425,290	2,493,613	1.5
Male householder, no wife present..................	594,455	736,626	776,561	2.0
Female householder, no husband present........	1,448,510	1,688,664	1,717,052	1.2
Nonfamily households...	3,582,821	3,898,619	4,060,451	0.9
Householder living alone...................................	2,708,308	3,001,307	3,099,766	1.0
Householder not living alone..............................	874,513	897,312	960,685	0.7
Housing Characteristics				
Total housing units...	12,214,549	13,682,976	13,988,399	1.0
Occupied housing units	11,502,870	12,406,475	12,896,357	0.8
Owner occupied..	6,546,334	6,903,175	6,910,823	0.4
Renter occupied..	4,956,536	5,503,300	5,985,534	1.4
Average household size.......................................	2.87	2.94	2.97	0.2
Financial Characteristics				
Median gross rent of renter-occupied housing	747	1,163	1,311	5.0
Median monthly owner costs for housing units with a mortgage	1,478	2,242	2,123	2.9
Median value of owner-occupied housing units...........................	211,500	370,900	449,100	7.5

Table CA-4. Migration, Origin, and Language

(Number, percent.)

Characteristic	State 2014	State 2015	State Percent change	U.S. 2014	U.S. 2015	U.S. Percent change
Residence 1 Year Ago						
Population 1 year and over	38,340,324	38,675,135	0.9	315,095,393	317,635,720	0.8
Same house...	85.7	86.5	X	85.1	85.3	X
Different house in the U.S...................................	13.5	12.6	X	14.3	14.1	X
Same county..	9.3	8.6	X	8.7	8.5	X
Different county..	4.2	4.1	X	5.6	5.6	X
Same state..	2.8	2.8	X	3.3	3.2	X
Different state...	1.3	1.3	X	2.3	2.4	X
Abroad...	0.8	0.9	X	0.6	0.7	X
Place of Birth						
Native born..	28,290,101	28,456,482	0.6	276,465,262	278,128,449	0.6
Male...	50.1	50.2	X	49.3	49.3	X
Female...	49.9	49.8	X	50.7	50.7	X
Foreign born..	10,512,399	10,688,336	1.7	42,391,794	43,290,372	2.1
Male...	48.5	48.2	X	48.7	48.6	X
Female...	51.5	51.8	X	51.3	51.4	X
Foreign born; naturalized U.S. citizen.................	5,154,783	5,314,136	3.1	19,984,738	20,697,103	3.6
Male...	46.2	45.9	X	45.9	45.9	X
Female...	53.8	54.1	X	54.1	54.1	X
Foreign born; not a U.S. citizen..........................	5,357,616	5,374,200	0.3	22,407,056	22,593,269	0.8
Male...	50.7	50.5	X	51.2	51.1	X
Female...	49.3	49.5	X	48.8	48.9	X
Entered 2010 or later..	8.6	11.2	X	12.3	15.6	X
Entered 2000 to 2009..	24.3	23.7	X	28.6	27.9	X
Entered before 2000...	67.1	65.0	X	59.1	56.5	X
World Region of Birth, Foreign						
Foreign-born population, excluding population born at sea	10,512,292	10,688,122	1.7	42,390,705	43,289,646	2.1
Europe...	6.4	6.4	X	11.2	11.1	X
Asia..	37.8	38.6	X	30.1	30.6	X
Africa...	1.6	1.8	X	4.6	4.8	X
Oceania..	0.7	0.7	X	0.6	0.6	X
Latin America..	52.1	51.2	X	51.6	51.1	X
North America..	1.3	1.3	X	1.9	1.9	X
Language Spoken at Home and Ability to Speak English						
Population 5 years and over................................	36,290,808	36,637,169	1.0	299,084,046	301,625,014	0.8
English only...	56.1	55.4	X	78.9	78.5	X
Language other than English...............................	43.9	44.6	X	21.1	21.5	X
Speaks English less than "very well".................	18.5	18.6	X	8.6	8.6	X

NA = Not available.
X = Not applicable.
- = Zero or rounds to zero.

Table CA-5. Median Income and Poverty Status, 2015

(Number, percent, except as noted.)

Characteristic	State Number	State Percent	U.S. Number	U.S. Percent
Median Income				
Households (dollars)....................	64,500	X	55,775	X
Families (dollars)	73,581	X	68,260	X
Below Poverty Level (All People)	5,891,678	15.3	46,153,077	14.7
Sex				
Male	2,705,197	14.3	20,599,407	13.4
Female	3,186,481	16.4	25,553,670	16.0
Age				
Under 18 years....................	1,901,505	21.2	15,000,273	20.7
Related children under 18 years....................	1,862,540	20.8	14,693,239	20.4
18 to 64 years	3,484,214	14.3	26,960,369	13.9
65 years and over	505,959	9.9	4,192,435	9.0

X = Not applicable.

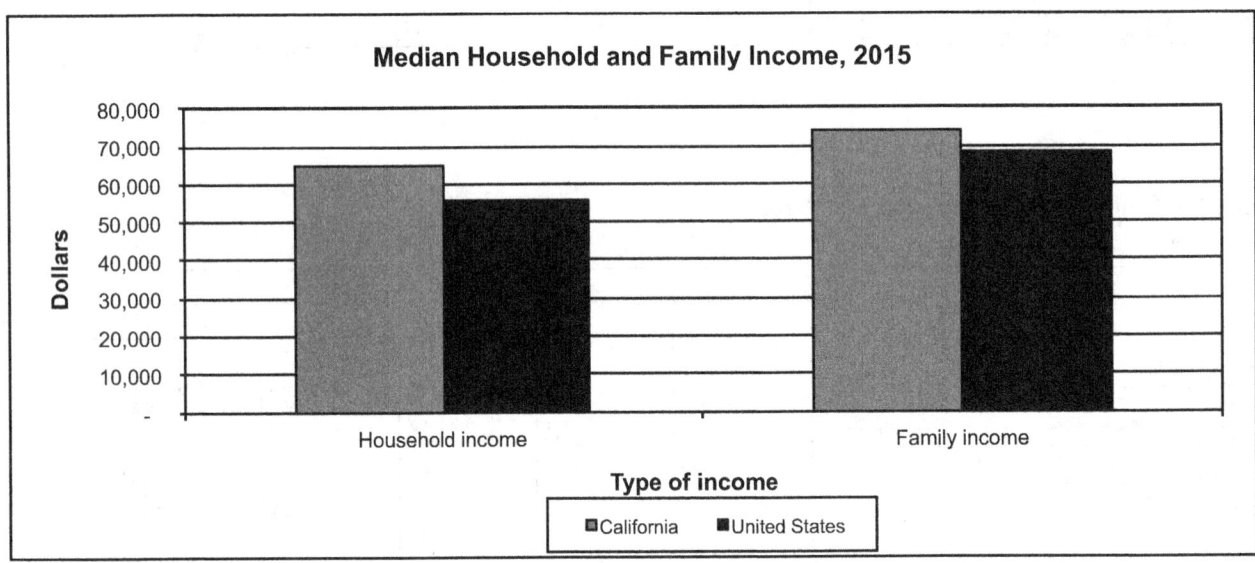

Median Household and Family Income, 2015

Table CA-6. Health Insurance Coverage Status for the Civilian Noninstitutionalized Population and Children Under 18 Years of Age

(Numbers in thousands, percent.)

Item	2007	2008	2009	2010	2011	2012	2013	2014	2015
Civilian Noninstitutionalized Population	36,295	36,161	36,377	36,816	37,162	37,524	37,832	38,297	38,650
Covered by Private or Public Insurance									
Number....................	29,682	29,730	29,818	29,990	30,436	30,815	31,331	33,531	35,332
Percent....................	81.8	82.2	82.0	81.5	81.9	82.1	82.8	87.6	91.4
Not Covered....................									
Number....................	6,613	6,431	6,559	6,835	6,726	6,709	6,500	4,767	3,317
Percent....................	18.2	17.8	18.0	18.5	18.1	17.9	17.2	12.4	8.6
Percent in the U.S. not covered....................	15.3	15.1	15.1	15.5	15.1	14.8	14.5	11.7	9.4
Children Under 18 Years of Age	9,423	9,348	9,423	9,289	9,252	9,223	9,158	9,135	9,103
Covered by Private or Public Insurance									
Number....................	8,410	8,337	8,532	8,456	8,507	8,503	8,485	8,638	8,801
Percent....................	89.3	89.2	90.5	91.0	92.0	92.1	92.6	94.6	96.7
Not Covered....................									
Number....................	1,013	1,011	891	833	745	720	673	497	302
Percent....................	10.7	10.8	9.5	9.0	8.0	7.9	7.4	5.4	3.3
Percent in the U.S. not covered....................	11.0	9.7	8.6	8.0	7.5	7.2	7.1	6.0	4.8

Table CA-7. Employment Status by Demographic Group, 2016

(Numbers in thousands, percent.)

Characteristic	Civilian noninstitutional population	Civilian labor force		Employed		Unemployed	
		Number	Percent of population	Number	Percent of population	Number	Percent of population
Total..	30,857	19,193	62.2	18,159	58.8	1,034	5.4
Sex							
Male..	15,070	10,581	70.2	10,028	66.5	552	5.2
Female	15,787	8,612	54.6	8,131	51.5	481	5.6
Race, Sex, and Hispanic Origin							
White	22,327	13,891	62.2	13,140	58.9	751	5.4
Male	11,058	7,847	71.0	7,449	67.4	398	5.1
Female	11,268	6,044	53.6	5,691	50.5	353	5.8
Black or African American........................	1,939	1,157	59.7	1,056	54.4	101	8.8
Male	921	574	62.4	516	56.0	58	10.2
Female	1,019	583	57.2	540	53.0	43	7.4
Hispanic or Latino ethnicity[1]	10,649	6,877	64.6	6,425	60.3	451	6.6
Male	5,282	3,973	75.2	3,738	70.8	235	5.9
Female	5,367	2,903	54.1	2,687	50.1	216	7.4
Age							
16 to 19 years....................................	2,075	581	28.0	478	23.0	104	17.8
20 to 24 years....................................	2,849	1,885	66.2	1,735	60.9	150	8.0
25 to 34 years....................................	5,586	4,457	79.8	4,197	75.1	260	5.8
35 to 44 years....................................	5,204	4,136	79.5	3,959	76.1	177	4.3
45 to 54 years....................................	5,222	4,110	78.7	3,945	75.5	165	4.0
55 to 64 years....................................	4,763	2,996	62.9	2,862	60.1	134	4.5
65 years and over	5,159	1,028	19.9	983	19.1	45	4.3

NOTE: Data in Table 7 are from the Current Population Survey (CPS) and do not match the estimates in Table 8. See notes and definitions for further information.
[1] May be of any race.

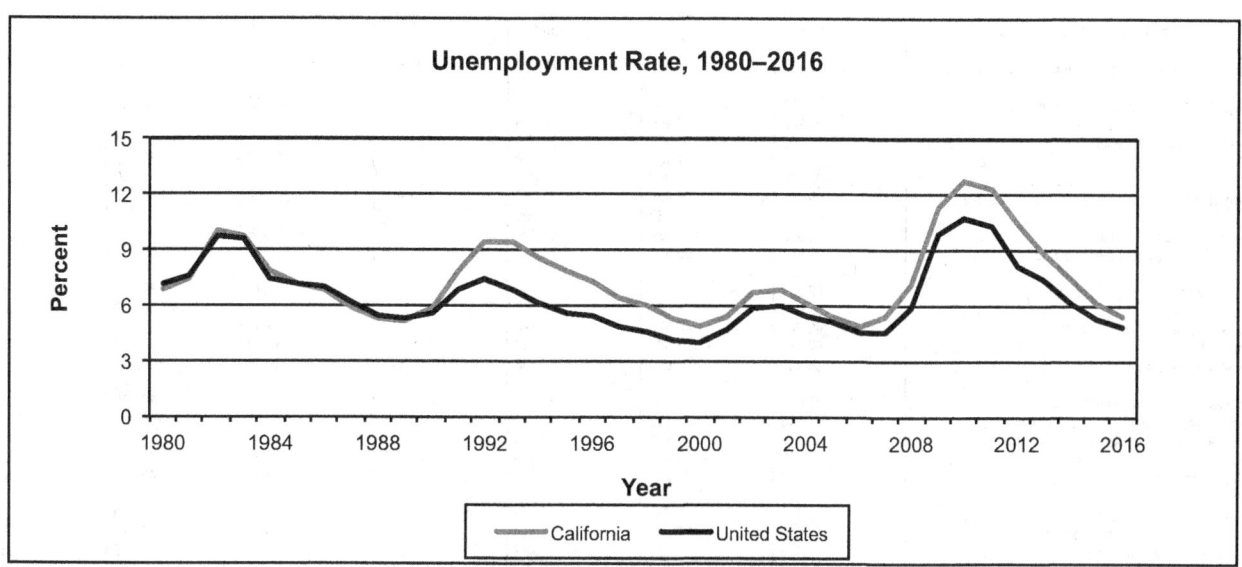

Table CA-8. Employment Status of the Civilian Noninstitutional Population Age 16 Years and Over

(Number, percent.)

Year	Civilian labor force	Civilian participation rate	Employed	Unemployed	Unemployment rate
2008..	18,178,123	65.8	16,854,482	1,323,641	7.3
2009..	18,215,140	65.2	16,182,572	2,032,568	11.2
2010..	18,336,271	64.2	16,091,945	2,244,326	12.2
2011..	18,415,100	63.5	16,258,133	2,156,967	11.7
2012..	18,551,413	63.1	16,627,835	1,923,578	10.4
2013..	18,670,058	62.7	17,001,033	1,669,025	8.9
2014..	18,827,925	62.4	17,418,042	1,409,883	7.5
2015..	18,981,770	62.2	17,798,614	1,183,156	6.2
2016..	19,102,726	62.3	18,065,043	1,037,683	5.4

Table CA-9. Employment and Average Wages by Industry

(Estimates through 2010 are based on the 2007 *North American Industry Classification System* [NAICS]. Estimates from 2011 onward are based on the 2012 NAICS.)

Industry	2009	2010	2011	2012	2013	2014	2015
	Number of Jobs						
Wage and Salary Employment by Industry..................	15,215,311	14,958,113	15,109,943	15,726,659	16,221,907	16,696,981	17,173,162
Farm Wage and Salary Employment..........................	161,057	167,173	163,477	158,790	165,882	180,222	179,440
Nonfarm Wage and Salary Employment....................	15,054,254	14,790,940	14,946,466	15,567,869	16,056,025	16,516,759	16,993,722
Private wage and salary employment........................	12,323,620	12,112,855	12,330,255	12,976,597	13,454,561	13,885,352	14,308,482
Forestry, fishing, and related activities........................	181,996	191,774	195,126	202,791	212,849	216,452	220,780
Mining...	23,953	24,372	26,290	28,048	27,858	28,597	26,219
Utilities...	60,043	57,109	58,292	59,386	58,934	57,872	57,600
Construction...	650,732	578,257	578,864	607,023	655,178	691,325	749,035
Manufacturing..	1,284,593	1,240,714	1,246,393	1,252,300	1,252,619	1,271,594	1,294,660
Durable goods manufacturing...............................	800,206	769,935	777,645	781,131	779,730	793,601	811,711
Nondurable goods manufacturing..........................	484,387	470,779	468,748	471,169	472,889	477,993	482,949
Wholesale trade	655,150	647,748	662,000	678,929	701,382	715,544	722,462
Retail trade..	1,546,027	1,526,808	1,550,561	1,582,568	1,613,810	1,643,658	1,675,045
Transportation and warehousing...............................	420,700	410,597	418,153	428,470	445,635	465,738	499,315
Information	435,872	426,557	430,873	434,346	446,949	460,760	487,002
Finance and insurance	556,700	532,879	541,683	553,120	552,516	550,475	560,606
Real estate and rental and leasing...........................	268,190	256,416	255,635	258,234	265,707	271,321	277,541
Professional, scientific, and technical services	1,040,957	1,032,268	1,068,397	1,116,103	1,152,308	1,184,378	1,215,406
Management of companies and enterprises..................	198,978	193,199	199,316	203,755	219,138	227,024	231,705
Administrative and waste services............................	854,210	863,137	888,260	940,979	989,531	1,035,046	1,065,505
Educational services	335,494	337,717	347,355	361,713	367,579	380,982	385,342
Health care and social assistance............................	1,470,249	1,501,079	1,522,010	1,843,849	1,983,750	2,046,843	2,131,469
Arts, entertainment, and recreation..........................	249,796	250,182	251,465	260,263	271,543	281,750	292,154
Accommodation and food services...........................	1,270,683	1,263,900	1,293,501	1,346,219	1,413,031	1,486,165	1,545,742
Other services, except public administration.................	819,297	778,142	796,081	818,501	824,244	869,828	870,894
Government and government enterprises........................	2,730,634	2,678,085	2,616,211	2,591,272	2,601,464	2,631,407	2,685,240
	Dollars						
Average Wages and Salaries by Industry	52,536	54,450	56,155	57,462	57,601	59,414	62,104
Average Farm Wages and Salaries	31,953	31,331	26,753	31,575	34,006	29,170	33,109
Average Nonfarm Wages and Salaries	52,756	54,711	56,476	57,726	57,845	59,744	62,410
Average private wages and salaries...........................	52,200	54,405	56,266	57,589	57,651	59,584	62,402
Forestry, fishing, and related activities........................	21,865	22,899	23,615	24,724	25,728	26,624	28,434
Mining...	114,351	131,186	129,586	135,288	135,964	138,907	138,023
Utilities...	100,915	103,320	108,064	110,932	117,337	118,310	127,705
Construction	55,175	55,858	57,232	58,949	59,059	60,300	63,062
Manufacturing..	69,753	74,238	76,505	79,002	79,512	83,047	85,564
Durable goods manufacturing...............................	77,552	85,624	88,798	90,609	90,378	95,056	97,407
Nondurable goods manufacturing..........................	56,868	55,617	56,112	59,760	61,597	63,107	65,657
Wholesale trade	63,683	65,910	68,396	70,038	70,527	73,458	77,368
Retail trade..	30,938	31,932	32,566	33,622	33,514	34,302	35,753
Transportation and warehousing...............................	46,940	48,576	49,776	51,257	51,831	52,754	53,966
Information..	92,574	101,596	107,897	114,760	134,269	138,163	147,550
Finance and insurance	89,059	94,010	97,188	102,697	103,202	109,400	114,130
Real estate and rental and leasing...........................	48,079	50,156	53,094	55,977	57,120	60,439	63,882
Professional, scientific, and technical services	86,685	91,109	94,876	103,618	98,971	105,266	113,000
Management of companies and enterprises..................	90,449	97,161	103,629	108,365	113,055	121,702	126,552
Administrative and waste services............................	36,802	38,027	39,140	40,627	40,037	40,759	42,656
Educational services	39,020	41,201	42,326	43,197	43,968	45,428	46,017
Health care and social assistance............................	52,462	53,459	54,825	49,337	47,352	47,939	49,666
Arts, entertainment, and recreation..........................	51,598	52,699	55,199	56,786	55,960	57,597	58,575
Accommodation and food services...........................	20,880	21,328	21,962	22,649	22,888	23,717	25,135
Other services, except public administration..................	28,770	30,171	30,720	31,213	31,864	32,513	34,035
Government and government enterprises........................	55,264	56,093	57,469	58,410	58,849	60,588	62,451

Table CA-10. Employment Characteristics by Family Type

(Number, percent.)

Family type and labor force status	2013 Total	2013 Families with own children under 18 years	2014 Total	2014 Families with own children under 18 years	2015 Total	2015 Families with own children under 18 years
All Families...................................	8,645,970	3,984,574	8,708,774	3,976,389	8,835,906	3,973,103
FAMILY TYPE AND LABOR FORCE STATUS						
Married-Couple Families.....................	6,160,314	2,753,934	6,185,858	2,754,933	6,342,293	2,783,907
Both husband and wife in labor force..................	50.5	60.2	50.0	59.9	49.0	59.7
Husband in labor force, wife not in labor force..........	25.8	33.8	26.5	34.0	26.2	33.9
Wife in labor force, husband not in labor force..........	7.4	3.8	7.6	4.1	7.5	3.9
Both husband and wife not in labor force...............	15.7	2.0	15.9	2.0	16.2	2.0
Other Families	2,485,656	1,230,640	2,522,916	1,221,456	2,493,613	1,189,196
Female householder, no husband present...............	69.5	72.4	69.4	71.9	68.9	71.3
In labor force	48.2	56.8	48.0	56.9	47.0	56.0
Not in labor force	21.3	15.6	21.4	15.0	21.8	15.2
Male householder, no wife present....................	30.5	27.6	30.6	28.1	31.1	28.7
In labor force	24.5	25.1	24.8	25.6	25.0	26.3
Not in labor force	6.0	2.5	5.8	2.5	6.1	2.5

Table CA-11. School Enrollment and Educational Attainment, 2015

(Number, percent.)

Item	State	U.S.
Enrollment		
Total population 3 years and over, enrolled in school	10,484,707	81,618,288
Enrolled in nursery school or preschool (percent)..................	5.7	6.0
Enrolled in kindergarten (percent)................................	5.0	5.0
Enrolled in elementary school, grades 1-8 (percent)...............	38.2	40.3
Enrolled in high school, grades 9-12 (percent)	20.6	20.9
Enrolled in college or graduate school (percent)..................	30.4	27.7
Attainment		
Total population 25 years and over	26,085,263	216,447,163
Less than ninth grade (percent)...................................	9.9	5.5
9th to 12th grade, no diploma (percent)...........................	7.9	7.3
High school graduate, including equivalency (percent).............	20.8	27.6
Some college, no degree (percent)................................	21.5	20.7
Associate's degree (percent)......................................	7.6	8.2
Bachelor's degree (percent)	20.3	19.0
Graduate or professional degree (percent).........................	12.0	11.6
High school graduate or higher (percent)..........................	82.2	87.1
Bachelor's degree or higher (percent).............................	32.3	30.6

Table CA-12. Public School Characteristics and Educational Indicators

(Number, percent; data derived from National Center of Education Statistics.)

Item	State	U.S.
Public Schools, 2014–2015 (except where noted)		
Number of school districts..	1,163	18,260
Number of schools..	10,303	98,373
Number of students	6,312,161	50,312,581
Number of teachers	267,685	3,132,351
Student-teacher ratio...	23.6	16.1
Expenditures per student (dollars), FY 2014........................	9,671	11,066
Four-year adjusted cohort graduation rate (ACGR)[1,2]	82.0	83.2
Students eligible for free or reduced-price lunch (percent).........	58.7	51.8
English language learners (percent)................................	22.4	9.4
Students age 3 to 21 served under IDEA, part B (percent)...........	11.3	13.0

Public Schools by Type	Number	Percent of state public schools
Total number of schools..	10,303	100.0
Regular	8,886	86.2
Special education	152	1.5
Vocational education	75	0.7
Alternative education...	1,190	11.6

NOTE: Every school is assigned only one school type based on its instructional emphasis.
[1] ACGR data represents a new method of calculating high-school completion rates and may not be comparable to previous years' data for Averaged Freshmen Graduation Rates (AFGR).
[2] The United States 4-year ACGRs were estimated using both the reported 4-year ACGR data from 49 states and the District of Columbia and using imputed data for Idaho. The estimate for American Indian/Alaska Native students also includes imputed data for Virginia.

Table CA-13. Reported Voting and Registration of the Voting-Age Population, November 2016

(Numbers in thousands, percent.)

Item	Total population	Total citizen population	Registered			Voted		
			Total registered	Percent registered (total population)	Percent registered (total citizen population)	Total voted	Percent voted (total population)	Percent voted (total citizen population)
U.S. Total	245,502	224,059	157,596	64.2	70.3	137,537	56.0	61.4
State Total...........................	29,894	24,890	16,096	53.8	64.7	14,416	48.2	57.9
Sex								
Male	14,604	12,131	7,663	52.5	63.2	6,833	46.8	56.3
Female	15,289	12,759	8,433	55.2	66.1	7,583	49.6	59.4
Race								
White alone..........................	21,592	18,104	12,084	56.0	66.7	10,908	50.5	60.3
White, non-Hispanic alone	12,480	11,954	8,732	70.0	73.0	8,020	64.3	67.1
Black alone...........................	1,849	1,768	1,018	55.0	57.6	856	46.3	48.4
Asian alone	4,838	3,585	2,080	43.0	58.0	1,859	38.4	51.9
Hispanic (of any race)	10,221	7,092	3,882	38.0	54.7	3,345	32.7	47.2
White alone or in combination	22,327	18,781	12,589	56.4	67.0	11,363	50.9	60.5
Black alone or in combination..........	2,111	2,007	1,161	55.0	57.9	990	46.9	49.3
Asian alone or in combination..........	5,066	3,798	2,243	44.3	59.0	2,007	39.6	52.8
Age								
18 to 24 years......................	3,760	3,308	1,656	44.0	50.1	1,411	37.5	42.7
25 to 34 years......................	5,742	4,579	2,795	48.7	61.0	2,379	41.4	51.9
35 to 44 years......................	5,145	3,797	2,412	46.9	63.5	2,074	40.3	54.6
45 to 64 years......................	9,835	8,252	5,581	56.8	67.6	5,124	52.1	62.1
65 years and over.................	5,412	4,955	3,651	67.5	73.7	3,429	63.4	69.2

Table CA-14. Crime

(Number, rate per 100,000. Data are derived from the FBI Uniform Crime Reports.)

Item	State			U.S. [1,2,3,4]		
	2014	2015	Percent change	2014	2015	Percent change
TOTAL POPULATION[5]...........................	38,792,291	39,144,818	0.9	318,907,401	321,418,820	0.8
VIOLENT CRIME						
Number........................	153,763	166,883	8.5	1,186,185	1,231,566	3.8
Rate	396.4	426.3	7.6	372.0	383.2	3.0
Murder and Nonnegligent Manslaughter						
Number........................	1,700	1,861	9.5	14,164	15,696	10.8
Rate	4.4	4.8	8.5	4.4	4.9	10.0
Rape[6]						
Number........................	11,578	12,811	10.6	118,027	124,047	5.1
Rate	29.8	32.7	9.7	37.0	38.6	4.3
Robbery						
Number........................	48,681	52,862	8.6	322,905	327,374	1.4
Rate	125.5	135.0	7.6	101.3	101.9	0.6
Aggravated Assault						
Number........................	91,804	99,349	8.2	731,089	764,449	4.6
Rate	236.7	253.8	7.2	229.2	237.8	3.7
PROPERTY CRIME						
Number........................	947,193	1,024,914	8.2	8,209,010	7,993,631	-2.6
Rate	2,441.7	2,618.3	7.2	2,574.1	2,487.0	-3.4
Burglary						
Number........................	202,669	197,404	-2.6	1,713,153	1,579,527	-7.8
Rate	522.4	504.3	-3.5	537.2	491.4	-8.5
Larceny-Theft						
Number........................	592,673	656,517	10.8	5,809,054	5,706,346	-1.8
Rate	1,527.8	1,677.1	9.8	1,821.5	1,775.4	-2.5
Motor Vehicle Theft						
Number........................	151,851	170,993	12.6	686,803	707,758	3.1
Rate	391.4	436.8	11.6	215.4	220.2	2.2

NOTE: Although arson data are included in the trend and clearance tables, sufficient data are not available to estimate totals for this offense. Therefore, no arson data are published in this table.

X = Not applicable.

- = Zero or rounds to zero.

[1] The crime figures have been adjusted.

[2] The data collection methodology for the offense of forcible rape used by the Minnesota state Uniform Crime Reporting (UCR) Program (with the exception of Minneapolis and St. Paul, Minnesota) does not comply with national UCR Program guidelines. Consequently, its figures for forcible rape and violent crime (of which forcible rape is a part) are not published in this table.

[3] Includes offenses reported by the Zoological Police and the Metro Transit Police.

[4] Because of changes in the state's reporting practices, figures are not comparable to previous years' data.

[5] Populations are U.S. Census Bureau provisional estimates as of July 1 of each year.

[6] The figures shown for the offense of rape were estimated using the revised Uniform Crime Reporting (UCR) definition of rape.

Table CA-15. State Government Finances, 2015

(Dollar amounts in thousands, percent distribution.)

Item	Dollars	Percent distribution
Total Revenue	332,456,557	100.0
General revenue	265,498,842	79.9
Intergovernmental revenue	82,907,118	24.9
Taxes	151,234,165	45.5
General sales	38,464,704	11.6
Selective sales	13,947,655	4.2
License taxes	9,420,863	2.8
Individual income tax	77,929,551	23.4
Corporate income tax	9,007,182	2.7
Other taxes	2,464,210	0.7
Current charges	21,373,082	6.4
Miscellaneous general revenue	9,984,477	3.0
Utility revenue	1,002,780	0.3
Liquor stores revenue	0	-
Insurance trust revenue[1]	65,954,935	19.8
Total Expenditure	330,502,626	100.0
Intergovernmental expenditure	97,968,655	29.6
Direct expenditure	232,533,971	70.4
Current operation	152,273,413	46.1
Capital outlay	10,183,475	3.1
Insurance benefits and repayments	57,750,839	17.5
Assistance and subsidies	4,930,538	1.5
Interest on debt	7,395,706	2.2
Exhibit: Salaries and wages	32,021,699	9.7
Total Expenditure	330,502,626	100.0
General expenditure	270,064,716	81.7
Intergovernmental expenditure	97,968,655	29.6
Direct expenditure	172,096,061	52.1
General expenditure, by function:		
Education	90,546,647	27.4
Public welfare	109,031,702	33.0
Hospitals	10,633,226	3.2
Health	8,648,877	2.6
Highways	10,529,860	3.2
Police protection	1,790,672	0.5
Correction	9,667,904	2.9
Natural resources	3,814,057	1.2
Parks and recreation	529,286	0.2
Governmental administration	7,485,654	2.3
Interest on general debt	7,168,706	2.2
Other and unallocable	10,218,125	3.1
Utility expenditure	2,687,071	0.8
Liquor stores expenditure	0	-
Insurance trust expenditure	57,750,839	17.5
Debt at End of Fiscal Year	151,715,007	X
Cash and Security Holdings	845,232,818	X

X = Not applicable.
- = Zero or rounds to zero.
[1] Within insurance trust revenue, net earnings of state retirement systems is a calculated statistic (the item code in the data file is X08), and thus can be positive or negative. Net earnings is the sum of earnings on investments plus gains on investments minus losses on investments. The change made in 2002 for asset valuation from book to market value in accordance with Statement 34 of the Governmental Accounting Standards Board is reflected in the calculated statistics.

Table CA-16. State Government Tax Collections, 2016

(Dollars in thousands, percent.)

Item	Dollars	Percent distribution
Total Taxes	155,231,252	100.0
Property taxes	2,513,157	1.6
Sales and gross receipts	53,365,753	34.4
General sales and gross receipts	39,189,007	25.2
Selective sales and gross receipts	14,176,746	9.1
Alcoholic beverages	368,699	0.2
Amusements	0	-
Insurance premiums	2,561,932	1.7
Motor fuels	5,000,539	3.2
Pari-mutuels	14,537	0.0
Public utilities	714,623	0.5
Tobacco products	840,034	0.5
Other selective sales	4,676,382	3.0
Licenses	8,551,427	5.5
Alcoholic beverages	57,406	-
Amusements	16,767	-
Corporations in general	75,066	-
Hunting and fishing	104,698	0.1
Motor vehicle	3,996,089	2.6
Motor vehicle operators	296,160	0.2
Public utilities	674,660	0.4
Occupation and business, NEC	3,303,576	2.1
Other licenses	27,005	-
Income taxes	90,655,530	58.4
Individual income	80,753,345	52.0
Corporation net income	9,902,185	6.4
Other taxes	145,385	0.1
Death and gift	0	-
Documentary and stock transfer	0	-
Severance	68,500	-
Taxes, NEC	76,885	-

- = Zero or rounds to zero.

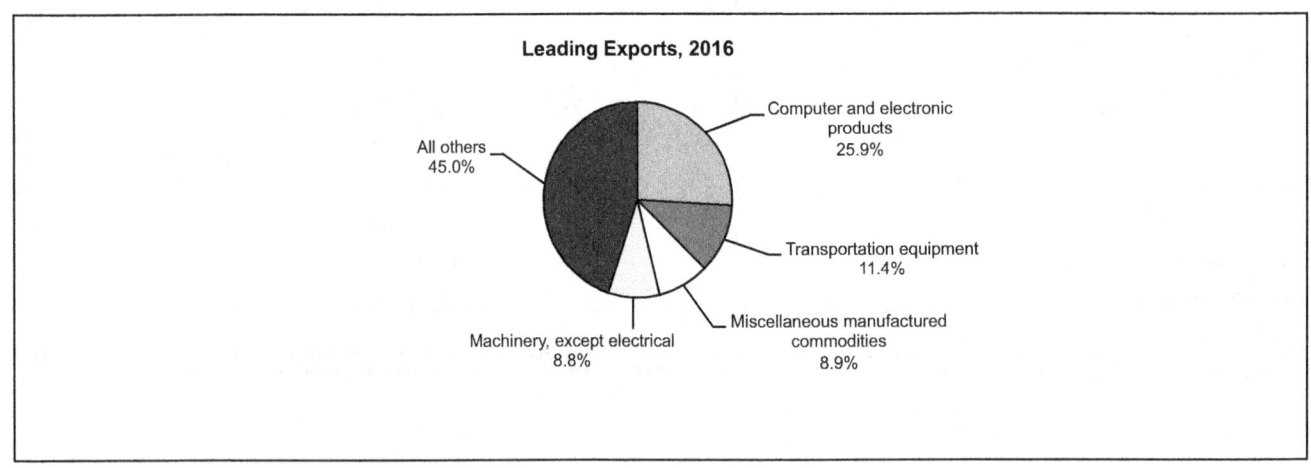

Leading Exports, 2016

- Computer and electronic products 25.9%
- All others 45.0%
- Transportation equipment 11.4%
- Miscellaneous manufactured commodities 8.9%
- Machinery, except electrical 8.8%

COLORADO

Facts and Figures

Location: Western United States; bordered on the N by Wyoming and Nebraska, on the E by Nebraska and Kansas, on the S by Oklahoma and New Mexico, and on the W by Utah; Colorado is one of the Four Corner states—at its SW corner it touches Arizona, New Mexico, and Utah

Area: 104,093 sq. mi. (269,601 sq. km.); rank—8th

Population: 5,540,545 (2016 est.); rank—21st

Principal Cities: capital—Denver; largest—Denver

Statehood: August 1, 1876; 38th state

U.S. Congress: 2 senators, 7 representatives

State Motto: *Nil sine numine* ("Nothing without providence")

State Songs: "Where the Columbines Grow"; "Rocky Mountain High"

State Nicknames: The Centennial State; Colorful Colorado

Abbreviations: CO; Colo.

State Symbols: flower—Rocky Mountain columbine; tree—Colorado blue spruce; bird—lark bunting

At a Glance

- With an increase in population of 10.2 percent, Colorado ranked 5th among the states in growth from 2010 to 2016.

- In 2015, 8.1 percent of Coloradans did not have health insurance, compared to 9.4 percent of the total U.S. population.

- At a rate of 15.4 per 100,000 population, the 2015 drug overdose death rate in Colorado was lower than the national average of 16.1 deaths per 100,000 population.

- In Colorado, 11.5 percent of the total population and 14.7 percent of persons under 18 years old lived below the poverty level in 2015, compared to nationwide poverty levels of 14.7 percent and 20.7 percent, respectively.

Table CO-1. Population by Age, Sex, Race, and Hispanic Origin

(Number, percent, except where noted.)

Sex, age, race, and Hispanic origin	2000	2010	2016 [1]	Average annual percent change, 2010–2016
Total Population...	4,301,261	5,029,196	5,540,545	0.6
Percent of total U.S. population	1.5	1.6	1.7	X
Sex				
Male..	2,165,983	2,520,662	2,785,818	0.7
Female	2,135,278	2,508,534	2,754,727	0.6
Age				
Under 5 years...	297,505	343,960	337,464	-0.1
5 to 19 years..	927,163	1,020,732	1,067,413	0.3
20 to 64 years..	2,660,520	3,114,879	3,392,144	0.6
65 years and over...	416,073	549,625	743,524	2.2
Median age (years)	34.3	36.1	36.6	0.1
Race and Hispanic Origin				
One race...				
White	3,560,005	4,450,623	4,846,441	0.6
Black...	165,063	214,919	248,833	1.0
American Indian and Alaska Native	44,241	78,144	88,197	0.8
Asian...	95,213	144,819	180,510	1.5
Native Hawaiian or Other Pacific Islander	4,621	8,420	10,602	1.6
Two or more races	122,187	132,271	165,962	1.6
Hispanic (of any race)..	735,601	1,078,225	1,181,219	0.6

X = Not applicable.
[1] Population figures for 2016 are July 1 estimates. The 2010 estimates are taken from the 2010 Census.

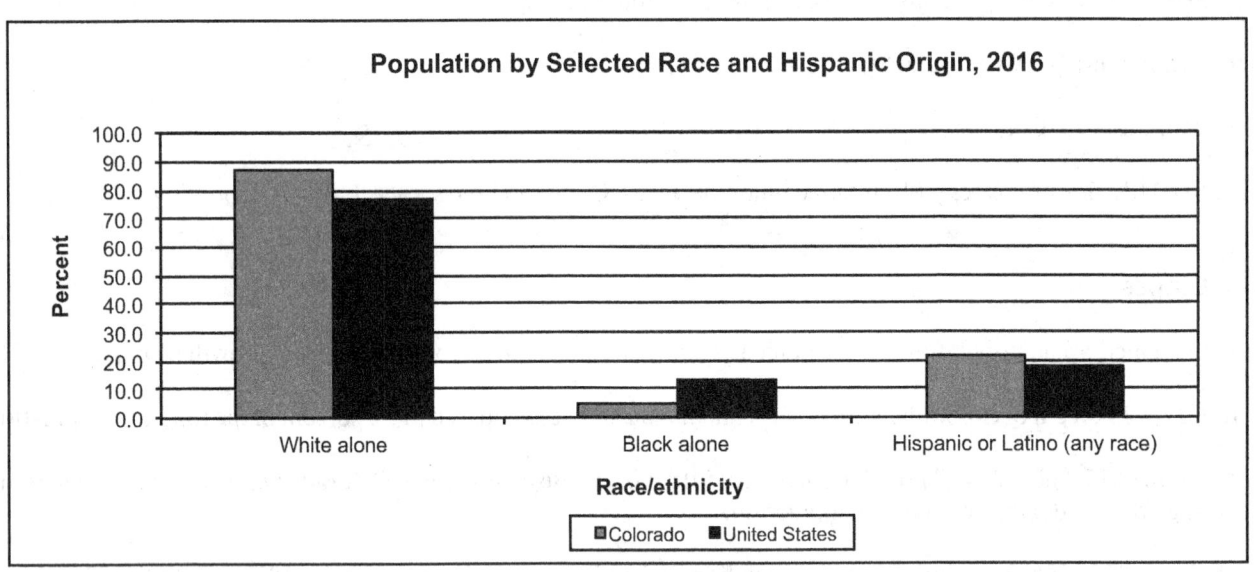

Population by Selected Race and Hispanic Origin, 2016

Table CO-2. Marital Status

(Number, percent distribution.)

Sex, age, race, and Hispanic origin	2000	2010	2015
Males, 15 Years and Over...	1,694,635	2,004,303	2,206,401
Never married	30.5	34.4	35.5
Now married, except separated...	56.6	51.7	50.8
Separated..	1.4	1.6	1.3
Widowed..	1.9	2.0	2.1
Divorced..	9.6	10.3	10.4
Females, 15 Years and Over..	1,690,734	2,017,425	2,199,719
Never married	23.4	26.9	27.9
Now married, except separated...	54.7	50.8	50.4
Separated..	1.8	2.0	1.6
Widowed..	7.6	7.0	6.4
Divorced..	12.5	13.3	13.7

Table CO-3. Households and Housing Characteristics

(Number, percent, dollars.)

Item	2000	2010	2015	Average annual percent change, 2000–2015
Total Households..	1,658,238	1,960,585	2,074,735	1.7
Family households..	1,084,461	1,258,885	1,331,861	1.5
Married-couple family.....................................	858,671	959,624	1,038,040	1.4
Other family..	225,790	299,261	293,821	2.0
Male householder, no wife present...................	66,811	90,518	93,024	2.6
Female householder, no husband present..........	158,979	208,743	200,797	1.8
Nonfamily households.......................................	573,777	701,700	742,874	2.0
Householder living alone.................................	435,778	555,080	564,757	2.0
Householder not living alone...........................	137,999	146,620	178,117	1.9
Housing Characteristics				
Total housing units..	1,808,037	2,214,262	2,309,122	1.8
Occupied housing units	1,658,238	1,960,585	2,074,735	1.7
Owner occupied..	1,116,173	1,292,792	1,322,618	1.2
Renter occupied...	542,101	667,793	752,117	2.6
Average household size......................................	2.53	2.52	2.57	0.1
Financial Characteristics				
Median gross rent of renter-occupied housing	671	863	1111	4.4
Median monthly owner costs for housing units with a mortgage	1,197	1,590	1,558	2.0
Median value of owner-occupied housing units	166,600	236,600	283,800	4.7

Table CO-4. Migration, Origin, and Language

(Number, percent.)

Characteristic	State 2014	State 2015	State Percent change	U.S. 2014	U.S. 2015	U.S. Percent change
Residence 1 Year Ago						
Population 1 year and over	5,293,943	5,393,067	1.9	315,095,393	317,635,720	0.8
Same house	80.5	81.7	X	85.1	85.3	X
Different house in the U.S.	18.8	17.7	X	14.3	14.1	X
Same county	9.5	8.6	X	8.7	8.5	X
Different county	9.3	9.1	X	5.6	5.6	X
Same state	5.2	4.9	X	3.3	3.2	X
Different state	4.1	4.2	X	2.3	2.4	X
Abroad	0.6	0.6	X	0.6	0.7	X
Place of Birth						
Native born	4,817,622	4,919,508	2.1	276,465,262	278,128,449	0.6
Male	50.4	50.3	X	49.3	49.3	X
Female	49.6	49.7	X	50.7	50.7	X
Foreign born	538,244	537,066	-0.2	42,391,794	43,290,372	2.1
Male	49.6	49.6	X	48.7	48.6	X
Female	50.4	50.4	X	51.3	51.4	X
Foreign born; naturalized U.S. citizen..............	214,373	207,694	-3.1	19,984,738	20,697,103	3.6
Male	45.5	44.2	X	45.9	45.9	X
Female	54.5	55.8	X	54.1	54.1	X
Foreign born; not a U.S. citizen........................	323,871	329,372	1.7	22,407,056	22,593,269	0.8
Male	52.3	52.9	X	51.2	51.1	X
Female	47.7	47.1	X	48.8	48.9	X
Entered 2010 or later	12.0	15.2	X	12.3	15.6	X
Entered 2000 to 2009	31.3	32.1	X	28.6	27.9	X
Entered before 2000..	56.7	52.8	X	59.1	56.5	X
World Region of Birth, Foreign						
Foreign-born population, excluding population born at sea	538,244	537,066	-0.2	42,390,705	43,289,646	2.1
Europe	14.6	13.4	X	11.2	11.1	X
Asia...	22.7	23.2	X	30.1	30.6	X
Africa	6.5	5.8	X	4.6	4.8	X
Oceania	0.7	0.7	X	0.6	0.6	X
Latin America	52.8	54.4	X	51.6	51.1	X
North America	2.6	2.5	X	1.9	1.9	X
Language Spoken at Home and Ability to Speak English						
Population 5 years and over................................	5,023,808	5,123,035	2.0	299,084,046	301,625,014	0.8
English only	82.8	82.8	X	78.9	78.5	X
Language other than English..............................	17.2	17.2	X	21.1	21.5	X
Speaks English less than "very well".................	6.2	6.2	X	8.6	8.6	X

NA = Not available.
X = Not applicable.
- = Zero or rounds to zero.

Table CO-5. Median Income and Poverty Status, 2015

(Number, percent, except as noted.)

Characteristic	State		U.S.	
	Number	Percent	Number	Percent
Median Income				
Households (dollars)...	63,909	X	55,775	X
Families (dollars)	78,384	X	68,260	X
Below Poverty Level (All People)	613,549	11.5	46,153,077	14.7
Sex				
Male	283,545	10.6	20,599,407	13.4
Female	330,004	12.3	25,553,670	16.0
Age				
Under 18 years...	182,541	14.7	15,000,273	20.7
Related children under 18 years..........................	177,098	14.4	14,693,239	20.4
18 to 64 years..	382,030	11.2	26,960,369	13.9
65 years and over	48,978	7.0	4,192,435	9.0

X = Not applicable.

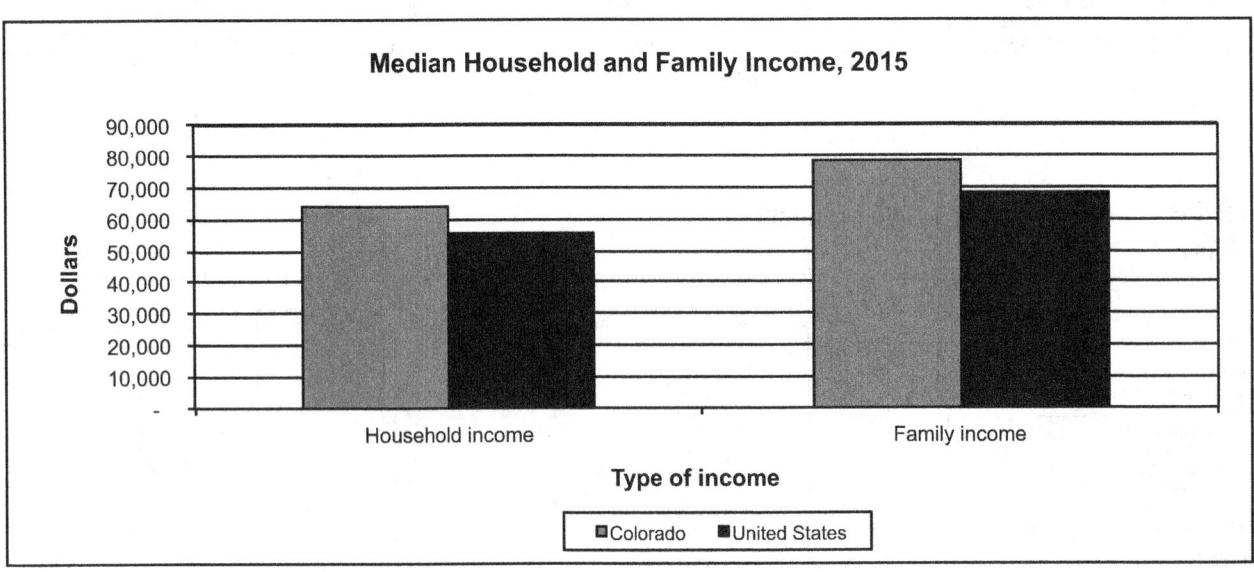

Median Household and Family Income, 2015

Table CO-6. Health Insurance Coverage Status for the Civilian Noninstitutionalized Population and Children Under 18 Years of Age

(Numbers in thousands, percent.)

Item	2007	2008	2009	2010	2011	2012	2013	2014	2015
Civilian Noninstitutionalized Population	4,877	4,853	4,930	4,957	5,025	5,095	5,173	5,266	5,367
Covered by Private or Public Insurance									
Number...	4,077	4,020	4,152	4,168	4,265	4,344	4,444	4,723	4,935
Percent...	83.6	82.8	84.2	84.1	84.9	85.3	85.9	89.7	91.9
Not Covered									
Number...	801	833	778	789	760	751	729	543	433
Percent...	16.4	17.2	15.8	15.9	15.1	14.7	14.1	10.3	8.1
Percent in the U.S. not covered..................................	15.3	15.1	15.1	15.5	15.1	14.8	14.5	11.7	9.4
Children Under 18 Years of Age	1,208	1,204	1,225	1,226	1,227	1,229	1,239	1,245	1,255
Covered by Private or Public Insurance									
Number...	1,051	1,031	1,101	1,102	1,111	1,120	1,137	1,175	1,202
Percent...	87.0	85.6	89.8	89.9	90.6	91.2	91.8	94.4	95.8
Not Covered									
Number...	157	173	124	124	116	109	102	70	52
Percent...	13.0	14.4	10.2	10.1	9.4	8.8	8.2	5.6	4.2
Percent in the U.S. not covered..................................	11.0	9.7	8.6	8.0	7.5	7.2	7.1	6.0	4.8

Table CO-7. Employment Status by Demographic Group, 2016

(Numbers in thousands, percent.)

Characteristic	Civilian noninstitutional population	Civilian labor force		Employed		Unemployed	
		Number	Percent of population	Number	Percent of population	Number	Percent of population
Total...	4,326	2,904	67.1	2,809	64.9	95	3.3
Sex							
Male..	2,141	1,600	74.7	1,553	72.5	48	3.0
Female...	2,185	1,304	59.7	1,256	57.5	48	3.6
Race, Sex, and Hispanic Origin							
White	3,852	2,583	67.0	2,500	64.9	82	3.2
Male..	1,904	1,423	74.7	1,382	72.6	41	2.9
Female...	1,948	1,159	59.5	1,119	57.4	41	3.5
Black or African American...................	185	129	69.7	123	66.4	6	4.8
Male..	NA	NA	NA	NA	NA	NA	NA
Female...	NA	NA	NA	NA	NA	NA	NA
Hispanic or Latino ethnicity[1]	790	535	67.6	510	64.5	25	4.7
Male..	402	321	79.8	309	76.9	12	3.7
Female...	388	214	55.0	200	51.6	13	6.2
Age							
16 to 19 years....................................	236	95	40.2	83	35.0	12	13.0
20 to 24 years....................................	351	274	78.1	262	74.8	12	4.2
25 to 34 years....................................	876	743	84.7	716	81.7	26	3.5
35 to 44 years....................................	740	620	83.7	601	81.2	19	3.1
45 to 54 years....................................	675	564	83.5	549	81.3	15	2.6
55 to 64 years....................................	682	459	67.3	451	66.2	8	1.7
65 years and over	766	150	19.6	147	19.2	4	2.5

NOTE: Data in Table 7 are from the Current Population Survey (CPS) and do not match the estimates in Table 8. See notes and definitions for further information.
[1] May be of any race.
NA = Not available.

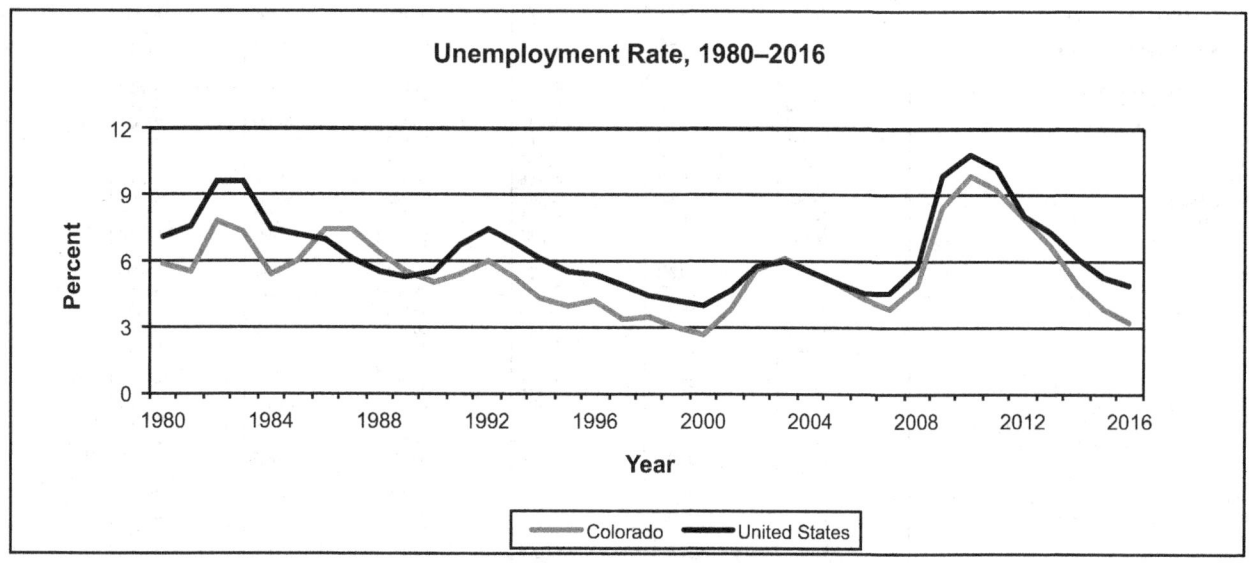

Unemployment Rate, 1980–2016

Colorado — United States

Table CO-8. Employment Status of the Civilian Noninstitutional Population Age 16 Years and Over

(Number, percent.)

Year	Civilian labor force	Civilian participation rate	Employed	Unemployed	Unemployment rate
2008..	2,716,625	72.1	2,585,243	131,382	4.8
2009..	2,722,982	70.9	2,524,443	198,539	7.3
2010..	2,724,417	70.4	2,486,404	238,013	8.7
2011..	2,736,079	69.7	2,507,265	228,814	8.4
2012..	2,759,437	69.1	2,542,267	217,170	7.9
2013..	2,780,536	68.3	2,590,651	189,885	6.8
2014..	2,815,200	67.9	2,674,635	140,565	5.0
2015..	2,828,529	66.7	2,718,698	109,831	3.9
2016..	2,891,046	66.9	2,795,233	95,813	3.3

Table CO-9. Employment and Average Wages by Industry

(Estimates through 2010 are based on the 2007 *North American Industry Classification System* [NAICS]. Estimates from 2011 onward are based on the 2012 NAICS.)

Industry	2009	2010	2011	2012	2013	2014	2015
				Number of Jobs			
Wage and Salary Employment by Industry..................	2,378,317	2,349,153	2,387,218	2,438,809	2,508,945	2,595,372	2,669,849
Farm Wage and Salary Employment.........................	12,051	12,592	11,877	11,957	12,763	11,975	11,633
Nonfarm Wage and Salary Employment....................	2,366,266	2,336,561	2,375,341	2,426,852	2,496,182	2,583,397	2,658,216
Private wage and salary employment....................	1,918,701	1,881,939	1,919,927	1,970,009	2,030,850	2,112,518	2,179,526
Forestry, fishing, and related activities....................	5,488	5,720	5,845	6,123	6,405	6,424	6,424
Mining........	23,957	24,046	27,602	30,067	30,282	33,680	30,419
Utilities........	8,314	8,179	8,138	8,045	7,842	8,148	8,210
Construction	137,215	119,224	115,869	119,294	131,491	146,265	152,528
Manufacturing........	129,910	125,597	129,321	132,160	132,867	136,528	141,078
Durable goods manufacturing........	84,546	81,212	84,036	86,437	86,028	88,175	90,297
Nondurable goods manufacturing........	45,364	44,385	45,285	45,723	46,839	48,353	50,781
Wholesale trade	94,124	91,240	92,201	94,601	97,135	100,420	103,748
Retail trade........	242,208	238,843	242,221	245,887	251,368	257,326	265,301
Transportation and warehousing........	63,294	60,733	61,863	63,946	66,496	69,434	71,561
Information........	74,819	71,749	72,474	69,954	69,965	70,179	70,597
Finance and insurance	103,474	101,650	102,496	104,569	107,617	108,848	111,434
Real estate and rental and leasing........	44,761	42,460	42,382	42,885	43,968	45,516	47,912
Professional, scientific, and technical services	172,355	169,405	173,677	179,917	190,520	198,317	206,122
Management of companies and enterprises........	28,562	28,834	29,920	31,811	34,657	35,489	36,525
Administrative and waste services........	133,804	134,717	138,793	146,734	150,022	155,419	158,590
Educational services	39,915	41,102	42,210	44,094	45,250	47,802	48,805
Health care and social assistance........	230,718	236,918	243,186	250,481	254,375	265,199	278,923
Arts, entertainment, and recreation........	45,369	45,525	46,188	47,374	47,922	49,702	51,312
Accommodation and food services........	220,179	219,411	227,117	234,160	243,440	252,637	263,107
Other services, except public administration........	120,235	116,586	118,424	117,907	119,228	125,185	126,930
Government and government enterprises........	447,565	454,622	455,414	456,843	465,332	470,879	478,690
				Dollars			
Average Wages and Salaries by Industry	47,217	48,437	49,664	51,260	51,654	53,442	54,900
Average Farm Wages and Salaries	37,691	31,724	33,979	38,509	40,726	41,821	40,872
Average Nonfarm Wages and Salaries	47,266	48,527	49,742	51,323	51,710	53,496	54,961
Average private wages and salaries........	47,435	48,818	50,192	52,033	52,340	54,244	55,745
Forestry, fishing, and related activities........	23,178	24,122	24,717	25,275	26,128	27,557	29,381
Mining........	91,131	100,276	105,864	104,927	109,964	113,847	115,803
Utilities........	82,161	87,151	91,745	100,647	90,933	93,545	96,924
Construction	48,063	48,815	49,856	51,118	51,966	54,567	56,221
Manufacturing........	59,663	61,761	63,371	64,040	64,245	67,023	68,360
Durable goods manufacturing........	64,831	67,851	69,995	70,900	71,194	73,717	76,012
Nondurable goods manufacturing........	50,031	50,616	51,081	51,073	51,481	54,818	54,754
Wholesale trade	66,652	69,688	72,904	75,091	75,691	78,933	80,972
Retail trade........	27,480	27,852	28,110	28,930	29,322	30,264	31,249
Transportation and warehousing........	45,074	46,330	47,504	49,648	52,102	54,520	55,661
Information........	79,079	83,611	85,856	90,251	92,109	97,855	96,236
Finance and insurance	70,633	73,432	76,342	79,736	81,358	84,896	89,899
Real estate and rental and leasing........	41,471	43,188	45,195	48,328	50,529	51,969	54,437
Professional, scientific, and technical services	78,582	81,097	82,811	85,508	86,369	88,620	90,355
Management of companies and enterprises........	119,237	127,324	133,543	155,549	127,658	136,933	145,515
Administrative and waste services........	34,641	35,348	36,061	36,857	35,890	37,175	38,919
Educational services	32,883	33,932	34,476	35,060	35,653	35,459	35,325
Health care and social assistance........	45,127	45,390	46,167	47,118	47,360	48,241	49,699
Arts, entertainment, and recreation........	33,732	33,516	34,359	34,755	35,796	37,060	39,548
Accommodation and food services........	19,341	19,774	20,449	21,119	21,662	22,491	23,591
Other services, except public administration........	30,878	31,973	32,522	34,166	35,166	35,854	37,378
Government and government enterprises........	46,540	47,324	47,846	48,262	48,962	50,136	51,390

Table CO-10. Employment Characteristics by Family Type

(Number, percent.)

Family type and labor force status	2013		2014		2015	
	Total	Families with own children under 18 years	Total	Families with own children under 18 years	Total	Families with own children under 18 years
All Families..	1,279,941	584,086	1,309,702	599,088	1,331,861	597,501
FAMILY TYPE AND LABOR FORCE STATUS						
Married-Couple Families......................................	982,202	411,595	1,000,145	421,101	1,038,040	435,028
Both husband and wife in labor force..............................	54.1	64.9	54.0	64.4	54.3	65.4
Husband in labor force, wife not in labor force	23.6	30.4	23.3	30.5	22.0	28.5
Wife in labor force, husband not in labor force	7.0	3.3	6.8	3.6	7.2	3.9
Both husband and wife not in labor force...........................	15.0	1.2	15.8	1.5	15.5	1.7
Other Families	297,739	172,491	309,557	177,987	293,821	162,473
Female householder, no husband present.............................	70.3	72.9	68.0	69.1	68.3	69.9
In labor force...	52.8	61.5	51.2	58.6	50.1	57.9
Not in labor force	17.5	11.4	16.8	10.5	18.2	11.9
Male householder, no wife present..................................	29.7	27.1	32.0	30.9	31.7	30.1
In labor force...	24.5	25.2	26.9	29.0	26.4	28.6
Not in labor force	5.2	1.9	5.1	1.9	5.3	1.5

Table CO-11. School Enrollment and Educational Attainment, 2015

(Number, percent.)

Item	State	U.S.
Enrollment		
Total population 3 years and over, enrolled in school	1,395,429	81,618,288
Enrolled in nursery school or preschool (percent)........................	6.2	6.0
Enrolled in kindergarten (percent)........................	4.9	5.0
Enrolled in elementary school, grades 1-8 (percent)........................	40.9	40.3
Enrolled in high school, grades 9-12 (percent)	20.0	20.9
Enrolled in college or graduate school (percent)........................	27.8	27.7
Attainment		
Total population 25 years and over	3,671,853	216,447,163
Less than ninth grade (percent)........................	3.7	5.5
9th to 12th grade, no diploma (percent)........................	5.1	7.3
High school graduate, including equivalency (percent)........................	21.7	27.6
Some college, no degree (percent)........................	22.0	20.7
Associate's degree (percent)........................	8.2	8.2
Bachelor's degree (percent)........................	24.8	19.0
Graduate or professional degree (percent)........................	14.5	11.6
High school graduate or higher (percent)........................	91.2	87.1
Bachelor's degree or higher (percent)........................	39.2	30.6

Table CO-12. Public School Characteristics and Educational Indicators

(Number, percent; data derived from National Center of Education Statistics.)

Item	State	U.S.
Public Schools, 2014–2015 (except where noted)		
Number of school districts........................	262	18,260
Number of schools........................	1,843	98,373
Number of students	889,006	50,312,581
Number of teachers	51,388	3,132,351
Student-teacher ratio	17.3	16.1
Expenditures per student (dollars), FY 2014........................	9,036	11,066
Four-year adjusted cohort graduation rate (ACGR)[1,2]	77.3	83.2
Students eligible for free or reduced-price lunch (percent)........................	41.6	51.8
English language learners (percent)........................	11.7	9.4
Students age 3 to 21 served under IDEA, part B (percent)........................	10.4	13.0

Public Schools by Type	Number	Percent of state public schools
Total number of schools........................	1,843	100.0
Regular	1,741	94.5
Special education	6	0.3
Vocational education	6	0.3
Alternative education........................	90	4.9

NOTE: Every school is assigned only one school type based on its instructional emphasis.
[1] ACGR data represents a new method of calculating high-school completion rates and may not be comparable to previous years' data for Averaged Freshmen Graduation Rates (AFGR).
[2] The United States 4-year ACGRs were estimated using both the reported 4-year ACGR data from 49 states and the District of Columbia and using imputed data for Idaho. The estimate for American Indian/Alaska Native students also includes imputed data for Virginia.

Table CO-13. Reported Voting and Registration of the Voting-Age Population, November 2016

(Numbers in thousands, percent.)

Item	Total population	Total citizen population	Registered				Voted		
			Total registered	Percent registered (total population)	Percent registered (total citizen population)		Total voted	Percent voted (total population)	Percent voted (total citizen population)
U.S. Total	245,502	224,059	157,596	64.2	70.3		137,537	56.0	61.4
State Total..........................	4,242	3,895	2,893	68.2	74.3		2,707	63.8	69.5
Sex									
Male	2,102	1,902	1,401	66.7	73.7		1,297	61.7	68.2
Female	2,140	1,994	1,492	69.7	74.8		1,410	65.9	70.7
Race									
White alone..........................	3,743	3,517	2,663	71.2	75.7		2,494	66.6	70.9
White, non-Hispanic alone	3,181	3,125	2,421	76.1	77.5		2,281	71.7	73.0
Black alone..........................	185	167	124	67.0	74.1		124	67.0	74.1
Asian alone..........................	170	104	39	22.7	37.0		35	20.5	33.4
Hispanic (of any race).....................	633	426	272	42.9	63.8		237	37.4	55.6
White alone or in combination	3,857	3,595	2,711	70.3	75.4		2,538	65.8	70.6
Black alone or in combination.......	188	170	127	67.6	74.6		127	67.6	74.6
Asian alone or in combination.......	188	122	52	27.5	42.2		44	23.5	36.1
Age									
18 to 24 years.....................	410	361	210	51.2	58.2		177	43.1	49.0
25 to 34 years.....................	922	851	596	64.7	70.1		535	58.0	62.9
35 to 44 years.....................	774	683	535	69.1	78.2		514	66.5	75.3
45 to 64 years.....................	1,342	1,243	914	68.1	73.6		867	64.6	69.7
65 years and over	794	757	638	80.4	84.3		614	77.3	81.1

B = Base is less than 75,000 and therefore too small to show the derived measure.

Table CO-14. Crime

(Number, rate per 100,000. Data are derived from the FBI Uniform Crime Reports.)

Item	State			U.S. [1,2,3,4]		
	2014	2015	Percent change	2014	2015	Percent change
TOTAL POPULATION[5]	5,355,588	5,456,574	1.9	318,907,401	321,418,820	0.8
VIOLENT CRIME						
Number.................................	16,487	17,515	6.2	1,186,185	1,231,566	3.8
Rate	307.8	321.0	4.3	372.0	383.2	3.0
Murder and Nonnegligent Manslaughter						
Number.................................	150	176	17.3	14,164	15,696	10.8
Rate	2.8	3.2	15.2	4.4	4.9	10.0
Rape[6]						
Number.................................	3,089	3,257	5.4	118,027	124,047	5.1
Rate	57.7	59.7	3.5	37.0	38.6	4.3
Robbery						
Number.................................	3,037	3,323	9.4	322,905	327,374	1.4
Rate	56.7	60.9	7.4	101.3	101.9	0.6
Aggravated Assault						
Number.................................	10,211	10,759	5.4	731,089	764,449	4.6
Rate	190.7	197.2	3.4	229.2	237.8	3.7
PROPERTY CRIME						
Number.................................	135,789	144,136	6.1	8,209,010	7,993,631	-2.6
Rate	2,535.5	2,641.5	4.2	2,574.1	2,487.0	-3.4
Burglary						
Number.................................	23,502	23,454	-0.2	1,713,153	1,579,527	-7.8
Rate	438.8	429.8	-2.1	537.2	491.4	-8.5
Larceny-Theft						
Number.................................	99,688	104,682	5.0	5,809,054	5,706,346	-1.8
Rate	1,861.4	1,918.5	3.1	1,821.5	1,775.4	-2.5
Motor Vehicle Theft						
Number.................................	12,599	16,000	27.0	686,803	707,758	3.1
Rate	235.2	293.2	24.6	215.4	220.2	2.2

NOTE: Although arson data are included in the trend and clearance tables, sufficient data are not available to estimate totals for this offense. Therefore, no arson data are published in this table.
X = Not applicable.
- = Zero or rounds to zero.
[1] The crime figures have been adjusted.
[2] The data collection methodology for the offense of forcible rape used by the Minnesota state Uniform Crime Reporting (UCR) Program (with the exception of Minneapolis and St. Paul, Minnesota) does not comply with national UCR Program guidelines. Consequently, its figures for forcible rape and violent crime (of which forcible rape is a part) are not published in this table.
[3] Includes offenses reported by the Zoological Police and the Metro Transit Police.
[4] Because of changes in the state's reporting practices, figures are not comparable to previous years' data.
[5] Populations are U.S. Census Bureau provisional estimates as of July 1 of each year.
[6] The figures shown for the offense of rape were estimated using the revised Uniform Crime Reporting (UCR) definition of rape.

Table CO-15. State Government Finances, 2015

(Dollar amounts in thousands, percent distribution.)

Item	Dollars	Percent distribution
Total Revenue	35,106,931	100.0
General revenue	28,839,683	82.1
Intergovernmental revenue	7,866,964	22.4
Taxes	12,797,117	36.5
General sales	2,817,773	8.0
Selective sales	1,976,239	5.6
License taxes	680,739	1.9
Individual income tax	6,360,629	18.1
Corporate income tax	669,054	1.9
Other taxes	292,683	0.8
Current charges	5,825,049	16.6
Miscellaneous general revenue	2,350,553	6.7
Utility revenue	0	-
Liquor stores revenue	0	-
Insurance trust revenue[1]	6,267,248	17.9
Total Expenditure	34,802,768	100.0
Intergovernmental expenditure	7,463,526	21.4
Direct expenditure	27,339,242	78.6
Current operation	18,540,378	53.3
Capital outlay	1,793,487	5.2
Insurance benefits and repayments	5,670,780	16.3
Assistance and subsidies	436,292	1.3
Interest on debt	898,305	2.6
Exhibit: Salaries and wages	4,860,013	14.0
Total Expenditure	34,802,768	100.0
General expenditure	29,118,685	83.7
Intergovernmental expenditure	7,463,526	21.4
Direct expenditure	21,655,159	62.2
General expenditure, by function:		
Education	10,824,727	31.1
Public welfare	7,910,755	22.7
Hospitals	3,053,876	8.8
Health	584,838	1.7
Highways	1,722,621	4.9
Police protection	236,328	0.7
Correction	1,052,356	3.0
Natural resources	308,195	0.9
Parks and recreation	95,885	0.3
Governmental administration	877,481	2.5
Interest on general debt	886,621	2.5
Other and unallocable	1,565,002	4.5
Utility expenditure	13,303	-
Liquor stores expenditure	0	-
Insurance trust expenditure	5,670,780	16.3
Debt at End of Fiscal Year	17,200,428	X
Cash and Security Holdings	76,870,758	X

X = Not applicable.
- = Zero or rounds to zero.
[1] Within insurance trust revenue, net earnings of state retirement systems is a calculated statistic (the item code in the data file is X08), and thus can be positive or negative. Net earnings is the sum of earnings on investments plus gains on investments minus losses on investments. The change made in 2002 for asset valuation from book to market value in accordance with Statement 34 of the Governmental Accounting Standards Board is reflected in the calculated statistics.

Table CO-16. State Government Tax Collections, 2016

(Dollars in thousands, percent.)

Item	Dollars	Percent distribution
Total Taxes	12,795,318	100.0
Property taxes..	0	-
Sales and gross receipts	4,897,029	38.3
General sales and gross receipts	2,840,173	22.2
Selective sales and gross receipts	2,056,856	16.1
Alcoholic beverages	43,407	0.3
Amusements	116,374	0.9
Insurance premiums..	277,647	2.2
Motor fuels	667,037	5.2
Pari-mutuels	620	-
Public utilities	11,650	0.1
Tobacco products...	201,187	1.6
Other selective sales	738,934	5.8
Licenses..	702,499	5.5
Alcoholic beverages	7,367	0.1
Amusements	821	-
Corporations in general...	19,541	0.2
Hunting and fishing..	79,664	0.6
Motor vehicle	504,010	3.9
Motor vehicle operators	36,751	0.3
Public utilities	14,717	0.1
Occupation and business, NEC	39,628	0.3
Other licenses	0	-
Income taxes..	7,111,711	55.6
Individual income...	6,485,602	50.7
Corporation net income	626,109	4.9
Other taxes...	84,079	0.7
Death and gift...	0	-
Documentary and stock transfer	0	-
Severance	84,079	0.7
Taxes, NEC	0	-

X = Not applicable.
- = Zero or rounds to zero.

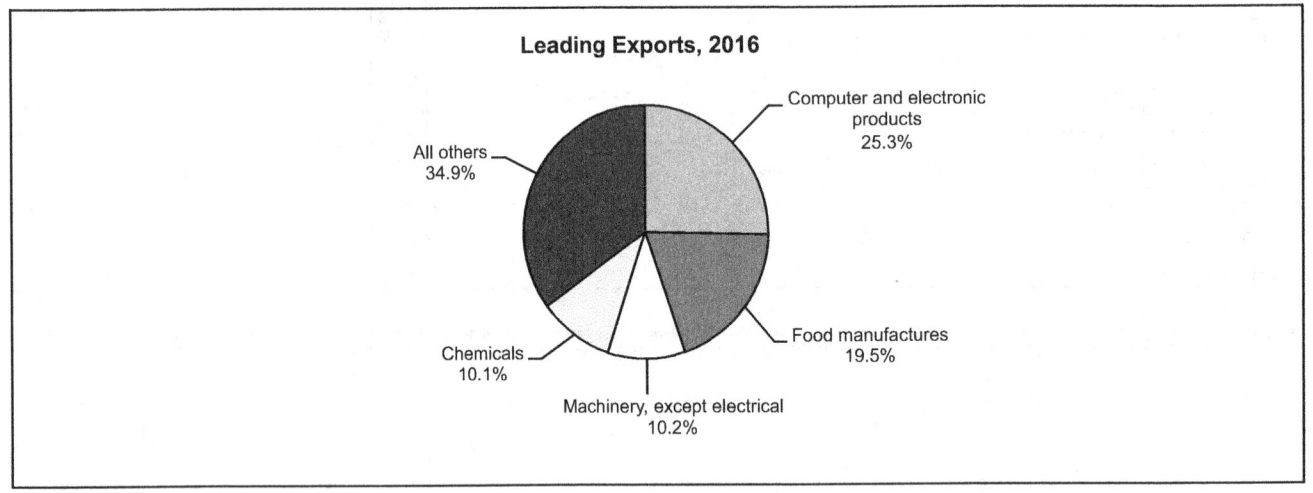

Leading Exports, 2016

Computer and electronic products 25.3%

Food manufactures 19.5%

Machinery, except electrical 10.2%

Chemicals 10.1%

All others 34.9%

CONNECTICUT

Facts and Figures

Location: Northeastern United States; bordered on the N by Massachusetts, on the E by Rhode Island, on the S by Long Island Sound, and on the W by New York

Area: 5,543 sq. mi. (14,357); rank—48th

Population: 3,576,452 (2016 est.); rank—29th

Principal Cities: capital—Hartford; largest—Bridgeport

Statehood: January 9, 1788; 5th state

U.S. Congress: 2 senators, 5 representatives

State Motto: *Qui transtulit sustinet* ("He who transplanted still sustains")

State Song: "Yankee Doodle"

State Nicknames: The Constitution State; The Nutmeg State

Abbreviations: CT; Conn.

State Symbols: flower—mountain laurel; tree—white oak; bird—American robin

At a Glance

- With an increase in population of just 0.1 percent, Connecticut experienced the smallest population growth among the states between 2010 and 2016.

- Connecticut's median household income in 2015 was $71,346, compared to the national median household income of $55,775.

- In 2015, 38.3 percent of Connecticut residents age 25 and older had a bachelor's degree or higher, which is the 5th highest percent in the country.

- Connecticut's per capita personal income in 2015 was $68,822, ranking second in the nation.

- The violent and property crime rates in Connecticut in 2015 were below the national average, at 218.5 and 1,812.0 incidents per 100,000 population respectively.

Table CT-1. Population by Age, Sex, Race, and Hispanic Origin

(Number, percent, except where noted.)

Sex, age, race, and Hispanic origin	2000	2010	2016 [1]	Average annual percent change, 2010–2016
Total Population..	3,405,565	3,574,097	3,576,452	-
Percent of total U.S. population	1.2	1.2	1.1	X
Sex				
Male..	1,649,319	1,739,614	1,745,615	-
Female	1,756,246	1,834,483	1,830,837	-
Age				
Under 5 years..	233,344	202,106	185,321	-0.5
5 to 19 years..	702,358	713,670	672,177	-0.4
20 to 64 years...	2,009,680	2,151,762	2,141,551	-
65 years and over..	470,183	506,559	577,403	0.9
Median age (years)	37.4	40.0	40.7	0.1
Race and Hispanic Origin				
One race..				
White	2,780,355	2,950,820	2,882,093	-0.1
Black...	309,843	392,131	421,023	0.5
American Indian and Alaska Native	9,639	16,734	19,140	0.9
Asian...	82,313	140,516	167,870	1.2
Native Hawaiian or Other Pacific Islander	1,366	3,491	3,815	0.6
Two or more races...	74,848	70,405	82,511	1.1
Hispanic (of any race)..	320,323	498,638	562,348	0.8

X = Not applicable.
[1] Population figures for 2016 are July 1 estimates. The 2010 estimates are taken from the 2010 Census.
- = Zero or rounds to zero.

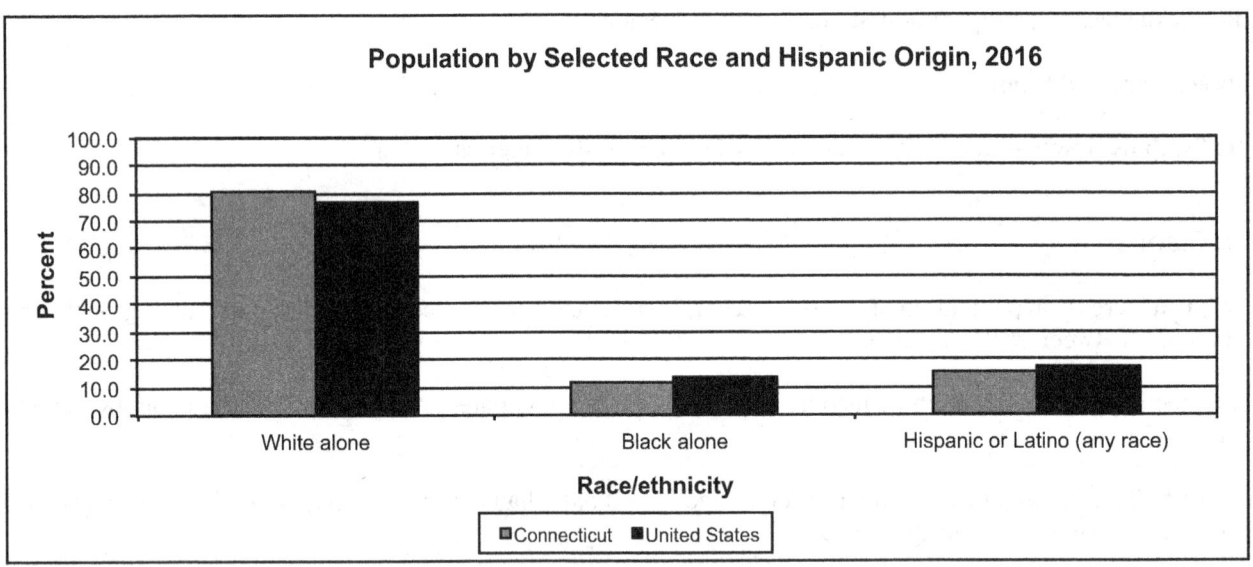

Population by Selected Race and Hispanic Origin, 2016

Table CT-2. Marital Status

(Number, percent distribution.)

Sex, age, race, and Hispanic origin	2000	2010	2015
Males, 15 Years and Over	1,284,881	1,399,329	1,435,144
Never married	30.0	36.3	38.2
Now married, except separated...	58.0	50.6	49.2
Separated...	1.3	1.1	1.1
Widowed...	2.7	2.7	2.5
Divorced..	7.9	9.3	8.9
Females, 15 Years and Over	1,411,369	1,512,492	1,536,805
Never married	24.5	29.9	32.6
Now married, except separated...	52.3	46.5	44.9
Separated...	1.8	1.8	1.6
Widowed...	10.8	9.3	8.7
Divorced..	10.5	12.5	12.3

Table CT-3. Households and Housing Characteristics

(Number, percent, dollars.)

Item	2000	2010	2015	Average annual percent change, 2000–2015
Total Households..	1,301,670	1,358,809	1,343,703	0.2
Family households..	881,170	890,770	876,188	-
Married-couple family..	676,467	656,629	647,589	-0.3
Other family...	204,703	234,141	228,599	0.8
Male householder, no wife present......................	47,292	58,325	58,006	1.5
Female householder, no husband present..............	157,411	175,816	170,593	0.6
Nonfamily households..	420,500	468,039	467,515	0.7
Householder living alone.....................................	334,224	384,382	382,401	1.0
Householder not living alone................................	76,276	83,657	85,114	0.8
Housing Characteristics				
Total housing units...	1,385,975	1,488,215	1,496,056	0.5
Occupied housing units	1,301,670	1,358,809	1,343,703	0.2
Owner occupied...	869,729	923,617	889,035	0.1
Renter occupied...	431,941	435,192	454,668	0.4
Average household size..	2.53	2.55	2.59	0.2
Financial Characteristics				
Median gross rent of renter-occupied housing	681	992	1,108	4.2
Median monthly owner costs for housing units with a mortgage	1,426	2,068	2,020	2.8
Median value of owner-occupied housing units	166,900	288,800	270,900	4.2

- = Zero or rounds to zero.

Table CT-4. Migration, Origin, and Language

(Number, percent.)

Characteristic	State			U.S.		
	2014	2015	Percent change	2014	2015	Percent change
Residence 1 Year Ago						
Population 1 year and over	3,558,915	3,554,844	-0.1	315,095,393	317,635,720	0.8
Same house	87.4	87.5	X	85.1	85.3	X
Different house in the U.S.	11.7	11.7	X	14.3	14.1	X
Same county	7.7	7.4	X	8.7	8.5	X
Different county	4	4.4	X	5.6	5.6	X
Same state	1.7	2.2	X	3.3	3.2	X
Different state	2.3	2.2	X	2.3	2.4	X
Abroad	0.8	0.8	X	0.6	0.7	X
Place of Birth						
Native born	3,104,758	3,071,238	-1.1	276,465,262	278,128,449	0.6
Male	48.7	48.8	X	49.3	49.3	X
Female	51.3	51.2	X	50.7	50.7	X
Foreign born	491,919	519,648	5.6	42,391,794	43,290,372	2.1
Male	49.5	48.9	X	48.7	48.6	X
Female	50.5	51.1	X	51.3	51.4	X
Foreign born; naturalized U.S. citizen.....................	235,905	253,505	7.5	19,984,738	20,697,103	3.6
Male	44.8	45.0	X	45.9	45.9	X
Female	55.2	55.0	X	54.1	54.1	X
Foreign born; not a U.S. citizen..............................	256,014	266,143	4.0	22,407,056	22,593,269	0.8
Male	53.9	52.6	X	51.2	51.1	X
Female	46.1	47.4	X	48.8	48.9	X
Entered 2010 or later...	14.3	17.0	X	12.3	15.6	X
Entered 2000 to 2009...	29.6	28.6	X	28.6	27.9	X
Entered before 2000..	56.1	54.3	X	59.1	56.5	X
World Region of Birth, Foreign						
Foreign-born population, excluding population born at sea	491,839	519,648	5.7	42,390,705	43,289,646	2.1
Europe	25.1	25.6	X	11.2	11.1	X
Asia...	25.2	24.3	X	30.1	30.6	X
Africa	4.6	3.9	X	4.6	4.8	X
Oceania	0.3	0.4	X	0.6	0.6	X
Latin America...	41.8	42.9	X	51.6	51.1	X
North America..	3.0	2.9	X	1.9	1.9	X
Language Spoken at Home and Ability to Speak English						
Population 5 years and over.....................................	3,407,815	3,404,358	-0.1	299,084,046	301,625,014	0.8
English only	78.2	77.6	X	78.9	78.5	X
Language other than English..................................	21.8	22.4	X	21.1	21.5	X
Speaks English less than "very well"......................	8.1	8.2	X	8.6	8.6	X

NA = Not available.
X = Not applicable.
- = Zero or rounds to zero.

Table CT-5. Median Income and Poverty Status, 2015

(Number, percent, except as noted.)

Characteristic	State		U.S.	
	Number	Percent	Number	Percent
Median Income				
Households (dollars)...............................	71,346	X	55,775	X
Families (dollars)	91,388	X	68,260	X
Below Poverty Level (All People)	366,909	10.5	46,153,077	14.7
Sex				
Male	163,704	9.7	20,599,407	13.4
Female	203,205	11.4	25,553,670	16.0
Age				
Under 18 years................................	109,293	14.5	15,000,273	20.7
Related children under 18 years..................	106,128	14.2	14,693,239	20.4
18 to 64 years................................	218,244	10.0	26,960,369	13.9
65 years and over	39,372	7.2	4,192,435	9.0

X = Not applicable.

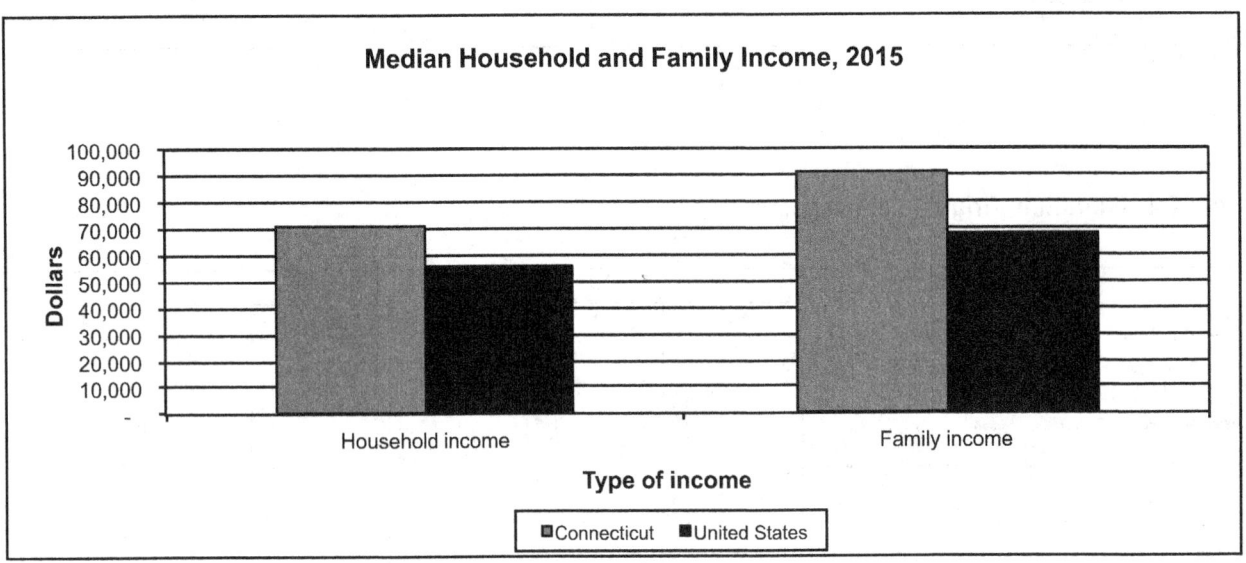

Median Household and Family Income, 2015

Table CT-6. Health Insurance Coverage Status for the Civilian Noninstitutionalized Population and Children Under 18 Years of Age

(Numbers in thousands, percent.)

Item	2007	2008	2009	2010	2011	2012	2013	2014	2015
Civilian Noninstitutionalized Population	3,476	3,441	3,457	3,520	3,523	3,535	3,541	3,541	3,538
Covered by Private or Public Insurance									
Number....................................	3,150	3,130	3,152	3,200	3,214	3,213	3,209	3,296	3,327
Percent....................................	90.6	91.0	91.2	90.9	91.2	90.9	90.6	93.1	94.0
Not Covered									
Number....................................	326	311	305	320	309	322	333	245	211
Percent....................................	9.4	9.0	8.8	9.1	8.8	9.1	9.4	6.9	6.0
Percent in the U.S. not covered................	15.3	15.1	15.1	15.5	15.1	14.8	14.5	11.7	9.4
Children Under 18 Years of Age	819	810	807	815	803	791	784	774	762
Covered by Private or Public Insurance									
Number....................................	776	770	777	791	780	761	751	745	737
Percent....................................	94.8	95.1	96.2	97.0	97.1	96.2	95.7	96.3	96.7
Not Covered									
Number....................................	43	40	30	24	23	30	34	29	25
Percent....................................	5.2	4.9	3.8	3.0	2.9	3.8	4.3	3.7	3.3
Percent in the U.S. not covered................	11.0	9.7	8.6	8.0	7.5	7.2	7.1	6.0	4.8

Table CT-7. Employment Status by Demographic Group, 2016

(Numbers in thousands, percent.)

Characteristic	Civilian noninstitutional population	Civilian labor force		Employed		Unemployed	
		Number	Percent of population	Number	Percent of population	Number	Percent of population
Total..	2,884	1,906	66.1	1,806	62.6	100	5.2
Sex							
Male..	1,385	986	71.2	933	67.4	53	5.4
Female..	1,499	919	61.3	873	58.2	47	5.1
Race, Sex, and Hispanic Origin							
White..	2,368	1,581	66.8	1,507	63.6	74	4.7
Male...	1,143	825	72.2	786	68.8	39	4.7
Female..	1,224	756	61.7	721	58.9	35	4.6
Black or African American.....................	309	188	60.8	167	54.2	20	10.8
Male...	142	90	63.6	78	55.1	12	13.3
Female..	167	97	58.4	89	53.4	8	8.5
Hispanic or Latino ethnicity[1]	415	290	70.0	268	64.7	22	7.6
Male...	194	148	76.1	138	71.0	10	6.8
Female..	220	142	64.6	130	59.2	12	8.4
Age							
16 to 19 years......................................	215	69	32.2	58	27.2	11	15.6
20 to 24 years......................................	201	136	67.7	125	62.4	11	7.9
25 to 34 years......................................	507	431	85.1	404	79.8	27	6.3
35 to 44 years......................................	371	317	85.3	304	81.9	13	4.0
45 to 54 years......................................	554	454	82.0	437	79.0	17	3.6
55 to 64 years......................................	490	358	73.0	341	69.6	17	4.8
65 years and over.................................	548	141	25.8	137	25.0	5	3.3

NOTE: Data in Table 7 are from the Current Population Survey (CPS) and do not match the estimates in Table 8. See notes and definitions for further information.
[1] May be of any race.

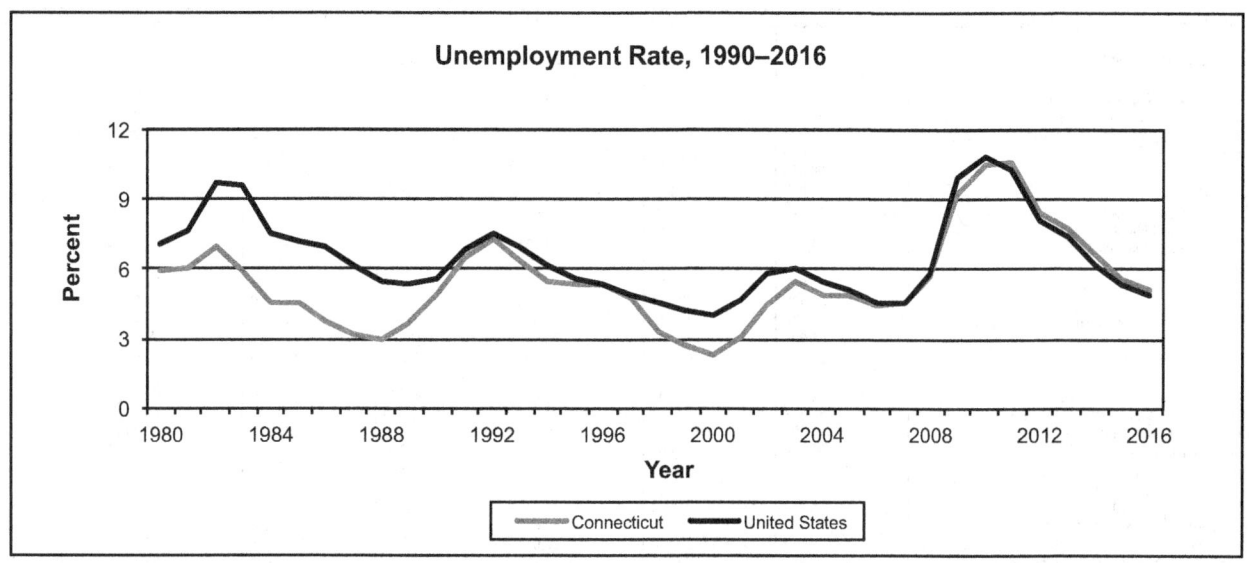

Table CT-8. Employment Status of the Civilian Noninstitutional Population Age 16 Years and Over

(Number, percent.)

Year	Civilian labor force	Civilian participation rate	Employed	Unemployed	Unemployment rate
2008..	1,881,454	69.0	1,774,681	106,773	5.7
2009..	1,891,077	68.8	1,740,971	150,106	7.9
2010..	1,911,712	68.3	1,737,449	174,263	9.1
2011..	1,914,775	67.7	1,745,967	168,808	8.8
2012..	1,888,336	66.4	1,730,695	157,641	8.3
2013..	1,872,031	65.5	1,726,875	145,156	7.8
2014..	1,886,398	65.8	1,761,610	124,788	6.6
2015..	1,888,001	65.7	1,781,517	106,484	5.6
2016..	1,891,792	65.9	1,795,519	96,273	5.1

Table CT-9. Employment and Average Wages by Industry

(Estimates through 2010 are based on the 2007 *North American Industry Classification System* [NAICS]. Estimates from 2011 onward are based on the 2012 NAICS.)

Industry	2009	2010	2011	2012	2013	2014	2015
				Number of Jobs			
Wage and Salary Employment by Industry..................	1,699,245	1,673,114	1,688,186	1,706,144	1,718,152	1,731,804	1,740,112
Farm Wage and Salary Employment.........................	4,449	4,395	4,806	4,775	5,463	5,478	5,458
Nonfarm Wage and Salary Employment....................	1,694,796	1,668,719	1,683,380	1,701,369	1,712,689	1,726,326	1,734,654
Private wage and salary employment.......................	1,425,527	1,403,233	1,422,376	1,439,674	1,451,008	1,465,127	1,474,937
Forestry, fishing, and related activities......................	744	697	688	661	680	707	692
Mining..	629	571	542	554	543	547	553
Utilities...	6,645	6,308	6,172	5,935	6,042	5,943	5,609
Construction	57,036	51,686	53,150	53,136	55,195	57,414	59,386
Manufacturing..	171,476	165,769	166,429	165,402	164,021	159,793	159,163
Durable goods manufacturing............................	132,089	127,381	128,567	128,740	127,608	124,402	123,778
Nondurable goods manufacturing.......................	39,387	38,388	37,862	36,662	36,413	35,391	35,385
Wholesale trade	65,531	62,988	63,707	63,505	63,421	63,381	62,807
Retail trade..	181,584	179,971	182,004	183,882	185,197	186,544	186,288
Transportation and warehousing...........................	40,828	39,809	41,081	41,819	42,551	43,717	45,286
Information	34,259	31,760	31,502	31,332	32,093	32,058	32,414
Finance and insurance	120,387	118,200	118,013	116,438	114,287	111,613	112,060
Real estate and rental and leasing........................	19,980	19,498	19,438	19,411	19,508	19,708	20,317
Professional, scientific, and technical services...........	88,641	86,845	88,750	90,300	91,094	96,019	96,416
Management of companies and enterprises..................	27,785	27,837	28,621	30,608	30,693	31,899	32,934
Administrative and waste services........................	77,454	78,348	81,570	84,698	85,669	86,366	88,499
Educational services	63,136	65,116	65,999	67,063	67,206	69,023	69,441
Health care and social assistance.........................	248,423	251,518	254,353	258,265	261,820	264,250	266,256
Arts, entertainment, and recreation........................	23,971	23,920	24,300	25,160	26,181	26,674	27,063
Accommodation and food services........................	111,355	110,791	114,006	118,413	122,133	124,696	125,134
Other services, except public administration..................	85,663	81,601	82,051	83,092	82,674	84,775	84,619
Government and government enterprises..........................	269,269	265,486	261,004	261,695	261,681	261,199	259,717
				Dollars			
Average Wages and Salaries by Industry	56,617	58,483	60,182	61,119	61,396	62,963	64,551
Average Farm Wages and Salaries	26,989	26,135	20,919	31,008	27,945	29,499	27,182
Average Nonfarm Wages and Salaries	56,695	58,568	60,294	61,204	61,502	63,069	64,669
Average private wages and salaries...................	57,404	59,670	61,400	62,554	62,753	64,301	65,807
Forestry, fishing, and related activities......................	22,973	23,735	24,028	25,442	25,859	26,358	28,042
Mining..	64,507	68,023	68,865	64,532	64,803	70,311	71,403
Utilities...	106,654	103,567	111,556	109,731	110,984	111,305	116,904
Construction	57,058	58,580	58,332	59,267	59,406	61,085	64,258
Manufacturing..	70,183	73,394	77,201	78,926	81,590	81,398	80,502
Durable goods manufacturing............................	69,668	72,978	76,322	78,603	81,647	82,106	80,816
Nondurable goods manufacturing.......................	71,911	74,775	80,186	80,058	81,389	78,911	79,406
Wholesale trade	78,943	81,517	83,379	85,380	85,982	87,722	92,692
Retail trade..	30,400	30,861	31,173	31,509	31,560	32,099	33,010
Transportation and warehousing...........................	45,774	46,347	47,312	47,933	46,991	47,757	48,639
Information	71,330	77,161	78,926	82,327	89,138	93,028	99,296
Finance and insurance	129,841	143,441	152,257	153,271	150,119	159,035	163,571
Real estate and rental and leasing........................	52,024	55,196	59,735	64,697	64,006	65,763	69,433
Professional, scientific, and technical services...............	84,807	88,279	89,660	91,718	92,646	95,859	98,993
Management of companies and enterprises..................	135,425	135,100	139,184	156,139	161,131	163,440	162,453
Administrative and waste services........................	38,424	40,008	40,829	41,269	40,827	43,017	44,101
Educational services	45,524	45,644	46,906	48,767	50,949	52,390	53,372
Health care and social assistance.........................	46,340	46,955	47,563	48,441	48,559	49,811	50,244
Arts, entertainment, and recreation........................	29,185	28,857	29,043	29,245	29,218	30,153	31,221
Accommodation and food services........................	19,772	20,298	20,614	21,234	21,364	22,055	23,303
Other services, except public administration..................	29,830	30,999	31,408	31,997	32,808	33,570	34,762
Government and government enterprises..........................	52,942	52,743	54,268	53,779	54,567	56,161	58,209

Table CT-10. Employment Characteristics by Family Type

(Number, percent.)

Family type and labor force status	2013		2014		2015	
	Total	Families with own children under 18 years	Total	Families with own children under 18 years	Total	Families with own children under 18 years
All Families..........................	890,293	384,072	881,355	378,078	876,188	365,594
FAMILY TYPE AND LABOR FORCE STATUS						
Married-Couple Families..........................	657,885	262,395	644,765	256,409	647,589	248,839
Both husband and wife in labor force..........	58.1	70.4	57.2	70.7	57.3	71.1
Husband in labor force, wife not in labor force..........	19.9	24.3	20.1	25.0	19.8	24.3
Wife in labor force, husband not in labor force..........	7.3	3.8	7.8	3.1	7.4	2.9
Both husband and wife not in labor force..........	14.0	1.1	14.9	1.2	14.6	1.2
Other Families	232,408	121,677	236,590	121,669	228,599	116,755
Female householder, no husband present..........	75.4	80.5	72.6	76.5	74.6	78.9
In labor force..........	55.7	67.8	55.5	65.7	55.3	69.0
Not in labor force	19.6	12.7	17.1	10.8	19.4	9.8
Male householder, no wife present..........	24.6	19.5	27.4	23.5	25.4	21.1
In labor force..........	19.6	17.9	22.6	21.7	20.9	19.8
Not in labor force	5.1	1.6	4.8	1.8	4.5	1.4

Table CT-11. School Enrollment and Educational Attainment, 2015

(Number, percent.)

Item	State	U.S.
Enrollment		
Total population 3 years and over, enrolled in school	913,807	81,618,288
Enrolled in nursery school or preschool (percent)..........	6.2	6.0
Enrolled in kindergarten (percent)..........	4.4	5.0
Enrolled in elementary school, grades 1-8 (percent)..........	37.9	40.3
Enrolled in high school, grades 9-12 (percent)..........	21.8	20.9
Enrolled in college or graduate school (percent)..........	29.6	27.7
Attainment		
Total population 25 years and over	2,474,718	216,447,163
Less than ninth grade (percent)..........	4.2	5.5
9th to 12th grade, no diploma (percent)..........	5.6	7.3
High school graduate, including equivalency (percent)..........	27.4	27.6
Some college, no degree (percent)..........	16.9	20.7
Associate's degree (percent)..........	7.6	8.2
Bachelor's degree (percent)..........	21.7	19.0
Graduate or professional degree (percent)..........	16.7	11.6
High school graduate or higher (percent)..........	90.2	87.1
Bachelor's degree or higher (percent)..........	38.3	30.6

Table CT-12. Public School Characteristics and Educational Indicators

(Number, percent; data derived from National Center of Education Statistics.)

Item	State	U.S.
Public Schools, 2014–2015 (except where noted)		
Number of school districts..........	205	18,260
Number of schools..........	1,299	98,373
Number of students..........	542,678	50,312,581
Number of teachers	42,062	3,132,351
Student-teacher ratio	12.9	16.1
Expenditures per student (dollars), FY 2014	18,401	11,066
Four-year adjusted cohort graduation rate (ACGR)[1,2]	87.2	83.2
Students eligible for free or reduced-price lunch (percent)..........	37.7	51.8
English language learners (percent)..........	6.6	9.4
Students age 3 to 21 served under IDEA, part B (percent)..........	13.5	13.0

Public Schools by Type	Number	Percent of state public schools
Total number of schools..........	1,299	100.0
Regular	1,053	81.1
Special education	134	10.3
Vocational education..........	17	1.3
Alternative education..........	95	7.3

NOTE: Every school is assigned only one school type based on its instructional emphasis.
[1] ACGR data represents a new method of calculating high-school completion rates and may not be comparable to previous years' data for Averaged Freshmen Graduation Rates (AFGR).
[2] The United States 4-year ACGRs were estimated using both the reported 4-year ACGR data from 49 states and the District of Columbia and using imputed data for Idaho. The estimate for American Indian/Alaska Native students also includes imputed data for Virginia.

Table CT-13. Reported Voting and Registration of the Voting-Age Population, November 2016

(Numbers in thousands, percent.)

Item	Total population	Total citizen population	Registered			Voted		
			Total registered	Percent registered (total population)	Percent registered (total citizen population)	Total voted	Percent voted (total population)	Percent voted (total citizen population)
U.S. Total	245,502	224,059	157,596	64.2	70.3	137,537	56.0	61.4
State Total..........................	2,759	2,483	1,763	63.9	71.0	1,586	57.5	63.9
Sex								
Male	1,321	1,182	798	60.4	67.5	718	54.4	60.7
Female	1,438	1,301	965	67.1	74.2	868	60.4	66.7
Race								
White alone........................	2,258	2,090	1,538	68.1	73.6	1,378	61.0	65.9
White, non-Hispanic alone	1,959	1,897	1,427	72.8	75.2	1,287	65.7	67.8
Black alone........................	297	266	157	53.0	59.2	142	47.9	53.5
Asian alone	143	83	31	(B)	(B)	29	(B)	(B)
Hispanic (of any race)......................	417	278	151	36.3	54.4	131	31.5	47.2
White alone or in combination	2,281	2,113	1,561	68.4	73.9	1,401	61.4	66.3
Black alone or in combination..........	324	293	185	57.0	63.0	170	52.3	57.9
Asian alone or in combination..........	148	88	36	(B)	(B)	34	(B)	(B)
Age								
18 to 24 years.....................	263	225	123	46.6	54.6	97	37.0	43.3
25 to 34 years.....................	505	425	279	55.2	65.5	244	48.4	57.5
35 to 44 years.....................	397	347	236	59.5	68.1	208	52.5	60.1
45 to 64 years.....................	1,034	943	700	67.7	74.3	636	61.5	67.4
65 years and over	560	544	425	75.9	78.2	400	71.4	73.6

B = Base is less than 75,000 and therefore too small to show the derived measure.

Table CT-14. Crime

(Number, rate per 100,000. Data are derived from the FBI Uniform Crime Reports.)

Item	State			U.S. [1,2,3,4]		
	2014	2015	Percent change	2014	2015	Percent change
TOTAL POPULATION[5]	3,594,762	3,590,886	-0.1	318,907,401	321,418,820	0.8
VIOLENT CRIME						
Number........................	8,575	7,845	-8.5	1,186,185	1,231,566	3.8
Rate	238.5	218.5	-8.4	372.0	383.2	3.0
Murder and Nonnegligent Manslaughter						
Number........................	89	117	31.5	14,164	15,696	10.8
Rate	2.5	3.3	31.6	4.4	4.9	10.0
Rape[6]						
Number........................	794	773	-2.6	118,027	124,047	5.1
Rate	22.1	21.5	-2.5	37.0	38.6	4.3
Robbery						
Number........................	3,172	2,892	-8.8	322,905	327,374	1.4
Rate	88.2	80.5	-8.7	101.3	101.9	0.6
Aggravated Assault						
Number........................	4,520	4,063	-10.1	731,089	764,449	4.6
Rate	125.7	113.1	-10.0	229.2	237.8	3.7
PROPERTY CRIME						
Number........................	69,326	65,066	-6.1	8,209,010	7,993,631	-2.6
Rate	1,928.5	1,812.0	-6.0	2,574.1	2,487.0	-3.4
Burglary						
Number........................	12,017	10,053	-16.3	1,713,153	1,579,527	-7.8
Rate	334.3	280.0	-16.3	537.2	491.4	-8.5
Larceny-Theft						
Number........................	51,195	48,675	-4.9	5,809,054	5,706,346	-1.8
Rate	1,424.2	1,355.5	-4.8	1,821.5	1,775.4	-2.5
Motor Vehicle Theft						
Number........................	6,114	6,338	3.7	686,803	707,758	3.1
Rate	170.1	176.5	3.8	215.4	220.2	2.2

NOTE: Although arson data are included in the trend and clearance tables, sufficient data are not available to estimate totals for this offense. Therefore, no arson data are published in this table.
X = Not applicable.
- = Zero or rounds to zero.
[1] The crime figures have been adjusted.
[2] The data collection methodology for the offense of forcible rape used by the Minnesota state Uniform Crime Reporting (UCR) Program (with the exception of Minneapolis and St. Paul, Minnesota) does not comply with national UCR Program guidelines. Consequently, its figures for forcible rape and violent crime (of which forcible rape is a part) are not published in this table.
[3] Includes offenses reported by the Zoological Police and the Metro Transit Police.
[4] Because of changes in the state's reporting practices, figures are not comparable to previous years' data.
[5] Populations are U.S. Census Bureau provisional estimates as of July 1 of each year.
[6] The figures shown for the offense of rape were estimated using the revised Uniform Crime Reporting (UCR) definition of rape.

Table CT-15. State Government Finances, 2015

(Dollar amounts in thousands, percent distribution.)

Item	Dollars	Percent distribution
Total Revenue	30,307,639	100.0
General revenue	26,635,794	87.9
Intergovernmental revenue	6,898,669	22.8
Taxes	16,224,696	53.5
General sales	4,082,787	13.5
Selective sales	2,472,098	8.2
License taxes	452,687	1.5
Individual income tax	8,182,071	27.0
Corporate income tax	689,685	2.3
Other taxes	345,368	1.1
Current charges	1,979,341	6.5
Miscellaneous general revenue	1,533,088	5.1
Utility revenue	35,331	0.1
Liquor stores revenue	0	-
Insurance trust revenue[1]	3,636,514	12.0
Total Expenditure	31,330,184	100.0
Intergovernmental expenditure	5,338,357	17.0
Direct expenditure	25,991,827	83.0
Current operation	17,162,581	54.8
Capital outlay	1,995,795	6.4
Insurance benefits and repayments	4,856,293	15.5
Assistance and subsidies	557,724	1.8
Interest on debt	1,419,434	4.5
Exhibit: Salaries and wages	4,583,568	14.6
Total Expenditure	31,330,184	100.0
General expenditure	25,749,941	82.2
Intergovernmental expenditure	5,338,357	17.0
Direct expenditure	20,411,584	65.1
General expenditure, by function:		
Education	7,874,421	25.1
Public welfare	7,677,002	24.5
Hospitals	1,416,472	4.5
Health	1,013,692	3.2
Highways	1,247,190	4.0
Police protection	242,755	0.8
Correction	708,469	2.3
Natural resources	204,319	0.7
Parks and recreation	114,852	0.4
Governmental administration	1,392,023	4.4
Interest on general debt	1,419,434	4.5
Other and unallocable	2,439,312	7.8
Utility expenditure	723,950	2.3
Liquor stores expenditure	0	-
Insurance trust expenditure	4,856,293	15.5
Debt at End of Fiscal Year	35,351,526	X
Cash and Security Holdings	49,792,991	X

X = Not applicable.
- = Zero or rounds to zero.
[1] Within insurance trust revenue, net earnings of state retirement systems is a calculated statistic (the item code in the data file is X08), and thus can be positive or negative. Net earnings is the sum of earnings on investments plus gains on investments minus losses on investments. The change made in 2002 for asset valuation from book to market value in accordance with Statement 34 of the Governmental Accounting Standards Board is reflected in the calculated statistics.

Table CT-16. State Government Tax Collections, 2016

(Dollars in thousands, percent.)

Item	Dollars	Percent distribution
Total Taxes	15,244,947	100.0
Property taxes	0	-
Sales and gross receipts	6,149,782	40.3
General sales and gross receipts	3,752,793	24.6
Selective sales and gross receipts	2,396,989	15.7
Alcoholic beverages	56,345	0.4
Amusements	305,057	2.0
Insurance premiums	208,895	1.4
Motor fuels	467,749	3.1
Pari-mutuels	6,876	-
Public utilities	298,858	2.0
Tobacco products	350,723	2.3
Other selective sales	702,486	4.6
Licenses	455,454	3.0
Alcoholic beverages	9,356	0.1
Amusements	230	-
Corporations in general	28,878	0.2
Hunting and fishing	5,200	-
Motor vehicle	224,287	1.5
Motor vehicle operators	48,719	0.3
Public utilities	675	-
Occupation and business, NEC	133,427	0.9
Other licenses	4,682	-
Income taxes	8,276,620	54.3
Individual income	7,557,153	49.6
Corporation net income	719,467	4.7
Other taxes	363,091	2.4
Death and gift	195,157	1.3
Documentary and stock transfer	167,132	1.1
Severance	0	-
Taxes, NEC	802	-

- = Zero or rounds to zero.
X = Not applicable.

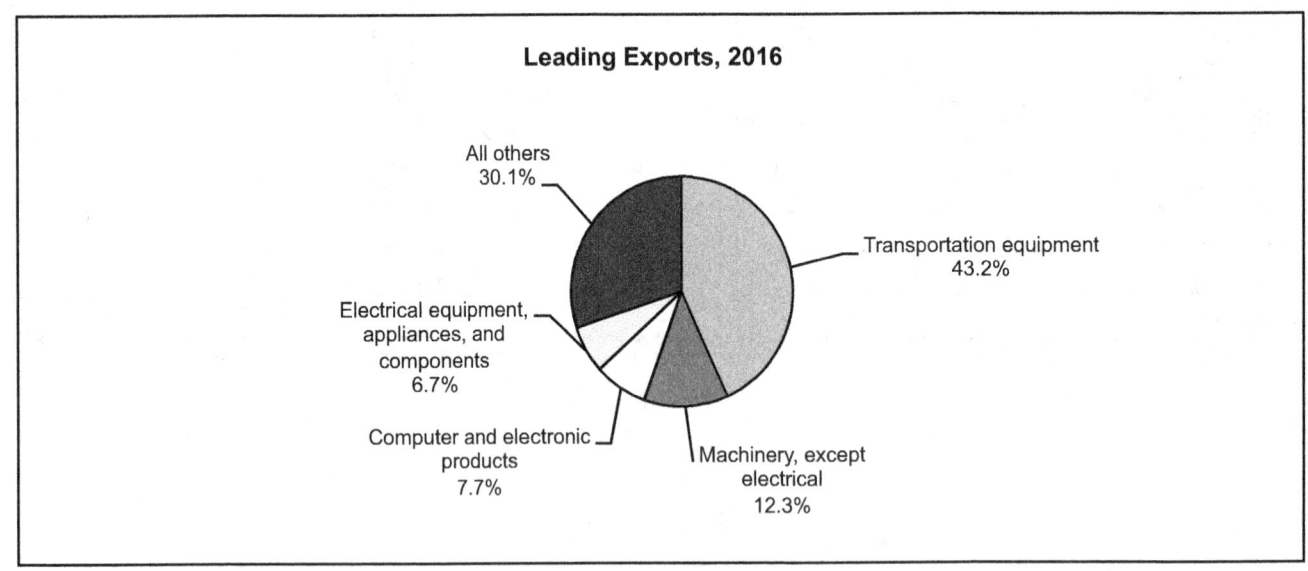

Leading Exports, 2016

All others 30.1%

Transportation equipment 43.2%

Electrical equipment, appliances, and components 6.7%

Computer and electronic products 7.7%

Machinery, except electrical 12.3%

DELAWARE

Facts and Figures

Location: Northeastern United States; bordered on the N by Pennsylvania, on the E by New Jersey, and on the S and W by Maryland

Area: 2,488 sq. mi. (6,447 sq. km.); rank—49th

Population: 952,065 (2016 est.); rank—45th

Principal Cities: capital—Dover; largest—Wilmington

Statehood: December 7, 1787; 1st state

U.S. Congress: 2 senators, 1 representative

State Motto: Liberty and Independence

State Song: "Our Delaware"

State Nickname: The First State

Abbreviations: DE; Del.

State Symbols: flower—peach blossom; tree—American holly; bird—blue hen chicken

At a Glance

- With an increase in population of 6.0 percent, Delaware ranked 16th among the states in growth from 2010 to 2016.

- In 2015, 5.9 percent of Delawareans did not have health insurance, compared to 9.4 percent of the total U.S. population.

- Delaware's violent crime rate in 2015 was 499.0 per 100,000 population, compared to 383.2 for the entire nation.

- Delaware's homeownership rate ranked second in the nation in 2016, with 73.0 percent of the population owning homes.

- In 2015, 12.4 percent of Delawareans lived below the poverty level, compared to 14.7 percent of the total U.S. population.

Table DE-1. Population by Age, Sex, Race, and Hispanic Origin

(Number, percent, except where noted.)

Sex, age, race, and Hispanic origin	2000	2010	2016 [1]	Average annual percent change, 2010–2016
Total Population..	783,600	897,934	952,065	0.4
Percent of total U.S. population	0.3	0.3	0.3	X
Sex				
Male..	380,541	434,939	460,670	0.4
Female	403,059	462,995	491,395	0.4
Age				
Under 5 years...	51,531	55,886	54,834	-0.1
5 to 19 years..	166,719	177,917	174,558	-0.1
20 to 64 years..	463,624	648,387	555,723	-0.9
65 years and over	101,726	129,277	166,950	1.8
Median age (years)	36.0	38.8	40.2	0.2
Race and Hispanic Origin				
One race..				
White	584,773	645,770	667,809	0.2
Black...	150,666	196,281	214,914	0.6
American Indian and Alaska Native	2,731	5,929	6,174	0.3
Asian...	16,259	29,342	37,846	1.8
Native Hawaiian or Other Pacific Islander	283	690	918	2.1
Two or more races	13,033	19,922	24,404	1.4
Hispanic (of any race)	37,277	76,137	87,152	0.9

X = Not applicable.
[1] Population figures for 2016 are July 1 estimates. The 2010 estimates are taken from the 2010 Census.
- = Zero or rounds to zero.

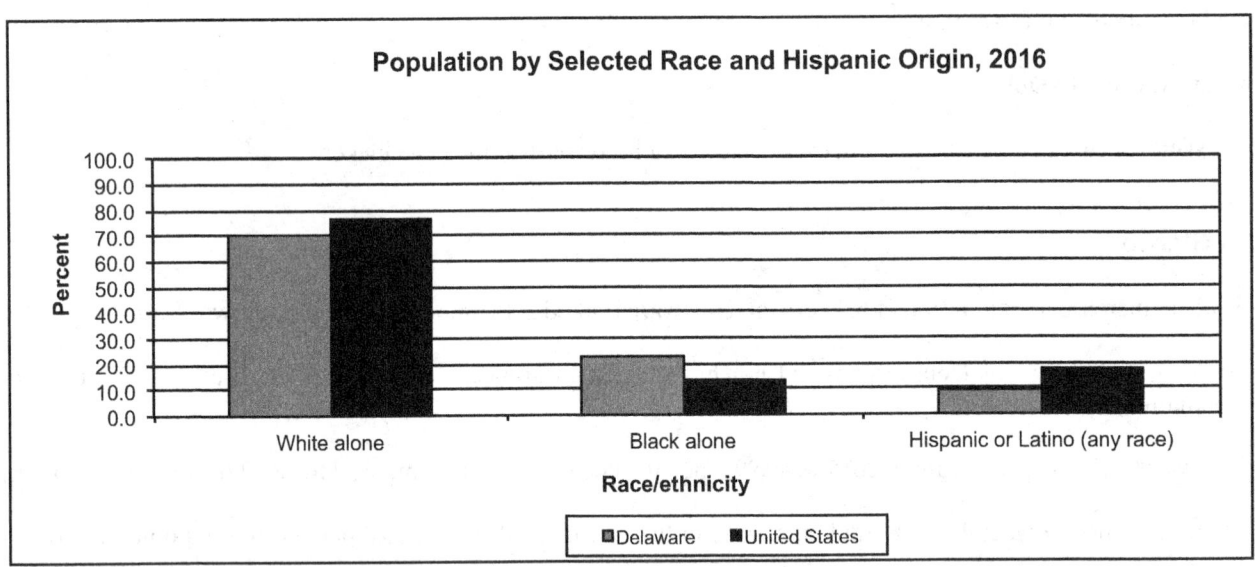

Table DE-2. Marital Status

(Number, percent distribution.)

Sex, age, race, and Hispanic origin	2000	2010	2015
Males, 15 Years and Over	296,619	350,025	372,263
Never married	29.4	35.3	36.6
Now married, except separated.............................	57.4	50.4	49.3
Separated...	1.8	1.9	1.3
Widowed...	2.8	2.9	3.1
Divorced...	8.7	9.4	9.7
Females, 15 Years and Over	324,042	380,618	404,268
Never married	25.3	30.8	31.3
Now married, except separated.............................	50.9	45.3	44.8
Separated...	2.2	2.0	2.1
Widowed...	10.7	9.8	9.3
Divorced...	10.9	12.1	12.5

Table DE-3. Households and Housing Characteristics

(Number, percent, dollars.)

Item	2000	2010	2015	Average annual percent change, 2000–2015
Total Households...	298,736	328,765	352,595	1.2
Family households..	204,590	221,233	235,385	1.0
Married-couple family..................................	153,136	161,575	170,416	0.8
Other family..	51,454	59,658	64,969	1.8
Male householder, no wife present................	12,468	14,124	16,183	2.0
Female householder, no husband present........	38,986	45,534	48,786	1.7
Nonfamily households	94,146	107,532	117,210	1.6
Householder living alone................................	74,639	86,990	93,824	1.7
Householder not living alone..........................	19,507	20,542	23,386	1.3
Housing Characteristics				
Total housing units...	343,072	406,489	421,734	1.5
Occupied housing units	298,736	328,765	352,595	1.2
Owner occupied	216,038	239,884	249,681	1.0
Renter occupied	86,698	88,881	102,914	1.2
Average household size......................................	2.54	2.66	2.61	0.2
Financial Characteristics				
Median gross rent of renter-occupied housing	639	952	1049	4.3
Median monthly owner costs for housing units with a mortgage	1,101	1,569	1,506	2.5
Median value of owner-occupied housing units	130,400	243,600	240,200	5.6

Table DE-4. Migration, Origin, and Language

(Number, percent.)

Characteristic	State 2014	State 2015	State Percent change	U.S. 2014	U.S. 2015	U.S. Percent change
Residence 1 Year Ago						
Population 1 year and over	924,770	935,813	1.2	315,095,393	317,635,720	0.8
Same house	87.7	85.6	X	85.1	85.3	X
Different house in the U.S.	11.8	13.9	X	14.3	14.1	X
Same county	7.3	7.9	X	8.7	8.5	X
Different county	4.5	6.1	X	5.6	5.6	X
Same state	1.0	1.3	X	3.3	3.2	X
Different state	3.5	4.8	X	2.3	2.4	X
Abroad	0.5	0.5	X	0.6	0.7	X
Place of Birth						
Native born	855,314	858,425	0.4	276,465,262	278,128,449	0.6
Male	48.5	48.4	X	49.3	49.3	X
Female	51.5	51.6	X	50.7	50.7	X
Foreign born	80,300	87,509	9.0	42,391,794	43,290,372	2.1
Male	49.1	48.4	X	48.7	48.6	X
Female	50.9	51.6	X	51.3	51.4	X
Foreign born; naturalized U.S. citizen.................	39,169	39,523	0.9	19,984,738	20,697,103	3.6
Male	49.2	44.0	X	45.9	45.9	X
Female	50.8	56.0	X	54.1	54.1	X
Foreign born; not a U.S. citizen	41,131	47,986	16.7	22,407,056	22,593,269	0.8
Male	49.1	52.1	X	51.2	51.1	X
Female	50.9	47.9	X	48.8	48.9	X
Entered 2010 or later	15.1	19.1	X	12.3	15.6	X
Entered 2000 to 2009	35.2	33	X	28.6	27.9	X
Entered before 2000.......................................	49.7	47.9	X	59.1	56.5	X
World Region of Birth, Foreign						
Foreign-born population, excluding population born at sea	80,300	87,509	9.0	42,390,705	43,289,646	2.1
Europe	13	10	X	11.2	11.1	X
Asia...	38.4	35.7	X	30.1	30.6	X
Africa...	8.9	12.2	X	4.6	4.8	X
Oceania..	0.0	0.0	X	0.6	0.6	X
Latin America..	38.2	41.3	X	51.6	51.1	X
North America...	1.4	1.2	X	1.9	1.9	X
Language Spoken at Home and Ability to Speak English						
Population 5 years and over...............................	879,604	890,489	1.2	299,084,046	301,625,014	0.8
English only	87.0	86.9	X	78.9	78.5	X
Language other than English............................	13.0	13.1	X	21.1	21.5	X
Speaks English less than "very well"...............	4.4	4.4	X	8.6	8.6	X

NA = Not available.
X = Not applicable.
- = Zero or rounds to zero.

Table DE-5. Median Income and Poverty Status, 2015

(Number, percent, except as noted.)

Characteristic	State		U.S.	
	Number	Percent	Number	Percent
Median Income				
Households (dollars)...........................	61,255	X	55,775	X
Families (dollars)	74,931	X	68,260	X
Below Poverty Level (All People)	114,360	12.4	46,153,077	14.7
Sex				
Male	49,867	11.2	20,599,407	13.4
Female	64,493	13.5	25,553,670	16.0
Age				
Under 18 years..............................	38,972	19.4	15,000,273	20.7
Related children under 18 years...........	38,298	19.1	14,693,239	20.4
18 to 64 years...............................	65,622	11.7	26,960,369	13.9
65 years and over	9,766	6.2	4,192,435	9.0

X = Not applicable.

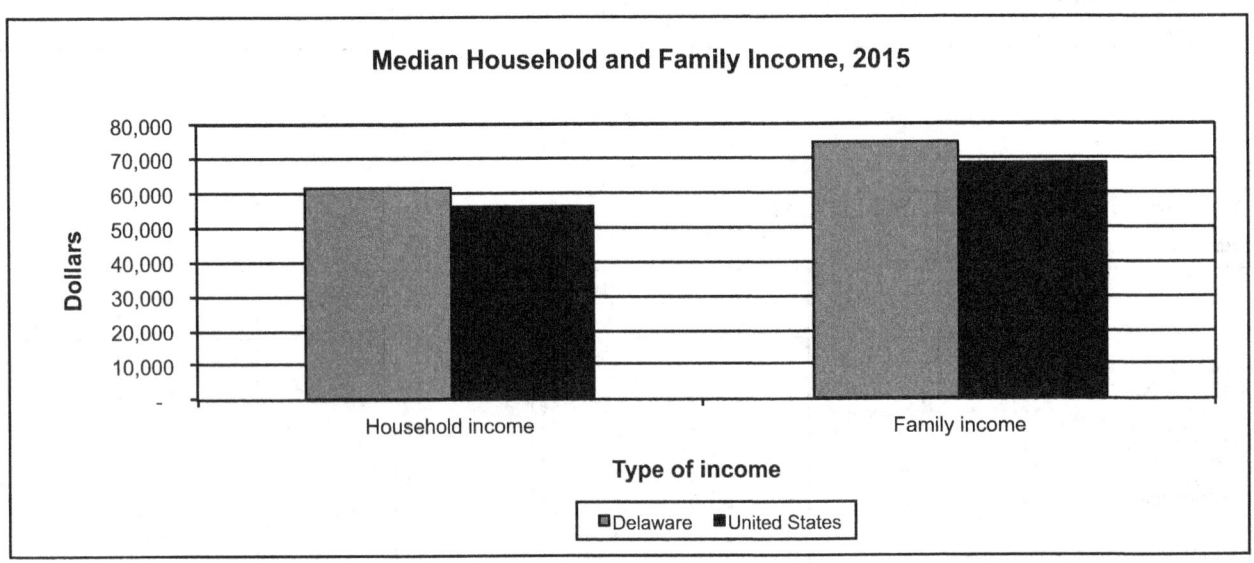

Table DE-6. Health Insurance Coverage Status for the Civilian Noninstitutionalized Population and Children Under 18 Years of Age

(Numbers in thousands, percent.)

Item	2007	2008	2009	2010	2011	2012	2013	2014	2015
Civilian Noninstitutionalized Population	863	856	869	885	892	903	912	921	931
Covered by Private or Public Insurance									
Number...	766	768	780	799	808	823	828	849	877
Percent...	88.8	89.7	89.8	90.3	90.6	91.2	90.9	92.2	94.1
Not Covered									
Number...	96	88	89	86	84	80	83	72	54
Percent...	11.2	10.3	10.2	9.7	9.4	8.8	9.1	7.8	5.9
Percent in the U.S. not covered.................	15.3	15.1	15.1	15.5	15.1	14.8	14.5	11.7	9.4
Children Under 18 Years of Age	209	206	207	206	204	204	203	203	204
Covered by Private or Public Insurance									
Number...	194	190	196	195	110	197	194	192	198
Percent...	92.5	92.2	94.5	94.7	95.4	96.5	95.5	94.3	97.0
Not Covered									
Number...	16	16	11	11	9	7	9	12	6
Percent...	7.5	7.8	5.5	5.3	4.6	3.5	4.5	5.7	3.0
Percent in the U.S. not covered.................	11.0	9.7	8.6	8.0	7.5	7.2	7.1	6.0	4.8

Table DE-7. Employment Status by Demographic Group, 2016

(Numbers in thousands, percent.)

Characteristic	Civilian noninstitutional population	Civilian labor force		Employed		Unemployed	
		Number	Percent of population	Number	Percent of population	Number	Percent of population
Total...	758	475	62.6	454	59.9	21	4.3
Sex							
Male..	359	243	67.7	233	64.8	10	4.2
Female.....................................	399	231	58.0	221	55.5	10	4.4
Race, Sex, and Hispanic Origin							
White.......................................	552	340	61.6	328	59.4	12	3.7
Male.....................................	265	179	67.5	173	65.3	6	3.4
Female..................................	288	162	56.1	155	53.9	6	3.9
Black or African American...................	160	108	67.3	101	63.1	7	6.2
Male.....................................	72	50	69.9	47	65.0	4	7.1
Female..................................	89	58	65.1	55	61.6	3	5.5
Hispanic or Latino ethnicity[1]	72	50	70.5	48	67.0	3	4.9
Male.....................................	33	27	79.8	25	75.4	2	5.7
Female..................................	38	24	62.4	23	59.9	1	4.1
Age							
16 to 19 years.............................	NA	NA	NA	NA	NA	NA	NA
20 to 24 years.............................	66	47	71.2	44	66.4	3	6.6
25 to 34 years.............................	120	103	85.6	97	80.7	6	5.9
35 to 44 years.............................	116	101	87.8	98	85.1	3	3.0
45 to 54 years.............................	124	102	82.5	99	79.8	3	3.2
55 to 64 years.............................	126	81	64.4	79	62.7	2	2.6
65 years and over..........................	168	28	16.9	27	16.3	1	3.5

NOTE: Data in Table 7 are from the Current Population Survey (CPS) and do not match the estimates in Table 8. See notes and definitions for further information.
[1] May be of any race.
NA = Not Available

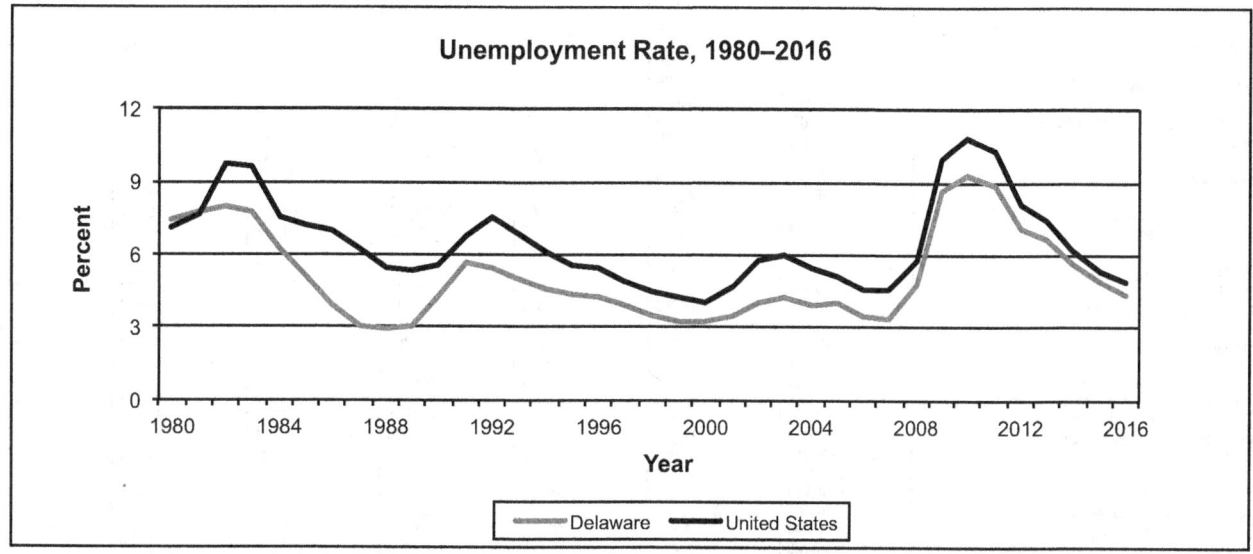

Table DE-8. Employment Status of the Civilian Noninstitutional Population Age 16 Years and Over

(Number, percent.)

Year	Civilian labor force	Civilian participation rate	Employed	Unemployed	Unemployment rate
2008...........................	447,041	65.9	424,914	22,127	4.9
2009...........................	437,500	63.8	401,312	36,188	8.3
2010...........................	434,419	62.0	397,869	36,550	8.4
2011...........................	443,346	62.3	410,086	33,260	7.5
2012...........................	445,708	61.9	413,589	32,119	7.2
2013...........................	442,518	60.7	412,766	29,752	6.7
2014...........................	453,631	61.4	427,708	25,923	5.7
2015...........................	467,472	62.4	444,578	22,894	4.9
2016...........................	472,676	62.5	451,973	20,703	4.4

Table DE-9. Employment and Average Wages by Industry

(Estimates through 2010 are based on the 2007 *North American Industry Classification System* [NAICS]. Estimates from 2011 onward are based on the 2012 NAICS.)

Industry	2009	2010	2011	2012	2013	2014	2015
	Number of Jobs						
Wage and Salary Employment by Industry	430,765	426,675	430,161	433,583	441,611	450,941	460,699
Farm Wage and Salary Employment	1,036	1,145	1,144	1,813	1,674	1,796	1,740
Nonfarm Wage and Salary Employment	429,729	425,530	429,017	431,770	439,937	449,145	458,959
Private wage and salary employment	358,077	352,593	356,226	357,982	365,798	375,026	384,392
Forestry, fishing, and related activities	(D)	(D)	(D)	(D)	(D)	(D)	(D)
Mining	(D)	(D)	(D)	(D)	(D)	(D)	(D)
Utilities	2,129	2,089	1,961	2,017	2,086	2,148	2,159
Construction	20,957	20,022	19,905	19,091	20,152	20,954	21,265
Manufacturing	27,984	26,163	25,694	25,783	25,378	25,708	27,073
Durable goods manufacturing	10,212	9,734	9,694	9,640	9,427	9,196	9,372
Nondurable goods manufacturing	17,772	16,429	16,000	16,143	15,951	16,512	17,701
Wholesale trade	13,356	12,552	12,548	12,527	12,257	12,040	11,854
Retail trade	50,475	50,338	51,057	51,111	51,886	52,837	53,345
Transportation and warehousing	10,215	9,977	10,182	10,513	11,758	12,948	14,432
Information	6,501	5,976	5,664	5,457	5,259	4,896	4,719
Finance and insurance	38,468	37,657	37,750	37,991	39,227	40,634	42,023
Real estate and rental and leasing	6,167	5,758	5,663	5,556	5,630	5,402	5,458
Professional, scientific, and technical services	24,567	24,038	26,160	27,434	28,716	29,134	28,648
Management of companies and enterprises	9,935	9,412	8,050	7,539	5,968	5,499	4,892
Administrative and waste services	21,526	21,310	22,071	22,024	23,900	25,499	26,812
Educational services	6,864	6,744	6,724	6,690	6,721	6,936	6,948
Health care and social assistance	56,397	57,303	58,554	59,885	61,973	64,172	66,887
Arts, entertainment, and recreation	8,225	8,842	9,115	8,883	9,736	10,055	10,209
Accommodation and food services	33,234	33,832	34,546	35,312	36,348	37,288	38,766
Other services, except public administration	20,662	20,122	20,001	19,573	18,135	18,207	18,212
Government and government enterprises	71,652	72,937	72,791	73,788	74,139	74,119	74,567
	Dollars						
Average Wages and Salaries by Industry	46,871	47,916	49,644	50,847	51,194	52,392	53,175
Average Farm Wages and Salaries	29,894	25,874	22,667	23,206	25,913	25,566	24,228
Average Nonfarm Wages and Salaries	46,912	47,976	49,716	50,963	51,290	52,499	53,285
Average private wages and salaries	46,893	48,407	50,301	51,627	51,913	53,216	53,994
Forestry, fishing, and related activities	(D)	(D)	(D)	(D)	(D)	(D)	(D)
Mining	(D)	(D)	(D)	(D)	(D)	(D)	(D)
Utilities	94,402	94,438	96,254	95,652	98,749	104,330	106,585
Construction	48,015	49,029	52,477	51,049	53,046	53,831	55,125
Manufacturing	57,876	56,998	56,139	57,102	57,909	59,581	64,065
Durable goods manufacturing	69,917	65,806	67,995	67,290	68,282	70,867	71,352
Nondurable goods manufacturing	50,958	51,780	48,955	51,018	51,779	53,296	60,207
Wholesale trade	72,043	76,846	82,546	81,336	79,124	83,265	79,870
Retail trade	25,556	25,789	25,994	26,182	26,439	27,184	28,287
Transportation and warehousing	42,941	42,993	43,843	46,018	45,476	46,313	45,956
Information	55,448	56,453	57,330	59,151	61,118	62,439	63,748
Finance and insurance	74,004	79,128	84,255	86,402	89,502	90,992	91,826
Real estate and rental and leasing	39,115	40,763	41,525	42,021	42,687	44,532	46,158
Professional, scientific, and technical services	80,684	85,445	89,452	97,514	94,592	100,173	107,041
Management of companies and enterprises	88,289	105,341	127,282	129,251	143,251	143,761	115,399
Administrative and waste services	30,947	32,400	32,720	33,686	33,751	35,345	36,520
Educational services	35,414	35,942	36,262	38,479	39,082	41,208	40,178
Health care and social assistance	46,776	47,286	48,729	49,744	49,855	50,972	52,000
Arts, entertainment, and recreation	27,662	28,400	30,712	30,178	27,713	27,120	27,189
Accommodation and food services	18,294	18,655	18,469	18,731	18,901	19,481	20,406
Other services, except public administration	27,768	28,477	28,825	30,106	32,565	33,262	34,575
Government and government enterprises	47,005	45,889	46,850	47,739	48,215	48,871	49,631

D = Not shown to avoid disclosure of confidential information, but the estimates for this item are included in the total.
L = Less than 10 jobs, but the estimates for this item are included in the total.

Table DE-10. Employment Characteristics by Family Type

(Number, percent.)

Family type and labor force status	2013 Total	2013 Families with own children under 18 years	2014 Total	2014 Families with own children under 18 years	2015 Total	2015 Families with own children under 18 years
All Families...	228,364	88,214	230,988	89,297	235,385	90,959
FAMILY TYPE AND LABOR FORCE STATUS						
Married-Couple Families...........................	164,733	55,941	163,350	55,964	170,416	57,755
Both husband and wife in labor force............	49.9	72.5	51.8	73.2	50.1	69.4
Husband in labor force, wife not in labor force	20.4	22.6	16.9	21.3	18.9	24.8
Wife in labor force, husband not in labor force	8.2	3.2	8.9	3.2	8.6	4.8
Both husband and wife not in labor force........	21.0	1.7	22.4	2.3	21.1	0.5
Other Families	63,631	32,273	67,638	33,333	64,969	33,204
Female householder, no husband present..........	77.0	77.2	73.2	77.5	75.1	77.9
In labor force	55.6	63.7	53.6	64.5	54.9	66.7
Not in labor force	21.4	13.5	19.6	13.0	20.2	11.2
Male householder, no wife present..................	23.0	22.8	26.8	22.5	24.9	22.1
In labor force	18.0	20.9	20.9	21.6	19.1	19.2
Not in labor force	5.1	2.0	5.9	0.9	5.8	2.9

Table DE-11. School Enrollment and Educational Attainment, 2015

(Number, percent.)

Item	State	U.S.
Enrollment		
Total population 3 years and over, enrolled in school	233,348	81,618,288
Enrolled in nursery school or preschool (percent)	5.9	6.0
Enrolled in kindergarten (percent)	4.9	5.0
Enrolled in elementary school, grades 1-8 (percent)................	38.7	40.3
Enrolled in high school, grades 9-12 (percent)	20.4	20.9
Enrolled in college or graduate school (percent)	30.2	27.7
Attainment		
Total population 25 years and over	652,636	216,447,163
Less than ninth grade (percent)	3.8	5.5
9th to 12th grade, no diploma (percent)	7.3	7.3
High school graduate, including equivalency (percent)	29.8	27.6
Some college, no degree (percent)	20.1	20.7
Associate's degree (percent)	8.1	8.2
Bachelor's degree (percent)	18.0	19.0
Graduate or professional degree (percent)...........................	12.9	11.6
High school graduate or higher (percent)	88.9	87.1
Bachelor's degree or higher (percent)	30.9	30.6

Table DE-12. Public School Characteristics and Educational Indicators

(Number, percent; data derived from National Center of Education Statistics.)

Item	State	U.S.
Public Schools, 2014–2015 (except where noted)		
Number of school districts...	46	18,260
Number of schools...	219	98,373
Number of students..	134,042	50,312,581
Number of teachers	9,649	3,132,351
Student-teacher ratio...	13.9	16.1
Expenditures per student (dollars), FY 2014........................	13,793	11,066
Four-year adjusted cohort graduation rate (ACGR)[1,2]	85.6	83.2
Students eligible for free or reduced-price lunch (percent).........	37.1	51.8
English language learners (percent).................................	6.6	9.4
Students age 3 to 21 served under IDEA, part B (percent)............	14.8	13.0

Public Schools by Type	Number	Percent of state public schools
Total number of schools...	219	100.0
Regular	194	88.6
Special education	13	5.9
Vocational education	6	2.7
Alternative education...	6	2.7

NOTE: Every school is assigned only one school type based on its instructional emphasis.
[1] ACGR data represents a new method of calculating high-school completion rates and may not be comparable to previous years' data for Averaged Freshmen Graduation Rates (AFGR).
[2] The United States 4-year ACGRs were estimated using both the reported 4-year ACGR data from 49 states and the District of Columbia and using imputed data for Idaho. The estimate for American Indian/Alaska Native students also includes imputed data for Virginia.

Table DE-13. Reported Voting and Registration of the Voting-Age Population, November 2016

(Numbers in thousands, percent.)

Item	Total population	Total citizen population	Registered			Voted		
			Total registered	Percent registered (total population)	Percent registered (total citizen population)	Total voted	Percent voted (total population)	Percent voted (total citizen population)
U.S. Total	245,502	224,059	157,596	64.2	70.3	137,537	56.0	61.4
State Total.............................	729	669	487	66.8	72.8	417	57.2	62.3
Sex								
Male	342	306	216	63.0	70.4	183	53.5	59.7
Female	387	362	271	70.1	74.8	234	60.4	64.5
Race								
White alone...........................	527	494	372	70.6	75.4	319	60.6	64.7
White, non-Hispanic alone	472	464	360	76.3	77.6	308	65.2	66.3
Black alone............................	148	144	96	64.9	66.5	82	55.1	56.5
Asian alone...........................	44	22	12	(B)	(B)	11	(B)	(B)
Hispanic (of any race).....................	66	39	19	(B)	(B)	14	(B)	(B)
White alone or in combination	535	501	378	70.7	75.5	323	60.3	64.4
Black alone or in combination.......	154	150	100	65.2	66.8	83	54.2	55.5
Asian alone or in combination.......	45	22	12	(B)	(B)	12	(B)	(B)
Age								
18 to 24 years..........................	82	69	44	(B)	(B)	29	(B)	(B)
25 to 34 years..........................	110	91	62	(B)	(B)	48	(B)	(B)
35 to 44 years..........................	115	102	77	66.4	75.0	62	54.0	61.1
45 to 64 years..........................	253	242	177	70.1	73.2	162	64.1	66.8
65 years and over	169	164	127	75.3	77.2	116	68.7	70.5

B = Base is less than 75,000 and therefore too small to show the derived measure.

Table DE-14. Crime

(Number, rate per 100,000. Data are derived from the FBI Uniform Crime Reports.)

Item	State			U.S. [1,2,3,4]		
	2014	2015	Percent change	2014	2015	Percent change
TOTAL POPULATION[5]	935,968	945,934	1.1	318,907,401	321,418,820	0.8
VIOLENT CRIME						
Number................................	4,568	4,720	3.3	1,186,185	1,231,566	3.8
Rate	488.1	499.0	2.2	372.0	383.2	3.0
Murder and Nonnegligent Manslaughter						
Number................................	50	63	26.0	14,164	15,696	10.8
Rate	5.3	6.7	24.7	4.4	4.9	10.0
Rape[6]						
Number................................	390	341	-12.6	118,027	124,047	5.1
Rate	41.7	36.0	-13.5	37.0	38.6	4.3
Robbery						
Number................................	1,271	1,235	-2.8	322,905	327,374	1.4
Rate	135.8	130.6	-3.9	101.3	101.9	0.6
Aggravated Assault						
Number................................	2,857	3,081	7.8	731,089	764,449	4.6
Rate	305.2	325.7	6.7	229.2	237.8	3.7
PROPERTY CRIME						
Number................................	27,915	25,455	-8.8	8,209,010	7,993,631	-2.6
Rate	2,982.5	2,691.0	-9.8	2,574.1	2,487.0	-3.4
Burglary						
Number................................	5,765	4,773	-17.2	1,713,153	1,579,527	-7.8
Rate	615.9	504.6	-18.1	537.2	491.4	-8.5
Larceny-Theft						
Number................................	20,885	19,501	-6.6	5,809,054	5,706,346	-1.8
Rate	2,231.4	2,061.6	-7.6	1,821.5	1,775.4	-2.5
Motor Vehicle Theft						
Number................................	1,265	1,181	-6.6	686,803	707,758	3.1
Rate	135.2	124.9	-7.6	215.4	220.2	2.2

NOTE: Although arson data are included in the trend and clearance tables, sufficient data are not available to estimate totals for this offense. Therefore, no arson data are published in this table.
X = Not applicable.
- = Zero or rounds to zero.
[1] The crime figures have been adjusted.
[2] The data collection methodology for the offense of forcible rape used by the Minnesota state Uniform Crime Reporting (UCR) Program (with the exception of Minneapolis and St. Paul, Minnesota) does not comply with national UCR Program guidelines. Consequently, its figures for forcible rape and violent crime (of which forcible rape is a part) are not published in this table.
[3] Includes offenses reported by the Zoological Police and the Metro Transit Police.
[4] Because of changes in the state's reporting practices, figures are not comparable to previous years' data.
[5] Populations are U.S. Census Bureau provisional estimates as of July 1 of each year.
[6] The figures shown for the offense of rape were estimated using the revised Uniform Crime Reporting (UCR) definition of rape.

Table DE-15. State Government Finances, 2015

(Dollar amounts in thousands, percent distribution.)

Item	Dollars	Percent distribution
Total Revenue	8,268,967	100.0
General revenue	7,573,457	91.6
Intergovernmental revenue	1,974,674	23.9
Taxes	3,513,916	42.5
General sales	0	-
Selective sales	498,557	6.0
License taxes	1,389,894	16.8
Individual income tax	1,140,248	13.8
Corporate income tax	400,746	4.8
Other taxes	84,471	1.0
Current charges	1,135,184	13.7
Miscellaneous general revenue	949,683	11.5
Utility revenue	21,273	0.3
Liquor stores revenue	0	-
Insurance trust revenue[1]	674,237	8.2
Total Expenditure	9,036,319	100.0
Intergovernmental expenditure	1,454,859	16.1
Direct expenditure	7,581,460	83.9
Current operation	5,725,555	63.4
Capital outlay	629,365	7.0
Insurance benefits and repayments	714,038	7.9
Assistance and subsidies	316,185	3.5
Interest on debt	196,317	2.2
Exhibit: Salaries and wages	1,411,796	15.6
Total Expenditure	9,036,319	100.0
General expenditure	8,199,548	90.7
Intergovernmental expenditure	1,454,859	16.1
Direct expenditure	6,744,689	74.6
General expenditure, by function:		
Education	3,025,239	33.5
Public welfare	2,323,157	25.7
Hospitals	44,119	0.5
Health	445,263	4.9
Highways	513,072	5.7
Police protection	133,120	1.5
Correction	302,261	3.3
Natural resources	90,199	1.0
Parks and recreation	46,003	0.5
Governmental administration	482,463	5.3
Interest on general debt	196,317	2.2
Other and unallocable	598,335	6.6
Utility expenditure	122,733	1.4
Liquor stores expenditure	0	-
Insurance trust expenditure	714,038	7.9
Debt at End of Fiscal Year	4,964,915	X
Cash and Security Holdings	13,122,886	X

X = Not applicable.
- = Zero or rounds to zero.
[1] Within insurance trust revenue, net earnings of state retirement systems is a calculated statistic (the item code in the data file is X08), and thus can be positive or negative. Net earnings is the sum of earnings on investments plus gains on investments minus losses on investments. The change made in 2002 for asset valuation from book to market value in accordance with Statement 34 of the Governmental Accounting Standards Board is reflected in the calculated statistics.

Table DE-16. State Government Tax Collections, 2016

(Dollars in thousands, percent.)

Item	Dollars	Percent distribution
Total Taxes	3,522,301	100.0
Property taxes	0	-
Sales and gross receipts	539,193	15.3
General sales and gross receipts	0	-
Selective sales and gross receipts	539,193	15.3
Alcoholic beverages	20,274	0.6
Amusements	0	-
Insurance premiums	96,279	2.7
Motor fuels	125,453	3.6
Pari-mutuels	69	0.0
Public utilities	55,394	1.6
Tobacco products	111,762	3.2
Other selective sales	129,962	3.7
Licenses	1,452,596	41.2
Alcoholic beverages	1,584	-
Amusements	306	-
Corporations in general	1,274,897	36.2
Hunting and fishing	3,030	0.1
Motor vehicle	54,287	1.5
Motor vehicle operators	6,738	0.2
Public utilities	0	-
Occupation and business, NEC	105,868	3.0
Other licenses	5,886	0.2
Income taxes	1,430,520	40.6
Individual income	1,112,368	31.6
Corporation net income	318,152	9.0
Other taxes	99,992	2.8
Death and gift	9,350	0.3
Documentary and stock transfer	89,527	2.5
Severance	0	-
Taxes, NEC	1,115	-

X = Not applicable.
- = Zero or rounds to zero.

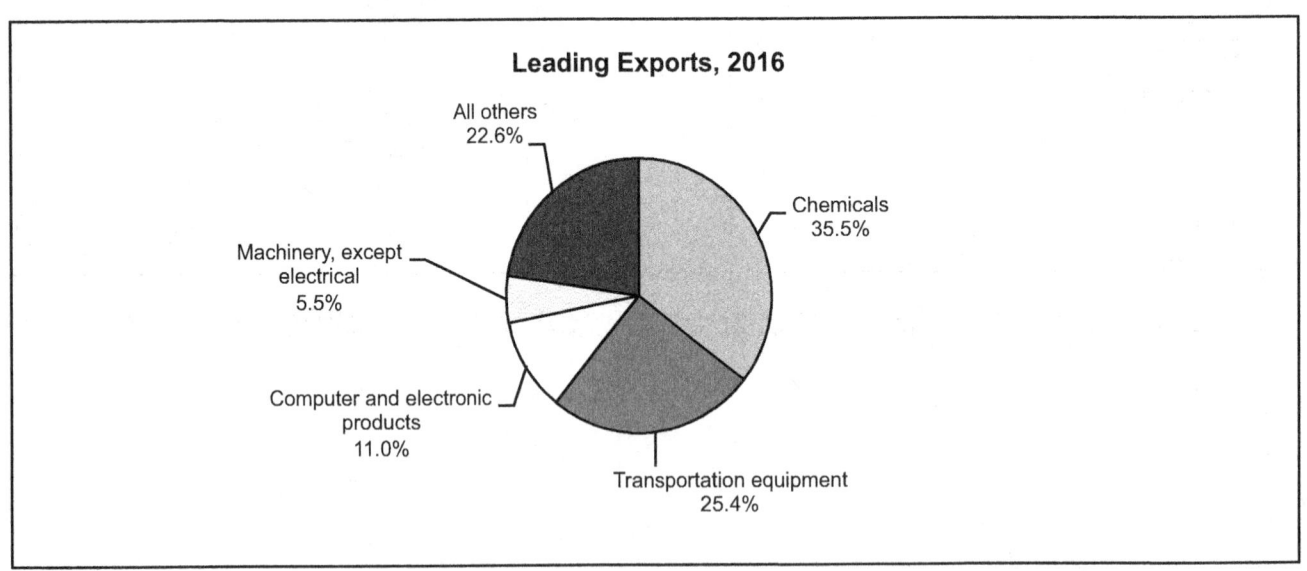

Leading Exports, 2016

All others 22.6%
Chemicals 35.5%
Machinery, except electrical 5.5%
Computer and electronic products 11.0%
Transportation equipment 25.4%

DISTRICT OF COLUMBIA

Facts and Figures:

Location: South Atlantic United States; bordered on the SE, NE, and NW by Maryland and on the SW by Virginia

Area: 68 sq. mi.

Population: 681,170 (2016 est.); rank—49th

Official Motto: Justitia omnibus ("Justice for All")

U.S. Congress: 1 delegate

Abbreviation: D.C.

Symbols: flower—American beauty rose; tree—scarlet oak; bird—wood thrush

At a Glance

- From 2010 to 2016, the population of the District of Columbia rose 13.2 percent, the highest increase in the country.

- The violent crime rate in the District of Columbia was 1,269.1 per 100,000 population in 2015, more than triple the national rate of 383.2 per 100,000.

- In 2015, The District of Columbia's property crime rate was the highest in the country at 4,676.2 per 100,000 population.

- Compared to the 50 states, the District of Columbia had the lowest percentage of people under 18 years of age (17.7 percent), and the third lowest percentage of people over age 65 (11.6 percent) in 2016.

- In 2015, 17.3 percent of all District of Columbia residents lived in poverty and 25.6 percent of children under 18 years of age lived in poverty.

Table DC-1. Population by Age, Sex, Race, and Hispanic Origin

(Number, percent, except where noted.)

Sex, age, race, and Hispanic origin	2000	2010	2016 [1]	Average annual percent change, 2010–2016
Total Population..	572,059	601,723	681,170	0.8
Percent of total U.S. population	0.2	0.2	0.2	X
Sex				
Male...	269,366	284,222	323,230	0.9
Female	302,693	317,501	357,940	0.8
Age				
Under 5 years..	32,536	32,613	43,507	2.1
5 to 19 years...	103,270	91,107	98,434	0.5
20 to 64 years...	366,355	409,194	460,538	0.8
65 years and over	69,898	68,809	78,691	0.9
Median age (years)	34.8	33.8	33.9	-
Race and Hispanic Origin				
One race...				
White	176,101	251,265	303,813	1.3
Black..	343,312	310,379	325,190	0.3
American Indian and Alaska Native	1,713	3,264	4,196	1.8
Asian..	15,189	21,705	28,251	1.9
Native Hawaiian or Other Pacific Islander	348	770	1041	2.2
Two or more races..	13,446	14,340	18,679	1.9
Hispanic (of any race)...	44,953	57,833	74,422	1.8

X = Not applicable.
- = Zero or rounds to zero.
[1] Population figures for 2016 are July 1 estimates. The 2010 estimates are taken from the 2010 Census.

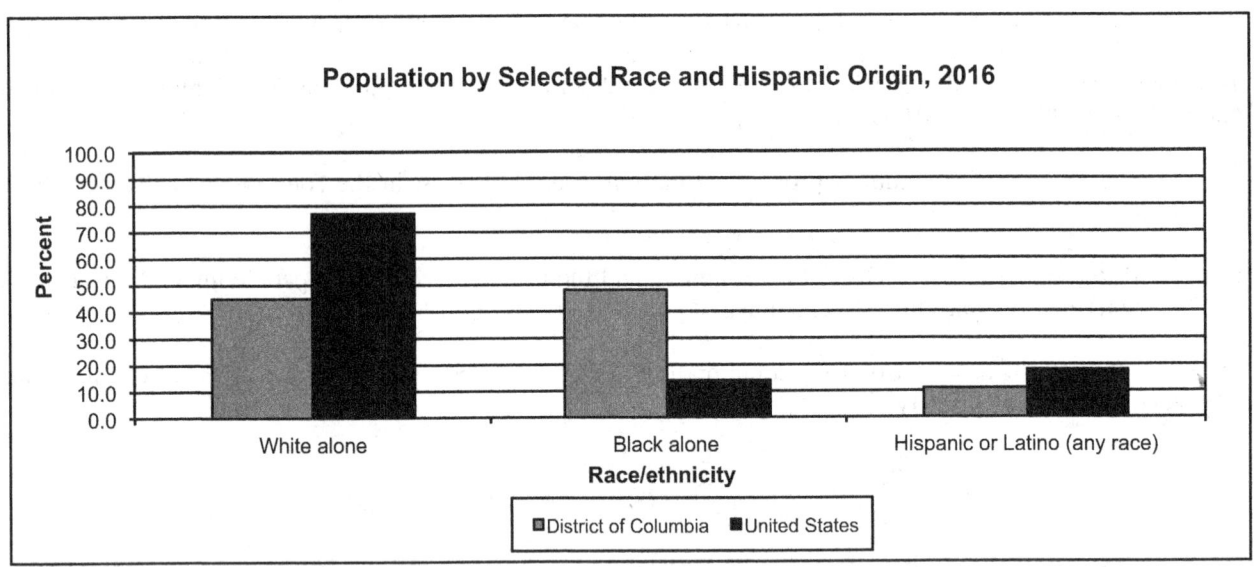

Table DC-2. Marital Status

(Number, percent distribution.)

Sex, age, race, and Hispanic origin	2000	2010	2015
Males, 15 Years and Over	219,706	243,152	267,946
Never married	51.2	58.9	57.4
Now married, except separated...	32.8	28.2	31.1
Separated..	3.9	2.4	2.3
Widowed..	3.4	2.1	2.2
Divorced..	8.7	8.4	7.1
Females, 15 Years and Over	254,711	277,203	302,000
Never married	46.0	55.8	53.6
Now married, except separated...	27.5	22.8	27.1
Separated..	4.4	3.1	2.1
Widowed..	11.6	7.5	6.8
Divorced..	10.6	10.8	10.4

Table DC-3. Households and Housing Characteristics

(Number, percent, dollars.)

Item	2000	2010	2015	Average annual percent change, 2000–2015
Total Households...	248,338	252,388	281,787	0.9
Family households...	114,166	101,519	125,178	0.6
Married-couple family...	56,631	57,275	71,857	1.8
Other family...	57,535	44,244	53,321	-0.5
Male householder, no wife present............................	10,503	8,740	10,834	0.2
Female householder, no husband present....................	47,032	35,504	42,487	-0.6
Nonfamily households...	134,172	150,869	156,609	1.1
Householder living alone...	108,744	121,036	118,347	0.6
Householder not living alone...	25,428	29,833	38,262	3.4
Housing Characteristics				
Total housing units...	274,845	296,836	309,596	0.8
Occupied housing units	248,338	252,388	281,787	0.9
Owner occupied...	101,214	107,193	112,555	0.7
Renter occupied...	147,124	145,195	169,232	1.0
Average household size...	2.16	2.24	2.24	0.2
Financial Characteristics				
Median gross rent of renter-occupied housing	618	1,198	1,417	8.6
Median monthly owner costs for housing units with a mortgage	1,291	2,297	2,312	5.3
Median value of owner-occupied housing units	157,200	426,900	551,300	16.7

Table DC-4. Migration, Origin, and Language

(Number, percent.)

Characteristic	State			U.S.		
	2014	2015	Percent change	2014	2015	Percent change
Residence 1 Year Ago						
Population 1 year and over	648,586	663,006	2.2	315,095,393	317,635,720	0.8
Same house	79.2	79.2	X	85.1	85.3	X
Different house in the U.S.	19.0	19.2	X	14.3	14.1	X
Same county	10.4	10.1	X	8.7	8.5	X
Different county	8.7	9.0	X	5.6	5.6	X
Same state	N/A	N/A	X	3.3	3.2	X
Different state	8.7	9.0	X	2.3	2.4	X
Abroad	1.8	1.6	X	0.6	0.7	X
Place of Birth						
Native born	566,944	577,111	1.8	276,465,262	278,128,449	0.6
Male	47.4	47.5	X	49.3	49.3	X
Female	52.6	52.5	X	50.7	50.7	X
Foreign born	91,949	95,117	3.4	42,391,794	43,290,372	2.1
Male	47.6	48.0	X	48.7	48.6	X
Female	52.4	52.0	X	51.3	51.4	X
Foreign born; naturalized U.S. citizen...............................	35,515	41,645	17.3	19,984,738	20,697,103	3.6
Male	42.0	45.4	X	45.9	45.9	X
Female	58.0	54.6	X	54.1	54.1	X
Foreign born; not a U.S. citizen...............................	56,434	53,472	-5.2	22,407,056	22,593,269	0.8
Male	51.1	50.0	X	51.2	51.1	X
Female	48.9	50.0	X	48.8	48.9	X
Entered 2010 or later	21.7	26.3	X	12.3	15.6	X
Entered 2000 to 2009...	35.5	27.4	X	28.6	27.9	X
Entered before 2000...	42.8	46.3	X	59.1	56.5	X
World Region of Birth, Foreign						
Foreign-born population, excluding population born at sea	91,949	95,117	3.4	42,390,705	43,289,646	2.1
Europe	20.0	18.1	X	11.2	11.1	X
Asia...	18.3	23.1	X	30.1	30.6	X
Africa...	15.9	14.6	X	4.6	4.8	X
Oceania...	0.9	1.3	X	0.6	0.6	X
Latin America...	43.1	40.3	X	51.6	51.1	X
North America...	2.0	2.7	X	1.9	1.9	X
Language Spoken at Home and Ability to Speak English						
Population 5 years and over...	616,130	628,998	2.1	299,084,046	301,625,014	0.8
English only...	82.2	82.6	X	78.9	78.5	X
Language other than English...	17.8	17.4	X	21.1	21.5	X
Speaks English less than "very well"............................	5.9	5.4	X	8.6	8.6	X

NA = Not available.
X = Not applicable.
- = Zero or rounds to zero.

Table DC-5. Median Income and Poverty Status, 2015

(Number, percent, except as noted.)

Characteristic	State Number	State Percent	U.S. Number	U.S. Percent
Median Income				
Households (dollars).........................	75,628	X	55,775	X
Families (dollars)	94,846	X	68,260	X
Below Poverty Level (All People)	110,500	17.3	46,153,077	14.7
Sex				
Male	48,884	16.1	20,599,407	13.4
Female	61,616	18.4	25,553,670	16.0
Age				
Under 18 years................	29,729	25.6	15,000,273	20.7
Related children under 18 years........	29,166	25.3	14,693,239	20.4
18 to 64 years................	69,604	15.5	26,960,369	13.9
65 years and over	11,167	15.2	4,192,435	9.0

X = Not applicable.

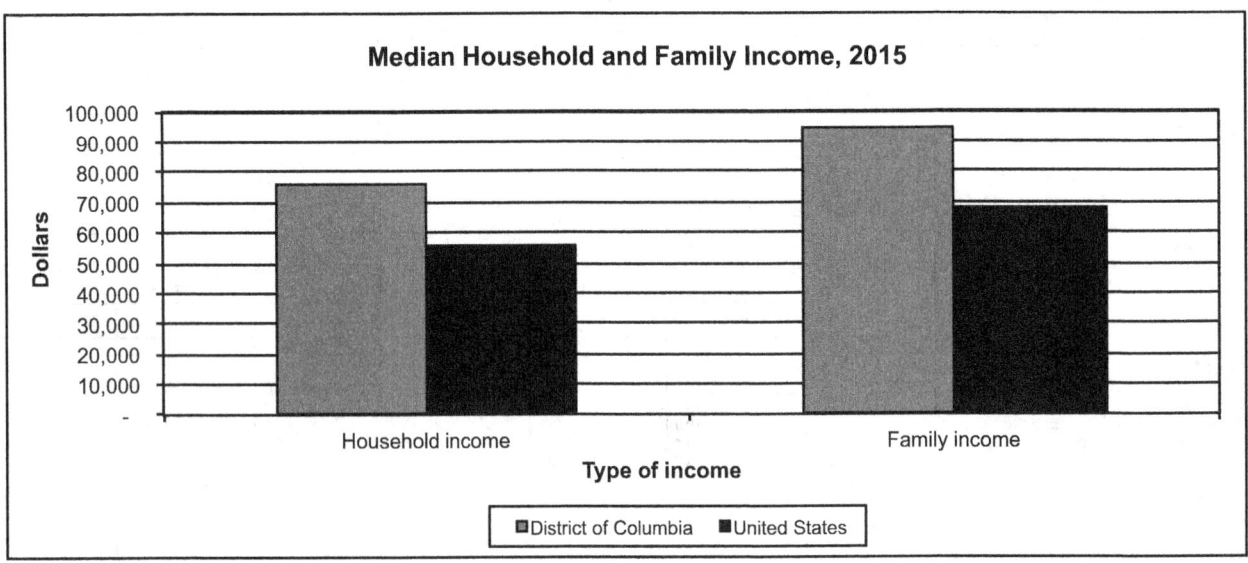

Median Household and Family Income, 2015

Table DC-6. Health Insurance Coverage Status for the Civilian Noninstitutionalized Population and Children Under 18 Years of Age

(Numbers in thousands, percent.)

Item	2007	2008	2009	2010	2011	2012	2013	2014	2015
Civilian Noninstitutionalized Population	582	580	589	594	608	621	636	648	661
Covered by Private or Public Insurance									
Number..........................	526	534	548	549	566	585	594	614	636
Percent...........................	90.5	92.1	93.0	92.4	93.1	94.1	93.3	94.7	96.2
Not Covered									
Number..........................	55	46	41	45	42	36	42	34	25
Percent...........................	9.5	7.9	7.0	7.6	6.9	5.9	6.7	5.3	3.8
Percent in the U.S. not covered................	15.3	15.1	15.1	15.5	15.1	14.8	14.5	11.7	9.4
Children Under 18 Years of Age	112	111	114	101	105	109	111	115	117
Covered by Private or Public Insurance									
Number..........................	105	106	111	99	101	107	109	112	116
Percent...........................	93.8	95.5	97.2	97.7	96.1	98.3	97.6	97.9	98.5
Not Covered									
Number..........................	7	5	3	2	4	2	3	2	2
Percent...........................	6.2	4.5	2.8	2.3	3.9	1.7	2.4	2.1	1.5
Percent in the U.S. not covered................	11.0	9.7	8.6	8.0	7.5	7.2	7.1	6.0	4.8

Table DC-7. Employment Status by Demographic Group, 2016

(Numbers in thousands, percent.)

Characteristic	Civilian noninstitutional population	Civilian labor force		Employed		Unemployed	
		Number	Percent of population	Number	Percent of population	Number	Percent of population
Total..............................	564	395	70.1	371	65.8	24	6.1
Sex							
Male.............................	262	194	74.2	182	69.6	12	6.2
Female	302	201	66.5	189	62.5	12	5.9
Race, Sex, and Hispanic Origin							
White	260	215	82.7	211	81.0	4	2.1
Male.............................	129	110	85.8	108	84.1	2	2.0
Female	131	105	79.7	102	78.0	2	2.2
Black or African American..................	259	147	56.8	129	49.9	18	12.2
Male.............................	113	69	60.7	60	52.6	9	13.4
Female	145	78	53.8	69	47.7	9	11.2
Hispanic or Latino ethnicity[1]	57	45	78.9	44	76.1	2	3.6
Male.............................	28	24	85.6	23	82.9	1	3.2
Female	29	21	72.5	20	69.5	1	4.0
Age							
16 to 19 years..................	NA	NA	NA	NA	NA	NA	NA
20 to 24 years..................	55	37	68.3	33	59.7	5	12.3
25 to 34 years..................	168	147	87.5	140	83.1	7	5.0
35 to 44 years..................	94	82	87.2	78	83.2	4	4.8
45 to 54 years..................	73	59	81.0	55	76.2	4	5.9
55 to 64 years..................	65	43	66.6	41	62.9	3	5.8
65 years and over..............	85	22	25.3	21	24.4	1	3.3

NOTE: Data in Table 7 are from the Current Population Survey (CPS) and do not match the estimates in Table 8. See notes and definitions for further information.
[1] May be of any race.
NA = Not available.

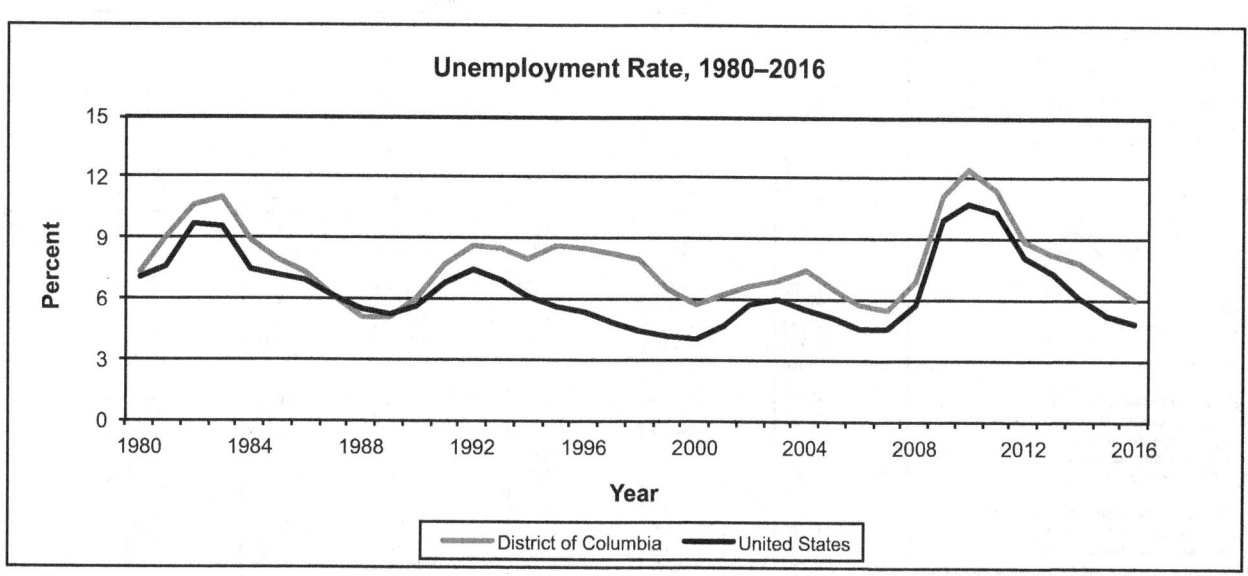

Table DC-8. Employment Status of the Civilian Noninstitutional Population Age 16 Years and Over

(Number, percent.)

Year	Civilian labor force	Civilian participation rate	Employed	Unemployed	Unemployment rate
2008..................	330,544	69.2	309,192	21,352	6.5
2009..................	335,672	69.1	304,500	31,172	9.3
2010..................	346,065	68.8	313,508	32,557	9.4
2011..................	350,778	67.9	315,171	35,607	10.2
2012..................	365,055	69.2	332,068	32,987	9.0
2013..................	373,835	69.6	342,061	31,774	8.5
2014..................	378,082	69.4	348,729	29,353	7.8
2015..................	388,388	70.1	361,544	26,844	6.9
2016..................	392,448	70.1	368,846	23,602	6.0

Table DC-9. Employment and Average Wages by Industry

(Estimates through 2010 are based on the 2007 *North American Industry Classification System* [NAICS]. Estimates from 2011 onward are based on the 2012 NAICS.)

Industry	2009	2010	2011	2012	2013	2014	2015
				Number of Jobs			
Wage and Salary Employment by Industry..................	723,857	732,179	744,088	749,686	759,102	767,860	776,441
Farm Wage and Salary Employment..........................	0	0	0	0	0	0	0
Nonfarm Wage and Salary Employment....................	723,857	732,179	744,088	749,686	759,102	767,860	776,441
Private wage and salary employment...........................	472,051	469,820	482,804	493,273	506,154	516,038	527,814
Forestry, fishing, and related activities........................	0	0	0	0	0	0	0
Mining..	0	0	0	0	0	0	0
Utilities..	2,459	1,832	1,830	1,850	1,891	1,920	2,005
Construction..	12,280	11,108	12,546	14,047	14,484	14,723	14,981
Manufacturing..	1,431	1,275	1,043	973	1,008	1,032	1,103
Durable goods manufacturing...........................	528	475	424	423	441	418	456
Nondurable goods manufacturing........................	903	800	619	550	567	614	647
Wholesale trade	4,674	4,801	4,647	4,974	4,870	4,939	4,872
Retail trade...	18,309	18,828	18,898	19,186	20,232	21,509	22,708
Transportation and warehousing..............................	4,102	4,119	4,120	4,070	4,031	4,157	4,598
Information	19,378	18,715	18,713	17,524	17,059	17,223	17,167
Finance and insurance	14,734	14,976	14,925	14,942	14,820	15,140	15,146
Real estate and rental and leasing............................	10,590	10,196	10,501	11,054	11,084	12,107	12,277
Professional, scientific, and technical services	102,937	101,714	103,664	107,412	108,715	109,588	112,981
Management of companies and enterprises....................	1,294	2,020	2,018	2,012	2,046	2,157	2,141
Administrative and waste services.............................	42,305	42,528	45,457	45,929	46,428	46,991	47,947
Educational services	49,750	49,162	50,566	50,229	55,716	56,583	57,232
Health care and social assistance.............................	58,018	59,897	61,598	62,734	64,596	65,183	66,155
Arts, entertainment, and recreation...........................	7,339	7,167	7,037	7,119	7,013	7,394	7,752
Accommodation and food services.............................	51,905	53,483	55,857	58,643	61,279	63,051	65,667
Other services, except public administration..................	70,546	67,999	69,384	70,575	70,882	72,341	73,082
Government and government enterprises......................	251,806	262,359	261,284	256,413	252,948	251,822	248,627
				Dollars			
Average Wages and Salaries by Industry	76,158	79,114	80,464	81,626	81,992	84,272	87,008
Average Farm Wages and Salaries	0	0	0	0	0	0	0
Average Nonfarm Wages and Salaries	76,158	79,114	80,464	81,626	81,992	84,272	87,008
Average private wages and salaries...........................	69,705	72,268	73,868	75,594	76,143	78,327	80,742
Forestry, fishing, and related activities	0	0	0	0	0	0	0
Mining..	0	0	0	0	0	0	0
Utilities..	93,792	85,298	91,295	91,640	98,335	98,391	103,181
Construction..	55,671	61,069	63,403	63,613	62,920	65,119	63,621
Manufacturing..	80,739	84,315	104,685	107,628	109,951	95,328	95,840
Durable goods manufacturing...........................	78,222	78,133	83,344	83,163	83,789	82,533	91,156
Nondurable goods manufacturing........................	82,212	87,986	119,302	126,444	130,300	104,039	99,142
Wholesale trade	97,086	100,871	107,664	114,085	116,518	120,436	121,038
Retail trade...	29,213	30,641	32,259	34,289	33,267	33,264	33,867
Transportation and warehousing..............................	65,249	66,051	70,447	73,459	73,247	75,991	74,031
Information	102,752	103,207	106,859	112,008	122,437	120,802	121,608
Finance and insurance	120,353	128,488	137,690	142,834	148,742	156,429	167,316
Real estate and rental and leasing............................	63,730	70,642	74,977	77,652	80,019	94,279	94,315
Professional, scientific, and technical services	112,647	117,447	120,097	122,664	122,655	126,658	128,775
Management of companies and enterprises....................	274,009	218,151	201,889	235,179	219,006	232,865	297,394
Administrative and waste services.............................	42,644	43,778	45,886	46,986	48,384	49,076	51,190
Educational services	44,323	45,211	45,669	47,289	47,199	47,698	51,015
Health care and social assistance.............................	55,594	56,769	57,529	58,171	57,753	60,384	62,701
Arts, entertainment, and recreation...........................	61,109	63,600	55,132	50,295	54,650	57,413	60,360
Accommodation and food services.............................	30,937	31,699	32,330	32,516	33,507	34,441	35,847
Other services, except public administration..................	70,026	74,691	77,255	78,567	81,692	83,461	86,781
Government and government enterprises......................	88,255	91,375	92,652	93,231	93,696	96,453	100,312

Table DC-10. Employment Characteristics by Family Type

(Number, percent.)

Family type and labor force status	2013 Total	2013 Families with own children under 18 years	2014 Total	2014 Families with own children under 18 years	2015 Total	2015 Families with own children under 18 years
All Families...	120,467	51,277	115,477	48,881	125,178	54,494
FAMILY TYPE AND LABOR FORCE STATUS						
Married-Couple Families	65,805	25,218	63,857	24,341	71,857	27,840
Both husband and wife in labor force............................	58.9	71.3	62.0	71.6	65.0	76.8
Husband in labor force, wife not in labor force	18.5	22.3	17.2	22.8	14.1	18.8
Wife in labor force, husband not in labor force	6.9	3.5	7.5	4.3	5.2	0.8
Both husband and wife not in labor force...................	13.2	1.3	13.2	1.3	12.2	2.5
Other Families	54,662	26,059	51,620	24,540	53,321	26,654
Female householder, no husband present............................	78.5	79.1	81.6	85.3	79.7	82.6
In labor force..	52.3	61.6	55.8	69.3	52.3	65.1
Not in labor force	26.1	17.5	25.8	16.0	27.4	17.5
Male householder, no wife present...........................	21.5	20.9	18.4	14.7	20.3	17.4
In labor force..	16.0	17.0	13.6	13.7	15.6	16.2
Not in labor force	5.5	4.0	4.8	1.0	4.7	1.2

Table DC-11. School Enrollment and Educational Attainment, 2015

(Number, percent.)

Item	District	U.S.
Enrollment		
Total population 3 years and over, enrolled in school	166,940	81,618,288
Enrolled in nursery school or preschool (percent)...	8.7	6.0
Enrolled in kindergarten (percent)...	4.1	5.0
Enrolled in elementary school, grades 1-8 (percent)............................	26.7	40.3
Enrolled in high school, grades 9-12 (percent)	14.7	20.9
Enrolled in college or graduate school (percent)..	45.8	27.7
Attainment		
Total population 25 years and over	472,884	216,447,163
Less than ninth grade (percent)...	4.3	5.5
9th to 12th grade, no diploma (percent)...	5.9	7.3
High school graduate, including equivalency (percent)........................	17.4	27.6
Some college, no degree (percent)...	12.7	20.7
Associate's degree (percent)	3.0	8.2
Bachelor's degree (percent)	23.8	19.0
Graduate or professional degree (percent)................................	32.9	11.6
High school graduate or higher (percent)	89.8	87.1
Bachelor's degree or higher (percent)	56.7	30.6

Table DC-12. Public School Characteristics and Educational Indicators

(Number, percent; data derived from National Center of Education Statistics.)

Item	District	U.S.
Public Schools, 2014–2015 (except where noted)		
Number of school districts...	64	18,260
Number of schools...	229	98,373
Number of students	80,958	50,312,581
Number of teachers	6,565	3,132,351
Student-teacher ratio	12.3	16.1
Expenditures per student (dollars), FY 2014.................................	20,577	11,066
Four-year adjusted cohort graduation rate (ACGR)[1,2]	68.5	83.2
Students eligible for free or reduced-price lunch (percent)...................	92.4	51.8
English language learners (percent)...	10.6	9.4
Students age 3 to 21 served under IDEA, part B (percent)................	15.0	13.0

Public Schools by Type	Number	Percent of D.C. public schools
Total number of schools...	229	100.0
Regular	215	93.9
Special education	4	1.7
Vocational education	0	-
Alternative education...	10	4.4

NOTE: Every school is assigned only one school type based on its instructional emphasis.

[1] ACGR data represents a new method of calculating high-school completion rates and may not be comparable to previous years' data for Averaged Freshmen Graduation Rates (AFGR).

[2] The United States 4-year ACGRs were estimated using both the reported 4-year ACGR data from 49 states and the District of Columbia and using imputed data for Idaho. The estimate for American Indian/Alaska Native students also includes imputed data for Virginia.

Table DC-13. Reported Voting and Registration of the Voting-Age Population, November 2016

(Numbers in thousands, percent.)

Item	Total population	Total citizen population	Registered			Voted		
			Total registered	Percent registered (total population)	Percent registered (total citizen population)	Total voted	Percent voted (total population)	Percent voted (total citizen population)
U.S. Total	245,502	224,059	157,596	64.2	70.3	137,537	56.0	61.4
State Total............................	553	512	420	75.9	82.1	380	68.7	74.3
Sex								
Male	255	237	190	74.8	80.4	168	66.1	71.0
Female	299	275	229	76.8	83.5	212	71.0	77.2
Race								
White alone..............................	264	243	209	79.5	86.3	194	73.7	80.0
White, non-Hispanic alone	231	222	195	84.6	88.2	181	78.6	81.9
Black alone.............................	250	238	184	73.9	77.5	162	64.8	68.0
Asian alone............................	27	18	14	(B)	(B)	13	(B)	(B)
Hispanic (of any race).....................	42	28	20	(B)	(B)	18	(B)	(B)
White alone or in combination	274	253	219	80.0	86.6	203	74.3	80.5
Black alone or in combination..........	259	247	192	74.2	77.7	169	65.4	68.4
Asian alone or in combination..........	29	20	16	(B)	(B)	15	(B)	(B)
Age								
18 to 24 years...................	59	55	40	(B)	(B)	34	(B)	(B)
25 to 34 years...................	179	164	130	72.9	79.6	120	67.1	73.3
35 to 44 years...................	91	80	70	(B)	(B)	64	(B)	(B)
45 to 64 years...................	139	131	110	79.5	84.2	99	71.4	75.7
65 years and over	86	82	70	(B)	(B)	63	(B)	(B)

B = Base is less than 75,000 and therefore too small to show the derived measure.

Table DC-14. Crime

(Number, rate per 100,000. Data are derived from the FBI Uniform Crime Reports.)

Item	District [1]			U.S. [1,2,3,4]		
	2014	2015	Percent change	2014	2015	Percent change
TOTAL POPULATION[5]	659,836	672,228	1.9	318,907,401	321,418,820	0.8
VIOLENT CRIME						
Number..............................	8,199	8,531	4.0	1,186,185	1,231,566	3.8
Rate	1,242.6	1,269.1	2.1	372.0	383.2	3.0
Murder and Nonnegligent Manslaughter						
Number..............................	105	162	54.3	14,164	15,696	10.8
Rate	15.9	24.1	51.4	4.4	4.9	10.0
Rape[6]						
Number..............................	472	494	4.7	118,027	124,047	5.1
Rate	71.5	73.5	2.7	37.0	38.6	4.3
Robbery						
Number..............................	3,497	3,742	7.0	322,905	327,374	1.4
Rate	530.0	556.7	5.0	101.3	101.9	0.6
Aggravated Assault						
Number..............................	4,125	4,133	0.2	731,089	764,449	4.6
Rate	625.2	614.8	-1.7	229.2	237.8	3.7
PROPERTY CRIME						
Number..............................	34,147	31,435	-7.9	8,209,010	7,993,631	-2.6
Rate	5,175.1	4,676.2	-9.6	2,574.1	2,487.0	-3.4
Burglary						
Number..............................	3,466	2,971	-14.3	1,713,153	1,579,527	-7.8
Rate	525.3	442.0	-15.9	537.2	491.4	-8.5
Larceny-Theft						
Number..............................	26,898	25,200	-6.3	5,809,054	5,706,346	-1.8
Rate	4,076.5	3,748.7	-8.0	1,821.5	1,775.4	-2.5
Motor Vehicle Theft						
Number..............................	3,783	3,264	-13.7	686,803	707,758	3.1
Rate	573.3	485.5	-15.3	215.4	220.2	2.2

NOTE: Although arson data are included in the trend and clearance tables, sufficient data are not available to estimate totals for this offense. Therefore, no arson data are published in this table.
X = Not applicable.
- = Zero or rounds to zero.
[1] Includes offenses reported by the Zoological Police and the Metro Transit Police.
[2] The crime figures have been adjusted.
[3] The data collection methodology for the offense of forcible rape used by the Minnesota state Uniform Crime Reporting (UCR) Program (with the exception of Minneapolis and St. Paul, Minnesota) does not comply with national UCR Program guidelines. Consequently, its figures for forcible rape and violent crime (of which forcible rape is a part) are not published in this table.
[4] Because of changes in the state's reporting practices, figures are not comparable to previous years' data.
[5] Populations are U.S. Census Bureau provisional estimates as of July 1 of each year.
[6] The figures shown for the offense of rape were estimated using the revised Uniform Crime Reporting (UCR) definition of rape.

Table DC-15. Local Government Finances, 2014

(Dollar amounts in thousands, percent distribution.)

Item	Dollars	Percent distribution
Total Revenue	14,712,741	100.0
General revenue	11,930,618	81.1
Intergovernmental revenue	3,789,766	25.8
Taxes	6,378,407	43.4
Property	2,070,974	14.1
Sales and gross receipts	1,600,421	10.9
Individual income tax	1,679,173	11.4
Corporate income tax	415,581	2.8
Motor vehicle license	36,083	0.2
Other taxes	576,175	3.9
Current charges	734,342	5.0
Miscellaneous general revenue	1,028,103	7.0
Utility revenue	1,005,169	6.8
Liquor stores revenue	0	-
Insurance trust revenue[1]	1,776,954	12.1
Total Expenditure	15,349,269	100.0
Intergovernmental expenditure	0	-
Direct expenditure	15,349,269	100.0
Current operation	11,644,460	75.9
Capital outlay	2,499,315	16.3
Insurance benefits and repayments	569,905	3.7
Assistance and subsidies	86,295	0.6
Interest on debt	549,294	3.6
Exhibit: Salaries and wages	3,612,416	23.5
Direct Expenditure	15,349,269	100.0
Direct expenditure by function:		
Direct general expenditure	11,960,017	77.9
Education	2,623,627	17.1
Public welfare	3,110,924	20.3
Hospitals	306,618	2.0
Health	453,749	3.0
Highways	767,495	5.0
Police protection	590,634	3.8
Correction	197,348	1.3
Natural resources	56,631	0.4
Parks and recreation	237,839	1.5
Governmental administration	502,043	3.3
Interest on general debt	533,313	3.5
Other and unallocable	656,350	4.3
Utility expenditure	2,819,347	18.4
Liquor stores expenditure	0	-
Insurance trust expenditure	569,905	3.7
Debt at End of Fiscal Year	13,087,235	X
Cash and Security Holdings	13,857,009	X

Note: At the time of publication, the Census Bureau had not yet released 2015 finance data for the District of Columbia.
X = Not applicable.
- = Zero or rounds to zero.
[1] Within insurance trust revenue, net earnings of state retirement systems is a calculated statistic (the item code in the data file is X08), and thus can be positive or negative. Net earnings is the sum of earnings on investments plus gains on investments minus losses on investments. The change made in 2002 for asset valuation from book to market value in accordance with Statement 34 of the Governmental Accounting Standards Board is reflected in the calculated statistics.

Table DC-16. District Government Tax Collections, 2016

(Dollars in thousands, percent.)

Item	Dollars	Percent distribution
Total Taxes	7,404,521	100.0
Property taxes..........	2,416,604	32.6
Sales and gross receipts	1,783,982	24.1
General sales and gross receipts	1,343,192	18.1
Selective sales and gross receipts	440,790	6.0
Alcoholic beverages	6,468	0.1
Amusements	0	-
Insurance premiums..........	106,887	1.4
Motor fuels	25,332	0.3
Pari-mutuels	0	-
Public utilities	186,498	2.5
Tobacco products..........	30,451	0.4
Other selective sales	85,154	1.2
Licenses..........	180,380	2.4
Alcoholic beverages	7,855	0.1
Amusements	0	-
Corporations in general..........	32,764	0.4
Hunting and fishing..........	94	-
Motor vehicle	36,751	0.5
Motor vehicle operators	5,079	0.1
Public utilities	0	-
Occupation and business, NEC	49,004	0.7
Other licenses	48,833	0.7
Income taxes..........	2,464,330	33.3
Individual income..........	1,907,862	25.8
Corporation net income	556,468	7.5
Other taxes..........	559,225	7.6
Death and gift..........	53,967	0.7
Documentary and stock transfer..........	444,194	6.0
Severance	0	-
Taxes, NEC..........	61,064	0.8

X = Not applicable.
- = Zero or rounds to zero.

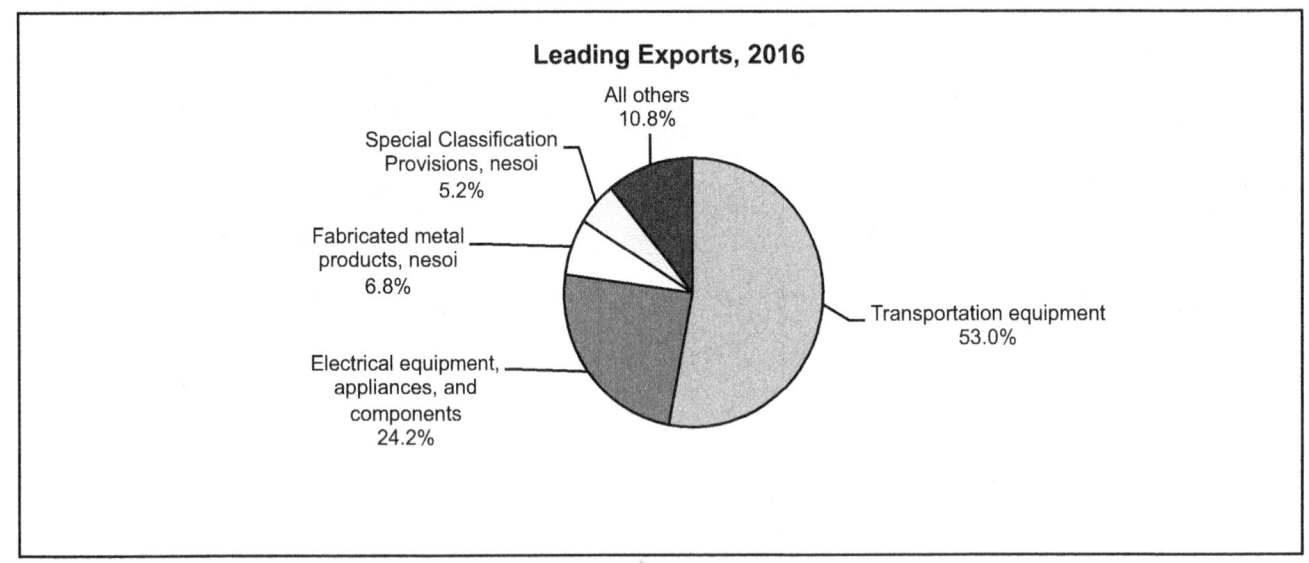

Leading Exports, 2016

All others 10.8%

Special Classification Provisions, nesoi 5.2%

Fabricated metal products, nesoi 6.8%

Electrical equipment, appliances, and components 24.2%

Transportation equipment 53.0%

FLORIDA

Facts and Figures

Location: Southeastern United States; bordered on the N by Georgia and Alabama, on the E by the Atlantic Ocean, on the S by the Straits of Florida, and on the W by Alabama and the Gulf of Mexico

Area: 65,757 sq. mi. (170,304 sq. km.); rank—22nd

Population: 20,612,439 (2016 est.); rank—3rd

Principal Cities: capital—Tallahassee; largest—Jacksonville

Statehood: March 3, 1845; 27th state

U.S. Congress: 2 senators, 27 representatives

State Motto: In God We Trust

State Song: "The Swanee River (Old Folks at Home)"

State Nickname: The Sunshine State

Abbreviations: FL; Fla.

State Symbols: flower—orange blossom; tree—Sabal palm (cabbage palm); bird—mockingbird

At a Glance

- With an increase in population of 9.6 percent, Florida ranked 6th among the states in growth from 2010 to 2016.

- Florida's violent crime rate in 2015 was 461.9 incidents per 100,000 population, compared to 383.2 for the entire nation.

- In 2016, Florida was once again the state with the largest percentage of its population in the 65 and older age group (19.9 percent).

- Florida ranked 6th among the states for the highest percent of Hispanic or Latino residents (24.9 percent) in 2016. Hispanic or Latino residents may be of any race.

- In 2015, 13.3 percent of all Florida residents were uninsured, compared to the national average of 9.4 percent.

Table FL-1. Population by Age, Sex, Race, and Hispanic Origin

(Number, percent, except where noted.)

Sex, age, race, and Hispanic origin	2000	2010	2016 [1]	Average annual percent change, 2010–2016
Total Population	15,982,378	18,801,310	20,612,439	0.6
Percent of total U.S. population	5.7	6.1	6.4	X
Sex				
Male	7,797,715	9,189,355	10,070,151	0.6
Female	8,184,663	9,611,955	10,542,288	0.6
Age				
Under 5 years	945,823	1,073,506	1,126,136	0.3
5 to 19 years	3,102,809	3,439,484	3,486,617	0.1
20 to 64 years	9,126,149	11,034,718	11,904,769	0.5
65 years and over	2,807,597	3,259,602	4,094,917	1.6
Median age (years)	38.7	40.7	42.1	0.2
Race and Hispanic Origin				
One race				
White	12,465,029	14,808,867	15,996,473	0.5
Black	2,335,505	3,078,067	3,471,950	0.8
American Indian and Alaska Native	53,541	89,119	102,439	0.9
Asian	266,256	474,199	587,722	1.5
Native Hawaiian or Other Pacific Islander	8,625	18,790	23,107	1.4
Two or more races	376,315	332,268	430,748	1.9
Hispanic (of any race)	2,682,715	4,301,853	5,126,975	1.2

X = Not applicable.
[1] Population figures for 2016 are July 1 estimates. The 2010 estimates are taken from the 2010 Census.

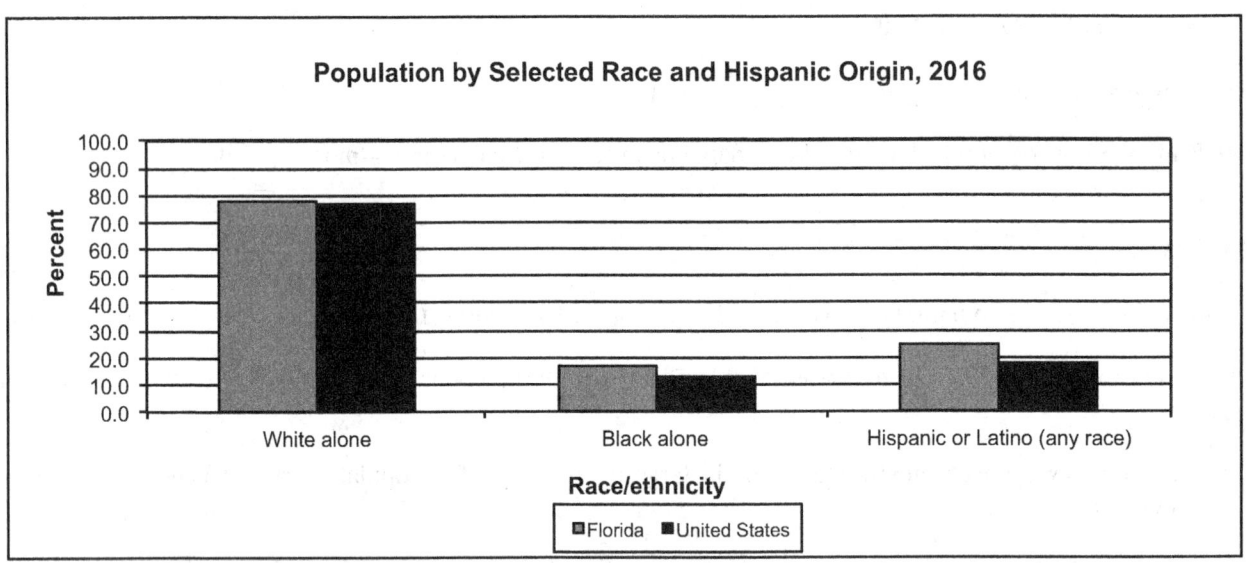

Population by Selected Race and Hispanic Origin, 2016

Legend: Florida, United States

Table FL-2. Marital Status

(Number, percent distribution.)

Sex, age, race, and Hispanic origin	2000	2010	2015
Males, 15 Years and Over	6,232,987	7,534,535	8,167,643
Never married	27.3	33.9	35.4
Now married, except separated	56.9	49.3	47.7
Separated	2.1	2.2	2.1
Widowed	3.2	3.2	3.2
Divorced	10.5	11.5	11.6
Females, 15 Years and Over	6,714,003	8,021,290	8,721,536
Never married	20.5	26.6	28.5
Now married, except separated	51.9	45.1	43.4
Separated	2.7	3.0	2.7
Widowed	12.3	10.8	10.7
Divorced	12.7	14.5	14.8

Table FL-3. Households and Housing Characteristics

(Number, percent, dollars.)

Item	2000	2010	2015	Average annual percent change, 2000–2015
Total Households..	6,337,929	7,035,068	7,463,184	1.2
Family households..	4,210,760	4,556,930	4,806,611	0.9
Married-couple family...	3,192,266	3,307,884	3,444,776	0.5
Other family..	1,018,494	1,249,046	1,361,835	2.2
Male householder, no wife present........................	259,924	313,305	359,661	2.6
Female householder, no husband present................	759,000	935,741	1,002,174	2.1
Nonfamily households..	2,127,169	2,478,138	2,656,573	1.7
Householder living alone.....................................	1,687,303	2,013,028	2,153,681	1.8
Householder not living alone................................	439,886	465,110	502,892	1.0
Housing Characteristics				
Total housing units...	7,302,947	8,994,091	9,210,287	1.7
Occupied housing units	6,337,929	7,035,068	7,463,184	1.2
Owner occupied..	4,441,799	4,794,130	4,760,071	0.5
Renter occupied...	1,896,130	2,240,938	2,703,113	2.8
Average household size...	2.46	2.62	2.66	0.5
Financial Characteristics				
Median gross rent of renter-occupied housing	641	947	1046	4.2
Median monthly owner costs for housing units with a mortgage	1,004	1,505	1,394	2.6
Median value of owner-occupied housing units	105,500	164,200	179,800	4.7

Table FL-4. Migration, Origin, and Language

(Number, percent.)

Characteristic	State 2014	State 2015	State Percent change	U.S. 2014	U.S. 2015	U.S. Percent change
Residence 1 Year Ago						
Population 1 year and over	19,683,763	20,068,392	2.0	315,095,393	317,635,720	0.8
Same house	83.9	83.9	X	85.1	85.3	X
Different house in the U.S.	15.2	15.1	X	14.3	14.1	X
Same county	9.3	9.0	X	8.7	8.5	X
Different county	5.9	6.1	X	5.6	5.6	X
Same state	3.1	3.1	X	3.3	3.2	X
Different state	2.8	2.9	X	2.3	2.4	X
Abroad..	1.0	1.1	X	0.6	0.7	X
Place of Birth						
Native born	15,919,782	16,185,032	1.7	276,465,262	278,128,449	0.6
Male	49.3	49.2	X	49.3	49.3	X
Female	50.7	50.8	X	50.7	50.7	X
Foreign born	3,973,515	4,086,240	2.8	42,391,794	43,290,372	2.1
Male	47.2	47.4	X	48.7	48.6	X
Female	52.8	52.6	X	51.3	51.4	X
Foreign born; naturalized U.S. citizen.......................	2,136,462	2,195,000	2.7	19,984,738	20,697,103	3.6
Male	44.1	44.4	X	45.9	45.9	X
Female	55.9	55.6	X	54.1	54.1	X
Foreign born; not a U.S. citizen................................	1,837,053	1,891,240	2.9	22,407,056	22,593,269	0.8
Male	50.8	50.8	X	51.2	51.1	X
Female	49.2	49.2	X	48.8	48.9	X
Entered 2010 or later	12.9	16.9	X	12.3	15.6	X
Entered 2000 to 2009	28.4	28.3	X	28.6	27.9	X
Entered before 2000...	58.7	54.8	X	59.1	56.5	X
World Region of Birth, Foreign						
Foreign-born population, excluding population born at sea	3,972,753	4,086,240	2.9	42,390,705	43,289,646	2.1
Europe	9.8	9.3	X	11.2	11.1	X
Asia..	10.6	10.9	X	30.1	30.6	X
Africa	1.6	1.8	X	4.6	4.8	X
Oceania	0.2	0.2	X	0.6	0.6	X
Latin America	75.1	75.1	X	51.6	51.1	X
North America	2.7	2.8	X	1.9	1.9	X
Language Spoken at Home and Ability to Speak English						
Population 5 years and over......................................	18,815,725	19,172,999	1.9	299,084,046	301,625,014	0.8
English only	71.7	71.0	X	78.9	78.5	X
Language other than English..................................	28.3	29.0	X	21.1	21.5	X
Speaks English less than "very well".......................	11.7	11.8	X	8.6	8.6	X

NA = Not available.
X = Not applicable.
- = Zero or rounds to zero.

Table FL-5. Median Income and Poverty Status, 2015

(Number, percent, except as noted.)

Characteristic	State		U.S.	
	Number	Percent	Number	Percent
Median Income				
Households (dollars)	49,426	X	55,775	X
Families (dollars)	59,339	X	68,260	X
Below Poverty Level (All People)	3,116,886	15.7	46,153,077	14.7
Sex				
Male	1,395,141	14.5	20,599,407	13.4
Female	1,721,745	16.8	25,553,670	16.0
Age				
Under 18 years	931,601	23.1	15,000,273	20.7
Related children under 18 years	914,206	22.8	14,693,239	20.4
18 to 64 years	1,786,129	15.0	26,960,369	13.9
65 years and over	399,156	10.3	4,192,435	9.0

X = Not applicable.

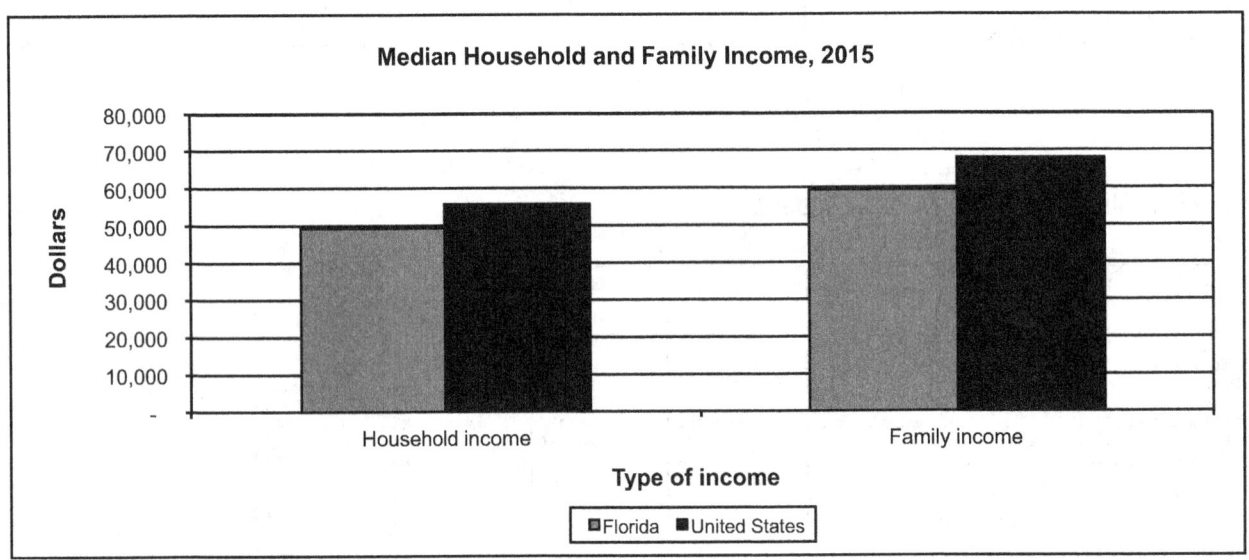

Table FL-6. Health Insurance Coverage Status for the Civilian Noninstitutionalized Population and Children Under 18 Years of Age

(Numbers in thousands, percent.)

Item	2007	2008	2009	2010	2011	2012	2013	2014	2015
Civilian Noninstitutionalized Population	18,074	17,996	18,193	18,534	18,752	19,011	19,245	19,583	19,960
Covered by Private or Public Insurance									
Number	14,426	14,247	14,397	14,593	14,841	15,195	15,392	16,338	17,299
Percent	79.8	79.2	79.1	78.7	79.1	79.9	80.0	83.4	86.7
Not Covered									
Number	3,648	3,749	3,795	3,941	3,911	3,816	3,853	3,245	2,662
Percent	20.2	20.8	20.9	21.3	20.9	20.1	20.0	16.6	13.3
Percent in the U.S. not covered	15.3	15.1	15.1	15.5	15.1	14.8	14.5	11.7	9.4
Children Under 18 Years of Age	4,084	3,996	4,051	3,990	3,987	3,991	4,020	4,046	4,093
Covered by Private or Public Insurance									
Number	3,298	3,295	3,450	3,483	3,512	3,555	3,575	3,668	3,810
Percent	80.8	82.5	85.2	87.3	88.1	89.1	88.9	90.7	93.1
Not Covered									
Number	785	701	601	507	475	436	445	378	284
Percent	19.2	17.5	14.8	12.7	11.9	10.9	11.1	9.3	6.9
Percent in the U.S. not covered	11.0	9.7	8.6	8.0	7.5	7.2	7.1	6.0	4.8

Table FL-7. Employment Status by Demographic Group, 2016

(Numbers in thousands, percent.)

Characteristic	Civilian noninstitutional population	Civilian labor force		Employed		Unemployed	
		Number	Percent of population	Number	Percent of population	Number	Percent of population
Total...	16,624	9,759	58.7	9,283	55.8	476	4.9
Sex							
Male	7,955	5,124	64.4	4,869	61.2	255	5.0
Female	8,669	4,636	53.5	4,414	50.9	222	4.8
Race, Sex, and Hispanic Origin							
White	13,344	7,703	57.7	7,372	55.2	331	4.3
Male	6,450	4,129	64.0	3,951	61.3	178	4.3
Female	6,894	3,574	51.8	3,421	49.6	153	4.3
Black or African American..........	2,555	1,590	62.2	1,464	57.3	126	7.9
Male	1,168	754	64.6	690	59.0	64	8.5
Female	1,387	836	60.3	774	55.8	62	7.4
Hispanic or Latino ethnicity[1]	4,214	2,608	61.9	2,490	59.1	119	4.5
Male	2,031	1,428	70.3	1,364	67.2	64	4.5
Female	2,184	1,180	54.1	1,126	51.6	54	4.6
Age							
16 to 19 years..........	1,018	277	27.2	229	22.5	48	17.4
20 to 24 years..........	1,263	856	67.8	791	62.6	66	7.7
25 to 34 years..........	2,538	2,058	81.1	1,948	76.8	110	5.3
35 to 44 years..........	2,365	1,940	82.0	1,865	78.8	75	3.9
45 to 54 years..........	2,948	2,311	78.4	2,227	75.6	83	3.6
55 to 64 years..........	2,677	1,649	61.6	1,586	59.3	63	3.8
65 years and over	3,815	669	17.5	638	16.7	32	4.7

NOTE: Data in Table 7 are from the Current Population Survey (CPS) and do not match the estimates in Table 8. See notes and definitions for further information.
[1] May be of any race.

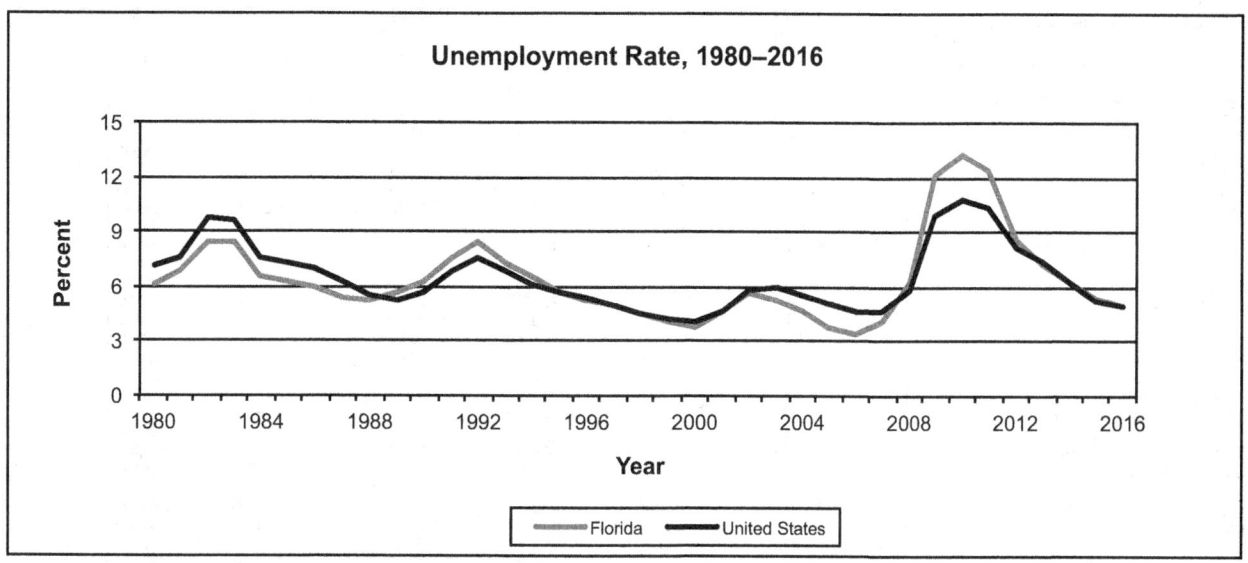

Table FL-8. Employment Status of the Civilian Noninstitutional Population Age 16 Years and Over

(Number, percent.)

Year	Civilian labor force	Civilian participation rate	Employed	Unemployed	Unemployment rate
2008..........	9,215,524	63.7	8,637,164	578,360	6.3
2009..........	9,094,825	62.3	8,148,123	946,702	10.4
2010..........	9,212,066	61.6	8,193,659	1,018,407	11.1
2011..........	9,300,542	61.0	8,371,638	928,904	10.0
2012..........	9,391,203	60.7	8,592,418	798,785	8.5
2013..........	9,460,552	60.2	8,771,158	689,394	7.3
2014..........	9,606,715	60.1	8,999,446	607,269	6.3
2015..........	9,675,328	59.3	9,153,264	522,064	5.4
2016..........	9,838,935	59.2	9,358,571	480,364	4.9

Table FL-9. Employment and Average Wages by Industry

(Estimates through 2010 are based on the 2007 *North American Industry Classification System* [NAICS]. Estimates from 2011 onward are based on the 2012 NAICS.)

Industry	2009	2010	2011	2012	2013	2014	2015
				Number of Jobs			
Wage and Salary Employment by Industry..................	7,635,641	7,528,307	7,612,793	7,767,188	7,939,949	8,196,734	8,470,602
Farm Wage and Salary Employment.........................	40,631	43,191	44,307	47,948	44,695	48,772	42,091
Nonfarm Wage and Salary Employment....................	7,595,010	7,485,116	7,568,486	7,719,240	7,895,254	8,147,962	8,428,511
Private wage and salary employment...........................	6,390,122	6,282,399	6,387,586	6,554,478	6,731,919	6,989,620	7,262,925
Forestry, fishing, and related activities........................	45,857	44,455	43,233	42,293	44,472	45,272	44,757
Mining..........	3,716	3,622	3,872	3,950	3,957	4,100	4,089
Utilities............	23,638	22,529	22,433	22,656	22,301	21,994	22,479
Construction	411,437	359,371	345,080	352,818	376,584	408,079	442,562
Manufacturing.........................	324,418	307,721	311,671	317,199	322,333	331,711	343,213
Durable goods manufacturing...........................	214,263	202,755	205,662	209,481	214,915	222,834	233,380
Nondurable goods manufacturing.....................	110,155	104,966	106,009	107,718	107,418	108,877	109,833
Wholesale trade	321,269	309,861	309,674	318,618	323,333	329,555	336,432
Retail trade........................	938,831	936,659	964,924	988,999	1,013,165	1,050,988	1,090,860
Transportation and warehousing........................	209,412	204,504	213,508	220,516	227,674	236,048	247,135
Information	143,046	135,784	134,653	134,183	134,306	137,011	136,311
Finance and insurance	334,266	330,180	339,871	350,784	355,323	362,838	373,492
Real estate and rental and leasing............................	161,894	154,982	156,010	164,934	169,995	175,098	181,581
Professional, scientific, and technical services	440,658	438,983	449,101	455,591	472,608	490,454	511,693
Management of companies and enterprises....................	80,006	78,208	81,039	83,695	91,063	94,224	97,003
Administrative and waste services..........................	541,264	537,734	533,392	545,876	563,070	590,262	623,004
Educational services	139,457	145,405	150,009	149,731	150,580	156,964	159,678
Health care and social assistance........................	922,775	936,182	951,342	972,164	989,676	1,013,948	1,051,455
Arts, entertainment, and recreation........................	186,835	186,688	191,629	197,725	199,810	210,555	218,730
Accommodation and food services........................	735,114	741,125	769,748	807,265	843,687	881,002	921,046
Other services, except public administration..................	426,229	408,406	416,397	425,481	427,982	449,517	457,405
Government and government enterprises.........................	1,204,888	1,202,717	1,180,900	1,164,762	1,163,335	1,158,342	1,165,586
				Dollars			
Average Wages and Salaries by Industry	42,020	42,895	43,672	44,580	45,138	46,202	47,686
Average Farm Wages and Salaries	29,540	28,152	23,921	21,475	28,280	23,692	26,771
Average Nonfarm Wages and Salaries	42,087	42,980	43,788	44,723	45,233	46,337	47,790
Average private wages and salaries...........................	41,067	42,058	42,978	44,087	44,615	45,736	47,268
Forestry, fishing, and related activities........................	21,104	22,306	23,079	24,274	24,558	25,040	26,966
Mining..........	56,308	59,880	60,928	68,082	64,267	66,343	67,514
Utilities............	80,117	80,205	84,360	86,092	88,025	92,431	95,384
Construction.........................	41,985	42,226	42,070	42,634	43,176	44,706	46,762
Manufacturing.........................	52,084	53,912	54,492	55,379	56,261	57,647	59,504
Durable goods manufacturing...........................	54,824	56,851	57,533	58,598	59,420	60,747	62,115
Nondurable goods manufacturing.....................	46,753	48,235	48,591	49,119	49,941	51,301	53,956
Wholesale trade	59,841	62,486	65,036	67,178	68,375	70,201	72,758
Retail trade........................	27,589	28,114	28,292	28,778	29,157	29,793	30,731
Transportation and warehousing........................	45,380	47,030	48,059	49,229	50,605	52,093	53,919
Information	60,863	63,375	66,555	68,867	70,734	72,991	76,062
Finance and insurance	65,426	68,266	71,159	73,603	75,464	79,037	81,736
Real estate and rental and leasing............................	38,877	40,442	41,850	43,126	44,265	46,630	48,657
Professional, scientific, and technical services	64,079	65,421	66,992	69,483	69,650	71,503	73,615
Management of companies and enterprises....................	85,656	91,269	95,597	106,264	101,673	104,288	106,910
Administrative and waste services..........................	32,929	33,461	34,065	34,699	34,654	35,361	36,561
Educational services	35,764	36,271	37,706	37,587	37,882	38,601	38,781
Health care and social assistance........................	45,245	45,937	46,896	47,757	48,216	49,206	50,984
Arts, entertainment, and recreation........................	36,007	36,617	37,261	38,368	38,148	38,980	40,846
Accommodation and food services........................	20,546	21,079	21,684	22,382	22,967	23,595	24,454
Other services, except public administration..................	28,614	29,707	29,821	30,600	31,585	32,415	33,729
Government and government enterprises.........................	47,499	47,792	48,167	48,302	48,813	49,966	51,044

Table FL-10. Employment Characteristics by Family Type

(Number, percent.)

Family type and labor force status	2013		2014		2015	
	Total	Families with own children under 18 years	Total	Families with own children under 18 years	Total	Families with own children under 18 years
All Families..	4,626,388	1,753,872	4,675,046	1,744,542	4,806,611	1,781,366
FAMILY TYPE AND LABOR FORCE STATUS						
Married-Couple Families....................................	3,334,383	1,109,448	3,361,738	1,094,773	3,444,776	1,117,422
Both husband and wife in labor force..........................	45.3	65.3	44.7	64.3	44.3	64.9
Husband in labor force, wife not in labor force	20.5	28.4	20.9	28.9	20.2	27.7
Wife in labor force, husband not in labor force	8.3	4.3	8.4	4.7	8.4	4.9
Both husband and wife not in labor force.......................	25.5	1.7	26.0	2.2	26.3	2.2
Other Families	1,292,005	644,424	1,313,308	649,769	1,361,835	663,944
Female householder, no husband present.........................	74.0	77.4	73.1	76.1	73.6	75.7
In labor force	52.2	63.9	51.7	63.4	51.4	63.3
Not in labor force	21.8	13.4	21.4	12.7	22.2	12.4
Male householder, no wife present..............................	26.0	22.6	26.9	23.9	26.4	24.3
In labor force	19.8	20.5	20.8	21.9	20.3	22.3
Not in labor force	6.2	2.1	6.1	2.1	6.1	2.0

Table FL-11. School Enrollment and Educational Attainment, 2015

(Number, percent.)

Item	State	U.S.
Enrollment		
Total population 3 years and over, enrolled in school	4,706,933	81,618,288
Enrolled in nursery school or preschool (percent)	6.1	6.0
Enrolled in kindergarten (percent)	4.7	5.0
Enrolled in elementary school, grades 1-8 (percent).........................	39.1	40.3
Enrolled in high school, grades 9-12 (percent)	20.9	20.9
Enrolled in college or graduate school (percent)...........................	29.2	27.7
Attainment		
Total population 25 years and over	14,394,281	216,447,163
Less than ninth grade (percent)	5.2	5.5
9th to 12th grade, no diploma (percent)	7.2	7.3
High school graduate, including equivalency (percent).......................	29.2	27.6
Some college, no degree (percent)	20.4	20.7
Associate's degree (percent)...	9.6	8.2
Bachelor's degree (percent)	18.2	19.0
Graduate or professional degree (percent)..................................	10.2	11.6
High school graduate or higher (percent)	87.6	87.1
Bachelor's degree or higher (percent)	28.4	30.6

Table FL-12. Public School Characteristics and Educational Indicators

(Number, percent; data derived from National Center of Education Statistics.)

Item	State	U.S.
Public Schools, 2014–2015 (except where noted)		
Number of school districts...	76	18,260
Number of schools...	4,319	98,373
Number of students	2,756,944	50,312,581
Number of teachers	180,442	3,132,351
Student-teacher ratio...	15.3	16.1
Expenditures per student (dollars), FY 2014	8,955	11,066
Four-year adjusted cohort graduation rate (ACGR)[1,2]	77.9	83.2
Students eligible for free or reduced-price lunch (percent)	58.4	51.8
English language learners (percent)..	9.2	9.4
Students age 3 to 21 served under IDEA, part B (percent)....................	13.2	13.0

Public Schools by Type	Number	Percent of state public schools
Total number of schools...	4,319	100.0
Regular	3,710	85.9
Special education...	179	4.1
Vocational education..	53	1.2
Alternative education...	377	8.7

NOTE: Every school is assigned only one school type based on its instructional emphasis.

[1] ACGR data represents a new method of calculating high-school completion rates and may not be comparable to previous years' data for Averaged Freshmen Graduation Rates (AFGR).

[2] The United States 4-year ACGRs were estimated using both the reported 4-year ACGR data from 49 states and the District of Columbia and using imputed data for Idaho. The estimate for American Indian/Alaska Native students also includes imputed data for Virginia.

Table FL-13. Reported Voting and Registration of the Voting-Age Population, November 2016

(Numbers in thousands, percent.)

Item	Total population	Total citizen population	Registered			Voted		
			Total registered	Percent registered (total population)	Percent registered (total citizen population)	Total voted	Percent voted (total population)	Percent voted (total citizen population)
U.S. Total	245,502	224,059	157,596	64.2	70.3	137,537	56.0	61.4
State Total...........................	16,202	14,428	9,604	59.3	66.6	8,578	52.9	59.5
Sex								
Male	7,736	6,868	4,377	56.6	63.7	3,920	50.7	57.1
Female	8,466	7,560	5,226	61.7	69.1	4,658	55.0	61.6
Race								
White alone........................	13,097	11,793	8,141	62.2	69.0	7,277	55.6	61.7
White, non-Hispanic alone	9,307	9,066	6,432	69.1	70.9	5,781	62.1	63.8
Black alone.........................	2,434	2,083	1,149	47.2	55.2	1,051	43.2	50.5
Asian alone	483	381	192	39.7	50.3	154	31.9	40.4
Hispanic (of any race).................	4,010	2,871	1,779	44.4	62.0	1,552	38.7	54.1
White alone or in combination	13,217	11,899	8,212	62.1	69.0	7,336	55.5	61.7
Black alone or in combination..........	2,496	2,135	1,184	47.4	55.4	1,077	43.2	50.4
Asian alone or in combination..........	525	424	212	40.4	50.1	170	32.3	40.0
Age								
18 to 24 years......................	1,589	1,413	728	45.8	51.5	527	33.1	37.3
25 to 34 years......................	2,582	2,245	1,357	52.5	60.5	1,157	44.8	51.6
35 to 44 years......................	2,505	1,985	1,315	52.5	66.3	1,144	45.7	57.6
45 to 64 years......................	5,661	5,091	3,446	60.9	67.7	3,171	56.0	62.3
65 years and over	3,865	3,694	2,758	71.4	74.7	2,578	66.7	69.8

Table FL-14. Crime

(Number, rate per 100,000. Data are derived from the FBI Uniform Crime Reports.)

Item	State			U.S. [1,2,3,4]		
	2014	2015	Percent change	2014	2015	Percent change
TOTAL POPULATION[5]	19,905,569	20,271,272	1.8	318,907,401	321,418,820	0.8
VIOLENT CRIME						
Number...........................	91,345	93,626	2.5	1,186,185	1,231,566	3.8
Rate	458.9	461.9	0.6	372.0	383.2	3.0
Murder and Nonnegligent Manslaughter						
Number...........................	982	1,041	6.0	14,164	15,696	10.8
Rate	4.9	5.1	4.1	4.4	4.9	10.0
Rape[6]						
Number...........................	7,132	7,553	5.9	118,027	124,047	5.1
Rate	35.8	37.3	4.0	37.0	38.6	4.3
Robbery						
Number...........................	21,621	21,137	-2.2	322,905	327,374	1.4
Rate	108.6	104.3	-4.0	101.3	101.9	0.6
Aggravated Assault						
Number...........................	61,610	63,895	3.7	731,089	764,449	4.6
Rate	309.5	315.2	1.8	229.2	237.8	3.7
PROPERTY CRIME						
Number...........................	583,774	570,270	-2.3	8,209,010	7,993,631	-2.6
Rate	2,932.7	2,813.2	-4.1	2,574.1	2,487.0	-3.4
Burglary						
Number...........................	121,379	109,268	-10.0	1,713,153	1,579,527	-7.8
Rate	609.8	539.0	-11.6	537.2	491.4	-8.5
Larceny-Theft						
Number...........................	426,197	420,341	-1.4	5,809,054	5,706,346	-1.8
Rate	2,141.1	2,073.6	-3.2	1,821.5	1,775.4	-2.5
Motor Vehicle Theft						
Number...........................	36,198	40,661	12.3	686,803	707,758	3.1
Rate	181.8	200.6	10.3	215.4	220.2	2.2

NOTE: Although arson data are included in the trend and clearance tables, sufficient data are not available to estimate totals for this offense. Therefore, no arson data are published in this table.

X = Not applicable.

- = Zero or rounds to zero.

[1] The crime figures have been adjusted.

[2] The data collection methodology for the offense of forcible rape used by the Minnesota state Uniform Crime Reporting (UCR) Program (with the exception of Minneapolis and St. Paul, Minnesota) does not comply with national UCR Program guidelines. Consequently, its figures for forcible rape and violent crime (of which forcible rape is a part) are not published in this table.

[3] Includes offenses reported by the Zoological Police and the Metro Transit Police.

[4] Because of changes in the state's reporting practices, figures are not comparable to previous years' data.

[5] Populations are U.S. Census Bureau provisional estimates as of July 1 of each year.

[6] The figures shown for the offense of rape were estimated using the revised Uniform Crime Reporting (UCR) definition of rape.

Table FL-15. State Government Finances, 2015

(Dollar amounts in thousands, percent distribution.)

Item	Dollars	Percent distribution
Total Revenue	91,563,525	100.0
General revenue	79,487,553	86.8
Intergovernmental revenue	26,270,941	28.7
Taxes	37,217,759	40.6
General sales	21,800,895	23.8
Selective sales	8,535,420	9.3
License taxes	2,138,834	2.3
Individual income tax	0	-
Corporate income tax	2,237,500	2.4
Other taxes	2,505,110	2.7
Current charges	8,972,049	9.8
Miscellaneous general revenue	7,026,804	7.7
Utility revenue	23,874	-
Liquor stores revenue	0	-
Insurance trust revenue[1]	12,052,098	13.2
Total Expenditure	87,374,452	100.0
Intergovernmental expenditure	19,173,628	21.9
Direct expenditure	68,200,824	78.1
Current operation	49,033,935	56.1
Capital outlay	6,500,958	7.4
Insurance benefits and repayments	9,524,697	10.9
Assistance and subsidies	2,034,784	2.3
Interest on debt	1,106,450	1.3
Exhibit: Salaries and wages	9,016,685	10.3
Total Expenditure	87,374,452	100.0
General expenditure	77,651,861	88.9
Intergovernmental expenditure	19,173,628	21.9
Direct expenditure	58,478,233	66.9
General expenditure, by function:		
Education	25,347,156	29.0
Public welfare	25,913,158	29.7
Hospitals	949,782	1.1
Health	3,706,839	4.2
Highways	7,600,460	8.7
Police protection	536,250	0.6
Correction	2,269,252	2.6
Natural resources	1,222,775	1.4
Parks and recreation	154,533	0.2
Governmental administration	2,439,153	2.8
Interest on general debt	1,106,450	1.3
Other and unallocable	6,406,053	7.3
Utility expenditure	197,894	0.2
Liquor stores expenditure	0	-
Insurance trust expenditure	9,524,697	10.9
Debt at End of Fiscal Year	33,315,277	X
Cash and Security Holdings	218,155,667	X

X = Not applicable.
- = Zero or rounds to zero.
[1] Within insurance trust revenue, net earnings of state retirement systems is a calculated statistic (the item code in the data file is X08), and thus can be positive or negative. Net earnings is the sum of earnings on investments plus gains on investments minus losses on investments. The change made in 2002 for asset valuation from book to market value in accordance with Statement 34 of the Governmental Accounting Standards Board is reflected in the calculated statistics.

Table FL-16. State Government Tax Collections, 2016

(Dollars in thousands, percent.)

Item	Dollars	Percent distribution
Total Taxes	37,640,420	100.0
Property taxes	20	-
Sales and gross receipts	30,429,302	80.8
General sales and gross receipts	22,291,157	59.2
Selective sales and gross receipts	8,138,145	21.6
Alcoholic beverages	396,418	1.1
Amusements	202,942	0.5
Insurance premiums	705,400	1.9
Motor fuels	2,611,492	6.9
Pari-mutuels	6,921	-
Public utilities	2,408,133	6.4
Tobacco products	1,223,029	3.2
Other selective sales	583,810	1.6
Licenses	2,241,468	6.0
Alcoholic beverages	9,132	-
Amusements	18,000	-
Corporations in general	315,059	0.8
Hunting and fishing	17,026	0.0
Motor vehicle	1,552,251	4.1
Motor vehicle operators	117,146	0.3
Public utilities	25,516	0.1
Occupation and business, NEC	177,077	0.5
Other licenses	10,261	-
Income taxes	2,272,230	6.0
Individual income	0	-
Corporation net income	2,272,230	6.0
Other taxes	2,697,400	7.2
Death and gift	140	-
Documentary and stock transfer	2,662,080	7.1
Severance	35,180	0.1
Taxes, NEC	0	-

X = Not applicable.
- = Zero or rounds to zero.

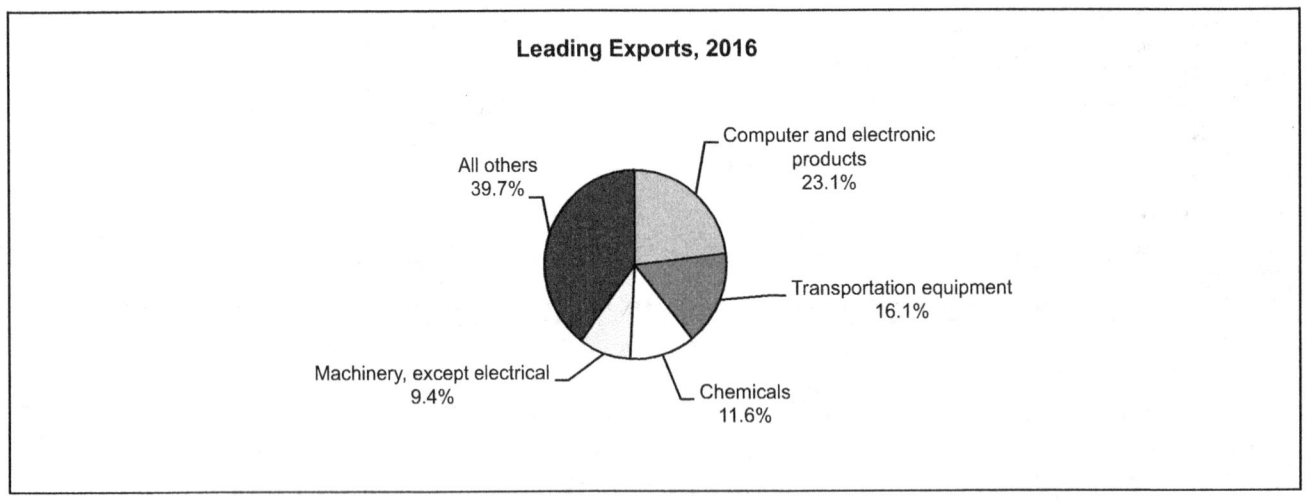

Leading Exports, 2016

Computer and electronic products 23.1%

Transportation equipment 16.1%

Chemicals 11.6%

Machinery, except electrical 9.4%

All others 39.7%

GEORGIA

Facts and Figures

Location: Southeastern United States; bordered on the N by Tennessee and North Carolina, on the E by South Carolina and the Atlantic Ocean, on the S by Florida, and on the W by Florida and Alabama

Area: 59,425 sq. mi. (153,909 sq. km.); rank—21st

Population: 10,310,371 (2016 est.); rank—8th

Principal Cities: capital—Atlanta; largest—Atlanta

Statehood: January 2, 1788; 4th state

U.S. Congress: 2 senators, 14 representatives

State Motto: Wisdom, Justice, and Moderation

State Song: "Georgia on My Mind"

State Nicknames: The Empire State of the South; The Peach State

Abbreviations: GA; Ga.

State Symbols: flower—Cherokee rose; tree—live oak; bird—brown thrasher

At a Glance

- With an increase in population of 6.4 percent, Georgia ranked 13th among the states in growth from 2010 to 2016.

- Georgia's median household income in 2014 was $51,244, and 17.0 percent of the population lived below the poverty level.

- In 2015, 13.9 percent of Georgians did not have health insurance, which was the third highest percent among the states.

- Georgia's violent crime rate was 378.3 per 100,000 population, compared to 383.2 for the U.S. as a whole in 2015.

- The property crime rate in Georgia in 2015 was 3,022.3 per 100,000 population, a rate that ranked 9th among the states.

Table GA-1. Population by Age, Sex, Race, and Hispanic Origin

(Number, percent, except where noted.)

Sex, age, race, and Hispanic origin	2000	2010	2016 [1]	Average annual percent change, 2010–2016
Total Population.....................................	8,186,453	9,687,653	10,310,371	0.4
Percent of total U.S. population	2.9	3.1	3.2	X
Sex				
Male..	4,027,113	4,729,171	5,020,465	0.4
Female	4,159,340	4,958,482	5,289,906	0.4
Age				
Under 5 years.....................................	595,150	686,785	660,839	-0.2
5 to 19 years.....................................	1,819,620	2,094,844	2,130,295	0.1
20 to 64 years....................................	4,986,408	5,873,989	6,164,575	0.3
65 years and over.................................	785,275	1,032,035	1,354,662	2.0
Median age (years)	33.4	35.3	36.5	0.2
Race and Hispanic Origin				
One race..				
White	5,327,281	6,144,931	6,311,001	0.2
Black...	2,349,542	2,993,927	3,301,809	0.6
American Indian and Alaska Native	21,737	48,599	52,365	0.5
Asian...	173,170	323,459	420,391	1.9
Native Hawaiian or Other Pacific Islander	4,246	10,454	11,942	0.9
Two or more races..................................	114,188	166,283	212,863	1.8
Hispanic (of any race).............................	435,227	911,863	972,698	0.4

X = Not applicable.
[1] Population figures for 2016 are July 1 estimates. The 2010 estimates are taken from the 2010 Census.

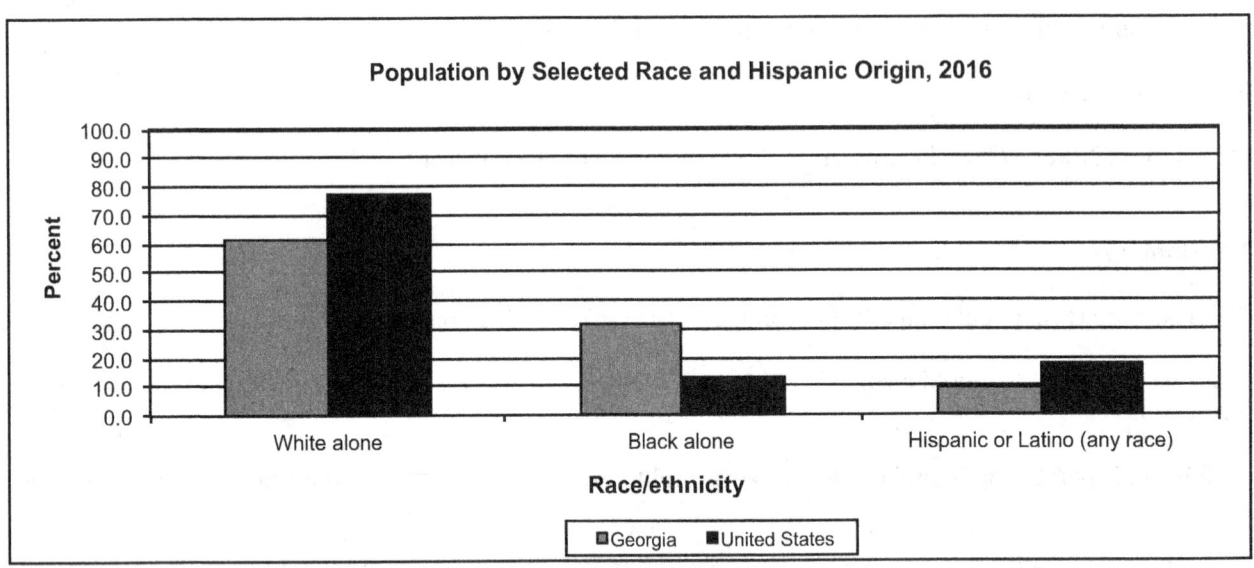

Population by Selected Race and Hispanic Origin, 2016

Georgia   United States

Table GA-2. Marital Status

(Number, percent distribution.)

Sex, age, race, and Hispanic origin	2000	2010	2015
Males, 15 Years and Over	3,092,736	3,683,258	3,916,665
Never married	30.4	35.4	36.7
Now married, except separated......................	56.5	50.5	49.1
Separated..	2.0	2.1	1.9
Widowed..	2.1	2.2	2.4
Divorced...	9.0	9.9	9.8
Females, 15 Years and Over	3,273,889	3,954,542	4,222,374
Never married	24.4	29.7	31.8
Now married, except separated......................	51.5	46.1	44.7
Separated..	2.7	2.9	2.5
Widowed..	9.8	8.6	8.4
Divorced...	11.6	12.7	12.7

Table GA-3. Households and Housing Characteristics

(Number, percent, dollars.)

Item	2000	2010	2015	Average annual percent change, 2000–2015
Total Households....................................	3,006,369	3,482,420	3,656,407	1.4
Family households....................................	2,111,647	2,385,969	2,466,415	1.1
Married-couple family............................	1,548,800	1,688,896	1,750,409	0.9
Other family...	562,847	697,073	716,006	1.8
Male householder, no wife present............	127,437	161,001	167,389	2.1
Female householder, no husband present.....	435,410	536,072	548,617	1.7
Nonfamily households..............................	894,722	1,096,451	1,189,992	2.2
Householder living alone.........................	710,523	921,005	983,496	2.6
Householder not living alone....................	184,199	175,446	206,496	0.8
Housing Characteristics				
Total housing units..................................	3,281,737	4,091,482	4,182,228	1.8
Occupied housing units	3,006,369	3,482,420	3,656,407	1.4
Owner occupied.....................................	2,029,154	2,304,165	2,261,166	0.8
Renter occupied.....................................	977,215	1,178,255	1,395,241	2.9
Average household size.............................	2.65	2.72	2.72	0.2
Financial Characteristics				
Median gross rent of renter-occupied housing	613	819	909	3.2
Median monthly owner costs for housing units with a mortgage	1,039	1,390	1,299	1.7
Median value of owner-occupied housing units	111,200	156,200	159,300	2.9

Table GA-4. Migration, Origin, and Language

(Number, percent.)

Characteristic	State			U.S.		
	2014	2015	Percent change	2014	2015	Percent change
Residence 1 Year Ago						
Population 1 year and over	9,970,167	10,088,525	1.2	315,095,393	317,635,720	0.8
Same house.......................................	84.3	84.2	X	85.1	85.3	X
Different house in the U.S.	15.2	15.3	X	14.3	14.1	X
Same county....................................	7.7	7.8	X	8.7	8.5	X
Different county...............................	7.5	7.5	X	5.6	5.6	X
Same state..................................	4.7	4.7	X	3.3	3.2	X
Different state.............................	2.7	2.8	X	2.3	2.4	X
Abroad..	0.5	0.6	X	0.6	0.7	X
Place of Birth						
Native born..	9,102,692	9,191,143	1.0	276,465,262	278,128,449	0.6
Male	48.6	48.5	X	49.3	49.3	X
Female	51.4	51.5	X	50.7	50.7	X
Foreign born	994,651	1,023,717	2.9	42,391,794	43,290,372	2.1
Male	50.2	50.4	X	48.7	48.6	X
Female	49.8	49.6	X	51.3	51.4	X
Foreign born; naturalized U.S. citizen.........	410,445	428,570	4.4	19,984,738	20,697,103	3.6
Male	47.6	47.6	X	45.9	45.9	X
Female	52.4	52.4	X	54.1	54.1	X
Foreign born; not a U.S. citizen	584,206	595,147	1.9	22,407,056	22,593,269	0.8
Male	52.1	52.5	X	51.2	51.1	X
Female	47.9	47.5	X	48.8	48.9	X
Entered 2010 or later	12.1	16.4	X	12.3	15.6	X
Entered 2000 to 2009	34.7	34.2	X	28.6	27.9	X
Entered before 2000.............................	53.2	49.4	X	59.1	56.5	X
World Region of Birth, Foreign						
Foreign-born population, excluding population born at sea	994,651	1,023,717	2.9	42,390,705	43,289,646	2.1
Europe..	9	8.9	X	11.2	11.1	X
Asia...	28.1	28.6	X	30.1	30.6	X
Africa...	9	10.1	X	4.6	4.8	X
Oceania...	0.4	0.4	X	0.6	0.6	X
Latin America....................................	51.4	50.1	X	51.6	51.1	X
North America...................................	2	2.0	X	1.9	1.9	X
Language Spoken at Home and Ability to Speak English						
Population 5 years and over........................	9,442,904	9,565,500	1.3	299,084,046	301,625,014	0.8
English only	86.4	86.0	X	78.9	78.5	X
Language other than English....................	13.6	14.0	X	21.1	21.5	X
Speaks English less than "very well"........	5.5	5.8	X	8.6	8.6	X

NA = Not available.
X = Not applicable.
- = Zero or rounds to zero.

Table GA-5. Median Income and Poverty Status, 2015

(Number, percent, except as noted.)

Characteristic	State Number	State Percent	U.S. Number	U.S. Percent
Median Income				
Households (dollars)...	51,244	X	55,775	X
Families (dollars)	61,250	X	68,260	X
Below Poverty Level (All People)	1,694,988	17.0	46,153,077	14.7
Sex				
Male	734,925	15.3	20,599,407	13.4
Female	960,063	18.7	25,553,670	16.0
Age				
Under 18 years..	603,354	24.5	15,000,273	20.7
Related children under 18 years..	595,328	24.2	14,693,239	20.4
18 to 64 years...	968,566	15.6	26,960,369	13.9
65 years and over	123,068	9.7	4,192,435	9.0

X = Not applicable.

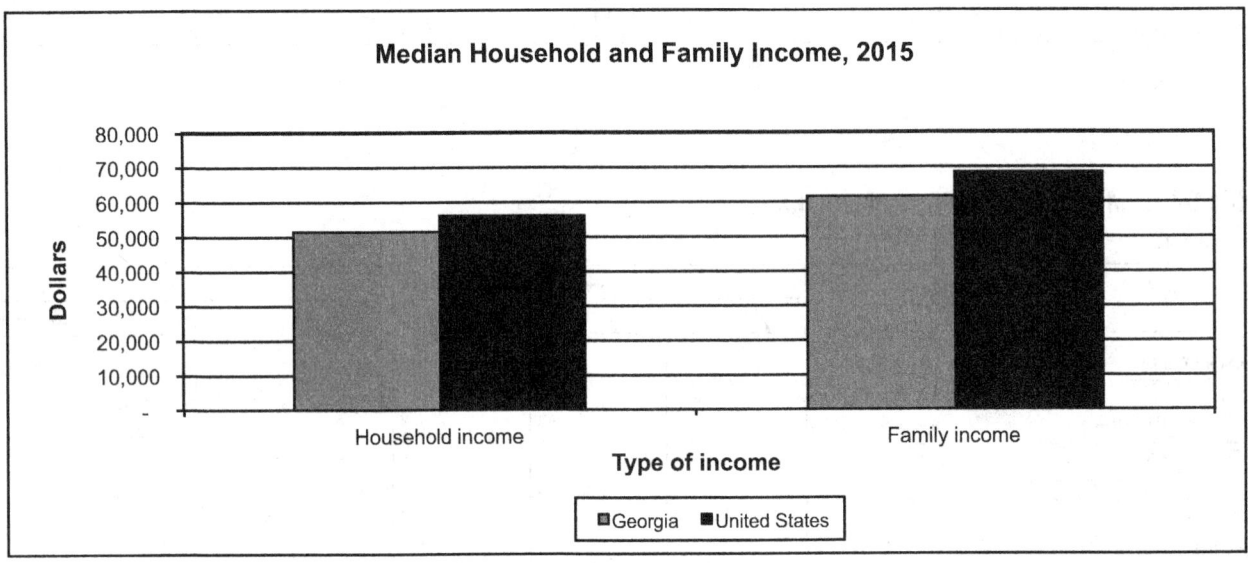

Median Household and Family Income, 2015

Table GA-6. Health Insurance Coverage Status for the Civilian Noninstitutionalized Population and Children Under 18 Years of Age

(Numbers in thousands, percent.)

Item	2007	2008	2009	2010	2011	2012	2013	2014	2015
Civilian Noninstitutionalized Population	9,493	9,473	9,594	9,520	9,620	9,719	9,801	9,907	10,024
Covered by Private or Public Insurance									
Number...	7,831	7,694	7,758	7,644	7,737	7,927	7,955	8,338	8,636
Percent..	82.5	81.2	80.9	80.3	80.4	81.6	81.2	84.2	86.1
Not Covered									
Number...	1,662	1,779	1,836	1,876	1,883	1,792	1,846	1,568	1,388
Percent..	17.5	18.8	19.1	19.7	19.6	18.4	18.8	15.8	13.9
Percent in the U.S. not covered..	15.3	15.1	15.1	15.5	15.1	14.8	14.5	11.7	9.4
Children Under 18 Years of Age	2,517	2,536	2,576	2,492	2,485	2,492	2,487	2,488	2,499
Covered by Private or Public Insurance									
Number...	2,228	2,245	2,295	2,248	2,248	2,272	2,249	2,299	2,333
Percent..	88.5	88.5	89.1	90.2	90.5	91.2	90.4	92.4	93.3
Not Covered									
Number...	289	291	281	244	237	220	238	189	166
Percent..	11.5	11.5	10.9	9.8	9.5	8.8	9.6	7.6	6.7
Percent in the U.S. not covered..	11.0	9.7	8.6	8.0	7.5	7.2	7.1	6.0	4.8

Table GA-7. Employment Status by Demographic Group, 2016

(Numbers in thousands, percent.)

Characteristic	Civilian noninstitutional population	Civilian labor force		Employed		Unemployed	
		Number	Percent of population	Number	Percent of population	Number	Percent of population
Total..	7,889	4,936	62.6	4,671	59.2	265	5.4
Sex							
Male..	3,733	2,572	68.9	2,446	65.5	126	4.9
Female..	4,155	2,364	56.9	2,226	53.6	139	5.9
Race, Sex, and Hispanic Origin							
White..	4,943	3,057	61.8	2,938	59.4	119	3.9
Male..	2,404	1,692	70.4	1,636	68.1	56	3.3
Female..	2,539	1,365	53.8	1,302	51.3	64	4.7
Black or African American...................	2,437	1,535	63.0	1,410	57.8	126	8.2
Male..	1,081	695	64.3	634	58.7	61	8.7
Female..	1,357	841	62.0	776	57.2	65	7.7
Hispanic or Latino ethnicity[1].............	712	508	71.3	488	68.5	20	4.0
Male..	352	294	83.3	286	81.2	8	2.6
Female..	360	214	59.5	202	56.0	13	5.9
Age							
16 to 19 years...................................	524	169	32.2	134	25.6	35	20.8
20 to 24 years...................................	693	462	66.6	412	59.4	50	10.8
25 to 34 years...................................	1,383	1,115	80.6	1,059	76.6	56	5.0
35 to 44 years...................................	1,350	1,096	81.2	1,047	77.6	50	4.5
45 to 54 years...................................	1,398	1,097	78.5	1,055	75.5	42	3.8
55 to 64 years...................................	1,231	763	62.0	739	60.0	24	3.2
65 years and over..............................	1,309	234	17.9	225	17.2	8	3.6

NOTE: Data in Table 7 are from the Current Population Survey (CPS) and do not match the estimates in Table 8. See notes and definitions for further information.
[1] May be of any race.

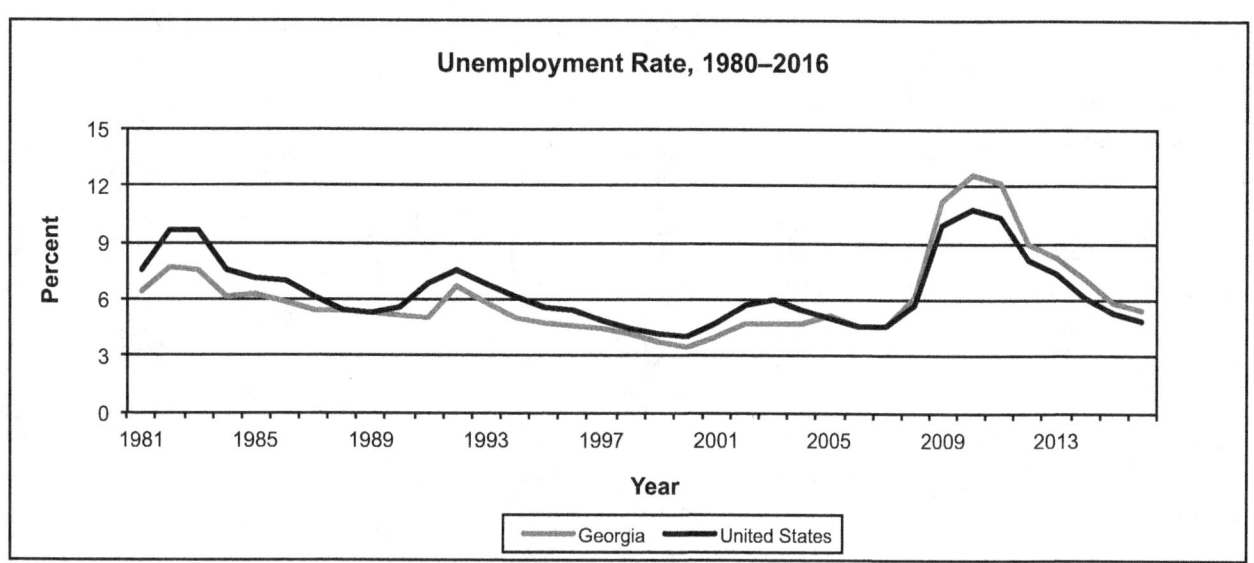

Table GA-8. Employment Status of the Civilian Noninstitutional Population Age 16 Years and Over

(Number, percent.)

Year	Civilian labor force	Civilian participation rate	Employed	Unemployed	Unemployment rate
2008..	4,879,253	67.8	4,575,010	304,243	6.2
2009..	4,787,749	65.6	4,311,854	475,895	9.9
2010..	4,696,676	64.1	4,202,052	494,624	10.5
2011..	4,748,754	64.3	4,263,305	485,449	10.2
2012..	4,788,068	63.9	4,349,796	438,272	9.2
2013..	4,759,506	62.8	4,369,349	390,157	8.2
2014..	4,753,765	62.0	4,416,715	337,050	7.1
2015..	4,770,873	61.3	4,490,931	279,942	5.9
2016..	4,920,464	62.4	4,656,255	264,209	5.4

Table GA-9. Employment and Average Wages by Industry

(Estimates through 2010 are based on the 2007 *North American Industry Classification System* [NAICS]. Estimates from 2011 onward are based on the 2012 NAICS.)

Industry	2009	2010	2011	2012	2013	2014	2015
	Number of Jobs						
Wage and Salary Employment by Industry..................	4,092,110	4,032,763	4,072,502	4,126,774	4,203,063	4,323,003	4,440,645
Farm Wage and Salary Employment.........................	16,478	13,636	14,838	16,206	15,271	16,194	15,830
Nonfarm Wage and Salary Employment....................	4,075,632	4,019,127	4,057,664	4,110,568	4,187,792	4,306,809	4,424,815
Private wage and salary employment......................	3,274,192	3,222,181	3,274,156	3,332,693	3,417,125	3,542,001	3,658,838
Forestry, fishing, and related activities..........................	14,306	14,805	14,690	14,653	15,125	15,368	15,829
Mining..	5,013	4,942	4,806	4,669	4,727	4,850	4,841
Utilities..	20,440	19,732	19,997	19,852	19,862	19,784	20,084
Construction..	174,395	155,028	150,622	145,738	150,324	161,142	170,210
Manufacturing...	359,759	346,225	351,357	354,831	357,742	367,306	378,283
Durable goods manufacturing.................................	161,508	155,689	161,622	166,766	171,269	176,714	182,851
Nondurable goods manufacturing...........................	198,251	190,536	189,735	188,065	186,473	190,592	195,432
Wholesale trade	201,361	197,322	198,615	202,702	206,198	211,734	218,692
Retail trade...	444,810	438,668	445,976	448,769	457,129	471,250	488,894
Transportation and warehousing.............................	162,930	160,849	165,961	169,258	170,483	177,512	185,659
Information	101,738	97,769	98,741	99,994	102,998	107,130	106,299
Finance and insurance	159,941	156,045	158,936	163,271	166,299	171,948	174,972
Real estate and rental and leasing..........................	60,040	57,446	57,580	57,577	58,538	60,818	63,894
Professional, scientific, and technical services	221,715	219,742	225,991	234,029	240,480	253,940	262,618
Management of companies and enterprises...................	52,595	52,900	54,025	57,404	59,654	62,521	66,043
Administrative and waste services...............................	247,561	258,039	268,355	275,207	291,043	306,634	315,094
Educational services	77,275	78,967	80,394	80,906	81,913	82,913	83,642
Health care and social assistance............................	394,014	402,244	407,869	417,568	430,252	438,167	454,449
Arts, entertainment, and recreation.........................	41,481	39,863	40,548	41,634	43,048	44,446	47,051
Accommodation and food services...........................	342,546	337,507	343,853	354,939	370,940	387,223	403,086
Other services, except public administration.................	192,272	184,088	185,840	189,692	190,370	197,315	199,198
Government and government enterprises.........................	801,440	796,946	783,508	777,875	770,667	764,808	765,977
	Dollars						
Average Wages and Salaries by Industry	43,754	44,924	46,117	47,359	47,783	49,086	50,519
Average Farm Wages and Salaries	18,976	23,010	18,899	26,483	21,153	24,200	26,412
Average Nonfarm Wages and Salaries	43,854	44,998	46,217	47,441	47,880	49,179	50,606
Average private wages and salaries........................	44,013	45,356	46,712	48,202	48,767	50,065	51,497
Forestry, fishing, and related activities.....................	29,486	31,431	31,569	32,753	33,480	34,166	35,122
Mining..	53,563	55,502	57,380	59,289	61,211	63,301	66,111
Utilities..	81,511	76,817	84,508	84,895	85,499	87,020	93,119
Construction..	45,390	46,572	47,166	48,783	49,805	51,763	53,901
Manufacturing...	48,931	51,832	53,727	54,856	55,927	56,948	57,851
Durable goods manufacturing.................................	52,027	54,799	57,080	57,108	58,464	59,786	60,842
Nondurable goods manufacturing...........................	46,409	49,407	50,870	52,858	53,597	54,317	55,054
Wholesale trade	65,262	67,625	69,932	71,417	72,526	74,059	76,205
Retail trade...	26,495	27,125	27,366	27,822	28,274	28,842	30,277
Transportation and warehousing.............................	48,523	51,026	52,737	54,234	56,346	58,858	59,500
Information	73,842	76,781	79,930	85,038	85,834	89,014	88,703
Finance and insurance	69,999	72,875	76,786	79,967	81,698	84,082	88,010
Real estate and rental and leasing..........................	44,679	46,344	49,001	51,107	51,894	53,703	55,171
Professional, scientific, and technical services	70,412	72,390	74,446	77,915	77,428	79,274	82,243
Management of companies and enterprises...................	85,428	88,926	94,492	100,262	99,235	106,110	110,236
Administrative and waste services...............................	34,147	34,546	34,975	35,600	35,733	36,386	37,840
Educational services	39,681	40,402	41,383	42,642	43,240	44,399	44,775
Health care and social assistance............................	44,262	44,689	45,725	47,027	47,596	48,422	50,097
Arts, entertainment, and recreation.........................	33,681	35,020	35,701	34,980	35,613	36,748	37,014
Accommodation and food services...........................	17,771	18,374	18,877	19,514	19,665	20,203	20,077
Other services, except public administration.................	28,400	29,578	29,795	30,194	31,089	31,734	33,124
Government and government enterprises.........................	43,205	43,552	44,148	44,181	43,946	45,076	46,348

Table GA-10. Employment Characteristics by Family Type

(Number, percent.)

Family type and labor force status	2013		2014		2015	
	Total	Families with own children under 18 years	Total	Families with own children under 18 years	Total	Families with own children under 18 years
All Families...	2,389,803	1,087,559	2,419,167	1,103,236	2,466,415	1,097,585
FAMILY TYPE AND LABOR FORCE STATUS						
Married-Couple Families..........................	1,672,704	692,412	1,684,808	702,051	1,750,409	714,312
Both husband and wife in labor force....................	51.6	65.2	50.7	63.8	50.3	63.8
Husband in labor force, wife not in labor force	23.2	29.0	24.3	30.0	24.0	30.3
Wife in labor force, husband not in labor force	7.7	3.8	8.2	4.3	7.9	3.9
Both husband and wife not in labor force...............	17.0	1.8	16.8	1.9	17.3	1.7
Other Families	717,099	395,147	734,359	401,185	716,006	383,273
Female householder, no husband present................	75.5	78.1	76.5	78.5	76.6	78.6
In labor force	53.8	64.7	54.1	65.2	53.6	65.7
Not in labor force	21.7	13.4	22.4	13.3	23.0	12.8
Male householder, no wife present..................	24.5	21.9	23.5	21.5	23.4	21.4
In labor force	19.3	19.9	18.2	19.4	17.7	18.8
Not in labor force	5.2	2.0	5.2	2.0	5.7	2.6

Table GA-11. School Enrollment and Educational Attainment, 2015

(Number, percent.)

Item	State	U.S.
Enrollment		
Total population 3 years and over, enrolled in school	2,760,000	81,618,288
Enrolled in nursery school or preschool (percent)..	6.3	6.0
Enrolled in kindergarten (percent)...	5.3	5.0
Enrolled in elementary school, grades 1-8 (percent)...	41.2	40.3
Enrolled in high school, grades 9-12 (percent)..	21.2	20.9
Enrolled in college or graduate school (percent)..	26.0	27.7
Attainment		
Total population 25 years and over	6,683,767	216,447,163
Less than ninth grade (percent)...	5.0	5.5
9th to 12th grade, no diploma (percent)	8.9	7.3
High school graduate, including equivalency (percent).......................................	28.1	27.6
Some college, no degree (percent)..	20.7	20.7
Associate's degree (percent)..	7.4	8.2
Bachelor's degree (percent)...	18.6	19.0
Graduate or professional degree (percent)...	11.3	11.6
High school graduate or higher (percent)	86.1	87.1
Bachelor's degree or higher (percent)...	29.9	30.6

Table GA-12. Public School Characteristics and Educational Indicators

(Number, percent; data derived from National Center of Education Statistics.)

Item	State	U.S.
Public Schools, 2014–2015 (except where noted)		
Number of school districts...	218	18,260
Number of schools...	2,329	98,373
Number of students..	1,744,437	50,312,581
Number of teachers..	111,470	3,132,351
Student-teacher ratio..	15.6	16.1
Expenditures per student (dollars), FY 2014...	9,236	11,066
Four-year adjusted cohort graduation rate (ACGR)[1,2]	78.8	83.2
Students eligible for free or reduced-price lunch (percent).................................	62.4	51.8
English language learners (percent)...	5.7	9.4
Students age 3 to 21 served under IDEA, part B (percent)...................................	11.2	13.0

Public Schools by Type	Number	Percent of state public schools
Total number of schools...	2,329	100.0
Regular	2,243	96.3
Special education...	19	0.8
Vocational education...	0	-
Alternative education...	67	2.9

NOTE: Every school is assigned only one school type based on its instructional emphasis.
[1] ACGR data represents a new method of calculating high-school completion rates and may not be comparable to previous years' data for Averaged Freshmen Graduation Rates (AFGR).
[2] The United States 4-year ACGRs were estimated using both the reported 4-year ACGR data from 49 states and the District of Columbia and using imputed data for Idaho. The estimate for American Indian/Alaska Native students also includes imputed data for Virginia.

Table GA-13. Reported Voting and Registration of the Voting-Age Population, November 2016

(Numbers in thousands, percent.)

Item	Total population	Total citizen population	Registered			Voted		
			Total registered	Percent registered (total population)	Percent registered (total citizen population)	Total voted	Percent voted (total population)	Percent voted (total citizen population)
U.S. Total	245,502	224,059	157,596	64.2	70.3	137,537	56.0	61.4
State Total.............................	7,626	7,048	4,892	64.1	69.4	4,246	55.7	60.2
Sex								
Male	3,623	3,317	2,237	61.7	67.4	1,908	52.7	57.5
Female	4,003	3,731	2,655	66.3	71.2	2,338	58.4	62.7
Race								
White alone...........................	4,798	4,453	3,179	66.2	71.4	2,786	58.1	62.6
White, non-Hispanic alone	4,184	4,142	3,028	72.4	73.1	2,643	63.2	63.8
Black alone...........................	2,325	2,255	1,552	66.8	68.8	1,346	57.9	59.7
Asian alone...........................	365	225	101	27.7	44.9	71	19.3	31.3
Hispanic (of any race)	680	335	168	24.8	50.2	161	23.6	47.9
White alone or in combination	4,872	4,526	3,224	66.2	71.2	2,815	57.8	62.2
Black alone or in combination.........	2,364	2,294	1,578	66.8	68.8	1,360	57.5	59.3
Asian alone or in combination.........	375	235	106	28.3	45.1	71	18.8	30.0
Age								
18 to 24 years........................	991	923	511	51.6	55.4	401	40.5	43.5
25 to 34 years........................	1,316	1,119	712	54.1	63.6	609	46.3	54.4
35 to 44 years........................	1,352	1,211	790	58.4	65.3	672	49.7	55.5
45 to 64 years........................	2,599	2,456	1,801	69.3	73.3	1,593	61.3	64.9
65 years and over	1,368	1,340	1,078	78.8	80.4	971	71.0	72.4

Table GA-14. Crime

(Number, rate per 100,000. Data are derived from the FBI Uniform Crime Reports.)

Item	State			U.S. [1,2,3,4]		
	2014	2015	Percent change	2014	2015	Percent change
TOTAL POPULATION[5]	10,097,132	10,214,860	1.2	318,907,401	321,418,820	0.8
VIOLENT CRIME						
Number..	38,955	38,643	-0.8	1,186,185	1,231,566	3.8
Rate..	385.8	378.3	-1.9	372.0	383.2	3.0
Murder and Nonnegligent Manslaughter						
Number..	607	615	1.3	14,164	15,696	10.8
Rate..	6.0	6.0	0.2	4.4	4.9	10.0
Rape[6]						
Number..	3,147	3,224	2.4	118,027	124,047	5.1
Rate..	31.2	31.6	1.3	37.0	38.6	4.3
Robbery						
Number..	12,786	12,247	-4.2	322,905	327,374	1.4
Rate..	126.6	119.9	-5.3	101.3	101.9	0.6
Aggravated Assault						
Number..	22,415	22,557	0.6	731,089	764,449	4.6
Rate..	222.0	220.8	-0.5	229.2	237.8	3.7
PROPERTY CRIME						
Number..	339,146	308,723	-9.0	8,209,010	7,993,631	-2.6
Rate..	3,358.8	3,022.3	-10.0	2,574.1	2,487.0	-3.4
Burglary						
Number..	78,029	66,374	-14.9	1,713,153	1,579,527	-7.8
Rate..	772.8	649.8	-15.9	537.2	491.4	-8.5
Larceny-Theft						
Number..	233,359	215,867	-7.5	5,809,054	5,706,346	-1.8
Rate..	2,311.1	2,113.3	-8.6	1,821.5	1,775.4	-2.5
Motor Vehicle Theft						
Number..	27,758	26,482	-4.6	686,803	707,758	3.1
Rate..	274.9	259.2	-5.7	215.4	220.2	2.2

NOTE: Although arson data are included in the trend and clearance tables, sufficient data are not available to estimate totals for this offense. Therefore, no arson data are published in this table.

X = Not applicable.

- = Zero or rounds to zero.

[1] The crime figures have been adjusted.

[2] The data collection methodology for the offense of forcible rape used by the Minnesota state Uniform Crime Reporting (UCR) Program (with the exception of Minneapolis and St. Paul, Minnesota) does not comply with national UCR Program guidelines. Consequently, its figures for forcible rape and violent crime (of which forcible rape is a part) are not published in this table.

[3] Includes offenses reported by the Zoological Police and the Metro Transit Police.

[4] Because of changes in the state's reporting practices, figures are not comparable to previous years' data.

[5] Populations are U.S. Census Bureau provisional estimates as of July 1 of each year.

[6] The figures shown for the offense of rape were estimated using the revised Uniform Crime Reporting (UCR) definition of rape.

Table GA-15. State Government Finances, 2015

(Dollar amounts in thousands, percent distribution.)

Item	Dollars	Percent distribution
Total Revenue	45,886,076	100.0
General revenue	39,507,686	86.1
Intergovernmental revenue	13,837,168	30.2
Taxes	19,732,308	43.0
General sales	5,256,592	11.5
Selective sales	2,299,273	5.0
License taxes	633,573	1.4
Individual income tax	9,678,524	21.1
Corporate income tax	1,000,536	2.2
Other taxes	863,810	1.9
Current charges	3,616,831	7.9
Miscellaneous general revenue	2,321,379	5.1
Utility revenue	5,952	-
Liquor stores revenue	0	-
Insurance trust revenue[1]	6,372,438	13.9
Total Expenditure	47,317,279	100.0
Intergovernmental expenditure	11,088,286	23.4
Direct expenditure	36,228,993	76.6
Current operation	24,905,979	52.6
Capital outlay	2,546,916	5.4
Insurance benefits and repayments	7,044,835	14.9
Assistance and subsidies	1,081,264	2.3
Interest on debt	649,999	1.4
Exhibit: Salaries and wages	6,167,929	13.0
Total Expenditure	47,317,279	100.0
General expenditure	40,236,787	85.0
Intergovernmental expenditure	11,088,286	23.4
Direct expenditure	29,148,501	61.6
General expenditure, by function:		
Education	17,864,354	37.8
Public welfare	12,197,038	25.8
Hospitals	1,189,939	2.5
Health	1,374,371	2.9
Highways	1,956,088	4.1
Police protection	373,798	0.8
Correction	1,484,986	3.1
Natural resources	514,200	1.1
Parks and recreation	206,090	0.4
Governmental administration	894,526	1.9
Interest on general debt	649,999	1.4
Other and unallocable	1,531,398	3.2
Utility expenditure	35,657	0.1
Liquor stores expenditure	0	-
Insurance trust expenditure	7,044,835	14.9
Debt at End of Fiscal Year	13,247,675	X
Cash and Security Holdings	103,083,887	X

X = Not applicable.
- = Zero or rounds to zero.

[1] Within insurance trust revenue, net earnings of state retirement systems is a calculated statistic (the item code in the data file is X08), and thus can be positive or negative. Net earnings is the sum of earnings on investments plus gains on investments minus losses on investments. The change made in 2002 for asset valuation from book to market value in accordance with Statement 34 of the Governmental Accounting Standards Board is reflected in the calculated statistics.

Table GA-16. State Government Tax Collections, 2016

(Dollars in thousands, percent.)

Item	Dollars	Percent distribution
Total Taxes	21,454,446	100.0
Property taxes..........................	961,780	4.5
Sales and gross receipts	8,408,456	39.2
General sales and gross receipts	5,480,196	25.5
Selective sales and gross receipts	2,928,260	13.6
Alcoholic beverages.........................	190,536	0.9
Amusements.........................	0	-
Insurance premiums.........................	428,700	2.0
Motor fuels.........................	1,655,028	7.7
Pari-mutuels.........................	0	-
Public utilities	0	-
Tobacco products.........................	219,870	1.0
Other selective sales	434,126	2.0
Licenses.........................	663,946	3.1
Alcoholic beverages.........................	3,983	-
Amusements.........................	0	-
Corporations in general.........................	51,050	0.2
Hunting and fishing.........................	26,569	0.1
Motor vehicle.........................	366,897	1.7
Motor vehicle operators	108,475	0.5
Public utilities	0	-
Occupation and business, NEC	82,123	0.4
Other licenses	24,849	0.1
Income taxes.........................	11,420,536	53.2
Individual income.........................	10,439,534	48.7
Corporation net income	981,002	4.6
Other taxes.........................	-272	-
Death and gift.........................	-414	-
Documentary and stock transfer	142	-
Severance	0	-
Taxes, NEC	0	-

X = Not applicable.
- = Zero or rounds to zero.

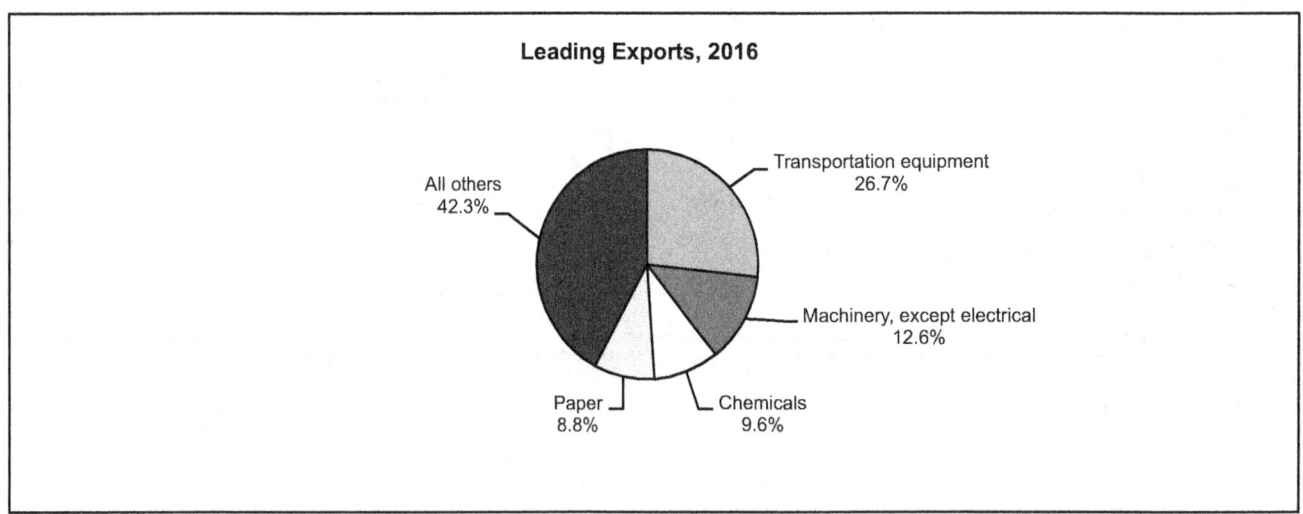

Leading Exports, 2016

All others 42.3%

Transportation equipment 26.7%

Machinery, except electrical 12.6%

Chemicals 9.6%

Paper 8.8%

HAWAII

Location: North Pacific Ocean

Area: 10,931 sq. mi. (28,311 sq. km.); rank—43rd

Population: 1,428,557 (2016 est.); rank—40th

Principal Cities: capital—Honolulu; largest—Honolulu

Statehood: August 21, 1959; 50th state

U.S. Congress: 2 senators, 2 representatives

State Motto: *Ua mau ke ea o ka'ina i ka pono* ("The life of the land is perpetuated in righteousness")

State Song: "Hawai'i Pono' (Hawaii's Own)"

State Nickname: The Aloha State

Abbreviations: HI

State Symbols: flower—native yellow hibiscus; tree—kukui (candlenut tree); bird—nene (Hawaiian goose)

At a Glance

- With an increase in population of 5.0 percent, Hawaii ranked 20th among the states in growth from 2010 to 2016.

- In 2015, 4.0 percent of Hawaiians did not have health insurance, compared to 9.4 percent of the total U.S. population.

- Hawaii had the second highest property crime rate in the country in 2015, with 3,796.2 incidents per 100,000 population.

- Hawaii had the highest proportion of state government employees to total residents in 2015, with 40.9 state employees per 1,000 residents, compared to the national average of 13.4 employees per 1,000 residents.

- Hawaii had the largest percent of Asian Alone residents in 2016, with 37.7 percent of its residents in this category.

Table HI-1. Population by Age, Sex, Race, and Hispanic Origin

(Number, percent, except where noted.)

Sex, age, race, and Hispanic origin	2000	2010	2016 [1]	Average annual percent change, 2010–2016
Total Population..	1,211,537	1,360,301	1,428,557	0.3
Percent of total U.S. population	0.4	0.4	0.4	X
Sex				
Male..	563,891	681,243	717,615	0.3
Female...	544,338	679,058	710,942	0.3
Age				
Under 5 years..	78,163	87,407	91,535	0.3
5 to 19 years...	249,088	250,894	247,502	-0.1
20 to 64 years...	723,685	826,868	845,558	0.1
65 years and over..	160,601	195,138	243,962	1.6
Median age (years)	36.2	38.6	38.6	-
Race and Hispanic Origin				
One race...				
White...	294,102	349,051	369,064	0.4
Black..	22,003	22,473	31,073	2.4
American Indian and Alaska Native	3,535	4,960	5,695	0.9
Asian..	503,868	531,633	539,050	0.1
Native Hawaiian or Other Pacific Islander	113,539	138,292	145,368	0.3
Two or more races..	259,343	313,892	338,307	0.5
Hispanic (of any race)..	87,699	133,342	148,148	0.7

X = Not applicable.
[1] Population figures for 2016 are July 1 estimates. The 2010 estimates are taken from the 2010 Census.

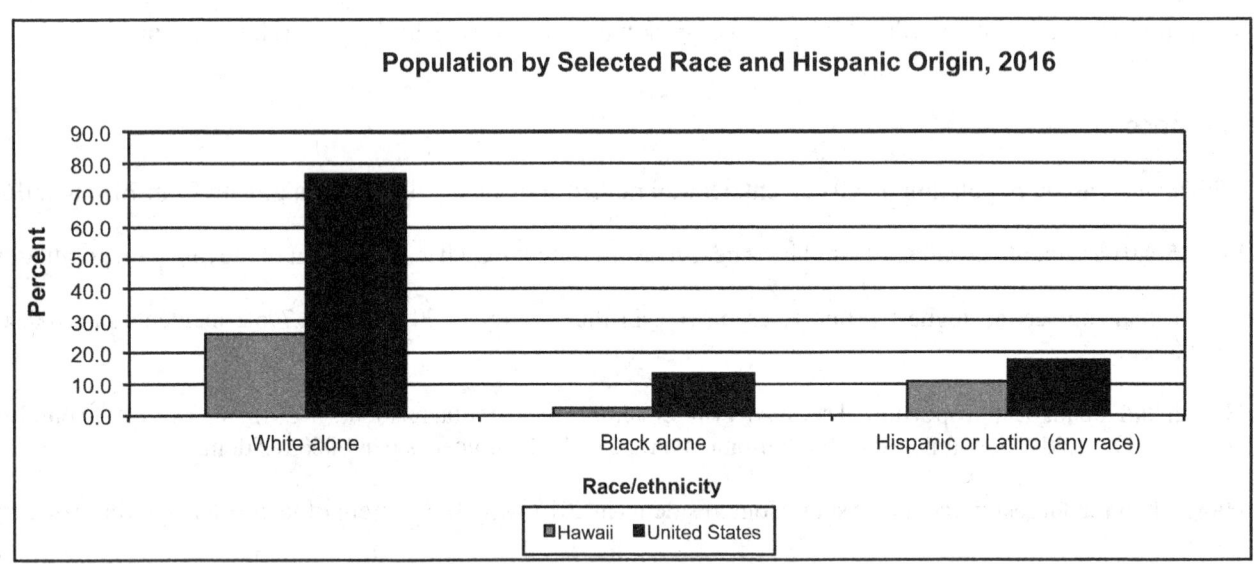

Table HI-2. Marital Status

(Number, percent distribution.)

Sex, age, race, and Hispanic origin	2000	2010	2015
Males, 15 Years and Over	481,768	554,154	590,393
Never married	34.6	37.8	37.7
Now married, except separated.................................	53.7	49.1	50.1
Separated...	1.4	1.2	1.3
Widowed...	2.2	2.7	2.7
Divorced...	8.1	9.2	8.3
Females, 15 Years and Over	484,107	556,915	577,908
Never married	25.9	28.7	29.3
Now married, except separated.................................	52.5	48.5	48.5
Separated...	1.7	1.8	1.5
Widowed...	9.8	10.1	9.9
Divorced...	10.0	11.0	10.8

Table HI-3. Households and Housing Characteristics

(Number, percent, dollars.)

Item	2000	2010	2015	Average annual percent change, 2000–2015
Total Households..	403,240	445,812	445,936	0.7
Family households	287,068	303,075	309,386	0.5
Married-couple family	216,077	224,402	232,451	0.5
Other family	70,991	78,673	76,935	(0.6
Male householder, no wife present..................	21,068	24,247	24,870	1.2
Female householder, no husband present........	49,923	54,426	52,065	0.3
Nonfamily households	116,172	142,737	136,550	1.2
Householder living alone...................................	88,153	108,872	104,220	1.2
Householder not living alone.............................	28,019	33,865	32,330	1.0
Housing Characteristics				
Total housing units...	460,542	519,992	532,413	1.0
Occupied housing units	403,240	445,812	445,936	0.7
Owner occupied	227,888	258,533	252,435	0.7
Renter occupied	175,352	187,279	193,501	0.7
Average household size......................................	2.92	2.96	3.11	0.4
Financial Characteristics				
Median gross rent of renter-occupied housing	779	1,291	1,500	6.2
Median monthly owner costs for housing units with a mortgage	1,636	2,240	2,248	2.5
Median value of owner-occupied housing units	272,700	525,400	566,900	7.2

Table HI-4. Migration, Origin, and Language

(Number, percent.)

Characteristic	State			U.S.		
	2014	2015	Percent change	2014	2015	Percent change
Residence 1 Year Ago						
Population 1 year and over	1,401,004	1,414,355	1.0	315,095,393	317,635,720	0.8
Same house	85.6	85.3	X	85.1	85.3	X
Different house in the U.S.	13.6	13.5	X	14.3	14.1	X
Same county	8.9	9.1	X	8.7	8.5	X
Different county	4.7	4.4	X	5.6	5.6	X
Same state	0.5	0.6	X	3.3	3.2	X
Different state	4.2	3.8	X	2.3	2.4	X
Abroad	0.9	1.3	X	0.6	0.7	X
Place of Birth						
Native born	1,169,289	1,178,189	0.8	276,465,262	278,128,449	0.6
Male	52.3	52.4	X	49.3	49.3	X
Female	47.7	47.6	X	50.7	50.7	X
Foreign born	250,272	253,414	1.3	42,391,794	43,290,372	2.1
Male	42.4	42.2	X	48.7	48.6	X
Female	57.6	57.8	X	51.3	51.4	X
Foreign born; naturalized U.S. citizen............	142,503	146,485	2.8	19,984,738	20,697,103	3.6
Male	41	42.4	X	45.9	45.9	X
Female	59	57.6	X	54.1	54.1	X
Foreign born; not a U.S. citizen....................	107,769	106,929	-0.8	22,407,056	22,593,269	0.8
Male	44.2	42.0	X	51.2	51.1	X
Female	55.8	58.0	X	48.8	48.9	X
Entered 2010 or later	11.3	15.3	X	12.3	15.6	X
Entered 2000 to 2009	27.8	22.9	X	28.6	27.9	X
Entered before 2000...................................	61	61.8	X	59.1	56.5	X
World Region of Birth, Foreign						
Foreign-born population, excluding population born at sea	250,272	253,414	1.3	42,390,705	43,289,646	2.1
Europe	4.2	4.9	X	11.2	11.1	X
Asia...	78.4	80.0	X	30.1	30.6	X
Africa	0.9	0.8	X	4.6	4.8	X
Oceania	10.8	7.4	X	0.6	0.6	X
Latin America...	4.1	5.7	X	51.6	51.1	X
North America..	1.7	1.2	X	1.9	1.9	X
Language Spoken at Home and Ability to Speak English						
Population 5 years and over...........................	1,328,554	1,339,510	0.8	299,084,046	301,625,014	0.8
English only	74.8	73.9	X	78.9	78.5	X
Language other than English..........................	25.2	26.1	X	21.1	21.5	X
Speaks English less than "very well"...............	12.8	12.4	X	8.6	8.6	X

NA = Not available.
X = Not applicable.
- = Zero or rounds to zero.

Table HI-5. Median Income and Poverty Status, 2015

(Number, percent, except as noted.)

Characteristic	State		U.S.	
	Number	Percent	Number	Percent
Median Income				
Households (dollars)..	73,486	X	55,775	X
Families (dollars)	83,823	X	68,260	X
Below Poverty Level (All People)	147,984	10.6	46,153,077	14.7
Sex				
Male	70,606	10.1	20,599,407	13.4
Female	77,378	11.1	25,553,670	16.0
Age				
Under 18 years..	43,438	14.2	15,000,273	20.7
Related children under 18 years................................	41,420	13.6	14,693,239	20.4
18 to 64 years..	86,303	10.1	26,960,369	13.9
65 years and over	18,243	7.8	4,192,435	9.0

X = Not applicable.

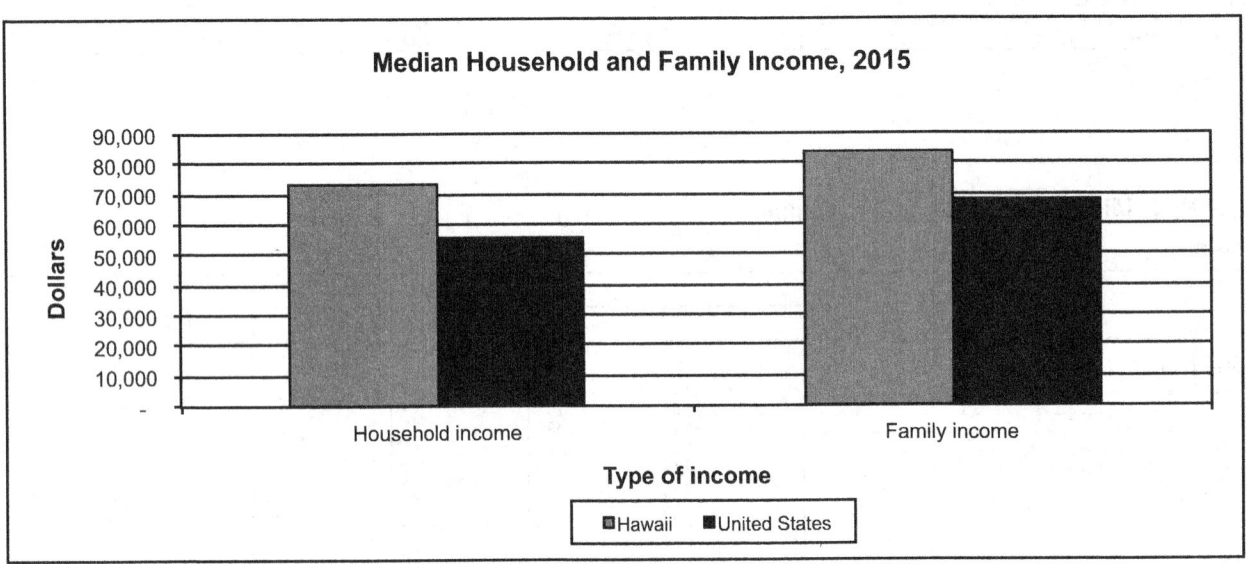

Table HI-6. Health Insurance Coverage Status for the Civilian Noninstitutionalized Population and Children Under 18 Years of Age

(Numbers in thousands, percent.)

Item	2007	2008	2009	2010	2011	2012	2013	2014	2015
Civilian Noninstitutionalized Population	1,267	1,237	1,232	1,316	1,326	1,342	1,345	1,368	1,375
Covered by Private or Public Insurance									
Number..	1,172	1,154	1,146	1,212	1,232	1,249	1,254	1,296	1,321
Percent..	92.5	93.3	93.0	92.1	92.9	93.1	93.3	94.7	96.0
Not Covered									
Number..	96	83	86	104	94	93	91	72	55
Percent..	7.5	6.7	7.0	7.9	7.1	6.9	6.7	5.3	4.0
Percent in the U.S. not covered.................................	15.3	15.1	15.1	15.5	15.1	14.8	14.5	11.7	9.4
Children Under 18 Years of Age	291	284	288	304	304	303	307	308	311
Covered by Private or Public Insurance									
Number..	277	274	281	293	293	293	298	298	306
Percent..	47.5	96.5	97.5	96.3	96.4	96.5	97.0	96.9	98.4
Not Covered									
Number..	14	10	7	11	11	10	9	10	5
Percent..	4.8	3.5	2.5	3.7	3.6	3.5	3.0	3.1	1.6
Percent in the U.S. not covered.................................	11.0	9.7	8.6	8.0	7.5	7.2	7.1	6.0	4.8

Table HI-7. Employment Status by Demographic Group, 2016

(Numbers in thousands, percent.)

Characteristic	Civilian noninstitutional population	Civilian labor force		Employed		Unemployed	
		Number	Percent of population	Number	Percent of population	Number	Percent of population
Total...................................	1,101	691	62.7	670	60.8	21	3.0
Sex							
Male.................................	539	365	67.6	354	65.6	11	2.9
Female	562	326	58.0	316	56.2	10	3.2
Race, Sex, and Hispanic Origin							
White.................................	226	135	59.6	130	57.6	5	3.4
Male.................................	114	75	65.7	73	63.9	2	2.8
Female	112	60	53.4	57	51.2	3	4.1
Black or African American....................	NA	NA	NA	NA	NA	NA	NA
Male.................................	NA	NA	NA	NA	NA	NA	NA
Female	NA	NA	NA	NA	NA	NA	NA
Hispanic or Latino ethnicity[1]	95	63	65.7	60	63.0	3	4.3
Male.................................	48	33	67.6	31	64.7	1	4.2
Female	47	30	63.8	29	60.9	1	4.4
Age							
16 to 19 years.......................	NA	NA	NA	NA	NA	NA	NA
20 to 24 years.......................	89	63	71.3	59	66.6	4	6.3
25 to 34 years.......................	198	159	80.0	153	77.1	6	3.5
35 to 44 years.......................	161	133	82.7	130	80.8	3	2.3
45 to 54 years.......................	171	141	82.1	138	80.5	3	1.9
55 to 64 years.......................	186	122	65.4	119	64.0	3	2.2
65 years and over	231	54	23.1	52	22.5	1	2.4

NOTE: Data in Table 7 are from the Current Population Survey (CPS) and do not match the estimates in Table 8. See notes and definitions for further information.
[1] May be of any race.
NA = Not available.

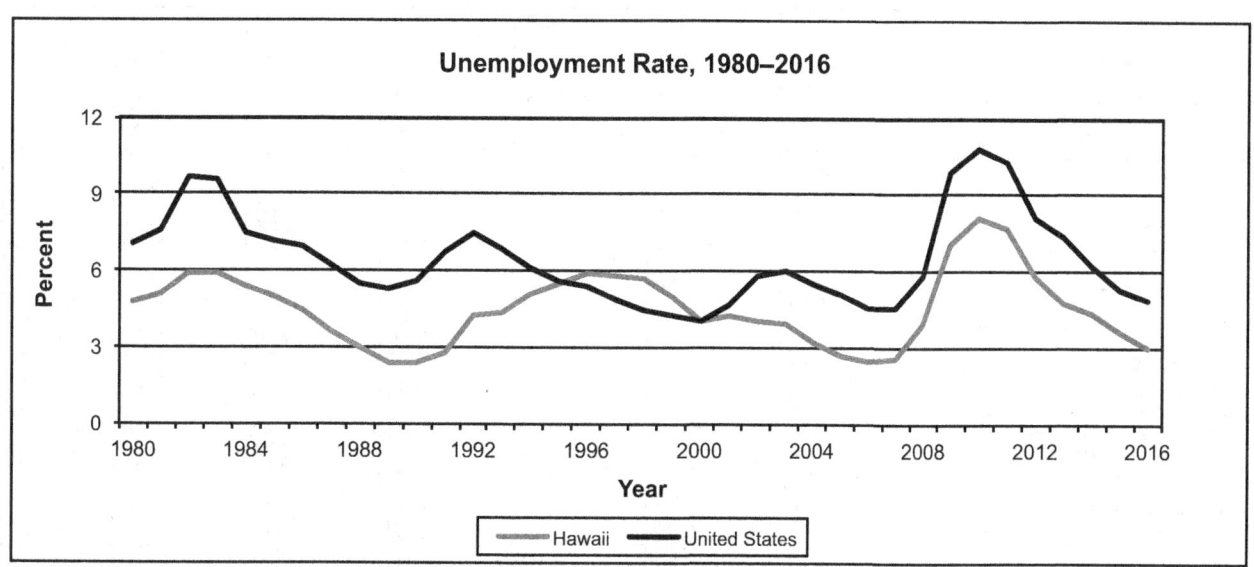

Table HI-8. Employment Status of the Civilian Noninstitutional Population Age 16 Years and Over

(Number, percent.)

Year	Civilian labor force	Civilian participation rate	Employed	Unemployed	Unemployment rate
2008............................	639,691	65.6	612,120	27,571	4.3
2009............................	631,690	64.3	586,522	45,168	7.2
2010............................	647,249	62.8	602,282	44,967	6.9
2011............................	660,253	62.6	615,319	44,934	6.8
2012............................	647,625	60.9	608,722	38,903	6.0
2013............................	650,708	60.6	619,088	31,620	4.9
2014............................	668,346	61.7	639,148	29,198	4.4
2015............................	677,439	62.0	652,939	24,500	3.6
2016............................	685,378	62.7	664,690	20,688	3.0

Table HI-9. Employment and Average Wages by Industry

(Estimates through 2010 are based on the 2007 *North American Industry Classification System* [NAICS]. Estimates from 2011 onward are based on the 2012 NAICS.)

Industry	2009	2010	2011	2012	2013	2014	2015
	Number of Jobs						
Wage and Salary Employment by Industry..................	667,763	661,830	669,911	681,247	693,899	703,401	714,856
Farm Wage and Salary Employment.........................	5,378	5,662	6,528	6,099	6,176	7,375	6,734
Nonfarm Wage and Salary Employment....................	662,385	656,168	663,383	675,148	687,723	696,026	708,122
Private wage and salary employment................................	481,121	474,096	481,281	492,070	504,956	512,970	522,758
Forestry, fishing, and related activities	1,295	1,311	1,425	1,473	1,521	1,543	1,565
Mining..	340	338	332	298	255	252	279
Utilities..	3,193	3,214	3,328	3,567	3,771	3,808	3,827
Construction	32,512	29,561	29,303	30,066	31,643	32,689	35,508
Manufacturing...	13,717	12,937	13,185	13,348	13,586	13,933	14,076
Durable goods manufacturing................................	4,155	3,789	3,884	3,619	3,630	3,595	3,699
Nondurable goods manufacturing..........................	9,562	9,148	9,301	9,729	9,956	10,338	10,377
Wholesale trade	17,993	17,774	17,535	17,745	17,824	17,798	18,085
Retail trade..	67,641	66,612	67,774	69,456	70,245	70,458	71,355
Transportation and warehousing...........................	23,865	23,311	23,979	25,107	25,981	26,568	27,347
Information	9,095	9,913	8,535	8,459	8,792	8,481	8,697
Finance and insurance	16,714	16,096	15,987	16,035	15,765	15,677	15,931
Real estate and rental and leasing........................	11,871	11,649	11,643	11,794	12,052	12,280	12,221
Professional, scientific, and technical services	25,052	24,414	24,519	24,603	24,599	24,561	24,701
Management of companies and enterprises..............	7,003	6,652	6,925	7,512	8,255	8,379	8,508
Administrative and waste services.........................	40,455	41,102	44,353	45,545	47,641	49,855	50,791
Educational services	15,774	15,833	15,852	16,284	16,067	15,772	15,738
Health care and social assistance.........................	61,416	61,978	62,194	62,827	64,986	65,795	67,890
Arts, entertainment, and recreation.......................	10,880	10,575	10,713	11,451	12,112	12,179	11,860
Accommodation and food services........................	91,008	90,463	93,079	96,479	99,678	101,763	103,168
Other services, except public administration..................	31,297	30,363	30,620	30,021	30,183	31,179	31,211
Government and government enterprises	181,264	182,072	182,102	183,078	182,767	183,056	185,364
	Dollars						
Average Wages and Salaries by Industry	42,725	43,253	44,020	45,042	45,452	46,687	48,371
Average Farm Wages and Salaries	33,110	29,919	24,880	39,574	39,499	33,674	38,951
Average Nonfarm Wages and Salaries	42,803	43,368	44,208	45,092	45,505	46,825	48,461
Average private wages and salaries...........................	39,267	39,954	40,553	41,663	42,371	43,483	45,347
Forestry, fishing, and related activities	21,108	21,963	22,354	23,050	24,218	24,553	26,868
Mining..	77,868	73,544	77,340	82,822	88,329	93,786	96,975
Utilities..	80,411	83,871	88,478	90,384	92,309	94,493	99,635
Construction	61,945	62,559	63,593	64,746	65,060	66,498	70,624
Manufacturing...	38,796	39,256	40,344	40,055	40,701	41,269	42,901
Durable goods manufacturing................................	47,807	48,285	50,970	49,978	50,886	53,290	55,125
Nondurable goods manufacturing..........................	34,881	35,516	35,907	36,364	36,988	37,089	38,544
Wholesale trade	48,009	48,192	49,750	51,348	52,585	54,236	55,799
Retail trade..	27,261	28,174	28,181	28,370	28,806	29,672	30,298
Transportation and warehousing...........................	40,848	42,035	43,518	44,751	46,384	48,220	50,676
Information	55,782	55,598	57,609	58,690	58,683	62,012	63,690
Finance and insurance	56,832	58,163	60,297	63,154	64,473	65,680	69,152
Real estate and rental and leasing........................	39,832	41,295	42,536	44,034	46,226	46,975	49,916
Professional, scientific, and technical services	62,075	63,147	63,535	65,854	66,763	68,329	69,868
Management of companies and enterprises..................	71,182	76,773	79,844	83,712	82,657	84,337	86,732
Administrative and waste services.........................	30,159	30,277	29,706	30,841	31,051	31,587	32,912
Educational services	32,304	32,971	33,631	34,032	34,599	34,871	35,221
Health care and social assistance.........................	45,247	45,564	46,663	47,926	48,290	49,734	51,501
Arts, entertainment, and recreation.......................	29,148	27,936	27,177	27,529	28,600	30,024	30,154
Accommodation and food services........................	28,357	29,403	30,461	31,808	32,581	33,742	35,376
Other services, except public administration..................	30,761	32,341	32,763	33,387	34,101	34,784	36,139
Government and government enterprises	52,189	52,257	53,868	54,306	54,164	56,191	57,241

Table HI-10. Employment Characteristics by Family Type

(Number, percent.)

Family type and labor force status	2013		2014		2015	
	Total	Families with own children under 18 years	Total	Families with own children under 18 years	Total	Families with own children under 18 years
All Families..	311,203	120,365	312,380	122,610	309,386	115,039
FAMILY TYPE AND LABOR FORCE STATUS						
Married-Couple Families...............................	235,190	91,038	230,278	89,744	232,451	87,488
Both husband and wife in labor force................	53.8	66.8	51.1	64.3	51.2	64.8
Husband in labor force, wife not in labor force........	21.0	28.8	21.9	28.9	22.0	29.6
Wife in labor force, husband not in labor force........	7.8	3.1	9.7	4.5	8.3	4.1
Both husband and wife not in labor force.............	17.1	1.1	17.3	2.3	17.6	1.3
Other Families	76,013	29,327	82,102	32,866	76,935	27,551
Female householder, no husband present.............	69.7	70.0	68.1	70.9	67.7	68.8
In labor force...	44.3	57.1	44.4	58.4	41.6	56.8
Not in labor force......................................	25.4	12.9	23.7	12.5	26.1	12.0
Male householder, no wife present....................	30.3	30.0	31.9	29.1	32.3	31.2
In labor force...	21.7	26.3	22.1	25.9	23.1	27.7
Not in labor force......................................	8.6	3.7	9.8	3.2	9.2	3.5

Table HI-11. School Enrollment and Educational Attainment, 2015

(Number, percent.)

Item	State	U.S.
Enrollment		
Total population 3 years and over, enrolled in school	330,445	81,618,288
Enrolled in nursery school or preschool (percent)	6.8	6.0
Enrolled in kindergarten (percent)	4.4	5.0
Enrolled in elementary school, grades 1-8 (percent)......................	39.5	40.3
Enrolled in high school, grades 9-12 (percent)............................	19.8	20.9
Enrolled in college or graduate school (percent)..........................	29.5	27.7
Attainment		
Total population 25 years and over	985,914	216,447,163
Less than ninth grade (percent)	4.1	5.5
9th to 12th grade, no diploma (percent)	5.1	7.3
High school graduate, including equivalency (percent).....................	27.1	27.6
Some college, no degree (percent)	21.6	20.7
Associate's degree (percent)...	10.7	8.2
Bachelor's degree (percent)	20.8	19.0
Graduate or professional degree (percent).................................	10.6	11.6
High school graduate or higher (percent)..................................	90.9	87.1
Bachelor's degree or higher (percent).....................................	31.4	30.6

Table HI-12. Public School Characteristics and Educational Indicators

(Number, percent; data derived from National Center of Education Statistics.)

Item	State	U.S.
Public Schools, 2014–2015 (except where noted)		
Number of school districts...	1	18,260
Number of schools..	289	98,373
Number of students...	182,384	50,312,581
Number of teachers...	11,663	3,132,351
Student-teacher ratio...	15.6	16.1
Expenditures per student (dollars), FY 2014.............................	12,400	11,066
Four-year adjusted cohort graduation rate (ACGR)[1,2]	81.6	83.2
Students eligible for free or reduced-price lunch (percent)	50.1	51.8
English language learners (percent)......................................	7.9	9.4
Students age 3 to 21 served under IDEA, part B (percent)................	10.5	13.0

Public Schools by Type	Number	Percent of state public schools
Total number of schools...	289	100.0
Regular	287	99.3
Special education	1	0.3
Vocational education	0	-
Alternative education...	1	0.3

NOTE: Every school is assigned only one school type based on its instructional emphasis.
[1] ACGR data represents a new method of calculating high-school completion rates and may not be comparable to previous years' data for Averaged Freshmen Graduation Rates (AFGR).
[2] The United States 4-year ACGRs were estimated using both the reported 4-year ACGR data from 49 states and the District of Columbia and using imputed data for Idaho. The estimate for American Indian/Alaska Native students also includes imputed data for Virginia.

Table HI-13. Reported Voting and Registration of the Voting-Age Population, November 2016

(Numbers in thousands, percent.)

Item	Total population	Total citizen population	Registered			Voted		
			Total registered	Percent registered (total population)	Percent registered (total citizen population)	Total voted	Percent voted (total population)	Percent voted (total citizen population)
U.S. Total	245,502	224,059	157,596	64.2	70.3	137,537	56.0	61.4
State Total.............................	1,064	974	530	49.8	54.4	460	43.3	47.3
Sex								
Male	519	476	249	48.0	52.3	215	41.5	45.2
Female	545	498	281	51.6	56.5	245	45.0	49.3
Race								
White alone............................	225	220	144	63.9	65.4	129	57.4	58.7
White, non-Hispanic alone	209	205	138	66.3	67.5	126	60.2	61.3
Black alone............................	24	24	16	(B)	(B)	15	(B)	(B)
Asian alone	492	417	206	41.8	49.3	182	37.0	43.6
Hispanic (of any race)	78	74	43	(B)	(B)	36	(B)	(B)
White alone or in combination	368	361	229	62.2	63.2	197	53.6	54.6
Black alone or in combination..........	31	30	19	(B)	(B)	17	(B)	(B)
Asian alone or in combination........	624	548	281	45.0	51.2	246	39.4	44.8
Age								
18 to 24 years..........................	115	108	38	33.4	35.6	23	20.4	21.7
25 to 34 years..........................	198	178	76	38.5	42.8	61	30.8	34.3
35 to 44 years..........................	161	148	79	49.3	53.6	69	42.8	46.6
45 to 64 years..........................	366	333	200	54.6	60.1	182	49.7	54.6
65 years and over	224	207	136	60.8	65.7	125	55.8	60.3

B = Base is less than 75,000 and therefore too small to show the derived measure.

Table HI-14. Crime

(Number, rate per 100,000. Data are derived from the FBI Uniform Crime Reports.)

Item	State			U.S. [1,2,3,4]		
	2014	2015	Percent change	2014	2015	Percent change
TOTAL POPULATION[5]	1,420,257	1,431,603	0.8	318,907,401	321,418,820	0.8
VIOLENT CRIME						
Number....................................	3,362	4,201	25.0	1,186,185	1,231,566	3.8
Rate	236.7	293.4	24.0	372.0	383.2	3.0
Murder and Nonnegligent Manslaughter						
Number....................................	20	19	-5.0	14,164	15,696	10.8
Rate	1.4	1.3	-5.8	4.4	4.9	10.0
Rape[6]						
Number....................................	548	561	2.4	118,027	124,047	5.1
Rate	38.6	39.2	1.6	37.0	38.6	4.3
Robbery						
Number....................................	952	1,203	26.4	322,905	327,374	1.4
Rate	67.0	84.0	25.4	101.3	101.9	0.6
Aggravated Assault						
Number....................................	1,842	2,418	31.3	731,089	764,449	4.6
Rate	129.7	168.9	30.2	229.2	237.8	3.7
PROPERTY CRIME						
Number....................................	46,022	54,346	18.1	8,209,010	7,993,631	-2.6
Rate	3,240.4	3,796.2	17.2	2,574.1	2,487.0	-3.4
Burglary						
Number....................................	7,470	6,557	-12.2	1,713,153	1,579,527	-7.8
Rate	526.0	458.0	-12.9	537.2	491.4	-8.5
Larceny-Theft						
Number....................................	33,003	42,010	27.3	5,809,054	5,706,346	-1.8
Rate	2,323.7	2,934.5	26.3	1,821.5	1,775.4	-2.5
Motor Vehicle Theft						
Number....................................	5,549	5,779	4.1	686,803	707,758	3.1
Rate	390.7	403.7	3.3	215.4	220.2	2.2

NOTE: Although arson data are included in the trend and clearance tables, sufficient data are not available to estimate totals for this offense. Therefore, no arson data are published in this table.
X = Not applicable.
- = Zero or rounds to zero.
[1] The crime figures have been adjusted.
[2] The data collection methodology for the offense of forcible rape used by the Minnesota state Uniform Crime Reporting (UCR) Program (with the exception of Minneapolis and St. Paul, Minnesota) does not comply with national UCR Program guidelines. Consequently, its figures for forcible rape and violent crime (of which forcible rape is a part) are not published in this table.
[3] Includes offenses reported by the Zoological Police and the Metro Transit Police.
[4] Because of changes in the state's reporting practices, figures are not comparable to previous years' data.
[5] Populations are U.S. Census Bureau provisional estimates as of July 1 of each year.
[6] The figures shown for the offense of rape were estimated using the revised Uniform Crime Reporting (UCR) definition of rape.

Table HI-15. State Government Finances, 2015

(Dollar amounts in thousands, percent distribution.)

Item	Dollars	Percent distribution
Total Revenue	13,065,465	100.0
General revenue	11,813,718	90.4
Intergovernmental revenue	2,697,519	20.6
Taxes	6,485,563	49.6
General sales	2,992,707	22.9
Selective sales	1,089,489	8.3
License taxes	252,431	1.9
Individual income tax	1,987,915	15.2
Corporate income tax	72,249	0.6
Other taxes	90,772	0.7
Current charges	1,715,453	13.1
Miscellaneous general revenue	915,183	7.0
Utility revenue	0	-
Liquor stores revenue	0	-
Insurance trust revenue[1]	1,251,747	9.6
Total Expenditure	12,337,211	100.0
Intergovernmental expenditure	267,863	2.2
Direct expenditure	12,069,348	97.8
Current operation	9,256,124	75.0
Capital outlay	1,004,240	8.1
Insurance benefits and repayments	1,281,912	10.4
Assistance and subsidies	183,559	1.5
Interest on debt	343,513	2.8
Exhibit: Salaries and wages	3,165,370	25.7
Total Expenditure	12,337,211	100.0
General expenditure	11,047,776	89.5
Intergovernmental expenditure	267,863	2.2
Direct expenditure	10,779,913	87.4
General expenditure, by function:		
Education	3,232,483	26.2
Public welfare	2,480,019	20.1
Hospitals	870,397	7.1
Health	538,736	4.4
Highways	549,795	4.5
Police protection	38,254	0.3
Correction	217,301	1.8
Natural resources	136,924	1.1
Parks and recreation	99,041	0.8
Governmental administration	487,579	4.0
Interest on general debt	343,513	2.8
Other and unallocable	2,053,734	16.6
Utility expenditure	7,523	0.1
Liquor stores expenditure	0	-
Insurance trust expenditure	1,281,912	10.4
Debt at End of Fiscal Year	8,757,730	X
Cash and Security Holdings	20,516,627	X

X = Not applicable.
- = Zero or rounds to zero.
[1] Within insurance trust revenue, net earnings of state retirement systems is a calculated statistic (the item code in the data file is X08), and thus can be positive or negative. Net earnings is the sum of earnings on investments plus gains on investments minus losses on investments. The change made in 2002 for asset valuation from book to market value in accordance with Statement 34 of the Governmental Accounting Standards Board is reflected in the calculated statistics.

Table HI-16. State Government Tax Collections, 2016

(Dollars in thousands, percent.)

Item	Dollars	Percent distribution
Total Taxes	6,919,035	100.0
Property taxes	0	-
Sales and gross receipts	4,315,902	62.4
General sales and gross receipts	3,206,154	46.3
Selective sales and gross receipts	1,109,748	16.0
Alcoholic beverages	50,590	0.7
Amusements	0	-
Insurance premiums	157,900	2.3
Motor fuels	92,591	1.3
Pari-mutuels	0	-
Public utilities	152,760	2.2
Tobacco products	124,890	1.8
Other selective sales	531,017	7.7
Licenses	263,130	3.8
Alcoholic beverages	0	-
Amusements	0	-
Corporations in general	1,765	-
Hunting and fishing	599	-
Motor vehicle	186,742	2.7
Motor vehicle operators	349	-
Public utilities	20,804	0.3
Occupation and business, NEC	41,566	0.6
Other licenses	11,305	0.2
Income taxes	2,224,299	32.1
Individual income	2,116,130	30.6
Corporation net income	108,169	1.6
Other taxes	115,704	1.7
Death and gift	49,613	0.7
Documentary and stock transfer	66,091	1.0
Severance	0	-
Taxes, NEC	0	-

X = Not applicable.
- = Zero or rounds to zero.

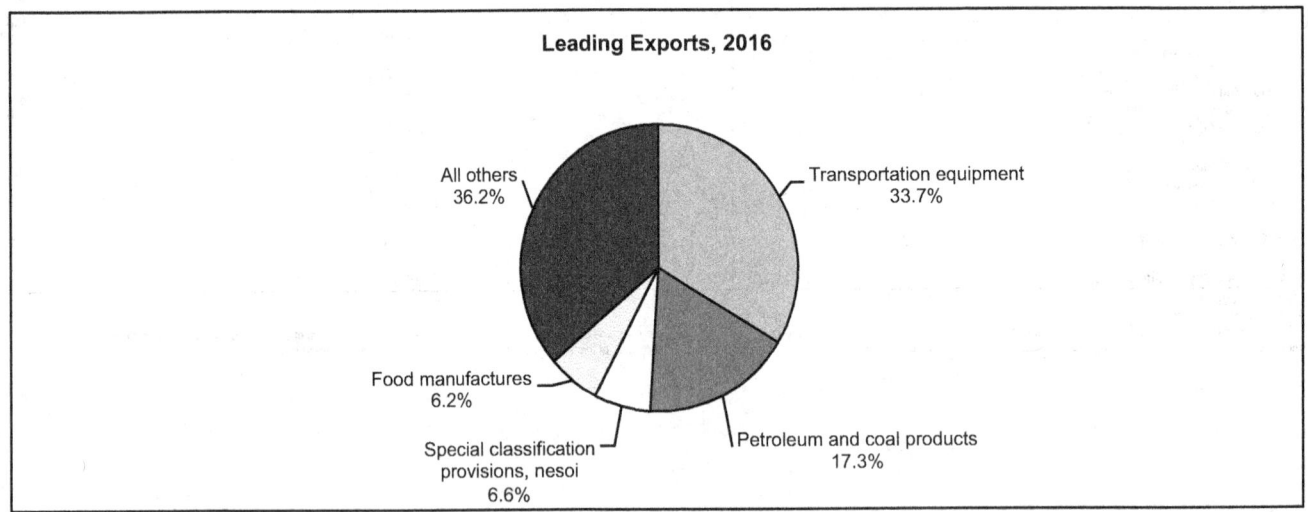

Leading Exports, 2016

- All others 36.2%
- Transportation equipment 33.7%
- Petroleum and coal products 17.3%
- Special classification provisions, nesoi 6.6%
- Food manufactures 6.2%

Facts and Figures

Location: Northwestern United States; bordered on the N by Canada, on the E by Montana and Wyoming, on the S by Nevada and Utah, and on the W by Washington and Oregon

Area: 83,568 sq. mi. (216,446 sq. km.); rank—14th

Population: 1,683,140 (2016 est.); rank—39th

Principal Cities: capital—Boise; largest—Boise

Statehood: July 3, 1890; 43rd state

U.S. Congress: 2 senators, 2 representatives

State Motto: *Esto perpetua* ("Let it be perpetual")

State Song: "Here We Have Idaho"

State Nickname: The Gem State

Abbreviations: ID

State Symbols: flower—syringa (mock orange); tree—Western white pine; bird—mountain bluebird

At a Glance

- With an increase in population of 7.4 percent, Idaho ranked 10th among the states in growth from 2010 to 2016.

- With 1,743.8 incidents per 100,000 population, Idaho had the 5th lowest property crime rate in the country in 2015.

- Idaho's violent crime rate in 2015 was 215.6 per 100,000 population, compared to 383.2 for the entire nation.

- With 26.0 percent of its population under age 18, Idaho ranked 3rd among the states for the highest percent children in 2016.

- Idaho's unemployment rate was lower than the national average in 2016, coming in at 3.7 percent compared to 4.9 for the entire country.

Table ID-1. Population by Age, Sex, Race, and Hispanic Origin

(Number, percent, except where noted.)

Sex, age, race, and Hispanic origin	2000	2010	2016 [1]	Average annual percent change, 2010–2016
Total Population	1,293,953	1,567,582	1,683,140	0.5
Percent of total U.S. population	0.5	0.5	0.5	X
Sex				
Male	648,660	785,324	843,532	0.5
Female	645,293	782,258	839,608	0.5
Age				
Under 5 years	97,643	121,772	115,289	-0.3
5 to 19 years	316,222	353,509	366,596	0.2
20 to 64 years	734,172	897,633	946,266	0.3
65 years and over	145,916	194,668	254,989	1.9
Median age (years)	33.2	34.6	36.2	0.3
Race and Hispanic Origin				
One race				
White	1,177,304	1,476,097	1,571,098	0.4
Black	5,456	10,950	14,183	1.8
American Indian and Alaska Native	17,645	25,782	29,457	0.9
Asian	11,889	20,034	24,815	1.5
Native Hawaiian or Other Pacific Islander	1,308	2,786	3,514	1.6
Two or more races	25,609	31,933	40,073	1.6
Hispanic (of any race)	101,690	182,424	207,743	0.9

X = Not applicable.
[1] Population figures for 2016 are July 1 estimates. The 2010 estimates are taken from the 2010 Census.

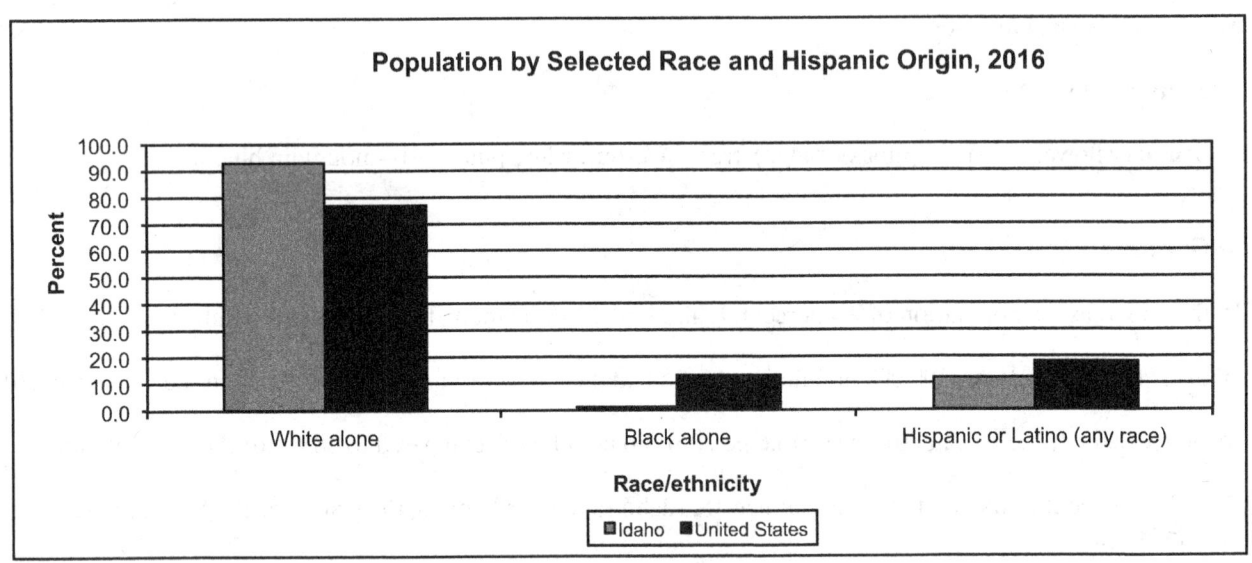

Population by Selected Race and Hispanic Origin, 2016

Table ID-2. Marital Status

(Number, percent distribution.)

Sex, age, race, and Hispanic origin	2000	2010	2015
Males, 15 Years and Over	493,045	602,308	642,880
Never married	26.1	28.3	31.3
Now married, except separated	61.0	57.0	54.4
Separated	1.0	1.4	1.4
Widowed	2.1	2.4	2.2
Divorced	9.9	10.9	10.7
Females, 15 Years and Over	498,579	608,900	651,812
Never married	19.6	22.4	25.5
Now married, except separated	59.0	55.3	52.4
Separated	1.3	1.6	1.4
Widowed	8.6	7.6	7.5
Divorced	11.4	13.1	13.2

Table ID-3. Households and Housing Characteristics

(Number, percent, dollars.)

Item	2000	2010	2015	Average annual percent change, 2000–2015
Total Households...	469,645	576,709	597,421	1.8
Family households...	333,588	401,806	400,347	1.3
Married-couple family..	276,511	322,129	320,853	1.1
Other family..	59,077	79,677	79,494	2.3
Male householder, no wife present............................	18,228	23,583	23,327	1.9
Female householder, no husband present...................	40,849	56,094	56,167	2.5
Nonfamily households...	134,057	174,903	197,074	3.1
Householder living alone...	105,175	139,909	162,423	3.6
Householder not living alone....................................	28,882	34,994	34,651	1.3
Housing Characteristics				
Total housing units..	527,824	668,634	692,482	2.1
Occupied housing units	469,645	576,709	597,421	1.8
Owner occupied..	339,960	401,532	411,958	1.4
Renter occupied...	129,685	175,177	185,463	2.9
Average household size...	2.69	2.67	2.72	0.1
Financial Characteristics				
Median gross rent of renter-occupied housing	515	683	770	3.3
Median monthly owner costs for housing units with a mortgage	887	1,187	1,170	2.1
Median value of owner-occupied housing units	106,300	165,100	176,300	4.4

- = Zero or rounds to zero.

Table ID-4. Migration, Origin, and Language

(Number, percent.)

Characteristic	State			U.S.		
	2014	2015	Percent change	2014	2015	Percent change
Residence 1 Year Ago						
Population 1 year and over	1,613,068	1,635,366	1.4	315,095,393	317,635,720	0.8
Same house	82.8	81.6	X	85.1	85.3	X
Different house in the U.S.	16.8	17.9	X	14.3	14.1	X
Same county	9.2	10.3	X	8.7	8.5	X
Different county	7.6	7.6	X	5.6	5.6	X
Same state	3.6	3.1	X	3.3	3.2	X
Different state	4.0	4.5	X	2.3	2.4	X
Abroad	0.4	0.6	X	0.6	0.7	X
Residence 1 Year Ago						
Native born	1,537,111	1,560,566	1.5	276,465,262	278,128,449	0.6
Male	50.0	50.1	X	49.3	49.3	X
Female	50.0	49.9	X	50.7	50.7	X
Foreign born	97,353	94,364	-3.1	42,391,794	43,290,372	2.1
Male	50.3	48.3	X	48.7	48.6	X
Female	49.7	51.7	X	51.3	51.4	X
Foreign born; naturalized U.S. citizen.........................	35,239	35,909	1.9	19,984,738	20,697,103	3.6
Male	46.0	43.3	X	45.9	45.9	X
Female	54.0	56.7	X	54.1	54.1	X
Foreign born; not a U.S. citizen................................	62,114	58,455	-5.9	22,407,056	22,593,269	0.8
Male	52.7	51.5	X	51.2	51.1	X
Female	47.3	48.5	X	48.8	48.9	X
Entered 2010 or later	11.3	18.7	X	12.3	15.6	X
Entered 2000 to 2009	29.6	24.8	X	28.6	27.9	X
Entered before 2000..	59.0	56.5	X	59.1	56.5	X
World Region of Birth, Foreign						
Foreign-born population, excluding population born at sea	97,353	94,364	-3.1	42,390,705	43,289,646	2.1
Europe	9.8	15.6	X	11.2	11.1	X
Asia..	20.3	19.9	X	30.1	30.6	X
Africa	2.6	2.8	X	4.6	4.8	X
Oceania	0.6	1.2	X	0.6	0.6	X
Latin America	60.8	55.8	X	51.6	51.1	X
North America	6.0	4.7	X	1.9	1.9	X
Language Spoken at Home and Ability to Speak English						
Population 5 years and over......................................	1,522,757	1,543,083	1.3	299,084,046	301,625,014	0.8
English only	89.7	89.8	X	78.9	78.5	X
Language other than English....................................	10.3	10.2	X	21.1	21.5	X
Speaks English less than "very well".........................	4.1	3.7	X	8.6	8.6	X

NA = Not available.
X = Not applicable.
- = Zero or rounds to zero.

Table ID-5. Median Income and Poverty Status, 2015

(Number, percent, except as noted.)

Characteristic	State		U.S.	
	Number	Percent	Number	Percent
Median Income				
Households (dollars)	48,275	X	55,775	X
Families (dollars)	60,081	X	68,260	X
Below Poverty Level (All People)	245,551	15.1	46,153,077	14.7
Sex				
Male	114,198	14.2	20,599,407	13.4
Female	131,353	16.1	25,553,670	16.0
Age				
Under 18 years	75,634	17.8	15,000,273	20.7
Related children under 18 years	73,263	17.4	14,693,239	20.4
18 to 64 years	149,239	15.6	26,960,369	13.9
65 years and over	20,678	8.7	4,192,435	9.0

X = Not applicable.

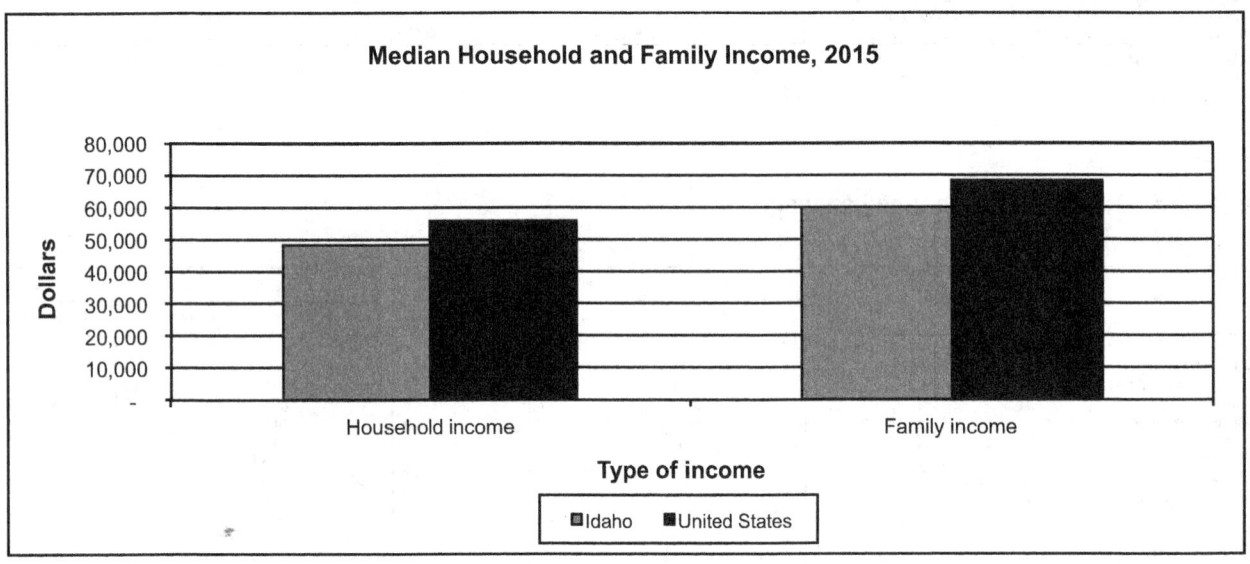

Table ID-6. Health Insurance Coverage Status for the Civilian Noninstitutionalized Population and Children Under 18 Years of Age

(Numbers in thousands, percent.)

Item	2007	2008	2009	2010	2011	2012	2013	2014	2015
Civilian Noninstitutionalized Population	1,501	1,499	1,521	1,552	1,566	1,576	1,592	1,613	1,632
Covered by Private or Public Insurance									
Number	1,292	1,232	1,256	1,276	1,307	1,321	1,335	1,394	1,452
Percent	86.1	82.2	82.6	82.3	83.5	83.8	83.8	86.4	89.0
Not Covered									
Number	209	267	264	275	259	255	257	219	180
Percent	13.9	17.8	17.4	17.7	16.5	16.2	16.2	13.6	11.0
Percent in the U.S. not covered	15.3	15.1	15.1	15.5	15.1	14.8	14.5	11.7	9.4
Children Under 18 Years of Age	415	413	418	428	427	424	426	431	431
Covered by Private or Public Insurance									
Number	369	357	371	383	388	388	388	397	406
Percent	89.0	86.4	88.8	89.5	90.9	91.5	91.1	92.2	94.2
Not Covered									
Number	46	56	47	45	39	36	38	34	25
Percent	11.0	13.6	11.2	10.5	9.1	8.5	8.9	7.8	5.8
Percent in the U.S. not covered	11.0	9.7	8.6	8.0	7.5	7.2	7.1	6.0	4.8

Table ID-7. Employment Status by Demographic Group, 2016

(Numbers in thousands, percent.)

Characteristic	Civilian noninstitutional population	Civilian labor force		Employed		Unemployed	
		Number	Percent of population	Number	Percent of population	Number	Percent of population
Total.................................	1,265	809	63.9	777	61.4	32	3.9
Sex							
Male	625	443	70.8	425	68.1	17	3.9
Female	640	366	57.2	352	55.0	14	3.9
Race, Sex, and Hispanic Origin							
White	1,200	765	63.8	736	61.4	29	3.8
Male	590	418	70.7	402	68.0	16	3.8
Female	609	348	57.1	335	54.9	13	3.7
Black or African American.............................	NA	NA	NA	NA	NA	NA	NA
Male	NA	NA	NA	NA	NA	NA	NA
Female	NA	NA	NA	NA	NA	NA	NA
Hispanic or Latino ethnicity[1]	151	112	74.0	106	70.6	5	4.7
Male	77	64	83.4	62	80.6	2	3.3
Female	74	48	64.3	44	60.2	3	6.4
Age							
16 to 19 years.................	87	36	41.9	32	37.3	4	11.0
20 to 24 years.................	114	88	77.4	84	73.2	5	5.4
25 to 34 years.................	215	179	83.1	172	79.9	7	3.9
35 to 44 years.................	201	167	83.2	163	81.3	4	2.3
45 to 54 years.................	204	171	83.7	165	80.8	6	3.5
55 to 64 years.................	193	124	63.9	119	61.6	4	3.6
65 years and over	252	45	17.7	43	17.0	2	3.8

NOTE: Data in Table 7 are from the Current Population Survey (CPS) and do not match the estimates in Table 8. See notes and definitions for further information.
[1] May be of any race.
NA = Not available.

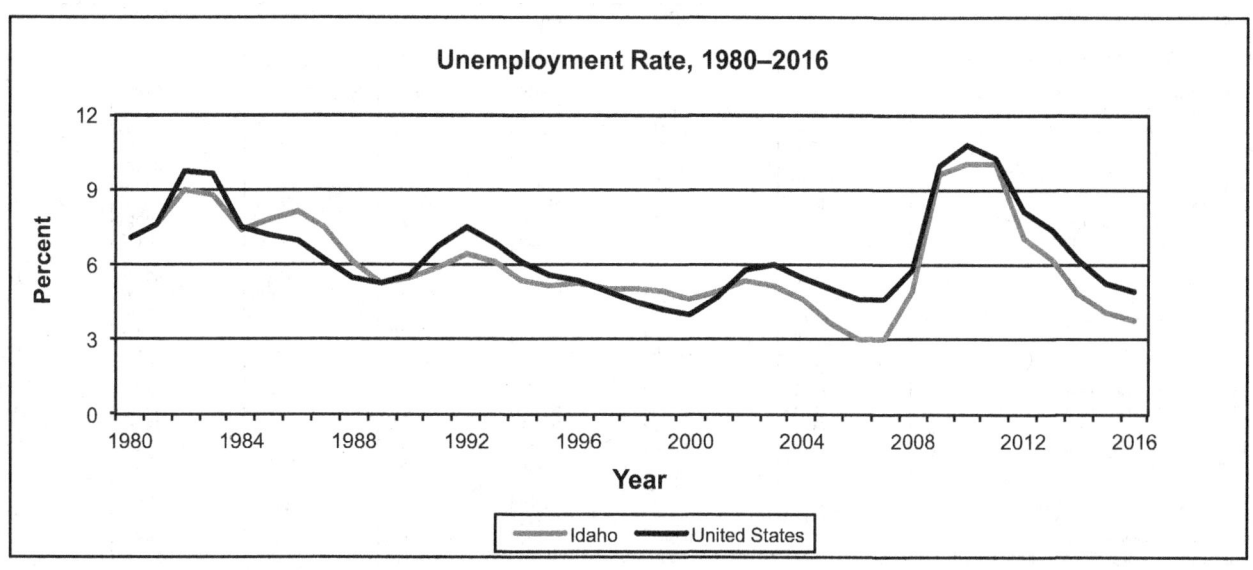

Unemployment Rate, 1980–2016

Table ID-8. Employment Status of the Civilian Noninstitutional Population Age 16 Years and Over

(Number, percent.)

Year	Civilian labor force	Civilian participation rate	Employed	Unemployed	Unemployment rate
2008..........................	755,153	66.6	716,653	38,500	5.1
2009..........................	757,131	65.8	690,722	66,409	8.8
2010..........................	761,056	65.3	692,826	68,230	9.0
2011..........................	765,178	64.9	701,466	63,712	8.3
2012..........................	769,617	64.5	713,981	55,636	7.2
2013..........................	772,513	63.9	724,955	47,558	6.2
2014..........................	781,390	63.6	743,574	37,816	4.8
2015..........................	797,475	63.9	764,463	33,012	4.1
2016..........................	814,571	64.0	783,434	31,137	3.8

Table ID-9. Employment and Average Wages by Industry

(Estimates through 2010 are based on the 2007 *North American Industry Classification System* [NAICS]. Estimates from 2011 onward are based on the 2012 NAICS.)

Industry	2009	2010	2011	2012	2013	2014	2015
				Number of Jobs			
Wage and Salary Employment by Industry..................	652,632	643,274	647,201	652,559	668,126	685,655	702,372
Farm Wage and Salary Employment.........................	14,323	14,489	16,704	16,505	16,402	17,624	17,001
Nonfarm Wage and Salary Employment....................	638,309	628,785	630,497	636,054	651,724	668,031	685,371
Private wage and salary employment.......................	509,438	500,211	503,690	509,535	525,045	540,591	557,077
Forestry, fishing, and related activities......................	7,659	7,821	7,758	7,854	8,202	8,405	8,589
Mining...	2,167	2,273	2,566	2,673	2,547	2,417	2,323
Utilities...	2,098	2,729	2,797	2,826	2,806	2,912	3,013
Construction	36,062	32,295	30,459	30,438	32,688	34,783	37,075
Manufacturing..	55,050	53,345	54,590	56,596	59,235	59,923	61,570
Durable goods manufacturing..............................	31,184	29,941	31,293	32,654	34,026	34,473	35,626
Nondurable goods manufacturing.........................	23,866	23,404	23,297	23,942	25,209	25,450	25,944
Wholesale trade	26,317	25,846	26,302	26,994	28,278	28,751	28,731
Retail trade...	77,553	75,641	75,663	77,087	78,600	80,368	83,463
Transportation and warehousing............................	18,402	18,127	18,374	18,648	18,726	19,437	20,378
Information	10,077	9,684	9,435	9,301	9,236	9,218	9,175
Finance and insurance	21,045	20,916	21,329	21,346	21,751	22,253	22,778
Real estate and rental and leasing.........................	7,518	7,013	6,836	6,698	6,843	6,978	7,309
Professional, scientific, and technical services	33,005	32,585	32,559	31,651	31,261	32,740	34,392
Management of companies and enterprises..................	6,721	5,865	5,874	5,918	5,435	5,480	5,642
Administrative and waste services	36,957	36,351	36,923	37,332	39,831	40,307	40,067
Educational services	10,039	10,375	10,723	11,059	11,166	11,447	11,848
Health care and social assistance.........................	73,382	76,047	77,176	77,871	80,873	83,581	86,183
Arts, entertainment, and recreation........................	8,706	8,642	8,558	9,056	9,342	9,790	9,690
Accommodation and food services	50,610	49,731	50,872	52,020	53,679	56,108	58,545
Other services, except public administration................	26,070	24,925	24,896	24,167	24,546	25,693	26,306
Government and government enterprises.........................	128,871	128,574	126,807	126,519	126,679	127,440	128,294
				Dollars			
Average Wages and Salaries by Industry	34,967	35,714	36,303	37,027	37,828	38,866	39,633
Average Farm Wages and Salaries	40,551	35,256	30,894	35,052	39,817	37,879	35,139
Average Nonfarm Wages and Salaries	34,842	35,724	36,446	37,079	37,778	38,892	39,744
Average private wages and salaries...........................	34,570	35,655	36,525	37,109	37,960	39,200	39,941
Forestry, fishing, and related activities......................	25,549	27,083	28,315	27,887	29,046	30,466	31,764
Mining...	57,861	67,840	69,004	71,415	76,038	76,522	71,355
Utilities...	65,166	73,492	74,966	76,801	78,930	81,007	82,894
Construction	37,487	38,972	39,360	39,975	39,813	40,034	40,758
Manufacturing..	48,113	50,800	51,716	52,014	54,780	59,982	56,947
Durable goods manufacturing..............................	54,396	58,643	58,199	57,967	62,228	69,794	63,609
Nondurable goods manufacturing.........................	39,905	40,766	43,009	43,895	44,728	46,690	47,799
Wholesale trade	45,769	47,305	48,824	49,681	50,896	53,225	56,767
Retail trade...	25,180	25,738	26,163	26,862	27,645	28,730	29,715
Transportation and warehousing............................	36,710	37,514	38,660	40,392	41,012	42,096	42,659
Information	41,868	42,458	44,329	46,949	46,886	48,156	48,791
Finance and insurance	47,376	48,496	49,418	52,464	53,872	55,643	57,892
Real estate and rental and leasing.........................	28,131	28,383	28,681	30,188	31,969	33,946	34,536
Professional, scientific, and technical services	54,645	56,415	58,029	57,115	59,096	59,286	61,372
Management of companies and enterprises..................	78,187	80,751	86,647	89,636	87,249	78,853	78,188
Administrative and waste services	26,033	26,577	26,985	27,048	27,075	27,818	29,579
Educational services	25,447	26,116	26,739	26,861	27,155	27,318	27,763
Health care and social assistance.........................	35,914	36,264	37,434	37,576	38,612	39,595	40,796
Arts, entertainment, and recreation........................	18,440	19,340	18,916	18,812	19,475	19,903	20,646
Accommodation and food services	14,505	14,960	15,284	15,873	16,013	16,613	17,305
Other services, except public administration................	23,525	24,398	24,761	26,061	26,891	27,537	28,529
Government and government enterprises.........................	35,914	35,992	36,132	36,957	37,025	37,587	38,890

Table ID-10. Employment Characteristics by Family Type

(Number, percent.)

Family type and labor force status	2013 Total	2013 Families with own children under 18 years	2014 Total	2014 Families with own children under 18 years	2015 Total	2015 Families with own children under 18 years
All Families...	410,061	190,524	406,767	180,018	400,347	175,338
FAMILY TYPE AND LABOR FORCE STATUS						
Married-Couple Families...............................	324,922	137,775	323,887	131,393	320,853	126,719
Both husband and wife in labor force................	48.9	60.1	48.7	61.0	48.4	62.7
Husband in labor force, wife not in labor force	25.1	34.6	23.9	33.6	23.1	31.9
Wife in labor force, husband not in labor force	7.5	3.2	6.8	3.0	7.2	3.2
Both husband and wife not in labor force...............	18.3	2.0	20.6	2.5	20.9	2.1
Other Families	85,139	52,749	82,880	48,625	79,494	48,619
Female householder, no husband present..................	67.6	67.1	66.7	67.9	70.7	70.7
In labor force...	46.1	53.4	47.8	53.1	49.7	57.6
Not in labor force	21.4	13.7	18.9	14.8	21.0	13.1
Male householder, no wife present........................	32.4	32.9	33.3	32.1	29.3	29.3
In labor force...	26.1	29.5	26.3	29.2	23.7	26.6
Not in labor force	6.4	3.3	7.0	2.9	5.7	2.7

Table ID-11. School Enrollment and Educational Attainment, 2015

(Number, percent.)

Item	State	U.S.
Enrollment		
Total population 3 years and over, enrolled in school	439,310	81,618,288
Enrolled in nursery school or preschool (percent)	4.4	6.0
Enrolled in kindergarten (percent)............................	5.4	5.0
Enrolled in elementary school, grades 1-8 (percent).........	44.8	40.3
Enrolled in high school, grades 9-12 (percent)...............	21.5	20.9
Enrolled in college or graduate school (percent)............	23.9	27.7
Attainment		
Total population 25 years and over	1,065,982	216,447,163
Less than ninth grade (percent)	3.7	5.5
9th to 12th grade, no diploma (percent)	6.3	7.3
High school graduate, including equivalency (percent).......	27.5	27.6
Some college, no degree (percent)	27.0	20.7
Associate's degree (percent)..................................	9.6	8.2
Bachelor's degree (percent)	17.8	19.0
Graduate or professional degree (percent)....................	8.2	11.6
High school graduate or higher (percent)	90.0	87.1
Bachelor's degree or higher (percent)	26.0	30.6

Table ID-12. Public School Characteristics and Educational Indicators

(Number, percent; data derived from National Center of Education Statistics.)

Item	State	U.S.
Public Schools, 2014–2015 (except where noted)		
Number of school districts.....................................	158	18,260
Number of schools...	742	98,373
Number of students..	290,885	50,312,581
Number of teachers	15,609	3,132,351
Student-teacher ratio	18.6	16.1
Expenditures per student (dollars), FY 2014	6,577	11,066
Four-year adjusted cohort graduation rate (ACGR)[1,2]	78.9	83.2
Students eligible for free or reduced-price lunch (percent)	48.5	51.8
English language learners (percent)	4.6	9.4
Students age 3 to 21 served under IDEA, part B (percent)......	9.8	13.0

Public Schools by Type	Number	Percent of state public schools
Total number of schools..	742	100.0
Regular	634	85.4
Special education..	18	2.4
Vocational education	12	1.6
Alternative education..	78	10.5

NOTE: Every school is assigned only one school type based on its instructional emphasis.
[1] ACGR data represents a new method of calculating high-school completion rates and may not be comparable to previous years' data for Averaged Freshmen Graduation Rates (AFGR).
[2] The United States 4-year ACGRs were estimated using both the reported 4-year ACGR data from 49 states and the District of Columbia and using imputed data for Idaho. The estimate for American Indian/Alaska Native students also includes imputed data for Virginia.
NA = Not available.

Table ID-13. Reported Voting and Registration of the Voting-Age Population, November 2016

(Numbers in thousands, percent.)

Item	Total population	Total citizen population	Registered			Voted		
			Total registered	Percent registered (total population)	Percent registered (total citizen population)	Total voted	Percent voted (total population)	Percent voted (total citizen population)
U.S. Total	245,502	224,059	157,596	64.2	70.3	137,537	56.0	61.4
State Total............................	1,224	1,150	790	64.5	68.7	714	58.3	62.1
Sex								
Male	607	571	386	63.5	67.5	346	57.0	60.6
Female	618	579	404	65.4	69.8	368	59.5	63.5
Race								
White alone............................	1,151	1,095	757	65.8	69.1	687	59.7	62.8
White, non-Hispanic alone	1,002	994	711	70.9	71.5	647	64.6	65.1
Black alone.............................	6	5	3	(B)	(B)	2	(B)	(B)
Asian alone	27	12	7	(B)	(B)	6	(B)	(B)
Hispanic (of any race).....................	163	114	55	33.5	48.0	49	29.9	42.9
White alone or in combination	1,175	1,118	770	65.5	68.9	698	59.3	62.4
Black alone or in combination.......	8	7	3	(B)	(B)	2	(B)	(B)
Asian alone or in combination.......	31	14	9	(B)	(B)	8	(B)	(B)
Age								
18 to 24 years............................	166	153	79	47.4	51.7	68	40.7	44.3
25 to 34 years............................	217	198	116	53.5	58.8	102	46.8	51.4
35 to 44 years............................	187	172	109	58.3	63.6	96	51.1	55.7
45 to 64 years............................	381	357	265	69.5	74.1	247	64.8	69.1
65 years and over	272	270	220	80.9	81.5	202	74.1	74.7

- = Zero or rounds to zero.
B = Base is less than 75,000 and therefore too small to show the derived measure.

Table ID-14. Crime

(Number, rate per 100,000. Data are derived from the FBI Uniform Crime Reports.)

Item	State			U.S. [1,2,3,4]		
	2014	2015	Percent change	2014	2015	Percent change
TOTAL POPULATION[5]	1,634,806	1,654,930	1.2	318,907,401	321,418,820	0.8
VIOLENT CRIME						
Number...............................	3,439	3,568	3.8	1,186,185	1,231,566	3.8
Rate	210.4	215.6	2.5	372.0	383.2	3.0
Murder and Nonnegligent Manslaughter						
Number...............................	32	32	0.0	14,164	15,696	10.8
Rate	2.0	1.9	-1.2	4.4	4.9	10.0
Rape[6]						
Number...............................	645	694	7.6	118,027	124,047	5.1
Rate	39.5	41.9	6.3	37.0	38.6	4.3
Robbery						
Number...............................	203	192	-5.4	322,905	327,374	1.4
Rate	12.4	11.6	-6.6	101.3	101.9	0.6
Aggravated Assault						
Number...............................	2,559	2,650	3.6	731,089	764,449	4.6
Rate	156.5	160.1	2.3	229.2	237.8	3.7
PROPERTY CRIME						
Number...............................	30,440	28,858	-5.2	8,209,010	7,993,631	-2.6
Rate	1,862.0	1,743.8	-6.3	2,574.1	2,487.0	-3.4
Burglary						
Number...............................	6,466	6,124	-5.3	1,713,153	1,579,527	-7.8
Rate	395.5	370.0	-6.4	537.2	491.4	-8.5
Larceny-Theft						
Number...............................	22,297	20,863	-6.4	5,809,054	5,706,346	-1.8
Rate	1,363.9	1,260.7	-7.6	1,821.5	1,775.4	-2.5
Motor Vehicle Theft						
Number...............................	1,677	1,871	11.6	686,803	707,758	3.1
Rate	102.6	113.1	10.2	215.4	220.2	2.2

NOTE: Although arson data are included in the trend and clearance tables, sufficient data are not available to estimate totals for this offense. Therefore, no arson data are published in this table.
X = Not applicable.
- = Zero or rounds to zero.
[1] The crime figures have been adjusted.
[2] The data collection methodology for the offense of forcible rape used by the Minnesota state Uniform Crime Reporting (UCR) Program (with the exception of Minneapolis and St. Paul, Minnesota) does not comply with national UCR Program guidelines. Consequently, its figures for forcible rape and violent crime (of which forcible rape is a part) are not published in this table.
[3] Includes offenses reported by the Zoological Police and the Metro Transit Police.
[4] Because of changes in the state's reporting practices, figures are not comparable to previous years' data.
[5] Populations are U.S. Census Bureau provisional estimates as of July 1 of each year.
[6] The figures shown for the offense of rape were estimated using the revised Uniform Crime Reporting (UCR) definition of rape.

Table ID-15. State Government Finances, 2015

(Dollar amounts in thousands, percent distribution.)

Item	Dollars	Percent distribution
Total Revenue	9,346,857	100.0
General revenue	7,925,198	84.8
Intergovernmental revenue	2,590,690	27.7
Taxes	3,976,017	42.5
General sales	1,463,802	15.7
Selective sales	477,478	5.1
License taxes	333,144	3.6
Individual income tax	1,478,368	15.8
Corporate income tax	217,082	2.3
Other taxes	6,143	0.1
Current charges	849,259	9.1
Miscellaneous general revenue	509,232	5.4
Utility revenue	0	-
Liquor stores revenue	145,953	1.6
Insurance trust revenue[1]	1,275,706	13.6
Total Expenditure	8,873,870	100.0
Intergovernmental expenditure	2,156,220	24.3
Direct expenditure	6,717,650	75.7
Current operation	4,860,097	54.8
Capital outlay	525,699	5.9
Insurance benefits and repayments	1,047,415	11.8
Assistance and subsidies	137,767	1.6
Interest on debt	146,672	1.7
Exhibit: Salaries and wages	1,322,544	14.9
Total Expenditure	8,873,870	100.0
General expenditure	7,713,895	86.9
Intergovernmental expenditure	2,156,220	24.3
Direct expenditure	5,557,675	62.6
General expenditure, by function:		
Education	2,817,674	31.8
Public welfare	2,304,073	26.0
Hospitals	53,417	0.6
Health	174,727	2.0
Highways	710,207	8.0
Police protection	58,108	0.7
Correction	273,000	3.1
Natural resources	240,186	2.7
Parks and recreation	35,345	0.4
Governmental administration	324,366	3.7
Interest on general debt	146,672	1.7
Other and unallocable	576,120	6.5
Utility expenditure	0	-
Liquor stores expenditure	112,560	1.3
Insurance trust expenditure	1,047,415	11.8
Debt at End of Fiscal Year	3,685,377	X
Cash and Security Holdings	23,151,748	X

X = Not applicable.
- = Zero or rounds to zero.
[1] Within insurance trust revenue, net earnings of state retirement systems is a calculated statistic (the item code in the data file is X08), and thus can be positive or negative. Net earnings is the sum of earnings on investments plus gains on investments minus losses on investments. The change made in 2002 for asset valuation from book to market value in accordance with Statement 34 of the Governmental Accounting Standards Board is reflected in the calculated statistics.

Table ID-16. State Government Tax Collections, 2016

(Dollars in thousands, percent.)

Item	Dollars	Percent distribution
Total Taxes	4,209,514	100.0
Property taxes..	0	-
Sales and gross receipts	2,121,094	50.4
General sales and gross receipts	1,559,332	37.0
Selective sales and gross receipts	561,762	13.3
Alcoholic beverages...	9,235	0.2
Amusements..	0	-
Insurance premiums..	87,727	2.1
Motor fuels	337,335	8.0
Pari-mutuels	3,666	0.1
Public utilities	1,876	-
Tobacco products..	50,574	1.2
Other selective sales	71,349	1.7
Licenses...	372,883	8.9
Alcoholic beverages...	1,662	-
Amusements..	289	-
Corporations in general.....................................	2,502	0.1
Hunting and fishing...	39,984	0.9
Motor vehicle..	177,260	4.2
Motor vehicle operators	11,187	0.3
Public utilities	57,166	1.4
Occupation and business, NEC	79,026	1.9
Other licenses	3,807	0.1
Income taxes..	1,710,234	40.6
Individual income..	1,521,238	36.1
Corporation net income	188,996	4.5
Other taxes..	5,303	0.1
Death and gift..	0	-
Documentary and stock transfer	0	-
Severance	5,303	0.1
Taxes, NEC	0	-

X = Not applicable.
- = Zero or rounds to zero.

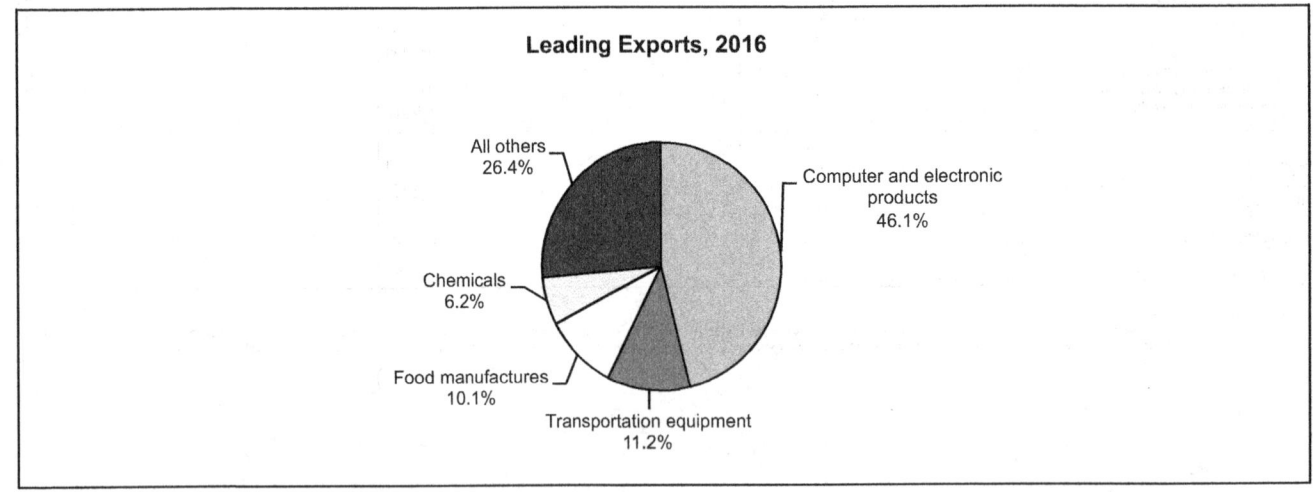

Leading Exports, 2016

All others 26.4%

Computer and electronic products 46.1%

Chemicals 6.2%

Food manufactures 10.1%

Transportation equipment 11.2%

Facts and Figures

Location: North central United States; bordered on the N by Wisconsin, on the E by Lake Michigan and Indiana, on the S by Kentucky, and on the W by Iowa and Missouri

Area: 57,913 sq. mi. (149,998 sq. km.); rank—25th

Population: 12,801,539 (2016 est.); rank—5th

Principal Cities: capital—Springfield; largest—Chicago

Statehood: December 3, 1818; 21st state

U.S. Congress: 2 senators, 18 representatives

State Motto: State Sovereignty, National Union

State Song: "Illinois"

State Nicknames: The Prairie State; The Land of Lincoln

Abbreviations: IL; Ill.

State Symbols: flower—native violet; tree—white oak; bird—cardinal

At a Glance

- Illinois was one of three states that experienced a population decline between 2010 and 2016, with a decrease in population of 0.2 percent.

- In 2015, Illinois employed 9.7 state government employees per 1,000 residents, which was the third lowest ratio in the country.

- The violent crime rate in Illinois in 2015 was 383.8 per 100,000 population, which was almost the same as the U.S. rate of 383.2 per 100,000 population.

- Illinois ranked 19th for median household income in 2015, with an income of $59,588.

- In 2015, 7.1 percent of Illinois residents did not have health insurance, compared to 9.4 percent of the entire U.S. population.

Table IL-1. Population by Age, Sex, Race, and Hispanic Origin

(Number, percent, except where noted.)

Sex, age, race, and Hispanic origin	2000	2010	2016 [1]	Average annual percent change, 2010–2016
Total Population......................................	12,419,293	12,830,632	12,801,539	-
Percent of total U.S. population	4.4	4.2	4.0	X
Sex				
Male...	6,080,336	6,292,276	6,291,791	-
Female	6,338,957	6,538,356	6,509,748	-
Age				
Under 5 years............................	876,549	835,557	772,511	-0.5
5 to 19 years............................	2,728,957	2,660,945	2,484,034	-0.4
20 to 64 years............................	7,313,762	7,724,917	7,673,730	-
65 years and over............................	1,500,025	1,609,213	1,871,264	1.0
Median age (years)	34.7	36.6	37.8	0.2
Race and Hispanic Origin				
One race..				
White	9,125,471	10,030,587	9,885,382	-0.1
Black..	1,878,875	1,903,458	1,877,776	-0.1
American Indian and Alaska Native	31,006	73,486	75,564	0.2
Asian..	423,603	604,399	708,794	1.1
Native Hawaiian or Other Pacific Islander	4,610	7,436	8,276	0.7
Two or more races............................	235,016	210,906	245,747	1.0
Hispanic (of any race)............................	1,530,262	2,073,054	2,181,439	0.3

X = Not applicable.
[1] Population figures for 2016 are July 1 estimates. The 2010 estimates are taken from the 2010 Census.
- = Zero or rounds to zero.

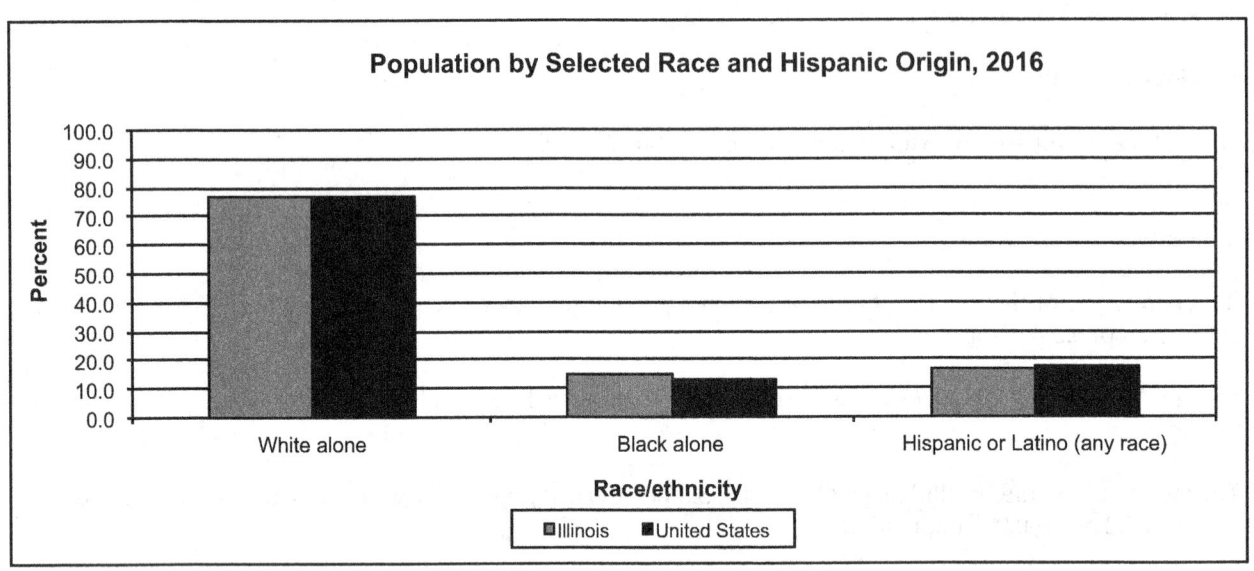

Table IL-2. Marital Status

(Number, percent distribution.)

Sex, age, race, and Hispanic origin	2000	2010	2015
Males, 15 Years and Over	4,685,982	4,977,964	5,063,925
Never married	31.9	37.2	38.3
Now married, except separated...................................	56.1	50.0	49.2
Separated..	1.6	1.4	1.4
Widowed..	2.5	2.6	2.5
Divorced..	7.9	8.8	8.5
Females, 15 Years and Over	5,021,855	5,289,803	5,348,903
Never married	26.1	31.1	32.8
Now married, except separated...................................	51.3	46.3	45.6
Separated..	2.0	2.1	1.9
Widowed..	10.7	9.5	8.8
Divorced..	9.9	11.0	10.8

Table IL-3. Households and Housing Characteristics

(Number, percent, dollars.)

Item	2000	2010	2015	Average annual percent change, 2000–2015
Total Households...	4,591,779	4,752,857	4,794,523	0.3
Family households...	3,105,513	3,133,813	3,099,463	-
Married-couple family.................................	2,353,892	2,301,009	2,285,540	-0.2
Other family...	751,621	832,804	813,923	0.6
Male householder, no wife present.............	187,903	220,197	213,962	0.9
Female householder, no husband present......	563,718	612,607	599,961	0.4
Nonfamily households.......................................	1,486,266	1,619,044	1,695,060	0.9
Householder living alone..............................	1,229,807	1,340,394	1,409,297	1.0
Householder not living alone........................	256,459	278,650	285,763	0.8
Housing Characteristics				
Total housing units..	4,885,615	5,297,077	5,317,618	0.6
Occupied housing units	4,591,779	4,752,857	4,794,523	0.3
Owner occupied...	3,088,884	3,219,338	3,129,641	0.1
Renter occupied...	1,502,895	1,533,519	1,664,882	0.7
Average household size.......................................	2.63	2.64	2.62	-
Financial Characteristics				
Median gross rent of renter-occupied housing	605	848	936	3.6
Median monthly owner costs for housing units with a mortgage	1,198	1,655	1,588	2.2
Median value of owner-occupied housing units.............	130,800	191,800	180,300	2.5

- = Zero or rounds to zero.

Table IL-4. Migration, Origin, and Language

(Number, percent.)

Characteristic	State			U.S.		
	2014	2015	Percent change	2014	2015	Percent change
Residence 1 Year Ago						
Population 1 year and over	12,730,206	12,706,393	-0.2	315,095,393	317,635,720	0.8
Same house	86.6	86.8	X	85.1	85.3	X
Different house in the U.S.	12.9	12.7	X	14.3	14.1	X
Same county	8.6	8.4	X	8.7	8.5	X
Different county	4.3	4.2	X	5.6	5.6	X
Same state	2.7	2.6	X	3.3	3.2	X
Different state	1.6	1.7	X	2.3	2.4	X
Abroad	0.5	0.5	X	0.6	0.7	X
Place of Birth						
Native born	11,096,177	11,033,839	-0.6	276,465,262	278,128,449	0.6
Male	48.9	49.0	X	49.3	49.3	X
Female	51.1	51.0	X	50.7	50.7	X
Foreign born	1,784,403	1,826,156	2.3	42,391,794	43,290,372	2.1
Male	50.1	49.8	X	48.7	48.6	X
Female	49.9	50.2	X	51.3	51.4	X
Foreign born; naturalized U.S. citizen.................	882,032	880,242	-0.2	19,984,738	20,697,103	3.6
Male	47.4	47.6	X	45.9	45.9	X
Female	52.6	52.4	X	54.1	54.1	X
Foreign born; not a U.S. citizen........................	902,371	945,914	4.8	22,407,056	22,593,269	0.8
Male	52.7	51.8	X	51.2	51.1	X
Female	47.3	48.2	X	48.8	48.9	X
Entered 2010 or later	10.0	13.0	X	12.3	15.6	X
Entered 2000 to 2009	26.2	27.4	X	28.6	27.9	X
Entered before 2000..	63.8	59.6	X	59.1	56.5	X
World Region of Birth, Foreign						
Foreign-born population, excluding population born at sea	1,784,403	1,826,156	2.3	42,390,705	43,289,646	2.1
Europe	20.7	20.0	X	11.2	11.1	X
Asia	29.7	29.2	X	30.1	30.6	X
Africa	3.1	4.0	X	4.6	4.8	X
Oceania	0.2	0.2	X	0.6	0.6	X
Latin America	45.3	45.7	X	51.6	51.1	X
North America	1.0	1.0	X	1.9	1.9	X
Language Spoken at Home and Ability to Speak English						
Population 5 years and over................................	12,091,454	12,080,329	-0.1	299,084,046	301,625,014	0.8
English only	77.4	77.0	X	78.9	78.5	X
Language other than English............................	22.6	23.0	X	21.1	21.5	X
Speaks English less than "very well".................	8.9	9.0	X	8.6	8.6	X

NA = Not available.
X = Not applicable.
- = Zero or rounds to zero.

Table IL-5. Median Income and Poverty Status, 2015

(Number, percent, except as noted.)

Characteristic	State		U.S.	
	Number	Percent	Number	Percent
Median Income				
Households (dollars)..	59,588	X	55,775	X
Families (dollars)	73,884	X	68,260	X
Below Poverty Level (All People)	1,703,258	13.6	46,153,077	14.7
Sex				
Male	754,336	12.3	20,599,407	13.4
Female	948,922	14.8	25,553,670	16.0
Age				
Under 18 years...	558,784	19.1	15,000,273	20.7
Related children under 18 years..	548,174	18.9	14,693,239	20.4
18 to 64 years..	995,263	12.6	26,960,369	13.9
65 years and over	149,211	8.5	4,192,435	9.0

X = Not applicable.

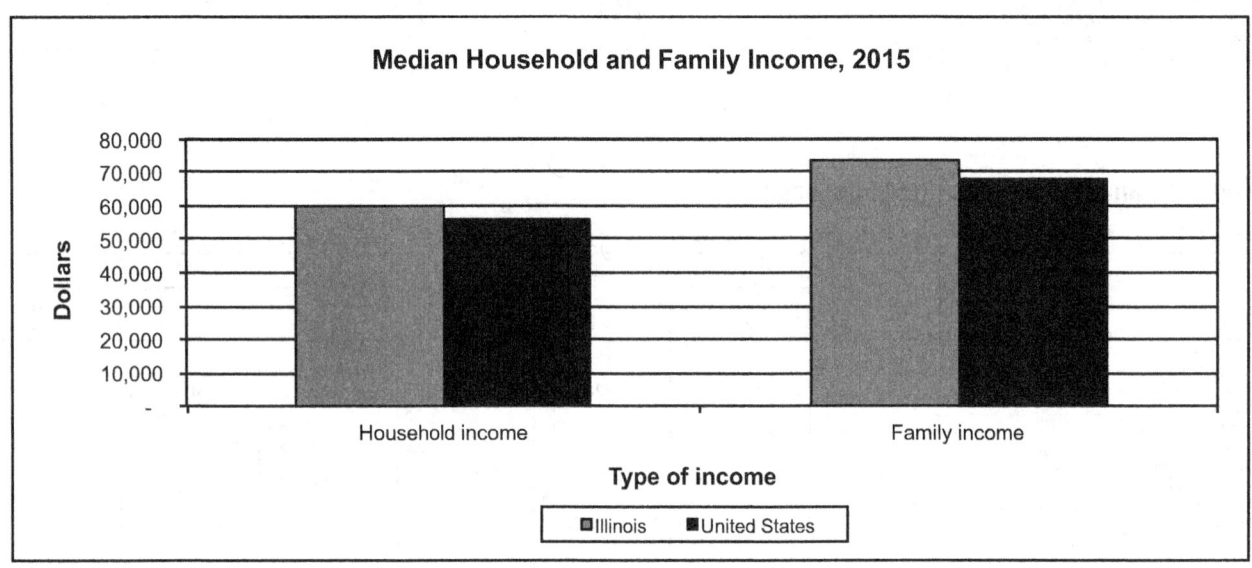

Table IL-6. Health Insurance Coverage Status for the Civilian Noninstitutionalized Population and Children Under 18 Years of Age

(Numbers in thousands, percent.)

Item	2007	2008	2009	2010	2011	2012	2013	2014	2015
Civilian Noninstitutionalized Population	12,688	12,709	12,720	12,673	12,689	12,698	12,705	12,702	12,680
Covered by Private or Public Insurance									
Number...	10,988	11,086	11,025	10,928	11,029	11,076	11,086	11,464	11,780
Percent..	86.6	87.2	86.7	86.2	86.9	87.2	87.3	90.3	92.9
Not Covered									
Number...	1,700	1,623	1,694	1,746	1,659	1,622	1,618	1,238	900
Percent..	13.4	12.8	13.3	13.8	13.1	12.8	12.7	9.7	7.1
Percent in the U.S. not covered............................	15.3	15.1	15.1	15.5	15.1	14.8	14.5	11.7	9.4
Children Under 18 Years of Age	3,180	3,176	3,168	3,122	3,092	3,059	3,018	2,981	2,956
Covered by Private or Public Insurance									
Number...	2,970	2,997	3,026	2,982	2,979	2,958	2,893	2,881	2,881
Percent..	93.4	94.4	95.5	95.5	96.3	96.7	95.8	96.7	97.5
Not Covered									
Number...	210	179	142	140	113	101	125	100	75
Percent..	6.6	5.6	4.5	4.5	3.7	3.3	4.2	3.3	2.5
Percent in the U.S. not covered............................	11.0	9.7	8.6	8.0	7.5	7.2	7.1	6.0	4.8

Table IL-7. Employment Status by Demographic Group, 2016

(Numbers in thousands, percent.)

Characteristic	Civilian noninstitutional population	Civilian labor force		Employed		Unemployed	
		Number	Percent of population	Number	Percent of population	Number	Percent of population
Total.................................	10,079	6,578	65.3	6,192	61.4	386	5.9
Sex							
Male..........................	4,871	3,478	71.4	3,274	67.2	204	5.9
Female	5,209	3,100	59.5	2,919	56.0	182	5.9
Race, Sex, and Hispanic Origin							
White	7,924	5,274	66.6	5,011	63.2	262	5.0
Male......................	3,880	2,835	73.1	2,693	69.4	142	5.0
Female	4,044	2,439	60.3	2,319	57.3	120	4.9
Black or African American..................	1,412	829	58.7	724	51.2	105	12.7
Male......................	627	380	60.7	326	52.0	54	14.2
Female	785	448	57.1	397	50.6	51	11.3
Hispanic or Latino ethnicity[1]	1,481	1,033	69.7	963	65.0	69	6.7
Male......................	734	586	79.9	547	74.5	40	6.8
Female	748	446	59.7	417	55.8	29	6.6
Age							
16 to 19 years	702	250	35.5	201	28.6	49	19.6
20 to 24 years	888	612	68.9	538	60.6	74	12.0
25 to 34 years	1,761	1,473	83.7	1,379	78.3	94	6.4
35 to 44 years	1,547	1,285	83.0	1,230	79.5	55	4.2
45 to 54 years	1,670	1,407	84.2	1,346	80.6	61	4.3
55 to 64 years	1,681	1,164	69.3	1,120	66.6	45	3.8
65 years and over	1,831	389	21.2	378	20.7	11	2.7

NOTE: Data in Table 7 are from the Current Population Survey (CPS) and do not match the estimates in Table 8. See notes and definitions for further information.
[1] May be of any race.

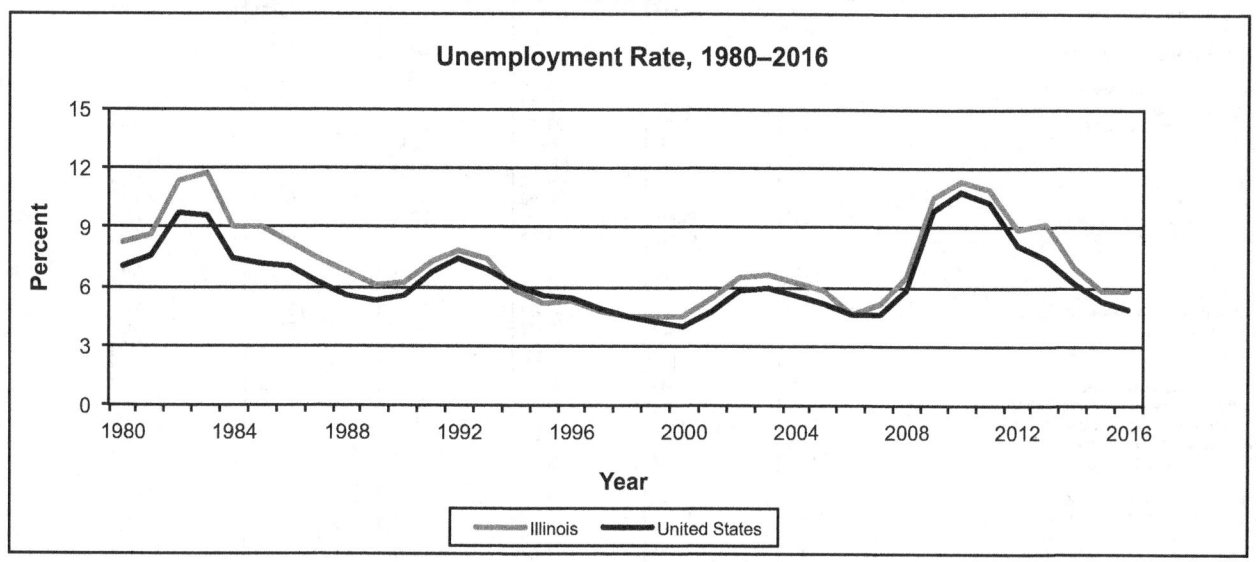

Unemployment Rate, 1980–2016

Table IL-8. Employment Status of the Civilian Noninstitutional Population Age 16 Years and Over

(Number, percent.)

Year	Civilian labor force	Civilian participation rate	Employed	Unemployed	Unemployment rate
2008............	6,657,227	67.8	6,238,611	418,616	6.3
2009............	6,618,658	67.0	5,943,229	675,429	10.2
2010............	6,625,321	66.9	5,937,047	688,274	10.4
2011............	6,586,893	66.2	5,948,366	638,527	9.7
2012............	6,584,691	65.9	5,993,148	591,543	9.0
2013............	6,561,142	65.5	5,964,580	596,562	9.1
2014............	6,515,198	64.8	6,053,884	461,314	7.1
2015............	6,512,386	64.7	6,126,307	386,079	5.9
2016............	6,539,008	65.2	6,154,867	384,141	5.9

Table IL-9. Employment and Average Wages by Industry

(Estimates through 2010 are based on the 2007 *North American Industry Classification System* [NAICS]. Estimates from 2011 onward are based on the 2012 NAICS.)

Industry	2009	2010	2011	2012	2013	2014	2015
	Number of Jobs						
Wage and Salary Employment by Industry.................	5,871,718	5,795,826	5,858,922	5,926,484	5,968,301	6,047,821	6,139,938
Farm Wage and Salary Employment.........................	15,410	17,706	16,970	15,801	12,669	11,709	14,742
Nonfarm Wage and Salary Employment....................	5,856,308	5,778,120	5,841,952	5,910,683	5,955,632	6,036,112	6,125,196
Private wage and salary employment........................	4,941,584	4,870,773	4,950,824	5,029,034	5,078,294	5,160,976	5,249,182
Forestry, fishing, and related activities.....................	4,603	4,187	4,305	4,637	4,828	5,940	5,460
Mining..	9,303	9,047	9,498	10,089	9,648	9,860	9,285
Utilities...	23,636	23,182	23,524	23,858	23,795	24,016	24,180
Construction	229,803	205,752	202,070	194,794	196,931	207,330	218,857
Manufacturing...	579,262	561,451	574,733	583,781	580,229	580,253	582,140
Durable goods manufacturing..............................	340,074	329,581	343,627	354,546	350,849	349,854	348,495
Nondurable goods manufacturing.........................	239,188	231,870	231,106	229,235	229,380	230,399	233,645
Wholesale trade	295,091	287,678	290,917	295,669	300,143	301,559	303,215
Retail trade...	606,114	593,731	601,359	602,374	603,976	610,071	619,647
Transportation and warehousing.................................	230,880	229,360	238,197	243,762	244,833	250,554	259,682
Information	106,949	101,711	100,348	100,489	98,983	99,399	101,054
Finance and insurance	298,337	292,989	291,710	294,508	293,630	292,479	300,759
Real estate and rental and leasing............................	78,014	74,360	73,522	73,672	75,540	76,839	78,947
Professional, scientific, and technical services	353,736	348,798	358,053	367,039	379,480	390,983	405,554
Management of companies and enterprises...................	95,285	96,403	98,255	102,790	103,688	103,297	94,759
Administrative and waste services.............................	348,253	364,158	382,452	401,441	412,508	428,650	428,916
Educational services	155,233	158,223	162,030	165,375	166,547	167,059	168,528
Health care and social assistance.............................	690,674	699,865	708,915	720,569	730,867	740,058	757,812
Arts, entertainment, and recreation...........................	78,632	77,506	77,620	79,972	80,931	82,972	85,267
Accommodation and food services.............................	445,295	441,380	448,443	459,908	469,331	477,937	495,503
Other services, except public administration................	312,484	300,992	304,873	304,307	302,406	311,720	309,617
Government and government enterprises	914,724	907,347	891,128	881,649	877,338	875,136	876,014
	Dollars						
Average Wages and Salaries by Industry	48,849	50,214	51,719	53,124	53,651	55,136	57,037
Average Farm Wages and Salaries	28,911	23,773	31,982	27,940	31,522	36,652	36,745
Average Nonfarm Wages and Salaries	48,902	50,295	51,776	53,191	53,698	55,172	57,086
Average private wages and salaries............................	49,150	50,613	52,178	53,603	54,040	55,695	57,774
Forestry, fishing, and related activities......................	28,771	27,859	28,307	28,371	27,438	30,260	32,698
Mining..	61,565	68,107	66,405	67,927	70,891	74,215	75,831
Utilities...	98,843	98,277	104,545	107,866	106,962	113,082	115,572
Construction	59,643	59,898	60,772	61,298	62,924	65,725	68,697
Manufacturing...	57,538	60,955	62,988	64,772	65,369	67,861	70,347
Durable goods manufacturing..............................	58,537	61,536	64,508	65,749	65,710	67,120	68,409
Nondurable goods manufacturing.........................	56,118	60,129	60,728	63,260	64,848	68,985	73,237
Wholesale trade	66,760	69,330	73,174	75,592	75,662	78,004	80,377
Retail trade...	26,390	27,210	27,773	28,484	28,859	29,263	30,409
Transportation and warehousing.................................	47,229	48,839	50,422	51,983	52,851	54,580	55,882
Information	67,179	68,659	72,819	74,851	77,546	79,787	82,938
Finance and insurance	89,540	91,325	97,207	101,064	99,776	105,519	110,710
Real estate and rental and leasing............................	49,136	51,686	53,536	56,404	58,405	61,017	65,003
Professional, scientific, and technical services	81,142	84,155	86,163	88,889	89,192	91,922	95,756
Management of companies and enterprises...................	107,430	114,260	117,316	121,284	123,511	124,622	129,847
Administrative and waste services.............................	33,789	34,729	34,896	35,554	35,255	36,705	38,879
Educational services	39,986	41,109	42,572	43,244	44,132	45,336	46,182
Health care and social assistance.............................	44,050	44,581	45,333	45,952	46,436	47,402	48,576
Arts, entertainment, and recreation...........................	33,771	34,647	35,643	37,029	36,957	36,451	38,791
Accommodation and food services.............................	18,807	19,335	20,021	20,802	21,150	21,632	22,786
Other services, except public administration................	32,337	33,681	34,527	34,999	35,986	37,579	38,943
Government and government enterprises	47,557	48,593	49,544	50,844	51,720	52,088	52,967

Table IL-10. Employment Characteristics by Family Type

(Number, percent.)

Family type and labor force status	2013		2014		2015	
	Total	Families with own children under 18 years	Total	Families with own children under 18 years	Total	Families with own children under 18 years
All Families..	3,128,369	1,383,676	3,086,335	1,350,738	3,099,463	1,348,476
FAMILY TYPE AND LABOR FORCE STATUS						
Married-Couple Families.................................	2,299,644	950,188	2,256,449	926,959	2,285,540	929,523
Both husband and wife in labor force.................	55.1	67.4	54.3	67.1	53.3	66.4
Husband in labor force, wife not in labor force	21.2	27.2	22.1	28.1	22.2	28.6
Wife in labor force, husband not in labor force	7.8	3.8	7.7	3.6	7.6	3.3
Both husband and wife not in labor force..............	15.5	1.4	15.9	1.3	16.2	1.4
Other Families.......................................	828,725	433,488	829,886	423,779	813,923	418,953
Female householder, no husband present..............	73.2	76.4	72.6	76.4	73.7	77.0
In labor force...................................	53.1	65.2	51.9	64.0	53.1	65.5
Not in labor force	20.1	11.1	20.6	12.5	20.6	11.5
Male householder, no wife present....................	26.8	23.6	27.4	23.6	26.3	23.0
In labor force...................................	21.5	21.9	21.6	21.7	20.8	21.5
Not in labor force	5.3	1.7	5.9	1.9	5.5	1.4

Table IL-11. School Enrollment and Educational Attainment, 2015

(Number, percent.)

Item	State	U.S.
Enrollment		
Total population 3 years and over, enrolled in school	3,325,495	81,618,288
Enrolled in nursery school or preschool (percent)	7.0	6.0
Enrolled in kindergarten (percent)	4.8	5.0
Enrolled in elementary school, grades 1-8 (percent)...............................	40.0	40.3
Enrolled in high school, grades 9-12 (percent)	20.9	20.9
Enrolled in college or graduate school (percent)..................................	27.3	27.7
Attainment		
Total population 25 years and over	8,661,938	216,447,163
Less than ninth grade (percent)..	5.3	5.5
9th to 12th grade, no diploma (percent)	6.2	7.3
High school graduate, including equivalency (percent).............................	26.7	27.6
Some college, no degree (percent)..	20.8	20.7
Associate's degree (percent)...	8.1	8.2
Bachelor's degree (percent)..	20.3	19.0
Graduate or professional degree (percent)..	12.7	11.6
High school graduate or higher (percent)	88.6	87.1
Bachelor's degree or higher (percent)..	32.9	30.6

Table IL-12. Public School Characteristics and Educational Indicators

(Number, percent; data derived from National Center of Education Statistics.)

Item	State	U.S.
Public Schools, 2014–2015 (except where noted)		
Number of school districts...	1,066	18,260
Number of schools...	4,201	98,373
Number of students	2,050,239	50,312,581
Number of teachers	132,456	3,132,351
Student-teacher ratio...	15.5	16.1
Expenditures per student (dollars), FY 2014......................................	13,213	11,066
Four-year adjusted cohort graduation rate (ACGR)[1,2]	85.6	83.2
Students eligible for free or reduced-price lunch (percent).......................	54.1	51.8
English language learners (percent)..	10.3	9.4
Students age 3 to 21 served under IDEA, part B (percent)..........................	14.4	13.0

Public Schools by Type	Number	Percent of state public schools
Total number of schools..	4,201	100.0
Regular	3,956	94.2
Special education	106	2.5
Vocational education	0	-
Alternative education..	139	3.3

NOTE: Every school is assigned only one school type based on its instructional emphasis.
[1] ACGR data represents a new method of calculating high-school completion rates and may not be comparable to previous years' data for Averaged Freshmen Graduation Rates (AFGR).
[2] The United States 4-year ACGRs were estimated using both the reported 4-year ACGR data from 49 states and the District of Columbia and using imputed data for Idaho. The estimate for American Indian/Alaska Native students also includes imputed data for Virginia.

Table IL-13. Reported Voting and Registration of the Voting-Age Population, November 2016

(Numbers in thousands, percent.)

Item	Total population	Total citizen population	Registered			Voted		
			Total registered	Percent registered (total population)	Percent registered (total citizen population)	Total voted	Percent voted (total population)	Percent voted (total citizen population)
U.S. Total	245,502	224,059	157,596	64.2	70.3	137,537	56.0	61.4
State Total	9,723	8,970	6,665	68.5	74.3	5,719	58.8	63.8
Sex								
Male	4,692	4,307	3,174	67.7	73.7	2,673	57.0	62.1
Female	5,031	4,663	3,490	69.4	74.9	3,046	60.6	65.3
Race								
White alone	7,647	7,100	5,391	70.5	75.9	4,636	60.6	65.3
White, non-Hispanic alone	6,297	6,153	4,839	76.8	78.6	4,174	66.3	67.8
Black alone	1,358	1,321	932	68.6	70.6	776	57.1	58.7
Asian alone	542	391	231	42.5	58.9	200	37.0	51.3
Hispanic (of any race)	1,490	1,073	634	42.5	59.1	527	35.4	49.2
White alone or in combination	7,711	7,165	5,438	70.5	75.9	4,679	60.7	65.3
Black alone or in combination	1,390	1,353	963	69.3	71.2	807	58.1	59.7
Asian alone or in combination	563	408	244	43.3	59.7	214	37.9	52.4
Age								
18 to 24 years	1,330	1,287	802	60.3	62.3	603	45.3	46.8
25 to 34 years	1,664	1,460	975	58.6	66.8	795	47.8	54.5
35 to 44 years	1,527	1,331	996	65.3	74.8	811	53.1	60.9
45 to 64 years	3,456	3,202	2,539	73.5	79.3	2,272	65.8	71.0
65 years and over	1,746	1,690	1,352	77.4	80.0	1,237	70.9	73.2

Table IL-14. Crime

(Number, rate per 100,000. Data are derived from the FBI Uniform Crime Reports.)

Item	State			U.S. [1,2,3,4]		
	2014	2015	Percent change	2014	2015	Percent change
TOTAL POPULATION[5]	12,882,189	12,859,995	-0.2	318,907,401	321,418,820	0.8
VIOLENT CRIME						
Number	47,775	49,354	3.3	1,186,185	1,231,566	3.8
Rate	370.9	383.8	3.5	372.0	383.2	3.0
Murder and Nonnegligent Manslaughter						
Number	690	744	7.8	14,164	15,696	10.8
Rate	5.4	5.8	8.0	4.4	4.9	10.0
Rape[6]						
Number	4,329	4,821	11.4	118,027	124,047	5.1
Rate	33.6	37.5	11.6	37.0	38.6	4.3
Robbery						
Number	15,271	14,910	-2.4	322,905	327,374	1.4
Rate	118.5	115.9	-2.2	101.3	101.9	0.6
Aggravated Assault						
Number	27,485	28,879	5.1	731,089	764,449	4.6
Rate	213.4	224.6	5.3	229.2	237.8	3.7
PROPERTY CRIME						
Number	269,647	255,729	-5.2	8,209,010	7,993,631	-2.6
Rate	2,093.2	1,988.6	-5.0	2,574.1	2,487.0	-3.4
Burglary						
Number	50,759	46,443	-8.5	1,713,153	1,579,527	-7.8
Rate	394.0	361.1	-8.3	537.2	491.4	-8.5
Larceny-Theft						
Number	201,003	191,634	-4.7	5,809,054	5,706,346	-1.8
Rate	1,560.3	1,490.2	-4.5	1,821.5	1,775.4	-2.5
Motor Vehicle Theft						
Number	17,885	17,652	-1.3	686,803	707,758	3.1
Rate	138.8	137.3	-1.1	215.4	220.2	2.2

NOTE: Although arson data are included in the trend and clearance tables, sufficient data are not available to estimate totals for this offense. Therefore, no arson data are published in this table.
X = Not applicable.
- = Zero or rounds to zero.
[1] The crime figures have been adjusted.
[2] The data collection methodology for the offense of forcible rape used by the Minnesota state Uniform Crime Reporting (UCR) Program (with the exception of Minneapolis and St. Paul, Minnesota) does not comply with national UCR Program guidelines. Consequently, its figures for forcible rape and violent crime (of which forcible rape is a part) are not published in this table.
[3] Includes offenses reported by the Zoological Police and the Metro Transit Police.
[4] Because of changes in the state's reporting practices, figures are not comparable to previous years' data.
[5] Populations are U.S. Census Bureau provisional estimates as of July 1 of each year.
[6] The figures shown for the offense of rape were estimated using the revised Uniform Crime Reporting (UCR) definition of rape.

Table IL-15. State Government Finances, 2015

(Dollar amounts in thousands, percent distribution.)

Item	Dollars	Percent distribution
Total Revenue	83,821,386	100.0
General revenue	69,991,182	83.5
Intergovernmental revenue	19,732,875	23.5
Taxes	40,821,385	48.7
General sales	10,489,152	12.5
Selective sales	7,152,130	8.5
License taxes	2,730,407	3.3
Individual income tax	15,913,816	19.0
Corporate income tax	4,054,267	4.8
Other taxes	481,613	0.6
Current charges	4,977,694	5.9
Miscellaneous general revenue	4,459,228	5.3
Utility revenue	0	-
Liquor stores revenue	0	-
Insurance trust revenue[1]	13,830,204	16.5
Total Expenditure	86,866,779	100.0
Intergovernmental expenditure	18,558,946	21.4
Direct expenditure	68,307,833	78.6
Current operation	39,503,201	45.5
Capital outlay	5,894,966	6.8
Insurance benefits and repayments	18,174,600	20.9
Assistance and subsidies	1,333,844	1.5
Interest on debt	3,401,222	3.9
Exhibit: Salaries and wages	8,260,564	9.5
Total Expenditure	86,866,779	100.0
General expenditure	68,692,179	79.1
Intergovernmental expenditure	18,558,946	21.4
Direct expenditure	50,133,233	57.7
General expenditure, by function:		
Education	17,895,093	20.6
Public welfare	22,671,203	26.1
Hospitals	1,403,131	1.6
Health	2,301,367	2.6
Highways	6,925,080	8.0
Police protection	462,803	0.5
Correction	1,458,695	1.7
Natural resources	306,754	0.4
Parks and recreation	287,312	0.3
Governmental administration	1,475,485	1.7
Interest on general debt	3,401,222	3.9
Other and unallocable	10,104,034	11.6
Utility expenditure	0	-
Liquor stores expenditure	0	-
Insurance trust expenditure	18,174,600	20.9
Debt at End of Fiscal Year	64,221,381	X
Cash and Security Holdings	180,403,562	X

X = Not applicable.
- = Zero or rounds to zero.
[1] Within insurance trust revenue, net earnings of state retirement systems is a calculated statistic (the item code in the data file is X08), and thus can be positive or negative. Net earnings is the sum of earnings on investments plus gains on investments minus losses on investments. The change made in 2002 for asset valuation from book to market value in accordance with Statement 34 of the Governmental Accounting Standards Board is reflected in the calculated statistics.

Table IL-16. State Government Tax Collections, 2016

(Dollars in thousands, percent.)

Item	Dollars	Percent distribution
Total Taxes	38,907,220	100.0
Property taxes	60,814	0.2
Sales and gross receipts	18,524,265	47.6
General sales and gross receipts	11,344,480	29.2
Selective sales and gross receipts	7,179,785	18.5
Alcoholic beverages	287,865	0.7
Amusements	787,519	2.0
Insurance premiums	424,959	1.1
Motor fuels	1,354,039	3.5
Pari-mutuels	6,420	-
Public utilities	1,585,911	4.1
Tobacco products	844,928	2.2
Other selective sales	1,888,144	4.9
Licenses	2,745,949	7.1
Alcoholic beverages	13,097	-
Amusements	15,442	-
Corporations in general	363,019	0.9
Hunting and fishing	40,354	0.1
Motor vehicle	1,695,934	4.4
Motor vehicle operators	116,222	0.3
Public utilities	4,723	-
Occupation and business, NEC	469,273	1.2
Other licenses	27,885	0.1
Income taxes	17,173,986	44.1
Individual income	13,806,525	35.5
Corporation net income	3,367,461	8.7
Other taxes	402,206	1.0
Death and gift	325,230	0.8
Documentary and stock transfer	76,976	0.2
Severance	0	-
Taxes, NEC	0	-

X = Not applicable.
- = Zero or rounds to zero.

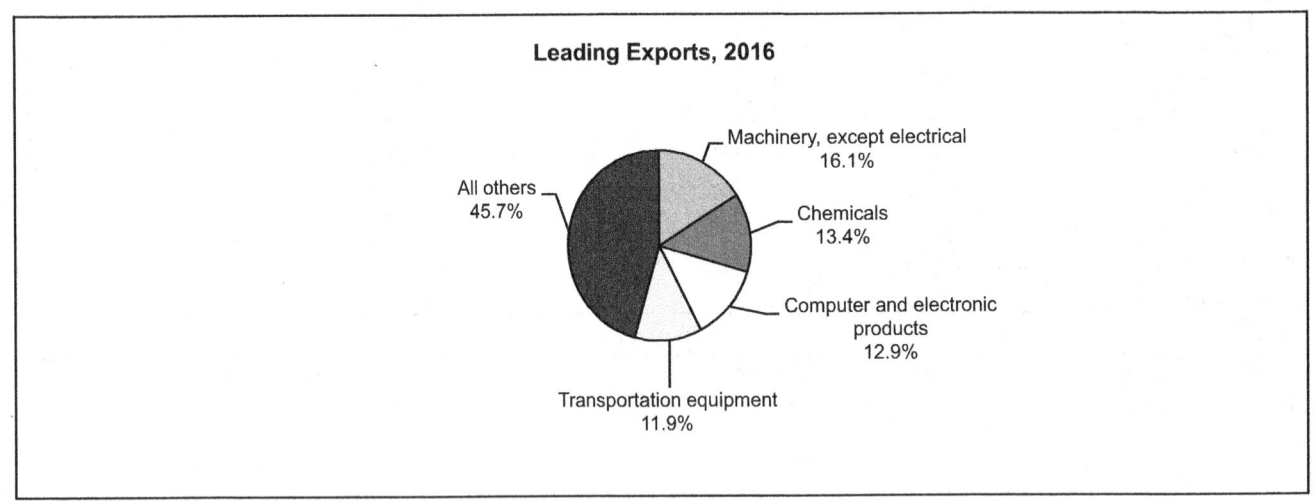

Leading Exports, 2016

Machinery, except electrical 16.1%
Chemicals 13.4%
Computer and electronic products 12.9%
Transportation equipment 11.9%
All others 45.7%

Facts and Figures

Location: East north central United States; bordered on the N by Michigan and Lake Michigan, on the E by Ohio, on the S by Kentucky, and on the W by Illinois

Area: 36,418 sq. mi. (94,321 sq. km.); rank—38th

Population: 6,633,053 (2016 est.); rank—17th

Principal Cities: capital—Indianapolis; largest—Indianapolis

Statehood: December 11, 1816; 19th state

U.S. Congress: 2 senators, 9 representatives

State Motto: The Crossroads of America

State Song: "On the Banks of the Wabash, Far Away"

State Nickname: The Hoosier State

Abbreviations: IN; Ind.

State Symbols: flower—peony; tree—tulip tree; bird—cardinal

At a Glance

- With an increase in population of 2.3 percent, Indiana ranked 32nd among the states in growth from 2010 to 2016.

- Indiana's violent crime rate in 2015 was 387.5 per 100,000 population, compared to 383.2 for the entire nation.

- The property crime rate in Indiana in 2015 was 2,596.0 per 100,000 population, ranking 27th in the nation.

- The median household income in Indiana in 2015 was $50,532, compared to the nationwide median of $55,775.

- Approximately 14.5 percent of all Indianans and 20.9 percent of children under 18 years of age lived in poverty in 2015.

Table IN-1. Population by Age, Sex, Race, and Hispanic Origin

(Number, percent, except where noted.)

Sex, age, race, and Hispanic origin	2000	2010	2016 [1]	Average annual percent change, 2010–2016
Total Population..	6,080,485	6,483,802	6,633,053	0.1
Percent of total U.S. population	2.2	2.1	2.1	X
Sex				
Male..	2,982,474	3,189,737	3,269,562	0.2
Female	3,098,011	3,294,065	3,363,491	0.1
Age				
Under 5 years...	423,215	434,075	421,987	-0.2
5 to 19 years...	1,340,171	1,372,507	1,335,425	-0.2
20 to 64 years...	3,564,268	3,836,112	3,884,078	0.1
65 years and over	752,831	841,108	991,563	1.1
Median age (years)	35.2	37.0	37.6	0.1
Race and Hispanic Origin				
One race..				
White	5,320,022	5,638,833	5,678,630	-
Black	510,034	603,797	641,409	0.4
American Indian and Alaska Native	15,815	24,487	26,875	0.6
Asian...	59,126	105,535	149,209	2.6
Native Hawaiian or Other Pacific Islander	2,005	3,532	4,214	1.2
Two or more races	75,672	107,618	132,716	1.5
Hispanic (of any race)...	214,536	403,234	449,871	0.7

X = Not applicable.
[1] Population figures for 2016 are July 1 estimates. The 2010 estimates are taken from the 2010 Census.

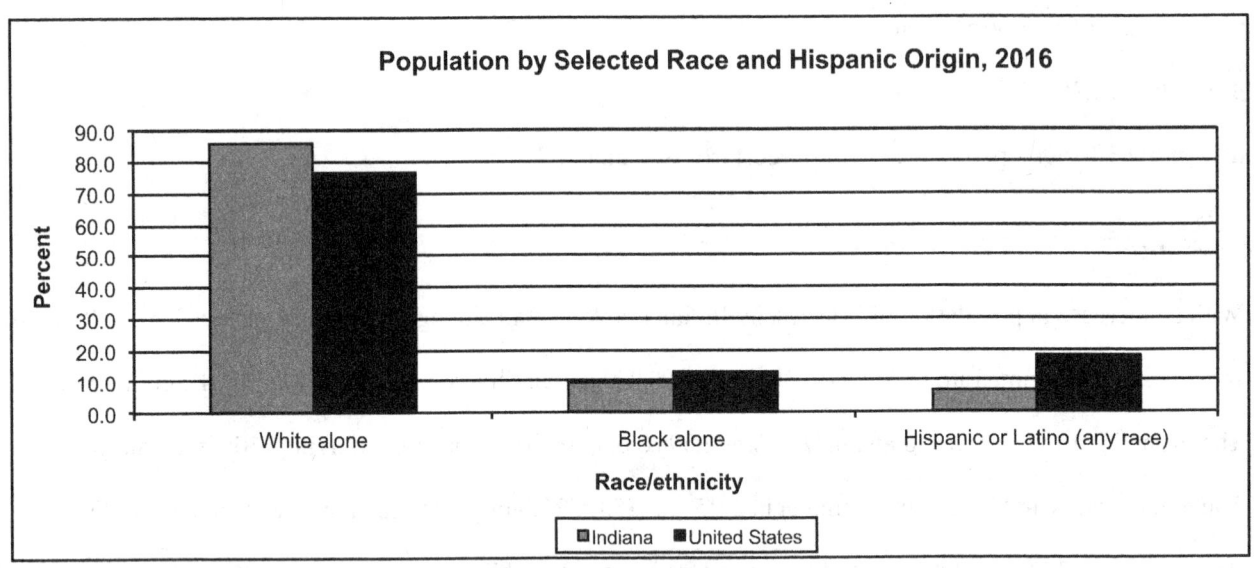

Table IN-2. Marital Status

(Number, percent distribution.)

Sex, age, race, and Hispanic origin	2000	2010	2015
Males, 15 Years and Over	2,308,917	2,513,953	2,586,612
Never married	27.9	32.6	34.5
Now married, except separated..................................	58.5	52.3	49.9
Separated..	1.3	1.1	1.2
Widowed..	2.4	2.5	2.7
Divorced..	10.0	11.4	11.7
Females, 15 Years and Over	2,462,123	2,644,068	2,728,149
Never married	22.0	26.7	28.6
Now married, except separated..................................	54.3	49.1	46.8
Separated..	1.5	1.8	1.5
Widowed..	10.6	9.2	9.3
Divorced..	11.6	13.2	13.9

Table IN-3. Households and Housing Characteristics

(Number, percent, dollars.)

Item	2000	2010	2015	Average annual percent change, 2000–2015
Total Households..	2,336,306	2,470,905	2,515,143	0.5
Family households..	1,602,501	1,656,386	1,633,695	0.1
Married-couple family....................................	1,251,458	1,236,518	1,213,558	-0.2
Other family..	351,043	419,868	420,137	1.3
Male householder, no wife present........................	91,671	110,663	118,626	2.0
Female householder, no husband present...............	259,372	309,205	301,511	1.1
Nonfamily households	733,805	814,519	881,448	1.3
Householder living alone..	605,428	678,460	730,975	1.4
Householder not living alone..................................	128,377	136,059	150,473	1.1
Housing Characteristics				
Total housing units..	2,532,319	2,797,172	2,841,450	0.8
Occupied housing units	2,336,306	2,470,905	2,515,143	0.5
Owner occupied	1,669,192	1,736,751	1,714,880	0.2
Renter occupied	667,144	734,154	800,263	1.3
Average household size..	2.53	2.55	2.56	0.1
Financial Characteristics				
Median gross rent of renter-occupied housing	521	683	758	3.0
Median monthly owner costs for housing units with a mortgage	869	1,090	1,089	1.7
Median value of owner-occupied housing units........................	94,300	123,300	131,000	2.6

Table IN-4. Migration, Origin, and Language

(Number, percent.)

Characteristic	State			U.S.		
	2014	2015	Percent change	2014	2015	Percent change
Residence 1 Year Ago						
Population 1 year and over	6,516,181	6,540,691	0.4	315,095,393	317,635,720	0.8
Same house	85.0	84.5	X	85.1	85.3	X
Different house in the U.S.	14.6	15.1	X	14.3	14.1	X
Same county	8.9	9.2	X	8.7	8.5	X
Different county	5.7	5.9	X	5.6	5.6	X
Same state..	3.6	3.6	X	3.3	3.2	X
Different state...	2.1	2.3	X	2.3	2.4	X
Abroad..	0.4	0.3	X	0.6	0.7	X
Place of Birth						
Native born	6,277,275	6,298,372	0.3	276,465,262	278,128,449	0.6
Male	49.1	49.1	X	49.3	49.3	X
Female	50.9	50.9	X	50.7	50.7	X
Foreign born	319,580	321,308	0.5	42,391,794	43,290,372	2.1
Male	50.3	50.8	X	48.7	48.6	X
Female	49.7	49.2	X	51.3	51.4	X
Foreign born; naturalized U.S. citizen.......................	123,697	123,109	-0.5	19,984,738	20,697,103	3.6
Male	47.8	47	X	45.9	45.9	X
Female	52.2	53	X	54.1	54.1	X
Foreign born; not a U.S. citizen................................	195,883	198,199	1.2	22,407,056	22,593,269	0.8
Male	51.9	53.1	X	51.2	51.1	X
Female	48.1	46.9	X	48.8	48.9	X
Entered 2010 or later	17.3	21.6	X	12.3	15.6	X
Entered 2000 to 2009	36.4	34.3	X	28.6	27.9	X
Entered before 2000..	46.3	44	X	59.1	56.5	X
World Region of Birth, Foreign						
Foreign-born population, excluding population born at sea	319,580	321,308	0.5	42,390,705	43,289,646	2.1
Europe	12.9	11.9	X	11.2	11.1	X
Asia..	34.7	33.7	X	30.1	30.6	X
Africa	5.3	6.3	X	4.6	4.8	X
Oceania..	0.4	0.5	X	0.6	0.6	X
Latin America..	44.5	45.4	X	51.6	51.1	X
North America...	2.2	2.2	X	1.9	1.9	X
Language Spoken at Home and Ability to Speak English						
Population 5 years and over.....................................	6,178,831	6,200,471	0.4	299,084,046	301,625,014	0.8
English only	92.1	91.6	X	78.9	78.5	X
Language other than English....................................	7.9	8.4	X	21.1	21.5	X
Speaks English less than "very well"..........................	3.1	3.3	X	8.6	8.6	X

NA = Not available.
X = Not applicable.
- = Zero or rounds to zero.

Table IN-5. Median Income and Poverty Status, 2015

(Number, percent, except as noted.)

Characteristic	State		U.S.	
	Number	Percent	Number	Percent
Median Income				
Households (dollars)...	50,532	X	55,775	X
Families (dollars)	63,165	X	68,260	X
Below Poverty Level (All People)	933,181	14.5	46,153,077	14.7
Sex				
Male	403,747	12.9	20,599,407	13.4
Female	529,434	16.2	25,553,670	16.0
Age				
Under 18 years...	322,520	20.9	15,000,273	20.7
Related children under 18 years..	315,007	20.5	14,693,239	20.4
18 to 64 years	543,910	13.8	26,960,369	13.9
65 years and over	66,751	7.2	4,192,435	9.0

X = Not applicable.

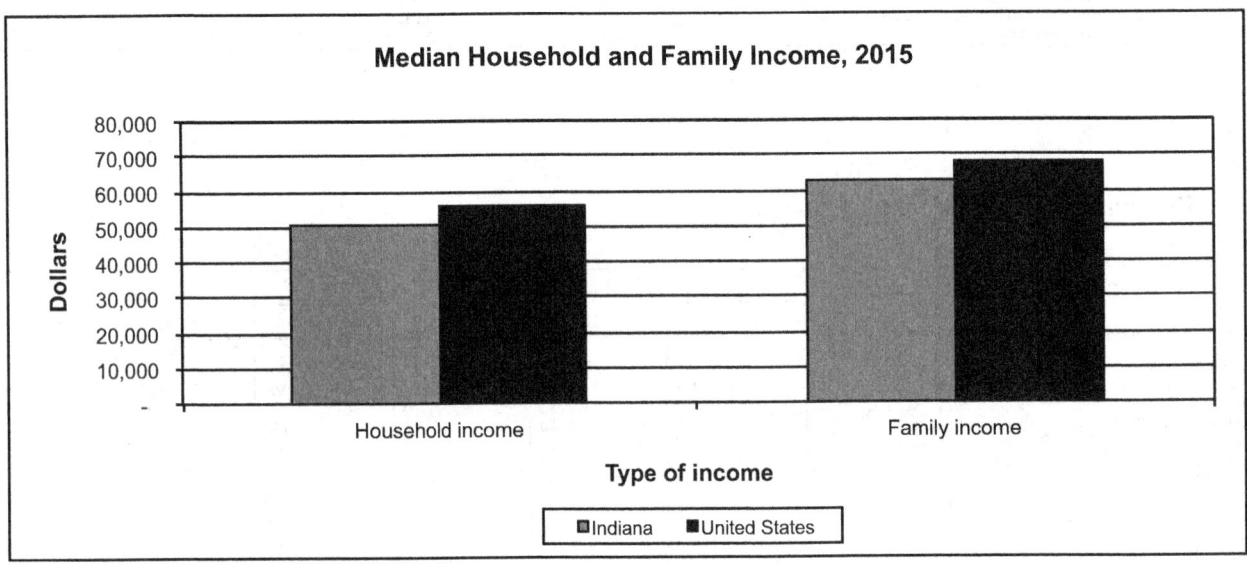

Median Household and Family Income, 2015

Table IN-6. Health Insurance Coverage Status for the Civilian Noninstitutionalized Population and Children Under 18 Years of Age

(Numbers in thousands, percent.)

Item	2007	2008	2009	2010	2011	2012	2013	2014	2015
Civilian Noninstitutionalized Population	6,263	6,271	6,316	6,391	6,418	6,437	6,472	6,498	6,520
Covered by Private or Public Insurance									
Number...	5,546	5,400	5,415	5,444	5,487	5,517	5,569	5,722	5,893
Percent..	88.6	86.1	85.7	85.2	85.5	85.7	86.0	88.1	90.4
Not Covered									
Number...	717	871	901	948	931	920	903	776	628
Percent..	11.4	13.9	14.3	14.8	14.5	14.3	14.0	11.9	9.6
Percent in the U.S. not covered..	15.3	15.1	15.1	15.5	15.1	14.8	14.5	11.7	9.4
Children Under 18 Years of Age	1,593	1,580	1,583	1,602	1,594	1,585	1,584	1,580	1,576
Covered by Private or Public Insurance									
Number...	1,511	1,420	1,443	1,459	1,465	1,451	1,454	1,466	1,470
Percent..	94.8	89.9	91.2	91.1	91.9	91.5	91.8	92.8	93.3
Not Covered									
Number...	83	160	140	143	129	134	130	113	106
Percent..	5.2	10.1	8.8	8.9	8.1	8.5	8.2	7.2	6.7
Percent in the U.S. not covered..	11.0	9.7	8.6	8.0	7.5	7.2	7.1	6.0	4.8

Table IN-7. Employment Status by Demographic Group, 2016

(Numbers in thousands, percent.)

Characteristic	Civilian noninstitutional population	Civilian labor force		Employed		Unemployed	
		Number	Percent of population	Number	Percent of population	Number	Percent of population
Total....................................	5,158	3,348	64.9	3,199	62.0	150	4.5
Sex							
Male..................................	2,501	1,764	70.5	1,687	67.4	77	4.4
Female................................	2,657	1,584	59.6	1,512	56.9	73	4.6
Race, Sex, and Hispanic Origin							
White	4,485	2,928	65.3	2,808	62.6	120	4.1
Male..............................	2,191	1,552	70.8	1,492	68.1	60	3.9
Female...........................	2,294	1,376	60.0	1,316	57.4	59	4.3
Black or African American..................	467	288	61.8	263	56.3	26	8.9
Male..............................	210	136	64.9	121	57.5	15	11.3
Female...........................	257	152	59.3	142	55.2	10	6.8
Hispanic or Latino ethnicity[1]	307	223	72.7	213	69.3	10	4.6
Male..............................	166	134	80.7	129	77.5	5	4.0
Female...........................	141	89	63.2	84	59.7	5	5.5
Age							
16 to 19 years......................	346	152	43.8	128	36.9	24	15.8
20 to 24 years......................	438	337	76.8	307	70.1	29	8.7
25 to 34 years......................	852	710	83.4	680	79.8	30	4.3
35 to 44 years......................	836	706	84.4	684	81.7	23	3.2
45 to 54 years......................	838	688	82.2	667	79.6	21	3.1
55 to 64 years......................	889	597	67.2	580	65.3	17	2.8
65 years and over	959	159	16.6	154	16.0	5	3.4

NOTE: Data in Table 7 are from the Current Population Survey (CPS) and do not match the estimates in Table 8. See notes and definitions for further information.
[1] May be of any race.

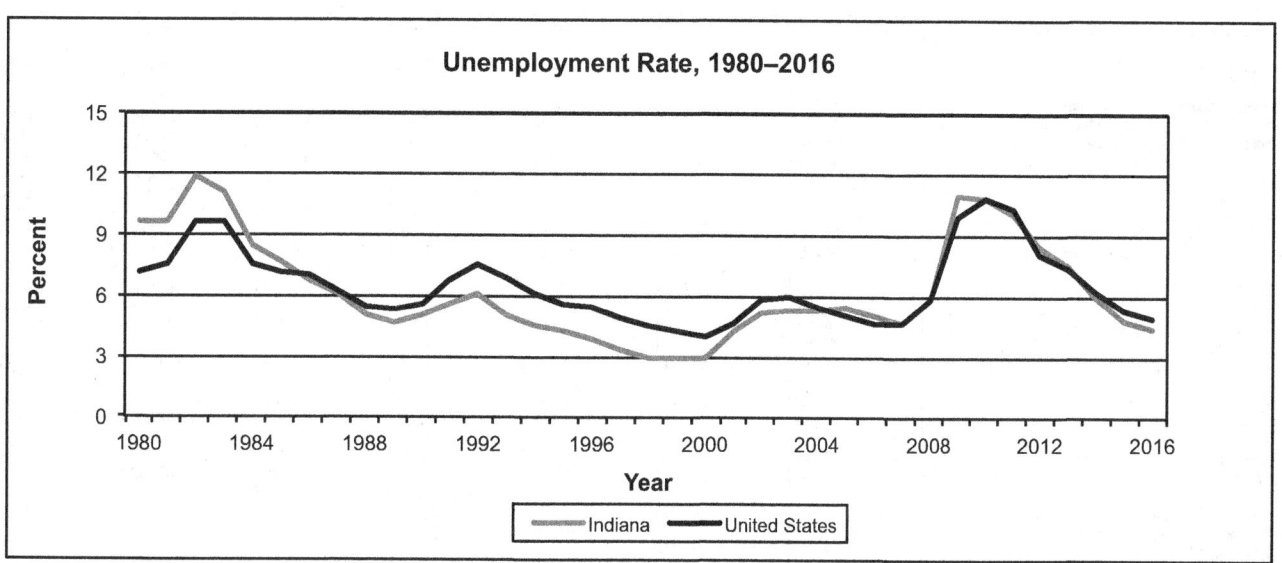

Table IN-8. Employment Status of the Civilian Noninstitutional Population Age 16 Years and Over

(Number, percent.)

Year	Civilian labor force	Civilian participation rate	Employed	Unemployed	Unemployment rate
2008..................	3,232,097	66.3	3,041,828	190,269	5.9
2009..................	3,193,989	65.1	2,864,985	329,004	10.3
2010..................	3,175,192	64.0	2,845,608	329,584	10.4
2011..................	3,181,991	63.6	2,891,945	290,046	9.1
2012..................	3,171,569	63.0	2,907,130	264,439	8.3
2013..................	3,193,427	63.0	2,948,941	244,486	7.7
2014..................	3,227,970	63.3	3,035,984	191,986	5.9
2015..................	3,265,761	63.7	3,109,217	156,544	4.8
2016..................	3,326,893	64.7	3,179,806	147,087	4.4

Table IN-9. Employment and Average Wages by Industry

(Estimates through 2010 are based on the 2007 *North American Industry Classification System* [NAICS]. Estimates from 2011 onward are based on the 2012 NAICS.)

Industry	2009	2010	2011	2012	2013	2014	2015
				Number of jobs			
Wage and Salary Employment by Industry..................	2,879,245	2,877,455	2,920,175	2,978,283	3,011,101	3,055,554	3,105,074
Farm Wage and Salary Employment..........................	10,437	13,906	10,519	13,757	12,390	11,533	10,443
Nonfarm Wage and Salary Employment.....................	2,868,808	2,863,549	2,909,656	2,964,526	2,998,711	3,044,021	3,094,631
Private wage and salary employment........................	2,406,895	2,405,359	2,458,273	2,517,691	2,555,724	2,600,626	2,651,516
Forestry, fishing, and related activities	3,185	3,278	3,208	3,329	3,475	4,124	3,961
Mining..	6,296	6,267	6,575	6,738	6,685	6,876	6,519
Utilities...	15,293	14,947	14,726	14,349	14,176	14,131	13,981
Construction..	126,070	119,771	123,954	128,784	126,941	126,449	130,297
Manufacturing...	442,733	448,663	464,482	482,763	492,411	507,753	519,478
Durable goods manufacturing.............................	309,316	314,365	330,539	346,500	352,165	363,453	373,484
Nondurable goods manufacturing........................	133,417	134,298	133,943	136,263	140,246	144,300	145,994
Wholesale trade	116,332	114,422	115,567	116,553	117,516	118,289	119,809
Retail trade..	312,887	307,231	310,875	315,024	318,730	321,552	327,318
Transportation and warehousing...........................	110,782	110,682	114,531	117,706	120,792	124,243	125,377
Information	37,771	35,749	34,348	35,761	35,780	35,602	33,628
Finance and insurance	98,258	97,329	97,963	98,102	97,796	99,278	101,074
Real estate and rental and leasing........................	34,348	32,591	32,846	33,065	33,293	33,569	34,029
Professional, scientific, and technical services	97,149	96,961	99,262	100,807	102,805	106,024	110,293
Management of companies and enterprises....................	27,524	27,006	28,093	29,166	31,072	32,154	33,392
Administrative and waste services.........................	139,285	152,708	163,966	171,602	176,038	185,187	188,555
Educational services	61,124	62,629	64,515	65,162	65,910	66,345	67,758
Health care and social assistance.........................	349,954	355,818	359,494	366,767	374,802	375,247	384,278
Arts, entertainment, and recreation.......................	43,793	42,464	41,427	41,459	41,663	41,159	41,141
Accommodation and food services........................	236,436	233,085	238,406	245,661	250,595	254,487	261,686
Other services, except public administration.................	147,675	143,758	144,035	144,893	145,244	148,157	148,942
Government and government enterprises..........................	461,913	458,190	451,383	446,835	442,987	443,395	443,115
				Dollars			
Average Wages and Salaries by Industry	38,725	39,774	40,837	41,862	42,366	43,262	44,634
Average Farm Wages and Salaries	30,931	24,289	30,764	27,411	32,031	36,281	36,912
Average Nonfarm Wages and Salaries	38,754	39,850	40,873	41,929	42,408	43,288	44,660
Average private wages and salaries...........................	38,991	40,217	41,357	42,485	42,967	43,925	45,360
Forestry, fishing, and related activities	21,493	22,556	22,949	23,871	24,382	29,069	30,762
Mining..	59,039	62,637	65,061	65,172	68,323	70,396	69,902
Utilities...	76,448	79,435	82,402	84,760	88,380	90,446	94,704
Construction..	47,268	50,359	52,407	54,951	54,397	53,349	54,567
Manufacturing...	54,007	55,999	57,054	57,976	58,055	59,427	60,851
Durable goods manufacturing.............................	53,451	55,347	56,700	57,944	57,401	58,713	60,334
Nondurable goods manufacturing........................	55,295	57,524	57,929	58,058	59,696	61,226	62,172
Wholesale trade	53,187	54,970	56,951	58,557	59,610	61,966	64,300
Retail trade..	23,685	24,430	24,776	25,317	25,501	26,172	27,152
Transportation and warehousing...........................	40,733	41,665	42,656	43,604	43,941	45,421	46,844
Information	49,352	50,410	52,148	54,123	55,515	56,550	57,977
Finance and insurance	54,211	56,339	59,236	62,095	63,149	65,585	68,413
Real estate and rental and leasing........................	33,623	35,242	36,677	38,009	39,001	41,571	42,883
Professional, scientific, and technical services	54,464	56,098	58,558	60,139	62,985	62,568	64,842
Management of companies and enterprises....................	74,933	79,027	84,392	86,302	88,130	90,644	94,290
Administrative and waste services.........................	27,736	27,898	28,418	28,731	29,165	29,568	30,344
Educational services	29,678	29,782	30,404	31,155	31,412	32,087	32,644
Health care and social assistance.........................	40,465	40,874	42,032	43,398	43,889	44,857	46,581
Arts, entertainment, and recreation.......................	31,531	32,644	32,800	33,021	33,369	33,809	35,032
Accommodation and food services........................	14,515	14,987	15,414	15,988	16,185	16,534	17,365
Other services, except public administration.................	26,457	27,572	28,044	28,939	29,668	30,629	31,856
Government and government enterprises..........................	37,520	37,920	38,236	38,795	39,189	39,552	40,468

Table IN-10. Employment Characteristics by Family Type

(Number, percent.)

Family type and labor force status	2013 Total	2013 Families with own children under 18 years	2014 Total	2014 Families with own children under 18 years	2015 Total	2015 Families with own children under 18 years
All Families	1,647,941	720,081	1,651,536	707,467	1,633,695	702,854
FAMILY TYPE AND LABOR FORCE STATUS						
Married-Couple Families	1,226,204	476,033	1,213,708	459,653	1,213,558	465,663
Both husband and wife in labor force	52.8	67.8	53.6	69.8	52.1	68.4
Husband in labor force, wife not in labor force	21.8	27.1	21.0	25.1	21.4	26.0
Wife in labor force, husband not in labor force	8.1	3.4	7.8	3.3	7.7	3.7
Both husband and wife not in labor force	17.1	1.5	17.6	1.8	18.1	1.5
Other Families	421,737	244,048	437,828	247,814	420,137	237,191
Female householder, no husband present	72.9	74.5	72.5	74.3	71.8	73.2
In labor force	51.4	61.0	52.3	62.3	50.9	60.9
Not in labor force	21.5	13.5	20.1	12.1	20.9	12.3
Male householder, no wife present	27.1	25.5	27.5	25.7	28.2	26.8
In labor force	21.3	22.6	21.8	23.7	22.4	24.2
Not in labor force	5.8	2.9	5.8	2.0	5.8	2.5

Table IN-11. School Enrollment and Educational Attainment, 2015

(Number, percent.)

Item	State	U.S.
Enrollment		
Total population 3 years and over, enrolled in school	1,693,308	81,618,288
Enrolled in nursery school or preschool (percent)	5.5	6.0
Enrolled in kindergarten (percent)	4.7	5.0
Enrolled in elementary school, grades 1-8 (percent)	42.3	40.3
Enrolled in high school, grades 9-12 (percent)	21.5	20.9
Enrolled in college or graduate school (percent)	26.1	27.7
Attainment		
Total population 25 years and over	4,363,573	216,447,163
Less than ninth grade (percent)	3.8	5.5
9th to 12th grade, no diploma (percent)	8.0	7.3
High school graduate, including equivalency (percent)	34.3	27.6
Some college, no degree (percent)	20.6	20.7
Associate's degree (percent)	8.3	8.2
Bachelor's degree (percent)	16.0	19.0
Graduate or professional degree (percent)	9.0	11.6
High school graduate or higher (percent)	88.2	87.1
Bachelor's degree or higher (percent)	24.9	30.6

Table IN-12. Public School Characteristics and Educational Indicators

(Number, percent; data derived from National Center of Education Statistics.)

Item	State	U.S.
Public Schools, 2014–2015 (except where noted)		
Number of school districts	411	18,260
Number of schools	1,910	98,373
Number of students	1,046,269	50,312,581
Number of teachers	56,547	3,132,351
Student-teacher ratio	18.5	16.1
Expenditures per student (dollars), FY 2014	9,396	11,066
Four-year adjusted cohort graduation rate (ACGR)[1,2]	87.1	83.2
Students eligible for free or reduced-price lunch (percent)	49.2	51.8
English language learners (percent)	5.6	9.4
Students age 3 to 21 served under IDEA, part B (percent)	16.3	13.0

Public Schools by Type	Number	Percent of state public schools
Total number of schools	1,910	100.0
Regular	1,852	97.0
Special education	22	1.2
Vocational education	28	1.5
Alternative education	8	0.4

NOTE: Every school is assigned only one school type based on its instructional emphasis.
[1] ACGR data represents a new method of calculating high-school completion rates and may not be comparable to previous years' data for Averaged Freshmen Graduation Rates (AFGR).
[2] The United States 4-year ACGRs were estimated using both the reported 4-year ACGR data from 49 states and the District of Columbia and using imputed data for Idaho. The estimate for American Indian/Alaska Native students also includes imputed data for Virginia.

Table IN-13. Reported Voting and Registration of the Voting-Age Population, November 2016

(Numbers in thousands, percent.)

Item	Total population	Total citizen population	Registered			Voted		
			Total registered	Percent registered (total population)	Percent registered (total citizen population)	Total voted	Percent voted (total population)	Percent voted (total citizen population)
U.S. Total	245,502	224,059	157,596	64.2	70.3	137,537	56.0	61.4
State Total............................	4,988	4,795	3,298	66.1	68.8	2,795	56.0	58.3
Sex								
Male	2,426	2,306	1,595	65.7	69.2	1,343	55.4	58.3
Female	2,562	2,490	1,704	66.5	68.4	1,452	56.6	58.3
Race								
White alone..............................	4,309	4,191	2,895	67.2	69.1	2,467	57.2	58.9
White, non-Hispanic alone	4,102	4,059	2,832	69.0	69.8	2,409	58.7	59.4
Black alone..............................	473	442	284	59.9	64.2	228	48.2	51.6
Asian alone	109	77	55	(B)	(B)	48	(B)	(B)
Hispanic (of any race).....................	224	138	69	30.9	50.1	63	28.3	46.0
White alone or in combination	4,378	4,260	2,949	67.4	69.2	2,513	57.4	59.0
Black alone or in combination..........	491	460	298	60.8	64.9	238	48.5	51.8
Asian alone or in combination..........	130	97	72	(B)	(B)	65	(B)	(B)
Age								
18 to 24 years..........................	618	587	338	54.7	57.6	252	40.8	43.0
25 to 34 years..........................	917	881	550	60.0	62.5	442	48.2	50.2
35 to 44 years..........................	758	713	492	65.0	69.0	426	56.2	59.7
45 to 64 years..........................	1,742	1,682	1,192	68.4	70.9	1,043	59.9	62.0
65 years and over	953	933	725	76.1	77.8	632	66.3	67.7

B = Base is less than 75,000 and therefore too small to show the derived measure.

Table IN-14. Crime

(Number, rate per 100,000. Data are derived from the FBI Uniform Crime Reports.)

Item	State			U.S. [1,2,3,4]		
	2014	2015	Percent change	2014	2015	Percent change
TOTAL POPULATION[5] ,..............................	6,597,880	6,619,680	0.3	318,907,401	321,418,820	0.8
VIOLENT CRIME						
Number..................................	24,105	25,653	6.4	1,186,185	1,231,566	3.8
Rate	365.3	387.5	6.1	372.0	383.2	3.0
Murder and Nonnegligent Manslaughter						
Number..................................	333	373	12.0	14,164	15,696	10.8
Rate	5.0	5.6	11.6	4.4	4.9	10.0
Rape[6]						
Number..................................	2,197	2,404	9.4	118,027	124,047	5.1
Rate	33.3	36.3	9.1	37.0	38.6	4.3
Robbery						
Number..................................	6,894	7,111	3.1	322,905	327,374	1.4
Rate	104.5	107.4	2.8	101.3	101.9	0.6
Aggravated Assault						
Number..................................	14,681	15,765	7.4	731,089	764,449	4.6
Rate	222.5	238.2	7.0	229.2	237.8	3.7
PROPERTY CRIME						
Number..................................	174,909	171,847	-1.8	8,209,010	7,993,631	-2.6
Rate	2,651.0	2,596.0	-2.1	2,574.1	2,487.0	-3.4
Burglary						
Number..................................	36,909	34,410	-6.8	1,713,153	1,579,527	-7.8
Rate	559.4	519.8	-7.1	537.2	491.4	-8.5
Larceny-Theft						
Number..................................	124,144	123,918	-0.2	5,809,054	5,706,346	-1.8
Rate	1,881.6	1,872.0	-0.5	1,821.5	1,775.4	-2.5
Motor Vehicle Theft						
Number..................................	13,856	13,519	-2.4	686,803	707,758	3.1
Rate	210.0	204.2	-2.8	215.4	220.2	2.2

NOTE: Although arson data are included in the trend and clearance tables, sufficient data are not available to estimate totals for this offense. Therefore, no arson data are published in this table.
X = Not applicable.
- = Zero or rounds to zero.
[1] The crime figures have been adjusted.
[2] The data collection methodology for the offense of forcible rape used by the Minnesota state Uniform Crime Reporting (UCR) Program (with the exception of Minneapolis and St. Paul, Minnesota) does not comply with national UCR Program guidelines. Consequently, its figures for forcible rape and violent crime (of which forcible rape is a part) are not published in this table.
[3] Includes offenses reported by the Zoological Police and the Metro Transit Police.
[4] Because of changes in the state's reporting practices, figures are not comparable to previous years' data.
[5] Populations are U.S. Census Bureau provisional estimates as of July 1 of each year.
[6] The figures shown for the offense of rape were estimated using the revised Uniform Crime Reporting (UCR) definition of rape.

Table IN-15. State Government Finances, 2015

(Dollar amounts in thousands, percent distribution.)

Item	Dollars	Percent distribution
Total Revenue	38,919,794	100.0
General revenue	35,036,133	90.0
Intergovernmental revenue	11,689,694	30.0
Taxes..	17,605,651	45.2
General sales..	7,279,604	18.7
Selective sales..	3,532,267	9.1
License taxes	641,788	1.6
Individual income tax..	5,232,977	13.4
Corporate income tax...	903,572	2.3
Other taxes..	15,443	0.0
Current charges	3,531,574	9.1
Miscellaneous general revenue	2,209,214	5.7
Utility revenue..	0	-
Liquor stores revenue	0	-
Insurance trust revenue[1]	3,883,661	10.0
Total Expenditure	37,579,629	100.0
Intergovernmental expenditure	9,548,136	25.4
Direct expenditure..	28,031,493	74.6
Current operation	20,661,061	55.0
Capital outlay	2,163,562	5.8
Insurance benefits and repayments	3,029,662	8.1
Assistance and subsidies..	1,170,064	3.1
Interest on debt	1,007,144	2.7
Exhibit: Salaries and wages..	4,369,859	11.6
Total Expenditure	37,579,629	100.0
General expenditure	34,549,589	91.9
Intergovernmental expenditure	9,548,136	25.4
Direct expenditure	25,001,453	66.5
General expenditure, by function:		
Education..	14,865,806	39.6
Public welfare	11,501,010	30.6
Hospitals...	158,234	0.4
Health..	569,675	1.5
Highways	2,581,632	6.9
Police protection	229,327	0.6
Correction	681,831	1.8
Natural resources..	343,124	0.9
Parks and recreation	81,929	0.2
Governmental administration	640,839	1.7
Interest on general debt	1,007,144	2.7
Other and unallocable	1,889,038	5.0
Utility expenditure..	378	-
Liquor stores expenditure	0	-
Insurance trust expenditure	3,029,662	8.1
Debt at End of Fiscal Year	22,463,710	X
Cash and Security Holdings......................................	58,168,989	X

X = Not applicable.
- = Zero or rounds to zero.
[1] Within insurance trust revenue, net earnings of state retirement systems is a calculated statistic (the item code in the data file is X08), and thus can be positive or negative. Net earnings is the sum of earnings on investments plus gains on investments minus losses on investments. The change made in 2002 for asset valuation from book to market value in accordance with Statement 34 of the Governmental Accounting Standards Board is reflected in the calculated statistics.

Table IN-16. State Government Tax Collections, 2016

(Dollars in thousands, percent.)

Item	Dollars	Percent distribution
Total Taxes	17,587,958	100.0
Property taxes	10,699	0.1
Sales and gross receipts	10,608,207	60.3
General sales and gross receipts	7,306,331	41.5
Selective sales and gross receipts	3,301,876	18.8
Alcoholic beverages	48,310	0.3
Amusements	578,829	3.3
Insurance premiums	235,024	1.3
Motor fuels	845,384	4.8
Pari-mutuels	1,958	-
Public utilities	214,976	1.2
Tobacco products	443,210	2.5
Other selective sales	934,185	5.3
Licenses	714,634	4.1
Alcoholic beverages	12,871	0.1
Amusements	5,912	-
Corporations in general	7,534	-
Hunting and fishing	19,362	0.1
Motor vehicle	294,209	1.7
Motor vehicle operators	237,329	1.3
Public utilities	0	-
Occupation and business, NEC	55,437	0.3
Other licenses	81,980	0.5
Income taxes	6,252,533	35.6
Individual income	5,218,166	29.7
Corporation net income	1,034,367	5.9
Other taxes	1,885	-
Death and gift	872	-
Documentary and stock transfer	0	-
Severance	1,013	-
Taxes, NEC	0	-

- = Zero or rounds to zero.

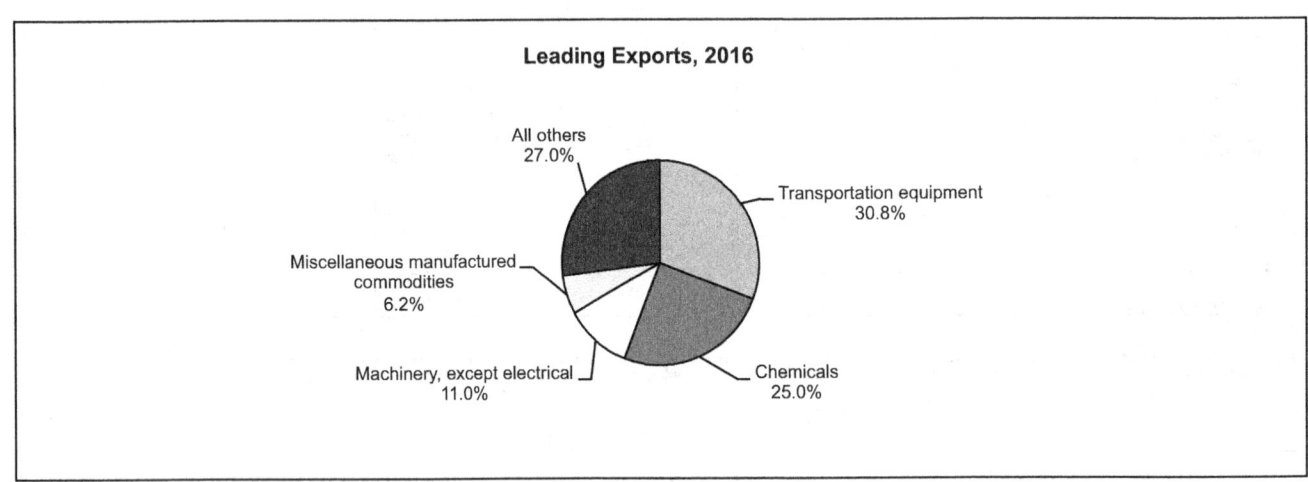

Leading Exports, 2016

All others 27.0%

Transportation equipment 30.8%

Miscellaneous manufactured commodities 6.2%

Machinery, except electrical 11.0%

Chemicals 25.0%

IOWA

Facts and Figures

Location: North central United States; bordered on the N by Minnesota, on the E by Wisconsin and Illinois, on the S by Missouri, and on the W by Nebraska and South Dakota

Area: 56,272 sq. mi. (145,743 sq. km.); rank—26th

Population: 3,134,693 (2016 est.); rank—30th

Principal Cities: capital—Des Moines; largest—Des Moines

Statehood: December 28, 1846; 29th state

U.S. Congress: 2 senators, 4 representatives

State Motto: Our Liberties We Prize and Our Rights We Will Maintain

State Song: "The Song of Iowa"

State Nickname: The Hawkeye State

Abbreviations: IA; Ia.

State Symbols: flower—wild prairie rose; tree—oak; bird—Eastern goldfinch

At a Glance

- With an increase in population of 2.9 percent, Iowa ranked 30th among the states in growth from 2010 to 2016.

- In 2015, Iowa's median household income was $54,736, and 12.2 percent of the population lived below the poverty level.

- Compared to 9.4 percent of the total U.S. population, 5.0 percent of Iowans did not have health insurance in 2015.

- Iowa's violent crime rate in 2015 was 286.1 per 100,000 population, compared to the rate of 383.2 for the United States as a whole.

- Iowa had the second highest percent of single-family homes in 2015, with 77.8 percent of housing units being one-unit attached or detached homes.

Table IA-1. Population by Age, Sex, Race, and Hispanic Origin

(Number, percent, except where noted.)

Sex, age, race, and Hispanic origin	2000	2010	2016 [1]	Average annual percent change, 2010–2016
Total Population	2,926,324	3,046,355	3,134,693	0.2
Percent of total U.S. population	1.0	1.0	1.0	X
Sex				
Male	1,435,515	1,508,319	1,559,119	0.2
Female	1,490,809	1,538,036	1,575,574	0.2
Age				
Under 5 years	188,413	202,123	199,415	-0.1
5 to 19 years	639,570	618,387	622,727	-
20 to 64 years	1,662,128	1,772,957	1,798,336	0.1
65 years and over	436,213	452,888	514,215	0.8
Median age (years)	36.6	38.1	38	-
Race and Hispanic Origin				
One race				
White	2,748,640	2,839,615	2,864,884	0.1
Black	61,853	91,695	114,874	1.6
American Indian and Alaska Native	8,989	13,563	15,924	1.1
Asian	36,635	54,232	78,735	2.8
Native Hawaiian or Other Pacific Islander	1,009	2,419	3,592	3.0
Two or more races	31,778	44,831	56,684	1.7
Hispanic (of any race)	82,473	156,932	182,606	1.0

X = Not applicable.
- = Zero or rounds to zero.
[1] Population figures for 2016 are July 1 estimates. The 2010 estimates are taken from the 2010 Census.

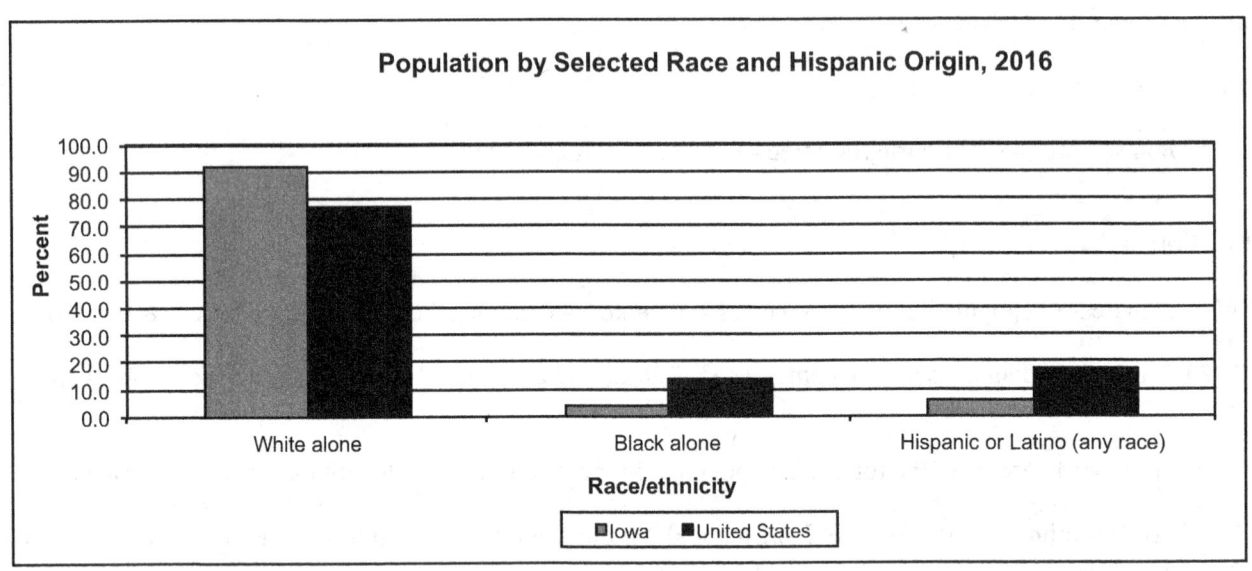

Population by Selected Race and Hispanic Origin, 2016

Table IA-2. Marital Status

(Number, percent distribution.)

Sex, age, race, and Hispanic origin	2000	2010	2015
Males, 15 Years and Over	1,126,566	1,199,509	1,240,310
Never married	28.2	31.3	32.7
Now married, except separated	59.8	55.2	53.3
Separated	0.9	1.1	1.0
Widowed	2.5	2.6	2.7
Divorced	8.5	9.7	10.2
Females, 15 Years and Over	1,198,297	1,250,612	1,278,344
Never married	21.8	24.7	26.5
Now married, except separated	55.8	52.4	50.9
Separated	1.1	1.5	1.5
Widowed	11.6	10.2	9.7
Divorced	9.6	11.2	11.4

Table IA-3. Households and Housing Characteristics

(Number, percent, dollars.)

Item	2000	2010	2015	Average annual percent change, 2000–2015
Total Households...	1,149,276	1,223,439	1,247,249	0.6
Family households...	769,684	793,768	796,799	0.2
Married-couple family....................................	633,254	633,602	628,004	-0.1
Other family...	136,430	160,166	168,795	1.6
Male householder, no wife present................	38,160	46,829	53,585	2.7
Female householder, no husband present.......	98,270	113,337	115,210	1.1
Nonfamily households.......................................	379,592	429,671	450,450	1.2
Householder living alone................................	313,083	349,736	362,532	1.1
Householder not living alone..........................	66,509	79,935	87,918	2.1
Housing Characteristics				
Total housing units..	1,232,511	1,337,563	1,369,379	0.7
Occupied housing units	1,149,276	1,223,439	1,247,249	0.6
Owner occupied...	831,419	885,284	881,480	0.4
Renter occupied..	317,857	338,155	365,769	1.0
Average household size....................................	2.46	2.41	2.42	-0.1
Financial Characteristics				
Median gross rent of renter-occupied housing	470	629	718	3.5
Median monthly owner costs for housing units with a mortgage	829	1,140	1,170	2.7
Median value of owner-occupied housing units...........	82,500	123,400	136,100	4.3

Table IA-4. Migration, Origin, and Language

(Number, percent.)

Characteristic	State			U.S.		
	2014	2015	Percent change	2014	2015	Percent change
Residence 1 Year Ago						
Population 1 year and over	3,067,872	3,081,446	0.4	315,095,393	317,635,720	0.8
Same house	84.6	84.3	X	85.1	85.3	X
Different house in the U.S.	15	15.3	X	14.3	14.1	X
Same county..	8.7	8.7	X	8.7	8.5	X
Different county	6.2	6.7	X	5.6	5.6	X
Same state	3.7	3.9	X	3.3	3.2	X
Different state	2.6	2.8	X	2.3	2.4	X
Abroad	0.5	0.3	X	0.6	0.7	X
Place of Birth						
Native born	2,953,805	2,975,178	0.7	276,465,262	278,128,449	0.6
Male	49.6	49.5	X	49.3	49.3	X
Female	50.4	50.5	X	50.7	50.7	X
Foreign born	153,321	148,721	-3.0	42,391,794	43,290,372	2.1
Male	52.5	50.7	X	48.7	48.6	X
Female	47.5	49.3	X	51.3	51.4	X
Foreign born; naturalized U.S. citizen........	54,750	55,685	1.7	19,984,738	20,697,103	3.6
Male	48.3	47.2	X	45.9	45.9	X
Female	51.7	52.8	X	54.1	54.1	X
Foreign born; not a U.S. citizen.................	98,571	93,036	-5.6	22,407,056	22,593,269	0.8
Male	54.9	52.8	X	51.2	51.1	X
Female	45.1	47.2	X	48.8	48.9	X
Entered 2010 or later	26.7	25.4	X	12.3	15.6	X
Entered 2000 to 2009	27.4	30.6	X	28.6	27.9	X
Entered before 2000.................................	45.9	44	X	59.1	56.5	X
World Region of Birth, Foreign						
Foreign-born population, excluding population born at sea	153,321	148,721	-3.0	42,390,705	43,289,646	2.1
Europe	12.8	12.9	X	11.2	11.1	X
Asia...	38.4	35.8	X	30.1	30.6	X
Africa	9.1	9.6	X	4.6	4.8	X
Oceania	1.0	0.9	X	0.6	0.6	X
Latin America...	37	39.3	X	51.6	51.1	X
North America..	1.6	1.5	X	1.9	1.9	X
Language Spoken at Home and Ability to Speak English						
Population 5 years and over........................	2,913,555	2,928,815	0.5	299,084,046	301,625,014	0.8
English only..	92.8	92.3	X	78.9	78.5	X
Language other than English......................	7.2	7.7	X	21.1	21.5	X
Speaks English less than "very well".........	3.0	3.3	X	8.6	8.6	X

NA = Not available.
X = Not applicable.
- = Zero or rounds to zero.

Table IA-5. Median Income and Poverty Status, 2015

(Number, percent, except as noted.)

Characteristic	State		U.S.	
	Number	Percent	Number	Percent
Median Income				
Households (dollars)	54,736	X	55,775	X
Families (dollars)	69,382	X	68,260	X
Below Poverty Level (All People)	367,414	12.2	46,153,077	14.7
Sex				
Male	163,093	10.9	20,599,407	13.4
Female	204,321	13.4	25,553,670	16.0
Age				
Under 18 years	105,540	14.8	15,000,273	20.7
Related children under 18 years	102,474	14.4	14,693,239	20.4
18 to 64 years	228,253	12.5	26,960,369	13.9
65 years and over	33,621	7.0	4,192,435	9.0

X = Not applicable.

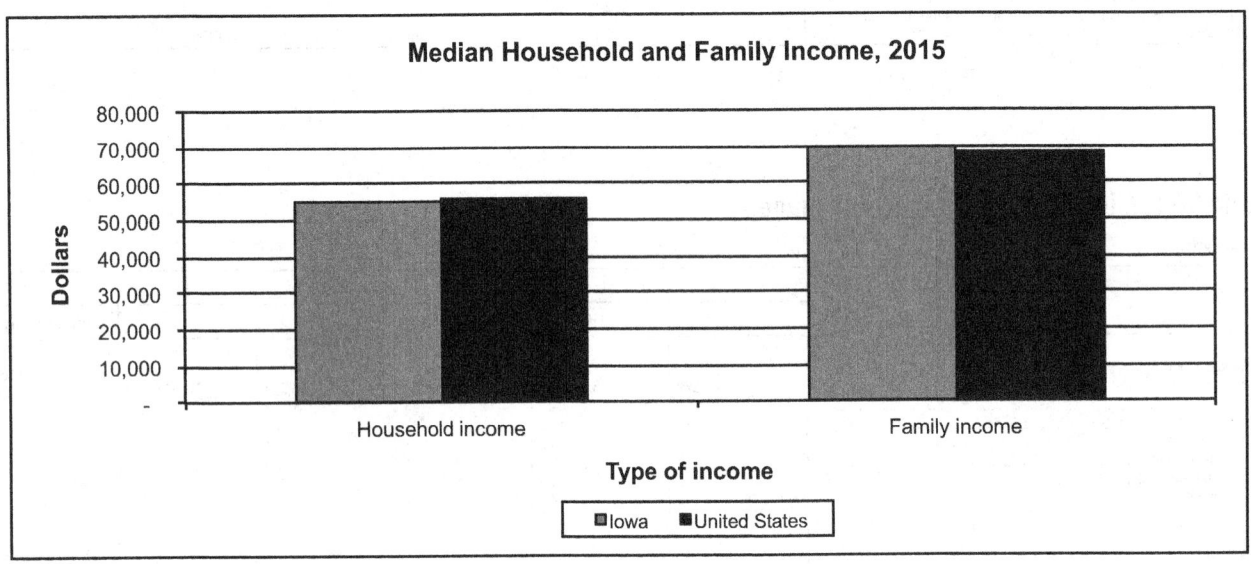

Table IA-6. Health Insurance Coverage Status for the Civilian Noninstitutionalized Population and Children Under 18 Years of Age

(Numbers in thousands, percent.)

Item	2007	2008	2009	2010	2011	2012	2013	2014	2015
Civilian Noninstitutionalized Population	2,970	2,951	2,957	3,005	3,017	3,029	3,045	3,063	3,080
Covered by Private or Public Insurance									
Number	2,695	2,683	2,702	2,725	2,748	2,775	2,798	2,874	2,925
Percent	90.7	90.9	91.4	90.7	91.1	91.6	91.9	93.8	95.0
Not Covered									
Number	275	268	255	280	269	254	248	189	155
Percent	9.3	9.1	8.6	9.3	8.9	8.4	8.1	6.2	5.0
Percent in the U.S. not covered	15.3	15.1	15.1	15.5	15.1	14.8	14.5	11.7	9.4
Children Under 18 Years of Age	709	708	707	722	722	720	721	723	726
Covered by Private or Public Insurance									
Number	675	668	675	693	690	691	692	700	701
Percent	95.2	94.4	95.4	96.0	95.6	96.0	95.9	96.8	96.5
Not Covered									
Number	34	40	32	29	32	29	30	23	26
Percent	4.8	5.6	4.6	4.0	4.4	4.0	4.1	3.2	3.5
Percent in the U.S. not covered	11.0	9.7	8.6	8.0	7.5	7.2	7.1	6.0	4.8

Table IA-7. Employment Status by Demographic Group, 2016

(Numbers in thousands, percent.)

Characteristic	Civilian noninstitutional population	Civilian labor force		Employed		Unemployed	
		Number	Percent of population	Number	Percent of population	Number	Percent of population
Total...	2,452	1,714	69.9	1,647	67.2	67	3.9
Sex							
Male..	1,208	899	74.4	860	71.2	39	4.3
Female...	1,244	815	65.5	787	63.2	28	3.4
Race, Sex, and Hispanic Origin							
White	2,283	1,604	70.3	1,547	67.8	57	3.6
Male..	1,118	835	74.7	802	71.7	33	4.0
Female...	1,165	769	66.0	745	63.9	24	3.1
Black or African American....................	NA	NA	NA	NA	NA	NA	NA
Male..	NA	NA	NA	NA	NA	NA	NA
Female...	NA	NA	NA	NA	NA	NA	NA
Hispanic or Latino ethnicity[1]	131	106	81.0	101	76.7	6	5.3
Male..	NA	NA	NA	NA	NA	NA	NA
Female...	NA	NA	NA	NA	NA	NA	NA
Age							
16 to 19 years....................................	144	76	53.0	71	49.0	6	7.4
20 to 24 years....................................	218	185	84.9	172	78.9	13	7.1
25 to 34 years....................................	445	389	87.4	373	83.9	15	4.0
35 to 44 years....................................	345	312	90.4	298	86.3	14	4.6
45 to 54 years....................................	387	336	86.8	328	84.8	8	2.3
55 to 64 years....................................	416	306	73.4	298	71.5	8	2.6
65 years and over	498	110	22.2	108	21.6	3	2.5

NOTE: Data in Table 7 are from the Current Population Survey (CPS) and do not match the estimates in Table 8. See notes and definitions for further information.
[1] May be of any race.
NA = Not available

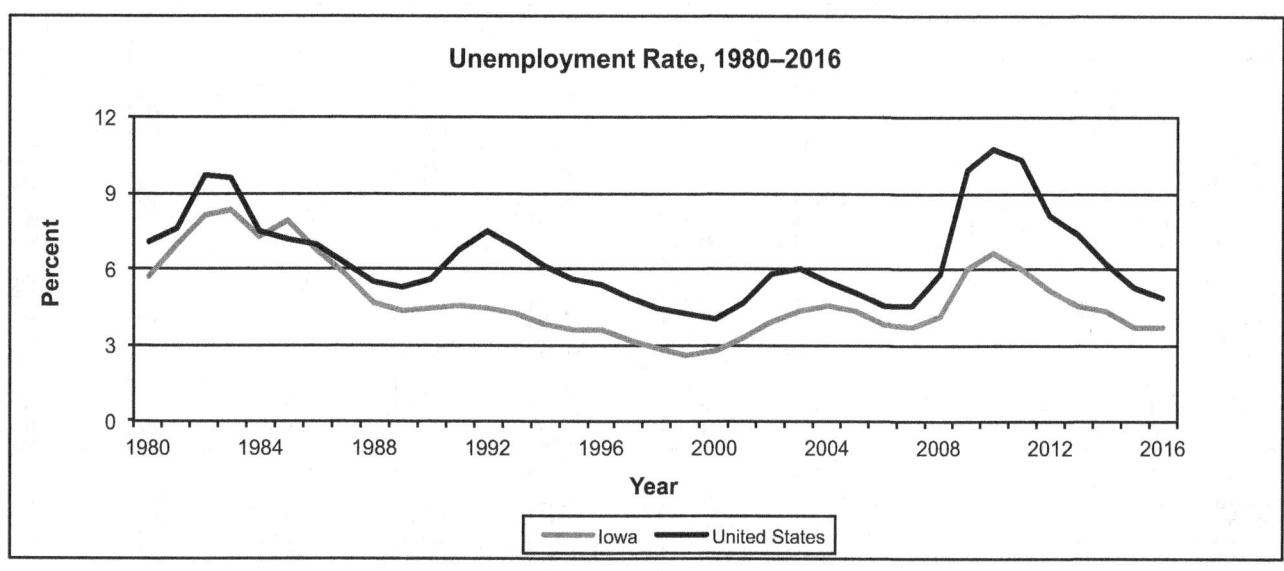

Table IA-8. Employment Status of the Civilian Noninstitutional Population Age 16 Years and Over

(Number, percent.)

Year	Civilian labor force	Civilian participation rate	Employed	Unemployed	Unemployment rate
2008..	1,679,293	72.4	1,608,695	70,598	4.2
2009..	1,687,411	72.3	1,579,248	108,163	6.4
2010..	1,678,281	71.2	1,577,447	100,834	6.0
2011..	1,662,376	70.0	1,570,177	92,199	5.5
2012..	1,649,169	69.0	1,565,874	83,295	5.1
2013..	1,672,399	69.5	1,593,027	79,372	4.7
2014..	1,697,712	70.1	1,626,270	71,442	4.2
2015..	1,701,329	69.9	1,638,868	62,461	3.7
2016..	1,700,683	69.6	1,638,288	62,395	3.7

Table IA-9. Employment and Average Wages by Industry

(Estimates through 2010 are based on the 2007 *North American Industry Classification System* [NAICS]. Estimates from 2011 onward are based on the 2012 NAICS.)

Industry	2009	2010	2011	2012	2013	2014	2015
				Number of jobs			
Wage and Salary Employment by Industry..................	1,547,457	1,537,132	1,553,036	1,571,483	1,593,351	1,608,122	1,625,722
Farm Wage and Salary Employment.........................	16,235	18,657	18,154	15,984	19,258	14,834	19,160
Nonfarm Wage and Salary Employment.....................	1,531,222	1,518,475	1,534,882	1,555,499	1,574,093	1,593,288	1,606,562
Private wage and salary employment..........................	1,261,085	1,249,767	1,266,721	1,288,057	1,306,874	1,325,609	1,339,472
Forestry, fishing, and related activities	6,324	7,158	7,147	7,852	8,555	7,636	7,430
Mining....................................	2,181	2,132	2,173	2,198	2,228	2,165	2,234
Utilities....................	7,008	6,783	6,606	6,499	6,456	6,483	6,577
Construction	67,987	63,735	64,427	66,519	69,761	76,323	80,216
Manufacturing.............................	203,640	201,225	206,405	211,033	214,693	217,215	216,574
Durable goods manufacturing...........................	117,789	116,692	122,278	126,649	128,861	130,922	129,102
Nondurable goods manufacturing....................	85,851	84,533	84,127	84,384	85,832	86,293	87,472
Wholesale trade	67,357	66,311	67,206	68,957	69,616	69,377	68,004
Retail trade.............................	177,576	174,321	175,949	177,344	177,477	178,344	181,755
Transportation and warehousing........................	55,431	54,648	56,493	57,341	59,388	59,963	60,980
Information	30,264	28,722	28,236	27,019	26,152	25,721	24,970
Finance and insurance	91,134	91,642	92,112	92,997	94,052	94,438	95,606
Real estate and rental and leasing....................	14,497	13,798	13,403	13,364	13,781	14,290	14,539
Professional, scientific, and technical services	42,979	43,025	43,670	45,168	46,975	48,737	49,729
Management of companies and enterprises..................	13,155	13,212	14,851	16,076	16,590	18,218	19,226
Administrative and waste services.....................	62,495	66,152	68,002	69,740	69,556	70,418	70,362
Educational services	37,923	39,090	39,998	40,429	40,596	40,499	41,028
Health care and social assistance............................	177,177	179,188	179,901	182,737	185,940	187,741	189,940
Arts, entertainment, and recreation...........................	20,769	19,971	20,442	19,793	18,702	18,801	19,025
Accommodation and food services..........................	113,450	110,772	112,115	115,218	118,639	119,825	121,579
Other services, except public administration..................	69,738	67,882	67,585	67,773	67,717	69,415	69,698
Government and government enterprises..........................	270,137	268,708	268,161	267,442	267,219	267,679	267,090
				Dollars			
Average Wages and Salaries by Industry	36,258	37,250	38,273	39,578	40,182	41,762	43,134
Average Farm Wages and Salaries	31,672	28,145	28,096	42,613	30,874	47,537	34,423
Average Nonfarm Wages and Salaries	36,306	37,362	38,393	39,547	40,296	41,708	43,238
Average private wages and salaries....................	35,857	37,111	38,256	39,501	40,222	41,717	43,277
Forestry, fishing, and related activities	24,023	24,648	25,413	26,997	26,857	29,712	30,781
Mining....................	42,630	43,583	45,470	45,574	46,949	51,842	53,932
Utilities....................	75,777	76,425	79,992	82,981	80,942	86,371	86,931
Construction	42,950	43,735	45,119	47,138	48,521	51,971	54,947
Manufacturing.........................	47,267	49,757	51,113	52,107	52,891	54,394	55,892
Durable goods manufacturing........................	49,665	52,486	54,504	55,164	55,990	57,394	58,766
Nondurable goods manufacturing........................	43,978	45,989	46,184	47,520	48,239	49,842	51,651
Wholesale trade	49,559	51,523	53,942	55,882	57,045	58,791	60,295
Retail trade......................	22,182	22,635	23,210	23,781	23,903	24,598	25,204
Transportation and warehousing........................	38,709	40,272	40,893	42,204	42,127	44,448	45,759
Information	43,565	45,224	46,721	47,045	49,011	50,825	52,979
Finance and insurance	55,516	58,991	61,202	63,338	65,913	68,242	71,503
Real estate and rental and leasing....................	35,808	37,438	39,333	41,090	41,116	42,777	44,767
Professional, scientific, and technical services	50,077	51,691	53,930	57,646	58,910	60,412	62,942
Management of companies and enterprises..................	69,742	70,049	71,652	76,962	75,656	77,913	81,838
Administrative and waste services.....................	25,612	26,356	26,249	27,279	27,732	28,544	29,624
Educational services	23,502	23,570	23,607	23,920	24,077	24,680	24,907
Health care and social assistance............................	35,825	36,348	37,394	38,157	38,393	39,417	41,322
Arts, entertainment, and recreation...........................	20,151	20,588	20,606	20,197	18,920	19,683	20,255
Accommodation and food services..........................	13,477	13,774	14,321	15,119	15,619	16,173	16,883
Other services, except public administration..................	24,675	25,679	26,453	27,591	28,515	29,456	30,953
Government and government enterprises..........................	38,403	38,528	39,042	39,766	40,659	41,660	43,039

Table IA-10. Employment Characteristics by Family Type

(Number, percent.)

Family type and labor force status	2013 Total	2013 Families with own children under 18 years	2014 Total	2014 Families with own children under 18 years	2015 Total	2015 Families with own children under 18 years
All Families..................................	793,749	345,493	796,909	348,223	796,799	340,225
FAMILY TYPE AND LABOR FORCE STATUS						
Married-Couple Families........................	625,107	238,739	632,094	245,038	628,004	235,322
Both husband and wife in labor force...............	59.2	78.5	59.6	78.2	58.4	77.5
Husband in labor force, wife not in labor force	16.1	17.5	16.6	17.9	16.8	18.4
Wife in labor force, husband not in labor force	7.3	2.9	7.2	2.8	7.1	2.6
Both husband and wife not in labor force........	16.9	0.9	16.6	1.2	17.1	1.2
Other Families	168,642	106,754	164,815	103,185	168,795	104,903
Female householder, no husband present................	68.6	70.3	67.0	67.5	68.3	68.9
In labor force..................................	51.5	60.4	51.4	58.6	53.0	61.1
Not in labor force	17.1	9.8	15.6	8.9	15.3	7.8
Male householder, no wife present................	31.4	29.7	33.0	32.5	31.7	31.1
In labor force..................................	25.7	26.2	27.1	30.2	26.6	28.7
Not in labor force	5.7	3.5	5.9	2.3	5.1	2.5

Table IA-11. School Enrollment and Educational Attainment, 2015

(Number, percent.)

Item	State	U.S.
Enrollment		
Total population 3 years and over, enrolled in school	809,269	81,618,288
Enrolled in nursery school or preschool (percent)...........	6.7	6.0
Enrolled in kindergarten (percent)........................	5.2	5.0
Enrolled in elementary school, grades 1-8 (percent)............	40.2	40.3
Enrolled in high school, grades 9-12 (percent)............	19.9	20.9
Enrolled in college or graduate school (percent)..........	28.0	27.7
Attainment		
Total population 25 years and over	2,074,504	216,447,163
Less than ninth grade (percent)	3.2	5.5
9th to 12th grade, no diploma (percent)	5.1	7.3
High school graduate, including equivalency (percent)........	32.1	27.6
Some college, no degree (percent)	21.4	20.7
Associate's degree (percent)	11.4	8.2
Bachelor's degree (percent)	18.2	19.0
Graduate or professional degree (percent)...........	8.7	11.6
High school graduate or higher (percent)	91.7	87.1
Bachelor's degree or higher (percent)..............	26.8	30.6

Table IA-12. Public School Characteristics and Educational Indicators

(Number, percent; data derived from National Center of Education Statistics.)

Item	State	U.S.
Public Schools, 2014–2015 (except where noted)		
Number of school districts........................	347	18,260
Number of schools................................	1,364	98,373
Number of students...............................	505,311	50,312,581
Number of teachers	35,684	3,132,351
Student-teacher ratio	14.2	16.1
Expenditures per student (dollars), FY 2014	10,647	11,066
Four-year adjusted cohort graduation rate (ACGR)[1,2]	90.8	83.2
Students eligible for free or reduced-price lunch (percent)........	40.7	51.8
English language learners (percent)................	5.1	9.4
Students age 3 to 21 served under IDEA, part B (percent)........	12.6	13.0

Public Schools by Type	Number	Percent of state public schools
Total number of schools........................	1,364	100.0
Regular	1,338	98.1
Special education	3	0.2
Vocational education............................	0	-
Alternative education...........................	23	1.7

NOTE: Every school is assigned only one school type based on its instructional emphasis.
[1] ACGR data represents a new method of calculating high-school completion rates and may not be comparable to previous years' data for Averaged Freshmen Graduation Rates (AFGR).
[2] The United States 4-year ACGRs were estimated using both the reported 4-year ACGR data from 49 states and the District of Columbia and using imputed data for Idaho. The estimate for American Indian/Alaska Native students also includes imputed data for Virginia.
- = Zero or rounds to zero.

Table IA-13. Reported Voting and Registration of the Voting-Age Population, November 2016

(Numbers in thousands, percent.)

Item	Total population	Total citizen population	Registered			Voted		
			Total registered	Percent registered (total population)	Percent registered (total citizen population)	Total voted	Percent voted (total population)	Percent voted (total citizen population)
U.S. Total	245,502	224,059	157,596	64.2	70.3	137,537	56.0	61.4
State Total..............................	2,394	2,292	1,657	69.2	72.3	1,454	60.7	63.4
Sex								
Male	1,172	1,111	780	66.5	70.2	673	57.4	60.6
Female	1,221	1,181	877	71.8	74.2	781	63.9	66.1
Race								
White alone............................	2,201	2,159	1,587	72.1	73.5	1,393	63.3	64.5
White, non-Hispanic alone	2,126	2,114	1,558	73.3	73.7	1,370	64.4	64.8
Black alone.............................	73	65	39	(B)	(B)	34	(B)	(B)
Asian alone.............................	66	30	15	(B)	(B)	13	(B)	(B)
Hispanic (of any race)......................	97	51	29	(B)	(B)	23	(B)	(B)
White alone or in combination	2,226	2,184	1,599	71.8	73.2	1,403	63.0	64.2
Black alone or in combination..........	84	76	39	(B)	(B)	34	(B)	(B)
Asian alone or in combination.........	68	32	17	(B)	(B)	13	(B)	(B)
Age								
18 to 24 years.............................	295	278	142	48.3	51.2	105	35.5	37.6
25 to 34 years.............................	450	405	305	67.8	75.2	241	53.6	59.5
35 to 44 years.............................	343	325	228	66.4	70.1	196	57.1	60.2
45 to 64 years.............................	768	754	545	71.0	72.3	499	65.0	66.2
65 years and over	538	529	436	81.2	82.4	413	76.8	78.0

B = Base is less than 75,000 and therefore too small to show the derived measure.

Table IA-14. Crime

(Number, rate per 100,000. Data are derived from the FBI Uniform Crime Reports.)

Item	State			U.S. [1,2,3,4]		
	2014	2015	Percent change	2014	2015	Percent change
TOTAL POPULATION[5]	3,109,481	3,123,899	0.5	318,907,401	321,418,820	0.8
VIOLENT CRIME						
Number..	8,484	8,936	5.3	1,186,185	1,231,566	3.8
Rate	272.8	286.1	4.8	372.0	383.2	3.0
Murder and Nonnegligent Manslaughter						
Number..	60	72	20.0	14,164	15,696	10.8
Rate	1.9	2.3	19.4	4.4	4.9	10.0
Rape[6]						
Number..	1,150	1,156	0.5	118,027	124,047	5.1
Rate	37.0	37.0	0.1	37.0	38.6	4.3
Robbery						
Number..	1,047	1,047	0.0	322,905	327,374	1.4
Rate	33.7	33.5	-0.5	101.3	101.9	0.6
Aggravated Assault						
Number..	6,227	6,661	7.0	731,089	764,449	4.6
Rate	200.3	213.2	6.5	229.2	237.8	3.7
PROPERTY CRIME						
Number..	65,100	63,957	-1.8	8,209,010	7,993,631	-2.6
Rate	2,093.6	2,047.3	-2.2	2,574.1	2,487.0	-3.4
Burglary						
Number..	14,363	14,892	3.7	1,713,153	1,579,527	-7.8
Rate	461.9	476.7	3.2	537.2	491.4	-8.5
Larceny-Theft						
Number..	46,594	44,723	-4.0	5,809,054	5,706,346	-1.8
Rate	1,498.4	1,431.6	-4.5	1,821.5	1,775.4	-2.5
Motor Vehicle Theft						
Number..	4,143	4,342	4.8	686,803	707,758	3.1
Rate	133.2	139.0	4.3	215.4	220.2	2.2

NOTE: Although arson data are included in the trend and clearance tables, sufficient data are not available to estimate totals for this offense. Therefore, no arson data are published in this table.
- = Zero or rounds to zero.
X = Not applicable.
[1] The crime figures have been adjusted.
[2] The data collection methodology for the offense of forcible rape used by the Minnesota state Uniform Crime Reporting (UCR) Program (with the exception of Minneapolis and St. Paul, Minnesota) does not comply with national UCR Program guidelines. Consequently, its figures for forcible rape and violent crime (of which forcible rape is a part) are not published in this table.
[3] Includes offenses reported by the Zoological Police and the Metro Transit Police.
[4] Because of changes in the state's reporting practices, figures are not comparable to previous years' data.
[5] Populations are U.S. Census Bureau provisional estimates as of July 1 of each year.
[6] The figures shown for the offense of rape were estimated using the revised Uniform Crime Reporting (UCR) definition of rape.

Table IA-15. State Government Finances, 2015

(Dollar amounts in thousands, percent distribution.)

Item	Dollars	Percent distribution
Total Revenue	23,478,092	100.0
General revenue	20,317,912	86.5
Intergovernmental revenue	6,547,949	27.9
Taxes	9,187,483	39.1
General sales	3,040,627	13.0
Selective sales	1,228,001	5.2
License taxes	874,778	3.7
Individual income tax	3,471,617	14.8
Corporate income tax	463,238	2.0
Other taxes	109,222	0.5
Current charges	3,263,620	13.9
Miscellaneous general revenue	1,318,860	5.6
Utility revenue	0	-
Liquor stores revenue	280,834	1.2
Insurance trust revenue[1]	2,879,346	12.3
Total Expenditure	22,760,938	100.0
Intergovernmental expenditure	5,225,016	23.0
Direct expenditure	17,535,922	77.0
Current operation	12,307,776	54.1
Capital outlay	2,040,995	9.0
Insurance benefits and repayments	2,388,037	10.5
Assistance and subsidies	582,635	2.6
Interest on debt	216,479	1.0
Exhibit: Salaries and wages	3,352,708	14.7
Total Expenditure	22,760,938	100.0
General expenditure	20,180,612	88.7
Intergovernmental expenditure	5,225,016	23.0
Direct expenditure	14,955,596	65.7
General expenditure, by function:		
Education	7,118,769	31.3
Public welfare	6,223,107	27.3
Hospitals	1,751,476	7.7
Health	261,541	1.1
Highways	2,076,439	9.1
Police protection	102,012	0.4
Correction	293,600	1.3
Natural resources	305,572	1.3
Parks and recreation	34,182	0.2
Governmental administration	576,090	2.5
Interest on general debt	216,479	1.0
Other and unallocable	1,221,345	5.4
Utility expenditure	0	-
Liquor stores expenditure	192,289	0.8
Insurance trust expenditure	2,388,037	10.5
Debt at End of Fiscal Year	6,120,464	X
Cash and Security Holdings	43,292,850	X

X = Not applicable.
- = Zero or rounds to zero.
[1] Within insurance trust revenue, net earnings of state retirement systems is a calculated statistic (the item code in the data file is X08), and thus can be positive or negative. Net earnings is the sum of earnings on investments plus gains on investments minus losses on investments. The change made in 2002 for asset valuation from book to market value in accordance with Statement 34 of the Governmental Accounting Standards Board is reflected in the calculated statistics.

Table IA-16. State Government Tax Collections, 2016

(Dollars in thousands, percent.)

Item	Dollars	Percent distribution
Total Taxes	9,558,563	100.0
Property taxes..........	1,410	-
Sales and gross receipts	4,591,421	48.0
General sales and gross receipts	3,162,854	33.1
Selective sales and gross receipts	1,428,567	14.9
Alcoholic beverages	22,423	0.2
Amusements..........	298,017	3.1
Insurance premiums..........	119,571	1.3
Motor fuels..........	689,693	7.2
Pari-mutuels	3,666	-
Public utilities	28,700	0.3
Tobacco products..........	227,901	2.4
Other selective sales	38,596	0.4
Licenses..........	925,958	9.7
Alcoholic beverages	15,468	0.2
Amusements..........	33,156	0.3
Corporations in general..........	46,695	0.5
Hunting and fishing..........	29,246	0.3
Motor vehicle..........	610,762	6.4
Motor vehicle operators..........	16,750	0.2
Public utilities	12,035	0.1
Occupation and business, NEC	153,278	1.6
Other licenses	8,568	0.1
Income taxes..........	3,930,190	41.1
Individual income..........	3,553,325	37.2
Corporation net income	376,865	3.9
Other taxes..........	109,584	1.1
Death and gift..........	88,759	0.9
Documentary and stock transfer	20,825	0.2
Severance	0	-
Taxes, NEC	0	-

X = Not applicable.
- = Zero or rounds to zero.

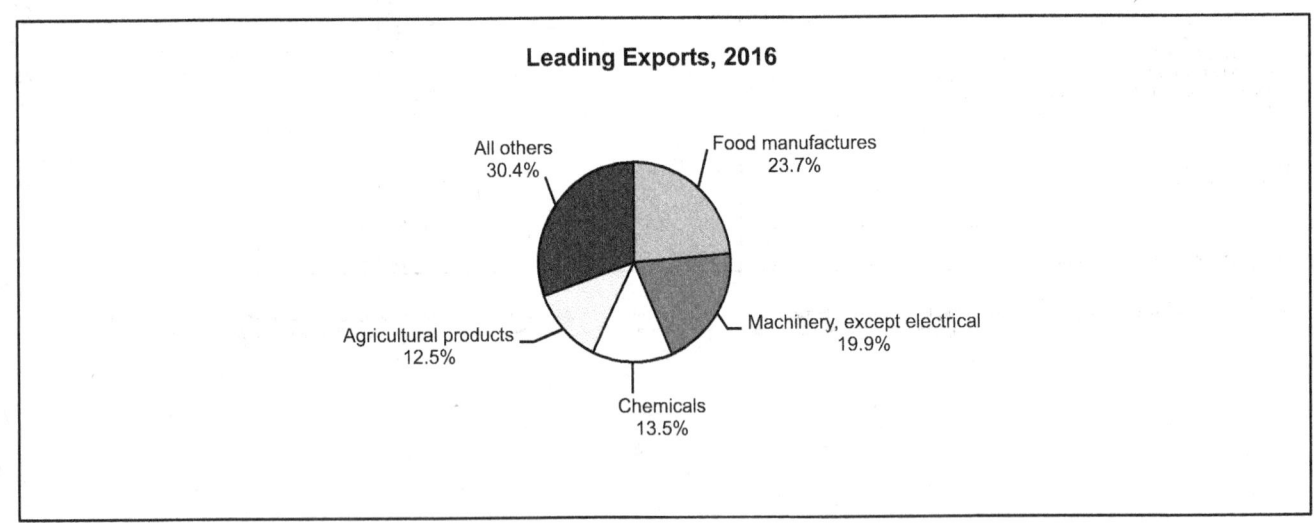

Leading Exports, 2016

All others 30.4%
Food manufactures 23.7%
Machinery, except electrical 19.9%
Chemicals 13.5%
Agricultural products 12.5%

Facts and Figures

Location: Central United States; bordered on the N by Nebraska, on the E by Missouri, on the S by Oklahoma, and on the W by Colorado

Area: 82,277 sq. mi. (213,096 sq. km.); rank—15th

Population: 2,907,289 (2016 est.); rank—35th

Principal Cities: capital—Topeka; largest—Wichita

Statehood: January 29, 1861; 34th state

U.S. Congress: 2 senators, 4 representatives

State Motto: *Ad astra per aspera* ("To the stars through difficulties")

State Song: "Home on the Range"

State Nicknames: The Sunflower State; The Jayhawk State

Abbreviations: KS; Kan.; Kans.

State Symbols: flower—wild native sunflower; tree—cottonwood; bird—Western meadowlark

At a Glance

- With an increase in population of 1.9 percent, Kansas ranked 34th among the states in growth from 2010 to 2016.

- In 2015, 9.1 percent of Kansans did not have health insurance, compared to 9.4 percent of the total U.S. population.

- Approximately 24.6 percent of Kansans were under 18 years old in 2016, the 6th highest percentage in the United States.

- Kansas's unemployment rate remained at 4.2 percent in 2016, compared to the national rate of 4.9 percent.

- In Kansas, 13.0 percent of the total population and 17.2 percent of children under age 18 lived in poverty in 2015, compared to that national averages of 14.7 percent and 20.7 percent respectively.

Table KS-1. Population by Age, Sex, Race, and Hispanic Origin

(Number, percent, except where noted.)

Sex, age, race, and Hispanic origin	2000	2010	2016 [1]	Average annual percent change, 2010–2016
Total Population..	2,688,418	2,853,118	2,907,289	0.1
Percent of total U.S. population	1.0	0.9	0.9	X
Sex				
Male...	1,328,474	1,415,408	1,447,759	0.1
Female	1,359,944	1,437,710	1,459,530	0.1
Age				
Under 5 years..	188,708	205,492	194,307	-0.3
5 to 19 years...	609,710	605,152	601,262	-
20 to 64 years...	1,533,771	1,666,358	1,674,727	-
65 years and over	356,229	376,116	436,993	1.0
Median age (years)	35.2	36.0	36.5	0.1
Race and Hispanic Origin				
One race...				
White..	2,313,944	2,501,057	2,518,720	-
Black...	154,198	173,298	179,599	0.2
American Indian and Alaska Native	24,936	33,044	34,616	0.3
Asian..	46,806	69,628	86,448	1.5
Native Hawaiian or Other Pacific Islander	1,313	2,864	3,235	0.8
Two or more races	56,496	73,227	84,671	1.0
Hispanic (of any race)..	188,252	311,460	338,481	0.5

X = Not applicable.
- = Zero or rounds to zero.
[1] Population figures for 2016 are July 1 estimates. The 2010 estimates are taken from the 2010 Census.

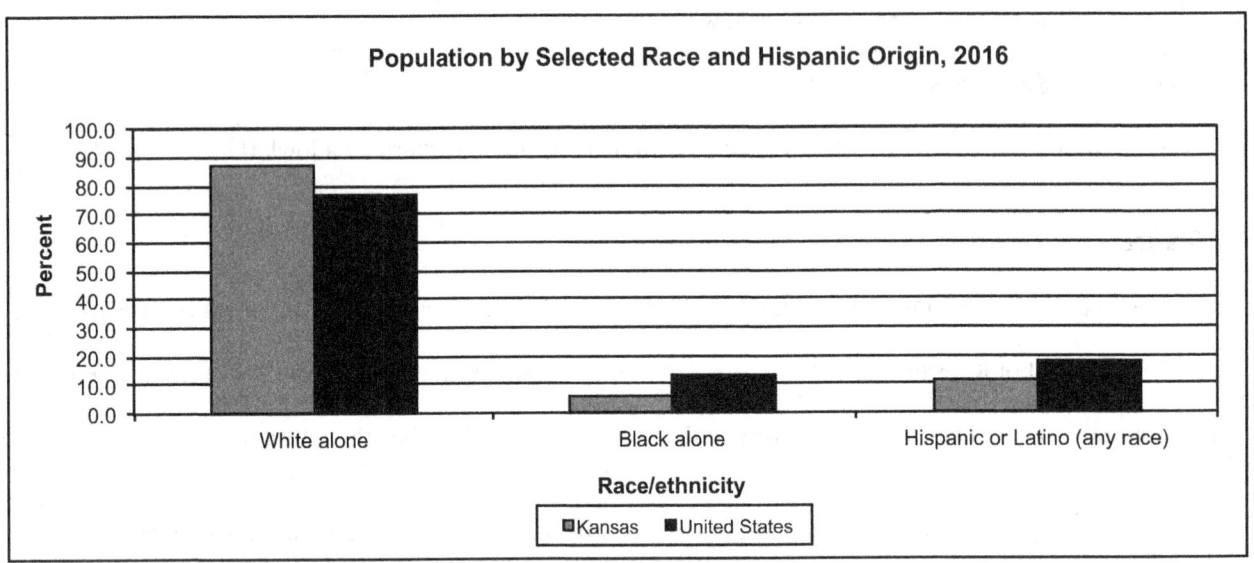

Population by Selected Race and Hispanic Origin, 2016

Kansas ■ United States

Table KS-2. Marital Status

(Number, percent distribution.)

Sex, age, race, and Hispanic origin	2000	2010	2015
Males, 15 Years and Over	1,025,114	1,106,102	1,144,771
Never married	27.4	31.6	33.6
Now married, except separated...............................	59.9	53.9	52.1
Separated..	1.1	1.4	1.1
Widowed..	2.3	2.6	2.6
Divorced..	9.2	10.5	10.6
Females, 15 Years and Over	1,075,542	1,145,453	1,167,789
Never married	20.8	25.1	26.5
Now married, except separated...............................	56.4	51.4	50.5
Separated..	1.3	1.7	1.6
Widowed..	10.6	9.2	9.3
Divorced..	10.9	12.6	12.1

Table KS-3. Households and Housing Characteristics

(Number, percent, dollars.)

Item	2000	2010	2015	Average annual percent change, 2000–2015
Total Households..	1,037,891	1,101,658	1,111,582	0.5
Family households..	701,547	721,592	720,780	0.2
Married-couple family...	567,924	559,199	560,633	-0.1
Other family...	133,623	162,393	160,147	1.3
Male householder, no wife present..................	36,962	46,692	50,370	2.4
Female householder, no husband present...........	96,661	115,701	109,777	0.9
Nonfamily households...	336,344	380,066	390,802	1.1
Householder living alone...................................	280,387	313,390	328,310	1.1
Householder not living alone..............................	55,957	66,676	62,492	0.8
Housing Characteristics				
Total housing units...	1,131,200	1,234,037	1,253,889	0.7
Occupied housing units	1,037,891	1,101,658	1,111,582	0.5
Owner occupied	718,703	749,907	738,336	0.2
Renter occupied..	319,188	351,751	373,246	1.1
Average household size..	2.51	2.52	2.55	0.1
Financial Characteristics				
Median gross rent of renter-occupied housing	498	682	782	3.8
Median monthly owner costs for housing units with a mortgage	888	1,239	1,279	2.9
Median value of owner-occupied housing units	83,500	127,300	141,200	4.6

Table KS-4. Migration, Origin, and Language

(Number, percent.)

Characteristic	State			U.S.		
	2014	2015	Percent change	2014	2015	Percent change
Residence 1 Year Ago						
Population 1 year and over	2,866,584	2,875,640	0.3	315,095,393	317,635,720	0.8
Same house..	83.0	83.7	X	85.1	85.3	X
Different house in the U.S.	16.5	15.7	X	14.3	14.1	X
Same county	9.7	9.1	X	8.7	8.5	X
Different county	6.8	6.6	X	5.6	5.6	X
Same state	3.5	3.4	X	3.3	3.2	X
Different state	3.4	3.2	X	2.3	2.4	X
Abroad...	0.5	0.6	X	0.6	0.7	X
Place of Birth						
Native born	2,699,601	2,705,921	0.2	276,465,262	278,128,449	0.6
Male..	49.6	49.7	X	49.3	49.3	X
Female...	50.4	50.3	X	50.7	50.7	X
Foreign born	204,420	205,720	0.6	42,391,794	43,290,372	2.1
Male..	51.3	51.3	X	48.7	48.6	X
Female...	48.7	48.7	X	51.3	51.4	X
Foreign born; naturalized U.S. citizen...............	77,384	77,110	-0.4	19,984,738	20,697,103	3.6
Male..	49.1	48	X	45.9	45.9	X
Female...	50.9	52	X	54.1	54.1	X
Foreign born; not a U.S. citizen......................	127,036	128,610	1.2	22,407,056	22,593,269	0.8
Male..	52.6	53.3	X	51.2	51.1	X
Female...	47.4	46.7	X	48.8	48.9	X
Entered 2010 or later	16.1	21	X	12.3	15.6	X
Entered 2000 to 2009	33.3	32.2	X	28.6	27.9	X
Entered before 2000..............................	50.6	46.8	X	59.1	56.5	X
World Region of Birth, Foreign						
Foreign-born population, excluding population born at sea	204,420	205,720	0.6	42,390,705	43,289,646	2.1
Europe	7.2	7.8	X	11.2	11.1	X
Asia...	29.9	31.1	X	30.1	30.6	X
Africa	6.5	7.4	X	4.6	4.8	X
Oceania..	0.7	0.2	X	0.6	0.6	X
Latin America.................................	54.3	51.7	X	51.6	51.1	X
North America................................	1.4	1.9	X	1.9	1.9	X
Language Spoken at Home and Ability to Speak English						
Population 5 years and over............................	2,704,673	2,714,575	0.4	299,084,046	301,625,014	0.8
English only	88.7	88.2	X	78.9	78.5	X
Language other than English...............	11.3	11.8	X	21.1	21.5	X
Speaks English less than "very well"..........	4.4	4.6	X	8.6	8.6	X

NA = Not available.
X = Not applicable.
- = Zero or rounds to zero.

Table KS-5. Median Income and Poverty Status, 2015

(Number, percent, except as noted.)

Characteristic	State Number	State Percent	U.S. Number	U.S. Percent
Median Income				
Households (dollars)...	53,906	X	55,775	X
Families (dollars)	69,401	X	68,260	X
Below Poverty Level (All People)	368,879	13.0	46,153,077	14.7
Sex				
Male	170,171	12.1	20,599,407	13.4
Female	198,708	13.9	25,553,670	16.0
Age				
Under 18 years..	122,329	17.2	15,000,273	20.7
Related children under 18 years................................	118,954	16.8	14,693,239	20.4
18 to 64 years..	216,734	12.7	26,960,369	13.9
65 years and over	29,816	7.3	4,192,435	9.0

X = Not applicable.

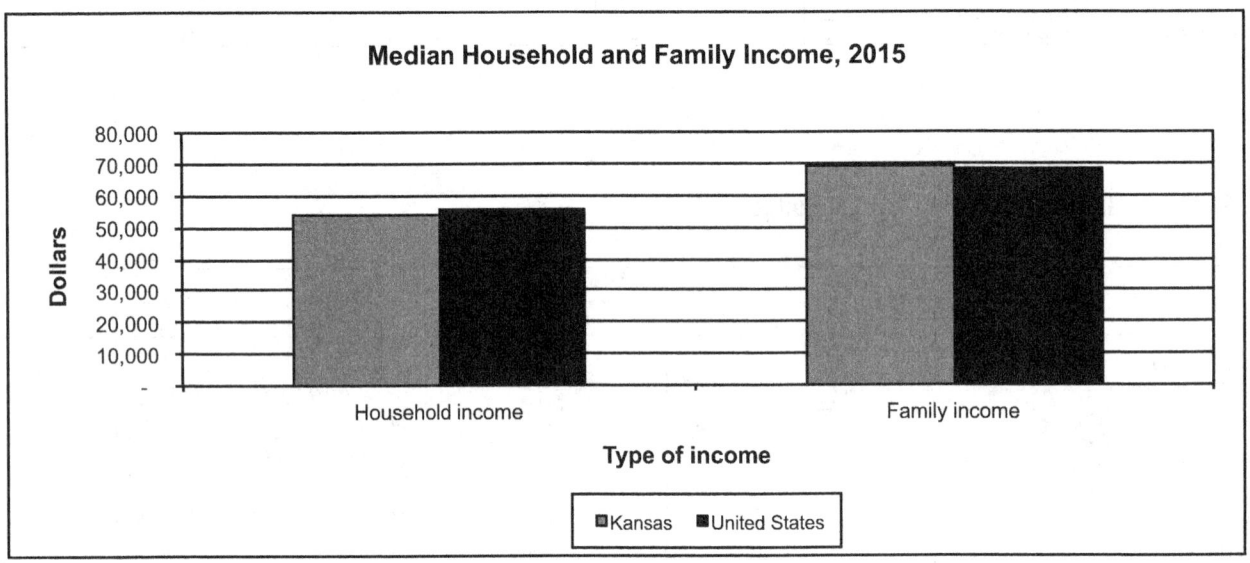

Table KS-6. Health Insurance Coverage Status for the Civilian Noninstitutionalized Population and Children Under 18 Years of Age

(Numbers in thousands, percent.)

Item	2007	2008	2009	2010	2011	2012	2013	2014	2015
Civilian Noninstitutionalized Population	2,722	2,739	2,757	2,804	2,814	2,825	2,837	2,845	2,850
Covered by Private or Public Insurance									
Number...	2,376	2,405	2,394	2,415	2,459	2,470	2,489	2,554	2,590
Percent..	87.3	87.8	86.8	86.1	87.4	87.4	87.7	89.8	90.9
Not Covered									
Number...	345	334	363	389	355	355	348	291	261
Percent..	12.7	12.2	13.2	13.9	12.6	12.6	12.3	10.2	9.1
Percent in the U.S. not covered...............................	15.3	15.1	15.1	15.5	15.1	14.8	14.5	11.7	9.4
Children Under 18 Years of Age	710	698	701	725	721	720	719	721	719
Covered by Private or Public Insurance									
Number...	655	640	643	665	675	672	675	681	682
Percent..	92.3	91.7	91.8	91.8	93.6	93.4	93.9	94.5	94.9
Not Covered									
Number...	54	58	58	60	46	48	44	39	37
Percent..	7.7	8.3	8.2	8.2	6.4	6.6	6.1	5.5	5.1
Percent in the U.S. not covered...............................	11.0	9.7	8.6	8.0	7.5	7.2	7.1	6.0	4.8

Table KS-7. Employment Status by Demographic Group, 2016

(Numbers in thousands, percent.)

Characteristic	Civilian noninstitutional population	Civilian labor force		Employed		Unemployed	
		Number	Percent of population	Number	Percent of population	Number	Percent of population
Total..................................	2,221	1,490	67.1	1,428	64.3	63	4.2
Sex							
Male................................	1,088	796	73.2	760	69.8	36	4.6
Female	1,133	694	61.3	668	59.0	26	3.8
Race, Sex, and Hispanic Origin							
White...............................	1,955	1,321	67.6	1,272	65.1	48	3.7
Male............................	960	708	73.8	680	70.8	29	4.1
Female.........................	995	612	61.5	593	59.6	20	3.2
Black or African American...................	133	87	65.5	78	58.6	9	10.4
Male............................	NA	NA	NA	NA	NA	NA	NA
Female.........................	NA	NA	NA	NA	NA	NA	NA
Hispanic or Latino ethnicity[1]	252	181	71.7	169	67.0	12	6.5
Male............................	133	107	80.7	99	74.9	8	7.2
Female.........................	120	74	61.7	70	58.3	4	5.6
Age							
16 to 19 years....................	165	71	43.2	65	39.3	6	8.9
20 to 24 years....................	184	140	76.1	128	69.8	12	8.4
25 to 34 years....................	382	328	85.7	315	82.5	12	3.8
35 to 44 years....................	351	303	86.4	294	83.9	9	2.9
45 to 54 years....................	349	292	83.5	281	80.4	11	3.8
55 to 64 years....................	376	260	69.0	250	66.4	10	3.8
65 years and over	414	97	23.4	94	22.8	2	2.5

NOTE: Data in Table 7 are from the Current Population Survey (CPS) and do not match the estimates in Table 8. See notes and definitions for further information.
[1] May be of any race.

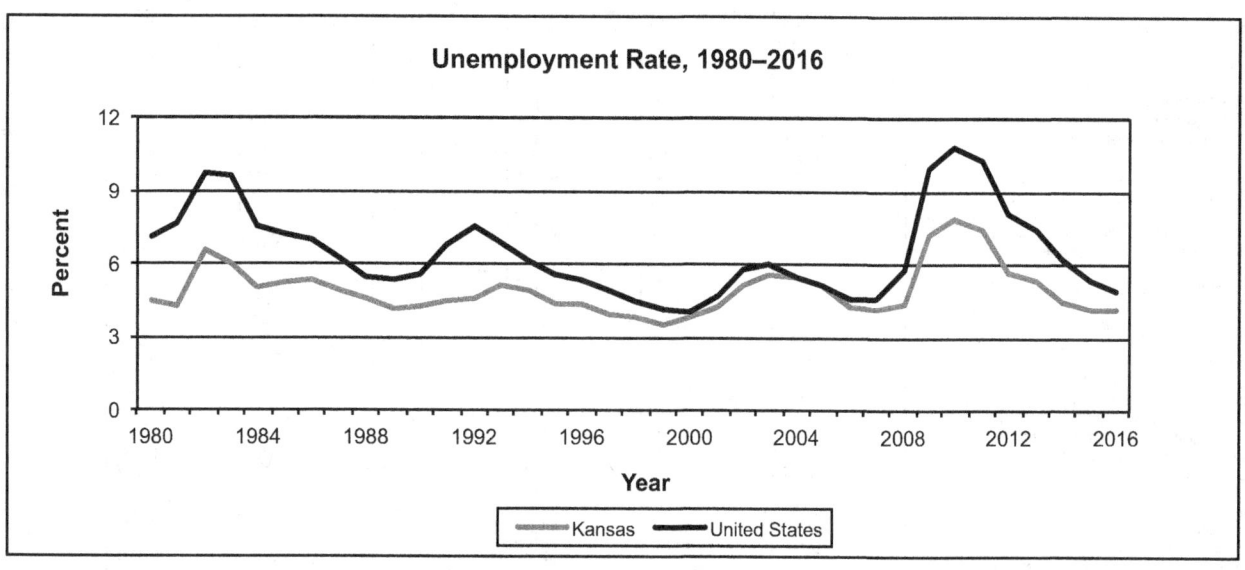

Table KS-8. Employment Status of the Civilian Noninstitutional Population Age 16 Years and Over

(Number, percent.)

Year	Civilian labor force	Civilian participation rate	Employed	Unemployed	Unemployment rate
2008..................................	1,499,676	71.0	1,430,628	69,048	4.6
2009..................................	1,518,207	71.3	1,413,873	104,334	6.9
2010..................................	1,500,764	69.8	1,394,958	105,806	7.1
2011..................................	1,491,087	69.0	1,394,082	97,005	6.5
2012..................................	1,483,574	68.2	1,398,474	85,100	5.7
2013..................................	1,485,405	68.0	1,406,374	79,031	5.3
2014..................................	1,494,188	68.0	1,425,970	68,218	4.6
2015..................................	1,499,009	67.9	1,435,884	63,125	4.2
2016..................................	1,484,001	67.1	1,422,122	61,879	4.2

Table KS-9. Employment and Average Wages by Industry

(Estimates through 2010 are based on the 2007 *North American Industry Classification System* [NAICS]. Estimates from 2011 onward are based on the 2012 NAICS.)

Industry	2009	2010	2011	2012	2013	2014	2015
	Number of jobs						
Wage and Salary Employment by Industry..................	1,428,186	1,408,765	1,418,264	1,433,367	1,448,151	1,471,837	1,481,514
Farm Wage and Salary Employment.........................	8,813	10,025	12,101	10,890	9,340	11,907	12,622
Nonfarm Wage and Salary Employment...................	1,419,373	1,398,740	1,406,163	1,422,477	1,438,811	1,459,930	1,468,892
Private wage and salary employment......................	1,118,961	1,094,999	1,106,362	1,124,558	1,141,223	1,163,349	1,173,674
Forestry, fishing, and related activities..................	3,953	4,109	4,252	4,516	4,773	4,882	4,908
Mining...	8,354	8,508	9,042	9,915	10,386	10,388	8,459
Utilities...	7,727	7,806	8,047	7,978	7,752	7,779	6,752
Construction..	60,862	56,276	54,590	56,641	58,496	61,430	62,549
Manufacturing..	167,618	160,410	161,271	163,133	163,197	162,463	161,361
Durable goods manufacturing......................	104,025	97,506	98,053	100,110	100,574	98,710	98,025
Nondurable goods manufacturing.................	63,593	62,904	63,218	63,023	62,623	63,753	63,336
Wholesale trade.......................................	61,444	59,761	59,691	59,135	60,126	61,672	60,487
Retail trade..	144,390	142,049	143,131	143,886	145,398	147,663	149,785
Transportation and warehousing....................	45,378	44,125	46,250	48,046	48,361	49,489	50,267
Information..	34,739	29,364	27,984	27,818	27,560	27,818	20,978
Finance and insurance...............................	58,316	58,166	60,146	60,950	61,406	62,483	63,861
Real estate and rental and leasing..................	15,112	14,719	14,965	14,103	14,261	14,821	15,437
Professional, scientific, and technical services.......	61,980	61,056	61,049	63,213	66,756	67,924	70,334
Management of companies and enterprises..........	13,455	15,189	13,982	13,640	15,197	18,630	27,602
Administrative and waste services..................	69,722	70,609	75,173	78,067	81,371	84,063	82,124
Educational services.................................	18,873	19,402	19,667	20,270	20,438	20,955	21,267
Health care and social assistance...................	165,145	164,960	167,438	169,645	170,837	172,378	177,636
Arts, entertainment, and recreation.................	13,406	13,360	13,859	15,628	16,049	16,307	16,445
Accommodation and food services..................	102,170	100,761	101,917	104,571	106,034	107,265	110,086
Other services, except public administration..........	66,317	64,369	63,908	63,403	62,825	64,939	63,336
Government and government enterprises...........	300,412	303,741	299,801	297,919	297,588	296,581	295,218
	Dollars						
Average Wages and Salaries by Industry..................	38,933	39,824	40,981	42,272	42,725	43,781	44,998
Average Farm Wages and Salaries..........................	41,618	35,036	35,637	43,617	41,780	41,678	40,193
Average Nonfarm Wages and Salaries....................	38,916	39,858	41,026	42,261	42,731	43,798	45,040
Average private wages and salaries.....................	39,208	40,334	41,577	43,025	43,547	44,693	46,001
Forestry, fishing, and related activities..................	22,500	23,914	23,865	24,595	25,014	25,876	27,631
Mining...	49,065	51,084	54,844	57,493	56,407	59,914	56,488
Utilities...	78,261	79,234	88,106	85,025	88,173	89,280	90,885
Construction..	43,447	45,615	46,003	48,169	48,736	50,524	51,720
Manufacturing..	50,043	52,096	53,520	53,791	54,589	55,249	56,821
Durable goods manufacturing......................	53,829	56,443	58,219	58,488	58,734	59,345	60,743
Nondurable goods manufacturing.................	43,850	45,358	46,231	46,331	47,931	48,907	50,753
Wholesale trade.......................................	56,671	59,193	60,022	63,446	63,104	65,326	66,364
Retail trade..	23,718	24,143	24,815	25,530	25,643	26,058	26,931
Transportation and warehousing....................	42,572	43,747	45,808	47,494	47,951	49,467	50,060
Information..	62,383	64,098	64,601	67,214	69,742	73,196	62,631
Finance and insurance...............................	55,589	57,763	61,308	66,244	66,715	69,560	71,802
Real estate and rental and leasing..................	32,643	33,854	35,347	36,215	36,989	38,421	40,610
Professional, scientific, and technical services.......	55,904	57,321	59,698	62,261	63,649	65,767	68,682
Management of companies and enterprises..........	79,841	81,016	87,709	95,045	93,023	94,580	104,901
Administrative and waste services..................	32,531	33,622	35,552	36,769	37,320	36,742	36,886
Educational services.................................	27,482	27,352	28,318	28,761	29,146	29,658	30,189
Health care and social assistance...................	37,966	38,680	39,476	40,901	40,839	41,501	42,703
Arts, entertainment, and recreation.................	17,230	17,779	18,343	20,532	20,972	20,908	21,563
Accommodation and food services..................	14,246	14,645	15,078	15,697	16,070	16,695	17,420
Other services, except public administration..........	25,840	26,783	27,722	28,545	29,416	30,325	31,788
Government and government enterprises...........	37,829	38,143	38,996	39,378	39,604	40,287	41,219

Table KS-10. Employment Characteristics by Family Type

(Number, percent.)

Family type and labor force status	2013 Total	2013 Families with own children under 18 years	2014 Total	2014 Families with own children under 18 years	2015 Total	2015 Families with own children under 18 years
All Families..	735,596	335,294	726,061	325,507	720,780	324,072
FAMILY TYPE AND LABOR FORCE STATUS						
Married-Couple Families................................	568,165	236,490	562,330	226,937	560,633	228,023
Both husband and wife in labor force....................	56.5	70.1	55.7	69.0	55.5	69.3
Husband in labor force, wife not in labor force........	21.2	25.4	21.3	26.5	21.2	25.3
Wife in labor force, husband not in labor force........	7.4	3.5	7.2	3.0	7.1	3.6
Both husband and wife not in labor force...............	14.6	0.9	15.9	1.4	15.6	1.3
Other Families	167,431	98,804	163,731	98,570	160,147	96,049
Female householder, no husband present................	71.1	72.8	68.8	70.1	68.5	70.9
In labor force..	51.7	60.6	50.4	59.2	51.2	59.8
Not in labor force	19.4	12.2	18.4	10.9	17.3	11.2
Male householder, no wife present.....................	28.9	27.2	31.2	29.9	31.5	29.1
In labor force..	24.3	25.8	26.5	28.1	25.5	26.4
Not in labor force	4.6	1.5	4.7	1.8	5.9	2.7

Table KS-11. School Enrollment and Educational Attainment, 2015

(Number, percent.)

Item	State	U.S.
Enrollment		
Total population 3 years and over, enrolled in school	783,366	81,618,288
Enrolled in nursery school or preschool (percent)........................	6.2	6.0
Enrolled in kindergarten (percent).......................................	5.4	5.0
Enrolled in elementary school, grades 1-8 (percent)......................	40.5	40.3
Enrolled in high school, grades 9-12 (percent)	20.9	20.9
Enrolled in college or graduate school (percent).........................	27.0	27.7
Attainment		
Total population 25 years and over	1,888,479	216,447,163
Less than ninth grade (percent)...	3.8	5.5
9th to 12th grade, no diploma (percent)	5.9	7.3
High school graduate, including equivalency (percent)....................	26.5	27.6
Some college, no degree (percent)	23.6	20.7
Associate's degree (percent)..	8.4	8.2
Bachelor's degree (percent)	20.4	19.0
Graduate or professional degree (percent)...............................	11.4	11.6
High school graduate or higher (percent)	90.3	87.1
Bachelor's degree or higher (percent)	31.7	30.6

Table KS-12. Public School Characteristics and Educational Indicators

(Number, percent; data derived from National Center of Education Statistics.)

Item	State	U.S.
Public Schools, 2014–2015 (except where noted)		
Number of school districts...	317	18,260
Number of schools...	1,337	98,373
Number of students..	497,275	50,312,581
Number of teachers	37,659	3,132,351
Student-teacher ratio	13.2	16.1
Expenditures per student (dollars), FY 2014.............................	10,240	11,066
Four-year adjusted cohort graduation rate (ACGR)[1,2]	85.7	83.2
Students eligible for free or reduced-price lunch (percent)..............	49.9	51.8
English language learners (percent)......................................	9.5	9.4
Students age 3 to 21 served under IDEA, part B (percent).................	14.0	13.0

Public Schools by Type	Number	Percent of state public schools
Total number of schools...	1,337	100.0
Regular	1,332	99.6
Special education...	4	0.3
Vocational education..	0	-
Alternative education...	1	0.1

NOTE: Every school is assigned only one school type based on its instructional emphasis.
[1] ACGR data represents a new method of calculating high-school completion rates and may not be comparable to previous years' data for Averaged Freshmen Graduation Rates (AFGR).
[2] The United States 4-year ACGRs were estimated using both the reported 4-year ACGR data from 49 states and the District of Columbia and using imputed data for Idaho. The estimate for American Indian/Alaska Native students also includes imputed data for Virginia.

Table KS-13. Reported Voting and Registration of the Voting-Age Population, November 2016

(Numbers in thousands, percent.)

Item	Total population	Total citizen population	Registered			Voted		
			Total registered	Percent registered (total population)	Percent registered (total citizen population)	Total voted	Percent voted (total population)	Percent voted (total citizen population)
U.S. Total	245,502	224,059	157,596	64.2	70.3	137,537	56.0	61.4
State Total..............................	2,142	2,029	1,438	67.1	70.9	1,243	58.0	61.3
Sex								
Male	1,048	992	671	64.0	67.6	570	54.4	57.5
Female	1,094	1,036	767	70.1	74.0	673	61.5	64.9
Race								
White alone................................	1,883	1,798	1,307	69.4	72.7	1,149	61.0	63.9
White, non-Hispanic alone	1,678	1,672	1,244	74.1	74.4	1,091	65.0	65.3
Black alone.................................	121	121	75	61.8	61.8	54	44.5	44.5
Asian alone.................................	59	31	15	(B)	(B)	7	(B)	(B)
Hispanic (of any race)	217	138	76	34.9	54.7	68	31.2	48.9
White alone or in combination	1,923	1,838	1,335	69.4	72.6	1,170	60.8	63.6
Black alone or in combination..........	136	136	82	60.4	60.4	56	41.2	41.2
Asian alone or in combination..........	64	36	19	(B)	(B)	11	(B)	(B)
Age								
18 to 24 years................................	269	254	126	46.7	49.5	91	33.8	35.8
25 to 34 years................................	402	362	219	54.5	60.5	184	45.9	50.8
35 to 44 years................................	328	314	240	73.2	76.4	210	63.9	66.7
45 to 64 years................................	719	682	502	69.9	73.7	445	61.8	65.2
65 years and over	424	417	350	82.6	84.1	314	73.9	75.2

B = Base is less than 75,000 and therefore too small to show the derived measure.

Table KS-14. Crime

(Number, rate per 100,000. Data are derived from the FBI Uniform Crime Reports.)

Item	State			U.S. 1,2,3,4		
	2014	2015	Percent change	2014	2015	Percent change
TOTAL POPULATION[5]	2,902,507	2,911,641	0.3	318,907,401	321,418,820	0.8
VIOLENT CRIME						
Number...	10,235	11,353	10.9	1,186,185	1,231,566	3.8
Rate	352.6	389.9	10.6	372.0	383.2	3.0
Murder and Nonnegligent Manslaughter						
Number...	92	128	39.1	14,164	15,696	10.8
Rate	3.2	4.4	38.7	4.4	4.9	10.0
Rape[6]						
Number...	1,483	1,615	8.9	118,027	124,047	5.1
Rate	51.1	55.5	8.6	37.0	38.6	4.3
Robbery						
Number...	1,361	1,818	33.6	322,905	327,374	1.4
Rate	46.9	62.4	33.2	101.3	101.9	0.6
Aggravated Assault						
Number...	7,299	7,792	6.8	731,089	764,449	4.6
Rate	251.5	267.6	6.4	229.2	237.8	3.7
PROPERTY CRIME						
Number...	80,029	79,199		8,209,010	7,993,631	-2.6
Rate	2,757.2	2,720.1	-1.3	2,574.1	2,487.0	-3.4
Burglary						
Number...	15,921	15,362	-3.5	1,713,153	1,579,527	-7.8
Rate	548.5	527.6	-3.8	537.2	491.4	-8.5
Larceny-Theft						
Number...	57,169	56,880	-0.5	5,809,054	5,706,346	-1.8
Rate	1,969.6	1,953.5	-0.8	1,821.5	1,775.4	-2.5
Motor Vehicle Theft						
Number...	6,939	6,957	0.3	686,803	707,758	3.1
Rate	239.1	238.9	-0.1	215.4	220.2	2.2

NOTE: Although arson data are included in the trend and clearance tables, sufficient data are not available to estimate totals for this offense. Therefore, no arson data are published in this table.
X = Not applicable.
- = Zero or rounds to zero.
[1] The crime figures have been adjusted.
[2] The data collection methodology for the offense of forcible rape used by the Minnesota state Uniform Crime Reporting (UCR) Program (with the exception of Minneapolis and St. Paul, Minnesota) does not comply with national UCR Program guidelines. Consequently, its figures for forcible rape and violent crime (of which forcible rape is a part) are not published in this table.
[3] Includes offenses reported by the Zoological Police and the Metro Transit Police.
[4] Because of changes in the state's reporting practices, figures are not comparable to previous years' data.
[5] Populations are U.S. Census Bureau provisional estimates as of July 1 of each year.
[6] The figures shown for the offense of rape were estimated using the revised Uniform Crime Reporting (UCR) definition of rape.

Table KS-15. State Government Finances, 2015

(Dollar amounts in thousands, percent distribution.)

Item	Dollars	Percent distribution
Total Revenue	17,950,851	100.0
General revenue	16,122,662	89.8
Intergovernmental revenue	3,948,181	22.0
Taxes	7,883,960	43.9
General sales	3,052,986	17.0
Selective sales	924,820	5.2
License taxes	378,193	2.1
Individual income tax	2,262,951	12.6
Corporate income tax	458,306	2.6
Other taxes	806,704	4.5
Current charges	3,231,057	18.0
Miscellaneous general revenue	1,059,464	5.9
Utility revenue	0	-
Liquor stores revenue	0	-
Insurance trust revenue[1]	1,828,189	10.2
Total Expenditure	18,043,289	100.0
Intergovernmental expenditure	4,849,983	26.9
Direct expenditure	13,193,306	73.1
Current operation	9,755,053	54.1
Capital outlay	1,131,153	6.3
Insurance benefits and repayments	1,972,913	10.9
Assistance and subsidies	158,368	0.9
Interest on debt	175,819	1.0
Exhibit: Salaries and wages	2,629,912	14.6
Total Expenditure	18,043,289	100.0
General expenditure	16,070,376	89.1
Intergovernmental expenditure	4,849,983	26.9
Direct expenditure	11,220,393	62.2
General expenditure, by function:		
Education	6,999,820	38.8
Public welfare	3,986,056	22.1
Hospitals	1,712,018	9.5
Health	131,796	0.7
Highways	1,298,356	7.2
Police protection	101,829	0.6
Correction	360,900	2.0
Natural resources	231,629	1.3
Parks and recreation	38,259	0.2
Governmental administration	430,112	2.4
Interest on general debt	175,819	1.0
Other and unallocable	603,782	3.3
Utility expenditure	0	-
Liquor stores expenditure	0	-
Insurance trust expenditure	1,972,913	10.9
Debt at End of Fiscal Year	7,581,462	X
Cash and Security Holdings	23,972,103	X

X = Not applicable.
- = Zero or rounds to zero.
[1] Within insurance trust revenue, net earnings of state retirement systems is a calculated statistic (the item code in the data file is X08), and thus can be positive or negative. Net earnings is the sum of earnings on investments plus gains on investments minus losses on investments. The change made in 2002 for asset valuation from book to market value in accordance with Statement 34 of the Governmental Accounting Standards Board is reflected in the calculated statistics.

Table KS-16. State Government Tax Collections, 2016

(Dollars in thousands, percent.)

Item	Dollars	Percent distribution
Total Taxes	8,058,949	100.0
Property taxes	663,841	8.2
Sales and gross receipts	4,324,953	53.7
General sales and gross receipts	3,240,354	40.2
Selective sales and gross receipts	1,084,599	13.5
Alcoholic beverages	133,709	1.7
Amusements	331	-
Insurance premiums	305,631	3.8
Motor fuels	450,633	5.6
Pari-mutuels	0	-
Public utilities	406	-
Tobacco products	146,552	1.8
Other selective sales	47,337	0.6
Licenses	396,648	4.9
Alcoholic beverages	3,672	-
Amusements	6,379	0.1
Corporations in general	27,173	0.3
Hunting and fishing	30,568	0.4
Motor vehicle	219,463	2.7
Motor vehicle operators	20,189	0.3
Public utilities	4,981	0.1
Occupation and business, NEC	81,617	1.0
Other licenses	2,606	-
Income taxes	2,623,779	32.6
Individual income	2,231,902	27.7
Corporation net income	391,877	4.9
Other taxes	49,728	0.6
Death and gift	1	-
Documentary and stock transfer	0	-
Severance	49,727	0.6
Taxes, NEC	0	-

- = Zero or rounds to zero.

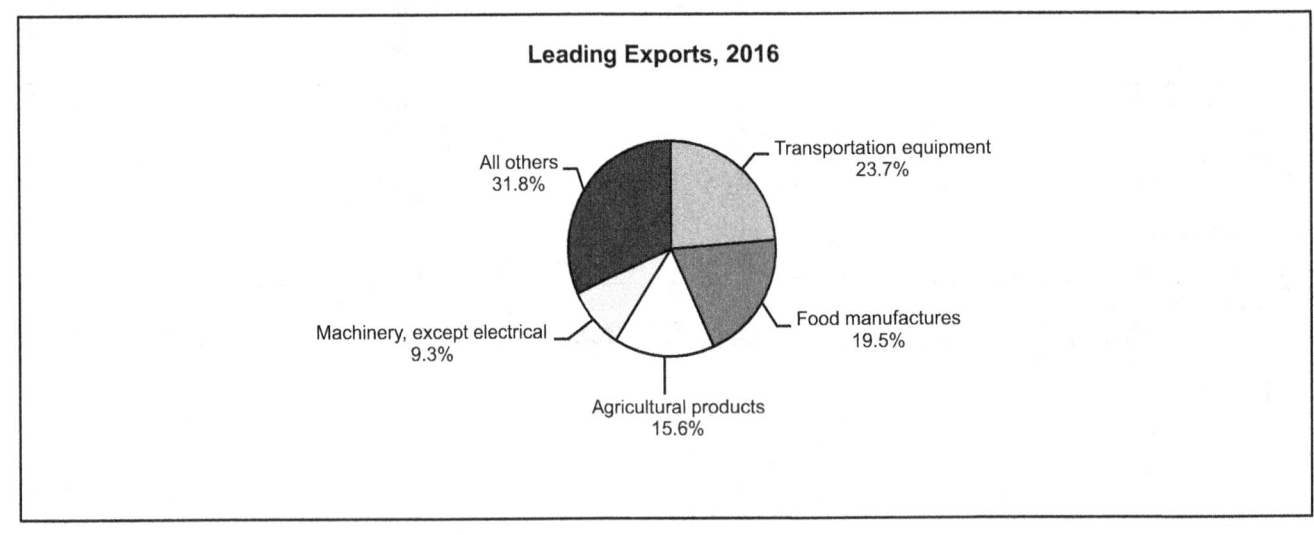

Leading Exports, 2016

- Transportation equipment 23.7%
- Food manufactures 19.5%
- Agricultural products 15.6%
- Machinery, except electrical 9.3%
- All others 31.8%

KENTUCKY

Facts and Figures

Location: East central United States; bordered on the N by Illinois, Indiana, and Ohio, on the E by West Virginia and Virginia, on the S by Tennessee, and on the W by Missouri and Illinois

Area: 40,409 sq. mi. (104,659 sq. km.); rank—37th

Population: 4,436,974 (2016 est.); rank—26th

Principal Cities: capital—Frankfort; largest—Lexington

Statehood: June 1, 1792; 15th state

U.S. Congress: 2 senators, 6 representatives

State Motto: United We Stand, Divided We Fall

State Song: "My Old Kentucky Home"

State Nickname: The Bluegrass State

Abbreviations: KY; Ky.

State Symbols: flower—goldenrod; tree—tulip poplar; bird—cardinal

At a Glance

- With an increase in population of 2.2 percent, Kentucky ranked 33rd among the states in growth from 2010 to 2016.

- Kentucky ranked third in the nation for the highest rate of drug overdose deaths in 2015, with 29.9 deaths per 100,000 population.

- In 2015, Kentucky's median household income was $45,215, the fifth lowest in the country, and 18.5 percent of the population lived below the poverty level.

- The property crime rate in Kentucky in 2015 was 2,177.6 per 100,000 population, compared to the U.S. rate of 2,487.0 per 100,000 population.

- In 2015, 6.0 percent of Kentucky residents did not have health insurance, compared to 9.4 percent of all U.S. residents.

Table KY-1. Population by Age, Sex, Race, and Hispanic Origin

(Number, percent, except where noted.)

Sex, age, race, and Hispanic origin	2000	2010	2016 [1]	Average annual percent change, 2010–2016
Total Population................................	4,041,769	4,339,367	4,436,974	0.1
Percent of total U.S. population	1.4	1.4	1.4	X
Sex				
Male..............	1,975,368	2,134,952	2,186,553	0.2
Female	2,066,401	2,204,425	2,250,421	0.1
Age				
Under 5 years...............	265,901	282,367	275,753	-0.1
5 to 19 years..................	847,743	863,837	849,140	-0.1
20 to 64 years..................	2,423,332	2,614,936	2,621,364	-
65 years and over..................	504,793	578,227	690,717	1.2
Median age (years)	35.9	38.1	38.7	0.1
Race and Hispanic Origin				
One race..................				
White	3,640,889	3,864,193	3,903,419	0.1
Black..................	295,994	342,804	367,591	0.5
American Indian and Alaska Native	8,616	12,105	13,297	0.6
Asian..................	29,744	50,177	66,230	2.0
Native Hawaiian or Other Pacific Islander	1,460	3,199	3,675	0.9
Two or more races	42,443	66,889	82,762	1.5
Hispanic (of any race)..................	59,939	138,618	155,520	0.8

X = Not applicable.
[1] Population figures for 2016 are July 1 estimates. The 2010 estimates are taken from the 2010 Census.
- = Zero or rounds to zero.

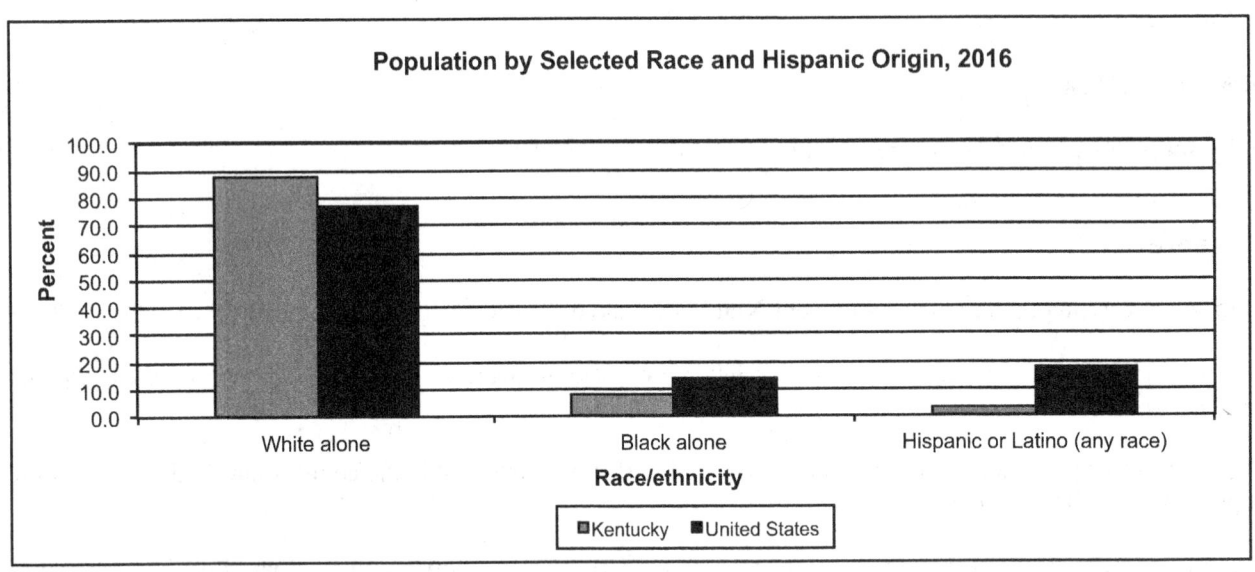

Population by Selected Race and Hispanic Origin, 2016

Table KY-2. Marital Status

(Number, percent distribution.)

Sex, age, race, and Hispanic origin	2000	2010	2015
Males, 15 Years and Over	1,551,174	1,702,020	1,746,997
Never married	25.9	30.8	31.6
Now married, except separated..................	59.9	52.0	50.4
Separated..................	1.5	2.1	1.8
Widowed..................	2.6	2.8	3.1
Divorced..................	10.2	12.3	13.1
Females, 15 Years and Over	1,665,993	1,794,164	1,841,808
Never married	19.7	24.2	25.6
Now married, except separated..................	55.0	48.9	48.0
Separated..................	2.1	2.6	2.5
Widowed..................	11.5	10.6	10.0
Divorced..................	11.8	13.7	13.9

Table KY-3. Households and Housing Characteristics

(Number, percent, dollars.)

Item	2000	2010	2015	Average annual percent change, 2000–2015
Total Households.....................................	1,590,647	1,684,348	1,716,168	0.5
Family households.............................	1,104,398	1,126,685	1,131,839	0.2
Married-couple family...................	857,944	833,872	828,120	-0.2
Other family.................................	246,454	292,813	303,719	1.5
Male householder, no wife present...	58,497	76,832	85,755	3.1
Female householder, no husband present...........................	187,957	215,981	217,964	1.1
Nonfamily households.......................	486,249	557,663	584,329	1.3
Householder living alone..................	414,095	470,103	488,517	1.2
Householder not living alone............	72,154	87,560	95,812	2.2
Housing Characteristics				
Total housing units...........................	1,750,927	1,928,617	1,957,133	0.8
Occupied housing units	1,590,647	1,684,348	1,716,168	0.5
Owner occupied.............................	1,125,397	1,156,292	1,138,253	0.1
Renter occupied.............................	465,250	528,056	577,915	1.6
Average household size......................	2.47	2.51	2.5	0.1
Financial Characteristics				
Median gross rent of renter-occupied housing	445	613	702	3.9
Median monthly owner costs for housing units with a mortgage	816	1,072	1,089	2.2
Median value of owner-occupied housing units...........................	86,700	121,600	130,000	3.3

Table KY-4. Migration, Origin, and Language

(Number, percent.)

Characteristic	State			U.S.		
	2014	2015	Percent change	2014	2015	Percent change
Residence 1 Year Ago						
Population 1 year and over	4,357,819	4,373,403	0.4	315,095,393	317,635,720	0.8
Same house	84.1	84.8	X	85.1	85.3	X
Different house in the U.S.	15.6	14.9	X	14.3	14.1	X
Same county	9.1	8.3	X	8.7	8.5	X
Different county	6.5	6.5	X	5.6	5.6	X
Same state	4.1	4.1	X	3.3	3.2	X
Different state	2.4	2.4	X	2.3	2.4	X
Abroad	0.3	0.4	X	0.6	0.7	X
Place of Birth						
Native born	4,251,417	4,267,756	0.4	276,465,262	278,128,449	0.6
Male	49.1	49.1	X	49.3	49.3	X
Female	50.9	50.9	X	50.7	50.7	X
Foreign born	162,040	157,336	-2.9	42,391,794	43,290,372	2.1
Male	53.1	50.2	X	48.7	48.6	X
Female	46.9	49.8	X	51.3	51.4	X
Foreign born; naturalized U.S. citizen.....	58,742	58,196	-0.9	19,984,738	20,697,103	3.6
Male	48.0	44.4	X	45.9	45.9	X
Female	52.0	55.6	X	54.1	54.1	X
Foreign born; not a U.S. citizen	103,298	99,140	-4.0	22,407,056	22,593,269	0.8
Male	56.0	53.6	X	51.2	51.1	X
Female	44.0	46.4	X	48.8	48.9	X
Entered 2010 or later	19.6	28.3	X	12.3	15.6	X
Entered 2000 to 2009	41.7	34.5	X	28.6	27.9	X
Entered before 2000...........................	38.7	37.2	X	59.1	56.5	X
World Region of Birth, Foreign						
Foreign-born population, excluding population born at sea	162,040	157,336	-2.9	42,390,705	43,289,646	2.1
Europe	14.0	15.1	X	11.2	11.1	X
Asia...	31.6	35.6	X	30.1	30.6	X
Africa	12.3	8.1	X	4.6	4.8	X
Oceania..	0.7	0.7	X	0.6	0.6	X
Latin America.................................	39.1	37.7	X	51.6	51.1	X
North America................................	2.3	2.8	X	1.9	1.9	X
Language Spoken at Home and Ability to Speak English						
Population 5 years and over...................	4,138,825	4,151,726	0.3	299,084,046	301,625,014	0.8
English only	94.8	94.7	X	78.9	78.5	X
Language other than English................	5.2	5.3	X	21.1	21.5	X
Speaks English less than "very well"...	2.3	2.1	X	8.6	8.6	X

NA = Not available.
X = Not applicable.
- = Zero or rounds to zero.

Table KY-5. Median Income and Poverty Status, 2015

(Number, percent, except as noted.)

Characteristic	State		U.S.	
	Number	Percent	Number	Percent
Median Income				
Households (dollars)...	45,215	X	55,775	X
Families (dollars)	56,187	X	68,260	X
Below Poverty Level (All People)	794,055	18.5	46,153,077	14.7
Sex				
Male	350,768	16.7	20,599,407	13.4
Female	443,287	20.2	25,553,670	16.0
Age				
Under 18 years..	256,106	25.9	15,000,273	20.7
Related children under 18 years...................	251,102	25.5	14,693,239	20.4
18 to 64 years	465,255	17.6	26,960,369	13.9
65 years and over	72,694	11.2	4,192,435	9.0

X = Not applicable.

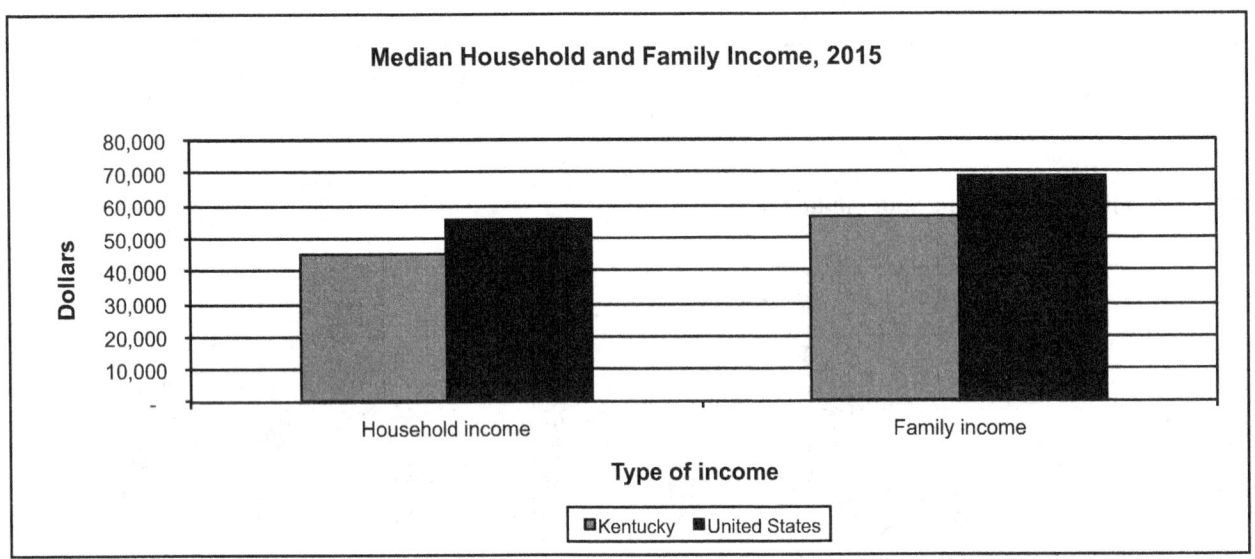

Table KY-6. Health Insurance Coverage Status for the Civilian Noninstitutionalized Population and Children Under 18 Years of Age

(Numbers in thousands, percent.)

Item	2007	2008	2009	2010	2011	2012	2013	2014	2015
Civilian Noninstitutionalized Population	4,207	4,188	4,225	4,243	4,284	4,293	4,312	4,329	4,343
Covered by Private or Public Insurance									
Number..	3,637	3,598	3,612	3,596	3,666	3,697	3,696	3,962	4,081
Percent...	86.4	85.9	85.5	84.7	85.6	86.1	85.7	91.5	94.0
Not Covered									
Number..	570	590	613	647	618	596	616	366	261
Percent...	13.6	14.1	14.5	15.3	14.4	13.9	14.3	8.5	6.0
Percent in the U.S. not covered......................................	15.3	15.1	15.1	15.5	15.1	14.8	14.5	11.7	9.4
Children Under 18 Years of Age	1,026	1,004	1,015	1,018	1,023	1,016	1,012	1,013	1,008
Covered by Private or Public Insurance									
Number..	944	934	951	957	961	960	953	969	965
Percent...	92.0	93.0	93.7	94.0	93.9	94.5	94.1	95.7	95.8
Not Covered									
Number..	82	70	64	61	62	56	60	43	43
Percent...	8.0	7.0	6.3	6.0	6.1	5.5	5.9	4.3	4.2
Percent in the U.S. not covered......................................	11.0	9.7	8.6	8.0	7.5	7.2	7.1	6.0	4.8

Table KY-7. Employment Status by Demographic Group, 2016

(Numbers in thousands, percent.)

Characteristic	Civilian noninstitutional population	Civilian labor force		Employed		Unemployed	
		Number	Percent of population	Number	Percent of population	Number	Percent of population
Total....................................	3,460	2,004	57.9	1,905	55.1	99	4.9
Sex							
Male...........................	1,667	1,056	63.4	1,000	59.9	57	5.4
Female	1,793	948	52.9	905	50.5	42	4.4
Race, Sex, and Hispanic Origin							
White..........................	3,099	1,791	57.8	1,705	55.0	85	4.8
Male.......................	1,491	940	63.0	892	59.8	48	5.1
Female	1,609	851	52.9	814	50.6	37	4.4
Black or African American..................	265	160	60.4	149	56.3	11	6.9
Male.......................	131	84	64.1	77	58.9	7	8.2
Female	135	77	56.9	72	53.8	4	5.4
Hispanic or Latino ethnicity[1]	92	65	70.8	60	65.2	5	7.9
Male.......................	NA	NA	NA	NA	NA	NA	NA
Female	NA	NA	NA	NA	NA	NA	NA
Age							
16 to 19 years................	230	80	34.7	69	29.8	11	13.9
20 to 24 years................	275	203	73.8	186	67.6	17	8.3
25 to 34 years................	548	430	78.4	407	74.2	23	5.3
35 to 44 years................	554	433	78.1	413	74.5	20	4.6
45 to 54 years................	570	426	74.7	411	72.1	15	3.5
55 to 64 years................	603	320	53.1	310	51.4	10	3.3
65 years and over	680	113	16.6	110	16.2	3	2.3

NOTE: Data in Table 7 are from the Current Population Survey (CPS) and do not match the estimates in Table 8. See notes and definitions for further information.
[1] May be of any race.
NA = Not available.

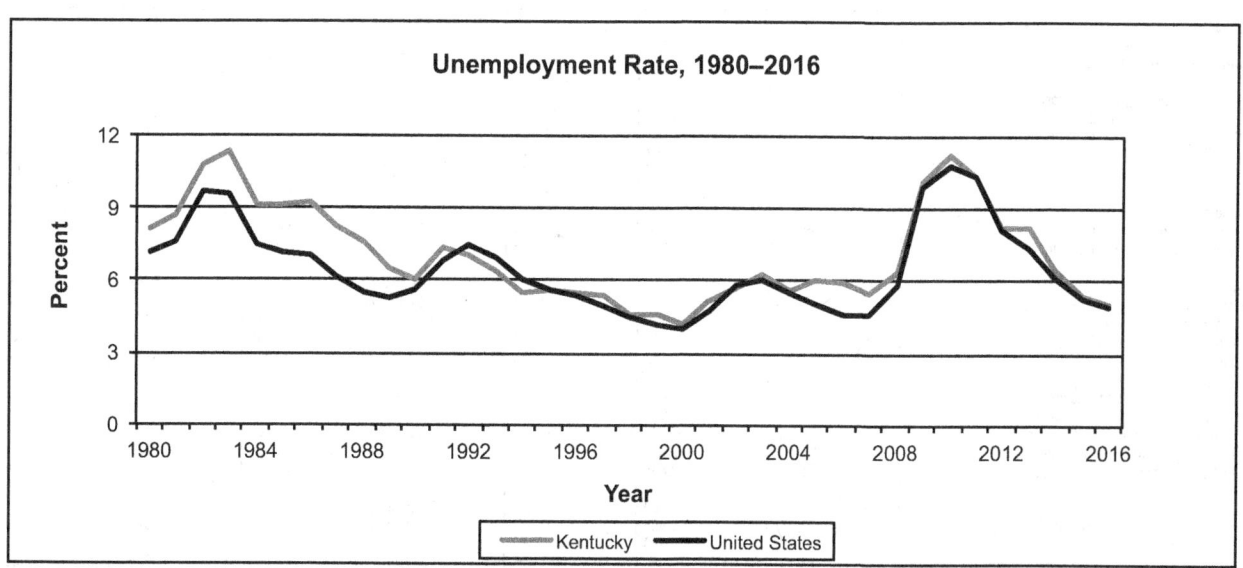

Table KY-8. Employment Status of the Civilian Noninstitutional Population Age 16 Years and Over

(Number, percent.)

Year	Civilian labor force	Civilian participation rate	Employed	Unemployed	Unemployment rate
2008............................	2,030,738	61.4	1,900,683	130,055	6.4
2009............................	2,060,162	61.9	1,847,126	213,036	10.3
2010............................	2,054,375	61.3	1,844,650	209,725	10.2
2011............................	2,056,410	61.0	1,862,928	193,482	9.4
2012............................	2,058,982	60.8	1,891,038	167,944	8.2
2013............................	2,058,186	60.4	1,892,027	166,159	8.1
2014............................	2,005,603	58.6	1,875,932	129,671	6.5
2015............................	1,953,393	56.8	1,847,938	105,455	5.4
2016............................	1,991,974	57.6	1,892,273	99,701	5.0

Table KY-9. Employment and Average Wages by Industry

(Estimates through 2010 are based on the 2007 *North American Industry Classification System* [NAICS]. Estimates from 2011 onward are based on the 2012 NAICS.)

Industry	2009	2010	2011	2012	2013	2014	2015
	Number of jobs						
Wage and Salary Employment by Industry..................	1,870,449	1,866,856	1,887,646	1,910,516	1,923,908	1,949,783	1,979,661
Farm Wage and Salary Employment.........................	12,629	12,662	14,003	14,781	13,660	14,615	16,632
Nonfarm Wage and Salary Employment....................	1,857,820	1,854,194	1,873,643	1,895,735	1,910,248	1,935,168	1,963,029
Private wage and salary employment.......................	1,482,972	1,470,901	1,492,161	1,523,431	1,542,651	1,572,666	1,605,288
Forestry, fishing, and related activities.....................	7,730	7,575	7,328	7,276	7,434	7,511	7,559
Mining..	23,299	21,800	22,623	20,295	17,189	16,235	13,698
Utilities..	6,502	6,422	6,514	6,566	6,512	6,624	6,569
Construction	77,475	70,257	69,768	69,366	70,046	74,852	77,622
Manufacturing...	213,054	209,255	212,914	223,357	229,626	235,074	241,640
Durable goods manufacturing.............................	127,343	124,981	128,840	138,706	143,808	149,164	155,651
Nondurable goods manufacturing........................	85,711	84,274	84,074	84,651	85,818	85,910	85,989
Wholesale trade	73,274	72,113	72,561	73,086	74,323	74,764	75,124
Retail trade..	204,733	202,117	202,920	204,597	204,821	206,669	211,304
Transportation and warehousing...............................	83,170	82,554	85,723	87,256	86,636	90,901	95,877
Information	27,202	26,221	26,881	26,593	26,325	26,360	25,340
Finance and insurance	71,038	69,631	70,162	72,204	73,802	74,992	76,764
Real estate and rental and leasing............................	19,176	18,605	18,260	18,249	18,641	18,604	18,911
Professional, scientific, and technical services	71,167	70,037	69,782	68,299	69,960	72,168	73,840
Management of companies and enterprises..................	19,705	19,462	20,013	20,526	20,570	20,677	19,972
Administrative and waste services.............................	83,508	91,904	98,934	105,185	111,676	119,153	122,832
Educational services	29,785	30,996	31,683	32,052	32,006	32,600	32,723
Health care and social assistance.............................	219,654	222,785	225,810	232,734	233,373	231,634	236,822
Arts, entertainment, and recreation...........................	19,783	18,924	18,557	19,842	20,265	20,291	21,271
Accommodation and food services............................	150,423	149,848	152,074	156,258	160,290	163,004	167,696
Other services, except public administration..................	82,294	80,395	79,654	79,690	79,156	80,553	79,724
Government and government enterprises	374,848	383,293	381,482	372,304	367,597	362,502	357,741
	Dollars						
Average Wages and Salaries by Industry	37,681	38,549	39,545	40,370	40,707	41,797	43,108
Average Farm Wages and Salaries	21,669	20,674	16,363	21,340	23,808	22,787	19,003
Average Nonfarm Wages and Salaries	37,790	38,671	39,719	40,519	40,828	41,941	43,312
Average private wages and salaries..........................	37,147	38,087	39,106	40,116	40,477	41,699	43,109
Forestry, fishing, and related activities.....................	25,278	26,307	26,425	26,931	27,634	28,278	29,556
Mining..	63,119	67,353	69,617	66,776	68,397	68,696	68,485
Utilities..	70,515	70,649	72,240	74,123	76,425	79,776	82,320
Construction	42,923	43,590	44,005	45,923	47,382	49,900	51,603
Manufacturing...	47,933	49,656	51,280	52,617	53,294	55,081	56,704
Durable goods manufacturing.............................	49,483	51,094	53,230	54,322	54,829	56,382	58,308
Nondurable goods manufacturing........................	45,629	47,524	48,293	49,822	50,722	52,823	53,800
Wholesale trade	50,863	51,758	53,664	54,842	55,085	57,408	60,110
Retail trade..	23,233	23,731	24,113	24,672	24,817	25,143	25,998
Transportation and warehousing...............................	46,193	47,845	47,677	48,895	49,391	50,533	51,763
Information	42,719	43,486	44,472	45,933	46,393	49,046	48,951
Finance and insurance	53,742	56,615	58,925	60,333	60,938	63,893	66,590
Real estate and rental and leasing............................	31,845	33,492	35,399	36,421	35,430	37,188	38,381
Professional, scientific, and technical services	49,616	51,062	52,835	55,096	56,280	57,915	60,413
Management of companies and enterprises..................	81,535	86,258	91,249	95,273	91,138	91,831	96,922
Administrative and waste services.............................	25,043	25,398	25,657	26,533	26,774	27,252	28,308
Educational services	23,426	23,885	24,247	24,718	25,027	24,750	24,969
Health care and social assistance.............................	40,066	40,782	41,992	42,903	43,448	44,561	46,576
Arts, entertainment, and recreation...........................	20,696	21,464	21,847	22,091	22,462	23,906	23,521
Accommodation and food services............................	14,738	15,143	15,498	16,063	16,167	16,841	17,566
Other services, except public administration..................	26,190	27,030	27,746	29,351	30,095	30,989	32,298
Government and government enterprises	40,336	40,914	42,116	42,164	42,302	42,990	44,224

Table KY-10. Employment Characteristics by Family Type

(Number, percent.)

Family type and labor force status	2013		2014		2015	
	Total	Families with own children under 18 years	Total	Families with own children under 18 years	Total	Families with own children under 18 years
All Families...	1,139,596	469,000	1,121,747	464,494	1,131,839	455,703
FAMILY TYPE AND LABOR FORCE STATUS						
Married-Couple Families....................................	833,340	305,408	826,087	307,360	828,120	300,055
Both husband and wife in labor force...................	48.4	66.3	48.5	65.6	46.7	65.2
Husband in labor force, wife not in labor force......	21.0	25.8	20.8	25.9	21.1	25.3
Wife in labor force, husband not in labor force......	8.9	4.3	9.0	4.5	9.5	5.5
Both husband and wife not in labor force..............	21.3	3.3	21.7	4.0	22.1	3.6
Other Families..	306,256	163,592	295,660	157,134	303,719	155,648
Female householder, no husband present.............	71.6	75.5	73.2	74.9	71.8	73.8
In labor force..	44.7	57.5	45.2	57.4	43.6	56.6
Not in labor force..	27.0	18.0	28.0	17.4	28.1	17.2
Male householder, no wife present......................	28.4	24.5	26.8	25.1	28.2	26.2
In labor force..	19.7	21.2	18.1	20.3	19.4	21.1
Not in labor force..	8.7	3.3	8.7	4.8	8.8	5.1

Table KY-11. School Enrollment and Educational Attainment, 2015

(Number, percent.)

Item	State	U.S.
Enrollment		
Total population 3 years and over, enrolled in school	1,062,437	81,618,288
Enrolled in nursery school or preschool (percent)	5.6	6.0
Enrolled in kindergarten (percent)	5.0	5.0
Enrolled in elementary school, grades 1-8 (percent).................................	42.5	40.3
Enrolled in high school, grades 9-12 (percent).................................	21.6	20.9
Enrolled in college or graduate school (percent).................................	25.2	27.7
Attainment		
Total population 25 years and over	2,988,790	216,447,163
Less than ninth grade (percent).................................	6.2	5.5
9th to 12th grade, no diploma (percent).................................	8.7	7.3
High school graduate, including equivalency (percent).................................	33.5	27.6
Some college, no degree (percent).................................	20.4	20.7
Associate's degree (percent).................................	7.9	8.2
Bachelor's degree (percent).................................	13.6	19.0
Graduate or professional degree (percent).................................	9.7	11.6
High school graduate or higher (percent).................................	85.1	87.1
Bachelor's degree or higher (percent).................................	23.3	30.6

Table KY-12. Public School Characteristics and Educational Indicators

(Number, percent; data derived from National Center of Education Statistics.)

Item	State	U.S.
Public Schools, 2014–2015 (except where noted)		
Number of school districts.................................	185	18,260
Number of schools.................................	1,548	98,373
Number of students.................................	688,640	50,312,581
Number of teachers.................................	41,586	3,132,351
Student-teacher ratio.................................	16.6	16.1
Expenditures per student (dollars), FY 2014.................................	9,411	11,066
Four-year adjusted cohort graduation rate (ACGR)[1,2]	88.0	83.2
Students eligible for free or reduced-price lunch (percent).................................	56.9	51.8
English language learners (percent).................................	3.0	9.4
Students age 3 to 21 served under IDEA, part B (percent).................................	14.2	13.0

Public Schools by Type	Number	Percent of state public schools
Total number of schools.................................	1,548	100.0
Regular	1,225	79.1
Special education.................................	8	0.5
Vocational education.................................	121	7.8
Alternative education.................................	194	12.5

NOTE: Every school is assigned only one school type based on its instructional emphasis.
[1] ACGR data represents a new method of calculating high-school completion rates and may not be comparable to previous years' data for Averaged Freshmen Graduation Rates (AFGR).
[2] The United States 4-year ACGRs were estimated using both the reported 4-year ACGR data from 49 states and the District of Columbia and using imputed data for Idaho. The estimate for American Indian/Alaska Native students also includes imputed data for Virginia.

Table KY-13. Reported Voting and Registration of the Voting-Age Population, November 2016

(Numbers in thousands, percent.)

Item	Total population	Total citizen population	Registered			Voted		
			Total registered	Percent registered (total population)	Percent registered (total citizen population)	Total voted	Percent voted (total population)	Percent voted (total citizen population)
U.S. Total	245,502	224,059	157,596	64.2	70.3	137,537	56.0	61.4
State Total...........................	3,348	3,246	2,253	67.3	69.4	1,850	55.3	57.0
Sex								
Male	1,614	1,550	1,035	64.1	66.8	861	53.3	55.5
Female	1,734	1,697	1,218	70.3	71.8	989	57.0	58.3
Race								
White alone............................	3,014	2,953	2,038	67.6	69.0	1,669	55.4	56.5
White, non-Hispanic alone	2,892	2,881	1,998	69.1	69.3	1,634	56.5	56.7
Black alone............................	250	231	187	74.9	81.2	159	63.7	69.1
Asian alone............................	28	14	3	(B)	(B)	3	(B)	(B)
Hispanic (of any race)	138	79	44	(B)	(B)	38	(B)	(B)
White alone or in combination	3,052	2,991	2,055	67.3	68.7	1,680	55.0	56.1
Black alone or in combination..........	281	262	210	74.5	80.0	175	62.3	66.9
Asian alone or in combination..........	36	23	8	(B)	(B)	8	(B)	(B)
Age								
18 to 24 years.....................	406	384	249	61.5	64.9	207	51.1	53.9
25 to 34 years.....................	530	496	336	63.3	67.7	273	51.5	55.1
35 to 44 years.....................	553	529	360	65.1	68.1	300	54.2	56.7
45 to 64 years.....................	1,244	1,229	853	68.6	69.4	703	56.6	57.2
65 years and over	615	609	455	73.9	74.7	366	59.5	60.2

B = Base is less than 75,000 and therefore too small to show the derived measure.

Table KY-14. Crime

(Number, rate per 100,000. Data are derived from the FBI Uniform Crime Reports.)

Item	State			U.S. [1,2,3,4]		
	2014	2015	Percent change	2014	2015	Percent change
TOTAL POPULATION[5]	4,412,617	4,425,092	0.3	318,907,401	321,418,820	0.8
VIOLENT CRIME						
Number..................................	9,495	9,676	1.9	1,186,185	1,231,566	3.8
Rate	215.2	218.7	1.6	372.0	383.2	3.0
Murder and Nonnegligent Manslaughter						
Number..................................	164	209	27.4	14,164	15,696	10.8
Rate	3.7	4.7	27.1	4.4	4.9	10.0
Rape[6]						
Number..................................	1,556	1,492	-4.1	118,027	124,047	5.1
Rate	35.3	33.7	-4.4	37.0	38.6	4.3
Robbery						
Number..................................	3,343	3,307	-1.1	322,905	327,374	1.4
Rate	75.8	74.7	-1.4	101.3	101.9	0.6
Aggravated Assault						
Number..................................	4,432	4,668	5.3	731,089	764,449	4.6
Rate	100.4	105.5	5.0	229.2	237.8	3.7
PROPERTY CRIME						
Number..................................	99,909	96,362	-3.6	8,209,010	7,993,631	-2.6
Rate	2,264.2	2,177.6	-3.8	2,574.1	2,487.0	-3.4
Burglary						
Number..................................	23,426	22,260	-5.0	1,713,153	1,579,527	-7.8
Rate	530.9	503.0	-5.2	537.2	491.4	-8.5
Larceny-Theft						
Number..................................	70,108	66,320	-5.4	5,809,054	5,706,346	-1.8
Rate	1,588.8	1,498.7	-5.7	1,821.5	1,775.4	-2.5
Motor Vehicle Theft						
Number..................................	6,375	7,782	22.1	686,803	707,758	3.1
Rate	144.5	175.9	21.7	215.4	220.2	2.2

NOTE: Although arson data are included in the trend and clearance tables, sufficient data are not available to estimate totals for this offense. Therefore, no arson data are published in this table.

X = Not applicable.

- = Zero or rounds to zero.

[1] The crime figures have been adjusted.

[2] The data collection methodology for the offense of forcible rape used by the Minnesota state Uniform Crime Reporting (UCR) Program (with the exception of Minneapolis and St. Paul, Minnesota) does not comply with national UCR Program guidelines. Consequently, its figures for forcible rape and violent crime (of which forcible rape is a part) are not published in this table.

[3] Includes offenses reported by the Zoological Police and the Metro Transit Police.

[4] Because of changes in the state's reporting practices, figures are not comparable to previous years' data.

[5] Populations are U.S. Census Bureau provisional estimates as of July 1 of each year.

[6] The figures shown for the offense of rape were estimated using the revised Uniform Crime Reporting (UCR) definition of rape.

Table KY-15. State Government Finances, 2015

(Dollar amounts in thousands, percent distribution.)

Item	Dollars	Percent distribution
Total Revenue	30,059,829	100.0
General revenue	26,633,530	88.6
Intergovernmental revenue	10,559,736	35.1
Taxes	11,597,983	38.6
General sales	3,267,331	10.9
Selective sales	2,183,120	7.3
License taxes	487,834	1.6
Individual income tax	4,069,501	13.5
Corporate income tax	751,910	2.5
Other taxes	838,287	2.8
Current charges	3,419,193	11.4
Miscellaneous general revenue	1,056,618	3.5
Utility revenue	0	-
Liquor stores revenue	0	-
Insurance trust revenue[1]	3,426,299	11.4
Total Expenditure	33,376,672	100.0
Intergovernmental expenditure	4,709,948	14.1
Direct expenditure	28,666,724	85.9
Current operation	20,382,646	61.1
Capital outlay	2,445,191	7.3
Insurance benefits and repayments	4,263,050	12.8
Assistance and subsidies	923,704	2.8
Interest on debt	652,133	2.0
Exhibit: Salaries and wages	4,217,499	12.6
Total Expenditure	33,376,672	100.0
General expenditure	29,113,622	87.2
Intergovernmental expenditure	4,709,948	14.1
Direct expenditure	24,403,674	73.1
General expenditure, by function:		
Education	9,681,710	29.0
Public welfare	10,918,824	32.7
Hospitals	1,422,065	4.3
Health	643,581	1.9
Highways	2,732,030	8.2
Police protection	195,408	0.6
Correction	532,798	1.6
Natural resources	338,503	1.0
Parks and recreation	99,791	0.3
Governmental administration	882,241	2.6
Interest on general debt	652,133	2.0
Other and unallocable	1,014,538	3.0
Utility expenditure	0	-
Liquor stores expenditure	0	-
Insurance trust expenditure	4,263,050	12.8
Debt at End of Fiscal Year	13,784,882	X
Cash and Security Holdings	42,027,997	X

X = Not applicable.
- = Zero or rounds to zero.
[1] Within insurance trust revenue, net earnings of state retirement systems is a calculated statistic (the item code in the data file is X08), and thus can be positive or negative. Net earnings is the sum of earnings on investments plus gains on investments minus losses on investments. The change made in 2002 for asset valuation from book to market value in accordance with Statement 34 of the Governmental Accounting Standards Board is reflected in the calculated statistics.

Table KY-16. State Government Tax Collections, 2016

(Dollars in thousands, percent.)

Item	Dollars	Percent distribution
Total Taxes	11,778,866	100.0
Property taxes	577,544	4.9
Sales and gross receipts	5,603,120	47.6
General sales and gross receipts	3,462,704	29.4
Selective sales and gross receipts	2,140,416	18.2
Alcoholic beverages	139,248	1.2
Amusements	229	-
Insurance premiums	145,250	1.2
Motor fuels	750,034	6.4
Pari-mutuels	4,993	-
Public utilities	64,681	0.5
Tobacco products	245,581	2.1
Other selective sales	790,400	6.7
Licenses	505,377	4.3
Alcoholic beverages	6,616	0.1
Amusements	324	-
Corporations in general	109,321	0.9
Hunting and fishing	28,455	0.2
Motor vehicle	207,617	1.8
Motor vehicle operators	16,836	0.1
Public utilities	0	-
Occupation and business, NEC	130,826	1.1
Other licenses	5,382	-
Income taxes	4,888,920	41.5
Individual income	4,282,080	36.4
Corporation net income	606,840	5.2
Other taxes	203,905	1.7
Death and gift	51,247	0.4
Documentary and stock transfer	3,255	-
Severance	149,403	1.3
Taxes, NEC	0	-

- = Zero or rounds to zero.

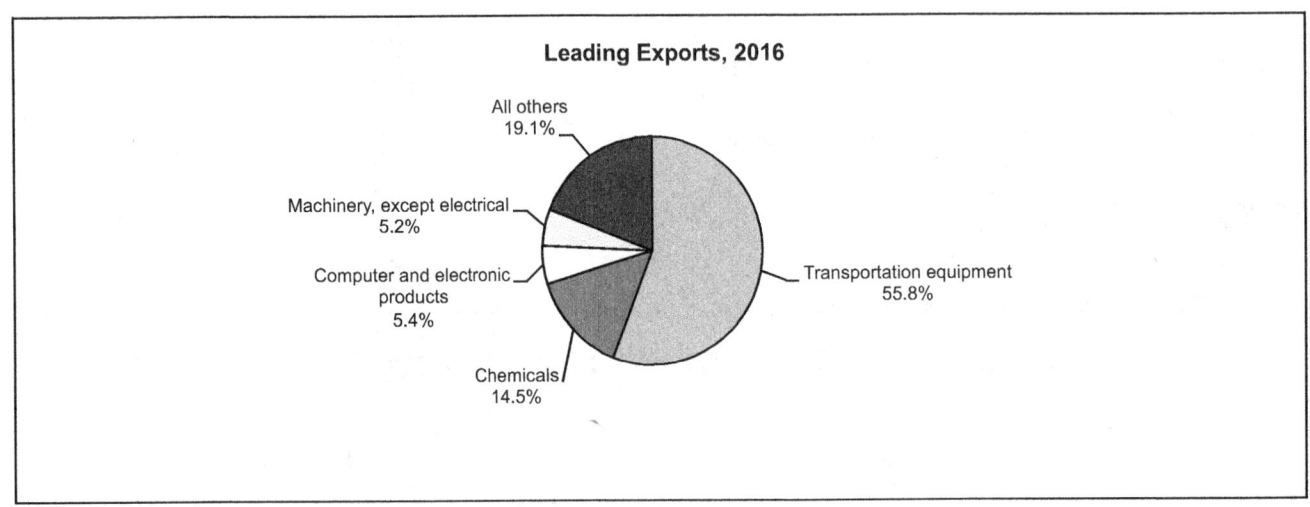

Leading Exports, 2016

All others 19.1%

Machinery, except electrical 5.2%

Computer and electronic products 5.4%

Chemicals 14.5%

Transportation equipment 55.8%

LOUISIANA

Location: South central United States; bordered on the N by Arkansas, on the E by Mississippi, on the S by the Gulf of Mexico, and on the W by Texas

Area: 51,840 sq. mi. (134,264 sq. km.); rank—31st

Population: 4,681,666 (2016 est.); rank—25th

Principal Cities: capital—Baton Rouge; largest—New Orleans

Statehood: April 30, 1812; 18th state

U.S. Congress: 2 senators, 6 representatives

State Motto: Union, Justice, Confidence

State Song: "Give Me Louisiana"

State Nicknames: The Pelican State; The Bayou State

Abbreviations: LA; La.

State Symbols: flower—magnolia; tree—bald cypress; bird—Eastern brown pelican

At a Glance

- With an increase in population of 3.3 percent, Louisiana ranked 29th in population growth from 2010 to 2016.

- Louisiana's median household income in 2015 was $45,727, and 19.6 percent of the population lived below the poverty level.

- In 2016, Louisiana had the third-highest percent of residents who identified as "Black or African-American Alone," with 32.6 percent of residents in this category.

- In 2015, 11.9 percent of Louisiana's population did not have health insurance, compared to 9.4 percent of the entire U.S. population.

- Louisianans consumed the most energy per capita in 2015, using 912.2 million Btu per person, compared to the U.S. average of 303.1 million Btu per capita.

Table LA-1. Population by Age, Sex, Race, and Hispanic Origin

(Number, percent, except where noted.)

Sex, age, race, and Hispanic origin	2000	2010	2016 [1]	Average annual percent change, 2010–2016
Total Population...........................	4,468,976	4,533,372	4,681,666	0.2
Percent of total U.S. population	1.6	1.5	1.4	X
Sex				
Male.............................	2,162,903	2,219,292	2,289,370	0.2
Female	2,306,073	2,314,080	2,392,296	0.2
Age				
Under 5 years..............................	317,392	314,260	310,601	-0.1
5 to 19 years.................................	1,050,637	939,977	918,934	-0.1
20 to 64 years.................................	2,584,018	2,721,278	2,777,688	0.1
65 years and over..............................	516,929	557,857	674,443	1.3
Median age (years)	34.0	35.8	36.6	0.1
Race and Hispanic Origin				
One race...				
White...	2,856,161	2,902,875	2,956,505	0.1
Black...	1,451,944	1,462,969	1,524,638	0.3
American Indian and Alaska Native	25,477	33,037	35,976	0.6
Asian...	54,758	71,829	85,006	1.1
Native Hawaiian or Other Pacific Islander	1,240	2,588	3,079	1.2
Two or more races	48,265	60,074	76,462	1.7
Hispanic (of any race).........................	107,738	200,653	236,152	1.1

X = Not applicable.

[1] Population figures for 2016 are July 1 estimates. The 2010 estimates are taken from the 2010 Census.

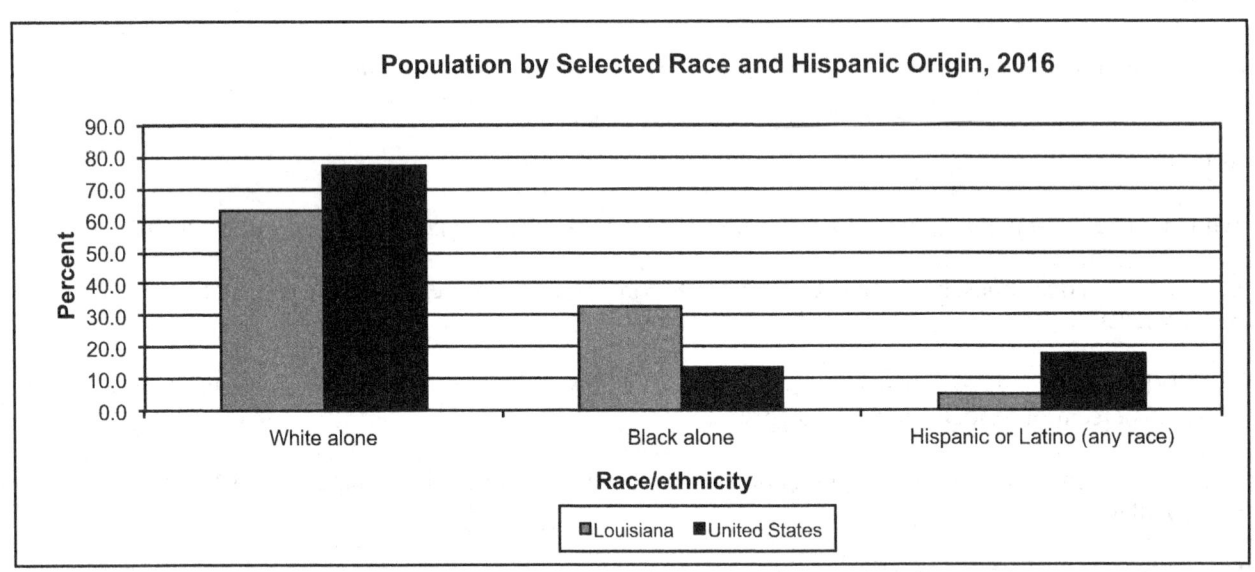

Population by Selected Race and Hispanic Origin, 2016

Table LA-2. Marital Status

(Number, percent distribution.)

Sex, age, race, and Hispanic origin	2000	2010	2015
Males, 15 Years and Over	1,648,133	1,751,556	1,806,873
Never married	31.2	37.0	38.7
Now married, except separated..............................	54.5	47.2	44.9
Separated..	2.2	2.2	2.1
Widowed..	2.8	2.8	3.3
Divorced..	9.2	10.8	11.0
Females, 15 Years and Over	1,828,247	1,861,490	1,934,046
Never married	26.3	30.8	32.7
Now married, except separated..............................	48.2	42.6	41.2
Separated..	2.9	3.2	3.0
Widowed..	11.5	10.1	10.2
Divorced..	11.1	13.3	12.9

Table LA-3. Households and Housing Characteristics

(Number, percent, dollars.)

Item	2000	2010	2015	Average annual percent change, 2000–2015
Total Households..	1,656,053	1,689,822	1,737,908	0.3
Family households..	1,156,438	1,129,117	1,108,586	-0.3
Married-couple family...	809,498	753,423	746,504	-0.5
Other family...	346,940	375,694	362,082	0.3
Male householder, no wife present......................	71,865	79,560	85,963	1.3
Female householder, no husband present.............	275,075	296,134	276,119	-
Nonfamily households..	499,615	560,705	629,322	1.7
Householder living alone......................................	419,200	468,853	533,824	1.8
Householder not living alone................................	80,415	91,852	95,498	1.3
Housing Characteristics				
Total housing units...	1,847,181	1,967,947	2,024,737	0.6
Occupied housing units	1,656,053	1,689,822	1,737,908	0.3
Owner occupied..	1,125,135	1,141,504	1,122,294	-
Renter occupied...	530,918	548,318	615,614	1.1
Average household size..	2.62	2.61	2.61	-
Financial Characteristics				
Median gross rent of renter-occupied housing	466	736	800	4.8
Median monthly owner costs for housing units with a mortgage	816	1,163	1,219	3.3
Median value of owner-occupied housing units	85,000	137,500	155,600	5.5

- = Zero or rounds to zero

Table LA-4. Migration, Origin, and Language

(Number, percent.)

Characteristic	State 2014	State 2015	State Percent change	U.S. 2014	U.S. 2015	U.S. Percent change
Residence 1 Year Ago						
Population 1 year and over	4,593,505	4,612,024	0.4	315,095,393	317,635,720	0.8
Same house	86.4	86.9	X	85.1	85.3	X
Different house in the U.S.	13.3	12.8	X	14.3	14.1	X
Same county	7.9	7.7	X	8.7	8.5	X
Different county	5.4	5.1	X	5.6	5.6	X
Same state	3.3	3.1	X	3.3	3.2	X
Different state	2.1	2.0	X	2.3	2.4	X
Abroad	0.3	0.3	X	0.6	0.7	X
Place of Birth						
Native born	4,455,399	4,484,355	0.6	276,465,262	278,128,449	0.6
Male	48.7	48.9	X	49.3	49.3	X
Female	51.3	51.1	X	50.7	50.7	X
Foreign born	194,277	186,369	-4.1	42,391,794	43,290,372	2.1
Male	52.9	49.9	X	48.7	48.6	X
Female	47.1	50.1	X	51.3	51.4	X
Foreign born; naturalized U.S. citizen...................	77,978	76,294	-2.2	19,984,738	20,697,103	3.6
Male	49.5	44.8	X	45.9	45.9	X
Female	50.5	55.2	X	54.1	54.1	X
Foreign born; not a U.S. citizen............................	116,299	110,075	-5.4	22,407,056	22,593,269	0.8
Male	55.1	53.5	X	51.2	51.1	X
Female	44.9	46.5	X	48.8	48.9	X
Entered 2010 or later	20.2	21.9	X	12.3	15.6	X
Entered 2000 to 2009	33.6	30.9	X	28.6	27.9	X
Entered before 2000..	46.3	47.2	X	59.1	56.5	X
World Region of Birth, Foreign						
Foreign-born population, excluding population born at sea	194,277	186,369	-4.1	42,390,705	43,289,646	2.1
Europe	7.8	9.7	X	11.2	11.1	X
Asia...	32.6	32.4	X	30.1	30.6	X
Africa	4.2	3.1	X	4.6	4.8	X
Oceania	0.5	0.3	X	0.6	0.6	X
Latin America..	53.4	52.7	X	51.6	51.1	X
North America..	1.4	1.8	X	1.9	1.9	X
Language Spoken at Home and Ability to Speak English						
Population 5 years and over...................................	4,344,222	4,365,879	0.5	299,084,046	301,625,014	0.8
English only	91.6	91.8	X	78.9	78.5	X
Language other than English.................................	8.4	8.2	X	21.1	21.5	X
Speaks English less than "very well"...................	3.0	2.8	X	8.6	8.6	X

NA = Not available.
X = Not applicable.
- = Zero or rounds to zero.

Table LA-5. Median Income and Poverty Status, 2015

(Number, percent, except as noted.)

Characteristic	State		U.S.	
	Number	Percent	Number	Percent
Median Income				
Households (dollars)................................	45,727	X	55,775	X
Families (dollars)	58,964	X	68,260	X
Below Poverty Level (All People)	889,946	19.6	46,153,077	14.7
Sex				
Male	377,757	17.2	20,599,407	13.4
Female	512,189	21.8	25,553,670	16.0
Age				
Under 18 years..	312,710	28.4	15,000,273	20.7
Related children under 18 years..............	308,911	28.1	14,693,239	20.4
18 to 64 years...	496,068	17.7	26,960,369	13.9
65 years and over	81,168	12.8	4,192,435	9.0

X = Not applicable.

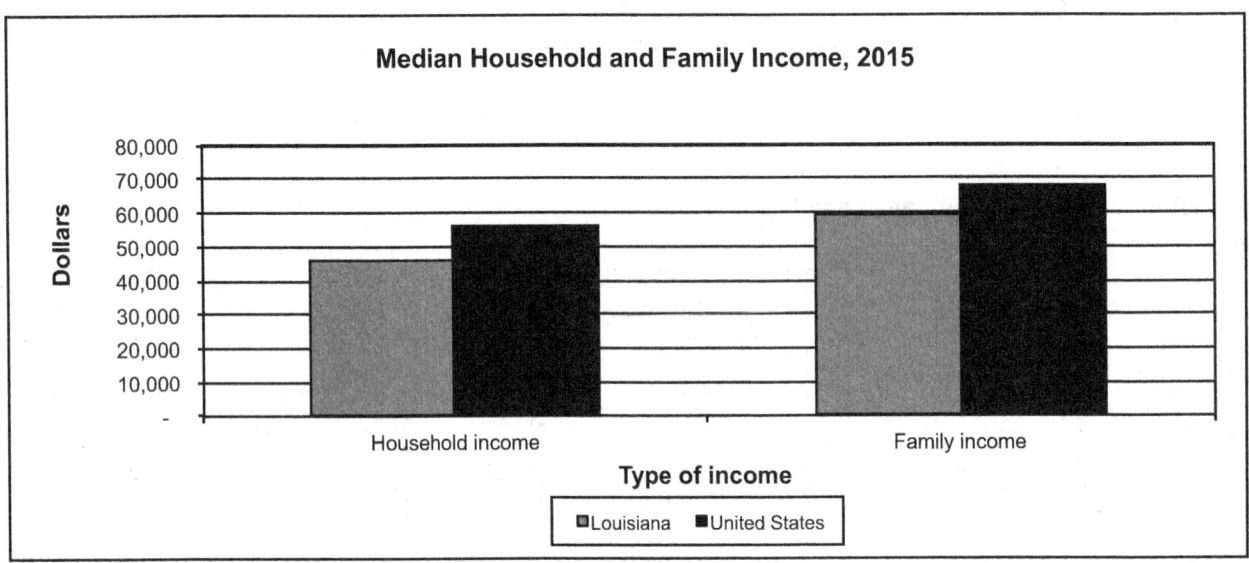

Table LA-6. Health Insurance Coverage Status for the Civilian Noninstitutionalized Population and Children Under 18 Years of Age

(Numbers in thousands, percent.)

Item	2007	2008	2009	2010	2011	2012	2013	2014	2015
Civilian Noninstitutionalized Population	4,197	4,313	4,392	4,440	4,473	4,499	4,523	4,548	4,567
Covered by Private or Public Insurance									
Number....................	3,421	3,546	3,629	3,649	3,689	3,739	3,772	3,876	4,022
Percent.....................	81.5	82.2	82.6	82.2	82.5	83.1	83.4	85.2	88.1
Not Covered									
Number....................	776	767	762	791	784	760	751	672	546
Percent.....................	18.5	17.8	17.4	17.8	17.5	16.9	16.6	14.8	11.9
Percent in the U.S. not covered..........................	15.3	15.1	15.1	15.5	15.1	14.8	14.5	11.7	9.4
Children Under 18 Years of Age	1,097	1,106	1,120	1,113	1,117	1,117	1,111	1,113	1,115
Covered by Private or Public Insurance									
Number....................	960	1,020	1,047	1,051	1,052	1,058	1,048	1,055	1,075
Percent.....................	87.5	92.2	93.5	94.5	94.2	94.7	94.3	94.8	96.4
Not Covered									
Number....................	137	86	73	62	65	59	63	58	40
Percent.....................	12.5	7.8	6.5	5.5	5.8	5.3	5.7	5.2	3.6
Percent in the U.S. not covered..........................	11.0	9.7	8.6	8.0	7.5	7.2	7.1	6.0	4.8

Table LA-7. Employment Status by Demographic Group, 2016

(Numbers in thousands, percent.)

Characteristic	Civilian noninstitutional population	Civilian labor force		Employed		Unemployed	
		Number	Percent of population	Number	Percent of population	Number	Percent of population
Total..	3,597	2,132	59.3	2,000	55.6	132	6.2
Sex							
Male..	1,706	1,097	64.3	1,024	60.0	73	6.6
Female	1,891	1,036	54.8	976	51.6	60	5.8
Race, Sex, and Hispanic Origin							
White	2,330	1,392	59.7	1,332	57.2	59	4.3
Male	1,130	756	66.9	721	63.8	35	4.6
Female	1,200	636	53.0	612	50.9	24	3.8
Black or African American........................	1,105	643	58.2	575	52.1	67	10.5
Male	494	284	57.4	249	50.5	34	12.1
Female	610	359	58.8	326	53.4	33	9.2
Hispanic or Latino ethnicity[1]	157	101	64.3	97	61.8	4	3.8
Male	82	64	78.1	62	75.6	2	3.3
Female	74	36	48.9	35	46.7	2	4.6
Age							
16 to 19 years....................................	250	74	29.4	59	23.4	15	20.3
20 to 24 years....................................	335	224	66.9	200	59.7	24	10.8
25 to 34 years....................................	632	500	79.1	464	73.4	36	7.2
35 to 44 years....................................	544	437	80.2	414	76.0	23	5.2
45 to 54 years....................................	590	454	77.0	438	74.3	16	3.4
55 to 64 years....................................	615	328	53.4	314	51.0	14	4.4
65 years and over	631	116	18.4	112	17.7	5	3.9

NOTE: Data in Table 7 are from the Current Population Survey (CPS) and do not match the estimates in Table 8. See notes and definitions for further information.
[1] May be of any race.

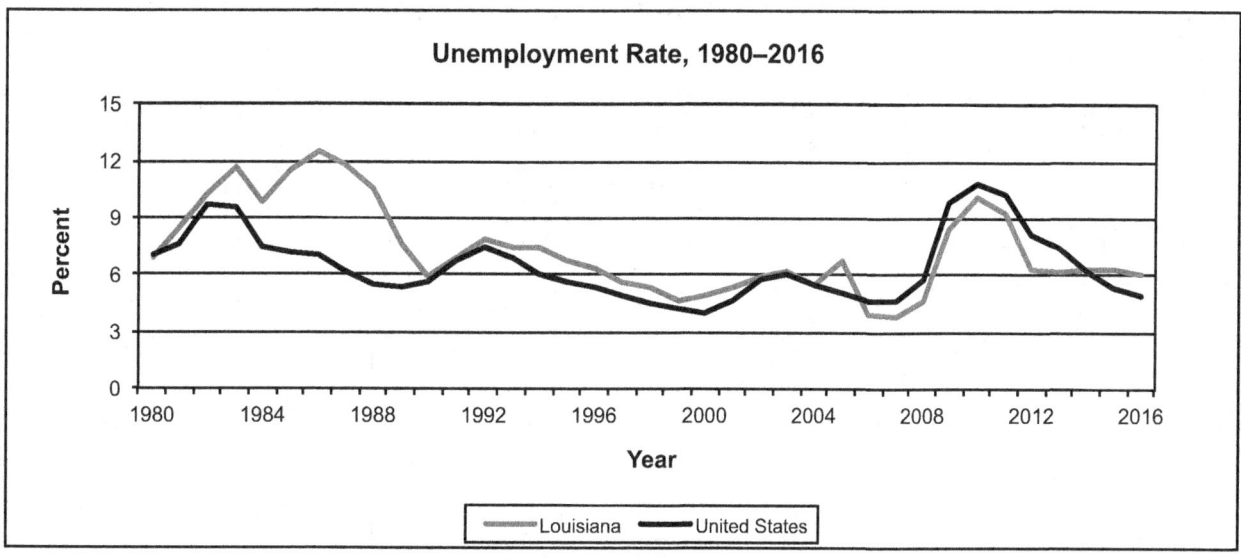

Table LA-8. Employment Status of the Civilian Noninstitutional Population Age 16 Years and Over

(Number, percent.)

Year	Civilian labor force	Civilian participation rate	Employed	Unemployed	Unemployment rate
2008..	2,084,835	62.2	1,982,381	102,454	4.9
2009..	2,064,768	60.9	1,923,884	140,884	6.8
2010..	2,086,076	60.7	1,919,852	166,224	8.0
2011..	2,073,217	59.6	1,911,021	162,196	7.8
2012..	2,080,664	59.4	1,932,880	147,784	7.1
2013..	2,106,424	59.7	1,964,634	141,790	6.7
2014..	2,156,737	60.8	2,018,593	138,144	6.4
2015..	2,160,195	60.5	2,025,102	135,093	6.3
2016..	2,121,230	59.1	1,992,125	129,105	6.1

Table LA-9. Employment and Average Wages by Industry

(Estimates through 2010 are based on the 2007 *North American Industry Classification System* [NAICS]. Estimates from 2011 onward are based on the 2012 NAICS.)

Industry	2009	2010	2011	2012	2013	2014	2015
				Number of jobs			
Wage and Salary Employment by Industry	2,004,363	1,984,467	1,998,993	2,018,389	2,039,085	2,067,420	2,075,222
Farm Wage and Salary Employment	8,875	8,911	8,286	7,181	6,553	6,186	8,839
Nonfarm Wage and Salary Employment	1,995,488	1,975,556	1,990,707	2,011,208	2,032,532	2,061,234	2,066,383
Private wage and salary employment	1,588,946	1,566,457	1,593,091	1,623,566	1,654,461	1,695,054	1,703,512
Forestry, fishing, and related activities	7,261	7,304	7,051	7,097	7,186	7,363	7,279
Mining	48,044	48,602	50,306	51,725	51,174	50,866	44,917
Utilities	9,524	9,479	9,340	9,152	9,155	8,838	8,608
Construction	136,973	125,118	125,873	130,242	135,129	143,188	144,319
Manufacturing	142,692	137,555	139,640	141,997	144,067	147,272	143,889
Durable goods manufacturing	74,532	69,642	71,160	73,105	74,637	77,226	73,116
Nondurable goods manufacturing	68,160	67,913	68,480	68,892	69,430	70,046	70,773
Wholesale trade	72,605	70,772	72,504	72,881	73,634	73,845	72,745
Retail trade	224,208	219,709	222,854	224,417	225,924	228,990	234,878
Transportation and warehousing	70,434	69,222	72,204	74,670	77,220	80,509	79,935
Information	24,777	24,578	23,757	24,909	26,672	26,104	26,741
Finance and insurance	58,689	60,308	61,953	60,800	60,708	61,167	60,810
Real estate and rental and leasing	31,441	30,904	31,743	32,294	33,418	32,636	31,905
Professional, scientific, and technical services	80,937	80,366	81,879	85,490	87,197	89,182	89,744
Management of companies and enterprises	24,196	23,872	24,369	25,122	25,286	25,225	23,707
Administrative and waste services	91,541	90,885	92,147	94,732	96,732	100,118	101,403
Educational services	36,785	38,979	39,227	40,441	42,662	43,174	43,713
Health care and social assistance	232,183	236,509	239,744	243,450	248,703	256,755	261,816
Arts, entertainment, and recreation	28,906	28,572	28,086	28,778	29,871	30,622	30,582
Accommodation and food services	168,117	167,498	174,173	179,508	184,721	191,898	198,958
Other services, except public administration	99,633	96,225	96,241	95,861	95,002	97,302	97,563
Government and government enterprises	406,542	409,099	397,616	387,642	378,071	366,180	362,871
				Dollars			
Average Wages and Salaries by Industry	41,075	42,163	43,107	44,118	44,851	46,172	46,784
Average Farm Wages and Salaries	18,067	18,508	17,143	29,539	25,584	21,314	24,827
Average Nonfarm Wages and Salaries	41,177	42,270	43,216	44,170	44,913	46,246	46,878
Average private wages and salaries	41,019	42,248	43,295	44,383	45,287	46,779	47,381
Forestry, fishing, and related activities	30,023	32,850	33,119	34,550	35,468	35,976	35,879
Mining	79,864	82,246	85,176	88,509	90,813	95,805	95,878
Utilities	73,547	72,441	76,686	78,373	80,350	84,586	87,718
Construction	51,097	51,294	51,890	52,386	53,495	56,608	58,586
Manufacturing	58,875	61,611	63,890	65,566	66,510	69,341	71,287
Durable goods manufacturing	51,531	54,357	56,757	57,752	58,515	60,834	60,722
Nondurable goods manufacturing	66,906	69,049	71,303	73,857	75,105	78,721	82,203
Wholesale trade	54,437	55,873	57,321	59,786	61,114	63,208	64,083
Retail trade	24,966	25,548	25,905	26,650	27,072	27,375	27,900
Transportation and warehousing	54,567	57,262	57,674	60,154	61,997	64,733	63,495
Information	48,091	49,796	51,441	51,791	49,794	52,508	53,261
Finance and insurance	52,484	55,181	58,956	60,180	61,992	65,782	66,065
Real estate and rental and leasing	42,430	45,940	48,219	48,317	49,085	50,064	49,324
Professional, scientific, and technical services	58,946	61,113	62,878	64,427	66,837	68,169	69,900
Management of companies and enterprises	65,123	67,220	70,947	73,255	79,415	78,434	80,885
Administrative and waste services	33,369	34,894	34,348	35,022	35,431	36,812	38,388
Educational services	32,440	33,063	34,316	34,579	34,644	34,824	34,272
Health care and social assistance	37,526	38,125	38,914	39,433	39,873	41,164	42,887
Arts, entertainment, and recreation	32,897	34,921	35,014	34,529	34,705	34,689	36,197
Accommodation and food services	18,158	18,791	18,987	19,510	19,852	20,380	21,119
Other services, except public administration	27,215	28,287	28,871	30,106	31,372	32,107	33,353
Government and government enterprises	41,795	42,355	42,896	43,275	43,275	43,780	44,517

Table LA-10. Employment Characteristics by Family Type

(Number, percent.)

Family type and labor force status	2013 Total	2013 Families with own children under 18 years	2014 Total	2014 Families with own children under 18 years	2015 Total	2015 Families with own children under 18 years
All Families..	1,129,437	484,007	1,109,475	468,474	1,108,586	471,898
FAMILY TYPE AND LABOR FORCE STATUS						
Married-Couple Families...	745,632	282,943	738,715	270,836	746,504	278,801
Both husband and wife in labor force...............................	49.3	66.0	47.4	63.4	48.0	65.2
Husband in labor force, wife not in labor force	25.3	28.8	24.9	30.0	24.8	28.3
Wife in labor force, husband not in labor force	7.8	3.4	8.8	4.4	8.2	4.5
Both husband and wife not in labor force............................	17.3	1.7	18.9	2.2	18.4	1.7
Other Families	383,805	201,064	370,760	197,638	362,082	193,097
Female householder, no husband present..........................	76.3	80.4	75.0	78.8	76.3	78.7
In labor force..	51.0	64.2	49.1	62.1	50.8	64.2
Not in labor force	25.3	16.2	26.0	16.6	25.4	14.6
Male householder, no wife present..................................	23.7	19.6	25.0	21.2	23.7	21.3
In labor force..	17.2	17.1	18.6	18.7	17.4	19.4
Not in labor force	6.5	2.5	6.4	2.6	6.4	1.8

Table LA-11. School Enrollment and Educational Attainment, 2015

(Number, percent.)

Item	State	U.S.
Enrollment		
Total population 3 years and over, enrolled in school	1,174,717	81,618,288
Enrolled in nursery school or preschool (percent)	7.0	6.0
Enrolled in kindergarten (percent)	5.2	5.0
Enrolled in elementary school, grades 1-8 (percent)..................................	43.3	40.3
Enrolled in high school, grades 9-12 (percent)..	20.8	20.9
Enrolled in college or graduate school (percent)......................................	23.7	27.7
Attainment		
Total population 25 years and over	3,095,255	216,447,163
Less than ninth grade (percent)	5.2	5.5
9th to 12th grade, no diploma (percent)..	10.2	7.3
High school graduate, including equivalency (percent)................................	34.1	27.6
Some college, no degree (percent)	21.1	20.7
Associate's degree (percent)...	6.1	8.2
Bachelor's degree (percent)..	15.2	19.0
Graduate or professional degree (percent)...	8.0	11.6
High school graduate or higher (percent)	84.6	87.1
Bachelor's degree or higher (percent)..	23.2	30.6

Table LA-12. Public School Characteristics and Educational Indicators

(Number, percent; data derived from National Center of Education Statistics.)

Item	State	U.S.
Public Schools, 2014–2015 (except where noted)		
Number of school districts..	139	18,260
Number of schools	1,383	98,373
Number of students	716,800	50,312,581
Number of teachers	46,340	3,132,351
Student-teacher ratio	15.5	16.1
Expenditures per student (dollars), FY 2014..	10,853	11,066
Four-year adjusted cohort graduation rate (ACGR)[1,2]	77.5	83.2
Students eligible for free or reduced-price lunch (percent)...........................	63.6	51.8
English language learners (percent)..	2.6	9.4
Students age 3 to 21 served under IDEA, part B (percent)............................	11.1	13.0

Public Schools by Type	Number	Percent of state public schools
Total number of schools...	1,383	100.0
Regular	1,334	96.5
Special education..	32	2.3
Vocational education..	12	0.9
Alternative education..	5	0.4

NOTE: Every school is assigned only one school type based on its instructional emphasis.
[1] ACGR data represents a new method of calculating high-school completion rates and may not be comparable to previous years' data for Averaged Freshmen Graduation Rates (AFGR).
[2] The United States 4-year ACGRs were estimated using both the reported 4-year ACGR data from 49 states and the District of Columbia and using imputed data for Idaho. The estimate for American Indian/Alaska Native students also includes imputed data for Virginia.

Table LA-13. Reported Voting and Registration of the Voting-Age Population, November 2016

(Numbers in thousands, percent.)

Item	Total population	Total citizen population	Registered			Voted		
			Total registered	Percent registered (total population)	Percent registered (total citizen population)	Total voted	Percent voted (total population)	Percent voted (total citizen population)
U.S. Total	245,502	224,059	157,596	64.2	70.3	137,537	56.0	61.4
State Total.............................	3,463	3,353	2,446	70.6	73.0	2,067	59.7	61.6
Sex								
Male	1,650	1,580	1,119	67.8	70.8	925	56.1	58.5
Female	1,813	1,773	1,327	73.2	74.8	1,142	63.0	64.4
Race								
White alone.................................	2,251	2,193	1,631	72.4	74.4	1,368	60.8	62.4
White, non-Hispanic alone	2,112	2,100	1,557	73.7	74.2	1,311	62.1	62.5
Black alone.................................	1,062	1,054	755	71.1	71.6	646	60.9	61.3
Asian alone	101	65	26	(B)	(B)	23	(B)	(B)
Hispanic (of any race)......................	174	121	99	56.7	81.5	82	47.2	67.9
White alone or in combination	2,275	2,216	1,652	72.6	74.6	1,386	60.9	62.5
Black alone or in combination...........	1,078	1,070	771	71.5	72.0	661	61.3	61.8
Asian alone or in combination...........	103	67	26	(B)	(B)	23	(B)	(B)
Age								
18 to 24 years.................................	458	453	283	61.7	62.5	225	49.2	49.8
25 to 34 years.................................	628	602	425	67.6	70.5	318	50.7	52.8
35 to 44 years.................................	536	510	348	64.9	68.2	308	57.4	60.4
45 to 64 years.................................	1,233	1,197	913	74.1	76.3	801	64.9	66.9
65 years and over	608	592	478	78.5	80.7	415	68.3	70.2

B = Base is less than 75,000 and therefore too small to show the derived measure.

Table LA-14. Crime

(Number, rate per 100,000. Data are derived from the FBI Uniform Crime Reports.)

Item	State			U.S. [1,2,3,4]		
	2014	2015	Percent change	2014	2015	Percent change
TOTAL POPULATION[5]	4,648,990	4,670,724	0.5	318,907,401	321,418,820	0.8
VIOLENT CRIME						
Number.................................	23,983	25,208	5.1	1,186,185	1,231,566	3.8
Rate	515.9	539.7	4.6	372.0	383.2	3.0
Murder and Nonnegligent Manslaughter						
Number.................................	476	481	1.1	14,164	15,696	10.8
Rate	10.2	10.3	0.6	4.4	4.9	10.0
Rape[6]						
Number.................................	1,382	1,723	24.7	118,027	124,047	5.1
Rate	29.7	36.9	24.1	37.0	38.6	4.3
Robbery						
Number.................................	5,725	5,550	-3.1	322,905	327,374	1.4
Rate	123.1	118.8	-3.5	101.3	101.9	0.6
Aggravated Assault						
Number.................................	16,400	17,454	6.4	731,089	764,449	4.6
Rate	352.8	373.7	5.9	229.2	237.8	3.7
PROPERTY CRIME						
Number.................................	161,192	156,629	-2.8	8,209,010	7,993,631	-2.6
Rate	3,467.2	3,353.4	-3.3	2,574.1	2,487.0	-3.4
Burglary						
Number.................................	38,541	35,453	-8.0	1,713,153	1,579,527	-7.8
Rate	829.0	759.0	-8.4	537.2	491.4	-8.5
Larceny-Theft						
Number.................................	113,251	111,435	-1.6	5,809,054	5,706,346	-1.8
Rate	2,436.0	2,385.8	-2.1	1,821.5	1,775.4	-2.5
Motor Vehicle Theft						
Number.................................	9,400	9,741	3.6	686,803	707,758	3.1
Rate	202.2	208.6	3.1	215.4	220.2	2.2

NOTE: Although arson data are included in the trend and clearance tables, sufficient data are not available to estimate totals for this offense. Therefore, no arson data are published in this table.
X = Not applicable.
- = Zero or rounds to zero.
[1] The crime figures have been adjusted.
[2] The data collection methodology for the offense of forcible rape used by the Minnesota state Uniform Crime Reporting (UCR) Program (with the exception of Minneapolis and St. Paul, Minnesota) does not comply with national UCR Program guidelines. Consequently, its figures for forcible rape and violent crime (of which forcible rape is a part) are not published in this table.
[3] Includes offenses reported by the Zoological Police and the Metro Transit Police.
[4] Because of changes in the state's reporting practices, figures are not comparable to previous years' data.
[5] Populations are U.S. Census Bureau provisional estimates as of July 1 of each year.
[6] The figures shown for the offense of rape were estimated using the revised Uniform Crime Reporting (UCR) definition of rape.

Table LA-15. State Government Finances, 2015

(Dollar amounts in thousands, percent distribution.)

Item	Dollars	Percent distribution
Total Revenue	28,060,553	100.0
General revenue	23,421,044	83.5
Intergovernmental revenue	9,910,427	35.3
Taxes	9,696,730	34.6
General sales	2,926,783	10.4
Selective sales	2,358,843	8.4
License taxes	386,358	1.4
Individual income tax	2,983,104	10.6
Corporate income tax	253,650	0.9
Other taxes	787,992	2.8
Current charges	1,821,455	6.5
Miscellaneous general revenue	1,992,432	7.1
Utility revenue	12,287	-
Liquor stores revenue	0	-
Insurance trust revenue[1]	4,627,222	16.5
Total Expenditure	31,155,710	100.0
Intergovernmental expenditure	5,726,498	18.4
Direct expenditure	25,429,212	81.6
Current operation	17,080,826	54.8
Capital outlay	2,014,988	6.5
Insurance benefits and repayments	4,621,061	14.8
Assistance and subsidies	857,856	2.8
Interest on debt	854,481	2.7
Exhibit: Salaries and wages	3,908,527	12.5
Total Expenditure	31,155,710	100.0
General expenditure	26,526,199	85.1
Intergovernmental expenditure	5,726,498	18.4
Direct expenditure	20,799,701	66.8
General expenditure, by function:		
Education	8,885,638	28.5
Public welfare	8,365,742	26.9
Hospitals	480,411	1.5
Health	538,631	1.7
Highways	1,611,669	5.2
Police protection	369,059	1.2
Correction	701,803	2.3
Natural resources	789,542	2.5
Parks and recreation	364,241	1.2
Governmental administration	985,127	3.2
Interest on general debt	854,481	2.7
Other and unallocable	2,579,855	8.3
Utility expenditure	8,450	-
Liquor stores expenditure	0	-
Insurance trust expenditure	4,621,061	14.8
Debt at End of Fiscal Year	17,593,764	X
Cash and Security Holdings	62,783,783	X

X = Not applicable.
- = Zero or rounds to zero.
[1] Within insurance trust revenue, net earnings of state retirement systems is a calculated statistic (the item code in the data file is X08), and thus can be positive or negative. Net earnings is the sum of earnings on investments plus gains on investments minus losses on investments. The change made in 2002 for asset valuation from book to market value in accordance with Statement 34 of the Governmental Accounting Standards Board is reflected in the calculated statistics.

Table LA-16. State Government Tax Collections, 2016

(Dollars in thousands, percent.)

Item	Dollars	Percent distribution
Total Taxes	9,309,673	100.0
Property taxes	62,273	0.7
Sales and gross receipts	5,352,907	57.5
General sales and gross receipts	3,186,614	34.2
Selective sales and gross receipts	2,166,293	23.3
Alcoholic beverages	63,356	0.7
Amusements	702,573	7.5
Insurance premiums	518,906	5.6
Motor fuels	622,234	6.7
Pari-mutuels	4,338	-
Public utilities	8,618	0.1
Tobacco products	121,200	1.3
Other selective sales	125,068	1.3
Licenses	400,191	4.3
Alcoholic beverages	0	-
Amusements	0	-
Corporations in general	106,104	1.1
Hunting and fishing	30,789	0.3
Motor vehicle	133,362	1.4
Motor vehicle operators	14,277	0.2
Public utilities	11,678	0.1
Occupation and business, NEC	99,581	1.1
Other licenses	4,400	-
Income taxes	3,038,035	32.6
Individual income	2,866,456	30.8
Corporation net income	171,579	1.8
Other taxes	456,267	4.9
Death and gift	0	-
Documentary and stock transfer	0	-
Severance	456,267	4.9
Taxes, NEC	0	-

- = Zero or rounds to zero.

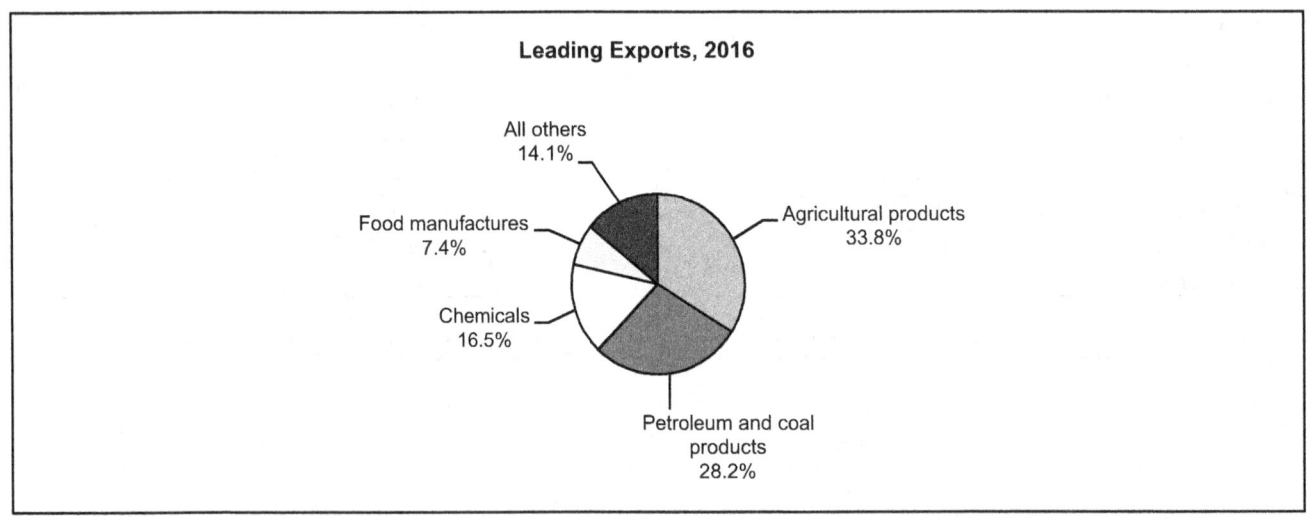

Leading Exports, 2016

All others 14.1%

Food manufactures 7.4%

Chemicals 16.5%

Agricultural products 33.8%

Petroleum and coal products 28.2%

MAINE

Facts and Figures

Location: Northeast corner of the United States; bordered on the N and E by New Brunswick, Canada; on the S by the Atlantic Ocean; on the W by New Hampshire; and on the NW by Quebec, Canada

Area: 35,385 sq. mi. (91,646 sq. km.); rank—39th

Population: 1,331,479 (2016 est.); rank—42nd

Principal Cities: capital—Augusta; largest—Portland

Statehood: March 15, 1820; 23rd state

U.S. Congress: 2 senators, 2 representatives

State Motto: *Dirigo* ("I lead")

State Song: "State of Maine Song"

State Nickname: The Pine Tree State

Abbreviations: ME; Me.

State Symbols: flower—white pinecone and tassel; tree—Eastern white pine; bird—chickadee

At a Glance

- With a population that grew 0.2 percent, Maine ranked 47th among the states in growth from 2010 to 2016.

- Maine had the highest percent of residents who identified as "White alone" in 2016, with 94.8 percent of its residents in this category.

- In the November 2016 election, Maine had the highest voter turnout among the states, with 71.3 percent of its population casting a ballot.

- With 19.4 percent of its population in the 65 and older age group, Maine ranked 2nd in this category in 2016.

- Maine's birth rate of 9.5 per 1,000 population was the third lowest in the country in 2015.

Table ME-1. Population by Age, Sex, Race, and Hispanic Origin

(Number, percent, except where noted.)

Sex, age, race, and Hispanic origin	2000	2010	2016 [1]	Average annual percent change, 2010–2016
Total Population............	1,274,923	1,328,361	1,331,479	-
Percent of total U.S. population	0.5	0.4	0.4	X
Sex				
Male...............	620,309	650,056	652,585	-
Female	654,614	678,305	678,894	-
Age				
Under 5 years............	70,726	69,520	65,068	-0.4
5 to 19 years............	264,729	241,439	222,719	-0.5
20 to 64 years............	756,036	806,322	786,009	-0.2
65 years and over	183,402	211,080	257,683	1.4
Median age (years)	38.6	42.7	44.6	0.3
Race and Hispanic Origin				
One race............				
White	1,236,014	1,269,764	1,262,168	-
Black............	6,760	16,269	20,025	1.4
American Indian and Alaska Native	7,098	8,771	9,329	0.4
Asian............	9,111	13,783	16,517	1.2
Native Hawaiian or Other Pacific Islander	382	377	500	2.0
Two or more races	12,647	19,397	22,940	1.1
Hispanic (of any race)	9,360	18,261	21,058	1.0

X = Not applicable.
- = Zero or rounds to zero.
[1] Population figures for 2016 are July 1 estimates. The 2010 estimates are taken from the 2010 Census.

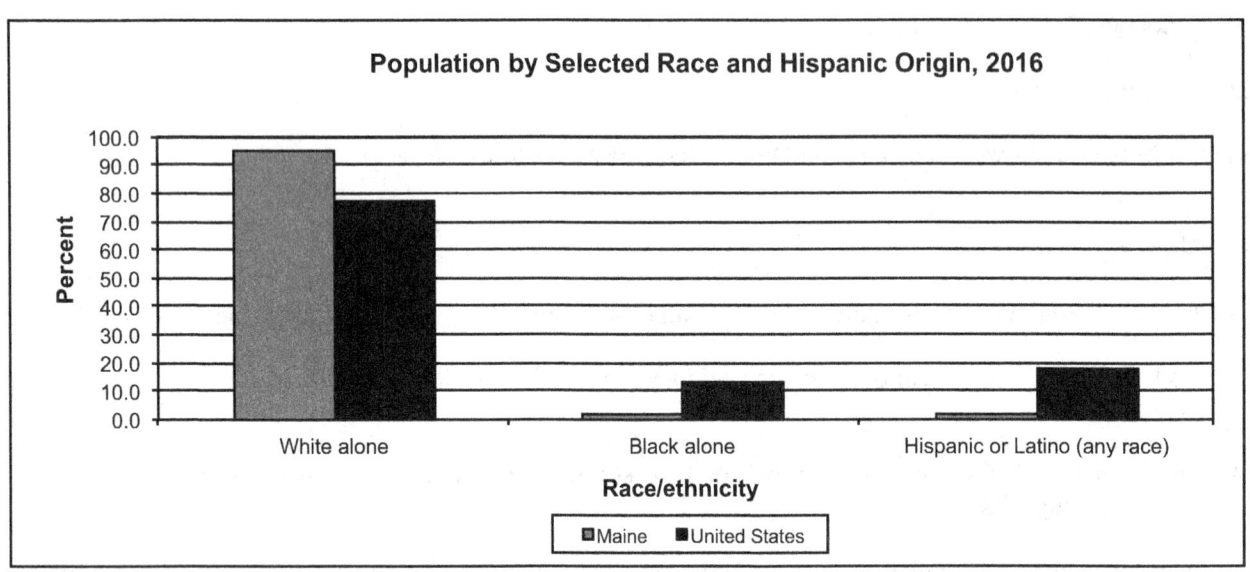

Population by Selected Race and Hispanic Origin, 2016

Legend: Maine / United States

Table ME-2. Marital Status

(Number, percent distribution.)

Sex, age, race, and Hispanic origin	2000	2010	2015
Males, 15 Years and Over	494,217	534,474	543,626
Never married	26.8	31.0	32.0
Now married, except separated............	58.8	52.5	51.4
Separated............	1.1	1.2	1.1
Widowed............	2.8	2.9	2.8
Divorced............	10.5	12.5	12.7
Females, 15 Years and Over	534,606	570,281	577,581
Never married	21.2	24.2	25.6
Now married, except separated............	54.1	49.3	48.0
Separated............	1.3	1.6	1.3
Widowed............	11.0	9.9	10.0
Divorced............	12.4	15.0	15.2

Table ME-3. Households and Housing Characteristics

(Number, percent, dollars.)

Item	2000	2010	2015	Average annual percent change, 2000–2015
Total Households...	518,200	545,417	545,226	0.3
Family households..	340,685	345,328	342,926	-
Married-couple family..............................	272,152	266,670	264,442	-0.2
Other family	68,533	78,658	78,484	1.0
Male householder, no wife present............	19,511	23,620	24,875	1.8
Female householder, no husband present......	49,022	55,038	53,609	0.6
Nonfamily households	177,515	200,089	202,300	0.9
Householder living alone............................	139,969	155,623	161,353	1.0
Householder not living alone......................	37,546	44,466	40,947	0.6
Housing Characteristics				
Total housing units......................................	651,901	722,217	729,392	0.8
Occupied housing units	518,200	545,417	545,226	0.3
Owner occupied	370,905	396,395	387,101	0.3
Renter occupied	147,295	149,022	158,125	0.5
Average household size...............................	2.39	2.37	2.37	-0.1
Financial Characteristics				
Median gross rent of renter-occupied housing	497	707	792	4.0
Median monthly owner costs for housing units with a mortgage	923	1,289	1,340	3.0
Median value of owner-occupied housing units..........	98,700	179,100	180,300	5.5

- = Zero or rounds to zero.

Table ME-4. Migration, Origin, and Language

(Number, percent.)

Characteristic	State			U.S.		
	2014	2015	Percent change	2014	2015	Percent change
Residence 1 Year Ago						
Population 1 year and over	1,317,638	1,317,444	-	315,095,393	317,635,720	0.8
Same house	86.4	85.6	X	85.1	85.3	X
Different house in the U.S.	13.2	14.1	X	14.3	14.1	X
Same county	7.3	8.7	X	8.7	8.5	X
Different county	5.9	5.4	X	5.6	5.6	X
Same state	2.9	3.2	X	3.3	3.2	X
Different state	3.0	2.3	X	2.3	2.4	X
Abroad...	0.4	0.3	X	0.6	0.7	X
Place of Birth						
Native born	1,280,403	1,284,634	0.8	276,465,262	278,128,449	0.6
Male	48.9	49.3	X	49.3	49.3	X
Female	51.1	50.7	X	50.7	50.7	X
Foreign born	49,686	44,694	0.8	42,391,794	43,290,372	2.1
Male	43.4	40.6	X	48.7	48.6	X
Female	56.6	59.4	X	51.3	51.4	X
Foreign born; naturalized U.S. citizen............	26,457	25,556	0.8	19,984,738	20,697,103	3.6
Male	44.8	39.7	X	45.9	45.9	X
Female	55.2	60.3	X	54.1	54.1	X
Foreign born; not a U.S. citizen..................	23,229	19,138	0.8	22,407,056	22,593,269	0.8
Male	41.8	41.7	X	51.2	51.1	X
Female	58.2	58.3	X	48.8	48.9	X
Entered 2010 or later	22.1	19.3	X	12.3	15.6	X
Entered 2000 to 2009	22.9	22.3	X	28.6	27.9	X
Entered before 2000..................................	55.0	58.4	X	59.1	56.5	X
World Region of Birth, Foreign						
Foreign-born population, excluding population born at sea	49,686	44,694	0.8	42,390,705	43,289,646	2.1
Europe	24.0	24.0	X	11.2	11.1	X
Asia..	28.4	30.0	X	30.1	30.6	X
Africa	16.0	13.0	X	4.6	4.8	X
Oceania	0.8	0.9	X	0.6	0.6	X
Latin America...	10.7	10.2	X	51.6	51.1	X
North America..	20.2	21.8	X	1.9	1.9	X
Language Spoken at Home and Ability to Speak English						
Population 5 years and over...........................	1,267,172	1,265,476	0.8	299,084,046	301,625,014	0.8
English only	93.2	93.9	X	78.9	78.5	X
Language other than English........................	6.8	6.1	X	21.1	21.5	X
Speaks English less than "very well"............	1.8	1.6	X	8.6	8.6	X

NA = Not available.
X = Not applicable.
- = Zero or rounds to zero.

Table ME-5. Median Income and Poverty Status, 2015

(Number, percent, except as noted.)

Characteristic	State Number	State Percent	U.S. Number	U.S. Percent
Median Income				
Households (dollars)..	51,494	X	55,775	X
Families (dollars)	64,651	X	68,260	X
Below Poverty Level (All People)	172,620	13.4	46,153,077	14.7
Sex				
Male	77,965	12.4	20,599,407	13.4
Female	94,655	14.3	25,553,670	16.0
Age				
Under 18 years...	43,343	17.4	15,000,273	20.7
Related children under 18 years...........................	41,042	16.6	14,693,239	20.4
18 to 64 years..	107,761	13.5	26,960,369	13.9
65 years and over	21,516	8.8	4,192,435	9.0

X = Not applicable.

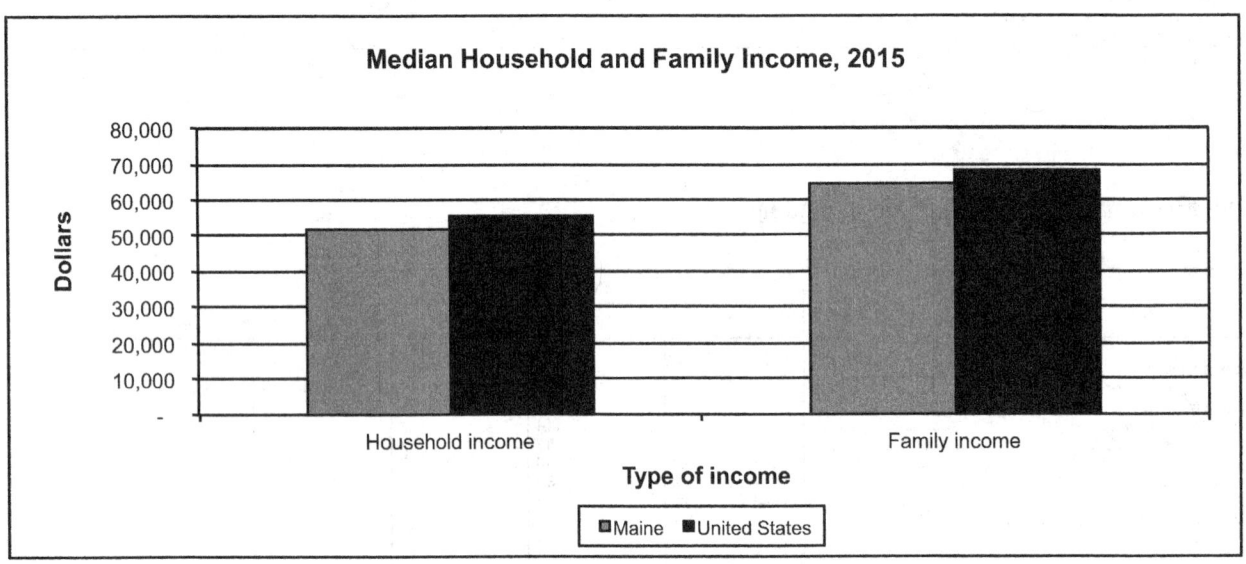

Table ME-6. Health Insurance Coverage Status for the Civilian Noninstitutionalized Population and Children Under 18 Years of Age

(Numbers in thousands, percent.)

Item	2007	2008	2009	2010	2011	2012	2013	2014	2015
Civilian Noninstitutionalized Population	1,313	1,299	1,301	1,313	1,314	1,316	1,314	1,316	1,315
Covered by Private or Public Insurance									
Number..	1,197	1,157	1,164	1,180	1,174	1,181	1,167	1,182	1,204
Percent..	91.2	89.1	89.5	89.8	89.3	89.8	88.8	89.9	91.6
Not Covered									
Number..	115	142	137	133	140	135	147	134	111
Percent..	8.8	10.9	10.5	10.1	10.7	10.2	11.2	10.1	8.4
Percent in the U.S. not covered..........................	15.3	15.1	15.1	15.5	15.1	14.8	14.5	11.7	9.4
Children Under 18 Years of Age	281	275	270	273	270	265	260	257	255
Covered by Private or Public Insurance									
Number..	268	255	255	262	256	253	244	241	241
Percent..	94.9	92.7	94.4	96.0	94.8	95.4	94.1	93.7	94.3
Not Covered									
Number..	14	20	15	11	14	12	15	16	14
Percent..	5.1	7.3	5.6	4.0	5.2	4.6	5.9	6.3	5.7
Percent in the U.S. not covered..........................	11.0	9.7	8.6	8.0	7.5	7.2	7.1	6.0	4.8

Table ME-7. Employment Status by Demographic Group, 2016

(Numbers in thousands, percent.)

Characteristic	Civilian noninstitutional population	Civilian labor force		Employed		Unemployed	
		Number	Percent of population	Number	Percent of population	Number	Percent of population
Total..................................	1,094	693	63.4	666	60.9	27	3.9
Sex							
Male..................................	530	365	68.8	350	65.9	15	4.1
Female................................	564	329	58.3	317	56.1	12	3.7
Race, Sex, and Hispanic Origin							
White	1,034	651	63.0	626	60.6	25	3.9
Male..................................	501	343	68.5	329	65.8	14	4.0
Female................................	533	308	57.9	297	55.7	12	3.8
Black or African American...................	NA	NA	NA	NA	NA	NA	NA
Male..................................	NA	NA	NA	NA	NA	NA	NA
Female................................	NA	NA	NA	NA	NA	NA	NA
Hispanic or Latino ethnicity[1]	NA	NA	NA	NA	NA	NA	NA
Male..................................	NA	NA	NA	NA	NA	NA	NA
Female................................	NA	NA	NA	NA	NA	NA	NA
Age							
16 to 19 years..........................	NA	NA	NA	NA	NA	NA	NA
20 to 24 years..........................	62	47	75.3	43	69.8	3	7.3
25 to 34 years..........................	150	120	80.4	116	77.2	5	3.9
35 to 44 years..........................	171	143	83.6	138	81.0	5	3.2
45 to 54 years..........................	197	162	82.1	158	79.9	4	2.7
55 to 64 years..........................	205	141	68.8	136	66.5	5	3.3
65 years and over	250	52	20.8	50	20.0	2	3.8

NOTE: Data in Table 7 are from the Current Population Survey (CPS) and do not match the estimates in Table 8. See notes and definitions for further information.
[1] May be of any race.
NA = Not available.

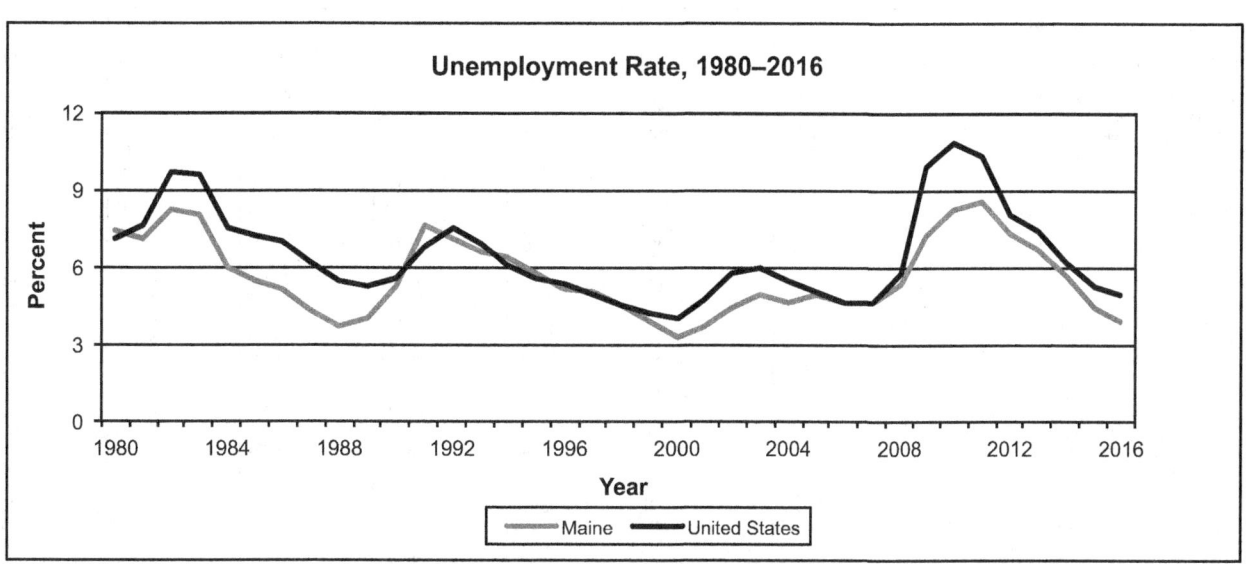

Unemployment Rate, 1980–2016

Table ME-8. Employment Status of the Civilian Noninstitutional Population Age 16 Years and Over

(Number, percent.)

Year	Civilian labor force	Civilian participation rate	Employed	Unemployed	Unemployment rate
2008..................................	701,646	66.0	663,158	38,488	5.5
2009..................................	696,219	65.4	639,954	56,265	8.1
2010..................................	695,182	64.8	638,630	56,552	8.1
2011..................................	699,281	64.8	644,085	55,196	7.9
2012..................................	702,799	64.9	650,249	52,550	7.5
2013..................................	707,623	65.2	660,662	46,961	6.6
2014..................................	696,578	63.9	657,302	39,276	5.6
2015..................................	679,756	62.3	649,855	29,901	4.4
2016..................................	690,624	63.1	664,010	26,614	3.9

Table ME-9. Employment and Average Wages by Industry

(Estimates through 2010 are based on the 2007 *North American Industry Classification System* [NAICS]. Estimates from 2011 onward are based on the 2012 NAICS.)

Industry	2009	2010	2011	2012	2013	2014	2015
				Number of jobs			
Wage and Salary Employment by Industry..................	2,004,363	1,984,467	1,998,993	2,018,389	2,039,085	2,067,420	2,075,222
Farm Wage and Salary Employment.........................	8,875	8,911	8,286	7,181	6,553	6,186	8,839
Nonfarm Wage and Salary Employment....................	1,995,488	1,975,556	1,990,707	2,011,208	2,032,532	2,061,234	2,066,383
Private wage and salary employment.....................	1,588,946	1,566,457	1,593,091	1,623,566	1,654,461	1,695,054	1,703,512
Forestry, fishing, and related activities.....................	7,261	7,304	7,051	7,097	7,186	7,363	7,279
Mining..	48,044	48,602	50,306	51,725	51,174	50,866	44,917
Utilities..	9,524	9,479	9,340	9,152	9,155	8,838	8,608
Construction...	136,973	125,118	125,873	130,242	135,129	143,188	144,319
Manufacturing..	142,692	137,555	139,640	141,997	144,067	147,272	143,889
Durable goods manufacturing............................	74,532	69,642	71,160	73,105	74,637	77,226	73,116
Nondurable goods manufacturing.......................	68,160	67,913	68,480	68,892	69,430	70,046	70,773
Wholesale trade	72,605	70,772	72,504	72,881	73,634	73,845	72,745
Retail trade..	224,208	219,709	222,854	224,417	225,924	228,990	234,878
Transportation and warehousing.........................	70,434	69,222	72,204	74,670	77,220	80,509	79,935
Information	24,777	24,578	23,757	24,909	26,672	26,104	26,741
Finance and insurance	58,689	60,308	61,953	60,800	60,708	61,167	60,810
Real estate and rental and leasing.....................	31,441	30,904	31,743	32,294	33,418	32,636	31,905
Professional, scientific, and technical services	80,937	80,366	81,879	85,490	87,197	89,182	89,744
Management of companies and enterprises...................	24,196	23,872	24,369	25,122	25,286	25,225	23,707
Administrative and waste services.............................	91,541	90,885	92,147	94,732	96,732	100,118	101,403
Educational services	36,785	38,979	39,227	40,441	42,662	43,174	43,713
Health care and social assistance..............................	232,183	236,509	239,744	243,450	248,703	256,755	261,816
Arts, entertainment, and recreation...........................	28,906	28,572	28,086	28,778	29,871	30,622	30,582
Accommodation and food services...........................	168,117	167,498	174,173	179,508	184,721	191,898	198,958
Other services, except public administration..................	99,633	96,225	96,241	95,861	95,002	97,302	97,563
Government and government enterprises.........................	406,542	409,099	397,616	387,642	378,071	366,180	362,871
				Dollars			
Average Wages and Salaries by Industry	41,075	42,163	43,107	44,118	44,851	46,172	46,784
Average Farm Wages and Salaries	18,067	18,508	17,143	29,539	25,584	21,314	24,827
Average Nonfarm Wages and Salaries	41,177	42,270	43,216	44,170	44,913	46,246	46,878
Average private wages and salaries.........................	41,019	42,248	43,295	44,383	45,287	46,779	47,381
Forestry, fishing, and related activities.....................	30,023	32,850	33,119	34,550	35,468	35,976	35,879
Mining..	79,864	82,246	85,176	88,509	90,813	95,805	95,878
Utilities..	73,547	72,441	76,686	78,373	80,350	84,586	87,718
Construction...	51,097	51,294	51,890	52,386	53,495	56,608	58,586
Manufacturing..	58,875	61,611	63,890	65,566	66,510	69,341	71,287
Durable goods manufacturing............................	51,531	54,357	56,757	57,752	58,515	60,834	60,722
Nondurable goods manufacturing.......................	66,906	69,049	71,303	73,857	75,105	78,721	82,203
Wholesale trade	54,437	55,873	57,321	59,786	61,114	63,208	64,083
Retail trade..	24,966	25,548	25,905	26,650	27,072	27,375	27,900
Transportation and warehousing.........................	54,567	57,262	57,674	60,154	61,997	64,733	63,495
Information	48,091	49,796	51,441	51,791	49,794	52,508	53,261
Finance and insurance	52,484	55,181	58,956	60,180	61,992	65,782	66,065
Real estate and rental and leasing.....................	42,430	45,940	48,219	48,317	49,085	50,064	49,324
Professional, scientific, and technical services	58,946	61,113	62,878	64,427	66,837	68,169	69,900
Management of companies and enterprises...................	65,123	67,220	70,947	73,255	79,415	78,434	80,885
Administrative and waste services.............................	33,369	34,894	34,348	35,022	35,431	36,812	38,388
Educational services	32,440	33,063	34,316	34,579	34,644	34,824	34,272
Health care and social assistance..............................	37,526	38,125	38,914	39,433	39,873	41,164	42,887
Arts, entertainment, and recreation...........................	32,897	34,921	35,014	34,529	34,705	34,689	36,197
Accommodation and food services...........................	18,158	18,791	18,987	19,510	19,852	20,380	21,119
Other services, except public administration..................	27,215	28,287	28,871	30,106	31,372	32,107	33,353
Government and government enterprises.........................	41,795	42,355	42,896	43,275	43,275	43,780	44,517

D = Not shown to avoid disclosure of confidential information, but the estimates for this item are included in the total.

Table ME-10. Employment Characteristics by Family Type

(Number, percent.)

Family type and labor force status	2013 Total	2013 Families with own children under 18 years	2014 Total	2014 Families with own children under 18 years	2015 Total	2015 Families with own children under 18 years
All Families..	338,609	126,751	342,108	128,896	342,926	126,257
FAMILY TYPE AND LABOR FORCE STATUS						
Married-Couple Families.................................	263,513	81,309	261,227	81,849	264,442	79,988
Both husband and wife in labor force...................	52.0	70.4	53.6	72.7	51.3	71.0
Husband in labor force, wife not in labor force..........	16.7	20.4	17.3	21.5	17.4	21.2
Wife in labor force, husband not in labor force..........	10.6	6.8	9.0	4.0	9.4	4.8
Both husband and wife not in labor force................	20.1	2.0	20.1	1.8	20.7	2.2
Other Families	75,096	45,442	80,881	47,047	78,484	46,269
Female householder, no husband present................	68.4	66.9	67.9	68.4	68.3	68.3
In labor force...	47.7	54.1	46.9	54.0	47.8	53.0
Not in labor force..	20.8	12.8	21.0	14.4	20.5	15.3
Male householder, no wife present........................	31.6	33.1	32.1	31.6	31.7	31.7
In labor force...	23.8	27.3	24.7	27.5	24.4	28.0
Not in labor force..	7.8	5.8	7.5	4.2	7.3	3.7

Table ME-11. School Enrollment and Educational Attainment, 2015

(Number, percent.)

Item	State	U.S.
Enrollment		
Total population 3 years and over, enrolled in school	289,749	81,618,288
Enrolled in nursery school or preschool (percent).........	4.8	6.0
Enrolled in kindergarten (percent)........................	4.9	5.0
Enrolled in elementary school, grades 1-8 (percent).......	39.3	40.3
Enrolled in high school, grades 9-12 (percent)............	22.5	20.9
Enrolled in college or graduate school (percent)..........	28.5	27.7
Attainment		
Total population 25 years and over	961,240	216,447,163
Less than ninth grade (percent)...........................	2.8	5.5
9th to 12th grade, no diploma (percent)...................	5.5	7.3
High school graduate, including equivalency (percent).....	32.7	27.6
Some college, no degree (percent)	19.2	20.7
Associate's degree (percent)..............................	9.7	8.2
Bachelor's degree (percent)...............................	19.5	19.0
Graduate or professional degree (percent).................	10.6	11.6
High school graduate or higher (percent)..................	91.7	87.1
Bachelor's degree or higher (percent).....................	30.1	30.6

Table ME-12. Public School Characteristics and Educational Indicators

(Number, percent; data derived from National Center of Education Statistics.)

Item	State	U.S.
Public Schools, 2014–2015 (except where noted)		
Number of school districts................................	261	18,260
Number of schools..	616	98,373
Number of students.......................................	182,470	50,312,581
Number of teachers	14,937	3,132,351
Student-teacher ratio	12.2	16.1
Expenditures per student (dollars), FY 2014..............	13,267	11,066
Four-year adjusted cohort graduation rate (ACGR)[1,2]	87.5	83.2
Students eligible for free or reduced-price lunch (percent)...	47.1	51.8
English language learners (percent).......................	2.9	9.4
Students age 3 to 21 served under IDEA, part B (percent)...	17.5	13.0

Public Schools by Type	Number	Percent of state public schools
Total number of schools...................................	616	100.0
Regular	588	95.5
Special education...	1	0.2
Vocational education......................................	27	4.4
Alternative education.....................................	0	-

NOTE: Every school is assigned only one school type based on its instructional emphasis.
[1] ACGR data represents a new method of calculating high-school completion rates and may not be comparable to previous years' data for Averaged Freshmen Graduation Rates (AFGR).
[2] The United States 4-year ACGRs were estimated using both the reported 4-year ACGR data from 49 states and the District of Columbia and using imputed data for Idaho. The estimate for American Indian/Alaska Native students also includes imputed data for Virginia.
- = Zero or rounds to zero.

Table ME-13. Reported Voting and Registration of the Voting-Age Population, November 2016

(Numbers in thousands, percent.)

Item	Total population	Total citizen population	Registered			Voted		
			Total registered	Percent registered (total population)	Percent registered (total citizen population)	Total voted	Percent voted (total population)	Percent voted (total citizen population)
U.S. Total	245,502	224,059	157,596	64.2	70.3	137,537	56.0	61.4
State Total..........................	1,058	1,038	830	78.5	80.0	754	71.3	72.7
Sex								
Male	510	500	388	76.1	77.5	347	68.1	69.3
Female	548	537	442	80.7	82.3	408	74.3	75.8
Race								
White alone.............................	1,001	988	793	79.2	80.3	720	71.9	72.9
White, non-Hispanic alone	982	972	786	80.1	80.9	713	72.6	73.3
Black alone..............................	13	10	9	(B)	(B)	7	(B)	(B)
Asian alone	11	8	6	(B)	(B)	5	(B)	(B)
Hispanic (of any race)	20	16	7	(B)	(B)	7	(B)	(B)
White alone or in combination	1,026	1,013	811	79.0	80.0	738	71.9	72.8
Black alone or in combination..........	17	14	9	(B)	(B)	7	(B)	(B)
Asian alone or in combination..........	13	9	7	(B)	(B)	6	(B)	(B)
Age								
18 to 24 years	101	100	63	61.7	62.4	49	48.8	49.4
25 to 34 years	157	154	109	69.2	70.8	95	60.4	61.8
35 to 44 years	146	139	107	73.3	76.9	97	66.4	69.6
45 to 64 years	421	418	354	83.9	84.6	327	77.5	78.2
65 years and over	232	227	198	85.4	87.3	186	80.3	82.0

B = Base is less than 75,000 and therefore too small to show the derived measure.

Table ME-14. Crime

(Number, rate per 100,000. Data are derived from the FBI Uniform Crime Reports.)

Item	State			U.S. 1,2,3,4		
	2014	2015	Percent change	2014	2015	Percent change
TOTAL POPULATION[5]	1,330,256	1,329,328	-0.1	318,907,401	321,418,820	0.8
VIOLENT CRIME						
Number......................................	1,698	1,729	1.8	1,186,185	1,231,566	3.8
Rate	127.6	130.1	1.9	372.0	383.2	3.0
Murder and Nonnegligent Manslaughter						
Number......................................	21	23	9.5	14,164	15,696	10.8
Rate	1.6	1.7	9.6	4.4	4.9	10.0
Rape[6]						
Number......................................	484	474	-2.1	118,027	124,047	5.1
Rate	36.4	35.7	-2.0	37.0	38.6	4.3
Robbery						
Number......................................	304	311	2.3	322,905	327,374	1.4
Rate	22.9	23.4	2.4	101.3	101.9	0.6
Aggravated Assault						
Number......................................	889	921	3.6	731,089	764,449	4.6
Rate	66.8	69.3	3.7	229.2	237.8	3.7
PROPERTY CRIME						
Number......................................	26,427	24,327	-7.9	8,209,010	7,993,631	-2.6
Rate	1,986.6	1,830.0	-7.9	2,574.1	2,487.0	-3.4
Burglary						
Number......................................	5,035	4,684	-7.0	1,713,153	1,579,527	-7.8
Rate	378.5	352.4	-6.9	537.2	491.4	-8.5
Larceny-Theft						
Number......................................	20,591	18,829	-8.6	5,809,054	5,706,346	-1.8
Rate	1,547.9	1,416.4	-8.5	1,821.5	1,775.4	-2.5
Motor Vehicle Theft						
Number......................................	801	814	1.6	686,803	707,758	3.1
Rate	60.2	61.2	1.7	215.4	220.2	2.2

NOTE: Although arson data are included in the trend and clearance tables, sufficient data are not available to estimate totals for this offense. Therefore, no arson data are published in this table.

X = Not applicable.

- = Zero or rounds to zero.

[1] The crime figures have been adjusted.

[2] The data collection methodology for the offense of forcible rape used by the Minnesota state Uniform Crime Reporting (UCR) Program (with the exception of Minneapolis and St. Paul, Minnesota) does not comply with national UCR Program guidelines. Consequently, its figures for forcible rape and violent crime (of which forcible rape is a part) are not published in this table.

[3] Includes offenses reported by the Zoological Police and the Metro Transit Police.

[4] Because of changes in the state's reporting practices, figures are not comparable to previous years' data.

[5] Populations are U.S. Census Bureau provisional estimates as of July 1 of each year.

[6] The figures shown for the offense of rape were estimated using the revised Uniform Crime Reporting (UCR) definition of rape.

Table ME-15. State Government Finances, 2015

(Dollar amounts in thousands, percent distribution.)

Item	Dollars	Percent distribution
Total Revenue	8,792,906	100.0
General revenue	8,008,750	91.1
Intergovernmental revenue	2,784,359	31.7
Taxes	4,064,075	46.2
General sales	1,280,298	14.6
Selective sales	718,753	8.2
License taxes	268,026	3.0
Individual income tax	1,533,130	17.4
Corporate income tax	168,966	1.9
Other taxes	94,902	1.1
Current charges	680,704	7.7
Miscellaneous general revenue	479,612	5.5
Utility revenue	8,744	0.1
Liquor stores revenue	33	-
Insurance trust revenue[1]	775,379	8.8
Total Expenditure	8,841,802	100.0
Intergovernmental expenditure	1,251,695	14.2
Direct expenditure	7,590,107	85.8
Current operation	5,748,786	65.0
Capital outlay	464,366	5.3
Insurance benefits and repayments	1,036,218	11.7
Assistance and subsidies	136,999	1.5
Interest on debt	203,738	2.3
Exhibit: Salaries and wages	1,058,702	12.0
Total Expenditure	8,841,802	100.0
General expenditure	7,784,997	88.0
Intergovernmental expenditure	1,251,695	14.2
Direct expenditure	6,533,302	73.9
General expenditure, by function:		
Education	2,081,683	23.5
Public welfare	2,917,467	33.0
Hospitals	51,676	0.6
Health	441,237	5.0
Highways	643,931	7.3
Police protection	79,612	0.9
Correction	155,673	1.8
Natural resources	172,174	1.9
Parks and recreation	7,616	0.1
Governmental administration	295,798	3.3
Interest on general debt	203,738	2.3
Other and unallocable	734,392	8.3
Utility expenditure	20,587	0.2
Liquor stores expenditure	0	-
Insurance trust expenditure	1,036,218	11.7
Debt at End of Fiscal Year	5,011,671	X
Cash and Security Holdings	18,629,874	X

X = Not applicable.
- = Zero or rounds to zero.
[1] Within insurance trust revenue, net earnings of state retirement systems is a calculated statistic (the item code in the data file is X08), and thus can be positive or negative. Net earnings is the sum of earnings on investments plus gains on investments minus losses on investments. The change made in 2002 for asset valuation from book to market value in accordance with Statement 34 of the Governmental Accounting Standards Board is reflected in the calculated statistics.

Table ME-16. State Government Tax Collections, 2016

(Dollars in thousands, percent.)

Item	Dollars	Percent distribution
Total Taxes	4,130,242	100.0
Property taxes	35,425	0.9
Sales and gross receipts	2,077,913	50.3
General sales and gross receipts	1,359,190	32.9
Selective sales and gross receipts	718,723	17.4
Alcoholic beverages	18,741	0.5
Amusements	53,255	1.3
Insurance premiums	102,528	2.5
Motor fuels	245,053	5.9
Pari-mutuels	1,562	-
Public utilities	21,674	0.5
Tobacco products	141,464	3.4
Other selective sales	134,446	3.3
Licenses	272,253	6.6
Alcoholic beverages	5,445	0.1
Amusements	590	-
Corporations in general	10,100	0.2
Hunting and fishing	16,731	0.4
Motor vehicle	108,845	2.6
Motor vehicle operators	10,935	0.3
Public utilities	0	-
Occupation and business, NEC	110,986	2.7
Other licenses	8,621	0.2
Income taxes	1,689,129	40.9
Individual income	1,551,637	37.6
Corporation net income	137,492	3.3
Other taxes	55,522	1.3
Death and gift	27,198	0.7
Documentary and stock transfer	28,324	0.7
Severance	0	-
Taxes, NEC	0	-

X = Not applicable.
- = Zero or rounds to zero.

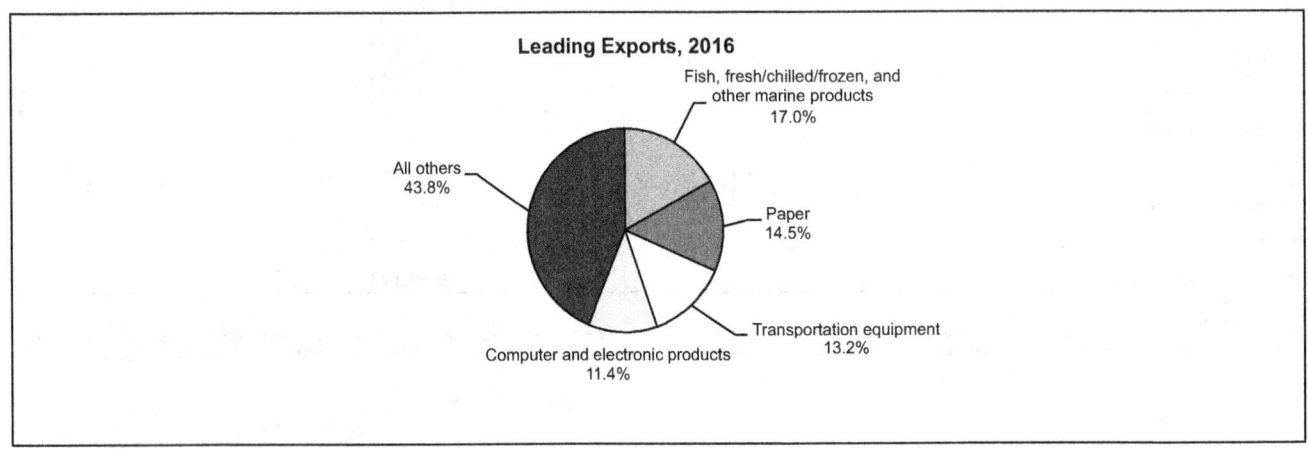

Leading Exports, 2016

Fish, fresh/chilled/frozen, and other marine products 17.0%

Paper 14.5%

Transportation equipment 13.2%

Computer and electronic products 11.4%

All others 43.8%

MARYLAND

Facts and Figures

Location: Eastern United States; bordered on the N by Pennsylvania, on the E by Delaware and the Atlantic Ocean, and on the S and W by Virginia and West Virginia

Area: 12,407 sq. mi. (32,133 sq. km.); rank—42nd

Population: 6,016,447 (2016 est.); rank—19th

Principal Cities: capital—Annapolis; largest—Baltimore

Statehood: April 28, 1788; 7th state

U.S. Congress: 2 senators, 8 representatives

State Motto: *Fatti maschii parole femine* ("Manly deeds, womanly words")

State Song: "Maryland, My Maryland"

State Nicknames: The Old Line State; The Free State

Abbreviations: MD; Md.

State Symbols: flower—black-eyed susan; tree—white oak; bird—Baltimore oriole

At a Glance

- With an increase in population of 4.2 percent, Maryland ranked 25th among the states in growth from 2010 to 2016.

- Maryland's 2015 median household income of $75,847 was the highest in the country, and its poverty rate of 9.7 percent was the second lowest among the states.

- Maryland's violent crime rate in 2015 was 457.2 per 100,000 population, compared to 383.2 for the entire nation.

- In 2015, 6.6 percent of all Marylanders were uninsured, compared to the national average of 9.4 percent.

- Approximately 30.7 percent of Marylanders self-identified their race as "Black or African American alone" in 2016, the 5th highest percentage in the country.

Table MD-1. Population by Age, Sex, Race, and Hispanic Origin

(Number, percent, except where noted.)

Sex, age, race, and Hispanic origin	2000	2010	2016 [1]	Average annual percent change, 2010–2016
Total Population................................	5,296,486	5,773,552	6,016,447	0.3
Percent of total U.S. population	1.9	1.9	1.9	X
Sex				
Male...	2,557,794	2,791,762	2,914,466	0.3
Female..	2,738,692	2,981,790	3,101,981	0.3
Age				
Under 5 years....................................	353,393	364,488	367,095	-
5 to 19 years....................................	1,139,572	1,152,138	1,135,936	-0.1
20 to 64 years..................................	3,204,214	3,549,284	3,637,206	0.2
65 years and over.............................	599,307	707,642	876,210	1.5
Median age (years)	36.0	38.0	38.5	0.1
Race and Hispanic Origin				
One race..				
White	3,391,308	3,542,379	3,567,397	-
Black	1,477,411	1,731,513	1,845,613	0.4
American Indian and Alaska Native	15,423	30,885	34,380	0.7
Asian	210,929	326,655	395,887	1.3
Native Hawaiian or Other Pacific Islander	2,303	5,391	6,460	1.2
Two or more races..............................	103,587	137,729	166,710	1.3
Hispanic (of any race).........................	227,916	493,811	586,801	1.2

X = Not applicable.
[1] Population figures for 2016 are July 1 estimates. The 2010 estimates are taken from the 2010 Census.

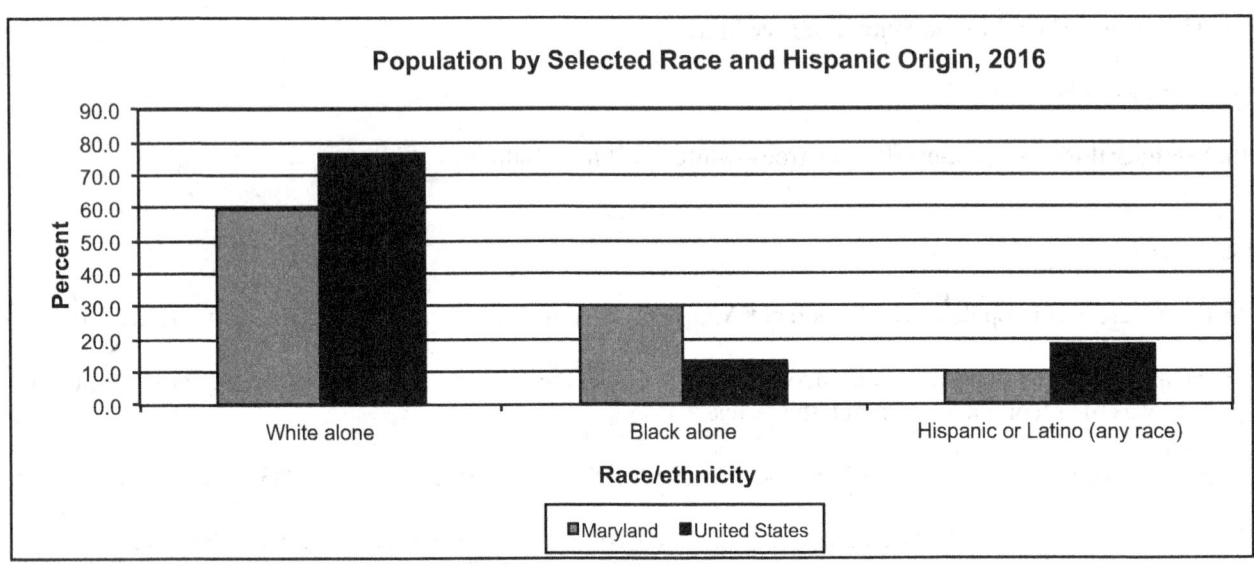

Table MD-2. Marital Status

(Number, percent distribution.)

Sex, age, race, and Hispanic origin	2000	2010	2015
Males, 15 Years and Over	1,972,921	2,232,162	2,340,835
Never married	31.0	36.8	37.6
Now married, except separated......................	56.3	50.2	49.5
Separated..	2.8	2.3	2.0
Widowed..	2.5	2.7	2.3
Divorced..	7.4	8.0	8.6
Females, 15 Years and Over	2,186,715	2,442,021	2,549,736
Never married	26.8	32.2	33.0
Now married, except separated......................	49.7	45.3	44.4
Separated..	3.4	2.9	2.5
Widowed..	10.1	9.0	8.6
Divorced..	10.1	10.7	11.5

Table MD-3. Households and Housing Characteristics

(Number, percent, dollars.)

Item	2000	2010	2015	Average annual percent change, 2000–2015
Total Households..	1,980,859	2,127,439	2,177,934	0.7
Family households	1,359,318	1,431,958	1,454,839	0.5
Married-couple family	994,549	1,022,613	1,042,467	0.3
Other family	364,789	409,345	412,372	0.9
Male householder, no wife present..............	84,893	104,112	108,262	1.8
Female householder, no husband present......	279,876	305,233	304,110	0.6
Nonfamily households	621,541	695,481	723,095	1.1
Householder living alone..............................	495,459	570,388	587,776	1.2
Householder not living alone.........................	126,082	125,093	135,319	0.5
Housing Characteristics				
Total housing units..	2,145,283	2,380,605	2,434,465	0.9
Occupied housing units	1,980,859	2,127,439	2,177,934	0.7
Owner occupied	1,341,751	1,426,267	1,436,159	0.5
Renter occupied	639,108	701,172	741,775	1.1
Average household size....................................	2.61	2.65	2.69	0.2
Financial Characteristics				
Median gross rent of renter-occupied housing	689	1,131	1,278	5.7
Median monthly owner costs for housing units with a mortgage	1,296	2,016	1,909	3.2
Median value of owner-occupied housing units	146,000	301,400	299,800	7.0

Table MD-4. Migration, Origin, and Language

(Number, percent.)

Characteristic	State			U.S.		
	2014	2015	Percent change	2014	2015	Percent change
Residence 1 Year Ago						
Population 1 year and over	5,911,235	5,934,005	0.4	315,095,393	317,635,720	0.8
Same house	86.1	85.6	X	85.1	85.3	X
Different house in the U.S.	13.1	13.6	X	14.3	14.1	X
Same county	7.6	7.8	X	8.7	8.5	X
Different county	5.5	5.8	X	5.6	5.6	X
Same state	2.8	3.0	X	3.3	3.2	X
Different state	2.7	2.8	X	2.3	2.4	X
Abroad	0.8	0.8	X	0.6	0.7	X
Place of Birth						
Native born	5,085,968	5,094,819	0.2	276,465,262	278,128,449	0.6
Male	48.5	48.5	X	49.3	49.3	X
Female	51.5	51.5	X	50.7	50.7	X
Foreign born	890,439	911,582	2.4	42,391,794	43,290,372	2.1
Male	48.4	48.7	X	48.7	48.6	X
Female	51.6	51.3	X	51.3	51.4	X
Foreign born; naturalized U.S. citizen............	434,791	447,550	3.4	19,984,738	20,697,103	3.6
Male	46.1	46.2	X	45.9	45.9	X
Female	53.9	53.8	X	54.1	54.1	X
Foreign born; not a U.S. citizen	455,648	464,032	1.8	22,407,056	22,593,269	0.8
Male	50.6	51.1	X	51.2	51.1	X
Female	49.4	48.9	X	48.8	48.9	X
Entered 2010 or later	14.4	17.5	X	12.3	15.6	X
Entered 2000 to 2009...................................	33.5	33.9	X	28.6	27.9	X
Entered before 2000......................................	52.1	48.6	X	59.1	56.5	X
World Region of Birth, Foreign						
Foreign-born population, excluding population born at sea	890,439	911,582	2.4	42,390,705	43,289,646	2.1
Europe	10.5	9.3	X	11.2	11.1	X
Asia...	33.1	33.4	X	30.1	30.6	X
Africa	16.1	16.6	X	4.6	4.8	X
Oceania	0.3	0.3	X	0.6	0.6	X
Latin America..	39.0	39.3	X	51.6	51.1	X
North America...	1.0	1.1	X	1.9	1.9	X
Language Spoken at Home and Ability to Speak English						
Population 5 years and over...........................	5,609,124	5,639,774	0.5	299,084,046	301,625,014	0.8
English only	82.9	81.5	X	78.9	78.5	X
Language other than English.........................	17.1	18.5	X	21.1	21.5	X
Speaks English less than "very well".........	6.4	6.9	X	8.6	8.6	X

NA = Not available.
X = Not applicable.
- = Zero or rounds to zero.

Table MD-5. Median Income and Poverty Status, 2015

(Number, percent, except as noted.)

Characteristic	State		U.S.	
	Number	Percent	Number	Percent
Median Income				
Households (dollars)...........................	75,847	X	55,775	X
Families (dollars)	91,567	X	68,260	X
Below Poverty Level (All People)	570,776	9.7	46,153,077	14.7
Sex				
Male	239,835	8.5	20,599,407	13.4
Female	330,941	10.9	25,553,670	16.0
Age				
Under 18 years.............................	175,124	13.2	15,000,273	20.7
Related children under 18 years...........	169,123	12.8	14,693,239	20.4
18 to 64 years..............................	335,667	9.0	26,960,369	13.9
65 years and over	59,985	7.3	4,192,435	9.0

X = Not applicable.

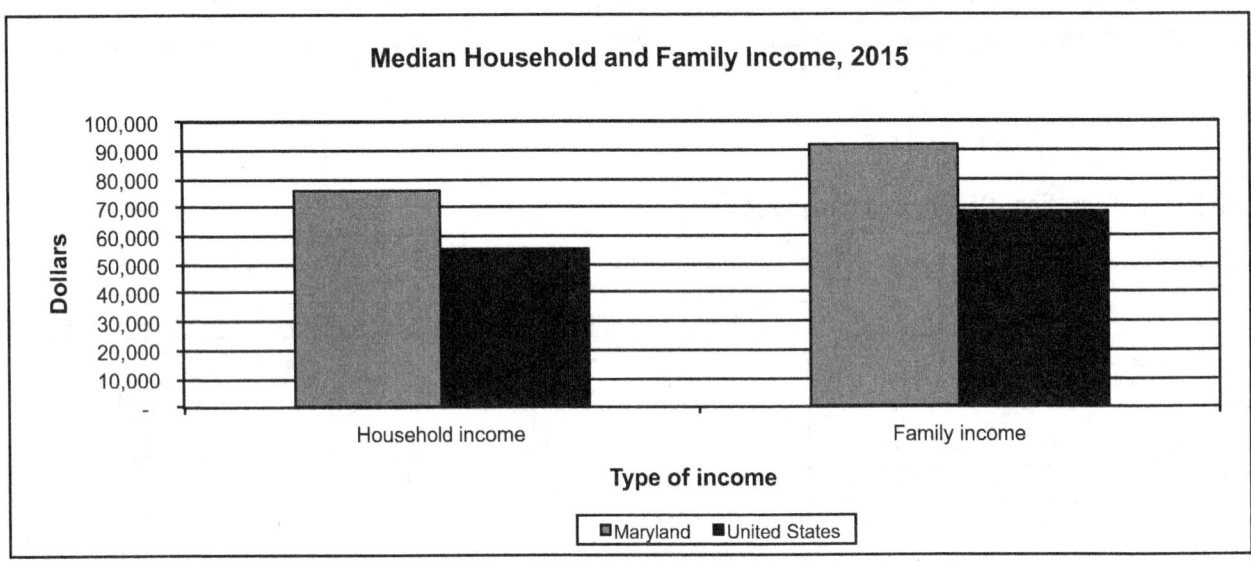

Table MD-6. Health Insurance Coverage Status for the Civilian Noninstitutionalized Population and Children Under 18 Years of Age

(Numbers in thousands, percent.)

Item	2007	2008	2009	2010	2011	2012	2013	2014	2015
Civilian Noninstitutionalized Population	5,565	5,530	5,590	5,688	5,737	5,788	5,834	5,886	5,909
Covered by Private or Public Insurance									
Number..	4,804	4,919	4,969	5,047	5,138	5,191	5,241	5,423	5,519
Percent..	86.3	89.0	88.9	88.7	89.6	89.7	89.8	92.1	93.4
Not Covered									
Number..	762	611	621	641	598	597	593	463	389
Percent..	13.7	11.0	11.1	11.3	10.4	10.3	10.2	7.9	6.6
Percent in the U.S. not covered................	15.3	15.1	15.1	15.5	15.1	14.8	14.5	11.7	9.4
Children Under 18 Years of Age	1,382	1,339	1,348	1,350	1,344	1,341	1,343	1,350	1,346
Covered by Private or Public Insurance									
Number..	1,237	1,269	1,283	1,286	1,283	1,290	1,284	1,307	1,294
Percent..	89.5	94.8	95.2	95.2	95.4	96.2	95.6	96.8	96.1
Not Covered									
Number..	146	70	65	64	61	51	59	43	52
Percent..	10.5	5.2	4.8	4.8	4.6	3.8	4.4	3.2	3.9
Percent in the U.S. not covered................	11.0	9.7	8.6	8.0	7.5	7.2	7.1	6.0	4.8

Table MD-7. Employment Status by Demographic Group, 2016

(Numbers in thousands, percent.)

Characteristic	Civilian noninstitutional population	Civilian labor force		Employed		Unemployed	
		Number	Percent of population	Number	Percent of population	Number	Percent of population
Total..	4,747	3,187	67.1	3,052	64.3	135	4.2
Sex							
Male...	2,246	1,630	72.6	1,568	69.8	62	3.8
Female...	2,501	1,557	62.2	1,484	59.3	73	4.7
Race, Sex, and Hispanic Origin							
White...	2,869	1,929	67.2	1,868	65.1	60	3.1
Male..	1,408	1,033	73.4	1,005	71.4	28	2.7
Female...	1,461	896	61.3	863	59.1	33	3.6
Black or African American...........................	1,414	933	66.0	869	61.5	63	6.8
Male..	630	436	69.2	408	64.8	27	6.3
Female...	784	497	63.4	461	58.8	36	7.2
Hispanic or Latino ethnicity[1]......................	399	308	77.2	291	73.0	17	5.4
Male..	207	183	88.4	176	85.0	7	3.9
Female...	191	125	65.2	115	60.1	10	7.7
Age							
16 to 19 years..	292	106	36.2	88	30.3	17	16.2
20 to 24 years..	391	294	75.1	271	69.4	23	7.7
25 to 34 years..	836	695	83.1	663	79.3	32	4.6
35 to 44 years..	733	626	85.5	601	82.1	25	4.0
45 to 54 years..	858	732	85.3	715	83.4	17	2.3
55 to 64 years..	820	552	67.2	538	65.6	13	2.4
65 years and over......................................	818	183	22.4	175	21.4	9	4.7

NOTE: Data in Table 7 are from the Current Population Survey (CPS) and do not match the estimates in Table 8. See notes and definitions for further information.
[1] May be of any race.

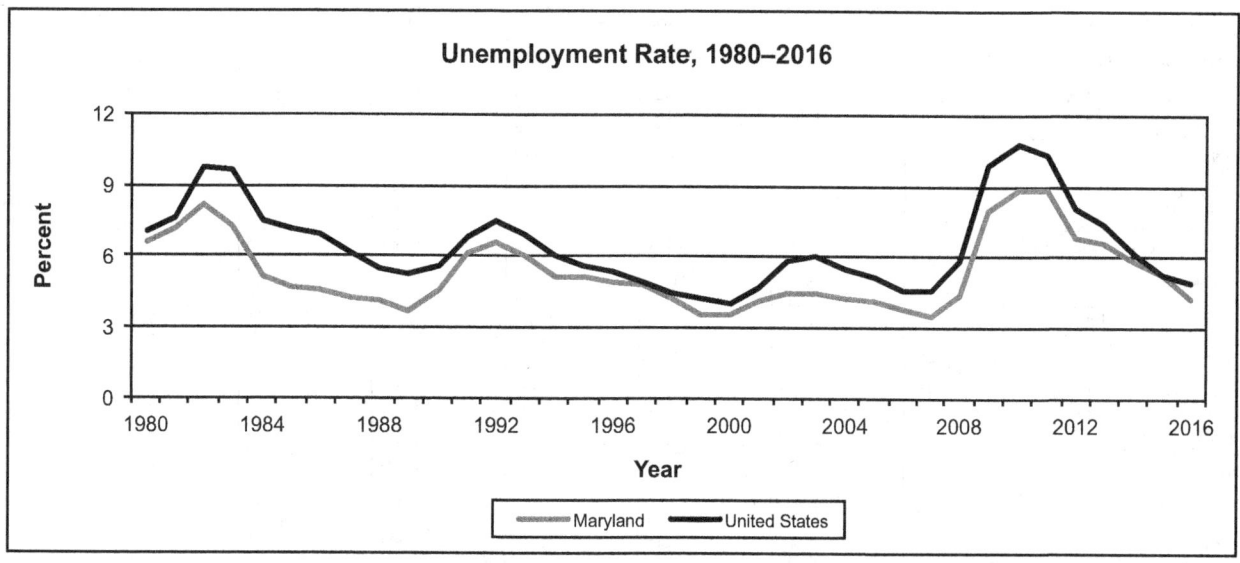

Table MD-8. Employment Status of the Civilian Noninstitutional Population Age 16 Years and Over

(Number, percent.)

Year	Civilian labor force	Civilian participation rate	Employed	Unemployed	Unemployment rate
2008..	3,001,953	68.9	2,874,987	126,966	4.2
2009..	3,032,700	69.0	2,820,245	212,455	7.0
2010..	3,073,826	68.5	2,838,492	235,334	7.7
2011..	3,096,561	68.0	2,872,084	224,477	7.2
2012..	3,120,678	67.8	2,903,673	217,005	7.0
2013..	3,127,825	67.3	2,921,375	206,450	6.6
2014..	3,128,296	66.8	2,946,520	181,776	5.8
2015..	3,151,929	66.8	2,988,101	163,828	5.2
2016..	3,170,011	67.1	3,034,131	135,880	4.3

Table MD-9. Employment and Average Wages by Industry

(Estimates through 2010 are based on the 2007 *North American Industry Classification System* [NAICS]. Estimates from 2011 onward are based on the 2012 NAICS.)

Industry	2009	2010	2011	2012	2013	2014	2015
				Number of jobs			
Wage and Salary Employment by Industry..................	2,645,643	2,625,019	2,650,584	2,685,280	2,702,959	2,728,522	2,767,317
Farm Wage and Salary Employment.........................	4,298	4,748	4,744	6,475	5,980	6,416	6,214
Nonfarm Wage and Salary Employment....................	2,641,345	2,620,271	2,645,840	2,678,805	2,696,979	2,722,106	2,761,103
Private wage and salary employment......................	2,083,705	2,056,337	2,078,218	2,109,420	2,128,533	2,155,027	2,193,577
Forestry, fishing, and related activities	2,180	2,209	2,019	1,977	2,022	2,060	2,124
Mining..	1,492	1,468	1,433	1,524	1,339	1,259	1,297
Utilities..	10,105	9,716	10,069	10,103	9,781	9,738	9,579
Construction	160,282	147,757	147,885	147,456	150,364	153,666	158,226
Manufacturing..	118,780	114,958	112,919	108,831	106,370	103,376	103,643
Durable goods manufacturing........................	63,908	61,488	60,189	57,860	56,302	53,714	54,436
Nondurable goods manufacturing....................	54,872	53,470	52,730	50,971	50,068	49,662	49,207
Wholesale trade	88,247	85,818	86,534	86,448	86,188	85,303	86,284
Retail trade...	281,096	279,657	283,148	286,405	286,608	289,186	291,677
Transportation and warehousing.......................	65,509	65,333	66,187	67,456	68,719	71,133	76,562
Information..	46,314	43,868	41,081	39,909	39,537	38,972	38,349
Finance and insurance	101,395	98,987	98,692	98,986	99,383	98,476	99,379
Real estate and rental and leasing....................	44,900	43,326	43,129	43,686	44,125	44,589	45,548
Professional, scientific, and technical services	227,485	226,313	231,104	235,966	237,301	241,056	243,456
Management of companies and enterprises..................	19,900	19,569	22,267	24,725	25,906	25,574	25,202
Administrative and waste services	141,583	144,151	147,539	152,558	156,700	159,818	164,484
Educational services	69,335	70,211	71,489	72,585	71,682	73,696	75,067
Health care and social assistance......................	324,924	329,856	334,550	342,513	346,073	350,187	359,235
Arts, entertainment, and recreation....................	35,909	36,331	36,622	38,209	42,311	44,530	45,950
Accommodation and food services....................	197,257	195,521	198,661	207,332	213,536	217,437	223,161
Other services, except public administration..................	147,012	141,288	142,890	142,751	140,588	144,971	144,354
Government and government enterprises......................	557,640	563,934	567,622	569,385	568,446	567,079	567,526
				Dollars			
Average Wages and Salaries by Industry	51,522	53,083	54,489	55,444	55,547	56,854	58,639
Average Farm Wages and Salaries	29,888	25,881	22,673	23,208	25,910	25,563	24,232
Average Nonfarm Wages and Salaries	51,557	53,132	54,546	55,522	55,612	56,927	58,717
Average private wages and salaries.....................	48,978	50,539	51,822	53,079	53,208	54,420	56,119
Forestry, fishing, and related activities....................	25,328	27,067	27,692	28,068	28,721	29,215	30,750
Mining..	53,965	56,032	61,075	61,333	60,153	62,712	61,488
Utilities..	96,582	107,343	110,167	118,943	115,073	114,520	122,096
Construction	53,772	55,076	56,025	56,907	57,117	59,179	61,012
Manufacturing..	64,833	67,998	68,822	70,363	70,981	72,306	75,281
Durable goods manufacturing........................	72,413	76,107	76,131	77,458	78,375	78,035	80,109
Nondurable goods manufacturing....................	56,004	58,674	60,478	62,309	62,665	66,109	69,940
Wholesale trade	68,334	70,739	72,939	74,437	75,214	77,445	79,659
Retail trade...	28,236	28,931	29,018	29,414	29,503	30,102	31,475
Transportation and warehousing.......................	45,932	48,006	49,931	50,370	50,288	52,829	53,975
Information..	70,547	74,193	78,548	80,343	83,120	85,281	86,354
Finance and insurance	78,477	82,529	85,537	93,568	93,248	96,557	100,331
Real estate and rental and leasing....................	51,187	55,401	56,579	57,971	58,007	60,631	62,824
Professional, scientific, and technical services	82,660	85,388	88,541	91,159	90,290	92,592	94,237
Management of companies and enterprises..................	97,666	107,421	106,413	105,241	107,488	111,088	116,214
Administrative and waste services	37,125	38,265	38,796	39,142	39,510	40,212	41,977
Educational services	42,894	43,382	45,531	47,145	47,629	49,007	49,851
Health care and social assistance......................	47,282	47,756	48,968	49,641	49,973	50,958	52,918
Arts, entertainment, and recreation....................	29,725	30,963	31,493	32,542	32,629	33,217	34,680
Accommodation and food services....................	19,506	19,965	20,481	20,951	21,265	21,871	22,844
Other services, except public administration..................	33,115	34,636	35,206	36,512	37,790	38,423	40,048
Government and government enterprises......................	61,195	62,587	64,521	64,574	64,616	66,456	68,757

Table MD-10. Employment Characteristics by Family Type

(Number, percent.)

Family type and labor force status	2013		2014		2015	
	Total	Families with own children under 18 years	Total	Families with own children under 18 years	Total	Families with own children under 18 years
All Families...	1,443,796	632,608	1,437,457	625,063	1,454,839	629,970
FAMILY TYPE AND LABOR FORCE STATUS						
Married-Couple Families..............................	1,022,394	423,061	1,013,543	415,627	1,042,467	429,625
Both husband and wife in labor force................	58.8	72.6	58.4	72.9	57.5	71.5
Husband in labor force, wife not in labor force.........	19.3	22.6	19.9	22.6	19.9	23.6
Wife in labor force, husband not in labor force.........	7.7	3.3	7.4	3.3	7.4	3.3
Both husband and wife not in labor force............	13.4	1.0	14.4	1.1	14.2	1.0
Other Families	421,402	209,547	423,914	209,436	412,372	200,345
Female householder, no husband present................	75.8	78.4	75.0	76.2	73.7	75.4
In labor force...................................	57.8	67.0	56.6	66.0	55.2	65.5
Not in labor force	17.9	11.4	18.4	10.2	18.6	9.9
Male householder, no wife present.....................	24.2	21.6	25.0	23.8	26.3	24.6
In labor force....................................	20.1	20.5	20.1	22.5	21.0	22.5
Not in labor force	4.1	1.1	4.9	1.3	5.3	2.2

Table MD-11. School Enrollment and Educational Attainment, 2015

(Number, percent.)

Item	State	U.S.
Enrollment		
Total population 3 years and over, enrolled in school	1,565,730	81,618,288
Enrolled in nursery school or preschool (percent).................................	6.5	6.0
Enrolled in kindergarten (percent)..	4.7	5.0
Enrolled in elementary school, grades 1-8 (percent)...............................	37.8	40.3
Enrolled in high school, grades 9-12 (percent)	19.8	20.9
Enrolled in college or graduate school (percent).................................	31.3	27.7
Attainment		
Total population 25 years and over	4,102,486	216,447,163
Less than ninth grade (percent)...	4.2	5.5
9th to 12th grade, no diploma (percent)...	6.1	7.3
High school graduate, including equivalency (percent).............................	25.1	27.6
Some college, no degree (percent)...	19.2	20.7
Associate's degree (percent)...	6.5	8.2
Bachelor's degree (percent)	21.1	19.0
Graduate or professional degree (percent).......................................	17.7	11.6
High school graduate or higher (percent)	89.6	87.1
Bachelor's degree or higher (percent)	38.8	30.6

Table MD-12. Public School Characteristics and Educational Indicators

(Number, percent; data derived from National Center of Education Statistics.)

Item	State	U.S.
Public Schools, 2014–2015 (except where noted)		
Number of school districts..	25	18,260
Number of schools..	1,438	98,373
Number of students...	874,514	50,312,581
Number of teachers	59,194	3,132,351
Student-teacher ratio	14.8	16.1
Expenditures per student (dollars), FY 2014	14,217	11,066
Four-year adjusted cohort graduation rate (ACGR)[1,2]	87.0	83.2
Students eligible for free or reduced-price lunch (percent).......................	45.0	51.8
English language learners (percent)...	6.9	9.4
Students age 3 to 21 served under IDEA, part B (percent).........................	11.9	13.0

Public Schools by Type	Number	Percent of state public schools
Total number of schools...	1,438	100.0
Regular	1,329	92.4
Special education	37	2.6
Vocational education	27	1.9
Alternative education...	45	3.1

NOTE: Every school is assigned only one school type based on its instructional emphasis.
[1] ACGR data represents a new method of calculating high-school completion rates and may not be comparable to previous years' data for Averaged Freshmen Graduation Rates (AFGR).
[2] The United States 4-year ACGRs were estimated using both the reported 4-year ACGR data from 49 states and the District of Columbia and using imputed data for Idaho. The estimate for American Indian/Alaska Native students also includes imputed data for Virginia.

Table MD-13. Reported Voting and Registration of the Voting-Age Population, November 2016

(Numbers in thousands, percent.)

Item	Total population	Total citizen population	Registered			Voted		
			Total registered	Percent registered (total population)	Percent registered (total citizen population)	Total voted	Percent voted (total population)	Percent voted (total citizen population)
U.S. Total	245,502	224,059	157,596	64.2	70.3	137,537	56.0	61.4
State Total..........................	4,623	4,158	3,114	67.3	74.9	2,737	59.2	65.8
Sex								
Male	2,203	1,963	1,454	66.0	74.1	1,253	56.9	63.8
Female	2,420	2,194	1,659	68.6	75.6	1,484	61.3	67.6
Race								
White alone........................	2,784	2,593	1,975	70.9	76.2	1,727	62.0	66.6
White, non-Hispanic alone...........	2,434	2,392	1,829	75.2	76.5	1,605	65.9	67.1
Black alone........................	1,386	1,289	954	68.9	74.0	858	61.9	66.6
Asian alone	349	213	147	42.0	69.1	117	33.4	54.9
Hispanic (of any race)................	450	250	170	37.9	68.2	148	32.8	59.1
White alone or in combination	2,820	2,629	2,002	71.0	76.2	1,752	62.1	66.6
Black alone or in combination..........	1,421	1,324	984	69.2	74.3	884	62.2	66.8
Asian alone or in combination..........	349	213	147	42.0	69.1	117	33.4	54.9
Age								
18 to 24 years......................	468	414	279	59.7	67.4	225	48.0	54.3
25 to 34 years......................	819	711	505	61.7	71.1	424	51.8	59.7
35 to 44 years......................	833	668	490	58.8	73.3	424	50.9	63.6
45 to 64 years......................	1,702	1,586	1,243	73.0	78.4	1,133	66.6	71.4
65 years and over	801	778	596	74.4	76.6	530	66.2	68.1

Table MD-14. Crime

(Number, rate per 100,000. Data are derived from the FBI Uniform Crime Reports.)

Item	State			U.S. 1,2,3,4		
	2014	2015	Percent change	2014	2015	Percent change
TOTAL POPULATION[5]	5,975,346	6,006,401	0.5	318,907,401	321,418,820	0.8
VIOLENT CRIME						
Number................................	26,767	27,462	2.6	1,186,185	1,231,566	3.8
Rate	448.0	457.2	2.1	372.0	383.2	3.0
Murder and Nonnegligent Manslaughter						
Number................................	362	516	42.5	14,164	15,696	10.8
Rate	6.1	8.6	41.8	4.4	4.9	10.0
Rape[6]						
Number................................	1,632	1,666	2.1	118,027	124,047	5.1
Rate	27.3	27.7	1.6	37.0	38.6	4.3
Robbery						
Number................................	9,565	9,863	3.1	322,905	327,374	1.4
Rate	160.1	164.2	2.6	101.3	101.9	0.6
Aggravated Assault						
Number................................	15,208	15,417	1.4	731,089	764,449	4.6
Rate	254.5	256.7	0.9	229.2	237.8	3.7
PROPERTY CRIME						
Number................................	150,390	139,048	-7.5	8,209,010	7,993,631	-2.6
Rate	2,516.8	2,315.0	-8.0	2,574.1	2,487.0	-3.4
Burglary						
Number................................	28,134	25,678	-8.7	1,713,153	1,579,527	-7.8
Rate	470.8	427.5	-9.2	537.2	491.4	-8.5
Larceny-Theft						
Number................................	109,140	100,219	-8.2	5,809,054	5,706,346	-1.8
Rate	1,826.5	1,668.5	-8.6	1,821.5	1,775.4	-2.5
Motor Vehicle Theft						
Number................................	13,116	13,151	0.3	686,803	707,758	3.1
Rate	219.5	218.9	-0.3	215.4	220.2	2.2

NOTE: Although arson data are included in the trend and clearance tables, sufficient data are not available to estimate totals for this offense. Therefore, no arson data are published in this table.

X = Not applicable.

- = Zero or rounds to zero.

[1] The crime figures have been adjusted.

[2] The data collection methodology for the offense of forcible rape used by the Minnesota state Uniform Crime Reporting (UCR) Program (with the exception of Minneapolis and St. Paul, Minnesota) does not comply with national UCR Program guidelines. Consequently, its figures for forcible rape and violent crime (of which forcible rape is a part) are not published in this table.

[3] Includes offenses reported by the Zoological Police and the Metro Transit Police.

[4] Because of changes in the state's reporting practices, figures are not comparable to previous years' data.

[5] Populations are U.S. Census Bureau provisional estimates as of July 1 of each year.

[6] The figures shown for the offense of rape were estimated using the revised Uniform Crime Reporting (UCR) definition of rape.

Table MD-15. State Government Finances, 2015

(Dollar amounts in thousands, percent distribution.)

Item	Dollars	Percent distribution
Total Revenue	43,222,344	100.0
General revenue	38,801,440	89.8
Intergovernmental revenue	12,342,856	28.6
Taxes..	20,001,304	46.3
General sales..	4,409,919	10.2
Selective sales..	4,040,399	9.3
License taxes..	851,466	2.0
Individual income tax..	8,346,145	19.3
Corporate income tax..	1,003,588	2.3
Other taxes...	1,349,787	3.1
Current charges	3,566,579	8.3
Miscellaneous general revenue	2,890,701	6.7
Utility revenue..	141,728	0.3
Liquor stores revenue	0	-
Insurance trust revenue[1]..	4,279,176	9.9
Total Expenditure	44,457,929	100.0
Intergovernmental expenditure	9,158,679	20.6
Direct expenditure...	35,299,250	79.4
Current operation	23,817,188	53.6
Capital outlay	2,931,179	6.6
Insurance benefits and repayments	5,502,970	12.4
Assistance and subsidies	1,879,014	4.2
Interest on debt...	1,168,899	2.6
Exhibit: Salaries and wages..	5,404,649	12.2
Total Expenditure	44,457,929	100.0
General expenditure	37,810,541	85.0
Intergovernmental expenditure	9,158,679	20.6
Direct expenditure..	28,651,862	64.4
General expenditure, by function:		
Education..	12,145,924	27.3
Public welfare	12,121,427	27.3
Hospitals..	535,929	1.2
Health..	2,205,886	5.0
Highways	2,521,117	5.7
Police protection	596,171	1.3
Correction	1,457,111	3.3
Natural resources..	540,507	1.2
Parks and recreation	165,902	0.4
Governmental administration	1,499,985	3.4
Interest on general debt	1,168,899	2.6
Other and unallocable	2,851,683	6.4
Utility expenditure...	1,144,418	2.6
Liquor stores expenditure	0	-
Insurance trust expenditure	5,502,970	12.4
Debt at End of Fiscal Year	26,592,571	X
Cash and Security Holdings	61,394,732	X

X = Not applicable.
- = Zero or rounds to zero.
[1] Within insurance trust revenue, net earnings of state retirement systems is a calculated statistic (the item code in the data file is X08), and thus can be positive or negative. Net earnings is the sum of earnings on investments plus gains on investments minus losses on investments. The change made in 2002 for asset valuation from book to market value in accordance with Statement 34 of the Governmental Accounting Standards Board is reflected in the calculated statistics.

Table MD-16. State Government Tax Collections, 2016

(Dollars in thousands, percent.)

Item	Dollars	Percent distribution
Total Taxes	20,894,199	100.0
Property taxes	748,389	3.6
Sales and gross receipts	8,939,430	42.8
General sales and gross receipts	4,504,242	21.6
Selective sales and gross receipts	4,435,188	21.2
Alcoholic beverages	31,627	0.2
Amusements	650,293	3.1
Insurance premiums	552,526	2.6
Motor fuels	1,017,769	4.9
Pari-mutuels	1,173	-
Public utilities	137,537	0.7
Tobacco products	395,266	1.9
Other selective sales	1,648,997	7.9
Licenses	884,363	4.2
Alcoholic beverages	1,446	-
Amusements	1,415	-
Corporations in general	103,860	0.5
Hunting and fishing	17,883	0.1
Motor vehicle	492,753	2.4
Motor vehicle operators	36,597	0.2
Public utilities	0	-
Occupation and business, NEC	228,582	1.1
Other licenses	1,827	-
Income taxes	9,646,537	46.2
Individual income	8,517,529	40.8
Corporation net income	1,129,008	5.4
Other taxes	675,480	3.2
Death and gift	261,922	1.3
Documentary and stock transfer	200,858	1.0
Severance	0	-
Taxes, NEC	212,700	1.0

X = Not applicable.
- = Zero or rounds to zero.

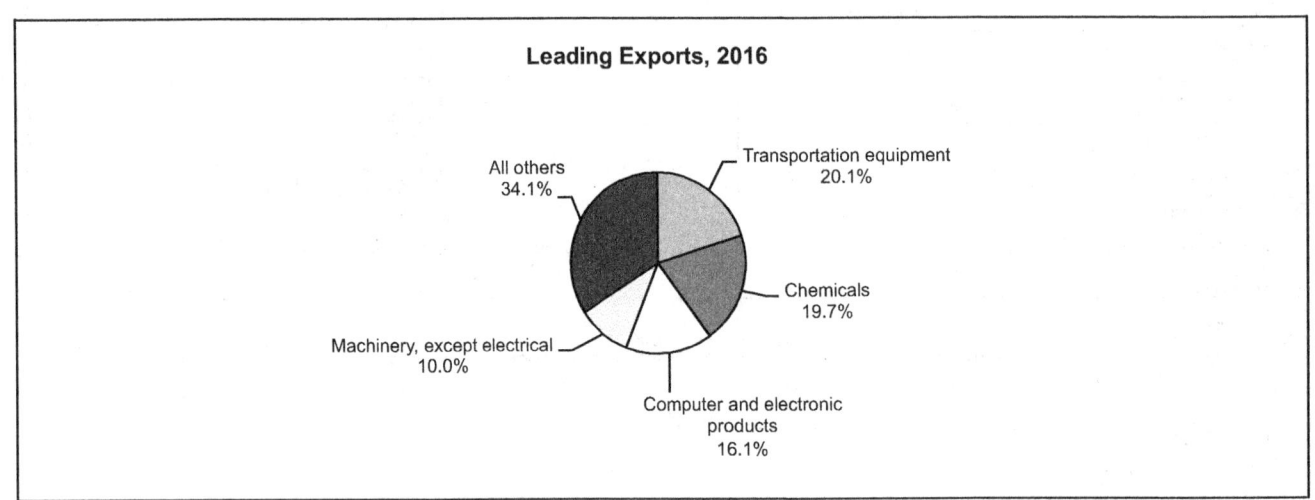

Leading Exports, 2016

All others 34.1%
Transportation equipment 20.1%
Chemicals 19.7%
Computer and electronic products 16.1%
Machinery, except electrical 10.0%

MASSACHUSETTS

Facts and Figures

Location: Northeastern United States; bordered on the N by Vermont and New Hampshire, on the E by the Atlantic Ocean, on the S by Connecticut and Rhode Island, and on the W by New York

Area: 10,555 sq. mi. (27,336 sq. km.); rank—44th

Population: 6,811,779 (2016 est.); rank—15th

Principal Cities: capital—Boston; largest—Boston

Statehood: February 6, 1788; 6th state

U.S. Congress: 2 senators, 9 representatives

State Motto: *Ense petit placidam sub libertate quietem* ("By the sword we seek peace, but peace only under liberty")

State Song: "All Hail to Massachusetts"

State Nickname: The Bay State

Abbreviations: MA; Mass.

State Symbols: flower—mayflower; tree—American elm; bird—chickadee

At a Glance

- With an increase in population of 4.0 percent, Massachusetts ranked 27th among the states in growth from 2010 to 2016.

- Massachusetts's median household income in 2015 was $70,628, the 7th highest in the country.

- Approximately 11.5 percent of the state's population lived below the poverty level in 2015, compared to 14.7 percent of the entire U.S. population.

- Massachusetts's violent crime rate in 2015 was 390.9 per 100,000 population, compared to 383.2 for the entire nation.

- Massachusetts's drug overdose death rate ranked 7th in the nation, with 25.7 deaths per 100,000 population.

Table MA-1. Population by Age, Sex, Race, and Hispanic Origin

(Number, percent, except where noted.)

Sex, age, race, and Hispanic origin	2000	2010	2016 [1]	Average annual percent change, 2010–2016
Total Population..	6,349,097	6,547,629	6,811,779	0.3
Percent of total U.S. population	2.3	2.1	2.1	X
Sex				
Male..	3,058,816	3,166,628	3,305,651	0.3
Female	3,290,281	3,381,001	3,506,128	0.2
Age				
Under 5 years..	397,268	367,087	361,376	-0.1
5 to 19 years...	1,277,845	1,254,056	1,222,640	-0.2
20 to 64 years...	3,813,822	4,023,762	4,153,799	0.2
65 years and over..	860,162	902,724	1,073,964	1.2
Median age (years)	36.5	39.1	39.4	-
Race and Hispanic Origin				
One race...				
White	5,367,286	5,524,937	5,570,872	0.1
Black...	343,454	504,365	587,417	1.0
American Indian and Alaska Native	15,015	29,944	32,988	0.6
Asian...	238,124	359,673	454,371	1.6
Native Hawaiian or Other Pacific Islander	2,489	5,971	6,975	1.1
Two or more races..	146,005	122,739	159,156	1.9
Hispanic (of any race)...	428,729	656,888	780,661	1.2

X = Not applicable.
[1] Population figures for 2016 are July 1 estimates. The 2010 estimates are taken from the 2010 Census.
- = Zero or rounds to zero.

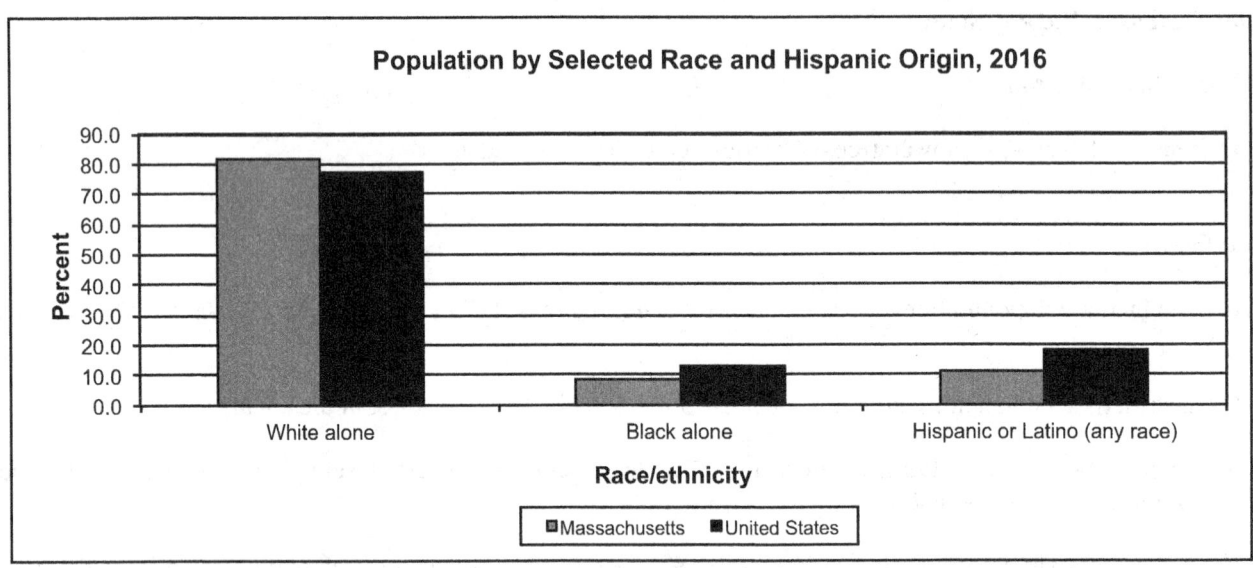

Population by Selected Race and Hispanic Origin, 2016

Legend: ▨ Massachusetts ■ United States

Table MA-2. Marital Status

(Number, percent distribution.)

Sex, age, race, and Hispanic origin	2000	2010	2015
Males, 15 Years and Over	2,412,349	2,579,221	2,716,576
Never married	33.9	38.7	40.4
Now married, except separated......................................	54.7	49.1	47.8
Separated..	1.6	1.6	1.3
Widowed..	2.7	2.7	2.4
Divorced..	7.0	8.0	8.1
Females, 15 Years and Over	2,679,020	2,819,768	2,941,597
Never married	28.5	33.2	34.5
Now married, except separated......................................	48.9	44.1	43.6
Separated..	2.3	2.4	2.1
Widowed..	10.8	9.1	8.6
Divorced..	9.5	11.1	11.2

Table MA-3. Households and Housing Characteristics

(Number, percent, dollars.)

Item	2000	2010	2015	Average annual percent change, 2000–2015
Total Households	2,443,580	2,520,419	2,559,951	0.3
Family households	1,576,696	1,590,257	1,613,404	0.2
Married-couple family	1,197,917	1,166,204	1,188,714	-0.1
Other family	378,779	424,053	424,690	0.8
Male householder, no wife present	88,835	100,400	105,294	1.2
Female householder, no husband present	289,944	323,653	319,396	0.7
Nonfamily households	866,884	930,162	946,547	0.6
Householder living alone	684,345	736,320	738,257	0.5
Householder not living alone	182,539	193,842	208,290	0.9
Housing Characteristics				
Total housing units	2,621,989	2,808,727	2,845,805	0.6
Occupied housing units	2,443,580	2,520,419	2,559,951	0.3
Owner occupied	1,508,052	1,568,382	1,579,953	0.3
Renter occupied	935,528	952,037	979,998	0.3
Average household size	2.51	2.51	2.56	0.1
Financial Characteristics				
Median gross rent of renter-occupied housing	684	1,009	1,164	4.7
Median monthly owner costs for housing units with a mortgage	1,353	2,036	2,048	3.4
Median value of owner-occupied housing units	185,700	334,100	352,100	6.0

Table MA-4. Migration, Origin, and Language

(Number, percent.)

Characteristic	State			U.S.		
	2014	2015	Percent change	2014	2015	Percent change
Residence 1 Year Ago						
Population 1 year and over	6,674,907	6,725,678	0.8	315,095,393	317,635,720	0.8
Same house	86.7	87.6	X	85.1	85.3	X
Different house in the U.S.	12.3	11.4	X	14.3	14.1	X
Same county	7.4	6.6	X	8.7	8.5	X
Different county	4.9	4.8	X	5.6	5.6	X
Same state	2.7	2.8	X	3.3	3.2	X
Different state	2.2	2.0	X	2.3	2.4	X
Abroad	1.1	1.0	X	0.6	0.7	X
Place of Birth						
Native born	5,685,127	5,698,469	0.2	276,465,262	278,128,449	0.6
Male	48.4	48.6	X	49.3	49.3	X
Female	51.6	51.4	X	50.7	50.7	X
Foreign born	1,060,281	1,095,953	3.4	42,391,794	43,290,372	2.1
Male	48.7	48.2	X	48.7	48.6	X
Female	51.3	51.8	X	51.3	51.4	X
Foreign born; naturalized U.S. citizen	554,211	572,765	3.3	19,984,738	20,697,103	3.6
Male	46.9	46.2	X	45.9	45.9	X
Female	53.1	53.8	X	54.1	54.1	X
Foreign born; not a U.S. citizen	506,070	523,188	3.4	22,407,056	22,593,269	0.8
Male	50.7	50.3	X	51.2	51.1	X
Female	49.3	49.7	X	48.8	48.9	X
Entered 2010 or later	16.6	19.7	X	12.3	15.6	X
Entered 2000 to 2009	28.9	28.2	X	28.6	27.9	X
Entered before 2000	54.4	52.1	X	59.1	56.5	X
World Region of Birth, Foreign						
Foreign-born population, excluding population born at sea	1,060,281	1,095,953	3.4	42,390,705	43,289,646	2.1
Europe	21.7	21.2	X	11.2	11.1	X
Asia	30.5	30.3	X	30.1	30.6	X
Africa	9.7	9.1	X	4.6	4.8	X
Oceania	0.4	0.3	X	0.6	0.6	X
Latin America	34.9	35.8	X	51.6	51.1	X
North America	2.8	3.2	X	1.9	1.9	X
Language Spoken at Home and Ability to Speak English						
Population 5 years and over	6,379,441	6,429,039	0.8	299,084,046	301,625,014	0.8
English only	77.4	77.0	X	78.9	78.5	X
Language other than English	22.6	23.0	X	21.1	21.5	X
Speaks English less than "very well"	8.9	9.0	X	8.6	8.6	X

NA = Not available.
X = Not applicable.
- = Zero or rounds to zero.

Table MA-5. Median Income and Poverty Status, 2015

(Number, percent, except as noted.)

Characteristic	State		U.S.	
	Number	Percent	Number	Percent
Median Income				
Households (dollars)....................................	70,628	X	55,775	X
Families (dollars)	90,590	X	68,260	X
Below Poverty Level (All People)	752,071	11.5	46,153,077	14.7
Sex				
Male	327,193	10.3	20,599,407	13.4
Female	424,878	12.6	25,553,670	16.0
Age				
Under 18 years....................................	202,513	14.8	15,000,273	20.7
Related children under 18 years....................	197,236	14.5	14,693,239	20.4
18 to 64 years....................................	457,090	10.9	26,960,369	13.9
65 years and over	92,468	9.2	4,192,435	9.0

X = Not applicable.

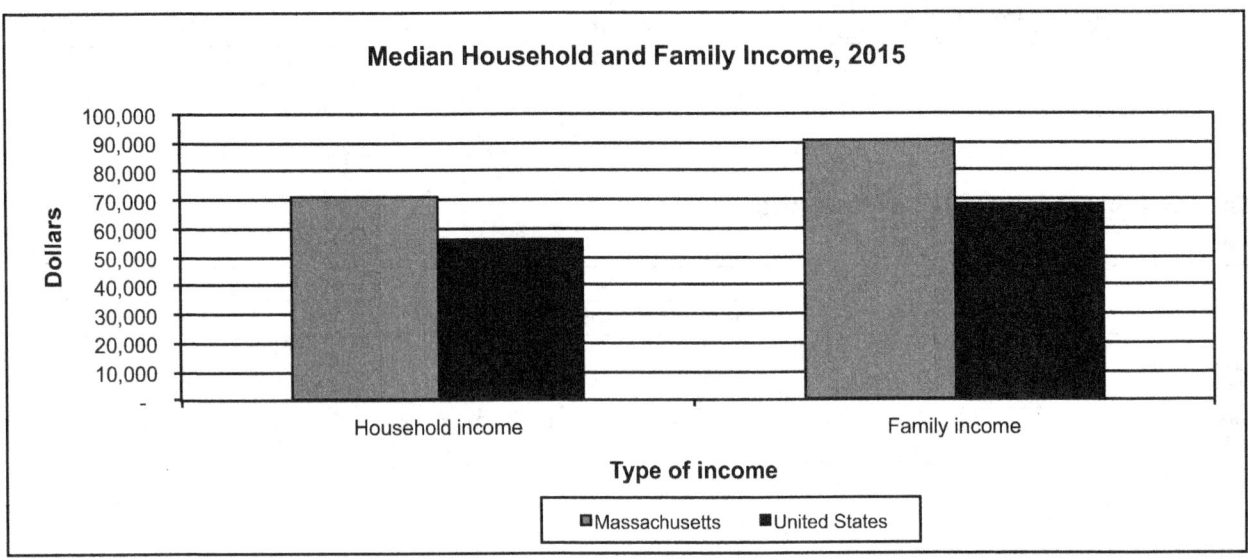

Table MA-6. Health Insurance Coverage Status for the Civilian Noninstitutionalized Population and Children Under 18 Years of Age

(Numbers in thousands, percent.)

Item	2007	2008	2009	2010	2011	2012	2013	2014	2015
Civilian Noninstitutionalized Population	6,340	6,399	6,496	6,478	6,508	6,567	6,614	6,668	6,718
Covered by Private or Public Insurance									
Number....................	6,000	6,135	6,225	6,192	6,231	6,313	6,367	6,450	6,529
Percent....................	94.6	95.9	95.8	95.6	95.7	96.1	96.3	96.7	97.2
Not Covered									
Number....................	340	264	271	286	277	254	247	219	189
Percent....................	5.4	4.1	4.2	4.4	4.3	3.9	3.7	3.3	2.8
Percent in the U.S. not covered....................	15.3	15.1	15.1	15.5	15.1	14.8	14.5	11.7	9.4
Children Under 18 Years of Age	1,435	1,427	1,431	1,415	1,402	1,398	1,389	1,387	1,384
Covered by Private or Public Insurance									
Number....................	1,392	1,397	1,411	1,393	1,378	1,378	1,368	1,366	1,368
Percent....................	97.0	97.9	98.6	98.5	98.3	98.6	98.5	98.5	98.9
Not Covered									
Number....................	43	30	20	22	24	20	21	21	16
Percent....................	3.0	2.1	1.4	1.5	1.7	1.4	1.5	1.5	1.1
Percent in the U.S. not covered....................	11.0	9.7	8.6	8.0	7.5	7.2	7.1	6.0	4.8

Table MA-7. Employment Status by Demographic Group, 2016

(Numbers in thousands, percent.)

Characteristic	Civilian noninstitutional population	Civilian labor force		Employed		Unemployed	
		Number	Percent of population	Number	Percent of population	Number	Percent of population
Total...................................	5,546	3,599	64.9	3,466	62.5	133	3.7
Sex							
Male..................................	2,656	1,866	70.3	1,791	67.4	75	4.0
Female...............................	2,891	1,733	60.0	1,675	58.0	58	3.3
Race, Sex, and Hispanic Origin							
White................................	4,595	2,993	65.1	2,888	62.9	105	3.5
Male..............................	2,207	1,549	70.2	1,492	67.6	57	3.7
Female...........................	2,389	1,445	60.5	1,397	58.5	48	3.3
Black or African American............	442	297	67.2	279	63.2	18	6.0
Male..............................	207	145	70.2	133	64.5	12	8.1
Female...........................	235	152	64.6	146	62.0	6	4.0
Hispanic or Latino ethnicity[1].........	549	351	63.9	328	59.7	23	6.5
Male..............................	247	173	69.8	157	63.6	15	8.9
Female...........................	302	178	59.0	171	56.6	8	4.2
Age							
16 to 19 years.......................	314	116	37.1	106	33.8	10	8.7
20 to 24 years.......................	477	322	67.4	303	63.4	19	6.0
25 to 34 years.......................	1,055	882	83.5	855	81.0	27	3.0
35 to 44 years.......................	783	658	83.9	636	81.1	22	3.3
45 to 54 years.......................	931	766	82.2	739	79.4	26	3.4
55 to 64 years.......................	883	611	69.3	592	67.0	20	3.2
65 years and over....................	1,103	245	22.2	236	21.4	9	3.8

NOTE: Data in Table 7 are from the Current Population Survey (CPS) and do not match the estimates in Table 8. See notes and definitions for further information.
[1] May be of any race.

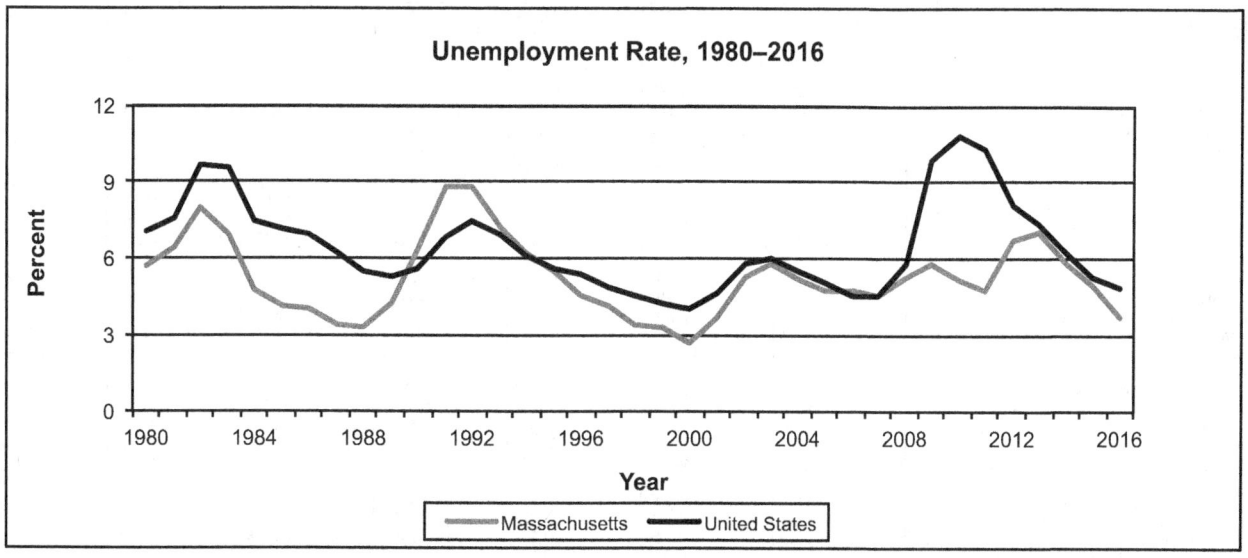

Table MA-8. Employment Status of the Civilian Noninstitutional Population Age 16 Years and Over

(Number, percent.)

Year	Civilian labor force	Civilian participation rate	Employed	Unemployed	Unemployment rate
2008..................................	3,452,468	66.6	3,261,408	191,060	5.5
2009..................................	3,470,382	66.3	3,189,010	281,372	8.1
2010..................................	3,480,083	66.3	3,190,818	289,265	8.3
2011..................................	3,469,308	65.5	3,217,754	251,554	7.3
2012..................................	3,486,326	65.2	3,254,060	232,266	6.7
2013..................................	3,513,565	65.0	3,277,801	235,764	6.7
2014..................................	3,557,362	65.2	3,353,138	204,224	5.7
2015..................................	3,569,956	64.9	3,392,107	177,849	5.0
2016..................................	3,588,610	64.9	3,455,827	132,783	3.7

Table MA-9. Employment and Average Wages by Industry

(Estimates through 2010 are based on the 2007 *North American Industry Classification System* [NAICS]. Estimates from 2011 onward are based on the 2012 NAICS.)

Industry	2009	2010	2011	2012	2013	2014	2015
	Number of jobs						
Wage and Salary Employment by Industry..................	3,306,898	3,304,140	3,343,033	3,423,005	3,476,147	3,543,338	3,608,821
Farm Wage and Salary Employment.........................	3,721	3,676	4,019	4,433	5,071	5,085	5,067
Nonfarm Wage and Salary Employment....................	3,303,177	3,300,464	3,339,014	3,418,572	3,471,076	3,538,253	3,603,754
Private wage and salary employment......................	2,850,798	2,845,946	2,888,245	2,965,379	3,015,357	3,076,773	3,141,864
Forestry, fishing, and related activities.........................	5,036	5,115	4,210	4,085	3,800	3,985	4,253
Mining..	1,220	1,048	1,002	866	886	930	986
Utilities...	10,211	10,429	10,451	10,267	10,056	10,683	10,438
Construction...	116,504	110,854	114,269	119,023	126,048	132,444	142,190
Manufacturing...	259,626	254,666	254,221	252,184	250,865	250,653	249,631
Durable goods manufacturing..................................	170,484	166,126	167,191	165,409	163,547	162,433	161,273
Nondurable goods manufacturing............................	89,142	88,540	87,030	86,775	87,318	88,220	88,358
Wholesale trade	128,478	123,456	123,874	122,217	123,976	124,587	124,257
Retail trade..	339,951	342,360	346,545	348,785	350,169	352,720	355,972
Transportation and warehousing................................	72,099	73,000	74,226	75,517	77,531	80,565	83,468
Information...	84,861	85,234	84,621	87,110	86,170	86,253	88,237
Finance and insurance	176,252	172,816	173,349	171,567	170,718	171,548	173,303
Real estate and rental and leasing............................	42,160	40,898	41,297	42,070	43,062	44,033	44,887
Professional, scientific, and technical services.............	254,759	250,884	258,899	268,035	276,265	285,437	295,829
Management of companies and enterprises..................	59,080	57,464	58,632	63,352	64,315	63,563	65,227
Administrative and waste services..............................	151,819	157,738	163,349	165,133	169,389	173,213	177,294
Educational services	183,451	182,605	186,522	189,831	193,479	195,388	199,113
Health care and social assistance..............................	498,889	510,540	516,969	557,896	571,075	587,863	607,133
Arts, entertainment, and recreation............................	48,393	49,664	49,970	51,282	52,834	55,094	57,303
Accommodation and food services.............................	255,108	260,069	267,253	276,731	284,008	289,926	295,025
Other services, except public administration.................	162,901	157,106	158,586	159,428	160,711	167,888	167,318
Government and government enterprises........................	452,379	454,518	450,769	453,193	455,719	461,480	461,890
	Dollars						
Average Wages and Salaries by Industry	55,004	56,761	58,578	59,533	60,405	62,646	65,196
Average Farm Wages and Salaries	26,987	26,132	20,922	31,008	27,949	29,503	27,183
Average Nonfarm Wages and Salaries	55,035	56,795	58,623	59,570	60,452	62,694	65,250
Average private wages and salaries............................	55,614	57,635	59,496	60,407	61,204	63,531	66,109
Forestry, fishing, and related activities.........................	48,619	52,543	53,152	55,342	54,144	49,341	49,237
Mining..	53,056	56,178	57,113	57,639	58,372	62,129	65,043
Utilities...	102,785	104,090	109,951	107,859	107,738	110,024	111,819
Construction...	61,052	62,129	63,257	65,175	66,430	68,662	71,160
Manufacturing...	69,209	75,209	77,549	79,518	79,825	83,378	86,043
Durable goods manufacturing..................................	75,675	83,890	86,718	89,043	88,688	91,996	92,864
Nondurable goods manufacturing............................	56,845	58,920	59,933	61,361	63,223	67,512	73,591
Wholesale trade	76,255	79,230	82,166	82,365	84,458	88,321	91,558
Retail trade..	27,587	27,797	27,912	28,323	28,923	30,077	31,364
Transportation and warehousing................................	43,323	44,006	45,351	46,412	46,569	48,158	49,648
Information...	84,632	92,042	95,864	97,039	97,452	103,372	108,059
Finance and insurance	110,370	114,551	119,326	124,434	126,301	136,232	144,150
Real estate and rental and leasing............................	54,798	60,242	63,222	66,495	69,829	72,789	73,189
Professional, scientific, and technical services.............	95,415	101,060	103,898	108,211	110,277	113,996	118,860
Management of companies and enterprises..................	101,482	104,229	123,029	115,667	118,769	126,628	140,175
Administrative and waste services..............................	38,287	38,530	39,805	41,054	41,125	42,264	44,320
Educational services	41,968	44,367	45,576	46,344	47,144	48,485	49,388
Health care and social assistance..............................	50,187	51,307	52,154	51,232	51,634	52,521	53,509
Arts, entertainment, and recreation............................	36,145	36,909	37,818	38,243	38,515	38,673	39,942
Accommodation and food services.............................	21,029	21,248	21,807	22,441	23,115	23,969	25,348
Other services, except public administration.................	30,032	31,067	31,816	32,767	33,341	34,113	35,444
Government and government enterprises........................	51,389	51,533	53,029	54,095	55,479	57,111	59,404

Table MA-10. Employment Characteristics by Family Type

(Number, percent.)

Family type and labor force status	2013 Total	2013 Families with own children under 18 years	2014 Total	2014 Families with own children under 18 years	2015 Total	2015 Families with own children under 18 years
All Families..	1,620,802	701,258	1,596,764	693,261	1,613,404	684,676
FAMILY TYPE AND LABOR FORCE STATUS						
Married-Couple Families...............................	1,190,249	482,070	1,169,707	475,565	1,188,714	474,202
Both husband and wife in labor force................................	58.5	72.1	59.2	73.1	57.7	72.5
Husband in labor force, wife not in labor force	18.4	22.1	18.4	22.5	18.1	22.0
Wife in labor force, husband not in labor force	7.7	3.7	7.5	3.3	7.7	3.4
Both husband and wife not in labor force................................	14.3	1.3	15.0	1.1	15.1	1.2
Other Families	430,553	219,188	427,057	217,696	424,690	210,474
Female householder, no husband present..........................	74.9	79.3	74.8	80.3	75.2	80.4
In labor force	53.2	62.7	54.1	66.5	53.7	66.2
Not in labor force	21.7	16.6	20.7	13.8	21.5	14.3
Male householder, no wife present..........................	25.1	20.7	25.2	19.7	24.8	19.6
In labor force	19.2	18.1	20.3	18.0	19.3	18.0
Not in labor force	5.9	2.6	4.9	1.7	5.5	1.6

Table MA-11. School Enrollment and Educational Attainment, 2015

(Number, percent.)

Item	State	U.S.
Enrollment		
Total population 3 years and over, enrolled in school	1,732,925	81,618,288
Enrolled in nursery school or preschool (percent)	6.3	6.0
Enrolled in kindergarten (percent)	4.3	5.0
Enrolled in elementary school, grades 1-8 (percent)................................	36.0	40.3
Enrolled in high school, grades 9-12 (percent)	19.6	20.9
Enrolled in college or graduate school (percent)................................	33.8	27.7
Attainment		
Total population 25 years and over	4,706,644	216,447,163
Less than ninth grade (percent)	4.5	5.5
9th to 12th grade, no diploma (percent)	5.2	7.3
High school graduate, including equivalency (percent)	25.2	27.6
Some college, no degree (percent)	15.9	20.7
Associate's degree (percent)	7.7	8.2
Bachelor's degree (percent)	23.1	19.0
Graduate or professional degree (percent)................................	18.4	11.6
High school graduate or higher (percent)	90.2	87.1
Bachelor's degree or higher (percent)	41.5	30.6

Table MA-12. Public School Characteristics and Educational Indicators

(Number, percent; data derived from National Center of Education Statistics.)

Item	State	U.S.
Public Schools, 2014–2015 (except where noted)		
Number of school districts................................	406	18,260
Number of schools................................	1,866	98,373
Number of students	955,844	50,312,581
Number of teachers	71,859	3,132,351
Student-teacher ratio	13.3	16.1
Expenditures per student (dollars), FY 2014................................	15,886	11,066
Four-year adjusted cohort graduation rate (ACGR)[1,2]	87.3	83.2
Students eligible for free or reduced-price lunch (percent)	39.9	51.8
English language learners (percent)	9.0	9.4
Students age 3 to 21 served under IDEA, part B (percent)................................	17.6	13.0

Public Schools by Type	Number	Percent of state public schools
Total number of schools................................	1,866	100.0
Regular	1,801	96.5
Special education	7	0.4
Vocational education	38	2.0
Alternative education................................	20	1.1

NOTE: Every school is assigned only one school type based on its instructional emphasis.
[1] ACGR data represents a new method of calculating high-school completion rates and may not be comparable to previous years' data for Averaged Freshmen Graduation Rates (AFGR).
[2] The United States 4-year ACGRs were estimated using both the reported 4-year ACGR data from 49 states and the District of Columbia and using imputed data for Idaho. The estimate for American Indian/Alaska Native students also includes imputed data for Virginia.

Table MA-13. Reported Voting and Registration of the Voting-Age Population, November 2016

(Numbers in thousands, percent.)

Item	Total population	Total citizen population	Registered			Voted		
			Total registered	Percent registered (total population)	Percent registered (total citizen population)	Total voted	Percent voted (total population)	Percent voted (total citizen population)
U.S. Total	245,502	224,059	157,596	64.2	70.3	137,537	56.0	61.4
State Total...........................	5,374	4,967	3,660	68.1	73.7	3,315	61.7	66.7
Sex								
Male	2,585	2,382	1,767	68.3	74.2	1,599	61.9	67.1
Female	2,788	2,585	1,893	67.9	73.2	1,715	61.5	66.4
Race								
White alone............................	4,464	4,260	3,229	72.3	75.8	2,919	65.4	68.5
White, non-Hispanic alone	4,083	3,969	3,078	75.4	77.5	2,789	68.3	70.3
Black alone............................	438	368	266	60.8	72.4	242	55.3	65.8
Asian alone...........................	353	238	128	36.3	53.8	121	34.2	50.8
Hispanic (of any race).................	500	397	199	39.8	50.1	177	35.4	44.6
White alone or in combination	4,573	4,357	3,263	71.4	74.9	2,950	64.5	67.7
Black alone or in combination..........	513	431	284	55.4	65.9	260	50.7	60.3
Asian alone or in combination.........	369	254	133	36.0	52.4	126	34.1	49.5
Age								
18 to 24 years.....................	596	555	298	50.0	53.6	238	39.9	42.8
25 to 34 years.....................	1,035	919	615	59.5	67.0	555	53.6	60.4
35 to 44 years.....................	811	696	506	62.4	72.6	475	58.6	68.3
45 to 64 years.....................	1,850	1,743	1,383	74.8	79.3	1,263	68.3	72.5
65 years and over	1,082	1,054	858	79.3	81.4	784	72.4	74.3

Table MA-14. Crime

(Number, rate per 100,000. Data are derived from the FBI Uniform Crime Reports.)

Item	State			U.S. [1,2,3,4]		
	2014	2015	Percent change	2014	2015	Percent change
TOTAL POPULATION[5]	6,755,124	6,794,422	0.6	318,907,401	321,418,820	0.8
VIOLENT CRIME						
Number..	26,689	26,562	-0.5	1,186,185	1,231,566	3.8
Rate	395.1	390.9	-1.1	372.0	383.2	3.0
Murder and Nonnegligent Manslaughter						
Number..	133	128	-3.8	14,164	15,696	10.8
Rate	2.0	1.9	-4.3	4.4	4.9	10.0
Rape[6]						
Number..	2,202	2,075	-5.8	118,027	124,047	5.1
Rate	32.6	30.5	-6.3	37.0	38.6	4.3
Robbery						
Number..	6,077	5,288	-13.0	322,905	327,374	1.4
Rate	90.0	77.8	-13.5	101.3	101.9	0.6
Aggravated Assault						
Number..	18,277	19,071	4.3	731,089	764,449	4.6
Rate	270.6	280.7	3.7	229.2	237.8	3.7
PROPERTY CRIME						
Number..	125,481	114,871	-8.5	8,209,010	7,993,631	-2.6
Rate	1,857.6	1,690.7	-9.0	2,574.1	2,487.0	-3.4
Burglary						
Number..	24,951	21,890	-12.3	1,713,153	1,579,527	-7.8
Rate	369.4	322.2	-12.8	537.2	491.4	-8.5
Larceny-Theft						
Number..	92,226	84,912	-7.9	5,809,054	5,706,346	-1.8
Rate	1,365.3	1,249.7	-8.5	1,821.5	1,775.4	-2.5
Motor Vehicle Theft						
Number..	8,304	8,069	-2.8	686,803	707,758	3.1
Rate	122.9	118.8	-3.4	215.4	220.2	2.2

NOTE: Although arson data are included in the trend and clearance tables, sufficient data are not available to estimate totals for this offense. Therefore, no arson data are published in this table.

X = Not applicable.

- = Zero or rounds to zero.

[1] The crime figures have been adjusted.

[2] The data collection methodology for the offense of forcible rape used by the Minnesota state Uniform Crime Reporting (UCR) Program (with the exception of Minneapolis and St. Paul, Minnesota) does not comply with national UCR Program guidelines. Consequently, its figures for forcible rape and violent crime (of which forcible rape is a part) are not published in this table.

[3] Includes offenses reported by the Zoological Police and the Metro Transit Police.

[4] Because of changes in the state's reporting practices, figures are not comparable to previous years' data.

[5] Populations are U.S. Census Bureau provisional estimates as of July 1 of each year.

[6] The figures shown for the offense of rape were estimated using the revised Uniform Crime Reporting (UCR) definition of rape.

Table MA-15. State Government Finances, 2015

(Dollar amounts in thousands, percent distribution.)

Item	Dollars	Percent distribution
Total Revenue	61,139,906	100.0
General revenue	51,975,677	85.0
Intergovernmental revenue	15,060,943	24.6
Taxes	26,973,576	44.1
General sales	5,803,934	9.5
Selective sales	2,470,238	4.0
License taxes	1,213,135	2.0
Individual income tax	14,491,903	23.7
Corporate income tax	2,227,381	3.6
Other taxes	766,985	1.3
Current charges	5,024,042	8.2
Miscellaneous general revenue	4,917,116	8.0
Utility revenue	840,340	1.4
Liquor stores revenue	0	-
Insurance trust revenue[1]	8,323,889	13.6
Total Expenditure	63,221,413	100.0
Intergovernmental expenditure	9,379,933	14.8
Direct expenditure	53,841,480	85.2
Current operation	36,705,062	58.1
Capital outlay	4,702,541	7.4
Insurance benefits and repayments	8,371,203	13.2
Assistance and subsidies	799,065	1.3
Interest on debt	3,263,609	5.2
Exhibit: Salaries and wages	6,857,279	10.8
Total Expenditure	63,221,413	100.0
General expenditure	51,341,206	81.2
Intergovernmental expenditure	9,379,933	14.8
Direct expenditure	41,961,273	66.4
General expenditure, by function:		
Education	13,192,076	20.9
Public welfare	18,790,185	29.7
Hospitals	545,674	0.9
Health	1,489,881	2.4
Highways	2,827,045	4.5
Police protection	903,465	1.4
Correction	1,102,746	1.7
Natural resources	419,951	0.7
Parks and recreation	250,829	0.4
Governmental administration	1,827,954	2.9
Interest on general debt	2,907,971	4.6
Other and unallocable	7,083,429	11.2
Utility expenditure	3,509,004	5.6
Liquor stores expenditure	0	-
Insurance trust expenditure	8,371,203	13.2
Debt at End of Fiscal Year	75,307,661	X
Cash and Security Holdings	100,232,700	X

X = Not applicable.
- = Zero or rounds to zero.

[1] Within insurance trust revenue, net earnings of state retirement systems is a calculated statistic (the item code in the data file is X08), and thus can be positive or negative. Net earnings is the sum of earnings on investments plus gains on investments minus losses on investments. The change made in 2002 for asset valuation from book to market value in accordance with Statement 34 of the Governmental Accounting Standards Board is reflected in the calculated statistics.

Table MA-16. State Government Tax Collections, 2016

(Dollars in thousands, percent.)

Item	Dollars	Percent distribution
Total Taxes	27,283,005	100.0
Property taxes	5,818	-
Sales and gross receipts	8,683,866	31.8
General sales and gross receipts	6,089,860	22.3
Selective sales and gross receipts	2,594,006	9.5
Alcoholic beverages	83,395	0.3
Amusements	66,844	0.2
Insurance premiums	406,796	1.5
Motor fuels	766,553	2.8
Pari-mutuels	1,326	-
Public utilities	24,929	0.1
Tobacco products	640,839	2.3
Other selective sales	603,324	2.2
Licenses	1,122,219	4.1
Alcoholic beverages	3,450	-
Amusements	14,916	0.1
Corporations in general	26,922	0.1
Hunting and fishing	5,532	-
Motor vehicle	464,428	1.7
Motor vehicle operators	99,051	0.4
Public utilities	0	-
Occupation and business, NEC	324,481	1.2
Other licenses	183,439	0.7
Income taxes	16,764,223	61.4
Individual income	14,430,331	52.9
Corporation net income	2,333,892	8.6
Other taxes	706,879	2.6
Death and gift	399,429	1.5
Documentary and stock transfer	307,450	1.1
Severance	0	-
Taxes, NEC	0	-

X = Not applicable.
- = Zero or rounds to zero.

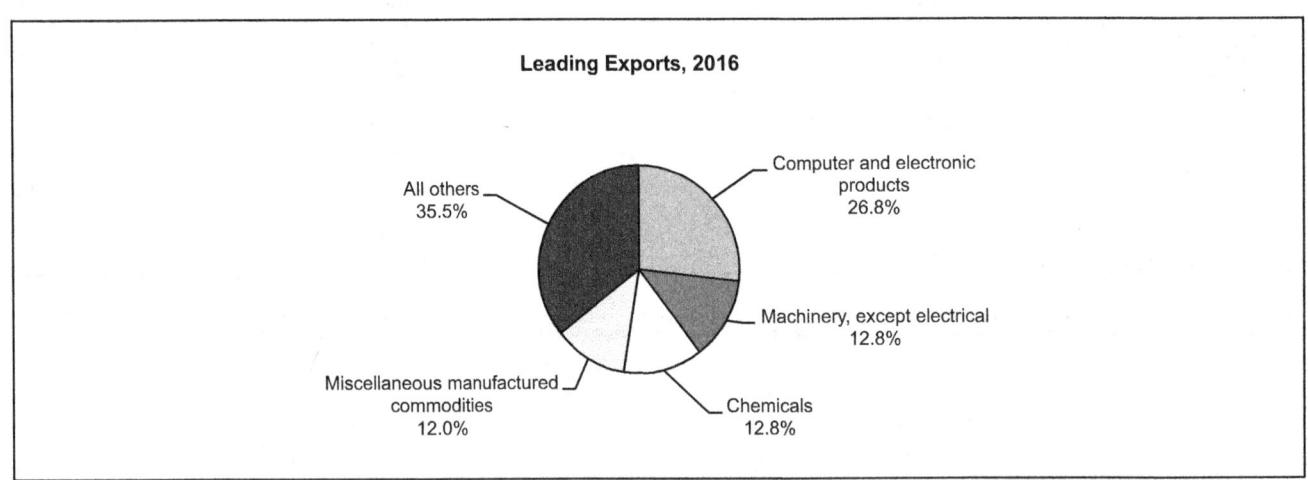

Leading Exports, 2016

- All others 35.5%
- Computer and electronic products 26.8%
- Machinery, except electrical 12.8%
- Chemicals 12.8%
- Miscellaneous manufactured commodities 12.0%

MICHIGAN

Facts and Figures

Location: East north central United States; bordered on the N by Lake Superior, on the E by Ontario, Canada, and Lakes Huron and Erie, on the S by Indiana and Ohio, and on the W by Wisconsin and Lake Michigan

Area: 96,716 sq. mi. (250,494 sq. km.); rank—11th

Population: 9,928,300 (2016 est.); rank—10th

Principal Cities: capital—Lansing; largest—Detroit

Statehood: January 26, 1837; 26th state

U.S. Congress: 2 senators, 14 representatives

State Motto: *Si quaeris peninsulam amoenam, circumspice* ("If you seek a pleasant peninsula, look about you")

State Song: "Michigan, My Michigan"

State Nicknames: The Wolverine State; The Great Lakes State

Abbreviations: MI; Mich.

State Symbols: flower—apple blossom; tree—Eastern white pine; bird—robin

At a Glance

- With an increase in population of 0.5 percent, Michigan ranked 45th among the states in growth from 2010 to 2016.

- In 2015, 6.1 percent of Michiganders did not have health insurance, compared to 9.4 percent of the total U.S. population.

- Michigan's violent crime rate in 2015 was 415.5 per 100,000 population, compared to the U.S. rate of 383.2 per 100,000 population.

- Approximately 15.8 percent of Michigan residents lived below the poverty level in 2015, compared to the national poverty rate of 14.7 percent.

- Michigan's unemployment rate of 4.9 percent ranked 21st in the nation in 2015.

Table MI-1. Population by Age, Sex, Race, and Hispanic Origin

(Number, percent, except where noted.)

Sex, age, race, and Hispanic origin	2000	2010	2016 [1]	Average annual percent change, 2010–2016
Total Population...	9,938,444	9,883,640	9,928,300	-
Percent of total U.S. population	3.5	3.2	3.1	X
Sex				
Male..	4,873,095	4,848,114	4,884,746	-
Female..	5,065,349	5,035,526	5,043,554	-
Age				
Under 5 years..	672,005	596,286	574,423	-0.2
5 to 19 years..	2,212,060	2,052,599	1,885,129	-0.5
20 to 64 years...	5,835,361	5,873,225	5,856,993	-
65 years and over...	1,219,018	1,361,530	1,611,755	1.1
Median age (years)	35.5	38.9	39.7	0.1
Race and Hispanic Origin				
One race..				
White..	7,966,053	7,949,497	7,902,903	-
Black..	1,412,742	1,416,067	1,406,212	-
American Indian and Alaska Native	58,479	68,396	72,252	0.4
Asian..	176,510	243,062	306,396	1.6
Native Hawaiian or Other Pacific Islander	2,692	3,442	3,948	0.9
Two or more races...	192,416	203,176	236,589	1.0
Hispanic (of any race)......................................	323,877	459,751	492,382	0.4

X = Not applicable.
- = Zero or rounds to zero.
[1] Population figures for 2016 are July 1 estimates. The 2010 estimates are taken from the 2010 Census.

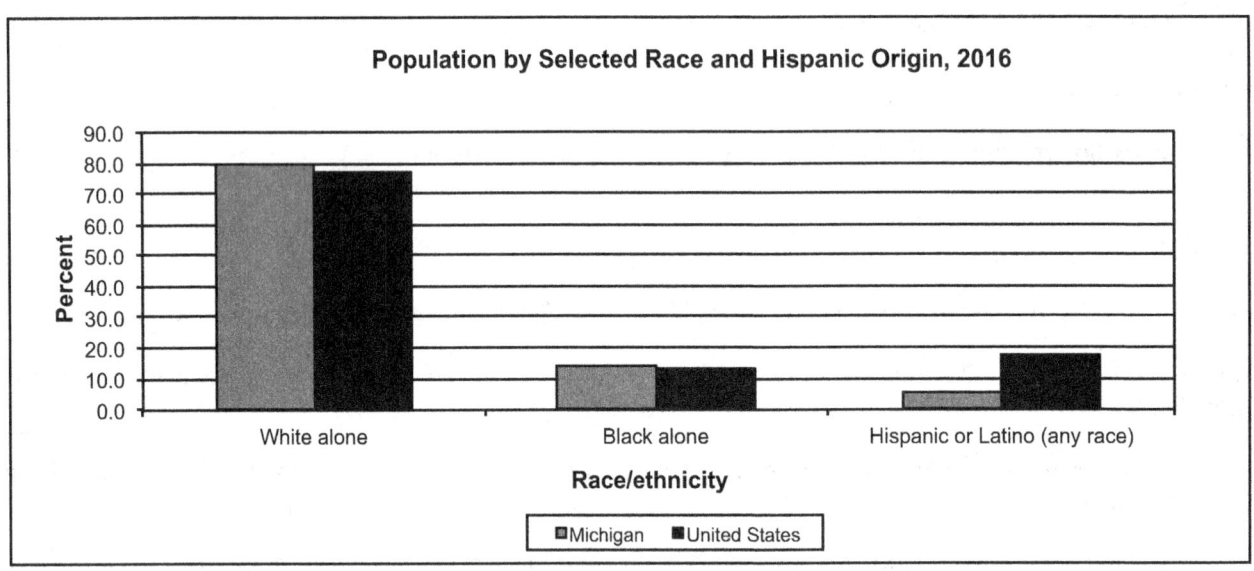

Population by Selected Race and Hispanic Origin, 2016

Table MI-2. Marital Status

(Number, percent distribution.)

Sex, age, race, and Hispanic origin	2000	2010	2015
Males, 15 Years and Over.....................................	3,761,881	3,875,107	3,954,251
Never married	30.8	34.9	36.6
Now married, except separated.............................	56.1	50.5	49.0
Separated..	1.3	1.3	1.2
Widowed..	2.5	2.7	2.7
Divorced..	9.3	10.6	10.5
Females, 15 Years and Over...................................	4,013,722	4,099,384	4,162,553
Never married	25.0	29.0	30.7
Now married, except separated.............................	51.8	47.2	46.3
Separated..	1.6	1.6	1.4
Widowed..	10.4	9.7	9.1
Divorced..	11.2	12.5	12.5

Table MI-3. Households and Housing Characteristics

(Number, percent, dollars.)

Item	2000	2010	2015	Average annual percent change, 2000–2015
Total Households...	3,785,661	3,806,621	3,858,532	0.1
Family households	2,575,699	2,508,780	2,479,724	-0.2
Married-couple family	1,947,610	1,845,094	1,821,803	-0.4
Other family	627,989	663,686	657,921	0.3
Male householder, no wife present..........................	154,187	168,337	182,054	1.2
Female householder, no husband present................	473,802	495,349	475,867	-
Nonfamily households	1,209,962	1,297,841	1,378,808	0.9
Householder living alone...	993,607	1,090,126	1,136,445	1.0
Householder not living alone...................................	216,335	207,715	242,363	0.8
Housing Characteristics				
Total housing units..	4,234,279	4,531,231	4,550,324	0.5
Occupied housing units	3,785,661	3,806,621	3,858,532	0.1
Owner occupied	2,793,124	2,769,474	2,717,217	-0.2
Renter occupied	992,537	1,037,147	1,141,315	1.0
Average household size...	2.56	2.53	2.51	-0.1
Financial Characteristics				
Median gross rent of renter-occupied housing	546	730	803	3.1
Median monthly owner costs for housing units with a mortgage	972	1,288	1,220	1.7
Median value of owner-occupied housing units..............	115,600	123,300	137,500	1.3

- = Zero or rounds to zero.

Table MI-4. Migration, Origin, and Language

(Number, percent.)

Characteristic	State			U.S.		
	2014	2015	Percent change	2014	2015	Percent change
Residence 1 Year Ago						
Population 1 year and over	9,795,659	9,811,416	0.2	315,095,393	317,635,720	0.8
Same house	85.1	85.6	X	85.1	85.3	X
Different house in the U.S.	14.4	14.0	X	14.3	14.1	X
Same county	9.0	9.0	X	8.7	8.5	X
Different county	5.4	5.0	X	5.6	5.6	X
Same state	3.9	3.6	X	3.3	3.2	X
Different state	1.5	1.5	X	2.3	2.4	X
Abroad	0.5	0.5	X	0.6	0.7	X
Place of Birth						
Native born	9,273,308	9,270,486	-	276,465,262	278,128,449	0.6
Male	49.1	49.2	X	49.3	49.3	X
Female	50.9	50.8	X	50.7	50.7	X
Foreign born	636,569	652,090	2.4	42,391,794	43,290,372	2.1
Male	48.7	49.1	X	48.7	48.6	X
Female	51.3	50.9	X	51.3	51.4	X
Foreign born; naturalized U.S. citizen.......................	328,337	342,465	4.3	19,984,738	20,697,103	3.6
Male	47.4	47.2	X	45.9	45.9	X
Female	52.6	52.8	X	54.1	54.1	X
Foreign born; not a U.S. citizen	308,232	309,625	0.5	22,407,056	22,593,269	0.8
Male	50.1	51.1	X	51.2	51.1	X
Female	49.9	48.9	X	48.8	48.9	X
Entered 2010 or later	17.5	20.8	X	12.3	15.6	X
Entered 2000 to 2009	27.0	26.4	X	28.6	27.9	X
Entered before 2000..	55.5	52.8	X	59.1	56.5	X
World Region of Birth, Foreign						
Foreign-born population, excluding population born at sea	636,569	652,090	2.4	42,390,705	43,289,646	2.1
Europe	19.8	20.6	X	11.2	11.1	X
Asia	50.1	50.7	X	30.1	30.6	X
Africa	4.5	4.3	X	4.6	4.8	X
Oceania	0.4	0.5	X	0.6	0.6	X
Latin America..	19.3	18.6	X	51.6	51.1	X
North America...	5.9	5.3	X	1.9	1.9	X
Language Spoken at Home and Ability to Speak English						
Population 5 years and over...	9,340,973	9,351,921	0.1	299,084,046	301,625,014	0.8
English only	90.8	90.5	X	78.9	78.5	X
Language other than English.....................................	9.2	9.5	X	21.1	21.5	X
Speaks English less than "very well"......................	3.4	3.4	X	8.6	8.6	X

NA = Not available.
X = Not applicable.
- = Zero or rounds to zero.

Table MI-5. Median Income and Poverty Status, 2015

(Number, percent, except as noted.)

Characteristic	State		U.S.	
	Number	Percent	Number	Percent
Median Income				
Households (dollars)..	51,084	X	55,775	X
Families (dollars)	63,893	X	68,260	X
Below Poverty Level (All People)	1,529,645	15.8	46,153,077	14.7
Sex				
Male	685,013	14.4	20,599,407	13.4
Female	844,632	17.1	25,553,670	16.0
Age				
Under 18 years..	485,920	22.4	15,000,273	20.7
Related children under 18 years........................	473,805	22.0	14,693,239	20.4
18 to 64 years..	923,969	15.4	26,960,369	13.9
65 years and over	119,756	7.8	4,192,435	9.0

X = Not applicable.

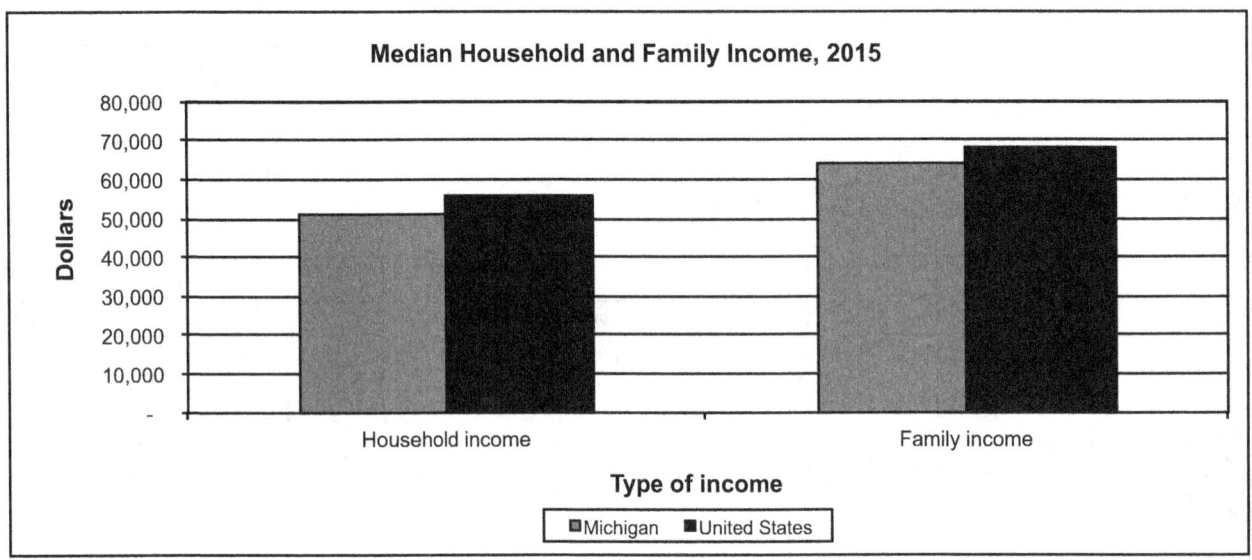

Median Household and Family Income, 2015

Table MI-6. Health Insurance Coverage Status for the Civilian Noninstitutionalized Population and Children Under 18 Years of Age

(Numbers in thousands, percent.)

Item	2007	2008	2009	2010	2011	2012	2013	2014	2015
Civilian Noninstitutionalized Population	9,927	9,866	9,835	9,764	9,762	9,773	9,784	9,799	9,811
Covered by Private or Public Insurance									
Number..	8,776	8,734	8,632	8,556	8,612	8,658	8,713	8,962	9,214
Percent..	88.4	88.5	87.8	87.6	88.2	88.6	89.0	91.5	93.9
Not Covered									
Number..	1,151	1,132	1,203	1,207	1,150	1,115	1,072	837	597
Percent..	11.6	11.5	12.2	12.4	11.8	11.4	11.0	8.5	6.1
Percent in the U.S. not covered........................	15.3	15.1	15.1	15.5	15.1	14.8	14.5	11.7	9.4
Children Under 18 Years of Age	2,419	2,389	2,343	2,331	2,290	2,264	2,240	2,220	2,204
Covered by Private or Public Insurance									
Number..	2,270	2,265	2,236	2,236	2,196	2,174	2,150	2,137	2,136
Percent..	93.8	94.8	95.4	95.9	95.9	96.0	96.0	96.2	96.9
Not Covered									
Number..	149	124	107	95	94	90	90	83	68
Percent..	6.2	5.2	4.6	4.1	4.1	4.0	4.0	3.8	3.1
Percent in the U.S. not covered........................	11.0	9.7	8.6	8.0	7.5	7.2	7.1	6.0	4.8

Table MI-7. Employment Status by Demographic Group, 2016

(Numbers in thousands, percent.)

Characteristic	Civilian noninstitutional population	Civilian labor force		Employed		Unemployed	
		Number	Percent of population	Number	Percent of population	Number	Percent of population
Total...	7,904	4,853	61.4	4,616	58.4	238	4.9
Sex							
Male..	3,824	2,566	67.1	2,443	63.9	123	4.8
Female	4,080	2,287	56.1	2,173	53.3	114	5.0
Race, Sex, and Hispanic Origin							
White	6,487	4,007	61.8	3,842	59.2	165	4.1
Male..	3,169	2,158	68.1	2,072	65.4	86	4.0
Female	3,318	1,850	55.7	1,771	53.4	79	4.3
Black or African American..................	1,053	595	56.5	535	50.8	60	10.1
Male..	475	273	57.5	243	51.1	30	11.1
Female	578	322	55.7	292	50.6	30	9.2
Hispanic or Latino ethnicity[1]	359	240	66.9	226	62.8	15	6.1
Male..	182	142	78.0	134	73.6	8	5.6
Female	177	98	55.4	91	51.6	7	6.9
Age							
16 to 19 years.................................	469	205	43.7	171	36.4	34	16.6
20 to 24 years.................................	711	544	76.5	499	70.1	46	8.4
25 to 34 years.................................	1,266	1,018	80.4	965	76.2	54	5.3
35 to 44 years.................................	1,137	917	80.6	885	77.8	32	3.4
45 to 54 years.................................	1,383	1,091	78.9	1,057	76.4	34	3.1
55 to 64 years.................................	1,358	808	59.5	781	57.5	27	3.3
65 years and over	1,580	271	17.1	259	16.4	12	4.5

NOTE: Data in Table 7 are from the Current Population Survey (CPS) and do not match the estimates in Table 8. See notes and definitions for further information.
[1] May be of any race.

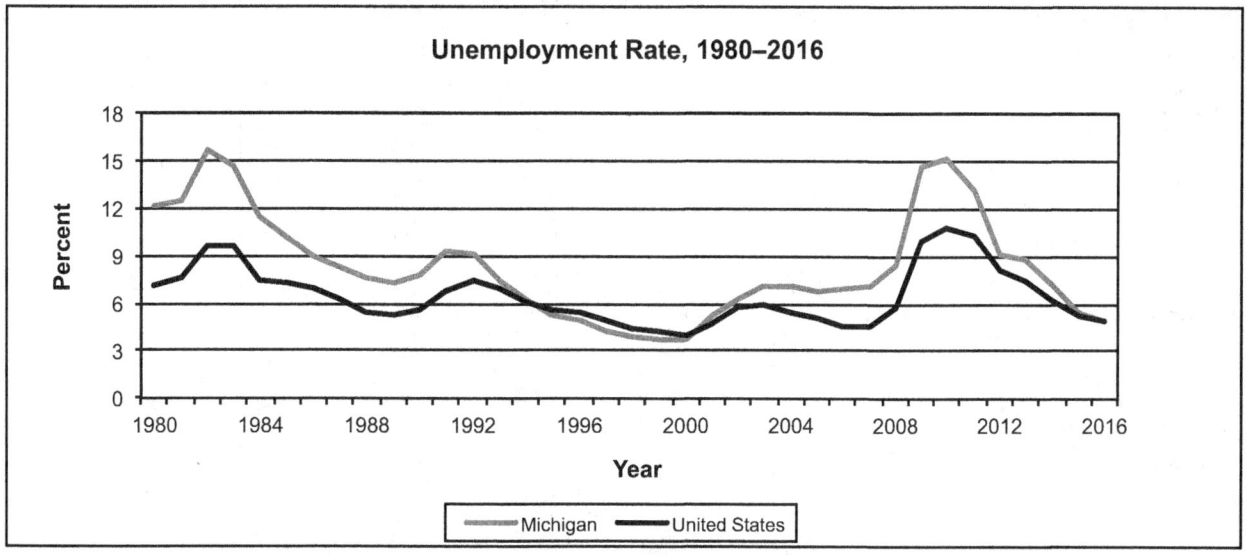

Unemployment Rate, 1980–2016

Table MI-8. Employment Status of the Civilian Noninstitutional Population Age 16 Years and Over

(Number, percent.)

Year	Civilian labor force	Civilian participation rate	Employed	Unemployed	Unemployment rate
2008..............................	4,921,466	63.3	4,529,289	392,177	8.0
2009..............................	4,903,544	63.1	4,233,803	669,741	13.7
2010..............................	4,798,954	62.0	4,194,041	604,913	12.6
2011..............................	4,685,164	60.5	4,198,349	486,815	10.4
2012..............................	4,672,484	60.0	4,246,233	426,251	9.1
2013..............................	4,729,625	60.5	4,311,262	418,363	8.8
2014..............................	4,754,282	60.6	4,408,144	346,138	7.3
2015..............................	4,750,627	60.3	4,492,989	257,638	5.4
2016..............................	4,836,760	61.3	4,599,049	237,711	4.9

Table MI-9. Employment and Average Wages by Industry

(Estimates through 2010 are based on the 2007 *North American Industry Classification System* [NAICS]. Estimates from 2011 onward are based on the 2012 NAICS.)

Industry	2009	2010	2011	2012	2013	2014	2015
	Number of jobs						
Wage and Salary Employment by Industry..................	3,960,001	3,940,724	4,031,623	4,104,082	4,181,596	4,257,161	4,329,598
Farm Wage and Salary Employment.........................	17,711	16,371	23,531	20,286	21,935	22,981	25,200
Nonfarm Wage and Salary Employment....................	3,942,290	3,924,353	4,008,092	4,083,796	4,159,661	4,234,180	4,304,398
Private wage and salary employment.....................	3,282,782	3,272,883	3,376,805	3,464,062	3,548,796	3,627,974	3,700,242
Forestry, fishing, and related activities..........	7,098	7,481	7,618	7,898	8,045	8,875	8,661
Mining...	5,561	5,612	5,913	6,302	6,484	6,643	6,005
Utilities...	20,272	19,474	19,333	19,213	19,365	19,771	19,895
Construction.....................................	131,041	124,543	128,953	132,074	137,367	145,615	151,862
Manufacturing...................................	469,534	479,048	513,120	538,454	547,834	569,120	587,498
Durable goods manufacturing................	345,976	353,580	382,995	406,032	412,375	429,747	444,462
Nondurable goods manufacturing...........	123,558	125,468	130,125	132,422	135,459	139,373	143,036
Wholesale trade.................................	153,245	150,997	155,751	159,920	164,529	168,419	170,466
Retail trade.......................................	458,391	449,725	452,316	453,205	458,709	464,369	470,398
Transportation and warehousing............	94,524	94,170	99,776	103,280	106,776	111,769	116,906
Information..	58,736	57,190	55,954	56,177	57,915	60,543	59,312
Finance and insurance	139,671	136,741	139,290	143,765	147,373	148,061	149,698
Real estate and rental and leasing.........	52,036	50,395	51,548	49,278	50,668	51,816	52,295
Professional, scientific, and technical services	223,066	224,981	237,367	249,951	270,882	278,962	289,641
Management of companies and enterprises...	48,696	48,151	50,856	52,135	54,692	55,232	56,437
Administrative and waste services..........	233,093	246,018	270,075	280,453	289,151	290,633	294,086
Educational services	74,666	76,014	76,787	76,794	78,788	79,985	81,195
Health care and social assistance..........	538,717	540,677	546,514	557,232	562,136	565,135	575,905
Arts, entertainment, and recreation........	53,743	51,945	48,367	47,539	48,681	49,679	50,921
Accommodation and food services.........	330,290	326,207	332,798	343,848	352,007	359,088	365,385
Other services, except public administration...	190,402	183,514	184,469	186,544	187,394	194,259	193,676
Government and government enterprises.........	659,508	651,470	631,287	619,734	610,865	606,206	604,156
	Dollars						
Average Wages and Salaries by Industry	42,951	43,857	45,179	46,222	46,643	47,997	49,590
Average Farm Wages and Salaries	33,092	27,814	24,677	36,899	31,996	35,884	36,622
Average Nonfarm Wages and Salaries	42,995	43,923	45,299	46,268	46,720	48,063	49,666
Average private wages and salaries...................	42,540	43,551	45,207	46,201	46,685	48,093	49,809
Forestry, fishing, and related activities.........	23,292	24,720	25,082	25,834	27,185	27,651	29,620
Mining...	62,470	73,773	74,828	73,509	73,413	77,204	75,759
Utilities...	89,202	93,779	98,214	102,212	104,109	109,032	112,232
Construction.....................................	49,012	50,539	52,002	53,193	53,624	55,592	57,323
Manufacturing...................................	58,590	59,733	62,190	62,793	62,524	63,563	65,081
Durable goods manufacturing................	61,131	62,237	65,296	65,336	64,900	65,884	67,415
Nondurable goods manufacturing...........	51,473	52,677	53,049	54,995	55,291	56,405	57,827
Wholesale trade.................................	61,416	64,302	66,990	67,788	67,338	69,912	71,170
Retail trade.......................................	25,110	25,629	26,030	26,398	26,510	27,356	28,492
Transportation and warehousing............	45,454	47,438	48,943	50,327	50,611	52,080	53,132
Information..	57,341	58,572	62,024	62,081	64,334	65,488	67,984
Finance and insurance	60,202	62,045	63,941	66,378	68,195	70,849	74,008
Real estate and rental and leasing.........	32,814	34,134	36,010	37,631	38,254	39,684	42,283
Professional, scientific, and technical services	70,178	70,759	73,177	74,389	75,939	77,812	80,486
Management of companies and enterprises...	99,942	103,207	113,271	116,160	110,684	119,925	122,505
Administrative and waste services..........	30,533	30,854	30,999	31,734	31,715	32,444	33,936
Educational services	28,059	28,493	28,356	29,869	29,911	30,783	31,092
Health care and social assistance..........	42,923	43,317	44,410	44,944	45,522	46,432	48,135
Arts, entertainment, and recreation........	30,437	30,502	30,263	31,950	32,597	33,120	33,898
Accommodation and food services.........	15,175	15,652	16,409	16,834	17,059	17,577	18,728
Other services, except public administration...	27,248	28,290	28,770	29,444	30,186	31,227	32,692
Government and government enterprises.........	45,262	45,793	45,795	46,645	46,923	47,887	48,788

Table MI-10. Employment Characteristics by Family Type

(Number, percent.)

Family type and labor force status	2013		2014		2015	
	Total	Families with own children under 18 years	Total	Families with own children under 18 years	Total	Families with own children under 18 years
All Families..	2,484,558	1,041,331	2,478,645	1,026,180	2,479,724	1,004,689
FAMILY TYPE AND LABOR FORCE STATUS						
Married-Couple Families..................................	1,809,823	675,621	1,808,447	670,411	1,821,803	658,920
Both husband and wife in labor force..................	49.5	66.7	48.9	67.2	48.4	67.0
Husband in labor force, wife not in labor force	20.0	26.0	20.2	26.2	20.7	26.3
Wife in labor force, husband not in labor force	8.8	5.0	8.8	4.3	8.5	4.5
Both husband and wife not in labor force............	21.4	2.1	22.1	2.3	22.1	2.0
Other Families	674,735	365,710	670,198	355,769	657,921	345,769
Female householder, no husband present..........	73.4	76.2	72.8	74.0	72.3	74.4
In labor force...	49.9	61.7	49.5	60.6	48.6	60.6
Not in labor force	23.5	14.5	23.3	13.4	23.7	13.8
Male householder, no wife present....................	26.6	23.8	27.2	26.0	27.7	25.6
In labor force...	19.9	21.0	20.0	22.7	20.5	22.7
Not in labor force	6.7	2.8	7.2	3.3	7.2	2.9

Table MI-11. School Enrollment and Educational Attainment, 2015

(Number, percent.)

Item	State	U.S.
Enrollment		
Total population 3 years and over, enrolled in school	2,495,741	81,618,288
Enrolled in nursery school or preschool (percent).................................	5.5	6.0
Enrolled in kindergarten (percent)..	4.6	5.0
Enrolled in elementary school, grades 1-8 (percent)............................	39.7	40.3
Enrolled in high school, grades 9-12 (percent)....................................	21.5	20.9
Enrolled in college or graduate school (percent).................................	28.7	27.7
Attainment		
Total population 25 years and over	6,728,347	216,447,163
Less than ninth grade (percent)...	3.0	5.5
9th to 12th grade, no diploma (percent)	6.9	7.3
High school graduate, including equivalency (percent).........................	29.4	27.6
Some college, no degree (percent)...	23.7	20.7
Associate's degree (percent)...	9.2	8.2
Bachelor's degree (percent)..	17.0	19.0
Graduate or professional degree (percent)..	10.8	11.6
High school graduate or higher (percent)	90.1	87.1
Bachelor's degree or higher (percent)..	27.8	30.6

Table MI-12. Public School Characteristics and Educational Indicators

(Number, percent; data derived from National Center of Education Statistics.)

Item	State	U.S.
Public Schools, 2014–2015 (except where noted)		
Number of school districts...	911	18,260
Number of schools...	3,496	98,373
Number of students	1,537,922	50,312,581
Number of teachers	85,038	3,132,351
Student-teacher ratio...	18.1	16.1
Expenditures per student (dollars), FY 2014.......................................	10,649	11,066
Four-year adjusted cohort graduation rate (ACGR)[1,2]	79.8	83.2
Students eligible for free or reduced-price lunch (percent)...................	46.6	51.8
English language learners (percent)..	5.2	9.4
Students age 3 to 21 served under IDEA, part B (percent).....................	12.9	13.0

Public Schools by Type	Number	Percent of state public schools
Total number of schools...	3,496	100.0
Regular	2,993	85.6
Special education	186	5.3
Vocational education	4	0.1
Alternative education...	313	9.0

NOTE: Every school is assigned only one school type based on its instructional emphasis.
[1] ACGR data represents a new method of calculating high-school completion rates and may not be comparable to previous years' data for Averaged Freshmen Graduation Rates (AFGR).
[2] The United States 4-year ACGRs were estimated using both the reported 4-year ACGR data from 49 states and the District of Columbia and using imputed data for Idaho. The estimate for American Indian/Alaska Native students also includes imputed data for Virginia.

Table MI-13. Reported Voting and Registration of the Voting-Age Population, November 2016

(Numbers in thousands, percent.)

Item	Total population	Total citizen population	Registered			Voted		
			Total registered	Percent registered (total population)	Percent registered (total citizen population)	Total voted	Percent voted (total population)	Percent voted (total citizen population)
U.S. Total	245,502	224,059	157,596	64.2	70.3	137,537	56.0	61.4
State Total............................	7,624	7,332	5,434	71.3	74.1	4,713	61.8	64.3
Sex								
Male	3,650	3,473	2,540	69.6	73.1	2,150	58.9	61.9
Female	3,974	3,859	2,893	72.8	75.0	2,563	64.5	66.4
Race								
White alone..........................	6,264	6,071	4,579	73.1	75.4	3,984	63.6	65.6
White, non-Hispanic alone	6,006	5,890	4,498	74.9	76.4	3,914	65.2	66.5
Black alone..........................	1,039	1,020	708	68.1	69.4	623	59.9	61.0
Asian alone	182	108	63	34.5	58.3	58	32.0	54.2
Hispanic (of any race)...............	288	206	101	35.0	49.0	74	25.7	36.0
White alone or in combination	6,365	6,167	4,648	73.0	75.4	4,021	63.2	65.2
Black alone or in combination.........	1,100	1,080	752	68.4	69.6	642	58.4	59.4
Asian alone or in combination.........	192	113	63	32.7	55.6	58	30.4	51.7
Age								
18 to 24 years......................	853	813	453	53.1	55.7	308	36.1	37.8
25 to 34 years......................	1,397	1,305	911	65.2	69.8	706	50.6	54.1
35 to 44 years......................	1,047	1,012	750	71.7	74.1	650	62.1	64.2
45 to 64 years......................	2,848	2,740	2,158	75.8	78.7	1,962	68.9	71.6
65 years and over	1,480	1,462	1,162	78.5	79.5	1,088	73.5	74.4

Table MI-14. Crime

(Number, rate per 100,000. Data are derived from the FBI Uniform Crime Reports.)

Item	State			U.S. [1,2,3,4]		
	2014	2015	Percent change	2014	2015	Percent change
TOTAL POPULATION[5]	9,916,306	9,922,576	0.1	318,907,401	321,418,820	0.8
VIOLENT CRIME						
Number..............................	42,555	41,231	-3.1	1,186,185	1,231,566	3.8
Rate	429.1	415.5	-3.2	372.0	383.2	3.0
Murder and Nonnegligent Manslaughter						
Number..............................	544	571	5.0	14,164	15,696	10.8
Rate	5.5	5.8	4.9	4.4	4.9	10.0
Rape[6]						
Number..............................	6,364	6,450	1.4	118,027	124,047	5.1
Rate	64.2	65.0	1.3	37.0	38.6	4.3
Robbery						
Number..............................	8,037	7,796	-3.0	322,905	327,374	1.4
Rate	81.0	78.6	-3.1	101.3	101.9	0.6
Aggravated Assault						
Number..............................	27,610	26,414	-4.3	731,089	764,449	4.6
Rate	278.4	266.2	-4.4	229.2	237.8	3.7
PROPERTY CRIME						
Number..............................	202,692	187,101	-7.7	8,209,010	7,993,631	-2.6
Rate	2,044.0	1,885.6	-7.8	2,574.1	2,487.0	-3.4
Burglary						
Number..............................	44,328	40,041	-9.7	1,713,153	1,579,527	-7.8
Rate	447.0	403.5	-9.7	537.2	491.4	-8.5
Larceny-Theft						
Number..............................	137,142	131,296	-4.3	5,809,054	5,706,346	-1.8
Rate	1,383.0	1,323.2	-4.3	1,821.5	1,775.4	-2.5
Motor Vehicle Theft						
Number..............................	21,222	15,764	-25.7	686,803	707,758	3.1
Rate	214.0	158.9	-25.8	215.4	220.2	2.2

NOTE: Although arson data are included in the trend and clearance tables, sufficient data are not available to estimate totals for this offense. Therefore, no arson data are published in this table.
X = Not applicable.
- = Zero or rounds to zero.
[1] The crime figures have been adjusted.
[2] The data collection methodology for the offense of forcible rape used by the Minnesota state Uniform Crime Reporting (UCR) Program (with the exception of Minneapolis and St. Paul, Minnesota) does not comply with national UCR Program guidelines. Consequently, its figures for forcible rape and violent crime (of which forcible rape is a part) are not published in this table.
[3] Includes offenses reported by the Zoological Police and the Metro Transit Police.
[4] Because of changes in the state's reporting practices, figures are not comparable to previous years' data.
[5] Populations are U.S. Census Bureau provisional estimates as of July 1 of each year.
[6] The figures shown for the offense of rape were estimated using the revised Uniform Crime Reporting (UCR) definition of rape.

Table MI-15. State Government Finances, 2015

(Dollar amounts in thousands, percent distribution.)

Item	Dollars	Percent distribution
Total Revenue	68,301,818	100.0
General revenue	59,727,638	87.4
Intergovernmental revenue	20,487,351	30.0
Taxes...	26,957,337	39.5
General sales..	9,211,783	13.5
Selective sales..	3,912,678	5.7
License taxes..	1,563,500	2.3
Individual income tax...	8,825,375	12.9
Corporate income tax...	1,185,568	1.7
Other taxes...	2,258,433	3.3
Current charges	8,252,294	12.1
Miscellaneous general revenue	4,030,656	5.9
Utility revenue...	0	-
Liquor stores revenue	1,021,890	1.5
Insurance trust revenue[1]	7,552,290	11.1
Total Expenditure	68,674,162	100.0
Intergovernmental expenditure	20,487,354	29.8
Direct expenditure..	48,186,808	70.2
Current operation	34,688,569	50.5
Capital outlay	2,011,610	2.9
Insurance benefits and repayments	8,764,283	12.8
Assistance and subsidies	1,226,344	1.8
Interest on debt..	1,496,002	2.2
Exhibit: Salaries and wages...	9,221,564	13.4
Total Expenditure	68,674,162	100.0
General expenditure	59,084,950	86.0
Intergovernmental expenditure	20,487,354	29.8
Direct expenditure..	38,597,596	56.2
General expenditure, by function:		
Education..	24,211,552	35.3
Public welfare	18,410,125	26.8
Hospitals...	3,422,936	5.0
Health...	1,350,074	2.0
Highways...	2,532,511	3.7
Police protection	470,963	0.7
Correction	1,888,120	2.7
Natural resources..	322,198	0.5
Parks and recreation	126,274	0.2
Governmental administration	1,011,686	1.5
Interest on general debt	1,496,002	2.2
Other and unallocable	3,842,509	5.6
Utility expenditure...	0	-
Liquor stores expenditure	824,929	1.2
Insurance trust expenditure	8,764,283	12.8
Debt at End of Fiscal Year	33,245,109	X
Cash and Security Holdings...	98,389,762	X

X = Not applicable.
- = Zero or rounds to zero.
[1] Within insurance trust revenue, net earnings of state retirement systems is a calculated statistic (the item code in the data file is X08), and thus can be positive or negative. Net earnings is the sum of earnings on investments plus gains on investments minus losses on investments. The change made in 2002 for asset valuation from book to market value in accordance with Statement 34 of the Governmental Accounting Standards Board is reflected in the calculated statistics.

Table MI-16. State Government Tax Collections, 2016

(Dollars in thousands, percent.)

Item	Dollars	Percent distribution
Total Taxes	27,436,607	100.0
Property taxes	2,034,013	7.4
Sales and gross receipts	13,239,133	48.3
General sales and gross receipts	9,163,542	33.4
Selective sales and gross receipts	4,075,591	14.9
Alcoholic beverages	157,242	0.6
Amusements	111,618	0.4
Insurance premiums	328,138	1.2
Motor fuels	1,028,780	3.7
Pari-mutuels	3,878	-
Public utilities	28,208	0.1
Tobacco products	947,194	3.5
Other selective sales	1,470,533	5.4
Licenses	1,660,663	6.1
Alcoholic beverages	17,469	0.1
Amusements	0	-
Corporations in general	23,703	0.1
Hunting and fishing	64,214	0.2
Motor vehicle	1,070,548	3.9
Motor vehicle operators	59,478	0.2
Public utilities	33,857	0.1
Occupation and business, NEC	162,626	0.6
Other licenses	228,768	0.8
Income taxes	10,202,060	37.2
Individual income	9,303,847	33.9
Corporation net income	898,213	3.3
Other taxes	300,738	1.1
Death and gift	23	-
Documentary and stock transfer	277,149	1.0
Severance	23,565	0.1
Taxes, NEC	1	-

- = Zero or rounds to zero.

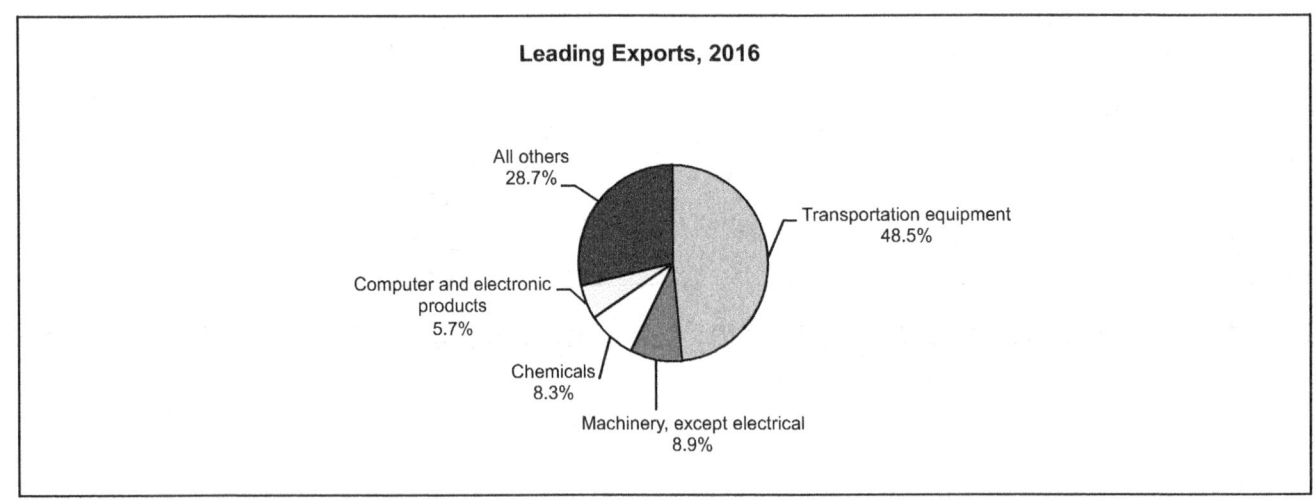

Leading Exports, 2016

All others 28.7%

Transportation equipment 48.5%

Computer and electronic products 5.7%

Chemicals 8.3%

Machinery, except electrical 8.9%

MINNESOTA

Facts and Figures

Location: North central United States; bordered on the N by Canada (Manitoba and Ontario), on the E by Lake Superior and Wisconsin, on the S by Iowa, and on the W by North Dakota and South Dakota

Area: 86,939 sq. mi. (225,171 sq. km.); rank—12th

Population: 5,519,952 (2016 est.); rank—22nd

Principal Cities: capital—St. Paul; largest—Minneapolis

Statehood: May 11, 1858; 32nd state

U.S. Congress: 2 senators, 8 representatives

State Motto: *L'Etoile du Nord* ("The Star of the North")

State Song: "Hail! Minnesota"

State Nicknames: The North Star State; The Land of 10,000 Lakes; The Gopher State

Abbreviations: MN; Minn.

State Symbols: flower—showy (pink and white) lady's slipper; tree—red (Norway) pine; bird—loon

At a Glance

- With an increase in population of 4.1 percent, Minnesota ranked 26th among the states in growth from 2010 to 2016.

- Minnesota's violent crime rate in 2015 was 242.6 per 100,000 population, compared to 383.2 for the entire nation.

- With a property crime rate of 2,222.1 per 100,000 population in 2015, Minnesota ranked 31st in the nation.

- Minnesota's median household income was $63,488 in 2015, which ranked 13th among the states.

- In 2015, 10.2 percent of all Minnesotans and 13.1 percent of children in Minnesota lived below the poverty level, compared to 14.7 percent of the entire U.S. population and 20.7 percent of all U.S. children.

Table MN-1. Population by Age, Sex, Race, and Hispanic Origin

(Number, percent, except where noted.)

Sex, age, race, and Hispanic origin	2000	2010	2016 [1]	Average annual percent change, 2010–2016
Total Population...	4,919,479	5,303,925	5,519,952	0.3
Percent of total U.S. population	1.7	1.7	1.7	X
Sex				
Male..	2,435,631	2,632,132	2,747,630	0.3
Female	2,483,848	2,671,793	2,772,322	0.2
Age				
Under 5 years..	329,594	355,504	352,504	-0.1
5 to 19 years...	1,105,251	1,075,707	1,076,397	-
20 to 64 years..	2,890,368	3,189,593	3,258,823	0.1
65 years and over	594,266	683,121	832,228	1.4
Median age (years)	35.4	37.4	37.9	0.1
Race and Hispanic Origin				
One race..				
White	4,400,282	4,623,461	4,691,265	0.1
Black..	171,731	280,949	344,322	1.4
American Indian and Alaska Native	54,967	67,325	73,970	0.6
Asian...	141,968	217,792	272,170	1.6
Native Hawaiian or Other Pacific Islander	1,979	2,958	3,761	1.7
Two or more races	82,742	111,440	134,464	1.3
Hispanic (of any race)..	143,382	264,432	289,422	0.6

X = Not applicable.
- = Zero or rounds to zero.
[1] Population figures for 2016 are July 1 estimates. The 2010 estimates are taken from the 2010 Census.

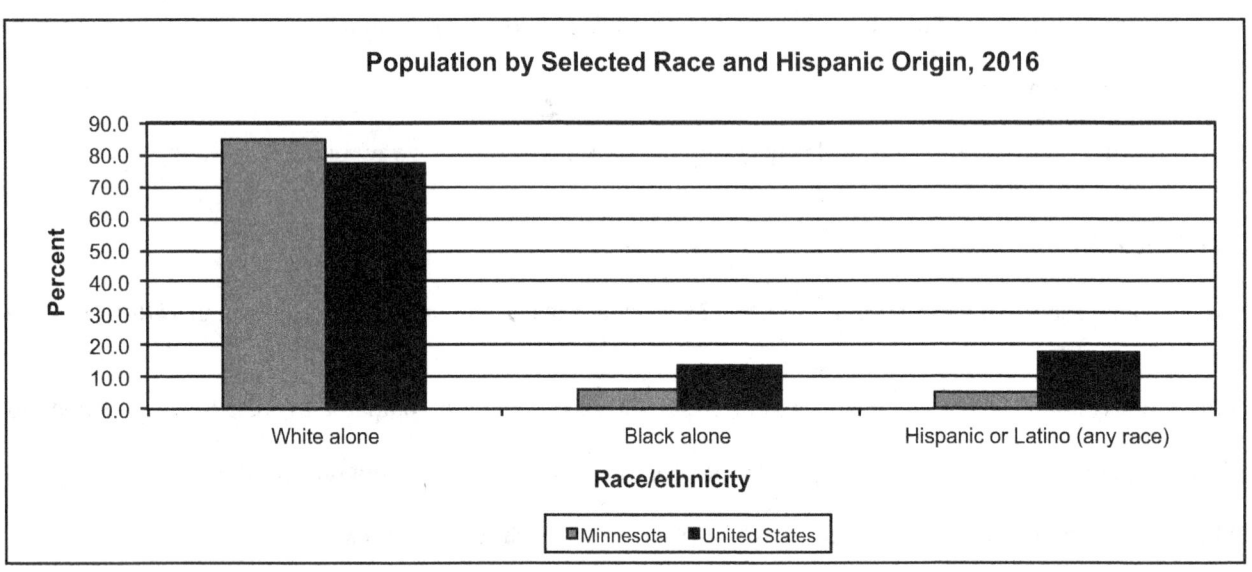

Table MN-2. Marital Status

(Number, percent distribution.)

Sex, age, race, and Hispanic origin	2000	2010	2015
Males, 15 Years and Over	1,889,936	2,090,940	2,181,651
Never married	31.3	34.6	34.9
Now married, except separated.................................	57.7	53.5	52.6
Separated..	0.9	0.9	1.0
Widowed..	2.1	2.2	2.4
Divorced...	8.0	8.7	9.1
Females, 15 Years and Over	1,967,819	2,155,042	2,239,109
Never married	25.0	28.2	28.7
Now married, except separated.................................	55.0	51.5	51.1
Separated..	1.2	1.2	1.2
Widowed..	9.4	8.4	7.8
Divorced...	9.5	10.7	11.3

Table MN-3. Households and Housing Characteristics

(Number, percent, dollars.)

Item	2000	2010	2015	Average annual percent change, 2000–2015
Total Households...	1,895,127	2,091,548	2,147,262	0.9
Family households..	1,255,141	1,353,758	1,383,950	0.7
Married-couple family.....................................	1,018,245	1,069,000	1,091,358	0.5
Other family..	236,986	284,758	292,592	1.6
Male householder, no wife present...................	68,114	87,757	95,250	2.7
Female householder, no husband present...........	168,782	197,001	197,342	1.1
Nonfamily households..	639,986	737,790	763,312	1.3
Householder living alone..................................	509,468	591,124	609,618	1.3
Householder not living alone............................	130,518	146,666	153,694	1.2
Housing Characteristics				
Total housing units..	2,065,946	2,348,242	2,397,081	1.1
Occupied housing units	1,895,127	2,091,548	2,147,262	0.9
Owner occupied..	1,412,865	1,527,328	1,523,273	0.5
Renter occupied..	482,262	564,220	623,989	2.0
Average household size.......................................	2.52	2.47	2.49	-0.1
Financial Characteristics				
Median gross rent of renter-occupied housing	566	764	888	3.8
Median monthly owner costs for housing units with a mortgage	1,044	1,503	1,459	2.7
Median value of owner-occupied housing units	122,400	194,300	200,000	4.2

Table MN-4. Migration, Origin, and Language

(Number, percent.)

Characteristic	State			U.S.		
	2014	2015	Percent change	2014	2015	Percent change
Residence 1 Year Ago						
Population 1 year and over	5,385,219	5,419,822	0.6	315,095,393	317,635,720	0.8
Same house	85.7	85.2	X	85.1	85.3	X
Different house in the U.S.	13.8	14.2	X	14.3	14.1	X
Same county	7.2	7.6	X	8.7	8.5	X
Different county	6.6	6.6	X	5.6	5.6	X
Same state	4.7	4.6	X	3.3	3.2	X
Different state	2.0	2.0	X	2.3	2.4	X
Abroad	0.6	0.6	X	0.6	0.7	X
Place of Birth						
Native born	5,029,116	5,032,409	0.2	276,465,262	278,128,449	0.6
Male	49.8	49.8	X	49.3	49.3	X
Female	50.2	50.2	X	50.7	50.7	X
Foreign born	428,057	457,185	6.1	42,391,794	43,290,372	2.1
Male	48.6	48.8	X	48.7	48.6	X
Female	51.4	51.2	X	51.3	51.4	X
Foreign born; naturalized U.S. citizen................	215,143	224,718	3.5	19,984,738	20,697,103	3.6
Male	45.5	45.7	X	45.9	45.9	X
Female	54.5	54.3	X	54.1	54.1	X
Foreign born; not a U.S. citizen......................	212,914	232,467	8.9	22,407,056	22,593,269	0.8
Male	51.7	51.8	X	51.2	51.1	X
Female	48.3	48.2	X	48.8	48.9	X
Entered 2010 or later	17.2	23.5	X	12.3	15.6	X
Entered 2000 to 2009	33.6	33.8	X	28.6	27.9	X
Entered before 2000......................................	49.3	42.7	X	59.1	56.5	X
World Region of Birth, Foreign						
Foreign-born population, excluding population born at sea	428,057	457,185	6.1	42,390,705	43,289,646	2.1
Europe	10.8	10.5	X	11.2	11.1	X
Asia	38.0	38.8	X	30.1	30.6	X
Africa	22.0	22.0	X	4.6	4.8	X
Oceania	0.5	0.6	X	0.6	0.6	X
Latin America...	25.6	25.1	X	51.6	51.1	X
North America	2.9	3.1	X	1.9	1.9	X
Language Spoken at Home and Ability to Speak English						
Population 5 years and over.............................	5,109,770	5,138,667	0.7	299,084,046	301,625,014	0.8
English only	88.9	88.5	X	78.9	78.5	X
Language other than English..........................	11.1	11.5	X	21.1	21.5	X
Speaks English less than "very well"..............	4.5	4.8	X	8.6	8.6	X

NA = Not available.
X = Not applicable.
- = Zero or rounds to zero.

Table MN-5. Median Income and Poverty Status, 2015

(Number, percent, except as noted.)

Characteristic	State		U.S.	
	Number	Percent	Number	Percent
Median Income				
Households (dollars)...	63,488	X	55,775	X
Families (dollars)	79,893	X	68,260	X
Below Poverty Level (All People)	546,431	10.2	46,153,077	14.7
Sex				
Male	247,529	9.3	20,599,407	13.4
Female	298,902	11.1	25,553,670	16.0
Age				
Under 18 years..	165,399	13.1	15,000,273	20.7
Related children under 18 years........................	159,073	12.7	14,693,239	20.4
18 to 64 years..	327,258	9.8	26,960,369	13.9
65 years and over	53,774	6.9	4,192,435	9.0

X = Not applicable.

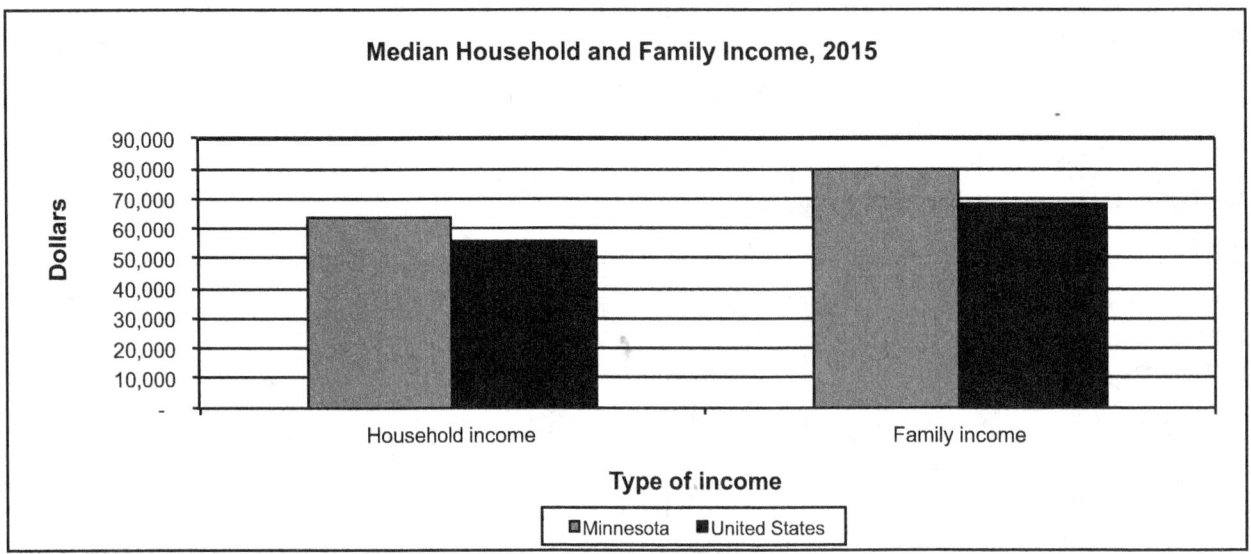

Table MN-6. Health Insurance Coverage Status for the Civilian Noninstitutionalized Population and Children Under 18 Years of Age

(Numbers in thousands, percent.)

Item	2007	2008	2009	2010	2011	2012	2013	2014	2015
Civilian Noninstitutionalized Population	5,190	5,151	5,197	5,252	5,287	5,320	5,363	5,398	5,432
Covered by Private or Public Insurance									
Number..	4,758	4,704	4,724	4,776	4,819	4,895	4,923	5,081	5,187
Percent...	91.7	91.3	90.9	90.9	91.2	92.0	91.8	94.1	95.5
Not Covered									
Number..	433	447	473	476	467	425	440	317	245
Percent...	8.3	8.7	9.1	9.1	8.8	8.0	8.2	5.9	4.5
Percent in the U.S. not covered........................	15.3	15.1	15.1	15.5	15.1	14.8	14.5	11.7	9.4
Children Under 18 Years of Age	1,246	1,248	1,256	1,281	1,276	1,276	1,280	1,281	1,281
Covered by Private or Public Insurance									
Number..	1,167	1,169	1,173	1,197	1,196	1,208	1,208	1,232	1,242
Percent...	93.6	93.7	93.4	93.4	93.7	94.6	94.4	96.2	96.9
Not Covered									
Number..	80	79	83	84	80	68	72	49	39
Percent...	6.4	6.3	6.6	6.6	6.3	5.4	5.6	3.8	3.1
Percent in the U.S. not covered........................	11.0	9.7	8.6	8.0	7.5	7.2	7.1	6.0	4.8

Table MN-7. Employment Status by Demographic Group, 2016

(Numbers in thousands, percent.)

Characteristic	Civilian noninstitutional population	Civilian labor force		Employed		Unemployed	
		Number	Percent of population	Number	Percent of population	Number	Percent of population
Total...................................	4,320	2,985	69.1	2,870	66.4	116	3.9
Sex							
Male.................................	2,133	1,571	73.7	1,501	70.4	70	4.5
Female	2,188	1,415	64.7	1,369	62.6	46	3.2
Race, Sex, and Hispanic Origin							
White	3,781	2,628	69.5	2,550	67.4	78	3.0
Male.................................	1,867	1,393	74.6	1,343	71.9	49	3.5
Female	1,914	1,235	64.5	1,207	63.0	28	2.3
Black or African American..................	231	150	64.9	137	59.1	13	8.8
Male.................................	NA	NA	NA	NA	NA	NA	NA
Female	NA	NA	NA	NA	NA	NA	NA
Hispanic or Latino ethnicity[1]	238	175	73.7	166	69.8	9	5.3
Male.................................	128	104	81.4	97	75.9	7	6.7
Female	NA	NA	NA	NA	NA	NA	NA
Age							
16 to 19 years......................	292	147	50.3	132	45.2	15	10.1
20 to 24 years......................	312	228	73.1	213	68.2	15	6.7
25 to 34 years......................	715	628	87.9	600	84.0	28	4.5
35 to 44 years......................	738	647	87.8	628	85.1	20	3.0
45 to 54 years......................	696	607	87.3	595	85.5	13	2.1
55 to 64 years......................	722	538	74.4	521	72.1	17	3.1
65 years and over	846	190	22.5	181	21.4	9	4.7

NOTE: Data in Table 7 are from the Current Population Survey (CPS) and do not match the estimates in Table 8. See notes and definitions for further information.
[1] May be of any race.
NA = Not available.

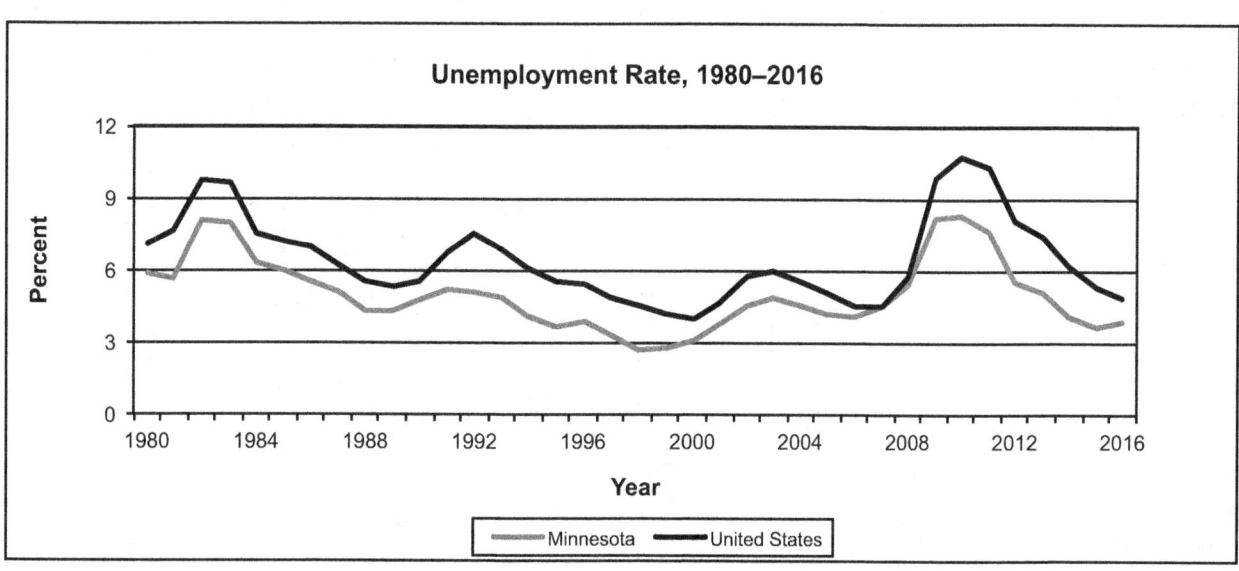

Unemployment Rate, 1980–2016

Minnesota ——— United States

Table MN-8. Employment Status of the Civilian Noninstitutional Population Age 16 Years and Over

(Number, percent.)

Year	Civilian labor force	Civilian participation rate	Employed	Unemployed	Unemployment rate
2008................................	2,925,088	72.2	2,766,342	158,746	5.4
2009................................	2,941,976	72.0	2,713,426	228,550	7.8
2010................................	2,938,795	71.4	2,721,194	217,601	7.4
2011................................	2,946,279	71.0	2,755,264	191,015	6.5
2012................................	2,958,273	70.6	2,793,143	165,130	5.6
2013................................	2,971,523	70.3	2,824,970	146,553	4.9
2014................................	2,982,750	70.1	2,858,592	124,158	4.2
2015................................	3,010,367	70.2	2,898,864	111,503	3.7
2016................................	3,001,131	69.5	2,884,091	117,040	3.9

Table MN-9. Employment and Average Wages by Industry

(Estimates through 2010 are based on the 2007 *North American Industry Classification System* [NAICS]. Estimates from 2011 onward are based on the 2012 NAICS.)

Industry	2009	2010	2011	2012	2013	2014	2015
	Number of jobs						
Wage and Salary Employment by Industry	2,728,923	2,710,413	2,751,062	2,791,399	2,834,955	2,875,681	2,923,079
Farm Wage and Salary Employment	19,099	19,300	16,872	17,591	15,802	14,250	17,516
Nonfarm Wage and Salary Employment	2,709,824	2,691,113	2,734,190	2,773,808	2,819,153	2,861,431	2,905,563
Private wage and salary employment	2,291,368	2,270,160	2,319,008	2,357,002	2,401,595	2,441,903	2,483,959
Forestry, fishing, and related activities	5,532	5,641	5,690	5,798	5,955	6,048	6,306
Mining	4,423	5,220	5,810	6,247	6,219	6,370	6,166
Utilities	12,728	12,687	12,804	12,707	13,012	12,863	12,788
Construction	97,771	90,671	94,676	97,751	103,549	110,611	118,007
Manufacturing	300,072	292,370	301,283	305,864	307,543	312,309	317,539
Durable goods manufacturing	188,561	183,344	190,230	194,502	195,236	198,700	202,729
Nondurable goods manufacturing	111,511	109,026	111,053	111,362	112,307	113,609	114,810
Wholesale trade	126,932	124,076	126,500	129,085	131,037	132,561	133,465
Retail trade	284,476	279,971	282,854	285,208	288,710	290,862	295,411
Transportation and warehousing	78,346	77,029	79,920	80,009	81,238	84,094	86,628
Information	55,745	54,209	53,837	53,788	53,354	52,704	51,731
Finance and insurance	137,922	138,165	141,385	141,764	144,280	142,070	145,016
Real estate and rental and leasing	37,546	36,727	36,722	39,859	40,629	40,155	40,115
Professional, scientific, and technical services	127,270	124,504	129,110	131,609	136,965	142,126	146,632
Management of companies and enterprises	69,828	70,684	72,685	74,841	77,025	78,767	78,192
Administrative and waste services	114,413	122,093	130,351	132,790	133,969	134,784	134,934
Educational services	66,198	69,338	70,428	70,303	71,140	71,567	72,598
Health care and social assistance	392,435	395,140	398,404	408,369	421,266	429,338	438,478
Arts, entertainment, and recreation	38,718	37,778	38,199	39,228	39,869	40,746	42,185
Accommodation and food services	202,416	199,613	203,511	207,865	211,963	215,318	218,910
Other services, except public administration	138,597	134,244	134,839	133,917	133,872	138,610	138,858
Government and government enterprises	418,456	420,953	415,182	416,806	417,558	419,528	421,604
	Dollars						
Average Wages and Salaries by Industry	44,381	45,845	46,935	48,502	49,254	50,753	52,632
Average Farm Wages and Salaries	33,149	28,320	25,319	39,306	32,721	36,717	37,003
Average Nonfarm Wages and Salaries	44,460	45,970	47,068	48,560	49,347	50,823	52,726
Average private wages and salaries	44,595	46,448	47,650	49,342	50,096	51,589	53,589
Forestry, fishing, and related activities	24,420	25,876	26,890	28,609	28,962	29,359	30,671
Mining	63,502	73,542	81,400	82,203	84,172	85,524	79,699
Utilities	81,770	86,368	90,398	92,774	97,249	99,321	102,117
Construction	51,601	51,868	53,460	55,587	57,333	58,954	61,512
Manufacturing	53,523	56,323	57,524	58,737	59,561	61,095	63,202
Durable goods manufacturing	57,355	60,747	61,812	63,090	64,227	65,819	67,825
Nondurable goods manufacturing	47,044	48,883	50,180	51,133	51,450	52,835	55,039
Wholesale trade	66,612	69,521	71,757	74,404	76,006	76,975	79,135
Retail trade	23,967	24,455	24,875	25,382	25,971	27,220	28,235
Transportation and warehousing	43,962	44,513	45,971	47,922	48,279	50,159	51,166
Information	60,081	62,140	66,104	65,018	66,777	69,527	72,258
Finance and insurance	74,562	77,753	82,032	89,504	88,625	92,771	96,827
Real estate and rental and leasing	43,229	44,982	46,890	51,848	53,610	55,039	58,234
Professional, scientific, and technical services	71,648	74,546	76,168	79,009	81,014	83,864	85,915
Management of companies and enterprises	94,838	110,411	109,612	112,101	112,835	115,280	120,493
Administrative and waste services	30,915	31,341	31,646	32,349	32,276	33,899	36,013
Educational services	29,170	28,883	29,377	30,198	30,084	30,664	30,675
Health care and social assistance	42,044	43,185	43,483	44,686	44,933	45,825	47,982
Arts, entertainment, and recreation	28,669	31,639	31,662	31,457	32,290	32,537	34,023
Accommodation and food services	15,532	15,909	16,547	17,102	17,478	18,233	19,570
Other services, except public administration	26,589	27,073	27,910	28,884	29,985	30,956	32,257
Government and government enterprises	43,720	43,395	43,818	44,139	45,041	46,362	47,641

Table MN-10. Employment Characteristics by Family Type

(Number, percent.)

Family type and labor force status	2013		2014		2015	
	Total	Families with own children under 18 years	Total	Families with own children under 18 years	Total	Families with own children under 18 years
All Families..	1,372,189	617,391	1,362,032	603,414	1,383,950	613,580
FAMILY TYPE AND LABOR FORCE STATUS						
Married-Couple Families..........................	1,077,897	436,434	1,068,394	428,952	1,091,358	433,140
Both husband and wife in labor force......................	61.0	75.7	60.6	77.1	60.1	77.3
Husband in labor force, wife not in labor force..........	15.7	19.4	15.7	18.5	15.9	18.2
Wife in labor force, husband not in labor force..........	7.3	3.7	7.5	3.6	7.2	3.2
Both husband and wife not in labor force.................	15.6	1.0	16.3	0.8	16.1	0.9
Other Families...................................	294,292	180,957	293,638	174,462	292,592	180,440
Female householder, no husband present..................	70.8	74.0	69.4	71.5	67.4	69.8
In labor force......................................	55.8	64.0	52.5	60.0	52.4	60.4
Not in labor force..................................	15.0	10.0	16.9	11.5	15.1	9.4
Male householder, no wife present.......................	29.2	26.0	30.6	28.5	32.6	30.2
In labor force......................................	24.6	24.7	25.4	26.3	27.8	28.1
Not in labor force..................................	4.6	1.3	5.2	2.2	4.7	2.1

Table MN-11. School Enrollment and Educational Attainment, 2015

(Number, percent.)

Item	State	U.S.
Enrollment		
Total population 3 years and over, enrolled in school	1,382,373	81,618,288
Enrolled in nursery school or preschool (percent)	6.5	6.0
Enrolled in kindergarten (percent)	4.9	5.0
Enrolled in elementary school, grades 1-8 (percent)........	41.3	40.3
Enrolled in high school, grades 9-12 (percent)	21.3	20.9
Enrolled in college or graduate school (percent)...........	26.0	27.7
Attainment		
Total population 25 years and over	3,700,935	216,447,163
Less than ninth grade (percent)	3.0	5.5
9th to 12th grade, no diploma (percent)	4.2	7.3
High school graduate, including equivalency (percent)......	25.4	27.6
Some college, no degree (percent)	21.5	20.7
Associate's degree (percent)	11.2	8.2
Bachelor's degree (percent)	22.9	19.0
Graduate or professional degree (percent)	11.8	11.6
High school graduate or higher (percent)	92.8	87.1
Bachelor's degree or higher (percent)	34.7	30.6

Table MN-12. Public School Characteristics and Educational Indicators

(Number, percent; data derived from National Center of Education Statistics.)

Item	State	U.S.
Public Schools, 2014–2015 (except where noted)		
Number of school districts.................................	554	18,260
Number of schools...	2,435	98,373
Number of students	857,235	50,312,581
Number of teachers	55,690	3,132,351
Student-teacher ratio.....................................	15.4	16.1
Expenditures per student (dollars), FY 2014...............	11,427	11,066
Four-year adjusted cohort graduation rate (ACGR)[1,2]	81.9	83.2
Students eligible for free or reduced-price lunch (percent)	38.3	51.8
English language learners (percent).......................	7.2	9.4
Students age 3 to 21 served under IDEA, part B (percent)...	14.6	13.0

Public Schools by Type	Number	Percent of state public schools
Total number of schools...................................	2,435	100.0
Regular	1,674	68.7
Special education	283	11.6
Vocational education	9	0.4
Alternative education.....................................	469	19.3

NOTE: Every school is assigned only one school type based on its instructional emphasis.
[1] ACGR data represents a new method of calculating high-school completion rates and may not be comparable to previous years' data for Averaged Freshmen Graduation Rates (AFGR).
[2] The United States 4-year ACGRs were estimated using both the reported 4-year ACGR data from 49 states and the District of Columbia and using imputed data for Idaho. The estimate for American Indian/Alaska Native students also includes imputed data for Virginia.

Table MN-13. Reported Voting and Registration of the Voting-Age Population, November 2016

(Numbers in thousands, percent.)

Item	Total population	Total citizen population	Registered			Voted		
			Total registered	Percent registered (total population)	Percent registered (total citizen population)	Total voted	Percent voted (total population)	Percent voted (total citizen population)
U.S. Total	245,502	224,059	157,596	64.2	70.3	137,537	56.0	61.4
State Total............................	4,190	3,985	3,055	72.9	76.7	2,738	65.3	68.7
Sex								
Male	2,063	1,952	1,457	70.6	74.6	1,312	63.6	67.2
Female	2,127	2,033	1,598	75.1	78.6	1,426	67.1	70.2
Race								
White alone...........................	3,614	3,506	2,723	75.4	77.7	2,457	68.0	70.1
White, non-Hispanic alone	3,425	3,405	2,680	78.2	78.7	2,417	70.6	71.0
Black alone..........................	193	169	126	65.3	74.7	112	58.0	66.3
Asian alone..........................	172	124	79	46.1	63.7	64	37.4	51.6
Hispanic (of any race)................	255	136	54	21.0	39.6	50	19.4	36.6
White alone or in combination	3,671	3,563	2,756	75.1	77.4	2,489	67.8	69.9
Black alone or in combination.........	201	176	134	66.6	75.8	120	59.6	67.7
Asian alone or in combination.........	196	148	97	49.8	65.7	82	42.1	55.6
Age								
18 to 24 years......................	524	476	297	56.7	62.4	260	49.6	54.7
25 to 34 years......................	708	674	491	69.3	72.8	435	61.4	64.5
35 to 44 years......................	684	625	476	69.7	76.2	438	64.1	70.1
45 to 64 years......................	1,503	1,441	1,158	77.1	80.3	1,047	69.7	72.6
65 years and over	772	769	633	82.0	82.3	558	72.3	72.6

Table MN-14. Crime

(Number, rate per 100,000. Data are derived from the FBI Uniform Crime Reports.)

Item	State [1]			U.S. [1,2,3,4]		
	2014	2015	Percent change	2014	2015	Percent change
TOTAL POPULATION[5]	5,457,125	5,489,594	0.6	318,907,401	321,418,820	0.8
VIOLENT CRIME						
Number..........................	12,505	13,319	6.5	1,186,185	1,231,566	3.8
Rate	229.1	242.6	5.9	372.0	383.2	3.0
Murder and Nonnegligent Manslaughter						
Number..........................	88	133	51.1	14,164	15,696	10.8
Rate	1.6	2.4	50.2	4.4	4.9	10.0
Rape[6]						
Number..........................	2,001	2,321	16.0	118,027	124,047	5.1
Rate	36.7	42.3	15.3	37.0	38.6	4.3
Robbery						
Number..........................	3,687	3,771	2.3	322,905	327,374	1.4
Rate	67.6	68.7	1.7	101.3	101.9	0.6
Aggravated Assault						
Number..........................	6,729	7,094	5.4	731,089	764,449	4.6
Rate	123.3	129.2	4.8	229.2	237.8	3.7
PROPERTY CRIME						
Number..........................	125,377	121,984	-2.7	8,209,010	7,993,631	-2.6
Rate	2,297.5	2,222.1	-3.3	2,574.1	2,487.0	-3.4
Burglary						
Number..........................	20,773	19,299	-7.1	1,713,153	1,579,527	-7.8
Rate	380.7	351.6	-7.6	537.2	491.4	-8.5
Larceny-Theft						
Number..........................	96,237	94,704	-1.6	5,809,054	5,706,346	-1.8
Rate	1,763.5	1,725.2	-2.2	1,821.5	1,775.4	-2.5
Motor Vehicle Theft						
Number..........................	8,367	7,981	-4.6	686,803	707,758	3.1
Rate	153.3	145.4	-5.2	215.4	220.2	2.2

NOTE: Although arson data are included in the trend and clearance tables, sufficient data are not available to estimate totals for this offense. Therefore, no arson data are published in this table.

X = Not applicable.

- = Zero or rounds to zero.

[1] The data collection methodology for the offense of forcible rape used by the Minnesota state Uniform Crime Reporting (UCR) Program (with the exception of Minneapolis and St. Paul, Minnesota) does not comply with national UCR Program guidelines. Consequently, its figures for forcible rape and violent crime (of which forcible rape is a part) are not published in this table.

[2] The crime figures have been adjusted.

[3] Includes offenses reported by the Zoological Police and the Metro Transit Police.

[4] Because of changes in the state's reporting practices, figures are not comparable to previous years' data.

[5] Populations are U.S. Census Bureau provisional estimates as of July 1 of each year.

[6] The figures shown for the offense of rape were estimated using the revised Uniform Crime Reporting (UCR) definition of rape.

Table MN-15. State Government Finances, 2015

(Dollar amounts in thousands, percent distribution.)

Item	Dollars	Percent distribution
Total Revenue	47,407,059	100.0
General revenue	40,470,072	85.4
Intergovernmental revenue	11,253,891	23.7
Taxes	24,479,856	51.6
General sales	5,483,791	11.6
Selective sales	4,469,620	9.4
License taxes	1,392,055	2.9
Individual income tax	10,370,047	21.9
Corporate income tax	1,476,629	3.1
Other taxes	1,287,714	2.7
Current charges	2,542,414	5.4
Miscellaneous general revenue	2,193,911	4.6
Utility revenue	101638	0.2
Liquor stores revenue	0	-
Insurance trust revenue[1]	6,835,349	14.4
Total Expenditure	43,406,909	100.0
Intergovernmental expenditure	12,827,108	29.6
Direct expenditure	30,579,801	70.4
Current operation	21,679,716	49.9
Capital outlay	1,923,983	4.4
Insurance benefits and repayments	5,310,474	12.2
Assistance and subsidies	1,091,983	2.5
Interest on debt	573,645	1.3
Exhibit: Salaries and wages	5,319,902	12.3
Total Expenditure	43,406,909	100.0
General expenditure	37,734,379	86.9
Intergovernmental expenditure	12,827,108	29.6
Direct expenditure	24,907,271	57.4
General expenditure, by function:		
Education	14,305,318	33.0
Public welfare	13,108,732	30.2
Hospitals	306,356	0.7
Health	489,107	1.1
Highways	2,974,584	6.9
Police protection	438,971	1.0
Correction	574,822	1.3
Natural resources	717,179	1.7
Parks and recreation	289,419	0.7
Governmental administration	1,121,595	2.6
Interest on general debt	570,730	1.3
Other and unallocable	2,837,566	6.5
Utility expenditure	362,056	0.8
Liquor stores expenditure	0	-
Insurance trust expenditure	5,310,474	12.2
Debt at End of Fiscal Year	16,755,784	X
Cash and Security Holdings	83,315,096	X

X = Not applicable.
- = Zero or rounds to zero.
[1] Within insurance trust revenue, net earnings of state retirement systems is a calculated statistic (the item code in the data file is X08), and thus can be positive or negative. Net earnings is the sum of earnings on investments plus gains on investments minus losses on investments. The change made in 2002 for asset valuation from book to market value in accordance with Statement 34 of the Governmental Accounting Standards Board is reflected in the calculated statistics.

Table MN-16. State Government Tax Collections, 2016

(Dollars in thousands, percent.)

Item	Dollars	Percent distribution
Total Taxes	25,189,128	100.0
Property taxes	849,824	3.4
Sales and gross receipts	10,120,647	40.2
General sales and gross receipts	5,583,910	22.2
Selective sales and gross receipts	4,536,737	18.0
Alcoholic beverages	88,352	0.4
Amusements	56,310	0.2
Insurance premiums	457,876	1.8
Motor fuels	901,156	3.6
Pari-mutuels	522	-
Public utilities	54	-
Tobacco products	650,042	2.6
Other selective sales	2,382,425	9.5
Licenses	1,426,235	5.7
Alcoholic beverages	2,580	-
Amusements	1,161	-
Corporations in general	8,201	
Hunting and fishing	64,581	0.3
Motor vehicle	741,938	2.9
Motor vehicle operators	47,452	0.2
Public utilities	934	-
Occupation and business, NEC	499,122	2.0
Other licenses	60,266	0.2
Income taxes	12,248,267	48.6
Individual income	10,732,570	42.6
Corporation net income	1,515,697	6.0
Other taxes	544,155	2.2
Death and gift	182,499	0.7
Documentary and stock transfer	226,485	0.9
Severance	49,711	0.2
Taxes, NEC	85,460	0.3

- = Zero or rounds to zero.

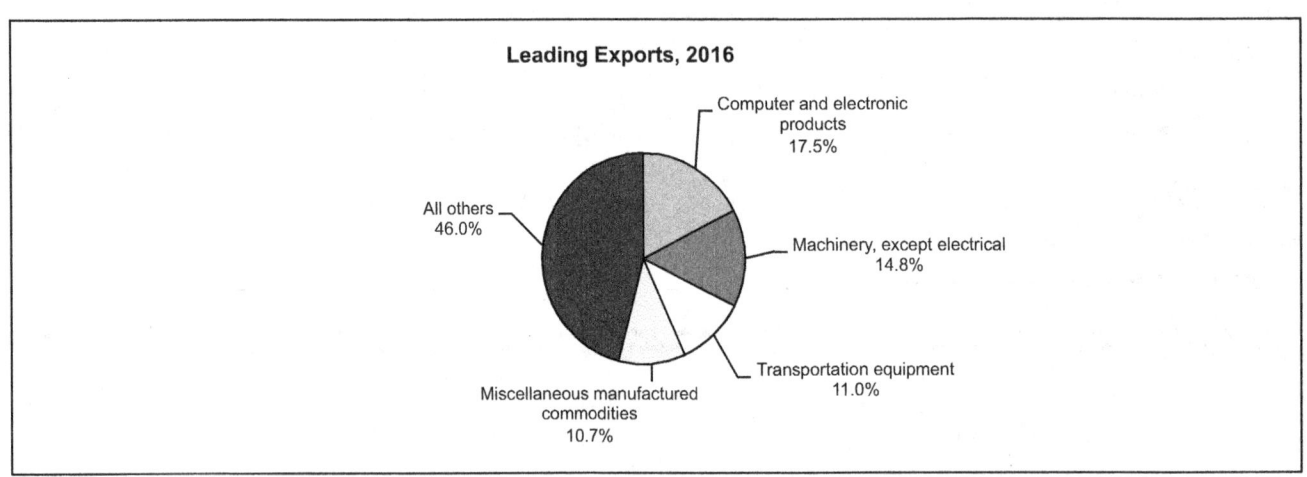

Leading Exports, 2016

Computer and electronic products 17.5%

Machinery, except electrical 14.8%

Transportation equipment 11.0%

Miscellaneous manufactured commodities 10.7%

All others 46.0%

MISSISSIPPI

Facts and Figures

Location: South central United States; bordered on the N by Tennessee, on the E by Alabama, on the S by Louisiana and the Gulf of Mexico, and on the W by Arkansas and Louisiana

Area: 48,430 sq. mi. (125,434 sq. km.); rank—32nd

Population: 2,988726 (2016 est.); rank—32nd

Principal Cities: capital—Jackson; largest—Jackson

Statehood: December 10, 1817; 20th state

U.S. Congress: 2 senators, 4 representatives

State Motto: *Virtute et armis* ("By valor and arms")

State Song: "Go, Mississippi"

State Nicknames: The Magnolia State; The Hospitality State

Abbreviations: MS; Miss.

State Symbols: flower—magnolia blossom; tree—Southern magnolia; bird—mockingbird

At a Glance

- With an increase in population of 0.7 percent, Mississippi ranked 42nd among the states in growth from 2010 to 2016.

- In 2015, Mississippi had the lowest median household income in the country ($40,593) and the highest percent of population living the below the poverty level (22.0 percent).

- In 2015, 12.7 percent of Mississippians did not have health insurance, compared to 9.4 percent of the total U.S. population.

- Mississippi had the third highest traffic fatality rate in 2015, with 1.70 deaths per 100 million vehicle miles.

- In 2015, 20.8 percent of Mississippians had a bachelor's degree or higher, which was the second lowest percentage among states.

Table MS-1. Population by Age, Sex, Race, and Hispanic Origin

(Number, percent, except where noted.)

Sex, age, race, and Hispanic origin	2000	2010	2016 [1]	Average annual percent change, 2010–2016
Total Population..	2,844,658	2,967,297	2,988,726	-
Percent of total U.S. population	1.0	1.0	0.9	X
Sex				
Male..	1,373,554	1,441,240	1,448,792	-
Female	1,471,104	1,526,057	1,539,934	0.1
Age				
Under 5 years..	204,364	210,956	188,701	-0.7
5 to 19 years..	668,850	638,539	615,372	-0.2
20 to 64 years..	1,627,921	1,737,395	1,733,712	-
65 years and over..	343,523	380,407	450,941	1.2
Median age (years)	33.8	36.0	37.1	0.2
Race and Hispanic Origin				
One race..				
White	1,746,099	1,789,391	1,772,995	-0.1
Black..	1,033,809	1,103,101	1,127,116	0.1
American Indian and Alaska Native	11,652	16,837	17,985	0.4
Asian..	18,626	26,477	31,969	1.3
Native Hawaiian or Other Pacific Islander	667	1,700	1,810	0.4
Two or more races..	20,021	29,791	36,851	1.5
Hispanic (of any race)..	39,569	85,107	91,448	0.5

X = Not applicable.
- = Zero or rounds to zero.
[1] Population figures for 2016 are July 1 estimates. The 2010 estimates are taken from the 2010 Census.

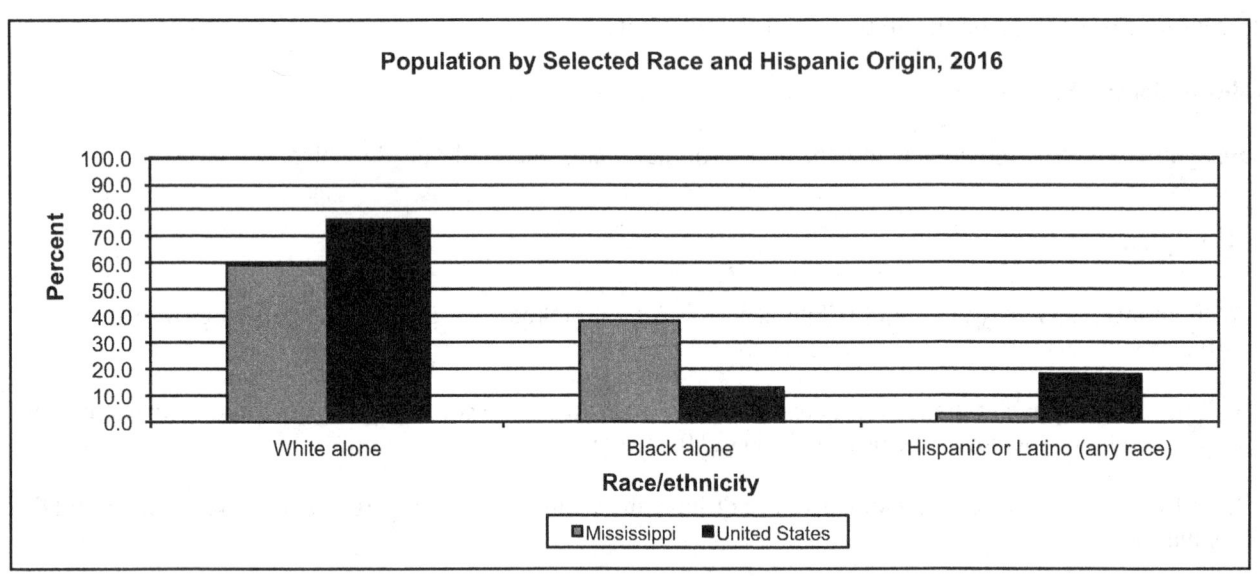

Table MS-2. Marital Status

(Number, percent distribution.)

Sex, age, race, and Hispanic origin	2000	2010	2015
Males, 15 Years and Over	1,046,252	1,121,265	1,143,411
Never married	30.6	34.9	37.3
Now married, except separated..	54.6	48.3	46.0
Separated..	2.4	2.5	2.7
Widowed..	2.9	2.7	3.0
Divorced..	9.5	11.7	10.9
Females, 15 Years and Over	1,157,363	1,224,423	1,244,736
Never married	25.1	29.8	32.0
Now married, except separated..	48.6	43.8	41.9
Separated..	3.2	3.4	3.0
Widowed..	12.5	10.8	10.6
Divorced..	10.6	12.3	12.4

Table MS-3. Households and Housing Characteristics

(Number, percent, dollars.)

Item	2000	2010	2015	Average annual percent change, 2000–2015
Total Households...	1,046,434	1,079,999	1,104,371	0.4
Family households..	747,159	746,115	743,154	-
Married-couple family..	520,884	501,571	485,198	-0.5
Other family..	226,315	244,544	257,956	0.9
Male householder, no wife present.................................	45,610	51,400	56,528	1.6
Female householder, no husband present.......................	180,705	193,144	201,428	0.8
Nonfamily households...	299,275	333,884	361,217	1.4
Householder living alone..	257,708	293,185	313,780	1.5
Householder not living alone...	41,567	40,699	47,437	0.9
Housing Characteristics				
Total housing units...	1,161,953	1,276,441	1,300,932	0.8
Occupied housing units	1,046,434	1,079,999	1,104,371	0.4
Owner occupied..	756,967	753,374	744,203	-0.1
Renter occupied...	289,467	326,625	360,168	1.6
Average household size..	2.63	2.66	2.62	-
Financial Characteristics				
Median gross rent of renter-occupied housing	439	672	724	4.3
Median monthly owner costs for housing units with a mortgage	762	1,043	1,083	2.8
Median value of owner-occupied housing units....................	71,400	100,100	112,700	3.9

- = Zero or rounds to zero.

Table MS-4. Migration, Origin, and Language

(Number, percent.)

Characteristic	State 2014	State 2015	State Percent change	U.S. 2014	U.S. 2015	U.S. Percent change
Residence 1 Year Ago						
Population 1 year and over	2,957,658	2,959,289	0.1	315,095,393	317,635,720	0.8
Same house	86.4	86.3	X	85.1	85.3	X
Different house in the U.S...	13.4	13.4	X	14.3	14.1	X
Same county	7.0	7.6	X	8.7	8.5	X
Different county	6.3	5.8	X	5.6	5.6	X
Same state	3.8	3.5	X	3.3	3.2	X
Different state	2.5	2.3	X	2.3	2.4	X
Abroad	0.3	0.3	X	0.6	0.7	X
Place of Birth						
Native born	2,928,929	2,920,075	-0.3	276,465,262	278,128,449	0.6
Male	48.6	48.3	X	49.3	49.3	X
Female	51.4	51.7	X	50.7	50.7	X
Foreign born	65,150	72,258	10.9	42,391,794	43,290,372	2.1
Male	52.7	53.7	X	48.7	48.6	X
Female	47.3	46.3	X	51.3	51.4	X
Foreign born; naturalized U.S. citizen.................................	23,340	24,140	3.4	19,984,738	20,697,103	3.6
Male	41.7	46.7	X	45.9	45.9	X
Female	58.3	53.3	X	54.1	54.1	X
Foreign born; not a U.S. citizen..	41,810	48,118	15.1	22,407,056	22,593,269	0.8
Male	58.8	57.3	X	51.2	51.1	X
Female	41.2	42.7	X	48.8	48.9	X
Entered 2010 or later	16.5	21.8	X	12.3	15.6	X
Entered 2000 to 2009	35.2	37.9	X	28.6	27.9	X
Entered before 2000...	48.4	40.3	X	59.1	56.5	X
World Region of Birth, Foreign						
Foreign-born population, excluding population born at sea	65,150	72,258	10.9	42,390,705	43,289,646	2.1
Europe	11.1	11.0	X	11.2	11.1	X
Asia	31.6	28.7	X	30.1	30.6	X
Africa	2.9	6.0	X	4.6	4.8	X
Oceania	0.3	0.7	X	0.6	0.6	X
Latin America	52.1	51.5	X	51.6	51.1	X
North America	2.0	2.2	X	1.9	1.9	X
Language Spoken at Home and Ability to Speak English						
Population 5 years and over..	2,802,072	2,803,484	0.1	299,084,046	301,625,014	0.8
English only	96.3	96.1	X	78.9	78.5	X
Language other than English...	3.7	3.9	X	21.1	21.5	X
Speaks English less than "very well"................................	1.5	1.7	X	8.6	8.6	X

NA = Not available.
X = Not applicable.
- = Zero or rounds to zero.

Table MS-5. Median Income and Poverty Status, 2015

(Number, percent, except as noted.)

Characteristic	State		U.S.	
	Number	Percent	Number	Percent
Median Income				
Households (dollars)...	40,593	X	55,775	X
Families (dollars)	50,069	X	68,260	X
Below Poverty Level (All People)	637,128	22.0	46,153,077	14.7
Sex				
Male	276,030	19.9	20,599,407	13.4
Female	361,098	23.9	25,553,670	16.0
Age				
Under 18 years...	224,273	31.3	15,000,273	20.7
Related children under 18 years..	222,507	31.1	14,693,239	20.4
18 to 64 years..	359,317	20.5	26,960,369	13.9
65 years and over	53,538	12.5	4,192,435	9.0

X = Not applicable.

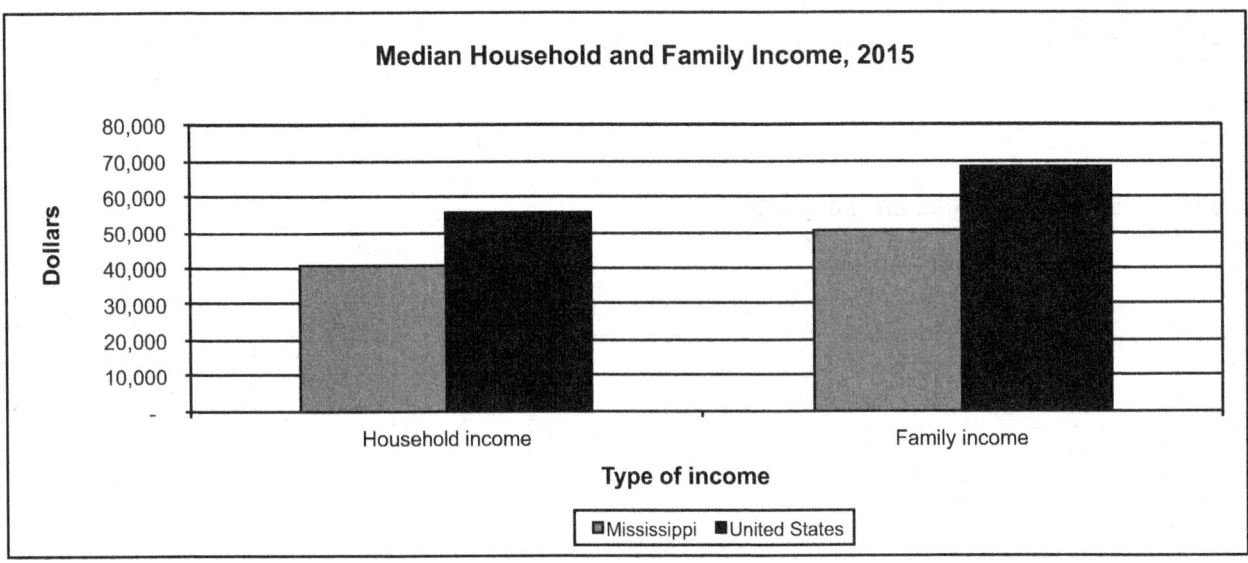

Table MS-6. Health Insurance Coverage Status for the Civilian Noninstitutionalized Population and Children Under 18 Years of Age

(Numbers in thousands, percent.)

Item	2007	2008	2009	2010	2011	2012	2013	2014	2015
Civilian Noninstitutionalized Population	2,903	2,868	2,880	2,903	2,912	2,918	2,925	2,927	2,928
Covered by Private or Public Insurance									
Number...	2,358	2,355	2,366	2,375	2,395	2,421	2,425	2,503	2,556
Percent...	81.2	82.1	82.1	81.8	82.3	83.0	82.9	85.5	87.3
Not Covered									
Number...	545	513	514	528	516	497	500	424	372
Percent...	18.8	17.9	17.9	18.2	17.7	17.0	17.1	14.5	12.7
Percent in the U.S. not covered...	15.3	15.1	15.1	15.5	15.1	14.8	14.5	11.7	9.4
Children Under 18 Years of Age	778	763	764	752	750	746	734	730	726
Covered by Private or Public Insurance									
Number...	684	666	685	688	689	691	678	691	696
Percent...	87.9	87.3	89.7	91.6	91.9	92.7	92.4	94.7	96.0
Not Covered									
Number...	94	97	79	64	61	55	56	39	29
Percent...	12.1	12.7	10.3	8.4	8.1	7.3	7.6	5.3	4.0
Percent in the U.S. not covered...	11.0	9.7	8.6	8.0	7.5	7.2	7.1	6.0	4.8

Table MS-7. Employment Status by Demographic Group, 2016

(Numbers in thousands, percent.)

Characteristic	Civilian noninstitutional population	Civilian labor force		Employed		Unemployed	
		Number	Percent of population	Number	Percent of population	Number	Percent of population
Total..................................	2,290	1,281	56.0	1,208	52.7	74	5.7
Sex							
Male..................................	1,076	654	60.8	615	57.2	39	6.0
Female	1,214	627	51.7	593	48.8	34	5.5
Race, Sex, and Hispanic Origin							
White	1,399	778	55.7	744	53.2	35	4.5
Male..............................	678	422	62.2	403	59.4	19	4.5
Female	720	356	49.5	341	47.3	16	4.4
Black or African American..................	825	466	56.4	429	52.0	36	7.8
Male..............................	368	213	58.0	194	52.8	19	9.0
Female	457	252	55.2	235	51.4	17	6.8
Hispanic or Latino ethnicity[1]	51	33	64.6	30	59.5	3	7.8
Male..............................	NA	NA	NA	NA	NA	NA	NA
Female	NA	NA	NA	NA	NA	NA	NA
Age							
16 to 19 years......................	172	41	23.8	32	18.7	9	21.3
20 to 24 years......................	199	129	64.9	116	58.5	13	9.9
25 to 34 years......................	348	271	78.0	255	73.2	17	6.2
35 to 44 years......................	382	310	81.0	294	77.0	16	5.0
45 to 54 years......................	383	266	69.4	255	66.7	10	3.9
55 to 64 years......................	379	202	53.4	195	51.5	7	3.6
65 years and over	428	63	14.7	60	14.1	2	3.7

NOTE: Data in Table 7 are from the Current Population Survey (CPS) and do not match the estimates in Table 8. See notes and definitions for further information.
[1] May be of any race.
NA = Not available.

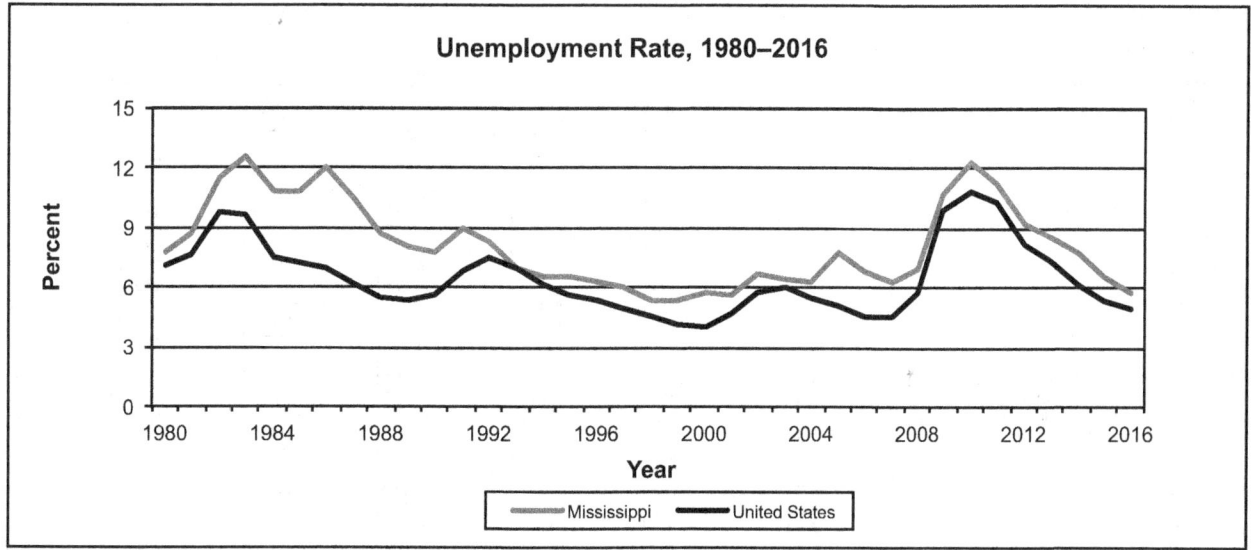

Table MS-8. Employment Status of the Civilian Noninstitutional Population Age 16 Years and Over

(Number, percent.)

Year	Civilian labor force	Civilian participation rate	Employed	Unemployed	Unemployment rate
2008..................................	1,306,772	59.8	1,220,991	85,781	6.6
2009..................................	1,269,219	57.7	1,148,930	120,289	9.5
2010..................................	1,306,608	58.6	1,170,879	135,729	10.4
2011..................................	1,342,808	59.8	1,208,747	134,061	10.0
2012..................................	1,317,447	58.4	1,198,914	118,533	9.0
2013..................................	1,271,436	56.1	1,161,814	109,622	8.6
2014..................................	1,249,288	54.9	1,154,812	94,476	7.6
2015..................................	1,272,657	55.8	1,189,646	83,011	6.5
2016..................................	1,280,432	56.0	1,205,779	74,653	5.8

Table MS-9. Employment and Average Wages by Industry

(Estimates through 2010 are based on the 2007 *North American Industry Classification System* [NAICS]. Estimates from 2011 onward are based on the 2012 NAICS.)

Industry	2009	2010	2011	2012	2013	2014	2015
	Number of jobs						
Wage and Salary Employment by Industry	1,178,539	1,167,548	1,167,750	1,175,222	1,179,604	1,194,267	1,202,838
Farm Wage and Salary Employment	9,888	9,928	9,232	8,188	6,950	12,119	9,375
Nonfarm Wage and Salary Employment	1,168,651	1,157,620	1,158,518	1,167,034	1,172,654	1,182,148	1,193,463
Private wage and salary employment	883,873	875,525	879,098	887,597	895,874	906,773	918,974
Forestry, fishing, and related activities	7,697	7,876	7,713	7,678	7,846	7,902	7,897
Mining	5,668	5,694	6,131	6,316	6,174	6,248	5,038
Utilities	7,715	7,731	7,732	7,727	7,870	7,826	7,876
Construction	53,942	51,418	50,376	49,784	52,723	50,467	47,269
Manufacturing	141,499	136,124	135,464	137,136	136,974	139,687	141,823
Durable goods manufacturing	90,681	87,349	88,072	90,805	90,645	93,613	94,674
Nondurable goods manufacturing	50,818	48,775	47,392	46,331	46,329	46,074	47,149
Wholesale trade	35,107	34,389	34,455	34,377	34,284	34,235	34,672
Retail trade	135,253	133,467	134,290	134,635	134,549	136,797	139,188
Transportation and warehousing	39,489	39,098	39,862	40,163	41,039	42,657	44,770
Information	12,815	12,296	11,901	12,586	12,806	13,247	13,620
Finance and insurance	34,123	33,883	34,062	34,154	33,497	33,171	33,203
Real estate and rental and leasing	12,389	11,678	11,650	11,703	11,754	11,756	11,775
Professional, scientific, and technical services	32,227	31,911	31,934	31,488	30,883	31,240	31,043
Management of companies and enterprises	9,818	9,752	10,141	10,222	10,777	10,660	10,616
Administrative and waste services	46,666	51,166	52,650	55,598	57,935	60,441	63,845
Educational services	18,638	19,703	19,407	19,893	19,830	19,613	19,963
Health care and social assistance	118,464	120,803	121,991	122,856	123,697	124,974	127,627
Arts, entertainment, and recreation	12,264	12,119	10,897	11,271	11,593	11,325	11,422
Accommodation and food services	108,855	106,890	109,049	111,098	113,104	115,255	118,389
Other services, except public administration	51,244	49,527	49,393	48,912	48,539	49,272	48,938
Government and government enterprises	284,778	282,095	279,420	279,437	276,780	275,375	274,489
	Dollars						
Average Wages and Salaries by Industry	34,513	35,263	35,917	36,920	37,469	38,005	38,603
Average Farm Wages and Salaries	18,066	18,508	17,142	29,392	25,584	21,320	24,826
Average Nonfarm Wages and Salaries	34,653	35,407	36,067	36,973	37,540	38,176	38,711
Average private wages and salaries	33,953	34,729	35,553	36,667	37,287	37,946	38,410
Forestry, fishing, and related activities	28,129	29,873	30,641	31,621	32,620	33,845	35,499
Mining	64,195	65,836	69,826	75,055	75,775	78,680	79,157
Utilities	66,200	67,401	68,280	71,131	71,800	73,995	77,878
Construction	40,896	41,481	42,488	44,732	46,679	47,282	47,217
Manufacturing	41,175	42,258	43,689	45,037	45,853	47,600	48,300
Durable goods manufacturing	42,808	43,860	45,283	46,421	47,294	49,031	49,457
Nondurable goods manufacturing	38,263	39,390	40,728	42,323	43,033	44,691	45,978
Wholesale trade	48,140	48,932	50,419	52,042	53,074	54,613	56,276
Retail trade	22,955	23,700	24,019	24,676	25,035	25,351	25,871
Transportation and warehousing	39,509	40,811	41,670	43,359	43,708	44,504	45,553
Information	40,345	42,223	44,087	44,872	46,409	47,721	46,125
Finance and insurance	47,186	48,982	50,212	52,499	54,720	55,841	57,558
Real estate and rental and leasing	29,225	30,787	31,879	33,464	33,496	34,834	35,646
Professional, scientific, and technical services	51,773	52,189	53,082	54,815	55,788	55,949	57,897
Management of companies and enterprises	70,903	73,202	77,953	81,444	80,302	82,949	84,821
Administrative and waste services	25,020	25,805	25,556	26,400	27,643	27,764	27,900
Educational services	24,635	24,899	26,663	27,719	28,519	28,832	27,554
Health care and social assistance	38,524	38,852	39,724	40,719	40,626	40,999	41,683
Arts, entertainment, and recreation	24,411	24,653	24,216	23,884	23,866	23,609	24,253
Accommodation and food services	17,561	18,042	18,409	18,615	18,774	18,926	19,016
Other services, except public administration	24,909	26,222	26,465	27,730	28,645	29,568	30,558
Government and government enterprises	36,824	37,512	37,683	37,943	38,358	38,933	39,720

Table MS-10. Employment Characteristics by Family Type

(Number, percent.)

Family type and labor force status	2013		2014		2015	
	Total	Families with own children under 18 years	Total	Families with own children under 18 years	Total	Families with own children under 18 years
All Families...	745,079	310,168	736,864	305,343	743,154	308,522
FAMILY TYPE AND LABOR FORCE STATUS						
Married-Couple Families..................................	487,648	176,292	480,622	173,656	485,198	175,460
Both husband and wife in labor force................................	47.4	67.9	48.6	67.6	47.3	67.5
Husband in labor force, wife not in labor force	21.1	23.4	21.8	24.9	21.4	24.0
Wife in labor force, husband not in labor force	10.7	6.0	9.1	4.4	9.4	5.4
Both husband and wife not in labor force................................	20.5	2.5	20.5	3.1	21.6	3.0
Other Families	257,431	133,876	256,242	131,687	257,956	133,062
Female householder, no husband present.........................	79.2	84.2	78.3	79.4	78.1	80.1
In labor force..................................	51.9	67.5	49.7	63.7	50.3	63.9
Not in labor force	27.3	16.7	28.6	15.7	27.8	16.2
Male householder, no wife present........................	20.8	15.8	21.7	20.6	21.9	19.9
In labor force..................................	13.5	13.7	16.0	18.3	15.7	17.8
Not in labor force	7.3	2.1	5.7	2.3	6.2	2.1

Table MS-11. School Enrollment and Educational Attainment, 2015

(Number, percent.)

Item	State	U.S.
Enrollment		
Total population 3 years and over, enrolled in school	796,722	81,618,288
Enrolled in nursery school or preschool (percent)................................	6.1	6.0
Enrolled in kindergarten (percent)................................	5.8	5.0
Enrolled in elementary school, grades 1-8 (percent)................................	41.8	40.3
Enrolled in high school, grades 9-12 (percent)	20.8	20.9
Enrolled in college or graduate school (percent)................................	25.4	27.7
Attainment		
Total population 25 years and over	1,952,337	216,447,163
Less than ninth grade (percent)................................	5.8	5.5
9th to 12th grade, no diploma (percent)	10.8	7.3
High school graduate, including equivalency (percent)................................	31.0	27.6
Some college, no degree (percent)................................	22.4	20.7
Associate's degree (percent)................................	9.2	8.2
Bachelor's degree (percent)	13.0	19.0
Graduate or professional degree (percent)................................	7.9	11.6
High school graduate or higher (percent)	83.5	87.1
Bachelor's degree or higher (percent)	20.8	30.6

Table MS-12. Public School Characteristics and Educational Indicators

(Number, percent; data derived from National Center of Education Statistics.)

Item	State	U.S.
Public Schools, 2014–2015 (except where noted)		
Number of school districts................................	157	18,260
Number of schools................................	1,071	98,373
Number of students	490,917	50,312,581
Number of teachers	32,311	3,132,351
Student-teacher ratio................................	15.2	16.1
Expenditures per student (dollars), FY 2014	8,265	11,066
Four-year adjusted cohort graduation rate (ACGR)[1,2]	80.8	83.2
Students eligible for free or reduced-price lunch (percent)................................	73.7	51.8
English language learners (percent)................................	1.6	9.4
Students age 3 to 21 served under IDEA, part B (percent)................................	13.5	13.0

Public Schools by Type	Number	Percent of state public schools
Total number of schools................................	1,071	100.0
Regular	914	85.3
Special education................................	1	0.1
Vocational education................................	91	8.5
Alternative education................................	65	6.1

NOTE: Every school is assigned only one school type based on its instructional emphasis.

[1] ACGR data represents a new method of calculating high-school completion rates and may not be comparable to previous years' data for Averaged Freshmen Graduation Rates (AFGR).

[2] The United States 4-year ACGRs were estimated using both the reported 4-year ACGR data from 49 states and the District of Columbia and using imputed data for Idaho. The estimate for American Indian/Alaska Native students also includes imputed data for Virginia.

Table MS-13. Reported Voting and Registration of the Voting-Age Population, November 2016

(Numbers in thousands, percent.)

Item	Total population	Total citizen population	Registered			Voted		
			Total registered	Percent registered (total population)	Percent registered (total citizen population)	Total voted	Percent voted (total population)	Percent voted (total citizen population)
U.S. Total	245,502	224,059	157,596	64.2	70.3	137,537	56.0	61.4
State Total.............................	2,203	2,170	1,725	78.3	79.5	1,470	66.7	67.7
Sex								
Male	1,026	1,010	780	76.0	77.2	657	64.0	65.0
Female	1,177	1,160	945	80.3	81.5	813	69.1	70.1
Race								
White alone.............................	1,377	1,355	1,070	77.7	79.0	918	66.7	67.8
White, non-Hispanic alone	1,345	1,339	1,056	78.5	78.8	907	67.4	67.7
Black alone..............................	782	777	632	80.9	81.4	537	68.7	69.1
Asian alone	18	13	8	(B)	(B)	6	(B)	(B)
Hispanic (of any race)	41	23	18	(B)	(B)	15	(B)	(B)
White alone or in combination	1,394	1,371	1,081	77.6	78.9	923	66.2	67.3
Black alone or in combination..........	791	786	639	80.8	81.3	544	68.8	69.2
Asian alone or in combination..........	22	18	10	(B)	(B)	6	(B)	(B)
Age								
18 to 24 years.....................	283	279	170	60.0	60.9	130	46.1	46.7
25 to 34 years.....................	356	345	262	73.7	76.1	203	57.0	58.9
35 to 44 years.....................	368	358	278	75.4	77.6	245	66.5	68.4
45 to 64 years.....................	763	758	635	83.1	83.8	557	72.9	73.5
65 years and over	433	431	380	87.9	88.4	335	77.3	77.7

B = Base is less than 75,000 and therefore too small to show the derived measure.

Table MS-14. Crime

(Number, rate per 100,000. Data are derived from the FBI Uniform Crime Reports.)

Item	State			U.S. [1,2,3,4]		
	2014	2015	Percent change	2014	2015	Percent change
TOTAL POPULATION[5]	2,993,443	2,992,333	-	318,907,401	321,418,820	0.8
VIOLENT CRIME						
Number...........................	8,331	8,254	-0.9	1,186,185	1,231,566	3.8
Rate	278.3	275.8	-0.9	372.0	383.2	3.0
Murder and Nonnegligent Manslaughter						
Number...........................	259	259	-	14,164	15,696	10.8
Rate	8.7	8.7	-	4.4	4.9	10.0
Rape[6]						
Number...........................	1,082	1,203	11.2	118,027	124,047	5.1
Rate	36.1	40.2	11.2	37.0	38.6	4.3
Robbery						
Number...........................	2,405	2,294	-4.6	322,905	327,374	1.4
Rate	80.3	76.7	-4.6	101.3	101.9	0.6
Aggravated Assault						
Number...........................	4,585	4,498	-1.9	731,089	764,449	4.6
Rate	153.2	150.3	-1.9	229.2	237.8	3.7
PROPERTY CRIME						
Number...........................	86,887	84,790	-2.4	8,209,010	7,993,631	-2.6
Rate	2,902.6	2,833.6	-2.4	2,574.1	2,487.0	-3.4
Burglary						
Number...........................	23,898	24,799	3.8	1,713,153	1,579,527	-7.8
Rate	798.3	828.8	3.8	537.2	491.4	-8.5
Larceny-Theft						
Number...........................	58,515	55,748	-4.7	5,809,054	5,706,346	-1.8
Rate	1,954.8	1,863.0	-4.7	1,821.5	1,775.4	-2.5
Motor Vehicle Theft						
Number...........................	4,474	4,243	-5.2	686,803	707,758	3.1
Rate	149.5	141.8	-5.1	215.4	220.2	2.2

NOTE: Although arson data are included in the trend and clearance tables, sufficient data are not available to estimate totals for this offense. Therefore, no arson data are published in this table.

X = Not applicable.

- = Zero or rounds to zero.

[1] The crime figures have been adjusted.

[2] The data collection methodology for the offense of forcible rape used by the Minnesota state Uniform Crime Reporting (UCR) Program (with the exception of Minneapolis and St. Paul, Minnesota) does not comply with national UCR Program guidelines. Consequently, its figures for forcible rape and violent crime (of which forcible rape is a part) are not published in this table.

[3] Includes offenses reported by the Zoological Police and the Metro Transit Police.

[4] Because of changes in the state's reporting practices, figures are not comparable to previous years' data.

[5] Populations are U.S. Census Bureau provisional estimates as of July 1 of each year.

[6] The figures shown for the offense of rape were estimated using the revised Uniform Crime Reporting (UCR) definition of rape.

Table MS-15. State Government Finances, 2015

(Dollar amounts in thousands, percent distribution.)

Item	Dollars	Percent distribution
Total Revenue	21,139,337	100.0
General revenue	18,496,169	87.5
Intergovernmental revenue	7,944,619	37.6
Taxes	7,902,885	37.4
General sales	3,422,774	16.2
Selective sales	1,451,003	6.9
License taxes	606,432	2.9
Individual income tax	1,783,438	8.4
Corporate income tax	534,547	2.5
Other taxes	104,691	0.5
Current charges	2,200,149	10.4
Miscellaneous general revenue	448,516	2.1
Utility revenue	0	-
Liquor stores revenue	312,934	1.5
Insurance trust revenue[1]	2,330,234	11.0
Total Expenditure	21,110,405	100.0
Intergovernmental expenditure	5,138,598	24.3
Direct expenditure	15,971,807	75.7
Current operation	11,510,324	54.5
Capital outlay	1,376,772	6.5
Insurance benefits and repayments	2,526,839	12.0
Assistance and subsidies	346,575	1.6
Interest on debt	211,297	1.0
Exhibit: Salaries and wages	2,519,256	11.9
Total Expenditure	21,110,405	100.0
General expenditure	18,325,018	86.8
Intergovernmental expenditure	5,138,598	24.3
Direct expenditure	13,186,420	62.5
General expenditure, by function:		
Education	5,791,535	27.4
Public welfare	6,228,236	29.5
Hospitals	1,257,672	6.0
Health	358,244	1.7
Highways	1,327,966	6.3
Police protection	162,829	0.8
Correction	371,359	1.8
Natural resources	331,887	1.6
Parks and recreation	62,572	0.3
Governmental administration	473,864	2.2
Interest on general debt	211,297	1.0
Other and unallocable	1,747,557	8.3
Utility expenditure	2,300	-
Liquor stores expenditure	256,248	1.2
Insurance trust expenditure	2,526,839	12.0
Debt at End of Fiscal Year	7,470,450	X
Cash and Security Holdings	33,083,013	X

X = Not applicable.
= Zero or rounds to zero.

[1] Within insurance trust revenue, net earnings of state retirement systems is a calculated statistic (the item code in the data file is X08), and thus can be positive or negative. Net earnings is the sum of earnings on investments plus gains on investments minus losses on investments. The change made in 2002 for asset valuation from book to market value in accordance with Statement 34 of the Governmental Accounting Standards Board is reflected in the calculated statistics.

Table MS-16. State Government Tax Collections, 2016

(Dollars in thousands, percent.)

Item	Dollars	Percent distribution
Total Taxes	7,660,391	100.0
Property taxes...	26,725	0.3
Sales and gross receipts	4,777,794	62.4
General sales and gross receipts	3,297,760	43.0
Selective sales and gross receipts	1,480,034	19.3
Alcoholic beverages..	42,352	0.6
Amusements..	133,847	1.7
Insurance premiums..	317,659	4.1
Motor fuels	443,578	5.8
Pari-mutuels...	0	-
Public utilities	1,602	-
Tobacco products...	145,931	1.9
Other selective sales	395,065	5.2
Licenses...	553,510	7.2
Alcoholic beverages...	1,306	-
Amusements..	35,337	0.5
Corporations in general...	144,283	1.9
Hunting and fishing..	2,731	-
Motor vehicle	158,029	2.1
Motor vehicle operators...	15,272	0.2
Public utilities	7,292	0.1
Occupation and business, NEC	129,892	1.7
Other licenses	59,368	0.8
Income taxes..	2,263,164	29.5
Individual income...	1,800,053	23.5
Corporation net income	463,111	6.0
Other taxes..	39,198	0.5
Death and gift..	4	-
Documentary and stock transfer	0	-
Severance	39,194	0.5
Taxes, NEC..	0	-

- = Zero or rounds to zero.

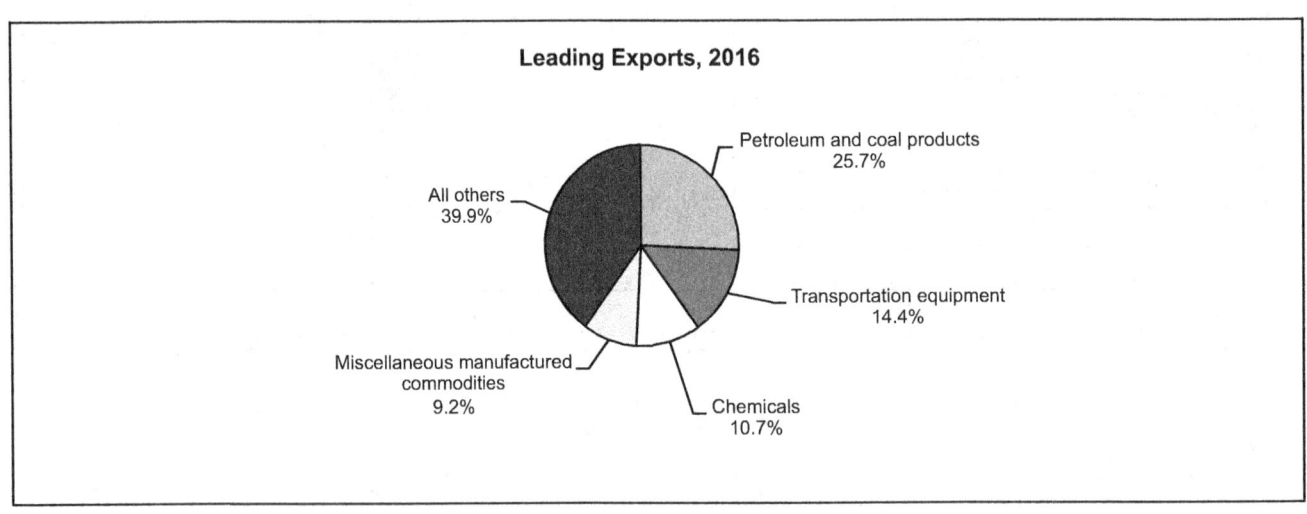

Leading Exports, 2016

Petroleum and coal products 25.7%

Transportation equipment 14.4%

Chemicals 10.7%

Miscellaneous manufactured commodities 9.2%

All others 39.9%

Facts and Figures

Location: Central United States; bordered on the N by Iowa, on the E by Illinois, Kentucky, and Tennessee, on the S by Arkansas, and on the W by Oklahoma, Kansas, and Nebraska

Area: 69,704 sq. mi. (180,533 sq. km.); rank—21st

Population: 6,093,000 (2016 est.); rank—18th

Principal Cities: capital—Jefferson City; largest—Kansas City

Statehood: August 10, 1821; 24th state

U.S. Congress: 2 senators, 8 representatives

State Motto: *Salus populi suprema lex esto* ("The welfare of the people shall be the supreme law")

State Song: "Missouri Waltz"

State Nickname: The Show Me State

Abbreviations: MO; Mo

State Symbols: flower—hawthorn; tree—flowering dogwood; bird—Eastern bluebird

At a Glance

- With an increase in population of 1.7 percent, Missouri ranked 36th among the states in growth from 2010 to 2016.

- In 2015, 9.8 percent of Missourians did not have health insurance, which was slightly above the national average of 9.4 percent.

- Missouri's violent crime rate was 497.4 per 100,000 population in 2015, compared to the U.S. rate of 383.2 per 100,000 population.

- Missouri's median household income of $50,238 ranked 37th in the country in 2015.

- In Missouri in 2015, 14.8 percent of residents lived below the poverty level, which was slightly above the national average of 14.7 percent; 20.2 percent of Missouri children lived in poverty, which was slightly lower than the national average of 20.7 percent.

Table MO-1. Population by Age, Sex, Race, and Hispanic Origin

(Number, percent, except where noted.)

Sex, age, race, and Hispanic origin	2000	2010	2016 [1]	Average annual percent change, 2010–2016
Total Population...	5,595,211	5,988,927	6,093,000	0.1
Percent of total U.S. population	2.0	1.9	1.9	X
Sex				
Male..	2,720,177	2,933,477	2,992,035	0.1
Female..	2,875,034	3,055,450	3,100,965	0.1
Age				
Under 5 years..	269,898	390,237	373,958	-0.3
5 to 19 years...	1,224,274	1,211,174	1,169,708	-0.2
20 to 64 years...	3,245,660	3,549,222	3,571,313	-
65 years and over.......................................	755,379	838,294	978,021	1.0
Median age (years)	36.1	37.9	38.4	0.1
Race and Hispanic Origin				
One race..				
White	4,748,083	5,038,407	5,071,682	-
Black	629,391	700,178	720,905	0.2
American Indian and Alaska Native	25,076	30,595	33,877	0.7
Asian...	61,595	100,213	121,812	1.3
Native Hawaiian or Other Pacific Islander	3,178	7,178	9,117	1.7
Two or more races...	82,061	112,356	135,607	1.3
Hispanic (of any race).....................................	118,592	223,421	250,476	0.8

X = Not applicable.
[1] Population figures for 2016 are July 1 estimates. The 2010 estimates are taken from the 2010 Census.
- = Zero or rounds to zero.

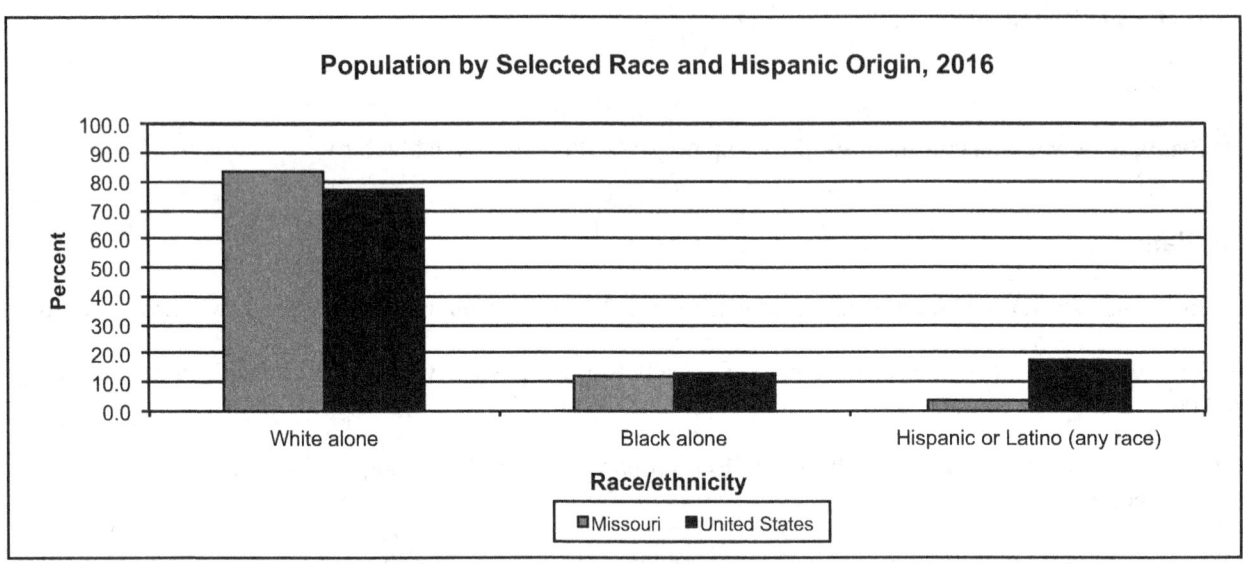

Table MO-2. Marital Status

(Number, percent distribution.)

Sex, age, race, and Hispanic origin	2000	2010	2015
Males, 15 Years and Over	2,114,280	2,332,888	2,395,744
Never married	27.8	32.1	33.5
Now married, except separated...	58.0	52.5	50.6
Separated...	1.6	1.7	1.6
Widowed...	2.6	2.6	2.9
Divorced...	10.0	11.0	11.4
Females, 15 Years and Over	2,300,111	2,492,198	2,535,714
Never married	22.1	26.8	27.8
Now married, except separated...	53.1	48.2	47.1
Separated...	2.0	2.2	2.0
Widowed...	11.3	10.0	9.9
Divorced...	11.5	12.8	13.3

Table MO-3. Households and Housing Characteristics

(Number, percent, dollars.)

Item	2000	2010	2015	Average annual percent change, 2000–2015
Total Households...	2,194,594	2,350,628	2,374,180	0.5
Family households	1,476,516	1,524,078	1,519,299	0.2
Married-couple family................................	1,140,866	1,146,501	1,137,014	-
Other family	335,650	377,577	382,285	0.9
Male householder, no wife present............	81,890	99,807	101,913	1.6
Female householder, no husband present.......	253,760	277,770	280,372	0.7
Nonfamily households	718,078	826,550	854,881	1.3
Householder living alone............................	599,808	689,361	704,910	1.2
Householder not living alone......................	118,270	137,189	149,971	1.8
Housing Characteristics				
Total housing units..	2,442,017	2,714,017	2,746,644	0.8
Occupied housing units	2,194,594	2,350,628	2,374,180	0.5
Owner occupied...	1,542,149	1,621,371	1,570,137	0.1
Renter occupied...	652,445	729,257	804,043	1.5
Average household size.....................................	2.48	2.48	2.49	-
Financial Characteristics				
Median gross rent of renter-occupied housing	484	682	763	3.8
Median monthly owner costs for housing units with a mortgage	861	1,182	1,200	2.6
Median value of owner-occupied housing units	89,900	139,000	147,800	4.3

- = Zero or rounds to zero

Table MO-4. Migration, Origin, and Language

(Number, percent.)

Characteristic	State			U.S.		
	2014	2015	Percent change	2014	2015	Percent change
Residence 1 Year Ago						
Population 1 year and over	5,992,195	6,015,580	0.4	315,095,393	317,635,720	0.8
Same house..	84.1	84.1	X	85.1	85.3	X
Different house in the U.S.	15.5	15.6	X	14.3	14.1	X
Same county..	8.9	8.6	X	8.7	8.5	X
Different county	6.7	7.0	X	5.6	5.6	X
Same state..	4.1	4.3	X	3.3	3.2	X
Different state	2.6	2.6	X	2.3	2.4	X
Abroad...	0.3	0.4	X	0.6	0.7	X
Place of Birth						
Native born...	5,838,467	5,840,911	-	276,465,262	278,128,449	0.6
Male	49.0	49.0	X	49.3	49.3	X
Female	51.0	51.0	X	50.7	50.7	X
Foreign born	225,122	242,761	7.8	42,391,794	43,290,372	2.1
Male	48.4	49.6	X	48.7	48.6	X
Female	51.6	50.4	X	51.3	51.4	X
Foreign born; naturalized U.S. citizen....................	102,996	107,781	4.6	19,984,738	20,697,103	3.6
Male	46	47.0	X	45.9	45.9	X
Female	54	53.0	X	54.1	54.1	X
Foreign born; not a U.S. citizen............................	122,126	134,980	10.5	22,407,056	22,593,269	0.8
Male	50.4	51.6	X	51.2	51.1	X
Female	49.6	48.4	X	48.8	48.9	X
Entered 2010 or later	17.5	23.5	X	12.3	15.6	X
Entered 2000 to 2009	32	31.9	X	28.6	27.9	X
Entered before 2000..	50.5	44.6	X	59.1	56.5	X
World Region of Birth, Foreign						
Foreign-born population, excluding population born at sea	225,122	242,761	7.8	42,390,705	43,289,646	2.1
Europe	18.7	16.2	X	11.2	11.1	X
Asia..	39	39.5	X	30.1	30.6	X
Africa..	8.8	10.0	X	4.6	4.8	X
Oceania...	0.8	0.9	X	0.6	0.6	X
Latin America...	29.9	31.1	X	51.6	51.1	X
North America..	2.8	2.3	X	1.9	1.9	X
Language Spoken at Home and Ability to Speak English						
Population 5 years and over....................................	5,691,365	5,709,302	0.3	299,084,046	301,625,014	0.8
English only	94.4	94.0	X	78.9	78.5	X
Language other than English............................	5.6	6.0	X	21.1	21.5	X
Speaks English less than "very well"..................	1.9	2.1	X	8.6	8.6	X

NA = Not available.
X = Not applicable.
- = Zero or rounds to zero.

Table MO-5. Median Income and Poverty Status, 2015

(Number, percent, except as noted.)

Characteristic	State		U.S.	
	Number	Percent	Number	Percent
Median Income				
Households (dollars)..	50,238	X	55,775	X
Families (dollars)	62,989	X	68,260	X
Below Poverty Level (All People)	875,495	14.8	46,153,077	14.7
Sex				
Male	383,187	13.3	20,599,407	13.4
Female	492,308	16.3	25,553,670	16.0
Age				
Under 18 years...	275,711	20.2	15,000,273	20.7
Related children under 18 years.....................	269,546	19.9	14,693,239	20.4
18 to 64 years..	522,013	14.4	26,960,369	13.9
65 years and over	77,771	8.5	4,192,435	9.0

X = Not applicable.

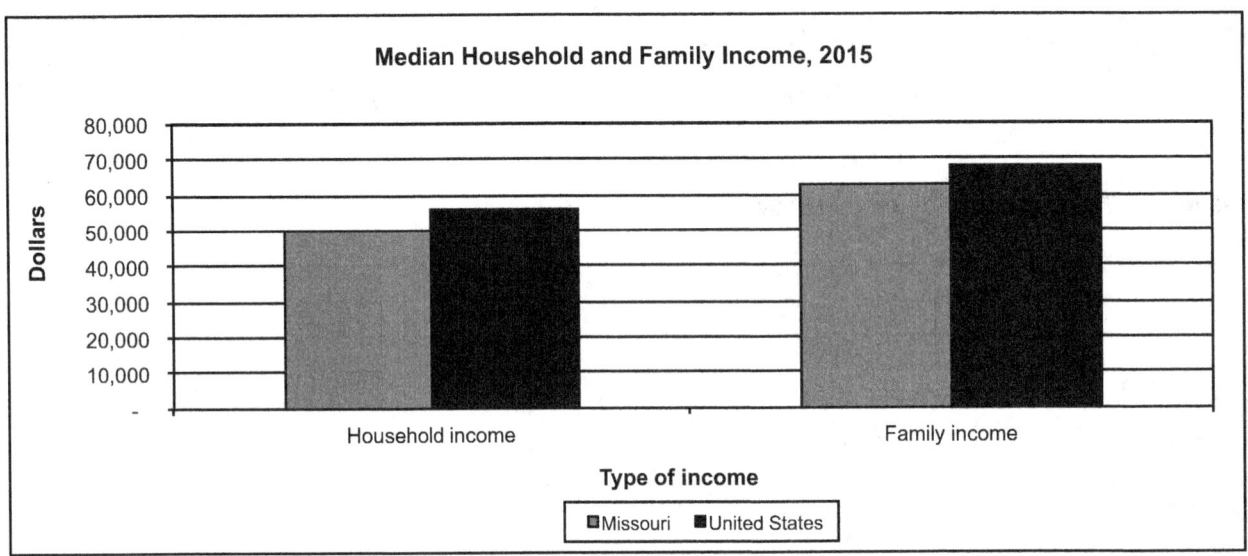

Table MO-6. Health Insurance Coverage Status for the Civilian Noninstitutionalized Population and Children Under 18 Years of Age

(Numbers in thousands, percent.)

Item	2007	2008	2009	2010	2011	2012	2013	2014	2015
Civilian Noninstitutionalized Population	5,791	5,795	5,871	5,880	5,899	5,909	5,931	5,951	5,969
Covered by Private or Public Insurance									
Number..	5,062	5,040	5,098	5,106	5,092	5,108	5,158	5,257	5,386
Percent..	87.4	87.0	86.8	86.8	86.3	86.4	87.0	88.3	90.2
Not Covered									
Number..	729	755	773	774	807	801	773	694	583
Percent..	12.6	13.0	13.2	13.2	13.7	13.6	13.0	11.7	9.8
Percent in the U.S. not covered........................	15.3	15.1	15.1	15.5	15.1	14.8	14.5	11.7	9.4
Children Under 18 Years of Age	1,442	1,418	1,427	1,414	1,409	1,400	1,395	1,388	1,388
Covered by Private or Public Insurance									
Number..	1,291	1,317	1,329	1,326	1,314	1,302	1,297	1,288	1,308
Percent..	89.6	92.9	93.1	93.8	93.3	93.0	93.0	92.8	94.3
Not Covered									
Number..	150	101	98	88	95	98	98	100	80
Percent..	10.4	7.1	6.9	6.2	6.7	7.0	7.0	7.2	5.7
Percent in the U.S. not covered........................	11.0	9.7	8.6	8.0	7.5	7.2	7.1	6.0	4.8

Table MO-7. Employment Status by Demographic Group, 2016

(Numbers in thousands, percent.)

Characteristic	Civilian noninstitutional population	Civilian labor force		Employed		Unemployed	
		Number	Percent of population	Number	Percent of population	Number	Percent of population
Total...	4,774	3,142	65.8	3,002	62.9	140	4.4
Sex							
Male..	2,302	1,640	71.2	1,568	68.1	72	4.4
Female...	2,472	1,502	60.8	1,434	58.0	68	4.5
Race, Sex, and Hispanic Origin							
White...	4,047	2,657	65.7	2,558	63.2	99	3.7
Male..	1,970	1,397	70.9	1,347	68.4	50	3.6
Female...	2,077	1,260	60.7	1,211	58.3	49	3.9
Black or African American....................	526	369	70.1	335	63.8	33	9.0
Male..	236	182	77.1	164	69.5	18	9.9
Female...	290	187	64.5	172	59.2	15	8.2
Hispanic or Latino ethnicity[1]...............	176	123	69.9	115	65.4	8	6.5
Male..	103	73	70.9	68	66.1	5	6.8
Female...	NA	NA	NA	NA	NA	NA	NA
Age							
16 to 19 years.....................................	319	150	47.0	128	40.0	22	14.8
20 to 24 years.....................................	357	291	81.6	268	75.0	24	8.1
25 to 34 years.....................................	815	695	85.3	664	81.5	31	4.4
35 to 44 years.....................................	748	654	87.5	634	84.8	20	3.1
45 to 54 years.....................................	809	651	80.5	630	77.9	20	3.1
55 to 64 years.....................................	769	510	66.3	493	64.1	17	3.4
65 years and over................................	959	191	20.0	186	19.4	6	3.0

NOTE: Data in Table 7 are from the Current Population Survey (CPS) and do not match the estimates in Table 8. See notes and definitions for further information.
[1] May be of any race.

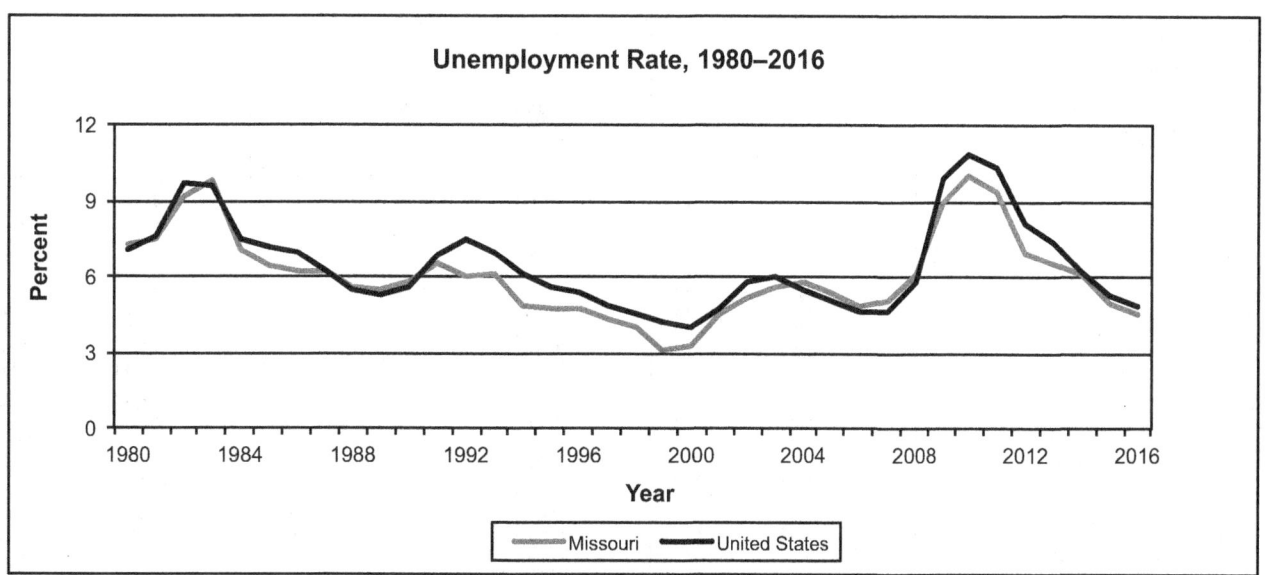

Table MO-8. Employment Status of the Civilian Noninstitutional Population Age 16 Years and Over

(Number, percent.)

Year	Civilian labor force	Civilian participation rate	Employed	Unemployed	Unemployment rate
2008..........................	3,028,857	66.2	2,842,845	186,012	6.1
2009..........................	3,049,563	66.1	2,766,711	282,852	9.3
2010..........................	3,056,484	66.0	2,763,535	292,949	9.6
2011..........................	3,047,786	65.6	2,789,224	258,562	8.5
2012..........................	3,016,161	64.6	2,806,121	210,040	7.0
2013..........................	3,011,601	64.2	2,809,402	202,199	6.7
2014..........................	3,051,812	64.7	2,863,982	187,830	6.2
2015..........................	3,113,760	65.6	2,958,176	155,584	5.0
2016..........................	3,111,517	65.4	2,970,702	140,815	4.5

Table MO-9. Employment and Average Wages by Industry

(Estimates through 2010 are based on the 2007 *North American Industry Classification System* [NAICS]. Estimates from 2011 onward are based on the 2012 NAICS.)

Industry	2009	2010	2011	2012	2013	2014	2015
	Number of jobs						
Wage and Salary Employment by Industry..................	2,790,120	2,740,634	2,746,857	2,780,514	2,810,852	2,837,229	2,887,885
Farm Wage and Salary Employment..........................	8,242	8,829	8,837	9,093	8,677	7,131	9,971
Nonfarm Wage and Salary Employment....................	2,781,878	2,731,805	2,738,020	2,771,421	2,802,175	2,830,098	2,877,914
Private wage and salary employment........................	2,282,190	2,240,686	2,256,882	2,295,033	2,326,343	2,357,466	2,406,875
Forestry, fishing, and related activities.......................	4,688	4,981	5,193	5,345	5,445	5,527	5,505
Mining..	4,134	4,092	4,017	3,977	3,947	3,896	3,927
Utilities..	12,660	12,598	12,342	12,178	12,119	11,960	11,874
Construction	124,503	109,953	106,573	107,737	111,078	113,175	117,334
Manufacturing..	255,588	243,578	246,598	248,802	252,913	256,196	261,615
Durable goods manufacturing............................	146,739	140,283	143,252	144,099	147,841	152,324	157,291
Nondurable goods manufacturing......................	108,849	103,295	103,346	104,703	105,072	103,872	104,324
Wholesale trade	119,186	116,870	116,686	117,932	119,052	121,458	120,921
Retail trade...	305,985	301,596	303,962	305,050	304,313	307,717	314,263
Transportation and warehousing...............................	91,794	86,674	87,879	89,822	92,360	94,359	97,963
Information	62,337	56,220	53,691	52,910	52,592	52,340	50,188
Finance and insurance	122,106	123,768	124,921	128,691	127,917	127,984	128,456
Real estate and rental and leasing............................	38,683	37,059	35,893	35,570	35,129	35,697	36,540
Professional, scientific, and technical services...........	126,291	122,549	125,025	131,529	133,752	137,293	147,048
Management of companies and enterprises..................	59,966	61,608	63,490	60,618	63,607	66,125	65,537
Administrative and waste services	134,519	140,834	147,222	147,489	151,886	155,409	159,635
Educational services	61,530	62,344	63,677	66,101	66,258	66,460	66,803
Health care and social assistance.............................	344,129	348,759	353,844	374,109	381,468	382,617	393,057
Arts, entertainment, and recreation............................	43,699	43,270	41,831	42,200	43,383	43,836	41,814
Accommodation and food services............................	233,031	230,869	230,909	234,248	239,127	244,000	252,497
Other services, except public administration.................	137,361	133,064	133,129	130,725	129,997	131,417	131,898
Government and government enterprises.........................	499,688	491,119	481,138	476,388	475,832	472,632	471,039
	Dollars						
Average Wages and Salaries by Industry	40,780	41,606	42,468	43,689	44,070	45,318	46,582
Average Farm Wages and Salaries	32,975	28,913	29,635	43,328	31,234	49,283	33,201
Average Nonfarm Wages and Salaries	40,803	41,647	42,509	43,690	44,109	45,308	46,628
Average private wages and salaries...........................	41,087	42,027	42,969	44,313	44,707	45,976	47,326
Forestry, fishing, and related activities........................	28,255	27,100	25,296	26,109	26,629	27,229	28,229
Mining..	61,166	59,740	69,748	70,236	68,208	69,630	69,565
Utilities..	77,395	79,462	82,736	83,300	85,828	89,328	91,066
Construction	49,472	49,284	49,632	51,253	51,650	53,421	55,282
Manufacturing..	50,270	51,024	52,096	54,027	54,666	56,871	58,207
Durable goods manufacturing............................	52,455	52,567	54,371	55,507	57,337	59,846	60,443
Nondurable goods manufacturing......................	47,325	48,929	48,942	51,991	50,908	52,510	54,835
Wholesale trade	57,497	58,982	60,352	62,205	62,181	64,513	66,297
Retail trade...	24,936	25,401	25,560	26,246	26,417	26,897	27,822
Transportation and warehousing...............................	42,746	44,020	44,841	46,161	47,194	48,447	49,061
Information	62,295	65,216	68,196	72,441	70,527	71,270	74,798
Finance and insurance	58,954	62,040	65,040	69,142	69,348	71,673	74,985
Real estate and rental and leasing............................	34,270	35,498	36,568	38,759	39,107	40,577	42,917
Professional, scientific, and technical services	67,577	67,988	68,786	71,289	71,063	72,643	76,092
Management of companies and enterprises...................	79,269	89,358	90,863	96,026	97,530	102,871	100,885
Administrative and waste services	30,528	31,376	31,852	32,331	32,893	33,924	34,378
Educational services	31,700	32,086	32,843	34,077	34,968	35,938	36,199
Health care and social assistance.................................	41,227	41,652	42,603	42,519	42,699	43,057	44,546
Arts, entertainment, and recreation............................	35,209	35,694	37,875	38,164	40,048	40,120	42,370
Accommodation and food services............................	16,069	16,560	16,887	17,261	17,540	18,112	19,103
Other services, except public administration.................	27,424	28,259	28,907	30,025	30,695	31,623	33,000
Government and government enterprises.........................	39,502	39,913	40,351	40,688	41,189	41,976	43,060

Table MO-10. Employment Characteristics by Family Type

(Number, percent.)

Family type and labor force status	2013		2014		2015	
	Total	Families with own children under 18 years	Total	Families with own children under 18 years	Total	Families with own children under 18 years
All Families...	1,523,085	645,682	1,503,886	629,862	1,519,299	633,503
FAMILY TYPE AND LABOR FORCE STATUS						
Married-Couple Families..	1,133,983	426,596	1,119,785	417,923	1,137,014	423,324
Both husband and wife in labor force..........................	52.1	68.6	52.1	70.2	52.6	70.9
Husband in labor force, wife not in labor force..........	19.9	25.0	19.2	23.5	19.1	23.4
Wife in labor force, husband not in labor force..........	8.8	3.9	8.9	4.2	8.6	3.9
Both husband and wife not in labor force..................	18.9	2.2	19.8	2.1	19.2	1.5
Other Families	389,102	219,086	384,101	211,939	382,285	210,179
Female householder, no husband present...................	74.1	76.4	73.1	72.8	73.3	74.8
In labor force..	53.9	64.6	50.4	59.4	51.8	62.4
Not in labor force	20.2	11.7	22.7	13.4	21.5	12.4
Male householder, no wife present..........................	25.9	23.6	26.9	27.2	26.7	25.2
In labor force..	19.7	21.4	21.2	24.2	20.3	22.6
Not in labor force	6.2	2.2	5.7	3.0	6.4	2.7

Table MO-11. School Enrollment and Educational Attainment, 2015

(Number, percent.)

Item	State	U.S.
Enrollment		
Total population 3 years and over, enrolled in school	1,511,239	81,618,288
Enrolled in nursery school or preschool (percent).................................	5.9	6.0
Enrolled in kindergarten (percent)...	5.3	5.0
Enrolled in elementary school, grades 1-8 (percent).............................	40.7	40.3
Enrolled in high school, grades 9-12 (percent)	21.0	20.9
Enrolled in college or graduate school (percent)..................................	27.0	27.7
Attainment		
Total population 25 years and over	4,097,212	216,447,163
Less than ninth grade (percent)..	3.6	5.5
9th to 12th grade, no diploma (percent)	7.5	7.3
High school graduate, including equivalency (percent).........................	31.0	27.6
Some college, no degree (percent)...	22.4	20.7
Associate's degree (percent)	7.7	8.2
Bachelor's degree (percent)	17.3	19.0
Graduate or professional degree (percent)...	10.6	11.6
High school graduate or higher (percent)	88.9	87.1
Bachelor's degree or higher (percent)	27.8	30.6

Table MO-12. Public School Characteristics and Educational Indicators

(Number, percent; data derived from National Center of Education Statistics.)

Item	State	U.S.
Public Schools, 2014–2015 (except where noted)		
Number of school districts...	567	18,260
Number of schools..	2,414	98,373
Number of students..	917,785	50,312,581
Number of teachers	67,356	3,132,351
Student-teacher ratio..	13.6	16.1
Expenditures per student (dollars), FY 2014..	9,938	11,066
Four-year adjusted cohort graduation rate (ACGR)[1,2]	87.8	83.2
Students eligible for free or reduced-price lunch (percent)	51.3	51.8
English language learners (percent)...	3.0	9.4
Students age 3 to 21 served under IDEA, part B (percent).....................	13.6	13.0

Public Schools by Type	Number	Percent of state public schools
Total number of schools...	2,414	100.0
Regular	2,235	92.6
Special education..	53	2.2
Vocational education..	64	2.7
Alternative education...	62	2.6

NOTE: Every school is assigned only one school type based on its instructional emphasis.
[1] ACGR data represents a new method of calculating high-school completion rates and may not be comparable to previous years' data for Averaged Freshmen Graduation Rates (AFGR).
[2] The United States 4-year ACGRs were estimated using both the reported 4-year ACGR data from 49 states and the District of Columbia and using imputed data for Idaho. The estimate for American Indian/Alaska Native students also includes imputed data for Virginia.

Table MO-13. Reported Voting and Registration of the Voting-Age Population, November 2016

(Numbers in thousands, percent.)

Item	Total population	Total citizen population	Registered			Voted		
			Total registered	Percent registered (total population)	Percent registered (total citizen population)	Total voted	Percent voted (total population)	Percent voted (total citizen population)
U.S. Total	245,502	224,059	157,596	64.2	70.3	137,537	56.0	61.4
State Total.............................	4,626	4,486	3,333	72.1	74.3	2,906	62.8	64.8
Sex								
Male	2,231	2,159	1,534	68.8	71.1	1,328	59.5	61.5
Female	2,395	2,328	1,799	75.1	77.3	1,577	65.9	67.8
Race								
White alone.............................	3,957	3,860	2,886	72.9	74.8	2,529	63.9	65.5
White, non-Hispanic alone	3,808	3,779	2,832	74.4	75.0	2,485	65.2	65.8
Black alone.............................	491	491	385	78.4	78.4	325	66.2	66.2
Asian alone	77	34	21	(B)	(B)	21	(B)	(B)
Hispanic (of any race)	160	93	59	(B)	(B)	50	(B)	(B)
White alone or in combination	4,015	3,919	2,898	72.2	73.9	2,538	63.2	64.8
Black alone or in combination..........	532	532	414	77.9	77.9	348	65.5	65.5
Asian alone or in combination..........	81	38	25	(B)	(B)	25	(B)	(B)
Age								
18 to 24 years.............................	565	540	326	57.7	60.4	259	45.9	48.0
25 to 34 years.............................	757	734	497	65.6	67.7	404	53.4	55.1
35 to 44 years.............................	753	692	473	62.9	68.4	418	55.5	60.4
45 to 64 years.............................	1,537	1,519	1,184	77.0	77.9	1,065	69.3	70.1
65 years and over	1,013	1,002	854	84.2	85.2	759	74.9	75.8

B = Base is less than 75,000 and therefore too small to show the derived measure.

Table MO-14. Crime

(Number, rate per 100,000. Data are derived from the FBI Uniform Crime Reports.)

Item	State			U.S. [1,2,3,4]		
	2014	2015	Percent change	2014	2015	Percent change
TOTAL POPULATION[5]	6,063,827	6,083,672	0.3	318,907,401	321,418,820	0.8
VIOLENT CRIME						
Number....................................	26,882	30,261	12.6	1,186,185	1,231,566	3.8
Rate	443.3	497.4	12.2	372.0	383.2	3.0
Murder and Nonnegligent Manslaughter						
Number....................................	404	502	24.3	14,164	15,696	10.8
Rate	6.7	8.3	23.9	4.4	4.9	10.0
Rape[6]						
Number....................................	2,403	2,553	6.2	118,027	124,047	5.1
Rate	39.6	42.0	5.9	37.0	38.6	4.3
Robbery						
Number....................................	5,592	6,376	14.0	322,905	327,374	1.4
Rate	92.2	104.8	13.6	101.3	101.9	0.6
Aggravated Assault						
Number....................................	18,483	20,830	12.7	731,089	764,449	4.6
Rate	304.8	342.4	12.3	229.2	237.8	3.7
PROPERTY CRIME						
Number....................................	176,436	173,642	-1.6	8,209,010	7,993,631	-2.6
Rate	2,909.6	2,854.2	-1.9	2,574.1	2,487.0	-3.4
Burglary						
Number....................................	35,293	34,006	-3.6	1,713,153	1,579,527	-7.8
Rate	582.0	559.0	-4.0	537.2	491.4	-8.5
Larceny-Theft						
Number....................................	124,769	122,637	-1.7	5,809,054	5,706,346	-1.8
Rate	2,057.6	2,015.8	-2.0	1,821.5	1,775.4	-2.5
Motor Vehicle Theft						
Number....................................	16,374	16,999	3.8	686,803	707,758	3.1
Rate	270.0	279.4	3.5	215.4	220.2	2.2

NOTE: Although arson data are included in the trend and clearance tables, sufficient data are not available to estimate totals for this offense. Therefore, no arson data are published in this table.

X = Not applicable.

- = Zero or rounds to zero.

[1] The crime figures have been adjusted.

[2] The data collection methodology for the offense of forcible rape used by the Minnesota state Uniform Crime Reporting (UCR) Program (with the exception of Minneapolis and St. Paul, Minnesota) does not comply with national UCR Program guidelines. Consequently, its figures for forcible rape and violent crime (of which forcible rape is a part) are not published in this table.

[3] Includes offenses reported by the Zoological Police and the Metro Transit Police.

[4] Because of changes in the state's reporting practices, figures are not comparable to previous years' data.

[5] Populations are U.S. Census Bureau provisional estimates as of July 1 of each year.

[6] The figures shown for the offense of rape were estimated using the revised Uniform Crime Reporting (UCR) definition of rape.

Table MO-15. State Government Finances, 2015

(Dollar amounts in thousands, percent distribution.)

Item	Dollars	Percent distribution
Total Revenue	34,610,377	100.0
General revenue	28,038,945	81.0
Intergovernmental revenue	10,736,241	31.0
Taxes	11,956,143	34.5
General sales	3,380,034	9.8
Selective sales	1,704,177	4.9
License taxes	547,993	1.6
Individual income tax	5,856,131	16.9
Corporate income tax	425,776	1.2
Other taxes	42,032	0.1
Current charges	2,914,544	8.4
Miscellaneous general revenue	2,432,017	7.0
Utility revenue	0	-
Liquor stores revenue	0	-
Insurance trust revenue[1]	6,571,432	19.0
Total Expenditure	32,468,396	100.0
Intergovernmental expenditure	5,987,018	18.4
Direct expenditure	26,481,378	81.6
Current operation	18,613,167	57.3
Capital outlay	1,364,116	4.2
Insurance benefits and repayments	5,112,644	15.7
Assistance and subsidies	615,372	1.9
Interest on debt	776,079	2.4
Exhibit: Salaries and wages	3,885,344	12.0
Total Expenditure	32,468,396	100.0
General expenditure	27,355,752	84.3
Intergovernmental expenditure	5,987,018	18.4
Direct expenditure	21,368,734	65.8
General expenditure, by function:		
Education	9,629,687	29.7
Public welfare	8,399,342	25.9
Hospitals	1,795,171	5.5
Health	1,740,525	5.4
Highways	1,470,145	4.5
Police protection	232,679	0.7
Correction	812,003	2.5
Natural resources	295,526	0.9
Parks and recreation	59,137	0.2
Governmental administration	530,179	1.6
Interest on general debt	776,079	2.4
Other and unallocable	1,615,279	5.0
Utility expenditure	0	-
Liquor stores expenditure	0	-
Insurance trust expenditure	5,112,644	15.7
Debt at End of Fiscal Year	19,350,325	X
Cash and Security Holdings	75,049,226	X

X = Not applicable.
- = Zero or rounds to zero.
[1] Within insurance trust revenue, net earnings of state retirement systems is a calculated statistic (the item code in the data file is X08), and thus can be positive or negative. Net earnings is the sum of earnings on investments plus gains on investments minus losses on investments. The change made in 2002 for asset valuation from book to market value in accordance with Statement 34 of the Governmental Accounting Standards Board is reflected in the calculated statistics.

Table MO-16. State Government Tax Collections, 2016

(Dollars in thousands, percent.)

Item	Dollars	Percent distribution
Total Taxes	12,245,169	100.0
Property taxes	30,892	0.3
Sales and gross receipts	5,302,264	43.3
General sales and gross receipts	3,536,396	28.9
Selective sales and gross receipts	1,765,868	14.4
Alcoholic beverages	36,849	0.3
Amusements	367,814	3.0
Insurance premiums	400,734	3.3
Motor fuels	717,178	5.9
Pari-mutuels	0	-
Public utilities	0	-
Tobacco products	101,944	0.8
Other selective sales	141,349	1.2
Licenses	547,326	4.5
Alcoholic beverages	5,359	-
Amusements	1,799	-
Corporations in general	13,430	0.1
Hunting and fishing	34,369	0.3
Motor vehicle	289,124	2.4
Motor vehicle operators	17,356	0.1
Public utilities	19,842	0.2
Occupation and business, NEC	143,496	1.2
Other licenses	22,551	0.2
Income taxes	6,352,437	51.9
Individual income	6,023,701	49.2
Corporation net income	328,736	2.7
Other taxes	12,250	0.1
Death and gift	56	-
Documentary and stock transfer	12,102	0.1
Severance	9	-
Taxes, NEC	83	-

- = Zero or rounds to zero.

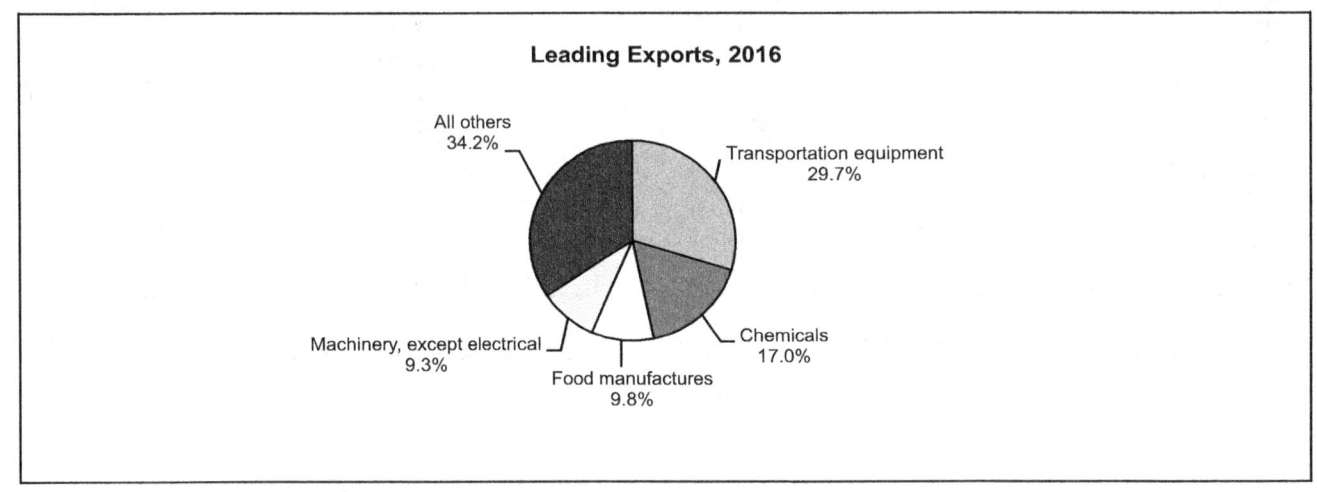

Leading Exports, 2016

All others 34.2%

Transportation equipment 29.7%

Chemicals 17.0%

Food manufactures 9.8%

Machinery, except electrical 9.3%

MONTANA

Facts and Figures

Location: Northwestern United States; bordered on the N by Canada (British Columbia, Alberta, and Saskatchewan), on the E by North Dakota and South Dakota, on the S by Idaho and Wyoming, and on the W by Idaho

Area: 147,042 sq. mi. (380,838 sq. km.); rank—4th

Population: 1,042,520 (2016 est.); rank—44th

Principal Cities: capital—Helena; largest—Billings

Statehood: November 8, 1889; 41st state

U.S. Congress: 2 senators, 1 representative

State Motto: *Oro y plata* ("Gold and silver")

State Song: "Montana"

State Nicknames: The Treasure State; Big Sky Country

Abbreviations: MT; Mont.

State Symbols: flower—bitterroot; tree—ponderosa pine; bird—Western meadowlark

At a Glance

- With an increase in population of 5.4 percent, Montana ranked 17th among the states in growth from 2010 to 2016.

- Montana had the second highest rate of traffic fatalities in 2015, with 1.81 deaths per 100 million vehicle miles.

- In 2016, 17.7 percent of Montana residents were in the 65 and older age group, a percentage that ranked 5th in the country.

- Approximately 0.6 percent of Montana residents self-identified as "Black or African-American alone" in 2016, which was the lowest percentage among all the states.

Table MT-1. Population by Age, Sex, Race, and Hispanic Origin

(Number, percent, except where noted.)

Sex, age, race, and Hispanic origin	2000	2010	2016 [1]	Average annual percent change, 2010–2016
Total Population...	902,195	989,415	1,042,520	0.3
Percent of total U.S. population	0.3	0.3	0.3	X
Sex				
Male..	449,480	496,667	524,775	0.4
Female..	452,715	492,748	517,745	0.3
Age				
Under 5 years...	54,869	62,423	63,029	0.1
5 to 19 years...	202,571	188,613	190,474	0.1
20 to 64 years..	523,806	591,637	603,977	0.1
65 years and over...	120,949	146,742	185,040	1.6
Median age (years)	37.5	39.8	39.8	-
Race and Hispanic Origin				
One race..				
White	817,229	891,529	929,802	0.3
Black...	2,692	4,215	6,034	2.7
American Indian and Alaska Native	56,068	63,495	69,073	0.5
Asian...	4,691	6,379	8,486	2.1
Native Hawaiian or Other Pacific Islander	470	734	931	1.7
Two or more races	15,730	23,063	28,194	1.4
Hispanic (of any race)......................................	18,081	31,018	37,840	1.4

X = Not applicable.
[1] Population figures for 2016 are July 1 estimates. The 2010 estimates are taken from the 2010 Census.
- = Zero or rounds to zero.

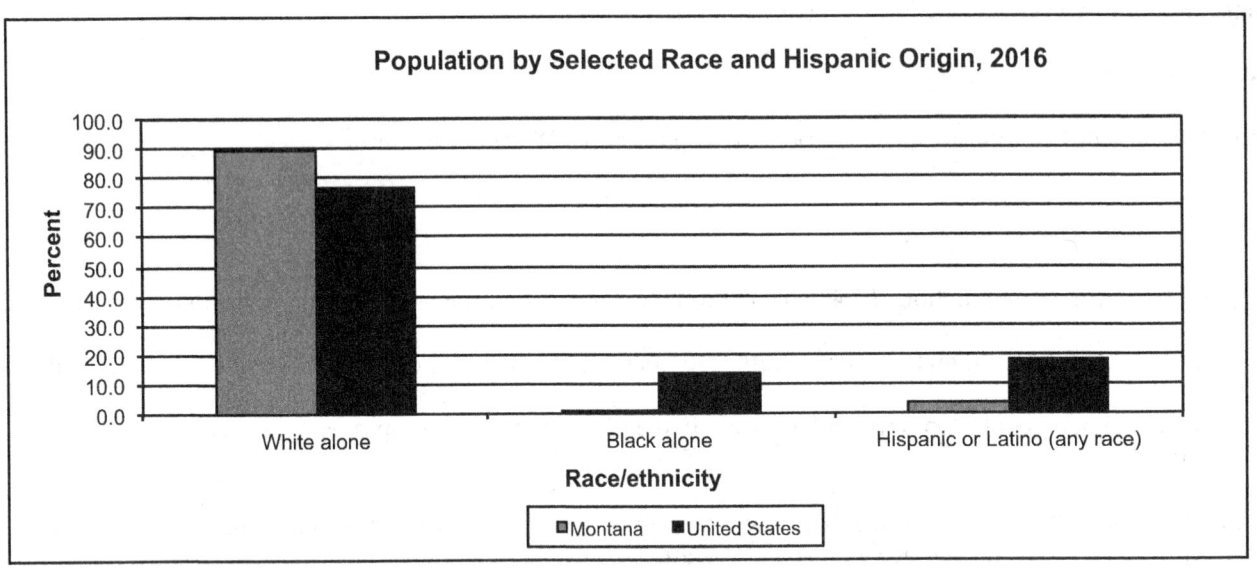

Population by Selected Race and Hispanic Origin, 2016

Table MT-2. Marital Status

(Number, percent distribution.)

Sex, age, race, and Hispanic origin	2000	2010	2015
Males, 15 Years and Over	353,801	404,179	423,623
Never married	27.7	30.5	33.3
Now married, except separated..............................	58.3	53.4	50.6
Separated..	1.2	1.5	1.2
Widowed...	2.6	2.3	3.2
Divorced...	10.2	12.4	11.7
Females, 15 Years and Over	362,114	403,766	420,815
Never married	20.4	23.5	25.0
Now married, except separated..............................	56.3	52.9	50.7
Separated..	1.3	1.6	1.1
Widowed...	10.4	9.7	8.9
Divorced...	11.6	12.3	14.2

Table MT-3. Households and Housing Characteristics

(Number, percent, dollars.)

Item	2000	2010	2015	Average annual percent change, 2000–2015
Total Households...	358,667	402,747	414,804	1.0
Family households...	237,407	255,199	253,101	0.4
Married-couple family...	192,067	203,500	202,848	0.4
Other family...	45,340	51,699	50,253	0.7
Male householder, no wife present.................	13,324	16,926	15,601	1.1
Female householder, no husband present.........	32,016	34,773	34,652	0.5
Nonfamily households...	121,260	147,548	161,703	2.2
Householder living alone.....................................	98,422	119,762	130,665	2.2
Householder not living alone.............................	22,838	27,786	31,038	2.4
Housing Characteristics				
Total housing units...	412,633	483,006	494,222	1.3
Occupied housing units	358,667	402,747	414,804	1.0
Owner occupied...	247,723	280,633	276,490	0.8
Renter occupied...	110,944	122,114	138,314	1.6
Average household size..	2.45	2.39	2.42	-0.1
Financial Characteristics				
Median gross rent of renter-occupied housing	447	642	763	4.7
Median monthly owner costs for housing units with a mortgage	863	1,217	1,316	3.5
Median value of owner-occupied housing units...........................	99,500	181,200	209,500	7.4

Table MT-4. Migration, Origin, and Language

(Number, percent.)

Characteristic	State			U.S.		
	2014	2015	Percent change	2014	2015	Percent change
Residence 1 Year Ago						
Population 1 year and over	1,012,169	1,019,646	0.7	315,095,393	317,635,720	0.8
Same house	83.5	83.9	X	85.1	85.3	X
Different house in the U.S.	16.2	15.8	X	14.3	14.1	X
Same county	8.9	8.3	X	8.7	8.5	X
Different county	7.3	7.5	X	5.6	5.6	X
Same state	3.6	3.3	X	3.3	3.2	X
Different state	3.7	4.2	X	2.3	2.4	X
Abroad	0.3	0.3	X	0.6	0.7	X
Place of Birth						
Native born	999,697	1,011,593	1.2	276,465,262	278,128,449	0.6
Male	50.3	50.4	X	49.3	49.3	X
Female	49.7	49.6	X	50.7	50.7	X
Foreign born	23,882	21,356	-10.6	42,391,794	43,290,372	2.1
Male	42.4	44.8	X	48.7	48.6	X
Female	57.6	55.2	X	51.3	51.4	X
Foreign born; naturalized U.S. citizen.................	11,410	11,373	-0.3	19,984,738	20,697,103	3.6
Male	41.7	40.7	X	45.9	45.9	X
Female	58.3	59.3	X	54.1	54.1	X
Foreign born; not a U.S. citizen.................	12,472	9,983	-20.0	22,407,056	22,593,269	0.8
Male	43.0	49.5	X	51.2	51.1	X
Female	57.0	50.5	X	48.8	48.9	X
Entered 2010 or later	15.7	21.1	X	12.3	15.6	X
Entered 2000 to 2009	23.6	19.1	X	28.6	27.9	X
Entered before 2000...........................	60.7	59.8	X	59.1	56.5	X
World Region of Birth, Foreign						
Foreign-born population, excluding population born at sea	23,882	21,356	-10.6	42,390,705	43,289,646	2.1
Europe	27.6	22.8	X	11.2	11.1	X
Asia...	27.9	25.9	X	30.1	30.6	X
Africa	2.9	4.4	X	4.6	4.8	X
Oceania	1.3	2.3	X	0.6	0.6	X
Latin America..................................	23.1	21.7	X	51.6	51.1	X
North America..................................	17.1	22.9	X	1.9	1.9	X
Language Spoken at Home and Ability to Speak English						
Population 5 years and over...........................	963,804	972,529	0.9	299,084,046	301,625,014	0.8
English only	96.1	95.8	X	78.9	78.5	X
Language other than English...........................	3.9	4.2	X	21.1	21.5	X
Speaks English less than "very well"..........	0.8	0.9	X	8.6	8.6	X

NA = Not available.
X = Not applicable.
- = Zero or rounds to zero.

Table MT-5. Median Income and Poverty Status, 2015

(Number, percent, except as noted.)

Characteristic	State		U.S.	
	Number	Percent	Number	Percent
Median Income				
Households (dollars)..............................	49,509	X	55,775	X
Families (dollars)	64,061	X	68,260	X
Below Poverty Level (All People)	147,287	14.6	46,153,077	14.7
Sex				
Male	69,482	13.8	20,599,407	13.4
Female	77,805	15.5	25,553,670	16.0
Age				
Under 18 years................................	42,837	19.4	15,000,273	20.7
Related children under 18 years.........	41,479	18.9	14,693,239	20.4
18 to 64 years.................................	91,157	14.9	26,960,369	13.9
65 years and over	13,293	7.6	4,192,435	9.0

X = Not applicable.

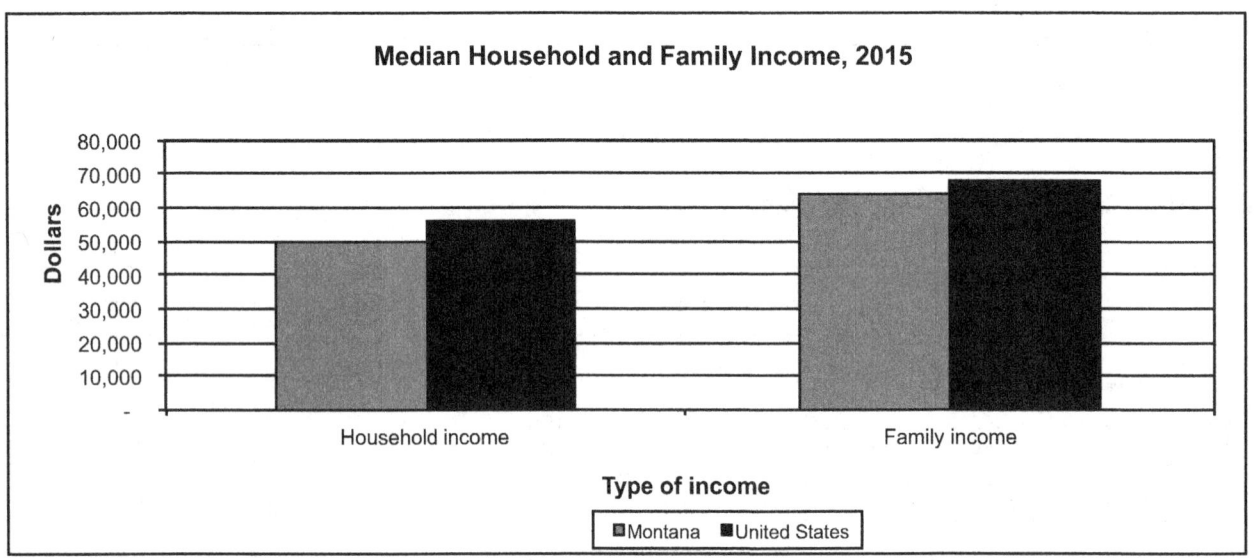

Median Household and Family Income, 2015

Table MT-6. Health Insurance Coverage Status for the Civilian Noninstitutionalized Population and Children Under 18 Years of Age

(Numbers in thousands, percent.)

Item	2007	2008	2009	2010	2011	2012	2013	2014	2015
Civilian Noninstitutionalized Population	939	950	958	976	983	990	999	1,008	1,017
Covered by Private or Public Insurance									
Number...	772	775	783	807	804	811	835	865	899
Percent...	84.4	81.6	81.8	82.7	81.7	82.0	83.5	85.8	88.4
Not Covered									
Number...	146	175	174	169	180	179	165	143	119
Percent...	15.6	18.4	18.2	17.3	18.3	18.0	16.5	14.2	11.6
Percent in the U.S. not covered.................	15.3	15.1	15.1	15.5	15.1	14.8	14.5	11.7	9.4
Children Under 18 Years of Age	219	222	220	221	222	219	223	224	225
Covered by Private or Public Insurance									
Number...	191	190	192	193	196	195	201	206	208
Percent...	85.5	85.6	87.1	87.6	88.5	88.9	89.9	91.8	92.4
Not Covered									
Number...	28	32	28	28	26	24	22	18	17
Percent...	12.6	14.4	12.9	12.4	11.5	11.1	10.1	8.2	7.6
Percent in the U.S. not covered.................	11.0	9.7	8.6	8.0	7.5	7.2	7.1	6.0	4.8

Table MT-7. Employment Status by Demographic Group, 2016

(Numbers in thousands, percent.)

Characteristic	Civilian noninstitutional population	Civilian labor force		Employed		Unemployed	
		Number	Percent of population	Number	Percent of population	Number	Percent of population
Total...	823	522	63.4	500	60.7	22	4.2
Sex							
Male..	411	277	67.5	264	64.3	13	4.6
Female.......................................	413	245	59.3	236	57.1	9	3.8
Race, Sex, and Hispanic Origin							
White...	764	484	63.3	464	60.8	19	4.0
Male......................................	382	257	67.4	246	64.5	11	4.3
Female...................................	382	226	59.2	218	57.1	8	3.6
Black or African American................	NA	NA	NA	NA	NA	NA	NA
Male......................................	NA	NA	NA	NA	NA	NA	NA
Female...................................	NA	NA	NA	NA	NA	NA	NA
Hispanic or Latino ethnicity[1].............	22	16	71.4	15	67.3	1	6.2
Male......................................	NA	NA	NA	NA	NA	NA	NA
Female...................................	NA	NA	NA	NA	NA	NA	NA
Age							
16 to 19 years.............................	52	25	48.1	22	42.8	3	11.1
20 to 24 years.............................	71	51	71.8	47	66.2	4	7.8
25 to 34 years.............................	133	112	84.6	107	80.8	5	4.5
35 to 44 years.............................	114	100	87.6	97	85.0	3	2.9
45 to 54 years.............................	122	98	80.6	95	77.8	3	3.5
55 to 64 years.............................	152	101	66.1	98	64.3	3	2.9
65 years and over	180	35	19.5	34	18.9	1	3.1

NOTE: Data in Table 7 are from the Current Population Survey (CPS) and do not match the estimates in Table 8. See notes and definitions for further information.
[1] May be of any race.
NA = Not available.

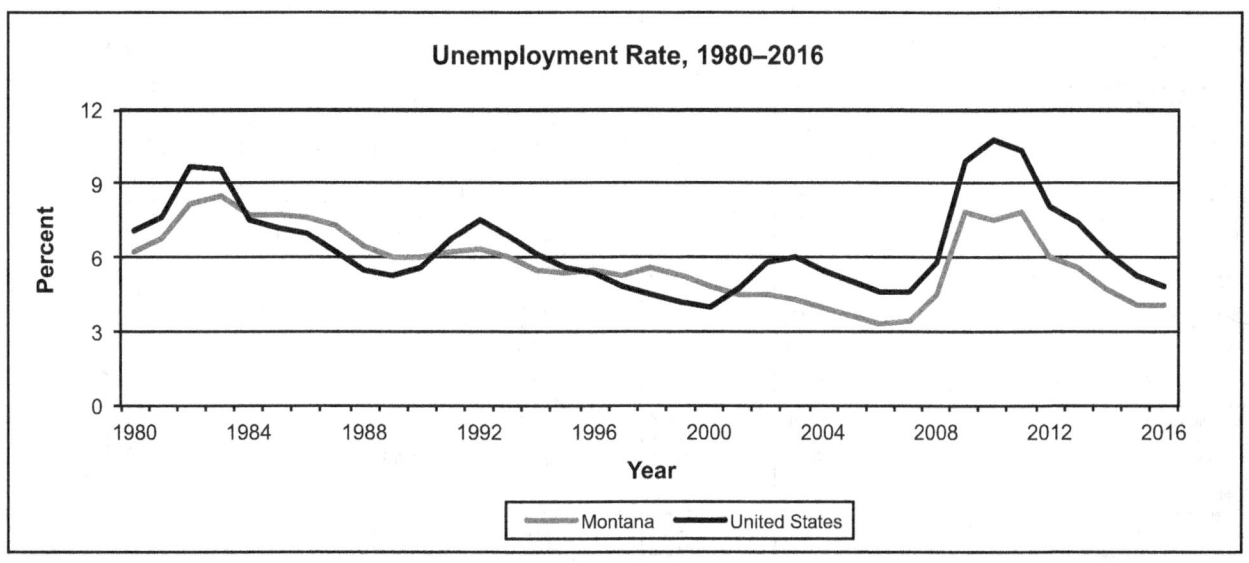

Table MT-8. Employment Status of the Civilian Noninstitutional Population Age 16 Years and Over

(Number, percent.)

Year	Civilian labor force	Civilian participation rate	Employed	Unemployed	Unemployment rate
2008...	509,163	67.0	483,347	25,816	5.1
2009...	501,014	65.3	466,713	34,301	6.8
2010...	500,525	64.4	463,998	36,527	7.3
2011...	501,225	63.9	466,403	34,822	6.9
2012...	506,446	63.9	476,115	30,331	6.0
2013...	513,255	64.1	485,456	27,799	5.4
2014...	515,947	63.9	491,938	24,009	4.7
2015...	522,727	64.0	501,186	21,541	4.1
2016...	526,404	63.9	504,573	21,831	4.1

Table MT-9. Employment and Average Wages by Industry

(Estimates through 2010 are based on the 2007 *North American Industry Classification System* [NAICS]. Estimates from 2011 onward are based on the 2012 NAICS.)

Industry	2009	2010	2011	2012	2013	2014	2015
	Number of jobs						
Wage and Salary Employment by Industry..................	452,084	447,718	451,920	460,613	467,095	470,632	479,586
Farm Wage and Salary Employment..........................	4,706	4,761	5,488	6,667	6,626	6,407	6,868
Nonfarm Wage and Salary Employment....................	447,378	442,957	446,432	453,946	460,469	464,225	472,718
Private wage and salary employment........................	351,326	345,850	350,399	358,791	365,367	368,908	376,992
Forestry, fishing, and related activities.....................	2,817	3,047	3,198	3,469	3,582	3,667	3,781
Mining..	6,489	6,831	7,558	8,719	8,828	8,522	7,564
Utilities...	3,067	3,046	3,116	3,197	3,179	3,157	3,080
Construction	25,111	23,500	23,437	23,752	24,790	25,661	27,153
Manufacturing..	17,333	16,331	16,849	17,576	18,353	18,902	19,139
Durable goods manufacturing..........................	10,020	9,394	9,743	10,621	11,113	11,557	11,718
Nondurable goods manufacturing.....................	7,313	6,937	7,106	6,955	7,240	7,345	7,421
Wholesale trade	16,125	15,727	15,713	16,330	17,131	17,017	17,627
Retail trade...	56,580	55,155	55,267	55,772	56,437	57,768	59,179
Transportation and warehousing........................	13,334	13,202	13,824	14,584	15,145	15,472	15,551
Information	7,474	7,397	7,227	6,942	6,907	6,417	6,365
Finance and insurance	16,570	16,201	16,263	15,701	15,947	16,064	16,180
Real estate and rental and leasing......................	5,622	5,304	5,234	5,250	5,399	5,413	5,706
Professional, scientific, and technical services	18,845	18,824	19,207	19,693	20,215	20,303	20,981
Management of companies and enterprises.................	1,570	1,695	2,009	2,057	1,973	1,962	2,067
Administrative and waste services	18,017	18,347	19,241	19,695	17,743	17,324	17,539
Educational services	5,308	5,363	5,540	5,687	5,920	6,049	6,234
Health care and social assistance.......................	59,204	59,951	59,953	62,082	63,385	64,032	65,183
Arts, entertainment, and recreation.....................	11,418	10,924	10,837	10,860	11,286	11,300	11,606
Accommodation and food services......................	45,968	45,094	45,957	47,431	49,028	49,372	51,388
Other services, except public administration.................	20,474	19,911	19,969	19,994	20,119	20,506	20,669
Government and government enterprises..........................	96,052	97,107	96,033	95,155	95,102	95,317	95,726
	Dollars						
Average Wages and Salaries by Industry	33,776	34,673	35,824	37,172	37,741	39,059	40,182
Average Farm Wages and Salaries	40,551	35,252	30,896	35,054	39,815	39,672	35,137
Average Nonfarm Wages and Salaries	33,705	34,667	35,884	37,203	37,711	39,051	40,255
Average private wages and salaries.......................	32,497	33,638	35,005	36,507	37,092	38,547	39,767
Forestry, fishing, and related activities.....................	26,529	26,362	27,187	28,548	29,435	31,059	33,315
Mining..	70,346	74,685	80,433	81,978	83,471	88,364	87,606
Utilities...	73,954	74,989	78,160	76,655	78,669	81,119	87,494
Construction	39,359	40,857	42,736	43,855	44,789	46,109	47,823
Manufacturing..	41,192	42,591	42,598	43,491	43,699	45,753	47,227
Durable goods manufacturing..........................	38,115	39,384	39,952	41,802	42,915	44,100	45,708
Nondurable goods manufacturing.....................	45,407	46,934	46,225	46,072	44,903	48,355	49,624
Wholesale trade	44,505	45,199	47,891	49,855	50,793	53,231	54,829
Retail trade...	23,482	24,210	24,685	25,341	25,851	26,870	27,684
Transportation and warehousing........................	41,826	43,784	46,810	48,339	49,394	51,574	51,354
Information	40,026	41,648	41,895	43,036	44,059	45,714	48,494
Finance and insurance	47,062	48,890	49,814	53,656	55,558	57,617	60,156
Real estate and rental and leasing......................	25,339	26,575	28,437	30,579	30,460	32,234	34,490
Professional, scientific, and technical services	48,016	49,657	51,753	57,585	54,414	57,885	59,337
Management of companies and enterprises.................	59,891	58,056	59,506	68,618	73,094	71,992	75,757
Administrative and waste services	25,585	27,095	27,847	29,310	28,769	30,154	32,092
Educational services	20,537	20,497	22,009	21,708	22,014	22,702	22,924
Health care and social assistance.......................	36,817	37,705	39,153	39,963	41,055	42,111	44,362
Arts, entertainment, and recreation.....................	19,233	19,450	20,234	20,298	21,066	22,690	23,290
Accommodation and food services......................	14,744	15,304	16,043	16,788	17,288	18,170	18,985
Other services, except public administration.................	23,714	24,646	25,399	26,287	26,992	27,969	29,237
Government and government enterprises..........................	38,121	38,329	39,093	39,827	40,090	41,003	42,177

Table MT-10. Employment Characteristics by Family Type

(Number, percent.)

Family type and labor force status	2013		2014		2015	
	Total	Families with own children under 18 years	Total	Families with own children under 18 years	Total	Families with own children under 18 years
All Families..	256,091	104,971	250,636	99,341	253,101	99,864
FAMILY TYPE AND LABOR FORCE STATUS						
Married-Couple Families.............................	199,251	70,607	198,955	69,152	202,848	70,742
Both husband and wife in labor force...............	51.6	67.2	52.5	69.9	51.2	68.1
Husband in labor force, wife not in labor force	20.2	27.1	19.2	24.9	19.5	25.3
Wife in labor force, husband not in labor force	8.6	3.5	8.0	3.1	8.8	3.8
Both husband and wife not in labor force...............	19.4	2.0	20.3	2.1	20.2	2.6
Other Families	56,840	34,364	51,681	30,189	50,253	29,122
Female householder, no husband present........................	66.6	69.5	65.5	63.2	69.0	68.5
In labor force..	50.9	56.6	46.0	50.2	46.4	53.0
Not in labor force	15.7	12.9	19.6	13.0	22.5	15.5
Male householder, no wife present..........................	33.4	30.5	34.5	36.8	31.0	31.5
In labor force..	26.3	27.3	29.0	34.8	23.6	27.6
Not in labor force	7.0	3.2	5.5	2.0	7.4	3.9

Table MT-11. School Enrollment and Educational Attainment, 2015

(Number, percent.)

Item	State	U.S.
Enrollment		
Total population 3 years and over, enrolled in school	233,966	81,618,288
Enrolled in nursery school or preschool (percent).................................	5.3	6.0
Enrolled in kindergarten (percent)..	5.6	5.0
Enrolled in elementary school, grades 1-8 (percent)............................	42.9	40.3
Enrolled in high school, grades 9-12 (percent)................................	20.9	20.9
Enrolled in college or graduate school (percent)...............................	25.4	27.7
Attainment		
Total population 25 years and over	706,329	216,447,163
Less than ninth grade (percent)	2.0	5.5
9th to 12th grade, no diploma (percent)	4.4	7.3
High school graduate, including equivalency (percent).........................	31.5	27.6
Some college, no degree (percent)	22.8	20.7
Associate's degree (percent)	8.6	8.2
Bachelor's degree (percent)	20.4	19.0
Graduate or professional degree (percent).....................................	10.2	11.6
High school graduate or higher (percent)	93.5	87.1
Bachelor's degree or higher (percent)..	30.6	30.6

Table MT-12. Public School Characteristics and Educational Indicators

(Number, percent; data derived from National Center of Education Statistics.)

Item	State	U.S.
Public Schools, 2014–2015 (except where noted)		
Number of school districts..	492	18,260
Number of schools..	824	98,373
Number of students..	144,532	50,312,581
Number of teachers	10,234	3,132,351
Student-teacher ratio	14.1	16.1
Expenditures per student (dollars), FY 2014.....................................	10,941	11,066
Four-year adjusted cohort graduation rate (ACGR)[1,2]	86.0	83.2
Students eligible for free or reduced-price lunch (percent)	43.6	51.8
English language learners (percent)...	2.3	9.4
Students age 3 to 21 served under IDEA, part B (percent).......................	11.8	13.0

Public Schools by Type	Number	Percent of state public schools
Total number of schools..	824	100.0
Regular	818	99.3
Special education..	2	0.2
Vocational education..	0	-
Alternative education..	4	0.5

NOTE: Every school is assigned only one school type based on its instructional emphasis.
[1] ACGR data represents a new method of calculating high-school completion rates and may not be comparable to previous years' data for Averaged Freshmen Graduation Rates (AFGR).
[2] The United States 4-year ACGRs were estimated using both the reported 4-year ACGR data from 49 states and the District of Columbia and using imputed data for Idaho. The estimate for American Indian/Alaska Native students also includes imputed data for Virginia.
- =Zero or rounds to zero.

Table MT-13. Reported Voting and Registration of the Voting-Age Population, November 2016

(Numbers in thousands, percent.)

Item	Total population	Total citizen population	Registered			Voted		
			Total registered	Percent registered (total population)	Percent registered (total citizen population)	Total voted	Percent voted (total population)	Percent voted (total citizen population)
U.S. Total	245,502	224,059	157,596	64.2	70.3	137,537	56.0	61.4
State Total.............................	798	790	581	72.8	73.5	521	65.2	65.9
Sex								
Male	399	396	287	71.9	72.5	256	64.0	64.6
Female	399	395	294	73.7	74.4	265	66.5	67.2
Race								
White alone..........................	738	735	542	73.4	73.8	492	66.7	67.0
White, non-Hispanic alone	721	718	532	73.8	74.1	483	67.0	67.3
Black alone...........................	5	3	2	(B)	(B)	2	(B)	(B)
Asian alone	7	5	3	(B)	(B)	2	(B)	(B)
Hispanic (of any race)......................	20	19	12	(B)	(B)	11	(B)	(B)
White alone or in combination	754	751	554	73.4	73.7	504	66.7	67.1
Black alone or in combination..........	8	5	4	(B)	(B)	4	(B)	(B)
Asian alone or in combination..........	8	7	3	(B)	(B)	3	(B)	(B)
Age								
18 to 24 years....................	97	95	51	(B)	(B)	38	(B)	(B)
25 to 34 years....................	131	129	83	63.2	64.4	65	49.8	50.7
35 to 44 years....................	114	113	84	73.6	74.3	77	67.2	67.8
45 to 64 years....................	274	272	212	77.4	77.9	199	72.5	73.0
65 years and over	182	182	151	82.9	82.9	142	78.1	78.1

- = Zero or rounds to zero.
B = Base is less than 75,000 and therefore too small to show the derived measure.

Table MT-14. Crime

(Number, rate per 100,000. Data are derived from the FBI Uniform Crime Reports.)

Item	State			U.S. [1,2,3,4]		
	2014	2015	Percent change	2014	2015	Percent change
TOTAL POPULATION[5]	1,023,252	1,032,949	0.9	318,907,401	321,418,820	0.8
VIOLENT CRIME						
Number..................................	3,361	3,611	7.4	1,186,185	1,231,566	3.8
Rate	328.5	349.6	6.4	372.0	383.2	3.0
Murder and Nonnegligent Manslaughter						
Number..................................	38	36	-5.3	14,164	15,696	10.8
Rate	3.7	3.5	-6.2	4.4	4.9	10.0
Rape[6]						
Number..................................	558	547	-2.0	118,027	124,047	5.1
Rate	54.5	53.0	-2.9	37.0	38.6	4.3
Robbery						
Number..................................	202	210	4.0	322,905	327,374	1.4
Rate	19.7	20.3	3.0	101.3	101.9	0.6
Aggravated Assault						
Number..................................	2,563	2,818	9.9	731,089	764,449	4.6
Rate	250.5	272.8	8.9	229.2	237.8	3.7
PROPERTY CRIME						
Number..................................	25,525	27,100	6.2	8,209,010	7,993,631	-2.6
Rate	2,494.5	2,623.6	5.2	2,574.1	2,487.0	-3.4
Burglary						
Number..................................	3,639	3,838	5.5	1,713,153	1,579,527	-7.8
Rate	355.6	371.6	4.5	537.2	491.4	-8.5
Larceny-Theft						
Number..................................	19,826	20,844	5.1	5,809,054	5,706,346	-1.8
Rate	1,937.5	2,017.9	4.1	1,821.5	1,775.4	-2.5
Motor Vehicle Theft						
Number..................................	2,060	2,418	17.4	686,803	707,758	3.1
Rate	201.3	234.1	16.3	215.4	220.2	2.2

NOTE: Although arson data are included in the trend and clearance tables, sufficient data are not available to estimate totals for this offense. Therefore, no arson data are published in this table.
X = Not applicable.
- = Zero or rounds to zero.
[1] Because of changes in the state's reporting practices, figures are not comparable to previous years' data.
[2] The crime figures have been adjusted.
[3] The crime figures for the offense of forcible rape used by the Minnesota state Uniform Crime Reporting (UCR) Program (with the exception of Minneapolis and St. Paul, Minnesota) does not comply with national UCR Program guidelines. Consequently, its figures for forcible rape and violent crime (of which forcible rape is a part) are not published in this table.
[4] Includes offenses reported by the Zoological Police and the Metro Transit Police.
[5] Populations are U.S. Census Bureau provisional estimates as of July 1 of each year.
[6] The figures shown for the offense of rape were estimated using the revised Uniform Crime Reporting (UCR) definition of rape.

Table MT-15. State Government Finances, 2015

(Dollar amounts in thousands, percent distribution.)

Item	Dollars	Percent distribution
Total Revenue	7,487,622	100.0
General revenue	6,276,612	83.8
Intergovernmental revenue	2,468,165	33.0
Taxes	2,843,465	38.0
General sales	0	-
Selective sales	603,200	8.1
License taxes	350,769	4.7
Individual income tax	1,180,478	15.8
Corporate income tax	168,039	2.2
Other taxes	540,979	7.2
Current charges	555,676	7.4
Miscellaneous general revenue	409,306	5.5
Utility revenue	0	-
Liquor stores revenue	89,312	1.2
Insurance trust revenue[1]	1,121,698	15.0
Total Expenditure	7,451,676	100.0
Intergovernmental expenditure	1,395,263	18.7
Direct expenditure	6,056,413	81.3
Current operation	4,194,612	56.3
Capital outlay	667,164	9.0
Insurance benefits and repayments	951,574	12.8
Assistance and subsidies	124,557	1.7
Interest on debt	118,506	1.6
Exhibit: Salaries and wages	1,078,555	14.5
Total Expenditure	7,451,676	100.0
General expenditure	6,406,607	86.0
Intergovernmental expenditure	1,395,263	18.7
Direct expenditure	5,011,344	67.3
General expenditure, by function:		
Education	1,997,896	26.8
Public welfare	1,545,178	20.7
Hospitals	55,639	0.7
Health	161,969	2.2
Highways	761,719	10.2
Police protection	57,872	0.8
Correction	214,638	2.9
Natural resources	215,945	2.9
Parks and recreation	21,897	0.3
Governmental administration	433,368	5.8
Interest on general debt	118,506	1.6
Other and unallocable	821,980	11.0
Utility expenditure	15,025	0.2
Liquor stores expenditure	78,470	1.1
Insurance trust expenditure	951,574	12.8
Debt at End of Fiscal Year	3,206,612	X
Cash and Security Holdings	18,620,346	X

X = Not applicable.
- = Zero or rounds to zero.
[1] Within insurance trust revenue, net earnings of state retirement systems is a calculated statistic (the item code in the data file is X08), and thus can be positive or negative. Net earnings is the sum of earnings on investments plus gains on investments minus losses on investments. The change made in 2002 for asset valuation from book to market value in accordance with Statement 34 of the Governmental Accounting Standards Board is reflected in the calculated statistics.

Table MT-16. State Government Tax Collections, 2016

(Dollars in thousands, percent.)

Item	Dollars	Percent distribution
Total Taxes	2,627,943	100.0
Property taxes	278,497	10.6
Sales and gross receipts	562,474	21.4
General sales and gross receipts	0	-
Selective sales and gross receipts	562,474	21.4
Alcoholic beverages	31,907	1.2
Amusements	60,392	2.3
Insurance premiums	98,463	3.7
Motor fuels	186,083	7.1
Pari-mutuels	44	-
Public utilities	43,995	1.7
Tobacco products	86,289	3.3
Other selective sales	55,301	2.1
Licenses	319,020	12.1
Alcoholic beverages	3,374	0.1
Amusements	7,576	0.3
Corporations in general	4,282	0.2
Hunting and fishing	32,517	1.2
Motor vehicle	144,973	5.5
Motor vehicle operators	8,573	0.3
Public utilities	12	-
Occupation and business, NEC	107,039	4.1
Other licenses	10,674	0.4
Income taxes	1,300,011	49.5
Individual income	1,181,042	44.9
Corporation net income	118,969	4.5
Other taxes	167,941	6.4
Death and gift	0	-
Documentary and stock transfer	0	-
Severance	164,373	6.3
Taxes, NEC	3,568	0.1

X = Not applicable.
- = Zero or rounds to zero.

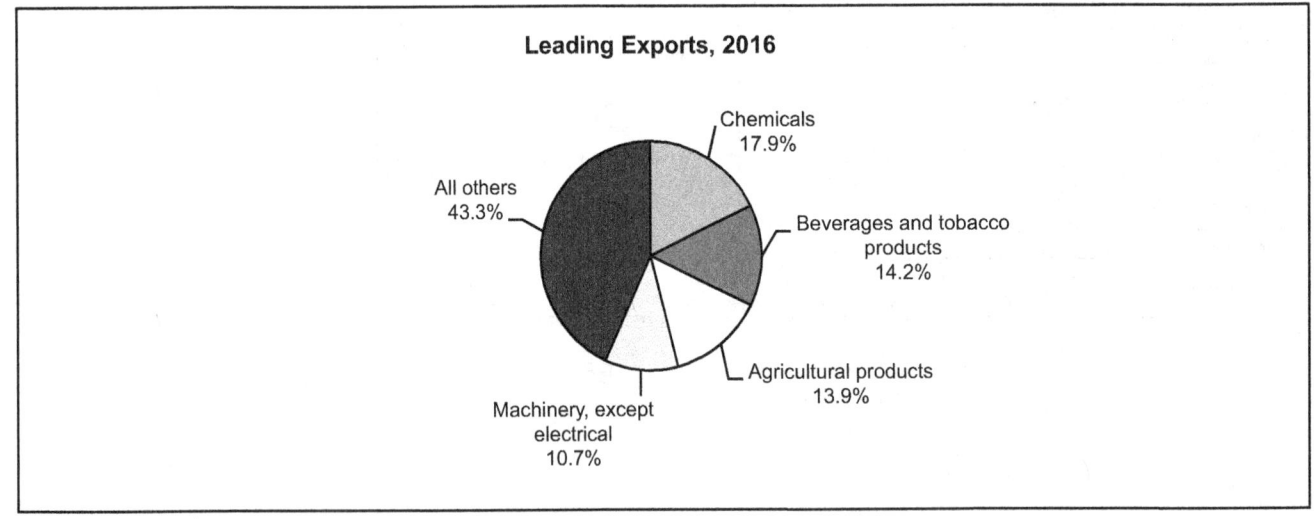

Leading Exports, 2016

Chemicals 17.9%
Beverages and tobacco products 14.2%
Agricultural products 13.9%
Machinery, except electrical 10.7%
All others 43.3%

NEBRASKA

Facts and Figures

Location: Central United States; bordered on the N by South Dakota, on the E by Iowa and Missouri, on the S by Kansas and Colorado, and on the W by Wyoming

Area: 77,354 sq. mi. (200,345 sq. km.); rank—16th

Population: 1,907,116 (2016 est.); rank—37th

Principal Cities: capital—Lincoln; largest—Omaha

Statehood: March 1, 1867; 37th state

U.S. Congress: 2 senators, 3 representatives

State Motto: Equality Before the Law

State Song: "Beautiful Nebraska"

State Nickname: The Cornhusker State

Abbreviations: NE; Nebr.; Neb.

State Symbols: flower—goldenrod; tree—cottonwood; bird—Western meadowlark

At a Glance

- With an increase in population of 4.4 percent, Nebraska ranked 24th among the states in growth from 2010 to 2016.

- In 2015, 8.2 percent of Nebraskans did not have health insurance, compared to 9.4 percent of the total U.S. population.

- The birth rate in Nebraska in 2015 was 14.1 births per 1,000 population, compared to the national average of 12.4 births per 1,000 population.

- Nebraska had the lowest rate of drug overdose deaths among the states in 2015, with 6.9 deaths per 100,000 population.

- The state's violent crime rate in 2015 was 274.9 per 100,000 population, compared to the national rate of 383.2 per 100,000 population.

Table NE-1. Population by Age, Sex, Race, and Hispanic Origin

(Number, percent, except where noted.)

Sex, age, race, and Hispanic origin	2000	2010	2016 [1]	Average annual percent change, 2010–2016
Total Population..	1,711,263	1,826,341	1,907,116	0.3
Percent of total U.S. population	0.6	0.6	0.6	X
Sex				
Male...	843,351	906,296	950,671	0.3
Female	867,912	920,045	956,445	0.2
Age				
Under 5 years...	117,048	131,908	132,809	-
5 to 19 years..	387,288	380,564	393,475	0.2
20 to 64 years..	974,732	1,067,192	1,094,088	0.2
65 years and over...	232,195	246,677	286,744	1.0
Median age (years)	35.3	36.2	36.3	-
Race and Hispanic Origin				
One race...				
White...	1,533,261	1,649,264	1,694,976	0.2
Black..	68,541	85,971	94,620	0.6
American Indian and Alaska Native	14,896	23,418	27,318	1.0
Asian...	21,931	33,322	47,282	2.6
Native Hawaiian or Other Pacific Islander	836	2,061	2,425	1.1
Two or more races	23,953	32,305	40,495	1.6
Hispanic (of any race)..	94,425	173,058	203,320	1.1

X = Not applicable.
- = Zero or rounds to zero.
[1] Population figures for 2016 are July 1 estimates. The 2010 estimates are taken from the 2010 Census.

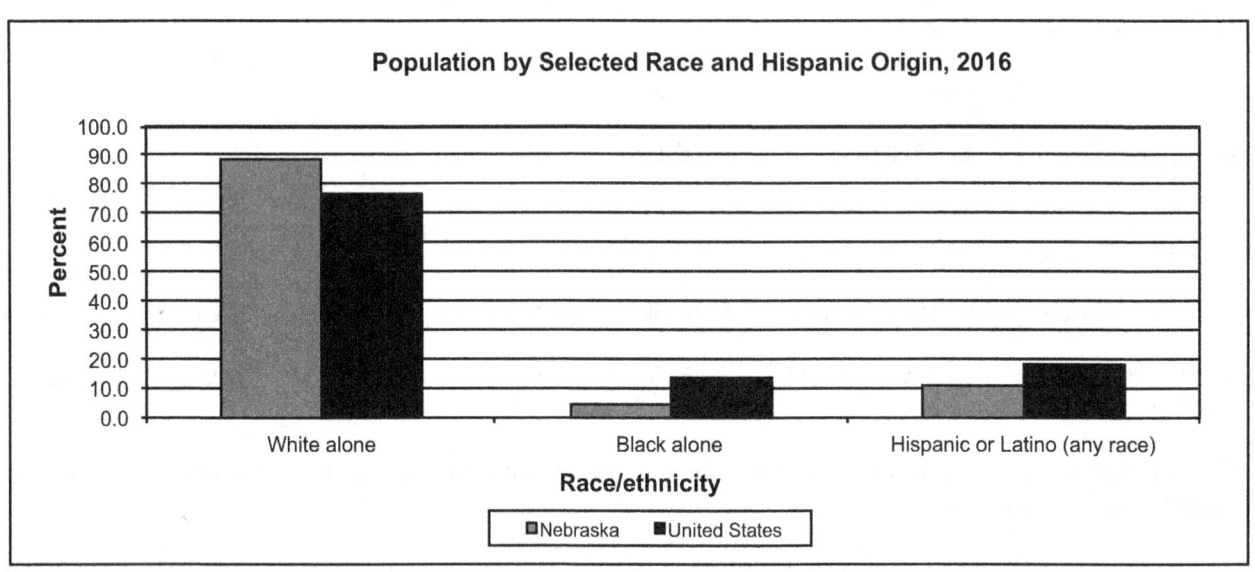

Table NE-2. Marital Status

(Number, percent distribution.)

Sex, age, race, and Hispanic origin	2000	2010	2015
Males, 15 Years and Over..	654,559	708,783	741,271
Never married	29.2	32.4	34.4
Now married, except separated....................................	59.1	54.0	52.2
Separated..	1.0	1.4	1.1
Widowed..	2.4	2.3	2.4
Divorced..	8.3	9.9	9.9
Females, 15 Years and Over.....................................	687,863	735,744	760,523
Never married	22.5	25.3	26.9
Now married, except separated....................................	55.7	52.7	51.3
Separated..	1.3	1.5	1.6
Widowed..	10.8	9.5	8.9
Divorced..	9.7	10.9	11.4

Table NE-3. Households and Housing Characteristics

(Number, percent, dollars.)

Item	2000	2010	2015	Average annual percent change, 2000–2015
Total Households...	666,184	719,304	744,159	0.8
Family households	443,411	468,407	469,797	0.4
Married-couple family	360,996	368,023	369,426	0.2
Other family	82,415	100,384	100,371	1.5
Male householder, no wife present....................	22,072	31,177	29,392	2.2
Female householder, no husband present...........	60,343	69,207	70,979	1.2
Nonfamily households	222,773	250,897	274,362	1.5
Householder living alone.....................................	183,550	205,263	223,076	1.4
Householder not living alone................................	39,223	45,634	51,286	2.1
Housing Characteristics				
Total housing units...	722,668	797,677	820,925	0.9
Occupied housing units	666,184	719,304	744,159	0.8
Owner occupied	449,317	484,649	490,394	0.6
Renter occupied	216,867	234,655	253,765	1.1
Average household size.......................................	2.49	2.47	2.48	-
Financial Characteristics				
Median gross rent of renter-occupied housing	491	669	750	3.5
Median monthly owner costs for housing units with a mortgage	895	1,218	1,269	2.8
Median value of owner-occupied housing units........	88,000	127,600	141,600	4.1

- = Zero or rounds to zero

Table NE-4. Migration, Origin, and Language

(Number, percent.)

Characteristic	State			U.S.		
	2014	2015	Percent change	2014	2015	Percent change
Residence 1 Year Ago						
Population 1 year and over	1,855,356	1,869,217	0.7	315,095,393	317,635,720	0.8
Same house	83.1	84.0	X	85.1	85.3	X
Different house in the U.S.....................................	16.4	15.5	X	14.3	14.1	X
Same county	10.0	9.0	X	8.7	8.5	X
Different county	6.4	6.4	X	5.6	5.6	X
Same state	3.6	3.6	X	3.3	3.2	X
Different state	2.8	2.8	X	2.3	2.4	X
Abroad	0.5	0.5	X	0.6	0.7	X
Place of Birth						
Native born	1,756,103	1,767,800	0.7	276,465,262	278,128,449	0.6
Male	49.6	49.6	X	49.3	49.3	X
Female	50.4	50.4	X	50.7	50.7	X
Foreign born	125,400	128,390	2.4	42,391,794	43,290,372	2.1
Male	51.3	50.8	X	48.7	48.6	X
Female	48.7	49.2	X	51.3	51.4	X
Foreign born; naturalized U.S. citizen....................	43,971	48,394	10.1	19,984,738	20,697,103	3.6
Male	50.5	48.9	X	45.9	45.9	X
Female	49.5	51.1	X	54.1	54.1	X
Foreign born; not a U.S. citizen............................	81,429	79,996	-1.8	22,407,056	22,593,269	0.8
Male	51.8	52.0	X	51.2	51.1	X
Female	48.2	48.0	X	48.8	48.9	X
Entered 2010 or later	18.5	23.9	X	12.3	15.6	X
Entered 2000 to 2009	35.1	30.8	X	28.6	27.9	X
Entered before 2000..	46.4	45.3	X	59.1	56.5	X
World Region of Birth, Foreign						
Foreign-born population, excluding population born at sea	125,400	128,390	2.4	42,390,705	43,289,646	2.1
Europe	7.3	6.5	X	11.2	11.1	X
Asia	27.7	28.0	X	30.1	30.6	X
Africa	7.4	9.3	X	4.6	4.8	X
Oceania	0.4	0.1	X	0.6	0.6	X
Latin America..	56.3	55.0	X	51.6	51.1	X
North America..	0.9	1.0	X	1.9	1.9	X
Language Spoken at Home and Ability to Speak English						
Population 5 years and over..................................	1,751,135	1,765,526	0.8	299,084,046	301,625,014	0.8
English only	89.4	88.9	X	78.9	78.5	X
Language other than English................................	10.6	11.1	X	21.1	21.5	X
Speaks English less than "very well".................	4.9	4.8	X	8.6	8.6	X

NA = Not available.
X = Not applicable.
- = Zero or rounds to zero.

Table NE-5. Median Income and Poverty Status, 2015

(Number, percent, except as noted.)

Characteristic	State		U.S.	
	Number	Percent	Number	Percent
Median Income				
Households (dollars)............................	54,996	X	55,775	X
Families (dollars)	71,039	X	68,260	X
Below Poverty Level (All People)	231,321	12.6	46,153,077	14.7
Sex				
Male	101,366	11.1	20,599,407	13.4
Female	129,955	14.0	25,553,670	16.0
Age				
Under 18 years............................	78,002	16.8	15,000,273	20.7
Related children under 18 years........................	74,836	16.3	14,693,239	20.4
18 to 64 years............................	133,652	12.0	26,960,369	13.9
65 years and over	19,667	7.4	4,192,435	9.0

X = Not applicable.

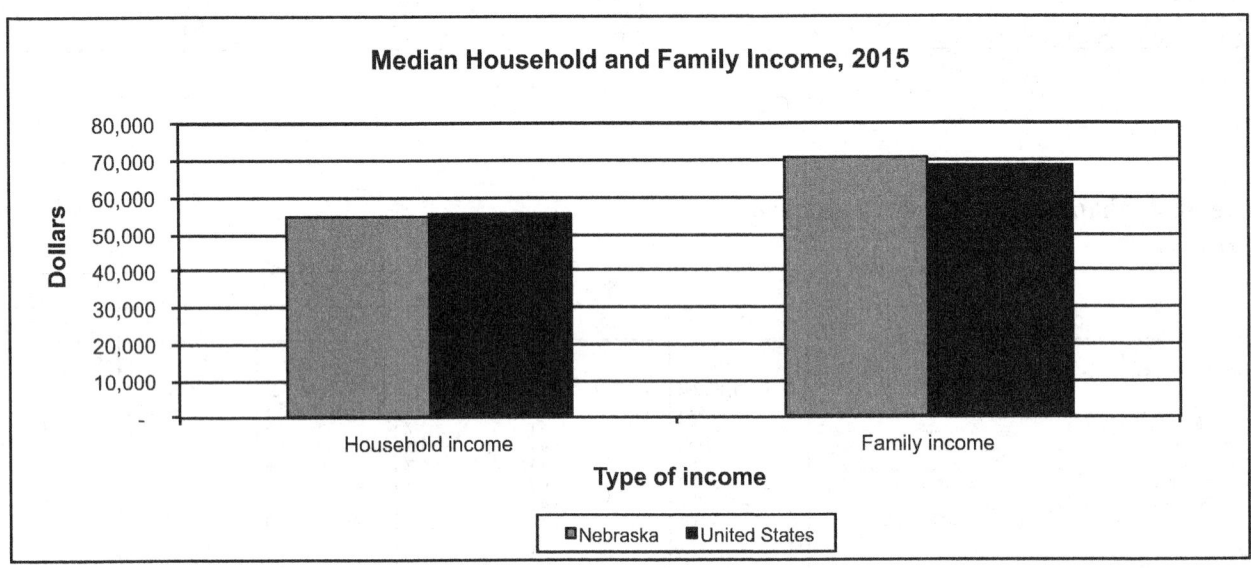

Table NE-6. Health Insurance Coverage Status for the Civilian Noninstitutionalized Population and Children Under 18 Years of Age

(Numbers in thousands, percent.)

Item	2007	2008	2009	2010	2011	2012	2013	2014	2015
Civilian Noninstitutionalized Population	1,753	1,750	1,763	1,802	1,814	1,827	1,841	1,854	1,866
Covered by Private or Public Insurance									
Number........................	1,522	1,555	1,553	1,594	1,607	1,621	1,632	1,674	1,713
Percent........................	86.8	88.9	88.1	88.5	88.6	88.7	88.7	90.3	91.8
Not Covered									
Number........................	232	195	210	208	207	206	209	179	154
Percent........................	13.2	11.1	11.9	11.5	11.4	11.3	11.3	9.7	8.2
Percent in the U.S. not covered........................	15.3	15.1	15.1	15.5	15.1	14.8	14.5	11.7	9.4
Children Under 18 Years of Age	452	445	445	459	459	461	463	467	469
Covered by Private or Public Insurance									
Number........................	407	414	417	433	432	433	437	442	445
Percent........................	90.0	93.0	93.7	94.4	94.1	94.0	94.5	94.7	94.7
Not Covered									
Number........................	45	31	28	26	27	28	25	25	25
Percent........................	10.0	7.0	6.3	5.6	5.9	6.0	5.5	5.3	5.3
Percent in the U.S. not covered........................	11.0	9.7	8.6	8.0	7.5	7.2	7.1	6.0	4.8

Table NE-7. Employment Status by Demographic Group, 2016

(Numbers in thousands, percent.)

Characteristic	Civilian noninstitutional population	Civilian labor force		Employed		Unemployed	
		Number	Percent of population	Number	Percent of population	Number	Percent of population
Total..	1,458	1,014	69.5	980	67.2	34	3.4
Sex							
Male..	719	534	74.2	512	71.2	21	4.0
Female	739	481	65.0	468	63.3	13	2.6
Race, Sex, and Hispanic Origin							
White	1,319	923	70.0	898	68.1	25	2.7
Male..	650	485	74.5	469	72.1	16	3.2
Female	669	438	65.6	429	64.1	10	2.2
Black or African American...................	NA	NA	NA	NA	NA	NA	NA
Male..	NA	NA	NA	NA	NA	NA	NA
Female	NA	NA	NA	NA	NA	NA	NA
Hispanic or Latino ethnicity[1]	141	104	73.9	99	70.4	5	4.7
Male..	72	59	81.7	56	77.6	3	5.0
Female	NA	NA	NA	NA	NA	NA	NA
Age							
16 to 19 years...................................	108	56	51.8	51	47.6	5	8.1
20 to 24 years...................................	134	106	78.8	100	74.7	6	5.3
25 to 34 years...................................	246	214	87.0	205	83.5	8	3.9
35 to 44 years...................................	228	204	89.4	199	87.2	5	2.5
45 to 54 years...................................	241	211	87.6	207	85.8	4	2.1
55 to 64 years...................................	237	169	71.2	164	69.4	4	2.6
65 years and over	265	55	20.8	53	20.2	2	3.3

NOTE: Data in Table 7 are from the Current Population Survey (CPS) and do not match the estimates in Table 8. See notes and definitions for further information.
[1] May be of any race.
NA = Not available.

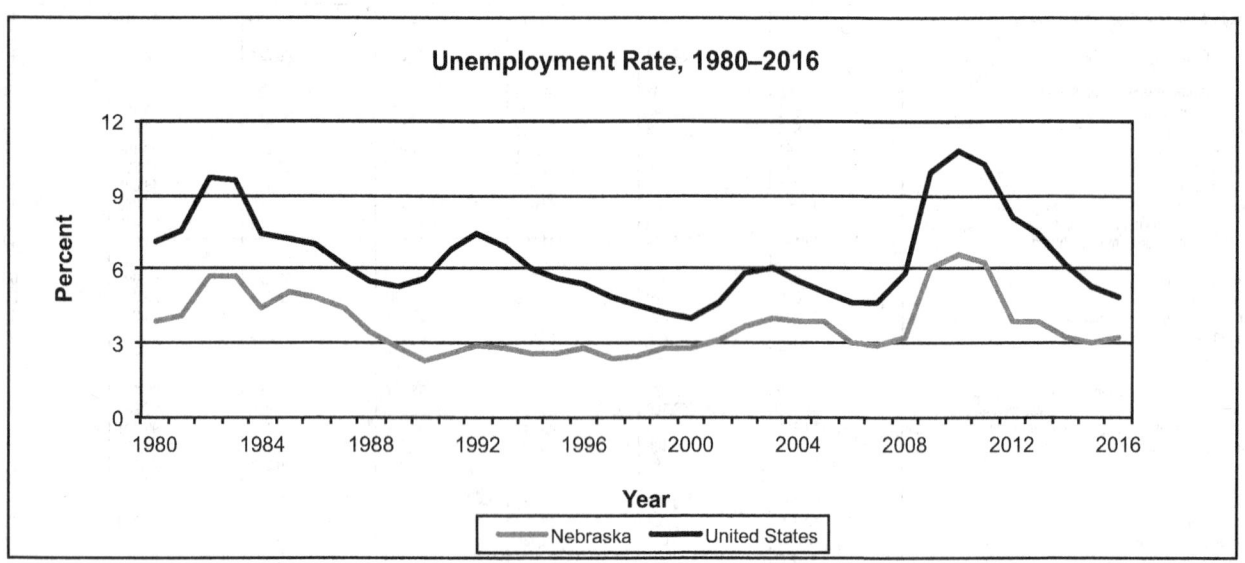

Table NE-8. Employment Status of the Civilian Noninstitutional Population Age 16 Years and Over

(Number, percent.)

Year	Civilian labor force	Civilian participation rate	Employed	Unemployed	Unemployment rate
2008...................	989,757	73.2	956,759	32,998	3.3
2009...................	991,583	72.7	945,648	45,935	4.6
2010...................	993,398	71.6	947,360	46,038	4.6
2011...................	1,003,256	71.6	959,059	44,197	4.4
2012...................	1,015,555	71.9	975,032	40,523	4.0
2013...................	1,019,345	71.6	980,779	38,566	3.8
2014...................	1,013,899	70.7	980,833	33,066	3.3
2015...................	1,012,973	70.1	982,707	30,266	3.0
2016...................	1,011,041	69.5	978,567	32,474	3.2

Table NE-9. Employment and Average Wages by Industry

(Estimates through 2010 are based on the 2007 *North American Industry Classification System* [NAICS]. Estimates from 2011 onward are based on the 2012 NAICS.)

Industry	2009	2010	2011	2012	2013	2014	2015
				Number of jobs			
Wage and Salary Employment by Industry..................	974,385	967,772	972,146	989,737	1,001,155	1,014,518	1,030,578
Farm Wage and Salary Employment.........................	11,597	12,992	13,694	12,116	12,293	12,168	16,088
Nonfarm Wage and Salary Employment.....................	962,788	954,780	958,452	977,621	988,862	1,002,350	1,014,490
Private wage and salary employment........................	786,548	777,635	783,995	804,150	815,559	828,358	840,035
Forestry, fishing, and related activities....................	4,884	5,124	5,339	5,698	6,119	6,023	5,573
Mining..	938	940	1,024	1,126	1,042	1,133	1,066
Utilities...	1,918	1,655	1,627	1,605	1,290	1,264	1,081
Construction...	48,447	43,128	41,742	43,439	45,497	47,473	50,109
Manufacturing...	93,460	91,682	93,694	95,092	96,556	97,532	97,423
Durable goods manufacturing............................	42,702	41,422	42,759	44,008	44,995	45,886	45,430
Nondurable goods manufacturing........................	50,758	50,260	50,935	51,084	51,561	51,646	51,993
Wholesale trade	41,486	40,670	41,035	41,536	42,139	43,131	42,500
Retail trade..	106,187	105,311	105,670	106,436	107,249	108,945	110,736
Transportation and warehousing...........................	51,764	50,377	51,583	52,338	52,583	53,073	54,103
Information...	17,516	16,932	17,199	17,199	17,220	17,071	17,566
Finance and insurance......................................	55,096	55,094	55,146	55,506	55,728	56,647	57,108
Real estate and rental and leasing.........................	9,449	9,199	9,189	9,053	9,226	9,344	9,614
Professional, scientific, and technical services.............	43,069	43,225	43,595	45,127	44,397	44,378	44,883
Management of companies and enterprises.................	17,167	17,157	16,670	16,742	19,340	20,413	22,119
Administrative and waste services........................	41,812	41,710	43,145	45,378	46,714	48,966	50,490
Educational services	18,081	18,596	18,526	18,554	18,137	18,338	18,795
Health care and social assistance.........................	109,980	111,890	113,063	120,611	122,136	123,124	124,024
Arts, entertainment, and recreation........................	12,909	12,425	12,436	13,018	13,392	13,740	14,287
Accommodation and food services.........................	69,641	69,035	69,962	71,714	72,950	73,821	74,660
Other services, except public administration................	42,744	43,485	43,350	43,978	43,844	43,942	43,898
Government and government enterprises.........................	176,240	177,145	174,457	173,471	173,303	173,992	174,455
				Dollars			
Average Wages and Salaries by Industry	38,038	38,771	39,719	40,899	41,499	42,812	44,385
Average Farm Wages and Salaries	41,694	34,064	35,259	41,844	40,724	42,548	40,103
Average Nonfarm Wages and Salaries	37,993	38,835	39,783	40,887	41,509	42,815	44,453
Average private wages and salaries........................	37,543	38,340	39,231	40,431	41,032	42,408	44,117
Forestry, fishing, and related activities....................	20,629	21,153	23,345	24,031	25,331	26,628	28,662
Mining..	43,741	45,847	47,741	51,673	52,363	53,194	54,452
Utilities...	96,738	88,526	90,719	91,398	86,072	111,397	108,795
Construction...	41,304	41,777	41,998	43,497	44,167	46,626	48,227
Manufacturing...	41,967	43,738	44,471	45,111	45,688	47,348	48,454
Durable goods manufacturing............................	44,120	46,189	47,894	48,084	48,854	50,450	51,038
Nondurable goods manufacturing........................	40,156	41,719	41,597	42,550	42,926	44,592	46,196
Wholesale trade	49,837	51,344	52,700	55,196	56,271	58,699	60,453
Retail trade..	23,018	23,890	23,919	24,791	25,152	25,638	26,431
Transportation and warehousing...........................	47,050	48,322	50,049	52,908	51,926	54,814	55,994
Information...	50,622	51,264	53,889	54,772	56,498	57,608	59,958
Finance and insurance......................................	52,782	54,886	57,209	59,309	61,257	62,732	65,493
Real estate and rental and leasing.........................	31,886	32,872	34,036	35,804	37,365	39,107	40,496
Professional, scientific, and technical services.............	57,520	58,580	59,560	62,018	60,869	61,965	64,644
Management of companies and enterprises.................	78,961	78,355	80,415	90,199	92,161	95,401	99,896
Administrative and waste services........................	29,135	29,106	29,927	31,167	32,394	34,200	36,032
Educational services	29,764	29,887	30,422	31,009	30,517	29,575	29,997
Health care and social assistance.........................	39,791	40,076	41,043	40,532	40,954	41,547	44,076
Arts, entertainment, and recreation........................	16,816	17,602	18,019	18,358	18,855	19,254	19,438
Accommodation and food services.........................	13,608	14,034	14,436	15,150	15,493	16,164	17,211
Other services, except public administration................	25,853	26,537	27,307	27,764	28,635	29,853	30,892
Government and government enterprises.........................	40,005	41,010	42,261	42,998	43,753	44,756	46,071

Table NE-10. Employment Characteristics by Family Type

(Number, percent.)

	2013		2014		2015	
Family type and labor force status	Total	Families with own children under 18 years	Total	Families with own children under 18 years	Total	Families with own children under 18 years
All Families...	475,000	212,719	479,357	217,321	469,797	214,069
FAMILY TYPE AND LABOR FORCE STATUS						
Married-Couple Families...............................	372,805	149,660	370,736	150,724	369,426	153,745
Both husband and wife in labor force....................	59.7	73.1	61.9	76.1	59.9	74.5
Husband in labor force, wife not in labor force	18.6	23.0	16.9	20.4	18.7	21.5
Wife in labor force, husband not in labor force	6.9	2.6	6.4	2.8	6.4	3.0
Both husband and wife not in labor force................	14.4	1.1	14.8	0.8	14.5	0.8
Other Families	102,195	63,059	108,621	66,597	100,371	60,324
Female householder, no husband present.................	69.9	72.8	71.8	74.6	70.7	73.2
In labor force..	53.7	63.2	57.3	66.1	54.5	65.1
Not in labor force	16.2	9.7	14.5	8.6	16.2	8.1
Male householder, no wife present.......................	30.1	27.2	28.2	25.4	29.3	26.8
In labor force..	25.9	25.9	24.4	23.8	24.5	25.0
Not in labor force	4.2	1.3	3.7	1.5	4.8	1.8

Table NE-11. School Enrollment and Educational Attainment, 2015

(Number, percent.)

Item	State	U.S.
Enrollment		
Total population 3 years and over, enrolled in school	505,827	81,618,288
Enrolled in nursery school or preschool (percent)................	6.6	6.0
Enrolled in kindergarten (percent)...............................	5.2	5.0
Enrolled in elementary school, grades 1-8 (percent)..............	40.8	40.3
Enrolled in high school, grades 9-12 (percent)..................	20.6	20.9
Enrolled in college or graduate school (percent)................	26.8	27.7
Attainment		
Total population 25 years and over	1,232,583	216,447,163
Less than ninth grade (percent).................................	3.9	5.5
9th to 12th grade, no diploma (percent).........................	5.1	7.3
High school graduate, including equivalency (percent)............	26.9	27.6
Some college, no degree (percent)	23.8	20.7
Associate's degree (percent)....................................	10.1	8.2
Bachelor's degree (percent)	19.8	19.0
Graduate or professional degree (percent).......................	10.4	11.6
High school graduate or higher (percent)	91.0	87.1
Bachelor's degree or higher (percent)	30.2	30.6

Table NE-12. Public School Characteristics and Educational Indicators

(Number, percent; data derived from National Center of Education Statistics.)

Item	State	U.S.
Public Schools, 2014–2015 (except where noted)		
Number of school districts......................................	284	18,260
Number of schools..	1,092	98,373
Number of students...	312,635	50,312,581
Number of teachers	22,988	3,132,351
Student-teacher ratio	13.6	16.1
Expenditures per student (dollars), FY 2014	11,877	11,066
Four-year adjusted cohort graduation rate (ACGR)[1,2]	88.9	83.2
Students eligible for free or reduced-price lunch (percent)	44.3	51.8
English language learners (percent).............................	5.6	9.4
Students age 3 to 21 served under IDEA, part B (percent)........	15.1	13.0

Public Schools by Type	Number	Percent of state public schools
Total number of schools...	1,092	100.0
Regular	1,016	93.0
Special education...	24	2.2
Vocational education..	0	-
Alternative education...	52	4.8

NOTE: Every school is assigned only one school type based on its instructional emphasis.
[1] ACGR data represents a new method of calculating high-school completion rates and may not be comparable to previous years' data for Averaged Freshmen Graduation Rates (AFGR).
[2] The United States 4-year ACGRs were estimated using both the reported 4-year ACGR data from 49 states and the District of Columbia and using imputed data for Idaho. The estimate for American Indian/Alaska Native students also includes imputed data for Virginia.
- =Zero or rounds to zero.

Table NE-13. Reported Voting and Registration of the Voting-Age Population, November 2016

(Numbers in thousands, percent.)

Item	Total population	Total citizen population	Registered			Voted		
			Total registered	Percent registered (total population)	Percent registered (total citizen population)	Total voted	Percent voted (total population)	Percent voted (total citizen population)
U.S. Total	245,502	224,059	157,596	64.2	70.3	137,537	56.0	61.4
State Total.............................	1,407	1,336	1,008	71.7	75.5	893	63.4	66.8
Sex								
Male	696	661	480	68.9	72.6	419	60.2	63.4
Female	711	676	529	74.3	78.2	474	66.6	70.1
Race								
White alone......	1,253	1,202	927	74.0	77.1	837	66.8	69.6
White, non-Hispanic alone...........	1,150	1,138	882	76.7	77.5	800	69.6	70.3
Black alone......	56	52	41	(B)	(B)	30	(B)	(B)
Asian alone	35	23	12	(B)	(B)	7	(B)	(B)
Hispanic (of any race)......	109	65	47	(B)	(B)	37	(B)	(B)
White alone or in combination	1,280	1,228	938	73.2	76.3	844	65.9	68.7
Black alone or in combination..........	63	58	42	(B)	(B)	31	(B)	(B)
Asian alone or in combination.........	35	23	12	(B)	(B)	7	(B)	(B)
Age								
18 to 24 years.....	190	180	115	60.5	63.8	95	50.1	52.9
25 to 34 years.....	258	238	162	62.5	68.0	130	50.4	54.8
35 to 44 years.....	212	191	146	69.1	76.5	131	62.0	68.7
45 to 64 years.....	454	438	341	75.1	77.9	306	67.3	69.8
65 years and over..........	293	290	245	83.5	84.4	230	78.6	79.5

B = Base is less than 75,000 and therefore too small to show the derived measure.
- = Zero or rounds to zero.

Table NE-14. Crime

(Number, rate per 100,000. Data are derived from the FBI Uniform Crime Reports.)

Item	State			U.S. [1,2,3,4]		
	2014	2015	Percent change	2014	2015	Percent change
TOTAL POPULATION[5]	1,882,980	1,896,190	0.7	318,907,401	321,418,820	0.8
VIOLENT CRIME						
Number...........	5,201	5,212	0.2	1,186,185	1,231,566	3.8
Rate	276.2	274.9	-0.5	372.0	383.2	3.0
Murder and Nonnegligent Manslaughter						
Number...........	53	62	17.0	14,164	15,696	10.8
Rate	2.8	3.3	16.2	4.4	-4.9	10.0
Rape[6]						
Number...........	878	873	-0.6	118,027	124,047	5.1
Rate	46.6	46.0	-1.3	37.0	38.6	4.3
Robbery						
Number...........	1,044	994	-4.8	322,905	327,374	1.4
Rate	55.4	52.4	-5.5	101.3	101.9	0.6
Aggravated Assault						
Number...........	3,226	3,283	1.8	731,089	764,449	4.6
Rate	171.3	173.1	1.1	229.2	237.8	3.7
PROPERTY CRIME						
Number...........	47,526	42,495	-10.6	8,209,010	7,993,631	-2.6
Rate	2,524.0	2,241.1	-11.2	2,574.1	2,487.0	-3.4
Burglary						
Number...........	7,936	6,422	-19.1	1,713,153	1,579,527	-7.8
Rate	421.5	338.7	-19.6	537.2	491.4	-8.5
Larceny-Theft						
Number...........	35,063	32,072	-8.5	5,809,054	5,706,346	-1.8
Rate	1,862.1	1,691.4	-9.2	1,821.5	1,775.4	-2.5
Motor Vehicle Theft						
Number...........	4,527	4,001	-11.6	686,803	707,758	3.1
Rate	240.4	211.0	-12.2	215.4	220.2	2.2

NOTE: Although arson data are included in the trend and clearance tables, sufficient data are not available to estimate totals for this offense. Therefore, no arson data are published in this table.
X = Not applicable.
- = Zero or rounds to zero.
[1] The crime figures have been adjusted.
[2] The data collection methodology for the offense of forcible rape used by the Minnesota state Uniform Crime Reporting (UCR) Program (with the exception of Minneapolis and St. Paul, Minnesota) does not comply with national UCR Program guidelines. Consequently, its figures for forcible rape and violent crime (of which forcible rape is a part) are not published in this table.
[3] Includes offenses reported by the Zoological Police and the Metro Transit Police.
[4] Because of changes in the state's reporting practices, figures are not comparable to previous years' data.
[5] Populations are U.S. Census Bureau provisional estimates as of July 1 of each year.
[6] The figures shown for the offense of rape were estimated using the revised Uniform Crime Reporting (UCR) definition of rape.

Table NE-15. State Government Finances, 2015

(Dollar amounts in thousands, percent distribution.)

Item	Dollars	Percent distribution
Total Revenue	11,361,675	100.0
General revenue	9,958,441	87.6
Intergovernmental revenue	3,033,641	26.7
Taxes	5,086,759	44.8
General sales	1,787,880	15.7
Selective sales	527,950	4.6
License taxes	172,391	1.5
Individual income tax	2,239,582	19.7
Corporate income tax	344,477	3.0
Other taxes	14,479	0.1
Current charges	1,037,248	9.1
Miscellaneous general revenue	800,793	7.0
Utility revenue	0	-
Liquor stores revenue	0	-
Insurance trust revenue[1]	1,403,234	12.4
Total Expenditure	10,850,904	100.0
Intergovernmental expenditure	2,303,467	21.2
Direct expenditure	8,547,437	78.8
Current operation	6,377,816	58.8
Capital outlay	899,819	8.3
Insurance benefits and repayments	1,032,616	9.5
Assistance and subsidies	182,289	1.7
Interest on debt	54,897	0.5
Exhibit: Salaries and wages	1,507,297	13.9
Total Expenditure	10,850,904	100.0
General expenditure	9,818,288	90.5
Intergovernmental expenditure	2,303,467	21.2
Direct expenditure	7,514,821	69.3
General expenditure, by function:		
Education	3,611,552	33.3
Public welfare	2,626,032	24.2
Hospitals	266,109	2.5
Health	532,776	4.9
Highways	800,388	7.4
Police protection	87,628	0.8
Correction	349,151	3.2
Natural resources	313,905	2.9
Parks and recreation	47,205	0.4
Governmental administration	216,806	2.0
Interest on general debt	54,897	0.5
Other and unallocable	911,839	8.4
Utility expenditure	0	-
Liquor stores expenditure	0	-
Insurance trust expenditure	1,032,616	9.5
Debt at End of Fiscal Year	1,809,126	X
Cash and Security Holdings	22,137,291	X

X = Not applicable.
- = Zero or rounds to zero.
[1] Within insurance trust revenue, net earnings of state retirement systems is a calculated statistic (the item code in the data file is X08), and thus can be positive or negative. Net earnings is the sum of earnings on investments plus gains on investments minus losses on investments. The change made in 2002 for asset valuation from book to market value in accordance with Statement 34 of the Governmental Accounting Standards Board is reflected in the calculated statistics.

Table NE-16. State Government Tax Collections, 2016

(Dollars in thousands, percent.)

Item	Dollars	Percent distribution
Total Taxes	5,117,133	100.0
Property taxes	123	-
Sales and gross receipts	2,362,718	46.2
General sales and gross receipts	1,783,498	34.9
Selective sales and gross receipts	579,220	11.3
Alcoholic beverages	30,520	0.6
Amusements	5,800	0.1
Insurance premiums	65,465	1.3
Motor fuels	342,004	6.7
Pari-mutuels	160	-
Public utilities	49,288	1.0
Tobacco products	61,258	1.2
Other selective sales	24,725	0.5
Licenses	185,082	3.6
Alcoholic beverages	648	-
Amusements	1,589	-
Corporations in general	16,213	0.3
Hunting and fishing	14,608	0.3
Motor vehicle	104,287	2.0
Motor vehicle operators	10,838	0.2
Public utilities	0	-
Occupation and business, NEC	35,843	0.7
Other licenses	1,056	-
Income taxes	2,552,391	49.9
Individual income	2,244,719	43.9
Corporation net income	307,672	6.0
Other taxes	16,819	0.3
Death and gift	0	-
Documentary and stock transfer	14,292	0.3
Severance	2,527	-
Taxes, NEC	0	-

- = Zero or rounds to zero.

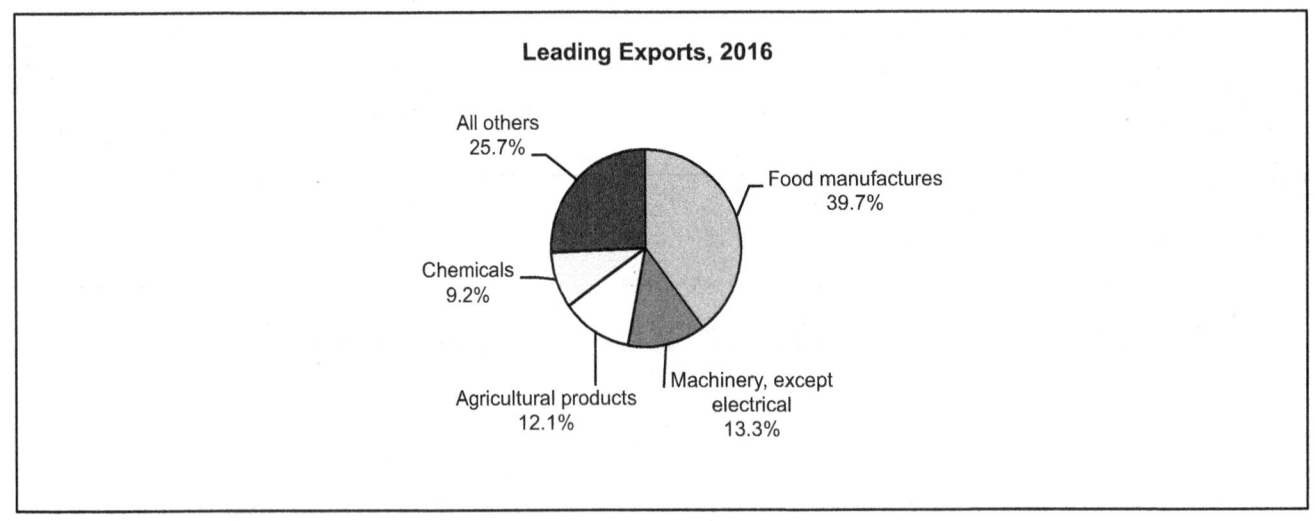

Leading Exports, 2016

All others 25.7%
Food manufactures 39.7%
Chemicals 9.2%
Agricultural products 12.1%
Machinery, except electrical 13.3%

NEVADA

Location: Western United States; bordered on the N by Oregon and Idaho, on the E by Utah and Arizona, on the S by Arizona and California, and on the W by California

Area: 110,561 sq. mi. (286,351 sq. km.); rank—7th

Population: 2,940,058 (2016 est.); rank—34th

Principal Cities: capital—Carson City; largest—Las Vegas

Statehood: October 31, 1864; 36th state

U.S. Congress: 2 senators, 4 representatives

State Motto: All for Our Country

State Song: "Home Means Nevada"

State Nicknames: The Silver State; The Sagebrush State

Abbreviations: NV; Nev.

State Symbols: flower—sagebrush; tree—single-leaf piñon and bristlecone pine; bird—mountain bluebird

At a Glance

- With an increase in population of 8.9 percent, Nevada ranked 7th among the states in growth from 2010 to 2016.

- In 2016, 5.7 percent of Nevadans were unemployed, compared to 4.9 percent of the total U.S. population.

- Nevada's violent crime rate in 2015 was 695.9 per 100,000 population, which ranked 3rd among the states. The national violent crime rate was 383.2 per 100,000 population.

- Approximately 28.5 percent of Nevadans self-identified their ethnicity as "Hispanic or Latino" in 2016, the 5th highest percentage in the country.

Table NV-1. Population by Age, Sex, Race, and Hispanic Origin

(Number, percent, except where noted.)

Sex, age, race, and Hispanic origin	2000	2010	2016 [1]	Average annual percent change, 2010–2016
Total Population..	1,998,257	2,700,551	2,940,058	0.6
Percent of total U.S. population	0.7	0.9	0.9	X
Sex				
Male..	1,018,051	1,363,616	1,473,997	0.5
Female	980,206	1,336,935	1,466,061	0.6
Age				
Under 5 years..	145,817	187,478	184,462	-0.1
5 to 19 years...	415,684	548,850	557,261	0.1
20 to 64 years...	1,217,827	1,639,864	1,757,193	0.4
65 years and over	218,929	324,359	441,142	2.3
Median age (years)	35.0	36.3	37.8	0.3
Race and Hispanic Origin				
One race...				
White	1,501,886	2,106,494	2,209,037	0.3
Black...	135,477	231,224	281,224	1.4
American Indian and Alaska Native	26,420	42,965	48,305	0.8
Asian...	90,266	203,478	254,432	1.6
Native Hawaiian or Other Pacific Islander	8,426	19,307	22,654	1.1
Two or more races..	76,428	97,083	124,406	1.8
Hispanic (of any race)...	393,970	741,200	836,626	0.8

X = Not applicable.
[1] Population figures for 2016 are July 1 estimates. The 2010 estimates are taken from the 2010 Census.

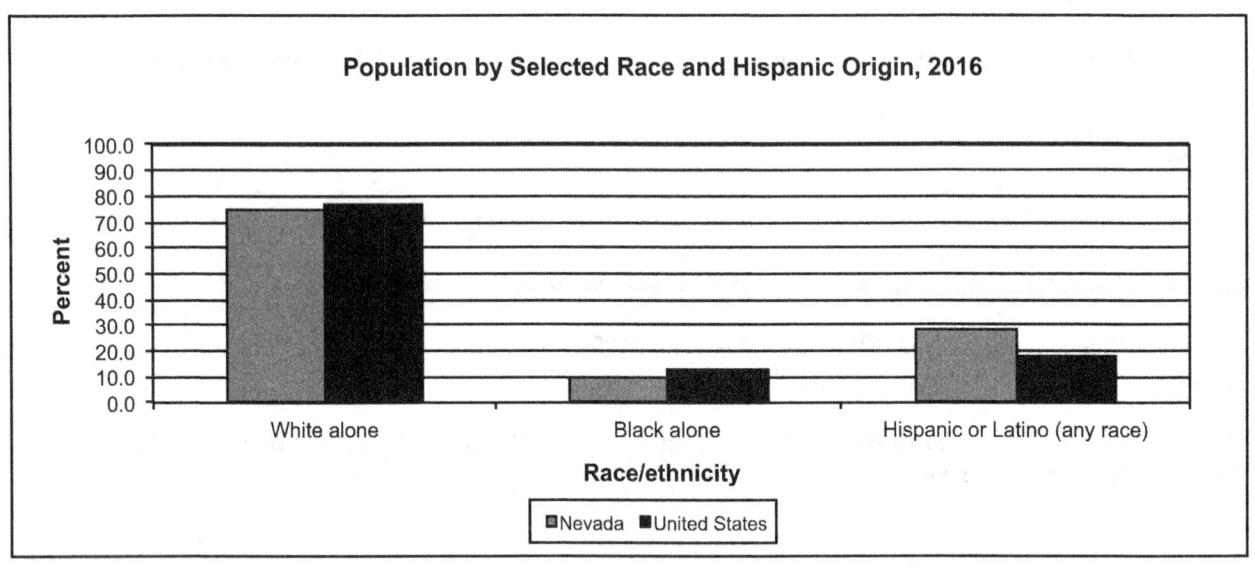

Table NV-2. Marital Status

(Number, percent distribution.)

Sex, age, race, and Hispanic origin	2000	2010	2015
Males, 15 Years and Over	792,317	1,081,514	1,163,719
Never married	28.8	35.0	37.1
Now married, except separated..	53.8	47.6	45.2
Separated...	2.0	2.0	2.2
Widowed...	2.5	2.9	2.7
Divorced...	12.9	12.5	12.7
Females, 15 Years and Over	771,263	1,069,123	1,169,176
Never married	20.9	27.2	29.5
Now married, except separated..	53.1	47.2	44.0
Separated...	2.7	2.8	2.6
Widowed...	8.6	8.0	8.2
Divorced...	14.7	14.8	15.7

Table NV-3. Households and Housing Characteristics

(Number, percent, dollars.)

Item	2000	2010	2015	Average annual percent change, 2000–2015
Total Households................................	751,165	989,811	1,042,065	2.6
Family households......................	498,333	639,686	659,355	2.2
Married-couple family..................	373,201	452,361	456,740	1.5
Other family........................	125,132	187,325	202,615	4.1
Male householder, no wife present.........	41,650	63,327	63,463	3.5
Female householder, no husband present....	83,482	123,998	139,152	4.4
Nonfamily households	252,832	350,125	382,710	3.4
Householder living alone...............	186,745	266,232	298,763	4.0
Householder not living alone...........	66,087	83,893	83,947	1.8
Housing Characteristics				
Total housing units....................	827,457	1,175,070	1,209,864	3.1
Occupied housing units	751,165	989,811	1,042,065	2.6
Owner occupied.......................	457,247	565,869	562,960	1.5
Renter occupied......................	293,918	423,942	479,105	4.2
Average household size.................	2.62	2.70	2.74	0.3
Financial Characteristics				
Median gross rent of renter-occupied housing	699	952	980	2.7
Median monthly owner costs for housing units with a mortgage	1,190	1,638	1,396	1.2
Median value of owner-occupied housing units	142,000	174,800	221,400	3.7

Table NV-4. Migration, Origin, and Language

(Number, percent.)

Characteristic	State			U.S.		
	2014	2015	Percent change	2014	2015	Percent change
Residence 1 Year Ago						
Population 1 year and over	2,806,170	2,859,489	1.9	315,095,393	317,635,720	0.8
Same house	79.7	80.1	X	85.1	85.3	X
Different house in the U.S.	19.8	19.2	X	14.3	14.1	X
Same county	14.4	13.6	X	8.7	8.5	X
Different county	5.5	5.6	X	5.6	5.6	X
Same state	0.8	0.9	X	3.3	3.2	X
Different state	4.6	4.8	X	2.3	2.4	X
Abroad	0.5	0.6	X	0.6	0.7	X
Place of Birth						
Native born	2,287,377	2,332,675	2.0	276,465,262	278,128,449	0.6
Male	51.1	50.7	X	49.3	49.3	X
Female	48.9	49.3	X	50.7	50.7	X
Foreign born	551,722	558,170	1.2	42,391,794	43,290,372	2.1
Male	46.9	47.2	X	48.7	48.6	X
Female	53.1	52.8	X	51.3	51.4	X
Foreign born; naturalized U.S. citizen......	249,730	261,316	4.6	19,984,738	20,697,103	3.6
Male	43.1	45.6	X	45.9	45.9	X
Female	56.9	54.4	X	54.1	54.1	X
Foreign born; not a U.S. citizen...........	301,992	296,854	-1.7	22,407,056	22,593,269	0.8
Male	50.1	48.7	X	51.2	51.1	X
Female	49.9	51.3	X	48.8	48.9	X
Entered 2010 or later	8.9	11.7	X	12.3	15.6	X
Entered 2000 to 2009	28.6	26.6	X	28.6	27.9	X
Entered before 2000...................	62.5	61.7	X	59.1	56.5	X
World Region of Birth, Foreign						
Foreign-born population, excluding population born at sea	551,722	558,170	1.2	42,390,705	43,289,646	2.1
Europe	7.0	7.9	X	11.2	11.1	X
Asia...............................	30.5	30.1	X	30.1	30.6	X
Africa	2.7	3.8	X	4.6	4.8	X
Oceania	0.7	0.4	X	0.6	0.6	X
Latin America.......................	57.4	56.2	X	51.6	51.1	X
North America.......................	1.7	1.6	X	1.9	1.9	X
Language Spoken at Home and Ability to Speak English						
Population 5 years and over.............	2,663,364	2,713,912	1.9	299,084,046	301,625,014	0.8
English only	69.3	69.8	X	78.9	78.5	X
Language other than English............	30.7	30.2	X	21.1	21.5	X
Speaks English less than "very well"....	12.3	12.2	X	8.6	8.6	X

NA = Not available.
X = Not applicable.
- = Zero or rounds to zero.

Table NV-5. Median Income and Poverty Status, 2015

(Number, percent, except as noted.)

Characteristic	State		U.S.	
	Number	Percent	Number	Percent
Median Income				
Households (dollars)	52,431	X	55,775	X
Families (dollars)	63,206	X	68,260	X
Below Poverty Level (All People)	418,243	14.7	46,153,077	14.7
Sex				
Male	194,549	13.7	20,599,407	13.4
Female	223,694	15.6	25,553,670	16.0
Age				
Under 18 years	137,348	20.9	15,000,273	20.7
Related children under 18 years	134,350	20.5	14,693,239	20.4
18 to 64 years	245,952	13.9	26,960,369	13.9
65 years and over	34,943	8.4	4,192,435	9.0

X = Not applicable.

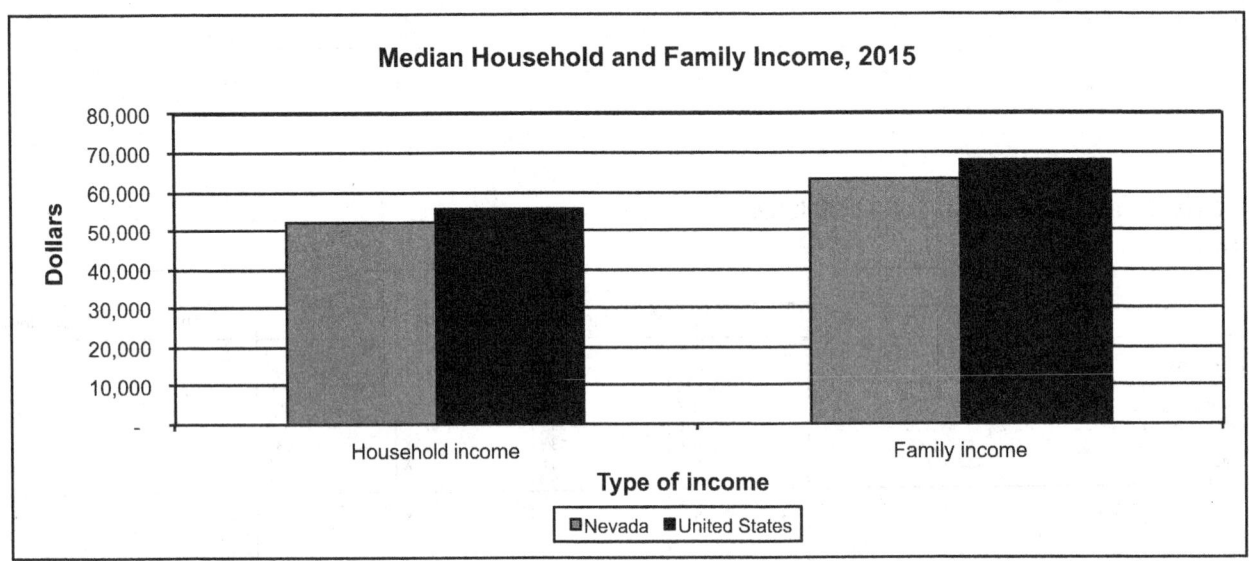

Median Household and Family Income, 2015

Table NV-6. Health Insurance Coverage Status for the Civilian Noninstitutionalized Population and Children Under 18 Years of Age

(Numbers in thousands, percent.)

Item	2007	2008	2009	2010	2011	2012	2013	2014	2015
Civilian Noninstitutionalized Population	2,568	2,568	2,610	2,669	2,687	2,724	2,757	2,806	2,856
Covered by Private or Public Insurance									
Number	2,126	2,020	2,038	2,065	2,098	2,121	2,187	2,379	2,505
Percent	82.8	78.7	78.1	77.4	78.1	77.8	79.3	84.8	87.7
Not Covered									
Number	441	548	572	604	589	603	570	427	351
Percent	17.2	21.3	21.9	22.6	21.9	22.2	20.7	15.2	12.3
Percent in the U.S. not covered	15.3	15.1	15.1	15.5	15.1	14.8	14.5	11.7	9.4
Children Under 18 Years of Age	660	667	682	664	662	663	661	662	668
Covered by Private or Public Insurance									
Number	566	532	561	549	155	553	563	598	617
Percent	85.7	79.8	82.2	82.6	83.8	83.4	85.1	90.4	92.4
Not Covered									
Number	94	135	121	115	107	110	99	64	50
Percent	14.3	20.2	17.8	17.4	16.2	16.6	14.9	9.6	7.6
Percent in the U.S. not covered	11.0	9.7	8.6	8.0	7.5	7.2	7.1	6.0	4.8

Table NV-15. State Government Finances, 2015

(Dollar amounts in thousands, percent distribution.)

Item	Dollars	Percent distribution
Total Revenue	16,439,338	100.0
General revenue	13,070,655	79.5
Intergovernmental revenue	4,147,557	25.2
Taxes	7,532,989	45.8
General sales..	4,080,507	24.8
Selective sales..	1,958,261	11.9
License taxes	649,333	3.9
Individual income tax...	0	-
Corporate income tax...	0	-
Other taxes...	844,888	5.1
Current charges	734,441	4.5
Miscellaneous general revenue	655,668	4.0
Utility revenue..	57,018	0.3
Liquor stores revenue	0	-
Insurance trust revenue[1]	3,311,665	20.1
Total Expenditure	14,720,817	100.0
Intergovernmental expenditure	4,336,630	29.5
Direct expenditure..	10,384,187	70.5
Current operation	6,844,988	46.5
Capital outlay	644,476	4.4
Insurance benefits and repayments	2,356,272	16.0
Assistance and subsidies	382,970	2.6
Interest on debt...	155,481	1.1
Exhibit: Salaries and wages..	1,594,288	10.8
Total Expenditure	14,720,817	100.0
General expenditure	12,303,598	83.6
Intergovernmental expenditure	4,336,630	29.5
Direct expenditure...	7,966,968	54.1
General expenditure, by function:		
Education..	4,738,862	32.2
Public welfare...	3,779,343	25.7
Hospitals...	252,160	1.7
Health...	351,866	2.4
Highways..	620,668	4.2
Police protection	97,800	0.7
Correction...	272,391	1.9
Natural resources...	99,767	0.7
Parks and recreation..	19,201	0.1
Governmental administration...	291,834	2.0
Interest on general debt...	153,289	1.0
Other and unallocable..	1,626,417	11.0
Utility expenditure..	60,947	0.4
Liquor stores expenditure	0	-
Insurance trust expenditure	2,356,272	16.0
Debt at End of Fiscal Year	3,351,972	X
Cash and Security Holdings	37,550,057	X

X = Not applicable.
- = Zero or rounds to zero.
[1] Within insurance trust revenue, net earnings of state retirement systems is a calculated statistic (the item code in the data file is X08), and thus can be positive or negative. Net earnings is the sum of earnings on investments plus gains on investments minus losses on investments. The change made in 2002 for asset valuation from book to market value in accordance with Statement 34 of the Governmental Accounting Standards Board is reflected in the calculated statistics.

Table NV-16. State Government Tax Collections, 2016

(Dollars in thousands, percent.)

Item	Dollars	Percent distribution
Total Taxes	8,025,046	100.0
Property taxes	280,055	3.5
Sales and gross receipts	6,347,777	79.1
General sales and gross receipts	4,266,267	53.2
Selective sales and gross receipts	2,081,510	25.9
Alcoholic beverages	45,098	0.6
Amusements	930,045	11.6
Insurance premiums	310,223	3.9
Motor fuels	315,897	3.9
Pari-mutuels	3	-
Public utilities	23,357	0.3
Tobacco products	174,663	2.2
Other selective sales	282,224	3.5
Licenses	651,067	8.1
Alcoholic beverages	0	-
Amusements	88,907	1.1
Corporations in general	75,726	0.9
Hunting and fishing	12,817	0.2
Motor vehicle	196,610	2.4
Motor vehicle operators	30,859	0.4
Public utilities	0	-
Occupation and business, NEC	242,794	3.0
Other licenses	3,354	-
Income taxes	0	-
Individual income	0	-
Corporation net income	0	-
Other taxes	746,147	9.3
Death and gift	0	-
Documentary and stock transfer	81,683	1.0
Severance	102,686	1.3
Taxes, NEC	561,778	7.0

X = Not applicable.
- = Zero or rounds to zero.

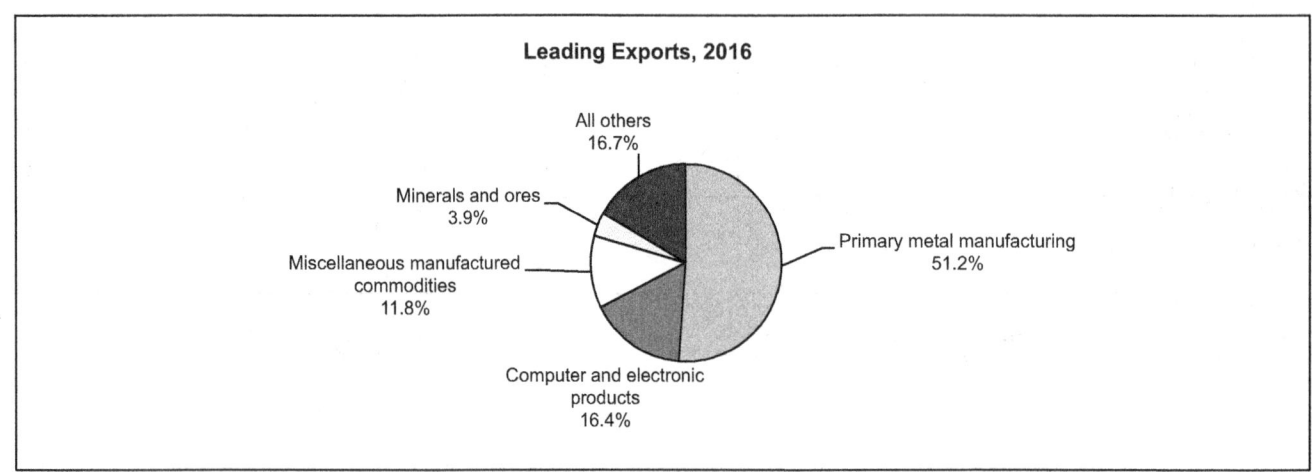

Leading Exports, 2016

All others 16.7%

Minerals and ores 3.9%

Miscellaneous manufactured commodities 11.8%

Primary metal manufacturing 51.2%

Computer and electronic products 16.4%

NEW HAMPSHIRE

Facts and Figures

Location: Northeastern United States; bordered on the N by Canada (Quebec), on the E by Maine, on the SE by the Atlantic Ocean, on the S by Massachusetts, and on the W by Vermont

Area: 9,350 sq. mi. (24,216 sq. km.); rank—46th

Population: 1,334,795 (2016 est.); rank—41st

Principal Cities: capital—Concord; largest—Manchester

Statehood: June 21, 1788; 9th state

U.S. Congress: 2 senators, 2 representatives

State Motto: Live Free or Die

State Song: "Old New Hampshire"

State Nickname: The Granite State

Abbreviations: NH; N.H.

State Symbols: flower—purple lilac; tree—white birch; bird—purple finch

At a Glance

- With an increase in population of 1.4 percent, New Hampshire ranked 40th among the states in growth from 2010 to 2016.

- New Hampshire's violent crime rate in 2015 was 199.3 per 100,000 population, the 4th lowest in the country, compared to a rate of 383.2 for the entire nation.

- The state's property crime rate, 1,745.7 per 100,000 population, ranked 46th in the country in 2015.

- New Hampshire's had the second highest rate of drug overdose deaths in 2015, with 34.3 deaths per 100,000 population.

- New Hampshire had the lowest birth rate in the country in 2015, with 9.3 births per 1,000 population.

Table NH-1. Population by Age, Sex, Race, and Hispanic Origin

(Number, percent, except where noted.)

Sex, age, race, and Hispanic origin	2000	2010	2016 [1]	Average annual percent change, 2010–2016
Total Population..	1,235,786	1,316,470	1,334,795	0.1
Percent of total U.S. population	0.4	0.4	0.4	X
Sex				
Male..	607,687	649,394	660,860	0.1
Female	628,099	667,076	673,935	0.1
Age				
Under 5 years..	75,685	69,806	64,200	-0.5
5 to 19 years..	268,480	255,996	233,213	-0.6
20 to 64 years..	743,651	812,400	810,578	-
65 years and over..	147,970	178,268	226,804	1.7
Median age (years)	37.1	41.1	43.0	0.3
Race and Hispanic Origin				
One race..				
White	1,186,851	1,248,321	1,251,893	-
Black..	9,035	16,365	20,266	1.5
American Indian and Alaska Native	2,964	3,530	3,926	0.7
Asian..	15,931	28,933	35,776	1.5
Native Hawaiian or Other Pacific Islander	371	532	670	1.6
Two or more races..	13,214	18,789	22,264	1.2
Hispanic (of any race)..	20,489	38,688	47,118	1.4

X = Not applicable.
- = Zero or rounds to zero.
[1] Population figures for 2016 are July 1 estimates. The 2010 estimates are taken from the 2010 Census.

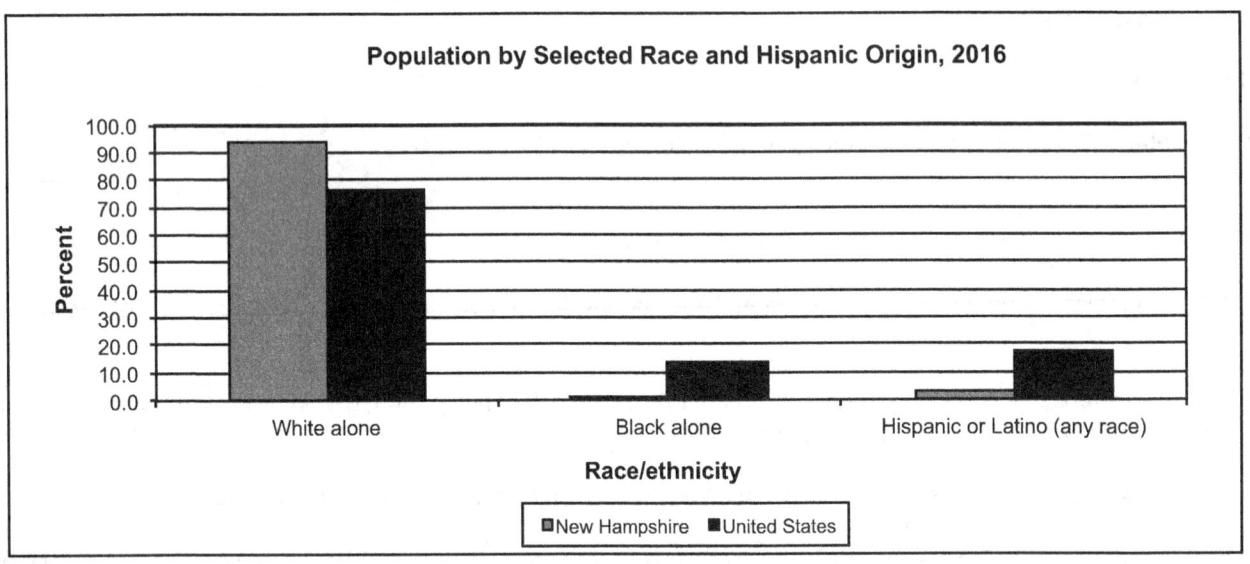

Table NH-2. Marital Status

(Number, percent distribution.)

Sex, age, race, and Hispanic origin	2000	2010	2015
Males, 15 Years and Over	476,409	529,439	548,584
Never married	27.7	30.5	33.4
Now married, except separated..	59.1	54.7	52.2
Separated..	1.2	1.3	0.9
Widowed..	2.4	2.6	2.6
Divorced..	9.6	10.9	11.0
Females, 15 Years and Over	502,232	555,698	569,020
Never married	22.3	25.4	26.4
Now married, except separated..	55.7	51.4	50.1
Separated..	1.5	1.3	1.3
Widowed..	9.2	8.6	8.4
Divorced..	11.3	13.4	13.8

Table NH-3. Households and Housing Characteristics

(Number, percent, dollars.)

Item	2000	2010	2015	Average annual percent change, 2000–2015
Total Households...	474,606	515,431	517,615	0.6
Family households..	323,651	344,057	341,473	0.4
Married-couple family...	262,438	274,195	268,944	0.2
Other family..	61,213	69,862	72,529	1.2
Male householder, no wife present........................	18,261	22,205	20,941	1.0
Female householder, no husband present.............	42,952	47,657	51,588	1.3
Nonfamily households..	150,955	171,374	176,142	1.1
Householder living alone..	116,014	130,327	135,510	1.1
Householder not living alone..................................	34,941	41,047	40,632	1.1
Housing Characteristics				
Total housing units..	547,024	614,996	622,604	0.9
Occupied housing units	474,606	515,431	517,615	0.6
Owner occupied..	330,700	369,448	366,739	0.7
Renter occupied...	143,906	145,983	150,876	0.3
Average household size...	2.53	2.48	2.49	-0.1
Financial Characteristics				
Median gross rent of renter-occupied housing	646	951	1017	3.8
Median monthly owner costs for housing units with a mortgage	1,226	1,853	1,828	3.3
Median value of owner-occupied housing units...........	133,300	243,000	244,500	5.6

Table NH-4. Migration, Origin, and Language

(Number, percent.)

Characteristic	State			U.S.		
	2014	2015	Percent change	2014	2015	Percent change
Residence 1 Year Ago						
Population 1 year and over	1,314,735	1,318,121	0.3	315,095,393	317,635,720	0.8
Same house	86.3	86.1	X	85.1	85.3	X
Different house in the U.S...	13.3	13.3	X	14.3	14.1	X
Same county	7.6	7.3	X	8.7	8.5	X
Different county	5.7	6.0	X	5.6	5.6	X
Same state..	2.6	2.0	X	3.3	3.2	X
Different state..	3.1	4.1	X	2.3	2.4	X
Abroad..	0.4	0.6	X	0.6	0.7	X
Place of Birth						
Native born...	1,247,281	1,250,649	0.3	276,465,262	278,128,449	0.6
Male..	49.6	49.5	X	49.3	49.3	X
Female...	50.4	50.5	X	50.7	50.7	X
Foreign born	79,532	79,959	0.5	42,391,794	43,290,372	2.1
Male	45.1	48.3	X	48.7	48.6	X
Female...	54.9	51.7	X	51.3	51.4	X
Foreign born; naturalized U.S. citizen........................	43,744	45,461	3.9	19,984,738	20,697,103	3.6
Male..	44	43.3	X	45.9	45.9	X
Female...	56	56.7	X	54.1	54.1	X
Foreign born; not a U.S. citizen.................................	35,788	34,498	-3.6	22,407,056	22,593,269	0.8
Male..	46.3	54.8	X	51.2	51.1	X
Female...	53.7	45.2	X	48.8	48.9	X
Entered 2010 or later	14.9	17.6	X	12.3	15.6	X
Entered 2000 to 2009	28.6	28.0	X	28.6	27.9	X
Entered before 2000...	56.6	54.4	X	59.1	56.5	X
World Region of Birth, Foreign						
Foreign-born population, excluding population born at sea	79,532	79,959	0.5	42,390,705	43,289,646	2.1
Europe..	23.7	25.4	X	11.2	11.1	X
Asia..	36.6	34.5	X	30.1	30.6	X
Africa..	7.2	6.4	X	4.6	4.8	X
Oceania..	0.5	0.2	X	0.6	0.6	X
Latin America...	20	20.9	X	51.6	51.1	X
North America..	11.9	12.6	X	1.9	1.9	X
Language Spoken at Home and Ability to Speak English						
Population 5 years and over..	1,261,731	1,267,099	0.4	299,084,046	301,625,014	0.8
English only	92.5	92.2	X	78.9	78.5	X
Language other than English......................................	7.5	7.8	X	21.1	21.5	X
Speaks English less than "very well"....................	2.4	2.2	X	8.6	8.6	X

NA = Not available.
X = Not applicable.
- = Zero or rounds to zero.

Table NH-5. Median Income and Poverty Status, 2015

(Number, percent, except as noted.)

Characteristic	State		U.S.	
	Number	Percent	Number	Percent
Median Income				
Households (dollars)..	70,303	X	55,775	X
Families (dollars)	85,873	X	68,260	X
Below Poverty Level (All People)	106,046	8.2	46,153,077	14.7
Sex				
Male	45,784	7.2	20,599,407	13.4
Female	60,262	9.2	25,553,670	16.0
Age				
Under 18 years..	27,592	10.7	15,000,273	20.7
Related children under 18 years...............................	26,146	10.2	14,693,239	20.4
18 to 64 years..	65,704	8.0	26,960,369	13.9
65 years and over	12,750	6.1	4,192,435	9.0

X = Not applicable.

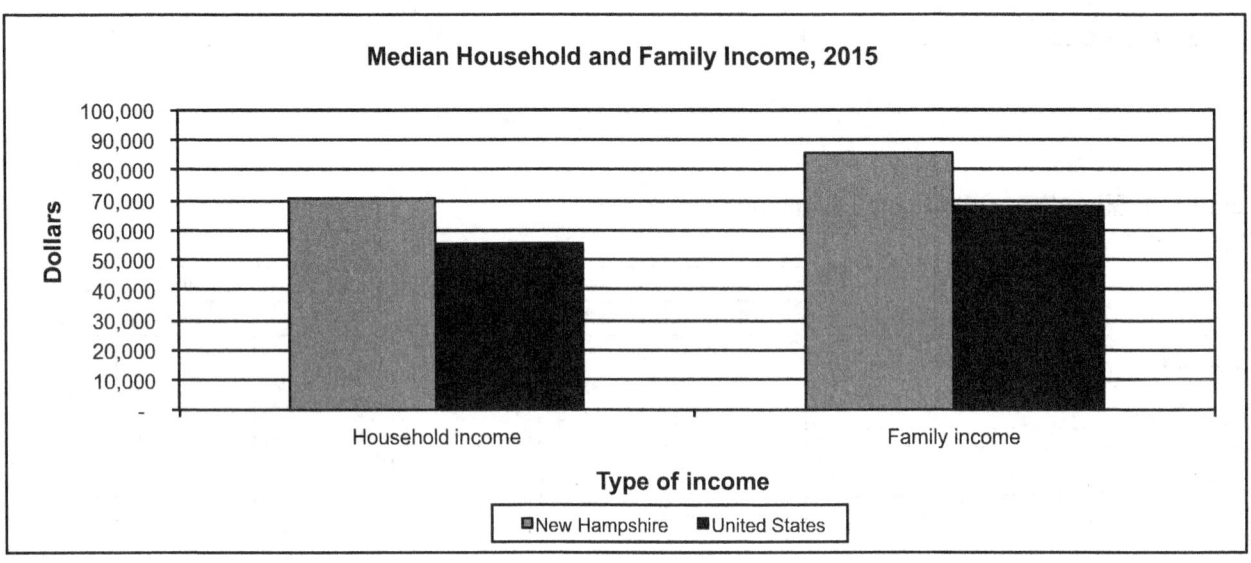

Median Household and Family Income, 2015

Table NH-6. Health Insurance Coverage Status for the Civilian Noninstitutionalized Population and Children Under 18 Years of Age

(Numbers in thousands, percent.)

Item	2007	2008	2009	2010	2011	2012	2013	2014	2015
Civilian Noninstitutionalized Population	1,314	1,299	1,309	1,303	1,304	1,306	1,309	1,312	1,314
Covered by Private or Public Insurance									
Number..	1,177	1,159	1,175	1,157	1,167	1,167	1,168	1,191	1,231
Percent..	89.5	89.2	89.8	88.9	89.5	89.4	89.3	90.8	93.7
Not Covered									
Number..	137	140	134	145	137	139	140	120	83
Percent..	10.5	10.8	10.2	11.1	10.5	10.6	10.7	9.2	6.3
Percent in the U.S. not covered....................	15.3	15.1	15.1	15.5	15.1	14.8	14.5	11.7	9.4
Children Under 18 Years of Age	296	293	289	286	279	275	271	267	263
Covered by Private or Public Insurance									
Number..	277	278	276	272	269	264	260	255	256
Percent..	93.5	94.9	95.3	95.2	96.3	96.0	96.2	95.6	97.3
Not Covered									
Number..	19	15	13	14	10	11	10	12	7
Percent..	6.5	5.1	4.7	4.8	3.7	4.0	3.8	4.4	2.7
Percent in the U.S. not covered....................	11.0	9.7	8.6	8.0	7.5	7.2	7.1	6.0	4.8

Table NH-7. Employment Status by Demographic Group, 2016

(Numbers in thousands, percent.)

Characteristic	Civilian noninstitutional population	Civilian labor force		Employed		Unemployed	
		Number	Percent of population	Number	Percent of population	Number	Percent of population
Total..................................	1,090	751	68.9	730	67.0	21	2.8
Sex							
Male..................................	535	397	74.1	384	71.8	12	3.1
Female	555	354	63.9	345	62.3	9	2.5
Race, Sex, and Hispanic Origin							
White	1,033	714	69.1	694	67.2	20	2.8
Male..............................	508	376	74.2	365	71.8	12	3.1
Female	526	337	64.2	330	62.7	8	2.4
Black or African American..................	NA	NA	NA	NA	NA	NA	NA
Male..............................	NA	NA	NA	NA	NA	NA	NA
Female	NA	NA	NA	NA	NA	NA	NA
Hispanic or Latino ethnicity[1]	NA	NA	NA	NA	NA	NA	NA
Male..............................	NA	NA	NA	NA	NA	NA	NA
Female	NA	NA	NA	NA	NA	NA	NA
Age							
16 to 19 years.....................	68	32	46.8	28	41.9	3	10.5
20 to 24 years.....................	85	69	81.4	67	78.1	3	4.2
25 to 34 years.....................	166	142	85.8	139	83.7	4	2.5
35 to 44 years.....................	149	128	85.8	126	84.6	2	1.4
45 to 54 years.....................	192	165	85.7	162	84.1	3	1.9
55 to 64 years.....................	214	158	74.1	154	72.3	4	2.7
65 years and over	216	56	26.0	54	24.9	2	4.1

NOTE: Data in Table 7 are from the Current Population Survey (CPS) and do not match the estimates in Table 8. See notes and definitions for further information.
[1] May be of any race.
NA = Not available.

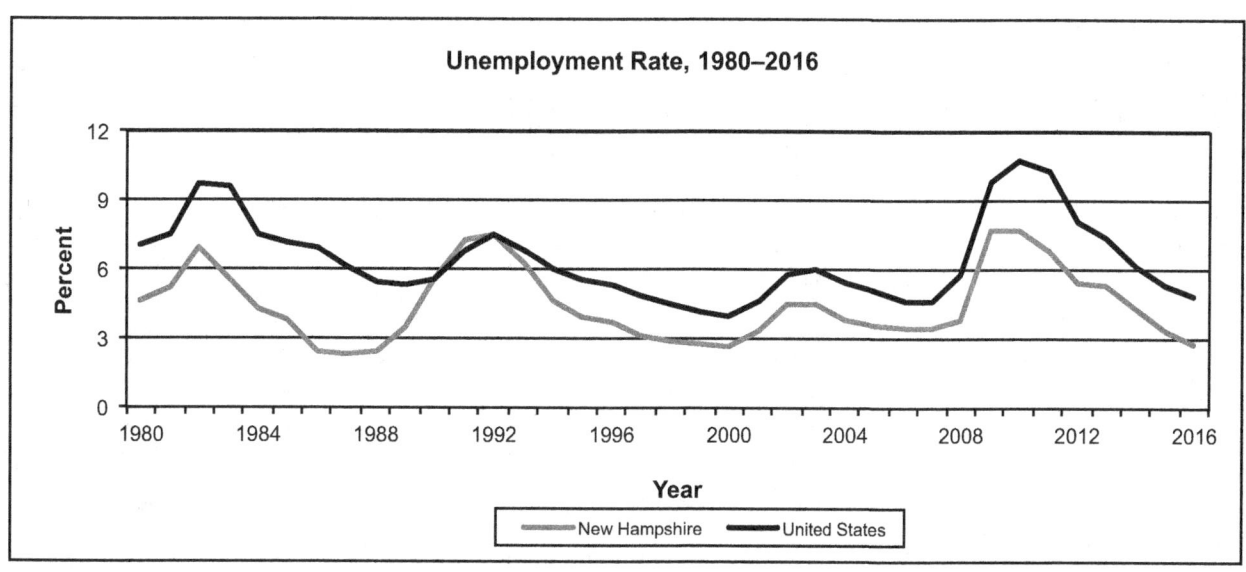

Unemployment Rate, 1980–2016

— New Hampshire   — United States

Table NH-8. Employment Status of the Civilian Noninstitutional Population Age 16 Years and Over

(Number, percent.)

Year	Civilian labor force	Civilian participation rate	Employed	Unemployed	Unemployment rate
2008..............................	742,781	70.7	714,104	28,677	3.9
2009..............................	744,227	70.4	697,802	46,425	6.2
2010..............................	738,257	69.9	695,135	43,122	5.8
2011..............................	736,302	69.5	696,532	39,770	5.4
2012..............................	741,031	69.5	700,290	40,741	5.5
2013..............................	741,937	69.2	704,196	37,741	5.1
2014..............................	740,609	68.6	708,896	31,713	4.3
2015..............................	741,192	68.4	715,727	25,465	3.4
2016..............................	748,563	68.7	727,420	21,143	2.8

Table NH-9. Employment and Average Wages by Industry

(Estimates through 2010 are based on the 2007 *North American Industry Classification System* [NAICS]. Estimates from 2011 onward are based on the 2012 NAICS.)

Industry	2009	2010	2011	2012	2013	2014	2015
	Number of jobs						
Wage and Salary Employment by Industry..................	635,883	630,596	634,658	640,890	647,438	655,973	665,995
Farm Wage and Salary Employment.........................	1,139	1,125	1,230	1,451	1,660	1,664	1,658
Nonfarm Wage and Salary Employment....................	634,744	629,471	633,428	639,439	645,778	654,309	664,337
Private wage and salary employment............................	538,473	531,746	538,117	544,521	551,094	559,252	569,899
Forestry, fishing, and related activities	795	765	737	751	788	826	816
Mining..................	510	490	494	500	531	532	526
Utilities.............	2,532	2,513	2,472	2,454	2,481	2,320	2,185
Construction.........................	23,697	22,170	22,857	22,835	23,197	23,857	24,853
Manufacturing......................	68,113	65,784	66,686	66,059	66,074	66,578	67,306
Durable goods manufacturing............................	51,987	50,303	51,179	50,205	49,884	49,938	50,169
Nondurable goods manufacturing........................	16,126	15,481	15,507	15,854	16,190	16,640	17,137
Wholesale trade	26,652	26,010	26,324	26,733	26,875	27,241	27,677
Retail trade........................	94,568	93,256	93,975	95,244	95,563	95,260	95,740
Transportation and warehousing.....................	12,383	12,198	12,432	12,569	12,623	13,035	13,502
Information	12,180	11,202	11,177	12,093	11,927	12,044	12,274
Finance and insurance	27,809	27,378	28,065	28,777	29,181	29,430	30,109
Real estate and rental and leasing............................	7,365	6,903	6,978	6,727	6,934	6,984	6,818
Professional, scientific, and technical services	29,989	29,523	30,174	30,706	32,006	32,696	33,680
Management of companies and enterprises....................	7,970	8,016	8,096	8,155	8,187	8,193	8,634
Administrative and waste services................................	25,888	27,515	28,836	29,985	30,708	33,229	34,800
Educational services	22,222	21,959	21,909	22,255	22,803	23,294	24,289
Health care and social assistance............................	84,751	85,344	85,456	85,964	86,774	87,527	89,220
Arts, entertainment, and recreation............................	11,084	11,225	11,342	11,342	11,391	11,163	11,456
Accommodation and food services...........................	51,518	51,733	52,394	53,589	55,240	56,273	57,469
Other services, except public administration..................	28,447	27,762	27,713	27,783	27,811	28,770	28,545
Government and government enterprises..........................	96,271	97,725	95,311	94,918	94,684	95,057	94,438
	Dollars						
Average Wages and Salaries by Industry	44,090	45,182	46,476	47,575	48,251	50,380	51,752
Average Farm Wages and Salaries	26,978	26,130	20,918	30,999	27,939	29,502	27,184
Average Nonfarm Wages and Salaries	44,121	45,216	46,526	47,612	48,303	50,434	51,814
Average private wages and salaries............................	44,564	45,946	47,269	48,526	49,219	51,544	52,883
Forestry, fishing, and related activities	33,722	36,197	37,312	44,023	40,786	45,105	47,180
Mining.........................	52,227	55,894	55,326	56,796	53,343	54,195	57,797
Utilities..................	87,753	87,825	96,454	94,513	94,655	102,359	103,123
Construction.........................	48,439	49,367	50,143	51,516	52,969	54,211	57,279
Manufacturing......................	58,273	61,916	63,203	63,505	64,635	66,258	66,891
Durable goods manufacturing............................	61,501	65,468	66,679	66,784	67,993	69,839	70,090
Nondurable goods manufacturing........................	47,867	50,375	51,731	53,122	54,291	55,513	57,524
Wholesale trade	70,819	74,712	77,816	80,552	82,165	84,833	90,564
Retail trade........................	26,159	26,731	27,391	27,940	28,485	29,674	30,755
Transportation and warehousing.....................	36,263	37,347	38,523	39,431	40,250	41,135	43,197
Information	69,345	75,234	74,492	75,495	78,953	91,556	82,763
Finance and insurance	74,213	78,077	81,359	84,488	85,898	94,501	94,668
Real estate and rental and leasing............................	43,648	41,118	47,289	45,040	46,133	47,655	50,861
Professional, scientific, and technical services	72,154	74,394	76,934	79,372	80,194	84,853	86,952
Management of companies and enterprises....................	76,927	80,800	82,358	97,866	89,768	106,426	106,638
Administrative and waste services................................	40,055	39,997	40,286	42,705	42,391	43,552	45,234
Educational services	39,281	40,004	40,808	41,711	42,730	43,902	44,666
Health care and social assistance............................	45,623	46,483	47,859	48,526	49,097	50,346	51,819
Arts, entertainment, and recreation............................	21,077	21,120	21,485	22,034	23,150	24,414	24,533
Accommodation and food services...........................	18,490	18,737	19,192	19,719	20,118	20,888	21,957
Other services, except public administration..................	28,958	30,106	30,744	31,644	32,725	33,254	34,902
Government and government enterprises..........................	41,646	41,243	42,327	42,368	42,968	43,898	45,361

Table NH-10. Employment Characteristics by Family Type

(Number, percent.)

Family type and labor force status	2013		2014		2015	
	Total	Families with own children under 18 years	Total	Families with own children under 18 years	Total	Families with own children under 18 years
All Families...	347,272	145,235	343,363	137,776	341,473	128,997
FAMILY TYPE AND LABOR FORCE STATUS						
Married-Couple Families..	272,206	102,397	268,440	94,424	268,944	91,828
Both husband and wife in labor force..............................	56.3	71.7	57.3	70.9	57.5	74.1
Husband in labor force, wife not in labor force....................	19.9	23.5	19.4	25.1	17.3	21.3
Wife in labor force, husband not in labor force....................	7.6	3.0	8.0	2.9	7.3	3.1
Both husband and wife not in labor force..........................	15.4	1.3	15.3	1.1	16.8	1.1
Other Families...	75,066	42,838	74,923	43,352	72,529	37,169
Female householder, no husband present............................	69.8	70.0	67.7	69.3	71.1	74.3
In labor force..	53.0	59.7	52.2	60.2	50.7	59.5
Not in labor force..	16.8	10.3	15.5	9.1	20.4	14.8
Male householder, no wife present.................................	30.2	30.0	32.3	30.7	28.9	25.7
In labor force..	24.2	26.5	27.7	29.3	22.4	23.9
Not in labor force..	6.0	3.5	4.6	1.4	6.4	1.8

Table NH-11. School Enrollment and Educational Attainment, 2015

(Number, percent.)

Item	State	U.S.
Enrollment		
Total population 3 years and over, enrolled in school	314,478	81,618,288
Enrolled in nursery school or preschool (percent)	5.6	6.0
Enrolled in kindergarten (percent).................................	4.7	5.0
Enrolled in elementary school, grades 1-8 (percent).................	37.8	40.3
Enrolled in high school, grades 9-12 (percent).....................	21.8	20.9
Enrolled in college or graduate school (percent)...................	30.1	27.7
Attainment		
Total population 25 years and over	937,214	216,447,163
Less than ninth grade (percent)	1.9	5.5
9th to 12th grade, no diploma (percent)	4.9	7.3
High school graduate, including equivalency (percent)..............	28.5	27.6
Some college, no degree (percent)	19.2	20.7
Associate's degree (percent)......................................	9.7	8.2
Bachelor's degree (percent).......................................	21.9	19.0
Graduate or professional degree (percent).........................	13.7	11.6
High school graduate or higher (percent)..........................	93.1	87.1
Bachelor's degree or higher (percent).............................	35.7	30.6

Table NH-12. Public School Characteristics and Educational Indicators

(Number, percent; data derived from National Center of Education Statistics.)

Item	State	U.S.
Public Schools, 2014–2015 (except where noted)		
Number of school districts..	296	18,260
Number of schools...	488	98,373
Number of students..	184,670	50,312,581
Number of teachers	14,773	3,132,351
Student-teacher ratio...	12.5	16.1
Expenditures per student (dollars), FY 2014.......................	14,601	11,066
Four-year adjusted cohort graduation rate (ACGR)[1,2]	88.1	83.2
Students eligible for free or reduced-price lunch (percent)........	29.0	51.8
English language learners (percent)...............................	2.0	9.4
Students age 3 to 21 served under IDEA, part B (percent)...........	15.7	13.0

Public Schools by Type	Number	Percent of state public schools
Total number of schools...	488	100.0
Regular	488	100.0
Special education	0	-
Vocational education	0	-
Alternative education...	0	-

NOTE: Every school is assigned only one school type based on its instructional emphasis.
[1] ACGR data represents a new method of calculating high-school completion rates and may not be comparable to previous years' data for Averaged Freshmen Graduation Rates (AFGR).
[2] The United States 4-year ACGRs were estimated using both the reported 4-year ACGR data from 49 states and the District of Columbia and using imputed data for Idaho. The estimate for American Indian/Alaska Native students also includes imputed data for Virginia.
- = Zero or rounds to zero.

Table NH-13. Reported Voting and Registration of the Voting-Age Population, November 2016

(Numbers in thousands, percent.)

Item	Total population	Total citizen population	Registered			Voted		
			Total registered	Percent registered (total population)	Percent registered (total citizen population)	Total voted	Percent voted (total population)	Percent voted (total citizen population)
U.S. Total	245,502	224,059	157,596	64.2	70.3	137,537	56.0	61.4
State Total...........................	1,044	1,012	763	73.1	75.4	698	66.9	69.0
Sex								
Male	509	494	359	70.6	72.7	327	64.3	66.2
Female	535	518	404	75.4	77.9	371	69.3	71.6
Race								
White alone........................	990	973	740	74.7	76.0	677	68.4	69.6
White, non-Hispanic alone	976	964	733	75.2	76.1	672	68.9	69.7
Black alone........................	11	9	5	(B)	(B)	5	(B)	(B)
Asian alone........................	27	16	9	(B)	(B)	9	(B)	(B)
Hispanic (of any race)	19	11	9	(B)	(B)	7	(B)	(B)
White alone or in combination	1,002	984	746	74.5	75.9	681	68.0	69.3
Black alone or in combination..........	16	13	8	(B)	(B)	5	(B)	(B)
Asian alone or in combination.........	28	17	11	(B)	(B)	11	(B)	(B)
Age								
18 to 24 years.....................	98	96	66	(B)	(B)	55	(B)	(B)
25 to 34 years.....................	157	149	103	65.4	68.8	89	56.9	59.8
35 to 44 years.....................	164	154	109	66.3	70.4	102	62.5	66.3
45 to 64 years.....................	396	386	310	78.1	80.1	287	72.3	74.2
65 years and over	228	225	175	76.9	77.8	165	72.3	73.2

B = Base is less than 75,000 and therefore too small to show the derived measure.

Table NH-14. Crime

(Number, rate per 100,000. Data are derived from the FBI Uniform Crime Reports.)

Item	State			U.S. [1,2,3,4]		
	2014	2015	Percent change	2014	2015	Percent change
TOTAL POPULATION[5]	1,327,996	1,330,608	0.2	318,907,401	321,418,820	0.8
VIOLENT CRIME						
Number.................................	2,625	2,652	1.0	1,186,185	1,231,566	3.8
Rate	197.7	199.3	0.8	372.0	383.2	3.0
Murder and Nonnegligent Manslaughter						
Number.................................	16	14	-12.5	14,164	15,696	10.8
Rate	1.2	1.1	-12.7	4.4	4.9	10.0
Rape[6]						
Number.................................	596	627	5.2	118,027	124,047	5.1
Rate	44.9	47.1	5.0	37.0	38.6	4.3
Robbery						
Number.................................	544	468	-14.0	322,905	327,374	1.4
Rate	41.0	35.2	-14.1	101.3	101.9	0.6
Aggravated Assault						
Number.................................	1,469	1,543	5.0	731,089	764,449	4.6
Rate	110.6	116.0	4.8	229.2	237.8	3.7
PROPERTY CRIME						
Number.................................	26,098	23,229	-11.0	8,209,010	7,993,631	-2.6
Rate	1,965.2	1,745.7	-11.2	2,574.1	2,487.0	-3.4
Burglary						
Number.................................	4,191	3,467	-17.3	1,713,153	1,579,527	-7.8
Rate	315.6	260.6	-17.4	537.2	491.4	-8.5
Larceny-Theft						
Number.................................	21,051	18,871	-10.4	5,809,054	5,706,346	-1.8
Rate	1,585.2	1,418.2	-10.5	1,821.5	1,775.4	-2.5
Motor Vehicle Theft						
Number.................................	856	891	4.1	686,803	707,758	3.1
Rate	64.5	67.0	3.9	215.4	220.2	2.2

NOTE: Although arson data are included in the trend and clearance tables, sufficient data are not available to estimate totals for this offense. Therefore, no arson data are published in this table.

X = Not applicable.

- = Zero or rounds to zero.

[1] The crime figures have been adjusted.

[2] The data collection methodology for the offense of forcible rape used by the Minnesota state Uniform Crime Reporting (UCR) Program (with the exception of Minneapolis and St. Paul, Minnesota) does not comply with national UCR Program guidelines. Consequently, its figures for forcible rape and violent crime (of which forcible rape is a part) are not published in this table.

[3] Includes offenses reported by the Zoological Police and the Metro Transit Police.

[4] Because of changes in the state's reporting practices, figures are not comparable to previous years' data.

[5] Populations are U.S. Census Bureau provisional estimates as of July 1 of each year.

[6] The figures shown for the offense of rape were estimated using the revised Uniform Crime Reporting (UCR) definition of rape.

Table NH-15. State Government Finances, 2015

(Dollar amounts in thousands, percent distribution.)

Item	Dollars	Percent distribution
Total Revenue	7,887,797	100.0
General revenue	6,406,102	81.2
Intergovernmental revenue	2,266,476	28.7
Taxes	2,487,737	31.5
General sales	0	-
Selective sales	970,102	12.3
License taxes	322,667	4.1
Individual income tax	96,038	1.2
Corporate income tax	576,679	7.3
Other taxes	522,251	6.6
Current charges	823,733	10.4
Miscellaneous general revenue	828,156	10.5
Utility revenue	0	-
Liquor stores revenue	631,280	8.0
Insurance trust revenue[1]	850,415	10.8
Total Expenditure	7,093,463	100.0
Intergovernmental expenditure	573,048	8.1
Direct expenditure	6,520,415	91.9
Current operation	4,878,497	68.8
Capital outlay	392,229	5.5
Insurance benefits and repayments	758,269	10.7
Assistance and subsidies	158,098	2.2
Interest on debt	333,322	4.7
Exhibit: Salaries and wages	1,068,976	15.1
Total Expenditure	7,093,463	100.0
General expenditure	5,831,133	82.2
Intergovernmental expenditure	573,048	8.1
Direct expenditure	5,258,085	74.1
General expenditure, by function:		
Education	1,331,713	18.8
Public welfare	2,112,515	29.8
Hospitals	54,295	0.8
Health	116,812	1.6
Highways	505,452	7.1
Police protection	63,624	0.9
Correction	106,824	1.5
Natural resources	73,930	1.0
Parks and recreation	28,555	0.4
Governmental administration	259,202	3.7
Interest on general debt	333,322	4.7
Other and unallocable	844,889	11.9
Utility expenditure	9,027	0.1
Liquor stores expenditure	495,034	7.0
Insurance trust expenditure	758,269	10.7
Debt at End of Fiscal Year	8,210,346	X
Cash and Security Holdings	14,682,474	X

X = Not applicable.
- = Zero or rounds to zero.
[1] Within insurance trust revenue, net earnings of state retirement systems is a calculated statistic (the item code in the data file is X08), and thus can be positive or negative. Net earnings is the sum of earnings on investments plus gains on investments minus losses on investments. The change made in 2002 for asset valuation from book to market value in accordance with Statement 34 of the Governmental Accounting Standards Board is reflected in the calculated statistics.

Table NH-16. State Government Tax Collections, 2016

(Dollars in thousands, percent.)

Item	Dollars	Percent distribution
Total Taxes	2,641,946	100.0
Property taxes	406,394	15.4
Sales and gross receipts	982,832	37.2
General sales and gross receipts	0	-
Selective sales and gross receipts	982,832	37.2
Alcoholic beverages	12,850	0.5
Amusements	427	-
Insurance premiums	113,473	4.3
Motor fuels	144,930	5.5
Pari-mutuels	922	-
Public utilities	58,206	2.2
Tobacco products	226,482	8.6
Other selective sales	425,542	16.1
Licenses	329,549	12.5
Alcoholic beverages	18,056	0.7
Amusements	288	-
Corporations in general	59,010	2.2
Hunting and fishing	11,742	0.4
Motor vehicle	116,127	4.4
Motor vehicle operators	5,849	0.2
Public utilities	16,989	0.6
Occupation and business, NEC	100,049	3.8
Other licenses	1,439	0.1
Income taxes	788,210	29.8
Individual income	87,973	3.3
Corporation net income	700,237	26.5
Other taxes	134,961	5.1
Death and gift	0	-
Documentary and stock transfer	134,961	5.1
Severance	0	-
Taxes, NEC	0	-

X = Not applicable.
- = Zero or rounds to zero.

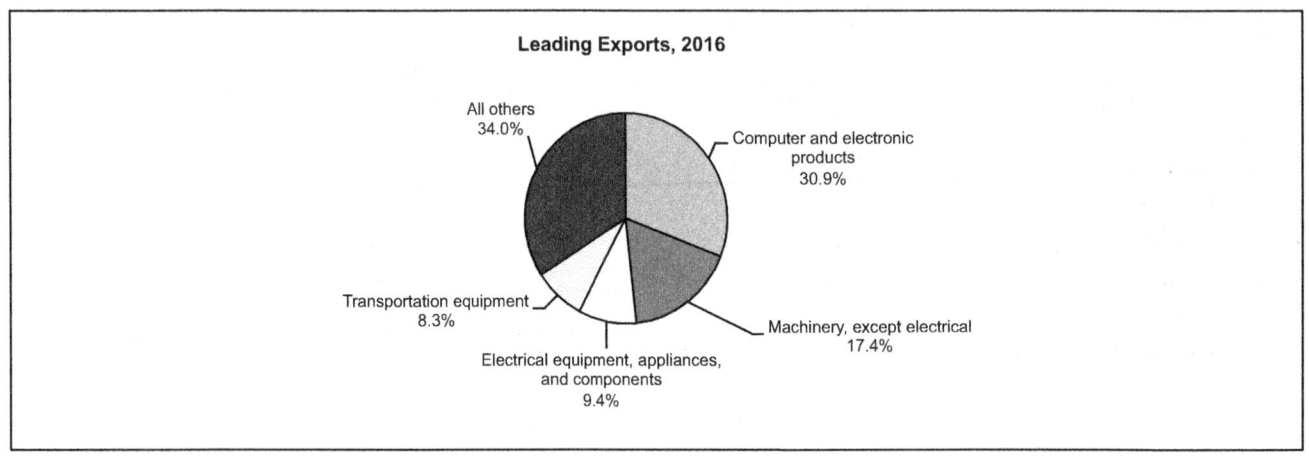

Leading Exports, 2016

- All others 34.0%
- Computer and electronic products 30.9%
- Machinery, except electrical 17.4%
- Electrical equipment, appliances, and components 9.4%
- Transportation equipment 8.3%

Facts and Figures

Location: Middle Atlantic region of the United States; bordered on the N and NE by New York, on the E by the Atlantic Ocean, on the S by Delaware Bay, and on the W by Delaware and Pennsylvania

Area: 8,721 sq. mi. (22,588 sq. km.); rank—47th

Population: 8,944,469 (2016 est.); rank—11th

Principal Cities: capital—Trenton; largest—Newark

Statehood: December 18, 1787; 3rd state

U.S. Congress: 2 senators, 12 representatives

State Motto: Liberty and Prosperity

State Song: None

State Nickname: The Garden State

Abbreviations: NJ; N.J.

State Symbols: flower—common meadow violet; tree—red oak; bird—Eastern goldfinch

At a Glance

- With an increase in population of 1.7 percent, New Jersey ranked 36th among the states in growth from 2010 to 2016.

- New Jersey's median household income was $72,222 in 2015, the second highest in the country.

- In 2015, 10.8 percent of the New Jersey's population lived below the poverty level, compared to 14.7 percent of the entire U.S. population.

- New Jersey's property crime rate of 1,626.5 incidents per 100,000 population, was the third lowest rate in the country in 2015.

- Approximately 37.6 percent of New Jersey residents had a bachelor's degree or more in 2015, the 6th highest percentage in the country.

Table NJ-1. Population by Age, Sex, Race, and Hispanic Origin

(Number, percent, except where noted.)

Sex, age, race, and Hispanic origin	2000	2010	2016 [1]	Average annual percent change, 2010–2016
Total Population...	8,414,350	8,791,894	8,944,469	0.1
Percent of total U.S. population	3.0	2.8	2.8	X
Sex				
Male..	4,082,813	4,279,600	4,367,744	0.1
Female	4,331,357	4,512,294	4,576,725	0.1
Age				
Under 5 years..	563,785	541,020	521,332	-0.2
5 to 19 years...	1,720,332	1,750,184	1,680,644	-0.2
20 to 64 years...	5,017,107	5,314,697	5,369,881	0.1
65 years and over	1,113,136	1,185,993	1,372,612	1.0
Median age (years)	36.7	39.0	39.7	0.1
Race and Hispanic Origin				
One race...				
White	6,104,705	6,546,498	6,473,721	-0.1
Black...	1,141,821	1,282,005	1,337,890	0.3
American Indian and Alaska Native	19,492	49,907	53,976	0.5
Asian..	480,276	746,212	877,077	1.1
Native Hawaiian or Other Pacific Islander	3,329	7,731	9,295	1.3
Two or more races	13,755	159,541	192,510	1.3
Hispanic (of any race)...	1,117,191	1,606,006	1,786,668	0.7

X = Not applicable.
[1] Population figures for 2016 are July 1 estimates. The 2010 estimates are taken from the 2010 Census.
- = Zero or rounds to zero.

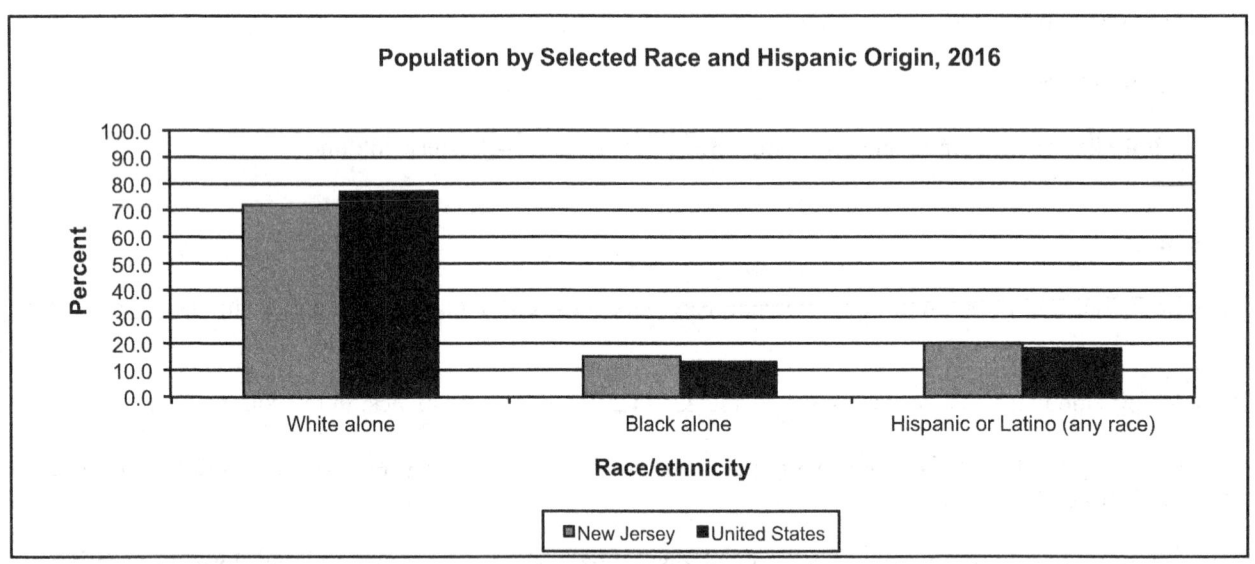

Table NJ-2. Marital Status

(Number, percent distribution.)

Sex, age, race, and Hispanic origin	2000	2010	2015
Males, 15 Years and Over	3,176,413	3,419,050	3,535,810
Never married	31.1	36.4	37.8
Now married, except separated...	57.7	52.1	51.2
Separated...	2.0	1.8	1.6
Widowed...	2.9	2.6	2.6
Divorced...	6.2	7.1	6.8
Females, 15 Years and Over	3,478,920	3,690,673	3,778,008
Never married	25.3	30.2	31.7
Now married, except separated...	51.8	47.6	46.7
Separated...	2.7	2.2	2.1
Widowed...	11.5	10.2	9.5
Divorced...	8.7	9.8	10.1

Table NJ-3. Households and Housing Characteristics

(Number, percent, dollars.)

Item	2000	2010	2015	Average annual percent change, 2000–2015
Total Households...	3,064,645	3,172,421	3,187,963	0.3
Family households	2,154,539	2,185,732	2,205,886	0.2
Married-couple family	1,638,322	1,614,230	1,632,061	-
Other family	516,217	571,502	573,825	0.7
Male householder, no wife present....................	129,205	154,036	156,240	1.4
Female householder, no husband present...........	387,012	417,466	417,585	0.5
Nonfamily households	910,106	986,689	982,077	0.5
Householder living alone.......................................	751,287	827,294	825,609	0.7
Householder not living alone.................................	158,819	159,395	156,468	-0.1
Housing Characteristics				
Total housing units...	3,310,275	3,554,909	3,593,722	0.6
Occupied housing units	3,064,645	3,172,421	3,187,963	0.3
Owner occupied	2,012,473	2,106,728	2,009,034	-
Renter occupied	1,053,172	1,065,693	1,178,929	0.8
Average household size..	2.68	2.72	2.75	0.2
Financial Characteristics				
Median gross rent of renter-occupied housing	751	1,114	1,214	4.1
Median monthly owner costs for housing units with a mortgage	1,560	2,370	2,349	3.4
Median value of owner-occupied housing units	170,800	339,200	322,600	5.9

- = Zero or rounds to zero

Table NJ-4. Migration, Origin, and Language

(Number, percent.)

Characteristic	State			U.S.		
	2014	2015	Percent change	2014	2015	Percent change
Residence 1 Year Ago						
Population 1 year and over	8,840,346	8,854,363	0.2	315,095,393	317,635,720	0.8
Same house	90.1	90.2	X	85.1	85.3	X
Different house in the U.S.	9.2	9.0	X	14.3	14.1	X
Same county	5.5	5.2	X	8.7	8.5	X
Different county	3.7	3.8	X	5.6	5.6	X
Same state	2.2	2.2	X	3.3	3.2	X
Different state	1.5	1.6	X	2.3	2.4	X
Abroad	0.7	0.7	X	0.6	0.7	X
Place of Birth						
Native born	6,977,441	6,980,688	-	276,465,262	278,128,449	0.6
Male	48.8	48.8	X	49.3	49.3	X
Female	51.2	51.2	X	50.7	50.7	X
Foreign born	1,960,734	1,977,325	0.8	42,391,794	43,290,372	2.1
Male	48.8	48.8	X	48.7	48.6	X
Female	51.2	51.2	X	51.3	51.4	X
Foreign born; naturalized U.S. citizen......................	1,066,460	1,091,687	2.4	19,984,738	20,697,103	3.6
Male	46.8	47.1	X	45.9	45.9	X
Female	53.2	52.9	X	54.1	54.1	X
Foreign born; not a U.S. citizen...............................	894,274	885,638	-1.0	22,407,056	22,593,269	0.8
Male	51.2	50.9	X	51.2	51.1	X
Female	48.8	49.1	X	48.8	48.9	X
Entered 2010 or later	12.1	14.8	X	12.3	15.6	X
Entered 2000 to 2009	29.6	28.5	X	28.6	27.9	X
Entered before 2000...	58.3	56.7	X	59.1	56.5	X
World Region of Birth, Foreign						
Foreign-born population, excluding population born at sea	1,960,734	1,977,257	0.8	42,390,705	43,289,646	2.1
Europe	15.6	15.4	X	11.2	11.1	X
Asia...	32.5	33.4	X	30.1	30.6	X
Africa	5.2	5.3	X	4.6	4.8	X
Oceania	0.2	0.2	X	0.6	0.6	X
Latin America..	45.7	44.8	X	51.6	51.1	X
North America	0.8	0.8	X	1.9	1.9	X
Language Spoken at Home and Ability to Speak English						
Population 5 years and over..	8,406,007	8,428,759	0.3	299,084,046	301,625,014	0.8
English only	69.4	69.2	X	78.9	78.5	X
Language other than English.................................	30.6	30.8	X	21.1	21.5	X
Speaks English less than "very well".................	12.2	12.1	X	8.6	8.6	X

NA = Not available.
X = Not applicable.
- = Zero or rounds to zero.

Table NJ-5. Median Income and Poverty Status, 2015

(Number, percent, except as noted.)

Characteristic	State		U.S.	
	Number	Percent	Number	Percent
Median Income				
Households (dollars).............................	72,222	X	55,775	X
Families (dollars)	90,245	X	68,260	X
Below Poverty Level (All People)	946,114	10.8	46,153,077	14.7
Sex				
Male	416,763	9.8	20,599,407	13.4
Female	529,351	11.7	25,553,670	16.0
Age				
Under 18 years............................	308,238	15.6	15,000,273	20.7
Related children under 18 years............	304,274	15.5	14,693,239	20.4
18 to 64 years	535,533	9.7	26,960,369	13.9
65 years and over	102,343	7.9	4,192,435	9.0

X = Not applicable.

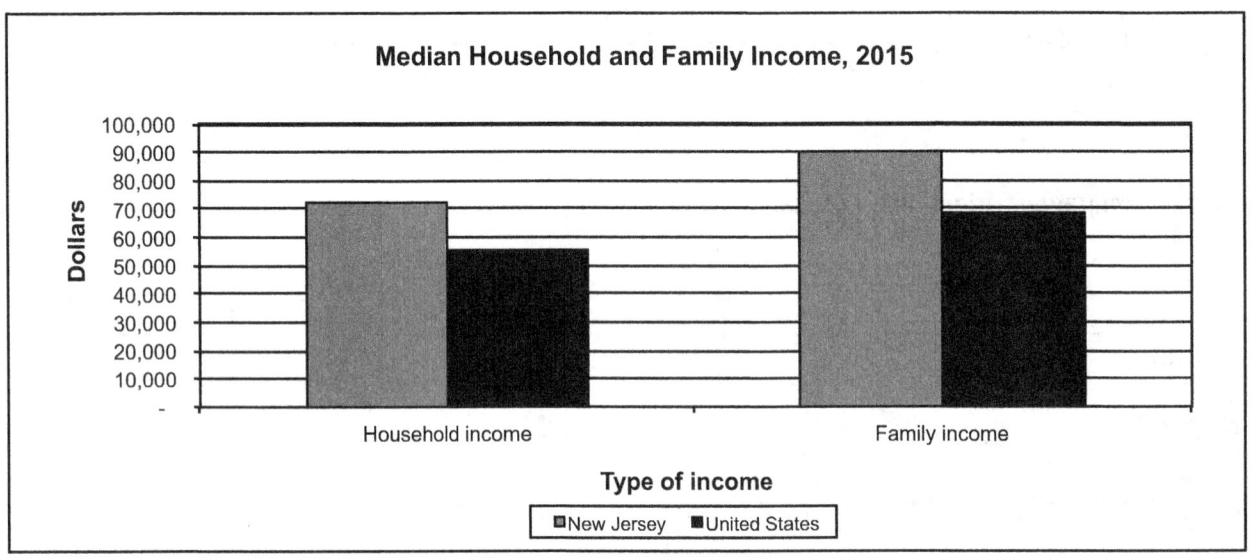

Table NJ-6. Health Insurance Coverage Status for the Civilian Noninstitutionalized Population and Children Under 18 Years of Age

(Numbers in thousands, percent.)

Item	2007	2008	2009	2010	2011	2012	2013	2014	2015
Civilian Noninstitutionalized Population	8,556	8,557	8,583	8,694	8,713	8,757	8,792	8,831	8,850
Covered by Private or Public Insurance									
Number............................	7,208	7,499	7,499	7,542	7,574	7,644	7,631	7,866	8,079
Percent............................	84.2	87.6	87.4	86.8	86.9	87.3	86.8	89.1	91.3
Not Covered									
Number............................	1,348	1,058	1,084	1,151	1,139	1,113	1,160	965	771
Percent............................	15.8	12.4	12.6	13.2	13.1	12.7	13.2	10.9	8.7
Percent in the U.S. not covered............................	15.3	15.1	15.1	15.5	15.1	14.8	14.5	11.7	9.4
Children Under 18 Years of Age	2,091	2,045	2,044	2,057	2,038	2,024	2,017	2,007	1,994
Covered by Private or Public Insurance									
Number............................	1,821	1,897	1,914	1,934	1,933	1,921	1,906	1,916	1,919
Percent............................	87.1	92.8	93.6	94.0	94.8	94.9	94.4	95.4	96.3
Not Covered									
Number............................	270	148	130	123	105	103	112	92	75
Percent............................	12.9	7.2	6.4	6.0	5.2	5.1	5.6	4.6	3.7
Percent in the U.S. not covered............................	11.0	9.7	8.6	8.0	7.5	7.2	7.1	6.0	4.8

Table NJ-7. Employment Status by Demographic Group, 2016

(Numbers in thousands, percent.)

Characteristic	Civilian noninstitutional population	Civilian labor force		Employed		Unemployed	
		Number	Percent of population	Number	Percent of population	Number	Percent of population
Total...	7,134	4,553	63.8	4,328	60.7	225	4.9
Sex							
Male..	3,430	2,444	71.3	2,331	68.0	113	4.6
Female	3,704	2,109	56.9	1,997	53.9	111	5.3
Race, Sex, and Hispanic Origin							
White	5,354	3,429	64.0	3,277	61.2	152	4.4
Male..	2,598	1,857	71.5	1,776	68.4	81	4.3
Female	2,756	1,572	57.0	1,501	54.5	71	4.5
Black or African American...................	1,006	618	61.5	573	57.0	45	7.3
Male..	453	295	65.1	272	60.0	23	7.8
Female	553	323	58.5	301	54.5	22	6.9
Hispanic or Latino ethnicity[1]	1,214	823	67.7	778	64.0	45	5.5
Male..	620	463	74.6	438	70.6	25	5.3
Female	594	360	60.6	339	57.1	21	5.7
Age							
16 to 19 years.................................	474	128	27.0	109	22.9	20	15.2
20 to 24 years.................................	565	379	67.1	341	60.3	38	10.1
25 to 34 years.................................	1,151	931	80.9	896	77.9	35	3.7
35 to 44 years.................................	1,110	923	83.2	889	80.1	34	3.7
45 to 54 years.................................	1,320	1,072	81.2	1,026	77.7	46	4.2
55 to 64 years.................................	1,140	784	68.8	745	65.4	39	5.0
65 years and over	1,375	336	24.5	322	23.5	14	4.1

NOTE: Data in Table 7 are from the Current Population Survey (CPS) and do not match the estimates in Table 8. See notes and definitions for further information.
[1] May be of any race.

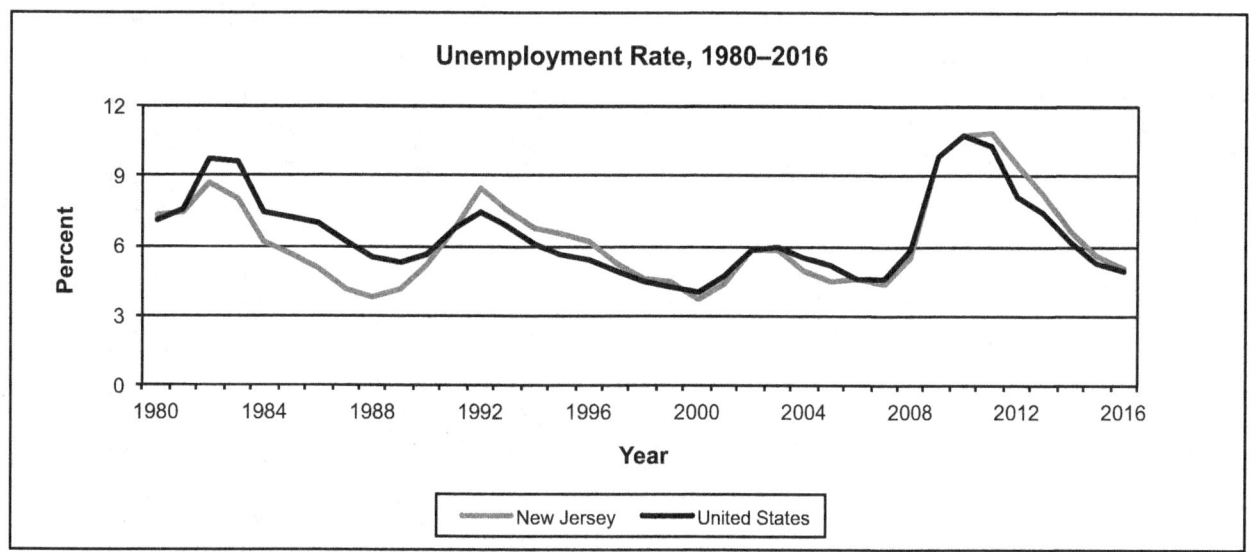

Table NJ-8. Employment Status of the Civilian Noninstitutional Population Age 16 Years and Over

(Number, percent.)

Year	Civilian labor force	Civilian participation rate	Employed	Unemployed	Unemployment rate
2008..	4,504,432	67.0	4,263,965	240,467	5.3
2009..	4,550,645	67.3	4,138,570	412,075	9.1
2010..	4,555,330	66.4	4,121,455	433,875	9.5
2011..	4,565,272	65.9	4,138,464	426,808	9.3
2012..	4,585,318	65.8	4,158,553	426,765	9.3
2013..	4,528,492	64.6	4,157,649	370,843	8.2
2014..	4,513,600	64.0	4,209,699	303,901	6.7
2015..	4,543,777	64.1	4,288,825	254,952	5.6
2016..	4,524,258	63.8	4,299,931	224,327	5.0

Table NJ-9. Employment and Average Wages by Industry

(Estimates through 2010 are based on the 2007 *North American Industry Classification System* [NAICS]. Estimates from 2011 onward are based on the 2012 NAICS.)

Industry	2009	2010	2011	2012	2013	2014	2015
	Number of jobs						
Wage and Salary Employment by Industry..................	3,968,683	3,911,956	3,908,751	3,940,169	3,980,038	4,012,486	4,061,802
Farm Wage and Salary Employment.........................	6,755	7,462	7,456	9,641	8,903	9,552	9,252
Nonfarm Wage and Salary Employment....................	3,961,928	3,904,494	3,901,295	3,930,528	3,971,135	4,002,934	4,052,550
Private wage and salary employment......................	3,301,848	3,256,067	3,276,766	3,312,574	3,352,598	3,385,928	3,440,722
Forestry, fishing, and related activities.....................	3,037	3,464	3,315	3,439	2,910	3,550	3,735
Mining..	1,492	1,371	1,307	1,250	1,317	1,412	1,388
Utilities...	11,778	14,341	13,592	13,806	13,671	13,659	14,210
Construction...	145,179	134,391	133,854	134,271	141,669	145,329	151,835
Manufacturing...	266,906	257,437	253,053	245,442	242,951	242,342	238,259
Durable goods manufacturing...........................	118,970	114,263	114,388	112,052	110,854	108,829	109,400
Nondurable goods manufacturing......................	147,936	143,174	138,665	133,390	132,097	133,513	128,859
Wholesale trade...	218,271	211,326	210,659	213,668	213,896	215,239	217,602
Retail trade..	443,249	441,175	445,246	447,763	451,981	458,307	464,982
Transportation and warehousing..........................	153,784	149,608	151,521	151,199	150,894	153,225	160,481
Information..	84,164	79,350	75,926	77,872	75,223	75,525	74,694
Finance and insurance	195,131	192,387	192,237	191,491	191,177	184,657	189,375
Real estate and rental and leasing........................	58,005	55,748	54,517	54,159	55,627	55,923	56,994
Professional, scientific, and technical services..............	281,395	275,112	279,503	281,123	285,363	289,811	297,173
Management of companies and enterprises..................	75,762	72,815	77,388	79,566	83,332	79,016	80,000
Administrative and waste services.........................	235,025	240,344	250,387	260,990	262,583	269,004	274,445
Educational services	92,522	92,390	93,366	94,770	96,630	97,501	99,360
Health care and social assistance.........................	497,713	504,981	507,701	518,324	532,277	540,882	552,633
Arts, entertainment, and recreation........................	53,777	53,751	54,121	56,565	57,916	60,062	62,779
Accommodation and food services.........................	283,925	283,552	283,824	291,381	297,260	299,105	299,347
Other services, except public administration..................	200,733	192,524	195,249	195,495	195,921	201,379	201,430
Government and government enterprises.........................	660,080	648,427	624,529	617,954	618,537	617,006	611,828
	Dollars						
Average Wages and Salaries by Industry	54,135	55,537	56,716	57,893	58,804	59,960	61,765
Average Farm Wages and Salaries	29,888	25,882	22,672	23,208	25,912	25,565	24,232
Average Nonfarm Wages and Salaries	54,176	55,594	56,781	57,978	58,878	60,042	61,851
Average private wages and salaries........................	53,709	55,176	56,359	57,649	58,647	59,809	61,704
Forestry, fishing, and related activities.....................	24,229	24,154	24,570	24,839	27,722	27,317	28,003
Mining..	64,131	67,226	66,803	70,301	72,159	71,365	77,484
Utilities...	95,323	99,495	106,157	108,454	107,128	113,039	116,162
Construction...	59,744	60,652	61,692	62,322	63,794	64,995	67,618
Manufacturing...	71,209	74,032	74,960	75,933	77,277	79,949	77,029
Durable goods manufacturing...........................	63,644	65,848	67,957	68,934	69,701	72,152	73,698
Nondurable goods manufacturing......................	77,292	80,564	80,737	81,813	83,634	86,304	79,856
Wholesale trade...	73,835	76,702	79,448	81,054	82,364	85,229	87,490
Retail trade..	29,496	29,979	30,382	30,587	30,966	31,712	32,879
Transportation and warehousing..........................	46,900	48,334	49,237	50,274	51,604	52,512	54,148
Information..	83,232	86,149	89,556	92,818	96,261	98,999	102,634
Finance and insurance	97,105	104,134	106,878	108,745	110,970	115,923	120,798
Real estate and rental and leasing........................	51,013	54,137	54,173	58,976	58,604	60,340	63,656
Professional, scientific, and technical services..............	85,611	88,215	91,003	95,591	97,666	100,179	106,520
Management of companies and enterprises..................	124,639	132,531	136,935	146,319	150,460	151,791	159,388
Administrative and waste services.........................	36,574	37,216	38,164	38,590	39,172	39,742	40,818
Educational services	36,223	37,368	38,256	38,906	40,009	41,221	41,511
Health care and social assistance.........................	46,701	46,790	47,488	48,303	48,529	49,493	50,951
Arts, entertainment, and recreation........................	35,651	36,272	35,535	36,857	37,095	36,440	37,023
Accommodation and food services.........................	22,241	22,449	22,668	23,097	23,715	24,506	24,801
Other services, except public administration..................	30,364	31,331	31,680	32,249	32,980	33,471	34,745
Government and government enterprises.........................	56,515	57,692	58,999	59,740	60,131	61,322	62,679

Table NJ-10. Employment Characteristics by Family Type

(Number, percent.)

Family type and labor force status	2013		2014		2015	
	Total	Families with own children under 18 years	Total	Families with own children under 18 years	Total	Families with own children under 18 years
All Families...	2,207,108	985,032	2,194,075	971,317	2,205,886	966,402
FAMILY TYPE AND LABOR FORCE STATUS						
Married-Couple Families...	1,609,473	703,827	1,598,280	689,184	1,632,061	695,182
Both husband and wife in labor force................................	55.1	67.4	55.7	67.6	54.8	66.6
Husband in labor force, wife not in labor force	22.9	27.8	22.5	27.9	22.4	27.9
Wife in labor force, husband not in labor force	7.4	3.6	7.5	3.4	7.4	3.7
Both husband and wife not in labor force.............................	14.2	0.9	14.3	1.0	14.6	1.4
Other Families	597,635	281,205	595,795	282,133	573,825	271,220
Female householder, no husband present...............................	73.2	76.2	74.1	77.7	72.8	77.0
In labor force...	52.7	63.2	54.2	65.8	52.9	65.1
Not in labor force	20.5	13.0	19.9	11.9	19.9	12.0
Male householder, no wife present.....................................	26.8	23.8	25.9	22.3	27.2	23.0
In labor force...	21.0	21.4	20.9	21.0	21.8	20.8
Not in labor force	5.8	2.4	5.0	1.3	5.4	2.2

Table NJ-11. School Enrollment and Educational Attainment, 2014

(Number, percent.)

Item	State	U.S.
Enrollment		
Total population 3 years and over, enrolled in school	2,272,659	82,063,714
Enrolled in nursery school or preschool (percent)...........................	7.7	6.0
Enrolled in kindergarten (percent)...	4.9	5.1
Enrolled in elementary school, grades 1-8 (percent)........................	39.7	40.2
Enrolled in high school, grades 9-12 (percent)	21.3	20.7
Enrolled in college or graduate school (percent)...........................	26.5	28.0
Attainment		
Total population 25 years and over	6,127,931	213,725,624
Less than ninth grade (percent)	5.2	5.6
9th to 12th grade, no diploma (percent)	5.8	7.5
High school graduate, including equivalency (percent)......................	28.2	27.7
Some college, no degree (percent)	17.1	21.0
Associate's degree (percent)	6.4	8.2
Bachelor's degree (percent)	23.1	18.7
Graduate or professional degree (percent).................................	14.3	11.4
High school graduate or higher (percent)	89.1	86.9
Bachelor's degree or higher (percent).....................................	37.4	30.1

Table NJ-12. Public School Characteristics and Educational Indicators

(Number, percent; data derived from National Center of Education Statistics.)

Item	State	U.S.
Public Schools, 2014–2015 (except where noted)		
Number of school districts..	693	18,260
Number of schools...	2,571	98,373
Number of students..	1,400,579	50,312,581
Number of teachers	115,067	3,132,351
Student-teacher ratio	12.2	16.1
Expenditures per student (dollars), FY 2014..............................	18,780	11,066
Four-year adjusted cohort graduation rate (ACGR)[1,2]	89.7	83.2
Students eligible for free or reduced-price lunch (percent)	36.8	51.8
English language learners (percent)......................................	4.8	9.4
Students age 3 to 21 served under IDEA, part B (percent)..................	16.6	13.0

Public Schools by Type	Number	Percent of state public schools
Total number of schools...	2,571	100.0
Regular	2,374	92.3
Special education..	63	2.5
Vocational education...	55	2.1
Alternative education..	79	3.1

NOTE: Every school is assigned only one school type based on its instructional emphasis.
[1] ACGR data represents a new method of calculating high-school completion rates and may not be comparable to previous years' data for Averaged Freshmen Graduation Rates (AFGR).
[2] The United States 4-year ACGRs were estimated using both the reported 4-year ACGR data from 49 states and the District of Columbia and using imputed data for Idaho. The estimate for American Indian/Alaska Native students also includes imputed data for Virginia.

Table NJ-13. Reported Voting and Registration of the Voting-Age Population, November 2016

(Numbers in thousands, percent.)

Item	Total population	Total citizen population	Registered			Voted		
			Total registered	Percent registered (total population)	Percent registered (total citizen population)	Total voted	Percent voted (total population)	Percent voted (total citizen population)
U.S. Total	245,502	224,059	157,596	64.2	70.3	137,537	56.0	61.4
State Total............................	6,862	5,958	4,165	60.7	69.9	3,665	53.4	61.5
Sex								
Male	3,282	2,825	1,911	58.2	67.6	1,668	50.8	59.1
Female	3,580	3,132	2,255	63.0	72.0	1,997	55.8	63.7
Race								
White alone..........................	5,237	4,669	3,349	64.0	71.7	2,961	56.6	63.4
White, non-Hispanic alone	4,048	3,891	2,933	72.5	75.4	2,604	64.3	66.9
Black alone..........................	964	814	550	57.0	67.5	469	48.7	57.6
Asian alone..........................	579	399	220	38.0	55.2	211	36.4	52.9
Hispanic (of any race)	1,379	913	486	35.2	53.2	395	28.6	43.2
White alone or in combination	5,274	4,702	3,374	64.0	71.7	2,982	56.5	63.4
Black alone or in combination..........	977	824	553	56.7	67.2	469	48.0	56.9
Asian alone or in combination..........	602	422	238	39.6	56.4	229	38.0	54.2
Age								
18 to 24 years.....................	849	750	419	49.4	55.9	305	35.9	40.7
25 to 34 years.....................	1,046	814	507	48.5	62.3	426	40.7	52.3
35 to 44 years.....................	1,110	881	631	56.8	71.6	566	51.0	64.3
45 to 64 years.....................	2,474	2,196	1,615	65.3	73.5	1,472	59.5	67.0
65 years and over	1,383	1,317	994	71.8	75.4	896	64.8	68.0

Table NJ-14. Crime

(Number, rate per 100,000. Data are derived from the FBI Uniform Crime Reports.)

Item	State			U.S. [1,2,3,4]		
	2014	2015	Percent change	2014	2015	Percent change
TOTAL POPULATION[5]	8,938,844	8,958,013	0.2	318,907,401	321,418,820	0.8
VIOLENT CRIME						
Number..............................	23,319	22,879	-1.9	1,186,185	1,231,566	3.8
Rate	260.9	255.4	-2.1	372.0	383.2	3.0
Murder and Nonnegligent Manslaughter						
Number..............................	352	363	3.1	14,164	15,696	10.8
Rate	3.9	4.1	2.9	4.4	4.9	10.0
Rape[6]						
Number..............................	1,280	1,373	7.3	118,027	124,047	5.1
Rate	14.3	15.3	7.0	37.0	38.6	4.3
Robbery						
Number..............................	10,499	9,729	-7.3	322,905	327,374	1.4
Rate	117.5	108.6	-7.5	101.3	101.9	0.6
Aggravated Assault						
Number..............................	11,188	11,414	2.0	731,089	764,449	4.6
Rate	125.2	127.4	1.8	229.2	237.8	3.7
PROPERTY CRIME						
Number..............................	154,945	145,701	-6.0	8,209,010	7,993,631	-2.6
Rate	1,733.4	1,626.5	-6.2	2,574.1	2,487.0	-3.4
Burglary						
Number..............................	31,707	27,960	-11.8	1,713,153	1,579,527	-7.8
Rate	354.7	312.1	-12.0	537.2	491.4	-8.5
Larceny-Theft						
Number..............................	111,534	105,963	-5.0	5,809,054	5,706,346	-1.8
Rate	1,247.7	1,182.9	-5.2	1,821.5	1,775.4	-2.5
Motor Vehicle Theft						
Number..............................	11,704	11,778	0.6	686,803	707,758	3.1
Rate	130.9	131.5	0.4	215.4	220.2	2.2

NOTE: Although arson data are included in the trend and clearance tables, sufficient data are not available to estimate totals for this offense. Therefore, no arson data are published in this table.
X = Not applicable.
- = Zero or rounds to zero.
[1] The crime figures have been adjusted.
[2] The data collection methodology for the offense of forcible rape used by the Minnesota state Uniform Crime Reporting (UCR) Program (with the exception of Minneapolis and St. Paul, Minnesota) does not comply with national UCR Program guidelines. Consequently, its figures for forcible rape and violent crime (of which forcible rape is a part) are not published in this table.
[3] Includes offenses reported by the Zoological Police and the Metro Transit Police.
[4] Because of changes in the state's reporting practices, figures are not comparable to previous years' data.
[5] Populations are U.S. Census Bureau provisional estimates as of July 1 of each year.
[6] The figures shown for the offense of rape were estimated using the revised Uniform Crime Reporting (UCR) definition of rape.

Table NJ-15. State Government Finances, 2015

(Dollar amounts in thousands, percent distribution.)

Item	Dollars	Percent distribution
Total Revenue	69,746,902	100.0
General revenue	60,668,535	87.0
Intergovernmental revenue	18,015,768	25.8
Taxes	31,567,654	45.3
General sales	9,146,025	13.1
Selective sales	3,805,842	5.5
License taxes	1,553,255	2.2
Individual income tax	13,250,002	19.0
Corporate income tax	2,579,391	3.7
Other taxes	1,233,139	1.8
Current charges	6,377,825	9.1
Miscellaneous general revenue	4,707,288	6.7
Utility revenue	1,054,985	1.5
Liquor stores revenue	0	-
Insurance trust revenue[1]	8,023,382	11.5
Total Expenditure	71,442,152	100.0
Intergovernmental expenditure	12,470,093	17.5
Direct expenditure	58,972,059	82.5
Current operation	38,043,759	53.3
Capital outlay	4,618,297	6.5
Insurance benefits and repayments	12,753,952	17.9
Assistance and subsidies	1,459,669	2.0
Interest on debt	2,096,382	2.9
Exhibit: Salaries and wages	10,158,771	14.2
Total Expenditure	71,442,152	100.0
General expenditure	55,946,822	78.3
Intergovernmental expenditure	12,470,093	17.5
Direct expenditure	43,476,729	60.9
General expenditure, by function:		
Education	17,582,765	24.6
Public welfare	18,197,283	25.5
Hospitals	2,234,169	3.1
Health	1,347,935	1.9
Highways	3,375,735	4.7
Police protection	751,594	1.1
Correction	1,395,260	2.0
Natural resources	509,988	0.7
Parks and recreation	232,369	0.3
Governmental administration	1,829,841	2.6
Interest on general debt	2,094,912	2.9
Other and unallocable	6,394,971	9.0
Utility expenditure	2,741,378	3.8
Liquor stores expenditure	0	-
Insurance trust expenditure	12,753,952	17.9
Debt at End of Fiscal Year	66,923,327	X
Cash and Security Holdings	120,903,572	X

X = Not applicable.

- = Zero or rounds to zero.

[1] Within insurance trust revenue, net earnings of state retirement systems is a calculated statistic (the item code in the data file is X08), and thus can be positive or negative. Net earnings is the sum of earnings on investments plus gains on investments minus losses on investments. The change made in 2002 for asset valuation from book to market value in accordance with Statement 34 of the Governmental Accounting Standards Board is reflected in the calculated statistics.

Table NJ-16. State Government Tax Collections, 2016

(Dollars in thousands, percent.)

Item	Dollars	Percent distribution
Total Taxes...	31,546,720	100.0
Property taxes..	4,638	-
Sales and gross receipts	13,173,332	41.8
General sales and gross receipts	9,267,703	29.4
Selective sales and gross receipts	3,905,629	12.4
Alcoholic beverages..	138,799	0.4
Amusements..	209,417	0.7
Insurance premiums...	605,447	1.9
Motor fuels...	554,473	1.8
Pari-mutuels...	0	-
Public utilities...	964,738	3.1
Tobacco products..	677,216	2.1
Other selective sales	755,539	2.4
Licenses..	1,499,889	4.8
Alcoholic beverages..	4,199	-
Amusements..	42,181	0.1
Corporations in general...	247,721	0.8
Hunting and fishing..	14,062	-
Motor vehicle...	642,537	2.0
Motor vehicle operators..	55,873	0.2
Public utilities...	6,961	-
Occupation and business, NEC	485,336	1.5
Other licenses	1,019	-
Income taxes..	15,585,479	49.4
Individual income...	13,355,992	42.3
Corporation net income	2,229,487	7.1
Other taxes..	1,283,382	4.1
Death and gift..	769,688	2.4
Documentary and stock transfer	513,694	1.6
Severance	0	-
Taxes, NEC	0	-

X = Not applicable.
- = Zero or rounds to zero.

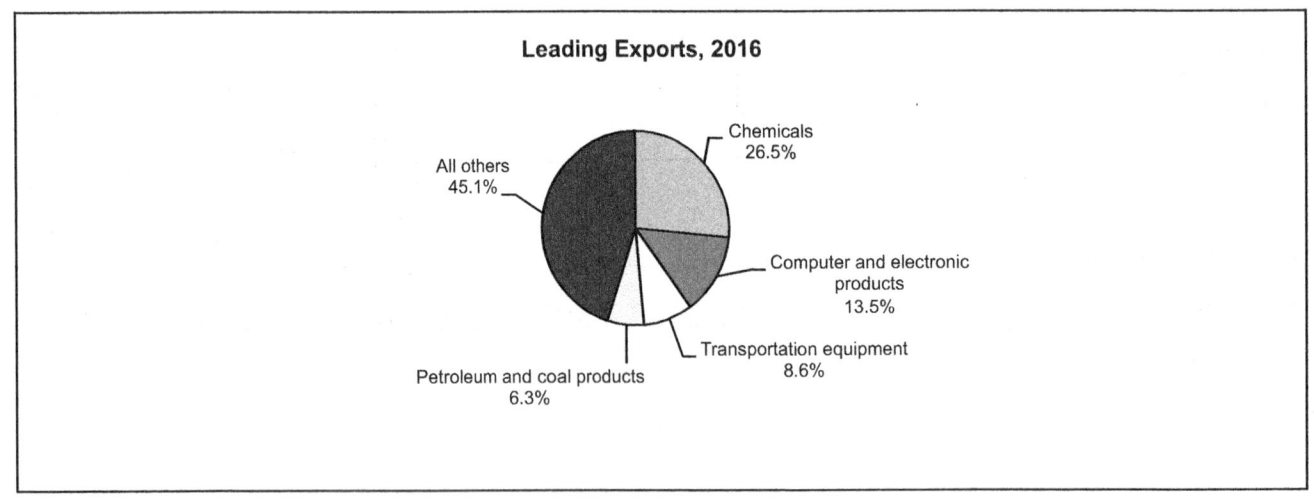

Leading Exports, 2016

Chemicals 26.5%

Computer and electronic products 13.5%

Transportation equipment 8.6%

Petroleum and coal products 6.3%

All others 45.1%

NEW MEXICO

Facts and Figures

Location: Southwestern United States; bordered on the N by Colorado, on the E by Oklahoma and Texas, on the S by Texas and Mexico, and on the W by Arizona; New Mexico is one of the Four Corner states—at its NW corner it touches Arizona, Colorado, and Utah

Area: 121,590 sq. mi. (314,915 sq. km.); rank—5th

Population: 2,081,015 (2016 est.); rank—36th

Principal Cities: capital—Santa Fe; largest—Albuquerque

Statehood: January 6, 1912; 47th state

U.S. Congress: 2 senators, 3 representatives

State Motto: *Crescit eundo* ("It grows as it goes")

State Song: "O, Fair New Mexico"

State Nickname: The Land of Enchantment

Abbreviations: NM; N. Mex.

State Symbols: flower—yucca; tree—piñon; bird—roadrunner

At a Glance

- With an increase in population of 1.1 percent, New Mexico ranked 41st among the states in growth from 2010 to 2016.

- In 2015, New Mexico's violent crime rate of 656.1 per 100,000 population was the 4th highest rate in the country, and its property crime rate of 3,697.4 per 100,000 population, was the 3rd highest in the country.

- With approximately 48.5 percent of its residents self-identifying as "Hispanic or Latino," New Mexico was the state with the highest percentage of this population in 2016.

- New Mexico had the 2nd highest percentage of residents living below the poverty line in 2015 (20.4 percent).

- In 2016, New Mexico had the highest unemployment rate of all the states (6.7 percent). The U.S. unemployment rate was 4.9 percent.

Table NM-1. Population by Age, Sex, Race, and Hispanic Origin

(Number, percent, except where noted.)

Sex, age, race, and Hispanic origin	2000	2010	2016 [1]	Average annual percent change, 2010–2016
Total Population..	1,819,046	2,059,179	2,081,015	0.1
Percent of total U.S. population	0.6	0.7	0.6	X
Sex				
Male..	894,317	1,017,421	1,030,663	0.1
Female...	924,729	1,041,758	1,050,352	0.1
Age				
Under 5 years..	130,628	144,981	128,950	-0.7
5 to 19 years...	434,231	434,860	416,308	-0.3
20 to 64 years...	1,041,962	1,207,083	1,193,331	-0.1
65 years and over..	212,225	272,255	342,426	1.6
Median age (years)	34.6	36.7	37.6	0.2
Race and Hispanic Origin				
One race..				
White..	1,214,253	1,720,992	1,718,307	-
Black...	34,343	49,006	52,133	0.4
American Indian and Alaska Native	173,483	208,890	219,953	0.3
Asian...	19,255	31,253	35,287	0.8
Native Hawaiian or Other Pacific Islander	1,503	3,132	3,293	0.3
Two or more races..	66,327	45,906	52,042	0.8
Hispanic (of any race)...	765,386	973,088	1,009,873	0.2

X = Not applicable.
- = Zero or rounds to zero.
[1] Population figures for 2016 are July 1 estimates. The 2010 estimates are taken from the 2010 Census.

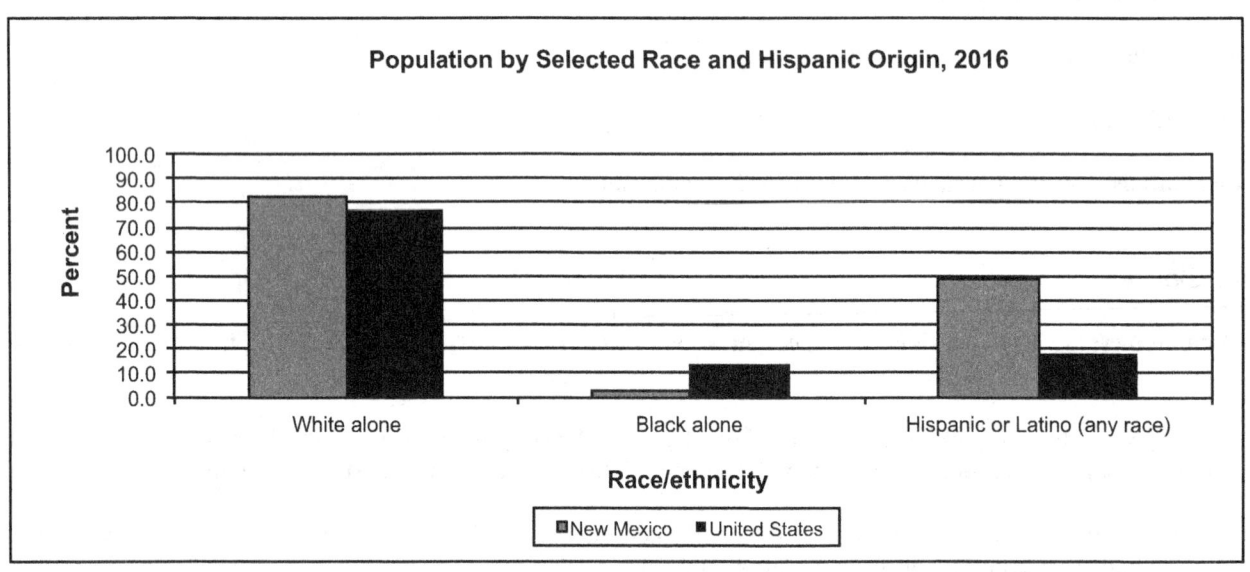

Population by Selected Race and Hispanic Origin, 2016

Table NM-2. Marital Status

(Number, percent distribution.)

Sex, age, race, and Hispanic origin	2000	2010	2015
Males, 15 Years and Over	677,967	801,901	821,541
Never married	30.5	35.4	37.4
Now married, except separated..	55.0	48.4	46.3
Separated...	1.6	1.6	1.5
Widowed...	2.6	2.6	3.0
Divorced...	10.4	11.9	11.9
Females, 15 Years and Over	720,529	833,357	847,448
Never married	24.7	29.9	30.9
Now married, except separated..	51.2	45.0	43.7
Separated...	2.0	2.6	2.1
Widowed...	9.4	8.5	9.0
Divorced...	12.8	14.1	14.3

Table NM-3. Households and Housing Characteristics

(Number, percent, dollars.)

Item	2000	2010	2015	Average annual percent change, 2000–2015
Total Households...	677,971	765,183	761,797	0.8
Family households..	466,515	501,092	485,404	0.3
Married-couple family..	341,818	349,344	341,876	-
Other family...	124,697	151,748	143,528	1.0
Male householder, no wife present...........................	35,075	49,041	44,002	1.7
Female householder, no husband present...................	89,622	102,707	99,526	0.7
Nonfamily households	211,456	264,091	276,393	2.0
Householder living alone...	172,181	216,704	232,741	2.3
Householder not living alone......................................	39,275	47,387	43,652	0.7
Housing Characteristics				
Total housing units...	780,579	902,242	914,979	1.1
Occupied housing units	677,971	765,183	761,797	0.8
Owner occupied..	474,445	519,864	513,843	0.6
Renter occupied..	203,526	245,319	247,954	1.5
Average household size...	2.63	2.64	2.68	0.1
Financial Characteristics				
Median gross rent of renter-occupied housing	503	699	783	3.7
Median monthly owner costs for housing units with a mortgage	929	1,202	1,214	2.0
Median value of owner-occupied housing units.......................	108,100	161,200	164,100	3.5

- = Zero or rounds to zero.

Table NM-4. Migration, Origin, and Language

(Number, percent.)

Characteristic	State			U.S.		
	2014	2015	Percent change	2014	2015	Percent change
Residence 1 Year Ago						
Population 1 year and over	2,060,189	2,060,441	-	315,095,393	317,635,720	0.8
Same house	85.9	85.8	X	85.1	85.3	X
Different house in the U.S.	13.7	13.8	X	14.3	14.1	X
Same county	7.8	8.8	X	8.7	8.5	X
Different county	5.9	5.0	X	5.6	5.6	X
Same state	2.5	2.3	X	3.3	3.2	X
Different state	3.3	2.7	X	2.3	2.4	X
Abroad	0.4	0.4	X	0.6	0.7	X
Place of Birth						
Native born	1,879,919	1,888,154	0.4	276,465,262	278,128,449	0.6
Male	49.8	49.6	X	49.3	49.3	X
Female	50.2	50.4	X	50.7	50.7	X
Foreign born	205,653	196,955	-4.2	42,391,794	43,290,372	2.1
Male	47.3	49.8	X	48.7	48.6	X
Female	52.7	50.2	X	51.3	51.4	X
Foreign born; naturalized U.S. citizen........................	75,607	71,581	-5.3	19,984,738	20,697,103	3.6
Male	43.7	47.8	X	45.9	45.9	X
Female	56.3	52.2	X	54.1	54.1	X
Foreign born; not a U.S. citizen................................	130,046	125,374	-3.6	22,407,056	22,593,269	0.8
Male	49.3	51.0	X	51.2	51.1	X
Female	50.7	49.0	X	48.8	48.9	X
Entered 2010 or later	8.4	13.7	X	12.3	15.6	X
Entered 2000 to 2009	29.9	27.2	X	28.6	27.9	X
Entered before 2000..	61.7	59.1	X	59.1	56.5	X
World Region of Birth, Foreign						
Foreign-born population, excluding population born at sea	205,653	196,955	-4.2	42,390,705	43,289,646	2.1
Europe	6.6	7.5	X	11.2	11.1	X
Asia	11.9	11.7	X	30.1	30.6	X
Africa	1.7	1.9	X	4.6	4.8	X
Oceania	0.3	0.3	X	0.6	0.6	X
Latin America...	77.9	76.9	X	51.6	51.1	X
North America..	1.7	1.7	X	1.9	1.9	X
Language Spoken at Home and Ability to Speak English						
Population 5 years and over...	1,950,156	1,950,879	-	299,084,046	301,625,014	0.8
English only	63.2	65.7	X	78.9	78.5	X
Language other than English..................................	36.8	34.3	X	21.1	21.5	X
Speaks English less than "very well".....................	9.1	8.6	X	8.6	8.6	X

NA = Not available.
X = Not applicable.
- = Zero or rounds to zero.

Table NM-5. Median Income and Poverty Status, 2015

(Number, percent, except as noted.)

Characteristic	State		U.S.	
	Number	Percent	Number	Percent
Median Income				
Households (dollars)...	45,382	X	55,775	X
Families (dollars)	56,207	X	68,260	X
Below Poverty Level (All People)	417,834	20.4	46,153,077	14.7
Sex				
Male	199,446	19.8	20,599,407	13.4
Female	218,388	21.1	25,553,670	16.0
Age				
Under 18 years..	141,053	28.6	15,000,273	20.7
Related children under 18 years................................	140,195	28.5	14,693,239	20.4
18 to 64 years..	240,613	19.6	26,960,369	13.9
65 years and over	36,168	11.1	4,192,435	9.0

X = Not applicable.

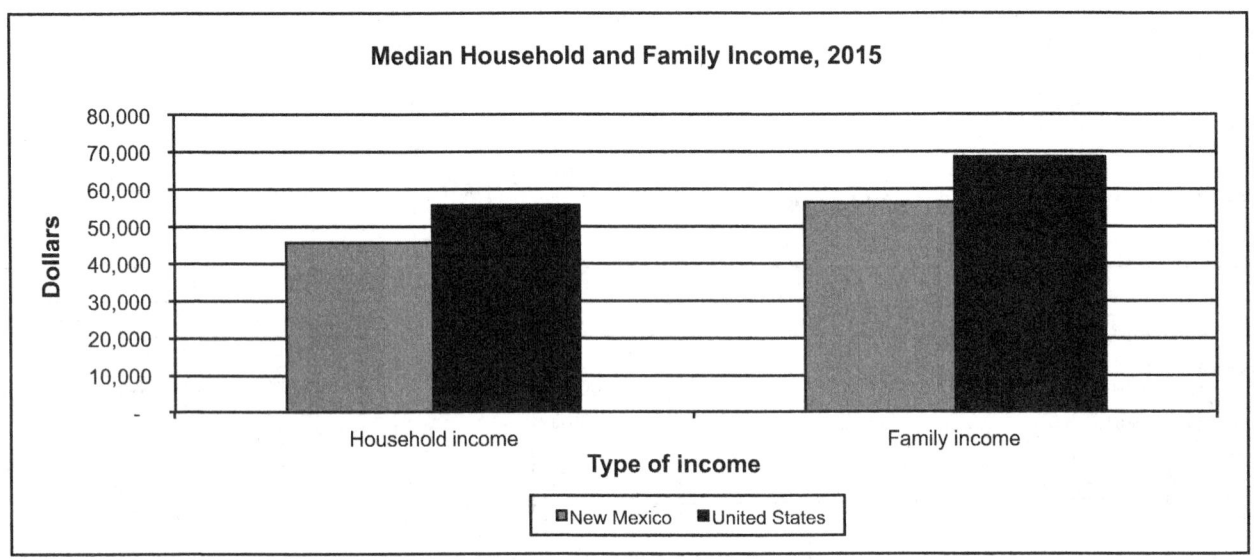

Median Household and Family Income, 2015

(New Mexico / United States)

Table NM-6. Health Insurance Coverage Status for the Civilian Noninstitutionalized Population and Children Under 18 Years of Age

(Numbers in thousands, percent.)

Item	2007	2008	2009	2010	2011	2012	2013	2014	2015
Civilian Noninstitutionalized Population	1,946	1,952	1,976	2,033	2,047	2,052	2,052	2,050	2,050
Covered by Private or Public Insurance									
Number..	1,509	1,533	1,586	1,634	1,641	1,674	1,669	1,753	1,826
Percent..	77.5	78.5	80.3	80.4	80.2	81.6	81.4	85.5	89.1
Not Covered									
Number..	437	419	390	399	406	378	382	298	224
Percent..	22.5	21.5	19.7	19.6	19.8	18.4	18.6	14.5	10.9
Percent in the U.S. not covered....................................	15.3	15.1	15.1	15.5	15.1	14.8	14.5	11.7	9.4
Children Under 18 Years of Age	495	501	514	518	517	515	507	499	498
Covered by Private or Public Insurance									
Number..	419	432	455	465	470	474	464	462	476
Percent..	84.5	86.2	88.6	89.8	90.8	92.0	91.5	92.7	95.5
Not Covered									
Number..	77	69	59	53	47	41	43	36	22
Percent..	15.5	13.8	11.4	10.2	9.2	8.0	8.5	7.3	4.5
Percent in the U.S. not covered....................................	11.0	9.7	8.6	8.0	7.5	7.2	7.1	6.0	4.8

Table NM-7. Employment Status by Demographic Group, 2016

(Numbers in thousands, percent.)

Characteristic	Civilian noninstitutional population	Civilian labor force		Employed		Unemployed	
		Number	Percent of population	Number	Percent of population	Number	Percent of population
Total..	1,611	933	57.9	870	54.0	63	6.8
Sex							
Male..	782	496	63.4	460	58.8	36	7.3
Female	829	437	52.7	410	49.5	27	6.1
Race, Sex, and Hispanic Origin							
White	1,258	738	58.7	698	55.5	40	5.4
Male...	612	397	64.7	373	61.0	23	5.8
Female	646	342	52.9	325	50.3	17	4.9
Black or African American................	40	26	65.9	26	64.6	1	2.1
Male...	NA	NA	NA	NA	NA	NA	NA
Female	NA	NA	NA	NA	NA	NA	NA
Hispanic or Latino ethnicity[1]	702	418	59.5	391	55.6	27	6.5
Male...	350	228	65.3	211	60.4	17	7.6
Female	352	190	53.8	180	51.0	10	5.3
Age							
16 to 19 years..............................	121	39	32.3	30	24.8	9	23.2
20 to 24 years..............................	143	98	68.7	85	59.8	13	12.9
25 to 34 years..............................	249	192	77.0	177	71.1	15	7.6
35 to 44 years..............................	242	189	78.2	179	73.9	11	5.7
45 to 54 years..............................	269	200	74.5	191	71.1	9	4.5
55 to 64 years..............................	264	156	58.8	150	56.6	6	3.8
65 years and over	323	59	18.3	58	17.9	1	2.0

NOTE: Data in Table 7 are from the Current Population Survey (CPS) and do not match the estimates in Table 8. See notes and definitions for further information.
[1] May be of any race.
NA = Not available.

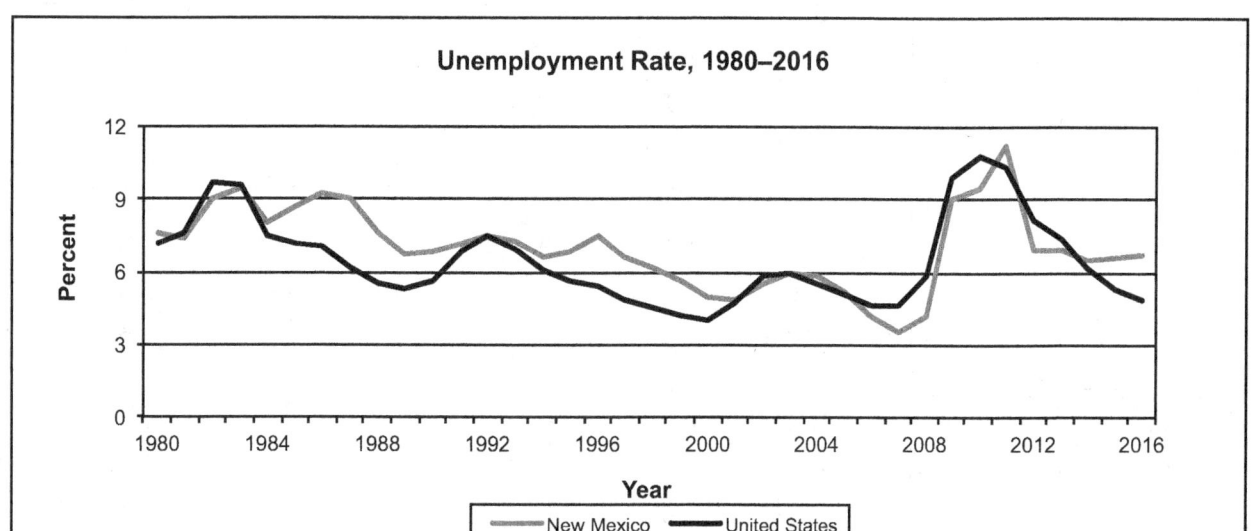

Table NM-8. Employment Status of the Civilian Noninstitutional Population Age 16 Years and Over

(Number, percent.)

Year	Civilian labor force	Civilian participation rate	Employed	Unemployed	Unemployment rate
2008..........................	944,548	63.0	902,411	42,137	4.5
2009..........................	940,352	62.0	869,491	70,861	7.5
2010..........................	936,088	60.0	860,154	75,934	8.1
2011..........................	930,356	58.8	860,305	70,051	7.5
2012..........................	928,739	58.4	862,556	66,183	7.1
2013..........................	923,685	57.8	859,428	64,257	7.0
2014..........................	921,380	57.5	859,305	62,075	6.7
2015..........................	919,889	57.2	859,242	60,647	6.6
2016..........................	927,355	57.6	864,912	62,443	6.7

Table NM-9. Employment and Average Wages by Industry

(Estimates through 2010 are based on the 2007 *North American Industry Classification System* [NAICS]. Estimates from 2011 onward are based on the 2012 NAICS.)

Industry	2009	2010	2011	2012	2013	2014	2015
	Number of jobs						
Wage and Salary Employment by Industry..................	849,122	837,320	837,281	839,789	846,896	852,861	859,738
Farm Wage and Salary Employment........................	6,958	6,547	6,608	6,934	7,671	6,789	7,461
Nonfarm Wage and Salary Employment....................	842,164	830,773	830,673	832,855	839,225	846,072	852,277
Private wage and salary employment....................	625,946	613,338	616,862	620,956	628,388	636,715	643,720
Forestry, fishing, and related activities........................	2,852	2,894	2,853	2,855	3,041	3,376	3,494
Mining...	17,513	18,257	21,087	23,836	25,820	27,655	25,355
Utilities..........................	4,615	4,373	4,367	4,386	4,446	4,418	4,384
Construction	50,023	45,408	43,593	42,366	43,493	43,967	44,542
Manufacturing...............................	30,077	28,990	29,533	29,693	29,105	28,012	27,780
Durable goods manufacturing....................	19,764	19,036	19,336	19,077	18,289	17,283	16,859
Nondurable goods manufacturing................	10,313	9,954	10,197	10,616	10,816	10,729	10,921
Wholesale trade	21,872	22,051	21,147	21,492	21,675	21,738	21,527
Retail trade...........................	93,060	90,594	91,002	91,809	92,741	93,541	94,479
Transportation and warehousing.................	18,301	17,581	18,364	19,226	19,285	19,787	20,188
Information....................	14,737	14,307	13,520	13,584	13,085	12,565	12,693
Finance and insurance	22,674	22,228	22,097	22,071	22,281	22,876	23,126
Real estate and rental and leasing.....................	10,371	9,966	9,900	9,880	10,129	10,229	10,275
Professional, scientific, and technical services..........	55,943	54,198	53,914	52,803	52,597	52,984	53,845
Management of companies and enterprises..................	5,080	4,956	5,075	4,990	5,081	5,056	5,178
Administrative and waste services....................	42,543	41,467	42,071	40,907	41,854	41,847	41,314
Educational services	10,040	10,371	10,383	10,383	10,284	10,233	10,373
Health care and social assistance.....................	101,920	103,549	105,215	107,065	108,261	109,852	114,601
Arts, entertainment, and recreation...................	8,781	8,654	8,561	8,964	9,068	8,993	9,513
Accommodation and food services...................	76,368	75,659	76,412	77,770	79,886	82,437	84,255
Other services, except public administration................	39,176	37,835	37,768	36,876	36,256	37,149	36,798
Government and government enterprises........................	216,218	217,435	213,811	211,899	210,837	209,357	208,557
	Dollars						
Average Wages and Salaries by Industry	39,170	40,055	40,860	41,684	41,823	42,958	43,553
Average Farm Wages and Salaries	36,463	34,082	34,113	35,560	36,285	39,502	34,126
Average Nonfarm Wages and Salaries	39,192	40,102	40,914	41,735	41,874	42,986	43,635
Average private wages and salaries...................	37,841	38,914	39,756	40,735	40,886	42,019	42,566
Forestry, fishing, and related activities.....................	21,081	21,622	22,354	22,930	23,486	23,535	24,631
Mining................................	66,775	75,899	72,749	74,014	74,235	77,687	76,434
Utilities....................	72,119	72,955	74,065	75,489	76,911	79,614	81,304
Construction	41,103	41,436	41,900	42,460	42,266	43,446	44,212
Manufacturing...........................	50,823	53,452	55,211	57,004	57,099	58,831	59,014
Durable goods manufacturing................	55,848	59,463	61,839	64,066	64,161	66,171	65,421
Nondurable goods manufacturing.............	41,193	41,957	42,642	44,313	45,158	47,008	49,124
Wholesale trade	48,970	50,275	50,579	51,466	51,584	53,341	54,335
Retail trade...........................	25,487	26,050	26,450	26,981	27,157	27,943	28,761
Transportation and warehousing...............	43,919	45,291	48,210	50,318	49,548	51,944	51,658
Information....................	43,838	43,098	45,756	47,461	47,524	49,765	52,565
Finance and insurance	50,522	52,571	55,061	57,334	58,650	59,669	61,905
Real estate and rental and leasing.....................	31,908	34,003	36,124	36,285	36,780	37,887	38,627
Professional, scientific, and technical services	68,006	70,555	71,296	72,666	72,442	75,261	76,753
Management of companies and enterprises..................	60,481	62,044	63,404	67,568	66,511	69,876	70,195
Administrative and waste services...................	32,696	32,968	34,471	34,970	34,681	34,674	35,177
Educational services	31,143	31,220	31,507	32,189	32,649	32,881	32,895
Health care and social assistance.....................	38,230	38,535	39,214	39,911	40,154	40,680	41,340
Arts, entertainment, and recreation...................	21,518	21,420	21,824	22,199	22,721	24,094	24,282
Accommodation and food services...................	16,788	17,113	17,425	17,920	18,306	18,898	19,426
Other services, except public administration................	25,207	26,095	26,578	27,630	28,065	28,683	29,615
Government and government enterprises........................	43,103	43,455	44,254	44,666	44,817	45,927	46,936

Table NM-10. Employment Characteristics by Family Type

(Number, percent.)

Family type and labor force status	2013		2014		2015	
	Total	Families with own children under 18 years	Total	Families with own children under 18 years	Total	Families with own children under 18 years
All Families...	482,570	210,516	487,117	205,222	485,404	199,125
FAMILY TYPE AND LABOR FORCE STATUS						
Married-Couple Families...........................	336,560	125,487	338,318	123,755	341,876	122,170
Both husband and wife in labor force....................	44.1	58.5	44.3	58.8	43.6	58.6
Husband in labor force, wife not in labor force	25.0	34.5	23.7	34.4	24.3	32.6
Wife in labor force, husband not in labor force	9.3	5.0	9.8	4.9	9.3	4.9
Both husband and wife not in labor force..................	21.2	1.8	22.1	1.9	21.6	3.4
Other Families	146,010	85,029	148,799	81,467	143,528	76,955
Female householder, no husband present.................	73.3	73.4	71.7	72.9	69.3	70.9
In labor force...................................	50.7	58.3	47.6	56.3	46.7	56.5
Not in labor force	22.6	15.1	24.1	16.6	22.6	14.4
Male householder, no wife present...................	26.7	26.6	28.3	27.1	30.7	29.1
In labor force...................................	18.9	22.8	21.8	24.1	23.3	26.7
Not in labor force	7.8	3.8	6.5	3.0	7.3	2.4

Table NM-11. School Enrollment and Educational Attainment, 2015

(Number, percent.)

Item	State	U.S.
Enrollment		
Total population 3 years and over, enrolled in school	545,265	81,618,288
Enrolled in nursery school or preschool (percent)	5.7	6.0
Enrolled in kindergarten (percent)	4.9	5.0
Enrolled in elementary school, grades 1-8 (percent).............................	42.0	40.3
Enrolled in high school, grades 9-12 (percent)	20.8	20.9
Enrolled in college or graduate school (percent).............................	26.6	27.7
Attainment		
Total population 25 years and over	1,377,548	216,447,163
Less than ninth grade (percent).............................	6.7	5.5
9th to 12th grade, no diploma (percent)	8.6	7.3
High school graduate, including equivalency (percent).............................	26.8	27.6
Some college, no degree (percent)	23.6	20.7
Associate's degree (percent).............................	7.7	8.2
Bachelor's degree (percent)	14.4	19.0
Graduate or professional degree (percent).............................	12.1	11.6
High school graduate or higher (percent)	84.6	87.1
Bachelor's degree or higher (percent).............................	26.5	30.6

Table NM-12. Public School Characteristics and Educational Indicators

(Number, percent; data derived from National Center of Education Statistics.)

Item	State	U.S.
Public Schools, 2014–2015 (except where noted)		
Number of school districts...	152	18,260
Number of schools...	885	98,373
Number of students	340,365	50,312,581
Number of teachers	22,411	3,132,351
Student-teacher ratio...	15.2	16.1
Expenditures per student (dollars), FY 2014...	9,403	11,066
Four-year adjusted cohort graduation rate (ACGR)[1,2]	68.6	83.2
Students eligible for free or reduced-price lunch (percent)...	62.6	51.8
English language learners (percent)...	14.6	9.4
Students age 3 to 21 served under IDEA, part B (percent)...	14.0	13.0

Public Schools by Type	Number	Percent of state public schools
Total number of schools...	885	100.0
Regular	847	95.7
Special education	5	0.6
Vocational education	1	0.1
Alternative education...	32	3.6

NOTE: Every school is assigned only one school type based on its instructional emphasis.
[1] ACGR data represents a new method of calculating high-school completion rates and may not be comparable to previous years' data for Averaged Freshmen Graduation Rates (AFGR).
[2] The United States 4-year ACGRs were estimated using both the reported 4-year ACGR data from 49 states and the District of Columbia and using imputed data for Idaho. The estimate for American Indian/Alaska Native students also includes imputed data for Virginia.

Table NM-13. Reported Voting and Registration of the Voting-Age Population, November 2016

(Numbers in thousands, percent.)

Item	Total population	Total citizen population	Registered			Voted		
			Total registered	Percent registered (total population)	Percent registered (total citizen population)	Total voted	Percent voted (total population)	Percent voted (total citizen population)
U.S. Total	245,502	224,059	157,596	64.2	70.3	137,537	56.0	61.4
State Total.............................	1,547	1,396	916	59.2	65.6	765	49.4	54.8
Sex								
Male	749	669	416	55.5	62.1	342	45.7	51.1
Female	798	727	500	62.7	68.8	423	53.0	58.2
Race								
White alone......................	1,183	1,053	722	61.1	68.6	620	52.4	58.8
White, non-Hispanic alone	554	543	420	75.8	77.3	376	67.8	69.2
Black alone......................	42	40	26	(B)	(B)	22	(B)	(B)
Asian alone	32	27	16	(B)	(B)	14	(B)	(B)
Hispanic (of any race)	705	571	340	48.3	59.6	276	39.1	48.2
White alone or in combination	1,211	1,074	738	61.0	68.7	635	52.4	59.1
Black alone or in combination..........	57	51	33	(B)	(B)	28	(B)	(B)
Asian alone or in combination..........	36	31	18	(B)	(B)	16	(B)	(B)
Age								
18 to 24 years.....................	241	223	120	49.7	53.8	91	37.8	40.9
25 to 34 years.....................	215	196	109	50.5	55.5	77	36.0	39.5
35 to 44 years.....................	233	183	117	50.2	63.8	94	40.3	51.2
45 to 64 years.....................	549	500	332	60.4	66.3	283	51.5	56.6
65 years and over	309	294	239	77.3	81.2	220	71.1	74.7

B = Base is less than 75,000 and therefore too small to show the derived measure.

Table NM-14. Crime

(Number, rate per 100,000. Data are derived from the FBI Uniform Crime Reports.)

Item	State			U.S. [1,2,3,4]		
	2014	2015	Percent change	2014	2015	Percent change
TOTAL POPULATION[5]	2,085,567	2,085,109	-	318,907,401	321,418,820	0.8
VIOLENT CRIME						
Number........................	12,465	13,681	9.8	1,186,185	1,231,566	3.8
Rate	597.7	656.1	9.8	372.0	383.2	3.0
Murder and Nonnegligent Manslaughter						
Number........................	101	117	15.8	14,164	15,696	10.8
Rate	4.8	5.6	15.9	4.4	4.9	10.0
Rape[6]						
Number........................	1,481	1,672	12.9	118,027	124,047	5.1
Rate	71.0	80.2	12.9	37.0	38.6	4.3
Robbery						
Number........................	2,086	2,485	19.1	322,905	327,374	1.4
Rate	100.0	119.2	19.2	101.3	101.9	0.6
Aggravated Assault						
Number........................	8,797	9,407	6.9	731,089	764,449	4.6
Rate	421.8	451.2	7.0	229.2	237.8	3.7
PROPERTY CRIME						
Number........................	73,877	77,094	4.4	8,209,010	7,993,631	-2.6
Rate	3,542.3	3,697.4	4.4	2,574.1	2,487.0	-3.4
Burglary						
Number........................	18,505	17,085	-7.7	1,713,153	1,579,527	-7.8
Rate	887.3	819.4	-7.7	537.2	491.4	-8.5
Larceny-Theft						
Number........................	49,082	51,483	4.9	5,809,054	5,706,346	-1.8
Rate	2,353.4	2,469.1	4.9	1,821.5	1,775.4	-2.5
Motor Vehicle Theft						
Number........................	6,290	8,526	35.5	686,803	707,758	3.1
Rate	301.6	408.9	35.6	215.4	220.2	2.2

NOTE: Although arson data are included in the trend and clearance tables, sufficient data are not available to estimate totals for this offense. Therefore, no arson data are published in this table.
X = Not applicable.
- = Zero or rounds to zero.
[1] The crime figures have been adjusted.
[2] The data collection methodology for the offense of forcible rape used by the Minnesota state Uniform Crime Reporting (UCR) Program (with the exception of Minneapolis and St. Paul, Minnesota) does not comply with national UCR Program guidelines. Consequently, its figures for forcible rape and violent crime (of which forcible rape is a part) are not published in this table.
[3] Includes offenses reported by the Zoological Police and the Metro Transit Police.
[4] Because of changes in the state's reporting practices, figures are not comparable to previous years' data.
[5] Populations are U.S. Census Bureau provisional estimates as of July 1 of each year.
[6] The figures shown for the offense of rape were estimated using the revised Uniform Crime Reporting (UCR) definition of rape.

Table NM-15. State Government Finances, 2015

(Dollar amounts in thousands, percent distribution.)

Item	Dollars	Percent distribution
Total Revenue	19,339,452	100.0
General revenue	17,340,442	89.7
Intergovernmental revenue	7,014,832	36.3
Taxes	6,009,443	31.1
General sales	2,256,088	11.7
Selective sales	739,601	3.8
License taxes	272,008	1.4
Individual income tax	1,381,254	7.1
Corporate income tax	249,947	1.3
Other taxes	1,110,545	5.7
Current charges	1,652,525	8.5
Miscellaneous general revenue	2,663,642	13.8
Utility revenue	0	-
Liquor stores revenue	0	-
Insurance trust revenue[1]	1,999,010	10.3
Total Expenditure	20,045,167	100.0
Intergovernmental expenditure	4,871,707	24.3
Direct expenditure	15,173,460	75.7
Current operation	11,204,039	55.9
Capital outlay	1,220,372	6.1
Insurance benefits and repayments	2,195,796	11.0
Assistance and subsidies	256,039	1.3
Interest on debt	297,214	1.5
Exhibit: Salaries and wages	2,473,403	12.3
Total Expenditure	20,045,167	100.0
General expenditure	17,849,371	89.0
Intergovernmental expenditure	4,871,707	24.3
Direct expenditure	12,977,664	64.7
General expenditure, by function:		
Education	5,825,058	29.1
Public welfare	5,610,951	28.0
Hospitals	1,098,722	5.5
Health	508,414	2.5
Highways	1,041,561	5.2
Police protection	147,721	0.7
Correction	456,801	2.3
Natural resources	219,334	1.1
Parks and recreation	58,584	0.3
Governmental administration	605,206	3.0
Interest on general debt	297,214	1.5
Other and unallocable	1,979,805	9.9
Utility expenditure	0	-
Liquor stores expenditure	0	-
Insurance trust expenditure	2,195,796	11.0
Debt at End of Fiscal Year	6,738,313	X
Cash and Security Holdings	43,852,693	X

X = Not applicable.
- = Zero or rounds to zero.
[1] Within insurance trust revenue, net earnings of state retirement systems is a calculated statistic (the item code in the data file is X08), and thus can be positive or negative. Net earnings is the sum of earnings on investments plus gains on investments minus losses on investments. The change made in 2002 for asset valuation from book to market value in accordance with Statement 34 of the Governmental Accounting Standards Board is reflected in the calculated statistics.

Table NM-16. State Government Tax Collections, 2016

(Dollars in thousands, percent.)

Item	Dollars	Percent distribution
Total Taxes	5,462,107	100.0
Property taxes	106,524	2.0
Sales and gross receipts	2,930,004	53.6
General sales and gross receipts	2,085,366	38.2
Selective sales and gross receipts	844,638	15.5
Alcoholic beverages	37,084	0.7
Amusements	73,000	1.3
Insurance premiums	214,688	3.9
Motor fuels	245,447	4.5
Pari-mutuels	1,298	-
Public utilities	29,552	0.5
Tobacco products	82,826	1.5
Other selective sales	160,743	2.9
Licenses	342,527	6.3
Alcoholic beverages	0	-
Amusements	653	-
Corporations in general	25,706	0.5
Hunting and fishing	25,738	0.5
Motor vehicle	234,806	4.3
Motor vehicle operators	12,325	0.2
Public utilities	1,720	-
Occupation and business, NEC	41,579	0.8
Other licenses	0	-
Income taxes	1,523,753	27.9
Individual income	1,409,811	25.8
Corporation net income	113,942	2.1
Other taxes	559,299	10.2
Death and gift	1	-
Documentary and stock transfer	0	-
Severance	559,296	10.2
Taxes, NEC	2	-

- = Zero or rounds to zero.

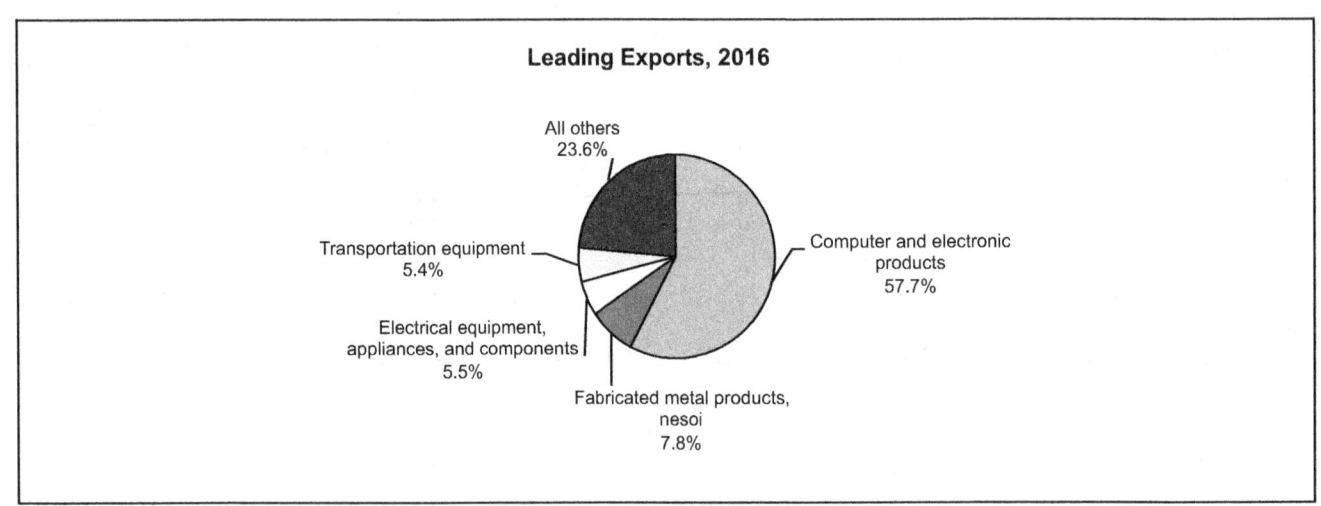

Leading Exports, 2016

All others 23.6%

Transportation equipment 5.4%

Electrical equipment, appliances, and components 5.5%

Fabricated metal products, nesoi 7.8%

Computer and electronic products 57.7%

Facts and Figures

Location: Northeastern United States; bordered on the N by Canada (Ontario and Quebec) and Lake Ontario; on the E by Vermont, Massachusetts, and Connecticut; on the S by New Jersey and Pennsylvania; and on the W by Pennsylvania, Lake Erie, Canada (Ontario), and Lake Ontario

Area: 54,556 sq. mi. (141,299 sq. km.); rank—27th

Population: 19,745,289 (2016 est.); rank—4th

Principal Cities: capital—Albany; largest—New York City

Statehood: July 26, 1788; 11th state

U.S. Congress: 2 senators, 27 representatives

State Motto: *Excelsior* ("Ever upward")

State Song: "I Love New York"

State Nickname: The Empire State

Abbreviations: NY; N.Y.

State Symbols: flower—rose; tree—sugar maple; bird—bluebird

At a Glance

- With an increase in population of 1.9 percent, New York ranked 34th among the states in growth from 2010 to 2016.

- In 2015, 7.1 percent of New Yorkers did not have health insurance, compared to 9.4 percent of the total U.S. population.

- New York had the second lowest homeownership rate in 2016, with 51.5 percent of residents owning homes.

- New York had the second lowest property crime rate in the country in 2015, at 1,406.6 incidents per 100,000 population.

- New York consumed the least energy per capita among all the states in 2015, using 188.6 million Btu per capita.

Table NY-1. Population by Age, Sex, Race, and Hispanic Origin

(Number, percent, except where noted.)

Sex, age, race, and Hispanic origin	2000	2010	2016 [1]	Average annual percent change, 2010–2016
Total Population..	18,976,457	19,378,102	19,745,289	0.1
Percent of total U.S. population	6.7	6.3	6.1	X
Sex				
Male..	9,146,748	9,377,147	9,587,365	0.1
Female..	9,829,709	10,000,955	10,157,924	0.1
Age				
Under 5 years..	1,239,417	1,155,822	1,160,057	-
5 to 19 years..	3,971,834	3,741,689	3,533,654	-0.3
20 to 64 years...	11,316,854	11,862,648	12,019,069	0.1
65 years and over..	2,448,352	2,617,943	3,032,509	1.0
Median age (years)	35.9	38.0	38.5	0.1
Race and Hispanic Origin				
One race..				
White...	12,893,689	13,901,661	13,797,556	-
Black...	3,014,385	3,378,047	3,488,119	0.2
American Indian and Alaska Native	82,461	183,046	191,449	0.3
Asian...	1,044,976	1,481,555	1,750,857	1.1
Native Hawaiian or Other Pacific Islander	8,818	24,000	26,489	0.6
Two or more races..	590,182	409,793	490,819	1.2
Hispanic (of any race)...	2,867,583	3,564,228	3,747,125	0.3

X = Not applicable.
[1] Population figures for 2016 are July 1 estimates. The 2010 estimates are taken from the 2010 Census.
- = Zero or rounds to zero.

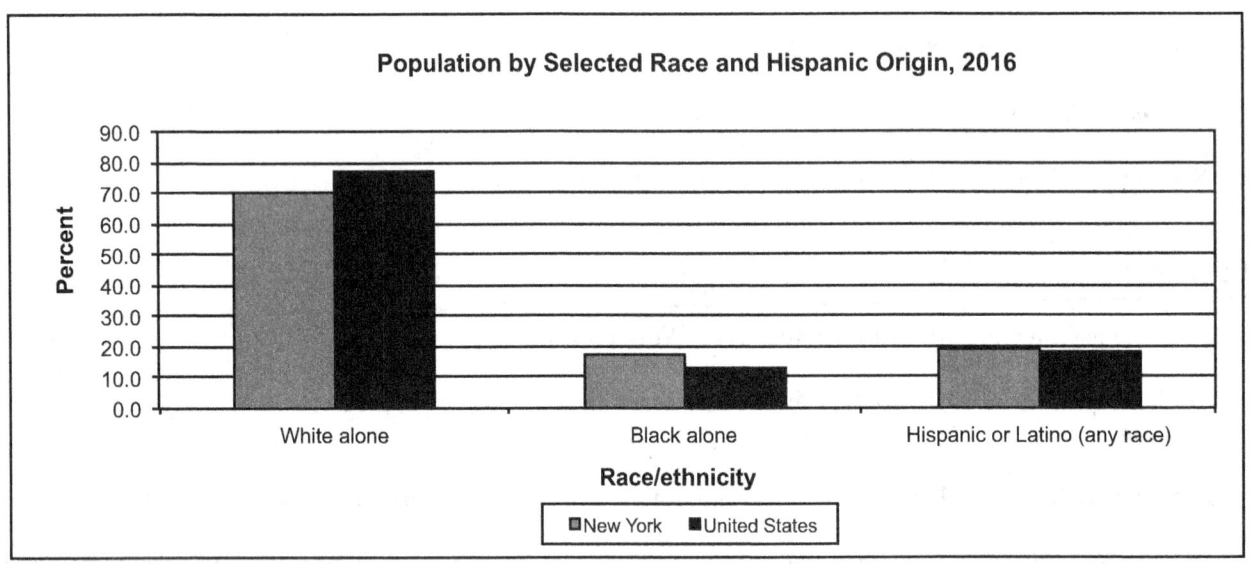

Population by Selected Race and Hispanic Origin, 2016

Legend: New York | United States

Table NY-2. Marital Status

(Number, percent distribution.)

Sex, age, race, and Hispanic origin	2000	2010	2015
Males, 15 Years and Over	7,125,715	7,586,733	7,832,354
Never married	34.7	40.5	41.7
Now married, except separated...	53.3	47.6	46.5
Separated..	2.7	2.2	2.0
Widowed...	2.8	2.6	2.5
Divorced...	6.5	7.2	7.3
Females, 15 Years and Over	7,932,161	8,283,542	8,480,063
Never married	29.0	34.8	36.3
Now married, except separated...	47.1	42.8	41.6
Separated..	3.7	3.1	3.0
Widowed...	11.2	9.6	8.8
Divorced...	8.9	9.7	10.4

Table NY-3. Households and Housing Characteristics

(Number, percent, dollars.)

Item	2000	2010	2015	Average annual percent change, 2000–2015
Total Households...	7,056,860	7,196,427	7,233,694	0.2
Family households	4,639,387	4,632,676	4,561,118	-0.1
Married-couple family	3,289,514	3,210,895	3,156,019	-0.3
Other family	1,349,873	1,421,781	1,405,099	0.3
Male householder, no wife present...............	311,697	355,236	359,454	1.0
Female householder, no husband present.......	1,038,176	1,066,545	1,045,645	-
Nonfamily households	2,417,473	2,563,751	2,672,576	0.7
Householder living alone..............................	1,982,742	2,089,816	2,175,753	0.6
Householder not living alone.......................	434,731	473,935	496,823	1.0
Housing Characteristics				
Total housing units......................................	7,679,301	8,108,211	8,207,161	0.5
Occupied housing units	7,056,860	7,196,427	7,233,694	0.2
Owner occupied	3,739,166	3,904,123	3,838,902	0.2
Renter occupied	3,317,694	3,292,304	3,394,792	0.2
Average household size...............................	2.61	2.61	2.66	0.1
Financial Characteristics				
Median gross rent of renter-occupied housing	627	1,020	1,173	5.8
Median monthly owner costs for housing units with a mortgage	1,357	1,963	2,009	3.2
Median value of owner-occupied housing units............................	148,700	296,500	293,500	6.5

- = Zero or rounds to zero.

Table NY-4. Migration, Origin, and Language

(Number, percent.)

Characteristic	State 2014	State 2015	State Percent change	U.S. 2014	U.S. 2015	U.S. Percent change
Residence 1 Year Ago						
Population 1 year and over	19,528,220	19,570,171	0.2	315,095,393	317,635,720	0.8
Same house	89.2	89.5	X	85.1	85.3	X
Different house in the U.S.	10.0	9.8	X	14.3	14.1	X
Same county	6.3	6.0	X	8.7	8.5	X
Different county	3.7	3.8	X	5.6	5.6	X
Same state	2.4	2.5	X	3.3	3.2	X
Different state	1.3	1.3	X	2.3	2.4	X
Abroad	0.8	0.8	X	0.6	0.7	X
Place of Birth						
Native born	15,280,758	15,265,704	-0.1	276,465,262	278,128,449	0.6
Male	48.9	49.0	X	49.3	49.3	X
Female	51.1	51.0	X	50.7	50.7	X
Foreign born	4,465,469	4,530,087	1.4	42,391,794	43,290,372	2.1
Male	47.1	47.2	X	48.7	48.6	X
Female	52.9	52.8	X	51.3	51.4	X
Foreign born; naturalized U.S. citizen........	2,416,184	2,502,783	3.6	19,984,738	20,697,103	3.6
Male	44.5	44.9	X	45.9	45.9	X
Female	55.5	55.1	X	54.1	54.1	X
Foreign born; not a U.S. citizen.................	2,049,285	2,027,304	-1.1	22,407,056	22,593,269	0.8
Male	50.1	50.1	X	51.2	51.1	X
Female	49.9	49.9	X	48.8	48.9	X
Entered 2010 or later	12.0	14.9	X	12.3	15.6	X
Entered 2000 to 2009	26.6	25.7	X	28.6	27.9	X
Entered before 2000..............................	61.4	59.4	X	59.1	56.5	X
World Region of Birth, Foreign						
Foreign-born population, excluding population born at sea	4,465,415	4,530,010	1.4	42,390,705	43,289,646	2.1
Europe	16.5	16.3	X	11.2	11.1	X
Asia...	28.3	29.3	X	30.1	30.6	X
Africa..	4.3	4.3	X	4.6	4.8	X
Oceania...	0.3	0.3	X	0.6	0.6	X
Latin America..	49.4	48.6	X	51.6	51.1	X
North America.......................................	1.2	1.2	X	1.9	1.9	X
Language Spoken at Home and Ability to Speak English						
Population 5 years and over........................	18,563,935	18,610,703	0.3	299,084,046	301,625,014	0.8
English only	69.6	69.1	X	78.9	78.5	X
Language other than English....................	30.4	30.9	X	21.1	21.5	X
Speaks English less than "very well"..........	13.8	13.5	X	8.6	8.6	X

NA = Not available.
X = Not applicable.
- = Zero or rounds to zero.

Table NY-5. Median Income and Poverty Status, 2015

(Number, percent, except as noted.)

Characteristic	State Number	State Percent	U.S. Number	U.S. Percent
Median Income				
Households (dollars)..	60,850	X	55,775	X
Families (dollars)	73,854	X	68,260	X
Below Poverty Level (All People)	2,970,032	15.4	46,153,077	14.7
Sex				
Male	1,306,073	14.0	20,599,407	13.4
Female	1,663,959	16.7	25,553,670	16.0
Age				
Under 18 years..	910,022	22.0	15,000,273	20.7
Related children under 18 years..	895,957	21.7	14,693,239	20.4
18 to 64 years...	1,739,054	14.2	26,960,369	13.9
65 years and over	320,956	11.2	4,192,435	9.0

X = Not applicable.

Median Household and Family Income, 2015

Table NY-6. Health Insurance Coverage Status for the Civilian Noninstitutionalized Population and Children Under 18 Years of Age

(Numbers in thousands, percent.)

Item	2007	2008	2009	2010	2011	2012	2013	2014	2015
Civilian Noninstitutionalized Population	19,062	19,207	19,264	19,134	19,208	19,317	19,400	19,500	19,556
Covered by Private or Public Insurance									
Number..	16,543	16,949	17,070	16,857	17,013	17,214	17,331	17,803	18,176
Percent..	86.8	88.2	88.6	88.1	88.6	89.1	89.3	91.3	92.9
Not Covered									
Number..	2,519	2,258	2,195	2,277	2,195	2,103	2,070	1,697	1,381
Percent..	13.2	11.8	11.4	11.9	11.4	10.9	10.7	8.7	7.1
Percent in the U.S. not covered...	15.3	15.1	15.1	15.5	15.1	14.8	14.5	11.7	9.4
Children Under 18 Years of Age	4,437	4,402	4,414	4,302	4,270	4,253	4,231	4,217	4,204
Covered by Private or Public Insurance									
Number..	4,042	4,147	4,209	4,094	4,089	4,085	4,060	4,080	4,101
Percent..	91.1	94.2	95.4	95.2	95.8	96.1	96.0	96.7	97.5
Not Covered									
Number..	395	255	205	208	181	168	171	138	104
Percent..	8.9	5.8	4.6	4.8	4.2	3.9	4.0	3.3	2.5
Percent in the U.S. not covered...	11.0	9.7	8.6	8.0	7.5	7.2	7.1	6.0	4.8

Table NY-7. Employment Status by Demographic Group, 2016

(Numbers in thousands, percent.)

Characteristic	Civilian noninstitutional population	Civilian labor force		Employed		Unemployed	
		Number	Percent of population	Number	Percent of population	Number	Percent of population
Total..	15,923	9,625	60.4	9,161	57.5	463	4.8
Sex							
Male	7,600	5,022	66.1	4,776	62.8	246	4.9
Female	8,323	4,603	55.3	4,386	52.7	218	4.7
Race, Sex, and Hispanic Origin							
White	11,380	6,919	60.8	6,626	58.2	294	4.2
Male	5,535	3,678	66.5	3,518	63.6	160	4.3
Female	5,845	3,241	55.5	3,107	53.2	134	4.1
Black or African American.............................	2,693	1,600	59.4	1,481	55.0	119	7.5
Male	1,201	758	63.1	698	58.2	59	7.8
Female	1,492	842	56.5	782	52.4	60	7.1
Hispanic or Latino ethnicity[1]	2,575	1,557	60.4	1,456	56.5	101	6.5
Male	1,233	872	70.7	817	66.3	55	6.3
Female	1,342	684	51.0	638	47.6	46	6.7
Age							
16 to 19 years	1,026	282	27.5	235	22.9	47	16.7
20 to 24 years	1,437	873	60.8	799	55.6	74	8.5
25 to 34 years	2,715	2,163	79.7	2,065	76.0	99	4.6
35 to 44 years	2,510	2,011	80.1	1,932	76.9	79	3.9
45 to 54 years	2,614	2,064	79.0	1,990	76.2	73	3.6
55 to 64 years	2,513	1,638	65.2	1,575	62.7	64	3.9
65 years and over	3,108	593	19.1	566	18.2	27	4.6

NOTE: Data in Table 7 are from the Current Population Survey (CPS) and do not match the estimates in Table 8. See notes and definitions for further information.
[1] May be of any race.

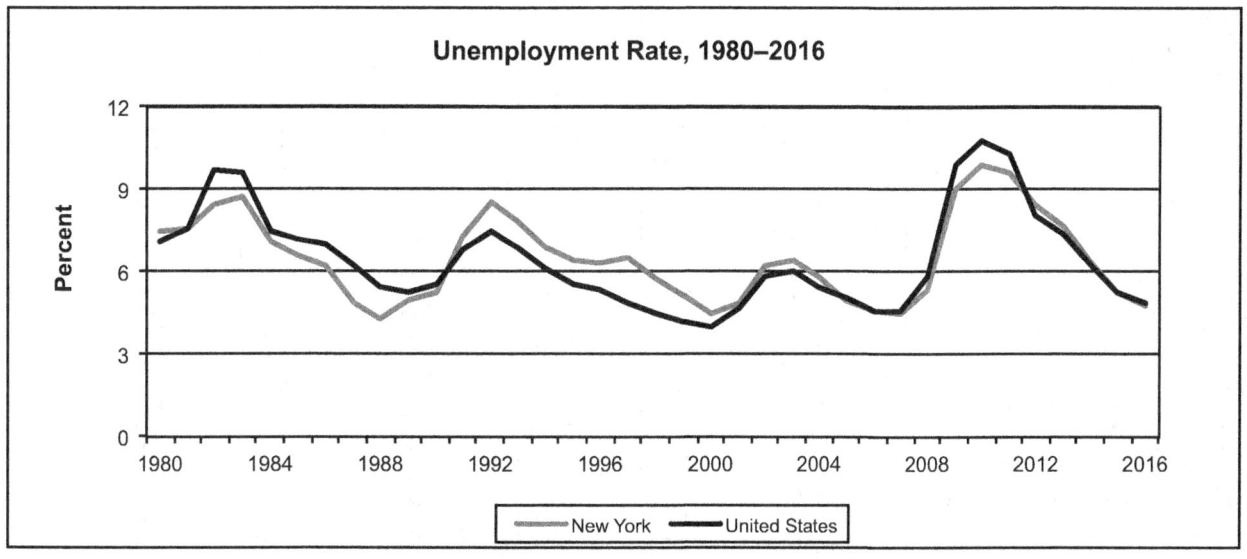

Unemployment Rate, 1980–2016

Table NY-8. Employment Status of the Civilian Noninstitutional Population Age 16 Years and Over

(Number, percent.)

Year	Civilian labor force	Civilian participation rate	Employed	Unemployed	Unemployment rate
2008..	9,664,773	63.3	9,139,080	525,693	5.4
2009..	9,647,485	62.8	8,844,486	802,999	8.3
2010..	9,595,362	62.4	8,769,723	825,639	8.6
2011..	9,517,361	61.4	8,728,057	789,304	8.3
2012..	9,617,611	61.7	8,797,832	819,779	8.5
2013..	9,636,411	61.4	8,893,628	742,783	7.7
2014..	9,595,304	60.8	8,989,429	605,875	6.3
2015..	9,679,321	61.1	9,166,246	513,075	5.3
2016..	9,584,450	60.6	9,121,323	463,127	4.8

Table NY-9. Employment and Average Wages by Industry

(Estimates through 2010 are based on the 2007 *North American Industry Classification System* [NAICS]. Estimates from 2011 onward are based on the 2012 NAICS.)

Industry	2009	2010	2011	2012	2013	2014	2015
	Number of jobs						
Wage and Salary Employment by Industry..................	8,751,639	8,718,528	8,821,283	8,939,979	9,055,889	9,226,937	9,388,514
Farm Wage and Salary Employment..........................	18,351	18,129	19,822	19,706	22,545	22,607	22,525
Nonfarm Wage and Salary Employment.....................	8,733,288	8,700,399	8,801,461	8,920,273	9,033,344	9,204,330	9,365,989
Private wage and salary employment..........................	7,206,984	7,168,895	7,312,652	7,452,244	7,575,321	7,750,548	7,909,983
Forestry, fishing, and related activities......................	5,301	5,345	5,391	5,254	5,313	5,569	5,693
Mining..	4,777	4,631	4,675	4,676	4,407	4,620	4,664
Utilities...	39,366	38,315	37,267	36,035	36,174	37,698	38,319
Construction..	339,990	317,506	318,184	323,895	336,773	352,480	370,305
Manufacturing..	477,620	457,778	459,173	459,362	456,608	453,325	455,717
Durable goods manufacturing............................	281,233	268,331	271,184	269,505	266,736	265,124	266,317
Nondurable goods manufacturing.......................	196,387	189,447	187,989	189,857	189,872	188,201	189,400
Wholesale trade	332,726	327,264	332,932	336,319	337,871	340,074	342,871
Retail trade...	878,224	884,321	901,923	921,567	934,586	950,811	954,409
Transportation and warehousing............................	230,528	224,163	228,998	231,209	232,195	240,346	249,757
Information..	253,281	252,642	257,252	261,262	261,361	265,671	267,104
Finance and insurance	510,089	502,625	517,633	516,586	511,664	520,874	528,109
Real estate and rental and leasing.........................	188,494	182,465	183,427	184,305	187,418	190,881	195,637
Professional, scientific, and technical services	571,617	560,249	580,444	604,138	619,278	635,101	656,645
Management of companies and enterprises..................	130,790	132,173	133,394	134,793	138,822	142,442	143,389
Administrative and waste services	410,727	417,543	431,659	442,334	454,993	461,879	475,512
Educational services	353,530	358,551	365,620	375,994	380,425	388,861	403,092
Health care and social assistance...........................	1,293,973	1,317,799	1,326,387	1,341,503	1,366,560	1,398,110	1,427,895
Arts, entertainment, and recreation..........................	143,138	142,852	143,714	150,204	157,399	162,671	165,742
Accommodation and food services..........................	579,272	599,088	629,802	659,089	687,788	714,887	737,244
Other services, except public administration.................	463,541	443,585	454,777	463,719	465,686	484,248	487,879
Government and government enterprises.........................	1,526,304	1,531,504	1,488,809	1,468,029	1,458,023	1,453,782	1,456,006
	Dollars						
Average Wages and Salaries by Industry	56,789	59,462	61,011	61,957	62,408	65,155	66,774
Average Farm Wages and Salaries	25,993	26,133	20,920	31,009	27,617	29,501	27,183
Average Nonfarm Wages and Salaries	56,854	59,532	61,101	62,025	62,494	65,242	66,870
Average private wages and salaries...........................	57,848	60,869	62,492	63,388	63,747	66,659	68,282
Forestry, fishing, and related activities......................	27,507	28,520	28,685	28,929	29,624	30,317	32,306
Mining..	55,458	58,276	67,428	63,465	60,336	65,252	64,907
Utilities...	92,548	97,923	102,987	108,836	106,107	107,822	110,560
Construction..	58,909	60,250	61,465	62,359	63,428	65,252	67,520
Manufacturing..	57,028	59,392	59,971	60,923	61,183	62,077	65,470
Durable goods manufacturing............................	60,550	62,753	64,380	66,008	66,343	66,891	70,319
Nondurable goods manufacturing.......................	51,984	54,632	53,612	53,705	53,933	55,295	58,652
Wholesale trade	68,548	71,647	73,724	77,717	76,846	79,564	82,965
Retail trade...	29,018	29,596	30,283	30,725	31,470	32,481	33,415
Transportation and warehousing............................	43,621	45,340	46,056	47,202	48,236	49,123	49,905
Information..	89,118	90,828	95,824	100,138	102,527	110,429	114,644
Finance and insurance	171,655	191,634	198,005	197,182	197,252	216,945	214,004
Real estate and rental and leasing.........................	51,638	54,724	56,793	59,690	60,054	63,838	66,701
Professional, scientific, and technical services	85,789	90,844	93,908	96,047	97,936	102,977	106,033
Management of companies and enterprises..................	121,419	143,384	145,794	144,086	142,751	143,605	148,958
Administrative and waste services	40,339	42,504	41,929	43,723	44,028	44,941	48,427
Educational services	40,455	41,226	42,461	43,671	44,761	46,102	49,200
Health care and social assistance...........................	43,644	44,362	45,170	45,851	46,580	47,451	48,088
Arts, entertainment, and recreation..........................	46,048	46,752	47,988	48,911	48,714	51,466	54,101
Accommodation and food services..........................	23,774	24,420	25,311	26,222	26,605	27,714	28,475
Other services, except public administration.................	31,823	33,121	33,598	34,696	35,746	36,399	38,103
Government and government enterprises.........................	52,160	53,272	54,272	55,109	55,984	57,692	59,195

Table NY-10. Employment Characteristics by Family Type

(Number, percent.)

Family type and labor force status	2013		2014		2015	
	Total	Families with own children under 18 years	Total	Families with own children under 18 years	Total	Families with own children under 18 years
All Families........................	4,584,095	1,980,127	4,592,706	1,938,644	4,561,118	1,918,562
FAMILY TYPE AND LABOR FORCE STATUS						
Married-Couple Families........................	3,158,468	1,303,725	3,147,131	1,269,381	3,156,019	1,261,456
Both husband and wife in labor force........................	52.6	64.6	53.0	65.5	51.9	65.5
Husband in labor force, wife not in labor force........................	21.7	28.3	21.5	28.1	21.3	27.4
Wife in labor force, husband not in labor force........................	8.7	4.8	8.6	4.6	8.7	4.7
Both husband and wife not in labor force........................	16.2	1.7	16.8	1.8	16.9	1.8
Other Families........................	1,425,627	676,402	1,445,575	669,263	1,405,099	657,106
Female householder, no husband present........................	74.5	78.9	74.6	77.9	74.4	77.1
In labor force........................	51.0	62.2	49.9	61.6	50.4	61.2
Not in labor force........................	23.5	16.7	24.7	16.3	24.0	16.0
Male householder, no wife present........................	25.5	21.1	25.4	22.1	25.6	22.9
In labor force........................	19.7	18.7	19.3	19.6	19.6	20.2
Not in labor force........................	5.9	2.4	6.1	2.5	6.0	2.7

Table NY-11. School Enrollment and Educational Attainment, 2015

(Number, percent.)

Item	State	U.S.
Enrollment		
Total population 3 years and over, enrolled in school........................	4,878,140	81,618,288
Enrolled in nursery school or preschool (percent)........................	6.2	6.0
Enrolled in kindergarten (percent)........................	4.7	5.0
Enrolled in elementary school, grades 1-8 (percent)........................	37.9	40.3
Enrolled in high school, grades 9-12 (percent)........................	20.4	20.9
Enrolled in college or graduate school (percent)........................	30.8	27.7
Attainment		
Total population 25 years and over........................	13,641,473	216,447,163
Less than ninth grade (percent)........................	6.6	5.5
9th to 12th grade, no diploma (percent)........................	7.4	7.3
High school graduate, including equivalency (percent)........................	26.5	27.6
Some college, no degree (percent)........................	16.0	20.7
Associate's degree (percent)........................	8.5	8.2
Bachelor's degree (percent)........................	20.0	19.0
Graduate or professional degree (percent)........................	15.0	11.6
High school graduate or higher (percent)........................	86.0	87.1
Bachelor's degree or higher (percent)........................	35.0	30.6

Table NY-12. Public School Characteristics and Educational Indicators

(Number, percent; data derived from National Center of Education Statistics.)

Item	State	U.S.
Public Schools, 2014–2015 (except where noted)		
Number of school districts........................	982	18,260
Number of schools........................	4,826	98,373
Number of students........................	2,741,185	50,312,581
Number of teachers........................	203,781	3,132,351
Student-teacher ratio........................	13.5	16.1
Expenditures per student (dollars), FY 2014........................	20,156	11,066
Four-year adjusted cohort graduation rate (ACGR)[1,2]........................	79.2	83.2
Students eligible for free or reduced-price lunch (percent)........................	50.9	51.8
English language learners (percent)........................	7.1	9.4
Students age 3 to 21 served under IDEA, part B (percent)........................	17.8	13.0

Public Schools by Type	Number	Percent of state public schools
Total number of schools........................	4,826	100.0
Regular........................	4,618	95.7
Special education........................	129	2.7
Vocational education........................	24	0.5
Alternative education........................	55	1.1

NOTE: Every school is assigned only one school type based on its instructional emphasis.
[1] ACGR data represents a new method of calculating high-school completion rates and may not be comparable to previous years' data for Averaged Freshmen Graduation Rates (AFGR).
[2] The United States 4-year ACGRs were estimated using both the reported 4-year ACGR data from 49 states and the District of Columbia and using imputed data for Idaho. The estimate for American Indian/Alaska Native students also includes imputed data for Virginia.

Table NY-13. Reported Voting and Registration of the Voting-Age Population, November 2016

(Numbers in thousands, percent.)

Item	Total population	Total citizen population	Registered				Voted		
			Total registered	Percent registered (total population)	Percent registered (total citizen population)		Total voted	Percent voted (total population)	Percent voted (total citizen population)
U.S. Total	245,502	224,059	157,596	64.2	70.3		137,537	56.0	61.4
State Total..........................	15,506	13,751	9,142	59.0	66.5		7,869	50.7	57.2
Sex									
Male	7,389	6,513	4,225	57.2	64.9		3,592	48.6	55.2
Female	8,116	7,238	4,917	60.6	67.9		4,277	52.7	59.1
Race									
White alone............................	11,101	10,159	6,997	63.0	68.9		6,049	54.5	59.5
White, non-Hispanic alone	9,270	8,870	6,264	67.6	70.6		5,418	58.4	61.1
Black alone............................	2,610	2,321	1,570	60.2	67.6		1,350	51.7	58.2
Asian alone............................	1,547	1,059	430	27.8	40.6		365	23.6	34.5
Hispanic (of any race)......................	2,346	1,735	1,044	44.5	60.2		878	37.4	50.6
White alone or in combination	11,193	10,241	7,040	62.9	68.7		6,089	54.4	59.5
Black alone or in combination..........	2,692	2,387	1,607	59.7	67.3		1,374	51.0	57.6
Asian alone or in combination...........	1,561	1,073	443	28.4	41.3		379	24.3	35.4
Age									
18 to 24 years.....................	1,756	1,590	832	47.4	52.3		607	34.6	38.2
25 to 34 years.....................	2,952	2,503	1,510	51.1	60.3		1,276	43.2	51.0
35 to 44 years.....................	2,528	2,092	1,363	53.9	65.1		1,153	45.6	55.1
45 to 64 years.....................	5,070	4,531	3,234	63.8	71.4		2,875	56.7	63.4
65 years and over	3,201	3,035	2,204	68.8	72.6		1,957	61.1	64.5

Table NY-14. Crime

(Number, rate per 100,000. Data are derived from the FBI Uniform Crime Reports.)

Item	State			U.S. [1,2,3,4]		
	2014	2015	Percent change	2014	2015	Percent change
TOTAL POPULATION[5]	19,748,858	19,795,791	0.2	318,907,401	321,418,820	0.8
VIOLENT CRIME						
Number..	75,972	75,165	-1.1	1,186,185	1,231,566	3.8
Rate	384.7	379.7	-1.3	372.0	383.2	3.0
Murder and Nonnegligent Manslaughter						
Number..	616	609	-1.1	14,164	15,696	10.8
Rate	3.1	3.1	-1.4	4.4	4.9	10.0
Rape[6]						
Number..	6,025	6,074	0.8	118,027	124,047	5.1
Rate	30.5	30.7	0.6	37.0	38.6	4.3
Robbery						
Number..	24,036	23,936	-0.4	322,905	327,374	1.4
Rate	121.7	120.9	-0.7	101.3	101.9	0.6
Aggravated Assault						
Number..	45,295	44,546	-1.7	731,089	764,449	4.6
Rate	229.4	225.0	-1.9	229.2	237.8	3.7
PROPERTY CRIME						
Number..	339,113	317,529	-6.4	8,209,010	7,993,631	-2.6
Rate	1,717.1	1,604.0	-6.6	2,574.1	2,487.0	-3.4
Burglary						
Number..	50,738	44,276	-12.7	1,713,153	1,579,527	-7.8
Rate	256.9	223.7	-12.9	537.2	491.4	-8.5
Larceny-Theft						
Number..	272,624	257,940	-5.4	5,809,054	5,706,346	-1.8
Rate	1,380.5	1,303.0	-5.6	1,821.5	1,775.4	-2.5
Motor Vehicle Theft						
Number..	15,751	15,313	-2.8	686,803	707,758	3.1
Rate	79.8	77.4	-3.0	215.4	220.2	2.2

NOTE: Although arson data are included in the trend and clearance tables, sufficient data are not available to estimate totals for this offense. Therefore, no arson data are published in this table.
X = Not applicable.
- = Zero or rounds to zero.
[1] The crime figures have been adjusted.
[2] The data collection methodology for the offense of forcible rape used by the Minnesota state Uniform Crime Reporting (UCR) Program (with the exception of Minneapolis and St. Paul, Minnesota) does not comply with national UCR Program guidelines. Consequently, its figures for forcible rape and violent crime (of which forcible rape is a part) are not published in this table.
[3] Includes offenses reported by the Zoological Police and the Metro Transit Police.
[4] Because of changes in the state's reporting practices, figures are not comparable to previous years' data.
[5] Populations are U.S. Census Bureau provisional estimates as of July 1 of each year.
[6] The figures shown for the offense of rape were estimated using the revised Uniform Crime Reporting (UCR) definition of rape.

Table NY-15. State Government Finances, 2015

(Dollar amounts in thousands, percent distribution.)

Item	Dollars	Percent distribution
Total Revenue	201,605,833	100.0
General revenue	156,803,800	77.8
Intergovernmental revenue	52,693,323	26.1
Taxes	78,205,405	38.8
General sales	13,104,421	6.5
Selective sales	10,828,096	5.4
License taxes	1,764,149	0.9
Individual income tax	43,713,484	21.7
Corporate income tax	5,084,187	2.5
Other taxes	3,711,068	1.8
Current charges	9,474,471	4.7
Miscellaneous general revenue	16,430,601	8.1
Utility revenue	8,673,969	4.3
Liquor stores revenue	0	-
Insurance trust revenue[1]	36,128,064	17.9
Total Expenditure	197,961,392	100.0
Intergovernmental expenditure	58,063,694	29.3
Direct expenditure	139,897,698	70.7
Current operation	89,297,327	45.1
Capital outlay	9,411,897	4.8
Insurance benefits and repayments	33,335,975	16.8
Assistance and subsidies	2,098,029	1.1
Interest on debt	5,754,470	2.9
Exhibit: Salaries and wages	17,549,717	8.9
Total Expenditure	197,961,392	100.0
General expenditure	151,013,834	76.3
Intergovernmental expenditure	58,063,694	29.3
Direct expenditure	92,950,140	47.0
General expenditure, by function:		
Education	42,460,614	21.4
Public welfare	58,344,171	29.5
Hospitals	4,948,173	2.5
Health	8,327,753	4.2
Highways	5,322,067	2.7
Police protection	918,892	0.5
Correction	3,284,138	1.7
Natural resources	473,507	0.2
Parks and recreation	726,422	0.4
Governmental administration	5,571,777	2.8
Interest on general debt	4,221,343	2.1
Other and unallocable	16,414,977	8.3
Utility expenditure	13,611,583	6.9
Liquor stores expenditure	0	-
Insurance trust expenditure	33,335,975	16.8
Debt at End of Fiscal Year	137,369,089	X
Cash and Security Holdings	537,876,819	X

X = Not applicable.
- = Zero or rounds to zero.
[1] Within insurance trust revenue, net earnings of state retirement systems is a calculated statistic (the item code in the data file is X08), and thus can be positive or negative. Net earnings is the sum of earnings on investments plus gains on investments minus losses on investments. The change made in 2002 for asset valuation from book to market value in accordance with Statement 34 of the Governmental Accounting Standards Board is reflected in the calculated statistics.

Table NY-16. State Government Tax Collections, 2016

(Dollars in thousands, percent.)

Item	Dollars	Percent distribution
Total Taxes	81,353,963	100.0
Property taxes	0	-
Sales and gross receipts	24,790,017	30.5
General sales and gross receipts	13,534,170	16.6
Selective sales and gross receipts	11,255,847	13.8
Alcoholic beverages	299,931	0.4
Amusements	1,231	-
Insurance premiums	1,539,422	1.9
Motor fuels	1,612,425	2.0
Pari-mutuels	19,778	-
Public utilities	914,309	1.1
Tobacco products	1,247,078	1.5
Other selective sales	5,621,673	6.9
Licenses	1,794,987	2.2
Alcoholic beverages	61,706	0.1
Amusements	0	-
Corporations in general	24,047	
Hunting and fishing	45,234	0.1
Motor vehicle	1,357,552	1.7
Motor vehicle operators	158,562	0.2
Public utilities	19,380	-
Occupation and business, NEC	127,046	0.2
Other licenses	1,460	-
Income taxes	50,690,443	62.3
Individual income	46,508,632	57.2
Corporation net income	4,181,811	5.1
Other taxes	4,078,516	5.0
Death and gift	1,364,261	1.7
Documentary and stock transfer	1,299,841	1.6
Severance	0	-
Taxes, NEC	1,414,414	1.7

X = Not applicable.
- = Zero or rounds to zero.

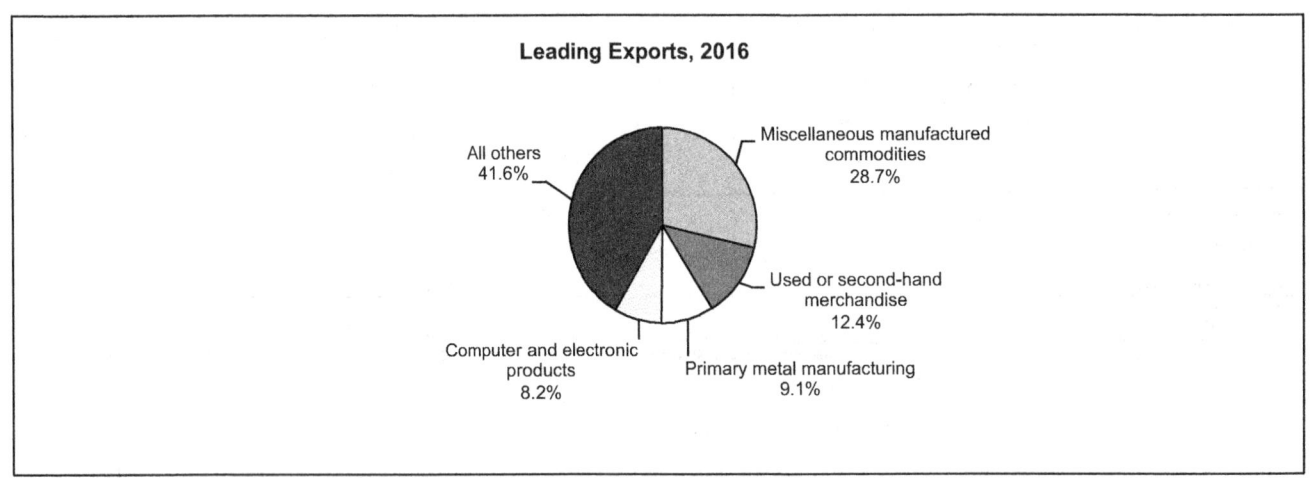

Leading Exports, 2016

All others 41.6%

Miscellaneous manufactured commodities 28.7%

Used or second-hand merchandise 12.4%

Primary metal manufacturing 9.1%

Computer and electronic products 8.2%

NORTH CAROLINA

Facts and Figures

Location: Southeastern United States; bordered on the N by Virginia, on the E by the Atlantic Ocean, on the S by South Carolina and Georgia, and on the W by Tennessee

Area: 53,819 sq. mi. (139,389 sq. km.); rank—28th

Population: 10,146,788 (2016 est.); rank—9th

Principal Cities: capital—Raleigh; largest—Charlotte

Statehood: November 21, 1789; 12th state

U.S. Congress: 2 senators, 13 representatives

State Motto: *Esse quam videri* ("To be rather than to seem")

State Song: "The Old North State"

State Nicknames: The Tar Heel State; The Old North State

Abbreviations: NC; N.C.

State Symbols: flower—flowering dogwood; tree—pine; bird—cardinal

At a Glance

- With an increase in population of 6.4 percent, North Carolina ranked 13th among the states in growth from 2010 to 2016.

- North Carolina's median household income in 2015 was $47,830, and 16.4 percent of the population lived below the poverty level.

- North Carolina's violent crime rate in 2015 was 347.0 per 100,000 population, compared to 383.2 for the entire nation.

- In 2015, 11.2 percent of North Carolinians did not have health insurance, compared to 9.4 percent of the entire U.S. population.

- North Carolina's unemployment rate of 5.1 percent ranked 17th in the nation in 2016.

Table NC-1. Population by Age, Sex, Race, and Hispanic Origin

(Number, percent, except where noted.)

Sex, age, race, and Hispanic origin	2000	2010	2016 [1]	Average annual percent change, 2010–2016
Total Population...	8,049,313	9,535,483	10,146,788	0.4
Percent of total U.S. population	2.9	3.1	3.1	X
Sex				
Male..	3,942,695	4,645,492	4,932,952	0.4
Female	4,106,618	4,889,991	5,213,836	0.4
Age				
Under 5 years...	539,509	632,040	606,310	-0.3
5 to 19 years..	1,653,851	1,926,640	1,962,581	0.1
20 to 64 years..	4,886,905	5,742,724	6,008,432	0.3
65 years and over	969,048	1,234,079	1,569,465	1.7
Median age (years)	35.3	37.4	38.7	0.2
Race and Hispanic Origin				
One race..				
White	5,804,656	6,898,296	7,206,071	0.3
Black..	1,737,545	2,088,362	2,252,403	0.5
American Indian and Alaska Native	99,551	147,566	158,476	0.5
Asian...	113,689	215,952	296,542	2.3
Native Hawaiian or Other Pacific Islander	3,983	10,309	12,623	1.4
Two or more races	103,260	174,998	220,673	1.6
Hispanic (of any race)...	378,963	830,172	932,221	0.8

X = Not applicable.
[1] Population figures for 2016 are July 1 estimates. The 2010 estimates are taken from the 2010 Census.

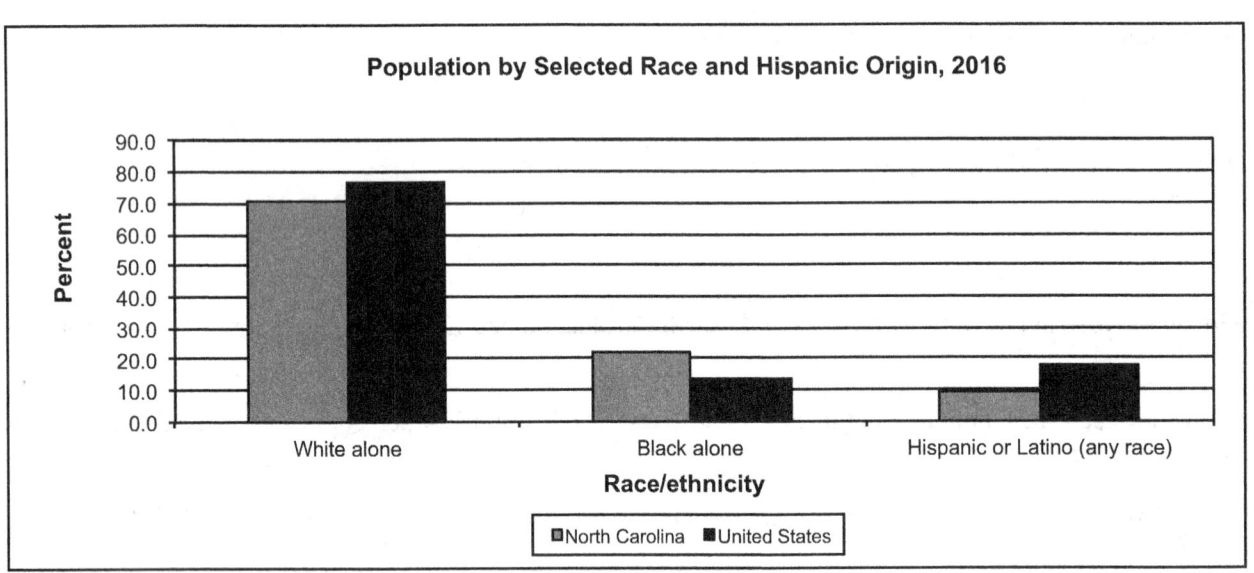

Population by Selected Race and Hispanic Origin, 2016

Table NC-2. Marital Status

(Number, percent distribution.)

Sex, age, race, and Hispanic origin	2000	2010	2015
Males, 15 Years and Over	3,092,380	3,678,950	3,924,333
Never married	28.2	33.3	34.7
Now married, except separated..................................	58.7	51.8	50.4
Separated..	2.7	2.9	2.5
Widowed..	2.4	2.5	2.7
Divorced..	8.1	9.6	9.7
Females, 15 Years and Over	3,301,327	3,975,748	4,222,510
Never married	22.0	27.3	29.0
Now married, except separated..................................	53.9	47.3	46.1
Separated..	3.3	3.5	3.1
Widowed..	10.9	9.8	9.4
Divorced..	9.9	12.1	12.4

Table NC-3. Households and Housing Characteristics

(Number, percent, dollars.)

Item	2000	2010	2015	Average annual percent change, 2000–2015
Total Households	3,132,012	3,670,859	3,843,745	1.5
Family households	2,158,869	2,441,916	2,506,215	1.1
Married-couple family	1,645,346	1,770,863	1,829,450	0.7
Other family	513,523	671,053	676,765	2.1
Male householder, no wife present	123,526	159,752	169,304	2.5
Female householder, no husband present	389,997	511,301	507,461	2.0
Nonfamily households	973,144	1,228,943	1,337,530	2.5
Householder living alone	795,271	1,022,017	1,106,806	2.6
Householder not living alone	177,873	206,926	230,724	2.0
Housing Characteristics				
Total housing units	3,523,944	4,333,479	4,491,090	1.8
Occupied housing units	3,132,012	3,670,859	3,843,745	1.5
Owner occupied	2,172,355	2,465,551	2,455,141	0.9
Renter occupied	959,658	1,205,308	1,388,604	3.0
Average household size	2.49	2.53	2.55	0.2
Financial Characteristics				
Median gross rent of renter-occupied housing	548	731	827	3.4
Median monthly owner costs for housing units with a mortgage	985	1,250	1,234	1.7
Median value of owner-occupied housing units	108,300	154,200	160,100	3.2

Table NC-4. Migration, Origin, and Language

(Number, percent.)

Characteristic	State 2014	State 2014	State Percent change	U.S. 2014	U.S. 2015	U.S. Percent change
Residence 1 Year Ago						
Population 1 year and over	9,832,152	9,927,547	1.0	315,095,393	317,635,720	0.8
Same house	84.7	84.4	X	85.1	85.3	X
Different house in the U.S.	14.8	15.2	X	14.3	14.1	X
Same county	8.4	8.4	X	8.7	8.5	X
Different county	6.4	6.7	X	5.6	5.6	X
Same state	3.5	3.6	X	3.3	3.2	X
Different state	2.9	3.1	X	2.3	2.4	X
Abroad	0.5	0.5	X	0.6	0.7	X
Place of Birth						
Native born	9,180,380	9,248,118	0.7	276,465,262	278,128,449	0.6
Male	48.5	48.5	X	49.3	49.3	X
Female	51.5	51.5	X	50.7	50.7	X
Foreign born	763,584	794,684	4.1	42,391,794	43,290,372	2.1
Male	50.5	51.2	X	48.7	48.6	X
Female	49.5	48.8	X	51.3	51.4	X
Foreign born; naturalized U.S. citizen	269,435	297,427	10.4	19,984,738	20,697,103	3.6
Male	47.3	47.2	X	45.9	45.9	X
Female	52.7	52.8	X	54.1	54.1	X
Foreign born; not a U.S. citizen	494,149	497,257	0.6	22,407,056	22,593,269	0.8
Male	52.2	53.7	X	51.2	51.1	X
Female	47.8	46.3	X	48.8	48.9	X
Entered 2010 or later	13.0	17.0	X	12.3	15.6	X
Entered 2000 to 2009	38.0	36.6	X	28.6	27.9	X
Entered before 2000	49.0	46.3	X	59.1	56.5	X
World Region of Birth, Foreign						
Foreign-born population, excluding population born at sea	763,584	794,515	4.1	42,390,705	43,289,646	2.1
Europe	9.9	11.1	X	11.2	11.1	X
Asia	25.8	26.4	X	30.1	30.6	X
Africa	6.4	6.0	X	4.6	4.8	X
Oceania	0.3	0.2	X	0.6	0.6	X
Latin America	55.3	53.6	X	51.6	51.1	X
North America	2.3	2.6	X	1.9	1.9	X
Language Spoken at Home and Ability to Speak English						
Population 5 years and over	9,342,422	9,443,944	1.1	299,084,046	301,625,014	0.8
English only	88.8	88.5	X	78.9	78.5	X
Language other than English	11.2	11.5	X	21.1	21.5	X
Speaks English less than "very well"	4.7	4.7	X	8.6	8.6	X

NA = Not available.
X = Not applicable.
- = Zero or rounds to zero.

Table NC-5. Median Income and Poverty Status, 2015

(Number, percent, except as noted.)

Characteristic	State		U.S.	
	Number	Percent	Number	Percent
Median Income				
Households (dollars)....................................	47,830	X	55,775	X
Families (dollars)	60,074	X	68,260	X
Below Poverty Level (All People)	1,607,835	16.4	46,153,077	14.7
Sex				
Male	709,633	14.9	20,599,407	13.4
Female	898,202	17.8	25,553,670	16.0
Age				
Under 18 years..	529,635	23.5	15,000,273	20.7
Related children under 18 years.................	519,690	23.2	14,693,239	20.4
18 to 64 years...	942,420	15.5	26,960,369	13.9
65 years and over	135,780	9.2	4,192,435	9.0

X = Not applicable.

Median Household and Family Income, 2015

Table NC-6. Health Insurance Coverage Status for the Civilian Noninstitutionalized Population and Children Under 18 Years of Age

(Numbers in thousands, percent.)

Item	2007	2008	2009	2010	2011	2012	2013	2014	2015
Civilian Noninstitutionalized Population	9,183	9,004	9,149	9,361	9,461	9,553	9,645	9,752	9,856
Covered by Private or Public Insurance									
Number...	7,673	7,570	7,679	7,791	7,916	7,970	8,136	8,476	8,753
Percent..	83.6	84.1	83.9	83.2	83.7	83.4	84.4	86.9	88.8
Not Covered									
Number...	1,510	1,434	1,471	1,570	1,545	1,583	1,509	1,276	1,103
Percent..	16.4	15.9	16.1	16.8	16.3	16.6	15.6	13.1	11.2
Percent in the U.S. not covered....................................	15.3	15.1	15.1	15.5	15.1	14.8	14.5	11.7	9.4
Children Under 18 Years of Age	2,247	2,237	2,271	2,281	2,287	2,282	2,281	2,287	2,283
Covered by Private or Public Insurance									
Number...	1,975	2,018	2,085	2,104	2,112	2,109	2,136	2,168	2,184
Percent..	87.9	90.2	91.8	92.3	92.4	92.4	93.7	94.8	95.6
Not Covered									
Number...	272	219	186	177	175	173	144	119	99
Percent..	12.1	9.8	8.2	7.7	7.6	7.6	6.3	5.2	4.4
Percent in the U.S. not covered....................................	11.0	9.7	8.6	8.0	7.5	7.2	7.1	6.0	4.8

Table NC-7. Employment Status by Demographic Group, 2016

(Numbers in thousands, percent.)

Characteristic	Civilian noninstitutional population	Civilian labor force		Employed		Unemployed	
		Number	Percent of population	Number	Percent of population	Number	Percent of population
Total...................................	7,892	4,873	61.7	4,628	58.6	245	5.0
Sex							
Male................................	3,738	2,551	68.2	2,429	65.0	121	4.8
Female.............................	4,154	2,323	55.9	2,199	52.9	124	5.3
Race, Sex, and Hispanic Origin							
White................................	5,662	3,492	61.7	3,352	59.2	140	4.0
Male..............................	2,736	1,896	69.3	1,822	66.6	75	3.9
Female...........................	2,927	1,596	54.5	1,530	52.3	66	4.1
Black or African American.................	1,690	1,031	61.0	948	56.1	83	8.1
Male..............................	752	473	62.9	434	57.7	39	8.2
Female...........................	938	558	59.5	514	54.8	44	7.9
Hispanic or Latino ethnicity[1]	701	499	71.1	473	67.5	26	5.1
Male..............................	355	299	84.3	293	82.5	6	2.1
Female...........................	346	200	57.6	181	52.1	19	9.6
Age							
16 to 19 years.....................	528	183	34.7	152	28.7	32	17.3
20 to 24 years.....................	670	467	69.6	416	62.1	50	10.8
25 to 34 years.....................	1,277	1,037	81.2	981	76.8	56	5.4
35 to 44 years.....................	1,245	1,041	83.7	1,004	80.6	38	3.6
45 to 54 years.....................	1,431	1,118	78.2	1,082	75.6	36	3.2
55 to 64 years.....................	1,236	743	60.1	721	58.3	23	3.1
65 years and over	1,505	284	18.8	273	18.1	11	3.7

NOTE: Data in Table 7 are from the Current Population Survey (CPS) and do not match the estimates in Table 8. See notes and definitions for further information.
[1] May be of any race.

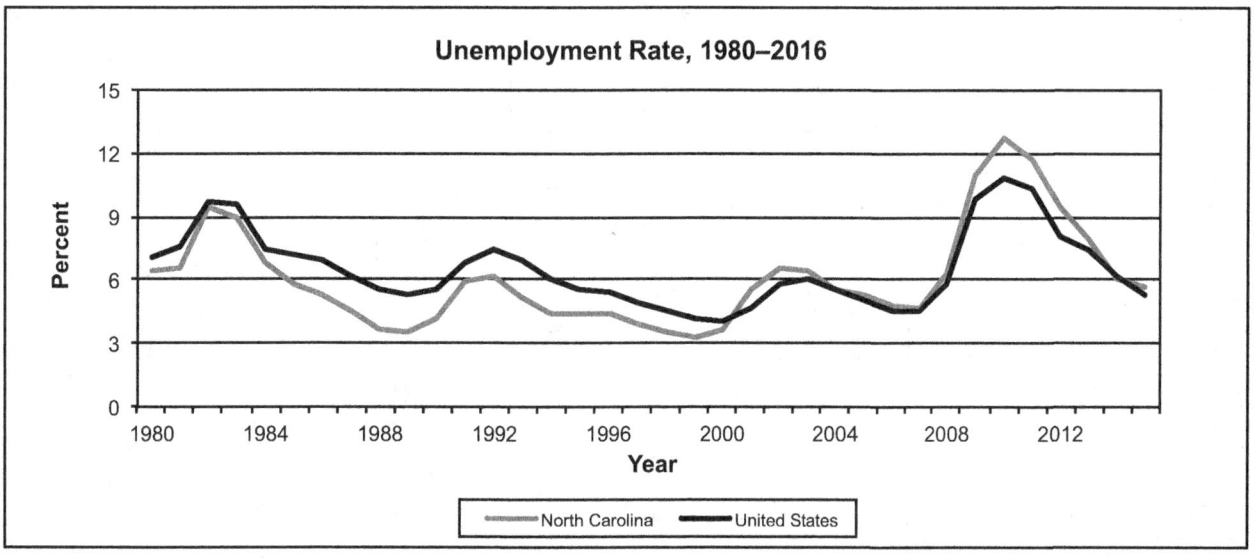

Table NC-8. Employment Status of the Civilian Noninstitutional Population Age 16 Years and Over

(Number, percent.)

Year	Civilian labor force	Civilian participation rate	Employed	Unemployed	Unemployment rate
2008............................	4,560,059	65.0	4,281,713	278,346	6.1
2009............................	4,570,789	64.2	4,087,105	483,684	10.6
2010............................	4,616,691	63.4	4,115,629	501,062	10.9
2011............................	4,633,072	62.5	4,157,543	475,529	10.3
2012............................	4,680,265	62.4	4,247,139	433,126	9.3
2013............................	4,683,022	61.7	4,310,817	372,205	7.9
2014............................	4,690,562	61.0	4,396,286	294,276	6.3
2015............................	4,769,245	61.2	4,495,473	273,772	5.7
2016............................	4,875,701	61.8	4,629,329	246,372	5.1

Table NC-9. Employment and Average Wages by Industry

(Estimates through 2010 are based on the 2007 *North American Industry Classification System* [NAICS]. Estimates from 2011 onward are based on the 2012 NAICS.)

Industry	2009	2010	2011	2012	2013	2014	2015
				Number of jobs			
Wage and Salary Employment by Industry.................	4,172,938	4,128,548	4,181,050	4,244,301	4,308,542	4,392,125	4,492,941
Farm Wage and Salary Employment........................	19,837	20,057	22,797	20,095	22,656	24,334	27,259
Nonfarm Wage and Salary Employment....................	4,153,101	4,108,491	4,158,253	4,224,206	4,285,886	4,367,791	4,465,682
Private wage and salary employment.............................	3,293,446	3,241,096	3,295,334	3,362,865	3,426,567	3,515,505	3,614,201
Forestry, fishing, and related activities........................	13,810	13,996	13,929	13,997	14,459	14,821	14,899
Mining..	3,421	3,017	3,040	3,004	2,934	2,812	2,770
Utilities..	12,657	12,313	12,304	12,273	12,460	13,645	14,045
Construction..	201,494	182,297	178,488	176,853	178,644	184,005	194,067
Manufacturing...	450,330	432,936	436,352	440,596	443,428	449,715	461,934
Durable goods manufacturing................................	233,201	222,477	226,917	234,532	236,280	240,318	248,678
Nondurable goods manufacturing..........................	217,129	210,459	209,435	206,064	207,148	209,397	213,256
Wholesale trade	168,535	165,441	168,607	172,285	174,621	177,543	179,450
Retail trade...	445,184	439,084	445,499	454,964	463,962	475,464	487,842
Transportation and warehousing................................	106,851	103,745	107,836	109,964	111,595	115,684	121,454
Information..	69,896	68,256	68,842	69,257	69,843	72,592	75,993
Finance and insurance	151,516	151,743	154,029	155,067	156,943	161,089	166,138
Real estate and rental and leasing............................	51,331	48,559	48,604	49,257	51,222	53,443	55,848
Professional, scientific, and technical services	182,963	183,086	190,459	197,032	201,517	209,273	220,692
Management of companies and enterprises..................	73,388	72,749	76,800	80,636	77,928	80,509	81,986
Administrative and waste services..............................	217,550	232,597	250,463	261,313	272,803	284,658	290,260
Educational services	86,193	87,415	88,363	90,080	92,049	94,282	96,191
Health care and social assistance.............................	470,860	465,494	463,670	470,654	480,627	485,569	492,656
Arts, entertainment, and recreation............................	57,458	56,604	57,296	58,883	60,873	62,147	63,831
Accommodation and food services.............................	340,542	338,374	345,164	359,131	372,524	384,135	398,054
Other services, except public administration..................	189,467	183,390	185,589	187,619	188,135	194,119	196,091
Government and government enterprises.........................	859,655	867,395	862,919	861,341	859,319	852,286	851,481
				Dollars			
Average Wages and Salaries by Industry	40,665	42,065	43,087	44,099	44,769	45,933	47,465
Average Farm Wages and Salaries	24,622	18,324	20,243	28,172	25,966	23,309	23,054
Average Nonfarm Wages and Salaries	40,742	42,181	43,212	44,175	44,868	46,060	47,614
Average private wages and salaries.............................	40,020	41,750	42,912	44,058	44,836	46,146	47,703
Forestry, fishing, and related activities........................	25,844	27,203	27,756	28,930	30,269	31,412	32,581
Mining..	51,542	43,917	46,912	47,012	48,191	50,369	56,453
Utilities..	76,161	81,537	82,987	86,362	93,359	91,112	92,587
Construction..	39,787	41,111	42,251	43,795	44,765	46,449	48,564
Manufacturing...	50,447	52,932	54,279	54,650	56,291	57,007	58,404
Durable goods manufacturing................................	53,609	56,561	58,246	59,132	61,205	61,041	62,275
Nondurable goods manufacturing..........................	47,050	49,095	49,981	49,550	50,686	52,379	53,891
Wholesale trade	57,805	60,718	62,852	64,500	65,970	68,445	70,630
Retail trade...	24,854	25,680	25,680	26,267	26,863	27,354	27,994
Transportation and warehousing................................	41,768	43,057	43,837	44,290	45,608	47,340	48,188
Information..	60,314	63,163	66,053	69,327	72,327	76,148	78,758
Finance and insurance	68,370	74,017	77,123	79,376	82,811	86,691	90,867
Real estate and rental and leasing............................	36,300	38,116	39,811	42,612	43,605	45,213	47,223
Professional, scientific, and technical services	63,110	66,542	68,385	71,276	71,331	73,882	76,360
Management of companies and enterprises..................	81,886	88,244	92,044	95,034	97,331	102,846	108,652
Administrative and waste services..............................	30,013	31,116	31,599	33,259	32,731	33,652	34,497
Educational services	33,859	34,773	36,045	36,333	37,172	37,950	38,148
Health care and social assistance.............................	39,735	40,675	41,939	42,963	43,659	44,680	46,084
Arts, entertainment, and recreation............................	30,129	30,254	31,298	31,785	31,964	33,168	34,324
Accommodation and food services.............................	15,856	16,515	16,852	17,441	17,612	18,078	18,783
Other services, except public administration..................	26,496	27,764	28,335	29,651	30,723	31,162	32,370
Government and government enterprises.........................	43,506	43,792	44,359	44,631	44,997	45,703	47,233

Table NC-10. Employment Characteristics by Family Type

(Number, percent.)

Family type and labor force status	2013		2014		2015	
	Total	Families with own children under 18 years	Total	Families with own children under 18 years	Total	Families with own children under 18 years
All Families..	2,474,802	1,048,744	2,483,732	1,054,151	2,506,215	1,056,067
FAMILY TYPE AND LABOR FORCE STATUS						
Married-Couple Families...........................	1,786,356	674,065	1,795,558	683,564	1,829,450	698,000
Both husband and wife in labor force....................	50.7	65.9	49.9	65.1	49.4	64.4
Husband in labor force, wife not in labor force..........	21.7	27.4	22.4	28.9	22.7	29.4
Wife in labor force, husband not in labor force..........	8.4	4.5	8.5	4.4	8.1	4.2
Both husband and wife not in labor force................	18.9	2.0	19.3	1.6	19.2	1.7
Other Families...................................	688,446	374,679	688,174	370,587	676,765	358,067
Female householder, no husband present.................	75.5	77.6	75.1	76.4	75.0	76.3
In labor force.......................................	53.6	64.3	52.5	63.8	51.5	63.5
Not in labor force...................................	21.9	13.3	22.6	12.5	23.4	12.8
Male householder, no wife present......................	24.5	22.4	24.9	23.6	25.0	23.7
In labor force.......................................	18.7	20.4	18.7	20.9	18.8	21.5
Not in labor force...................................	5.8	2.0	6.2	2.7	6.2	2.2

Table NC-11. School Enrollment and Educational Attainment, 2015

(Number, percent.)

Item	State	U.S.
Enrollment		
Total population 3 years and over, enrolled in school	2,507,958	81,618,288
Enrolled in nursery school or preschool (percent)................................	5.2	6.0
Enrolled in kindergarten (percent)................................	5.1	5.0
Enrolled in elementary school, grades 1-8 (percent)................................	41.0	40.3
Enrolled in high school, grades 9-12 (percent)	21.3	20.9
Enrolled in college or graduate school (percent)................................	27.5	27.7
Attainment		
Total population 25 years and over	6,762,644	216,447,163
Less than ninth grade (percent)................................	5.0	5.5
9th to 12th grade, no diploma (percent)	8.4	7.3
High school graduate, including equivalency (percent)................................	26.4	27.6
Some college, no degree (percent)	21.5	20.7
Associate's degree (percent)	9.2	8.2
Bachelor's degree (percent)	18.9	19.0
Graduate or professional degree (percent)................................	10.6	11.6
High school graduate or higher (percent)	86.6	87.1
Bachelor's degree or higher (percent)	29.4	30.6

Table NC-12. Public School Characteristics and Educational Indicators

(Number, percent; data derived from National Center of Education Statistics.)

Item	State	U.S.
Public Schools, 2014–2015 (except where noted)		
Number of school districts................................	287	18,260
Number of schools................................	2,594	98,373
Number of students	1,548,895	50,312,581
Number of teachers	99,320	3,132,351
Student-teacher ratio................................	15.6	16.1
Expenditures per student (dollars), FY 2014................................	8,287	11,066
Four-year adjusted cohort graduation rate (ACGR)[1,2]	85.6	83.2
Students eligible for free or reduced-price lunch (percent)	57.2	51.8
English language learners (percent)................................	6.3	9.4
Students age 3 to 21 served under IDEA, part B (percent)................................	12.7	13.0

Public Schools by Type	Number	Percent of state public schools
Total number of schools................................	2,594	100.0
Regular	2,485	95.8
Special education	23	0.9
Vocational education	8	0.3
Alternative education................................	78	3.0

NOTE: Every school is assigned only one school type based on its instructional emphasis.
[1] ACGR data represents a new method of calculating high-school completion rates and may not be comparable to previous years' data for Averaged Freshmen Graduation Rates (AFGR).
[2] The United States 4-year ACGRs were estimated using both the reported 4-year ACGR data from 49 states and the District of Columbia and using imputed data for Idaho. The estimate for American Indian/Alaska Native students also includes imputed data for Virginia.

Table NC-13. Reported Voting and Registration of the Voting-Age Population, November 2016

(Numbers in thousands, percent.)

Item	Total population	Total citizen population	Registered			Voted		
			Total registered	Percent registered (total population)	Percent registered (total citizen population)	Total voted	Percent voted (total population)	Percent voted (total citizen population)
U.S. Total	245,502	224,059	157,596	64.2	70.3	137,537	56.0	61.4
State Total.............................	7,631	6,960	5,194	68.1	74.6	4,700	61.6	67.5
Sex								
Male	3,596	3,243	2,414	67.1	74.4	2,181	60.6	67.2
Female	4,034	3,717	2,780	68.9	74.8	2,519	62.4	67.8
Race								
White alone...............................	5,480	4,997	3,776	68.9	75.6	3,412	62.3	68.3
White, non-Hispanic alone	4,740	4,679	3,595	75.8	76.8	3,253	68.6	69.5
Black alone................................	1,625	1,582	1,191	73.3	75.3	1,094	67.3	69.1
Asian alone	312	211	151	48.4	71.5	124	39.6	58.5
Hispanic (of any race)......................	804	350	208	25.9	59.6	186	23.1	53.1
White alone or in combination	5,564	5,072	3,823	68.7	75.4	3,453	62.1	68.1
Black alone or in combination..........	1,685	1,633	1,223	72.6	74.9	1,126	66.8	69.0
Asian alone or in combination.........	318	217	156	49.3	72.2	124	38.9	57.0
Age								
18 to 24 years............................	924	817	505	54.7	61.8	414	44.8	50.7
25 to 34 years............................	1,319	1,111	784	59.5	70.6	666	50.5	60.0
35 to 44 years............................	1,180	1,037	754	63.9	72.8	676	57.3	65.2
45 to 64 years............................	2,712	2,520	1,979	73.0	78.5	1,841	67.9	73.1
65 years and over	1,496	1,476	1,172	78.4	79.4	1,102	73.7	74.7

B = Base is less than 75,000 and therefore too small to show the derived measure.

Table NC-14. Crime

(Number, rate per 100,000. Data are derived from the FBI Uniform Crime Reports.)

Item	State			U.S. 1,2,3,4		
	2014	2015	Percent change	2014	2015	Percent change
TOTAL POPULATION[5]	9,940,387	10,042,802	1.0	318,907,401	321,418,820	0.8
VIOLENT CRIME						
Number...	32,718	34,852	6.5	1,186,185	1,231,566	3.8
Rate	329.1	347.0	5.4	372.0	383.2	3.0
Murder and Nonnegligent Manslaughter						
Number...	498	517	3.8	14,164	15,696	10.8
Rate	5.0	5.1	2.8	4.4	4.9	10.0
Rape[6]						
Number...	2,432	2,684	10.4	118,027	124,047	5.1
Rate	24.5	26.7	9.2	37.0	38.6	4.3
Robbery						
Number...	8,411	8,825	4.9	322,905	327,374	1.4
Rate	84.6	87.9	3.9	101.3	101.9	0.6
Aggravated Assault						
Number...	21,377	22,826	6.8	731,089	764,449	4.6
Rate	215.1	227.3	5.7	229.2	237.8	3.7
PROPERTY CRIME						
Number...	285,498	276,183	-3.3	8,209,010	7,993,631	-2.6
Rate	2,872.1	2,750.1	-4.2	2,574.1	2,487.0	-3.4
Burglary						
Number...	79,266	74,841	-5.6	1,713,153	1,579,527	-7.8
Rate	797.4	745.2	-6.5	537.2	491.4	-8.5
Larceny-Theft						
Number...	192,609	187,907	-2.4	5,809,054	5,706,346	-1.8
Rate	1,937.6	1,871.1	-3.4	1,821.5	1,775.4	-2.5
Motor Vehicle Theft						
Number...	13,623	13,435	-1.4	686,803	707,758	3.1
Rate	137.0	133.8	-2.4	215.4	220.2	2.2

NOTE: Although arson data are included in the trend and clearance tables, sufficient data are not available to estimate totals for this offense. Therefore, no arson data are published in this table.
X = Not applicable.
- = Zero or rounds to zero.
[1] The crime figures have been adjusted.
[2] The data collection methodology for the offense of forcible rape used by the Minnesota state Uniform Crime Reporting (UCR) Program (with the exception of Minneapolis and St. Paul, Minnesota) does not comply with national UCR Program guidelines. Consequently, its figures for forcible rape and violent crime (of which forcible rape is a part) are not published in this table.
[3] Includes offenses reported by the Zoological Police and the Metro Transit Police.
[4] Because of changes in the state's reporting practices, figures are not comparable to previous years' data.
[5] Populations are U.S. Census Bureau provisional estimates as of July 1 of each year.
[6] The figures shown for the offense of rape were estimated using the revised Uniform Crime Reporting (UCR) definition of rape.

Table NC-15. State Government Finances, 2015

(Dollar amounts in thousands, percent distribution.)

Item	Dollars	Percent distribution
Total Revenue	54,782,496	100.0
General revenue	49,675,292	90.7
Intergovernmental revenue	16,021,314	29.2
Taxes	25,062,544	45.7
General sales	6,862,578	12.5
Selective sales	3,849,600	7.0
License taxes	1,755,328	3.2
Individual income tax	11,197,650	20.4
Corporate income tax	1,330,223	2.4
Other taxes	67,165	0.1
Current charges	5,420,907	9.9
Miscellaneous general revenue	3,170,527	5.8
Utility revenue	35	-
Liquor stores revenue	0	-
Insurance trust revenue[1]	5,107,169	9.3
Total Expenditure	52,755,037	100.0
Intergovernmental expenditure	13,021,171	24.7
Direct expenditure	39,733,866	75.3
Current operation	28,894,134	54.8
Capital outlay	3,413,344	6.5
Insurance benefits and repayments	5,770,185	10.9
Assistance and subsidies	1,081,415	2.0
Interest on debt	574,788	1.1
Exhibit: Salaries and wages	7,675,687	14.5
Total Expenditure	52,755,037	100.0
General expenditure	46,840,193	88.8
Intergovernmental expenditure	13,021,171	24.7
Direct expenditure	33,819,022	64.1
General expenditure, by function:		
Education	20,020,108	37.9
Public welfare	13,568,795	25.7
Hospitals	1,846,648	3.5
Health	1,132,050	2.1
Highways	3,719,766	7.1
Police protection	676,300	1.3
Correction	1,207,307	2.3
Natural resources	506,529	1.0
Parks and recreation	184,526	0.3
Governmental administration	1,525,594	2.9
Interest on general debt	574,788	1.1
Other and unallocable	1,877,782	3.6
Utility expenditure	144,659	0.3
Liquor stores expenditure	0	-
Insurance trust expenditure	5,770,185	10.9
Debt at End of Fiscal Year	17,463,787	X
Cash and Security Holdings	115,552,345	X

X = Not applicable.
- = Zero or rounds to zero.
[1] Within insurance trust revenue, net earnings of state retirement systems is a calculated statistic (the item code in the data file is X08), and thus can be positive or negative. Net earnings is the sum of earnings on investments plus gains on investments minus losses on investments. The change made in 2002 for asset valuation from book to market value in accordance with Statement 34 of the Governmental Accounting Standards Board is reflected in the calculated statistics.

Table NC-16. State Government Tax Collections, 2016

(Dollars in thousands, percent.)

Item	Dollars	Percent distribution
Total Taxes	26,201,576	100.0
Property taxes	0	-
Sales and gross receipts	11,149,110	42.6
General sales and gross receipts	7,187,844	27.4
Selective sales and gross receipts	3,961,266	15.1
Alcoholic beverages	378,744	1.4
Amusements	-250	-
Insurance premiums	503,407	1.9
Motor fuels	1,936,102	7.4
Pari-mutuels	0	-
Public utilities	122	-
Tobacco products	286,286	1.1
Other selective sales	856,855	3.3
Licenses	1,869,060	7.1
Alcoholic beverages	25,140	0.1
Amusements	199	-
Corporations in general	609,410	2.3
Hunting and fishing	33,578	0.1
Motor vehicle	714,464	2.7
Motor vehicle operators	134,435	0.5
Public utilities	20,097	0.1
Occupation and business, NEC	306,808	1.2
Other licenses	24,929	0.1
Income taxes	13,109,468	50.0
Individual income	12,042,957	46.0
Corporation net income	1,066,511	4.1
Other taxes	73,938	0.3
Death and gift	4,493	-
Documentary and stock transfer	67,484	0.3
Severance	1,961	-
Taxes, NEC	0	-

X = Not applicable.
- = Zero or rounds to zero.

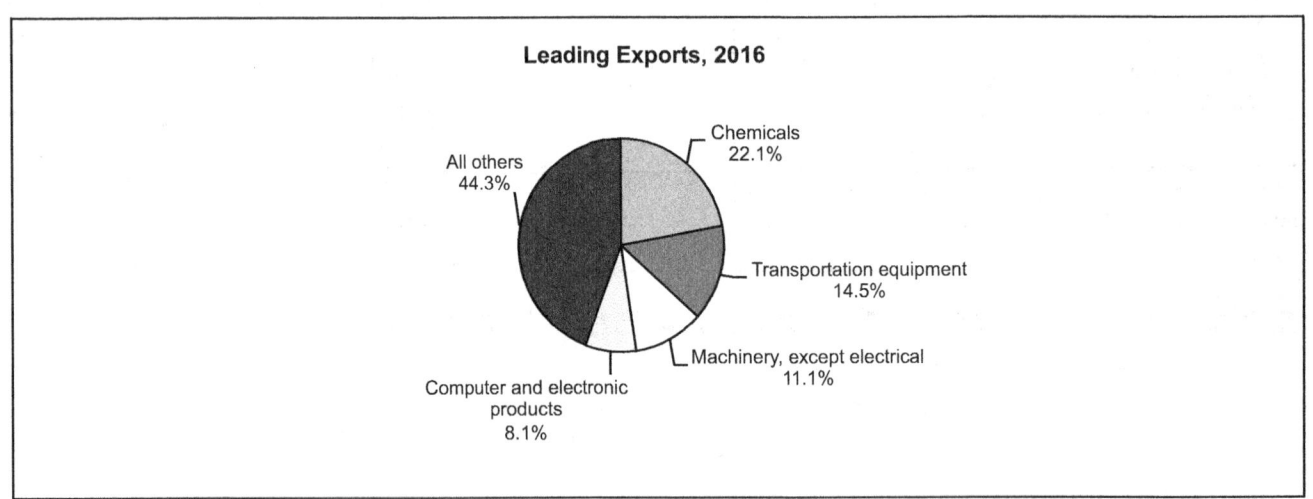

Leading Exports, 2016

Chemicals 22.1%
All others 44.3%
Transportation equipment 14.5%
Machinery, except electrical 11.1%
Computer and electronic products 8.1%

NORTH DAKOTA

Facts and Figures

Location: North central United States; bordered on the N by Canada (Manitoba and Saskatchewan), on the E by Minnesota, on the S by South Dakota, and on the W by Montana

Area: 70,700 sq. mi. (183,112 sq. km.); rank—19th

Population: 757,952 (2016 est.); rank—47th

Principal Cities: capital—Bismarck; largest—Fargo

Statehood: November 2, 1889; 39th state

U.S. Congress: 2 senators, 1 representative

State Motto: Liberty and Union, Now and Forever, One and Inseparable

State Song: "North Dakota Hymn"

State Nicknames: The Peace Garden State; The Flickertail State; The Rough Rider State

Abbreviations: ND; N.D.; N. Dak.

State Symbols: flower—wild prairie rose; tree—American elm; bird—Western meadowlark

At a Glance

- With an increase in population of 12.7 percent, North Dakota ranked 2nd for population growth between 2010 and 2016.

- In 2015, 7.8 percent of North Dakotans did not have health insurance, compared to 9.4 percent of the total U.S. population.

- North Dakota had the 3rd highest birth rate in the country in 2015 (15.0 births per 1,000 population).

- In 2016, 3.2 percent of North Dakotans were unemployed, which was the 4th lowest unemployment rate in the country.

- North Dakota had the second lowest childhood poverty rate in 2015, with 12.1 percent of children under 18 years old living in poverty. The national average was 20.7 percent.

Table ND-1. Population by Age, Sex, Race, and Hispanic Origin

(Number, percent, except where noted.)

Sex, age, race, and Hispanic origin	2000	2010	2016 [1]	Average annual percent change, 2010–2016
Total Population	642,200	672,591	757,952	0.8
Percent of total U.S. population	0.2	0.2	0.2	X
Sex				
Male	320,524	339,864	388,974	0.9
Female	321,676	332,727	368,978	0.7
Age				
Under 5 years	39,400	44,595	55,236	1.5
5 to 19 years	144,064	127,340	143,619	0.8
20 to 64 years	364,258	403,179	449,098	0.7
65 years and over	94,478	97,477	109,999	0.8
Median age (years)	36.2	37.0	34.8	-0.4
Race and Hispanic Origin				
One race				
White	593,181	609,136	665,977	0.6
Black	3,916	8,248	22,356	10.7
American Indian and Alaska Native	31,329	36,948	41,596	0.8
Asian	3,606	7,032	11,561	4.0
Native Hawaiian or Other Pacific Islander	230	334	566	4.3
Two or more races	7,398	10,893	15,896	2.9
Hispanic (of any race)	7,786	14,407	27,538	5.7

X = Not applicable.
[1] Population figures for 2016 are July 1 estimates. The 2010 estimates are taken from the 2010 Census.

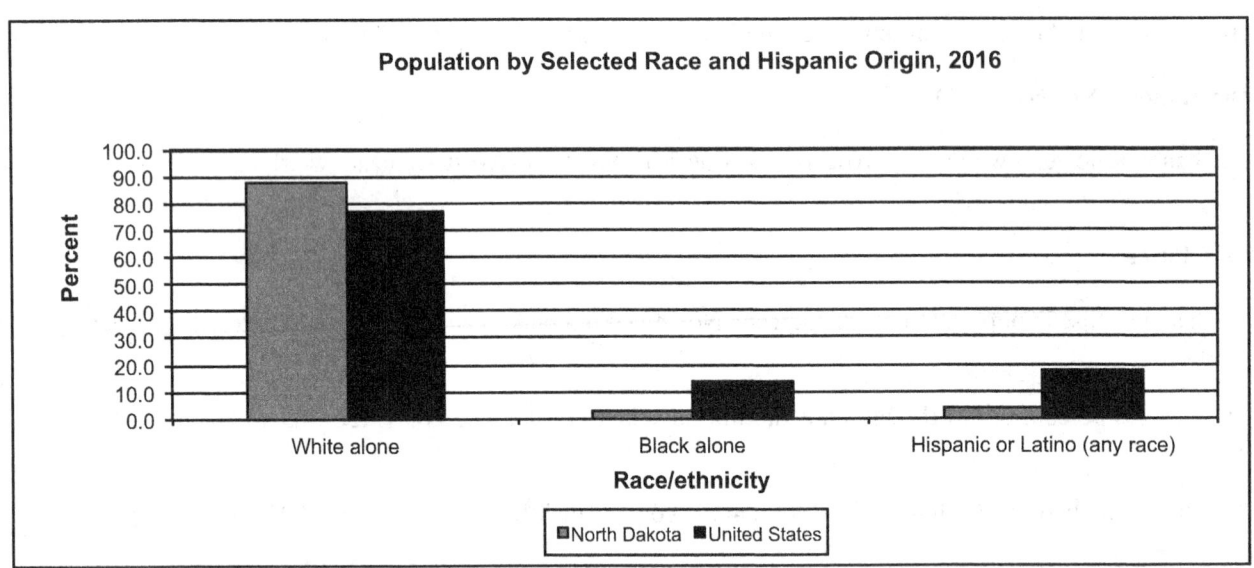

Population by Selected Race and Hispanic Origin, 2016

Table ND-2. Marital Status

(Number, percent distribution.)

Sex, age, race, and Hispanic origin	2000	2010	2015
Males, 15 Years and Over	253,900	278,276	314,948
Never married	32.0	35.8	36.9
Now married, except separated	57.5	53.1	51.2
Separated	0.6	0.6	0.9
Widowed	2.5	2.1	2.0
Divorced	7.3	8.4	9.0
Females, 15 Years and Over	258,381	271,462	296,712
Never married	23.2	26.6	27.7
Now married, except separated	56.0	52.5	51.9
Separated	0.8	0.7	1.0
Widowed	11.7	10.1	9.2
Divorced	8.2	10.2	10.2

Table ND-3. Households and Housing Characteristics

(Number, percent, dollars.)

Item	2000	2010	2015	Average annual percent change, 2000–2015
Total Households...	257,252	280,412	313,475	1.5
Family households	166,150	171,945	188,210	0.9
Married-couple family	137,433	140,277	150,297	0.6
Other family	28,717	31,668	37,913	2.1
Male householder, no wife present............................	8,569	8,846	13,606	3.9
Female householder, no husband present....................	20,148	22,822	24,307	1.4
Nonfamily households	91,002	108,467	125,265	2.5
Householder living alone.......................................	75,420	87,883	95,388	1.8
Householder not living alone..................................	15,582	20,584	29,877	6.1
Housing Characteristics				
Total housing units...	289,677	318,099	362,889	1.7
Occupied housing units	257,252	280,412	313,475	1.5
Owner occupied	171,299	187,673	193,342	0.9
Renter occupied	85,853	92,739	120,133	2.7
Average household size..	2.41	2.32	2.33	-0.2
Financial Characteristics				
Median gross rent of renter-occupied housing	412	583	775	5.9
Median monthly owner costs for housing units with a mortgage	818	1,133	1,297	3.9
Median value of owner-occupied housing units...............	74,400	123,000	180,900	9.5

Table ND-4. Migration, Origin, and Language

(Number, percent.)

Characteristic	State 2014	State 2015	State Percent change	U.S. 2014	U.S. 2015	U.S. Percent change
Residence 1 Year Ago						
Population 1 year and over	729,874	745,291	2.1	315,095,393	317,635,720	0.8
Same house	82.5	81.6	X	85.1	85.3	X
Different house in the U.S.	17.0	17.9	X	14.3	14.1	X
Same county	8.4	8.9	X	8.7	8.5	X
Different county	8.6	9.0	X	5.6	5.6	X
Same state	3.3	3.3	X	3.3	3.2	X
Different state	5.4	5.7	X	2.3	2.4	X
Abroad	0.4	0.5	X	0.6	0.7	X
Place of Birth						
Native born	715,328	728,279	1.8	276,465,262	278,128,449	0.6
Male	51.0	51.3	X	49.3	49.3	X
Female	49.0	48.7	X	50.7	50.7	X
Foreign born	24,154	28,649	18.6	42,391,794	43,290,372	2.1
Male	48.5	50.9	X	48.7	48.6	X
Female	51.5	49.1	X	51.3	51.4	X
Foreign born; naturalized U.S. citizen..........................	9,390	12,582	34.0	19,984,738	20,697,103	3.6
Male	43.9	44.5	X	45.9	45.9	X
Female	56.1	55.5	X	54.1	54.1	X
Foreign born; not a U.S. citizen	14,764	16,067	8.8	22,407,056	22,593,269	0.8
Male	51.4	56.0	X	51.2	51.1	X
Female	48.6	44.0	X	48.8	48.9	X
Entered 2010 or later	24.6	40.5	X	12.3	15.6	X
Entered 2000 to 2009	38.2	25.5	X	28.6	27.9	X
Entered before 2000...	37.2	34.1	X	59.1	56.5	X
World Region of Birth, Foreign						
Foreign-born population, excluding population born at sea	24,154	28,649	18.6	42,390,705	43,289,646	2.1
Europe	16.5	21.5	X	11.2	11.1	X
Asia..	32.6	33.2	X	30.1	30.6	X
Africa..	24.6	19.8	X	4.6	4.8	X
Oceania...	0.5	0.2	X	0.6	0.6	X
Latin America..	14.0	15.2	X	51.6	51.1	X
North America...	11.9	10.1	X	1.9	1.9	X
Language Spoken at Home and Ability to Speak English						
Population 5 years and over......................................	689,505	704,756	2.2	299,084,046	301,625,014	0.8
English only	94.5	94.1	X	78.9	78.5	X
Language other than English.....................................	5.5	5.9	X	21.1	21.5	X
Speaks English less than "very well"..........................	1.5	1.9	X	8.6	8.6	X

NA = Not available.
X = Not applicable.
- = Zero or rounds to zero.

Table ND-5. Median Income and Poverty Status, 2015

(Number, percent, except as noted.)

Characteristic	State Number	State Percent	U.S. Number	U.S. Percent
Median Income				
Households (dollars)...	60,557	X	55,775	X
Families (dollars)	79,642	X	68,260	X
Below Poverty Level (All People)	80,170	11.0	46,153,077	14.7
Sex				
Male	36,666	9.8	20,599,407	13.4
Female	43,504	12.2	25,553,670	16.0
Age				
Under 18 years...	20,308	12.1	15,000,273	20.7
Related children under 18 years...	19,298	11.5	14,693,239	20.4
18 to 64 years...	50,796	11.0	26,960,369	13.9
65 years and over	9,066	8.9	4,192,435	9.0

X = Not applicable.

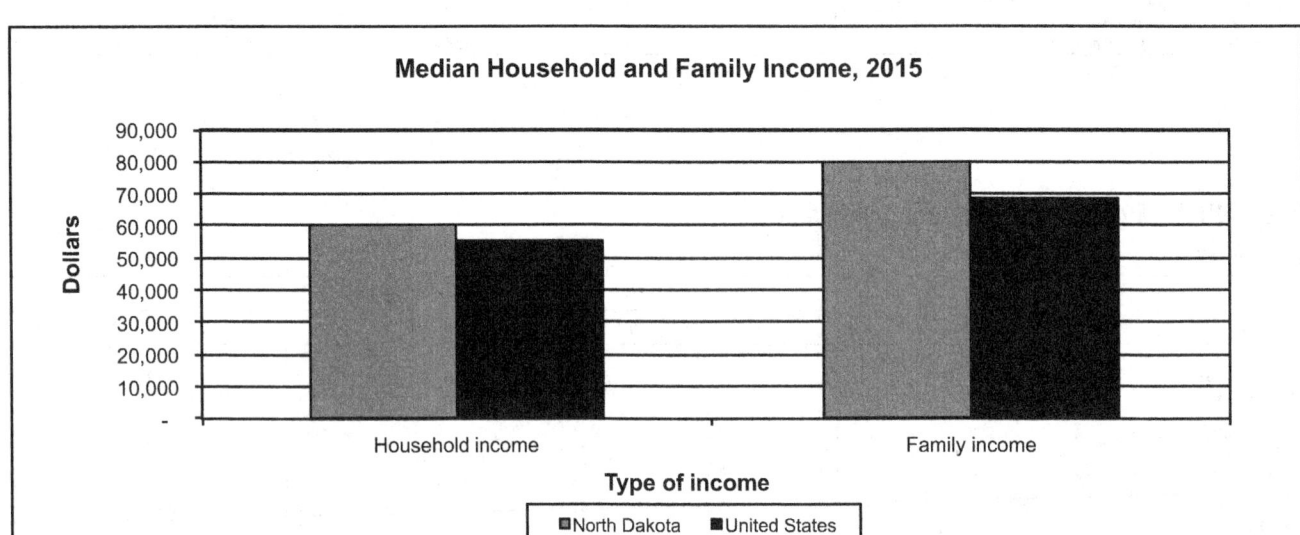

Median Household and Family Income, 2015

Table ND-6. Health Insurance Coverage Status for the Civilian Noninstitutionalized Population and Children Under 18 Years of Age

(Numbers in thousands, percent.)

Item	2007	2008	2009	2010	2011	2012	2013	2014	2015
Civilian Noninstitutionalized Population	615	624	630	661	669	685	708	724	741
Covered by Private or Public Insurance									
Number...	553	558	569	596	604	616	635	668	683
Percent...	90.0	89.4	90.3	90.2	90.2	90.0	89.6	92.1	92.2
Not Covered									
Number...	61	66	61	65	65	69	73	57	57
Percent...	10.0	10.6	9.7	9.8	9.8	10.0	10.4	7.9	7.8
Percent in the U.S. not covered...	15.3	15.1	15.1	15.5	15.1	14.8	14.5	11.7	9.4
Children Under 18 Years of Age	146	141	141	150	151	154	160	167	171
Covered by Private or Public Insurance									
Number...	135	130	133	140	141	143	148	156	158
Percent...	92.1	92.2	94.4	93.5	93.6	93.1	92.1	93.1	92.1
Not Covered									
Number...	11	11	8	10	10	11	13	12	13
Percent...	7.9	7.8	5.6	6.5	6.4	6.9	7.9	6.9	7.9
Percent in the U.S. not covered...	11.0	9.7	8.6	8.0	7.5	7.2	7.1	6.0	4.8

Table ND-7. Employment Status by Demographic Group, 2016

(Numbers in thousands, percent.)

Characteristic	Civilian noninstitutional population	Civilian labor force		Employed		Unemployed	
		Number	Percent of population	Number	Percent of population	Number	Percent of population
Total..	596	429	71.9	414	69.5	14	3.3
Sex							
Male...	305	234	76.8	225	73.9	9	3.7
Female	291	194	66.7	189	64.8	6	2.8
Race, Sex, and Hispanic Origin							
White	538	390	72.4	380	70.6	10	2.6
Male	278	214	76.9	207	74.4	7	3.2
Female	260	176	67.7	173	66.4	3	1.9
Black or African American.................................	NA	NA	NA	NA	NA	NA	NA
Male	NA	NA	NA	NA	NA	NA	NA
Female	NA	NA	NA	NA	NA	NA	NA
Hispanic or Latino ethnicity[1]	NA	NA	NA	NA	NA	NA	NA
Male	NA	NA	NA	NA	NA	NA	NA
Female	NA	NA	NA	NA	NA	NA	NA
Age							
16 to 19 years...	NA	NA	NA	NA	NA	NA	NA
20 to 24 years...	64	51	80.5	49	76.3	3	5.3
25 to 34 years...	119	102	86.0	99	83.2	3	3.3
35 to 44 years...	89	79	89.5	77	87.1	2	2.6
45 to 54 years...	93	81	87.0	78	84.4	2	3.0
55 to 64 years...	93	74	80.1	73	78.4	2	2.2
65 years and over	102	23	22.9	23	22.3	1	2.6

NOTE: Data in Table 7 are from the Current Population Survey (CPS) and do not match the estimates in Table 8. See notes and definitions for further information.
[1] May be of any race.
NA = Not available.

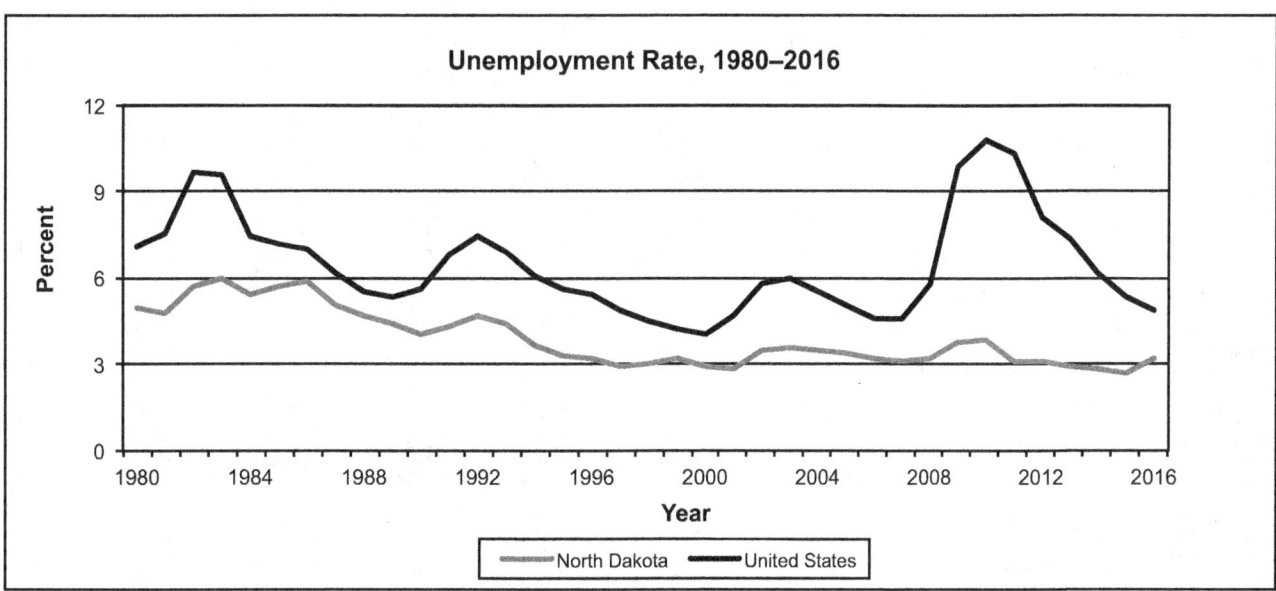

Table ND-8. Employment Status of the Civilian Noninstitutional Population Age 16 Years and Over

(Number, percent.)

Year	Civilian labor force	Civilian participation rate	Employed	Unemployed	Unemployment rate
2008..	371,025	74.4	359,333	11,692	3.2
2009..	368,665	73.2	353,455	15,210	4.1
2010..	378,342	72.6	364,053	14,289	3.8
2011..	388,634	72.9	375,153	13,481	3.5
2012..	397,812	73.0	385,596	12,216	3.1
2013..	406,602	72.7	394,833	11,769	2.9
2014..	415,286	72.6	404,147	11,139	2.7
2015..	414,344	71.0	403,058	11,286	2.7
2016..	416,227	71.5	403,067	13,160	3.2

Table ND-9. Employment and Average Wages by Industry

(Estimates through 2010 are based on the 2007 *North American Industry Classification System* [NAICS]. Estimates from 2011 onward are based on the 2012 NAICS.)

Industry	2009	2010	2011	2012	2013	2014	2015
	Number of jobs						
Wage and Salary Employment by Industry	383,754	392,470	413,535	447,582	463,457	480,912	470,976
Farm Wage and Salary Employment	4,382	4,729	5,316	6,260	6,607	7,292	5,149
Nonfarm Wage and Salary Employment	379,372	387,741	408,219	441,322	456,850	473,620	465,827
Private wage and salary employment	296,338	302,959	324,043	355,749	370,734	387,743	378,725
Forestry, fishing, and related activities	2,022	2,198	2,343	2,521	2,602	2,616	2,577
Mining	6,907	10,520	16,605	24,144	25,923	29,564	23,054
Utilities	3,384	3,417	3,418	3,506	3,593	3,702	3,831
Construction	21,557	21,995	25,050	30,299	33,288	35,720	34,930
Manufacturing	23,605	22,578	23,783	25,187	25,430	25,959	25,447
Durable goods manufacturing	15,494	14,626	15,842	16,955	17,233	17,642	17,086
Nondurable goods manufacturing	8,111	7,952	7,941	8,232	8,197	8,317	8,361
Wholesale trade	20,379	21,161	22,790	25,216	26,524	27,434	26,782
Retail trade	43,438	43,882	45,137	47,455	49,399	50,989	51,113
Transportation and warehousing	12,059	12,772	16,232	21,201	22,504	24,557	22,705
Information	7,509	7,307	7,135	6,960	6,820	6,839	6,613
Finance and insurance	16,751	17,011	17,373	17,446	17,928	18,527	18,870
Real estate and rental and leasing	3,565	3,660	4,116	4,728	5,210	5,852	5,737
Professional, scientific, and technical services	12,663	12,576	12,779	14,446	15,689	16,845	17,173
Management of companies and enterprises	4,298	4,330	4,470	4,765	5,133	5,292	5,338
Administrative and waste services	12,420	11,681	12,821	13,543	13,575	14,329	13,801
Educational services	3,743	3,969	3,953	4,027	4,174	4,119	4,212
Health care and social assistance	50,329	52,104	53,120	54,573	55,815	56,169	57,507
Arts, entertainment, and recreation	3,762	3,865	3,776	4,007	4,180	4,315	4,358
Accommodation and food services	30,575	30,674	31,887	34,279	35,241	36,399	36,288
Other services, except public administration	17,372	17,259	17,255	17,446	17,706	18,516	18,389
Government and government enterprises	83,034	84,782	84,176	85,573	86,116	85,877	87,102
	Dollars						
Average Wages and Salaries by Industry	35,531	37,612	41,103	45,121	46,841	49,910	49,795
Average Farm Wages and Salaries	40,400	37,200	36,634	45,112	39,939	40,952	38,826
Average Nonfarm Wages and Salaries	35,474	37,617	41,161	45,121	46,941	50,048	49,916
Average private wages and salaries	35,429	37,858	41,946	46,669	48,577	51,948	51,505
Forestry, fishing, and related activities	24,276	25,273	25,775	26,494	27,139	28,264	29,950
Mining	72,754	79,302	88,983	95,731	97,203	104,040	100,831
Utilities	76,924	78,500	81,955	82,096	86,456	90,560	95,230
Construction	44,760	46,472	51,147	56,417	60,155	64,861	64,919
Manufacturing	41,538	43,370	44,725	46,672	48,065	49,770	51,179
Durable goods manufacturing	42,510	44,130	45,391	47,343	48,611	49,985	50,766
Nondurable goods manufacturing	39,682	41,973	43,396	45,288	46,916	49,314	52,022
Wholesale trade	48,569	51,336	57,534	63,632	65,258	68,064	66,624
Retail trade	23,126	24,181	25,680	27,492	28,346	29,710	30,800
Transportation and warehousing	46,099	49,694	56,264	62,153	63,970	68,516	66,735
Information	47,543	49,062	50,886	54,447	55,754	58,394	59,859
Finance and insurance	45,314	46,713	49,871	52,930	54,118	56,331	59,317
Real estate and rental and leasing	30,636	34,617	44,213	50,412	53,413	59,654	56,584
Professional, scientific, and technical services	46,286	51,504	55,920	63,228	67,258	71,698	69,687
Management of companies and enterprises	59,978	63,706	65,947	69,339	69,949	76,648	81,419
Administrative and waste services	22,965	25,133	27,897	31,646	31,956	34,056	34,928
Educational services	21,283	20,986	21,706	22,538	22,472	23,659	23,335
Health care and social assistance	37,860	39,323	41,294	43,459	44,548	46,530	49,298
Arts, entertainment, and recreation	15,121	15,488	16,270	16,815	17,339	17,621	18,445
Accommodation and food services	13,252	14,010	15,305	17,313	18,464	19,555	19,918
Other services, except public administration	22,441	23,698	25,416	28,001	30,076	31,951	32,975
Government and government enterprises	35,635	36,758	38,139	38,682	39,896	41,472	43,007

Table ND-10. Employment Characteristics by Family Type

(Number, percent.)

Family type and labor force status	2013		2014		2015	
	Total	Families with own children under 18 years	Total	Families with own children under 18 years	Total	Families with own children under 18 years
All Families..	180,213	78,738	187,451	84,732	188,210	82,326
FAMILY TYPE AND LABOR FORCE STATUS						
Married-Couple Families..	145,079	57,092	148,667	59,010	150,297	58,631
Both husband and wife in labor force..........................	59.9	72.3	60.8	74.6	60.5	76.5
Husband in labor force, wife not in labor force	18.2	23.4	17.7	21.0	17.1	19.6
Wife in labor force, husband not in labor force...............	7.0	2.9	6.7	2.9	6.6	2.3
Both husband and wife not in labor force......................	14.5	1.3	14.9	1.5	15.3	0.9
Other Families	35,134	21,646	38,784	25,722	37,913	23,695
Female householder, no husband present......................	63.1	63.8	63.6	68.5	64.1	66.0
In labor force..	47.6	50.8	47.1	55.7	49.8	56.1
Not in labor force	15.4	13.0	16.5	12.8	14.3	9.9
Male householder, no wife present.............................	36.9	36.2	36.4	31.5	35.9	34.0
In labor force..	31.7	34.2	31.1	27.9	30.2	31.1
Not in labor force	5.2	2.0	5.3	3.6	5.7	2.9

Table ND-11. School Enrollment and Educational Attainment, 2015

(Number, percent.)

Item	State	U.S.
Enrollment		
Total population 3 years and over, enrolled in school	181,102	81,618,288
Enrolled in nursery school or preschool (percent)...................................	5.6	6.0
Enrolled in kindergarten (percent)..	5.1	5.0
Enrolled in elementary school, grades 1-8 (percent)................................	38.7	40.3
Enrolled in high school, grades 9-12 (percent)	19.2	20.9
Enrolled in college or graduate school (percent)....................................	31.4	27.7
Attainment		
Total population 25 years and over..	492,017	216,447,163
Less than ninth grade (percent)	3.7	5.5
9th to 12th grade, no diploma (percent)	3.8	7.3
High school graduate, including equivalency (percent)..............................	27.6	27.6
Some college, no degree (percent)	22.7	20.7
Associate's degree (percent)	13.1	8.2
Bachelor's degree (percent)	21.5	19.0
Graduate or professional degree (percent)..	7.7	11.6
High school graduate or higher (percent)	92.5	87.1
Bachelor's degree or higher (percent)...	29.1	30.6

Table ND-12. Public School Characteristics and Educational Indicators

(Number, percent; data derived from National Center of Education Statistics.)

Item	State	U.S.
Public Schools, 2014–2015 (except where noted)		
Number of school districts...	221	18,260
Number of schools..	513	98,373
Number of students...	106,586	50,312,581
Number of teachers	9,049	3,132,351
Student-teacher ratio	11.8	16.1
Expenditures per student (dollars), FY 2014...	12,032	11,066
Four-year adjusted cohort graduation rate (ACGR)[1,2]	86.6	83.2
Students eligible for free or reduced-price lunch (percent).........................	29.2	51.8
English language learners (percent)	3.0	9.4
Students age 3 to 21 served under IDEA, part B (percent)...........................	12.8	13.0

Public Schools by Type	Number	Percent of state public schools
Total number of schools..	513	100.0
Regular	470	91.6
Special education..	31	6.0
Vocational education..	12	2.3
Alternative education...	0	-

NOTE: Every school is assigned only one school type based on its instructional emphasis.
[1] ACGR data represents a new method of calculating high-school completion rates and may not be comparable to previous years' data for Averaged Freshmen Graduation Rates (AFGR).
[2] The United States 4-year ACGRs were estimated using both the reported 4-year ACGR data from 49 states and the District of Columbia and using imputed data for Idaho. The estimate for American Indian/Alaska Native students also includes imputed data for Virginia.
- = Zero or rounds to zero.

Table ND-13. Reported Voting and Registration of the Voting-Age Population, November 2016

(Numbers in thousands, percent.)

Item	Total population	Total citizen population	Registered			Voted		
			Total registered	Percent registered (total population)	Percent registered (total citizen population)	Total voted	Percent voted (total population)	Percent voted (total citizen population)
U.S. Total	245,502	224,059	157,596	64.2	70.3	137,537	56.0	61.4
State Total............................	583	564	424	72.8	75.2	362	62.1	64.2
Sex								
Male	298	288	216	72.6	75.0	182	61.1	63.2
Female	285	276	208	73.1	75.4	180	63.2	65.2
Race								
White alone............................	520	515	403	77.5	78.2	348	67.1	67.7
White, non-Hispanic alone	511	508	399	77.9	78.4	345	67.4	67.9
Black alone............................	15	9	4	(B)	(B)	3	(B)	(B)
Asian alone	11	3	2	(B)	(B)	2	(B)	(B)
Hispanic (of any race).......................	9	7	5	(B)	(B)	4	(B)	(B)
White alone or in combination	528	523	406	77.0	77.7	351	66.5	67.1
Black alone or in combination..........	15	10	4	(B)	(B)	3	(B)	(B)
Asian alone or in combination........	12	4	3	(B)	(B)	2	(B)	(B)
Age								
18 to 24 years.....................	79	78	47	(B)	(B)	37	(B)	(B)
25 to 34 years.....................	124	117	83	66.7	71.2	70	56.2	60.0
35 to 44 years.....................	90	87	65	(B)	(B)	56	(B)	(B)
45 to 64 years.....................	192	187	153	79.6	81.5	132	68.7	70.3
65 years and over	97	96	76	(B)	(B)	67	(B)	(B)

- = Zero or rounds to zero.
B = Base is less than 75,000 and therefore too small to show the derived measure.

Table ND-14. Crime

(Number, rate per 100,000. Data are derived from the FBI Uniform Crime Reports.)

Item	State			U.S. [1,2,3,4]		
	2014	2015	Percent change	2014	2015	Percent change
TOTAL POPULATION[5]	740,040	756,927	2.3	318,907,401	321,418,820	0.8
VIOLENT CRIME						
Number..................................	2,001	1,812	-9.4	1,186,185	1,231,566	3.8
Rate	270.4	239.4	-11.5	372.0	383.2	3.0
Murder and Nonnegligent Manslaughter						
Number..................................	23	21	-8.7	14,164	15,696	10.8
Rate	3.1	2.8	-10.7	4.4	4.9	10.0
Rape[6]						
Number..................................	382	345	-9.7	118,027	124,047	5.1
Rate	51.6	45.6	-11.7	37.0	38.6	4.3
Robbery						
Number..................................	175	148	-15.4	322,905	327,374	1.4
Rate	23.6	19.6	-17.3	101.3	101.9	0.6
Aggravated Assault						
Number..................................	1,421	1,298	-8.7	731,089	764,449	4.6
Rate	192.0	171.5	-10.7	229.2	237.8	3.7
PROPERTY CRIME						
Number..................................	15,857	16,020	1.0	8,209,010	7,993,631	-2.6
Rate	2,142.7	2,116.5	-1.2	2,574.1	2,487.0	-3.4
Burglary						
Number..................................	2,751	2,997	8.9	1,713,153	1,579,527	-7.8
Rate	371.7	395.9	6.5	537.2	491.4	-8.5
Larceny-Theft						
Number..................................	11,559	11,440		5,809,054	5,706,346	-1.8
Rate	1,561.9	1,511.4	-3.2	1,821.5	1,775.4	-2.5
Motor Vehicle Theft						
Number..................................	1,547	1,583	2.3	686,803	707,758	3.1
Rate	209.0	209.1	-	215.4	220.2	2.2

NOTE: Although arson data are included in the trend and clearance tables, sufficient data are not available to estimate totals for this offense. Therefore, no arson data are published in this table.
X = Not applicable.
- = Zero or rounds to zero.
[1] The crime figures have been adjusted.
[2] The data collection methodology for the offense of forcible rape used by the Minnesota state Uniform Crime Reporting (UCR) Program (with the exception of Minneapolis and St. Paul, Minnesota) does not comply with national UCR Program guidelines. Consequently, its figures for forcible rape and violent crime (of which forcible rape is a part) are not published in this table.
[3] Includes offenses reported by the Zoological Police and the Metro Transit Police.
[4] Because of changes in the state's reporting practices, figures are not comparable to previous years' data.
[5] Populations are U.S. Census Bureau provisional estimates as of July 1 of each year.
[6] The figures shown for the offense of rape were estimated using the revised Uniform Crime Reporting (UCR) definition of rape.

Table ND-15. State Government Finances, 2015

(Dollar amounts in thousands, percent distribution.)

Item	Dollars	Percent distribution
Total Revenue	9,883,423	100.0
General revenue	8,800,855	89.0
Intergovernmental revenue	1,677,677	17.0
Taxes	5,736,355	58.0
General sales	1,389,083	14.1
Selective sales	546,733	5.5
License taxes	225,540	2.3
Individual income tax	536,131	5.4
Corporate income tax	186,039	1.9
Other taxes	2,852,829	28.9
Current charges	783,804	7.9
Miscellaneous general revenue	603,019	6.1
Utility revenue	0	-
Liquor stores revenue	0	-
Insurance trust revenue[1]	1,082,568	11.0
Total Expenditure	8,250,765	100.0
Intergovernmental expenditure	2,555,758	31.0
Direct expenditure	5,695,007	69.0
Current operation	3,620,856	43.9
Capital outlay	1,111,740	13.5
Insurance benefits and repayments	712,142	8.6
Assistance and subsidies	168,609	2.0
Interest on debt	81,660	1.0
Exhibit: Salaries and wages	1,063,359	12.9
Total Expenditure	8,250,765	100.0
General expenditure	7,538,623	91.4
Intergovernmental expenditure	2,555,758	31.0
Direct expenditure	4,982,865	60.4
General expenditure, by function:		
Education	2,280,513	27.6
Public welfare	1,335,551	16.2
Hospitals	61,726	0.7
Health	153,008	1.9
Highways	1,224,581	14.8
Police protection	48,088	0.6
Correction	91,209	1.1
Natural resources	483,695	5.9
Parks and recreation	33,375	0.4
Governmental administration	182,708	2.2
Interest on general debt	81,660	1.0
Other and unallocable	1,562,509	18.9
Utility expenditure	0	-
Liquor stores expenditure	0	-
Insurance trust expenditure	712,142	8.6
Debt at End of Fiscal Year	2,063,788	X
Cash and Security Holdings	24,979,559	X

X = Not applicable.
- = Zero or rounds to zero.
[1] Within insurance trust revenue, net earnings of state retirement systems is a calculated statistic (the item code in the data file is X08), and thus can be positive or negative. Net earnings is the sum of earnings on investments plus gains on investments minus losses on investments. The change made in 2002 for asset valuation from book to market value in accordance with Statement 34 of the Governmental Accounting Standards Board is reflected in the calculated statistics.

Table ND-16. State Government Tax Collections, 2016

(Dollars in thousands, percent.)

Item	Dollars	Percent distribution
Total Taxes	3,709,105	100.0
Property taxes	3,910	0.1
Sales and gross receipts	1,496,824	40.4
General sales and gross receipts	1,017,269	27.4
Selective sales and gross receipts	479,555	12.9
Alcoholic beverages	9,026	0.2
Amusements	3,406	0.1
Insurance premiums	65,113	1.8
Motor fuels	196,837	5.3
Pari-mutuels	1,566	-
Public utilities	46,455	1.3
Tobacco products	30,757	0.8
Other selective sales	126,395	3.4
Licenses	204,055	5.5
Alcoholic beverages	381	-
Amusements	756	-
Corporations in general	0	-
Hunting and fishing	19,306	0.5
Motor vehicle	119,473	3.2
Motor vehicle operators	4,226	0.1
Public utilities	6	-
Occupation and business, NEC	59,907	1.6
Other licenses	0	-
Income taxes	454,194	12.2
Individual income	351,125	9.5
Corporation net income	103,069	2.8
Other taxes	1,550,122	41.8
Death and gift	0	-
Documentary and stock transfer	0	-
Severance	1,550,122	41.8
Taxes, NEC	0	-

- = Zero or rounds to zero.

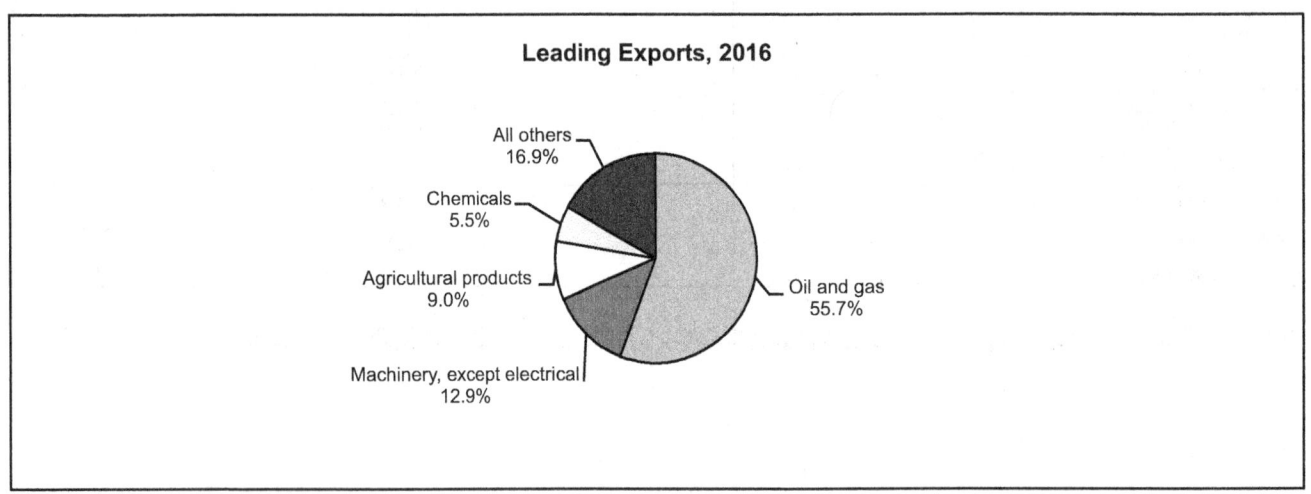

Leading Exports, 2016

All others 16.9%
Chemicals 5.5%
Agricultural products 9.0%
Machinery, except electrical 12.9%
Oil and gas 55.7%

OHIO

Facts and Figures

Location: East north central United States; bordered on the N by Michigan and Lake Erie, on the E by Pennsylvania and West Virginia, on the S by West Virginia and Kentucky, and on the W by Indiana

Area: 44,825 sq. mi. (116,096 sq. km.); rank—34th

Population: 11,614,373 (2016 est.); rank—7th

Principal Cities: capital—Columbus; largest—Columbus

Statehood: March 1, 1803; 17th state

U.S. Congress: 2 senators, 16 representatives

State Motto: With God, All Things Are Possible

State Song: "Beautiful Ohio"

State Nickname: The Buckeye State

Abbreviations: OH

State Symbols: flower—scarlet carnation; tree—Ohio buckeye; bird—cardinal

At a Glance

- With an increase in population of 0.7 percent, Ohio ranked 42nd among the states in growth from 2010 to 2016.

- Ohio's violent crime rate in 2015 was 291.9 per 100,000 population, compared to 383.2 for the entire nation.

- In 2015, 6.5 percent of Ohioans did not have health insurance, compared to 9.4 percent of the entire U.S. population.

- Ohio had the 3rd highest drug overdose death rate in 2015, with 29.9 deaths per 100,000 population.

- Approximately 0.3 percent of Ohio's population identified as "American Indian or Alaska Native Alone" in 2016, which was the second lowest percent among all states.

Table OH-1. Population by Age, Sex, Race, and Hispanic Origin

(Number, percent, except where noted.)

Sex, age, race, and Hispanic origin	2000	2010	2016 [1]	Average annual percent change, 2010–2016
Total Population................................	11,353,140	11,536,504	11,614,373	-
Percent of total U.S. population	4.0	3.7	3.6	X
Sex				
Male..	5,512,262	5,632,156	5,691,694	0.1
Female...	5,840,878	5,904,348	5,922,679	-
Age				
Under 5 years....................................	754,930	720,856	697,923	-0.2
5 to 19 years....................................	2,461,025	2,346,270	2,218,535	-0.3
20 to 64 years..................................	6,629,428	6,847,363	6,811,286	-
65 years and over..............................	1,507,757	1,622,015	1,886,629	1.0
Median age (years)	36.2	38.8	39.3	0.1
Race and Hispanic Origin				
One race...				
White...	9,645,453	9,664,524	9,576,321	-0.1
Black...	1,301,307	1,426,861	1,487,040	0.3
American Indian and Alaska Native........	24,486	29,674	32,364	0.6
Asian...	132,633	196,693	255,464	1.9
Native Hawaiian or Other Pacific Islander..	2,749	5,336	6,639	1.5
Two or more races..............................	157,885	213,416	256,545	1.3
Hispanic (of any race).........................	217,123	375,004	424,625	0.8

X = Not applicable.
- = Zero or rounds to zero.
[1] Population figures for 2016 are July 1 estimates. The 2010 estimates are taken from the 2010 Census.

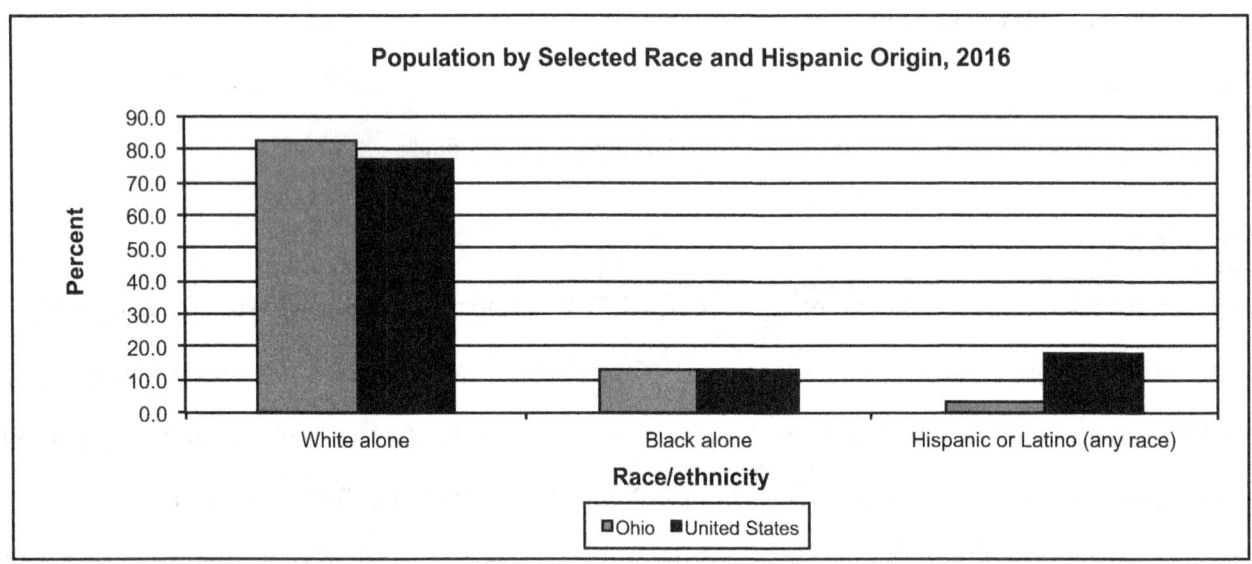

Population by Selected Race and Hispanic Origin, 2016

Ohio / United States

Table OH-2. Marital Status

(Number, percent distribution.)

Sex, age, race, and Hispanic origin	2000	2010	2015
Males, 15 Years and Over	4,281,736	4,487,900	4,577,925
Never married	29.2	33.5	35.2
Now married, except separated...........................	57.0	51.2	49.1
Separated..	1.4	1.7	1.6
Widowed..	2.7	2.9	2.9
Divorced..	9.7	10.8	11.2
Females, 15 Years and Over	4,670,985	4,809,613	4,873,524
Never married	23.5	27.9	29.2
Now married, except separated...........................	52.1	46.9	46.1
Separated..	1.7	2.1	1.9
Widowed..	11.1	10.1	9.7
Divorced..	11.5	12.9	13.0

Table OH-3. Households and Housing Characteristics

(Number, percent, dollars.)

Item	2000	2010	2015	Average annual percent change, 2000–2015
Total Households...	4,445,773	4,525,066	4,606,655	0.2
Family households...	2,993,023	2,960,107	2,922,095	-0.2
Married-couple family..	2,285,798	2,169,003	2,123,886	-0.5
Other family	707,225	791,104	798,209	0.9
Male householder, no wife present.............................	170,347	196,130	210,633	1.6
Female householder, no husband present...................	536,878	594,974	587,576	0.6
Nonfamily households	1,452,750	1,564,959	1,684,560	1.1
Householder living alone..	1,215,614	1,315,321	1,393,835	1.0
Householder not living alone...	237,136	249,638	290,725	1.5
Housing Characteristics				
Total housing units...	4,783,051	5,128,113	5,156,546	0.5
Occupied housing units	4,445,773	4,525,066	4,606,655	0.2
Owner occupied	3,072,522	3,095,197	3,013,093	-0.1
Renter occupied	1,373,251	1,429,869	1,593,562	1.1
Average household size...	2.49	2.48	2.45	-0.1
Financial Characteristics				
Median gross rent of renter-occupied housing	515	685	746	3.0
Median monthly owner costs for housing units with a mortgage	983	1,246	1,228	1.7
Median value of owner-occupied housing units......................	103,700	134,400	136,400	2.1

Table OH-4. Migration, Origin, and Language

(Number, percent.)

Characteristic	State			U.S.		
	2014	2015	Percent change	2014	2015	Percent change
Residence 1 Year Ago						
Population 1 year and over	11,464,891	11,482,142	0.2	315,095,393	317,635,720	0.8
Same house	85.0	84.7	X	85.1	85.3	X
Different house in the U.S.	14.7	14.9	X	14.3	14.1	X
Same county	9.5	9.7	X	8.7	8.5	X
Different county	5.1	5.3	X	5.6	5.6	X
Same state...	3.4	3.5	X	3.3	3.2	X
Different state..	1.7	1.8	X	2.3	2.4	X
Abroad	0.4	0.4	X	0.6	0.7	X
Place of Birth						
Native born	11,112,049	11,109,512	-	276,465,262	278,128,449	0.6
Male	48.9	48.9	X	49.3	49.3	X
Female	51.1	51.1	X	50.7	50.7	X
Foreign born	482,114	503,911	4.5	42,391,794	43,290,372	2.1
Male	49.4	49.1	X	48.7	48.6	X
Female	50.6	50.9	X	51.3	51.4	X
Foreign born; naturalized U.S. citizen..................................	240,565	255,342	6.1	19,984,738	20,697,103	3.6
Male	47.0	47.5	X	45.9	45.9	X
Female	53.0	52.5	X	54.1	54.1	X
Foreign born; not a U.S. citizen	241,549	248,569	2.9	22,407,056	22,593,269	0.8
Male	51.7	50.8	X	51.2	51.1	X
Female	48.3	49.2	X	48.8	48.9	X
Entered 2010 or later	20.0	25.8	X	12.3	15.6	X
Entered 2000 to 2009	31.5	29.2	X	28.6	27.9	X
Entered before 2000...	48.4	44.9	X	59.1	56.5	X
World Region of Birth, Foreign						
Foreign-born population, excluding population born at sea	482,114	503,911	4.5	42,390,705	43,289,646	2.1
Europe	21.6	22.3	X	11.2	11.1	X
Asia...	43.4	42.0	X	30.1	30.6	X
Africa	12.1	12.8	X	4.6	4.8	X
Oceania...	0.5	0.5	X	0.6	0.6	X
Latin America..	19.5	19.3	X	51.6	51.1	X
North America..	3.0	3.0	X	1.9	1.9	X
Language Spoken at Home and Ability to Speak English						
Population 5 years and over..	10,904,728	10,924,135	0.2	299,084,046	301,625,014	0.8
English only	93.4	93.1	X	78.9	78.5	X
Language other than English..	6.6	6.9	X	21.1	21.5	X
Speaks English less than "very well"................................	2.4	2.5	X	8.6	8.6	X

NA = Not available.
X = Not applicable.
- = Zero or rounds to zero.

Table OH-5. Median Income and Poverty Status, 2015

(Number, percent, except as noted.)

Characteristic	State		U.S.	
	Number	Percent	Number	Percent
Median Income				
Households (dollars).................................	51,075	X	55,775	X
Families (dollars)	65,176	X	68,260	X
Below Poverty Level (All People)	1,674,415	14.8	46,153,077	14.7
Sex				
Male	741,150	13.5	20,599,407	13.4
Female	933,265	16.1	25,553,670	16.0
Age				
Under 18 years.................................	550,270	21.3	15,000,273	20.7
Related children under 18 years................	539,084	20.9	14,693,239	20.4
18 to 64 years.................................	989,765	14.3	26,960,369	13.9
65 years and over	134,380	7.6	4,192,435	9.0

X = Not applicable.

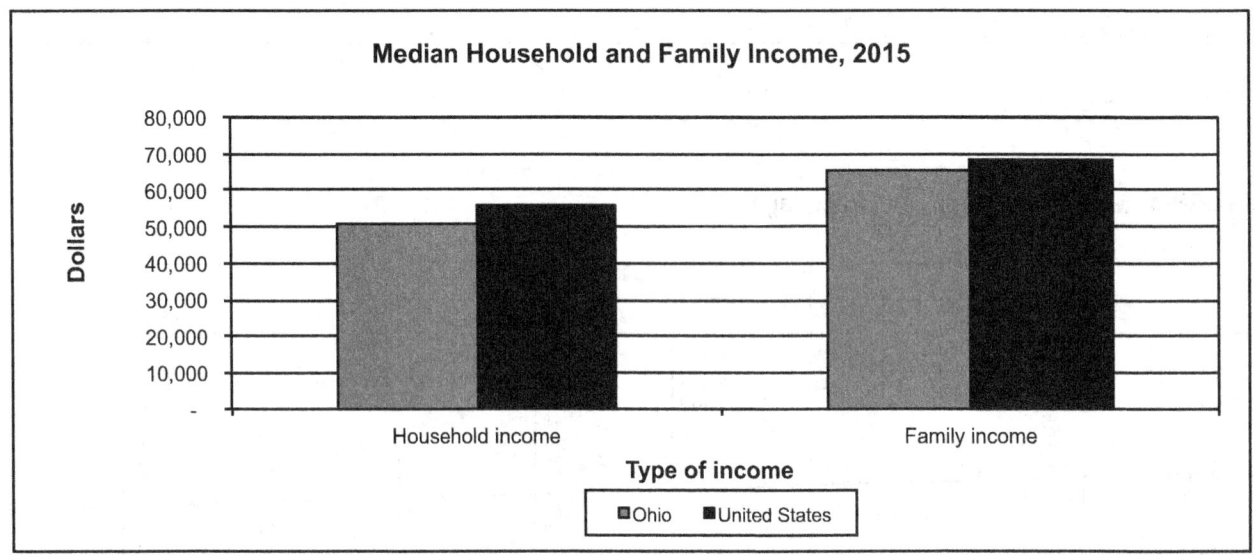

Median Household and Family Income, 2015

Table OH-6. Health Insurance Coverage Status for the Civilian Noninstitutionalized Population and Children Under 18 Years of Age

(Numbers in thousands, percent.)

Item	2007	2008	2009	2010	2011	2012	2013	2014	2015
Civilian Noninstitutionalized Population	11,300	11,296	11,352	11,359	11,369	11,372	11,398	11,421	11,442
Covered by Private or Public Insurance									
Number..	9,979	9,966	9,969	9,960	10,015	10,068	10,141	10,466	10,696
Percent..	88.3	88.2	87.8	87.7	88.1	88.5	89.0	91.6	93.5
Not Covered									
Number..	1,322	1,330	1,383	1,399	1,354	1,304	1,258	955	746
Percent..	11.7	11.8	12.2	12.3	11.9	11.5	11.0	8.4	6.5
Percent in the U.S. not covered......................	15.3	15.1	15.1	15.5	15.1	14.8	14.5	11.7	9.4
Children Under 18 Years of Age	2,790	2,728	2,710	2,715	2,688	2,657	2,645	2,631	2,627
Covered by Private or Public Insurance									
Number..	2,551	2,531	2,538	2,553	2,531	2,516	2,504	2,505	2,512
Percent..	91.4	92.8	93.6	94.0	94.2	94.7	94.7	95.2	95.6
Not Covered									
Number..	239	197	172	162	157	141	141	126	115
Percent..	8.6	7.2	6.4	6.0	5.8	5.3	5.3	4.8	4.4
Percent in the U.S. not covered......................	11.0	9.7	8.6	8.0	7.5	7.2	7.1	6.0	4.8

Table OH-7. Employment Status by Demographic Group, 2016

(Numbers in thousands, percent.)

Characteristic	Civilian noninstitutional population	Civilian labor force		Employed		Unemployed	
		Number	Percent of population	Number	Percent of population	Number	Percent of population
Total...	9,167	5,737	62.6	5,453	59.5	284	4.9
Sex							
Male...	4,419	3,012	68.2	2,855	64.6	157	5.2
Female...	4,748	2,725	57.4	2,598	54.7	127	4.7
Race, Sex, and Hispanic Origin							
White...	7,685	4,832	62.9	4,628	60.2	205	4.2
Male..	3,742	2,585	69.1	2,461	65.8	123	4.8
Female..	3,943	2,248	57.0	2,166	54.9	81	3.6
Black or African American....................	1,086	633	58.3	572	52.7	61	9.6
Male..	495	289	58.5	264	53.4	25	8.7
Female..	591	343	58.1	308	52.0	36	10.4
Hispanic or Latino ethnicity[1]	277	193	69.8	182	65.7	12	5.9
Male..	131	103	78.4	97	74.2	6	5.3
Female..	146	91	62.1	85	58.0	6	6.6
Age							
16 to 19 years...................................	601	280	46.7	235	39.2	45	16.0
20 to 24 years...................................	772	580	75.1	531	68.8	49	8.5
25 to 34 years...................................	1,497	1,239	82.8	1,170	78.1	69	5.6
35 to 44 years...................................	1,324	1,104	83.4	1,060	80.0	45	4.0
45 to 54 years...................................	1,465	1,173	80.0	1,137	77.6	36	3.1
55 to 64 years...................................	1,604	1,021	63.7	993	61.9	28	2.8
65 years and over	1,904	340	17.8	328	17.2	12	3.5

NOTE: Data in Table 7 are from the Current Population Survey (CPS) and do not match the estimates in Table 8. See notes and definitions for further information.
[1] May be of any race.

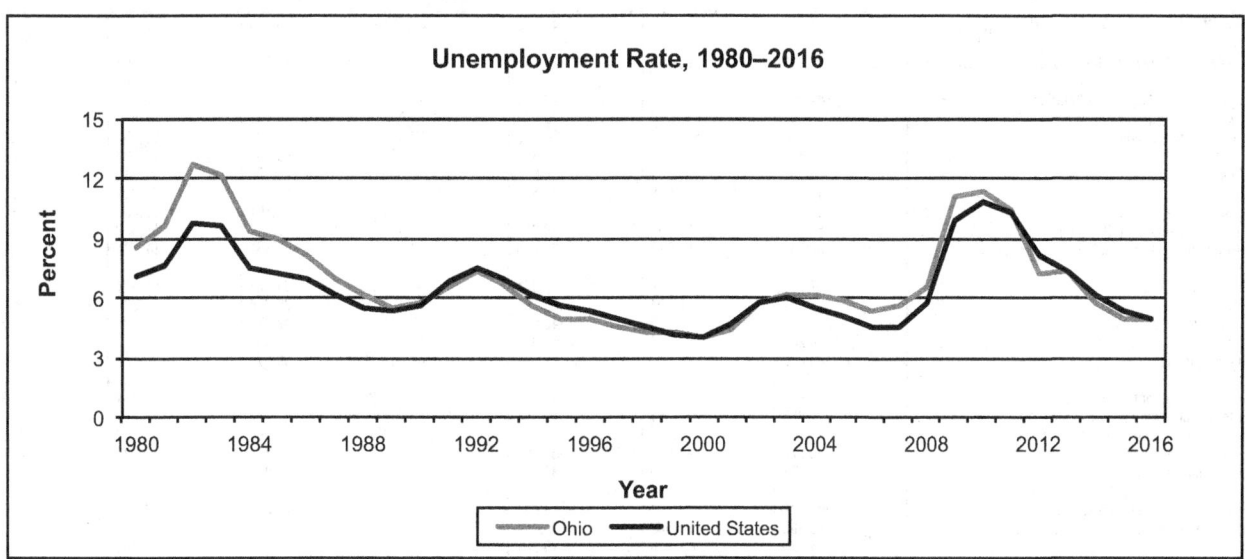

Table OH-8. Employment Status of the Civilian Noninstitutional Population Age 16 Years and Over

(Number, percent.)

Year	Civilian labor force	Civilian participation rate	Employed	Unemployed	Unemployment rate
2008..	5,965,166	66.8	5,580,843	384,323	6.4
2009..	5,906,768	66.0	5,297,098	609,670	10.3
2010..	5,846,886	65.2	5,247,050	599,836	10.3
2011..	5,771,469	64.1	5,261,238	510,231	8.8
2012..	5,706,059	63.2	5,284,522	421,537	7.4
2013..	5,717,133	63.1	5,290,147	426,986	7.5
2014..	5,702,698	62.7	5,372,754	329,944	5.8
2015..	5,700,344	62.5	5,423,019	277,325	4.9
2016..	5,713,088	62.5	5,430,790	282,298	4.9

Table OH-9. Employment and Average Wages by Industry

(Estimates through 2010 are based on the 2007 *North American Industry Classification System* [NAICS]. Estimates from 2011 onward are based on the 2012 NAICS.)

Industry	2009	2010	2011	2012	2013	2014	2015
	Number of jobs						
Wage and Salary Employment by Industry..................	5,232,886	5,168,965	5,228,768	5,319,551	5,371,183	5,444,825	5,525,739
Farm Wage and Salary Employment........................	13,609	13,347	13,254	19,593	16,081	12,576	18,013
Nonfarm Wage and Salary Employment....................	5,219,277	5,155,618	5,215,514	5,299,958	5,355,102	5,432,249	5,507,726
Private wage and salary employment...............................	4,380,207	4,330,575	4,407,972	4,500,698	4,559,821	4,637,480	4,712,491
Forestry, fishing, and related activities........................	4,457	4,603	4,600	4,885	5,111	5,250	5,357
Mining........................	11,450	10,897	11,375	12,214	12,134	14,388	13,724
Utilities........................	21,323	19,951	19,308	19,109	18,799	18,217	19,210
Construction........................	189,612	174,975	181,890	186,456	191,406	201,029	205,353
Manufacturing........................	630,766	621,524	638,976	657,622	663,376	675,125	686,892
Durable goods manufacturing........................	419,602	412,151	429,033	444,884	449,296	459,786	467,773
Nondurable goods manufacturing........................	211,164	209,373	209,943	212,738	214,080	215,339	219,119
Wholesale trade........................	223,539	218,050	219,727	225,351	228,901	233,996	237,166
Retail trade........................	569,531	557,113	560,667	564,908	567,546	571,007	575,637
Transportation and warehousing........................	169,009	163,061	168,395	172,494	175,384	180,789	190,047
Information........................	80,891	77,613	76,220	74,741	75,412	72,703	71,727
Finance and insurance........................	216,751	215,060	217,368	219,562	220,341	220,352	224,423
Real estate and rental and leasing........................	62,731	59,548	59,441	59,421	60,898	62,364	63,708
Professional, scientific, and technical services..............	243,161	241,100	247,909	244,260	246,524	250,425	252,677
Management of companies and enterprises....................	107,953	107,329	112,862	127,247	132,404	137,549	138,940
Administrative and waste services........................	271,590	280,657	295,144	306,110	313,943	324,918	328,030
Educational services........................	111,740	114,771	116,887	115,630	113,283	114,186	117,380
Health care and social assistance........................	731,170	741,552	747,221	759,706	770,270	776,822	790,708
Arts, entertainment, and recreation........................	64,234	63,363	63,984	68,684	74,247	76,250	78,120
Accommodation and food services........................	419,091	415,822	422,961	435,065	447,031	453,767	464,569
Other services, except public administration..................	251,208	243,586	243,037	247,233	242,811	248,343	248,823
Government and government enterprises..........................	839,070	825,043	807,542	799,260	795,281	794,769	795,235
	Dollars						
Average Wages and Salaries by Industry	41,171	42,314	43,685	44,984	45,520	46,837	48,007
Average Farm Wages and Salaries	29,241	23,163	29,747	27,100	30,897	35,465	36,272
Average Nonfarm Wages and Salaries	41,202	42,364	43,720	45,050	45,564	46,864	48,045
Average private wages and salaries............................	40,859	42,004	43,424	44,830	45,404	46,810	47,973
Forestry, fishing, and related activities........................	24,238	25,499	26,286	27,029	27,824	29,057	29,752
Mining........................	62,840	66,799	71,353	73,284	65,255	71,207	69,537
Utilities........................	82,786	84,183	86,823	88,802	90,586	93,316	96,921
Construction........................	47,321	47,918	49,698	51,542	52,933	54,941	56,841
Manufacturing........................	52,777	54,891	57,140	57,344	57,651	59,420	60,192
Durable goods manufacturing........................	53,805	56,068	58,310	58,473	58,744	60,469	60,797
Nondurable goods manufacturing........................	50,736	52,573	54,749	54,982	55,357	57,181	58,899
Wholesale trade........................	57,712	60,057	62,471	64,079	64,677	66,491	68,500
Retail trade........................	24,361	25,104	25,755	26,427	26,674	27,335	28,158
Transportation and warehousing........................	44,758	44,996	46,229	47,534	47,773	49,203	50,163
Information........................	56,231	58,350	60,318	61,957	63,636	64,870	67,016
Finance and insurance........................	60,650	62,838	65,057	66,644	69,375	72,182	74,550
Real estate and rental and leasing........................	35,861	37,738	39,534	41,312	42,397	44,414	46,020
Professional, scientific, and technical services..............	61,856	63,581	66,002	67,404	68,713	70,557	72,741
Management of companies and enterprises....................	86,548	93,529	96,478	108,034	104,995	108,768	106,499
Administrative and waste services........................	29,678	29,945	30,620	31,654	32,304	33,126	34,397
Educational services........................	29,377	29,459	30,074	30,567	30,841	31,077	31,239
Health care and social assistance........................	40,349	40,701	41,646	42,928	43,650	44,693	46,224
Arts, entertainment, and recreation........................	29,803	31,069	30,619	32,105	32,083	34,225	35,107
Accommodation and food services........................	14,823	15,198	15,701	16,370	16,712	17,290	18,076
Other services, except public administration..................	25,774	26,868	27,531	28,556	29,167	30,095	31,359
Government and government enterprises..........................	42,997	44,253	45,335	46,292	46,476	47,176	48,475

Table OH-10. Employment Characteristics by Family Type

(Number, percent.)

Family type and labor force status	2013		2014		2015	
	Total	Families with own children under 18 years	Total	Families with own children under 18 years	Total	Families with own children under 18 years
All Families...	2,923,404	1,232,209	2,914,550	1,218,710	2,922,095	1,218,342
FAMILY TYPE AND LABOR FORCE STATUS						
Married-Couple Families...	2,118,209	781,239	2,095,746	766,196	2,123,886	781,230
Both husband and wife in labor force.................................	52.3	69.7	52.6	69.9	52.0	69.8
Husband in labor force, wife not in labor force......................	20.3	24.3	20.1	24.5	20.0	24.1
Wife in labor force, husband not in labor force......................	8.6	3.8	8.3	4.1	8.6	4.0
Both husband and wife not in labor force............................	18.5	2.1	19.0	1.5	19.0	1.8
Other Families	805,195	450,970	818,804	452,514	798,209	437,112
Female householder, no husband present.............................	73.6	76.2	73.8	76.6	73.6	75.6
In labor force..	51.7	62.9	51.3	63.5	50.9	62.2
Not in labor force	21.9	13.3	22.5	13.1	22.7	13.3
Male householder, no wife present..................................	26.4	23.8	26.2	23.4	26.4	24.4
In labor force..	20.0	21.2	20.0	21.0	20.2	21.7
Not in labor force	6.4	2.6	6.2	2.4	6.2	2.7

Table OH-11. School Enrollment and Educational Attainment, 2015

(Number, percent.)

Item	State	U.S.
Enrollment		
Total population 3 years and over, enrolled in school	2,879,469	81,618,288
Enrolled in nursery school or preschool (percent)...................	6.0	6.0
Enrolled in kindergarten (percent)...................................	4.9	5.0
Enrolled in elementary school, grades 1-8 (percent).................	40.9	40.3
Enrolled in high school, grades 9-12 (percent)......................	21.7	20.9
Enrolled in college or graduate school (percent)....................	26.6	27.7
Attainment		
Total population 25 years and over	7,896,470	216,447,163
Less than ninth grade (percent)......................................	3.0	5.5
9th to 12th grade, no diploma (percent)..............................	7.3	7.3
High school graduate, including equivalency (percent)...............	33.7	27.6
Some college, no degree (percent)...................................	20.6	20.7
Associate's degree (percent)...	8.6	8.2
Bachelor's degree (percent)..	16.8	19.0
Graduate or professional degree (percent)...........................	10.0	11.6
High school graduate or higher (percent)............................	89.7	87.1
Bachelor's degree or higher (percent)...............................	26.8	30.6

Table OH-12. Public School Characteristics and Educational Indicators

(Number, percent; data derived from National Center of Education Statistics.)

Item	State	U.S.
Public Schools, 2014–2015 (except where noted)		
Number of school districts..	1,106	18,260
Number of schools..	3,631	98,373
Number of students	1,724,810	50,312,581
Number of teachers	106,526	3,132,351
Student-teacher ratio	16.2	16.1
Expenditures per student (dollars), FY 2014.........................	11,434	11,066
Four-year adjusted cohort graduation rate (ACGR)[1,2]	80.7	83.2
Students eligible for free or reduced-price lunch (percent)..........	45.1	51.8
English language learners (percent)..................................	2.6	9.4
Students age 3 to 21 served under IDEA, part B (percent)............	14.7	13.0

Public Schools by Type	Number	Percent of state public schools
Total number of schools..	3,631	100.0
Regular	3,517	96.9
Special education...	44	1.2
Vocational education..	70	1.9
Alternative education...	0	-

NOTE: Every school is assigned only one school type based on its instructional emphasis.
[1] ACGR data represents a new method of calculating high-school completion rates and may not be comparable to previous years' data for Averaged Freshmen Graduation Rates (AFGR).
[2] The United States 4-year ACGRs were estimated using both the reported 4-year ACGR data from 49 states and the District of Columbia and using imputed data for Idaho. The estimate for American Indian/Alaska Native students also includes imputed data for Virginia.

Table OH-13. Reported Voting and Registration of the Voting-Age Population, November 2016

(Numbers in thousands, percent.)

Item	Total population	Total citizen population	Registered			Voted		
			Total registered	Percent registered (total population)	Percent registered (total citizen population)	Total voted	Percent voted (total population)	Percent voted (total citizen population)
U.S. Total	245,502	224,059	157,596	64.2	70.3	137,537	56.0	61.4
State Total..............................	8,811	8,499	6,128	69.5	72.1	5,408	61.4	63.6
Sex								
Male	4,219	4,070	2,837	67.2	69.7	2,472	58.6	60.7
Female	4,593	4,429	3,291	71.7	74.3	2,936	63.9	66.3
Race								
White alone......	7,340	7,226	5,235	71.3	72.4	4,642	63.2	64.2
White, non-Hispanic alone	7,108	7,058	5,121	72.0	72.6	4,547	64.0	64.4
Black alone.......	1,031	977	722	70.0	73.9	637	61.8	65.2
Asian alone......	250	118	62	25.0	53.1	55	22.0	46.8
Hispanic (of any race).....................	277	173	119	43.1	68.9	100	36.2	57.8
White alone or in combination	7,496	7,371	5,319	71.0	72.2	4,696	62.6	63.7
Black alone or in combination..........	1,127	1,072	769	68.3	71.8	662	58.8	61.8
Asian alone or in combination.........	262	129	68	25.9	52.5	60	23.1	46.8
Age								
18 to 24 years.....................	1,075	1,060	576	53.6	54.3	425	39.6	40.1
25 to 34 years.....................	1,425	1,276	859	60.2	67.3	718	50.4	56.3
35 to 44 years.....................	1,325	1,270	884	66.7	69.6	792	59.8	62.3
45 to 64 years.....................	3,061	2,997	2,271	74.2	75.8	2,072	67.7	69.1
65 years and over	1,925	1,895	1,537	79.8	81.1	1,402	72.8	74.0

B = Base is less than 75,000 and therefore too small to show the derived measure.

Table OH-14. Crime

(Number, rate per 100,000. Data are derived from the FBI Uniform Crime Reports.)

Item	State			U.S. [1,2,3,4]		
	2014	2015	Percent change	2014	2015	Percent change
TOTAL POPULATION[5]	11,596,998	11,613,423	0.1	318,907,401	321,418,820	0.8
VIOLENT CRIME						
Number..........	33,130	33,898	2.3	1,186,185	1,231,566	3.8
Rate	285.7	291.9	2.2	372.0	383.2	3.0
Murder and Nonnegligent Manslaughter						
Number..........	464	500	7.8	14,164	15,696	10.8
Rate	4.0	4.3	7.6	4.4	4.9	10.0
Rape[6]						
Number..........	5,228	5,149	-1.5	118,027	124,047	5.1
Rate	45.1	44.3	-1.7	37.0	38.6	4.3
Robbery						
Number..........	12,780	12,554	-1.8	322,905	327,374	1.4
Rate	110.2	108.1	-1.9	101.3	101.9	0.6
Aggravated Assault						
Number..........	14,658	15,695	7.1	731,089	764,449	4.6
Rate	126.4	135.1	6.9	229.2	237.8	3.7
PROPERTY CRIME						
Number..........	322,517	300,525	-6.8	8,209,010	7,993,631	-2.6
Rate	2,781.0	2,587.7	-7.0	2,574.1	2,487.0	-3.4
Burglary						
Number..........	79,466	69,303	-12.8	1,713,153	1,579,527	-7.8
Rate	685.2	596.7	-12.9	537.2	491.4	-8.5
Larceny-Theft						
Number..........	224,942	213,993	-4.9	5,809,054	5,706,346	-1.8
Rate	1,939.7	1,842.6	-5.0	1,821.5	1,775.4	-2.5
Motor Vehicle Theft						
Number..........	18,109	17,229	-4.9	686,803	707,758	3.1
Rate	156.2	148.4	-5.0	215.4	220.2	2.2

NOTE: Although arson data are included in the trend and clearance tables, sufficient data are not available to estimate totals for this offense. Therefore, no arson data are published in this table.

X = Not applicable.

- = Zero or rounds to zero.

[1] The crime figures have been adjusted.

[2] The data collection methodology for the offense of forcible rape used by the Minnesota state Uniform Crime Reporting (UCR) Program (with the exception of Minneapolis and St. Paul, Minnesota) does not comply with national UCR Program guidelines. Consequently, its figures for forcible rape and violent crime (of which forcible rape is a part) are not published in this table.

[3] Includes offenses reported by the Zoological Police and the Metro Transit Police.

[4] Because of changes in the state's reporting practices, figures are not comparable to previous years' data.

[5] Populations are U.S. Census Bureau provisional estimates as of July 1 of each year.

[6] The figures shown for the offense of rape were estimated using the revised Uniform Crime Reporting (UCR) definition of rape.

Table OH-15. State Government Finances, 2015

(Dollar amounts in thousands, percent distribution.)

Item	Dollars	Percent distribution
Total Revenue	85,140,343	100.0
General revenue	65,381,404	76.8
Intergovernmental revenue	24,008,999	28.2
Taxes	28,297,156	33.2
General sales	11,900,176	14.0
Selective sales	5,314,229	6.2
License taxes	2,171,231	2.6
Individual income tax	8,882,973	10.4
Corporate income tax	2,586	0.0
Other taxes	25,961	0.0
Current charges	8,593,946	10.1
Miscellaneous general revenue	4,481,303	5.3
Utility revenue	0	-
Liquor stores revenue	1,079,367	1.3
Insurance trust revenue[1]	18,679,572	21.9
Total Expenditure	79,177,914	100.0
Intergovernmental expenditure	17,872,592	22.6
Direct expenditure	61,305,322	77.4
Current operation	36,815,156	46.5
Capital outlay	4,793,963	6.1
Insurance benefits and repayments	16,819,899	21.2
Assistance and subsidies	1,605,740	2.0
Interest on debt	1,270,564	1.6
Exhibit: Salaries and wages	7,896,831	10.0
Total Expenditure	79,177,914	100.0
General expenditure	61,602,051	77.8
Intergovernmental expenditure	17,872,592	22.6
Direct expenditure	43,729,459	55.2
General expenditure, by function:		
Education	22,348,752	28.2
Public welfare	19,421,982	24.5
Hospitals	3,754,111	4.7
Health	2,373,209	3.0
Highways	4,015,891	5.1
Police protection	325,202	0.4
Correction	1,702,920	2.2
Natural resources	421,134	0.5
Parks and recreation	117,444	0.1
Governmental administration	1,862,953	2.4
Interest on general debt	1,270,564	1.6
Other and unallocable	3,987,889	5.0
Utility expenditure	0	-
Liquor stores expenditure	755,964	1.0
Insurance trust expenditure	16,819,899	21.2
Debt at End of Fiscal Year	33,108,954	X
Cash and Security Holdings	229,939,266	X

X = Not applicable.
- = Zero or rounds to zero.
[1] Within insurance trust revenue, net earnings of state retirement systems is a calculated statistic (the item code in the data file is X08), and thus can be positive or negative. Net earnings is the sum of earnings on investments plus gains on investments minus losses on investments. The change made in 2002 for asset valuation from book to market value in accordance with Statement 34 of the Governmental Accounting Standards Board is reflected in the calculated statistics.

Table OH-16. State Government Tax Collections, 2016

(Dollars in thousands, percent.)

Item	Dollars	Percent distribution
Total Taxes	28,694,883	100.0
Property taxes	0	-
Sales and gross receipts	18,231,167	63.5
General sales and gross receipts	12,226,504	42.6
Selective sales and gross receipts	6,004,663	20.9
Alcoholic beverages	100,712	0.4
Amusements	269,267	0.9
Insurance premiums	579,408	2.0
Motor fuels	1,855,699	6.5
Pari-mutuels	5,628	-
Public utilities	1,156,646	4.0
Tobacco products	1,008,798	3.5
Other selective sales	1,028,505	3.6
Licenses	2,223,747	7.7
Alcoholic beverages	42,501	0.1
Amusements	37,833	0.1
Corporations in general	237,487	0.8
Hunting and fishing	37,695	0.1
Motor vehicle	769,085	2.7
Motor vehicle operators	78,821	0.3
Public utilities	27,863	0.1
Occupation and business, NEC	943,758	3.3
Other licenses	48,704	0.2
Income taxes	8,202,432	28.6
Individual income	8,169,197	28.5
Corporation net income	33,235	0.1
Other taxes	37,537	0.1
Death and gift	2,154	-
Documentary and stock transfer	0	-
Severance	35,383	0.1
Taxes, NEC	0	-

X = Not applicable.
- = Zero or rounds to zero.

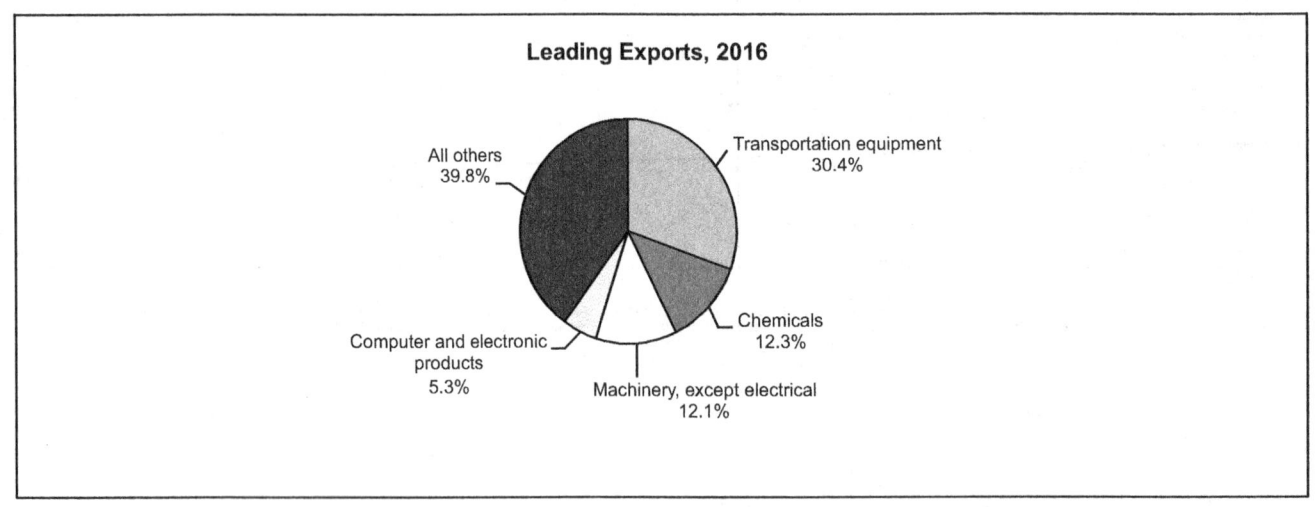

Leading Exports, 2016

All others 39.8%

Transportation equipment 30.4%

Chemicals 12.3%

Machinery, except electrical 12.1%

Computer and electronic products 5.3%

OKLAHOMA

Facts and Figures

Location: West south central United States; bordered on the N by Colorado and Kansas, on the E by Missouri and Arkansas, on the S by Texas, and on the W by Texas and New Mexico

Area: 69,898 sq. mi. (181,036 sq. km.); rank—20th

Population: 3,923,561 (2016 est.); rank—28th

Principal Cities: capital—Oklahoma City; largest—Oklahoma City

Statehood: November 16, 1907; 46th state

U.S. Congress: 2 senators, 5 representatives

State Motto: *Labor omnia vincit* ("Labor conquers all things")

State Song: "Oklahoma!"

State Nickname: The Sooner State

Abbreviations: OK; Okla.

State Symbols: flower—mistletoe; tree—redbud; bird—scissor-tailed flycatcher

At a Glance

- With an increase in population of 4.6 percent, Oklahoma ranked 22nd among the states in growth from 2010 to 2016.

- Oklahoma's median household income in 2015 was $48,568, and 16.1 percent of the population lived below the poverty level.

- In 2015, 13.9 percent of Oklahomans did not have health insurance, making it the state with the 3rd highest percent of uninsured residents.

- Oklahoma's violent crime rate in 2015 was 422.0 per 100,000 population, compared to 383.2 for the entire nation.

- The state ranked 14th for property crime rate in 2015, with a rate of 2,885.9 incidents per 100,000 population.

Table OK-1. Population by Age, Sex, Race, and Hispanic Origin

(Number, percent, except where noted.)

Sex, age, race, and Hispanic origin	2000	2010	2016 [1]	Average annual percent change, 2010–2016
Total Population	3,450,654	3,751,351	3,923,561	0.3
Percent of total U.S. population	1.2	1.2	1.2	X
Sex				
Male	1,695,895	1,856,977	1,943,903	0.3
Female	1,754,759	1,894,374	1,979,658	0.3
Age				
Under 5 years	236,353	264,126	266,910	0.1
5 to 19 years	765,927	777,484	798,437	0.2
20 to 64 years	1,992,424	2,203,027	2,268,076	0.2
65 years and over	455,950	506,714	590,138	1.0
Median age (years)	35.5	36.2	36.4	-
Race and Hispanic Origin				
One race				
White	2,628,434	2,851,510	2,925,602	0.2
Black	260,968	284,332	304,465	0.4
American Indian and Alaska Native	273,230	335,664	360,158	0.5
Asian	46,767	67,126	88,156	2.0
Native Hawaiian or Other Pacific Islander	2,372	5,354	7,102	2.0
Two or more races	155,985	207,365	238,078	0.9
Hispanic (of any race)	179,304	351,542	403,938	0.9

X = Not applicable.
- = Zero or rounds to zero.
[1] Population figures for 2016 are July 1 estimates. The 2010 estimates are taken from the 2010 Census.

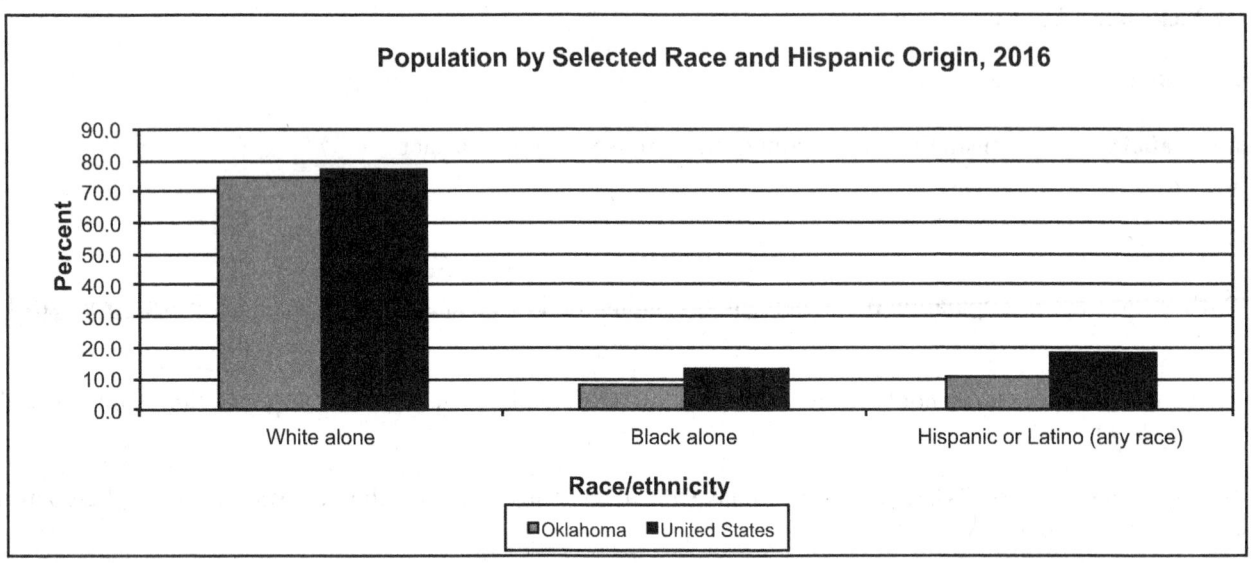

Table OK-2. Marital Status

(Number, percent distribution.)

Sex, age, race, and Hispanic origin	2000	2010	2015
Males, 15 Years and Over	1,318,729	1,457,860	1,526,608
Never married	25.8	30.7	32.2
Now married, except separated	59.5	52.2	50.6
Separated	1.6	1.8	1.8
Widowed	2.5	3.0	3.3
Divorced	10.6	12.3	12.0
Females, 15 Years and Over	1,398,823	1,521,546	1,581,844
Never married	19.1	23.8	24.9
Now married, except separated	55.3	49.7	48.5
Separated	1.9	2.7	2.1
Widowed	11.1	10.1	9.9
Divorced	12.5	13.7	14.5

Table OK-3. Households and Housing Characteristics

(Number, percent, dollars.)

Item	2000	2010	2015	Average annual percvent change, 2000–2015
Total Households...	1,342,293	1,432,959	1,465,951	0.6
Family households...	921,750	954,622	969,588	0.3
Married-couple family...	717,611	709,256	713,308	-
Other family..	204,139	245,366	256,280	1.7
Male householder, no wife present........................	51,564	62,855	77,752	3.4
Female householder, no husband present..............	152,575	182,511	178,528	1.1
Nonfamily households...	420,543	478,337	496,363	1.2
Householder living alone...	358,560	400,840	411,001	1.0
Householder not living alone...................................	61,983	77,497	85,362	2.5
Housing Characteristics				
Total housing units...	1,514,400	1,666,205	1,711,515	0.9
Occupied housing units	1,342,293	1,432,959	1,465,951	0.6
Owner occupied..	918,259	971,378	957,858	0.3
Renter occupied...	424,034	461,581	508,093	1.3
Average household size..	2.49	2.55	2.59	0.3
Financial Characteristics				
Median gross rent of renter-occupied housing	456	659	759	4.4
Median monthly owner costs for housing units with a mortgage	764	1,089	1,159	3.4
Median value of owner-occupied housing units	70,700	111,400	126,800	5.3

Table OK-4. Migration, Origin, and Language

(Number, percent.)

Characteristic	State			U.S.		
	2014	2015	Percent change	2014	2015	Percent change
Residence 1 Year Ago						
Population 1 year and over	3,827,288	3,864,908	1.0	315,095,393	317,635,720	0.8
Same house..	82.3	82.9	X	85.1	85.3	X
Different house in the U.S.	17.3	16.7	X	14.3	14.1	X
Same county...	10.0	9.4	X	8.7	8.5	X
Different county	7.3	7.3	X	5.6	5.6	X
Same state...	4.4	4.4	X	3.3	3.2	X
Different state..	2.9	2.9	X	2.3	2.4	X
Abroad	0.4	0.5	X	0.6	0.7	X
Place of Birth						
Native born..	3,651,386	3,675,988	0.7	276,465,262	278,128,449	0.6
Male	49.4	49.4	X	49.3	49.3	X
Female	50.6	50.6	X	50.7	50.7	X
Foreign born	226,665	235,350	3.8	42,391,794	43,290,372	2.1
Male	50.9	52.4	X	48.7	48.6	X
Female	49.1	47.6	X	51.3	51.4	X
Foreign born; naturalized U.S. citizen....................	73,438	78,382	6.7	19,984,738	20,697,103	3.6
Male	45.4	47.8	X	45.9	45.9	X
Female	54.6	52.2	X	54.1	54.1	X
Foreign born; not a U.S. citizen..............................	153,227	156,968	2.4	22,407,056	22,593,269	0.8
Male	53.6	54.7	X	51.2	51.1	X
Female	46.4	45.3	X	48.8	48.9	X
Entered 2010 or later	16.7	19.7	X	12.3	15.6	X
Entered 2000 to 2009	35.3	33.0	X	28.6	27.9	X
Entered before 2000...	47.9	47.2	X	59.1	56.5	X
World Region of Birth, Foreign						
Foreign-born population, excluding population born at sea	226,665	235,350	3.8	42,390,705	43,289,646	2.1
Europe	7.7	6.1	X	11.2	11.1	X
Asia	27.1	27.1	X	30.1	30.6	X
Africa	4.2	4.2	X	4.6	4.8	X
Oceania	0.7	0.7	X	0.6	0.6	X
Latin America..	58.7	60.1	X	51.6	51.1	X
North America...	1.7	1.8	X	1.9	1.9	X
Language Spoken at Home and Ability to Speak English						
Population 5 years and over.......................................	3,614,253	3,648,387	0.9	299,084,046	301,625,014	0.8
English only	90.0	89.9	X	78.9	78.5	X
Language other than English..................................	10.0	10.1	X	21.1	21.5	X
Speaks English less than "very well".................	4.2	4.1	X	8.6	8.6	X

NA = Not available.
X = Not applicable.
- = Zero or rounds to zero.

Table OK-5. Median Income and Poverty Status, 2015

(Number, percent, except as noted.)

Characteristic	State		U.S.	
	Number	Percent	Number	Percent
Median Income				
Households (dollars)..	48,568	X	55,775	X
Families (dollars)	60,215	X	68,260	X
Below Poverty Level (All People)	610,828	16.1	46,153,077	14.7
Sex				
Male	272,140	14.6	20,599,407	13.4
Female	338,688	17.6	25,553,670	16.0
Age				
Under 18 years..	208,993	22.2	15,000,273	20.7
Related children under 18 years..	204,623	21.8	14,693,239	20.4
18 to 64 years..	355,008	15.5	26,960,369	13.9
65 years and over	46,827	8.4	4,192,435	9.0

X = Not applicable.

Median Household and Family Income, 2015

Table OK-6. Health Insurance Coverage Status for the Civilian Noninstitutionalized Population and Children Under 18 Years of Age

(Numbers in thousands, percent.)

Item	2007	2008	2009	2010	2011	2012	2013	2014	2015
Civilian Noninstitutionalized Population	3,551	3,550	3,590	3,677	3,710	3,733	3,770	3,798	3,830
Covered by Private or Public Insurance									
Number..	2,920	2,858	2,919	2,984	3,017	3,048	3,104	3,214	3,298
Percent..	82.2	80.5	81.3	81.1	81.3	81.6	82.3	84.6	86.1
Not Covered									
Number..	631	692	672	694	694	685	666	584	533
Percent..	17.8	19.5	18.7	18.9	18.7	18.4	17.7	15.4	13.9
Percent in the U.S. not covered..	15.3	15.1	15.1	15.5	15.1	14.8	14.5	11.7	9.4
Children Under 18 Years of Age	920	903	919	929	934	935	946	950	958
Covered by Private or Public Insurance									
Number..	804	786	816	836	834	841	851	868	887
Percent..	87.4	87.0	88.8	90.0	89.4	89.9	90.0	91.3	92.6
Not Covered									
Number..	116	117	103	93	100	94	95	82	71
Percent..	12.6	13.0	11.2	10.0	10.6	10.1	10.0	8.7	7.4
Percent in the U.S. not covered..	11.0	9.7	8.6	8.0	7.5	7.2	7.1	6.0	4.8

Table OK-7. Employment Status by Demographic Group, 2016

(Numbers in thousands, percent.)

Characteristic	Civilian noninstitutional population	Civilian labor force		Employed		Unemployed	
		Number	Percent of population	Number	Percent of population	Number	Percent of population
Total...	3,006	1,836	61.1	1,743	58.0	93	5.1
Sex							
Male..	1,455	1,006	69.1	952	65.4	54	5.4
Female..	1,551	830	53.5	791	51.0	39	4.7
Race, Sex, and Hispanic Origin							
White..	2,345	1,418	60.5	1,359	58.0	59	4.2
Male..	1,148	794	69.2	758	66.0	36	4.6
Female..	1,198	624	52.1	601	50.2	23	3.6
Black or African American................................	209	132	62.9	121	58.0	10	7.9
Male..	100	71	70.8	67	66.9	4	5.5
Female..	109	61	55.6	54	49.6	7	10.7
Hispanic or Latino ethnicity[1]............................	307	211	68.6	200	65.1	11	5.1
Male..	157	130	82.6	126	79.8	5	3.5
Female..	150	81	53.9	75	49.8	6	7.7
Age							
16 to 19 years..	201	67	33.1	57	28.6	9	13.8
20 to 24 years..	241	169	70.1	150	62.2	19	11.2
25 to 34 years..	569	445	78.2	422	74.1	24	5.3
35 to 44 years..	460	369	80.2	352	76.5	17	4.6
45 to 54 years..	460	350	76.1	340	73.7	11	3.1
55 to 64 years..	507	314	61.9	304	59.9	10	3.2
65 years and over.......................................	567	122	21.6	118	20.9	4	3.2

NOTE: Data in Table 7 are from the Current Population Survey (CPS) and do not match the estimates in Table 8. See notes and definitions for further information.
[1] May be of any race.

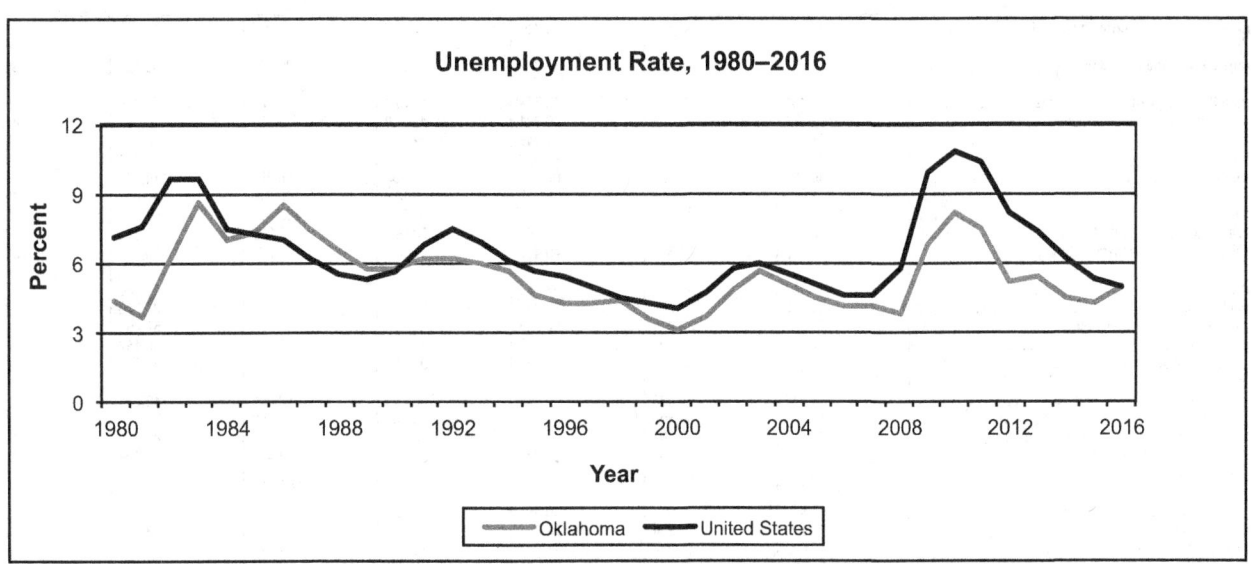

Unemployment Rate, 1980–2016

Table OK-8. Employment Status of the Civilian Noninstitutional Population Age 16 Years and Over

(Number, percent.)

Year	Civilian labor force	Civilian participation rate	Employed	Unemployed	Unemployment rate
2008..	1,746,466	63.7	1,681,081	65,385	3.7
2009..	1,764,432	63.6	1,652,023	112,409	6.4
2010..	1,768,284	62.4	1,648,138	120,146	6.8
2011..	1,772,666	61.8	1,668,418	104,248	5.9
2012..	1,804,071	62.3	1,709,352	94,719	5.3
2013..	1,806,829	61.8	1,710,781	96,048	5.3
2014..	1,797,934	61.0	1,717,136	80,798	4.5
2015..	1,842,049	61.9	1,763,844	78,205	4.2
2016..	1,828,415	61.2	1,739,362	89,053	4.9

Table OK-9. Employment and Average Wages by Industry

(Estimates through 2010 are based on the 2007 *North American Industry Classification System* [NAICS]. Estimates from 2011 onward are based on the 2012 NAICS.)

Industry	2009	2010	2011	2012	2013	2014	2015
				Number of jobs			
Wage and Salary Employment by Industry..................	1,625,164	1,607,228	1,626,838	1,658,230	1,680,348	1,700,578	1,706,632
Farm Wage and Salary Employment.........................	11,383	9,486	8,747	10,449	11,413	9,772	5,799
Nonfarm Wage and Salary Employment....................	1,613,781	1,597,742	1,618,091	1,647,781	1,668,935	1,690,806	1,700,833
Private wage and salary employment..........................	1,234,356	1,217,262	1,246,015	1,279,703	1,298,410	1,321,362	1,328,050
Forestry, fishing, and related activities.....................	4,212	4,251	4,130	4,162	4,337	4,456	4,526
Mining..	42,592	43,111	50,919	57,807	59,588	61,330	53,599
Utilities..	11,447	11,230	11,189	11,729	11,722	12,021	12,095
Construction..	72,370	69,905	70,483	72,396	77,103	77,763	79,242
Manufacturing..	131,768	125,135	132,136	137,832	139,057	142,066	139,494
Durable goods manufacturing.............................	87,555	81,854	87,932	94,796	96,168	98,841	96,563
Nondurable goods manufacturing........................	44,213	43,281	44,204	43,036	42,889	43,225 v	42,931
Wholesale trade...	56,978	55,821	58,496	60,705	62,269	63,687	60,479
Retail trade..	172,027	169,991	171,988	174,845	176,309	180,001	184,645
Transportation and warehousing............................	44,480	42,000	43,231	45,200	46,618	47,581	52,040
Information...	26,503	24,994	24,136	22,697	21,846	21,724	21,081
Finance and insurance	58,385	57,750	57,873	59,163	58,807	59,792	60,195
Real estate and rental and leasing...........................	23,035	22,115	22,073	22,001	22,592	21,092	21,027
Professional, scientific, and technical services..............	64,185	63,383	65,317	66,561	67,573	68,303	69,801
Management of companies and enterprises...................	14,539	15,166	14,927	16,060	16,599	18,681	18,688
Administrative and waste services...........................	92,237	93,387	94,939	96,612	96,290	98,630	98,200
Educational services	19,596	19,777	20,547	21,250	21,444	21,821	21,799
Health care and social assistance...........................	181,105	183,837	184,533	186,385	188,117	188,301	191,980
Arts, entertainment, and recreation...........................	14,105	13,970	14,136	14,464	14,773	15,058	16,171
Accommodation and food services..........................	127,333	125,460	129,416	133,551	137,576	141,583	146,001
Other services, except public administration..................	77,459	75,979	75,546	76,283	75,790	77,472	76,987
Government and government enterprises....................	379,425	380,480	372,076	368,078	370,525	369,444	372,783
				Dollars			
Average Wages and Salaries by Industry	37,650	38,833	40,713	42,320	43,044	44,403	45,045
Average Farm Wages and Salaries	23,337	27,828	33,019	33,722	25,527	33,064	38,063
Average Nonfarm Wages and Salaries	37,751	38,898	40,754	42,374	43,164	44,469	45,069
Average private wages and salaries...........................	37,474	38,759	40,931	42,728	43,653	45,041	45,577
Forestry, fishing, and related activities.....................	21,742	22,833	23,246	23,891	24,698	26,261	27,538
Mining..	81,198	85,025	94,953	92,215	94,907	96,641	103,002
Utilities..	80,288	79,827	82,921	92,093	96,384	114,248	99,720
Construction..	39,593	41,614	42,402	44,697	46,819	47,947	49,609
Manufacturing..	45,752	47,765	49,511	51,889	53,176	55,125	55,467
Durable goods manufacturing.............................	47,447	49,574	51,569	53,968	55,323	57,283	57,070
Nondurable goods manufacturing........................	42,395	44,345	45,415	47,310	48,361	50,190	51,862
Wholesale trade...	50,563	50,360	52,455	54,912	55,682	57,950	59,105
Retail trade..	24,319	25,245	25,930	26,940	27,354	27,856	28,276
Transportation and warehousing............................	47,242	50,314	52,898	54,375	55,574	57,560	56,538
Information...	47,087	47,992	51,793	53,056	55,035	56,452	56,930
Finance and insurance	48,510	50,313	52,455	55,152	56,767	59,913	60,454
Real estate and rental and leasing...........................	34,147	36,421	39,358	47,054	42,091	42,735	43,188
Professional, scientific, and technical services..............	52,049	54,206	55,769	59,349	60,962	62,058	62,908
Management of companies and enterprises...................	71,776	75,002	96,091	88,111	88,731	81,844	88,672
Administrative and waste services...........................	30,413	30,992	31,745	33,134	33,411	34,596	35,868
Educational services	29,553	29,888	30,105	30,590	31,214	32,267	31,389
Health care and social assistance...........................	37,898	38,644	40,066	41,354	42,016	43,387	45,062
Arts, entertainment, and recreation...........................	27,188	27,834	28,697	31,205	31,308	33,802	35,175
Accommodation and food services..........................	14,845	15,544	15,977	16,707	16,974	17,524	18,021
Other services, except public administration..................	25,231	26,408	27,342	28,447	29,424	30,216	31,409
Government and government enterprises....................	38,655	39,344	40,163	41,145	41,451	42,422	43,259

Table OK-10. Employment Characteristics by Family Type

(Number, percent.)

Family type and labor force status	2013 Total	2013 Families with own children under 18 years	2014 Total	2014 Families with own children under 18 years	2015 Total	2015 Families with own children under 18 years
All Families	956,517	415,825	963,008	418,186	969,588	417,301
FAMILY TYPE AND LABOR FORCE STATUS						
Married-Couple Families	702,897	271,793	707,265	274,441	713,308	274,692
Both husband and wife in labor force	48.7	62.4	48.7	62.3	48.5	62.7
Husband in labor force, wife not in labor force	24.9	30.9	24.6	30.9	23.9	30.2
Wife in labor force, husband not in labor force	8.0	4.2	8.3	4.5	8.2	4.2
Both husband and wife not in labor force	18.2	2.3	18.4	2.3	18.7	2.3
Other Families	253,620	144,032	255,743	143,745	256,280	142,609
Female householder, no husband present	71.2	73.8	71.4	73.9	69.7	71.8
In labor force	48.4	57.5	48.2	58.2	47.6	57.5
Not in labor force	22.8	16.3	23.2	15.7	22.0	14.3
Male householder, no wife present	28.8	26.2	28.6	26.1	30.3	28.2
In labor force	22.2	23.1	22.3	23.2	23.6	25.1
Not in labor force	6.6	3.1	6.3	2.9	6.7	3.1

Table OK-11. School Enrollment and Educational Attainment, 2015

(Number, percent.)

Item	State	U.S.
Enrollment		
Total population 3 years and over, enrolled in school	1,025,729	81,618,288
Enrolled in nursery school or preschool (percent)	7.0	6.0
Enrolled in kindergarten (percent)	5.5	5.0
Enrolled in elementary school, grades 1-8 (percent)	42.3	40.3
Enrolled in high school, grades 9-12 (percent)	20.5	20.9
Enrolled in college or graduate school (percent)	24.7	27.7
Attainment		
Total population 25 years and over	2,557,863	216,447,163
Less than ninth grade (percent)	4.3	5.5
9th to 12th grade, no diploma (percent)	8.4	7.3
High school graduate, including equivalency (percent)	31.6	27.6
Some college, no degree (percent)	23.7	20.7
Associate's degree (percent)	7.4	8.2
Bachelor's degree (percent)	16.5	19.0
Graduate or professional degree (percent)	8.1	11.6
High school graduate or higher (percent)	87.3	87.1
Bachelor's degree or higher (percent)	24.6	30.6

Table OK-12. Public School Characteristics and Educational Indicators

(Number, percent; data derived from National Center of Education Statistics.)

Item	State	U.S.
Public Schools, 2014–2015 (except where noted)		
Number of school districts	600	18,260
Number of schools	1,796	98,373
Number of students	688,511	50,312,581
Number of teachers	42,073	3,132,351
Student-teacher ratio	16.4	16.1
Expenditures per student (dollars), FY 2014	7,995	11,066
Four-year adjusted cohort graduation rate (ACGR)[1,2]	82.5	83.2
Students eligible for free or reduced-price lunch (percent)	60.9	51.8
English language learners (percent)	7.1	9.4
Students age 3 to 21 served under IDEA, part B (percent)	15.3	13.0

Public Schools by Type	Number	Percent of state public schools
Total number of schools	1,796	100.0
Regular	1,791	99.7
Special education	4	0.2
Vocational education	0	-
Alternative education	1	0.1

NOTE: Every school is assigned only one school type based on its instructional emphasis.
[1] ACGR data represents a new method of calculating high-school completion rates and may not be comparable to previous years' data for Averaged Freshmen Graduation Rates (AFGR).
[2] The United States 4-year ACGRs were estimated using both the reported 4-year ACGR data from 49 states and the District of Columbia and using imputed data for Idaho. The estimate for American Indian/Alaska Native students also includes imputed data for Virginia.
- = Zero or rounds to zero.

Table OK-13. Reported Voting and Registration of the Voting-Age Population, November 2016

(Numbers in thousands, percent.)

Item	Total population	Total citizen population	Registered			Voted		
			Total registered	Percent registered (total population)	Percent registered (total citizen population)	Total voted	Percent voted (total population)	Percent voted (total citizen population)
U.S. Total	245,502	224,059	157,596	64.2	70.3	137,537	56.0	61.4
State Total.............................	2,923	2,746	1,861	63.7	67.8	1,555	53.2	56.6
Sex								
Male	1,417	1,330	890	62.8	66.9	735	51.8	55.2
Female	1,507	1,416	971	64.5	68.6	820	54.4	57.9
Race								
White alone.............................	2,289	2,158	1,470	64.2	68.1	1,263	55.2	58.5
White, non-Hispanic alone	2,038	2,029	1,416	69.5	69.8	1,227	60.2	60.5
Black alone..............................	198	178	139	70.2	77.8	102	51.7	57.3
Asian alone..............................	81	56	37	(B)	(B)	28	(B)	(B)
Hispanic (of any race)................	280	150	68	24.2	45.2	50	17.9	33.4
White alone or in combination	2,380	2,250	1,520	63.9	67.6	1,300	54.6	57.8
Black alone or in combination..........	214	195	149	69.3	76.2	109	50.7	55.8
Asian alone or in combination..........	87	62	40	(B)	(B)	28	(B)	(B)
Age								
18 to 24 years..........................	316	303	144	45.8	47.6	102	32.4	33.7
25 to 34 years..........................	563	502	324	57.6	64.6	241	42.8	48.0
35 to 44 years..........................	504	457	291	57.8	63.8	240	47.5	52.5
45 to 64 years..........................	944	892	636	67.4	71.3	553	58.6	62.0
65 years and over......................	597	593	465	78.0	78.5	419	70.2	70.7

B = Base is less than 75,000 and therefore too small to show the derived measure.

Table OK-14. Crime

(Number, rate per 100,000. Data are derived from the FBI Uniform Crime Reports.)

Item	State			U.S. [1,2,3,4]		
	2014	2015	Percent change	2014	2015	Percent change
TOTAL POPULATION[5]	3,879,610	3,911,338	0.8	318,907,401	321,418,820	0.8
VIOLENT CRIME						
Number................................	16,052	16,506	2.8	1,186,185	1,231,566	3.8
Rate	413.8	422.0	2.0	372.0	383.2	3.0
Murder and Nonnegligent Manslaughter						
Number................................	180	234	30.0	14,164	15,696	10.8
Rate	4.6	6.0	28.9	4.4	4.9	10.0
Rape[6]						
Number................................	1,862	1,849	-0.7	118,027	124,047	5.1
Rate	48.0	47.3	-1.5	37.0	38.6	4.3
Robbery						
Number................................	3,073	3,005	-2.2	322,905	327,374	1.4
Rate	79.2	76.8	-3.0	101.3	101.9	0.6
Aggravated Assault						
Number................................	10,937	11,418	4.4	731,089	764,449	4.6
Rate	281.9	291.9	3.6	229.2	237.8	3.7
PROPERTY CRIME						
Number................................	117,445	112,878	-3.9	8,209,010	7,993,631	-2.6
Rate	3,027.2	2,885.9	-4.7	2,574.1	2,487.0	-3.4
Burglary						
Number................................	29,963	28,406	-5.2	1,713,153	1,579,527	-7.8
Rate	772.3	726.2	-6.0	537.2	491.4	-8.5
Larceny-Theft						
Number................................	76,719	74,022	-3.5	5,809,054	5,706,346	-1.8
Rate	1,977.5	1,892.5	-4.3	1,821.5	1,775.4	-2.5
Motor Vehicle Theft						
Number................................	10,763	10,450	-2.9	686,803	707,758	3.1
Rate	277.4	267.2	-3.7	215.4	220.2	2.2

NOTE: Although arson data are included in the trend and clearance tables, sufficient data are not available to estimate totals for this offense. Therefore, no arson data are published in this table.
X = Not applicable.
- = Zero or rounds to zero.
[1] The crime figures have been adjusted.
[2] The data collection methodology for the offense of forcible rape used by the Minnesota state Uniform Crime Reporting (UCR) Program (with the exception of Minneapolis and St. Paul, Minnesota) does not comply with national UCR Program guidelines. Consequently, its figures for forcible rape and violent crime (of which forcible rape is a part) are not published in this table.
[3] Includes offenses reported by the Zoological Police and the Metro Transit Police.
[4] Because of changes in the state's reporting practices, figures are not comparable to previous years' data.
[5] Populations are U.S. Census Bureau provisional estimates as of July 1 of each year.
[6] The figures shown for the offense of rape were estimated using the revised Uniform Crime Reporting (UCR) definition of rape.

Table OK-15. State Government Finances, 2015

(Dollar amounts in thousands, percent distribution.)

Item	Dollars	Percent distribution
Total Revenue	24,938,838	100.0
General revenue	21,572,037	86.5
Intergovernmental revenue	7,169,356	28.7
Taxes	9,303,462	37.3
General sales	2,682,008	10.8
Selective sales	1,350,080	5.4
License taxes	1,055,808	4.2
Individual income tax	3,252,290	13.0
Corporate income tax	388,530	1.6
Other taxes	574,746	2.3
Current charges	2,726,030	10.9
Miscellaneous general revenue	2,373,189	9.5
Utility revenue	679,827	2.7
Liquor stores revenue	0	-
Insurance trust revenue[1]	2,686,974	10.8
Total Expenditure	24,069,520	100.0
Intergovernmental expenditure	4,342,470	18.0
Direct expenditure	19,727,050	82.0
Current operation	13,855,899	57.6
Capital outlay	2,237,971	9.3
Insurance benefits and repayments	2,686,786	11.2
Assistance and subsidies	488,798	2.0
Interest on debt	457,596	1.9
Exhibit: Salaries and wages	3,335,552	13.9
Total Expenditure	24,069,520	100.0
General expenditure	20,506,596	85.2
Intergovernmental expenditure	4,342,470	18.0
Direct expenditure	16,164,126	67.2
General expenditure, by function:		
Education	7,735,783	32.1
Public welfare	6,502,889	27.0
Hospitals	281,280	1.2
Health	908,033	3.8
Highways	2,101,894	8.7
Police protection	230,542	1.0
Correction	571,220	2.4
Natural resources	277,842	1.2
Parks and recreation	93,079	0.4
Governmental administration	723,923	3.0
Interest on general debt	383,198	1.6
Other and unallocable	696,913	2.9
Utility expenditure	876,138	3.6
Liquor stores expenditure	0	-
Insurance trust expenditure	2,686,786	11.2
Debt at End of Fiscal Year	8,899,021	X
Cash and Security Holdings	44,043,407	X

X = Not applicable.
- = Zero or rounds to zero.
[1] Within insurance trust revenue, net earnings of state retirement systems is a calculated statistic (the item code in the data file is X08), and thus can be positive or negative. Net earnings is the sum of earnings on investments plus gains on investments minus losses on investments. The change made in 2002 for asset valuation from book to market value in accordance with Statement 34 of the Governmental Accounting Standards Board is reflected in the calculated statistics.

Table OK-16. State Government Tax Collections, 2016

(Dollars in thousands, percent.)

Item	Dollars	Percent distribution
Total Taxes	8,491,187	100.0
Property taxes	0	-
Sales and gross receipts	3,778,399	44.5
General sales and gross receipts	2,471,242	29.1
Selective sales and gross receipts	1,307,157	15.4
Alcoholic beverages	120,099	1.4
Amusements	20,963	0.2
Insurance premiums	322,604	3.8
Motor fuels	463,962	5.5
Pari-mutuels	1,162	-
Public utilities	46,168	0.5
Tobacco products	316,471	3.7
Other selective sales	15,728	0.2
Licenses	1,039,167	12.2
Alcoholic beverages	1,224	-
Amusements	156,410	1.8
Corporations in general	55,082	0.6
Hunting and fishing	21,082	0.2
Motor vehicle	719,518	8.5
Motor vehicle operators	26,963	0.3
Public utilities	471	-
Occupation and business, NEC	57,692	0.7
Other licenses	725	-
Income taxes	3,324,653	39.2
Individual income	2,996,870	35.3
Corporation net income	327,783	3.9
Other taxes	348,968	4.1
Death and gift	273	-
Documentary and stock transfer	17,871	0.2
Severance	330,824	3.9
Taxes, NEC	0	-

X = Not applicable.
- = Zero or rounds to zero.

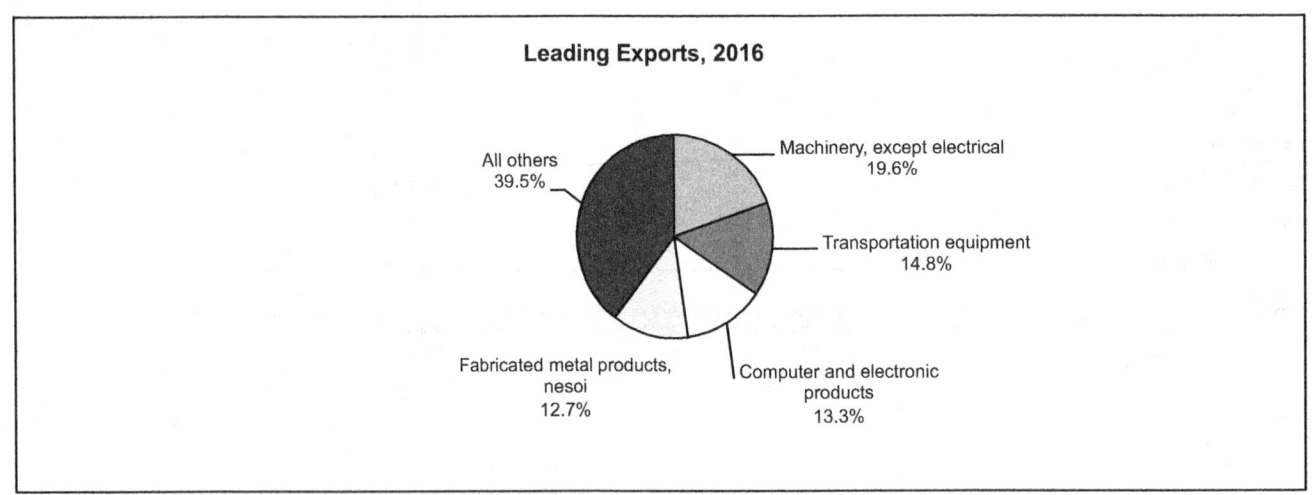

Leading Exports, 2016

- All others 39.5%
- Machinery, except electrical 19.6%
- Transportation equipment 14.8%
- Computer and electronic products 13.3%
- Fabricated metal products, nesoi 12.7%

OREGON

Facts and Figures

Location: Northwestern United States; bordered on the N by Washington, on the E by Idaho, on the S by Nevada and California, and on the W by the Pacific Ocean

Area: 98,381 sq. mi. (254,805 sq. km.); rank—9th

Population: 4,093,465 (2016 est.); rank—27th

Principal Cities: capital—Salem; largest—Portland

Statehood: February 14, 1859; 33rd state

U.S. Congress: 2 senators, 5 representatives

State Motto: She Flies With Her Own Wings

State Song: "Oregon, My Oregon"

State Nickname: The Beaver State

Abbreviations: OR; Oreg.

State Symbols: flower—Oregon grape; tree—Douglas fir; bird—Western meadowlark

At a Glance

- With an increase in population of 6.8 percent, Oregon ranked 12th among the states in growth from 2010 to 2016.

- In 2015, 7.0 percent of Oregonians did not have health insurance, compared to 9.4 percent of the total U.S. population.

- Oregon's violent crime rate in 2015 was 259.8 per 100,000 population, compared to 383.2 for the entire nation.

- Oregon tied with Texas as the state with the largest percent change in real GDP from 2014 to 2015, with an increase of 4.5 percent.

- The median household income in Oregon was $54,148 in 2015, and the poverty rate was 15.4 percent.

Table OR-1. Population by Age, Sex, Race, and Hispanic Origin

(Number, percent, except where noted.)

Sex, age, race, and Hispanic origin	2000	2010	2016 [1]	Average annual percent change, 2010–2016
Total Population..	3,421,399	3,831,074	4,093,465	0.4
Percent of total U.S. population	1.2	1.2	1.3	X
Sex				
Male..	1,696,550	1,896,002	2,027,010	0.4
Female	1,724,849	1,935,072	2,066,455	0.4
Age				
Under 5 years...	223,005	237,556	235,800	-
5 to 19 years..	720,999	734,627	730,739	-
20 to 64 years..	2,039,218	2,325,358	2,438,048	0.3
65 years and over...	438,177	533,533	688,878	1.8
Median age (years)	36.3	38.4	39.3	0.1
Race and Hispanic Origin				
One race...				
White...	2,961,623	3,403,252	3,578,285	0.3
Black...	55,662	74,414	86,539	1.0
American Indian and Alaska Native	45,211	66,784	73,274	0.6
Asian...	101,350	145,009	183,054	1.6
Native Hawaiian or Other Pacific Islander	7,976	14,649	18,249	1.5
Two or more races...	104,745	126,966	154,064	1.3
Hispanic (of any race)...	275,314	467,030	522,571	0.7

X = Not applicable.
[1] Population figures for 2016 are July 1 estimates. The 2010 estimates are taken from the 2010 Census.

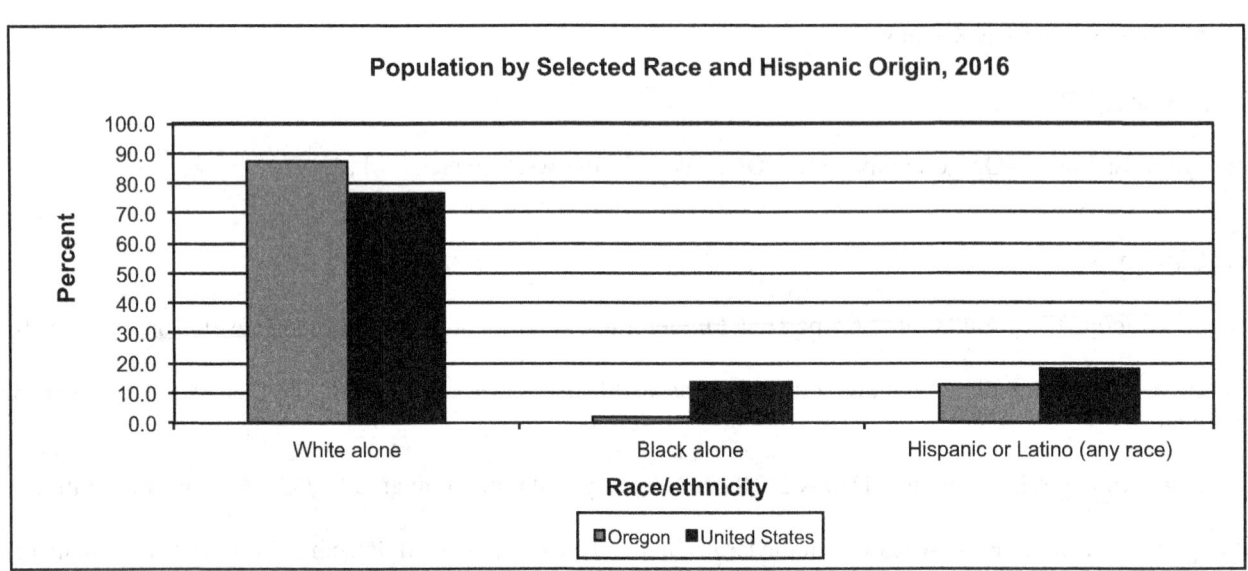

Population by Selected Race and Hispanic Origin, 2016

Table OR-2. Marital Status

(Number, percent distribution.)

Sex, age, race, and Hispanic origin	2000	2010	2015
Males, 15 Years and Over	1,336,805	1,533,177	1,629,953
Never married	28.5	32.6	34.7
Now married, except separated...	57.1	51.4	49.7
Separated..	1.5	1.6	1.6
Widowed...	2.4	2.7	2.4
Divorced..	10.6	11.8	11.5
Females, 15 Years and Over	1,385,329	1,588,428	1,687,036
Never married	21.9	25.8	27.4
Now married, except separated...	53.9	48.9	47.6
Separated..	1.9	1.9	2.0
Widowed...	9.6	8.5	8.1
Divorced..	12.7	14.9	14.9

Table OR-3. Households and Housing Characteristics

(Number, percent, dollars.)

Item	2000	2010	2015	Average annual percent change, 2000–2015
Total Households..	1,333,723	1,507,137	1,553,205	1.1
Family households..	877,671	963,362	978,396	0.8
Married-couple family...	692,532	733,095	749,945	0.6
Other family...	185,139	230,267	228,451	1.6
Male householder, no wife present.........................	54,357	65,972	67,975	1.7
Female householder, no husband present................	130,782	164,295	160,476	1.5
Nonfamily households..	456,032	543,775	574,809	1.7
Householder living alone..	347,624	416,500	433,632	1.6
Householder not living alone..................................	108,428	127,275	141,177	2.0
Housing Characteristics				
Total housing units...	1,452,709	1,676,476	1,718,509	1.2
Occupied housing units	1,333,723	1,507,137	1,553,205	1.1
Owner occupied..	856,951	942,674	948,891	0.7
Renter occupied..	476,772	564,463	604,314	1.8
Average household size...	2.51	2.49	2.54	0.1
Financial Characteristics				
Median gross rent of renter-occupied housing	620	816	943	3.5
Median monthly owner costs for housing units with a mortgage ...	1,125	1,577	1,534	2.4
Median value of owner-occupied housing units.............	152,100	244,500	264,100	4.9

- = Zero or rounds to zero.

Table OR-4. Migration, Origin, and Language

(Number, percent.)

Characteristic	State			U.S.		
	2014	2015	Percent change	2014	2015	Percent change
Residence 1 Year Ago						
Population 1 year and over	3,927,857	3,985,712	1.5	315,095,393	317,635,720	0.8
Same house	81.4	82.2	X	85.1	85.3	X
Different house in the U.S.	18.0	17.2	X	14.3	14.1	X
Same county	10.5	10.1	X	8.7	8.5	X
Different county	7.5	7.1	X	5.6	5.6	X
Same state	4.0	3.6	X	3.3	3.2	X
Different state	3.5	3.5	X	2.3	2.4	X
Abroad	0.6	0.6	X	0.6	0.7	X
Place of Birth						
Native born	3,576,587	3,631,684	1.5	276,465,262	278,128,449	0.6
Male	49.4	49.6	X	49.3	49.3	X
Female	50.6	50.4	X	50.7	50.7	X
Foreign born	393,652	397,293	0.9	42,391,794	43,290,372	2.1
Male	49.9	48.3	X	48.7	48.6	X
Female	50.1	51.7	X	51.3	51.4	X
Foreign born; naturalized U.S. citizen............................	159,830	167,977	5.1	19,984,738	20,697,103	3.6
Male	45.9	45.4	X	45.9	45.9	X
Female	54.1	54.6	X	54.1	54.1	X
Foreign born; not a U.S. citizen....................................	233,822	229,316	-1.9	22,407,056	22,593,269	0.8
Male	52.7	50.5	X	51.2	51.1	X
Female	47.3	49.5	X	48.8	48.9	X
Entered 2010 or later	13.3	15.2	X	12.3	15.6	X
Entered 2000 to 2009	27.3	28.4	X	28.6	27.9	X
Entered before 2000...	59.4	56.4	X	59.1	56.5	X
World Region of Birth, Foreign						
Foreign-born population, excluding population born at sea	393,652	397,244	0.9	42,390,705	43,289,646	2.1
Europe	14.6	13.8	X	11.2	11.1	X
Asia	30.0	32.1	X	30.1	30.6	X
Africa	4.1	3.6	X	4.6	4.8	X
Oceania	1.7	2.3	X	0.6	0.6	X
Latin America	45.7	44.8	X	51.6	51.1	X
North America	3.8	3.5	X	1.9	1.9	X
Language Spoken at Home and Ability to Speak English						
Population 5 years and over...	3,743,771	3,799,838	1.5	299,084,046	301,625,014	0.8
English only	84.5	84.9	X	78.9	78.5	X
Language other than English.......................................	15.5	15.1	X	21.1	21.5	X
Speaks English less than "very well"..........................	6.1	6.0	X	8.6	8.6	X

NA = Not available.
X = Not applicable.
- = Zero or rounds to zero.

Table OR-5. Median Income and Poverty Status, 2015

(Number, percent, except as noted.)

Characteristic	State Number	State Percent	U.S. Number	U.S. Percent
Median Income				
Households (dollars)...	54,148	X	55,775	X
Families (dollars)	66,287	X	68,260	X
Below Poverty Level (All People)	607,029	15.4	46,153,077	14.7
Sex				
Male	278,457	14.3	20,599,407	13.4
Female	328,572	16.4	25,553,670	16.0
Age				
Under 18 years..	170,659	20.3	15,000,273	20.7
Related children under 18 years........................	164,856	19.7	14,693,239	20.4
18 to 64 years..	388,659	15.8	26,960,369	13.9
65 years and over	47,711	7.3	4,192,435	9.0

X = Not applicable.

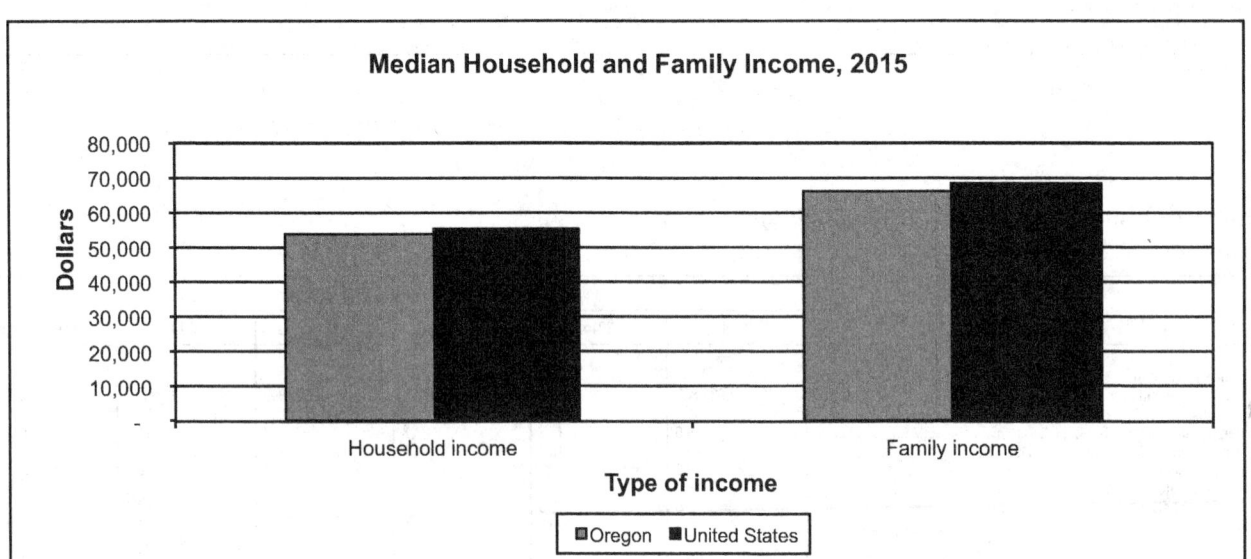

Median Household and Family Income, 2015

Table OR-6. Health Insurance Coverage Status for the Civilian Noninstitutionalized Population and Children Under 18 Years of Age

(Numbers in thousands, percent.)

Item	2007	2008	2009	2010	2011	2012	2013	2014	2015
Civilian Noninstitutionalized Population	3,762	3,746	3,780	3,799	3,833	3,860	3,893	3,931	3,991
Covered by Private or Public Insurance									
Number...	3,130	3,132	3,137	3,148	3,230	3,284	3,322	3,549	3,711
Percent...	83.2	83.6	83.0	82.9	84.3	85.1	85.3	90.3	93.0
Not Covered									
Number...	632	614	643	652	602	576	571	383	280
Percent...	16.8	16.4	17.0	17.1	15.7	14.9	14.7	9.7	7.0
Percent in the U.S. not covered.........................	15.3	15.1	15.1	15.5	15.1	14.8	14.5	11.7	9.4
Children Under 18 Years of Age	864	865	871	865	861	860	858	857	859
Covered by Private or Public Insurance									
Number...	772	755	781	789	798	805	808	818	828
Percent...	89.4	87.3	89.6	91.2	92.7	93.6	94.2	95.4	96.4
Not Covered									
Number...	92	110	90	76	63	55	50	39	31
Percent...	10.6	12.7	10.4	8.8	7.3	6.4	5.8	4.6	3.6
Percent in the U.S. not covered.........................	11.0	9.7	8.6	8.0	7.5	7.2	7.1	6.0	4.8

Table OR-7. Employment Status by Demographic Group, 2016

(Numbers in thousands, percent.)

Characteristic	Civilian noninstitutional population	Civilian labor force		Employed		Unemployed	
		Number	Percent of population	Number	Percent of population	Number	Percent of population
Total...	3,274	2,061	63.0	1,960	59.9	101	4.9
Sex							
Male...	1,599	1,092	68.3	1,040	65.0	52	4.8
Female......................................	1,675	969	57.8	920	54.9	49	5.1
Race, Sex, and Hispanic Origin							
White..	2,909	1,833	63.0	1,743	59.9	90	4.9
Male......................................	1,417	966	68.2	920	65.0	46	4.7
Female...................................	1,492	867	58.1	822	55.1	45	5.1
Black or African American.................	NA	NA	NA	NA	NA	NA	NA
Male......................................	NA	NA	NA	NA	NA	NA	NA
Female...................................	NA	NA	NA	NA	NA	NA	NA
Hispanic or Latino ethnicity[1]............	372	276	74.1	260	69.9	16	5.7
Male......................................	192	162	84.7	155	80.7	8	4.7
Female...................................	181	114	62.8	106	58.4	8	7.0
Age							
16 to 19 years............................	204	69	33.8	55	27.0	14	20.0
20 to 24 years............................	260	186	71.4	168	64.5	18	9.6
25 to 34 years............................	547	444	81.1	427	78.1	17	3.7
35 to 44 years............................	532	448	84.3	431	81.1	17	3.8
45 to 54 years............................	532	431	81.1	414	77.9	17	4.0
55 to 64 years............................	545	351	64.5	338	62.0	13	3.8
65 years and over........................	654	132	20.1	126	19.3	6	4.3

NOTE: Data in Table 7 are from the Current Population Survey (CPS) and do not match the estimates in Table 8. See notes and definitions for further information.
[1] May be of any race.
NA = Not available.

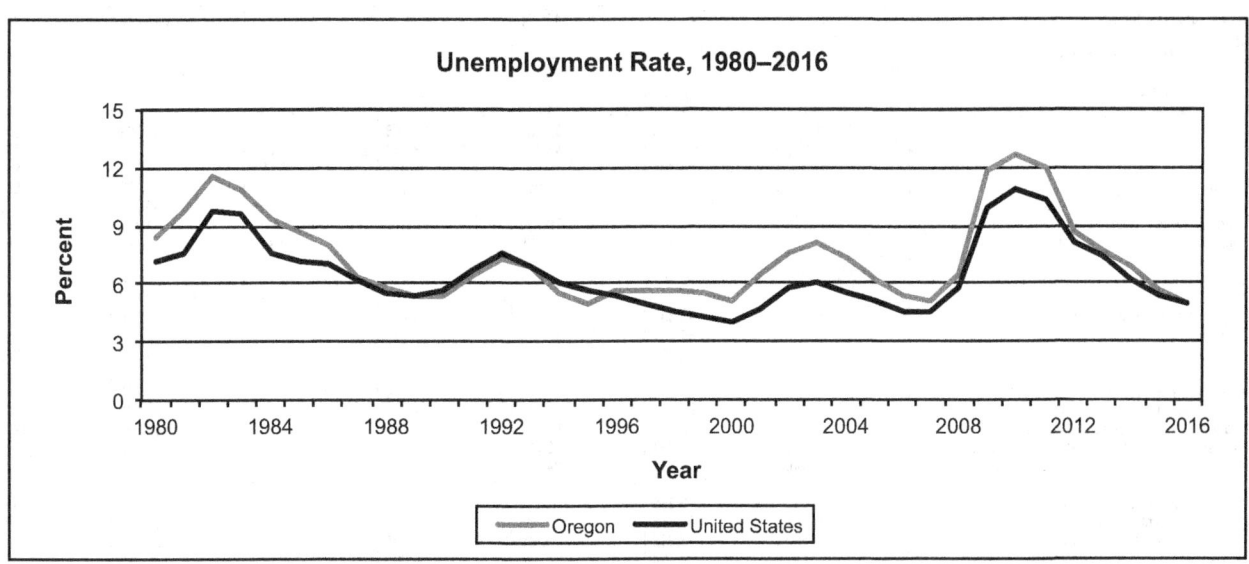

Table OR-8. Employment Status of the Civilian Noninstitutional Population Age 16 Years and Over

(Number, percent.)

Year	Civilian labor force	Civilian participation rate	Employed	Unemployed	Unemployment rate
2008...................................	1,955,121	65.8	1,827,352	127,769	6.5
2009...................................	1,976,638	65.7	1,753,682	222,956	11.3
2010...................................	1,984,039	65.4	1,773,076	210,963	10.6
2011...................................	1,993,889	65.1	1,804,320	189,569	9.5
2012...................................	1,954,098	63.1	1,781,428	172,670	8.8
2013...................................	1,909,842	61.0	1,759,197	150,645	7.9
2014...................................	1,939,396	61.1	1,807,328	132,068	6.8
2015...................................	1,969,466	61.1	1,857,114	112,352	5.7
2016...................................	2,055,114	62.6	1,954,821	100,293	4.9

Table OR-9. Employment and Average Wages by Industry

(Estimates through 2010 are based on the 2007 *North American Industry Classification System* [NAICS]. Estimates from 2011 onward are based on the 2012 NAICS.)

Industry	2009	2010	2011	2012	2013	2014	2015
	Number of jobs						
Wage and Salary Employment by Industry..................	1,706,492	1,678,186	1,698,810	1,718,785	1,751,577	1,800,801	1,851,888
Farm Wage and Salary Employment.........................	33,075	33,244	34,088	29,669	30,222	29,615	24,153
Nonfarm Wage and Salary Employment....................	1,673,417	1,644,942	1,664,722	1,689,116	1,721,355	1,771,186	1,827,735
Private wage and salary employment........................	1,374,595	1,356,999	1,381,021	1,409,712	1,445,880	1,493,610	1,545,553
Forestry, fishing, and related activities.....................	19,944	20,169	20,326	21,221	22,330	22,500	22,772
Mining..	1,676	1,575	1,599	1,593	1,527	1,546	1,699
Utilities...	4,714	4,547	4,493	4,562	4,497	4,512	4,484
Construction...	75,981	68,531	69,440	71,097	75,541	81,513	84,509
Manufacturing...	166,965	163,410	167,925	171,659	174,829	179,219	185,647
Durable goods manufacturing............................	117,693	114,735	118,525	121,560	123,110	125,956	130,098
Nondurable goods manufacturing......................	49,272	48,675	49,400	50,099	51,719	53,263	55,549
Wholesale trade	75,863	73,300	74,302	75,498	71,665	72,657	73,999
Retail trade..	185,855	184,201	185,899	188,350	192,672	197,498	203,587
Transportation and warehousing............................	49,669	48,087	49,465	50,159	50,989	53,066	55,137
Information...	33,111	32,195	32,211	32,685	32,343	32,173	33,134
Finance and insurance	58,705	57,616	58,421	58,520	58,939	59,198	59,485
Real estate and rental and leasing........................	26,067	24,663	24,003	23,887	24,309	24,792	25,562
Professional, scientific, and technical services..............	70,759	70,660	74,108	77,335	80,546	84,657	87,934
Management of companies and enterprises..................	30,745	30,540	30,416	30,471	37,980	40,227	42,953
Administrative and waste services	80,216	81,422	83,914	88,489	91,299	95,420	98,590
Educational services	41,263	42,221	43,183	44,275	44,999	45,408	46,122
Health care and social assistance..........................	207,429	212,055	215,042	218,341	223,046	230,142	240,980
Arts, entertainment, and recreation........................	22,217	21,848	22,117	21,927	22,651	23,540	24,058
Accommodation and food services.........................	142,304	141,444	144,365	148,991	154,582	160,134	168,228
Other services, except public administration.................	81,112	78,515	79,792	80,652	81,136	85,408	86,673
Government and government enterprises..........................	298,822	287,943	283,701	279,404	275,475	277,576	282,182
	Dollars						
Average Wages and Salaries by Industry	40,994	42,277	43,571	44,891	45,775	47,230	49,206
Average Farm Wages and Salaries	28,732	25,141	24,770	27,520	30,498	29,986	34,908
Average Nonfarm Wages and Salaries	41,236	42,623	43,956	45,196	46,043	47,519	49,395
Average private wages and salaries...........................	40,755	42,020	43,434	44,770	45,535	47,016	48,966
Forestry, fishing, and related activities.....................	29,739	30,138	31,864	33,363	34,444	36,231	38,353
Mining..	45,626	45,495	48,465	48,140	50,623	51,238	53,625
Utilities...	84,524	84,344	86,873	88,623	89,596	93,672	96,377
Construction...	47,123	48,111	50,056	51,509	52,432	54,132	54,398
Manufacturing...	55,216	59,174	61,887	63,860	63,526	65,669	67,414
Durable goods manufacturing............................	60,934	66,381	70,040	72,368	71,848	74,715	76,489
Nondurable goods manufacturing......................	41,559	42,186	42,325	43,216	43,716	44,275	46,161
Wholesale trade	63,001	66,361	69,521	71,480	63,131	65,046	67,544
Retail trade..	26,404	26,954	27,250	27,842	28,276	29,027	29,881
Transportation and warehousing............................	41,822	43,339	43,976	44,938	45,252	46,928	47,749
Information...	63,373	64,701	67,657	67,715	69,181	72,599	75,434
Finance and insurance	60,697	62,536	63,993	67,420	69,661	71,298	76,185
Real estate and rental and leasing........................	31,869	33,209	34,232	35,534	36,261	38,235	40,352
Professional, scientific, and technical services..............	58,839	61,322	63,515	66,357	67,693	70,496	73,742
Management of companies and enterprises..................	74,982	76,406	80,987	84,350	107,059	112,192	121,880
Administrative and waste services	30,195	30,231	30,706	31,637	32,057	33,338	34,848
Educational services	23,240	23,739	24,354	25,147	25,693	26,072	26,502
Health care and social assistance..........................	42,336	42,884	44,251	45,234	45,945	46,992	49,192
Arts, entertainment, and recreation........................	24,601	26,152	25,383	28,092	27,225	27,583	28,890
Accommodation and food services.........................	17,602	18,022	18,548	19,324	19,812	20,545	21,571
Other services, except public administration.................	27,300	28,390	28,815	29,892	30,680	31,273	32,732
Government and government enterprises..........................	43,451	45,465	46,499	47,347	48,710	50,224	51,746

Table OR-10. Employment Characteristics by Family Type

(Number, percent.)

Family type and labor force status	2013 Total	2013 Families with own children under 18 years	2014 Total	2014 Families with own children under 18 years	2015 Total	2015 Families with own children under 18 years
All Families	961,197	405,368	960,100	398,763	978,396	396,731
FAMILY TYPE AND LABOR FORCE STATUS						
Married-Couple Families	731,763	276,074	724,465	267,628	749,945	272,127
Both husband and wife in labor force	49.2	65.1	49.1	66.0	48.8	65.6
Husband in labor force, wife not in labor force	20.7	28.3	21.0	27.9	20.0	27.0
Wife in labor force, husband not in labor force	8.6	4.3	8.5	4.3	8.2	4.9
Both husband and wife not in labor force	21.1	2.0	21.4	1.8	21.8	1.8
Other Families	229,434	129,294	235,635	131,135	228,451	124,604
Female householder, no husband present	71.1	73.7	69.7	72.0	70.2	73.2
In labor force	48.9	59.7	48.5	57.8	49.7	61.0
Not in labor force	22.1	14.0	21.2	14.2	20.5	12.1
Male householder, no wife present	28.9	26.3	30.3	28.0	29.8	26.8
In labor force	22.5	23.5	24.1	25.1	23.5	24.5
Not in labor force	6.5	2.8	6.3	2.9	6.2	2.4

Table OR-11. School Enrollment and Educational Attainment, 2015

(Number, percent.)

Item	State	U.S.
Enrollment		
Total population 3 years and over, enrolled in school	950,559	81,618,288
Enrolled in nursery school or preschool (percent)	6.1	6.0
Enrolled in kindergarten (percent)	4.9	5.0
Enrolled in elementary school, grades 1-8 (percent)	39.7	40.3
Enrolled in high school, grades 9-12 (percent)	21.4	20.9
Enrolled in college or graduate school (percent)	27.9	27.7
Attainment		
Total population 25 years and over	2,804,461	216,447,163
Less than ninth grade (percent)	3.7	5.5
9th to 12th grade, no diploma (percent)	6.3	7.3
High school graduate, including equivalency (percent)	23.4	27.6
Some college, no degree (percent)	25.8	20.7
Associate's degree (percent)	8.8	8.2
Bachelor's degree (percent)	20.2	19.0
Graduate or professional degree (percent)	12.0	11.6
High school graduate or higher (percent)	90.0	87.1
Bachelor's degree or higher (percent)	32.2	30.6

Table OR-12. Public School Characteristics and Educational Indicators

(Number, percent; data derived from National Center of Education Statistics.)

Item	State	U.S.
Public Schools, 2014–2015 (except where noted)		
Number of school districts	220	18,260
Number of schools	1,242	98,373
Number of students	601,318	50,312,581
Number of teachers	27,850	3,132,351
Student-teacher ratio	21.6	16.1
Expenditures per student (dollars), FY 2014	9,959	11,066
Four-year adjusted cohort graduation rate (ACGR)[1,2]	73.8	83.2
Students eligible for free or reduced-price lunch (percent)	52.9	51.8
English language learners (percent)	8.7	9.4
Students age 3 to 21 served under IDEA, part B (percent)	13.8	13.0

Public Schools by Type	Number	Percent of state public schools
Total number of schools	1,242	100.0
Regular	1,209	97.3
Special education	1	0.1
Vocational education	0	-
Alternative education	32	2.6

NOTE: Every school is assigned only one school type based on its instructional emphasis.
[1] ACGR data represents a new method of calculating high-school completion rates and may not be comparable to previous years' data for Averaged Freshmen Graduation Rates (AFGR).
[2] The United States 4-year ACGRs were estimated using both the reported 4-year ACGR data from 49 states and the District of Columbia and using imputed data for Idaho. The estimate for American Indian/Alaska Native students also includes imputed data for Virginia.
- = Zero or rounds to zero.

Table OR-13. Reported Voting and Registration of the Voting-Age Population, November 2016

(Numbers in thousands, percent.)

Item	Total population	Total citizen population	Registered			Voted		
			Total registered	Percent registered (total population)	Percent registered (total citizen population)	Total voted	Percent voted (total population)	Percent voted (total citizen population)
U.S. Total	245,502	224,059	157,596	64.2	70.3	137,537	56.0	61.4
State Total.............................	3,185	2,929	2,147	67.4	73.3	1,942	61.0	66.3
Sex								
Male	1,567	1,431	1,052	67.1	73.5	952	60.7	66.5
Female	1,618	1,497	1,095	67.7	73.2	990	61.2	66.1
Race								
White alone....................	2,808	2,644	1,961	69.9	74.2	1,790	63.7	67.7
White, non-Hispanic alone	2,466	2,448	1,836	74.4	75.0	1,684	68.3	68.8
Black alone....................	57	41	28	(B)	(B)	23	(B)	(B)
Asian alone....................	145	92	53	(B)	(B)	47	(B)	(B)
Hispanic (of any race).....................	371	223	142	38.3	63.8	122	32.9	54.9
White alone or in combination	2,907	2,737	2,030	69.8	74.2	1,850	63.6	67.6
Black alone or in combination..........	82	65	44	(B)	(B)	37	(B)	(B)
Asian alone or in combination..........	172	116	77	44.8	66.4	66	38.3	56.7
Age								
18 to 24 years.................	345	320	202	58.3	63.0	156	45.2	48.8
25 to 34 years.................	577	504	341	59.1	67.8	275	47.6	54.6
35 to 44 years.................	521	442	344	66.2	77.9	320	61.4	72.3
45 to 64 years.................	1,044	977	724	69.3	74.0	679	65.1	69.5
65 years and over	698	685	536	76.9	78.2	512	73.4	74.7

B = Base is less than 75,000 and therefore too small to show the derived measure.

Table OR-14. Crime

(Number, rate per 100,000. Data are derived from the FBI Uniform Crime Reports.)

Item	State			U.S. [1,2,3,4]		
	2014	2015	Percent change	2014	2015	Percent change
TOTAL POPULATION[5]	3,971,202	4,028,977	1.5	318,907,401	321,418,820	0.8
VIOLENT CRIME						
Number........................	10,294	10,468	1.7	1,186,185	1,231,566	3.8
Rate	259.2	259.8	0.2	372.0	383.2	3.0
Murder and Nonnegligent Manslaughter						
Number........................	84	99	17.9	14,164	15,696	10.8
Rate	2.1	2.5	16.2	4.4	4.9	10.0
Rape[6]						
Number........................	1,620	1,593	-1.7	118,027	124,047	5.1
Rate	40.8	39.5	-3.1	37.0	38.6	4.3
Robbery						
Number........................	2,270	2,146	-5.5	322,905	327,374	1.4
Rate	57.2	53.3	-6.8	101.3	101.9	0.6
Aggravated Assault						
Number........................	6,320	6,630	4.9	731,089	764,449	4.6
Rate	159.1	164.6	3.4	229.2	237.8	3.7
PROPERTY CRIME						
Number........................	123,142	118,719	-3.6	8,209,010	7,993,631	-2.6
Rate	3,100.9	2,946.6	-5.0	2,574.1	2,487.0	-3.4
Burglary						
Number........................	18,690	18,336	-1.9	1,713,153	1,579,527	-7.8
Rate	470.6	455.1	-3.3	537.2	491.4	-8.5
Larceny-Theft						
Number........................	94,177	89,836	-4.6	5,809,054	5,706,346	-1.8
Rate	2,371.5	2,229.7	-6.0	1,821.5	1,775.4	-2.5
Motor Vehicle Theft						
Number........................	10,275	10,547	2.6	686,803	707,758	3.1
Rate	258.7	261.8	1.2	215.4	220.2	2.2

NOTE: Although arson data are included in the trend and clearance tables, sufficient data are not available to estimate totals for this offense. Therefore, no arson data are published in this table.
X = Not applicable.
- = Zero or rounds to zero.
[1] The crime figures have been adjusted.
[2] The data collection methodology for the offense of forcible rape used by the Minnesota state Uniform Crime Reporting (UCR) Program (with the exception of Minneapolis and St. Paul, Minnesota) does not comply with national UCR Program guidelines. Consequently, its figures for forcible rape and violent crime (of which forcible rape is a part) are not published in this table.
[3] Includes offenses reported by the Zoological Police and the Metro Transit Police.
[4] Because of changes in the state's reporting practices, figures are not comparable to previous years' data.
[5] Populations are U.S. Census Bureau provisional estimates as of July 1 of each year.
[6] The figures shown for the offense of rape were estimated using the revised Uniform Crime Reporting (UCR) definition of rape.

Table OR-15. State Government Finances, 2015

(Dollar amounts in thousands, percent distribution.)

Item	Dollars	Percent distribution
Total Revenue	35,086,418	100.0
General revenue	28,163,913	80.3
Intergovernmental revenue	11,033,172	31.4
Taxes	10,577,079	30.1
General sales	0	-
Selective sales	1,498,647	4.3
License taxes	988,932	2.8
Individual income tax	7,309,115	20.8
Corporate income tax	621,727	1.8
Other taxes	158,658	0.5
Current charges	4,433,796	12.6
Miscellaneous general revenue	2,119,866	6.0
Utility revenue	743	-
Liquor stores revenue	544,756	1.6
Insurance trust revenue[1]	6,377,006	18.2
Total Expenditure	32,225,752	100.0
Intergovernmental expenditure	6,209,293	19.3
Direct expenditure	26,016,459	80.7
Current operation	18,355,472	57.0
Capital outlay	1,426,922	4.4
Insurance benefits and repayments	5,264,467	16.3
Assistance and subsidies	571,040	1.8
Interest on debt	398,558	1.2
Exhibit: Salaries and wages	3,915,565	12.2
Total Expenditure	32,225,752	100.0
General expenditure	26,665,443	82.7
Intergovernmental expenditure	6,209,293	19.3
Direct expenditure	20,456,150	63.5
General expenditure, by function:		
Education	8,292,900	25.7
Public welfare	10,039,321	31.2
Hospitals	2,130,460	6.6
Health	467,328	1.5
Highways	1,360,696	4.2
Police protection	198,401	0.6
Correction	775,064	2.4
Natural resources	524,247	1.6
Parks and recreation	94,949	0.3
Governmental administration	1,343,855	4.2
Interest on general debt	398,558	1.2
Other and unallocable	1,039,664	3.2
Utility expenditure	28,845	0.1
Liquor stores expenditure	266,997	0.8
Insurance trust expenditure	5,264,467	16.3
Debt at End of Fiscal Year	13,061,182	X
Cash and Security Holdings	83,270,290	X

X = Not applicable.
- = Zero or rounds to zero.
[1] Within insurance trust revenue, net earnings of state retirement systems is a calculated statistic (the item code in the data file is X08), and thus can be positive or negative. Net earnings is the sum of earnings on investments plus gains on investments minus losses on investments. The change made in 2002 for asset valuation from book to market value in accordance with Statement 34 of the Governmental Accounting Standards Board is reflected in the calculated statistics.

Table OR-16. State Government Tax Collections, 2016

(Dollars in thousands, percent.)

Item	Dollars	Percent distribution
Total Taxes	11,043,311	100.0
Property taxes	20,587	0.2
Sales and gross receipts	1,532,190	13.9
General sales and gross receipts	0	-
Selective sales and gross receipts	1,532,190	13.9
Alcoholic beverages	18,375	0.2
Amusements	0	-
Insurance premiums	86,283	0.8
Motor fuels	517,757	4.7
Pari-mutuels	1,980	-
Public utilities	96,970	0.9
Tobacco products	268,808	2.4
Other selective sales	542,017	4.9
Licenses	1,048,709	9.5
Alcoholic beverages	4,543	-
Amusements	2,834	-
Corporations in general	34,825	0.3
Hunting and fishing	53,978	0.5
Motor vehicle	539,474	4.9
Motor vehicle operators	37,973	0.3
Public utilities	14,577	0.1
Occupation and business, NEC	353,372	3.2
Other licenses	7,133	0.1
Income taxes	8,299,887	75.2
Individual income	7,690,019	69.6
Corporation net income	609,868	5.5
Other taxes	141,938	1.3
Death and gift	125,969	1.1
Documentary and stock transfer	2,379	-
Severance	13,590	0.1
Taxes, NEC	0	-

X = Not applicable.
- = Zero or rounds to zero.

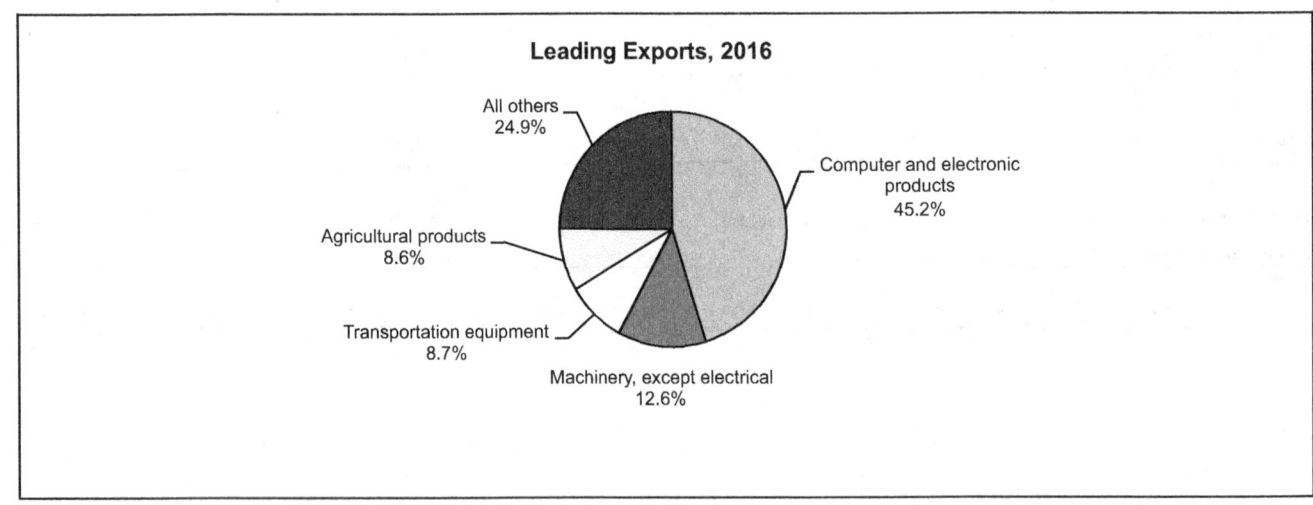

Leading Exports, 2016

All others 24.9%

Computer and electronic products 45.2%

Agricultural products 8.6%

Transportation equipment 8.7%

Machinery, except electrical 12.6%

PENNSYLVANIA

Facts and Figures

Location: Northeastern United States; bordered on the N by Lake Erie and New York, on the E by New York and New Jersey, on the S by Delaware, Maryland, and West Virginia, and on the W by West Virginia and Ohio

Area: 46,055 sq. mi. (119,283 sq. km.); rank—33rd

Population: 12,784,227 (2016 est.); rank—6th

Principal Cities: capital—Harrisburg; largest—Philadelphia

Statehood: December 12, 1787; 2nd state

U.S. Congress: 2 senators, 18 representatives

State Motto: Virtue, Liberty, and Independence

State Song: "Pennsylvania"

State Nicknames: The Keystone State; The Quaker State

Abbreviations: PA; Penn.

State Symbols: flower—mountain laurel; tree—Eastern hemlock; bird—ruffed grouse

At a Glance

- With an increase in population of 0.6 percent, Pennsylvania ranked 44th among the states in growth from 2010 to 2016.

- Pennsylvania's median household income in 2015 was $55,702, and 13.2 percent of the population lived below the poverty level.

- Approximately 6.4 percent of Pennsylvanians did not have health insurance in 2015, compared to the national rate of 9.4 percent.

- Pennsylvania's violent crime rate in 2015 was 315.1 per 100,000 population, compared to 383.2 for the entire nation.

- The unemployment rate in Pennsylvania was 5.4 percent in 2016, compared to the national unemployment rate of 4.9 percent.

Table PA-1. Population by Age, Sex, Race, and Hispanic Origin

(Number, percent, except where noted.)

Sex, age, race, and Hispanic origin	2000	2010	2016 [1]	Average annual percent change, 2010–2016
Total Population..	12,281,054	12,702,379	12,784,227	-
Percent of total U.S. population	4.4	4.1	4.0	X
Sex				
Male..	5,929,663	6,190,363	6,261,194	0.1
Female	6,351,391	6,512,016	6,523,033	-
Age				
Under 5 years...	727,804	729,538	711,765	-0.2
5 to 19 years..	2,542,780	2,449,852	2,309,216	-0.4
20 to 64 years..	7,091,305	7,563,682	7,539,525	-
65 years and over...	1,919,165	1,959,307	2,223,721	0.8
Median age (years)	38.0	40.1	40.7	0.1
Race and Hispanic Origin				
One race...				
White	10,484,203	10,663,774	10,531,113	-0.1
Black	1,224,612	1,431,826	1,505,204	0.3
American Indian and Alaska Native	18,348	39,735	46,770	1.1
Asian..	219,813	358,195	442,652	1.5
Native Hawaiian or Other Pacific Islander	3,417	7,115	9,265	1.9
Two or more races	142,224	201,734	249,223	1.5
Hispanic (of any race)...	394,088	758,058	900,814	1.2

X = Not applicable.
[1] Population figures for 2016 are July 1 estimates. The 2010 estimates are taken from the 2010 Census.
- = Zero or rounds to zero.

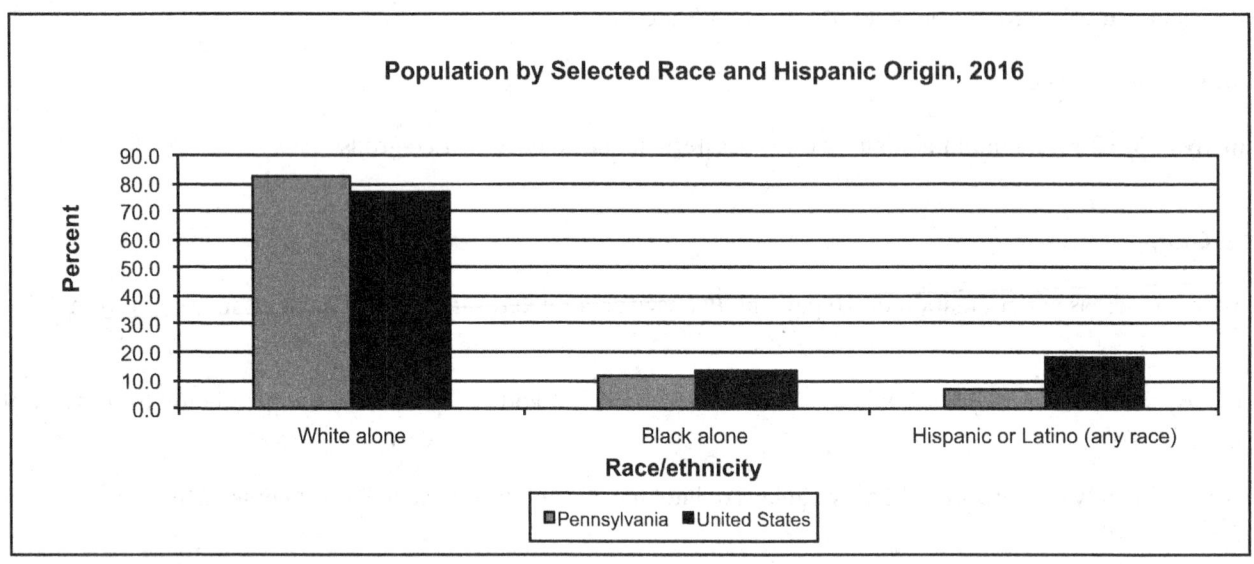

Table PA-2. Marital Status

(Number, percent distribution.)

Sex, age, race, and Hispanic origin	2000	2010	2015
Males, 15 Years and Over	4,686,277	5,031,761	5,130,670
Never married	30.1	35.9	36.9
Now married, except separated....................................	57.4	50.6	49.4
Separated...	1.9	2.0	2.0
Widowed...	3.3	3.1	3.0
Divorced...	7.3	8.5	8.8
Females, 15 Years and Over	5,175,436	5,406,494	5,459,046
Never married	24.6	29.8	30.8
Now married, except separated....................................	51.5	46.2	45.8
Separated...	2.4	2.7	2.4
Widowed...	12.7	11.2	10.3
Divorced...	8.8	10.2	10.6

Table PA-3. Households and Housing Characteristics

(Number, percent, dollars.)

Item	2000	2010	2015	Average annual percent change, 2000–2015
Total Households..	4,777,003	4,936,030	4,956,037	0.2
Family households..	3,208,388	3,197,710	3,204,295	-
Married-couple family...	2,467,673	2,381,094	2,366,755	-0.3
Other family...	740,715	816,616	837,540	0.9
Male householder, no wife present......................	186,022	215,082	228,064	1.5
Female householder, no husband present.............	554,693	601,534	609,476	0.7
Nonfamily households..	1,568,615	1,738,320	1,751,742	0.8
Householder living alone..	1,320,941	1,458,055	1,446,822	0.6
Householder not living alone..................................	247,674	280,265	304,920	1.5
Housing Characteristics				
Total housing units..	5,249,750	5,568,820	5,603,051	0.4
Occupied housing units	4,777,003	4,936,030	4,956,037	0.2
Owner occupied...	3,406,337	3,461,678	3,405,756	-
Renter occupied...	1,370,666	1,474,352	1,550,281	0.9
Average household size..	2.48	2.49	2.50	0.1
Financial Characteristics				
Median gross rent of renter-occupied housing	531	763	868	4.2
Median monthly owner costs for housing units with a mortgage	1,010	1,390	1,414	2.7
Median value of owner-occupied housing units	97,000	165,500	170,600	5.1

- = Zero or rounds to zero.

Table PA-4. Migration, Origin, and Language

(Number, percent.)

Characteristic	State			U.S.		
	2014	2015	Percent change	2014	2015	Percent change
Residence 1 Year Ago						
Population 1 year and over	12,645,888	12,662,192	0.1	315,095,393	317,635,720	0.8
Same house	87.8	87.7	X	85.1	85.3	X
Different house in the U.S.	11.7	11.8	X	14.3	14.1	X
Same county	7.2	7.3	X	8.7	8.5	X
Different county	4.5	4.5	X	5.6	5.6	X
Same state	2.6	2.6	X	3.3	3.2	X
Different state	1.8	1.8	X	2.3	2.4	X
Abroad	0.5	0.5	X	0.6	0.7	X
Place of Birth						
Native born	11,965,509	11,965,344	-	276,465,262	278,128,449	0.6
Male	48.9	49.0	X	49.3	49.3	X
Female	51.1	51.0	X	50.7	50.7	X
Foreign born	821,700	837,159	1.9	42,391,794	43,290,372	2.1
Male	48.9	48.0	X	48.7	48.6	X
Female	51.1	52.0	X	51.3	51.4	X
Foreign born; naturalized U.S. citizen............................	419,991	440,198	4.8	19,984,738	20,697,103	3.6
Male	45.4	45.9	X	45.9	45.9	X
Female	54.6	54.1	X	54.1	54.1	X
Foreign born; not a U.S. citizen.....................................	401,709	396,961	-1.2	22,407,056	22,593,269	0.8
Male	52.5	50.4	X	51.2	51.1	X
Female	47.5	49.6	X	48.8	48.9	X
Entered 2010 or later	17.5	21.8	X	12.3	15.6	X
Entered 2000 to 2009	31.5	28.8	X	28.6	27.9	X
Entered before 2000...	51.0	49.4	X	59.1	56.5	X
World Region of Birth, Foreign						
Foreign-born population, excluding population born at sea	821,700	837,159	1.9	42,390,705	43,289,646	2.1
Europe	20.0	20.9	X	11.2	11.1	X
Asia	39.2	40.2	X	30.1	30.6	X
Africa	7.2	7.9	X	4.6	4.8	X
Oceania	0.5	0.3	X	0.6	0.6	X
Latin America..	31.3	28.7	X	51.6	51.1	X
North America	1.8	1.9	X	1.9	1.9	X
Language Spoken at Home and Ability to Speak English						
Population 5 years and over..	12,075,749	12,087,611	0.1	299,084,046	301,625,014	0.8
English only	89.2	89.1	X	78.9	78.5	X
Language other than English.....................................	10.8	10.9	X	21.1	21.5	X
Speaks English less than "very well".......................	4.2	4.1	X	8.6	8.6	X

NA = Not available.
X = Not applicable.
- = Zero or rounds to zero.

Table PA-5. Median Income and Poverty Status, 2015

(Number, percent, except as noted.)

Characteristic	State		U.S.	
	Number	Percent	Number	Percent
Median Income				
Households (dollars)...............................	55,702	X	55,775	X
Families (dollars)	70,194	X	68,260	X
Below Poverty Level (All People)	1,629,995	13.2	46,153,077	14.7
Sex				
Male	719,852	11.9	20,599,407	13.4
Female	910,143	14.3	25,553,670	16.0
Age				
Under 18 years.................................	512,793	19.4	15,000,273	20.7
Related children under 18 years...........	498,942	19.0	14,693,239	20.4
18 to 64 years.................................	953,490	12.5	26,960,369	13.9
65 years and over	163,712	7.8	4,192,435	9.0

X = Not applicable.

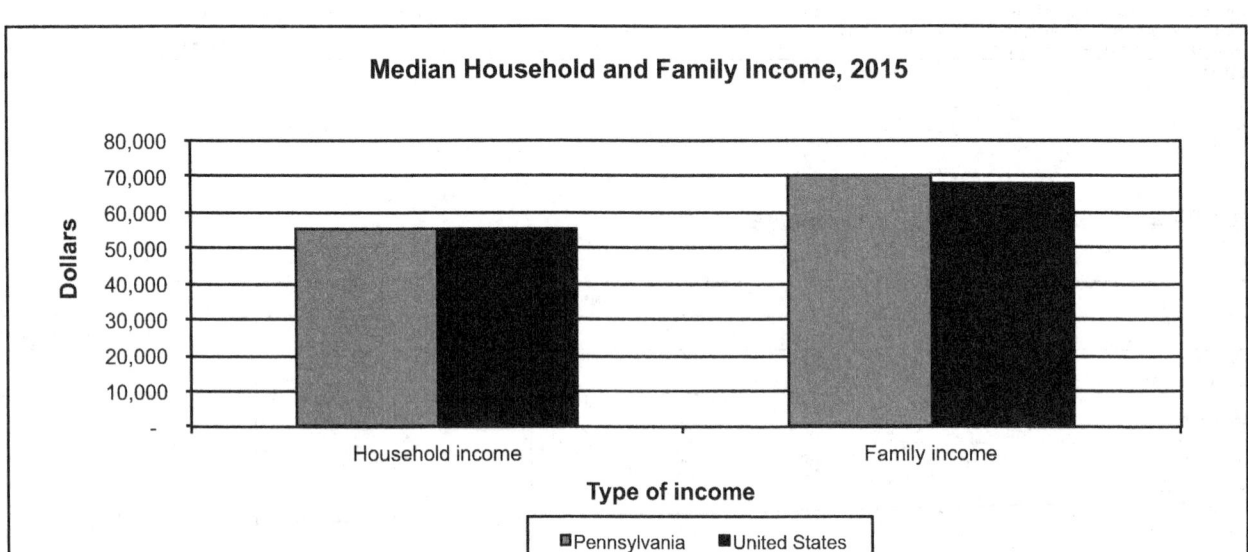

Table PA-6. Health Insurance Coverage Status for the Civilian Noninstitutionalized Population and Children Under 18 Years of Age

(Numbers in thousands, percent.)

Item	2007	2008	2009	2010	2011	2012	2013	2014	2015
Civilian Noninstitutionalized Population	12,313	12,209	12,366	12,506	12,540	12,559	12,569	12,583	12,599
Covered by Private or Public Insurance									
Number..	11,138	11,058	11,146	11,235	11,275	11,335	11,347	11,518	11,797
Percent..	90.5	90.6	90.1	89.8	89.9	90.2	90.3	91.5	93.6
Not Covered									
Number..	1,176	1,151	1,220	1,271	1,265	1,224	1,222	1,065	802
Percent..	9.5	9.4	9.9	10.2	10.1	9.8	9.7	8.5	6.4
Percent in the U.S. not covered..............	15.3	15.1	15.1	15.5	15.1	14.8	14.5	11.7	9.4
Children Under 18 Years of Age	2,775	2,757	2,766	2,778	2,755	2,731	2,709	2,693	2,685
Covered by Private or Public Insurance									
Number..	2,568	2,588	2,619	2,634	2,606	2,592	2,562	2,554	2,574
Percent..	92.6	93.9	94.7	94.8	94.6	94.9	94.6	94.8	95.9
Not Covered									
Number..	207	169	147	144	149	139	147	139	111
Percent..	7.4	6.1	5.3	5.2	5.4	5.1	5.4	5.2	4.1
Percent in the U.S. not covered..............	11.0	9.7	8.6	8.0	7.5	7.2	7.1	6.0	4.8

Table PA-7. Employment Status by Demographic Group, 2016

(Numbers in thousands, percent.)

Characteristic	Civilian noninstitutional population	Civilian labor force		Employed		Unemployed	
		Number	Percent of population	Number	Percent of population	Number	Percent of population
Total..	10,272	6,507	63.3	6,144	59.8	362	5.6
Sex							
Male...	4,947	3,387	68.5	3,191	64.5	195	5.8
Female......................................	5,325	3,120	58.6	2,953	55.5	167	5.3
Race, Sex, and Hispanic Origin							
White..	8,619	5,520	64.0	5,249	60.9	271	4.9
Male.....................................	4,184	2,905	69.4	2,748	65.7	157	5.4
Female..................................	4,435	2,615	59.0	2,501	56.4	114	4.3
Black or African American...............	1,100	654	59.5	579	52.7	75	11.4
Male.....................................	499	310	62.1	278	55.8	31	10.1
Female..................................	601	344	57.3	301	50.1	43	12.6
Hispanic or Latino ethnicity[1]...........	606	386	63.7	340	56.1	46	11.9
Male.....................................	298	206	69.2	184	61.8	22	10.7
Female..................................	308	179	58.3	156	50.5	24	13.2
Age							
16 to 19 years.............................	672	289	42.9	241	35.8	48	16.5
20 to 24 years.............................	891	673	75.5	618	69.3	56	8.3
25 to 34 years.............................	1,611	1,349	83.7	1,271	78.9	78	5.8
35 to 44 years.............................	1,410	1,190	84.4	1,136	80.6	54	4.6
45 to 54 years.............................	1,621	1,337	82.5	1,279	78.9	58	4.3
55 to 64 years.............................	1,866	1,228	65.8	1,177	63.1	51	4.1
65 years and over	2,200	441	20.1	423	19.2	19	4.2

NOTE: Data in Table 7 are from the Current Population Survey (CPS) and do not match the estimates in Table 8. See notes and definitions for further information.
[1] May be of any race.

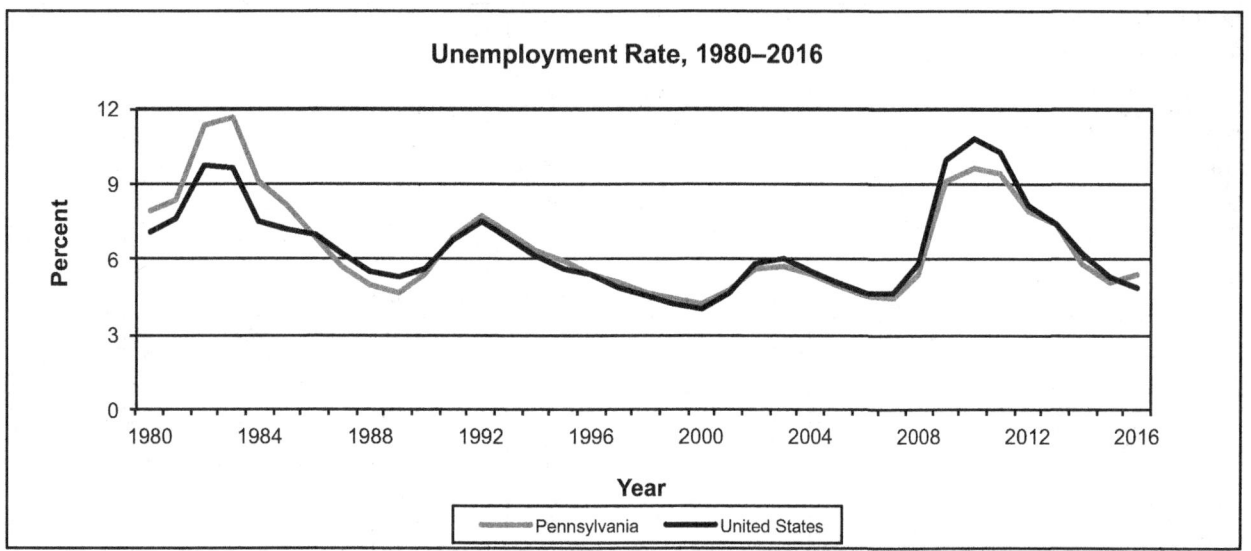

Table PA-8. Employment Status of the Civilian Noninstitutional Population Age 16 Years and Over

(Number, percent.)

Year	Civilian labor force	Civilian participation rate	Employed	Unemployed	Unemployment rate
2008....................................	6,451,535	65.2	6,109,645	341,890	5.3
2009....................................	6,400,263	64.4	5,885,351	514,912	8.0
2010....................................	6,380,949	63.5	5,840,887	540,062	8.5
2011....................................	6,395,506	63.2	5,888,745	506,761	7.9
2012....................................	6,463,922	63.6	5,957,326	506,596	7.8
2013....................................	6,440,444	63.2	5,964,726	475,718	7.4
2014....................................	6,391,421	62.6	6,015,668	375,753	5.9
2015....................................	6,423,903	62.8	6,093,858	330,045	5.1
2016....................................	6,471,990	63.3	6,120,029	351,961	5.4

Table PA-9. Employment and Average Wages by Industry

(Estimates through 2010 are based on the 2007 *North American Industry Classification System* [NAICS]. Estimates from 2011 onward are based on the 2012 NAICS.)

Industry	2009	2010	2011	2012	2013	2014	2015
	Number of jobs						
Wage and Salary Employment by Industry..................	5,815,187	5,800,496	5,861,034	5,912,279	5,937,016	5,991,194	6,038,056
Farm Wage and Salary Employment.........................	16,793	18,550	18,537	24,201	22,349	21,096	23,224
Nonfarm Wage and Salary Employment....................	5,798,394	5,781,946	5,842,497	5,888,078	5,914,667	5,970,098	6,014,832
Private wage and salary employment.........................	4,975,830	4,957,801	5,036,964	5,100,434	5,125,629	5,188,236	5,240,294
Forestry, fishing, and related activities.........................	7,748	7,731	7,593	7,718	8,022	8,049	7,737
Mining.........................	21,564	25,848	32,342	35,920	34,990	36,722	32,894
Utilities.........................	21,760	21,783	22,294	22,301	22,007	21,466	24,202
Construction.........................	235,035	223,895	229,814	232,554	232,295	237,517	241,267
Manufacturing.........................	576,220	561,041	565,728	567,803	564,204	567,899	568,236
Durable goods manufacturing.........................	346,345	334,786	342,332	347,894	346,367	346,525	346,274
Nondurable goods manufacturing.........................	229,875	226,255	223,396	219,909	217,837	221,374	221,962
Wholesale trade.........................	227,873	224,861	228,920	228,862	226,516	227,084	225,649
Retail trade.........................	635,555	631,232	635,275	639,409	637,557	638,390	638,251
Transportation and warehousing.........................	212,526	210,572	218,061	220,940	224,443	231,189	242,232
Information.........................	99,962	93,215	91,430	90,627	88,568	85,317	85,049
Finance and insurance.........................	263,703	260,349	260,840	262,121	263,489	266,878	266,132
Real estate and rental and leasing.........................	63,421	60,369	59,870	59,878	60,325	62,196	63,397
Professional, scientific, and technical services..............	310,826	305,774	311,117	319,572	327,022	331,404	338,124
Management of companies and enterprises..................	113,152	117,434	123,139	129,662	133,362	132,894	132,422
Administrative and waste services.........................	256,959	270,583	286,042	288,106	294,257	301,232	311,407
Educational services	236,136	239,701	243,178	244,157	245,178	248,859	251,020
Health care and social assistance.........................	895,370	907,448	916,185	930,944	937,060	953,348	965,556
Arts, entertainment, and recreation.........................	88,300	90,711	93,278	94,475	93,138	92,680	93,657
Accommodation and food services.........................	411,967	414,217	420,749	432,263	442,671	448,410	455,095
Other services, except public administration..................	297,753	291,037	291,109	293,122	290,525	296,702	297,967
Government and government enterprises.........................	822,564	824,145	805,533	787,644	789,038	781,862	774,538
	Dollars						
Average Wages and Salaries by Industry	43,766	44,793	46,072	47,382	48,057	49,486	51,044
Average Farm Wages and Salaries	29,024	25,883	22,671	23,208	25,613	27,360	24,232
Average Nonfarm Wages and Salaries	43,809	44,854	46,147	47,481	48,142	49,565	51,148
Average private wages and salaries.........................	43,678	44,787	46,161	47,650	48,301	49,777	51,313
Forestry, fishing, and related activities.........................	24,122	25,568	26,147	27,188	28,128	29,170	30,613
Mining.........................	61,548	68,015	72,605	75,476	77,784	83,030	81,285
Utilities.........................	92,714	94,538	100,369	101,831	103,329	109,284	109,586
Construction.........................	51,768	53,064	54,644	56,072	56,824	58,769	60,146
Manufacturing.........................	51,508	53,641	55,206	56,368	56,679	58,555	59,552
Durable goods manufacturing.........................	51,557	54,110	56,157	56,861	57,304	59,341	60,112
Nondurable goods manufacturing.........................	51,434	52,947	53,748	55,588	55,685	57,324	58,679
Wholesale trade.........................	63,449	65,507	68,674	70,815	72,479	76,274	77,307
Retail trade.........................	24,506	25,000	25,322	25,693	25,799	26,246	27,315
Transportation and warehousing.........................	39,509	40,491	41,478	42,324	42,923	44,451	45,687
Information.........................	60,631	63,458	65,693	67,456	69,093	70,688	73,620
Finance and insurance.........................	69,876	72,026	74,969	78,979	80,538	84,367	87,442
Real estate and rental and leasing.........................	43,774	46,475	48,629	51,142	51,226	54,085	56,570
Professional, scientific, and technical services..............	75,318	77,461	78,975	82,317	82,785	84,898	87,704
Management of companies and enterprises..................	98,074	101,107	106,940	114,448	115,056	120,850	130,132
Administrative and waste services.........................	30,896	31,121	31,323	31,967	32,329	32,856	33,723
Educational services	38,445	39,346	40,162	41,265	42,140	42,716	43,537
Health care and social assistance.........................	41,758	42,242	43,221	44,213	44,912	45,826	47,476
Arts, entertainment, and recreation.........................	29,250	30,290	32,022	32,260	32,576	33,425	34,650
Accommodation and food services.........................	16,261	16,635	17,153	17,727	18,259	18,775	19,554
Other services, except public administration..................	27,081	28,046	28,670	29,445	30,225	31,081	32,268
Government and government enterprises.........................	44,601	45,255	46,057	46,392	47,106	48,155	50,031

Table PA-10. Employment Characteristics by Family Type

(Number, percent.)

Family type and labor force status	2013		2014		2015	
	Total	Families with own children under 18 years	Total	Families with own children under 18 years	Total	Families with own children under 18 years
All Families...	3,152,234	1,253,201	3,173,379	1,256,610	3,204,295	1,252,169
FAMILY TYPE AND LABOR FORCE STATUS						
Married-Couple Families..	2,354,778	845,149	2,352,767	841,562	2,366,755	830,337
Both husband and wife in labor force..............................	53.1	69.3	53.0	70.0	52.1	69.7
Husband in labor force, wife not in labor force	20.0	24.9	19.8	24.7	20.0	24.8
Wife in labor force, husband not in labor force	8.3	3.7	8.4	3.8	8.3	3.7
Both husband and wife not in labor force............................	18.3	1.8	18.9	1.5	19.0	1.6
Other Families	797,456	408,052	820,612	415,048	837,540	421,832
Female householder, no husband present.........................	73.8	76.0	72.6	75.1	72.8	75.0
In labor force..	51.2	62.6	49.2	59.6	48.6	60.0
Not in labor force	22.6	13.4	23.4	15.5	24.2	15.0
Male householder, no wife present..............................	26.2	24.0	27.4	24.9	27.2	25.0
In labor force..	19.6	21.3	20.5	22.2	20.7	22.6
Not in labor force	6.6	2.8	6.9	2.7	6.5	2.4

Table PA-11. School Enrollment and Educational Attainment, 2015

(Number, percent.)

Item	State	U.S.
Enrollment		
Total population 3 years and over, enrolled in school	2,999,437	81,618,288
Enrolled in nursery school or preschool (percent)..................................	6.1	6.0
Enrolled in kindergarten (percent)..	4.7	5.0
Enrolled in elementary school, grades 1-8 (percent)...............................	39.6	40.3
Enrolled in high school, grades 9-12 (percent)...................................	21.2	20.9
Enrolled in college or graduate school (percent)..................................	28.4	27.7
Attainment		
Total population 25 years and over	8,895,727	216,447,163
Less than ninth grade (percent)..	3.3	5.5
9th to 12th grade, no diploma (percent)	7.0	7.3
High school graduate, including equivalency (percent).............................	35.7	27.6
Some college, no degree (percent)	16.0	20.7
Associate's degree (percent)	8.3	8.2
Bachelor's degree (percent)	18.1	19.0
Graduate or professional degree (percent)..	11.6	11.6
High school graduate or higher (percent)	89.7	87.1
Bachelor's degree or higher (percent)..	29.7	30.6

Table PA-12. Public School Characteristics and Educational Indicators

(Number, percent; data derived from Nativonal Center of Education Statistics.)

Item	State	U.S.
Public Schools, 2014–2015 (except where noted)		
Number of school districts...	796	18,260
Number of schools...	3,055	98,373
Number of students	1,743,160	50,312,581
Number of teachers	122,030	3,132,351
Student-teacher ratio	14.3	16.1
Expenditures per student (dollars), FY 2014......................................	13,824	11,066
Four-year adjusted cohort graduation rate (ACGR)[1,2]	84.8	83.2
Students eligible for free or reduced-price lunch (percent)........................	45.6	51.8
English language learners (percent)..	3.0	9.4
Students age 3 to 21 served under IDEA, part B (percent).........................	17.1	13.0

Public Schools by Type	Number	Percent of state public schools
Total number of schools..	3,055	100.0
Regular	2,959	96.9
Special education	4	0.1
Vocational education	85	2.8
Alternative education...	7	0.2

NOTE: Every school is assigned only one school type based on its instructional emphasis.
[1] ACGR data represents a new method of calculating high-school completion rates and may not be comparable to previous years' data for Averaged Freshmen Graduation Rates (AFGR).
[2] The United States 4-year ACGRs were estimated using both the reported 4-year ACGR data from 49 states and the District of Columbia and using imputed data for Idaho. The estimate for American Indian/Alaska Native students also includes imputed data for Virginia.

Table PA-13. Reported Voting and Registration of the Voting-Age Population, November 2016

(Numbers in thousands, percent.)

Item	Total population	Total citizen population	Registered			Voted		
			Total registered	Percent registered (total population)	Percent registered (total citizen population)	Total voted	Percent voted (total population)	Percent voted (total citizen population)
U.S. Total	245,502	224,059	157,596	64.2	70.3	137,537	56.0	61.4
State Total............................	9,980	9,596	6,909	69.2	72.0	6,008	60.2	62.6
Sex								
Male	4,808	4,589	3,199	66.5	69.7	2,793	58.1	60.9
Female	5,172	5,007	3,709	71.7	74.1	3,215	62.2	64.2
Race								
White alone........................	8,435	8,203	5,916	70.1	72.1	5,153	61.1	62.8
White, non-Hispanic alone	8,022	7,884	5,716	71.3	72.5	4,991	62.2	63.3
Black alone........................	1,071	1,007	751	70.1	74.5	637	59.5	63.2
Asian alone	311	223	138	44.4	61.8	135	43.3	60.3
Hispanic (of any race)	544	443	279	51.2	62.9	229	42.1	51.7
White alone or in combination	8,524	8,292	5,958	69.9	71.9	5,190	60.9	62.6
Black alone or in combination..........	1,152	1,088	805	69.9	74.0	692	60.1	63.6
Asian alone or in combination..........	325	238	147	45.2	61.8	144	44.2	60.4
Age								
18 to 24 years.....................	1,193	1,130	720	60.4	63.7	581	48.7	51.4
25 to 34 years.....................	1,649	1,525	1,026	62.2	67.3	837	50.8	54.9
35 to 44 years.....................	1,425	1,351	983	69.0	72.8	865	60.7	64.1
45 to 64 years.....................	3,471	3,382	2,536	73.1	75.0	2,294	66.1	67.8
65 years and over	2,243	2,208	1,643	73.3	74.4	1,431	63.8	64.8

Table PA-14. Crime

(Number, rate per 100,000. Data are derived from the FBI Uniform Crime Reports.)

Item	State			U.S. [1,2,3,4]		
	2014	2015	Percent change	2014	2015	Percent change
TOTAL POPULATION[5]	12,793,767	12,802,503	0.1	318,907,401	321,418,820	0.8
VIOLENT CRIME						
Number........................	40,298	40,339	0.1	1,186,185	1,231,566	3.8
Rate	315.0	315.1	-	372.0	383.2	3.0
Murder and Nonnegligent Manslaughter						
Number........................	610	658	7.9	14,164	15,696	10.8
Rate	4.8	5.1	7.8	4.4	4.9	10.0
Rape[6]						
Number........................	3,839	4,305	12.1	118,027	124,047	5.1
Rate	30.0	33.6	12.1	37.0	38.6	4.3
Robbery						
Number........................	13,545	13,003	-4.0	322,905	327,374	1.4
Rate	105.9	101.6	-4.1	101.3	101.9	0.6
Aggravated Assault						
Number........................	22,304	22,373	0.3	731,089	764,449	4.6
Rate	174.3	174.8	0.2	229.2	237.8	3.7
PROPERTY CRIME						
Number........................	246,982	232,085	-6.0	8,209,010	7,993,631	-2.6
Rate	1,930.5	1,812.8	-6.1	2,574.1	2,487.0	-3.4
Burglary						
Number........................	45,718	39,664	-13.2	1,713,153	1,579,527	-7.8
Rate	357.3	309.8	-13.3	537.2	491.4	-8.5
Larceny-Theft						
Number........................	188,211	180,287	-4.2	5,809,054	5,706,346	-1.8
Rate	1,471.1	1,408.2	-4.3	1,821.5	1,775.4	-2.5
Motor Vehicle Theft						
Number........................	13,053	12,134	-7.0	686,803	707,758	3.1
Rate	102.0	94.8	-7.1	215.4	220.2	2.2

NOTE: Although arson data are included in the trend and clearance tables, sufficient data are not available to estimate totals for this offense. Therefore, no arson data are published in this table.

X = Not applicable.

- = Zero or rounds to zero.

[1] The crime figures have been adjusted.

[2] The data collection methodology for the offense of forcible rape used by the Minnesota state Uniform Crime Reporting (UCR) Program (with the exception of Minneapolis and St. Paul, Minnesota) does not comply with national UCR Program guidelines. Consequently, its figures for forcible rape and violent crime (of which forcible rape is a part) are not published in this table.

[3] Includes offenses reported by the Zoological Police and the Metro Transit Police.

[4] Because of changes in the state's reporting practices, figures are not comparable to previous years' data.

[5] Populations are U.S. Census Bureau provisional estimates as of July 1 of each year.

[6] The figures shown for the offense of rape were estimated using the revised Uniform Crime Reporting (UCR) definition of rape.

Table PA-15. State Government Finances, 2015

(Dollar amounts in thousands, percent distribution.)

Item	Dollars	Percent distribution
Total Revenue	90,830,702	100.0
General revenue	74,729,881	82.3
Intergovernmental revenue	23,065,920	25.4
Taxes	36,110,311	39.8
General sales	9,865,270	10.9
Selective sales	8,504,539	9.4
License taxes	2,222,062	2.4
Individual income tax	11,488,974	12.6
Corporate income tax	2,510,136	2.8
Other taxes	1,519,330	1.7
Current charges	10,527,926	11.6
Miscellaneous general revenue	5,025,724	5.5
Utility revenue	0	-
Liquor stores revenue	1,862,270	2.1
Insurance trust revenue[1]	14,238,551	15.7
Total Expenditure	89,577,939	100.0
Intergovernmental expenditure	19,407,646	21.7
Direct expenditure	70,170,293	78.3
Current operation	46,974,310	52.4
Capital outlay	7,096,723	7.9
Insurance benefits and repayments	12,451,377	13.9
Assistance and subsidies	2,213,982	2.5
Interest on debt	1,433,901	1.6
Exhibit: Salaries and wages	9,908,104	11.1
Total Expenditure	89,577,939	100.0
General expenditure	75,364,303	84.1
Intergovernmental expenditure	19,407,646	21.7
Direct expenditure	55,956,657	62.5
General expenditure, by function:		
Education	23,442,663	26.2
Public welfare	24,749,412	27.6
Hospitals	4,228,219	4.7
Health	3,042,955	3.4
Highways	7,746,006	8.6
Police protection	1,037,183	1.2
Correction	2,061,391	2.3
Natural resources	665,218	0.7
Parks and recreation	320,836	0.4
Governmental administration	2,996,767	3.3
Interest on general debt	1,433,901	1.6
Other and unallocable	3,639,752	4.1
Utility expenditure	4	-
Liquor stores expenditure	1,762,255	-
Insurance trust expenditure	12,451,377	13.9
Debt at End of Fiscal Year	47,052,095	X
Cash and Security Holdings	128,274,927	X

X = Not applicable.
- = Zero or rounds to zero.
[1] Within insurance trust revenue, net earnings of state retirement systems is a calculated statistic (the item code in the data file is X08), and thus can be positive or negative. Net earnings is the sum of earnings on investments plus gains on investments minus losses on investments. The change made in 2002 for asset valuation from book to market value in accordance with Statement 34 of the Governmental Accounting Standards Board is reflected in the calculated statistics.

Table PA-16. State Government Tax Collections, 2016

(Dollars in thousands, percent.)

Item	Dollars	Percent distribution
Total Taxes	37,394,589	100.0
Property taxes	43,124	0.1
Sales and gross receipts	19,284,374	51.6
General sales and gross receipts	10,221,593	27.3
Selective sales and gross receipts	9,062,781	24.2
Alcoholic beverages	373,004	1.0
Amusements	1,395,968	3.7
Insurance premiums	820,513	2.2
Motor fuels	2,971,950	7.9
Pari-mutuels	10,350	-
Public utilities	1,310,130	3.5
Tobacco products	962,110	2.6
Other selective sales	1,218,756	3.3
Licenses	2,159,170	5.8
Alcoholic beverages	17,741	-
Amusements	11,820	-
Corporations in general	80,943	0.2
Hunting and fishing	74,654	0.2
Motor vehicle	900,127	2.4
Motor vehicle operators	71,765	0.2
Public utilities	80,661	0.2
Occupation and business, NEC	901,143	2.4
Other licenses	20,316	0.1
Income taxes	14,388,463	38.5
Individual income	11,932,232	31.9
Corporation net income	2,456,231	6.6
Other taxes	1,519,458	4.1
Death and gift	933,140	2.5
Documentary and stock transfer	562,623	1.5
Severance	0	-
Taxes, NEC	23,695	0.1

X = Not applicable.
- = Zero or rounds to zero.

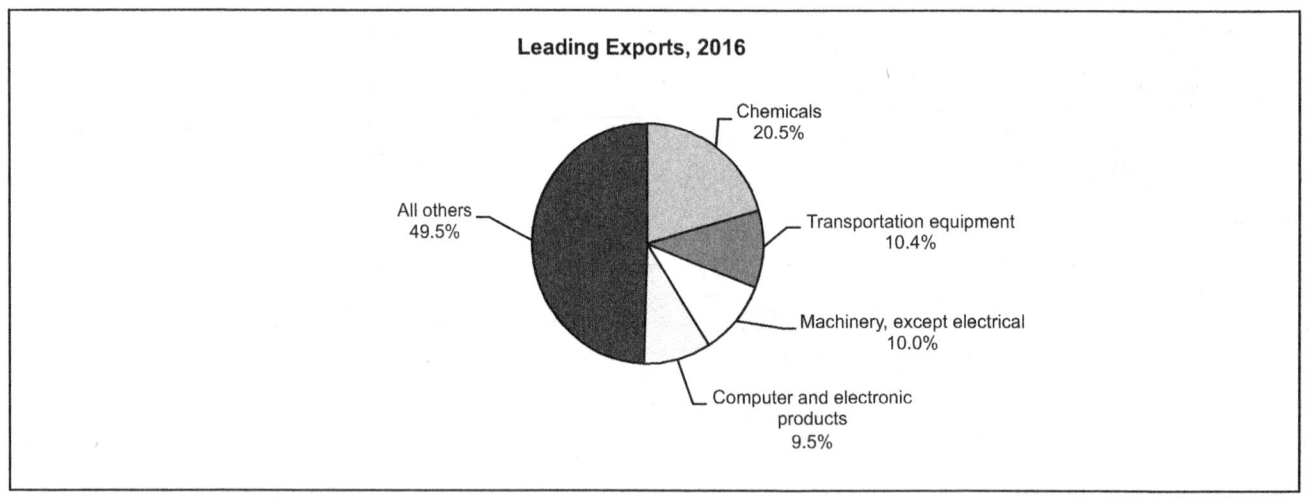

Leading Exports, 2016

Chemicals 20.5%
Transportation equipment 10.4%
Machinery, except electrical 10.0%
Computer and electronic products 9.5%
All others 49.5%

Facts and Figures

Location: Eastern United States; bordered on the N by Massachusetts, on the E by Massachusetts and the Atlantic Ocean, on the S by Block Island Sound and the Atlantic Ocean, and on the W by Connecticut

Area: 1,545 sq. mi. (4,002 sq. km.); rank—50th

Population: 1,056,426 (2016 est.); rank—43rd

Principal Cities: capital—Providence; largest—Providence

Statehood: May 29, 1790; 13th state

U.S. Congress: 2 senators, 2 representatives

State Motto: Hope

State Song: "Rhode Island"

State Nickname: The Ocean State

Abbreviations: RI; R.I.

State Symbols: flower—violet; tree—red maple; bird—Rhode Island red

At a Glance

- With an increase in population of 0.4 percent, Rhode Island ranked 46th among the states in growth from 2010 to 2016.

- In 2015, 5.7 percent of Rhode Islanders did not have health insurance, compared to 9.4 percent of the total U.S. population.

- Rhode Island's violent crime rate in 2015 was 242.5 per 100,000 population, compared to 383.2 for the entire nation.

- The state's median income in 2015 was $58,073, and 13.9 percent of its residents lived below the poverty level.

- In 2016, 19.7 percent of Rhode Island's population was under 18 years old, and 16.5 percent of its population was 65 years or older, compared to the national averages of 22.8 percent and 15.4 percent respectively.

Table RI-1. Population by Age, Sex, Race, and Hispanic Origin

(Number, percent, except where noted.)

Sex, age, race, and Hispanic origin	2000	2010	2016 [1]	Average annual percent change, 2010–2016
Total Population..............................	1,048,319	1,052,567	1,056,426	-
Percent of total U.S. population	0.4	0.3	0.3	X
Sex				
Male....................................	503,635	508,400	513,081	0.1
Female	544,684	544,167	543,345	-
Age				
Under 5 years................................	63,896	57,448	54,708	-0.3
5 to 19 years................................	218,720	204,310	188,797	-0.5
20 to 64 years................................	613,301	638,928	638,957	-
65 years and over	152,402	151,881	173,964	0.9
Median age (years)	36.7	39.4	40.0	0.1
Race and Hispanic Origin				
One race...................................				
White	891,191	910,253	892,045	-0.1
Black....................................	46,908	75,073	85,355	0.9
American Indian and Alaska Native	5,121	9,173	10,576	1.0
Asian....................................	23,665	31,768	37,629	1.2
Native Hawaiian or Other Pacific Islander	567	1,602	1,970	1.4
Two or more races.........................	28,251	24,698	28,851	1.1
Hispanic (of any race)......................	90,820	137,169	157,352	0.9

X = Not applicable.
- = Zero or rounds to zero.
[1] Population figures for 2016 are July 1 estimates. The 2010 estimates are taken from the 2010 Census.

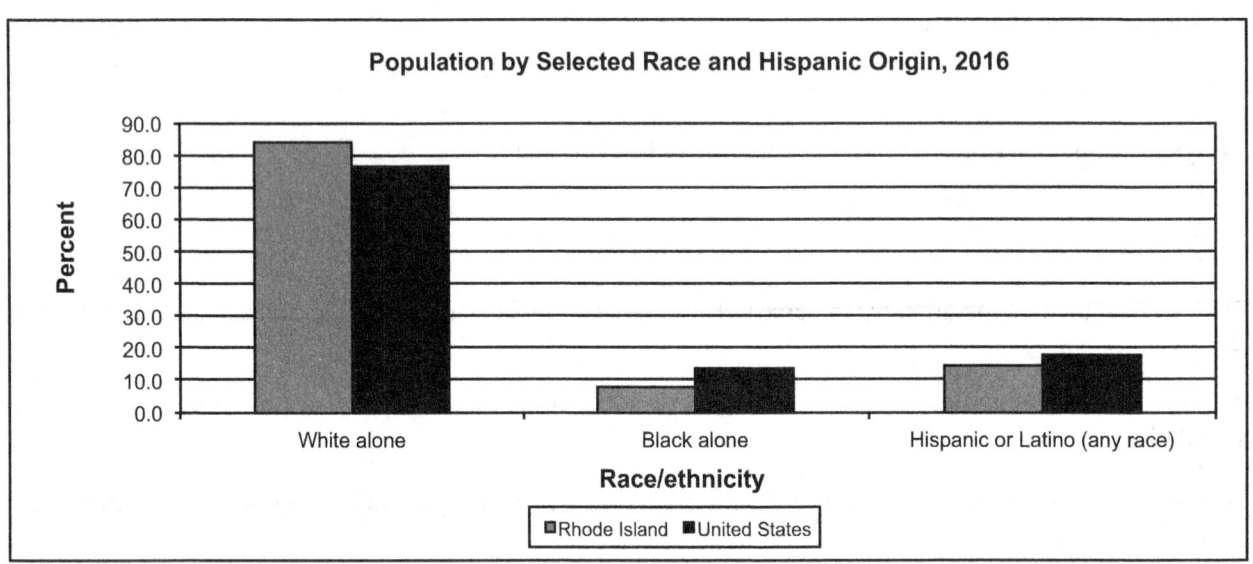

Population by Selected Race and Hispanic Origin, 2016

Table RI-2. Marital Status

(Number, percent distribution.)

Sex, age, race, and Hispanic origin	2000	2010	2015
Males, 15 Years and Over	396,396	414,628	422,625
Never married	32.5	39.8	40.1
Now married, except separated................................	54.9	45.2	46.5
Separated..	1.5	1.6	1.3
Widowed...	3.0	3.1	2.5
Divorced...	8.0	10.3	9.5
Females, 15 Years and Over	445,107	456,425	460,046
Never married	27.1	32.4	34.1
Now married, except separated................................	48.5	41.8	40.9
Separated..	2.3	2.4	2.1
Widowed...	11.5	10.4	9.6
Divorced...	10.7	13.0	13.3

Table RI-3. Households and Housing Characteristics

(Number, percent, dollars.)

Item	2000	2010	2015	Average annual percent change, 2000–2015
Total Households...	408,424	402,295	407,484	-
Family households	265,398	246,028	250,262	-0.4
Married-couple family	196,757	173,848	174,967	-0.7
Other family	68,641	72,180	75,295	0.6
Male householder, no wife present.............................	16,032	17,525	18,302	0.9
Female householder, no husband present.....................	52,609	54,655	56,993	0.6
Nonfamily households	143,026	156,267	157,222	0.7
Householder living alone..	116,678	125,371	129,553	0.7
Householder not living alone.....................................	26,348	30,896	27,669	0.3
Housing Characteristics				
Total housing units..	439,837	463,416	462,555	0.3
Occupied housing units	408,424	402,295	407,484	-
Owner occupied	245,156	244,516	240,618	-0.1
Renter occupied	163,268	157,779	166,866	0.1
Average household size..	2.47	2.51	2.49	0.1
Financial Characteristics				
Median gross rent of renter-occupied housing	553	868	938	4.6
Median monthly owner costs for housing units with a mortgage	1,205	1,837	1,730	2.9
Median value of owner-occupied housing units	133,000	254,500	241,000	5.4

- = Zero or rounds to zero.

Table RI-4. Migration, Origin, and Language

(Number, percent.)

Characteristic	State			U.S.		
	2014	2015	Percent change	2014	2015	Percent change
Residence 1 Year Ago						
Population 1 year and over	1,045,791	1,045,062	-0.1	315,095,393	317,635,720	0.8
Same house	86.7	86.2	X	85.1	85.3	X
Different house in the U.S.	12.6	13.0	X	14.3	14.1	X
Same county	8.0	7.8	X	8.7	8.5	X
Different county	4.6	5.3	X	5.6	5.6	X
Same state	1.5	1.6	X	3.3	3.2	X
Different state	3.1	3.7	X	2.3	2.4	X
Abroad	0.7	0.7	X	0.6	0.7	X
Place of Birth						
Native born	913,940	913,974	-	276,465,262	278,128,449	0.6
Male	48.4	48.3	X	49.3	49.3	X
Female	51.6	51.7	X	50.7	50.7	X
Foreign born	141,233	142,324	0.8	42,391,794	43,290,372	2.1
Male	48.8	49.3	X	48.7	48.6	X
Female	51.2	50.7	X	51.3	51.4	X
Foreign born; naturalized U.S. citizen...................................	72,884	77,381	6.2	19,984,738	20,697,103	3.6
Male	46.8	44.8	X	45.9	45.9	X
Female	53.2	55.2	X	54.1	54.1	X
Foreign born; not a U.S. citizen	68,349	64,943	-5.0	22,407,056	22,593,269	0.8
Male	51.0	54.5	X	51.2	51.1	X
Female	49.0	45.5	X	48.8	48.9	X
Entered 2010 or later...	14.1	16.9	X	12.3	15.6	X
Entered 2000 to 2009..	24.3	22.4	X	28.6	27.9	X
Entered before 2000..	61.6	60.6	X	59.1	56.5	X
World Region of Birth, Foreign						
Foreign-born population, excluding population born at sea	141,233	142,324	0.8	42,390,705	43,289,646	2.1
Europe	21.9	21.9	X	11.2	11.1	X
Asia..	20.4	19.1	X	30.1	30.6	X
Africa..	11.7	12.6	X	4.6	4.8	X
Oceania..	0.1	0.2	X	0.6	0.6	X
Latin America..	44.5	43.8	X	51.6	51.1	X
North America..	1.2	2.4	X	1.9	1.9	X
Language Spoken at Home and Ability to Speak English						
Population 5 years and over..	1,000,317	1,001,905	0.2	299,084,046	301,625,014	0.8
English only	79.0	77.8	X	78.9	78.5	X
Language other than English...	21.0	22.2	X	21.1	21.5	X
Speaks English less than "very well"...................................	8.4	8.2	X	8.6	8.6	X

NA = Not available.
X = Not applicable.
- = Zero or rounds to zero.

Table RI-5. Median Income and Poverty Status, 2015

(Number, percent, except as noted.)

Characteristic	State		U.S.	
	Number	Percent	Number	Percent
Median Income				
Households (dollars)..	58,073	X	55,775	X
Families (dollars)	76,623	X	68,260	X
Below Poverty Level (All People)	141,035	13.9	46,153,077	14.7
Sex				
Male	62,131	12.6	20,599,407	13.4
Female	78,904	15.1	25,553,670	16.0
Age				
Under 18 years...	40,566	19.4	15,000,273	20.7
Related children under 18 years......................	39,877	19.1	14,693,239	20.4
18 to 64 years...	83,685	13.0	26,960,369	13.9
65 years and over	16,784	10.3	4,192,435	9.0

X = Not applicable.

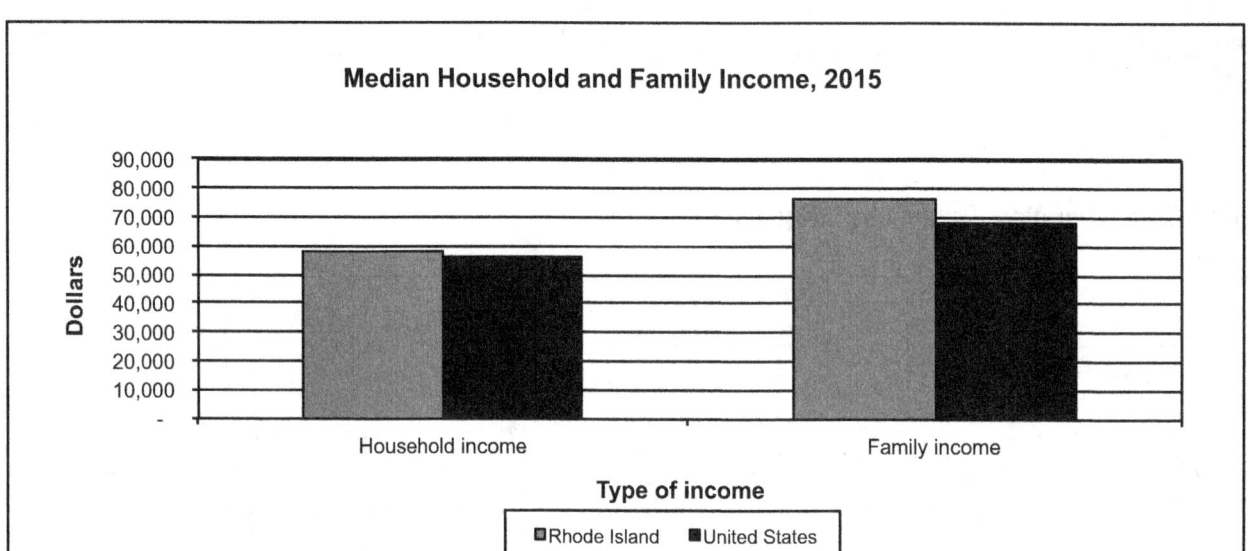

Table RI-6. Health Insurance Coverage Status for the Civilian Noninstitutionalized Population and Children Under 18 Years of Age

(Numbers in thousands, percent.)

Item	2007	2008	2009	2010	2011	2012	2013	2014	2015
Civilian Noninstitutionalized Population	1,044	1,030	1,035	1,037	1,035	1,035	1,036	1,040	1,041
Covered by Private or Public Insurance									
Number...	931	922	919	911	923	920	916	963	982
Percent...	89.2	89.5	88.7	87.8	89.2	88.9	88.4	92.6	94.3
Not Covered									
Number...	113	108	117	126	112	115	120	77	59
Percent...	10.8	10.5	11.3	12.2	10.8	11.1	11.6	7.4	5.7
Percent in the U.S. not covered...................	15.3	15.1	15.1	15.5	15.1	14.8	14.5	11.7	9.4
Children Under 18 Years of Age	238	228	227	224	219	217	212	212	211
Covered by Private or Public Insurance									
Number...	217	215	215	212	211	207	201	205	204
Percent...	91.2	94.3	94.6	94.4	96.0	95.5	94.6	96.7	96.6
Not Covered									
Number...	21	13	12	12	8	10	12	7	7
Percent...	8.8	5.7	5.4	5.6	4.0	4.5	5.4	3.3	3.4
Percent in the U.S. not covered...................	11.0	9.7	8.6	8.0	7.5	7.2	7.1	6.0	4.8

Table RI-7. Employment Status by Demographic Group, 2016

(Numbers in thousands, percent.)

Characteristic	Civilian noninstitutional population	Civilian labor force		Employed		Unemployed	
		Number	Percent of population	Number	Percent of population	Number	Percent of population
Total...	859	551	64.2	522	60.7	30	5.4
Sex							
Male..	410	282	68.7	263	64.2	18	6.5
Female	449	269	60.0	258	57.5	11	4.1
Race, Sex, and Hispanic Origin							
White	737	472	64.1	448	60.8	24	5.1
Male	355	243	68.4	228	64.2	15	6.1
Female	381	229	60.0	220	57.6	9	4.0
Black or African American.........................	62	41	66.0	38	61.5	3	6.9
Male	29	19	67.3	18	61.2	2	9.0
Female	33	21	64.8	20	61.5	1	5.0
Hispanic or Latino ethnicity[1]	121	78	64.1	71	58.5	7	8.7
Male	62	44	70.5	40	64.0	4	9.2
Female	59	34	57.4	31	52.7	3	8.2
Age							
16 to 19 years......................................	56	24	43.9	20	36.8	4	16.2
20 to 24 years......................................	66	49	74.2	45	67.5	4	9.0
25 to 34 years......................................	143	118	82.5	113	78.8	5	4.5
35 to 44 years......................................	135	111	82.2	104	77.3	7	6.0
45 to 54 years......................................	137	109	79.4	106	77.4	3	2.5
55 to 64 years......................................	156	105	67.6	100	64.4	5	4.7
65 years and over	167	35	21.0	33	20.0	2	4.6

NOTE: Data in Table 7 are from the Current Population Survey (CPS) and do not match the estimates in Table 8. See notes and definitions for further information.
[1] May be of any race.

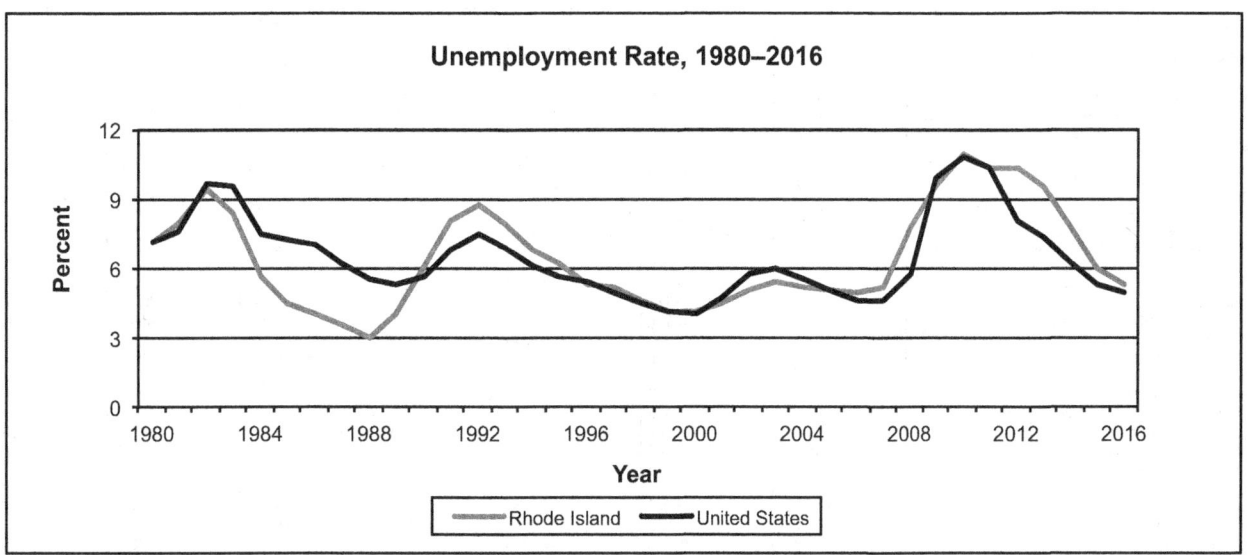

Table RI-8. Employment Status of the Civilian Noninstitutional Population Age 16 Years and Over

(Number, percent.)

Year	Civilian labor force	Civilian participation rate	Employed	Unemployed	Unemployment rate
2008..	570,328	68.0	525,941	44,387	7.8
2009..	567,280	67.4	504,951	62,329	11.0
2010..	566,704	67.3	503,216	63,488	11.2
2011..	560,056	66.4	498,248	61,808	11.0
2012..	558,392	66.0	500,316	58,076	10.4
2013..	557,256	65.7	505,686	51,570	9.3
2014..	555,955	65.3	513,217	42,738	7.7
2015..	554,558	64.9	521,434	33,124	6.0
2016..	552,219	64.4	522,812	29,407	5.3

Table RI-9. Employment and Average Wages by Industry

(Estimates through 2010 are based on the 2007 *North American Industry Classification System* [NAICS]. Estimates from 2011 onward are based on the 2012 NAICS.)

Industry	2009	2010	2011	2012	2013	2014	2015
	Number of jobs						
Wage and Salary Employment by Industry..................	477,603	474,551	476,085	477,784	484,147	491,907	498,383
Farm Wage and Salary Employment.........................	509	503	550	536	614	615	613
Nonfarm Wage and Salary Employment.....................	477,094	474,048	475,535	477,248	483,533	491,292	497,770
Private wage and salary employment...........................	403,679	400,945	403,274	405,810	411,806	419,463	426,262
Forestry, fishing, and related activities	561	(D)	(D)	554	(D)	(D)	(D)
Mining..	194	(D)	(D)	188	(D)	(D)	(D)
Utilities...	1,119	1,129	1,077	1,058	1,060	1,057	1,082
Construction..	17,988	16,521	16,174	16,499	16,584	16,948	17,431
Manufacturing..	41,845	40,396	40,424	39,708	40,128	40,911	41,242
Durable goods manufacturing..............................	26,913	25,810	25,856	25,343	25,595	26,120	26,032
Nondurable goods manufacturing.........................	14,932	14,586	14,568	14,365	14,533	14,791	15,210
Wholesale trade	16,228	15,882	16,237	16,897	16,768	16,918	17,021
Retail trade..	47,839	47,320	47,336	47,323	46,934	47,576	48,449
Transportation and warehousing................................	9,186	9,138	9,628	9,776	9,780	9,962	10,282
Information	10,156	10,009	10,169	9,597	9,096	8,872	8,631
Finance and insurance	24,133	24,082	23,896	24,199	24,722	25,069	25,544
Real estate and rental and leasing............................	6,232	5,801	5,814	5,919	6,050	6,072	6,138
Professional, scientific, and technical services	21,474	21,116	21,166	21,673	22,174	23,007	24,036
Management of companies and enterprises...................	9,212	9,331	9,858	10,536	11,343	12,015	12,574
Administrative and waste services.............................	22,480	23,405	23,676	24,326	25,565	26,292	27,317
Educational services	24,838	24,973	25,627	24,316	24,266	25,324	25,856
Health care and social assistance.............................	78,394	79,709	79,212	79,609	81,445	81,281	81,345
Arts, entertainment, and recreation............................	7,770	7,695	7,609	7,725	8,489	8,923	9,066
Accommodation and food services............................	41,805	42,246	42,849	44,369	45,426	46,617	47,528
Other services, except public administration.................	22,225	21,449	21,779	21,538	21,264	21,821	21,901
Government and government enterprises.........................	73,415	73,103	72,261	71,438	71,727	71,829	71,508
	Dollars						
Average Wages and Salaries by Industry	43,817	45,317	46,299	47,464	48,458	49,946	51,321
Average Farm Wages and Salaries	26,974	26,113	20,902	31,032	27,930	29,517	27,189
Average Nonfarm Wages and Salaries	43,835	45,338	46,328	47,483	48,484	49,971	51,351
Average private wages and salaries............................	42,139	43,685	44,682	45,921	47,067	48,719	50,042
Forestry, fishing, and related activities	37,111	(D)	(D)	41,554	(D)	(D)	(D)
Mining..	48,572	(D)	(D)	51,410	(D)	(D)	(D)
Utilities...	85,203	86,734	93,879	92,194	96,742	97,839	98,657
Construction..	52,391	52,554	53,804	54,496	55,199	56,067	57,703
Manufacturing..	48,833	51,041	52,632	53,620	55,338	56,682	57,835
Durable goods manufacturing..............................	49,811	52,539	54,280	55,210	56,999	58,021	58,862
Nondurable goods manufacturing.........................	47,069	48,391	49,708	50,815	52,413	54,318	56,076
Wholesale trade	61,234	64,825	65,422	67,073	69,417	70,389	70,935
Retail trade..	27,132	28,172	27,725	28,214	28,639	29,806	31,076
Transportation and warehousing................................	38,686	39,818	40,412	41,144	41,924	43,009	43,499
Information	61,340	62,978	65,805	68,741	67,782	70,540	71,955
Finance and insurance	69,872	75,615	80,297	84,148	86,563	93,574	93,640
Real estate and rental and leasing............................	36,848	38,977	40,027	41,607	42,631	44,237	46,459
Professional, scientific, and technical services	62,925	65,445	66,415	67,376	69,320	72,313	74,481
Management of companies and enterprises...................	95,202	104,262	106,265	114,488	116,746	122,375	124,016
Administrative and waste services.............................	31,089	31,604	32,214	33,175	34,543	35,355	36,108
Educational services	38,480	39,490	39,443	40,698	42,279	42,584	42,798
Health care and social assistance.............................	41,648	42,326	43,277	43,680	44,101	45,144	47,026
Arts, entertainment, and recreation............................	26,505	27,019	28,049	28,795	29,425	31,261	33,890
Accommodation and food services............................	17,804	18,208	18,761	19,364	19,968	20,667	21,764
Other services, except public administration.................	27,687	28,887	28,995	29,803	31,003	31,970	33,285
Government and government enterprises.........................	53,160	54,401	55,518	56,353	56,621	57,285	59,153

D = Not shown to avoid disclosure of confidential information, but the estimates for this item are included in the total.

Table RI-10. Employment Characteristics by Family Type

(Number, percent.)

Family type and labor force status	2013		2014		2015	
	Total	Families with own children under 18 years	Total	Families with own children under 18 years	Total	Families with own children under 18 years
All Families...	259,863	108,073	256,077	108,359	250,262	105,051
FAMILY TYPE AND LABOR FORCE STATUS						
Married-Couple Families..............................	180,930	66,807	178,127	66,035	174,967	65,193
Both husband and wife in labor force......................	56.3	71.6	56.9	74.2	56.7	74.9
Husband in labor force, wife not in labor force..........	18.6	22.6	16.5	19.2	17.2	18.2
Wife in labor force, husband not in labor force.........	8.8	4.4	9.0	4.7	7.8	4.3
Both husband and wife not in labor force..................	15.5	0.9	17.6	1.8	17.2	2.2
Other Families	78,933	41,266	77,950	42,324	75,295	39,858
Female householder, no husband present...................	73.1	78.1	74.0	77.7	75.7	80.1
In labor force	52.7	61.9	52.9	64.8	54.9	67.1
Not in labor force	20.4	16.2	21.1	12.9	20.8	13.0
Male householder, no wife present..........................	26.9	21.9	26.0	22.3	24.3	19.9
In labor force	20.1	19.8	20.6	19.8	19.9	18.6
Not in labor force	6.8	2.1	5.3	2.5	4.4	1.3

Table RI-11. School Enrollment and Educational Attainment, 2015

(Number, percent.)

Item	State	U.S.
Enrollment		
Total population 3 years and over, enrolled in school	262,347	81,618,288
Enrolled in nursery school or preschool (percent)...........................	4.9	6.0
Enrolled in kindergarten (percent)...	4.7	5.0
Enrolled in elementary school, grades 1-8 (percent)........................	35.9	40.3
Enrolled in high school, grades 9-12 (percent)	17.8	20.9
Enrolled in college or graduate school (percent)...........................	36.6	27.7
Attainment		
Total population 25 years and over	730,083	216,447,163
Less than ninth grade (percent)	5.5	5.5
9th to 12th grade, no diploma (percent)	6.8	7.3
High school graduate, including equivalency (percent)......................	28.0	27.6
Some college, no degree (percent)	18.5	20.7
Associate's degree (percent)	8.5	8.2
Bachelor's degree (percent)	19.3	19.0
Graduate or professional degree (percent)..................................	13.4	11.6
High school graduate or higher (percent)	87.7	87.1
Bachelor's degree or higher (percent)	32.7	30.6

Table RI-12. Public School Characteristics and Educational Indicators

(Number, percent; data derived from National Center of Education Statistics.)

Item	State	U.S.
Public Schools, 2014–2015 (except where noted)		
Number of school districts...	63	18,260
Number of schools...	307	98,373
Number of students..	141,959	50,312,581
Number of teachers	9,471	3,132,351
Student-teacher ratio	15.0	16.1
Expenditures per student (dollars), FY 2014................................	15,372	11,066
Four-year adjusted cohort graduation rate (ACGR)[1,2]	83.2	83.2
Students eligible for free or reduced-price lunch (percent)................	46.8	51.8
English language learners (percent)..	7.3	9.4
Students age 3 to 21 served under IDEA, part B (percent)...................	16.5	13.0

Public Schools by Type	Number	Percent of state public schools
Total number of schools...	307	100.0
Regular	291	94.8
Special education...	1	0.3
Vocational education..	10	3.3
Alternative education...	5	1.6

NOTE: Every school is assigned only one school type based on its instructional emphasis.
[1] ACGR data represents a new method of calculating high-school completion rates and may not be comparable to previous years' data for Averaged Freshmen Graduation Rates (AFGR).
[2] The United States 4-year ACGRs were estimated using both the reported 4-year ACGR data from 49 states and the District of Columbia and using imputed data for Idaho. The estimate for American Indian/Alaska Native students also includes imputed data for Virginia.

Table RI-13. Reported Voting and Registration of the Voting-Age Population, November 2016

(Numbers in thousands, percent.)

Item	Total population	Total citizen population	Registered			Voted		
			Total registered	Percent registered (total population)	Percent registered (total citizen population)	Total voted	Percent voted (total population)	Percent voted (total citizen population)
U.S. Total	245,502	224,059	157,596	64.2	70.3	137,537	56.0	61.4
State Total..............................	836	766	538	64.4	70.3	464	55.5	60.6
Sex								
Male	404	369	253	62.7	68.6	213	52.8	57.8
Female	432	397	285	66.0	71.8	251	58.1	63.2
Race								
White alone...............................	699	664	467	66.7	70.3	403	57.7	60.7
White, non-Hispanic alone	599	588	417	69.5	70.9	363	60.5	61.7
Black alone...............................	63	58	42	(B)	(B)	34	(B)	(B)
Asian alone	37	16	9	(B)	(B)	9	(B)	(B)
Hispanic (of any race).....................	132	98	67	(B)	(B)	57	(B)	(B)
White alone or in combination	707	672	472	66.8	70.3	407	57.6	60.6
Black alone or in combination..........	69	64	47	(B)	(B)	38	(B)	(B)
Asian alone or in combination..........	39	18	10	(B)	(B)	10	(B)	(B)
Age								
18 to 24 years..............................	81	69	43	(B)	(B)	34	(B)	(B)
25 to 34 years..............................	148	137	93	62.7	67.6	74	49.7	53.6
35 to 44 years..............................	145	125	95	65.1	75.9	78	53.4	62.2
45 to 64 years..............................	284	263	184	64.8	69.9	169	59.5	64.2
65 years and over	178	172	124	69.7	72.0	111	62.4	64.4

B = Base is less than 75,000 and therefore too small to show the derived measure.

Table RI-14. Crime

(Number, rate per 100,000. Data are derived from the FBI Uniform Crime Reports.)

Item	State			U.S. [1,2,3,4]		
	2014	2015	Percent change	2014	2015	Percent change
TOTAL POPULATION[5]	1,054,907	1,056,298	0.1	318,907,401	321,418,820	0.8
VIOLENT CRIME						
Number..	2,320	2,562	10.4	1,186,185	1,231,566	3.8
Rate	219.9	242.5	10.3	372.0	383.2	3.0
Murder and Nonnegligent Manslaughter						
Number..	26	29	11.5	14,164	15,696	10.8
Rate	2.5	2.7	11.4	4.4	4.9	10.0
Rape[6]						
Number..	366	459	25.4	118,027	124,047	5.1
Rate	34.7	43.5	25.2	37.0	38.6	4.3
Robbery						
Number..	530	556	4.9	322,905	327,374	1.4
Rate	50.2	52.6	4.8	101.3	101.9	0.6
Aggravated Assault						
Number..	1,398	1,518	8.6	731,089	764,449	4.6
Rate	132.5	143.7	8.4	229.2	237.8	3.7
PROPERTY CRIME						
Number..	22,982	20,043	-12.8	8,209,010	7,993,631	-2.6
Rate	2,178.6	1,897.5	-12.9	2,574.1	2,487.0	-3.4
Burglary						
Number..	4,830	3,947	-18.3	1,713,153	1,579,527	-7.8
Rate	457.9	373.7	-18.4	537.2	491.4	-8.5
Larceny-Theft						
Number..	16,317	14,707	-9.9	5,809,054	5,706,346	-1.8
Rate	1,546.8	1,392.3	-10.0	1,821.5	1,775.4	-2.5
Motor Vehicle Theft						
Number..	1,835	1,389	-24.3	686,803	707,758	3.1
Rate	173.9	131.5	-24.4	215.4	220.2	2.2

NOTE: Although arson data are included in the trend and clearance tables, sufficient data are not available to estimate totals for this offense. Therefore, no arson data are published in this table.
X = Not applicable.
- = Zero or rounds to zero.
[1] The crime figures have been adjusted.
[2] The data collection methodology for the offense of forcible rape used by the Minnesota state Uniform Crime Reporting (UCR) Program (with the exception of Minneapolis and St. Paul, Minnesota) does not comply with national UCR Program guidelines. Consequently, its figures for forcible rape and violent crime (of which forcible rape is a part) are not published in this table.
[3] Includes offenses reported by the Zoological Police and the Metro Transit Police.
[4] Because of changes in the state's reporting practices, figures are not comparable to previous years' data.
[5] Populations are U.S. Census Bureau provisional estimates as of July 1 of each year.
[6] The figures shown for the offense of rape were estimated using the revised Uniform Crime Reporting (UCR) definition of rape.

Table RI-15. State Government Finances, 2015

(Dollar amounts in thousands, percent distribution.)

Item	Dollars	Percent distribution
Total Revenue	8,404,622	100.0
General revenue	7,364,385	87.6
Intergovernmental revenue	2,466,598	29.3
Taxes	3,196,673	38.0
General sales	959,513	11.4
Selective sales	661,010	7.9
License taxes	120,832	1.4
Individual income tax	1,215,368	14.5
Corporate income tax	176,336	2.1
Other taxes	63,614	0.8
Current charges	789,919	9.4
Miscellaneous general revenue	911,195	10.8
Utility revenue	24,588	0.3
Liquor stores revenue	0	-
Insurance trust revenue[1]	1,015,649	12.1
Total Expenditure	8,676,551	100.0
Intergovernmental expenditure	1,226,790	14.1
Direct expenditure	7,449,761	85.9
Current operation	4,941,610	57.0
Capital outlay	477,367	5.5
Insurance benefits and repayments	1,354,270	15.6
Assistance and subsidies	157,315	1.8
Interest on debt	519,199	6.0
Exhibit: Salaries and wages	1,246,305	14.4
Total Expenditure	8,676,551	100.0
General expenditure	7,171,900	82.7
Intergovernmental expenditure	1,226,790	14.1
Direct expenditure	5,945,110	68.5
General expenditure, by function:		
Education	2,052,694	23.7
Public welfare	2,672,489	30.8
Hospitals	65,951	0.8
Health	170,838	2.0
Highways	317,439	3.7
Police protection	81,869	0.9
Correction	191,023	2.2
Natural resources	57,629	0.7
Parks and recreation	34,105	0.4
Governmental administration	386,131	4.5
Interest on general debt	518,163	6.0
Other and unallocable	623,569	7.2
Utility expenditure	150,381	1.7
Liquor stores expenditure	0	-
Insurance trust expenditure	1,354,270	15.6
Debt at End of Fiscal Year	9,004,835	X
Cash and Security Holdings	16,790,546	X

X = Not applicable.
- = Zero or rounds to zero.
[1] Within insurance trust revenue, net earnings of state retirement systems is a calculated statistic (the item code in the data file is X08), and thus can be positive or negative. Net earnings is the sum of earnings on investments plus gains on investments minus losses on investments. The change made in 2002 for asset valuation from book to market value in accordance with Statement 34 of the Governmental Accounting Standards Board is reflected in the calculated statistics.

Table RI-16. State Government Tax Collections, 2016

(Dollars in thousands, percent.)

Item	Dollars	Percent distribution
Total Taxes	3,265,727	100.0
Property taxes	2,544	0.1
Sales and gross receipts	1,665,438	51.0
General sales and gross receipts	973,585	29.8
Selective sales and gross receipts	691,853	21.2
Alcoholic beverages	20,399	0.6
Amusements	0	-
Insurance premiums	113,993	3.5
Motor fuels	90,032	2.8
Pari-mutuels	1,070	-
Public utilities	103,971	3.2
Tobacco products	144,403	4.4
Other selective sales	217,985	6.7
Licenses	120,936	3.7
Alcoholic beverages	72	-
Amusements	197	-
Corporations in general	5,131	0.2
Hunting and fishing	1,988	0.1
Motor vehicle	45,359	1.4
Motor vehicle operators	4,911	0.2
Public utilities	0	-
Occupation and business, NEC	58,915	1.8
Other licenses	4,363	0.1
Income taxes	1,380,463	42.3
Individual income	1,236,194	37.9
Corporation net income	144,269	4.4
Other taxes	96,346	3.0
Death and gift	75,288	2.3
Documentary and stock transfer	21,058	0.6
Severance	0	-
Taxes, NEC	0	-

X = Not applicable.
- = Zero or rounds to zero.

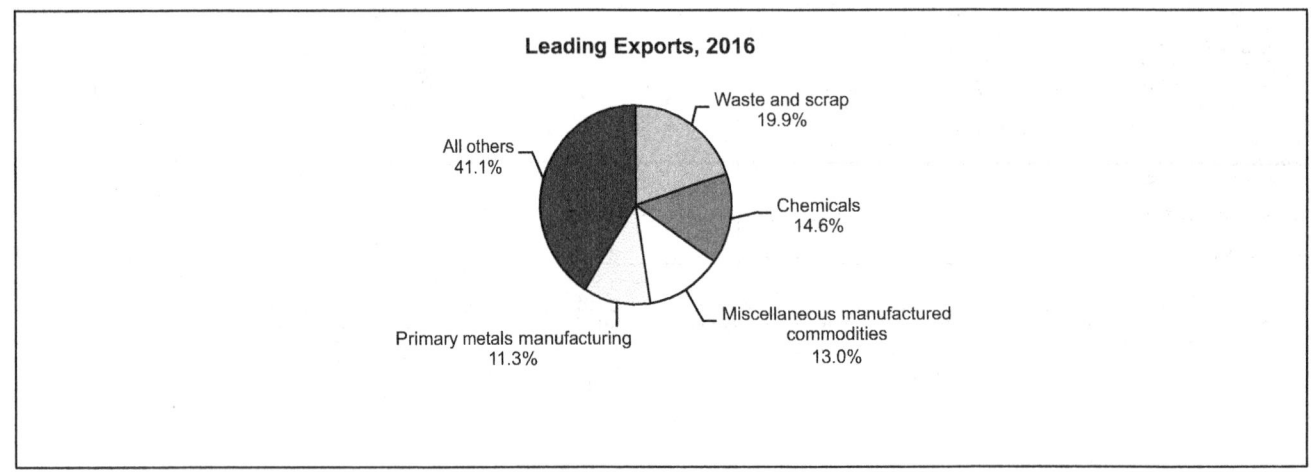

Leading Exports, 2016

Waste and scrap 19.9%
Chemicals 14.6%
Miscellaneous manufactured commodities 13.0%
Primary metals manufacturing 11.3%
All others 41.1%

Facts and Figures

Location: Southeastern United States; bordered on the N by North Carolina, on the E by the Atlantic Ocean, on the S by the Atlantic Ocean and Georgia, and on the W by Georgia

Area: 32,020 sq. mi. (82,932 sq. km.); rank—40th

Population: 4,961,119 (2016 est.); rank—23rd

Principal Cities: capital—Columbia; largest—Columbia

Statehood: May 23, 1788; 8th state

U.S. Congress: 2 senators, 7 representatives

State Mottoes: *Animis opibusque parati* ("Prepared in mind and resources"); *Dum spiro, spero* ("While I breathe, I hope")

State Songs: "Carolina"; "South Carolina on My Mind"

State Nickname: The Palmetto State

Abbreviations: SC; S.C.

State Symbols: flower—yellow jessamine; tree—cabbage palmetto; bird—Carolina wren

At a Glance

- With an increase in population of 7.3 percent, South Carolina ranked 11th among the states in growth from 2010 to 2016.

- South Carolina's median household income in 2015 was $47,238, and 16.6 percent of the population lived below the poverty level.

- South Carolina's violent crime rate in 2015 was 504.5 incidents per 100,000 population, which ranked 8th in the nation.

- In 2015, 10.9 percent of South Carolinians did not have health insurance, compared to 9.4 percent of the total U.S. population.

- South Carolina had the highest rate of traffic fatalities in the U.S. in 2015, with 1.89 deaths per 100 million vehicle miles driven.

Table SC-1. Population by Age, Sex, Race, and Hispanic Origin

(Number, percent, except where noted.)

Sex, age, race, and Hispanic origin	2000	2010	2016 [1]	Average annual percent change, 2010–2016
Total Population..	4,012,013	4,625,364	4,961,119	0.5
Percent of total U.S. population	1.4	1.5	1.5	X
Sex				
Male...	1,948,929	2,250,101	2,407,934	0.4
Female...	2,063,083	2,375,263	2,553,185	0.5
Age				
Under 5 years..	264,679	302,297	293,134	-0.2
5 to 19 years...	871,099	922,128	935,491	0.1
20 to 64 years..	2,390,901	2,769,065	2,902,262	0.3
65 years and over...	485,333	631,874	830,232	2.0
Median age (years)	35.4	37.9	39.2	0.2
Race and Hispanic Origin				
One race..				
White..	2,695,560	3,164,143	3,396,931	0.5
Black...	1,185,216	1,302,865	1,362,579	0.3
American Indian and Alaska Native	13,718	24,665	26,923	0.6
Asian...	36,014	61,247	79,941	1.9
Native Hawaiian or Other Pacific Islander	1,628	3,957	4,698	1.2
Two or more races..	39,950	68,487	90,047	2.0
Hispanic (of any race)...	95,076	243,923	274,596	0.8

X = Not applicable.

[1] Population figures for 2016 are July 1 estimates. The 2010 estimates are taken from the 2010 Census.

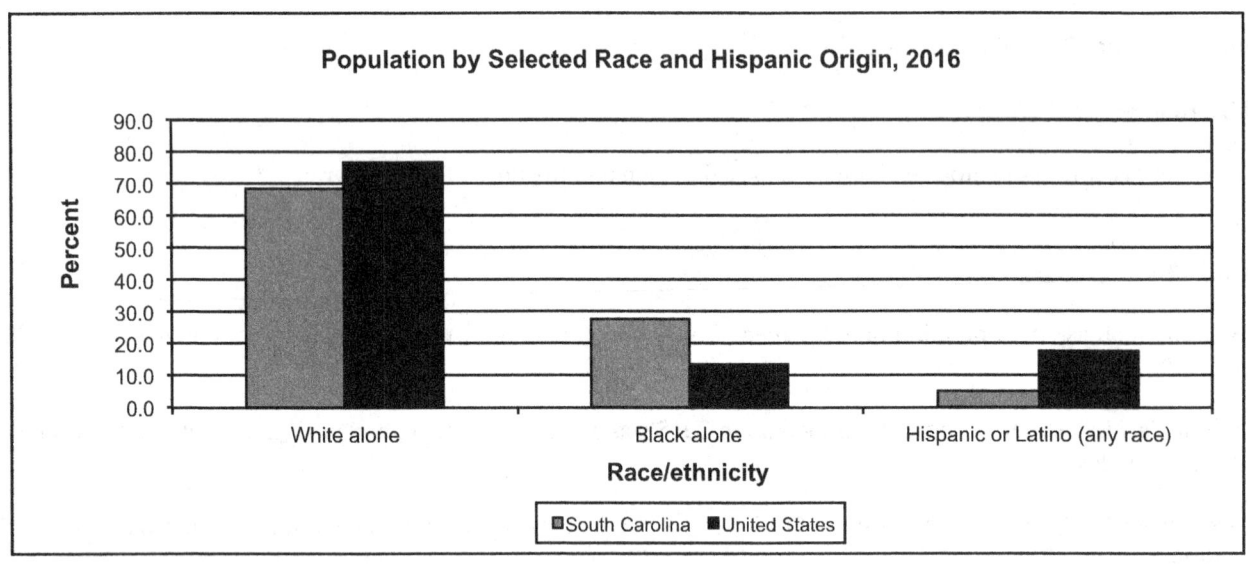

Table SC-2. Marital Status

(Number, percent distribution.)

Sex, age, race, and Hispanic origin	2000	2010	2015
Males, 15 Years and Over	1,516,125	1,797,441	1,925,137
Never married..	28.8	35.2	35.6
Now married, except separated...	57.3	49.4	48.7
Separated...	2.8	3.0	2.6
Widowed...	2.7	2.8	2.9
Divorced...	8.3	9.5	10.1
Females, 15 Years and Over	1,652,793	1,939,054	2,069,688
Never married..	23.4	29.1	29.8
Now married, except separated...	51.4	45.2	44.5
Separated...	3.8	3.9	3.6
Widowed...	11.5	10.6	10.2
Divorced...	9.9	11.2	11.9

Table SC-3. Households and Housing Characteristics

(Number, percent, dollars.)

Item	2000	2010	2015	Average annual percent change, 2000–2015
Total Households...	1,533,854	1,761,393	1,857,768	1.4
Family households..	1,072,822	1,180,687	1,220,885	0.9
Married-couple family................................	783,142	827,387	867,390	0.7
Other family...	289,680	353,300	353,495	1.5
Male householder, no wife present.............	62,722	77,062	81,853	2.0
Female householder, no husband present......	226,958	276,238	271,642	1.3
Nonfamily households...................................	461,032	580,706	636,883	2.5
Householder living alone............................	383,142	489,995	536,679	2.7
Householder not living alone.......................	77,890	90,711	100,204	1.9
Housing Characteristics				
Total housing units......................................	1,753,670	2,140,337	2,210,150	1.7
Occupied housing units	1,533,854	1,761,393	1,857,768	1.4
Owner occupied..	1,107,617	1,210,160	1,265,627	1.0
Renter occupied.......................................	426,237	551,233	592,141	2.6
Average household size.................................	2.53	2.55	2.56	0.1
Financial Characteristics				
Median gross rent of renter-occupied housing	510	728	819	4.0
Median monthly owner costs for housing units with a mortgage	894	1,177	1,168	2.0
Median value of owner-occupied housing units...........................	94,900	138,100	148,600	3.8

Table SC-4. Migration, Origin, and Language

(Number, percent.)

Characteristic	State 2014	State 2015	Percent change	U.S. 2014	U.S. 2015	Percent change
Residence 1 Year Ago						
Population 1 year and over..........................	4,780,659	4,839,984	1.2	315,095,393	317,635,720	0.8
Same house	84.6	84.8	X	85.1	85.3	X
Different house in the U.S.	15.0	14.7	X	14.3	14.1	X
Same county	8.2	8.1	X	8.7	8.5	X
Different county	6.8	6.7	X	5.6	5.6	X
Same state	3.2	3.1	X	3.3	3.2	X
Different state	3.6	3.5	X	2.3	2.4	X
Abroad	0.4	0.4	X	0.6	0.7	X
Place of Birth						
Native born	4,603,929	4,663,397	1.3	276,465,262	278,128,449	0.6
Male	48.5	48.6	X	49.3	49.3	X
Female	51.5	51.4	X	50.7	50.7	X
Foreign born	228,553	232,749	1.8	42,391,794	43,290,372	2.1
Male	51.7	51.4	X	48.7	48.6	X
Female	48.3	48.6	X	51.3	51.4	X
Foreign born; naturalized U.S. citizen............	86,647	92,001	6.2	19,984,738	20,697,103	3.6
Male	46.0	46.5	X	45.9	45.9	X
Female	54.0	53.5	X	54.1	54.1	X
Foreign born; not a U.S. citizen....................	141,906	140,748	-0.8	22,407,056	22,593,269	0.8
Male	55.1	54.5	X	51.2	51.1	X
Female	44.9	45.5	X	48.8	48.9	X
Entered 2010 or later	16.5	18.1	X	12.3	15.6	X
Entered 2000 to 2009	33.9	34.9	X	28.6	27.9	X
Entered before 2000	49.6	47.0	X	59.1	56.5	X
World Region of Birth, Foreign						
Foreign-born population, excluding population born at sea	228,553	232,749	1.8	42,390,705	43,289,646	2.1
Europe	16.2	15.8	X	11.2	11.1	X
Asia	23.5	25.1	X	30.1	30.6	X
Africa	5.1	3.8	X	4.6	4.8	X
Oceania	1.0	1.0	X	0.6	0.6	X
Latin America..	51.4	51.0	X	51.6	51.1	X
North America..	2.9	3.4	X	1.9	1.9	X
Language Spoken at Home and Ability to Speak English						
Population 5 years and over...........................	4,545,554	4,608,658	1.4	299,084,046	301,625,014	0.8
English only	93.2	93.2	X	78.9	78.5	X
Language other than English........................	6.8	6.8	X	21.1	21.5	X
Speaks English less than "very well"..............	2.9	2.7	X	8.6	8.6	X

NA = Not available.
X = Not applicable.
- = Zero or rounds to zero.

Table SC-5. Median Income and Poverty Status, 2015

(Number, percent, except as noted.)

Characteristic	State		U.S.	
	Number	Percent	Number	Percent
Median Income				
Households (dollars)..	47,238	X	55,775	X
Families (dollars)	59,282	X	68,260	X
Below Poverty Level (All People)	790,715	16.6	46,153,077	14.7
Sex				
Male	345,502	15.1	20,599,407	13.4
Female	445,213	18.1	25,553,670	16.0
Age				
Under 18 years..	256,179	24.0	15,000,273	20.7
Related children under 18 years..............................	253,279	23.8	14,693,239	20.4
18 to 64 years..	462,522	15.9	26,960,369	13.9
65 years and over	72,014	9.3	4,192,435	9.0

X = Not applicable.

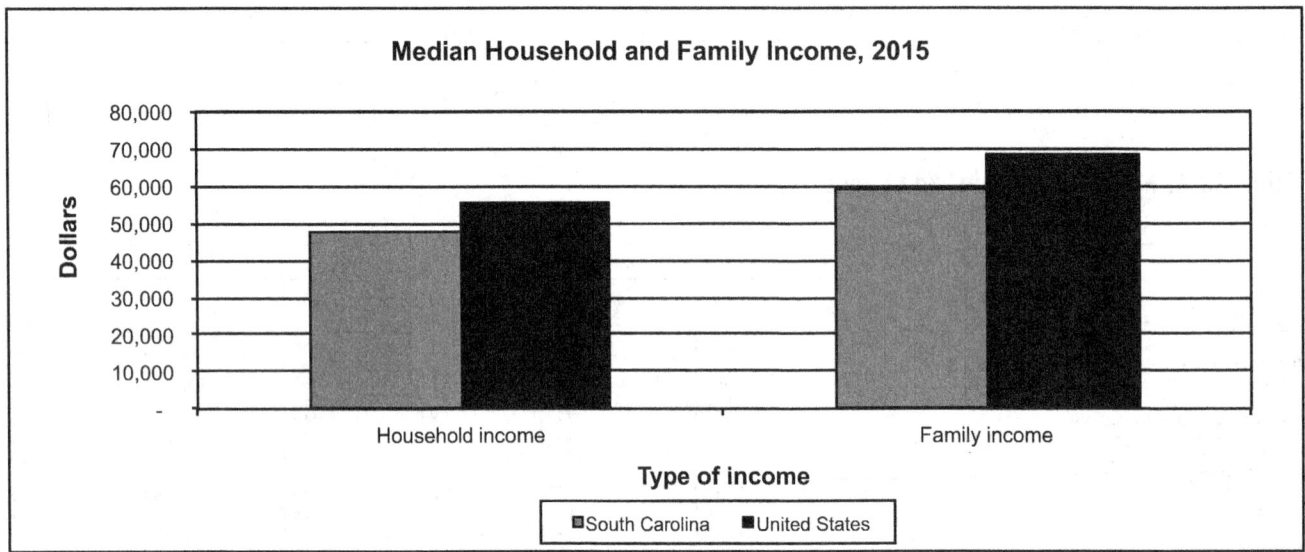

Table SC-6. Health Insurance Coverage Status for the Civilian Noninstitutionalized Population and Children Under 18 Years of Age

(Numbers in thousands, percent.)

Item	2007	2008	2009	2010	2011	2012	2013	2014	2015
Civilian Noninstitutionalized Population	4,384	4,373	4,454	4,537	4,579	4,623	4,678	4,734	4,801
Covered by Private or Public Insurance									
Number...	3,664	3,612	3,705	3,742	3,813	3,845	3,939	4,092	4,278
Percent...	83.6	82.6	83.2	82.5	83.3	83.2	84.2	86.4	89.1
Not Covered									
Number...	721	761	750	795	766	778	739	642	523
Percent...	16.4	17.4	16.8	17.5	16.7	16.8	15.8	13.6	10.9
Percent in the U.S. not covered...............................	15.3	15.1	15.1	15.5	15.1	14.8	14.5	11.7	9.4
Children Under 18 Years of Age	1,070	1,064	1,078	1,078	1,079	1,078	1,077	1,081	1,087
Covered by Private or Public Insurance									
Number...	918	930	971	976	988	989	1,004	1,021	1,042
Percent...	85.8	87.4	90.0	90.6	91.6	91.7	93.3	94.5	95.9
Not Covered									
Number...	152	134	107	102	91	89	73	60	44
Percent...	14.2	12.6	10.0	9.4	8.4	8.3	6.7	5.5	4.1
Percent in the U.S. not covered...............................	11.0	9.7	8.6	8.0	7.5	7.2	7.1	6.0	4.8

Table SC-7. Employment Status by Demographic Group, 2016

(Numbers in thousands, percent.)

Characteristic	Civilian noninstitutional population	Civilian labor force		Employed		Unemployed	
		Number	Percent of population	Number	Percent of population	Number	Percent of population
Total...	3,880	2,316	59.7	2,203	56.8	113	4.9
Sex							
Male...	1,832	1,188	64.9	1,122	61.3	66	5.6
Female..	2,048	1,127	55.1	1,081	52.8	47	4.2
Race, Sex, and Hispanic Origin							
White..	2,737	1,641	60.0	1,575	57.5	66	4.0
Male..	1,327	878	66.2	840	63.3	39	4.4
Female..	1,410	763	54.1	735	52.1	28	3.6
Black or African American.........................	1,018	599	58.8	554	54.4	45	7.5
Male..	453	274	60.5	247	54.6	27	9.8
Female..	565	324	57.4	307	54.3	18	5.5
Hispanic or Latino ethnicity[1]	181	129	71.2	124	68.7	5	3.6
Male..	99	83	83.5	81	81.0	2	2.9
Female..	NA	NA	NA	NA	NA	NA	NA
Age							
16 to 19 years......................................	237	78	33.1	67	28.5	11	14.0
20 to 24 years......................................	290	208	71.9	189	65.3	19	9.2
25 to 34 years......................................	646	518	80.2	490	75.9	28	5.4
35 to 44 years......................................	602	508	84.3	487	80.8	21	4.2
45 to 54 years......................................	647	482	74.4	466	72.0	16	3.3
55 to 64 years......................................	662	396	59.8	383	57.8	13	3.4
65 years and over..................................	796	125	15.7	121	15.2	4	3.4

NOTE: Data in Table 7 are from the Current Population Survey (CPS) and do not match the estimates in Table 8. See notes and definitions for further information.
[1] May be of any race.

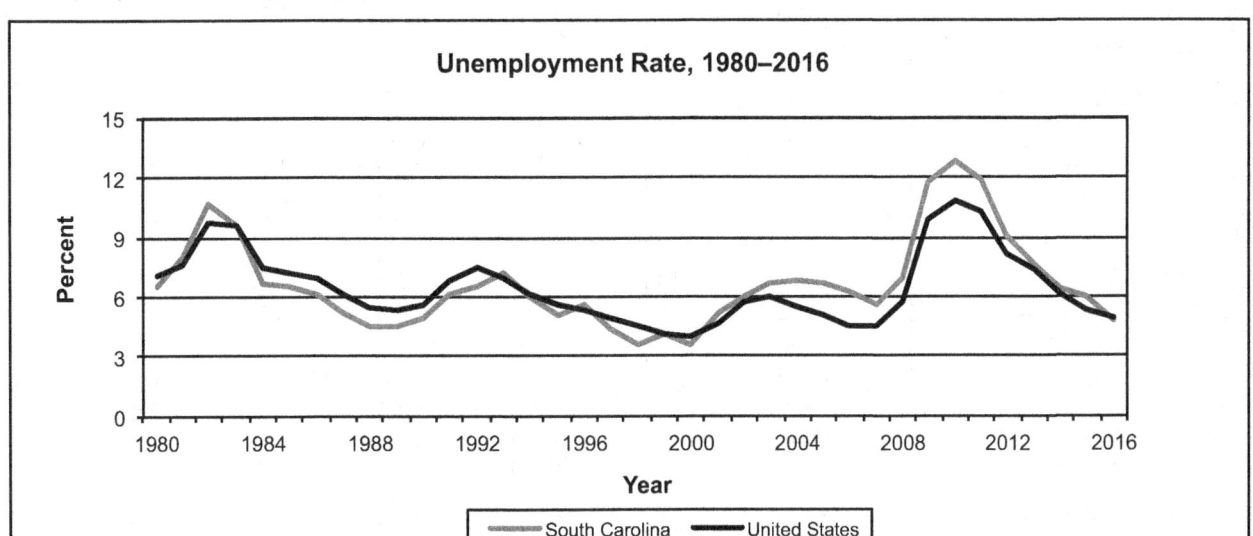

Unemployment Rate, 1980–2016

Table SC-8. Employment Status of the Civilian Noninstitutional Population Age 16 Years and Over

(Number, percent.)

Year	Civilian labor force	Civilian participation rate	Employed	Unemployed	Unemployment rate
2008..	2,142,232	62.3	1,996,409	145,823	6.8
2009..	2,152,745	61.7	1,910,670	242,075	11.2
2010..	2,155,668	60.5	1,915,045	240,623	11.2
2011..	2,175,523	60.2	1,945,900	229,623	10.6
2012..	2,184,113	59.7	1,983,506	200,607	9.2
2013..	2,189,368	59.1	2,022,444	166,924	7.6
2014..	2,216,782	58.9	2,074,277	142,505	6.4
2015..	2,257,077	59.0	2,122,573	134,504	6.0
2016..	2,297,807	59.1	2,186,740	111,067	4.8

Table SC-9. Employment and Average Wages by Industry

(Estimates through 2010 are based on the 2007 *North American Industry Classification System* [NAICS]. Estimates from 2011 onward are based on the 2012 NAICS.)

Industry	2009	2010	2011	2012	2013	2014	2015
	Number of jobs						
Wage and Salary Employment by Industry..................	1,910,184	1,893,730	1,914,988	1,948,461	1,986,153	2,033,961	2,089,696
Farm Wage and Salary Employment........................	7,860	6,516	6,818	6,839	7,785	6,085	7,511
Nonfarm Wage and Salary Employment....................	1,902,324	1,887,214	1,908,170	1,941,622	1,978,368	2,027,876	2,082,185
Private wage and salary employment...................	1,499,967	1,489,053	1,516,171	1,546,120	1,579,045	1,627,358	1,676,529
Forestry, fishing, and related activities........................	6,783	6,969	6,956	6,788	6,985	7,090	7,217
Mining..................	1,340	1,244	1,233	1,194	1,141	1,157	1,237
Utilities..................	12,437	12,045	11,919	12,134	12,212	12,349	12,348
Construction..................	92,454	82,725	79,200	79,917	82,269	84,960	89,140
Manufacturing..................	214,792	208,218	216,506	221,565	225,157	230,606	236,292
Durable goods manufacturing..................	118,300	114,252	121,053	126,092	129,343	133,648	137,664
Nondurable goods manufacturing..................	96,492	93,966	95,453	95,473	95,814	96,958	98,628
Wholesale trade..................	65,674	64,002	64,839	65,968	66,736	68,475	71,098
Retail trade..................	227,172	225,247	227,520	228,228	232,852	238,915	243,483
Transportation and warehousing..................	47,672	46,695	48,112	50,228	52,711	56,561	60,751
Information..................	27,227	25,849	25,898	25,782	26,431	26,468	26,961
Finance and insurance..................	70,184	68,631	68,662	69,519	70,593	70,410	70,805
Real estate and rental and leasing..................	28,605	26,555	26,246	25,968	26,808	27,841	28,730
Professional, scientific, and technical services..............	74,276	75,363	79,777	80,404	82,512	85,644	88,999
Management of companies and enterprises..................	14,523	14,302	15,060	15,890	16,489	17,042	16,678
Administrative and waste services..................	115,344	128,991	136,229	141,908	144,982	153,489	158,091
Educational services..................	28,262	29,068	29,771	30,408	30,766	32,094	32,623
Health care and social assistance..................	168,487	172,670	174,493	177,766	181,144	186,040	193,152
Arts, entertainment, and recreation..................	27,041	26,104	26,540	26,925	27,467	28,178	29,154
Accommodation and food services..................	183,910	182,600	185,411	191,160	196,777	202,176	211,109
Other services, except public administration..................	93,784	91,775	91,799	94,368	95,013	97,863	98,661
Government and government enterprises..................	402,357	398,161	391,999	395,502	399,323	400,518	405,656
	Dollars						
Average Wages and Salaries by Industry	37,763	38,744	39,660	40,568	41,030	42,032	43,223
Average Farm Wages and Salaries	18,426	22,862	18,819	27,893	19,497	23,973	26,451
Average Nonfarm Wages and Salaries	37,843	38,799	39,734	40,613	41,115	42,086	43,284
Average private wages and salaries..................	36,713	37,874	38,899	39,852	40,326	41,353	42,565
Forestry, fishing, and related activities..................	29,288	31,339	31,412	32,821	33,417	35,096	35,973
Mining..................	43,021	48,069	50,693	53,295	55,280	57,723	69,375
Utilities..................	73,910	78,467	80,476	81,359	84,787	87,517	92,254
Construction..................	40,494	41,966	42,924	44,652	45,391	47,206	48,854
Manufacturing..................	48,757	51,213	52,826	54,010	54,946	56,942	58,320
Durable goods manufacturing..................	50,340	53,305	55,296	56,367	57,308	59,783	60,779
Nondurable goods manufacturing..................	46,816	48,670	49,693	50,895	51,759	53,025	54,888
Wholesale trade..................	54,547	56,032	58,169	60,469	61,250	63,889	65,479
Retail trade..................	24,805	25,444	25,493	25,932	26,208	26,480	27,170
Transportation and warehousing..................	38,961	40,407	41,085	41,985	41,871	42,405	43,345
Information..................	50,807	52,156	52,169	53,764	55,522	57,917	59,102
Finance and insurance..................	53,880	55,040	57,379	59,410	60,478	61,779	64,839
Real estate and rental and leasing..................	33,497	34,622	36,197	37,772	39,105	40,789	42,333
Professional, scientific, and technical services..............	57,679	59,895	61,264	63,738	64,093	65,665	67,613
Management of companies and enterprises..................	65,731	66,808	69,614	72,730	71,579	71,896	74,345
Administrative and waste services..................	32,074	32,834	33,706	33,429	32,883	33,536	34,096
Educational services..................	27,627	27,885	28,713	29,372	29,990	30,565	30,885
Health care and social assistance..................	39,979	41,315	42,285	43,250	43,661	44,820	46,285
Arts, entertainment, and recreation..................	20,055	20,290	20,964	21,158	21,022	21,380	22,454
Accommodation and food services..................	16,337	16,917	17,364	18,005	18,275	18,578	19,273
Other services, except public administration..................	26,411	27,468	28,051	28,366	29,633	30,307	31,604
Government and government enterprises..................	42,055	42,256	42,964	43,588	44,234	45,064	46,254

Table SC-10. Employment Characteristics by Family Type

(Number, percent.)

Family type and labor force status	2013 Total	2013 Families with own children under 18 years	2014 Total	2014 Families with own children under 18 years	2015 Total	2015 Families with own children under 18 years
All Families....................................	1,195,104	479,885	1,197,456	463,567	1,220,885	475,168
FAMILY TYPE AND LABOR FORCE STATUS						
Married-Couple Families........................	840,762	298,898	843,169	284,325	867,390	299,238
Both husband and wife in labor force..............	47.8	66.4	47.5	66.6	47.1	66.4
Husband in labor force, wife not in labor force..........	21.3	26.1	21.8	27.5	21.7	27.6
Wife in labor force, husband not in labor force..........	9.4	4.8	8.5	4.4	8.4	3.7
Both husband and wife not in labor force.............	21.2	2.5	22.2	1.5	22.3	2.1
Other Families	354,342	180,987	354,287	179,242	353,495	175,930
Female householder, no husband present................	77.1	80.1	76.5	79.5	76.8	79.5
In labor force.................................	52.2	65.8	50.8	65.6	52.3	65.8
Not in labor force.............................	24.9	14.2	25.7	13.9	24.5	13.8
Male householder, no wife present..................	22.9	19.9	23.5	20.5	23.2	20.5
In labor force.................................	16.7	17.9	17.5	18.4	17.2	18.6
Not in labor force	6.2	2.0	6.1	2.0	5.9	1.8

Table SC-11. School Enrollment and Educational Attainment, 2015

(Number, percent.)

Item	State	U.S.
Enrollment		
Total population 3 years and over, enrolled in school	1,198,207	81,618,288
Enrolled in nursery school or preschool (percent)	5.0	6.0
Enrolled in kindergarten (percent)................................	6.1	5.0
Enrolled in elementary school, grades 1-8 (percent)...................	40.8	40.3
Enrolled in high school, grades 9-12 (percent)	21.5	20.9
Enrolled in college or graduate school (percent)......................	26.5	27.7
Attainment		
Total population 25 years and over	3,319,832	216,447,163
Less than ninth grade (percent)	4.4	5.5
9th to 12th grade, no diploma (percent)	9.2	7.3
High school graduate, including equivalency (percent)...................	29.4	27.6
Some college, no degree (percent)	20.7	20.7
Associate's degree (percent)	9.4	8.2
Bachelor's degree (percent)	17.3	19.0
Graduate or professional degree (percent)...........................	9.5	11.6
High school graduate or higher (percent)	86.3	87.1
Bachelor's degree or higher (percent).............................	26.8	30.6

Table SC-12. Public School Characteristics and Educational Indicators

(Number, percent; data derived from National Center of Education Statistics.)

Item	State	U.S.
Public Schools, 2014–2015 (except where noted)		
Number of school districts...	102	18,260
Number of schools...	1,244	98,373
Number of students	756,523	50,312,581
Number of teachers	49,475	3,132,351
Student-teacher ratio	15.3	16.1
Expenditures per student (dollars), FY 2014.........................	9,608	11,066
Four-year adjusted cohort graduation rate (ACGR)[1,2]	80.3	83.2
Students eligible for free or reduced-price lunch (percent)...............	55.9	51.8
English language learners (percent).................................	5.7	9.4
Students age 3 to 21 served under IDEA, part B (percent)................	13.1	13.0

Public Schools by Type	Number	Percent of state public schools
Total number of schools...	1,244	100.0
Regular	1,181	94.9
Special education	9	0.7
Vocational education	42	3.4
Alternative education...	12	1.0

NOTE: Every school is assigned only one school type based on its instructional emphasis.
[1] ACGR data represents a new method of calculating high-school completion rates and may not be comparable to previous years' data for Averaged Freshmen Graduation Rates (AFGR).
[2] The United States 4-year ACGRs were estimated using both the reported 4-year ACGR data from 49 states and the District of Columbia and using imputed data for Idaho. The estimate for American Indian/Alaska Native students also includes imputed data for Virginia.

Table SC-13. Reported Voting and Registration of the Voting-Age Population, November 2016

(Numbers in thousands, percent.)

Item	Total population	Total citizen population	Registered				Voted		
			Total registered	Percent registered (total population)	Percent registered (total citizen population)		Total voted	Percent voted (total population)	Percent voted (total citizen population)
U.S. Total	245,502	224,059	157,596	64.2	70.3		137,537	56.0	61.4
State Total................................	3,733	3,598	2,575	69.0	71.6		2,233	59.8	62.1
Sex									
Male	1,774	1,709	1,145	64.6	67.0		992	55.9	58.0
Female	1,959	1,889	1,430	73.0	75.7		1,241	63.4	65.7
Race									
White alone..............................	2,621	2,516	1,760	67.1	70.0		1,529	58.3	60.8
White, non-Hispanic alone	2,477	2,459	1,736	70.1	70.6		1,513	61.1	61.5
Black alone...............................	975	964	720	73.8	74.6		628	64.4	65.2
Asian alone	62	48	35	(B)	(B)		29	(B)	(B)
Hispanic (of any race).................	175	76	39	(B)	(B)		31	(B)	(B)
White alone or in combination	2,662	2,557	1,795	67.4	70.2		1,554	58.4	60.8
Black alone or in combination...........	997	986	735	73.8	74.6		640	64.3	65.0
Asian alone or in combination...........	62	48	35	(B)	(B)		29	(B)	(B)
Age									
18 to 24 years...........................	341	332	185	54.5	55.9		146	42.7	43.9
25 to 34 years...........................	635	585	366	57.7	62.6		288	45.4	49.3
35 to 44 years...........................	642	587	409	63.7	69.7		346	53.9	58.9
45 to 64 years...........................	1,301	1,281	951	73.1	74.2		860	66.1	67.1
65 years and over	815	812	663	81.3	81.6		594	72.9	73.1

B = Base is less than 75,000 and therefore too small to show the derived measure.

Table SC-14. Crime

(Number, rate per 100,000. Data are derived from the FBI Uniform Crime Reports.)

Item	State			U.S. [1,2,3,4]		
	2014	2015	Percent change	2014	2015	Percent change
TOTAL POPULATION[5]	4,829,160	4,896,146	1.4	318,907,401	321,418,820	0.8
VIOLENT CRIME						
Number..	24,038	24,700	2.8	1,186,185	1,231,566	3.8
Rate	497.8	504.5	1.3	372.0	383.2	3.0
Murder and Nonnegligent Manslaughter						
Number..	322	399	23.9	14,164	15,696	10.8
Rate	6.7	8.1	22.2	4.4	4.9	10.0
Rape[6]						
Number..	2,185	2,297	5.1	118,027	124,047	5.1
Rate	45.2	46.9	3.7	37.0	38.6	4.3
Robbery						
Number..	4,018	3,931	-2.2	322,905	327,374	1.4
Rate	83.2	80.3	-3.5	101.3	101.9	0.6
Aggravated Assault						
Number..	17,513	18,073	3.2	731,089	764,449	4.6
Rate	362.7	369.1	1.8	229.2	237.8	3.7
PROPERTY CRIME						
Number..	168,281	161,245	-4.2	8,209,010	7,993,631	-2.6
Rate	3,484.7	3,293.3	-5.5	2,574.1	2,487.0	-3.4
Burglary						
Number..	37,163	34,551	-7.0	1,713,153	1,579,527	-7.8
Rate	769.6	705.7	-8.3	537.2	491.4	-8.5
Larceny-Theft						
Number..	118,173	113,724	-3.8	5,809,054	5,706,346	-1.8
Rate	2,447.1	2,322.7	-5.1	1,821.5	1,775.4	-2.5
Motor Vehicle Theft						
Number..	12,945	12,970	0.2	686,803	707,758	3.1
Rate	268.1	264.9	-1.2	215.4	220.2	2.2

NOTE: Although arson data are included in the trend and clearance tables, sufficient data are not available to estimate totals for this offense. Therefore, no arson data are published in this table.
X = Not applicable.
- = Zero or rounds to zero.
[1] The crime figures have been adjusted.
[2] The data collection methodology for the offense of forcible rape used by the Minnesota state Uniform Crime Reporting (UCR) Program (with the exception of Minneapolis and St. Paul, Minnesota) does not comply with national UCR Program guidelines. Consequently, its figures for forcible rape and violent crime (of which forcible rape is a part) are not published in this table.
[3] Includes offenses reported by the Zoological Police and the Metro Transit Police.
[4] Because of changes in the state's reporting practices, figures are not comparable to previous years' data.
[5] Populations are U.S. Census Bureau provisional estimates as of July 1 of each year.
[6] The figures shown for the offense of rape were estimated using the revised Uniform Crime Reporting (UCR) definition of rape.

Table SC-15. State Government Finances, 2015

(Dollar amounts in thousands, percent distribution.)

Item	Dollars	Percent distribution
Total Revenue	29,546,888	100.0
General revenue	24,695,871	83.6
Intergovernmental revenue	8,443,093	28.6
Taxes	9,620,534	32.6
General sales	3,568,788	12.1
Selective sales	1,322,830	4.5
License taxes	524,285	1.8
Individual income tax	3,695,701	12.5
Corporate income tax	410,931	1.4
Other taxes	97,999	0.3
Current charges	4,760,058	16.1
Miscellaneous general revenue	1,872,186	6.3
Utility revenue	1,983,216	6.7
Liquor stores revenue	0	-
Insurance trust revenue[1]	2,867,801	9.7
Total Expenditure	30,551,967	100.0
Intergovernmental expenditure	5,955,882	19.5
Direct expenditure	24,596,085	80.5
Current operation	18,212,302	59.6
Capital outlay	1,343,941	4.4
Insurance benefits and repayments	3,302,627	10.8
Assistance and subsidies	1,105,484	3.6
Interest on debt	631,731	2.1
Exhibit: Salaries and wages	3,872,842	12.7
Total Expenditure	30,551,967	100.0
General expenditure	25,421,331	83.2
Intergovernmental expenditure	5,955,882	19.5
Direct expenditure	19,465,449	63.7
General expenditure, by function:		
Education	9,225,130	30.2
Public welfare	7,398,432	24.2
Hospitals	1,657,101	5.4
Health	1,132,870	3.7
Highways	1,259,022	4.1
Police protection	174,707	0.6
Correction	510,461	1.7
Natural resources	211,338	0.7
Parks and recreation	111,859	0.4
Governmental administration	631,923	2.1
Interest on general debt	357,902	1.2
Other and unallocable	2,750,586	9.0
Utility expenditure	1,828,009	6.0
Liquor stores expenditure	0	-
Insurance trust expenditure	3,302,627	10.8
Debt at End of Fiscal Year	15,122,266	X
Cash and Security Holdings	40,178,972	X

X = Not applicable.
- = Zero or rounds to zero.
[1] Within insurance trust revenue, net earnings of state retirement systems is a calculated statistic (the item code in the data file is X08), and thus can be positive or negative. Net earnings is the sum of earnings on investments plus gains on investments minus losses on investments. The change made in 2002 for asset valuation from book to market value in accordance with Statement 34 of the Governmental Accounting Standards Board is reflected in the calculated statistics.

Table SC-16. State Government Tax Collections, 2016

(Dollars in thousands, percent.)

Item	Dollars	Percent distribution
Total Taxes	9,551,052	100.0
Property taxes	32,670	0.3
Sales and gross receipts	4,620,807	48.4
General sales and gross receipts	3,268,415	34.2
Selective sales and gross receipts	1,352,392	14.2
Alcoholic beverages	173,138	1.8
Amusements	42,530	0.4
Insurance premiums	246,059	2.6
Motor fuels	565,405	5.9
Pari-mutuels	0	-
Public utilities	29,158	0.3
Tobacco products	27,264	0.3
Other selective sales	268,838	2.8
Licenses	499,053	5.2
Alcoholic beverages	12,591	0.1
Amusements	1,266	-
Corporations in general	88,702	0.9
Hunting and fishing	18,284	0.2
Motor vehicle	240,551	2.5
Motor vehicle operators	8,686	0.1
Public utilities	10,487	0.1
Occupation and business, NEC	100,076	1.0
Other licenses	18,410	0.2
Income taxes	4,309,831	45.1
Individual income	3,869,342	40.5
Corporation net income	440,489	4.6
Other taxes	88,691	0.9
Death and gift	0	-
Documentary and stock transfer	88,691	0.9
Severance	0	-
Taxes, NEC	0	-

X = Not applicable.
- = Zero or rounds to zero.

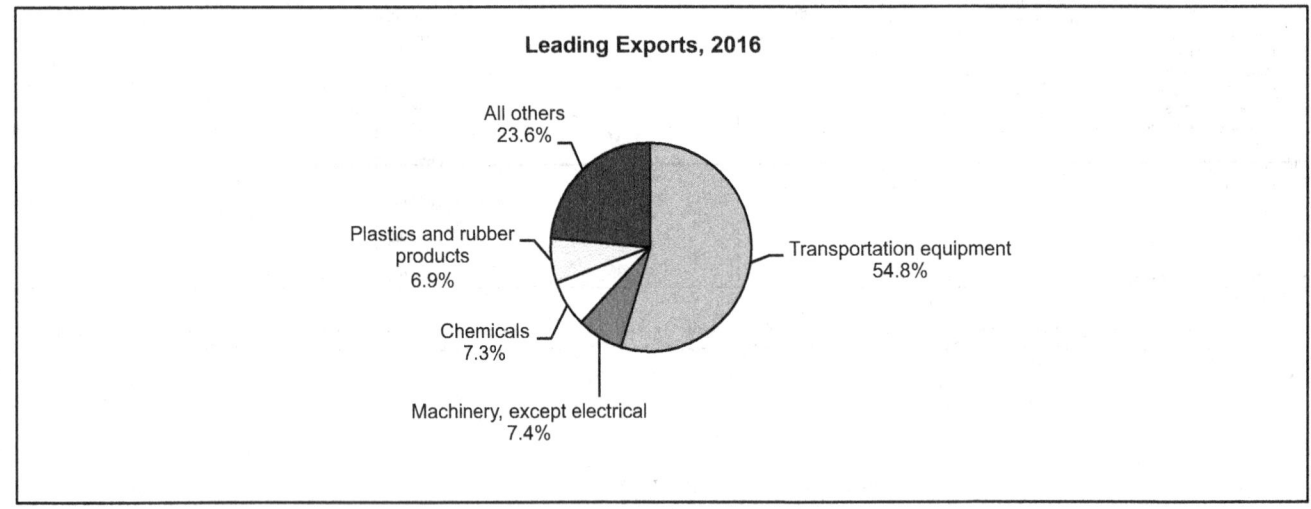

Leading Exports, 2016

All others 23.6%
Plastics and rubber products 6.9%
Chemicals 7.3%
Machinery, except electrical 7.4%
Transportation equipment 54.8%

SOUTH DAKOTA

Facts and Figures

Location: North central United States; bordered on the N by North Dakota, on the E by Minnesota and Iowa, on the S by Nebraska, and on the W by Wyoming and Montana

Area: 77,117 sq. mi. (199,731 sq. km.); rank—17th

Population: 865,454 (2016 est.); rank—46th

Principal Cities: capital—Pierre; largest—Sioux Falls

Statehood: November 2, 1889; 40th state

U.S. Congress: 2 senators, 1 representative

State Motto: Under God the People Rule

State Song: "Hail, South Dakota"

State Nickname: The Mount Rushmore State

Abbreviations: SD; S.D.; S. Dak.

State Symbols: flower—pasqueflower; tree—Black Hills spruce; bird—ring-necked pheasant

At a Glance

- With an increase in population of 6.3 percent, South Dakota ranked 15th among the states in growth from 2010 to 2016.

- In 2015, 10.2 percent of South Dakotans did not have health insurance, compared to 9.4 percent of the total U.S. population.

- South Dakota's violent crime rate in 2015 was 383.1 incidents per 100,000 population, compared to 383.2 for the entire nation.

- South Dakota's median income in 2014 was $53,017, and 13.7 percent of its residents lived below the poverty level.

- In 2015, South Dakota had the lowest unemployment rate in the country, with 2.8 percent of the population unemployed.

Table SD-1. Population by Age, Sex, Race, and Hispanic Origin

(Number, percent, except where noted.)

Sex, age, race, and Hispanic origin	2000	2010	2016 [1]	Average annual percent change, 2010–2016
Total Population...	754,844	814,180	865,454	0.4
Percent of total U.S. population	0.4	0.3	0.3	X
Sex				
Male..................	374,558	407,381	436,272	0.4
Female	380,286	406,799	429,182	0.3
Age				
Under 5 years..................................	51,069	59,621	61,369	0.2
5 to 19 years...	176,412	167,119	175,157	0.3
20 to 64 years...	419,232	470,859	490,123	0.3
65 years and over...	108,131	116,581	138,805	1.2
Median age (years)	35.6	36.9	37.0	-
Race and Hispanic Origin				
One race..				
White	669,404	706,690	737,070	0.3
Black..	4,685	10,533	17,302	4.0
American Indian and Alaska Native	62,283	72,782	77,711	0.4
Asian..	4,378	7,775	12,767	4.0
Native Hawaiian or Other Pacific Islander	261	517	656	1.7
Two or more races	10,156	15,883	19,948	1.6
Hispanic (of any race)...................................	10,903	23,699	32,169	2.2

X = Not applicable.
[1] Population figures for 2016 are July 1 estimates. The 2010 estimates are taken from the 2010 Census.
- = Zero or rounds to zero.

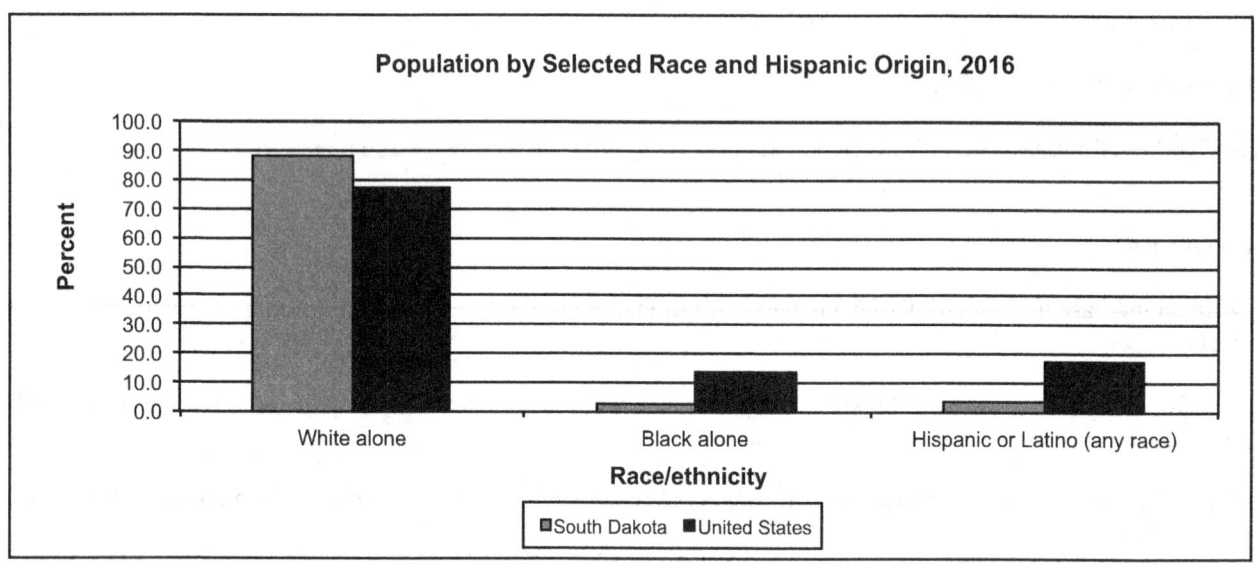

Population by Selected Race and Hispanic Origin, 2016

Table SD-2. Marital Status

(Number, percent distribution.)

Sex, age, race, and Hispanic origin	2000	2010	2015
Males, 15 Years and Over......................................	289,858	322,689	341,300
Never married	29.8	33.5	34.3
Now married, except separated................................	58.2	52.5	52.1
Separated..	1.0	0.9	1.1
Widowed..	2.4	2.8	2.8
Divorced...	8.5	10.3	9.8
Females, 15 Years and Over	299,754	325,640	341,534
Never married	22.5	26.0	26.5
Now married, except separated................................	55.9	52.1	52.0
Separated..	1.1	1.0	1.3
Widowed..	11.4	9.5	9.2
Divorced...	9.0	11.4	11.0

Table SD-3. Households and Housing Characteristics

(Number, percent, dollars.)

Item	2000	2010	2015	Average annual percent change, 2000–2015
Total Households...	290,245	318,955	339,437	1.1
Family households..	194,330	204,029	217,013	0.8
Married-couple family...................................	157,391	161,534	170,511	0.6
Other family...	36,939	42,495	46,502	1.7
Male householder, no wife present...............	10,734	12,526	14,182	2.1
Female householder, no husband present.......	26,205	29,969	32,320	1.6
Nonfamily households......................................	95,915	114,926	122,424	1.8
Householder living alone................................	80,040	95,610	100,383	1.7
Householder not living alone..........................	15,875	19,316	22,041	2.6
Housing Characteristics				
Total housing units..	323,208	364,031	380,307	1.2
Occupied housing units	290,245	318,955	339,437	1.1
Owner occupied..	197,940	216,821	231,452	1.1
Renter occupied..	92,305	102,134	107,985	1.1
Average household size....................................	2.50	2.45	2.43	-0.2
Financial Characteristics				
Median gross rent of renter-occupied housing	426	591	675	3.9
Median monthly owner costs for housing units with a mortgage	828	1,151	1,225	3.2
Median value of owner-occupied housing units..	79,600	129,700	152,800	6.1

Table SD-4. Migration, Origin, and Language

(Number, percent.)

Characteristic	State			U.S.		
	2014	2015	Percent change	2014	2015	Percent change
Residence 1 Year Ago						
Population 1 year and over	842,076	848,285	0.7	315,095,393	317,635,720	0.8
Same house	83.3	82.8	X	85.1	85.3	X
Different house in the U.S.	16.4	16.9	X	14.3	14.1	X
Same county	8.6	8.7	X	8.7	8.5	X
Different county	7.8	8.2	X	5.6	5.6	X
Same state	4.4	5.1	X	3.3	3.2	X
Different state	3.3	3.2	X	2.3	2.4	X
Abroad	0.4	0.3	X	0.6	0.7	X
Place of Birth						
Native born	828,548	830,624	0.3	276,465,262	278,128,449	0.6
Male	50.1	50.3	X	49.3	49.3	X
Female	49.9	49.7	X	50.7	50.7	X
Foreign born	24,627	27,845	13.1	42,391,794	43,290,372	2.1
Male	49.4	49.7	X	48.7	48.6	X
Female	50.6	50.3	X	51.3	51.4	X
Foreign born; naturalized U.S. citizen.................................	11,301	10,426	-7.7	19,984,738	20,697,103	3.6
Male	49.1	41.4	X	45.9	45.9	X
Female	50.9	58.6	X	54.1	54.1	X
Foreign born; not a U.S. citizen...	13,326	17,419	30.7	22,407,056	22,593,269	0.8
Male	49.6	54.7	X	51.2	51.1	X
Female	50.4	45.3	X	48.8	48.9	X
Entered 2010 or later	24.0	26.6	X	12.3	15.6	X
Entered 2000 to 2009	36.0	40.1	X	28.6	27.9	X
Entered before 2000...	40.0	33.3	X	59.1	56.5	X
World Region of Birth, Foreign						
Foreign-born population, excluding population born at sea	24,627	27,845	13.1	42,390,705	43,289,646	2.1
Europe	12.8	17.5	X	11.2	11.1	X
Asia...	37.6	38.6	X	30.1	30.6	X
Africa	23.3	18.7	X	4.6	4.8	X
Oceania	0.4	0.5	X	0.6	0.6	X
Latin America...	20.7	20.2	X	51.6	51.1	X
North America..	5.1	4.4	X	1.9	1.9	X
Language Spoken at Home and Ability to Speak English						
Population 5 years and over..	792,820	798,872	0.8	299,084,046	301,625,014	0.8
English only	94.3	93.4	X	78.9	78.5	X
Language other than English...	5.7	6.6	X	21.1	21.5	X
Speaks English less than "very well"..................................	1.7	2.4	X	8.6	8.6	X

NA = Not available.
X = Not applicable.
- = Zero or rounds to zero.

Table SD-5. Median Income and Poverty Status, 2015

(Number, percent, except as noted.)

Characteristic	State		U.S.	
	Number	Percent	Number	Percent
Median Income				
Households (dollars)..	53,017	X	55,775	X
Families (dollars)	67,643	X	68,260	X
Below Poverty Level (All People)	114,071	13.7	46,153,077	14.7
Sex				
Male	50,410	12.1	20,599,407	13.4
Female	63,661	15.4	25,553,670	16.0
Age				
Under 18 years..	37,247	18.1	15,000,273	20.7
Related children under 18 years...................	36,009	17.6	14,693,239	20.4
18 to 64 years...	66,190	13.3	26,960,369	13.9
65 years and over	10,634	8.3	4,192,435	9.0

X = Not applicable.

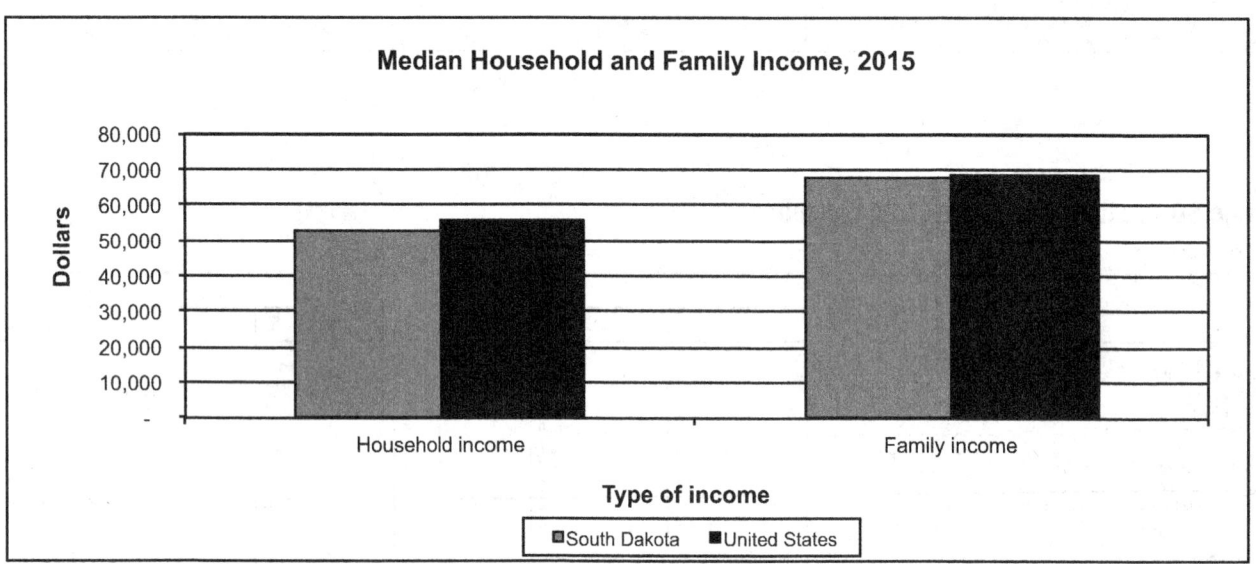

Median Household and Family Income, 2015

Table SD-6. Health Insurance Coverage Status for the Civilian Noninstitutionalized Population and Children Under 18 Years of Age

(Numbers in thousands, percent.)

Item	2007	2008	2009	2010	2011	2012	2013	2014	2015
Civilian Noninstitutionalized Population	788	784	793	798	806	816	827	835	841
Covered by Private or Public Insurance									
Number..	708	692	689	699	710	722	734	753	755
Percent...	89.9	88.3	86.9	87.6	88.1	88.5	88.7	90.2	89.8
Not Covered									
Number..	80	92	104	99	96	94	93	82	86
Percent...	10.1	11.7	13.1	12.4	11.9	11.5	11.3	9.8	10.2
Percent in the U.S. not covered..................................	15.3	15.1	15.1	15.5	15.1	14.8	14.5	11.7	9.4
Children Under 18 Years of Age	198	196	195	201	201	203	207	210	209
Covered by Private or Public Insurance									
Number..	183	179	180	184	189	191	194	198	195
Percent...	92.0	91.3	92.4	91.7	94.0	94.2	93.7	94.3	93.3
Not Covered									
Number..	16	17	15	17	12	12	13	12	14
Percent...	8.0	8.7	7.6	8.3	6.0	5.8	6.3	5.7	6.7
Percent in the U.S. not covered..................................	11.0	9.7	8.6	8.0	7.5	7.2	7.1	6.0	4.8

Table SD-7. Employment Status by Demographic Group, 2016

(Numbers in thousands, percent.)

Characteristic	Civilian noninstitutional population	Civilian labor force		Employed		Unemployed	
		Number	Percent of population	Number	Percent of population	Number	Percent of population
Total...	656	452	68.9	440	67.0	13	2.8
Sex							
Male..	326	243	74.4	235	72.1	7	3.0
Female...	330	210	63.6	204	61.9	5	2.6
Race, Sex, and Hispanic Origin							
White..	576	403	70.0	397	69.0	6	1.5
Male..	289	217	75.0	213	73.8	4	1.6
Female...	287	187	65.0	184	64.1	3	1.4
Black or African American...........................	NA	NA	NA	NA	NA	NA	NA
Male..	NA	NA	NA	NA	NA	NA	NA
Female...	NA	NA	NA	NA	NA	NA	NA
Hispanic or Latino ethnicity[1]	NA	NA	NA	NA	NA	NA	NA
Male..	NA	NA	NA	NA	NA	NA	NA
Female...	NA	NA	NA	NA	NA	NA	NA
Age							
16 to 19 years...	NA	NA	NA	NA	NA	NA	NA
20 to 24 years...	58	45	77.4	43	72.9	3	5.8
25 to 34 years...	112	96	85.0	93	83.0	2	2.4
35 to 44 years...	93	79	85.6	77	82.9	3	3.1
45 to 54 years...	101	86	85.1	84	83.7	1	1.6
55 to 64 years...	115	87	75.2	85	74.1	1	1.5
65 years and over....................................	132	38	28.5	37	28.1	1	1.3

NOTE: Data in Table 7 are from the Current Population Survey (CPS) and do not match the estimates in Table 8. See notes and definitions for further information.
[1] May be of any race.
NA = Not available.
... = Fewer than 500 persons

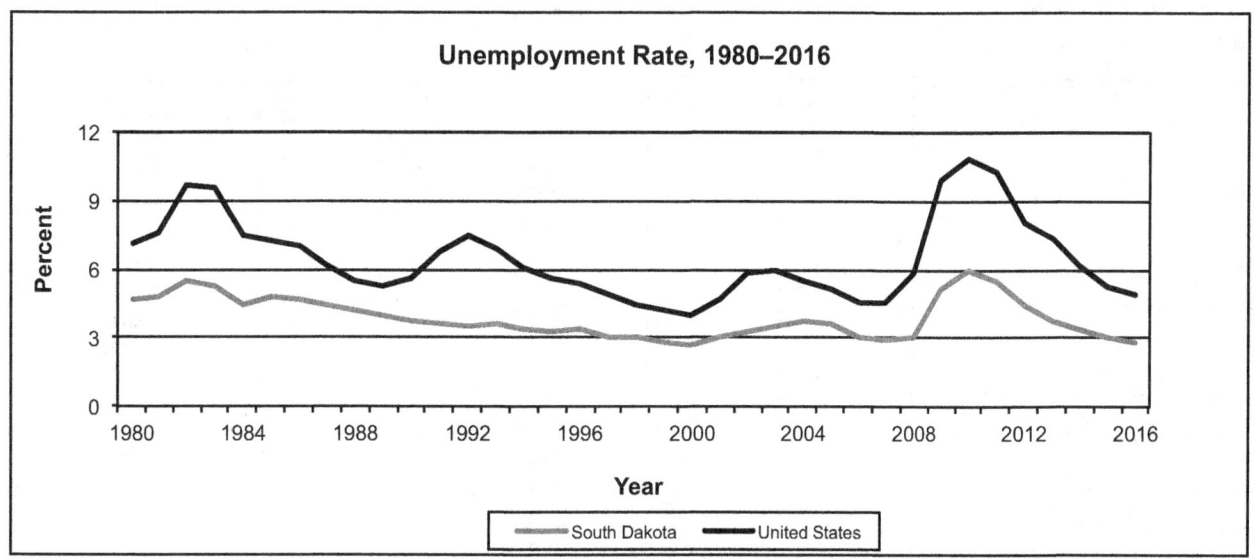

Table SD-8. Employment Status of the Civilian Noninstitutional Population Age 16 Years and Over

(Number, percent.)

Year	Civilian labor force	Civilian participation rate	Employed	Unemployed	Unemployment rate
2008..	446,618	73.0	432,925	13,693	3.1
2009..	446,010	72.2	423,993	22,017	4.9
2010..	441,339	71.3	419,355	21,984	5.0
2011..	440,934	70.6	420,054	20,880	4.7
2012..	442,575	70.0	423,651	18,924	4.3
2013..	444,880	69.4	428,075	16,805	3.8
2014..	448,631	69.3	433,203	15,428	3.4
2015..	452,300	69.4	438,077	14,223	3.1
2016..	453,069	69.0	440,299	12,770	2.8

Table SD-9. Employment and Average Wages by Industry

(Estimates through 2010 are based on the 2007 *North American Industry Classification System* [NAICS]. Estimates from 2011 onward are based on the 2012 NAICS.)

Industry	2009	2010	2011	2012	2013	2014	2015
	Number of jobs						
Wage and Salary Employment by Industry..................	423,601	423,507	427,833	435,383	438,456	444,762	447,859
Farm Wage and Salary Employment.........................	4,580	4,943	5,557	6,845	6,298	6,367	4,908
Nonfarm Wage and Salary Employment....................	419,021	418,564	422,276	428,538	432,158	438,395	442,951
Private wage and salary employment................................	334,632	332,795	337,194	344,515	348,091	353,955	358,641
Forestry, fishing, and related activities.........................	1,962	2,098	2,269	2,397	2,471	2,430	2,427
Mining..	836	818	833	850	846	816	837
Utilities...	2,112	2,091	2,071	1,969	1,950	1,967	1,996
Construction..	21,839	20,828	20,785	20,749	21,090	21,854	22,767
Manufacturing..	37,808	37,011	39,268	41,233	41,574	42,447	42,652
Durable goods manufacturing..............................	24,785	24,021	25,887	27,217	27,515	28,482	28,537
Nondurable goods manufacturing...........................	13,023	12,990	13,381	14,016	14,059	13,965	14,115
Wholesale trade	18,476	18,663	19,061	19,589	19,978	20,899	21,215
Retail trade	50,351	49,973	50,646	51,489	51,641	52,252	53,312
Transportation and warehousing.........................	10,617	10,333	10,479	10,515	10,534	11,247	11,524
Information..	6,709	6,544	6,398	6,208	6,025	6,060	5,885
Finance and insurance	27,150	26,042	25,503	26,149	27,134	27,137	26,905
Real estate and rental and leasing............................	3,701	3,462	3,517	3,543	3,626	3,729	3,811
Professional, scientific, and technical services	11,212	11,272	11,266	11,652	12,545	12,484	12,610
Management of companies and enterprises...................	3,475	3,625	3,768	4,146	4,235	4,572	4,936
Administrative and waste services............................	12,567	12,884	13,812	13,622	13,100	13,386	13,317
Educational services	7,545	7,865	7,997	8,104	8,055	8,063	8,306
Health care and social assistance............................	56,046	57,069	57,510	59,106	59,945	60,068	60,908
Arts, entertainment, and recreation............................	6,566	6,504	6,413	6,341	6,190	6,402	6,610
Accommodation and food services...........................	36,826	36,847	37,315	38,241	38,703	39,290	39,787
Other services, except public administration..................	18,834	18,866	18,283	18,612	18,449	18,852	18,836
Government and government enterprises.........................	84,389	85,769	85,082	84,023	84,067	84,440	84,310
	Dollars						
Average Wages and Salaries by Industry	32,944	33,919	35,003	36,217	36,833	38,260	39,658
Average Farm Wages and Salaries	40,406	37,203	36,398	44,444	39,940	40,978	38,828
Average Nonfarm Wages and Salaries	32,863	33,880	34,985	36,085	36,788	38,220	39,667
Average private wages and salaries............................	32,525	33,657	34,925	36,128	36,967	38,521	40,056
Forestry, fishing, and related activities.........................	23,087	24,440	25,071	25,315	26,679	25,863	27,415
Mining..	46,587	49,593	55,685	57,316	55,965	58,808	60,777
Utilities...	61,659	64,924	67,059	69,450	73,256	74,710	76,286
Construction..	37,577	38,080	38,984	39,931	40,942	42,886	44,987
Manufacturing..	38,300	39,903	41,466	42,175	42,447	44,511	45,441
Durable goods manufacturing..............................	38,694	40,469	42,403	42,836	43,536	45,259	45,996
Nondurable goods manufacturing...........................	37,549	38,856	39,654	40,891	40,316	42,986	44,319
Wholesale trade	45,399	46,650	48,908	51,352	52,927	54,992	56,262
Retail trade	22,043	23,091	23,733	24,552	25,168	26,198	27,030
Transportation and warehousing.........................	37,739	39,275	41,193	42,125	42,862	43,978	44,955
Information..	39,243	39,903	41,823	42,780	43,368	44,834	45,799
Finance and insurance	44,054	45,799	48,149	49,764	50,336	52,962	56,374
Real estate and rental and leasing............................	25,476	26,755	28,105	29,600	30,639	32,329	34,785
Professional, scientific, and technical services	44,371	46,507	49,104	51,609	49,921	52,681	56,395
Management of companies and enterprises...................	74,839	88,726	88,046	89,076	91,577	92,716	93,532
Administrative and waste services............................	24,377	25,307	25,533	26,958	27,166	29,194	29,969
Educational services	23,551	24,601	24,242	24,522	24,861	25,031	24,814
Health care and social assistance............................	39,429	40,059	41,621	43,112	44,281	45,810	47,772
Arts, entertainment, and recreation............................	17,894	17,705	17,929	17,945	18,285	18,834	19,718
Accommodation and food services...........................	13,446	13,964	14,396	14,984	15,522	16,076	17,297
Other services, except public administration..................	23,019	23,597	25,062	25,613	27,009	28,115	29,510
Government and government enterprises.........................	34,203	34,746	35,224	35,908	36,047	36,958	38,015

Table SD-10. Employment Characteristics by Family Type

(Number, percent.)

Family type and labor force status	2013 Total	2013 Families with own children under 18 years	2014 Total	2014 Families with own children under 18 years	2015 Total	2015 Families with own children under 18 years
All Families..	213,838	94,183	210,903	88,396	217,013	94,326
FAMILY TYPE AND LABOR FORCE STATUS						
Married-Couple Families...........................	166,793	62,905	165,397	59,765	170,511	64,388
Both husband and wife in labor force....................	62.3	79.6	61.7	78.8	61.1	78.4
Husband in labor force, wife not in labor force........	15.5	15.6	16.2	17.2	16.2	18.3
Wife in labor force, husband not in labor force........	6.9	3.1	7.0	2.7	6.5	1.9
Both husband and wife not in labor force...............	14.9	1.4	15.1	1.3	15.8	1.3
Other Families	47,045	31,278	45,506	28,631	46,502	29,938
Female householder, no husband present.............	67.4	69.9	68.7	73.3	69.5	70.4
In labor force.....................................	51.0	58.5	51.7	61.6	53.7	62.3
Not in labor force..............................	16.4	11.4	17.0	11.7	15.8	8.1
Male householder, no wife present.................	32.6	30.1	31.3	26.7	30.5	29.6
In labor force.....................................	25.6	26.9	26.8	26.0	26.2	27.6
Not in labor force..............................	7.0	3.2	4.5	0.7	4.3	2.0

Table SD-11. School Enrollment and Educational Attainment, 2015

(Number, percent.)

Item	State	U.S.
Enrollment		
Total population 3 years and over, enrolled in school	212,152	81,618,288
Enrolled in nursery school or preschool (percent)...........................	6.6	6.0
Enrolled in kindergarten (percent)..............................	5.8	5.0
Enrolled in elementary school, grades 1-8 (percent).........................	42.1	40.3
Enrolled in high school, grades 9-12 (percent).............................	20.3	20.9
Enrolled in college or graduate school (percent)...........................	25.2	27.7
Attainment		
Total population 25 years and over	563,108	216,447,163
Less than ninth grade (percent)...............................	3.4	5.5
9th to 12th grade, no diploma (percent)............................	5.4	7.3
High school graduate, including equivalency (percent).......................	31.2	27.6
Some college, no degree (percent)	21.3	20.7
Associate's degree (percent)	11.1	8.2
Bachelor's degree (percent)	19.6	19.0
Graduate or professional degree (percent).............................	7.9	11.6
High school graduate or higher (percent)	91.1	87.1
Bachelor's degree or higher (percent)................................	27.5	30.6

Table SD-12. Public School Characteristics and Educational Indicators

(Number, percent; data derived from National Center of Education Statistics.)

Item	State	U.S.
Public Schools, 2014–2015 (except where noted)		
Number of school districts..................................	170	18,260
Number of schools.......................................	698	98,373
Number of students	133,040	50,312,581
Number of teachers	9,618	3,132,351
Student-teacher ratio	13.8	16.1
Expenditures per student (dollars), FY 2014......................	9,036	11,066
Four-year adjusted cohort graduation rate (ACGR)[1,2]	83.9	83.2
Students eligible for free or reduced-price lunch (percent)...............	39.5	51.8
English language learners (percent)............................	3.5	9.4
Students age 3 to 21 served under IDEA, part B (percent)................	14.3	13.0

Public Schools by Type	Number	Percent of state public schools
Total number of schools..................................	698	100.0
Regular	654	93.7
Special education......................................	12	1.7
Vocational education....................................	4	0.6
Alternative education....................................	28	4.0

NOTE: Every school is assigned only one school type based on its instructional emphasis.
[1] ACGR data represents a new method of calculating high-school completion rates and may not be comparable to previous years' data for Averaged Freshmen Graduation Rates (AFGR).
[2] The United States 4-year ACGRs were estimated using both the reported 4-year ACGR data from 49 states and the District of Columbia and using imputed data for Idaho. The estimate for American Indian/Alaska Native students also includes imputed data for Virginia.

Table SD-13. Reported Voting and Registration of the Voting-Age Population, November 2016

(Numbers in thousands, percent.)

Item	Total population	Total citizen population	Registered			Voted		
			Total registered	Percent registered (total population)	Percent registered (total citizen population)	Total voted	Percent voted (total population)	Percent voted (total citizen population)
U.S. Total	245,502	224,059	157,596	64.2	70.3	137,537	56.0	61.4
State Total	631	612	437	69.3	71.4	362	57.3	59.1
Sex								
Male	314	304	213	68.0	70.3	171	54.6	56.5
Female	318	309	224	70.6	72.6	191	60.0	61.7
Race								
White alone	560	551	406	72.5	73.6	340	60.7	61.6
White, non-Hispanic alone	546	543	402	73.6	74.0	336	61.6	61.9
Black alone	11	8	4	(B)	(B)	3	(B)	(B)
Asian alone	9	2	-	(B)	(B)	-	(B)	(B)
Hispanic (of any race)	21	15	8	(B)	(B)	7	(B)	(B)
White alone or in combination	565	557	410	72.6	73.7	343	60.7	61.6
Black alone or in combination	12	9	6	(B)	(B)	5	(B)	(B)
Asian alone or in combination	9	2	-	(B)	(B)	-	(B)	(B)
Age								
18 to 24 years	84	81	41	(B)	(B)	26	(B)	(B)
25 to 34 years	103	98	63	(B)	(B)	50	(B)	(B)
35 to 44 years	94	90	61	(B)	(B)	52	(B)	(B)
45 to 64 years	230	224	177	76.7	78.8	147	63.7	65.4
65 years and over	119	119	95	79.9	79.9	88	73.9	73.9

- = Zero or rounds to zero.
B = Base is less than 75,000 and therefore too small to show the derived measure.

Table SD-14. Crime

(Number, rate per 100,000. Data are derived from the FBI Uniform Crime Reports.)

Item	State			U.S. [1,2,3,4]		
	2014	2015	Percent change	2014	2015	Percent change
TOTAL POPULATION [5]	853,304	858,469	0.6	318,907,401	321,418,820	0.8
VIOLENT CRIME						
Number	2,801	3,289	17.4	1,186,185	1,231,566	3.8
Rate	328.3	383.1	16.7	372.0	383.2	3.0
Murder and Nonnegligent Manslaughter						
Number	23	32	39.1	14,164	15,696	10.8
Rate	2.7	3.7	38.3	4.4	4.9	10.0
Rape [6]						
Number	478	495	3.6	118,027	124,047	5.1
Rate	56.0	57.7	2.9	37.0	38.6	4.3
Robbery						
Number	199	216	8.5	322,905	327,374	1.4
Rate	23.3	25.2	7.9	101.3	101.9	0.6
Aggravated Assault						
Number	2,101	2,546	21.2	731,089	764,449	4.6
Rate	246.2	296.6	20.5	229.2	237.8	3.7
PROPERTY CRIME						
Number	16,036	16,680	4.0	8,209,010	7,993,631	-2.6
Rate	1,879.3	1,943.0	3.4	2,574.1	2,487.0	-3.4
Burglary						
Number	2,817	2,960	5.1	1,713,153	1,579,527	-7.8
Rate	330.1	344.8	4.4	537.2	491.4	-8.5
Larceny-Theft						
Number	12,209	12,532	2.6	5,809,054	5,706,346	-1.8
Rate	1,430.8	1,459.8	2.0	1,821.5	1,775.4	-2.5
Motor Vehicle Theft						
Number	1,010	1,188	17.6	686,803	707,758	3.1
Rate	118.4	138.4	16.9	215.4	220.2	2.2

NOTE: Although arson data are included in the trend and clearance tables, sufficient data are not available to estimate totals for this offense. Therefore, no arson data are published in this table.
X = Not applicable.
- = Zero or rounds to zero.
[1] The crime figures have been adjusted.
[2] The data collection methodology for the offense of forcible rape used by the Minnesota state Uniform Crime Reporting (UCR) Program (with the exception of Minneapolis and St. Paul, Minnesota) does not comply with national UCR Program guidelines. Consequently, its figures for forcible rape and violent crime (of which forcible rape is a part) are not published in this table.
[3] Includes offenses reported by the Zoological Police and the Metro Transit Police.
[4] Because of changes in the state's reporting practices, figures are not comparable to previous years' data.
[5] Populations are U.S. Census Bureau provisional estimates as of July 1 of each year.
[6] The figures shown for the offense of rape were estimated using the revised Uniform Crime Reporting (UCR) definition of rape.

Table SD-15. State Government Finances, 2015

(Dollar amounts in thousands, percent distribution.)

Item	Dollars	Percent distribution
Total Revenue	4,875,457	100.0
General revenue	4,169,927	85.5
Intergovernmental revenue	1,498,716	30.7
Taxes	1,674,108	34.3
General sales	970,784	19.9
Selective sales	401,898	8.2
License taxes	288,796	5.9
Individual income tax	0	-
Corporate income tax	4,334	0.1
Other taxes	8,296	0.2
Current charges	374,044	7.7
Miscellaneous general revenue	623,059	12.8
Utility revenue	0	-
Liquor stores revenue	0	-
Insurance trust revenue[1]	705,530	14.5
Total Expenditure	4,715,528	100.0
Intergovernmental expenditure	772,034	16.4
Direct expenditure	3,943,494	83.6
Current operation	2,612,051	55.4
Capital outlay	586,595	12.4
Insurance benefits and repayments	548,872	11.6
Assistance and subsidies	87,888	1.9
Interest on debt	108,088	2.3
Exhibit: Salaries and wages	732,261	15.5
Total Expenditure	4,715,528	100.0
General expenditure	4,166,656	88.4
Intergovernmental expenditure	772,034	16.4
Direct expenditure	3,394,622	72.0
General expenditure, by function:		
Education	1,316,817	27.9
Public welfare	1,037,395	22.0
Hospitals	23,648	0.5
Health	191,962	4.1
Highways	605,572	12.8
Police protection	45,483	1.0
Correction	125,983	2.7
Natural resources	209,860	4.5
Parks and recreation	45,255	1.0
Governmental administration	183,906	3.9
Interest on general debt	108,088	2.3
Other and unallocable	272,687	5.8
Utility expenditure	0	-
Liquor stores expenditure	0	-
Insurance trust expenditure	548,872	11.6
Debt at End of Fiscal Year	3,286,231	X
Cash and Security Holdings	16,436,064	X

X = Not applicable.
- = Zero or rounds to zero.
[1] Within insurance trust revenue, net earnings of state retirement systems is a calculated statistic (the item code in the data file is X08), and thus can be positive or negative. Net earnings is the sum of earnings on investments plus gains on investments minus losses on investments. The change made in 2002 for asset valuation from book to market value in accordance with Statement 34 of the Governmental Accounting Standards Board is reflected in the calculated statistics.

Table SD-16. State Government Tax Collections, 2016

(Dollars in thousands, percent.)

Item	Dollars	Percent distribution
Total Taxes	1,747,550	100.0
Property taxes	0	-
Sales and gross receipts	1,440,041	82.4
General sales and gross receipts	968,787	55.4
Selective sales and gross receipts	471,254	27.0
Alcoholic beverages	16,656	1.0
Amusements	9,256	0.5
Insurance premiums	86,879	5.0
Motor fuels	186,990	10.7
Pari-mutuels	388	-
Public utilities	3,624	0.2
Tobacco products	63,082	3.6
Other selective sales	104,379	6.0
Licenses	268,227	15.3
Alcoholic beverages	530	-
Amusements	6,617	0.4
Corporations in general	5,194	0.3
Hunting and fishing	30,699	1.8
Motor vehicle	89,045	5.1
Motor vehicle operators	5,346	0.3
Public utilities	0	-
Occupation and business, NEC	107,967	6.2
Other licenses	22,829	1.3
Income taxes	32,684	1.9
Individual income	0	-
Corporation net income	32,684	1.9
Other taxes	6,598	0.4
Death and gift	0	-
Documentary and stock transfer	194	-
Severance	6,404	0.4
Taxes, NEC	0	-

X = Not applicable.
- = Zero or rounds to zero.

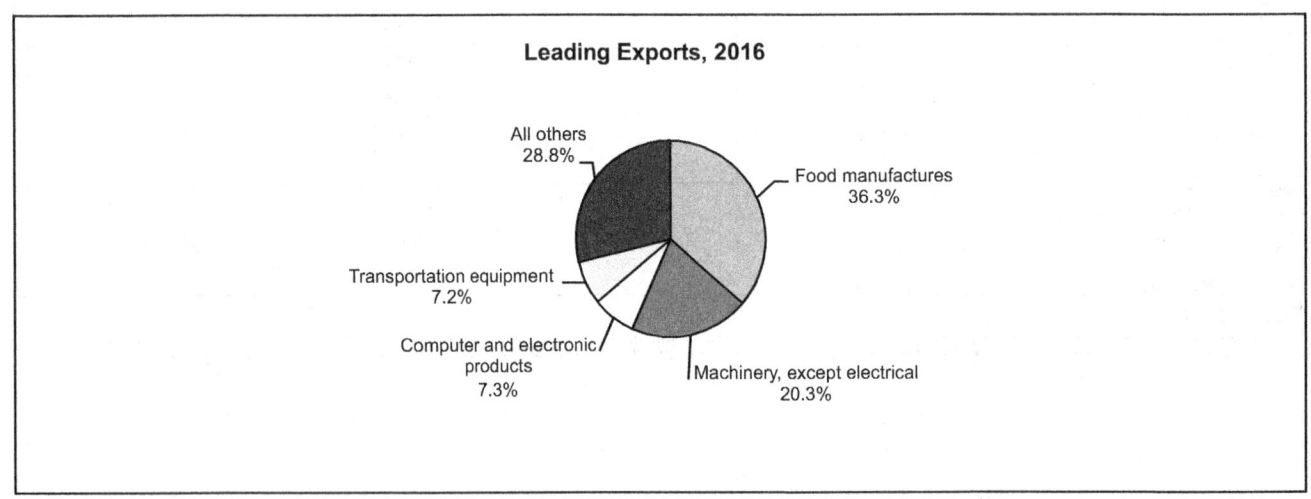

Leading Exports, 2016

All others 28.8%
Food manufactures 36.3%
Transportation equipment 7.2%
Computer and electronic products 7.3%
Machinery, except electrical 20.3%

TENNESSEE

Facts and Figures

Location: South central United States; bordered on the N by Kentucky and Virginia, on the E by North Carolina, on the S by Georgia, Alabama, and Mississippi, and on the W by Arkansas and Missouri

Area: 42,143 sq. mi. (109,151 sq. km.); rank—36th

Population: 6,651,194 (2016 est.); rank—16th

Principal Cities: capital—Nashville; largest—Nashville

Statehood: June 1, 1796; 16th state

U.S. Congress: 2 senators, 9 representatives

State Motto: Agriculture and Commerce

State Song: "The Tennessee Waltz"

State Nickname: The Volunteer State

Abbreviations: TN; Tenn.

State Symbols: flower—iris; tree—yellow poplar (tulip poplar); bird—mockingbird

At a Glance

- With an increase in population of 4.8 percent, Tennessee ranked 21st among the states in growth from 2010 to 2016.

- Tennessee's median household income in 2015 was $47,275, and 16.7 percent of the population lived below the poverty level.

- In 2015, 10.3 percent of Tennesseans did not have health insurance, compared to 9.4 percent of the total U.S. population.

- Tennessee's violent crime rate in 2015 was 612.1 per 100,000 population, compared to 383.2 for the entire nation; this was the 5th highest rate in the country.

- Tennessee's unemployment rate of 4.8 percent ranked 26th among the states in 2016 and was slightly lower than the national rate of 4.9 percent.

Table TN-1. Population by Age, Sex, Race, and Hispanic Origin

(Number, percent, except where noted.)

Sex, age, race, and Hispanic origin	2000	2010	2016 [1]	Average annual percent change, 2010–2016
Total Population...	5,689,283	6,346,105	6,651,194	0.3
Percent of total U.S. population	2.0	2.1	2.1	X
Sex				
Male..	2,770,275	3,093,504	3,242,515	0.3
Female..	2,919,008	3,252,601	3,408,679	0.3
Age				
Under 5 years..	374,880	407,813	407,599	-
5 to 19 years...	1,186,152	1,268,308	1,257,166	-0.1
20 to 64 years...	3,424,940	3,816,522	3,939,377	0.2
65 years and over..	703,311	853,462	1,047,052	1.4
Median age (years)	35.9	38.0	38.7	0.1
Race and Hispanic Origin				
One race..				
White	4,563,310	5,056,311	5,234,030	0.2
Black	932,809	1,068,010	1,137,075	0.4
American Indian and Alaska Native	15,152	26,256	29,866	0.9
Asian	56,662	93,897	120,219	1.8
Native Hawaiian or Other Pacific Islander	2,205	5,426	6,432	1.2
Two or more races	63,109	96,205	123,572	1.8
Hispanic (of any race)...	123,838	301,090	348,725	1.0

X = Not applicable.
[1] Population figures for 2016 are July 1 estimates. The 2010 estimates are taken from the 2010 Census.

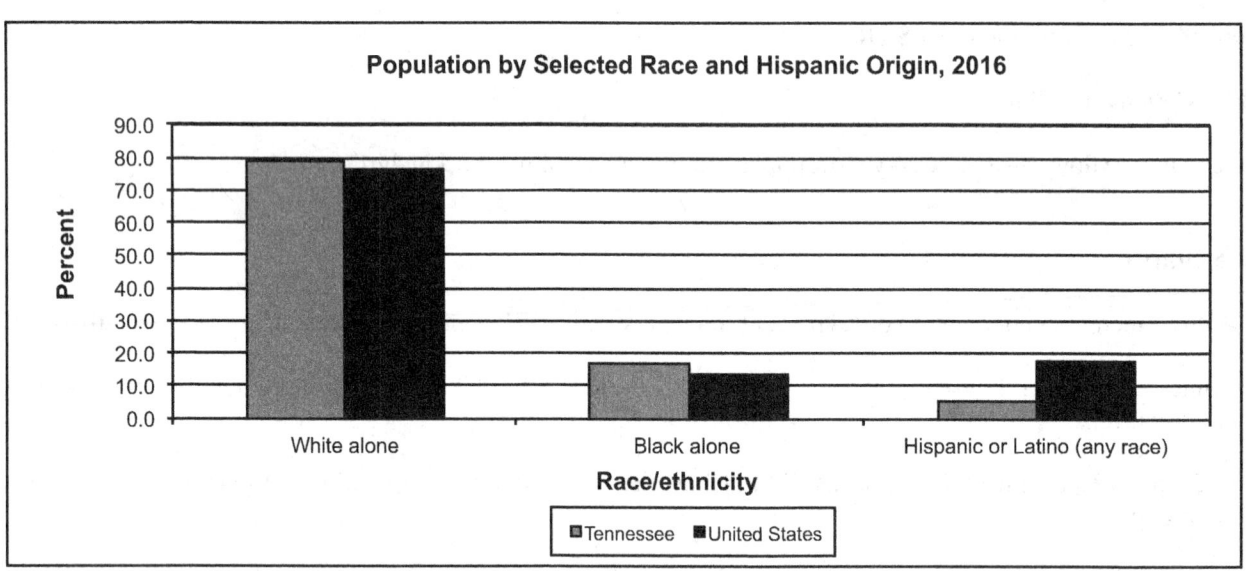

Population by Selected Race and Hispanic Origin, 2016

Table TN-2. Marital Status

(Number, percent distribution.)

Sex, age, race, and Hispanic origin	2000	2010	2015
Males, 15 Years and Over	2,169,327	2,461,573	2,586,068
Never married	26.6	31.4	33.0
Now married, except separated..............................	58.9	52.2	50.6
Separated..	1.7	2.1	1.8
Widowed..	2.5	2.7	2.8
Divorced..	10.4	11.7	11.8
Females, 15 Years and Over	2,353,303	2,652,823	2,777,189
Never married	20.7	25.3	27.4
Now married, except separated..............................	53.6	47.9	46.6
Separated..	2.3	2.7	2.5
Widowed..	11.2	10.3	9.8
Divorced..	12.2	13.7	13.7

Table TN-3. Households and Housing Characteristics

(Number, percent, dollars.)

Item	2000	2010	2015	Average annual percent change, 2000–2015
Total Households...	2,232,905	2,440,663	2,530,260	0.9
Family households..	1,547,835	1,644,896	1,675,678	0.6
Married-couple family.....................................	1,173,960	1,195,406	1,213,001	0.2
Other family...	373,875	449,490	462,677	1.6
Male householder, no wife present..............	85,976	106,616	119,587	2.6
Female householder, no husband present......	287,899	342,874	343,090	1.3
Nonfamily households...	685,070	795,767	854,582	1.6
Householder living alone.................................	576,401	675,565	709,111	1.5
Householder not living alone...........................	108,669	120,202	145,471	2.3
Housing Characteristics				
Total housing units...	2,439,443	2,815,087	2,892,407	1.2
Occupied housing units	2,232,905	2,440,663	2,530,260	0.9
Owner occupied..	1,561,363	1,662,768	1,665,498	0.4
Renter occupied...	671,542	777,895	864,762	1.9
Average household size.......................................	2.48	2.54	2.55	0.2
Financial Characteristics				
Median gross rent of renter-occupied housing	505	697	785	3.7
Median monthly owner costs for housing units with a mortgage	882	1,161	1,167	2.2
Median value of owner-occupied housing units	93,000	139,000	150,600	4.1

Table TN-4. Migration, Origin, and Language

(Number, percent.)

Characteristic	State			U.S.		
	2014	2015	Percent change	2014	2015	Percent change
Residence 1 Year Ago						
Population 1 year and over	6,471,445	6,522,259	0.8	315,095,393	317,635,720	0.8
Same house	84.4	84.9	X	85.1	85.3	X
Different house in the U.S.	15.1	14.8	X	14.3	14.1	X
Same county	9.1	8.6	X	8.7	8.5	X
Different county	6.1	6.2	X	5.6	5.6	X
Same state	3.3	3.2	X	3.3	3.2	X
Different state	2.8	3.0	X	2.3	2.4	X
Abroad	0.4	0.4	X	0.6	0.7	X
Place of Birth						
Native born	6,228,094	6,268,729	0.7	276,465,262	278,128,449	0.6
Male	48.6	48.6	X	49.3	49.3	X
Female	51.4	51.4	X	50.7	50.7	X
Foreign born	321,258	331,570	3.2	42,391,794	43,290,372	2.1
Male	51.7	51.6	X	48.7	48.6	X
Female	48.3	48.4	X	51.3	51.4	X
Foreign born; naturalized U.S. citizen............	115,725	120,762	4.4	19,984,738	20,697,103	3.6
Male	47.1	46.4	X	45.9	45.9	X
Female	52.9	53.6	X	54.1	54.1	X
Foreign born; not a U.S. citizen....................	205,533	210,808	2.6	22,407,056	22,593,269	0.8
Male	54.3	54.6	X	51.2	51.1	X
Female	45.7	45.4	X	48.8	48.9	X
Entered 2010 or later	16.5	22.7	X	12.3	15.6	X
Entered 2000 to 2009	39.5	36.3	X	28.6	27.9	X
Entered before 2000..................................	44.0	41.0	X	59.1	56.5	X
World Region of Birth, Foreign						
Foreign-born population, excluding population born at sea	321,258	331,513	3.2	42,390,705	43,289,646	2.1
Europe	10.5	9.7	X	11.2	11.1	X
Asia	30.1	30.0	X	30.1	30.6	X
Africa	9.8	11.4	X	4.6	4.8	X
Oceania	0.5	0.4	X	0.6	0.6	X
Latin America..	46.5	44.7	X	51.6	51.1	X
North America..	2.5	3.9	X	1.9	1.9	X
Language Spoken at Home and Ability to Speak English						
Population 5 years and over..........................	6,150,997	6,201,062	0.8	299,084,046	301,625,014	0.8
English only	93.0	93.1	X	78.9	78.5	X
Language other than English.......................	7.0	6.9	X	21.1	21.5	X
Speaks English less than "very well"............	2.9	2.9	X	8.6	8.6	X

NA = Not available.
X = Not applicable.
- = Zero or rounds to zero.

Table TN-5. Median Income and Poverty Status, 2015

(Number, percent, except as noted.)

Characteristic	State		U.S.	
	Number	Percent	Number	Percent
Median Income				
Households (dollars)...	47,275	X	55,775	X
Families (dollars)	57,830	X	68,260	X
Below Poverty Level (All People)	1,077,900	16.7	46,153,077	14.7
Sex				
Male	483,282	15.5	20,599,407	13.4
Female	594,618	17.9	25,553,670	16.0
Age				
Under 18 years...	355,175	24.2	15,000,273	20.7
Related children under 18 years...............................	348,522	23.8	14,693,239	20.4
18 to 64 years...	625,459	15.7	26,960,369	13.9
65 years and over	97,266	9.8	4,192,435	9.0

X = Not applicable.

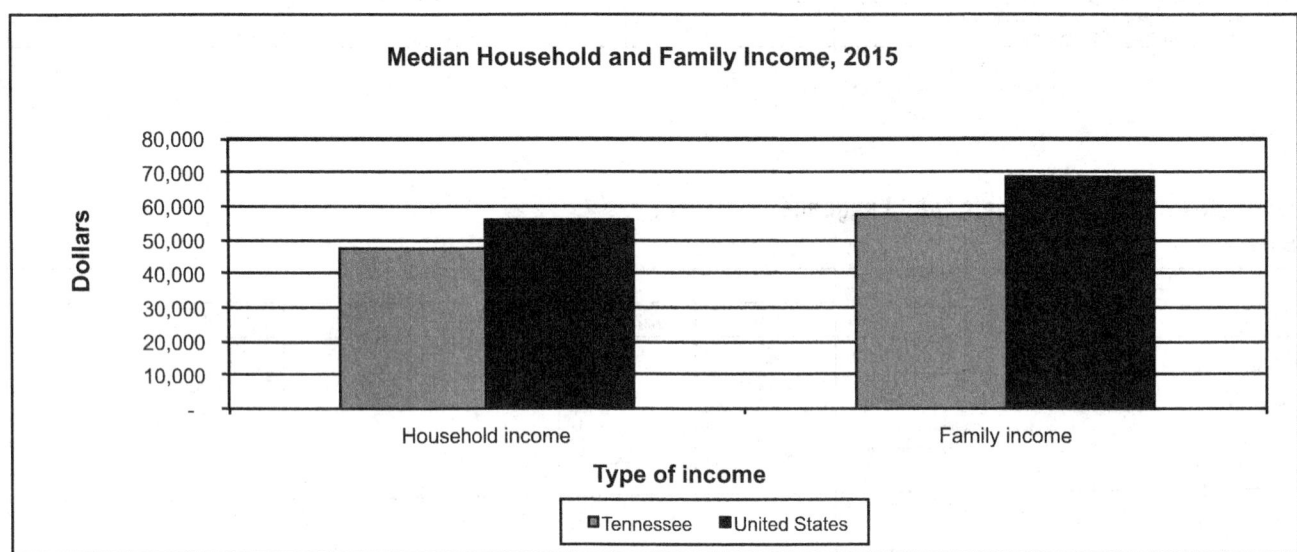

Table TN-6. Health Insurance Coverage Status for the Civilian Noninstitutionalized Population and Children Under 18 Years of Age

(Numbers in thousands, percent.)

Item	2007	2008	2009	2010	2011	2012	2013	2014	2015
Civilian Noninstitutionalized Population	6,150	6,113	6,188	6,260	6,302	6,355	6,395	6,449	6,496
Covered by Private or Public Insurance									
Number...	5,268	5,279	5,305	5,361	5,380	5,473	5,508	5,672	5,829
Percent..	85.6	86.4	85.7	85.6	85.4	86.1	86.1	88.0	89.7
Not Covered									
Number...	883	834	883	899	923	882	887	776	667
Percent..	14.4	13.6	14.3	14.4	14.6	13.9	13.9	12.0	10.3
Percent in the U.S. not covered................................	15.3	15.1	15.1	15.5	15.1	14.8	14.5	11.7	9.4
Children Under 18 Years of Age	1,479	1,476	1,488	1,493	1,488	1,490	1,490	1,490	1,491
Covered by Private or Public Insurance									
Number...	1,344	1,370	1,401	1,414	1,403	1,405	1,404	1,412	1,429
Percent..	90.9	92.8	94.1	94.7	94.3	94.3	94.3	94.8	95.8
Not Covered									
Number...	135	106	87	79	85	85	85	78	62
Percent..	9.1	7.2	5.9	5.3	5.7	5.7	5.7	5.2	4.2
Percent in the U.S. not covered................................	11.0	9.7	8.6	8.0	7.5	7.2	7.1	6.0	4.8

Table TN-7. Employment Status by Demographic Group, 2016

(Numbers in thousands, percent.)

Characteristic	Civilian noninstitutional population	Civilian labor force		Employed		Unemployed	
		Number	Percent of population	Number	Percent of population	Number	Percent of population
Total..	5,221	3,147	60.3	3,000	57.4	147	4.7
Sex							
Male..................................	2,494	1,680	67.4	1,606	64.4	74	4.4
Female	2,728	1,467	53.8	1,394	51.1	73	5.0
Race, Sex, and Hispanic Origin							
White	4,165	2,470	59.3	2,376	57.1	94	3.8
Male................................	2,015	1,354	67.2	1,301	64.6	52	3.9
Female	2,149	1,117	51.9	1,075	50.0	41	3.7
Black or African American..........	845	532	63.0	485	57.4	47	8.9
Male................................	379	249	65.7	231	60.9	18	7.2
Female	465	283	60.8	254	54.5	29	10.4
Hispanic or Latino ethnicity[1]	241	163	67.5	156	65.0	6	3.8
Male................................	134	110	82.1	108	80.2	3	2.3
Female	NA	NA	NA	NA	NA	NA	NA
Age							
16 to 19 years......................	299	115	38.3	98	32.9	16	14.1
20 to 24 years......................	427	314	73.4	286	66.8	28	8.9
25 to 34 years......................	965	766	79.4	725	75.1	41	5.4
35 to 44 years......................	761	613	80.5	590	77.5	23	3.8
45 to 54 years......................	842	632	75.1	612	72.7	20	3.2
55 to 64 years......................	885	517	58.4	504	57.0	13	2.5
65 years and over	1,043	191	18.3	185	17.8	6	3.0

NOTE: Data in Table 7 are from the Current Population Survey (CPS) and do not match the estimates in Table 8. See notes and definitions for further information.
[1] May be of any race.

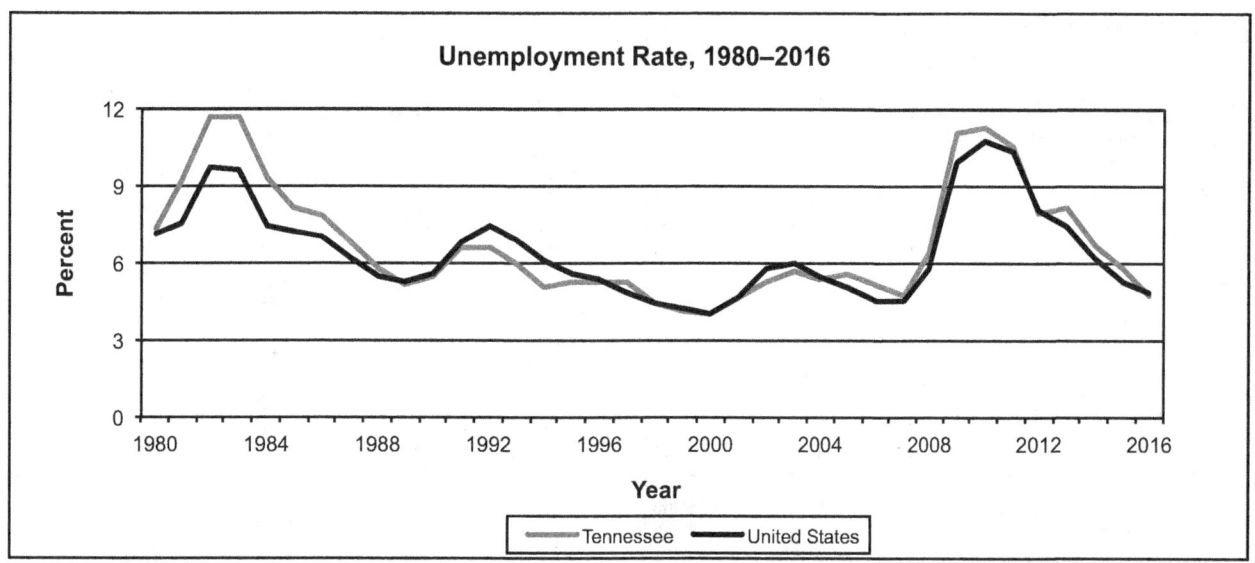

Table TN-8. Employment Status of the Civilian Noninstitutional Population Age 16 Years and Over

(Number, percent.)

Year	Civilian labor force	Civilian participation rate	Employed	Unemployed	Unemployment rate
2008..................................	3,054,785	63.4	2,853,746	201,039	6.6
2009..................................	3,052,678	62.7	2,733,113	319,565	10.5
2010..................................	3,090,795	62.7	2,792,063	298,732	9.7
2011..................................	3,125,307	62.8	2,844,662	280,645	9.0
2012..................................	3,103,047	61.8	2,860,355	242,692	7.8
2013..................................	3,077,048	60.7	2,837,898	239,150	7.8
2014..................................	3,046,632	59.6	2,847,777	198,855	6.5
2015..................................	3,062,775	59.3	2,886,024	176,751	5.8
2016..................................	3,135,102	60.1	2,984,259	150,843	4.8

Table TN-9. Employment and Average Wages by Industry

(Estimates through 2010 are based on the 2007 *North American Industry Classification System* [NAICS]. Estimates from 2011 onward are based on the 2012 NAICS.)

Industry	2009	2010	2011	2012	2013	2014	2015
				Number of jobs			
Wage and Salary Employment by Industry..................	2,727,279	2,711,898	2,757,216	2,807,608	2,848,078	2,905,771	2,976,108
Farm Wage and Salary Employment.........................	8,408	8,430	9,323	9,901	9,150	9,927	11,141
Nonfarm Wage and Salary Employment....................	2,718,871	2,703,468	2,747,893	2,797,707	2,838,928	2,895,844	2,964,967
Private wage and salary employment............................	2,266,947	2,246,595	2,294,109	2,348,606	2,390,888	2,450,409	2,522,162
Forestry, fishing, and related activities.......................	4,480	4,540	4,605	4,727	4,878	5,037	5,081
Mining..	3,228	3,549	3,594	3,427	3,424	3,430	3,458
Utilities..	3,558	3,357	3,317	3,356	3,342	3,380	3,366
Construction..	110,827	104,531	107,959	107,909	106,798	109,475	115,678
Manufacturing..	310,554	300,059	304,299	313,975	318,867	325,265	332,827
Durable goods manufacturing..............................	183,430	177,816	183,657	194,398	198,948	205,407	210,733
Nondurable goods manufacturing..........................	127,124	122,243	120,642	119,577	119,919	119,858	122,094
Wholesale trade	121,884	117,444	118,044	121,161	122,872	123,754	121,607
Retail trade..	311,717	309,757	312,756	315,571	317,385	323,501	328,403
Transportation and warehousing............................	132,538	130,188	135,002	140,699	144,274	147,394	155,455
Information..	46,324	44,369	43,265	42,797	43,474	43,353	43,450
Finance and insurance	108,289	108,367	107,288	108,421	106,845	109,228	111,170
Real estate and rental and leasing..........................	34,437	32,875	31,812	32,379	33,608	35,193	37,211
Professional, scientific, and technical services..............	109,334	108,118	110,449	111,968	115,065	120,947	129,212
Management of companies and enterprises..................	25,390	26,059	28,992	31,563	35,228	37,312	41,472
Administrative and waste services...........................	162,158	171,006	186,036	195,552	204,974	217,073	224,684
Educational services	51,628	53,094	53,946	55,170	56,295	57,628	58,633
Health care and social assistance...........................	324,266	329,629	336,314	343,825	347,917	350,658	361,027
Arts, entertainment, and recreation.........................	30,649	30,079	30,218	30,709	31,688	32,875	34,819
Accommodation and food services..........................	236,154	234,262	238,955	248,139	256,131	265,373	274,947
Other services, except public administration..................	139,532	135,312	137,258	137,258	137,823	139,533	139,662
Government and government enterprises.........................	451,924	456,873	453,784	449,101	448,040	445,435	442,805
				Dollars			
Average Wages and Salaries by Industry	39,586	41,009	41,873	43,404	43,573	44,701	46,176
Average Farm Wages and Salaries	21,668	20,674	16,362	21,339	23,808	23,229	19,002
Average Nonfarm Wages and Salaries	39,641	41,072	41,960	43,482	43,637	44,774	46,278
Average private wages and salaries...........................	39,808	41,447	42,358	44,051	44,113	45,214	46,831
Forestry, fishing, and related activities.......................	21,602	23,088	23,885	24,682	24,951	25,878	26,590
Mining..	56,958	63,573	61,486	64,423	63,487	67,906	68,225
Utilities..	60,820	61,568	63,014	63,793	65,517	67,999	70,791
Construction..	42,511	44,279	45,586	47,136	47,570	49,914	52,820
Manufacturing..	48,656	51,858	52,863	54,730	54,673	56,301	57,325
Durable goods manufacturing..............................	47,765	50,735	51,742	54,263	53,212	55,136	56,255
Nondurable goods manufacturing..........................	49,943	53,491	54,569	55,490	57,097	58,299	59,172
Wholesale trade	55,406	57,520	59,664	62,067	61,572	64,264	67,281
Retail trade..	25,991	27,018	27,724	28,107	27,882	28,633	29,520
Transportation and warehousing............................	45,848	48,093	49,515	50,159	50,675	51,270	52,516
Information..	52,112	54,019	57,049	59,041	58,964	61,817	62,876
Finance and insurance	62,824	66,041	68,054	72,399	72,250	74,927	76,002
Real estate and rental and leasing..........................	36,610	38,115	39,888	42,139	42,655	44,668	46,651
Professional, scientific, and technical services..............	61,413	64,655	66,004	70,898	70,550	72,036	75,723
Management of companies and enterprises..................	73,553	82,130	83,137	99,412	98,318	97,015	100,532
Administrative and waste services...........................	30,857	31,373	31,170	32,675	33,174	32,317	33,064
Educational services	33,400	33,449	34,279	35,343	35,917	36,262	36,289
Health care and social assistance...........................	43,933	44,813	45,546	46,389	46,669	47,777	49,686
Arts, entertainment, and recreation.........................	37,431	40,000	41,602	44,197	44,140	47,206	53,703
Accommodation and food services..........................	17,087	17,692	18,050	18,452	18,329	18,862	19,571
Other services, except public administration..................	27,062	28,128	28,797	30,223	30,632	32,000	33,365
Government and government enterprises.........................	38,804	39,227	39,947	40,502	41,093	42,356	43,128

Table TN-10. Employment Characteristics by Family Type

(Number, percent.)

Family type and labor force status	2013		2014		2015	
	Total	Families with own children under 18 years	Total	Families with own children under 18 years	Total	Families with own children under 18 years
All Families...	1,658,071	677,544	1,655,480	684,060	1,675,678	675,024
FAMILY TYPE AND LABOR FORCE STATUS						
Married-Couple Families..........................	1,208,430	439,638	1,198,174	447,165	1,213,001	438,614
Both husband and wife in labor force......................	48.6	64.3	48.0	64.3	48.6	65.9
Husband in labor force, wife not in labor force	22.4	28.6	23.2	29.2	22.8	27.3
Wife in labor force, husband not in labor force	9.1	4.7	9.1	4.2	8.5	4.5
Both husband and wife not in labor force.................	19.8	2.2	19.8	2.3	19.6	2.2
Other Families	449,641	237,906	457,306	236,895	462,677	236,410
Female householder, no husband present........................	74.1	75.6	74.9	77.9	74.2	75.9
In labor force...	50.5	60.9	49.8	61.8	49.6	61.5
Not in labor force	23.6	14.7	25.1	16.2	24.5	14.4
Male householder, no wife present........................	25.9	24.4	25.1	22.1	25.8	24.1
In labor force..	19.8	21.9	18.2	19.5	18.7	20.8
Not in labor force	6.1	2.6	7.0	2.6	7.1	3.3

Table TN-11. School Enrollment and Educational Attainment, 2015

(Number, percent.)

Item	State	U.S.
Enrollment		
Total population 3 years and over, enrolled in school	1,565,318	81,618,288
Enrolled in nursery school or preschool (percent)...	5.5	6.0
Enrolled in kindergarten (percent)...	4.8	5.0
Enrolled in elementary school, grades 1-8 (percent).............................	42.7	40.3
Enrolled in high school, grades 9-12 (percent).............................	21.5	20.9
Enrolled in college or graduate school (percent).............................	25.6	27.7
Attainment		
Total population 25 years and over	4,473,487	216,447,163
Less than ninth grade (percent)...	5.3	5.5
9th to 12th grade, no diploma (percent)...	8.6	7.3
High school graduate, including equivalency (percent).............................	33.1	27.6
Some college, no degree (percent)...	20.5	20.7
Associate's degree (percent)...	6.7	8.2
Bachelor's degree (percent)...	16.1	19.0
Graduate or professional degree (percent).............................	9.6	11.6
High school graduate or higher (percent).............................	86.1	87.1
Bachelor's degree or higher (percent).............................	25.7	30.6

Table TN-12. Public School Characteristics and Educational Indicators

(Number, percent; data derived from National Center of Education Statistics.)

Item	State	U.S.
Public Schools, 2014–2015 (except where noted)		
Number of school districts...	146	18,260
Number of schools...	1,851	98,373
Number of students..	995,475	50,312,581
Number of teachers	65,341	3,132,351
Student-teacher ratio	15.2	16.1
Expenditures per student (dollars), FY 2014	8,662	11,066
Four-year adjusted cohort graduation rate (ACGR)[1,2]	87.9	83.2
Students eligible for free or reduced-price lunch (percent)......	55.9	51.8
English language learners (percent)...................................	3.7	9.4
Students age 3 to 21 served under IDEA, part B (percent).......	13.1	13.0

Public Schools by Type	Number	Percent of state public schools
Total number of schools...	1,851	100.0
Regular	1,796	97.0
Special education	16	0.9
Vocational education	17	0.9
Alternative education..	22	1.2

NOTE: Every school is assigned only one school type based on its instructional emphasis.
[1] ACGR data represents a new method of calculating high-school completion rates and may not be comparable to previous years' data for Averaged Freshmen Graduation Rates (AFGR).
[2] The United States 4-year ACGRs were estimated using both the reported 4-year ACGR data from 49 states and the District of Columbia and using imputed data for Idaho. The estimate for American Indian/Alaska Native students also includes imputed data for Virginia.

Table TN-13. Reported Voting and Registration of the Voting-Age Population, November 2016

(Numbers in thousands, percent.)

Item	Total population	Total citizen population	Registered			Voted		
			Total registered	Percent registered (total population)	Percent registered (total citizen population)	Total voted	Percent voted (total population)	Percent voted (total citizen population)
U.S. Total	245,502	224,059	157,596	64.2	70.3	137,537	56.0	61.4
State Total............................	5,057	4,872	3,251	64.3	66.7	2,630	52.0	54.0
Sex								
Male	2,418	2,316	1,505	62.2	65.0	1,218	50.4	52.6
Female	2,639	2,556	1,746	66.2	68.3	1,412	53.5	55.3
Race								
White alone............................	4,014	3,893	2,640	65.8	67.8	2,176	54.2	55.9
White, non-Hispanic alone	3,808	3,783	2,601	68.3	68.7	2,148	56.4	56.8
Black alone............................	814	800	519	63.8	64.9	402	49.4	50.3
Asian alone	132	82	42	(B)	(B)	29	(B)	(B)
Hispanic (of any race)......................	221	125	40	18.0	31.8	27	12.3	21.7
White alone or in combination	4,093	3,972	2,679	65.5	67.4	2,199	53.7	55.4
Black alone or in combination..........	828	814	525	63.4	64.5	404	48.8	49.7
Asian alone or in combination.........	148	98	48	(B)	(B)	32	(B)	(B)
Age								
18 to 24 years......................	523	503	235	45.0	46.8	156	29.9	31.1
25 to 34 years......................	971	903	520	53.5	57.6	379	39.1	42.0
35 to 44 years......................	777	741	513	66.0	69.2	411	52.9	55.5
45 to 64 years......................	1,720	1,674	1,187	69.0	70.9	1,008	58.6	60.2
65 years and over	1,065	1,052	797	74.8	75.7	676	63.4	64.2

B = Base is less than 75,000 and therefore too small to show the derived measure.

Table TN-14. Crime

(Number, rate per 100,000. Data are derived from the FBI Uniform Crime Reports.)

Item	State			U.S. [1,2,3,4]		
	2014	2015	Percent change	2014	2015	Percent change
TOTAL POPULATION[5]	6,547,779	6,600,299	0.8	318,907,401	321,418,820	0.8
VIOLENT CRIME						
Number..	39,989	40,400	1.0	1,186,185	1,231,566	3.8
Rate	610.7	612.1	0.2	372.0	383.2	3.0
Murder and Nonnegligent Manslaughter						
Number..	369	406	10.0	14,164	15,696	10.8
Rate	5.6	6.2	9.2	4.4	4.9	10.0
Rape[6]						
Number..	2,595	2,676	3.1	118,027	124,047	5.1
Rate	39.6	40.5	2.3	37.0	38.6	4.3
Robbery						
Number..	7,268	7,474	2.8	322,905	327,374	1.4
Rate	111.0	113.2	2.0	101.3	101.9	0.6
Aggravated Assault						
Number..	29,757	29,844	0.3	731,089	764,449	4.6
Rate	454.5	452.2	-0.5	229.2	237.8	3.7
PROPERTY CRIME						
Number..	200,911	193,796	-3.5	8,209,010	7,993,631	-2.6
Rate	3,068.4	2,936.2	-4.3	2,574.1	2,487.0	-3.4
Burglary						
Number..	46,798	43,247	-7.6	1,713,153	1,579,527	-7.8
Rate	714.7	655.2	-8.3	537.2	491.4	-8.5
Larceny-Theft						
Number..	141,464	137,679	-2.7	5,809,054	5,706,346	-1.8
Rate	2,160.5	2,086.0	-3.5	1,821.5	1,775.4	-2.5
Motor Vehicle Theft						
Number..	12,649	12,870	1.7	686,803	707,758	3.1
Rate	193.2	195.0	0.9	215.4	220.2	2.2

NOTE: Although arson data are included in the trend and clearance tables, sufficient data are not available to estimate totals for this offense. Therefore, no arson data are published in this table.
X = Not applicable.
- = Zero or rounds to zero.
[1] The crime figures have been adjusted.
[2] The data collection methodology for the offense of forcible rape used by the Minnesota state Uniform Crime Reporting (UCR) Program (with the exception of Minneapolis and St. Paul, Minnesota) does not comply with national UCR Program guidelines. Consequently, its figures for forcible rape and violent crime (of which forcible rape is a part) are not published in this table.
[3] Includes offenses reported by the Zoological Police and the Metro Transit Police.
[4] Because of changes in the state's reporting practices, figures are not comparable to previous years' data.
[5] Populations are U.S. Census Bureau provisional estimates as of July 1 of each year.
[6] The figures shown for the offense of rape were estimated using the revised Uniform Crime Reporting (UCR) definition of rape.

Table TN-15. State Government Finances, 2015

(Dollar amounts in thousands, percent distribution.)

Item	Dollars	Percent distribution
Total Revenue	30,806,454	100.0
General revenue	27,632,347	89.7
Intergovernmental revenue	10,568,128	34.3
Taxes	12,698,496	41.2
General sales	6,548,032	21.3
Selective sales	2,648,689	8.6
License taxes	1,502,770	4.9
Individual income tax	302,196	1.0
Corporate income tax	1,400,973	4.5
Other taxes	295,836	1.0
Current charges	2,134,527	6.9
Miscellaneous general revenue	2,231,196	7.2
Utility revenue	0	-
Liquor stores revenue	0	-
Insurance trust revenue[1]	3,174,107	10.3
Total Expenditure	31,957,529	100.0
Intergovernmental expenditure	7,233,618	22.6
Direct expenditure	24,723,911	77.4
Current operation	18,580,912	58.1
Capital outlay	1,538,331	4.8
Insurance benefits and repayments	3,177,122	9.9
Assistance and subsidies	1,191,350	3.7
Interest on debt	236,196	0.7
Exhibit: Salaries and wages	3,853,504	12.1
Total Expenditure	31,957,529	100.0
General expenditure	28,780,407	90.1
Intergovernmental expenditure	7,233,618	22.6
Direct expenditure	21,546,789	67.4
General expenditure, by function:		
Education	10,260,470	32.1
Public welfare	11,420,314	35.7
Hospitals	409,917	1.3
Health	656,123	2.1
Highways	1,572,450	4.9
Police protection	258,724	0.8
Correction	941,977	2.9
Natural resources	304,603	1.0
Parks and recreation	90,137	0.3
Governmental administration	876,655	2.7
Interest on general debt	236,196	0.7
Other and unallocable	1,752,841	5.5
Utility expenditure	0	-
Liquor stores expenditure	0	-
Insurance trust expenditure	3,177,122	9.9
Debt at End of Fiscal Year	6,025,074	X
Cash and Security Holdings	60,822,627	X

X = Not applicable.
- = Zero or rounds to zero.
[1] Within insurance trust revenue, net earnings of state retirement systems is a calculated statistic (the item code in the data file is X08), and thus can be positive or negative. Net earnings is the sum of earnings on investments plus gains on investments minus losses on investments. The change made in 2002 for asset valuation from book to market value in accordance with Statement 34 of the Governmental Accounting Standards Board is reflected in the calculated statistics.

Table TN-16. State Government Tax Collections, 2016

(Dollars in thousands, percent.)

Item	Dollars	Percent distribution
Total Taxes	13,386,169	100.0
Property taxes..	0	-
Sales and gross receipts	9,704,247	72.5
General sales and gross receipts	7,006,376	52.3
Selective sales and gross receipts	2,697,871	20.2
Alcoholic beverages	174,340	1.3
Amusements	0	-
Insurance premiums....................................	885,037	6.6
Motor fuels	897,608	6.7
Pari-mutuels	0	-
Public utilities	8,268	0.1
Tobacco products......................................	263,739	2.0
Other selective sales	468,879	3.5
Licenses...	1,516,966	11.3
Alcoholic beverages	1,467	-
Amusements	254	-
Corporations in general................................	773,374	5.8
Hunting and fishing......................................	38,848	0.3
Motor vehicle	301,635	2.3
Motor vehicle operators	56,063	0.4
Public utilities	6,108	-
Occupation and business, NEC	330,149	2.5
Other licenses	9,068	0.1
Income taxes...	1,862,601	13.9
Individual income..	323,952	2.4
Corporation net income	1,538,649	11.5
Other taxes..	302,355	2.3
Death and gift...	62,471	0.5
Documentary and stock transfer....................	219,188	1.6
Severance	1,444	-
Taxes, NEC...	19,252	0.1

X = Not applicable.
- = Zero or rounds to zero.

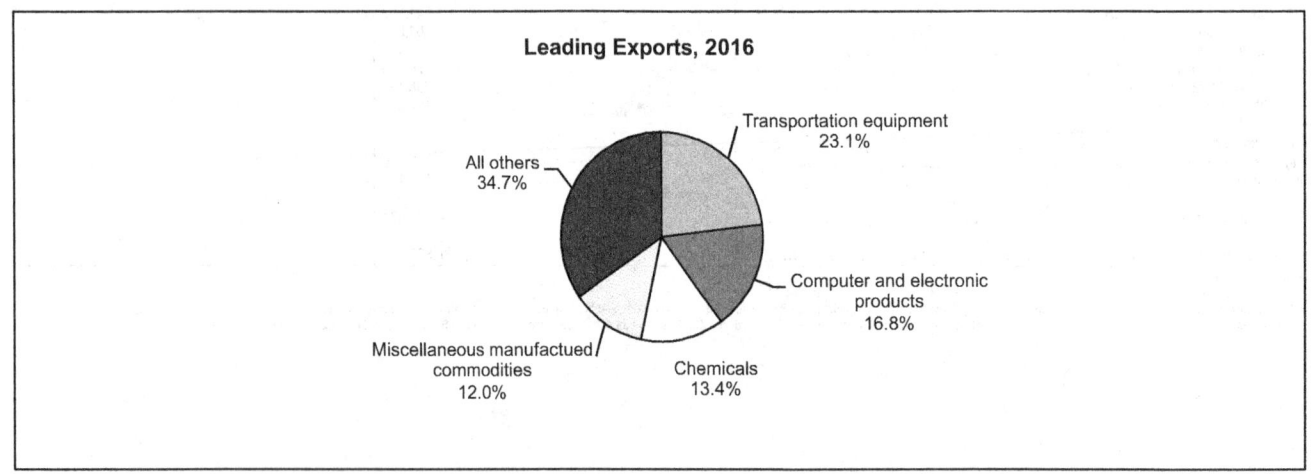

Leading Exports, 2016

Transportation equipment 23.1%
All others 34.7%
Computer and electronic products 16.8%
Miscellaneous manufactued commodities 12.0%
Chemicals 13.4%

TEXAS

Facts and Figures

Location: West South Central United States; bordered on the N by Oklahoma, on the E by Arkansas and Louisiana, on the S by Mexico and the Gulf of Mexico, and on the W by Mexico and New Mexico

Area: 268,581 sq. mi. (695,621 sq. km.); rank—2nd

Population: 27,862,596 (2016 est.); rank—2nd

Principal Cities: capital—Austin; largest—Houston

Statehood: December 29, 1845; 28th state

U.S. Congress: 2 senators, 36 representatives

State Motto: Friendship

State Song: "Texas, Our Texas"

State Nickname: The Lone Star State

Abbreviations: TX; Tex.

State Symbols: flower—bluebonnet; tree—pecan; bird—mockingbird

At a Glance

- With an increase in population of 10.8 percent, Texas ranked 3rd among the states in growth from 2010 to 2016.

- In 2016, Texas ranked second for the highest percent of its population under 18 years old (26.2 percent).

- Texas's median household income in 2015 was $55,653, and 15.9 percent of the population lived below the poverty level.

- In 2015, 17.1 percent of Texans did not have health insurance, making it the state with the highest percent of uninsured residents.

- Texas ranked 17th among states for its violent and property crime rates in 2015, which were 412.2 and 2,831.3 per 100,000 population respectively.

Table TX-1. Population by Age, Sex, Race, and Hispanic Origin

(Number, percent, except where noted.)

Sex, age, race, and Hispanic origin	2000	2010	2016 [1]	Average annual percent change, 2010–2016
Total Population................................	20,851,820	25,145,561	27,862,596	0.7
Percent of total U.S. population	7.4	8.1	8.6	X
Sex				
Male................................	10,352,910	12,472,280	13,831,432	0.7
Female	10,498,910	12,673,281	14,031,164	0.7
Age				
Under 5 years................................	1,625,628	1,928,473	2,019,171	0.3
5 to 19 years................................	4,291,608	5,693,241	6,037,969	0.4
20 to 64 years................................	12,233,052	14,921,961	16,452,216	0.6
65 years and over................................	2,072,532	2,601,886	3,353,240	1.8
Median age (years)	32.3	33.6	34.5	0.2
Race and Hispanic Origin				
One race........................				
White................................	14,799,505	20,389,793	22,135,668	0.5
Black................................	2,404,566	3,070,440	3,515,215	0.9
American Indian and Alaska Native	118,362	251,209	283,393	0.8
Asian................................	562,319	1,000,473	1,350,474	2.2
Native Hawaiian or Other Pacific Islander	14,434	31,242	39,079	1.6
Two or more races........................	514,633	402,404	538,767	2.1
Hispanic (of any race)........................	6,699,666	9,578,505	10,881,124	0.8

X = Not applicable.
[1] Population figures for 2016 are July 1 estimates. The 2010 estimates are taken from the 2010 Census.

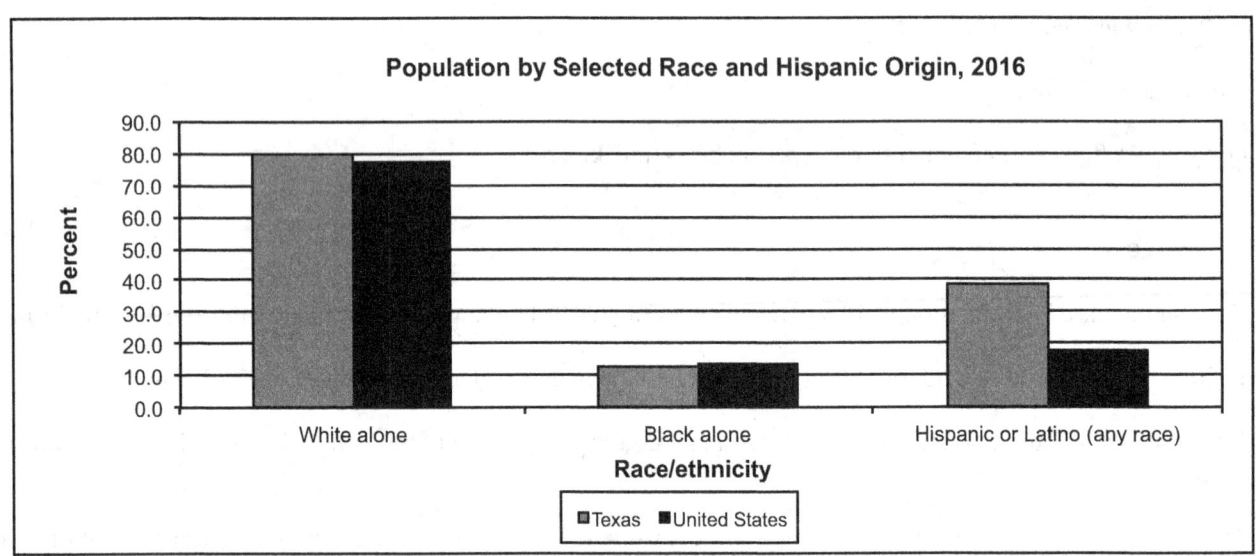

Population by Selected Race and Hispanic Origin, 2016

Table TX-2. Marital Status

(Number, percent distribution.)

Sex, age, race, and Hispanic origin	2000	2010	2015
Males, 15 Years and Over	7,820,248	9,587,343	10,558,177
Never married	28.6	34.6	36.0
Now married, except separated........................	58.8	51.6	50.3
Separated........................	2.0	2.3	2.1
Widowed........................	2.1	2.2	2.2
Divorced........................	8.5	9.4	9.4
Females, 15 Years and Over	8,117,395	9,903,147	10,888,388
Never married........................	22.6	27.6	29.6
Now married, except separated........................	54.3	48.5	47.3
Separated........................	2.9	3.3	3.0
Widowed........................	9.1	8.1	7.9
Divorced........................	11.0	12.5	12.2

Table TX-3. Households and Housing Characteristics

(Number, percent, dollars.)

Item	2000	2010	2015	Average annual percent change, 2000–2015
Total Households..	7,393,354	8,738,664	9,421,412	1.8
Family households..............................	5,247,794	6,091,590	6,520,909	1.6
Married-couple family.........................	3,989,741	4,386,996	4,709,478	1.2
Other family....................................	1,258,053	1,704,594	1,811,431	2.9
Male householder, no wife present............	320,464	436,727	489,774	3.5
Female householder, no husband present......	937,489	1,267,867	1,321,657	2.7
Nonfamily households............................	2,145,560	2,647,074	2,900,503	2.3
Householder living alone.......................	1,752,141	2,166,469	2,379,887	2.4
Householder not living alone...................	393,419	480,605	520,616	2.2
Housing Characteristics				
Total housing units..............................	8,157,575	9,996,209	10,588,236	2.0
Occupied housing units	7,393,354	8,738,664	9,421,412	1.8
Owner occupied................................	4,716,959	5,555,903	5,752,826	1.5
Renter occupied................................	2,676,395	3,182,761	3,668,586	2.5
Average household size...........................	2.74	2.82	2.85	0.3
Financial Characteristics				
Median gross rent of renter-occupied housing	574	801	932	4.2
Median monthly owner costs for housing units with a mortgage	986	1,402	1,453	3.2
Median value of owner-occupied housing units...........	82,500	128,100	152,000	5.6

Table TX-4. Migration, Origin, and Language

(Number, percent.)

	State			U.S.		
Characteristic	2014	2015	Percent change	2014	2015	Percent change
Residence 1 Year Ago						
Population 1 year and over	26,588,600	27,092,848	1.9	315,095,393	317,635,720	0.8
Same house	83.3	83.9	X	85.1	85.3	X
Different house in the U.S.	15.9	15.3	X	14.3	14.1	X
Same county	9.8	9.3	X	8.7	8.5	X
Different county	6.1	6.0	X	5.6	5.6	X
Same state	4.1	4.0	X	3.3	3.2	X
Different state	2.0	2.0	X	2.3	2.4	X
Abroad	0.8	0.8	X	0.6	0.7	X
Place of Birth						
Native born	22,434,530	22,797,819	1.6	276,465,262	278,128,449	0.6
Male	49.5	49.5	X	49.3	49.3	X
Female	50.5	50.5	X	50.7	50.7	X
Foreign born	4,522,428	4,671,295	3.3	42,391,794	43,290,372	2.1
Male	50.3	50.1	X	48.7	48.6	X
Female	49.7	49.9	X	51.3	51.4	X
Foreign born; naturalized U.S. citizen...........	1,579,958	1,673,484	5.9	19,984,738	20,697,103	3.6
Male	47.6	47.2	X	45.9	45.9	X
Female	52.4	52.8	X	54.1	54.1	X
Foreign born; not a U.S. citizen	2,942,470	2,997,811	1.9	22,407,056	22,593,269	0.8
Male	51.7	51.7	X	51.2	51.1	X
Female	48.3	48.3	X	48.8	48.9	X
Entered 2010 or later	12.8	16.3	X	12.3	15.6	X
Entered 2000 to 2009	30.6	30.4	X	28.6	27.9	X
Entered before 2000..........................	56.6	53.3	X	59.1	56.5	X
World Region of Birth, Foreign						
Foreign-born population, excluding population born at sea	4,522,428	4,671,295	3.3	42,390,705	43,289,646	2.1
Europe	4.4	4.1	X	11.2	11.1	X
Asia	20.3	21.1	X	30.1	30.6	X
Africa	4.2	4.7	X	4.6	4.8	X
Oceania	0.3	0.3	X	0.6	0.6	X
Latin America................................	69.9	68.7	X	51.6	51.1	X
North America	1.0	1.2	X	1.9	1.9	X
Language Spoken at Home and Ability to Speak English						
Population 5 years and over.......................	25,010,570	25,502,406	2.0	299,084,046	301,625,014	0.8
English only	64.5	64.6	X	78.9	78.5	X
Language other than English....................	35.5	35.4	X	21.1	21.5	X
Speaks English less than "very well"...........	14.4	14.3	X	8.6	8.6	X

NA = Not available.
X = Not applicable.
- = Zero or rounds to zero.

Table TX-5. Median Income and Poverty Status, 2015

(Number, percent, except as noted.)

Characteristic	State		U.S.	
	Number	Percent	Number	Percent
Median Income				
Households (dollars)	55,653	X	55,775	X
Families (dollars)	65,316	X	68,260	X
Below Poverty Level (All People)	4,255,517	15.9	46,153,077	14.7
Sex				
Male	1,900,782	14.4	20,599,407	13.4
Female	2,354,735	17.3	25,553,670	16.0
Age				
Under 18 years	1,637,308	23.0	15,000,273	20.7
Related children under 18 years	1,613,692	22.7	14,693,239	20.4
18 to 64 years	2,295,867	13.8	26,960,369	13.9
65 years and over	322,342	10.3	4,192,435	9.0

X = Not applicable.

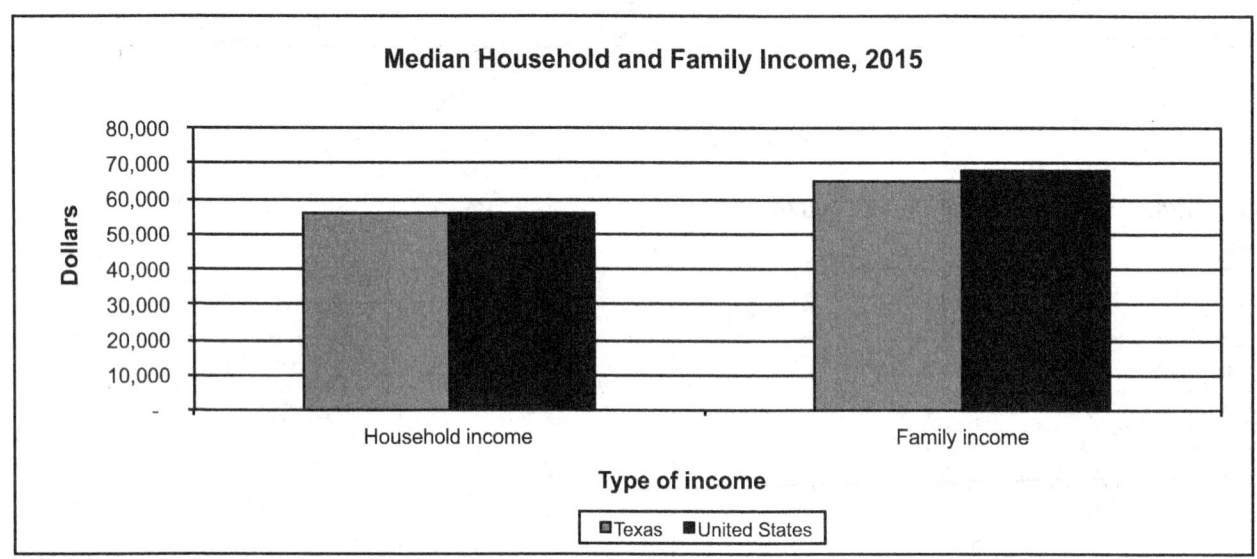

Median Household and Family Income, 2015

Table TX-6. Health Insurance Coverage Status for the Civilian Noninstitutionalized Population and Children Under 18 Years of Age

(Numbers in thousands, percent.)

Item	2007	2008	2009	2010	2011	2012	2013	2014	2015
Civilian Noninstitutionalized Population	23,704	23,827	24,292	24,779	25,197	25,584	25,977	26,486	26,990
Covered by Private or Public Insurance									
Number	17,742	18,082	18,508	18,904	19,408	19,822	20,228	21,438	22,375
Percent	74.8	75.9	76.2	76.3	77.0	77.5	77.9	80.9	82.9
Not Covered									
Number	5,962	5,745	5,783	5,875	5,790	5,762	5,748	5,047	4,615
Percent	25.2	24.1	23.8	23.7	23.0	22.5	22.1	19.1	17.1
Percent in the U.S. not covered	15.3	15.1	15.1	15.5	15.1	14.8	14.5	11.7	9.4
Children Under 18 Years of Age	6,720	6,714	6,878	6,876	6,947	6,972	7,029	7,107	7,198
Covered by Private or Public Insurance									
Number	5,285	5,518	5,758	5,880	6,030	6,109	6,140	6,323	6,516
Percent	78.6	82.2	83.7	85.5	86.8	87.6	87.4	89.0	90.5
Not Covered									
Number	1,435	1,196	1,120	996	917	863	888	784	682
Percent	21.4	17.8	16.3	14.5	13.2	12.4	12.6	11.0	9.5
Percent in the U.S. not covered	11.0	9.7	8.6	8.0	7.5	7.2	7.1	6.0	4.8

Table TX-7. Employment Status by Demographic Group, 2016

(Numbers in thousands, percent.)

Characteristic	Civilian noninstitutional population	Civilian labor force		Employed		Unemployed	
		Number	Percent of population	Number	Percent of population	Number	Percent of population
Total................................	20,939	13,344	63.7	12,735	60.8	609	4.6
Sex							
Male................................	10,177	7,407	72.8	7,054	69.3	352	4.8
Female	10,762	5,937	55.2	5,681	52.8	256	4.3
Race, Sex, and Hispanic Origin							
White................................	16,773	10,621	63.3	10,177	60.7	445	4.2
Male...............................	8,197	5,987	73.0	5,727	69.9	259	4.3
Female.............................	8,576	4,635	54.0	4,449	51.9	185	4.0
Black or African American..............	2,560	1,668	65.1	1,552	60.6	116	6.9
Male...............................	1,177	816	69.3	745	63.3	71	8.7
Female.............................	1,383	852	61.6	807	58.4	45	5.3
Hispanic or Latino ethnicity[1]	7,474	4,869	65.1	4,633	62.0	236	4.9
Male...............................	3,744	2,870	76.6	2,732	73.0	138	4.8
Female.............................	3,731	1,999	53.6	1,901	50.9	99	4.9
Age							
16 to 19 years.......................	1,573	500	31.8	422	26.8	78	15.6
20 to 24 years.......................	1,927	1,337	69.4	1,226	63.6	110	8.3
25 to 34 years.......................	4,001	3,192	79.8	3,044	76.1	148	4.6
35 to 44 years.......................	3,609	2,974	82.4	2,881	79.8	93	3.1
45 to 54 years.......................	3,339	2,666	79.8	2,578	77.2	88	3.3
55 to 64 years.......................	3,158	2,046	64.8	1,978	62.6	67	3.3
65 years and over	3,331	630	18.9	606	18.2	24	3.8

NOTE: Data in Table 7 are from the Current Population Survey (CPS) and do not match the estimates in Table 8. See notes and definitions for further information.
[1] May be of any race.

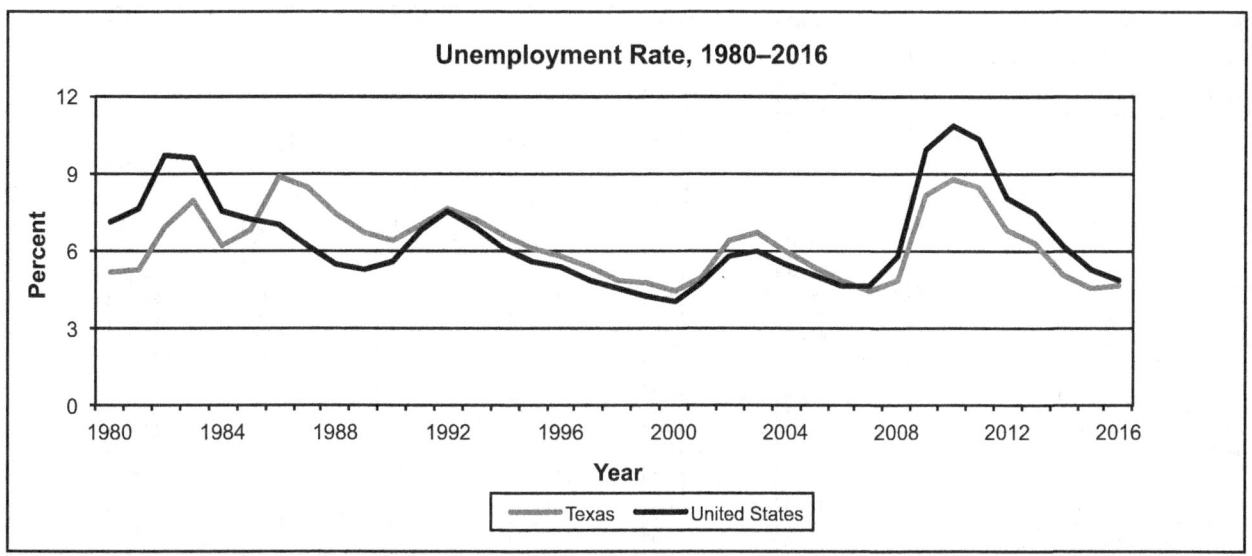

Table TX-8. Employment Status of the Civilian Noninstitutional Population Age 16 Years and Over

(Number, percent.)

Year	Civilian labor force	Civilian participation rate	Employed	Unemployed	Unemployment rate
2008................................	11,664,390	65.8	11,104,115	560,275	4.8
2009................................	11,910,799	65.8	11,008,903	901,896	7.6
2010................................	12,241,970	65.9	11,244,632	997,338	8.1
2011................................	12,504,498	65.9	11,535,095	969,403	7.8
2012................................	12,682,204	65.6	11,830,356	851,848	6.7
2013................................	12,891,255	65.4	12,090,501	800,754	6.2
2014................................	13,022,851	64.7	12,358,703	664,148	5.1
2015................................	13,078,304	63.7	12,494,350	583,954	4.5
2016................................	13,284,623	63.7	12,671,801	612,822	4.6

Table TX-9. Employment and Average Wages by Industry

(Estimates through 2010 are based on the 2007 *North American Industry Classification System* [NAICS]. Estimates from 2011 onward are based on the 2012 NAICS.)

Industry	2009	2010	2011	2012	2013	2014	2015
	Number of jobs						
Wage and Salary Employment by Industry..................	10,812,718	10,790,781	11,042,608	11,367,650	11,670,732	12,028,094	12,305,468
Farm Wage and Salary Employment.........................	48,340	43,326	41,977	43,718	47,503	47,110	49,030
Nonfarm Wage and Salary Employment....................	10,764,378	10,747,455	11,000,631	11,323,932	11,623,229	11,980,984	12,256,438
Private wage and salary employment........................	8,780,593	8,727,604	9,009,609	9,353,987	9,648,041	9,995,823	10,241,726
Forestry, fishing, and related activities........................	30,158	31,560	31,740	32,099	32,346	33,114	33,427
Mining..........................	203,253	202,972	233,875	268,335	287,841	304,031	268,425
Utilities..........................	48,050	48,301	49,010	48,693	48,981	49,022	49,455
Construction..........................	626,602	585,279	583,161	602,678	631,784	669,947	701,478
Manufacturing..........................	838,585	811,201	837,535	864,226	875,064	888,537	879,369
Durable goods manufacturing..........................	537,366	515,892	543,773	569,119	578,553	589,975	577,702
Nondurable goods manufacturing..........................	301,219	295,309	293,762	295,107	296,511	298,562	301,667
Wholesale trade	503,182	499,769	517,723	542,974	564,650	581,723	599,154
Retail trade..........................	1,159,277	1,146,645	1,171,735	1,197,956	1,227,715	1,264,248	1,307,146
Transportation and warehousing..........................	376,664	374,170	390,327	406,563	417,198	433,783	452,799
Information..........................	205,543	195,789	195,887	197,235	201,252	203,279	201,054
Finance and insurance	458,406	463,249	476,380	492,851	507,099	517,398	533,924
Real estate and rental and leasing..........................	182,637	175,546	178,925	183,940	192,392	200,908	205,205
Professional, scientific, and technical services	570,470	573,982	593,233	627,780	653,097	683,752	713,867
Management of companies and enterprises....................	77,097	79,375	83,406	89,976	93,917	111,745	116,664
Administrative and waste services	622,682	633,308	675,365	707,501	727,828	762,307	775,548
Educational services	148,381	153,578	159,028	162,971	165,827	169,692	173,531
Health care and social assistance..........................	1,155,391	1,195,195	1,225,814	1,263,159	1,295,178	1,325,805	1,378,404
Arts, entertainment, and recreation..........................	111,693	111,953	111,488	113,104	118,658	125,667	131,343
Accommodation and food services..........................	906,035	903,182	938,896	981,693	1,028,314	1,070,233	1,117,385
Other services, except public administration..................	556,487	542,550	556,081	570,253	578,900	600,632	603,548
Government and government enterprises..........................	1,983,785	2,019,851	1,991,022	1,969,945	1,975,188	1,985,161	2,014,712
	Dollars						
Average Wages and Salaries by Industry	45,091	46,505	48,285	50,075	50,665	52,660	53,769
Average Farm Wages and Salaries	24,163	26,295	32,493	31,875	26,301	31,683	38,167
Average Nonfarm Wages and Salaries	45,185	46,587	48,345	50,146	50,764	52,743	53,832
Average private wages and salaries..........................	45,509	47,138	49,063	51,115	51,698	53,775	54,801
Forestry, fishing, and related activities..........................	23,843	24,942	25,081	26,051	26,238	27,442	28,611
Mining..........................	111,423	117,497	122,069	120,617	119,742	123,979	125,100
Utilities..........................	88,499	89,996	90,259	98,762	97,642	100,436	104,051
Construction..........................	48,316	49,192	50,919	54,213	55,702	58,586	60,534
Manufacturing..........................	60,222	63,180	65,894	68,245	68,525	71,113	72,802
Durable goods manufacturing..........................	62,226	65,431	68,311	70,111	70,295	73,116	74,113
Nondurable goods manufacturing..........................	56,647	59,247	61,421	64,647	65,071	67,153	70,291
Wholesale trade	64,828	67,898	71,407	74,567	74,148	77,185	78,398
Retail trade..........................	26,361	27,147	27,896	28,850	29,084	30,004	30,722
Transportation and warehousing..........................	50,372	53,307	55,297	58,744	58,285	60,022	61,536
Information..........................	66,778	67,351	70,676	73,399	75,305	76,706	79,783
Finance and insurance	65,169	68,427	71,429	74,499	75,762	79,571	82,471
Real estate and rental and leasing..........................	43,750	46,074	49,458	52,884	53,963	57,305	58,296
Professional, scientific, and technical services	73,561	76,558	79,513	81,892	83,831	86,530	88,414
Management of companies and enterprises....................	94,093	99,994	106,975	114,364	113,568	123,477	124,005
Administrative and waste services	35,056	36,050	36,958	38,354	38,964	40,653	41,799
Educational services	35,061	35,885	36,896	37,520	38,686	39,025	39,859
Health care and social assistance..........................	40,400	40,936	41,703	42,343	42,564	43,910	45,407
Arts, entertainment, and recreation..........................	31,722	31,561	32,486	33,892	32,989	33,657	35,550
Accommodation and food services..........................	17,680	18,279	18,876	19,569	19,879	20,539	21,233
Other services, except public administration..................	26,901	28,025	28,847	30,041	31,114	32,325	33,405
Government and government enterprises..........................	43,749	44,204	45,096	45,543	46,202	47,547	48,904

Table TX-10. Employment Characteristics by Family Type

(Number, percent.)

Family type and labor force status	2013 Total	2013 Families with own children under 18 years	2014 Total	2014 Families with own children under 18 years	2015 Total	2015 Families with own children under 18 years
All Families...	6,322,542	3,033,950	6,386,885	3,036,494	6,520,909	3,076,309
FAMILY TYPE AND LABOR FORCE STATUS						
Married-Couple Families..	4,552,753	2,049,461	4,582,954	2,049,534	4,709,478	2,092,503
Both husband and wife in labor force................................	50.4	59.2	49.9	59.2	49.3	58.6
Husband in labor force, wife not in labor force	28.4	35.6	28.7	36.0	28.5	36.0
Wife in labor force, husband not in labor force	6.9	3.4	6.7	3.2	6.9	3.5
Both husband and wife not in labor force................................	14.0	1.6	14.7	1.6	14.7	1.5
Other Families	1,769,789	984,489	1,803,931	986,960	1,811,431	983,806
Female householder, no husband present................................	74.0	77.9	73.5	77.4	73.0	76.6
In labor force..	54.2	64.9	53.1	63.6	52.9	63.4
Not in labor force	19.7	13.0	20.4	13.8	20.1	13.2
Male householder, no wife present........................	26.0	22.1	26.5	22.6	27.0	23.4
In labor force..	21.0	20.1	21.3	20.7	22.2	21.7
Not in labor force	5.1	2.0	5.1	1.8	4.8	1.8

Table TX-11. School Enrollment and Educational Attainment, 2015

(Number, percent.)

Item	State	U.S.
Enrollment		
Total population 3 years and over, enrolled in school	7,540,957	81,618,288
Enrolled in nursery school or preschool (percent)	6.0	6.0
Enrolled in kindergarten (percent)................................	5.6	5.0
Enrolled in elementary school, grades 1-8 (percent)................................	43.4	40.3
Enrolled in high school, grades 9-12 (percent)................................	21.1	20.9
Enrolled in college or graduate school (percent)................................	23.9	27.7
Attainment		
Total population 25 years and over	17,472,861	216,447,163
Less than ninth grade (percent)................................	8.9	5.5
9th to 12th grade, no diploma (percent)................................	8.7	7.3
High school graduate, including equivalency (percent)................................	25.3	27.6
Some college, no degree (percent)................................	21.8	20.7
Associate's degree (percent)	6.9	8.2
Bachelor's degree (percent)................................	18.7	19.0
Graduate or professional degree (percent)................................	9.7	11.6
High school graduate or higher (percent)	82.4	87.1
Bachelor's degree or higher (percent)................................	28.4	30.6

Table TX-12. Public School Characteristics and Educational Indicators

(Number, percent; data derived from National Center of Education Statistics.)

Item	State	U.S.
Public Schools, 2014–2015 (except where noted)		
Number of school districts................................	1,244	18,260
Number of schools................................	8,798	98,373
Number of students	5,233,765	50,312,581
Number of teachers	342,257	3,132,351
Student-teacher ratio	15.3	16.1
Expenditures per student (dollars), FY 2014................................	8,602	11,066
Four-year adjusted cohort graduation rate (ACGR)[1,2]	89.0	83.2
Students eligible for free or reduced-price lunch (percent)................................	58.8	51.8
English language learners (percent)................................	15.4	9.4
Students age 3 to 21 served under IDEA, part B (percent)................................	8.6	13.0

Public Schools by Type	Number	Percent of state public schools
Total number of schools................................	8,798	100.0
Regular	7,818	88.9
Special education................................	13	0.1
Vocational education	0	-
Alternative education................................	967	11.0

NOTE: Every school is assigned only one school type based on its instructional emphasis.
[1] ACGR data represents a new method of calculating high-school completion rates and may not be comparable to previous years' data for Averaged Freshmen Graduation Rates (AFGR).
[2] The United States 4-year ACGRs were estimated using both the reported 4-year ACGR data from 49 states and the District of Columbia and using imputed data for Idaho. The estimate for American Indian/Alaska Native students also includes imputed data for Virginia.

Table TX-13. Reported Voting and Registration of the Voting-Age Population, November 2016

(Numbers in thousands, percent.)

Item	Total population	Total citizen population	Registered			Voted		
			Total registered	Percent registered (total population)	Percent registered (total citizen population)	Total voted	Percent voted (total population)	Percent voted (total citizen population)
U.S. Total	245,502	224,059	157,596	64.2	70.3	137,537	56.0	61.4
State Total.............................	20,172	17,378	11,724	58.1	67.5	9,626	47.7	55.4
Sex								
Male	9,775	8,325	5,479	56.0	65.8	4,465	45.7	53.6
Female	10,397	9,053	6,245	60.1	69.0	5,162	49.6	57.0
Race								
White alone..............................	16,095	13,909	9,306	57.8	66.9	7,700	47.8	55.4
White, non-Hispanic alone	9,534	9,383	6,822	71.6	72.7	5,905	61.9	62.9
Black alone...............................	2,458	2,358	1,724	70.2	73.1	1,349	54.9	57.2
Asian alone..............................	1,110	715	418	37.7	58.5	338	30.4	47.3
Hispanic (of any race)...................	6,923	4,781	2,654	38.3	55.5	1,938	28.0	40.5
White alone or in combination	16,291	14,101	9,436	57.9	66.9	7,807	47.9	55.4
Black alone or in combination..........	2,576	2,473	1,812	70.3	73.3	1,417	55.0	57.3
Asian alone or in combination..........	1,135	736	440	38.7	59.7	356	31.3	48.3
Age								
18 to 24 years...........................	2,542	2,175	1,036	40.8	47.6	694	27.3	31.9
25 to 34 years...........................	3,950	3,186	1,918	48.6	60.2	1,483	37.5	46.5
35 to 44 years...........................	3,764	3,008	2,033	54.0	67.6	1,617	42.9	53.7
45 to 64 years...........................	6,450	5,743	4,181	64.8	72.8	3,579	55.5	62.3
65 years and over	3,465	3,265	2,556	73.7	78.3	2,254	65.0	69.0

Table TX-14. Crime

(Number, rate per 100,000. Data are derived from the FBI Uniform Crime Reports.)

Item	State			U.S. [1,2,3,4]		
	2014	2015	Percent change	2014	2015	Percent change
TOTAL POPULATION[5]	26,979,078	27,469,114	1.8	318,907,401	321,418,820	0.8
VIOLENT CRIME						
Number..................................	109,711	113,227	3.2	1,186,185	1,231,566	3.8
Rate	406.7	412.2	1.4	372.0	383.2	3.0
Murder and Nonnegligent Manslaughter						
Number..................................	1,192	1,316	10.4	14,164	15,696	10.8
Rate	4.4	4.8	8.4	4.4	4.9	10.0
Rape[6]						
Number..................................	11,636	12,250	5.3	118,027	124,047	5.1
Rate	43.1	44.6	3.4	37.0	38.6	4.3
Robbery						
Number..................................	31,021	31,934	2.9	322,905	327,374	1.4
Rate	115.0	116.3	1.1	101.3	101.9	0.6
Aggravated Assault						
Number..................................	65,862	67,727	2.8	731,089	764,449	4.6
Rate	244.1	246.6	1.0	229.2	237.8	3.7
PROPERTY CRIME						
Number..................................	813,515	777,739	-4.4	8,209,010	7,993,631	-2.6
Rate	3,015.4	2,831.3	-6.1	2,574.1	2,487.0	-3.4
Burglary						
Number..................................	168,085	153,054	-8.9	1,713,153	1,579,527	-7.8
Rate	623.0	557.2	-10.6	537.2	491.4	-8.5
Larceny-Theft						
Number..................................	577,018	557,200	-3.4	5,809,054	5,706,346	-1.8
Rate	2,138.8	2,028.5	-5.2	1,821.5	1,775.4	-2.5
Motor Vehicle Theft						
Number..................................	68,412	67,485	-1.4	686,803	707,758	3.1
Rate	253.6	245.7	-3.1	215.4	220.2	2.2

NOTE: Although arson data are included in the trend and clearance tables, sufficient data are not available to estimate totals for this offense. Therefore, no arson data are published in this table.
X = Not applicable.
- = Zero or rounds to zero.
[1] The crime figures have been adjusted.
[2] The data collection methodology for the offense of forcible rape used by the Minnesota state Uniform Crime Reporting (UCR) Program (with the exception of Minneapolis and St. Paul, Minnesota) does not comply with national UCR Program guidelines. Consequently, its figures for forcible rape and violent crime (of which forcible rape is a part) are not published in this table.
[3] Includes offenses reported by the Zoological Police and the Metro Transit Police.
[4] Because of changes in the state's reporting practices, figures are not comparable to previous years' data.
[5] Populations are U.S. Census Bureau provisional estimates as of July 1 of each year.
[6] The figures shown for the offense of rape were estimated using the revised Uniform Crime Reporting (UCR) definition of rape.

Table TX-15. State Government Finances, 2015

(Dollar amounts in thousands, percent distribution.)

Item	Dollars	Percent distribution
Total Revenue	138,669,933	100.0
General revenue	124,039,294	89.4
Intergovernmental revenue	43,863,312	31.6
Taxes	55,086,438	39.7
General sales	33,664,187	24.3
Selective sales	13,989,995	10.1
License taxes	3,426,885	2.5
Individual income tax	0	-
Corporate income tax	0	-
Other taxes	4,005,371	2.9
Current charges	14,091,904	10.2
Miscellaneous general revenue	10,997,640	7.9
Utility revenue	0	-
Liquor stores revenue	0	-
Insurance trust revenue[1]	14,630,639	10.6
Total Expenditure	138,658,997	100.0
Intergovernmental expenditure	29,951,157	21.6
Direct expenditure	108,707,840	78.4
Current operation	77,201,719	55.7
Capital outlay	9,310,276	6.7
Insurance benefits and repayments	17,934,328	12.9
Assistance and subsidies	2,673,958	1.9
Interest on debt	1,587,559	1.1
Exhibit: Salaries and wages	17,580,372	12.7
Total Expenditure	138,658,997	100.0
General expenditure	120,724,669	87.1
Intergovernmental expenditure	29,951,157	21.6
Direct expenditure	90,773,512	65.5
General expenditure, by function:		
Education	52,321,669	37.7
Public welfare	35,961,689	25.9
Hospitals	6,048,942	4.4
Health	2,661,393	1.9
Highways	8,445,801	6.1
Police protection	1,013,704	0.7
Correction	3,848,268	2.8
Natural resources	1,214,701	0.9
Parks and recreation	163,302	0.1
Governmental administration	2,048,722	1.5
Interest on general debt	1,587,559	1.1
Other and unallocable	5,408,919	3.9
Utility expenditure	0	-
Liquor stores expenditure	0	-
Insurance trust expenditure	17,934,328	12.9
Debt at End of Fiscal Year	48,237,511	X
Cash and Security Holdings	329,246,316	X

X = Not applicable.
- = Zero or rounds to zero.
[1] Within insurance trust revenue, net earnings of state retirement systems is a calculated statistic (the item code in the data file is X08), and thus can be positive or negative. Net earnings is the sum of earnings on investments plus gains on investments minus losses on investments. The change made in 2002 for asset valuation from book to market value in accordance with Statement 34 of the Governmental Accounting Standards Board is reflected in the calculated statistics.

Table TX-16. State Government Tax Collections, 2016

(Dollars in thousands, percent.)

Item	Dollars	Percent distribution
Total Taxes	52,132,817	100.0
Property taxes	0	-
Sales and gross receipts	46,370,774	88.9
General sales and gross receipts	32,131,385	61.6
Selective sales and gross receipts	14,239,389	27.3
Alcoholic beverages	1,191,961	2.3
Amusements	29,780	0.1
Insurance premiums	2,171,362	4.2
Motor fuels	3,500,210	6.7
Pari-mutuels	6,954	-
Public utilities	605,487	1.2
Tobacco products	1,479,863	2.8
Other selective sales	5,253,772	10.1
Licenses	3,414,335	6.5
Alcoholic beverages	74,711	0.1
Amusements	19,874	-
Corporations in general	137,109	0.3
Hunting and fishing	110,051	0.2
Motor vehicle	2,227,996	4.3
Motor vehicle operators	137,372	0.3
Public utilities	20,542	-
Occupation and business, NEC	517,411	1.0
Other licenses	169,269	0.3
Income taxes	0	-
Individual income	0	-
Corporation net income	0	-
Other taxes	2,347,708	4.5
Death and gift	0	-
Documentary and stock transfer	0	-
Severance	2,347,708	4.5
Taxes, NEC	0	-

X = Not applicable.
- = Zero or rounds to zero.

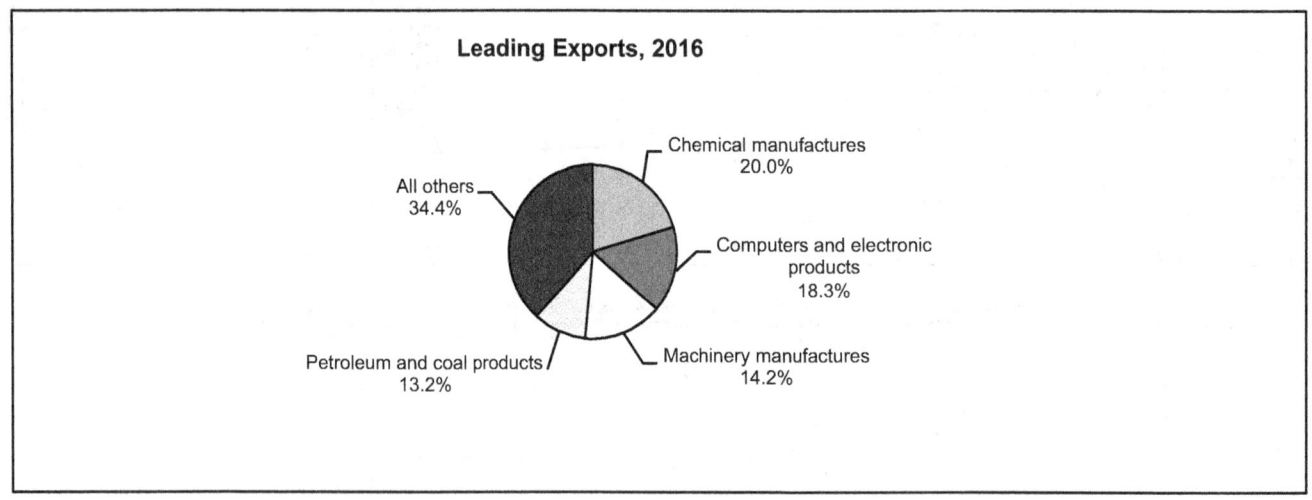

Leading Exports, 2016

Chemical manufactures 20.0%
Computers and electronic products 18.3%
Machinery manufactures 14.2%
Petroleum and coal products 13.2%
All others 34.4%

Facts and Figures

Location: Western United States; bordered on the N by Idaho and Wyoming, on the E by Colorado, on the S by Arizona, and on the W by Nevada; Utah is one of the Four Corner states—at its SE corner it touches Arizona, Colorado, and New Mexico

Area: 84,899 sq. mi. (219,887 sq. km.); rank—13th

Population: 3,051,217 (2016 est.); rank—31st

Principal Cities: capital—Salt Lake City; largest—Salt Lake City

Statehood: January 4, 1896; 45th state

U.S. Congress: 2 senators, 4 representatives

State Motto: Industry

State Song: "Utah, We Love Thee"

State Nickname: The Beehive State

Abbreviations: UT

State Symbols: flower—sego lily; tree—blue spruce; bird—California seagull

At a Glance

- With an increase in population of 10.4 percent, Utah ranked 4th among the states in growth from 2010 to 2016.

- Utah's violent crime rate in 2015 was 236.0 per 100,000 population, compared to 383.2 for the entire nation.

- Of all the states, Utah had the highest percent children in 2016, with 30.2 percent of its population under age 18.

- Utah also has the highest birth rate among states in 2015, at a rate of 17.0 births per 1,000 population.

- In 2015, 10.5 percent of Utahns did not have health insurance, compared to 9.4 percent of the total U.S. population.

Table UT-1. Population by Age, Sex, Race, and Hispanic Origin

(Number, percent, except where noted.)

Sex, age, race, and Hispanic origin	2000	2010	2016 [1]	Average annual percent change, 2010–2016
Total Population..	2,233,169	2,763,885	3,051,217	0.6
Percent of total U.S. population	0.8	0.9	0.9	X
Sex				
Male..	1,119,031	1,388,317	1,535,894	0.7
Female	1,114,138	1,375,568	1,515,323	0.6
Age				
Under 5 years...	209,378	263,924	253,450	-0.2
5 to 19 years..	601,599	698,613	758,625	0.5
20 to 64 years..	1,231,970	1,551,886	1,717,978	0.7
65 years and over...	190,222	249,462	321,164	1.8
Median age (years)	27.1	29.2	30.8	0.3
Race and Hispanic Origin				
One race..				
White..	1,992,975	2,547,328	2,778,175	0.6
Black...	17,657	33,864	41,418	1.4
American Indian and Alaska Native	29,684	40,729	47,514	1.0
Asian..	37,108	57,800	77,033	2.1
Native Hawaiian or Other Pacific Islander	15,145	26,049	31,502	1.3
Two or more races	47,185	58,114	75,575	1.9
Hispanic (of any race).....................................	201,559	370,870	420,440	0.8

X = Not applicable.
[1] Population figures for 2016 are July 1 estimates. The 2010 estimates are taken from the 2010 Census.

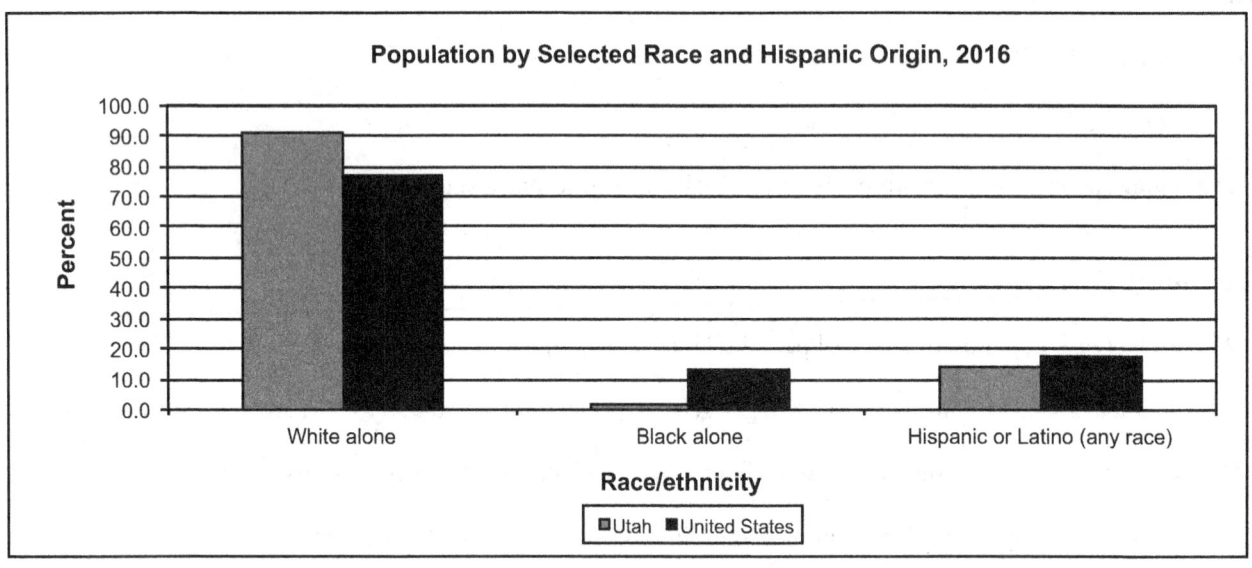

Table UT-2. Marital Status

(Number, percent distribution.)

Sex, age, race, and Hispanic origin	2000	2010	2015
Males, 15 Years and Over	813,693	1,014,706	1,111,888
Never married..	30.6	31.3	33.2
Now married, except separated...................................	59.5	58.0	55.7
Separated..	1.1	1.3	1.4
Widowed..	1.6	1.8	1.7
Divorced..	7.3	7.6	8.0
Females, 15 Years and Over	852,995	1,019,010	1,116,485
Never married..	25.2	25.8	26.7
Now married, except separated...................................	58.0	56.6	54.9
Separated..	1.4	1.6	1.7
Widowed..	6.6	5.8	5.9
Divorced..	8.8	10.1	10.7

Table UT-3. Households and Housing Characteristics

(Number, percent, dollars.)

Item	2000	2010	2015	Average annual percent change, 2000–2015
Total Households	701,281	880,025	930,980	2.2
Family households	535,294	665,964	693,181	2.0
Married-couple family	442,931	543,212	564,803	1.8
Other family	92,363	122,752	128,378	2.6
Male householder, no wife present	26,422	37,258	39,778	3.4
Female householder, no husband present	65,941	85,494	88,600	2.3
Nonfamily households	165,987	214,061	237,799	2.9
Householder living alone	124,756	164,863	184,180	3.2
Householder not living alone	41,231	49,198	53,619	2.0
Housing Characteristics				
Total housing units	768,594	981,821	1,038,065	2.3
Occupied housing units	701,281	880,025	930,980	2.2
Owner occupied	501,547	615,142	641,215	1.9
Renter occupied	188,734	264,883	289,765	3.6
Average household size	3.13	3.10	3.17	0.1
Financial Characteristics				
Median gross rent of renter-occupied housing	597	796	925	3.7
Median monthly owner costs for housing units with a mortgage	1,102	1,433	1,408	1.9
Median value of owner-occupied housing units	146,100	217,200	234,600	4.0

Table UT-4. Migration, Origin, and Language

(Number, percent.)

Characteristic	State 2014	State 2015	State Percent change	U.S. 2014	U.S. 2015	U.S. Percent change
Residence 1 Year Ago						
Population 1 year and over	2,894,001	2,947,423	1.8	315,095,393	317,635,720	0.8
Same house	83.2	82.6	X	85.1	85.3	X
Different house in the U.S.	16.1	16.6	X	14.3	14.1	X
Same county	9.7	10.2	X	8.7	8.5	X
Different county	6.4	6.3	X	5.6	5.6	X
Same state	3.3	3.0	X	3.3	3.2	X
Different state	3.1	3.3	X	2.3	2.4	X
Abroad	0.7	0.8	X	0.6	0.7	X
Place of Birth						
Native born	2,692,985	2,751,452	2.2	276,465,262	278,128,449	0.6
Male	50.4	50.5	X	49.3	49.3	X
Female	49.6	49.5	X	50.7	50.7	X
Foreign born	249,917	244,467	-2.2	42,391,794	43,290,372	2.1
Male	49.1	48.0	X	48.7	48.6	X
Female	50.9	52.0	X	51.3	51.4	X
Foreign born; naturalized U.S. citizen	95,039	95,513	0.5	19,984,738	20,697,103	3.6
Male	45.3	46.2	X	45.9	45.9	X
Female	54.7	53.8	X	54.1	54.1	X
Foreign born; not a U.S. citizen	154,878	148,954	-3.8	22,407,056	22,593,269	0.8
Male	51.5	49.2	X	51.2	51.1	X
Female	48.5	50.8	X	48.8	48.9	X
Entered 2010 or later	13.4	14.7	X	12.3	15.6	X
Entered 2000 to 2009	32.7	31.6	X	28.6	27.9	X
Entered before 2000	53.9	53.7	X	59.1	56.5	X
World Region of Birth, Foreign						
Foreign-born population, excluding population born at sea	249,831	244,413	-2.2	42,390,705	43,289,646	2.1
Europe	9.5	9.3	X	11.2	11.1	X
Asia	21.7	20.0	X	30.1	30.6	X
Africa	3.2	3.4	X	4.6	4.8	X
Oceania	3.5	3.4	X	0.6	0.6	X
Latin America	59.0	60.5	X	51.6	51.1	X
North America	3.1	3.3	X	1.9	1.9	X
Language Spoken at Home and Ability to Speak English						
Population 5 years and over	2,693,093	2,745,950	2.0	299,084,046	301,625,014	0.8
English only	85.3	85.2	X	78.9	78.5	X
Language other than English	14.7	14.8	X	21.1	21.5	X
Speaks English less than "very well"	5.1	4.8	X	8.6	8.6	X

NA = Not available.
X = Not applicable.
- = Zero or rounds to zero.

Table UT-5. Median Income and Poverty Status, 2015

(Number, percent, except as noted.)

Characteristic	State		U.S.	
	Number	Percent	Number	Percent
Median Income				
Households (dollars)	62,912	X	55,775	X
Families (dollars)	71,594	X	68,260	X
Below Poverty Level (All People)	331,854	11.3	46,153,077	14.7
Sex				
Male	152,901	10.4	20,599,407	13.4
Female	178,953	12.2	25,553,670	16.0
Age				
Under 18 years	115,994	12.9	15,000,273	20.7
Related children under 18 years	112,203	12.5	14,693,239	20.4
18 to 64 years	195,074	11.2	26,960,369	13.9
65 years and over	20,786	6.8	4,192,435	9.0

X = Not applicable.

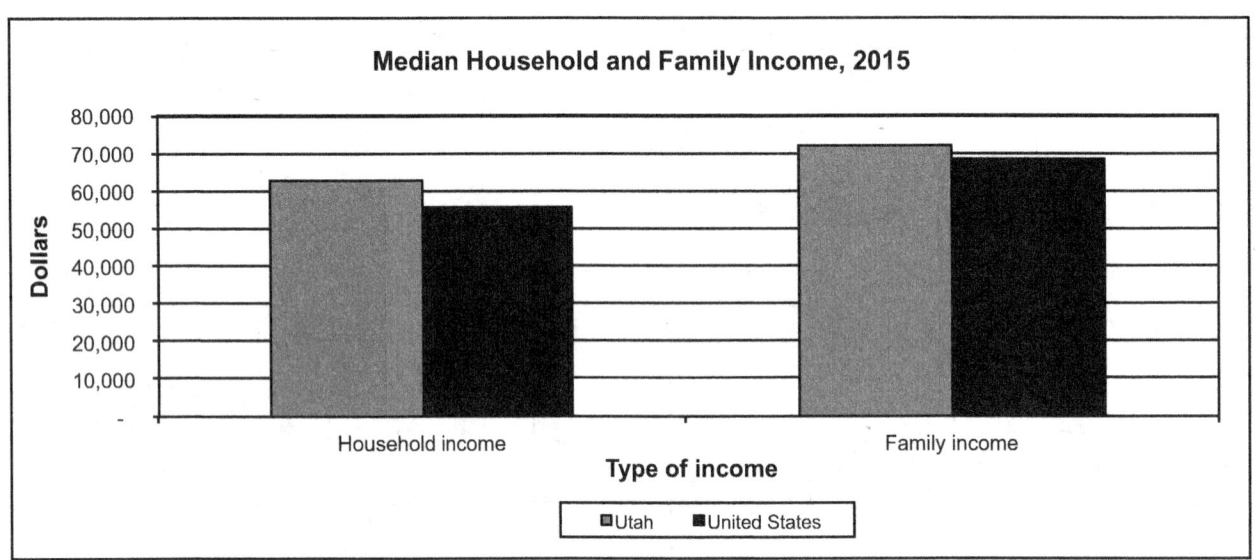

Table UT-6. Health Insurance Coverage Status for the Civilian Noninstitutionalized Population and Children Under 18 Years of Age

(Numbers in thousands, percent.)

Item	2007	2008	2009	2010	2011	2012	2013	2014	2015
Civilian Noninstitutionalized Population	2,657	2,705	2,755	2,750	2,790	2,829	2,874	2,916	2,971
Covered by Private or Public Insurance									
Number	2,317	2,286	2,354	2,328	2,364	2,420	2,472	2,551	2,660
Percent	87.2	84.5	85.4	84.7	84.7	85.5	86.0	87.5	89.5
Not Covered									
Number	340	419	401	422	426	409	402	366	311
Percent	12.8	15.5	14.6	15.3	15.3	14.5	14.0	12.5	10.5
Percent in the U.S. not covered	15.3	15.1	15.1	15.5	15.1	14.8	14.5	11.7	9.4
Children Under 18 Years of Age	832	849	869	870	878	884	894	902	909
Covered by Private or Public Insurance									
Number	746	738	780	775	781	794	809	818	844
Percent	89.6	86.9	89.7	89.1	88.9	89.9	90.5	90.6	92.8
Not Covered									
Number	87	111	89	95	97	90	85	85	65
Percent	10.4	13.1	10.3	10.9	11.1	10.1	9.5	9.4	7.2
Percent in the U.S. not covered	11.0	9.7	8.6	8.0	7.5	7.2	7.1	6.0	4.8

Table UT-7. Employment Status by Demographic Group, 2016

(Numbers in thousands, percent.)

Characteristic	Civilian noninstitutional population	Civilian labor force		Employed		Unemployed	
		Number	Percent of population	Number	Percent of population	Number	Percent of population
Total...................................	2,194	1,509	68.8	1,455	66.3	54	3.6
Sex							
Male.............................	1,089	855	78.5	823	75.6	32	3.7
Female...........................	1,105	654	59.2	632	57.2	22	3.4
Race, Sex, and Hispanic Origin							
White.............................	2,049	1,403	68.5	1,353	66.0	50	3.6
Male...........................	1,015	795	78.3	765	75.4	30	3.7
Female.........................	1,034	608	58.8	588	56.9	21	3.4
Black or African American............	NA	NA	NA	NA	NA	NA	NA
Male...........................	NA	NA	NA	NA	NA	NA	NA
Female.........................	NA	NA	NA	NA	NA	NA	NA
Hispanic or Latino ethnicity[1]	259	193	74.5	187	72.0	7	3.3
Male...........................	131	111	84.6	107	81.6	4	3.6
Female.........................	128	82	64.1	79	62.1	3	3.0
Age							
16 to 19 years.....................	175	92	52.7	84	48.1	8	8.7
20 to 24 years.....................	239	194	81.3	185	77.5	9	4.7
25 to 34 years.....................	453	369	81.4	356	78.6	13	3.5
35 to 44 years.....................	411	339	82.5	329	80.1	10	2.8
45 to 54 years.....................	314	256	81.7	249	79.4	7	2.8
55 to 64 years.....................	273	196	71.6	191	69.8	5	2.7
65 years and over	329	63	19.0	61	18.4	2	2.9

NOTE: Data in Table 7 are from the Current Population Survey (CPS) and do not match the estimates in Table 8. See notes and definitions for further information.
[1] May be of any race.
NA = Not available.

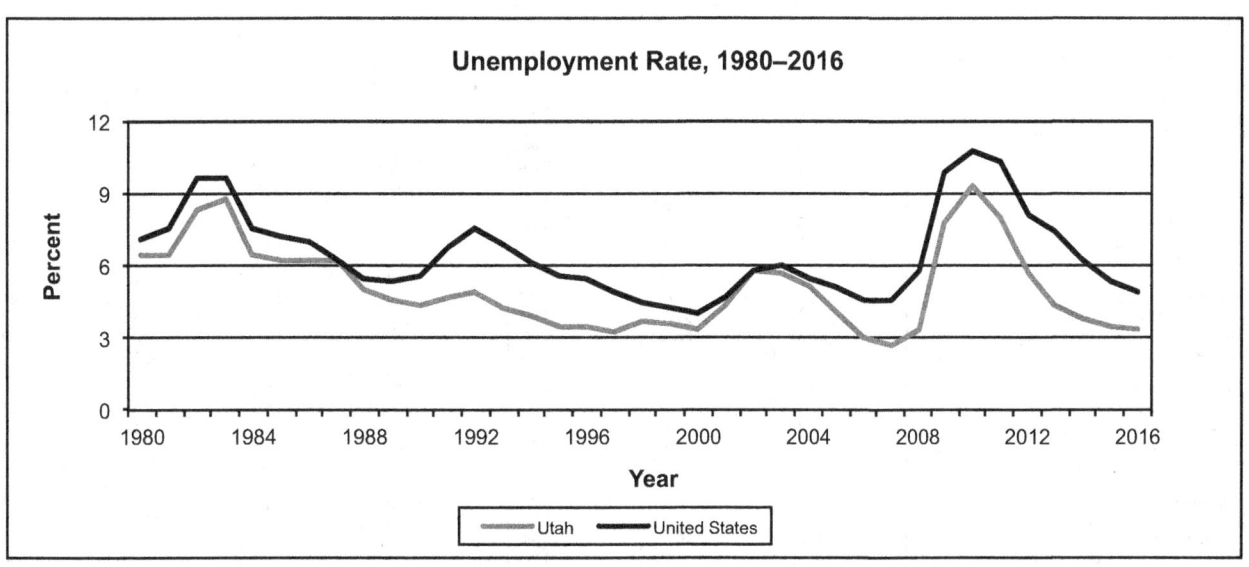

Table UT-8. Employment Status of the Civilian Noninstitutional Population Age 16 Years and Over

(Number, percent.)

Year	Civilian labor force	Civilian participation rate	Employed	Unemployed	Unemployment rate
2008...................................	1,371,201	70.9	1,322,089	49,112	3.6
2009...................................	1,365,850	69.2	1,266,009	99,841	7.3
2010...................................	1,356,097	68.8	1,249,814	106,283	7.8
2011...................................	1,350,444	67.8	1,259,337	91,107	6.7
2012...................................	1,373,479	67.7	1,299,289	74,190	5.4
2013...................................	1,409,366	68.2	1,344,637	64,729	4.6
2014...................................	1,431,553	68.0	1,377,013	54,540	3.8
2015...................................	1,464,404	68.1	1,412,473	51,931	3.5
2016...................................	1,511,465	68.7	1,459,703	51,762	3.4

Table UT-9. Employment and Average Wages by Industry

(Estimates through 2010 are based on the 2007 *North American Industry Classification System* [NAICS]. Estimates from 2011 onward are based on the 2012 NAICS.)

Industry	2009	2010	2011	2012	2013	2014	2015
				Number of jobs			
Wage and Salary Employment by Industry..................	1,247,431	1,236,311	1,264,381	1,304,870	1,343,013	1,382,315	1,430,866
Farm Wage and Salary Employment........................	4,542	4,745	4,476	4,495	4,798	4,502	4,373
Nonfarm Wage and Salary Employment....................	1,242,889	1,231,566	1,259,905	1,300,375	1,338,215	1,377,813	1,426,493
Private wage and salary employment.....................	1,011,265	997,121	1,020,488	1,059,033	1,097,208	1,135,166	1,181,597
Forestry, fishing, and related activities........................	1,371	1,382	1,411	1,399	1,457	1,532	1,557
Mining...	10,662	10,369	11,591	12,491	12,129	12,175	10,329
Utilities..	4,139	4,062	4,019	4,019	3,908	3,888	3,912
Construction..	73,800	67,530	67,266	71,313	75,629	80,837	86,806
Manufacturing..	112,331	110,393	113,016	115,985	118,052	120,017	123,008
Durable goods manufacturing.............................	73,502	71,733	74,019	76,623	77,818	79,018	81,630
Nondurable goods manufacturing.........................	38,829	38,660	38,997	39,362	40,234	40,999	41,378
Wholesale trade...	45,522	44,172	46,251	47,996	48,477	48,862	50,204
Retail trade...	143,178	139,248	139,834	144,940	148,947	152,841	159,333
Transportation and warehousing.............................	44,386	43,080	44,833	46,519	47,197	48,666	51,519
Information..	28,436	28,116	28,416	30,228	31,306	32,174	33,246
Finance and insurance	55,602	53,446	54,102	55,221	57,640	59,449	63,161
Real estate and rental and leasing.........................	17,323	16,682	17,015	17,167	18,063	18,630	19,007
Professional, scientific, and technical services..............	66,312	65,836	68,730	73,021	79,029	83,621	88,701
Management of companies and enterprises....................	17,635	16,754	16,750	17,283	17,408	18,137	18,333
Administrative and waste services............................	65,471	69,047	73,449	76,498	80,362	82,675	86,436
Educational services	37,853	39,457	40,824	41,897	42,774	44,094	45,945
Health care and social assistance............................	116,697	119,309	121,459	124,302	130,157	132,733	138,848
Arts, entertainment, and recreation...........................	17,730	17,730	18,097	19,338	19,689	20,240	21,327
Accommodation and food services..........................	94,422	93,791	96,180	100,007	104,624	108,629	113,101
Other services, except public administration..................	58,395	56,717	57,245	59,409	60,360	65,966	66,824
Government and government enterprises..........................	231,624	234,445	239,417	241,342	241,007	242,647	244,896
				Dollars			
Average Wages and Salaries by Industry	39,193	40,162	41,133	42,235	42,720	43,836	45,204
Average Farm Wages and Salaries	37,687	31,728	33,979	38,508	40,724	41,817	40,873
Average Nonfarm Wages and Salaries	39,199	40,195	41,158	42,248	42,727	43,843	45,217
Average private wages and salaries..........................	39,016	40,267	41,399	42,717	43,172	44,368	45,751
Forestry, fishing, and related activities........................	24,968	26,643	27,033	28,332	30,161	31,581	31,815
Mining...	66,881	70,891	73,980	77,015	78,053	79,323	80,526
Utilities..	83,110	87,123	87,897	86,758	88,995	91,002	93,356
Construction..	41,060	42,905	43,829	44,926	44,270	45,690	47,279
Manufacturing..	49,054	50,928	51,694	52,677	53,225	54,527	56,223
Durable goods manufacturing.............................	52,697	54,659	55,543	56,039	56,348	57,749	59,120
Nondurable goods manufacturing.........................	42,158	44,005	44,389	46,134	47,184	48,318	50,509
Wholesale trade...	54,545	55,801	58,745	60,119	62,397	62,829	64,047
Retail trade...	25,954	26,845	27,289	28,418	28,798	29,775	31,210
Transportation and warehousing.............................	42,147	43,785	44,554	45,251	46,443	47,482	48,633
Information..	50,212	53,734	58,043	60,623	61,454	65,104	69,360
Finance and insurance	53,344	56,012	58,663	62,936	63,491	66,093	69,895
Real estate and rental and leasing.........................	35,202	36,755	38,877	40,301	40,685	42,834	46,283
Professional, scientific, and technical services..............	59,975	60,901	62,894	63,719	63,512	66,872	67,970
Management of companies and enterprises....................	70,347	80,450	78,821	86,187	85,400	84,967	86,489
Administrative and waste services............................	28,479	28,844	29,670	30,448	31,387	32,174	32,993
Educational services	26,508	27,428	28,027	28,354	28,946	29,823	30,566
Health care and social assistance............................	38,479	38,540	39,328	40,169	40,556	41,403	42,109
Arts, entertainment, and recreation...........................	24,361	25,106	25,161	25,039	26,527	26,838	27,698
Accommodation and food services..........................	16,040	16,480	16,968	17,597	17,738	18,393	19,404
Other services, except public administration..................	38,154	40,191	41,259	43,246	43,927	43,383	44,831
Government and government enterprises..........................	39,994	39,884	40,135	40,190	40,699	41,383	42,640

Table UT-10. Employment Characteristics by Family Type

(Number, percent.)

Family type and labor force status	2013 Total	2013 Families with own children under 18 years	2014 Total	2014 Families with own children under 18 years	2015 Total	2015 Families with own children under 18 years
All Families	677,332	352,191	688,140	351,950	693,181	346,662
FAMILY TYPE AND LABOR FORCE STATUS						
Married-Couple Families	551,975	283,134	563,526	281,444	564,803	278,527
Both husband and wife in labor force	49.9	54.1	51.8	57.5	50.3	56.3
Husband in labor force, wife not in labor force	31.2	41.1	29.7	39.5	30.3	40.0
Wife in labor force, husband not in labor force	5.9	3.5	5.3	2.3	5.0	2.0
Both husband and wife not in labor force	12.6	1.1	13.2	0.8	13.9	1.4
Other Families	125,357	69,057	124,614	70,506	128,378	68,135
Female householder, no husband present	69.0	70.6	69.7	72.9	69.0	71.4
In labor force	51.1	58.7	50.2	61.8	49.3	60.7
Not in labor force	17.9	11.9	19.5	11.1	19.7	10.6
Male householder, no wife present	31.0	29.4	30.3	27.1	31.0	28.6
In labor force	25.0	28.3	24.7	25.1	25.7	26.4
Not in labor force	5.9	1.2	5.6	2.0	5.3	2.2

Table UT-11. School Enrollment and Educational Attainment, 2015

(Number, percent.)

Item	State	U.S.
Enrollment		
Total population 3 years and over, enrolled in school	954,586	81,618,288
Enrolled in nursery school or preschool (percent)	6.2	6.0
Enrolled in kindergarten (percent)	5.1	5.0
Enrolled in elementary school, grades 1-8 (percent)	43.1	40.3
Enrolled in high school, grades 9-12 (percent)	20.9	20.9
Enrolled in college or graduate school (percent)	24.6	27.7
Attainment		
Total population 25 years and over	1,741,949	216,447,163
Less than ninth grade (percent)	2.9	5.5
9th to 12th grade, no diploma (percent)	5.6	7.3
High school graduate, including equivalency (percent)	24.2	27.6
Some college, no degree (percent)	26.3	20.7
Associate's degree (percent)	9.2	8.2
Bachelor's degree (percent)	21.1	19.0
Graduate or professional degree (percent)	10.7	11.6
High school graduate or higher (percent)	91.5	87.1
Bachelor's degree or higher (percent)	31.8	30.6

Table UT-12. Public School Characteristics and Educational Indicators

(Number, percent; data derived from National Center of Education Statistics.)

Item	State	U.S.
Public Schools, 2014–2015 (except where noted)		
Number of school districts	148	18,260
Number of schools	1,020	98,373
Number of students	635,577	50,312,581
Number of teachers	27,374	3,132,351
Student-teacher ratio	23.2	16.1
Expenditures per student (dollars), FY 2014	6,546	11,066
Four-year adjusted cohort graduation rate (ACGR)[1,2]	84.8	83.2
Students eligible for free or reduced-price lunch (percent)	36.9	51.8
English language learners (percent)	6.3	9.4
Students age 3 to 21 served under IDEA, part B (percent)	12.2	13.0

Public Schools by Type	Number	Percent of state public schools
Total number of schools	1,020	100.0
Regular	920	90.2
Special education	69	6.8
Vocational education	4	0.4
Alternative education	27	2.6

NOTE: Every school is assigned only one school type based on its instructional emphasis.
[1] ACGR data represents a new method of calculating high-school completion rates and may not be comparable to previous years' data for Averaged Freshmen Graduation Rates (AFGR).
[2] The United States 4-year ACGRs were estimated using both the reported 4-year ACGR data from 49 states and the District of Columbia and using imputed data for Idaho. The estimate for American Indian/Alaska Native students also includes imputed data for Virginia.

Table UT-13. Reported Voting and Registration of the Voting-Age Population, November 2016

(Numbers in thousands, percent.)

Item	Total population	Total citizen population	Registered			Voted		
			Total registered	Percent registered (total population)	Percent registered (total citizen population)	Total voted	Percent voted (total population)	Percent voted (total citizen population)
U.S. Total	245,502	224,059	157,596	64.2	70.3	137,537	56.0	61.4
State Total............................	2,096	1,969	1,398	66.7	71.0	1,234	58.9	62.7
Sex								
Male	1,043	983	700	67.1	71.3	613	58.7	62.4
Female	1,053	986	698	66.3	70.8	621	59.0	63.0
Race								
White alone............................	1,955	1,852	1,339	68.5	72.3	1,181	60.4	63.8
White, non-Hispanic alone	1,737	1,731	1,265	72.8	73.0	1,115	64.2	64.4
Black alone.............................	20	16	8	(B)	(B)	7	(B)	(B)
Asian alone............................	44	27	19	(B)	(B)	19	(B)	(B)
Hispanic (of any race)......................	245	148	94	38.5	63.8	86	35.0	58.1
White alone or in combination	1,977	1,874	1,348	68.2	71.9	1,190	60.2	63.5
Black alone or in combination..........	32	27	13	(B)	(B)	12	(B)	(B)
Asian alone or in combination..........	49	32	19	(B)	(B)	19	(B)	(B)
Age								
18 to 24 years......................	342	326	171	50.0	52.4	142	41.6	43.6
25 to 34 years......................	416	388	243	58.5	62.7	201	48.3	51.8
35 to 44 years......................	416	373	276	66.3	73.9	243	58.5	65.2
45 to 64 years......................	586	549	432	73.7	78.7	393	67.0	71.5
65 years and over	336	333	276	82.0	82.9	255	75.8	76.6

B = Base is less than 75,000 and therefore too small to show the derived measure.

Table UT-14. Crime

(Number, rate per 100,000. Data are derived from the FBI Uniform Crime Reports.)

Item	State			U.S. [1,2,3,4]		
	2014	2015	Percent change	2014	2015	Percent change
TOTAL POPULATION[5]	2,944,498	2,995,919	1.7	318,907,401	321,418,820	0.8
VIOLENT CRIME						
Number.......................................	6,464	7,071	9.4	1,186,185	1,231,566	3.8
Rate	219.5	236.0	7.5	372.0	383.2	3.0
Murder and Nonnegligent Manslaughter						
Number.......................................	66	54	-18.2	14,164	15,696	10.8
Rate	2.2	1.8	-19.6	4.4	4.9	10.0
Rape[6]						
Number.......................................	1,547	1,645	6.3	118,027	124,047	5.1
Rate	52.5	54.9	4.5	37.0	38.6	4.3
Robbery						
Number.......................................	1,313	1,326	1.0	322,905	327,374	1.4
Rate	44.6	44.3	-0.7	101.3	101.9	0.6
Aggravated Assault						
Number.......................................	3,538	4,046	14.4	731,089	764,449	4.6
Rate	120.2	135.1	12.4	229.2	237.8	3.7
PROPERTY CRIME						
Number.......................................	85,473	89,278	4.5	8,209,010	7,993,631	-2.6
Rate	2,902.8	2,980.0	2.7	2,574.1	2,487.0	-3.4
Burglary						
Number.......................................	11,656	12,468	7.0	1,713,153	1,579,527	-7.8
Rate	395.9	416.2	5.1	537.2	491.4	-8.5
Larceny-Theft						
Number.......................................	66,487	68,103	2.4	5,809,054	5,706,346	-1.8
Rate	2,258.0	2,273.2	0.7	1,821.5	1,775.4	-2.5
Motor Vehicle Theft						
Number.......................................	7,330	8,707	18.8	686,803	707,758	3.1
Rate	248.9	290.6	16.7	215.4	220.2	2.2

NOTE: Although arson data are included in the trend and clearance tables, sufficient data are not available to estimate totals for this offense. Therefore, no arson data are published in this table.
X = Not applicable.
- = Zero or rounds to zero.
[1] The crime figures have been adjusted.
[2] The data collection methodology for the offense of forcible rape used by the Minnesota state Uniform Crime Reporting (UCR) Program (with the exception of Minneapolis and St. Paul, Minnesota) does not comply with national UCR Program guidelines. Consequently, its figures for forcible rape and violent crime (of which forcible rape is a part) are not published in this table.
[3] Includes offenses reported by the Zoological Police and the Metro Transit Police.
[4] Because of changes in the state's reporting practices, figures are not comparable to previous years' data.
[5] Populations are U.S. Census Bureau provisional estimates as of July 1 of each year.
[6] The figures shown for the offense of rape were estimated using the revised Uniform Crime Reporting (UCR) definition of rape.

Table UT-15. State Government Finances, 2015

(Dollar amounts in thousands, percent distribution.)

Item	Dollars	Percent distribution
Total Revenue	18,621,543	100.0
General revenue	15,665,711	84.1
Intergovernmental revenue	4,207,318	22.6
Taxes	6,703,356	36.0
General sales	1,882,901	10.1
Selective sales	883,823	4.7
License taxes	280,021	1.5
Individual income tax	3,157,718	17.0
Corporate income tax	368,681	2.0
Other taxes	130,212	0.7
Current charges	3,705,464	19.9
Miscellaneous general revenue	1,049,573	5.6
Utility revenue	0	-
Liquor stores revenue	334,840	1.8
Insurance trust revenue[1]	2,620,992	14.1
Total Expenditure	17,916,963	100.0
Intergovernmental expenditure	3,344,201	18.7
Direct expenditure	14,572,762	81.3
Current operation	10,726,625	59.9
Capital outlay	1,234,984	6.9
Insurance benefits and repayments	1,693,244	9.5
Assistance and subsidies	680,449	3.8
Interest on debt	237,460	1.3
Exhibit: Salaries and wages	3,072,396	17.1
Total Expenditure	17,916,963	100.0
General expenditure	15,983,565	89.2
Intergovernmental expenditure	3,344,201	18.7
Direct expenditure	12,639,364	70.5
General expenditure, by function:		
Education	7,371,045	41.1
Public welfare	3,245,210	18.1
Hospitals	1,442,435	8.1
Health	379,151	2.1
Highways	905,259	5.1
Police protection	138,041	0.8
Correction	326,545	1.8
Natural resources	174,952	1.0
Parks and recreation	44,056	0.2
Governmental administration	617,330	3.4
Interest on general debt	237,460	1.3
Other and unallocable	1,102,081	6.2
Utility expenditure	0	-
Liquor stores expenditure	240,154	1.3
Insurance trust expenditure	1,693,244	9.5
Debt at End of Fiscal Year	7,479,978	X
Cash and Security Holdings	32,765,194	X

X = Not applicable.
- = Zero or rounds to zero.
[1] Within insurance trust revenue, net earnings of state retirement systems is a calculated statistic (the item code in the data file is X08), and thus can be positive or negative. Net earnings is the sum of earnings on investments plus gains on investments minus losses on investments. The change made in 2002 for asset valuation from book to market value in accordance with Statement 34 of the Governmental Accounting Standards Board is reflected in the calculated statistics.

Table UT-16. State Government Tax Collections, 2016

(Dollars in thousands, percent.)

Item	Dollars	Percent distribution
Total Taxes	7,082,961	100.0
Property taxes	0	-
Sales and gross receipts	3,031,819	42.8
General sales and gross receipts	2,083,671	29.4
Selective sales and gross receipts	948,148	13.4
Alcoholic beverages	51,563	0.7
Amusements	0	-
Insurance premiums	133,157	1.9
Motor fuels	419,727	5.9
Pari-mutuels	0	-
Public utilities	24,351	0.3
Tobacco products	119,717	1.7
Other selective sales	199,633	2.8
Licenses	290,426	4.1
Alcoholic beverages	2,669	-
Amusements	0	-
Corporations in general	586	-
Hunting and fishing	29,813	0.4
Motor vehicle	184,078	2.6
Motor vehicle operators	15,414	0.2
Public utilities	0	-
Occupation and business, NEC	53,264	0.8
Other licenses	4,602	0.1
Income taxes	3,707,893	52.3
Individual income	3,374,535	47.6
Corporation net income	333,358	4.7
Other taxes	52,823	0.7
Death and gift	0	-
Documentary and stock transfer	0	-
Severance	52,823	0.7
Taxes, NEC	0	-

X = Not applicable.
- = Zero or rounds to zero.

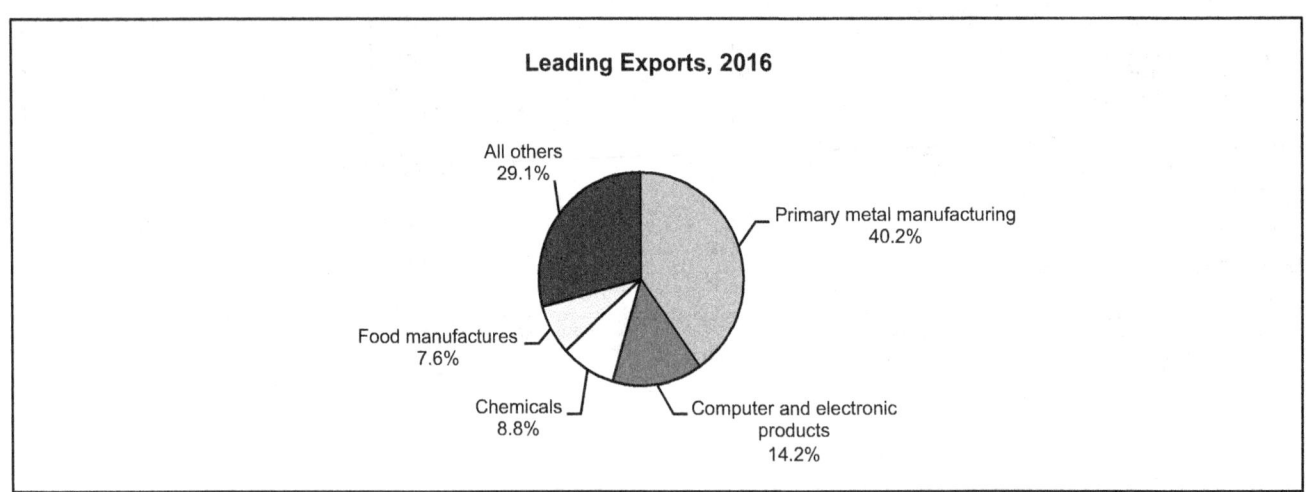

Leading Exports, 2016

All others 29.1%
Primary metal manufacturing 40.2%
Food manufactures 7.6%
Chemicals 8.8%
Computer and electronic products 14.2%

VERMONT

Facts and Figures

Location: Northeastern United States; bordered on the N by Canada (Quebec), on the E by New Hampshire, on the S by Massachusetts, and on the W by New York

Area: 9,614 sq. mi. (24,901 sq. km.); rank—45th

Population: 624,594 (2016 est.); rank—50th

Principal Cities: capital—Montpelier; largest—Burlington

Statehood: March 4, 1791; the 14th state

U.S. Congress: 2 senators, 1 representative

State Motto: Freedom and Unity

State Song: "These Green Mountains"

State Nickname: The Green Mountain State

Abbreviations: VT; Vt.

State Symbols: flower—red clover; tree—sugar maple; bird—hermit thrush

At a Glance

- Vermont's was one of three states that experienced a decrease in population between 2010 and 2015, with a drop of 0.2 percent.

- Vermont's median household income in 2015 was $56,990, and 10.2 percent of the population lived below the poverty level.

- Vermont's violent and property crime rates in 2015 were the lowest in the nation at 118.0 and 1,406.6 incidents per 100,000 population respectively.

- In 2015, 3.8 percent of Vermonters did not have health insurance, which was the second lowest percent in the country.

- Vermont had the second lowest percent of its population under age 18 in 2016, with 19.0 percent of its residents in this age group. It also had the second lowest birth rate, with 9.4 births per 100,000 population.

Table VT-1. Population by Age, Sex, Race, and Hispanic Origin

(Number, percent, except where noted.)

Sex, age, race, and Hispanic origin	2000	2010	2016 [1]	Average annual percent change, 2010–2016
Total Population...	608,827	625,741	624,594	-
Percent of total U.S. population	0.2	0.2	0.2	X
Sex				
Male..	298,337	308,206	308,466	-
Female..	310,490	317,535	316,128	-
Age				
Under 5 years..	33,989	31,952	30,641	-0.3
5 to 19 years...	132,268	118,323	108,525	-0.5
20 to 64 years...	365,060	384,388	372,496	-0.2
65 years and over..	77,510	91,078	112,932	1.5
Median age (years)	37.7	41.5	42.7	0.2
Race and Hispanic Origin				
One race...				
White	589,208	598,592	590,869	-0.1
Black..	3,063	6,456	8,147	1.6
American Indian and Alaska Native	2,420	2,308	2,426	0.3
Asian..	5,217	8,069	11,079	2.3
Native Hawaiian or Other Pacific Islander	141	175	260	3.0
Two or more races...	7,335	10,141	11,813	1.0
Hispanic (of any race)...	5,504	9,962	11,651	1.1

X = Not applicable.
- = Zero or rounds to zero.
[1] Population figures for 2016 are July 1 estimates. The 2010 estimates are taken from the 2010 Census.

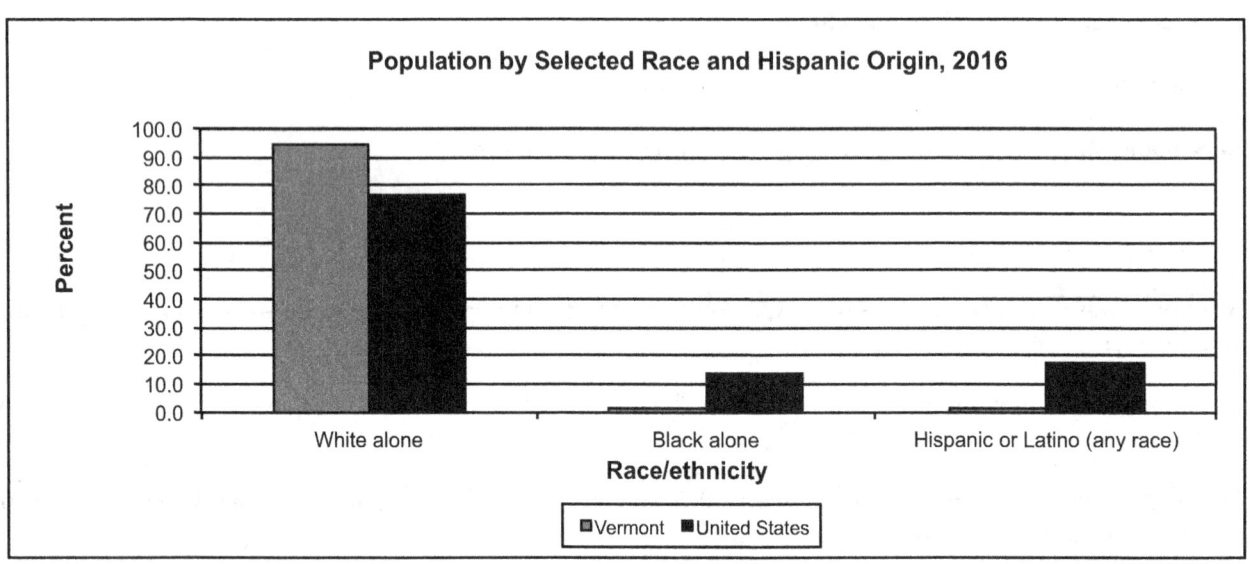

Population by Selected Race and Hispanic Origin, 2016

Legend: Vermont, United States

Table VT-2. Marital Status

(Number, percent distribution.)

Sex, age, race, and Hispanic origin	2000	2010	2015
Males, 15 Years and Over	236,517	254,288	258,397
Never married	29.7	34.2	35.1
Now married, except separated......................................	57.1	51.3	49.9
Separated...	1.2	1.3	0.9
Widowed...	2.4	2.5	2.5
Divorced...	9.6	10.7	11.6
Females, 15 Years and Over	251,764	266,860	270,727
Never married	23.9	27.7	28.5
Now married, except separated......................................	53.3	49.7	47.9
Separated...	1.4	1.4	1.2
Widowed...	10.0	8.2	8.5
Divorced...	11.5	13.0	13.9

Table VT-3. Households and Housing Characteristics

(Number, percent, dollars.)

Item	2000	2010	2015	Average annual percent change, 2000–2015
Total Households	240,634	256,922	254,865	0.4
Family households	157,763	159,846	152,379	-0.2
Married-couple family	126,413	125,678	123,509	-0.2
Other family	31,350	34,168	28,870	-0.5
Male householder, no wife present	9,078	10,887	8,643	-0.3
Female householder, no husband present	22,272	23,281	20,227	-0.6
Nonfamily households	82,871	97,076	102,486	1.6
Householder living alone	63,112	75,243	77,314	1.5
Householder not living alone	19,759	21,833	25,172	1.8
Housing Characteristics				
Total housing units	294,382	322,698	326,874	0.7
Occupied housing units	240,634	256,922	254,865	0.4
Owner occupied	169,784	180,847	180,212	0.4
Renter occupied	70,850	76,075	74,653	0.4
Average household size	2.44	2.34	2.36	-0.2
Financial Characteristics				
Median gross rent of renter-occupied housing	553	823	923	4.5
Median monthly owner costs for housing units with a mortgage	1,021	1,445	1,530	3.3
Median value of owner-occupied housing units	111,500	216,800	223,700	6.7

- = Zero or rounds to zero

Table VT-4. Migration, Origin, and Language

(Number, percent.)

Characteristic	State			U.S.		
	2014	2015	Percent change	2014	2015	Percent change
Residence 1 Year Ago						
Population 1 year and over	620,898	619,952	-0.2	315,095,393	317,635,720	0.8
Same house	86.5	85.9	X	85.1	85.3	X
Different house in the U.S.	13.3	13.4	X	14.3	14.1	X
Same county	7.1	7.6	X	8.7	8.5	X
Different county	6.2	5.8	X	5.6	5.6	X
Same state	2.5	2.4	X	3.3	3.2	X
Different state	3.6	3.4	X	2.3	2.4	X
Abroad	0.2	0.7	X	0.6	0.7	X
Place of Birth						
Native born	600,984	597,795	-0.5	276,465,262	278,128,449	0.6
Male	49.4	49.3	X	49.3	49.3	X
Female	50.6	50.7	X	50.7	50.7	X
Foreign born	25,578	28,247	10.4	42,391,794	43,290,372	2.1
Male	44.8	48.8	X	48.7	48.6	X
Female	55.2	51.2	X	51.3	51.4	X
Foreign born; naturalized U.S. citizen	13,360	15,464	15.7	19,984,738	20,697,103	3.6
Male	41.7	47.8	X	45.9	45.9	X
Female	58.3	52.2	X	54.1	54.1	X
Foreign born; not a U.S. citizen	12,218	12,783	4.6	22,407,056	22,593,269	0.8
Male	48.1	50.1	X	51.2	51.1	X
Female	51.9	49.9	X	48.8	48.9	X
Entered 2010 or later	18.5	21.9	X	12.3	15.6	X
Entered 2000 to 2009	26.8	24.6	X	28.6	27.9	X
Entered before 2000	54.7	53.6	X	59.1	56.5	X
World Region of Birth, Foreign						
Foreign-born population, excluding population born at sea	25,578	28,247	10.4	42,390,705	43,289,646	2.1
Europe	31.5	32.3	X	11.2	11.1	X
Asia	34.7	29.0	X	30.1	30.6	X
Africa	6.0	9.3	X	4.6	4.8	X
Oceania	0.4	1.4	X	0.6	0.6	X
Latin America	10.5	10.8	X	51.6	51.1	X
North America	16.9	17.3	X	1.9	1.9	X
Language Spoken at Home and Ability to Speak English						
Population 5 years and over	595,681	595,870	-	299,084,046	301,625,014	0.8
English only	95.0	93.9	X	78.9	78.5	X
Language other than English	5.0	6.1	X	21.1	21.5	X
Speaks English less than "very well"	1.3	1.5	X	8.6	8.6	X

NA = Not available.
X = Not applicable.
- = Zero or rounds to zero.

Table VT-5. Median Income and Poverty Status, 2015

(Number, percent, except as noted.)

Characteristic	State		U.S.	
	Number	Percent	Number	Percent
Median Income				
Households (dollars)................................	56,990	X	55,775	X
Families (dollars)	75,595	X	68,260	X
Below Poverty Level (All People)	61,314	10.2	46,153,077	14.7
Sex				
Male	27,316	9.3	20,599,407	13.4
Female	33,998	11.1	25,553,670	16.0
Age				
Under 18 years................................	15,469	13.3	15,000,273	20.7
Related children under 18 years................	14,376	12.4	14,693,239	20.4
18 to 64 years................................	38,837	10.3	26,960,369	13.9
65 years and over	7,008	6.6	4,192,435	9.0

X = Not applicable.

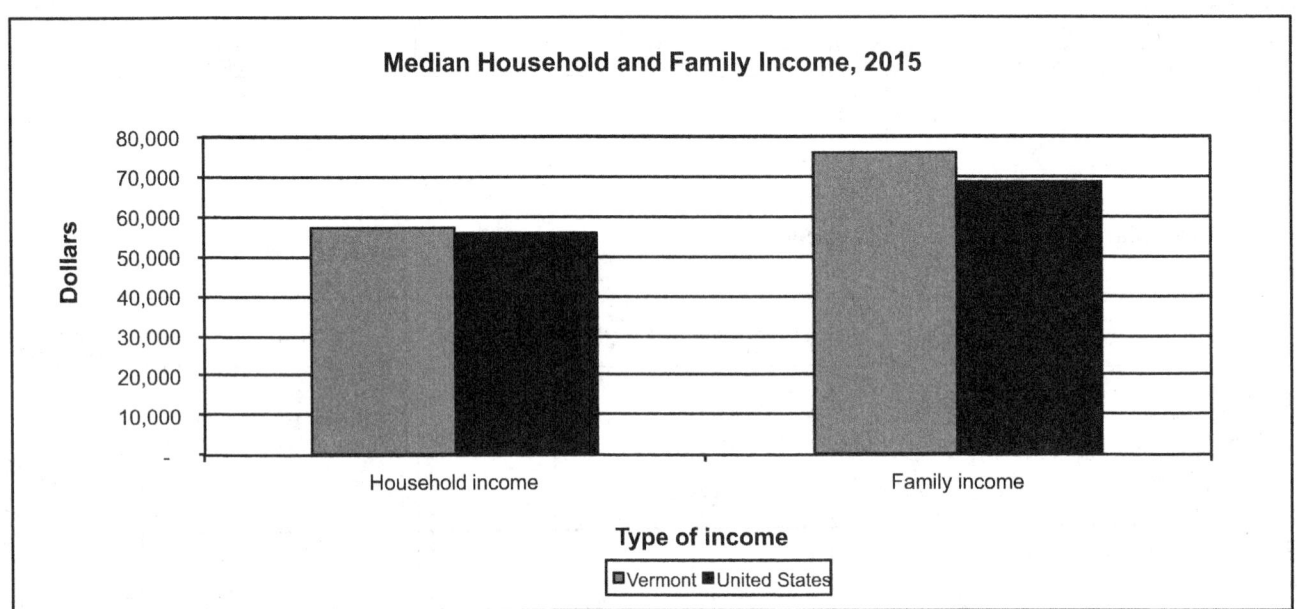

Table VT-6. Health Insurance Coverage Status for the Civilian Noninstitutionalized Population and Children Under 18 Years of Age

(Numbers in thousands, percent.)

Item	2007	2008	2009	2010	2011	2012	2013	2014	2015
Civilian Noninstitutionalized Population	614	615	615	620	620	620	621	620	620
Covered by Private or Public Insurance									
Number................................	545	559	562	570	579	580	576	590	596
Percent................................	88.8	90.9	91.4	92.0	93.4	93.5	92.8	95.0	96.2
Not Covered									
Number................................	69	56	53	50	41	40	45	31	24
Percent................................	11.2	9.1	8.6	8.0	6.6	6.5	7.2	5.0	3.8
Percent in the U.S. not covered................	15.3	15.1	15.1	15.5	15.1	14.8	14.5	11.7	9.4
Children Under 18 Years of Age	129	129	126	130	126	124	124	121	120
Covered by Private or Public Insurance									
Number................................	117	124	122	127	123	121	120	119	119
Percent................................	90.6	96.1	96.8	98.0	97.6	97.2	96.9	97.8	99.0
Not Covered									
Number................................	12	5	4	3	3	3	4	3	1
Percent................................	9.4	3.9	3.2	2.0	2.4	2.8	3.1	2.2	1.0
Percent in the U.S. not covered................	11.0	9.7	8.6	8.0	7.5	7.2	7.1	6.0	4.8

Table VT-7. Employment Status by Demographic Group, 2016

(Numbers in thousands, percent.)

Characteristic	Civilian noninstitutional population	Civilian labor force		Employed		Unemployed	
		Number	Percent of population	Number	Percent of population	Number	Percent of population
Total................................	516	346	67.1	335	65.0	11	3.3
Sex							
Male..................................	252	180	71.3	173	68.7	7	3.7
Female	264	167	63.2	162	61.4	5	2.8
Race, Sex, and Hispanic Origin							
White	488	330	67.6	319	65.4	11	3.2
Male..............................	238	170	71.6	164	69.0	6	3.6
Female	250	160	63.7	155	62.0	5	2.8
Black or African American...........	NA	NA	NA	NA	NA	NA	NA
Male..............................	NA	NA	NA	NA	NA	NA	NA
Female	NA	NA	NA	NA	NA	NA	NA
Hispanic or Latino ethnicity[1]	NA	NA	NA	NA	NA	NA	NA
Male..............................	NA	NA	NA	NA	NA	NA	NA
Female	NA	NA	NA	NA	NA	NA	NA
Age							
16 to 19 years.....................	35	16	47.2	15	42.2	2	10.5
20 to 24 years.....................	40	31	76.8	29	72.6	2	5.5
25 to 34 years.....................	73	60	81.9	58	79.0	2	3.3
35 to 44 years.....................	75	66	87.5	64	85.3	2	2.4
45 to 54 years.....................	82	70	85.8	69	84.0	2	2.1
55 to 64 years.....................	100	73	72.7	71	71.1	2	2.2
65 years and over.................	111	31	27.7	30	26.7	1	3.6

NOTE: Data in Table 7 are from the Current Population Survey (CPS) and do not match the estimates in Table 8. See notes and definitions for further information.
[1] May be of any race.
NA = Not available.

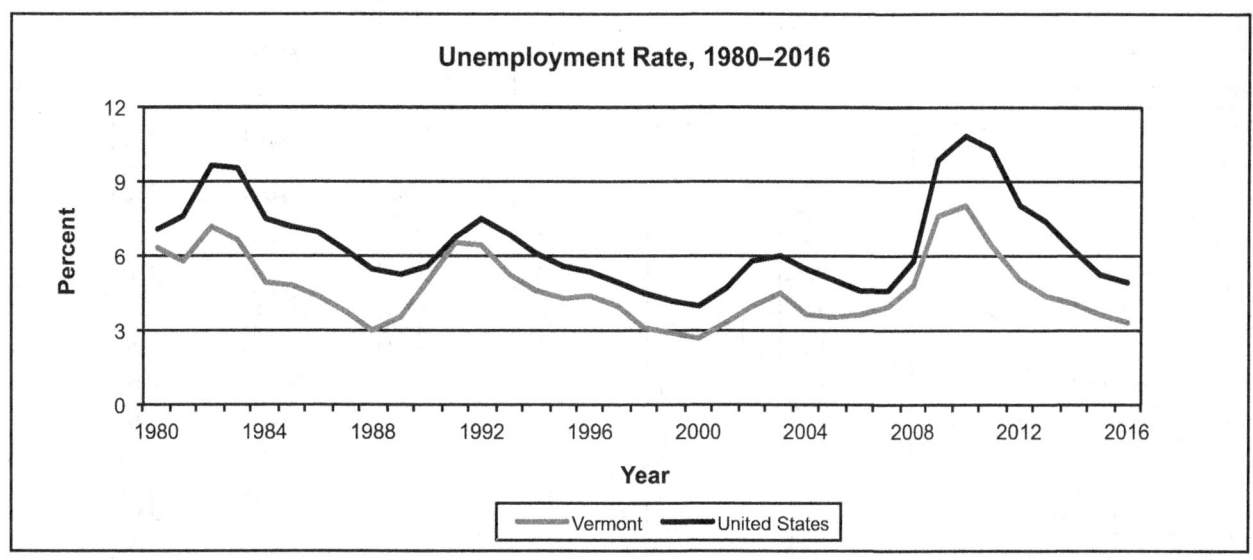

Table VT-8. Employment Status of the Civilian Noninstitutional Population Age 16 Years and Over

(Number, percent.)

Year	Civilian labor force	Civilian participation rate	Employed	Unemployed	Unemployment rate
2008..	354,899	70.3	338,273	16,626	4.7
2009..	359,836	71.0	336,104	23,732	6.6
2010..	359,402	70.8	337,488	21,914	6.1
2011..	358,108	70.2	338,463	19,645	5.5
2012..	354,849	69.4	337,247	17,602	5.0
2013..	351,342	68.5	335,856	15,486	4.4
2014..	347,898	67.6	334,044	13,854	4.0
2015..	344,414	66.8	331,824	12,590	3.7
2016..	344,892	66.9	333,640	11,252	3.3

Table VT-9. Employment and Average Wages by Industry

(Estimates through 2010 are based on the 2007 *North American Industry Classification System* [NAICS]. Estimates from 2011 onward are based on the 2012 NAICS.)

Industry	2009	2010	2011	2012	2013	2014	2015
	Number of jobs						
Wage and Salary Employment by Industry.................	310,971	310,614	313,625	318,425	320,279	323,603	325,821
Farm Wage and Salary Employment........................	2,276	2,249	2,458	2,581	2,953	2,961	2,950
Nonfarm Wage and Salary Employment....................	308,695	308,365	311,167	315,844	317,326	320,642	322,871
Private wage and salary employment................................	251,544	250,945	253,909	258,182	259,517	262,235	264,593
Forestry, fishing, and related activities........................	917	916	917	861	884	923	923
Mining...	650	594	611	648	621	600	645
Utilities...	1,756	1,800	1,801	1,828	1,790	1,727	1,548
Construction...	14,399	14,031	14,524	14,625	14,508	15,192	15,544
Manufacturing..	31,154	30,832	30,939	31,968	31,743	31,231	30,967
Durable goods manufacturing.............................	22,091	21,781	21,618	21,753	21,221	20,382	19,696
Nondurable goods manufacturing.........................	9,063	9,051	9,321	10,215	10,522	10,849	11,271
Wholesale trade	9,676	9,592	9,647	9,244	9,256	9,289	9,339
Retail trade..	38,854	38,351	38,366	37,945	38,053	38,284	38,237
Transportation and warehousing............................	6,763	6,808	7,139	7,073	6,994	7,005	6,882
Information	5,509	5,357	4,962	4,671	4,680	4,765	4,637
Finance and insurance	9,375	9,324	9,360	9,294	9,187	9,250	9,235
Real estate and rental and leasing........................	3,159	3,027	3,031	3,065	3,138	3,149	3,016
Professional, scientific, and technical services	13,452	13,698	13,780	14,182	14,190	13,974	14,310
Management of companies and enterprises................	778	893	1,418	1,962	1,949	2,081	2,219
Administrative and waste services...........................	8,421	8,803	9,682	10,243	10,483	10,754	11,065
Educational services	13,636	13,742	14,048	14,245	14,195	14,526	14,778
Health care and social assistance...........................	47,665	47,666	47,776	48,899	49,598	50,049	50,851
Arts, entertainment, and recreation.........................	3,867	3,887	3,934	4,038	4,084	4,260	4,184
Accommodation and food services..........................	28,151	28,708	28,910	29,585	30,459	31,086	32,079
Other services, except public administration.................	13,362	12,916	13,064	13,806	13,705	14,090	14,134
Government and government enterprises........................	57,151	57,420	57,258	57,662	57,809	58,407	58,278
	Dollars						
Average Wages and Salaries by Industry	37,984	38,739	39,484	40,197	41,244	42,193	43,360
Average Farm Wages and Salaries	26,989	26,127	20,925	31,010	27,945	29,501	27,185
Average Nonfarm Wages and Salaries	38,065	38,831	39,630	40,272	41,368	42,310	43,507
Average private wages and salaries...........................	37,300	38,150	39,033	39,764	40,835	41,771	42,969
Forestry, fishing, and related activities........................	26,812	28,238	29,029	29,085	29,719	31,189	32,038
Mining...	55,369	55,712	54,218	52,637	54,477	55,887	57,352
Utilities...	87,911	92,310	92,697	95,712	98,065	104,387	123,178
Construction...	41,160	42,686	43,298	43,671	45,399	46,231	46,949
Manufacturing..	51,653	53,101	53,794	54,254	54,663	55,294	55,947
Durable goods manufacturing.............................	56,001	57,389	58,377	58,802	59,099	59,234	59,899
Nondurable goods manufacturing.........................	41,054	42,783	43,164	44,458	45,715	47,892	49,041
Wholesale trade	51,342	52,495	54,632	56,324	56,590	56,468	59,013
Retail trade..	25,371	25,962	26,746	26,590	27,460	28,385	29,426
Transportation and warehousing............................	36,388	37,165	37,737	38,143	38,703	40,308	40,465
Information	45,152	45,131	49,247	48,895	51,420	53,809	56,210
Finance and insurance	61,393	62,199	64,146	66,034	67,665	69,790	73,157
Real estate and rental and leasing........................	32,406	33,341	34,480	36,126	37,860	38,495	39,637
Professional, scientific, and technical services	59,932	63,900	64,654	65,961	68,812	70,897	73,590
Management of companies and enterprises................	77,548	78,473	78,311	77,929	81,898	87,230	86,152
Administrative and waste services...........................	30,430	28,713	29,240	31,724	34,536	36,631	36,087
Educational services	31,360	30,534	30,781	31,171	32,382	33,235	33,487
Health care and social assistance...........................	37,527	38,416	39,199	40,066	41,161	42,031	43,513
Arts, entertainment, and recreation.........................	22,819	23,383	23,538	23,915	25,252	25,695	25,139
Accommodation and food services..........................	19,657	19,782	20,617	21,093	21,812	22,626	23,743
Other services, except public administration.................	24,678	25,538	26,040	26,778	27,775	28,382	29,808
Government and government enterprises........................	41,434	41,806	42,280	42,549	43,761	44,729	45,951

Table VT-10. Employment Characteristics by Family Type

(Number, percent.)

Family type and labor force status	2013		2014		2015	
	Total	Families with own children under 18 years	Total	Families with own children under 18 years	Total	Families with own children under 18 years
All Families..	155,933	60,395	160,392	65,545	152,379	58,593
FAMILY TYPE AND LABOR FORCE STATUS						
Married-Couple Families..........................	123,176	40,361	124,116	42,593	123,509	41,961
Both husband and wife in labor force.................................	57.7	75.4	59.5	76.6	57.1	75.8
Husband in labor force, wife not in labor force	15.6	18.1	15.3	17.7	15.2	17.7
Wife in labor force, husband not in labor force	8.3	4.1	8.5	3.6	9.1	4.2
Both husband and wife not in labor force................................	17.2	1.5	16.8	2.1	16.6	1.5
Other Families	32,757	20,034	36,276	22,952	28,870	16,632
Female householder, no husband present...........................	70.4	71.0	68.4	70.6	70.1	68.6
In labor force....................................	50.1	55.0	49.1	58.0	50.8	57.8
Not in labor force	20.3	16.0	19.3	12.6	19.2	10.9
Male householder, no wife present........................	29.6	29.0	31.6	29.4	29.9	31.4
In labor force....................................	22.5	24.5	25.4	26.4	21.9	25.3
Not in labor force	7.1	4.5	6.2	2.9	8.1	6.0

Table VT-11. School Enrollment and Educational Attainment, 2015

(Number, percent.)

Item	State	U.S.
Enrollment		
Total population 3 years and over, enrolled in school	150,285	81,618,288
Enrolled in nursery school or preschool (percent)	5.2	6.0
Enrolled in kindergarten (percent)...	3.7	5.0
Enrolled in elementary school, grades 1-8 (percent)...........................	35.6	40.3
Enrolled in high school, grades 9-12 (percent)................................	20.9	20.9
Enrolled in college or graduate school (percent).............................	34.6	27.7
Attainment		
Total population 25 years and over	438,654	216,447,163
Less than ninth grade (percent)	2.8	5.5
9th to 12th grade, no diploma (percent)	5.5	7.3
High school graduate, including equivalency (percent)......................	29.0	27.6
Some college, no degree (percent)	17.1	20.7
Associate's degree (percent)	8.6	8.2
Bachelor's degree (percent)	22.3	19.0
Graduate or professional degree (percent)..................................	14.6	11.6
High school graduate or higher (percent)	91.7	87.1
Bachelor's degree or higher (percent)......................................	36.9	30.6

Table VT-12. Public School Characteristics and Educational Indicators

(Number, percent; data derived from National Center of Education Statistics.)

Item	State	U.S.
Public Schools, 2014–2015 (except where noted)		
Number of school districts..	360	18,260
Number of schools..	316	98,373
Number of students...	87,311	50,312,581
Number of teachers	8,276	3,132,351
Student-teacher ratio	10.6	16.1
Expenditures per student (dollars), FY 2014	18,066	11,066
Four-year adjusted cohort graduation rate (ACGR)[1,2]	87.7	83.2
Students eligible for free or reduced-price lunch (percent).................	39.1	51.8
English language learners (percent)...	1.7	9.4
Students age 3 to 21 served under IDEA, part B (percent)..................	16.0	13.0

Public Schools by Type	Number	Percent of state public schools
Total number of schools..	316	100.0
Regular	300	94.9
Special education...	0	-
Vocational education	15	4.7
Alternative education	1	0.3

NOTE: Every school is assigned only one school type based on its instructional emphasis.
[1] ACGR data represents a new method of calculating high-school completion rates and may not be comparable to previous years' data for Averaged Freshmen Graduation Rates (AFGR).
[2] The United States 4-year ACGRs were estimated using both the reported 4-year ACGR data from 49 states and the District of Columbia and using imputed data for Idaho. The estimate for American Indian/Alaska Native students also includes imputed data for Virginia.
- = Zero or rounds to zero.

Table VT-13. Reported Voting and Registration of the Voting-Age Population, November 2016

(Numbers in thousands, percent.)

Item	Total population	Total citizen population	Registered			Voted		
			Total registered	Percent registered (total population)	Percent registered (total citizen population)	Total voted	Percent voted (total population)	Percent voted (total citizen population)
U.S. Total	245,502	224,059	157,596	64.2	70.3	137,537	56.0	61.4
State Total	500	488	351	70.2	71.9	305	61.0	62.5
Sex								
Male	246	241	166	67.6	69.0	144	58.4	59.7
Female	254	248	185	72.8	74.7	161	63.6	65.2
Race								
White alone.............................	468	464	339	72.5	73.0	293	62.7	63.2
White, non-Hispanic alone	464	460	336	72.4	73.0	290	62.6	63.1
Black alone.............................	5	4	2	(B)	(B)	1	(B)	(B)
Asian alone	13	7	4	(B)	(B)	4	(B)	(B)
Hispanic (of any race)	5	4	3	(B)	(B)	3	(B)	(B)
White alone or in combination	479	476	344	71.8	72.3	298	62.3	62.8
Black alone or in combination..........	7	6	3	(B)	(B)	2	(B)	(B)
Asian alone or in combination..........	15	9	5	(B)	(B)	5	(B)	(B)
Age								
18 to 24 years.............................	57	55	34	(B)	(B)	26	(B)	(B)
25 to 34 years.............................	77	75	43	(B)	(B)	35	(B)	(B)
35 to 44 years.............................	72	70	50	(B)	(B)	42	(B)	(B)
45 to 64 years.............................	181	177	133	73.7	75.3	118	65.0	66.5
65 years and over	112	111	91	81.0	82.2	85	75.9	77.1

B = Base is less than 75,000 and therefore too small to show the derived measure.
- = Zero or rounds to zero.

Table VT-14. Crime

(Number, rate per 100,000. Data are derived from the FBI Uniform Crime Reports.)

Item	State			U.S. [1,2,3,4]		
	2014	2015	Percent change	2014	2015	Percent change
TOTAL POPULATION[5]	626,767	626,042	-0.1	318,907,401	321,418,820	0.8
VIOLENT CRIME						
Number.............................	643	739	14.9	1,186,185	1,231,566	3.8
Rate	102.6	118.0	15.1	372.0	383.2	3.0
Murder and Nonnegligent Manslaughter						
Number.............................	10	10	0.0	14,164	15,696	10.8
Rate	1.6	1.6	0.1	4.4	4.9	10.0
Rape[6]						
Number.............................	117	136	16.2	118,027	124,047	5.1
Rate	18.7	21.7	16.4	37.0	38.6	4.3
Robbery						
Number.............................	72	101	40.3	322,905	327,374	1.4
Rate	11.5	16.1	40.4	101.3	101.9	0.6
Aggravated Assault						
Number.............................	444	492	10.8	731,089	764,449	4.6
Rate	70.8	78.6	10.9	229.2	237.8	3.7
PROPERTY CRIME						
Number.............................	9,721	8,806	-9.4	8,209,010	7,993,631	-2.6
Rate	1,551.0	1,406.6	-9.3	2,574.1	2,487.0	-3.4
Burglary						
Number.............................	2,092	1,968	-5.9	1,713,153	1,579,527	-7.8
Rate	333.8	314.4	-5.8	537.2	491.4	-8.5
Larceny-Theft						
Number.............................	7,375	6,660	-9.7	5,809,054	5,706,346	-1.8
Rate	1,176.7	1,063.8	-9.6	1,821.5	1,775.4	-2.5
Motor Vehicle Theft						
Number.............................	254	178	-29.9	686,803	707,758	3.1
Rate	40.5	28.4	-29.8	215.4	220.2	2.2

NOTE: Although arson data are included in the trend and clearance tables, sufficient data are not available to estimate totals for this offense. Therefore, no arson data are published in this table.
X = Not applicable.
- = Zero or rounds to zero.
[1] The crime figures have been adjusted.
[2] The data collection methodology for the offense of forcible rape used by the Minnesota state Uniform Crime Reporting (UCR) Program (with the exception of Minneapolis and St. Paul, Minnesota) does not comply with national UCR Program guidelines. Consequently, its figures for forcible rape and violent crime (of which forcible rape is a part) are not published in this table.
[3] Includes offenses reported by the Zoological Police and the Metro Transit Police.
[4] Because of changes in the state's reporting practices, figures are not comparable to previous years' data.
[5] Populations are U.S. Census Bureau provisional estimates as of July 1 of each year.
[6] The figures shown for the offense of rape were estimated using the revised Uniform Crime Reporting (UCR) definition of rape.

Table VT-15. State Government Finances, 2015

(Dollar amounts in thousands, percent distribution.)

Item	Dollars	Percent distribution
Total Revenue	6,325,712	100.0
General revenue	6,008,737	95.0
Intergovernmental revenue	2,107,303	33.3
Taxes	3,043,152	48.1
General sales	366,667	5.8
Selective sales	659,521	10.4
License taxes	111,527	1.8
Individual income tax	709,310	11.2
Corporate income tax	112,643	1.8
Other taxes	1,083,484	17.1
Current charges	552,293	8.7
Miscellaneous general revenue	305,989	4.8
Utility revenue	0	-
Liquor stores revenue	54,320	0.9
Insurance trust revenue[1]	262,655	4.2
Total Expenditure	6,469,338	100.0
Intergovernmental expenditure	1,614,414	25.0
Direct expenditure	4,854,924	75.0
Current operation	3,974,674	61.4
Capital outlay	267,028	4.1
Insurance benefits and repayments	375,570	5.8
Assistance and subsidies	151,339	2.3
Interest on debt	86,313	1.3
Exhibit: Salaries and wages	886,462	13.7
Total Expenditure	6,469,338	100.0
General expenditure	6,036,238	93.3
Intergovernmental expenditure	1,614,414	25.0
Direct expenditure	4,421,824	68.4
General expenditure, by function:		
Education	2,534,073	39.2
Public welfare	1,728,547	26.7
Hospitals	18578	0.3
Health	318,421	4.9
Highways	501,722	7.8
Police protection	103,861	1.6
Correction	145,536	2.2
Natural resources	105,956	1.6
Parks and recreation	14,513	0.2
Governmental administration	182,663	2.8
Interest on general debt	86,313	1.3
Other and unallocable	296,055	4.6
Utility expenditure	314	-
Liquor stores expenditure	57,216	0.9
Insurance trust expenditure	375,570	5.8
Debt at End of Fiscal Year	3,340,624	X
Cash and Security Holdings	8,103,900	X

X = Not applicable.
- = Zero or rounds to zero.
[1] Within insurance trust revenue, net earnings of state retirement systems is a calculated statistic (the item code in the data file is X08), and thus can be positive or negative. Net earnings is the sum of earnings on investments plus gains on investments minus losses on investments. The change made in 2002 for asset valuation from book to market value in accordance with Statement 34 of the Governmental Accounting Standards Board is reflected in the calculated statistics.

Table VT-16. State Government Tax Collections, 2016

(Dollars in thousands, percent.)

Item	Dollars	Percent distribution
Total Taxes	3,085,865	100.0
Property taxes	1,056,323	34.2
Sales and gross receipts	1,031,257	33.4
General sales and gross receipts	371,365	12.0
Selective sales and gross receipts	659,892	21.4
Alcoholic beverages	25,025	0.8
Amusements	0	-
Insurance premiums	59,055	1.9
Motor fuels	77,404	2.5
Pari-mutuels	0	-
Public utilities	9,012	0.3
Tobacco products	80,418	2.6
Other selective sales	408,978	13.3
Licenses	117,328	3.8
Alcoholic beverages	431	-
Amusements	26	-
Corporations in general	3,444	0.1
Hunting and fishing	7,833	0.3
Motor vehicle	71,626	2.3
Motor vehicle operators	9,550	0.3
Public utilities	0	-
Occupation and business, NEC	20,955	0.7
Other licenses	3,463	0.1
Income taxes	828,322	26.8
Individual income	729,986	23.7
Corporation net income	98,336	3.2
Other taxes	52,635	1.7
Death and gift	12,509	0.4
Documentary and stock transfer	35,627	1.2
Severance	0	-
Taxes, NEC	4,499	0.1

X = Not applicable.
- = Zero or rounds to zero.

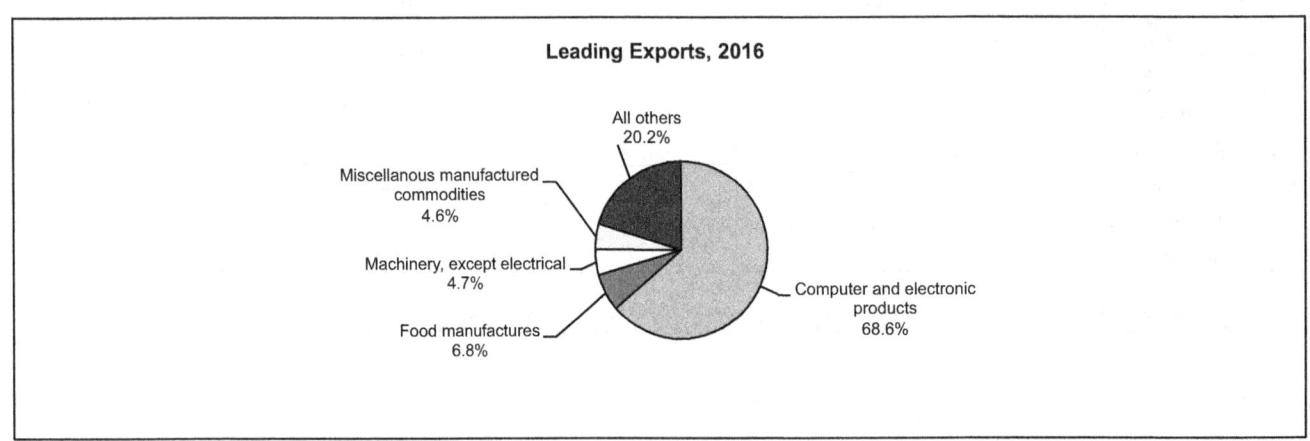

Leading Exports, 2016

All others 20.2%

Miscellanous manufactured commodities 4.6%

Machinery, except electrical 4.7%

Food manufactures 6.8%

Computer and electronic products 68.6%

VIRGINIA

Facts and Figures

Location: Eastern United States; bordered on the N and NE by Maryland and the District of Columbia, on the E by the Atlantic Ocean, on the S by North Carolina and Tennessee, and on the W by Kentucky and West Virginia

Area: 42,774 sq. mi. (110,785 sq. km.); rank—35th

Population: 8,411,808 (2016 est.); rank—12th

Principal Cities: capital—Richmond; largest—Virginia Beach

Statehood: June 25, 1788; 10th state

U.S. Congress: 2 senators, 11 representatives

State Motto: *Sic semper tyrannis* ("Thus always to tyrants")

State Song: "Our Great Virginia" and "Sweet Virginia Breeze"

State Nickname: The Old Dominion State

Abbreviations: VA; Va.

State Symbols: flower—flowering dogwood; tree—flowering dogwood; bird—cardinal

At a Glance

- With an increase in population of 5.1 percent, Virginia ranked 19th among the states in growth from 2010 to 2016.

- Virginia's violent crime rate (195.6 incidents per 100,000 population) was the 3rd lowest in the country in 2015.

- In 2016, 4.0 percent of Virginians were unemployed, compared to 4.9 percent of the total U.S. population.

- Virginia's median household income in 2015 was $66,262, and 11.2 percent of the population lived below the poverty level.

- In 2016, 6.6 percent of Virginians identified as "Asian alone," ranking it 8th among the states in this category.

Table VA-1. Population by Age, Sex, Race, and Hispanic Origin

(Number, percent, except where noted.)

Sex, age, race, and Hispanic origin	2000	2010	2016 [1]	Average annual percent change, 2010–2016
Total Population...	7,078,515	8,001,024	8,411,808	0.3
Percent of total U.S. population	2.5	2.6	2.6	X
Sex				
Male..	3,471,895	3,925,983	4,136,814	0.3
Female...	3,606,620	4,075,041	4,274,994	0.3
Age				
Under 5 years..	461,982	509,625	510,501	-
5 to 19 years...	1,475,104	1,574,060	1,582,028	-
20 to 64 years...	4,349,096	4,940,402	5,090,535	0.2
65 years and over...	79,233	976,937	1,228,744	1.6
Median age (years)	35.7	37.5	38.1	0.1
Race and Hispanic Origin				
One race...				
White	5,120,110	5,725,432	5,891,553	0.2
Black..	1,390,293	1,579,414	1,664,523	0.3
American Indian and Alaska Native	21,172	41,525	45,510	0.6
Asian..	261,025	449,149	555,515	1.5
Native Hawaiian or Other Pacific Islander	3,946	8,201	9,407	0.9
Two or more races...	143,069	197,303	245,300	1.5
Hispanic (of any race)..	329,540	660,501	766,004	1.0

X = Not applicable.
[1] Population figures for 2016 are July 1 estimates. The 2010 estimates are taken from the 2010 Census.
- = Zero or rounds to zero.

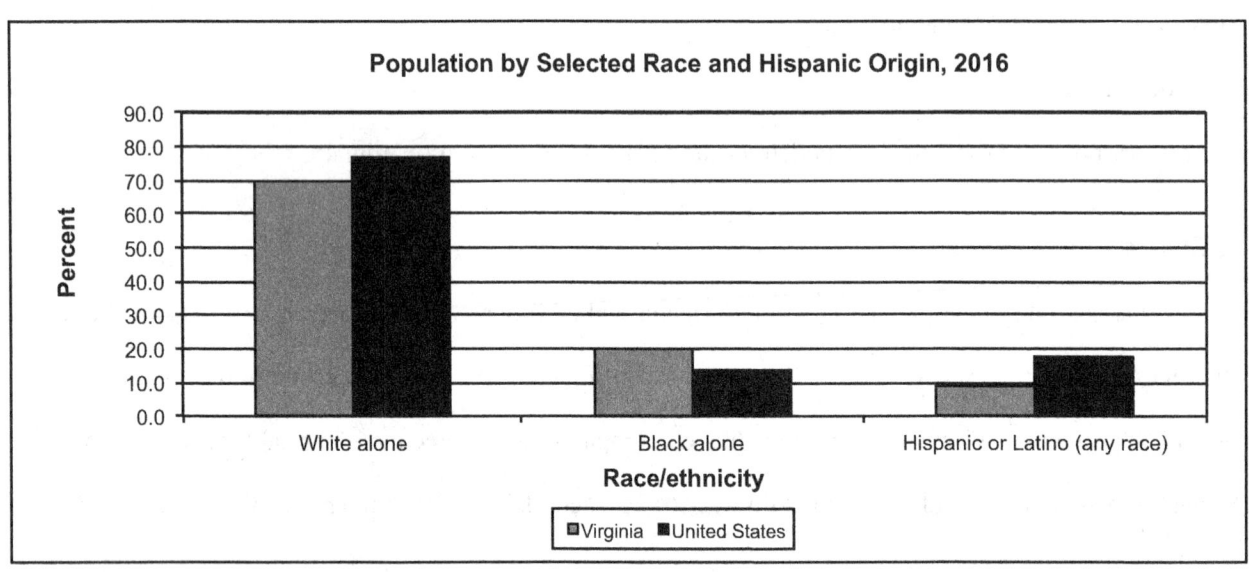

Table VA-2. Marital Status

(Number, percent distribution.)

Sex, age, race, and Hispanic origin	2000	2010	2015
Males, 15 Years and Over......................................	2,724,334	3,156,115	3,331,211
Never married..	29.1	34.2	35.3
Now married, except separated.................................	58.2	52.6	51.2
Separated..	2.6	2.3	2.2
Widowed..	2.3	2.3	2.5
Divorced..	7.9	8.5	8.8
Females, 15 Years and Over...................................	2,899,294	3,331,264	3,495,647
Never married..	23.5	28.0	29.6
Now married, except separated.................................	53.4	49.0	47.2
Separated..	3.2	2.9	2.8
Widowed..	9.9	8.7	8.4
Divorced..	10.0	11.4	12.0

Table VA-3. Households and Housing Characteristics

(Number, percent, dollars.)

Item	2000	2010	2015	Average annual percent change, 2000–2015
Total Households...	2,699,173	2,992,732	3,106,895	1.0
Family households	1,847,796	2,013,520	2,054,857	0.7
Married-couple family	1,426,044	1,517,627	1,549,808	0.6
Other family	421,752	495,893	505,049	1.3
Male householder, no wife present........................	101,462	124,273	135,352	2.2
Female householder, no husband present...............	320,290	371,620	369,697	1.0
Nonfamily households	851,377	979,212	1,052,038	1.6
Householder living alone...	676,907	794,535	842,558	1.6
Householder not living alone...................................	174,470	184,677	209,480	1.3
Housing Characteristics				
Total housing units..	2,904,192	3,368,674	3,468,952	1.3
Occupied housing units	2,699,173	2,992,732	3,106,895	1.0
Owner occupied	1,837,939	2,025,240	2,019,869	0.7
Renter occupied	861,234	967,492	1,087,026	1.7
Average household size..	2.54	2.60	2.62	0.2
Financial Characteristics				
Median gross rent of renter-occupied housing	650	1,019	1,144	5.1
Median monthly owner costs for housing units with a mortgage	1,144	1,728	1,692	3.2
Median value of owner-occupied housing units	125,400	249,100	257,800	7.0

Table VA-4. Migration, Origin, and Language

(Number, percent.)

Characteristic	State			U.S.		
	2014	2015	Percent change	2014	2015	Percent change
Residence 1 Year Ago						
Population 1 year and over	8,224,054	8,283,737	0.7	315,095,393	317,635,720	0.8
Same house	83.8	83.9	X	85.1	85.3	X
Different house in the U.S.	15.3	15.2	X	14.3	14.1	X
Same county	6.9	6.8	X	8.7	8.5	X
Different county	8.4	8.4	X	5.6	5.6	X
Same state	5.2	5.1	X	3.3	3.2	X
Different state	3.2	3.4	X	2.3	2.4	X
Abroad	0.9	0.8	X	0.6	0.7	X
Place of Birth						
Native born	7,320,669	7,364,367	0.6	276,465,262	278,128,449	0.6
Male	49.3	49.4	X	49.3	49.3	X
Female	50.7	50.6	X	50.7	50.7	X
Foreign born	1,005,620	1,018,626	1.3	42,391,794	43,290,372	2.1
Male	48.0	48.0	X	48.7	48.6	X
Female	52.0	52.0	X	51.3	51.4	X
Foreign born; naturalized U.S. citizen.......................	496,809	519,086	4.5	19,984,738	20,697,103	3.6
Male	46.3	46.1	X	45.9	45.9	X
Female	53.7	53.9	X	54.1	54.1	X
Foreign born; not a U.S. citizen	508,811	499,540	-1.8	22,407,056	22,593,269	0.8
Male	49.7	50.0	X	51.2	51.1	X
Female	50.3	50.0	X	48.8	48.9	X
Entered 2010 or later	14.7	18.2	X	12.3	15.6	X
Entered 2000 to 2009	33.5	31.1	X	28.6	27.9	X
Entered before 2000..	51.8	50.7	X	59.1	56.5	X
World Region of Birth, Foreign						
Foreign-born population, excluding population born at sea	1,005,620	1,018,626	1.3	42,390,705	43,289,646	2.1
Europe	10.0	10.1	X	11.2	11.1	X
Asia	41.9	42.0	X	30.1	30.6	X
Africa	10.4	10.4	X	4.6	4.8	X
Oceania	0.3	0.2	X	0.6	0.6	X
Latin America	35.9	35.8	X	51.6	51.1	X
North America	1.4	1.5	X	1.9	1.9	X
Language Spoken at Home and Ability to Speak English						
Population 5 years and over..	7,818,739	7,872,076	0.7	299,084,046	301,625,014	0.8
English only	84.4	84.1	X	78.9	78.5	X
Language other than English...................................	15.6	15.9	X	21.1	21.5	X
Speaks English less than "very well"......................	5.6	5.9	X	8.6	8.6	X

NA = Not available.
X = Not applicable.
- = Zero or rounds to zero.

Table VA-5. Median Income and Poverty Status, 2015

(Number, percent, except as noted.)

Characteristic	State		U.S.	
	Number	Percent	Number	Percent
Median Income				
Households (dollars)	66,262	X	55,775	X
Families (dollars)	80,403	X	68,260	X
Below Poverty Level (All People)	909,346	11.2	46,153,077	14.7
Sex				
Male	395,736	10.0	20,599,407	13.4
Female	513,610	12.3	25,553,670	16.0
Age				
Under 18 years	272,829	14.8	15,000,273	20.7
Related children under 18 years	266,602	14.5	14,693,239	20.4
18 to 64 years	552,124	10.8	26,960,369	13.9
65 years and over	84,393	7.3	4,192,435	9.0

X = Not applicable.

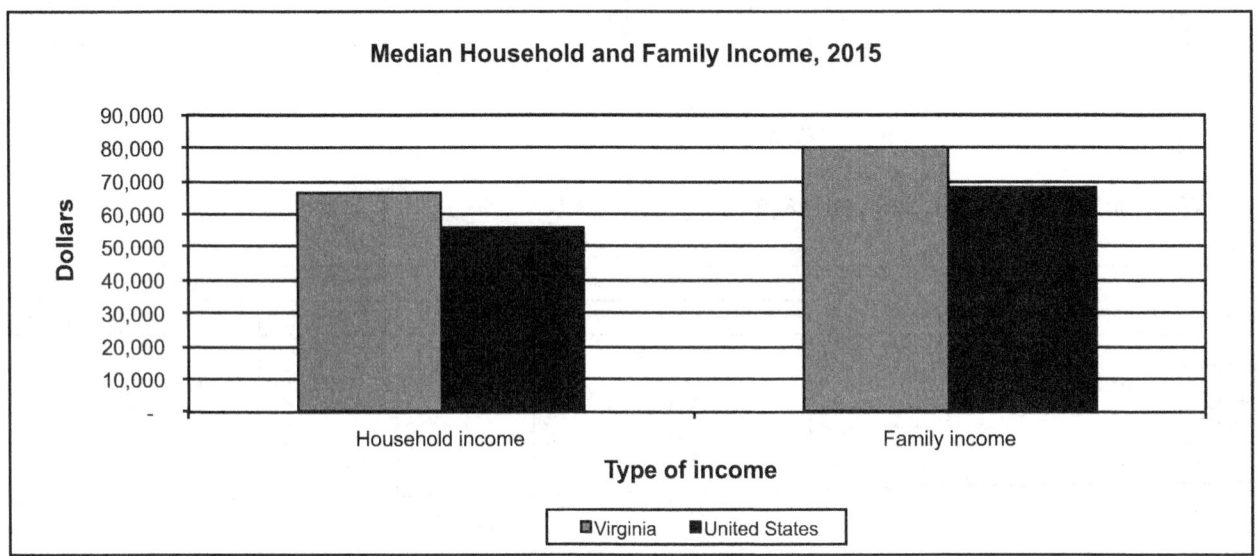

Median Household and Family Income, 2015

Table VA-6. Health Insurance Coverage Status for the Civilian Noninstitutionalized Population and Children Under 18 Years of Age

(Numbers in thousands, percent.)

Item	2007	2008	2009	2010	2011	2012	2013	2014	2015
Civilian Noninstitutionalized Population	7,684	7,520	7,644	7,807	7,887	7,973	8,054	8,115	8,163
Covered by Private or Public Insurance									
Number	6,548	6,621	6,736	6,787	6,904	6,974	7,064	7,231	7,416
Percent	85.2	88.0	88.1	86.9	87.5	87.5	87.7	89.1	90.9
Not Covered									
Number	1,135	899	908	1,020	983	999	991	884	746
Percent	14.8	12.0	11.9	13.1	12.5	12.5	12.3	10.9	9.1
Percent in the U.S. not covered	15.3	15.1	15.1	15.5	15.1	14.8	14.5	11.7	9.4
Children Under 18 Years of Age	1,833	1,815	1,843	1,850	1,849	1,852	1,862	1,865	1,867
Covered by Private or Public Insurance									
Number	1,646	1,677	1,721	1,729	1,741	1,748	1,760	1,758	1,776
Percent	89.8	92.4	93.4	93.4	94.1	94.4	94.6	94.3	95.1
Not Covered									
Number	187	138	122	121	108	104	101	107	91
Percent	10.2	7.6	6.6	6.6	5.9	5.6	5.4	5.7	4.9
Percent in the U.S. not covered	11.0	9.7	8.6	8.0	7.5	7.2	7.1	6.0	4.8

Table VA-7. Employment Status by Demographic Group, 2016

(Numbers in thousands, percent.)

Characteristic	Civilian noninstitutional population	Civilian labor force		Employed		Unemployed	
		Number	Percent of population	Number	Percent of population	Number	Percent of population
Total................................	6,558	4,218	64.3	4,047	61.7	171	4.1
Sex							
Male....................	3,148	2,225	70.7	2,135	67.8	91	4.1
Female..................	3,410	1,992	58.4	1,912	56.1	80	4.0
Race, Sex, and Hispanic Origin							
White............................	4,688	2,991	63.8	2,898	61.8	93	3.1
Male.....................	2,301	1,618	70.3	1,563	67.9	55	3.4
Female...................	2,388	1,373	57.5	1,335	55.9	38	2.8
Black or African American...............	1,241	794	64.0	738	59.4	56	7.1
Male.....................	566	386	68.1	360	63.6	25	6.6
Female...................	675	408	60.5	377	55.9	31	7.5
Hispanic or Latino ethnicity[1]	536	395	73.7	382	71.3	13	3.2
Male.....................	263	221	84.0	215	81.5	6	2.9
Female...................	272	174	63.8	168	61.5	6	3.6
Age							
16 to 19 years...........	420	146	34.8	122	29.1	24	16.4
20 to 24 years...........	544	374	68.7	348	64.0	26	6.9
25 to 34 years...........	1,106	937	84.7	901	81.5	36	3.8
35 to 44 years...........	1,092	910	83.4	878	80.5	32	3.5
45 to 54 years...........	1,112	909	81.7	880	79.1	29	3.2
55 to 64 years...........	1,035	675	65.2	658	63.6	16	2.4
65 years and over	1,250	267	21.4	259	20.7	9	3.2

NOTE: Data in Table 7 are from the Current Population Survey (CPS) and do not match the estimates in Table 8. See notes and definitions for further information.
[1] May be of any race.

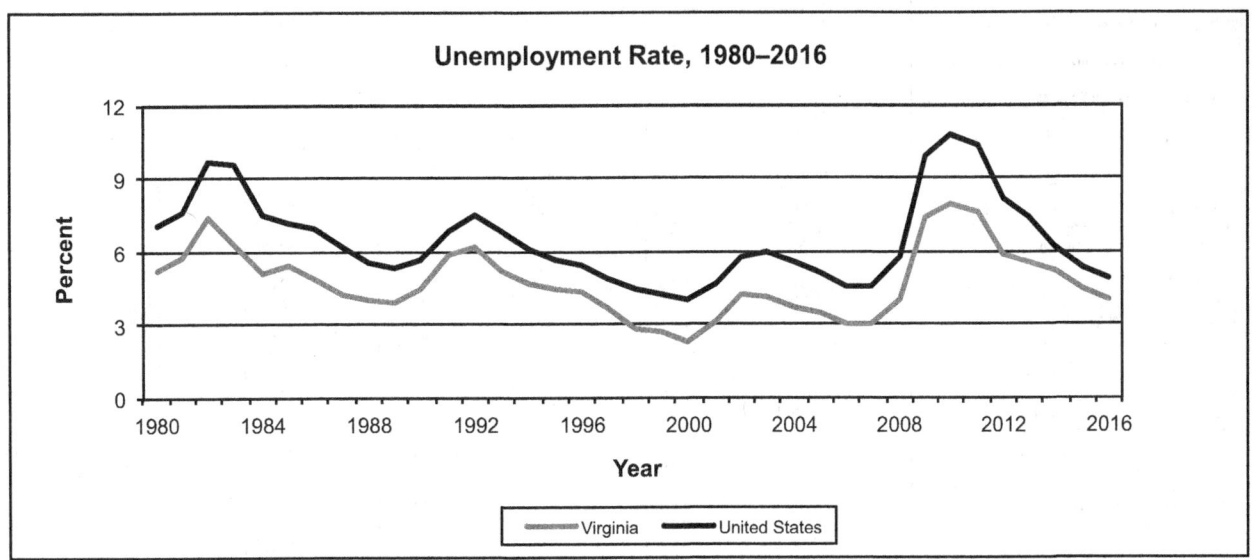

Table VA-8. Employment Status of the Civilian Noninstitutional Population Age 16 Years and Over

(Number, percent.)

Year	Civilian labor force	Civilian participation rate	Employed	Unemployed	Unemployment rate
2008..................	4,133,443	69.7	3,970,428	163,015	3.9
2009..................	4,118,171	68.6	3,842,516	275,655	6.7
2010..................	4,157,658	67.7	3,860,386	297,272	7.1
2011..................	4,211,802	67.4	3,934,326	277,476	6.6
2012..................	4,225,252	66.8	3,969,890	255,362	6.0
2013..................	4,239,491	66.3	3,998,244	241,247	5.7
2014..................	4,257,986	66.0	4,036,280	221,706	5.2
2015..................	4,240,470	65.2	4,051,908	188,562	4.4
2016..................	4,240,403	64.8	4,070,260	170,143	4.0

Table VA-9. Employment and Average Wages by Industry

(Estimates through 2010 are based on the 2007 *North American Industry Classification System* [NAICS]. Estimates from 2011 onward are based on the 2012 NAICS.)

Industry	2009	2010	2011	2012	2013	2014	2015
	Number of jobs						
Wage and Salary Employment by Industry..................	3,882,412	3,856,908	3,887,761	3,929,899	3,948,870	3,974,046	4,050,089
Farm Wage and Salary Employment.........................	9,829	13,123	10,306	10,499	11,678	14,301	12,948
Nonfarm Wage and Salary Employment....................	3,872,583	3,843,785	3,877,455	3,919,400	3,937,192	3,959,745	4,037,141
Private wage and salary employment.................................	2,999,017	2,969,478	3,006,948	3,047,333	3,069,001	3,091,552	3,165,120
Forestry, fishing, and related activities........................	5,551	5,595	5,590	5,734	5,966	6,101	6,751
Mining..	8,489	8,590	9,056	9,035	8,071	7,463	6,845
Utilities..	11,450	10,913	10,889	10,636	10,536	10,646	10,786
Construction...	199,662	189,854	184,070	182,079	182,178	183,419	189,695
Manufacturing..	239,421	230,597	230,796	231,785	231,357	232,063	233,733
Durable goods manufacturing.................................	137,120	132,359	134,326	136,484	136,575	137,524	138,405
Nondurable goods manufacturing...........................	102,301	98,238	96,470	95,301	94,782	94,539	95,328
Wholesale trade..	114,290	110,633	112,724	111,825	111,819	111,416	111,356
Retail trade..	404,813	401,843	406,083	409,506	414,124	417,390	421,952
Transportation and warehousing..................................	103,622	102,637	104,716	105,616	106,079	108,540	115,856
Information...	81,309	76,295	74,414	71,794	71,229	71,691	69,824
Finance and insurance	124,978	124,280	128,507	131,529	134,049	135,871	139,122
Real estate and rental and leasing.............................	56,129	53,022	52,239	52,751	53,091	52,792	53,915
Professional, scientific, and technical services	381,746	386,006	394,529	399,057	397,523	392,570	402,634
Management of companies and enterprises..................	74,763	74,000	73,350	76,427	75,619	73,985	74,229
Administrative and waste services..............................	193,804	196,706	203,608	207,894	210,367	216,813	226,963
Educational services	70,018	70,756	72,872	73,093	73,593	72,336	73,998
Health care and social assistance...............................	374,295	381,213	388,288	397,629	406,261	410,904	423,331
Arts, entertainment, and recreation.............................	47,118	47,530	47,976	49,187	50,403	50,174	53,486
Accommodation and food services..............................	298,551	296,559	303,457	312,039	318,214	323,633	334,819
Other services, except public administration..................	209,008	202,449	203,784	209,717	208,522	213,745	215,825
Government and government enterprises..........................	873,566	874,307	870,507	872,067	868,191	868,193	872,021
	Dollars						
Average Wages and Salaries by Industry	49,362	50,987	52,049	53,011	53,314	54,329	55,663
Average Farm Wages and Salaries	24,546	18,204	20,289	28,277	25,881	22,657	22,975
Average Nonfarm Wages and Salaries	49,425	51,098	52,133	53,077	53,396	54,443	55,768
Average private wages and salaries.............................	48,412	50,172	51,348	52,428	52,813	53,766	55,124
Forestry, fishing, and related activities........................	26,116	27,991	28,521	29,317	30,037	31,513	32,892
Mining..	61,542	67,459	70,589	68,526	69,184	71,090	69,102
Utilities..	93,822	100,102	100,708	101,456	101,266	105,964	105,655
Construction...	45,500	47,616	48,596	49,022	49,649	50,994	52,508
Manufacturing..	51,096	53,483	54,522	55,473	56,302	58,491	59,829
Durable goods manufacturing.................................	52,877	55,240	57,124	57,996	59,101	61,896	63,453
Nondurable goods manufacturing...........................	48,709	51,117	50,900	51,859	52,268	53,537	54,568
Wholesale trade..	66,969	69,186	72,261	72,571	73,653	75,497	78,101
Retail trade..	25,848	26,508	26,802	27,384	27,695	28,229	28,979
Transportation and warehousing..................................	45,673	47,035	47,866	49,864	51,111	52,060	51,762
Information...	78,319	80,769	81,830	84,358	88,040	92,779	97,560
Finance and insurance	72,296	75,393	78,453	83,257	83,606	86,021	89,639
Real estate and rental and leasing.............................	43,332	45,318	46,814	48,776	49,590	51,442	53,928
Professional, scientific, and technical services	89,770	93,389	96,078	97,683	98,141	99,125	100,999
Management of companies and enterprises..................	98,672	103,180	107,477	112,182	112,749	114,579	121,621
Administrative and waste services..............................	35,289	37,015	37,811	38,668	38,574	39,291	40,546
Educational services	40,701	39,811	38,189	38,461	38,861	39,158	38,965
Health care and social assistance...............................	44,025	44,698	45,820	46,634	47,036	48,030	49,060
Arts, entertainment, and recreation.............................	26,005	27,246	26,488	27,248	27,179	28,275	28,855
Accommodation and food services..............................	17,940	18,492	18,883	19,446	19,736	20,299	21,053
Other services, except public administration..................	33,723	35,138	35,612	36,167	36,908	37,792	39,125
Government and government enterprises..........................	52,901	54,245	54,845	55,344	55,456	56,853	58,105

Table VA-10. Employment Characteristics by Family Type

(Number, percent.)

Family type and labor force status	2013 Total	2013 Families with own children under 18 years	2014 Total	2014 Families with own children under 18 years	2015 Total	2015 Families with own children under 18 years
All Families..	2,049,184	887,364	2,051,042	901,080	2,054,857	882,330
FAMILY TYPE AND LABOR FORCE STATUS						
Married-Couple Families..	1,530,934	622,543	1,536,661	635,484	1,549,808	620,930
Both husband and wife in labor force.............................	54.8	67.3	54.8	67.2	54.0	67.4
Husband in labor force, wife not in labor force	21.9	27.9	22.2	27.8	22.1	27.5
Wife in labor force, husband not in labor force	7.3	3.3	7.5	3.5	7.5	3.5
Both husband and wife not in labor force.........................	15.6	1.3	15.5	1.5	15.7	1.3
Other Families	518,250	264,821	514,381	265,596	505,049	261,400
Female householder, no husband present.........................	74.4	77.9	74.1	76.6	73.2	76.5
In labor force..	54.1	65.1	53.6	64.3	53.2	64.9
Not in labor force...	20.3	12.7	20.5	12.3	20.0	11.6
Male householder, no wife present................................	25.6	22.1	25.9	23.4	26.8	23.5
In labor force..	20.4	20.5	20.7	21.8	21.6	21.6
Not in labor force...	5.2	1.7	5.3	1.6	5.2	1.9

Table VA-11. School Enrollment and Educational Attainment, 2015

(Number, percent.)

Item	State	U.S.
Enrollment		
Total population 3 years and over, enrolled in school	2,143,693	81,618,288
Enrolled in nursery school or preschool (percent)...............................	5.8	6.0
Enrolled in kindergarten (percent)..	5.1	5.0
Enrolled in elementary school, grades 1-8 (percent)............................	38.6	40.3
Enrolled in high school, grades 9-12 (percent)..................................	20.0	20.9
Enrolled in college or graduate school (percent)................................	30.5	27.7
Attainment		
Total population 25 years and over	5,685,318	216,447,163
Less than ninth grade (percent)	4.5	5.5
9th to 12th grade, no diploma (percent)...	6.6	7.3
High school graduate, including equivalency (percent)..........................	24.6	27.6
Some college, no degree (percent)..	19.8	20.7
Associate's degree (percent)..	7.5	8.2
Bachelor's degree (percent)...	21.3	19.0
Graduate or professional degree (percent).......................................	15.7	11.6
High school graduate or higher (percent)	88.9	87.1
Bachelor's degree or higher (percent)..	37.0	30.6

Table VA-12. Public School Characteristics and Educational Indicators

(Number, percent; data derived from National Center of Education Statistics.)

Item	State	U.S.
Public Schools, 2014–2015 (except where noted)		
Number of school districts..	222	18,260
Number of schools..	2,134	98,373
Number of students	1,280,381	50,312,581
Number of teachers	89,968	3,132,351
Student-teacher ratio	14.2	16.1
Expenditures per student (dollars), FY 2014	10,955	11,066
Four-year adjusted cohort graduation rate (ACGR)[1,2]	85.7	83.2
Students eligible for free or reduced-price lunch (percent).......................	40.2	51.8
English language learners (percent)...	7.7	9.4
Students age 3 to 21 served under IDEA, part B (percent)........................	12.7	13.0

Public Schools by Type	Number	Percent of state public schools
Total number of schools..	2,134	100.0
Regular	1,866	87.4
Special education	53	2.5
Vocational education..	90	4.2
Alternative education...	125	5.9

NOTE: Every school is assigned only one school type based on its instructional emphasis.
[1] ACGR data represents a new method of calculating high-school completion rates and may not be comparable to previous years' data for Averaged Freshmen Graduation Rates (AFGR).
[2] The United States 4-year ACGRs were estimated using both the reported 4-year ACGR data from 49 states and the District of Columbia and using imputed data for Idaho. The estimate for American Indian/Alaska Native students also includes imputed data for Virginia.

Table VA-13. Reported Voting and Registration of the Voting-Age Population, November 2016

(Numbers in thousands, percent.)

Item	Total population	Total citizen population	Registered			Voted		
			Total registered	Percent registered (total population)	Percent registered (total citizen population)	Total voted	Percent voted (total population)	Percent voted (total citizen population)
U.S. Total	245,502	224,059	157,596	64.2	70.3	137,537	56.0	61.4
State Total..........................	6,343	5,829	4,399	69.4	75.5	3,973	62.6	68.2
Sex								
Male	3,026	2,778	2,023	66.9	72.8	1,806	59.7	65.0
Female	3,317	3,052	2,376	71.6	77.9	2,168	65.3	71.0
Race								
White alone..........................	4,459	4,172	3,218	72.2	77.1	2,891	64.8	69.3
White, non-Hispanic alone...........	3,976	3,885	3,009	75.7	77.5	2,702	68.0	69.6
Black alone..........................	1,189	1,136	817	68.7	71.9	738	62.0	64.9
Asian alone	462	300	219	47.4	73.0	210	45.4	69.9
Hispanic (of any race)......................	606	342	240	39.5	70.1	219	36.2	64.2
White alone or in combination	4,571	4,285	3,298	72.1	77.0	2,967	64.9	69.2
Black alone or in combination..........	1,256	1,203	851	67.8	70.8	768	61.2	63.9
Asian alone or in combination..........	513	351	261	50.9	74.3	251	49.1	71.7
Age								
18 to 24 years......................	819	737	501	61.1	67.9	447	54.6	60.7
25 to 34 years......................	1,118	993	640	57.2	64.4	549	49.1	55.3
35 to 44 years......................	982	833	651	66.3	78.1	573	58.3	68.8
45 to 64 years......................	2,144	2,023	1,612	75.2	79.7	1,500	70.0	74.2
65 years and over	1,279	1,244	996	77.8	80.0	903	70.6	72.6

Table VA-14. Crime

(Number, rate per 100,000. Data are derived from the FBI Uniform Crime Reports.)

Item	State			U.S. [1,2,3,4]		
	2014	2015	Percent change	2014	2015	Percent change
TOTAL POPULATION[5]	8,328,098	8,382,993	0.7	318,907,401	321,418,820	0.8
VIOLENT CRIME						
Number..........................	16,522	16,399	-0.7	1,186,185	1,231,566	3.8
Rate	198.4	195.6	-1.4	372.0	383.2	3.0
Murder and Nonnegligent Manslaughter						
Number..........................	350	383	9.4	14,164	15,696	10.8
Rate	4.2	4.6	8.7	4.4	4.9	10.0
Rape[6]						
Number..........................	2,416	2,340	-3.1	118,027	124,047	5.1
Rate	29.0	27.9	-3.8	37.0	38.6	4.3
Robbery						
Number..........................	4,294	4,441	3.4	322,905	327,374	1.4
Rate	51.6	53.0	2.7	101.3	101.9	0.6
Aggravated Assault						
Number..........................	9,462	9,235	-2.4	731,089	764,449	4.6
Rate	113.6	110.2	-3.0	229.2	237.8	3.7
PROPERTY CRIME						
Number..........................	161,934	156,470	-3.4	8,209,010	7,993,631	-2.6
Rate	1,944.4	1,866.5	-4.0	2,574.1	2,487.0	-3.4
Burglary						
Number..........................	23,210	21,340	-8.1	1,713,153	1,579,527	-7.8
Rate	278.7	254.6	-8.7	537.2	491.4	-8.5
Larceny-Theft						
Number..........................	131,001	127,019	-3.0	5,809,054	5,706,346	-1.8
Rate	1,573.0	1,515.2	-3.7	1,821.5	1,775.4	-2.5
Motor Vehicle Theft						
Number..........................	7,723	8,111	5.0	686,803	707,758	3.1
Rate	92.7	96.8	4.3	215.4	220.2	2.2

NOTE: Although arson data are included in the trend and clearance tables, sufficient data are not available to estimate totals for this offense. Therefore, no arson data are published in this table.

X = Not applicable.

- = Zero or rounds to zero.

[1] The crime figures have been adjusted.

[2] The data collection methodology for the offense of forcible rape used by the Minnesota state Uniform Crime Reporting (UCR) Program (with the exception of Minneapolis and St. Paul, Minnesota) does not comply with national UCR Program guidelines. Consequently, its figures for forcible rape and violent crime (of which forcible rape is a part) are not published in this table.

[3] Includes offenses reported by the Zoological Police and the Metro Transit Police.

[4] Because of changes in the state's reporting practices, figures are not comparable to previous years' data.

[5] Populations are U.S. Census Bureau provisional estimates as of July 1 of each year.

[6] The figures shown for the offense of rape were estimated using the revised Uniform Crime Reporting (UCR) definition of rape.

Table VA-15. State Government Finances, 2015

(Dollar amounts in thousands, percent distribution.)

Item	Dollars	Percent distribution
Total Revenue	51,920,942	100.0
General revenue	44,324,730	85.4
Intergovernmental revenue	10,177,643	19.6
Taxes	20,536,885	39.6
General sales	3,793,215	7.3
Selective sales	2,701,872	5.2
License taxes	829,279	1.6
Individual income tax	11,903,945	22.9
Corporate income tax	817,851	1.6
Other taxes	490,723	0.9
Current charges	9,422,799	18.1
Miscellaneous general revenue	4,187,403	8.1
Utility revenue	0	-
Liquor stores revenue	736,558	1.4
Insurance trust revenue[1]	6,859,654	13.2
Total Expenditure	53,184,660	100.0
Intergovernmental expenditure	12,479,548	23.5
Direct expenditure	40,705,112	76.5
Current operation	29,127,478	54.8
Capital outlay	3,155,734	5.9
Insurance benefits and repayments	5,625,552	10.6
Assistance and subsidies	1,704,493	3.2
Interest on debt	1,091,855	2.1
Exhibit: Salaries and wages	7,162,424	13.5
Total Expenditure	53,184,660	100.0
General expenditure	46,846,314	88.1
Intergovernmental expenditure	12,479,548	23.5
Direct expenditure	34,366,766	64.6
General expenditure, by function:		
Education	15,834,457	29.8
Public welfare	11,248,106	21.1
Hospitals	4,416,753	8.3
Health	1,443,520	2.7
Highways	4,900,426	9.2
Police protection	586,570	1.1
Correction	1,806,022	3.4
Natural resources	264,995	0.5
Parks and recreation	126,753	0.2
Governmental administration	1,550,881	2.9
Interest on general debt	1,091,855	2.1
Other and unallocable	3,575,976	6.7
Utility expenditure	119165	0.2
Liquor stores expenditure	593,629	1.1
Insurance trust expenditure	5,625,552	10.6
Debt at End of Fiscal Year	28,231,613	X
Cash and Security Holdings	109,224,043	X

X = Not applicable.
- = Zero or rounds to zero.
[1] Within insurance trust revenue, net earnings of state retirement systems is a calculated statistic (the item code in the data file is X08), and thus can be positive or negative. Net earnings is the sum of earnings on investments plus gains on investments minus losses on investments. The change made in 2002 for asset valuation from book to market value in accordance with Statement 34 of the Governmental Accounting Standards Board is reflected in the calculated statistics.

Table VA-16. State Government Tax Collections, 2016

(Dollars in thousands, percent.)

Item	Dollars	Percent distribution
Total Taxes	21,219,757	100.0
Property taxes	30,367	0.1
Sales and gross receipts	6,886,378	32.5
General sales and gross receipts	3,931,717	18.5
Selective sales and gross receipts	2,954,661	13.9
Alcoholic beverages	268,547	1.3
Amusements	83	-
Insurance premiums	491,495	2.3
Motor fuels	895,589	4.2
Pari-mutuels	0	-
Public utilities	121,749	0.6
Tobacco products	178,847	0.8
Other selective sales	998,351	4.7
Licenses	826,306	3.9
Alcoholic beverages	13,297	0.1
Amusements	129	-
Corporations in general	61,138	0.3
Hunting and fishing	27,763	0.1
Motor vehicle	477,126	2.2
Motor vehicle operators	40,558	0.2
Public utilities	0	-
Occupation and business, NEC	202,087	1.0
Other licenses	4,208	-
Income taxes	12,990,685	61.2
Individual income	12,237,996	57.7
Corporation net income	752,689	3.5
Other taxes	486,021	2.3
Death and gift	222	-
Documentary and stock transfer	368,747	1.7
Severance	2,468	-
Taxes, NEC	114,584	0.5

- = Zero or rounds to zero.

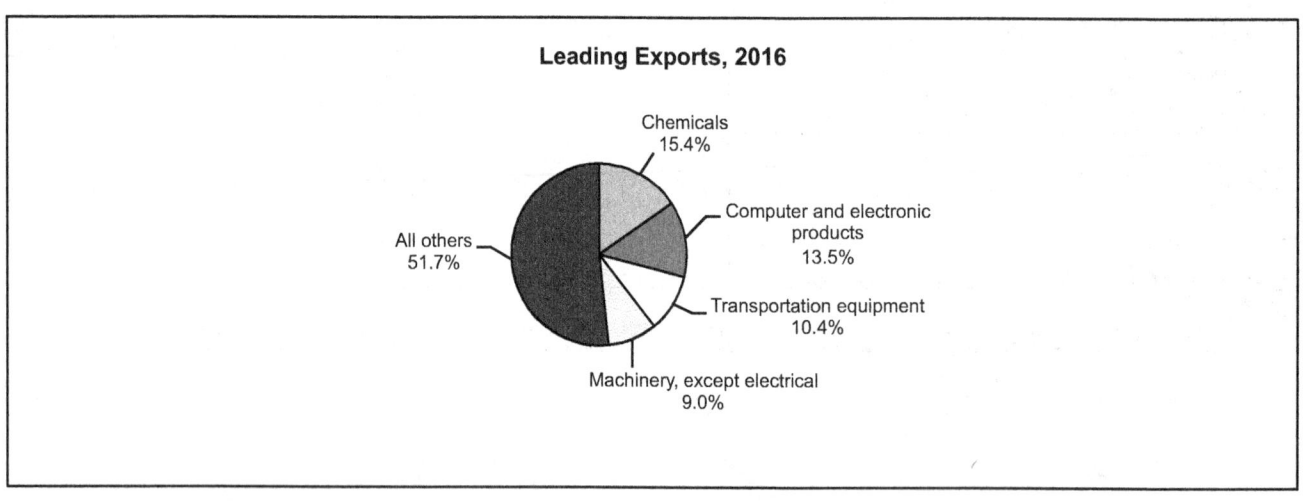

Leading Exports, 2016

Facts and Figures

Location: Northwestern United States; bordered on the N by Canada (British Columbia), on the E by Idaho, on the S by Oregon, and on the W by the Pacific Ocean

Area: 71,300 sq. mi. (184,665 sq. km.); rank—18th

Population: 7,288,000 (2016 est.); rank—13th

Principal Cities: capital—Olympia; largest—Seattle

Statehood: November 11, 1889; 42nd state

U.S. Congress: 2 senators, 10 representatives

State Motto: *Alki* ("By and by")

State Song: "Washington, My Home"

State Nickname: The Evergreen State

Abbreviations: WA; Wash.

State Symbols: flower—coast rhododendron; tree—Western hemlock; bird—willow goldfinch

At a Glance

- With an increase in population of 8.4 percent, Washington ranked 8th among the states in growth from 2010 to 2016.

- Washington's median household income in 2015 was $64,129, and 12.2 percent of the population lived below the poverty level.

- In 2015, 6.6 percent of Washingtonians did not have health insurance, compared to 9.4 percent of the total U.S. population.

- Washington had the 4th highest property crime rate in the country in 2015 (3,463.8 incidents per 100,000 population).

- Approximately 34.2 percent of Washingtonians had a bachelor's degree or more in 2015, compared to 30.6 percent of all U.S. residents.

Table WA-1. Population by Age, Sex, Race, and Hispanic Origin

(Number, percent, except where noted.)

Sex, age, race, and Hispanic origin	2000	2010	2016 [1]	Average annual percent change, 2010–2016
Total population	5,894,121	6,724,540	7,288,000	0.5
Percent of total U.S. population	2.1	2.2	2.3	X
Sex				
Male	2,934,300	3,349,707	3,641,400	0.5
Female	2,959,821	3,374,833	3,646,600	0.5
Age				
Under 5 years	394,306	439,657	455,339	0.2
5 to 19 years	1,288,713	1,330,238	1,347,117	0.1
20 to 64 years	3,548,954	4,126,968	4,404,481	0.4
65 years and over	662,148	827,677	1,081,063	1.9
Median age (years)	35.9	37.3	37.7	0.1
Race and Hispanic origin				
One race				
White	4,821,823	5,535,262	5,830,144	0.3
Black	190,267	252,333	301,955	1.2
American Indian and Alaska Native	93,301	122,649	138,489	0.8
Asian	322,335	491,685	625,138	1.7
Native Hawaiian or Other Pacific Islander	23,953	43,505	54,702	1.6
Two or more races	213,519	279,106	337,572	1.3
Hispanic (of any race)	441,509	776,539	907,000	1.1

X = Not applicable.
[1] Population figures for 2016 are July 1 estimates. The 2010 estimates are taken from the 2010 Census.

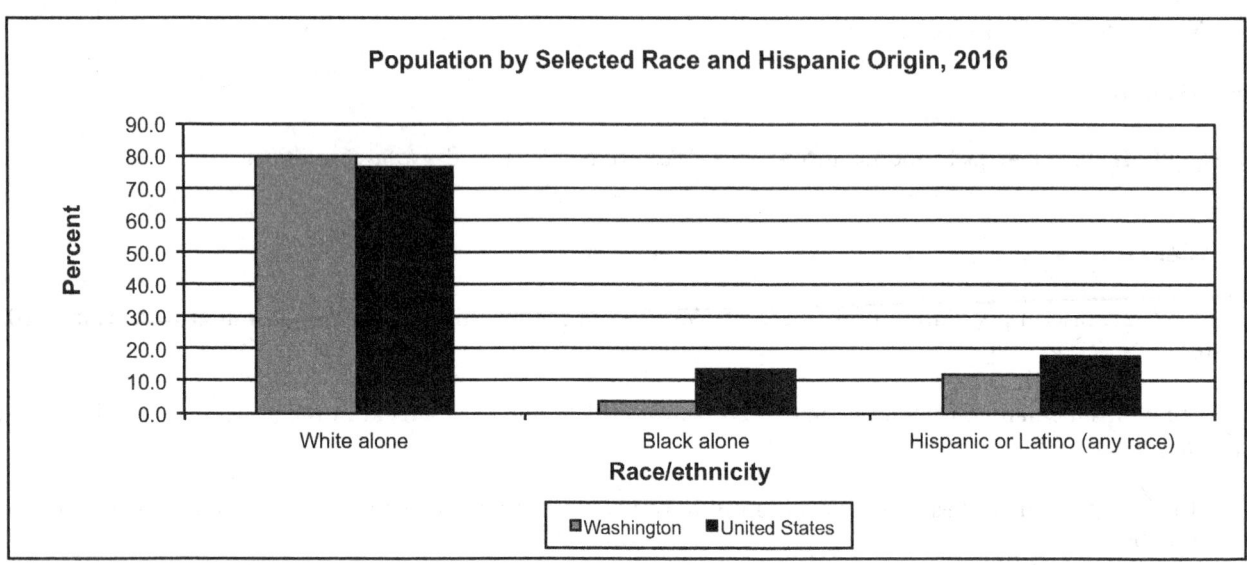

Population by Selected Race and Hispanic Origin, 2016

Table WA-2. Marital Status

(Number, percent distribution.)

Sex, age, race, and Hispanic origin	2000	2010	2015
Males, 15 Years and Over	2,287,431	2,686,801	2,900,227
Never married	29.8	33.8	34.9
Now married, except separated	56.6	52.0	51.0
Separated	1.4	1.6	1.3
Widowed	2.1	2.1	2.2
Divorced	10.1	10.5	10.7
Females, 15 Years and Over	2,352,091	2,746,158	2,928,587
Never married	22.8	26.4	27.6
Now married, except separated	54.1	50.6	49.6
Separated	1.8	2.1	1.8
Widowed	8.6	7.8	7.4
Divorced	12.7	13.2	13.5

Table WA-3. Households and Housing Characteristics

(Number, percent, dollars.)

Item	2000	2010	2015	Average annual percent change, 2000–2015
Total Households...	2,271,398	2,606,863	2,728,573	1.3
Family households...	1,499,127	1,681,386	1,760,593	1.2
Married-couple family..	1,181,995	1,297,240	1,363,817	1.0
Other family..	317,132	384,146	396,776	1.7
Male householder, no wife present...........................	92,514	114,187	122,653	2.2
Female householder, no husband present...................	224,618	269,959	274,123	1.5
Nonfamily households..	772,271	925,477	967,980	1.7
Householder living alone..	594,325	731,452	736,390	1.6
Householder not living alone.....................................	117,946	194,025	231,590	6.4
Housing Characteristics				
Total housing units..	2,451,075	2,888,594	2,991,584	1.5
Occupied housing units	2,271,398	2,606,863	2,728,573	1.3
Owner occupied..	1,467,009	1,644,939	1,703,269	1.1
Renter occupied...	804,389	961,924	1,025,304	1.8
Average household size..	2.53	2.53	2.58	0.1
Financial Characteristics				
Median gross rent of renter-occupied housing	663	908	1,080	4.2
Median monthly owner costs for housing units with a mortgage	1,268	1,736	1,704	2.3
Median value of owner-occupied housing units	168,300	271,800	284,000	4.6

Table WA-4. Migration, Origin, and Language

(Number, percent.)

Characteristic	State			U.S.		
	2014	2015	Percent change	2014	2015	Percent change
Residence 1 Year Ago						
Population 1 year and over	6,979,369	7,089,143	1.6	315,095,393	317,635,720	0.8
Same house	82.5	81.5	X	85.1	85.3	X
Different house in the U.S.	16.6	17.6	X	14.3	14.1	X
Same county	10.4	10.9	X	8.7	8.5	X
Different county	6.2	6.7	X	5.6	5.6	X
Same state	3.0	3.4	X	3.3	3.2	X
Different state	3.2	3.3	X	2.3	2.4	X
Abroad	1.0	0.9	X	0.6	0.7	X
Place of Birth						
Native born	6,116,784	6,190,193	1.2	276,465,262	278,128,449	0.6
Male	50.2	50.3	X	49.3	49.3	X
Female	49.8	49.7	X	50.7	50.7	X
Foreign born	944,746	980,158	3.7	42,391,794	43,290,372	2.1
Male	48.5	48.4	X	48.7	48.6	X
Female	51.5	51.6	X	51.3	51.4	X
Foreign born; naturalized U.S. citizen.................	437,379	458,313	4.8	19,984,738	20,697,103	3.6
Male	45.1	45.5	X	45.9	45.9	X
Female	54.9	54.5	X	54.1	54.1	X
Foreign born; not a U.S. citizen........................	507,367	521,845	2.9	22,407,056	22,593,269	0.8
Male	51.4	51.0	X	51.2	51.1	X
Female	48.6	49.0	X	48.8	48.9	X
Entered 2010 or later	14.9	17.5	X	12.3	15.6	X
Entered 2000 to 2009	29.9	28.4	X	28.6	27.9	X
Entered before 2000.......................................	55.2	54.1	X	59.1	56.5	X
World Region of Birth, Foreign						
Foreign-born population, excluding population born at sea	944,746	980,158	3.7	42,390,705	43,289,646	2.1
Europe	16.4	15.4	X	11.2	11.1	X
Asia	41.8	42.4	X	30.1	30.6	X
Africa	5.5	5.0	X	4.6	4.8	X
Oceania	1.6	1.8	X	0.6	0.6	X
Latin America..	29.9	30.9	X	51.6	51.1	X
North America	4.8	4.4	X	1.9	1.9	X
Language Spoken at Home and Ability to Speak English						
Population 5 years and over...............................	6,617,324	6,725,680	1.6	299,084,046	301,625,014	0.8
English only	81.2	80.7	X	78.9	78.5	X
Language other than English............................	18.8	19.3	X	21.1	21.5	X
Speaks English less than "very well"..................	7.6	7.5	X	8.6	8.6	X

NA = Not available.
X = Not applicable.
- = Zero or rounds to zero.

Table WA-5. Median Income and Poverty Status, 2015

(Number, percent, except as noted.)

Characteristic	State		U.S.	
	Number	Percent	Number	Percent
Median Income				
Households (dollars)...............................	64,129	X	55,775	X
Families (dollars)	76,954	X	68,260	X
Below Poverty Level (All People)	857,801	12.2	46,153,077	14.7
Sex				
Male	394,995	11.3	20,599,407	13.4
Female	462,806	13.1	25,553,670	16.0
Age				
Under 18 years...................................	246,076	15.5	15,000,273	20.7
Related children under 18 years..........	236,697	15.0	14,693,239	20.4
18 to 64 years...................................	536,148	12.1	26,960,369	13.9
65 years and over	75,577	7.4	4,192,435	9.0

X = Not applicable.

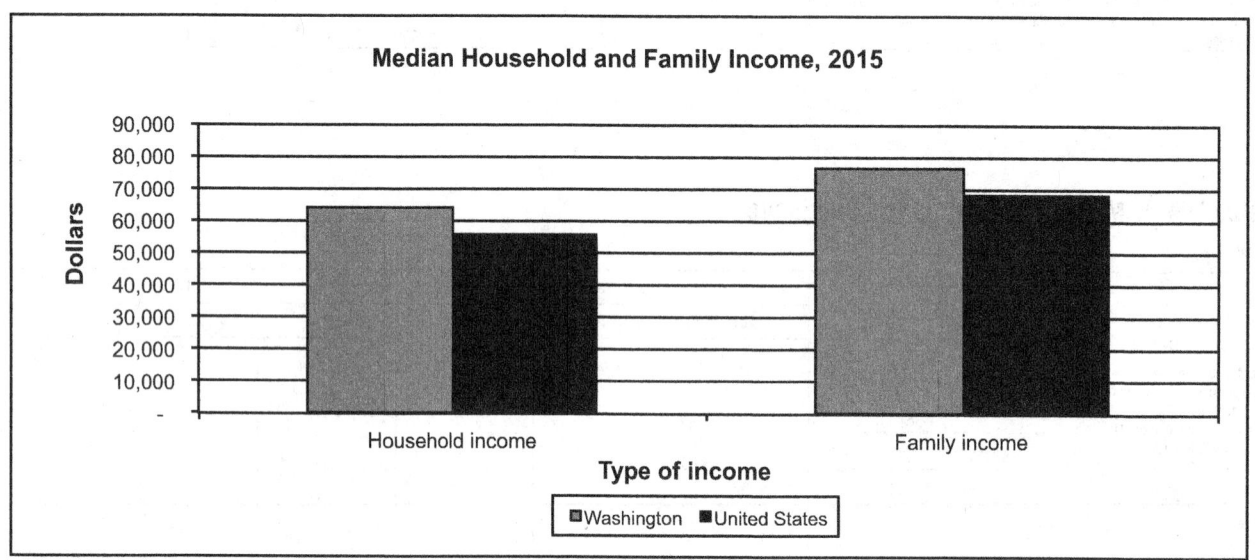

Median Household and Family Income, 2015

Table WA-6. Health Insurance Coverage Status for the Civilian Noninstitutionalized Population and Children Under 18 Years of Age

(Numbers in thousands, percent.)

Item	2007	2008	2009	2010	2011	2012	2013	2014	2015
Civilian Noninstitutionalized Population	6,509	6,428	6,546	6,638	6,717	6,793	6,864	6,955	7,067
Covered by Private or Public Insurance									
Number.........................	5,773	5,586	5,669	5,692	5,764	5,848	5,904	6,312	6,599
Percent..........................	88.7	86.9	86.6	85.8	85.8	86.1	86.0	90.8	93.4
Not Covered									
Number.........................	737	842	878	946	952	945	960	643	468
Percent..........................	11.3	13.1	13.4	14.2	14.2	13.9	14.0	9.2	6.6
Percent in the U.S. not covered..........	15.3	15.1	15.1	15.5	15.1	14.8	14.5	11.7	9.4
Children Under 18 Years of Age	1,558	1,541	1,570	1,583	1,578	1,584	1,595	1,601	1,611
Covered by Private or Public Insurance									
Number.........................	1,452	1,411	1,462	1,481	1,481	1,493	1,500	1,526	1,568
Percent..........................	93.2	91.6	93.1	93.6	93.8	94.2	94.1	95.3	97.4
Not Covered									
Number.........................	106	130	108	102	97	91	95	75	43
Percent..........................	6.8	8.4	6.9	6.4	6.2	5.8	5.9	4.7	2.6
Percent in the U.S. not covered...........	11.0	9.7	8.6	8.0	7.5	7.2	7.1	6.0	4.8

Table WA-7. Employment Status by Demographic Group, 2016

(Numbers in thousands, percent.)

Characteristic	Civilian noninstitutional population	Civilian labor force		Employed		Unemployed	
		Number	Percent of population	Number	Percent of population	Number	Percent of population
Total..	5,709	3,639	63.7	3,441	60.3	199	5.5
Sex							
Male..................	2,810	1,930	68.7	1,817	64.7	113	5.8
Female	2,899	1,710	59.0	1,624	56.0	86	5.0
Race, Sex, and Hispanic Origin							
White	4,618	2,930	63.4	2,775	60.1	155	5.3
Male..................	2,281	1,568	68.8	1,481	64.9	87	5.5
Female	2,338	1,362	58.3	1,294	55.4	68	5.0
Black or African American............	213	149	69.9	140	65.7	9	6.1
Male..................	122	87	71.7	80	65.6	7	8.4
Female	91	62	67.6	60	65.7	2	2.8
Hispanic or Latino ethnicity[1]	630	450	71.3	415	65.9	34	7.6
Male	331	259	78.2	240	72.5	19	7.3
Female	299	191	63.7	175	58.6	15	8.1
Age							
16 to 19 years....................	369	137	37.1	109	29.5	28	20.5
20 to 24 years....................	464	347	74.7	315	67.9	32	9.1
25 to 34 years....................	1,002	814	81.3	768	76.6	46	5.7
35 to 44 years....................	945	785	83.0	752	79.6	32	4.1
45 to 54 years....................	920	746	81.1	720	78.2	27	3.6
55 to 64 years....................	964	630	65.3	603	62.6	26	4.2
65 years and over	1,045	181	17.3	174	16.6	7	4.0

NOTE: Data in Table 7 are from the Current Population Survey (CPS) and do not match the estimates in Table 8. See notes and definitions for further information.
[1] May be of any race.

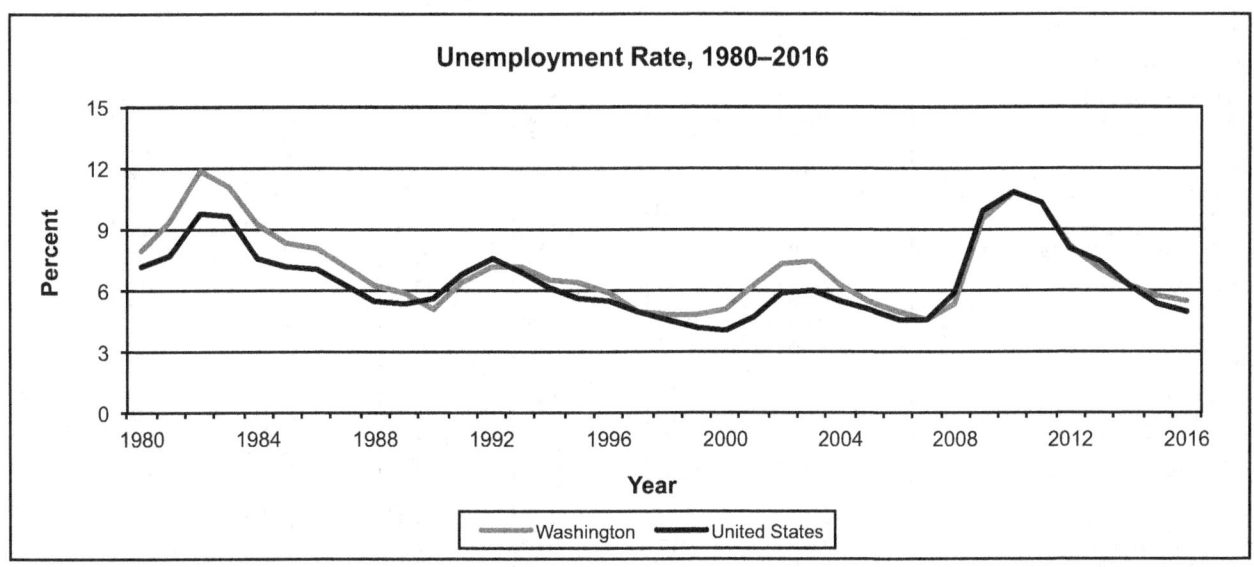

Unemployment Rate, 1980–2016

Table WA-8. Employment Status of the Civilian Noninstitutional Population Age 16 Years and Over

(Number, percent.)

Year	Civilian labor force	Civilian participation rate	Employed	Unemployed	Unemployment rate
2008...	3,478,577	68.4	3,291,309	187,268	5.4
2009...	3,535,200	68.3	3,211,649	323,551	9.2
2010...	3,511,326	66.9	3,160,544	350,782	10.0
2011...	3,461,428	65.2	3,140,190	321,238	9.3
2012...	3,472,727	64.5	3,190,421	282,306	8.1
2013...	3,464,760	63.6	3,220,860	243,900	7.0
2014...	3,492,866	63.2	3,278,975	213,891	6.1
2015...	3,544,242	63.0	3,343,992	200,250	5.7
2016...	3,643,881	63.7	3,445,880	198,001	5.4

Table WA-9. Employment and Average Wages by Industry

(Estimates through 2010 are based on the 2007 *North American Industry Classification System* [NAICS]. Estimates from 2011 onward are based on the 2012 NAICS.)

Industry	2009	2010	2011	2012	2013	2014	2015
	Number of jobs						
Wage and Salary Employment by Industry..................	3,048,125	2,999,842	3,032,727	3,131,758	3,199,080	3,283,925	3,361,613
Farm Wage and Salary Employment.........................	47,502	48,035	47,192	56,397	53,379	53,512	51,721
Nonfarm Wage and Salary Employment....................	3,000,623	2,951,807	2,985,535	3,075,361	3,145,701	3,230,413	3,309,892
Private wage and salary employment.......................	2,369,673	2,319,349	2,360,090	2,454,780	2,526,500	2,609,307	2,679,466
Forestry, fishing, and related activities.......................	28,607	28,107	28,654	30,087	30,879	31,534	31,914
Mining..	2,367	2,202	2,203	2,157	2,162	2,245	2,402
Utilities..	4,768	4,862	4,869	4,913	4,823	4,838	4,943
Construction...	166,311	144,998	140,274	142,919	153,393	165,274	179,164
Manufacturing..	265,911	258,156	269,066	280,497	286,551	288,598	291,104
Durable goods manufacturing..............................	190,346	183,710	193,099	204,382	209,168	209,511	211,158
Nondurable goods manufacturing..........................	75,565	74,446	75,967	76,115	77,383	79,087	79,946
Wholesale trade...	122,973	120,709	122,227	124,439	127,634	131,104	133,708
Retail trade...	314,065	310,747	315,418	322,037	332,130	345,814	358,991
Transportation and warehousing...........................	87,025	84,401	86,962	89,112	90,314	94,277	97,985
Information..	103,812	102,749	104,479	105,441	106,435	109,617	114,400
Finance and insurance....................................	97,019	93,514	93,666	94,470	96,354	98,163	98,968
Real estate and rental and leasing.......................	49,547	46,258	45,605	45,786	47,274	48,640	50,306
Professional, scientific, and technical services..............	163,577	163,696	169,212	173,025	176,928	184,576	190,071
Management of companies and enterprises..................	32,185	31,808	33,264	36,318	38,894	39,998	41,936
Administrative and waste services........................	132,671	133,747	139,790	142,804	147,555	152,226	159,775
Educational services	49,013	50,092	51,661	52,465	53,533	54,958	56,510
Health care and social assistance.........................	331,053	333,346	336,277	380,054	393,137	402,753	398,868
Arts, entertainment, and recreation.......................	46,588	45,930	46,035	46,361	46,967	47,823	48,657
Accommodation and food services........................	225,937	222,720	226,645	232,731	242,327	252,306	263,402
Other services, except public administration................	146,244	141,307	143,783	149,164	149,210	154,563	156,362
Government and government enterprises	630,950	632,458	625,445	620,581	619,201	621,106	630,426
	Dollars						
Average Wages and Salaries by Industry	48,014	49,331	51,102	52,427	53,356	55,333	57,057
Average Farm Wages and Salaries	27,782	25,207	24,384	26,968	29,471	28,663	33,953
Average Nonfarm Wages and Salaries	48,334	49,724	51,525	52,894	53,761	55,775	57,418
Average private wages and salaries........................	48,127	49,670	51,765	53,256	54,099	56,218	57,910
Forestry, fishing, and related activities.......................	30,641	32,454	33,778	35,280	34,955	35,237	35,557
Mining..	53,312	56,234	59,754	60,992	63,154	64,057	68,084
Utilities..	83,430	77,220	81,842	83,774	85,783	87,781	93,343
Construction...	51,482	51,797	52,850	53,666	54,405	55,720	57,744
Manufacturing..	62,985	65,248	68,424	69,790	71,735	75,443	74,884
Durable goods manufacturing..............................	69,037	72,098	75,726	76,892	79,341	84,325	83,308
Nondurable goods manufacturing..........................	47,741	48,344	49,864	50,720	51,176	51,912	52,635
Wholesale trade	62,268	64,372	66,787	69,458	69,087	71,004	73,213
Retail trade...	30,788	31,524	32,583	34,579	36,211	38,857	42,109
Transportation and warehousing...........................	48,061	49,501	51,800	53,517	54,373	55,207	56,618
Information..	106,864	111,515	121,687	135,539	137,016	150,328	150,847
Finance and insurance....................................	71,176	70,271	73,164	77,437	79,404	81,918	85,473
Real estate and rental and leasing.......................	36,830	38,891	40,355	42,764	44,171	46,135	47,881
Professional, scientific, and technical services	72,733	76,310	77,843	80,651	82,598	85,689	86,010
Management of companies and enterprises..................	89,717	100,074	104,038	107,164	106,965	109,022	108,957
Administrative and waste services........................	39,795	41,750	43,187	43,627	43,553	44,649	46,207
Educational services	27,634	28,476	28,921	29,735	30,523	30,843	31,095
Health care and social assistance.........................	44,282	45,373	46,623	43,923	43,892	44,860	48,238
Arts, entertainment, and recreation.......................	28,002	27,651	27,570	27,851	30,575	32,714	33,550
Accommodation and food services........................	19,124	20,105	21,133	22,729	22,703	23,026	23,944
Other services, except public administration................	29,383	30,477	31,963	32,568	33,818	33,669	34,844
Government and government enterprises	49,111	49,919	50,617	51,460	52,382	53,913	55,329

Table WA-10. Employment Characteristics by Family Type

(Number, percent.)

Family type and labor force status	2013 Total	2013 Families with own children under 18 years	2014 Total	2014 Families with own children under 18 years	2015 Total	2015 Families with own children under 18 years
All Families	1,705,112	755,115	1,712,570	739,472	1,760,593	760,914
FAMILY TYPE AND LABOR FORCE STATUS						
Married-Couple Families	1,309,075	526,959	1,316,747	521,639	1,363,817	539,460
Both husband and wife in labor force	50.8	62.5	50.7	61.5	50.0	61.8
Husband in labor force, wife not in labor force	23.5	31.8	23.8	32.7	23.2	31.9
Wife in labor force, husband not in labor force	7.7	3.8	7.9	4.2	7.7	4.3
Both husband and wife not in labor force	17.4	1.5	17.6	1.7	18.0	1.6
Other Families	396,037	228,156	395,823	217,833	396,776	221,454
Female householder, no husband present	68.9	70.4	69.6	70.4	69.1	70.6
In labor force	49.2	55.7	50.2	56.9	48.7	57.0
Not in labor force	19.7	14.7	19.4	13.5	20.4	13.7
Male householder, no wife present	31.1	29.6	30.4	29.6	30.9	29.4
In labor force	25.0	26.2	24.2	27.0	24.8	26.9
Not in labor force	6.1	3.4	6.2	2.6	6.1	2.5

Table WA-11. School Enrollment and Educational Attainment, 2015

(Number, percent.)

Item	State	U.S.
Enrollment		
Total population 3 years and over, enrolled in school	1,728,161	81,618,288
Enrolled in nursery school or preschool (percent)	5.9	6.0
Enrolled in kindergarten (percent)	5.6	5.0
Enrolled in elementary school, grades 1-8 (percent)	40.7	40.3
Enrolled in high school, grades 9-12 (percent)	21.3	20.9
Enrolled in college or graduate school (percent)	26.5	27.7
Attainment		
Total population 25 years and over	4,889,314	216,447,163
Less than ninth grade (percent)	3.9	5.5
9th to 12th grade, no diploma (percent)	5.2	7.3
High school graduate, including equivalency (percent)	23.1	27.6
Some college, no degree (percent)	24.0	20.7
Associate's degree (percent)	9.6	8.2
Bachelor's degree (percent)	21.7	19.0
Graduate or professional degree (percent)	12.5	11.6
High school graduate or higher (percent)	90.8	87.1
Bachelor's degree or higher (percent)	34.2	30.6

Table WA-12. Public School Characteristics and Educational Indicators

(Number, percent; data derived from National Center of Education Statistics.)

Item	State	U.S.
Public Schools, 2014–2015 (except where noted)		
Number of school districts	322	18,260
Number of schools	2,398	98,373
Number of students	1,073,638	50,312,581
Number of teachers	59,555	3,132,351
Student-teacher ratio	18.0	16.1
Expenditures per student (dollars), FY 2014	10,305	11,066
Four-year adjusted cohort graduation rate (ACGR)[1,2]	78.2	83.2
Students eligible for free or reduced-price lunch (percent)	46.0	51.8
English language learners (percent)	10.0	9.4
Students age 3 to 21 served under IDEA, part B (percent)	12.4	13.0

Public Schools by Type	Number	Percent of state public schools
Total number of schools	2,398	100.0
Regular	1,966	82.0
Special education	94	3.9
Vocational education	20	0.8
Alternative education	318	13.3

NOTE: Every school is assigned only one school type based on its instructional emphasis.
[1] ACGR data represents a new method of calculating high-school completion rates and may not be comparable to previous years' data for Averaged Freshmen Graduation Rates (AFGR).
[2] The United States 4-year ACGRs were estimated using both the reported 4-year ACGR data from 49 states and the District of Columbia and using imputed data for Idaho. The estimate for American Indian/Alaska Native students also includes imputed data for Virginia.

Table WA-13. Reported Voting and Registration of the Voting-Age Population, November 2016

(Numbers in thousands, percent.)

Item	Total population	Total citizen population	Registered			Voted		
			Total registered	Percent registered (total population)	Percent registered (total citizen population)	Total voted	Percent voted (total population)	Percent voted (total citizen population)
U.S. Total	245,502	224,059	157,596	64.2	70.3	137,537	56.0	61.4
State Total............................	5,592	5,104	3,906	69.9	76.5	3,382	60.5	66.3
Sex								
Male	2,765	2,497	1,852	67.0	74.2	1,525	55.2	61.1
Female	2,827	2,607	2,055	72.7	78.8	1,857	65.7	71.2
Race								
White alone............................	4,628	4,353	3,403	73.5	78.2	3,027	65.4	69.5
White, non-Hispanic alone	4,059	3,965	3,164	77.9	79.8	2,842	70.0	71.7
Black alone..................................	201	184	116	57.7	63.2	78	38.8	42.6
Asian alone.................................	426	239	190	44.6	79.6	165	38.7	69.0
Hispanic (of any race).....................	656	465	292	44.6	62.9	219	33.4	47.2
White alone or in combination	4,775	4,500	3,503	73.4	77.8	3,093	64.8	68.7
Black alone or in combination..........	239	222	137	57.4	61.9	85	35.5	38.3
Asian alone or in combination..........	470	283	224	47.7	79.4	188	40.1	66.7
Age								
18 to 24 years.....................	646	594	351	54.4	59.1	273	42.2	45.9
25 to 34 years.....................	987	848	587	59.4	69.2	460	46.5	54.2
35 to 44 years.....................	1,014	876	676	66.7	77.2	564	55.6	64.4
45 to 64 years.....................	1,986	1,859	1,523	76.7	81.9	1,366	68.8	73.5
65 years and over	958	927	769	80.3	83.0	720	75.1	77.6

Table WA-14. Crime

(Number, rate per 100,000. Data are derived from the FBI Uniform Crime Reports.)

Item	State			U.S. [1,2,3,4]		
	2014	2015	Percent change	2014	2015	Percent change
TOTAL POPULATION[5]	7,063,166	7,170,351	1.5	318,907,401	321,418,820	0.8
VIOLENT CRIME						
Number..............................	20,185	20,394	1.0	1,186,185	1,231,566	3.8
Rate	285.8	284.4	-0.5	372.0	383.2	3.0
Murder and Nonnegligent Manslaughter						
Number..............................	178	211	18.5	14,164	15,696	10.8
Rate	2.5	2.9	16.8	4.4	4.9	10.0
Rape[6]						
Number..............................	2,780	2,705	-2.7	118,027	124,047	5.1
Rate	39.4	37.7	-4.2	37.0	38.6	4.3
Robbery						
Number..............................	5,641	5,449	-3.4	322,905	327,374	1.4
Rate	79.9	76.0	-4.8	101.3	101.9	0.6
Aggravated Assault						
Number..............................	11,586	12,029	3.8	731,089	764,449	4.6
Rate	164.0	167.8	2.3	229.2	237.8	3.7
PROPERTY CRIME						
Number..............................	261,257	248,369	-4.9	8,209,010	7,993,631	-2.6
Rate	3,698.9	3,463.8	-6.4	2,574.1	2,487.0	-3.4
Burglary						
Number..............................	55,381	50,993	-7.9	1,713,153	1,579,527	-7.8
Rate	784.1	711.2	-9.3	537.2	491.4	-8.5
Larceny-Theft						
Number..............................	175,317	170,509	-2.7	5,809,054	5,706,346	-1.8
Rate	2,482.1	2,378.0	-4.2	1,821.5	1,775.4	-2.5
Motor Vehicle Theft						
Number..............................	30,559	26,867	-12.1	686,803	707,758	3.1
Rate	432.7	374.7	-13.4	215.4	220.2	2.2

NOTE: Although arson data are included in the trend and clearance tables, sufficient data are not available to estimate totals for this offense. Therefore, no arson data are published in this table.
X = Not applicable.
- = Zero or rounds to zero.
[1] The crime figures have been adjusted.
[2] The data collection methodology for the offense of forcible rape used by the Minnesota state Uniform Crime Reporting (UCR) Program (with the exception of Minneapolis and St. Paul, Minnesota) does not comply with national UCR Program guidelines. Consequently, its figures for forcible rape and violent crime (of which forcible rape is a part) are not published in this table.
[3] Includes offenses reported by the Zoological Police and the Metro Transit Police.
[4] Because of changes in the state's reporting practices, figures are not comparable to previous years' data.
[5] Populations are U.S. Census Bureau provisional estimates as of July 1 of each year.
[6] The figures shown for the offense of rape were estimated using the revised Uniform Crime Reporting (UCR) definition of rape.

Table WA-15. State Government Finances, 2015

(Dollar amounts in thousands, percent distribution.)

Item	Dollars	Percent distribution
Total Revenue	50,247,419	100.0
General revenue	41,439,464	82.5
Intergovernmental revenue	13,333,571	26.5
Taxes	20,644,454	41.1
General sales	12,517,831	24.9
Selective sales	3,723,403	7.4
License taxes	1,396,989	2.8
Individual income tax	0	-
Corporate income tax	0	-
Other taxes	3,006,231	6.0
Current charges	5,027,944	10.0
Miscellaneous general revenue	2,433,495	4.8
Utility revenue	0	-
Liquor stores revenue	0	-
Insurance trust revenue[1]	8,807,955	17.5
Total Expenditure	51,091,651	100.0
Intergovernmental expenditure	11,017,998	21.6
Direct expenditure	40,073,653	78.4
Current operation	26,803,623	52.5
Capital outlay	3,222,596	6.3
Insurance benefits and repayments	7,006,868	13.7
Assistance and subsidies	1,625,567	3.2
Interest on debt	1,414,999	2.8
Exhibit: Salaries and wages	7,468,727	14.6
Total Expenditure	51,091,651	100.0
General expenditure	43,901,116	85.9
Intergovernmental expenditure	11,017,998	21.6
Direct expenditure	32,883,118	64.4
General expenditure, by function:		
Education	17,087,813	33.4
Public welfare	11,477,978	22.5
Hospitals	2,556,697	5.0
Health	2,672,952	5.2
Highways	2,884,151	5.6
Police protection	383,449	0.8
Correction	1,016,931	2.0
Natural resources	1,000,159	2.0
Parks and recreation	138,015	0.3
Governmental administration	1,148,488	2.2
Interest on general debt	1,414,999	2.8
Other and unallocable	2,119,484	4.1
Utility expenditure	183,667	0.4
Liquor stores expenditure	0	-
Insurance trust expenditure	7,006,868	13.7
Debt at End of Fiscal Year	32,231,967	X
Cash and Security Holdings	103,134,515	X

X = Not applicable.
- = Zero or rounds to zero.
[1] Within insurance trust revenue, net earnings of state retirement systems is a calculated statistic (the item code in the data file is X08), and thus can be positive or negative. Net earnings is the sum of earnings on investments plus gains on investments minus losses on investments. The change made in 2002 for asset valuation from book to market value in accordance with Statement 34 of the Governmental Accounting Standards Board is reflected in the calculated statistics.

Table WA-16. State Government Tax Collections, 2016

(Dollars in thousands, percent.)

Item	Dollars	Percent distribution
Total Taxes	22,280,088	100.0
Property taxes	2,062,065	9.3
Sales and gross receipts	17,636,031	79.2
General sales and gross receipts	13,560,382	60.9
Selective sales and gross receipts	4,075,649	18.3
Alcoholic beverages	347,642	1.6
Amusements	0	-
Insurance premiums	534,663	2.4
Motor fuels	1,457,933	6.5
Pari-mutuels	1,840	-
Public utilities	489,225	2.2
Tobacco products	450,805	2.0
Other selective sales	793,541	3.6
Licenses	1,461,200	6.6
Alcoholic beverages	143,858	0.6
Amusements	6,630	-
Corporations in general	35,739	0.2
Hunting and fishing	43,864	0.2
Motor vehicle	603,519	2.7
Motor vehicle operators	119,671	0.5
Public utilities	22,587	0.1
Occupation and business, NEC	323,654	1.5
Other licenses	161,678	0.7
Income taxes	0	-
Individual income	0	-
Corporation net income	0	-
Other taxes	1,120,792	5.0
Death and gift	136,035	0.6
Documentary and stock transfer	945,026	4.2
Severance	39,731	0.2
Taxes, NEC	0	-

X = Not applicable.
- = Zero or rounds to zero.

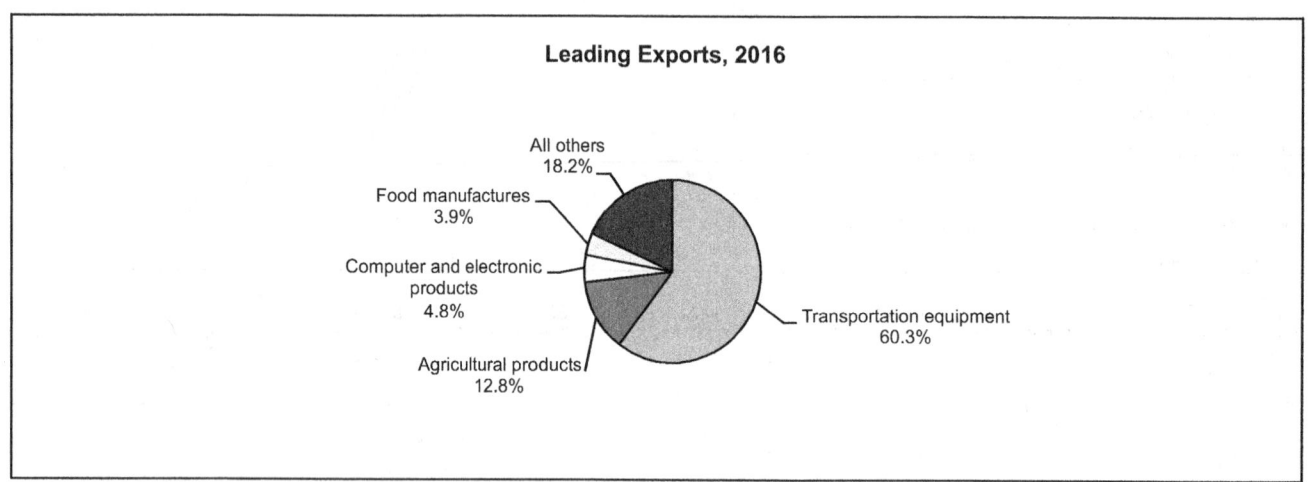

Leading Exports, 2016

All others 18.2%
Food manufactures 3.9%
Computer and electronic products 4.8%
Agricultural products 12.8%
Transportation equipment 60.3%

Facts and Figures

Location: East central United States; bordered on the N by Ohio and Pennsylvania, on the E by Pennsylvania, Maryland, and Virginia, on the S by Virginia and Kentucky, and on the W by Kentucky and Ohio

Area: 24,230 sq. mi. (62,755 sq. km.); rank—41st

Population: 1,831,102 (2016 est.); rank—38th

Principal Cities: capital—Charleston; largest—Charleston

Statehood: June 20, 1863; 35th state

U.S. Congress: 2 senators, 3 representatives

State Motto: *Montani semper liberi* (Mountaineers are always free)

State Songs: "West Virginia Hills"; "This Is My West Virginia"; "West Virginia, My Home Sweet Home"

State Nickname: The Mountain State

Abbreviations: WV; W. Va.

State Symbols: flower—rhododendron (great laurel); tree—sugar maple; bird—cardinal

At a Glance

- West Virginia experienced the largest population decline among the states from 2010 to 2016, with its population falling 1.2 percent.

- West Virginia's median household income was $42,019 in 2015, the 3rd lowest among the states, and 17.9 percent of the population lived below the poverty level.

- At a rate more than twice the national average, West Virginia had the highest rate of drug overdose deaths in 2015 (41.5 deaths per 100,000 residents).

- West Virginia had the lowest percent of residents that self-identified as "Hispanic or Latino" in 2016, with just 1.5 percent of its population in this category.

- West Virginia had the highest homeownership rate of all the states in 2016, with 74.8 percent of residents owning homes.

Table WV-1. Population by Age, Sex, Race, and Hispanic Origin

(Number, percent, except where noted.)

Sex, age, race, and Hispanic origin	2000	2010	2016 [1]	Average annual percent change, 2010–2016
Total Population..	1,808,344	1,852,994	1,831,102	-0.1
Percent of total U.S. population	0.6	0.6	0.6	X
Sex				
Male..	879,170	913,586	905,943	-0.1
Female...	929,174	939,408	925,159	-0.1
Age				
Under 5 years..	101,805	104,060	101,019	-0.2
5 to 19 years..	352,910	335,153	317,999	-0.3
20 to 64 years..	1,076,734	1,116,377	1,068,567	-0.3
65 years and over...	276,895	297,404	343,517	1.0
Median age (years)	38.9	41.3	42.2	0.1
Race and Hispanic Origin				
One race...				
White	1,718,777	1,746,513	1,713,756	-0.1
Black	57,232	63,885	65,929	0.2
American Indian and Alaska Native	3,606	3,975	4,503	0.8
Asian	9,434	12,637	15,385	1.4
Native Hawaiian or Other Pacific Islander	400	485	591	1.4
Two or more races	15,788	25,499	30,938	1.3
Hispanic (of any race).....................................	12,279	23,679	28,295	1.2

X = Not applicable.
- = Zero or rounds to zero.
[1] Population figures for 2016 are July 1 estimates. The 2010 estimates are taken from the 2010 Census.

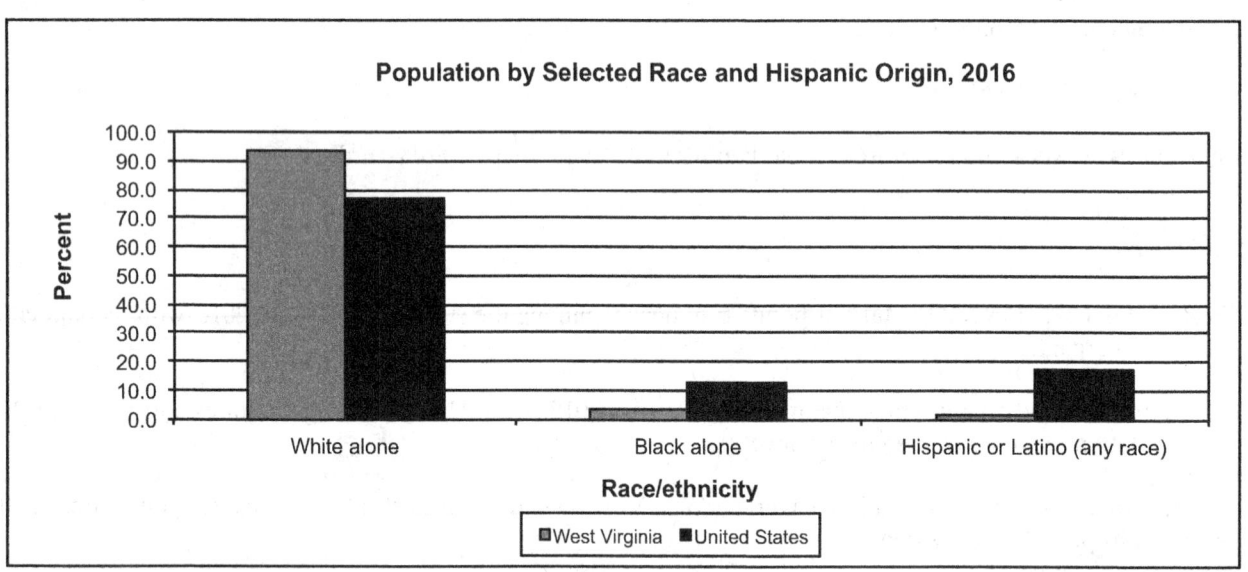

Population by Selected Race and Hispanic Origin, 2016

Table WV-2. Marital Status

(Number, percent distribution.)

Sex, age, race, and Hispanic origin	2000	2010	2015
Males, 15 Years and Over	710,443	750,542	750,821
Never married	25.4	30.3	31.3
Now married, except separated........................	59.9	52.1	49.6
Separated..	1.3	1.6	1.4
Widowed..	3.2	3.4	3.7
Divorced..	10.1	12.6	14.0
Females, 15 Years and Over	768,858	785,182	781,058
Never married	19.1	22.6	24.5
Now married, except separated........................	54.7	49.7	47.9
Separated..	1.6	1.7	1.8
Widowed..	13.9	12.8	11.8
Divorced..	10.8	13.2	13.9

Table WV-3. Households and Housing Characteristics

(Number, percent, dollars.)

Item	2000	2010	2015	Average annual percent change, 2000–2015
Total Households..	736,481	741,940	734,536	-
Family households	504,055	485,652	471,947	-0.4
Married-couple family	397,499	372,301	351,328	-0.8
Other family	106,556	113,351	120,619	0.9
Male householder, no wife present................	27,436	28,515	35,814	2.0
Female householder, no husband present.......	79,120	84,836	84,805	0.5
Nonfamily households	232,426	256,288	262,589	0.9
Householder living alone..............................	199,587	219,848	222,639	0.8
Householder not living alone........................	32,839	36,440	39,950	1.4
Housing Characteristics				
Total housing units...	844,623	882,213	885,539	0.3
Occupied housing units	736,481	741,940	734,536	-
Owner occupied	553,699	553,429	531,151	-0.3
Renter occupied	182,782	188,511	203,385	0.8
Average household size....................................	2.40	2.43	2.44	0.1
Financial Characteristics				
Median gross rent of renter-occupied housing	401	571	675	4.6
Median monthly owner costs for housing units with a mortgage	713	918	972	2.4
Median value of owner-occupied housing units	72,800	95,100	112,100	3.6

- = Zero or rounds to zero

Table WV-4. Migration, Origin, and Language

(Number, percent.)

Characteristic	State 2014	State 2015	State Percent change	U.S. 2014	U.S. 2015	U.S. Percent change
Residence 1 Year Ago						
Population 1 year and over	1,831,414	1,823,753	-0.4	315,095,393	317,635,720	0.8
Same house	88.3	88.3	X	85.1	85.3	X
Different house in the U.S.	11.5	11.5	X	14.3	14.1	X
Same county	6.4	6.3	X	8.7	8.5	X
Different county	5.1	5.2	X	5.6	5.6	X
Same state	2.5	2.9	X	3.3	3.2	X
Different state	2.6	2.3	X	2.3	2.4	X
Abroad	0.2	0.2	X	0.6	0.7	X
Place of Birth						
Native born	1,824,919	1,814,606	-0.6	276,465,262	278,128,449	0.6
Male	49.4	49.2	X	49.3	49.3	X
Female	50.6	50.8	X	50.7	50.7	X
Foreign born	25,407	29,522	16.2	42,391,794	43,290,372	2.1
Male	48.9	50.7	X	48.7	48.6	X
Female	51.1	49.3	X	51.3	51.4	X
Foreign born; naturalized U.S. citizen............................	12,651	15,430	22.0	19,984,738	20,697,103	3.6
Male	37.4	43.6	X	45.9	45.9	X
Female	62.6	56.4	X	54.1	54.1	X
Foreign born; not a U.S. citizen..................................	12,756	14,092	10.5	22,407,056	22,593,269	0.8
Male	60.3	58.5	X	51.2	51.1	X
Female	39.7	41.5	X	48.8	48.9	X
Entered 2010 or later	23.9	27.0	X	12.3	15.6	X
Entered 2000 to 2009	23.1	17.9	X	28.6	27.9	X
Entered before 2000	53.0	55.2	X	59.1	56.5	X
World Region of Birth, Foreign						
Foreign-born population, excluding population born at sea	25,407	29,522	16.2	42,390,705	43,289,646	2.1
Europe	18.1	26.0	X	11.2	11.1	X
Asia..	47.4	43.3	X	30.1	30.6	X
Africa	8.5	4.1	X	4.6	4.8	X
Oceania	0.7	0.8	X	0.6	0.6	X
Latin America...	21.6	22.0	X	51.6	51.1	X
North America..	3.7	3.9	X	1.9	1.9	X
Language Spoken at Home and Ability to Speak English						
Population 5 years and over..	1,747,774	1,742,174	-0.3	299,084,046	301,625,014	0.8
English only	98.0	97.4	X	78.9	78.5	X
Language other than English.......................................	2.0	2.6	X	21.1	21.5	X
Speaks English less than "very well"...........................	0.6	0.7	X	8.6	8.6	X

NA = Not available.
X = Not applicable.
- = Zero or rounds to zero.

Table WV-5. Median Income and Poverty Status, 2015

(Number, percent, except as noted.)

Characteristic	State		U.S.	
	Number	Percent	Number	Percent
Median Income				
Households (dollars)..	42,019	X	55,775	X
Families (dollars)	53,463	X	68,260	X
Below Poverty Level (All People)	321,583	17.9	46,153,077	14.7
Sex				
Male	141,783	16.1	20,599,407	13.4
Female	179,800	19.7	25,553,670	16.0
Age				
Under 18 years...	93,524	25.2	15,000,273	20.7
Related children under 18 years.............................	90,727	24.6	14,693,239	20.4
18 to 64 years..	200,102	18.3	26,960,369	13.9
65 years and over	27,957	8.5	4,192,435	9.0

X = Not applicable.

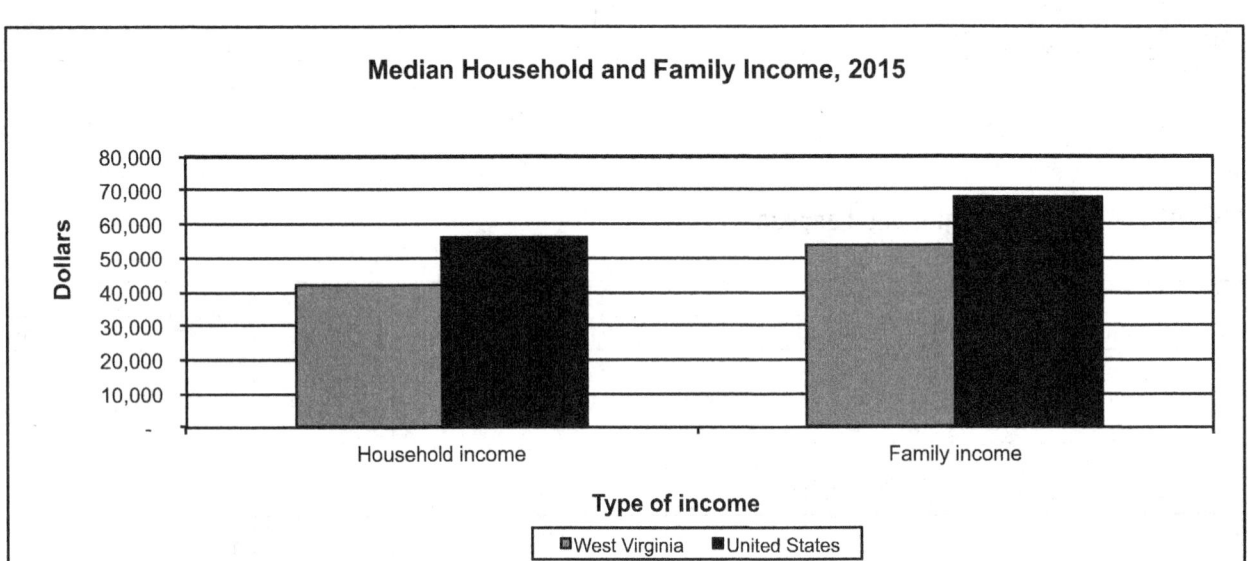

Median Household and Family Income, 2015

Table WV-6. Health Insurance Coverage Status for the Civilian Noninstitutionalized Population and Children Under 18 Years of Age

(Numbers in thousands, percent.)

Item	2007	2008	2009	2010	2011	2012	2013	2014	2015
Civilian Noninstitutionalized Population	1,795	1,788	1,793	1,823	1,826	1,827	1,825	1,821	1,816
Covered by Private or Public Insurance									
Number..	1,541	1,505	1,539	1,557	1,554	1,563	1,570	1,665	1,707
Percent..	85.9	84.2	85.8	85.4	85.1	85.6	86.0	91.4	94.0
Not Covered									
Number..	254	283	254	266	272	264	255	156	108
Percent..	14.1	15.8	14.2	14.6	14.9	14.4	14.0	8.6	6.0
Percent in the U.S. not covered..............................	15.3	15.1	15.1	15.5	15.1	14.8	14.5	11.7	9.4
Children Under 18 Years of Age	394	385	383	385	385	383	381	382	378
Covered by Private or Public Insurance									
Number..	376	359	362	367	368	368	361	371	368
Percent..	95.4	93.2	94.5	95.5	95.6	96.1	94.7	97.0	97.2
Not Covered									
Number..	18	26	21	18	17	15	20	11	11
Percent..	4.6	6.8	5.5	4.5	4.4	3.9	5.3	3.0	2.8
Percent in the U.S. not covered..............................	11.0	9.7	8.6	8.0	7.5	7.2	7.1	6.0	4.8

Table WV-7. Employment Status by Demographic Group, 2016

(Numbers in thousands, percent.)

Characteristic	Civilian noninstitutional population	Civilian labor force		Employed		Unemployed	
		Number	Percent of population	Number	Percent of population	Number	Percent of population
Total..	1,481	787	53.2	740	49.9	48	6.1
Sex							
Male	721	422	58.4	393	54.5	29	6.8
Female	760	366	48.1	347	45.6	19	5.2
Race, Sex, and Hispanic Origin							
White	1,393	743	53.3	698	50.1	45	6.0
Male	681	400	58.7	373	54.8	27	6.7
Female	713	343	48.2	325	45.6	18	5.3
Black or African American............	50	25	50.3	24	46.9	2	6.6
Male	NA	NA	NA	NA	NA	NA	NA
Female	NA	NA	NA	NA	NA	NA	NA
Hispanic or Latino ethnicity[1]	NA	NA	NA	NA	NA	NA	NA
Male	NA	NA	NA	NA	NA	NA	NA
Female	NA	NA	NA	NA	NA	NA	NA
Age							
16 to 19 years.............................	94	26	28.1	20	21.6	6	22.9
20 to 24 years.............................	110	73	66.1	65	59.3	8	10.3
25 to 34 years.............................	214	163	76.4	150	70.1	14	8.3
35 to 44 years.............................	219	165	75.4	155	71.1	10	5.8
45 to 54 years.............................	238	168	70.7	162	68.2	6	3.7
55 to 64 years.............................	263	139	52.7	135	51.3	4	2.6
65 years and over	344	53	15.5	52	15.1	1	2.6

NOTE: Data in Table 7 are from the Current Population Survey (CPS) and do not match the estimates in Table 8. See notes and definitions for further information.
[1] May be of any race.
NA = Not available.

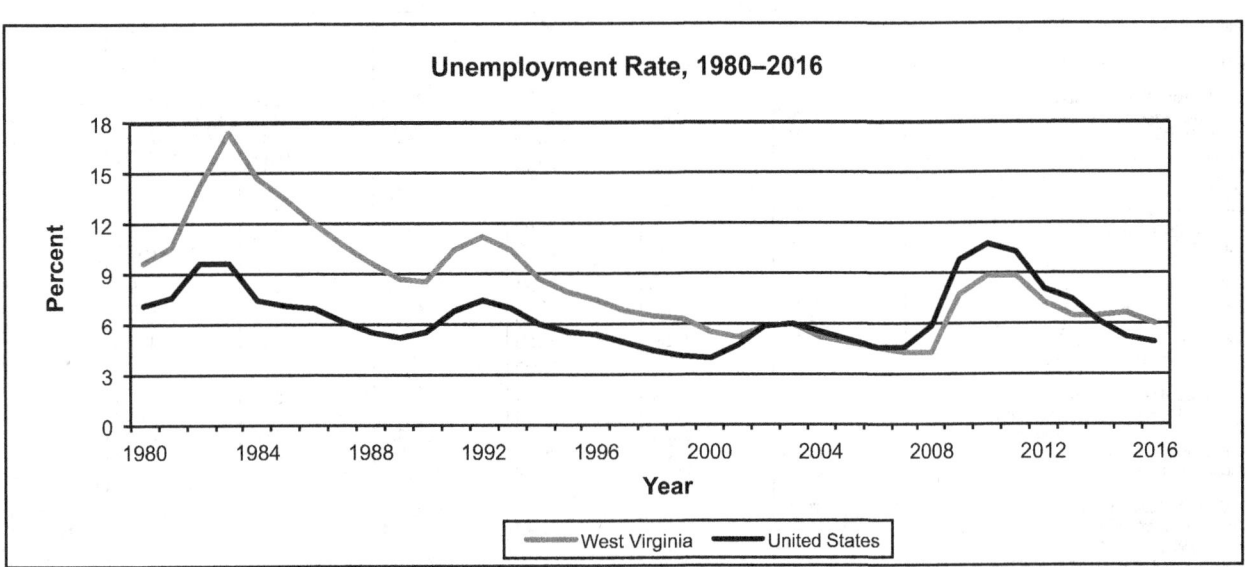

Unemployment Rate, 1980–2016

Table WV-8. Employment Status of the Civilian Noninstitutional Population Age 16 Years and Over

(Number, percent.)

Year	Civilian labor force	Civilian participation rate	Employed	Unemployed	Unemployment rate
2008....................................	812,905	56.1	777,560	35,345	4.3
2009....................................	814,027	56.0	751,165	62,862	7.7
2010....................................	811,125	54.9	740,910	70,215	8.7
2011....................................	807,021	54.3	741,972	65,049	8.1
2012....................................	807,595	54.3	747,092	60,503	7.5
2013....................................	798,953	53.8	745,081	53,872	6.7
2014....................................	789,850	53.2	737,479	52,371	6.6
2015....................................	785,049	53.0	732,146	52,903	6.7
2016....................................	783,470	53.2	736,427	47,043	6.0

Table WV-9. Employment and Average Wages by Industry

(Estimates through 2010 are based on the 2007 *North American Industry Classification System* [NAICS]. Estimates from 2011 onward are based on the 2012 NAICS.)

Industry	2009	2010	2011	2012	2013	2014	2015
	Number of jobs						
Wage and Salary Employment by Industry..................	736,679	734,594	742,909	751,541	743,781	740,524	734,428
Farm Wage and Salary Employment........................	1,286	1,289	1,425	1,699	1,570	1,703	1,911
Nonfarm Wage and Salary Employment....................	735,393	733,305	741,484	749,842	742,211	738,821	732,517
Private wage and salary employment.......................	576,089	570,952	580,200	587,347	583,874	582,102	577,336
Forestry, fishing, and related activities........................	1,426	1,366	1,275	1,371	1,368	1,412	1,476
Mining...	28,948	29,238	32,888	32,729	30,876	29,192	24,956
Utilities...	6,195	5,630	5,438	5,307	5,178	5,204	5,051
Construction...	35,861	33,900	34,056	36,717	35,394	34,732	33,265
Manufacturing...	50,761	49,150	49,573	49,157	48,409	47,828	47,718
Durable goods manufacturing.............................	30,944	29,639	29,957	29,582	29,090	28,882	28,642
Nondurable goods manufacturing........................	19,817	19,511	19,616	19,575	19,319	18,946	19,076
Wholesale trade...	23,557	23,047	23,386	23,612	23,020	22,742	22,329
Retail trade..	88,333	87,389	87,872	88,416	88,334	87,541	87,427
Transportation and warehousing..........................	19,484	19,153	19,728	19,289	20,228	20,882	21,581
Information...	10,467	10,314	10,386	9,633	9,515	9,589	9,555
Finance and insurance.....................................	20,920	20,642	20,409	20,236	19,946	19,652	19,282
Real estate and rental and leasing........................	7,299	7,123	6,885	6,843	6,812	6,970	6,954
Professional, scientific, and technical services..............	24,471	24,682	25,270	25,744	26,145	26,368	26,086
Management of companies and enterprises.................	5,431	5,471	5,696	6,687	6,490	6,382	6,407
Administrative and waste services........................	30,405	30,861	32,270	32,721	32,763	34,663	35,002
Educational services..	8,474	8,730	8,931	9,136	8,936	8,882	8,905
Health care and social assistance........................	107,362	108,948	110,492	113,227	114,116	114,068	115,680
Arts, entertainment, and recreation........................	9,308	9,566	7,278	7,643	7,715	7,759	7,686
Accommodation and food services........................	63,456	63,160	65,983	67,086	67,316	66,962	67,298
Other services, except public administration...............	33,931	32,582	32,384	31,793	31,313	31,274	30,678
Government and government enterprises......................	159,304	162,353	161,284	162,495	158,337	156,719	155,181
	Dollars						
Average Wages and Salaries by Industry	36,268	37,130	38,527	39,193	39,658	40,641	41,172
Average Farm Wages and Salaries	21,660	20,673	16,368	21,335	23,806	23,230	19,006
Average Nonfarm Wages and Salaries	36,294	37,159	38,569	39,234	39,692	40,681	41,230
Average private wages and salaries........................	35,792	36,907	38,525	39,316	39,591	40,603	41,090
Forestry, fishing, and related activities........................	24,074	25,908	26,776	27,804	27,808	28,998	29,534
Mining..	72,218	73,366	78,870	79,263	80,149	80,892	78,837
Utilities..	76,085	77,026	80,493	80,681	81,299	85,137	88,959
Construction..	44,052	47,228	46,985	50,851	51,951	53,528	53,370
Manufacturing..	47,923	49,970	51,707	52,779	53,068	55,054	55,835
Durable goods manufacturing.............................	44,992	46,545	48,413	49,993	49,653	51,395	51,596
Nondurable goods manufacturing........................	52,500	55,174	56,737	56,990	58,210	60,632	62,200
Wholesale trade...	49,149	49,830	51,241	51,732	52,206	54,973	55,912
Retail trade...	22,492	23,164	23,730	24,146	24,414	24,668	25,658
Transportation and warehousing..........................	46,166	46,766	48,622	50,359	48,905	50,275	50,004
Information...	43,584	46,260	48,484	48,644	47,613	48,779	51,167
Finance and insurance	41,281	42,460	46,724	46,077	47,647	49,382	50,868
Real estate and rental and leasing........................	30,684	34,944	34,984	36,326	36,530	37,814	37,925
Professional, scientific, and technical services..............	48,022	50,523	50,654	53,053	53,754	55,169	56,109
Management of companies and enterprises.................	64,239	67,657	81,774	70,876	69,869	72,385	73,950
Administrative and waste services........................	25,280	26,578	28,499	29,063	29,582	31,296	31,906
Educational services..	22,594	23,401	24,330	24,583	24,743	24,673	24,855
Health care and social assistance........................	36,875	37,127	37,833	38,796	39,617	40,985	42,623
Arts, entertainment, and recreation........................	20,751	22,179	19,387	19,334	19,102	19,319	19,999
Accommodation and food services........................	15,308	15,907	17,203	17,656	17,665	18,039	18,865
Other services, except public administration...............	24,030	25,371	26,040	26,813	27,722	28,218	28,972
Government and government enterprises........................	38,108	38,045	38,728	38,937	40,066	40,972	41,752

Table WV-10. Employment Characteristics by Family Type

(Number, percent.)

Family type and labor force status	2013		2014		2015	
	Total	Families with own children under 18 years	Total	Families with own children under 18 years	Total	Families with own children under 18 years
All Families...	479,389	177,583	471,865	167,580	471,947	172,703
FAMILY TYPE AND LABOR FORCE STATUS						
Married-Couple Families..	355,958	113,167	354,686	108,911	351,328	112,219
Both husband and wife in labor force..............................	41.3	60.9	41.6	61.6	39.5	60.7
Husband in labor force, wife not in labor force	22.5	30.0	22.2	28.2	22.1	30.0
Wife in labor force, husband not in labor force	10.3	5.0	9.9	5.5	10.7	5.3
Both husband and wife not in labor force..............................	25.7	4.1	26.3	4.6	27.1	3.6
Other Families	123,431	64,416	117,179	58,669	120,619	60,484
Female householder, no husband present...........................	70.1	70.3	71.6	70.4	70.3	70.5
In labor force..	40.1	49.8	41.6	51.1	40.9	52.1
Not in labor force	30.0	20.5	30.0	19.3	29.4	18.4
Male householder, no wife present..........................	29.9	29.7	28.4	29.6	29.7	29.5
In labor force..	20.3	24.0	17.5	23.7	18.2	23.8
Not in labor force	9.6	5.6	10.9	5.9	11.5	5.7

Table WV-11. School Enrollment and Educational Attainment, 2015

(Number, percent.)

Item	State	U.S.
Enrollment		
Total population 3 years and over, enrolled in school	399,802	81,618,288
Enrolled in nursery school or preschool (percent)..	5.1	6.0
Enrolled in kindergarten (percent)...	5.5	5.0
Enrolled in elementary school, grades 1-8 (percent)..	42.2	40.3
Enrolled in high school, grades 9-12 (percent)...	21.1	20.9
Enrolled in college or graduate school (percent)...	26.1	27.7
Attainment		
Total population 25 years and over	1,300,347	216,447,163
Less than ninth grade (percent)...	4.5	5.5
9th to 12th grade, no diploma (percent)..	9.5	7.3
High school graduate, including equivalency (percent).....................................	40.7	27.6
Some college, no degree (percent)..	18.8	20.7
Associate's degree (percent)...	6.9	8.2
Bachelor's degree (percent)	11.7	19.0
Graduate or professional degree (percent)...	7.9	11.6
High school graduate or higher (percent)	86.0	87.1
Bachelor's degree or higher (percent)...	19.6	30.6

Table WV-12. Public School Characteristics and Educational Indicators

(Number, percent; data derived from National Center of Education Statistics.)

Item	State	U.S.
Public Schools, 2014–2015 (except where noted)		
Number of school districts..	57	18,260
Number of schools..	745	98,373
Number of students	280,310	50,312,581
Number of teachers	20,029	3,132,351
Student-teacher ratio...	14.0	16.1
Expenditures per student (dollars), FY 2014..	11,371	11,066
Four-year adjusted cohort graduation rate (ACGR)[1,2]	86.5	83.2
Students eligible for free or reduced-price lunch (percent).....................................	46.1	51.8
English language learners (percent)...	1.0	9.4
Students age 3 to 21 served under IDEA, part B (percent).....................................	15.8	13.0

Public Schools by Type	Number	Percent of state public schools
Total number of schools..	745	100.0
Regular	682	91.5
Special education	3	0.4
Vocational education	30	4.0
Alternative education...	30	4.0

NOTE: Every school is assigned only one school type based on its instructional emphasis.
[1] ACGR data represents a new method of calculating high-school completion rates and may not be comparable to previous years' data for Averaged Freshmen Graduation Rates (AFGR).
[2] The United States 4-year ACGRs were estimated using both the reported 4-year ACGR data from 49 states and the District of Columbia and using imputed data for Idaho. The estimate for American Indian/Alaska Native students also includes imputed data for Virginia.

Table WV-13. Reported Voting and Registration of the Voting-Age Population, November 2016

(Numbers in thousands, percent.)

Item	Total population	Total citizen population	Registered			Voted		
			Total registered	Percent registered (total population)	Percent registered (total citizen population)	Total voted	Percent voted (total population)	Percent voted (total citizen population)
U.S. Total	245,502	224,059	157,596	64.2	70.3	137,537	56.0	61.4
State Total.............................	1,434	1,425	913	63.6	64.1	723	50.4	50.8
Sex								
Male	695	688	428	61.5	62.1	335	48.2	48.7
Female	739	736	485	65.6	65.9	388	52.5	52.7
Race								
White alone.............................	1,350	1,347	865	64.0	64.2	682	50.5	50.7
White, non-Hispanic alone	1,340	1,339	860	64.2	64.2	679	50.7	50.7
Black alone..............................	48	47	27	(B)	(B)	24	(B)	(B)
Asian alone	10	7	4	(B)	(B)	3	(B)	(B)
Hispanic (of any race)	13	9	4	(B)	(B)	3	(B)	(B)
White alone or in combination	1,371	1,368	880	64.2	64.3	695	50.7	50.8
Black alone or in combination.........	55	55	30	(B)	(B)	25	(B)	(B)
Asian alone or in combination..........	14	11	8	(B)	(B)	6	(B)	(B)
Age								
18 to 24 years.........................	155	153	78	50.3	50.7	50	32.2	32.5
25 to 34 years.........................	226	225	141	62.3	62.7	98	43.5	43.8
35 to 44 years.........................	206	204	116	56.3	57.1	96	46.6	47.2
45 to 64 years.........................	513	509	329	64.2	64.7	268	52.2	52.6
65 years and over	334	334	249	74.3	74.5	211	63.1	63.3

B = Base is less than 75,000 and therefore too small to show the derived measure.

Table WV-14. Crime

(Number, rate per 100,000. Data are derived from the FBI Uniform Crime Reports.)

Item	State			U.S. [1,2,3,4]		
	2014	2015	Percent change	2014	2015	Percent change
TOTAL POPULATION[5]	1,848,751	1,844,128	-0.3	318,907,401	321,418,820	0.8
VIOLENT CRIME						
Number..	5,850	6,231	6.5	1,186,185	1,231,566	3.8
Rate...	316.4	337.9	6.8	372.0	383.2	3.0
Murder and Nonnegligent Manslaughter						
Number..	84	70	-16.7	14,164	15,696	10.8
Rate...	4.5	3.8	-16.5	4.4	4.9	10.0
Rape[6]						
Number..	594	672	13.1	118,027	124,047	5.1
Rate...	32.1	36.4	13.4	37.0	38.6	4.3
Robbery						
Number..	655	760	16.0	322,905	327,374	1.4
Rate...	35.4	41.2	16.3	101.3	101.9	0.6
Aggravated Assault						
Number..	4,517	4,729	4.7	731,089	764,449	4.6
Rate...	244.3	256.4	5.0	229.2	237.8	3.7
PROPERTY CRIME						
Number..	38,282	37,251	-2.7	8,209,010	7,993,631	-2.6
Rate...	2,070.7	2,020.0	-2.4	2,574.1	2,487.0	-3.4
Burglary						
Number..	9,368	9,170	-2.1	1,713,153	1,579,527	-7.8
Rate...	506.7	497.3	-1.9	537.2	491.4	-8.5
Larceny-Theft						
Number..	26,954	25,842	-4.1	5,809,054	5,706,346	-1.8
Rate...	1,458.0	1,401.3	-3.9	1,821.5	1,775.4	-2.5
Motor Vehicle Theft						
Number..	1,960	2,239	14.2	686,803	707,758	3.1
Rate...	106.0	121.4	14.5	215.4	220.2	2.2

NOTE: Although arson data are included in the trend and clearance tables, sufficient data are not available to estimate totals for this offense. Therefore, no arson data are published in this table.
X = Not applicable.
- = Zero or rounds to zero.
[1] The crime figures have been adjusted.
[2] The data collection methodology for the offense of forcible rape used by the Minnesota state Uniform Crime Reporting (UCR) Program (with the exception of Minneapolis and St. Paul, Minnesota) does not comply with national UCR Program guidelines. Consequently, its figures for forcible rape and violent crime (of which forcible rape is a part) are not published in this table.
[3] Includes offenses reported by the Zoological Police and the Metro Transit Police.
[4] Because of changes in the state's reporting practices, figures are not comparable to previous years' data.
[5] Populations are U.S. Census Bureau provisional estimates as of July 1 of each year.
[6] The figures shown for the offense of rape were estimated using the revised Uniform Crime Reporting (UCR) definition of rape.

Table WV-15. State Government Finances, 2015

(Dollar amounts in thousands, percent distribution.)

Item	Dollars	Percent distribution
Total Revenue	14,387,594	100.0
General revenue	13,075,676	90.9
Intergovernmental revenue	4,654,167	32.3
Taxes	5,565,985	38.7
General sales	1,293,327	9.0
Selective sales	1,325,996	9.2
License taxes	138,918	1.0
Individual income tax	1,932,457	13.4
Corporate income tax	188,758	1.3
Other taxes	686,529	4.8
Current charges	1,618,611	11.3
Miscellaneous general revenue	1,236,913	8.6
Utility revenue	2,190	-
Liquor stores revenue	93,951	0.7
Insurance trust revenue[1]	1,215,777	8.5
Total Expenditure	13,538,528	100.0
Intergovernmental expenditure	2,344,701	17.3
Direct expenditure	11,193,827	82.7
Current operation	8,506,711	62.8
Capital outlay	834,617	6.2
Insurance benefits and repayments	1,424,382	10.5
Assistance and subsidies	246,791	1.8
Interest on debt	181,326	1.3
Exhibit: Salaries and wages	1,795,008	13.3
Total Expenditure	13,538,528	100.0
General expenditure	12,034,960	88.9
Intergovernmental expenditure	2,344,701	17.3
Direct expenditure	9,690,259	71.6
General expenditure, by function:		
Education	4,154,300	30.7
Public welfare	4,393,172	32.4
Hospitals	134,596	1.0
Health	309,414	2.3
Highways	1,065,058	7.9
Police protection	76,847	0.6
Correction	290,060	2.1
Natural resources	243,022	1.8
Parks and recreation	45,737	0.3
Governmental administration	456,483	3.4
Interest on general debt	181,326	1.3
Other and unallocable	684,945	5.1
Utility expenditure	2,780	-
Liquor stores expenditure	76,406	0.6
Insurance trust expenditure	1,424,382	10.5
Debt at End of Fiscal Year	7,123,763	X
Cash and Security Holdings	22,054,573	X

X = Not applicable.
- = Zero or rounds to zero.
[1] Within insurance trust revenue, net earnings of state retirement systems is a calculated statistic (the item code in the data file is X08), and thus can be positive or negative. Net earnings is the sum of earnings on investments plus gains on investments minus losses on investments. The change made in 2002 for asset valuation from book to market value in accordance with Statement 34 of the Governmental Accounting Standards Board is reflected in the calculated statistics.

Table WV-16. State Government Tax Collections, 2016

(Dollars in thousands, percent.)

Item	Dollars	Percent distribution
Total Taxes	5,127,970	100.0
Property taxes	6,957	0.1
Sales and gross receipts	2,566,690	50.1
General sales and gross receipts	1,286,833	25.1
Selective sales and gross receipts	1,279,857	25.0
Alcoholic beverages	17,936	0.3
Amusements	43,545	0.8
Insurance premiums	158,315	3.1
Motor fuels	396,010	7.7
Pari-mutuels	2,282	-
Public utilities	120,406	2.3
Tobacco products	100,273	2.0
Other selective sales	441,090	8.6
Licenses	128,478	2.5
Alcoholic beverages	995	-
Amusements	3,192	0.1
Corporations in general	986	-
Hunting and fishing	12,096	0.2
Motor vehicle	4,295	0.1
Motor vehicle operators	95,314	1.9
Public utilities	442	-
Occupation and business, NEC	9,928	0.2
Other licenses	1,230	-
Income taxes	1,990,391	38.8
Individual income	1,845,711	36.0
Corporation net income	144,680	2.8
Other taxes	435,454	8.5
Death and gift	0	-
Documentary and stock transfer	10,631	0.2
Severance	424,823	8.3
Taxes, NEC	0	-

- = Zero or rounds to zero.

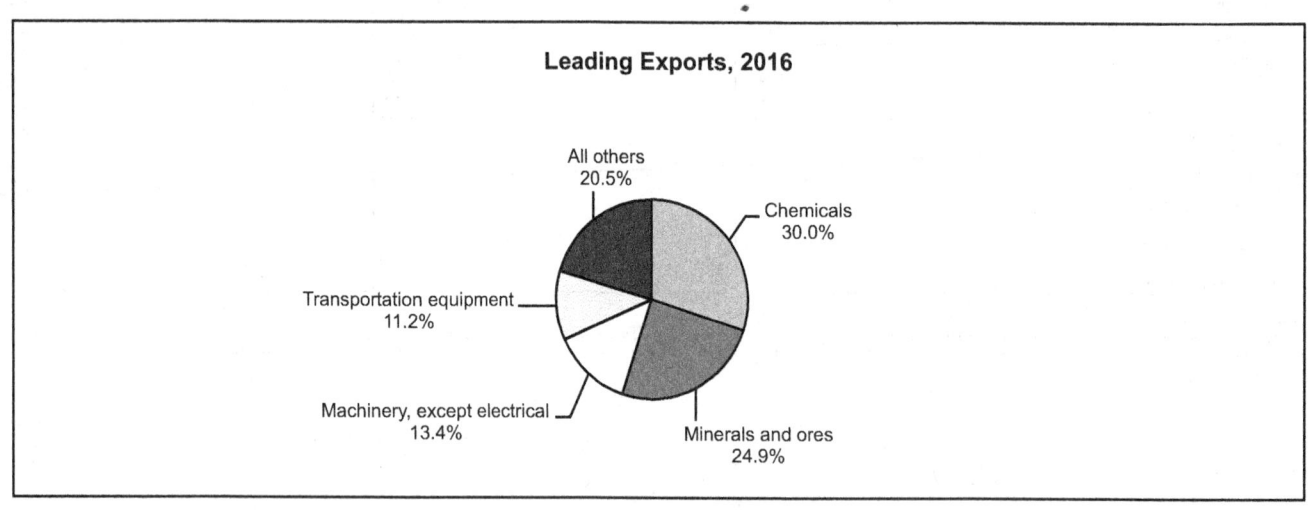

Leading Exports, 2016

All others 20.5%

Chemicals 30.0%

Transportation equipment 11.2%

Machinery, except electrical 13.4%

Minerals and ores 24.9%

WISCONSIN

Facts and Figures

Location: North central United States; bordered on the N by Michigan and Lake Superior, on the E by Lake Michigan, on the S by Illinois, and on the W by Iowa and Minnesota

Area: 65,498 sq. mi. (169,639 sq. km.); rank—23rd

Population: 5,778,708 (2016 est.); rank—20th

Principal Cities: capital—Madison; largest—Milwaukee

Statehood: May 29, 1848; 30th state

U.S. Congress: 2 senators, 8 representatives

State Motto: Forward

State Song: "On, Wisconsin!"

State Nickname: The Badger State

Abbreviations: WI; Wis.; Wisc.

State Symbols: flower—wood violet; tree—sugar maple; bird—robin

At a Glance

- With an increase in population of 1.6 percent, Wisconsin ranked 39th among the states in growth from 2010 to 2016.

- Wisconsin's violent crime rate in 2015 was 305.8 per 100,000 population, compared to 383.2 for the entire nation.

- Wisconsin's median household income in 2015 was $55,638, and 12.1 percent of the population lived below the poverty level.

- In the November 2016 election, 68.7 percent of Wisconsin's eligible voters cast ballots, making it third in the nation for voter turnout.

- The unemployment rate in Wisconsin in 2016 was 4.1 percent, compared to the national rate of 4.9 percent.

Table WI-1. Population by Age, Sex, Race, and Hispanic Origin

(Number, percent, except where noted.)

Sex, age, race, and Hispanic origin	2000	2010	2016 [1]	Average annual percent change, 2010–2016
Total Population...	5,363,675	5,686,986	5,778,708	0.1
Percent of total U.S. population	1.9	1.8	1.8	X
Sex				
Male..	2,649,041	2,822,400	2,873,426	0.1
Female..	2,714,634	2,864,586	2,905,282	0.1
Age				
Under 5 years..	342,340	358,443	336,906	-0.4
5 to 19 years...	1,189,753	1,143,753	1,105,793	-0.2
20 to 64 years...	3,129,029	3,407,476	3,407,591	-
65 years and over..	702,553	777,314	928,418	1.2
Median age (years)	36.0	38.5	39.3	0.1
Race and Hispanic Origin				
One race..				
White..	4,769,857	5,036,923	5,057,070	-
Black...	304,460	367,021	381,807	0.3
American Indian and Alaska Native....................................	47,228	60,100	65,597	0.6
Asian...	88,763	131,828	163,622	1.5
Native Hawaiian or Other Pacific Islander	1,630	2,505	3,050	1.4
Two or more races..	66,895	88,609	107,562	1.3
Hispanic (of any race)...	192,291	349,366	387,666	0.7

X = Not applicable.
[1] Population figures for 2016 are July 1 estimates. The 2010 estimates are taken from the 2010 Census.

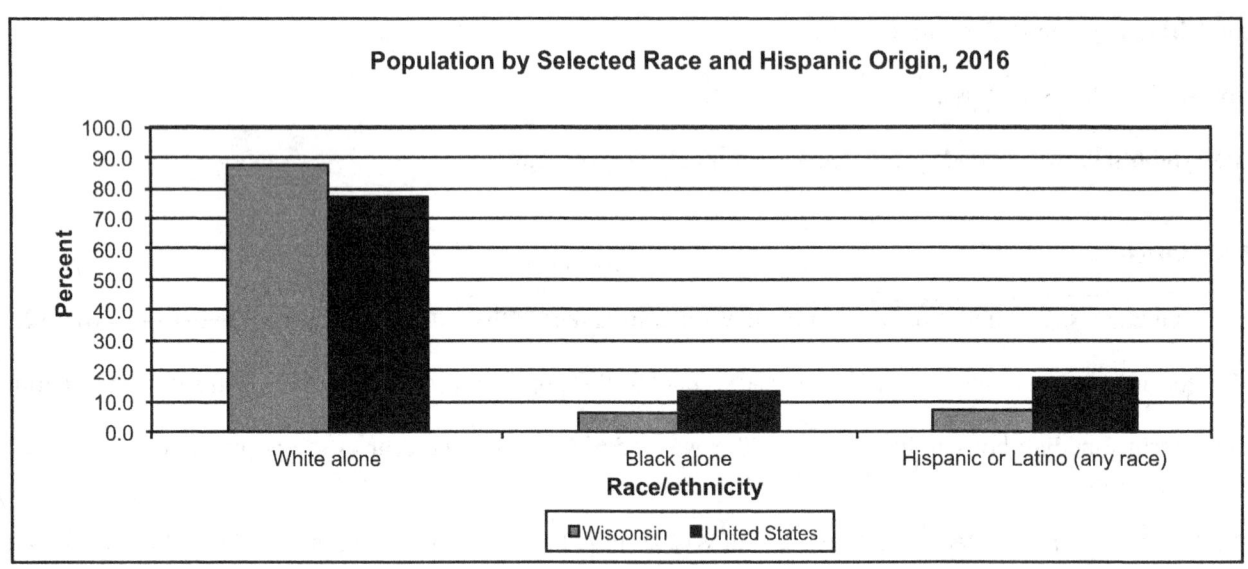

Population by Selected Race and Hispanic Origin, 2016

Table WI-2. Marital Status

(Number, percent distribution.)

Sex, age, race, and Hispanic origin	2000	2010	2015
Males, 15 Years and Over	2,072,397	2,261,022	2,321,002
Never married	30.2	34.1	35.4
Now married, except separated...	57.9	52.1	51.4
Separated...	1.1	1.0	0.9
Widowed..	2.4	2.6	2.5
Divorced..	8.4	10.2	9.8
Females, 15 Years and Over	2,167,164	2,328,733	2,382,885
Never married	24.3	28.1	28.9
Now married, except separated...	54.6	50.1	49.5
Separated...	1.3	1.2	1.3
Widowed..	10.2	9.2	8.7
Divorced..	9.7	11.4	11.5

Table WI-3. Households and Housing Characteristics

(Number, percent, dollars.)

Item	2000	2010	2015	Average annual percent change, 2000–2015
Total Households...	2,084,544	2,279,532	2,319,538	0.8
Family households...	1,386,815	1,453,332	1,469,666	0.4
Married-couple family......................................	1,108,597	1,125,314	1,137,483	0.2
Other family..	278,218	328,018	332,183	1.3
Male householder, no wife present................	77,918	96,237	103,803	2.2
Female householder, no husband present........	200,300	231,781	228,380	0.9
Nonfamily households..	697,729	826,200	849,872	1.5
Householder living alone..................................	557,875	669,106	674,147	1.4
Householder not living alone............................	139,854	157,094	175,725	1.7
Housing Characteristics				
Total housing units...	2,321,144	2,625,477	2,656,669	1.0
Occupied housing units	2,084,544	2,279,532	2,319,538	0.8
Owner occupied..	1,426,361	1,566,039	1,549,143	0.6
Renter occupied...	658,183	713,493	770,395	1.1
Average household size..	2.50	2.43	2.42	-0.2
Financial Characteristics				
Median gross rent of renter-occupied housing	540	715	792	3.1
Median monthly owner costs for housing units with a mortgage	1,024	1,404	1,359	2.2
Median value of owner-occupied housing units	112,200	169,400	168,300	3.3

Table WI-4. Migration, Origin, and Language

(Number, percent.)

Characteristic	State			U.S.		
	2014	2015	Percent change	2014	2015	Percent change
Residence 1 Year Ago						
Population 1 year and over	5,692,727	5,708,201	0.3	315,095,393	317,635,720	0.8
Same house...	85.5	85.7	X	85.1	85.3	X
Different house in the U.S.................................	14.2	14.0	X	14.3	14.1	X
Same county..	8.5	8.6	X	8.7	8.5	X
Different county...	5.6	5.3	X	5.6	5.6	X
Same state...	3.5	3.5	X	3.3	3.2	X
Different state...	2.1	1.9	X	2.3	2.4	X
Abroad..	0.3	0.3	X	0.6	0.7	X
Place of Birth						
Native born...	5,477,407	5,492,356	0.3	276,465,262	278,128,449	0.6
Male...	49.6	49.7	X	49.3	49.3	X
Female..	50.4	50.3	X	50.7	50.7	X
Foreign born...	280,157	278,981	-0.4	42,391,794	43,290,372	2.1
Male...	50.9	49.9	X	48.7	48.6	X
Female..	49.1	50.1	X	51.3	51.4	X
Foreign born; naturalized U.S. citizen...................	124,687	126,745	1.7	19,984,738	20,697,103	3.6
Male...	47.5	46.8	X	45.9	45.9	X
Female..	52.5	53.2	X	54.1	54.1	X
Foreign born; not a U.S. citizen..........................	155,470	152,236	-2.1	22,407,056	22,593,269	0.8
Male...	53.6	52.5	X	51.2	51.1	X
Female..	46.4	47.5	X	48.8	48.9	X
Entered 2010 or later...	14.9	17.4	X	12.3	15.6	X
Entered 2000 to 2009...	31.7	30.9	X	28.6	27.9	X
Entered before 2000..	53.4	51.7	X	59.1	56.5	X
World Region of Birth, Foreign						
Foreign-born population, excluding population born at sea	280,157	278,943	-0.4	42,390,705	43,289,646	2.1
Europe..	18.2	15.7	X	11.2	11.1	X
Asia..	34.6	36.1	X	30.1	30.6	X
Africa..	3.5	4.2	X	4.6	4.8	X
Oceania..	0.4	0.5	X	0.6	0.6	X
Latin America..	40.9	41.1	X	51.6	51.1	X
North America..	2.4	2.4	X	1.9	1.9	X
Language Spoken at Home and Ability to Speak English						
Population 5 years and over.....................................	5,418,476	5,434,494	0.3	299,084,046	301,625,014	0.8
English only...	91.3	91.3	X	78.9	78.5	X
Language other than English..................................	8.7	8.7	X	21.1	21.5	X
Speaks English less than "very well".........................	3.3	3.1	X	8.6	8.6	X

NA = Not available.
X = Not applicable.
- = Zero or rounds to zero.

Table WI-5. Median Income and Poverty Status, 2015

(Number, percent, except as noted.)

Characteristic	State Number	State Percent	U.S. Number	U.S. Percent
Median Income				
Households (dollars)....................................	55,638	X	55,775	X
Families (dollars)	70,870	X	68,260	X
Below Poverty Level (All People)	677,964	12.1	46,153,077	14.7
Sex				
Male	305,493	11.0	20,599,407	13.4
Female	372,471	13.1	25,553,670	16.0
Age				
Under 18 years..	207,438	16.4	15,000,273	20.7
Related children under 18 years...................	200,400	15.9	14,693,239	20.4
18 to 64 years...	408,546	11.7	26,960,369	13.9
65 years and over	61,980	7.1	4,192,435	9.0

X = Not applicable.

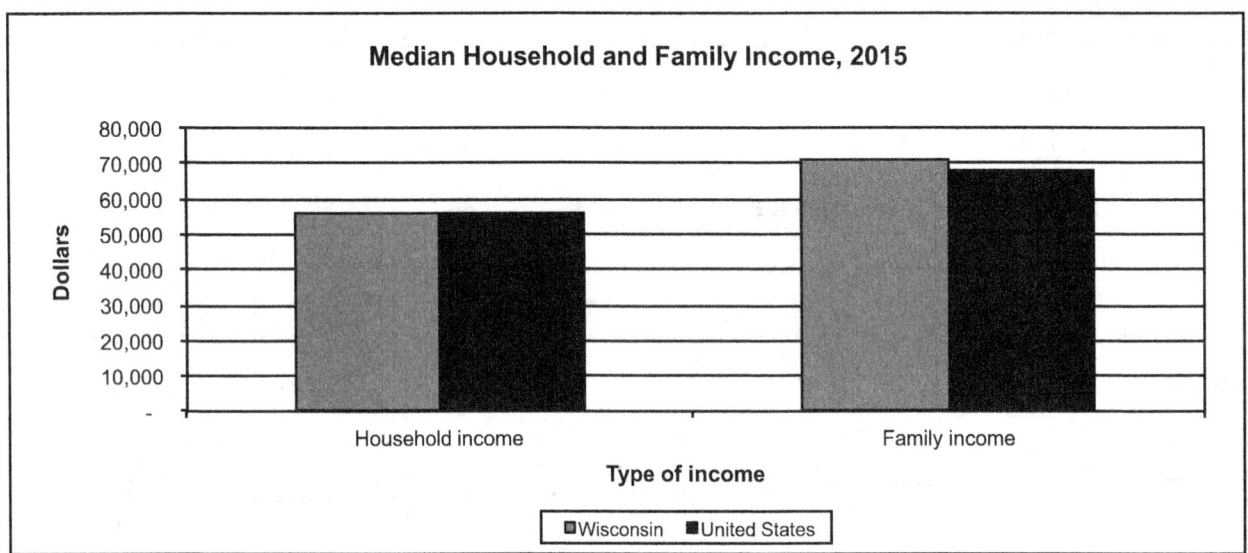

Table WI-6. Health Insurance Coverage Status for the Civilian Noninstitutionalized Population and Children Under 18 Years of Age

(Numbers in thousands, percent.)

Item	2007	2008	2009	2010	2011	2012	2013	2014	2015
Civilian Noninstitutionalized Population	5,473	5,540	5,566	5,613	5,634	5,652	5,669	5,685	5,699
Covered by Private or Public Insurance									
Number..	5,023	5,034	5,045	5,084	5,127	5,146	5,151	5,267	5,376
Percent...	91.8	90.9	90.6	90.6	91.0	91.0	90.9	92.7	94.3
Not Covered									
Number...	451	506	521	529	507	506	518	418	323
Percent...	8.2	9.1	9.4	9.4	9.0	9.0	9.1	7.3	5.7
Percent in the U.S. not covered.....................	15.3	15.1	15.1	15.5	15.1	14.8	14.5	11.7	9.4
Children Under 18 Years of Age	1,329	1,309	1,303	1,334	1,323	1,315	1,305	1,298	1,290
Covered by Private or Public Insurance									
Number...	1,252	1,241	1,238	1,267	1,265	1,253	1,243	1,240	1,244
Percent...	94.2	94.8	95.0	95.0	95.6	95.3	95.3	95.6	96.4
Not Covered									
Number...	77	68	65	67	58	62	61	58	46
Percent...	5.8	5.2	5.0	5.0	4.4	4.7	4.7	4.4	3.6
Percent in the U.S. not covered.....................	11.0	9.7	8.6	8.0	7.5	7.2	7.1	6.0	4.8

Table WI-7. Employment Status by Demographic Group, 2016

(Numbers in thousands, percent.)

Characteristic	Civilian noninstitutional population	Civilian labor force		Employed		Unemployed	
		Number	Percent of population	Number	Percent of population	Number	Percent of population
Total...................................	4,575	3,129	68.4	2,999	65.6	129	4.1
Sex							
Male..................................	2,247	1,632	72.6	1,555	69.2	77	4.7
Female..............................	2,328	1,497	64.3	1,444	62.0	53	3.5
Race, Sex, and Hispanic Origin							
White.................................	4,065	2,780	68.4	2,674	65.8	105	3.8
Male...............................	2,028	1,475	72.7	1,414	69.7	61	4.1
Female............................	2,038	1,305	64.0	1,260	61.8	45	3.4
Black or African American......................	255	167	65.5	149	58.6	18	10.6
Male...............................	NA	NA	NA	NA	NA	NA	NA
Female............................	142	92	65.2	86	60.7	6	6.9
Hispanic or Latino ethnicity[1]............................	313	222	71.1	215	68.7	7	3.3
Male...............................	151	119	78.5	114	75.3	5	4.0
Female............................	162	104	64.1	101	62.5	3	2.5
Age							
16 to 19 years......................	296	158	53.3	143	48.3	15	9.3
20 to 24 years......................	404	317	78.3	300	74.3	16	5.2
25 to 34 years......................	738	651	88.2	619	84.0	31	4.8
35 to 44 years......................	653	594	90.9	574	87.8	20	3.4
45 to 54 years......................	767	678	88.4	657	85.6	21	3.2
55 to 64 years......................	835	577	69.1	558	66.8	19	3.4
65 years and over..................	882	155	17.6	149	16.9	6	4.1

NOTE: Data in Table 7 are from the Current Population Survey (CPS) and do not match the estimates in Table 8. See notes and definitions for further information.
[1] May be of any race.
NA = Not available.

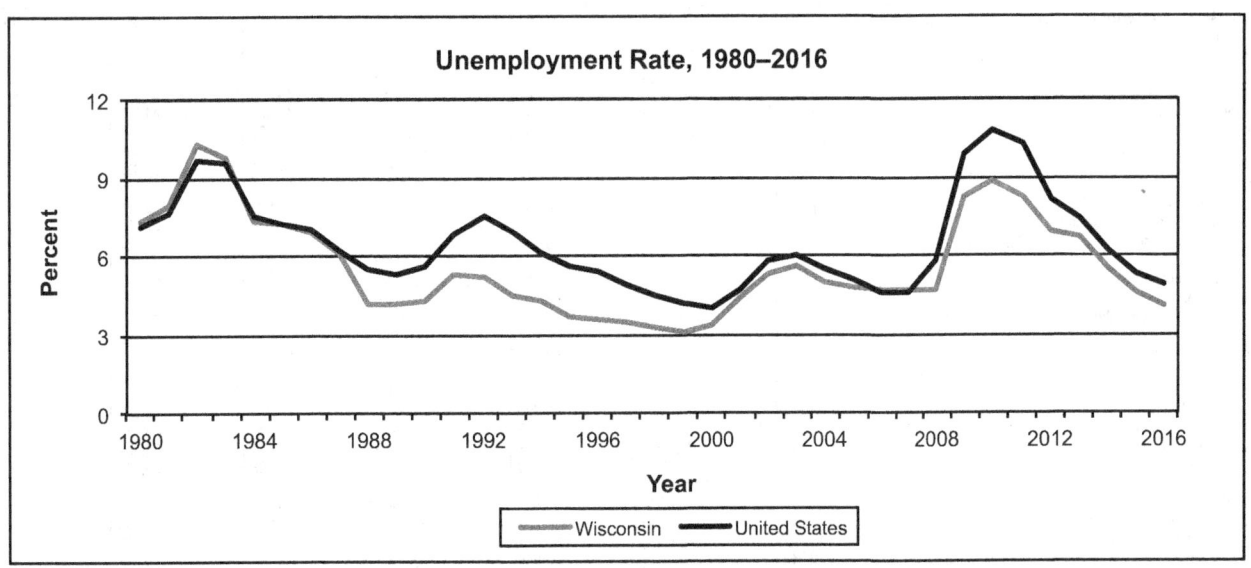

Unemployment Rate, 1980–2016

Table WI-8. Employment Status of the Civilian Noninstitutional Population Age 16 Years and Over

(Number, percent.)

Year	Civilian labor force	Civilian participation rate	Employed	Unemployed	Unemployment rate
2008..	3,091,796	70.4	2,940,438	151,358	4.9
2009..	3,100,348	70.2	2,834,335	266,013	8.6
2010..	3,081,512	69.5	2,814,393	267,119	8.7
2011..	3,079,759	69.0	2,840,996	238,763	7.8
2012..	3,074,339	68.5	2,857,673	216,666	7.0
2013..	3,083,790	68.4	2,876,037	207,753	6.7
2014..	3,086,365	68.1	2,918,966	167,399	5.4
2015..	3,095,376	68.0	2,952,797	142,579	4.6
2016..	3,120,229	68.3	2,991,033	129,196	4.1

Table WI-9. Employment and Average Wages by Industry

(Estimates through 2010 are based on the 2007 *North American Industry Classification System* [NAICS]. Estimates from 2011 onward are based on the 2012 NAICS.)

Industry	2009	2010	2011	2012	2013	2014	2015
				Number of jobs			
Wage and Salary Employment by Industry..................	2,803,897	2,783,755	2,812,907	2,842,635	2,876,051	2,914,062	2,945,802
Farm Wage and Salary Employment.........................	22,424	23,031	24,276	21,305	25,245	24,495	22,635
Nonfarm Wage and Salary Employment....................	2,781,473	2,760,724	2,788,631	2,821,330	2,850,806	2,889,567	2,923,167
Private wage and salary employment......................	2,345,448	2,323,123	2,355,343	2,387,430	2,416,575	2,453,303	2,489,111
Forestry, fishing, and related activities........................	5,486	5,557	5,578	5,712	5,854	5,911	6,135
Mining...	2,308	2,227	2,304	2,752	3,009	3,407	3,452
Utilities...	11,273	11,109	10,915	10,898	10,707	10,418	10,536
Construction...	106,717	98,034	95,771	96,380	101,451	106,427	112,357
Manufacturing...	436,994	431,403	445,485	456,419	458,076	465,418	468,191
Durable goods manufacturing..............................	264,058	258,744	270,621	279,646	279,725	283,711	284,991
Nondurable goods manufacturing...........................	172,936	172,659	174,864	176,773	178,351	181,707	183,200
Wholesale trade	116,798	113,409	115,044	117,367	119,588	121,021	122,799
Retail trade..	302,813	296,621	297,919	297,985	301,047	305,283	307,550
Transportation and warehousing...........................	91,547	89,378	91,362	91,784	91,793	93,509	96,697
Information	48,034	46,788	47,127	46,684	47,297	48,071	49,034
Finance and insurance	132,906	130,118	130,001	130,577	129,039	126,733	127,244
Real estate and rental and leasing........................	26,615	25,428	24,964	24,840	25,079	25,044	25,489
Professional, scientific, and technical services	97,674	94,602	96,965	99,420	100,639	102,189	105,573
Management of companies and enterprises.................	46,415	47,160	50,751	53,040	55,773	59,407	62,436
Administrative and waste services..........................	119,373	130,961	138,846	140,724	144,528	148,097	146,861
Educational services	52,473	54,201	54,618	54,899	55,696	55,892	56,337
Health care and social assistance...........................	358,704	361,709	362,986	368,624	374,464	379,807	385,226
Arts, entertainment, and recreation........................	35,235	35,260	35,476	36,233	36,490	37,121	38,334
Accommodation and food services	220,468	218,215	218,718	222,340	226,413	228,614	233,982
Other services, except public administration.................	133,615	130,943	130,513	130,752	129,632	130,934	130,878
Government and government enterprises..........................	436,025	437,601	433,288	433,900	434,231	436,264	434,056
				Dollars			
Average Wages and Salaries by Industry	39,474	40,422	41,602	42,664	43,375	44,399	45,966
Average Farm Wages and Salaries	33,748	28,870	25,615	37,348	32,305	36,210	37,100
Average Nonfarm Wages and Salaries	39,520	40,519	41,741	42,704	43,473	44,468	46,035
Average private wages and salaries.......................	39,490	40,625	41,946	43,123	43,899	44,919	46,556
Forestry, fishing, and related activities.....................	27,863	29,792	30,804	32,071	33,101	34,280	36,341
Mining..	53,342	56,983	60,082	61,402	61,606	67,119	63,706
Utilities...	93,330	92,556	95,991	98,022	103,598	101,366	103,197
Construction ....,...	49,089	50,045	51,184	52,695	54,210	56,128	58,012
Manufacturing...	49,336	51,880	53,186	54,179	54,822	55,956	57,097
Durable goods manufacturing..............................	50,436	53,644	55,199	55,979	56,508	57,686	58,391
Nondurable goods manufacturing...........................	47,656	49,236	50,072	51,331	52,178	53,254	55,085
Wholesale trade	53,200	55,134	57,417	59,268	60,139	61,663	63,697
Retail trade..	23,192	23,777	24,195	24,580	24,931	25,502	26,674
Transportation and warehousing...........................	38,876	39,590	40,775	42,488	42,927	44,533	45,205
Information	52,588	54,116	56,217	58,850	61,297	65,520	69,686
Finance and insurance	57,489	59,726	62,547	65,831	67,041	69,144	72,939
Real estate and rental and leasing........................	33,373	33,052	34,178	34,946	35,699	37,055	39,361
Professional, scientific, and technical services	58,269	59,580	61,708	64,035	64,974	67,233	70,029
Management of companies and enterprises.................	78,310	84,527	87,346	89,600	91,843	93,649	97,060
Administrative and waste services..........................	26,352	26,420	27,198	27,341	28,127	28,554	29,933
Educational services	32,051	32,839	34,248	35,117	35,728	35,963	36,475
Health care and social assistance...........................	42,414	42,772	43,881	44,684	45,321	45,242	46,844
Arts, entertainment, and recreation........................	27,096	28,018	29,107	28,451	29,872	30,760	29,996
Accommodation and food services	13,376	13,830	14,314	14,945	15,187	15,746	16,585
Other services, except public administration.................	25,247	26,280	26,949	27,640	28,432	29,368	30,746
Government and government enterprises..........................	39,680	39,956	40,622	40,399	41,103	41,936	43,048

Table WI-10. Employment Characteristics by Family Type

(Number, percent.)

Family type and labor force status	2013 Total	2013 Families with own children under 18 years	2014 Total	2014 Families with own children under 18 years	2015 Total	2015 Families with own children under 18 years
All Families...	1,458,482	619,727	1,481,237	633,240	1,469,666	618,822
FAMILY TYPE AND LABOR FORCE STATUS						
Married-Couple Families............................	1,124,707	420,513	1,128,553	416,204	1,137,483	422,095
Both husband and wife in labor force.....................	58.0	75.4	57.3	75.6	56.8	75.1
Husband in labor force, wife not in labor force	16.1	19.8	16.5	19.6	16.1	19.2
Wife in labor force, husband not in labor force	7.9	3.4	8.2	3.7	8.2	4.0
Both husband and wife not in labor force.................	17.6	1.1	18.1	1.2	18.4	1.4
Other Families	333,775	199,214	352,684	217,036	332,183	196,727
Female householder, no husband present................	69.9	72.5	67.7	69.4	68.8	69.6
In labor force..	51.8	61.4	50.1	58.1	51.1	59.2
Not in labor force..	18.1	11.1	17.6	11.3	17.6	10.3
Male householder, no wife present......................	30.1	27.5	32.3	30.6	31.2	30.4
In labor force...	24.9	25.0	26.6	27.9	25.5	27.9
Not in labor force	5.3	2.5	5.7	2.7	5.7	2.5

Table WI-11. School Enrollment and Educational Attainment, 2015

(Number, percent.)

Item	State	U.S.
Enrollment		
Total population 3 years and over, enrolled in school	1,429,175	81,618,288
Enrolled in nursery school or preschool (percent)	5.3	6.0
Enrolled in kindergarten (percent)...........................	5.9	5.0
Enrolled in elementary school, grades 1-8 (percent)...........	40.6	40.3
Enrolled in high school, grades 9-12 (percent)...............	21.0	20.9
Enrolled in college or graduate school (percent).............	27.2	27.7
Attainment		
Total population 25 years and over	3,918,997	216,447,163
Less than ninth grade (percent).............................	3.0	5.5
9th to 12th grade, no diploma (percent).....................	5.6	7.3
High school graduate, including equivalency (percent).........	31.2	27.6
Some college, no degree (percent)	21.3	20.7
Associate's degree (percent)................................	10.5	8.2
Bachelor's degree (percent).................................	18.9	19.0
Graduate or professional degree (percent)...................	9.4	11.6
High school graduate or higher (percent)	91.4	87.1
Bachelor's degree or higher (percent).......................	28.4	30.6

Table WI-12. Public School Characteristics and Educational Indicators

(Number, percent; data derived from National Center of Education Statistics.)

Item	State	U.S.
Public Schools, 2014–2015 (except where noted)		
Number of school districts...................................	466	18,260
Number of schools...	2,255	98,373
Number of students	871,432	50,312,581
Number of teachers	58,376	3,132,351
Student-teacher ratio..	14.9	16.1
Expenditures per student (dollars), FY 2014.................	11,345	11,066
Four-year adjusted cohort graduation rate (ACGR)[1,2]	88.4	83.2
Students eligible for free or reduced-price lunch (percent)...	41.5	51.8
English language learners (percent)..........................	4.9	9.4
Students age 3 to 21 served under IDEA, part B (percent)......	13.8	13.0

Public Schools by Type	Number	Percent of state public schools
Total number of schools......................................	2,255	100.0
Regular	2,146	95.2
Special education..	11	0.5
Vocational education...	6	0.3
Alternative education..	92	4.1

NOTE: Every school is assigned only one school type based on its instructional emphasis.
[1] ACGR data represents a new method of calculating high-school completion rates and may not be comparable to previous years' data for Averaged Freshmen Graduation Rates (AFGR).
[2] The United States 4-year ACGRs were estimated using both the reported 4-year ACGR data from 49 states and the District of Columbia and using imputed data for Idaho. The estimate for American Indian/Alaska Native students also includes imputed data for Virginia.

Table WI-13. Reported Voting and Registration of the Voting-Age Population, November 2016

(Numbers in thousands, percent.)

Item	Total population	Total citizen population	Registered			Voted		
			Total registered	Percent registered (total population)	Percent registered (total citizen population)	Total voted	Percent voted (total population)	Percent voted (total citizen population)
U.S. Total	245,502	224,059	157,596	64.2	70.3	137,537	56.0	61.4
State Total........................	4,465	4,354	3,323	74.4	76.3	3,068	68.7	70.5
Sex								
Male	2,193	2,132	1,584	72.2	74.3	1,468	66.9	68.8
Female	2,272	2,222	1,739	76.5	78.3	1,600	70.4	72.0
Race								
White alone.......................	4,079	3,998	3,130	76.7	78.3	2,897	71.0	72.5
White, non-Hispanic alone	3,792	3,776	3,009	79.4	79.7	2,796	73.7	74.0
Black alone......................	205	197	101	49.3	51.2	92	45.1	46.8
Asian alone	118	95	50	(B)	(B)	45	(B)	(B)
Hispanic (of any race)	329	260	136	41.2	52.1	111	33.8	42.8
White alone or in combination	4,129	4,049	3,165	76.6	78.2	2,923	70.8	72.2
Black alone or in combination..........	241	233	122	50.5	52.2	104	43.4	44.8
Asian alone or in combination..........	129	106	62	48.0	58.3	57	43.8	53.3
Age								
18 to 24 years.....................	547	530	269	49.2	50.7	249	45.6	47.1
25 to 34 years....................	704	678	436	62.0	64.3	370	52.6	54.6
35 to 44 years....................	724	701	573	79.1	81.8	527	72.7	75.2
45 to 64 years....................	1,520	1,479	1,236	81.3	83.5	1,169	76.9	79.0
65 years and over	970	966	809	83.4	83.8	753	77.6	77.9

B = Base is less than 75,000 and therefore too small to show the derived measure.

Table WI-14. Crime

(Number, rate per 100,000. Data are derived from the FBI Uniform Crime Reports.)

Item	State			U.S. [1,2,3,4]		
	2014	2015	Percent change	2014	2015	Percent change
TOTAL POPULATION[5]	5,759,432	5,771,337	0.2	318,907,401	321,418,820	0.8
VIOLENT CRIME						
Number..........................	16,763	17,647	5.3	1,186,185	1,231,566	3.8
Rate	291.1	305.8	5.1	372.0	383.2	3.0
Murder and Nonnegligent Manslaughter						
Number..........................	159	240	50.9	14,164	15,696	10.8
Rate	2.8	4.2	50.6	4.4	4.9	10.0
Rape[6]						
Number..........................	1,677	1,780	6.1	118,027	124,047	5.1
Rate	29.1	30.8	5.9	37.0	38.6	4.3
Robbery						
Number..........................	5,101	5,232	2.6	322,905	327,374	1.4
Rate	88.6	90.7	2.4	101.3	101.9	0.6
Aggravated Assault						
Number..........................	9,826	10,395	5.8	731,089	764,449	4.6
Rate	170.6	180.1	5.6	229.2	237.8	3.7
PROPERTY CRIME						
Number..........................	120,535	113,924	-5.5	8,209,010	7,993,631	-2.6
Rate	2,092.8	1,974.0	-5.7	2,574.1	2,487.0	-3.4
Burglary						
Number..........................	21,375	19,554	-8.5	1,713,153	1,579,527	-7.8
Rate	371.1	338.8	-8.7	537.2	491.4	-8.5
Larceny-Theft						
Number..........................	89,255	83,385	-6.6	5,809,054	5,706,346	-1.8
Rate	1,549.7	1,444.8	-6.8	1,821.5	1,775.4	-2.5
Motor Vehicle Theft						
Number..........................	9,905	10,985	10.9	686,803	707,758	3.1
Rate	172.0	190.3	10.7	215.4	220.2	2.2

NOTE: Although arson data are included in the trend and clearance tables, sufficient data are not available to estimate totals for this offense. Therefore, no arson data are published in this table.
X = Not applicable.
- = Zero or rounds to zero.
[1] The crime figures have been adjusted.
[2] The data collection methodology for the offense of forcible rape used by the Minnesota state Uniform Crime Reporting (UCR) Program (with the exception of Minneapolis and St. Paul, Minnesota) does not comply with national UCR Program guidelines. Consequently, its figures for forcible rape and violent crime (of which forcible rape is a part) are not published in this table.
[3] Includes offenses reported by the Zoological Police and the Metro Transit Police.
[4] Because of changes in the state's reporting practices, figures are not comparable to previous years' data.
[5] Populations are U.S. Census Bureau provisional estimates as of July 1 of each year.
[6] The figures shown for the offense of rape were estimated using the revised Uniform Crime Reporting (UCR) definition of rape.

Table WI-15. State Government Finances, 2015

(Dollar amounts in thousands, percent distribution.)

Item	Dollars	Percent distribution
Total Revenue	42,099,547	100.0
General revenue	33,475,661	79.5
Intergovernmental revenue	9,440,463	22.4
Taxes	17,019,026	40.4
General sales	4,892,126	11.6
Selective sales	2,754,971	6.5
License taxes	1,026,575	2.4
Individual income tax	7,069,248	16.8
Corporate income tax	1,032,411	2.5
Other taxes	243,695	0.6
Current charges	4,056,608	9.6
Miscellaneous general revenue	2,959,564	7.0
Utility revenue	0	-
Liquor stores revenue	0	-
Insurance trust revenue[1]	8,623,886	20.5
Total Expenditure	40,314,538	100.0
Intergovernmental expenditure	10,387,801	25.8
Direct expenditure	29,926,737	74.2
Current operation	20,485,353	50.8
Capital outlay	2,159,362	5.4
Insurance benefits and repayments	5,701,576	14.1
Assistance and subsidies	658,214	1.6
Interest on debt	922,232	2.3
Exhibit: Salaries and wages	4,288,010	10.6
Total Expenditure	40,314,538	100.0
General expenditure	34,521,686	85.6
Intergovernmental expenditure	10,387,801	25.8
Direct expenditure	24,133,885	59.9
General expenditure, by function:		
Education	11,757,644	29.2
Public welfare	10,227,923	25.4
Hospitals	1,568,137	3.9
Health	674,063	1.7
Highways	2,509,882	6.2
Police protection	125,981	0.3
Correction	1,141,779	2.8
Natural resources	702,500	1.7
Parks and recreation	29,356	0.1
Governmental administration	773,012	1.9
Interest on general debt	922,232	2.3
Other and unallocable	4,089,177	10.1
Utility expenditure	91,276	0.2
Liquor stores expenditure	0	-
Insurance trust expenditure	5,701,576	14.1
Debt at End of Fiscal Year	22,086,615	X
Cash and Security Holdings	115,173,453	X

X = Not applicable.
- = Zero or rounds to zero.
[1] Within insurance trust revenue, net earnings of state retirement systems is a calculated statistic (the item code in the data file is X08), and thus can be positive or negative. Net earnings is the sum of earnings on investments plus gains on investments minus losses on investments. The change made in 2002 for asset valuation from book to market value in accordance with Statement 34 of the Governmental Accounting Standards Board is reflected in the calculated statistics.

Table WI-16. State Government Tax Collections, 2016

(Dollars in thousands, percent.)

Item	Dollars	Percent distribution
Total Taxes	17,607,733	100.0
Property taxes	170,537	1.0
Sales and gross receipts	7,721,707	43.9
General sales and gross receipts	5,058,789	28.7
Selective sales and gross receipts	2,662,918	15.1
Alcoholic beverages	58,970	0.3
Amusements	201	-
Insurance premiums	196,543	1.1
Motor fuels	1,043,282	5.9
Pari-mutuels	0	-
Public utilities	326,990	1.9
Tobacco products	649,538	3.7
Other selective sales	387,394	2.2
Licenses	1,151,656	6.5
Alcoholic beverages	1,823	-
Amusements	545	-
Corporations in general	20,357	0.1
Hunting and fishing	67,572	0.4
Motor vehicle	493,293	2.8
Motor vehicle operators	40,113	0.2
Public utilities	88,707	0.5
Occupation and business, NEC	437,933	2.5
Other licenses	1,313	-
Income taxes	8,473,461	48.1
Individual income	7,486,676	42.5
Corporation net income	986,785	5.6
Other taxes	90,372	0.5
Death and gift	1,745	-
Documentary and stock transfer	65,154	0.4
Severance	10,562	0.1
Taxes, NEC	12,911	0.1

- = Zero or rounds to zero.

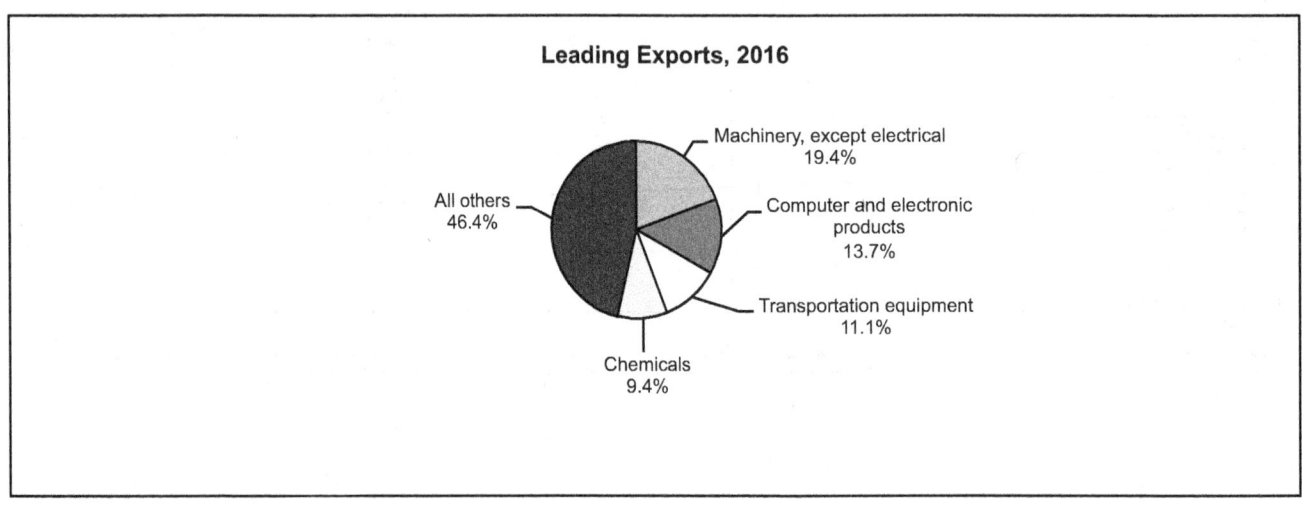

Leading Exports, 2016

Machinery, except electrical 19.4%

Computer and electronic products 13.7%

Transportation equipment 11.1%

Chemicals 9.4%

All others 46.4%

Facts and Figures

Location: Western United States; bordered on the N by Montana, on the E by South Dakota and Nebraska, on the S by Colorado and Utah, and on the W by Utah and Idaho

Area: 97,814 sq. mi. (253,336 sq. km.); rank—10th

Population: 585,501 (2016 est.); rank—51st

Principal Cities: capital—Cheyenne; largest—Cheyenne

Statehood: July 10, 1890; 44th state

U.S. Congress: 2 senators, 1 representative

State Motto: Equal Rights

State Song: "Wyoming"

State Nicknames: The Equality State; The Cowboy State

Abbreviations: WY; Wyo.

State Symbols: flower—Indian paintbrush; tree—cottonwood; bird—Western meadowlark

At a Glance

- With an increase in population of 3.9 percent, Wyoming ranked 28th among the states in growth from 2010 to 2016.

- Wyoming's violent crime rate in 2015 was 222.1 per 100,000 population, compared to the U.S. rate of 383.2 per 100,000 population.

- Wyoming's median household income in 2015 was $60,214, and 11.1 percent of the population lived below the poverty level.

- Wyoming had the 5th lowest childhood poverty rate in the country in 2015, with 13.2 percent of children under 18 years of age living in poverty.

- In 2015, 11.5 percent of Wyoming residents did not have health insurance, compared to 9.4 percent of total U.S. residents.

Table WY-1. Population by Age, Sex, Race, and Hispanic Origin

(Number, percent, except where noted.)

Sex, age, race, and Hispanic origin	2000	2010	2016 [1]	Average annual percent change, 2010–2016
Total Population	493,782	563,626	585,501	0.2
Percent of total U.S. population	0.2	0.2	0.2	X
Sex				
Male	248,374	287,437	298,942	0.3
Female	245,408	276,189	286,559	0.2
Age				
Under 5 years	30,940	40,203	38,145	-0.3
5 to 19 years	114,406	111,310	115,581	0.2
20 to 64 years	290,743	342,023	343,963	-
65 years and over	57,693	70,090	87,812	1.6
Median age (years)	36.2	36.8	37.1	0.1
Race and Hispanic Origin				
One race				
White	454,670	529,110	543,387	0.2
Black	3,722	5,135	7,753	3.2
American Indian and Alaska Native	11,133	14,457	15,762	0.6
Asian	2,771	4,649	5,856	1.6
Native Hawaiian or Other Pacific Islander	302	521	673	1.8
Two or more races	8,883	9,754	12,070	1.5
Hispanic (of any race)	31,669	52,112	58,413	0.8

X = Not applicable.
- = Zero or rounds to zero.
[1] Population figures for 2016 are July 1 estimates. The 2010 estimates are taken from the 2010 Census.

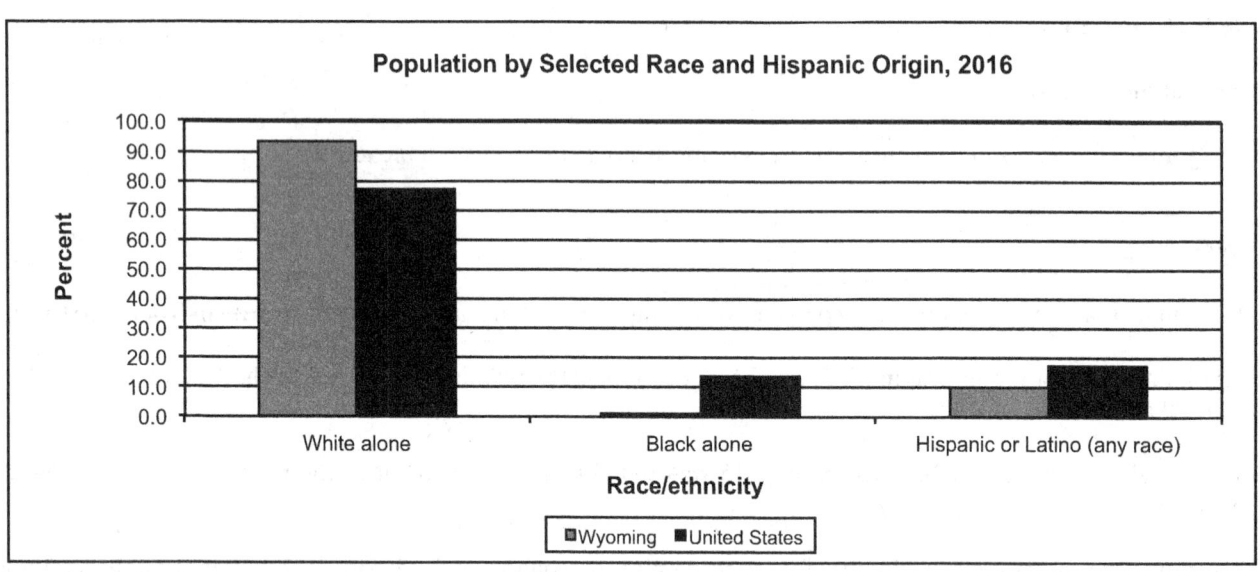

Population by Selected Race and Hispanic Origin, 2016

Table WY-2. Marital Status

(Number, percent distribution.)

Sex, age, race, and Hispanic origin	2000	2010	2015
Males, 15 Years and Over	195,412	228,725	234,851
Never married	26.6	29.0	30.9
Now married, except separated	58.8	56.2	53.5
Separated	1.0	1.3	1.1
Widowed	2.3	2.4	2.5
Divorced	11.3	11.2	12.0
Females, 15 Years and Over	195,433	220,169	233,206
Never married	20.0	20.7	25.2
Now married, except separated	57.5	55.1	52.5
Separated	1.3	2.0	1.6
Widowed	9.2	8.6	8.5
Divorced	12.0	13.6	12.2

Table WY-3. Households and Housing Characteristics

(Number, percent, dollars.)

Item	2000	2010	2015	Average annual percent change, 2000–2015
Total Households...	193,608	222,803	228,937	1.2
Family households	130,497	147,394	145,470	0.8
Married-couple family	106,179	119,756	117,245	0.7
Other family	24,318	27,638	28,225	1.1
Male householder, no wife present...................	7,481	7,804	11,821	3.9
Female householder, no husband present.........	16,837	19,834	16,404	-0.2
Nonfamily households	63,111	75,409	83,467	2.2
Householder living alone	50,980	61,775	68,358	2.3
Householder not living alone	12,131	13,634	15,109	1.6
Housing Characteristics				
Total housing units..	223,854	262,286	269,469	1.4
Occupied housing units	193,608	222,803	228,937	1.2
Owner occupied	135,514	155,278	155,575	1.0
Renter occupied	58,094	67,525	73,362	1.8
Average household size...	2.48	2.47	2.5	0.1
Financial Characteristics				
Median gross rent of renter-occupied housing	437	693	815	5.8
Median monthly owner costs for housing units with a mortgage	825	1,300	1,364	4.4
Median value of owner-occupied housing units	96,600	180,100	212,500	8.0

Table WY-4. Migration, Origin, and Language

(Number, percent.)

Characteristic	State			U.S.		
	2014	2015	Percent change	2014	2015	Percent change
Residence 1 Year Ago						
Population 1 year and over	577,782	579,102	0.2	315,095,393	317,635,720	0.8
Same house	82.3	82.0	X	85.1	85.3	X
Different house in the U.S.	17.4	17.5	X	14.3	14.1	X
Same county	10.2	8.4	X	8.7	8.5	X
Different county	7.2	9.1	X	5.6	5.6	X
Same state	2.7	2.9	X	3.3	3.2	X
Different state	4.5	6.2	X	2.3	2.4	X
Abroad	0.3	0.5	X	0.6	0.7	X
Place of Birth						
Native born	561,675	564,108	0.4	276,465,262	278,128,449	0.6
Male	51.0	50.7	X	49.3	49.3	X
Female	49.0	49.3	X	50.7	50.7	X
Foreign born	22,478	21,999	-2.1	42,391,794	43,290,372	2.1
Male	48.9	42.0	X	48.7	48.6	X
Female	51.1	58.0	X	51.3	51.4	X
Foreign born; naturalized U.S. citizen...............	7,778	8,500	9.3	19,984,738	20,697,103	3.6
Male	43.8	43.4	X	45.9	45.9	X
Female	56.2	56.6	X	54.1	54.1	X
Foreign born; not a U.S. citizen	14,700	13,499	-8.2	22,407,056	22,593,269	0.8
Male	51.6	41.1	X	51.2	51.1	X
Female	48.4	58.9	X	48.8	48.9	X
Entered 2010 or later	13.5	16.7	X	12.3	15.6	X
Entered 2000 to 2009	36.3	36.2	X	28.6	27.9	X
Entered before 2000..	50.2	47.1	X	59.1	56.5	X
World Region of Birth, Foreign						
Foreign-born population, excluding population born at sea	22,478	21,999	-2.1	42,390,705	43,289,646	2.1
Europe	17.3	12.4	X	11.2	11.1	X
Asia	17.7	18.9	X	30.1	30.6	X
Africa	5.4	5.3	X	4.6	4.8	X
Oceania	3.1	0.6	X	0.6	0.6	X
Latin America	51.3	58.8	X	51.6	51.1	X
North America	5.2	4.1	X	1.9	1.9	X
Language Spoken at Home and Ability to Speak English						
Population 5 years and over..................................	546,224	547,957	0.3	299,084,046	301,625,014	0.8
English only	93.0	92.5	X	78.9	78.5	X
Language other than English................................	7.0	7.5	X	21.1	21.5	X
Speaks English less than "very well"...............	2.0	2.5	X	8.6	8.6	X

NA = Not available.
X = Not applicable.
- = Zero or rounds to zero.

Table WY-5. Median Income and Poverty Status, 2015

(Number, percent, except as noted.)

Characteristic	State Number	State Percent	U.S. Number	U.S. Percent
Median Income				
Households (dollars)..	60,214	X	55,775	X
Families (dollars)	75,540	X	68,260	X
Below Poverty Level (All People)	63,425	11.1	46,153,077	14.7
Sex				
Male	27,535	9.6	20,599,407	13.4
Female	35,890	12.6	25,553,670	16.0
Age				
Under 18 years...	18,154	13.2	15,000,273	20.7
Related children under 18 years........................	17,689	12.9	14,693,239	20.4
18 to 64 years............................	38,846	11.0	26,960,369	13.9
65 years and over	6,425	8.0	4,192,435	9.0

X = Not applicable.

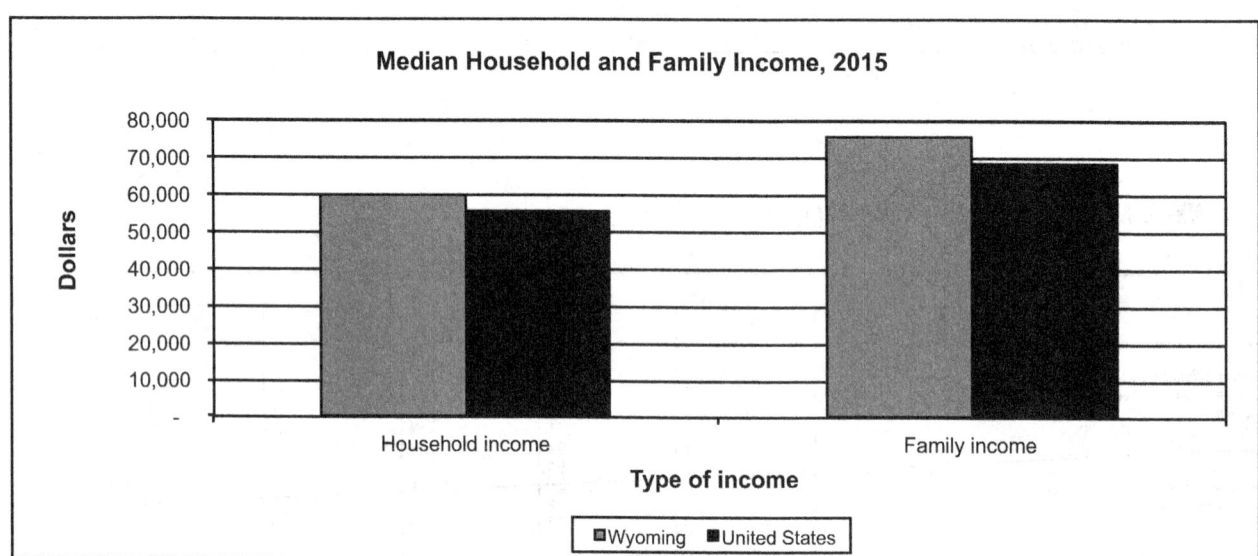

Median Household and Family Income, 2015

Table WY-6. Health Insurance Coverage Status for the Civilian Noninstitutionalized Population and Children Under 18 Years of Age

(Numbers in thousands, percent.)

Item	2007	2008	2009	2010	2011	2012	2013	2014	2015
Civilian Noninstitutionalized Population	518	523	534	555	559	567	573	575	577
Covered by Private or Public Insurance									
Number..	447	451	453	472	473	480	496	506	510
Percent..	86.4	86.2	84.8	85.1	84.6	84.6	86.6	88.0	88.5
Not Covered									
Number..	70	72	81	83	86	87	77	69	66
Percent..	13.6	13.8	15.2	14.9	15.4	15.4	13.4	12.0	11.5
Percent in the U.S. not covered..	15.3	15.1	15.1	15.5	15.1	14.8	14.5	11.7	9.4
Children Under 18 Years of Age	127	127	128	136	135	136	139	137	139
Covered by Private or Public Insurance									
Number..	115	116	117	125	123	123	131	129	128
Percent..	90.4	91.3	91.0	92.1	91.4	90.7	94.3	94.1	92.2
Not Covered									
Number..	12	11	11	11	12	13	8	8	11
Percent..	9.6	8.7	9.0	7.9	8.6	9.3	5.7	5.9	7.8
Percent in the U.S. not covered..	11.0	9.7	8.6	8.0	7.5	7.2	7.1	6.0	4.8

Table WY-7. Employment Status by Demographic Group, 2016

(Numbers in thousands, percent.)

Characteristic	Civilian noninstitutional population	Civilian labor force		Employed		Unemployed	
		Number	Percent of population	Number	Percent of population	Number	Percent of population
Total...	453	303	66.8	286	63.2	17	5.4
Sex							
Male...	229	167	72.9	156	68.3	11	6.4
Female.....................................	224	136	60.6	130	58.0	6	4.3
Race, Sex, and Hispanic Origin							
White..	426	284	66.6	269	63.1	15	5.2
Male.....................................	216	156	72.5	147	68.0	10	6.2
Female.................................	211	128	60.5	123	58.1	5	4.0
Black or African American...............	NA	NA	NA	NA	NA	NA	NA
Male.....................................	NA	NA	NA	NA	NA	NA	NA
Female.................................	NA	NA	NA	NA	NA	NA	NA
Hispanic or Latino ethnicity[1]	36	25	69.5	23	64.6	2	6.9
Male.....................................	19	14	76.1	13	69.3	1	8.9
Female.................................	17	11	62.1	10	59.4	1	4.3
Age							
16 to 19 years...........................	31	13	43.6	11	37.0	2	15.1
20 to 24 years...........................	40	30	75.3	28	70.0	2	7.0
25 to 34 years...........................	76	63	82.8	59	78.3	3	5.3
35 to 44 years...........................	73	64	88.3	61	83.9	3	4.8
45 to 54 years...........................	67	56	84.5	54	80.9	2	4.3
55 to 64 years...........................	84	57	68.2	55	65.0	3	4.7
65 years and over	84	20	23.2	19	22.1	1	4.6

NOTE: Data in Table 7 are from the Current Population Survey (CPS) and do not match the estimates in Table 8. See notes and definitions for further information.
[1] May be of any race.
NA = Not available.

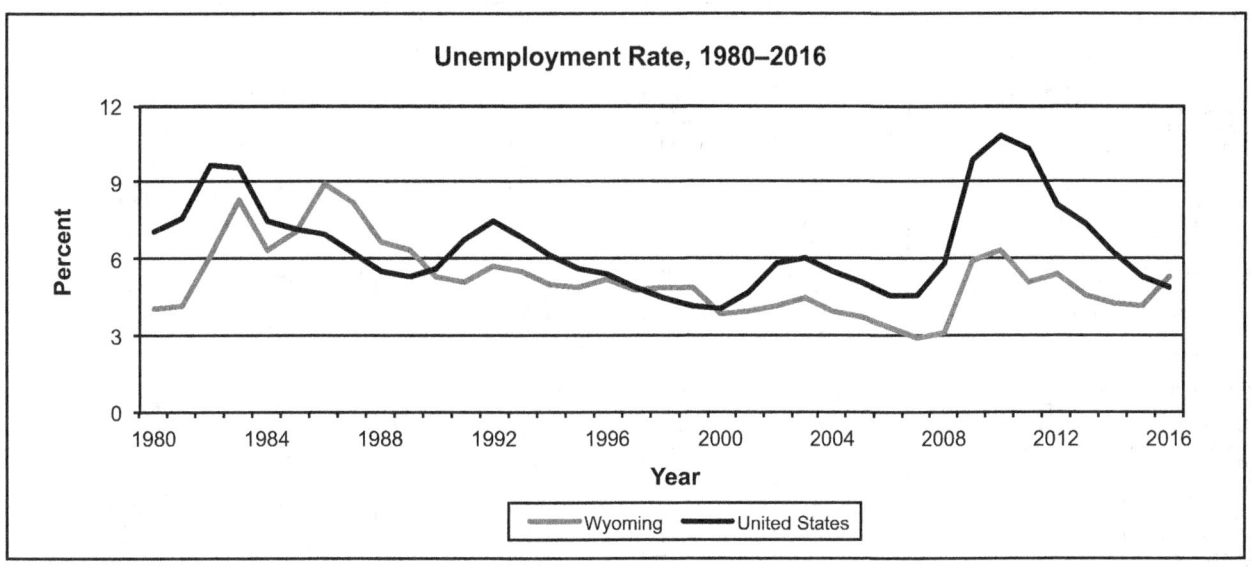

Unemployment Rate, 1980–2016

Table WY-8. Employment Status of the Civilian Noninstitutional Population Age 16 Years and Over

(Number, percent.)

Year	Civilian labor force	Civilian participation rate	Employed	Unemployed	Unemployment rate
2008...	293,279	71.4	284,310	8,969	3.1
2009...	300,120	71.8	281,150	18,970	6.3
2010...	303,297	70.4	283,744	19,553	6.4
2011...	306,815	70.2	289,019	17,796	5.8
2012...	307,425	69.2	291,076	16,349	5.3
2013...	306,571	68.3	292,157	14,414	4.7
2014...	306,933	68.1	294,207	12,726	4.1
2015...	306,012	67.7	293,262	12,750	4.2
2016...	302,331	67.0	286,373	15,958	5.3

Table WY-9. Employment and Average Wages by Industry

(Estimates through 2010 are based on the 2007 *North American Industry Classification System* [NAICS]. Estimates from 2011 onward are based on the 2012 NAICS.)

Industry	2009	2010	2011	2012	2013	2014	2015
				Number of jobs			
Wage and Salary Employment by Industry..................	294,731	290,162	294,099	298,341	299,528	304,005	302,286
Farm Wage and Salary Employment.........................	2,805	2,837	3,271	3,711	3,688	3,566	3,822
Nonfarm Wage and Salary Employment.....................	291,926	287,325	290,828	294,630	295,840	300,439	298,464
Private wage and salary employment................................	217,996	212,271	215,770	218,950	220,076	225,068	222,723
Forestry, fishing, and related activities........................	978	1,007	1,059	1,100	1,136	1,170	1,165
Mining...	25,346	24,908	27,207	27,550	26,461	27,112	23,737
Utilities..	2,493	2,483	2,488	2,471	2,484	2,489	2,536
Construction..	25,032	23,172	21,733	22,172	22,472	24,447	23,843
Manufacturing..	9,123	8,724	9,185	9,362	9,474	9,818	9,765
Durable goods manufacturing.............................	4,589	4,265	4,615	4,734	4,704	4,873	4,711
Nondurable goods manufacturing.........................	4,534	4,459	4,570	4,628	4,770	4,945	5,054
Wholesale trade	8,810	8,497	8,868	9,199	9,291	9,541	9,538
Retail trade...	31,156	29,755	29,460	29,699	30,026	30,036	31,015
Transportation and warehousing............................	11,668	11,385	12,016	12,111	12,294	13,076	13,079
Information	3,960	3,886	3,859	3,916	3,801	3,779	3,770
Finance and insurance	7,334	7,152	7,105	7,094	7,180	7,197	7,231
Real estate and rental and leasing.........................	4,223	4,033	4,076	4,153	4,426	4,528	4,366
Professional, scientific, and technical services..............	9,433	9,232	9,166	9,313	9,330	9,604	9,442
Management of companies and enterprises..................	773	857	866	956	1,032	1,014	1,025
Administrative and waste services.........................	7,378	7,278	7,909	7,909	7,916	7,954	8,135
Educational services	1,983	2,142	2,083	2,030	2,123	2,133	2,158
Health care and social assistance...........................	23,587	23,870	24,044	24,111	24,393	24,476	24,645
Arts, entertainment, and recreation.........................	2,799	2,793	2,801	2,853	2,923	3,033	3,177
Accommodation and food services..........................	30,431	30,043	30,447	31,241	31,863	32,486	33,106
Other services, except public administration.................	11,489	11,054	11,398	11,710	11,451	11,175	10,990
Government and government enterprises..........................	73,930	75,054	75,058	75,680	75,764	75,371	75,741
				Dollars			
Average Wages and Salaries by Industry	41,376	42,637	44,004	45,367	45,834	47,357	47,173
Average Farm Wages and Salaries	40,550	35,261	30,896	35,050	39,813	39,672	35,142
Average Nonfarm Wages and Salaries	41,384	42,710	44,151	45,497	45,909	47,449	47,327
Average private wages and salaries..........................	40,902	42,521	44,285	45,815	46,227	47,973	47,482
Forestry, fishing, and related activities........................	21,254	22,578	23,634	23,854	24,601	25,896	26,707
Mining...	74,292	77,942	80,828	83,346	85,574	88,929	88,771
Utilities..	78,791	81,406	84,357	84,537	85,601	88,845	92,220
Construction	45,596	48,358	48,404	50,107	51,132	52,293	51,843
Manufacturing..	51,070	53,031	56,164	57,207	58,905	62,321	64,635
Durable goods manufacturing.............................	45,498	47,162	48,594	50,149	50,915	53,648	53,945
Nondurable goods manufacturing.........................	56,710	58,645	63,809	64,428	66,785	70,869	74,599
Wholesale trade	53,720	55,487	57,547	59,035	59,490	64,165	61,140
Retail trade...	25,303	25,986	26,741	28,026	27,857	28,552	28,941
Transportation and warehousing............................	51,283	53,371	55,223	56,910	56,493	58,529	58,028
Information	38,917	40,008	41,844	43,088	44,294	45,875	47,071
Finance and insurance	47,839	49,407	51,114	54,107	55,111	57,847	59,963
Real estate and rental and leasing.........................	36,300	38,945	43,084	45,350	46,634	48,924	47,468
Professional, scientific, and technical services	52,370	53,947	55,967	58,626	59,364	62,471	61,884
Management of companies and enterprises..................	95,712	103,484	105,253	114,444	113,453	100,090	103,578
Administrative and waste services.........................	29,151	29,010	32,106	31,829	31,912	32,603	33,492
Educational services	27,349	27,347	29,051	29,993	29,549	29,735	28,065
Health care and social assistance...........................	38,342	39,342	40,526	42,027	41,543	42,549	43,872
Arts, entertainment, and recreation.........................	21,581	21,410	21,486	21,420	22,086	23,813	23,897
Accommodation and food services..........................	18,246	18,516	18,991	19,883	20,713	21,215	21,847
Other services, except public administration.................	29,027	31,360	31,613	32,806	33,459	33,200	34,036
Government and government enterprises..........................	42,804	43,246	43,766	44,576	44,985	45,884	46,872

Table WY-10. Employment Characteristics by Family Type

(Number, percent.)

Family type and labor force status	2013		2014		2015	
	Total	Families with own children under 18 years	Total	Families with own children under 18 years	Total	Families with own children under 18 years
All Families..	148,556	64,587	148,660	63,332	145,470	63,698
FAMILY TYPE AND LABOR FORCE STATUS						
Married-Couple Families......................................	118,017	45,915	116,668	45,397	117,245	45,664
Both husband and wife in labor force..........................	57.6	70.9	57.7	68.0	56.4	68.9
Husband in labor force, wife not in labor force................	19.8	25.6	19.8	26.8	20.3	26.3
Wife in labor force, husband not in labor force...............	7.1	1.9	7.2	4.5	6.7	3.5
Both husband and wife not in labor force......................	14.9	1.3	15.3	0.6	16.3	1.1
Other Families	30,539	18,672	31,992	17,935	28,225	18,034
Female householder, no husband present.......................	66.3	70.4	62.0	64.0	58.1	56.7
In labor force...	49.2	60.8	45.4	51.7	45.0	49.4
Not in labor force...	17.1	9.7	16.6	12.3	13.1	7.3
Male householder, no wife present............................	33.7	29.6	38.0	36.0	41.9	43.3
In labor force...	28.6	28.0	30.2	32.8	35.8	40.4
Not in labor force...	5.1	1.5	7.8	3.2	6.1	3.0

Table WY-11. School Enrollment and Educational Attainment, 2015

(Number, percent.)

Item	State	U.S.
Enrollment		
Total population 3 years and over, enrolled in school	148,772	81,618,288
Enrolled in nursery school or preschool (percent)..................................	6.8	6.0
Enrolled in kindergarten (percent)..	5.5	5.0
Enrolled in elementary school, grades 1-8 (percent)...............................	42.4	40.3
Enrolled in high school, grades 9-12 (percent)....................................	19.1	20.9
Enrolled in college or graduate school (percent)..................................	26.2	27.7
Attainment		
Total population 25 years and over	388,747	216,447,163
Less than ninth grade (percent)	2.0	5.5
9th to 12th grade, no diploma (percent)..	5.8	7.3
High school graduate, including equivalency (percent).............................	28.8	27.6
Some college, no degree (percent)	26.3	20.7
Associate's degree (percent)...	10.9	8.2
Bachelor's degree (percent)..	17.3	19.0
Graduate or professional degree (percent)..	9.0	11.6
High school graduate or higher (percent)	92.2	87.1
Bachelor's degree or higher (percent)..	26.2	30.6

Table WY-12. Public School Characteristics and Educational Indicators

(Number, percent; data derived from National Center of Education Statistics.)

Item	State	U.S.
Public Schools, 2014–2015 (except where noted)		
Number of school districts..	61	18,260
Number of schools..	367	98,373
Number of students...	94,067	50,312,581
Number of teachers...	7,615	3,132,351
Student-teacher ratio	12.4	16.1
Expenditures per student (dollars), FY 2014	15,903	11,066
Four-year adjusted cohort graduation rate (ACGR)[1,2]	79.3	83.2
Students eligible for free or reduced-price lunch (percent).......................	37.6	51.8
English language learners (percent)..	2.9	9.4
Students age 3 to 21 served under IDEA, part B (percent)..........................	NA	13.0

Public Schools by Type	Number	Percent of state public schools
Total number of schools...	367	100.0
Regular	342	93.2
Special education...	3	0.8
Vocational education..	0	-
Alternative education...	22	6.0

NOTE: Every school is assigned only one school type based on its instructional emphasis.
[1] ACGR data represents a new method of calculating high-school completion rates and may not be comparable to previous years' data for Averaged Freshmen Graduation Rates (AFGR).
[2] The United States 4-year ACGRs were estimated using both the reported 4-year ACGR data from 49 states and the District of Columbia and using imputed data for Idaho. The estimate for American Indian/Alaska Native students also includes imputed data for Virginia.
- = Zero or rounds to zero.
NA = Not available.

Table WY-13. Reported Voting and Registration of the Voting-Age Population, November 2016

(Numbers in thousands, percent.)

Item	Total population	Total citizen population	Registered			Voted		
			Total registered	Percent registered (total population)	Percent registered (total citizen population)	Total voted	Percent voted (total population)	Percent voted (total citizen population)
U.S. Total	245,502	224,059	157,596	64.2	70.3	137,537	56.0	61.4
State Total..............................	436	427	304	69.7	71.1	277	63.5	64.8
Sex								
Male	223	218	154	69.1	70.6	139	62.4	63.7
Female	213	209	150	70.3	71.7	138	64.7	66.0
Race								
White alone................................	405	399	284	70.2	71.2	260	64.3	65.3
White, non-Hispanic alone............	374	373	270	72.2	72.3	249	66.6	66.8
Black alone.................................	5	5	4	(B)	(B)	3	(B)	(B)
Asian alone	6	4	3	(B)	(B)	3	(B)	(B)
Hispanic (of any race).....................	32	26	15	(B)	(B)	12	(B)	(B)
White alone or in combination	409	404	289	70.5	71.6	264	64.6	65.5
Black alone or in combination..........	6	6	6	(B)	(B)	4	(B)	(B)
Asian alone or in combination..........	7	4	3	(B)	(B)	3	(B)	(B)
Age								
18 to 24 years.............................	57	55	33	(B)	(B)	30	(B)	(B)
25 to 34 years.............................	75	73	47	(B)	(B)	42	(B)	(B)
35 to 44 years.............................	70	68	46	(B)	(B)	40	(B)	(B)
45 to 64 years.............................	151	148	110	72.9	74.2	102	67.4	68.6
65 years and over	83	83	68	(B)	(B)	63	(B)	(B)

- = Zero or rounds to zero.
B = Base is less than 75,000 and therefore too small to show the derived measure.

Table WY-14. Crime

(Number, rate per 100,000. Data are derived from the FBI Uniform Crime Reports.)

Item	State			U.S. [1,2,3,4]		
	2014	2015	Percent change	2014	2015	Percent change
TOTAL POPULATION[5]	584,304	586,107	0.3	318,907,401	321,418,820	0.8
VIOLENT CRIME						
Number..	1,142	1,302	14.0	1,186,185	1,231,566	3.8
Rate	195.4	222.1	13.7	372.0	383.2	3.0
Murder and Nonnegligent Manslaughter						
Number..	16	16	-	14,164	15,696	10.8
Rate	2.7	2.7	-0.3	4.4	4.9	10.0
Rape[6]						
Number..	174	173	-0.6	118,027	124,047	5.1
Rate	29.8	29.5	-0.9	37.0	38.6	4.3
Robbery						
Number..	53	59	11.3	322,905	327,374	1.4
Rate	9.1	10.1	11.0	101.3	101.9	0.6
Aggravated Assault						
Number..	899	1,054	17.2	731,089	764,449	4.6
Rate	153.9	179.8	16.9	229.2	237.8	3.7
PROPERTY CRIME						
Number..	11,477	11,151	-2.8	8,209,010	7,993,631	-2.6
Rate	1,964.2	1,902.6	-3.1	2,574.1	2,487.0	-3.4
Burglary						
Number..	1,689	1,762	4.3	1,713,153	1,579,527	-7.8
Rate	289.1	300.6	4.0	537.2	491.4	-8.5
Larceny-Theft						
Number..	9,185	8,797	-4.2	5,809,054	5,706,346	-1.8
Rate	1,572.0	1,500.9	-4.5	1,821.5	1,775.4	-2.5
Motor Vehicle Theft						
Number..	603	592	-1.8	686,803	707,758	3.1
Rate	103.2	101.0	-2.1	215.4	220.2	2.2

NOTE: Although arson data are included in the trend and clearance tables, sufficient data are not available to estimate totals for this offense. Therefore, no arson data are published in this table.
X = Not applicable.
- = Zero or rounds to zero.
[1] The crime figures have been adjusted.
[2] The data collection methodology for the offense of forcible rape used by the Minnesota state Uniform Crime Reporting (UCR) Program (with the exception of Minneapolis and St. Paul, Minnesota) does not comply with national UCR Program guidelines. Consequently, its figures for forcible rape and violent crime (of which forcible rape is a part) are not published in this table.
[3] Includes offenses reported by the Zoological Police and the Metro Transit Police.
[4] Because of changes in the state's reporting practices, figures are not comparable to previous years' data.
[5] Populations are U.S. Census Bureau provisional estimates as of July 1 of each year.
[6] The figures shown for the offense of rape were estimated using the revised Uniform Crime Reporting (UCR) definition of rape.

Table WY-15. State Government Finances, 2015

(Dollar amounts in thousands, percent distribution.)

Item	Dollars	Percent distribution
Total Revenue	7,261,528	100.0
General revenue	6,045,155	83.2
Intergovernmental revenue	2,204,470	30.4
Taxes	2,356,323	32.4
General sales	811,105	11.2
Selective sales	183,745	2.5
License taxes	153,768	2.1
Individual income tax	0	-
Corporate income tax	0	-
Other taxes	1,207,705	16.6
Current charges	210,671	2.9
Miscellaneous general revenue	1,273,691	17.5
Utility revenue	0	-
Liquor stores revenue	112634	1.6
Insurance trust revenue[1]	1,103,739	15.2
Total Expenditure	6,391,491	100.0
Intergovernmental expenditure	2,097,456	32.8
Direct expenditure	4,294,035	67.2
Current operation	2,932,893	45.9
Capital outlay	490,914	7.7
Insurance benefits and repayments	761,738	11.9
Assistance and subsidies	74,100	1.2
Interest on debt	34,390	0.5
Exhibit: Salaries and wages	696,646	10.9
Total Expenditure	6,391,491	100.0
General expenditure	5,531,926	86.6
Intergovernmental expenditure	2,097,456	32.8
Direct expenditure	3,434,470	53.7
General expenditure, by function:		
Education	2,010,117	31.4
Public welfare	795,434	12.4
Hospitals	3,768	0.1
Health	266,544	4.2
Highways	543,113	8.5
Police protection	45,605	0.7
Correction	147,014	2.3
Natural resources	372,125	5.8
Parks and recreation	28,367	0.4
Governmental administration	335,222	5.2
Interest on general debt	34,390	0.5
Other and unallocable	950,227	14.9
Utility expenditure	0	-
Liquor stores expenditure	97827	1.5
Insurance trust expenditure	761,738	11.9
Debt at End of Fiscal Year	834,783	X
Cash and Security Holdings	30,028,125	X

X = Not applicable.
- = Zero or rounds to zero.
[1] Within insurance trust revenue, net earnings of state retirement systems is a calculated statistic (the item code in the data file is X08), and thus can be positive or negative. Net earnings is the sum of earnings on investments plus gains on investments minus losses on investments. The change made in 2002 for asset valuation from book to market value in accordance with Statement 34 of the Governmental Accounting Standards Board is reflected in the calculated statistics.

Table WY-16. State Government Tax Collections, 2016

(Dollars in thousands, percent.)

Item	Dollars	Percent distribution
Total Taxes	1,913,607	100.0
Property taxes	338,776	17.7
Sales and gross receipts	820,146	42.9
General sales and gross receipts	641,495	33.5
Selective sales and gross receipts	178,651	9.3
Alcoholic beverages	1,919	0.1
Amusements	0	-
Insurance premiums	27,991	1.5
Motor fuels	115,175	6.0
Pari-mutuels	1,963	0.1
Public utilities	4,823	0.3
Tobacco products	24,060	1.3
Other selective sales	2,720	0.1
Licenses	157,086	8.2
Alcoholic beverages	0	-
Amusements	0	-
Corporations in general	13,826	0.7
Hunting and fishing	33,919	1.8
Motor vehicle	76,448	4.0
Motor vehicle operators	2,303	0.1
Public utilities	0	-
Occupation and business, NEC	30,590	1.6
Other licenses	0	-
Income taxes	0	-
Individual income	0	-
Corporation net income	0	-
Other taxes	597,599	31.2
Death and gift	0	-
Documentary and stock transfer	0	-
Severance	593,959	31.0
Taxes, NEC	3,640	0.2

X = Not applicable.
- = Zero or rounds to zero.

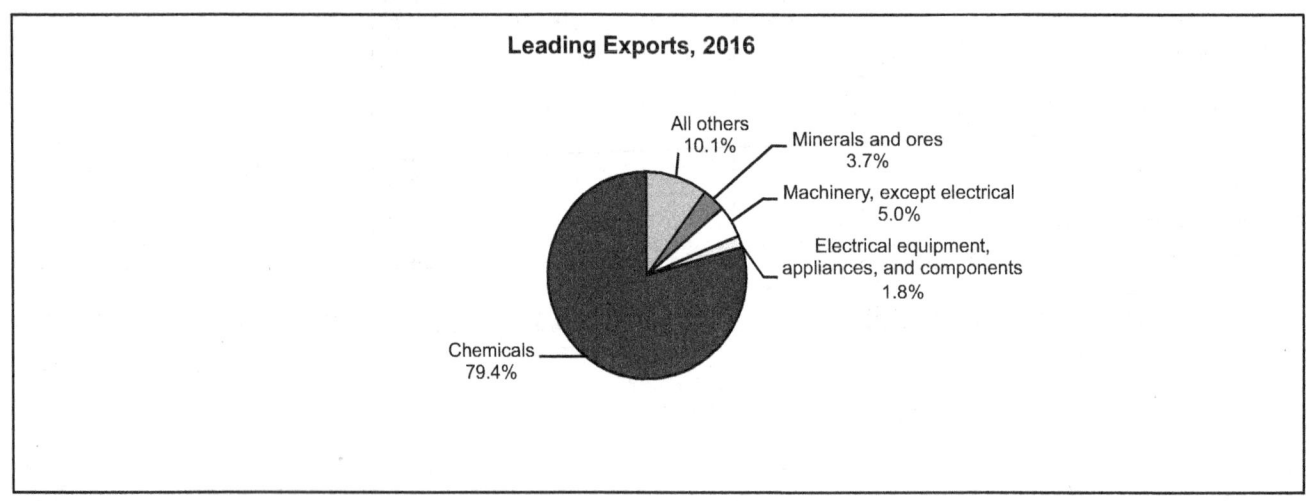

Leading Exports, 2016

All others 10.1%
Minerals and ores 3.7%
Machinery, except electrical 5.0%
Electrical equipment, appliances, and components 1.8%
Chemicals 79.4%

The state chapters in this book follow a standard plan of organization, and the same data sources are used for the tables and figures found in each chapter. These notes describe the standard data sources, which are presented by topic in the order in which they appear in each chapter. Definitions, brief descriptions of methodology, and sources of additional information are also provided.

Symbols used are included in the footnotes of the tables.

Table 1.
Source: U.S. Department of Commerce. U.S Census Bureau. 2000 and 2010 Decennial Census. Census statistics, 2016.
<http://factfinder.census.gov/>.

Population estimates data are accessed through American FactFinder from the U.S. Census Bureau, as well as from the Census Bureau itself. The data for average annual percent change, 2010–2016, were calculated by the editor.

Population estimates and the decennial census. Population data are estimates produced by the Census Bureau. The Bureau's Population Estimates Program (PEP) produces estimates of the population as of July 1 for each year following the most recently published decennial census (the actual physical count of the population made every ten years, which is described below). Existing data on births, deaths, and domestic and international immigration are used to update the decennial census base. PEP estimates are used to set federal funding allocations, update national surveys, and monitor recent demographic changes.

Noncitizens residing in the United States are included, regardless of their immigration status.

Persons temporarily away from their usual residence on Census Day (April 1), for reasons such as vacation or business trips, were counted as being at their usual residence. People who live at more than one residence during the week, month, or year were counted as being at the place in which they lived most of the year. However, people without a usual residence were counted as being where they were staying on Census Day.

Age, sex, race, and ethnicity. While estimates of the age and sex of the population are straightforward, estimates of race and ethnicity are not. Decennial census data on race and ethnicity are based on self-identification by the respondent, and the same respondent may answer differently on separate occasions. On the 2000 decennial census, respondents could report more than one race; in previous censuses, respondents had to identify themselves as belonging to only one race.

The Census Bureau treats Hispanic or Latino origin as a separate and distinct concept from race. Beginning with the 2000 census, a separate self-identification question was asked regarding Hispanic or Latino origin. Persons of Hispanic or Latino origin are those who classified themselves as belonging to one of the specific categories listed on the questionnaire—Mexican, Puerto Rican, Cuban, or Other Spanish/Hispanic origin (including those whose origins are from Spain, the Spanish-speaking countries of Central and South America, or the Dominican Republic). People who are Hispanic may be of any race, and people in each race group may be Hispanic. The overlap of race and Hispanic origin is a major comparability issue, because Hispanics may be of any race. For a further discussion of this issue, see: U.S. Census Bureau. *U.S. Census Bureau Guidance on the Presentation and Comparison of Race and Hispanic Origin Data.* (June 12, 2003.) <http://www.census.gov/population/www/socdemo/compraceho.html>.

Table 2.
Source: U.S. Department of Commerce. U.S Census Bureau. 2000 Decennial Census. American Community Survey, 2000, 2010, and 2015.
<http://factfinder.census.gov/>.

Data on marital status was tabulated for persons 15 years and over. Marital status was reported for each person as either "now married," "widowed," "divorced," "separated," or "never married." Individuals who were living together (unmarried people, people in commonlaw marriages) reported the marital status they considered most appropriate.

Now Married, Except Separated. Includes people whose current marriage has not ended through widowhood, divorce, or separation (regardless of previous marital history). The category may also include couples who live together or people in common-law marriages if they consider this category the most appropriate. In certain tabulations, currently married people are further classified as "spouse present" or "spouse absent."

Separated. Refers to people who were not living with their spouse due to marital discord.

Divorced. Indicates people who reported being divorced and had not remarried.

Widowed. Refers to people whose last marriage ended with the death of their spouse and who had not remarried.

Never married. The term applies to those who had never been legally married or people whose only marriage ended in an annulment.

Table 3.
Source: U.S. Department of Commerce. U.S Census Bureau. 2000 Decennial Census. American Community Survey, 2000, 2010, and 2015.
<http://factfinder.census.gov/>.

The annual data were obtained from the Census Bureau. The data for average annual percent change, 2000–2015, were calculated by the editor.

Households. A household comprises one or more persons occupying a single housing unit, such as a house, apartment, or a room occupied as separate living quarters. A household may consist of a person living alone, a single family, two or more families living together, or any other group of unrelated individuals sharing a housing unit.

Householder. The person, or one of the people, in whose name the home is owned, being bought, or rented. If there is no such person present, any household member 15 years old and over can serve as the householder for the purposes of the census.

Two types of householders are distinguished: a family householder and a nonfamily householder. A family householder is a householder living with one or more people related to him or her by birth, marriage, or adoption. The householder and all people in the household related to him are family members. A nonfamily householder is a householder living alone or with nonrelatives only.

Housing unit. A house, an apartment, a mobile home or trailer, a group of rooms, or a single room occupied as separate living quarters, or if vacant, intended for occupancy as separate living quarters.

Median gross rent. The monthly amount of contract rent plus the estimated average monthly cost of utilities (electricity, gas, water, and sewer) and fuels (oil, coal, kerosene, wood, etc.).

Median monthly owner costs for housing units with a mortgage. The sum of payments for mortgages, deeds of trust, contracts to purchase, or similar debts on the property (including payments for the first mortgage, second mortgages, home equity loans, and other junior mortgages); real estate taxes; fire, hazard, and flood insurance on the property; utilities (electricity, gas, water, and sewer); and fuels (oil, coal, kerosene, wood, etc.). It also includes, where appropriate, the monthly condominium fee for condominiums and mobile home costs (installment loan payments, personal property taxes, site rent, registration fees, and license fees). Selected monthly owner costs were tabulated for all owner-occupied units, and usually are shown separately for units "with a mortgage" and for units "not mortgaged."

Median value of owner-occupied housing units. Data for the median value of owner-occupied housing units are respondents' estimates of how much their property would sell for if it was currently on the market.

Table 4.
Source: U.S. Department of Commerce. U.S Census Bureau. American Community Survey, 2014 and 2015.
<http://factfinder.census.gov/>.

The annual data derives from Census estimates. The data for percent change were calculated by the editor.

Residence 1 year ago. The data on residence 1 year ago were derived from answers to Question 15, which were asked of the population 1 year and older. For the American Community Survey, people who had moved from another residence in the United States or Puerto Rico 1 year earlier were asked to report the exact address (number and street name); the name of the city, town, or post office; the name of the U.S. county; and the ZIP Code where they lived 1 year ago. People living outside the United States and Puerto Rico were asked to report the name of the foreign country or U.S. Island Area where they were living 1 year ago.

Native born. The native population includes anyone who was a U.S. citizen or a U.S. national at birth. This includes respondents who indicated they were born in the United States, Puerto Rico, a U.S. Island Area (such as Guam), or abroad of an American (U.S. citizen) parent or parents.

Foreign born. The foreign-born population includes anyone who was not a U.S. citizen or a U.S. national at birth. This includes respondents who indicated they were a U.S. citizen by naturalization or not a U.S. citizen.

Respondent's ability to speak English. Respondents who reported speaking a language other than English were asked to indicate their English-speaking ability based on one of the following categories: "Very well," "Well," "Not well," or "Not at all." Those who answered "Well," "Not well," or "Not at all" are sometimes referred as "Less than 'very well.'" Respondents were not instructed on how to interpret the response categories in this question. Households in which no one 14 and over speaks English only or speaks a language other than English at home and speaks English "very well" identifies households that may need English language assistance. This arises when no one 14 and over meets either of two conditions: (1) they speak English at home or (2) even though they speak another language, they also report that they speak English "very well."

Table 5.
Source: U.S. Department of Commerce. U.S Census Bureau. American Community Survey.
<http://factfinder.census.gov/>.

Median household income. Includes the income of the householder and all other individuals 15 years old and over in the household, whether they are related to the householder or not. Because many households consist of only one person, average household income is usually less than average family income. Total income is the sum of the amounts reported separately for wage or salary income; net self-employment income; interest, dividends, or net rental or royalty income or income from estates and trusts; Social Security or railroad retirement income; Supplemental Security Income (SSI); public assistance or welfare payments; retirement, survivor, or disability pensions; and all other income. Receipts from the following sources are not included as income: capital gains, money received from the sale of property (unless the recipient was engaged in the business of selling such property); the value of income "in kind" from food stamps, public housing subsidies, medical care, employer contributions for individuals, etc.; withdrawal of bank deposits; money borrowed; tax refunds; exchange of money between relatives living in the same household; gifts; and lump-sum inheritances, insurance payments, and other types of lump-sum receipts.

Median family income. The incomes of all members 15 years old and over related to the householder are summed and treated as a single amount.

Poverty. Following the Office of Management and Budget standards that have been in use since the late 1960s, the Census Bureau uses a set of money income thresholds that vary by family size and composition to determine the proportion of Americans in poverty. If a household's total income is less than the threshold for the applicable family size, age of householder, and number of children present in the family under 18 years of age, every individual in that household is considered to be living in poverty.

Table 6.
Source: U.S. Department of Commerce. U.S. Census Bureau. American Community Survey.
<http://factfinder.census.gov/>.

The data on health insurance coverage were derived from answers to Question 16 in the American Community Survey (ACS), which was asked of all respondents. Respondents were instructed to report their current coverage and to mark "yes" or "no" for each of the eight types of private and public insurance listed. Health insurance coverage in the ACS and other Census Bureau surveys define coverage to include plans and programs that provide comprehensive health coverage. Plans that provide insurance for specific conditions or situations such as cancer and long-term care policies are not considered coverage. Likewise, other types of insurance like dental, vision, life, and disability insurance are not considered health insurance coverage.

Private health insurance. Coverage through an employer or union, a plan purchased by an individual from a private company, or TRICARE or other military health care.

Public health insurance. Coverage includes the federal programs Medicare, Medicaid, and VA Health Care (provided through the Department of Veterans Affairs); the Children's Health Insurance Program (CHIP); and individual state health plans.

Table 7.
Source: U.S. Department of Labor. Bureau of Labor Statistics. Current Population Survey.
<http://www.bls.gov/cps/>.

Annual data on the labor force, employment, and unemployment for state and local areas are available from two major sources: the Current Population Survey (CPS) and the Local Area Unemployment Statistics (LAUS) program. In Table 7, the data are obtained from the CPS. The CPS is a monthly survey of approximately 60,000 households conducted by the Census Bureau for the Bureau of Labor Statistics. It provides comprehensive data on topics such as the labor force, employment, unemployment, and persons not in the labor force. The data for 2016 in Table 7 are preliminary, so the data may differ slightly from the final table when it is released, but it should be little changed.

Civilian noninstitutional population included are persons 16 years of age and older residing in the 50 States and the District of Columbia who are not inmates of institutions (for example, penal and mental facilities, homes for the aged), and who are not on active duty in the Armed Forces.

Civilian labor force includes all persons classified as employed or unemployed who are not inmates of institutions (for example, penal and mental facilities, homes for the aged), and who are not on active duty in the Armed Forces. Civilians 16 years of age and over in the noninstitutional population who are not classified as employed or unemployed are defined as not in the labor force.

Employment includes persons 16 years and over in the civilian noninstitutional population who, during the reference week, (a) did any work at all (at least 1 hour) as paid employees; worked in their own business, profession, or on their own farm, or worked 15 hours or more as unpaid workers in an enterprise operated by a member of the family; and (b) all those who were not working but who had jobs or businesses from which they were temporarily absent because of vacation, illness, bad weather, childcare problems, maternity or paternity leave, labor-management dispute, job training, or other family or personal reasons, whether or not they were paid for the time off or were seeking other jobs.

Unemployed persons. All civilians who were not employed (according to the above definition) during the reference week, but who were available for work—except for temporary illness—and who had made specific efforts to find employment sometime during the previous four weeks. Persons who did not look for work because they were on layoff are also counted as unemployed.

Unemployment rate. The number of unemployed as a percentage of the civilian labor force.

Table 8.
Source: U.S. Department of Labor. Bureau of Labor Statistics. Local Area Unemployment Statistics.
<http://www.bls.gov/lau/home.htm>.

The Local Area Unemployment Statistics (LAUS) program is a Federal-State cooperative effort in which monthly estimates of total employment and unemployment are prepared for approximately 7,300 areas.

The concepts and definitions underlying LAUS data come from the Current Population Survey (CPS), the household survey that is the official measure of the labor force for the nation. State monthly model estimates are controlled in "real time" to sum to national monthly labor force estimates from the CPS. These models combine current and historical data from the CPS, the Current Employment Statistics (CES) program, and State unemployment insurance (UI) systems. Estimates for seven large areas and their respective balances of State are also model-based. Estimates for the remainder of the substate labor market areas are produced through a building-block approach known as the "Handbook method." This procedure also uses data from several sources, including the CPS, the CES program, State UI systems, and the decennial census, to create estimates that are adjusted to the statewide measures of employment and unemployment. Below the labor market area level, estimates are prepared using disaggregation techniques based on inputs from the decennial census, annual population estimates, and current UI data.

Table 9.
Source: U.S. Department of Commerce. Bureau of Economic Analysis. <http://www.bea.gov/regional>.

In this table, the data by industry reflect the North American Industry Classification System (NAICS), a supply- or production-based system that replaced the Standard Industrial Classification (SIC) system in January 2003. Estimates of state employment and earnings by industry use NAICS. NAICS was adopted to more fully reflect the current composition of U.S. businesses and to establish a standard measure of industry classification throughout the United States, Canada, and Mexico, in accordance with the North American Free Trade Agreement, to enhance cross-border comparisons among these trading partners.

Wage and salary employment, also referred to as wage and salary jobs, measures the average annual number of full-time and part-time jobs in each area by place-of-work. All jobs for which wages and salaries are paid are counted. Full-time and part-time jobs are counted with equal weight. Jury and witness service, as well as paid employment of prisoners, are not counted as wage and salary employment; the payments for these activities are classified as "other labor income" in the personal income measure. Corporate directorships are counted as self-employment. This concept of employment differs from that in the Current Population Survey (CPS), which is the source of the employment data in the table on population and labor force. The CPS is a household survey. It counts each individual only once, no matter how many jobs the person holds, and it includes only civilian employment.

Wages and salaries consist of the monetary remuneration of employees, including corporate officer salaries and bonuses, commissions, pay-in-kind, incentive payments, and tips. It reflects the amount of payments disbursed, but not necessarily earned during the year. Wage and salary disbursements are measured before deductions, such as social security contributions and union dues. In recent years, stock options have become a point of discussion. Wage and salary disbursements include stock options of nonqualified plans at the time that they have been exercised by the individual. Stock options are reported in wage and salary disbursements. The value that is included in wages is the difference between the exercise price and the price that the stock options were granted. Average annual wages and salaries were calculated by the editor by dividing total wages and salaries paid during the year in each sector by total wage and salary employment in that sector.

Table 10.
Source: U.S. Department of Commerce. U.S. Census Bureau. American Community Survey, 2013, 2014, 2015.
<http://factfinder.census.gov/>.

Civilian labor force. (See definition under Table 7.)

Employment. (See definition under Table 7.)

Family. A family consists of a householder and one or more other people living in the same household who are related to the householder by birth, marriage, or adoption. All people in a household who are related to the householder are regarded as members of his or her family. A family household may contain people not related to the householder, but those people are not included as part of the householder's family in tabulations. Thus, the number of family households is equal to the number of families, but family households may include more members than do families. A household can contain only one family for purposes of tabulations. Not all households contain families since a household may be comprised of a group of unrelated people or of one person living alone – these are called nonfamily households. Families are classified by type as either a "married-couple family" or "other family" according to the sex of the householder and the presence of relatives. The data on family type are based on answers to questions on sex and relationship that were asked of all people.

Married-couple family. A family in which the householder and his or her spouse are listed as members of the same household.

Other family:

Male householder, no wife present. A family with a male householder and no spouse of householder present.

Female householder, no husband present. A family with a female householder and no spouse of householder present.

Table 11.
Source: U.S. Department of Commerce. U.S. Census Bureau. American Community Survey, 2015.
<http://www.census.gov/programs-surveys/acs.html>.

Data on school enrollment and educational attainment were derived from a sample of the population. Persons were classified as enrolled in school if they reported attending a "regular" public or private school (or college) during the year. The instructions were to "include only nursery school, kindergarten, elementary school, and schooling which would lead to a high school diploma or a college degree" as regular school. The Census Bureau defines a public school as "any school or college controlled and supported by a local, county, state, or federal government." Schools primarily supported and controlled by religious organizations or other private groups are defined as private schools.

Data on educational attainment are tabulated for the population 25 years old and over. The data were derived from a question that asked respondents for the highest level of school completed or the highest degree received. Persons who had passed a high school equivalency examination were considered high school graduates. Schooling received in foreign schools was to be reported as the equivalent grade or years in the regular American school system.

Vocational and technical training, such as barber school training; business, trade, technical, and vocational schools; or other training for a specific trade are specifically excluded.

High school graduate or more. This category includes persons whose highest degree was a high school diploma or its equivalent, and those who reported any level higher than a high school diploma.

Bachelor's degree or more. This category includes persons who have received bachelor's degrees, master's degrees, professional school degrees (such as law school or medical school degrees), and doctoral degrees.

Graduate degree or more. This category includes persons who have a master's degree, including the traditional MA and MS degrees and field-specific degrees, such as MSW, MEd, MBA, MLS, and MEng., or a professional school degree: medicine, dentistry, chiropractic, optometry, osteopathic medicine, pharmacy, podiatry, veterinary medicine, law, and theology.

Table 12.
Source: U.S. Department of Education, National Center for Education Statistics. *Common Core of Data.*
<http://nces.ed.gov/ccd/>.

The data are from the Common Core of Data (CCD), which is made up of a set of five surveys sent to state education departments. Most of the data are obtained from administrative records maintained by the state education agencies (SEAs). Statistical information is collected annually from approximately 100,000 public elementary and secondary schools and approximately 18,000 public school districts (including supervisory unions and regional education service agencies) in the 50 states, the District of Columbia, Department of Defense Schools, and the outlying areas. The SEAs compile CCD requested data into prescribed formats and transmit the information to NCES.

A school district or Local Education Agency (LEA) is the agency at the local level whose primary responsibility is to operate public schools or to contract for public school services.

The primary grades include pre-kindergarten through grade 4. Middle school grades included grades 5 through 8. High school grades include grades 9 through 12. Ungraded students are included in the total but are not separately listed. Some states have no ungraded students.

The student-teacher ratio is calculated by dividing the number of students in all schools by the number of full-time equivalent teachers employed by all schools and agencies.

Current expenditures per student are derived by dividing total current expenditures by the fall student membership count from the CCD. Current expenditures are comprised of expenditures for the day-to-day operation of schools and school districts for public elementary and secondary education, including expenditures for staff salaries and benefits, supplies, and purchased services. They exclude expenditures for construction, equipment, property, debt services, and programs outside of public elementary and secondary education, such as adult education and community services. Student membership consists of the count of students enrolled on or about October 1 and is comparable across all states. Data are for FY 2013; please see the NCES Web site for the exact beginning and ending dates of fiscal years for each state.

The 4-year adjusted cohort graduation rate (ACGR) is the number of students who graduate in 4 years with a regular high school diploma divided by the number of students who form the adjusted cohort for the graduating class. From the beginning of 9th grade (or the earliest high school grade), students who are entering that grade for the first time form a cohort that is "adjusted" by adding any students who subsequently transfer into the cohort and subtracting any students who subsequently transfer out, emigrate to another country, or die.

Students are eligible for free and reduced-price lunch under the National School Lunch Program, which was established by President Truman in 1946. The program is a federally assisted meal program operated in public and private nonprofit schools and residential child care centers and provides cash subsidies for free or reduced-price meals to students based on family size and income criteria. Participation in the National School Lunch Program depends on income, and eligibility is often used to estimate student needs.

An English language learner is an individual who, due to any of the reasons listed below, has enough difficulty speaking, reading, writing, or understanding the English language that it affects their ability to learn in an English-speaking classroom. Such an individual (1) was not born in the United States or has a native language other than English; (2) comes from environments where a language other than English is dominant; or (3) is an American Indian or Alaska Native and comes from environments where a language other than English has had a significant impact on the individual's level of English language proficiency.

Individuals with Disabilities Education Act (IDEA) is a federal law requiring services to children with disabilities throughout the nation. IDEA governs how states and public agencies provide early intervention, special education, and related services to eligible infants, toddlers, children, and youth with disabilities. Infants and toddlers with disabilities (birth–age 2) and their families receive early intervention services under IDEA, Part C. Children and youth (ages 3–21) receive special education and related services under IDEA, Part B.

Public School Types

A regular school provides instruction and education services that does not focus primarily on special education, vocational/technical education, or alternative education, or on any of the particular themes associated with magnet/special program emphasis schools.

A special education school focuses primarily on special education—including instruction for students with any of the following conditions: autism, deaf-blindness, developmental delay, hearing impairment, mental retardation, multiple disabilities, orthopedic impairment, serious emotional disturbance, specific learning disability, speech or language impairment, traumatic brain injury, visual impairment, and other health impairments—and that adapts curriculum, materials, or instruction for students served.

A vocational education school focuses primarily on providing formal preparation for semiskilled, skilled, technical, or professional occupations for high school-age students who have opted to develop or expand their employment opportunities, often in lieu of preparing for college entry.

An alternative education school is an elementary/secondary school that (1) addresses needs of students that typically cannot be met in a regular school, (2) provides nontraditional education, (3) serves as an adjunct to a regular school, or (4) falls outside the categories of regular, special education, or vocational education.

Table 13.
Source: U.S. Department of Commerce. U.S. Census Bureau. November Supplement to the Current Population Survey (CPS). *Voting and Registration in the Election of November 2016.*
<https://www.census.gov/topics/public-sector/voting/data/tables.html >

Voter participation data are obtained from additional questions regarding voting and voter registration, which are added to the Current Population Survey each November. Because these data are from a sample of the noninstitutional population, they differ from the "official" tally of voter participation reported by the Clerk of the U.S. House of Representatives.

Voting, people eligible to register. The population of voting age includes a considerable number of people who meet the age requirement but cannot register and vote. People who are not citizens are not eligible to vote. Among citizens of voting age, some people are not permitted to vote because they have been committed to penal institutions, mental hospitals, or other institutions, or because they fail to meet state and local resident requirements for various reasons. The eligibility to register is governed by state laws, which differ in many respects.

Registration is the act of qualifying to vote by formally enrolling on a list of voters. People who have moved to another election district must take steps to have their names placed on the voting rolls in their new place of residence.

In a few states or parts of states, no formal registration is required. Voters merely present themselves at the polling place on Election Day with proof that they are of age and have met the appropriate residence requirements. Therefore, in these areas people who are citizens and of voting age, and who meet the residence requirement, would be considered as being registered.

Voter, reported participation. Voter participation data are derived from replies to the following question asked of people (excluding noncitizens) of voting age: "In any election some people are not able to vote because they are sick or busy, or have some other reason, and others do not want to vote. Did (this person) vote in the election held on November (date varies)?"

Those of voting age were classified as "voted" or "did not vote." In most tables, this "did not vote" class includes those reported as "did not vote," "do not know," noncitizens, and nonrespondents. Nonrespondents and people who reported that they did not know if they voted were included in the "did not vote" class because of the general over-reporting by respondents in the sample.

Voter, reported registration. The data on registration were obtained by tabulating replies to the following question for those people included in the category "did not vote." "Was (this person) registered to vote in the November (date varies) election?"

All people reported as having voted were assumed to have been registered. Therefore, the total registered population is obtained by combining the number of people who voted and people included in the category "did not vote," but who had registered.

Table 14.
Source: U.S. Department of Justice. Federal Bureau of Investigation. Uniform Crime Reports. *Crime in the United States, 2015.*
<https://ucr.fbi.gov/crime-in-the-u.s/2015/crime-in-the-u.s.-2015 >

The Uniform Crime Reports (UCR) Program, administered by the Federal Bureau of Investigation (FBI), was created in 1929 and collects information on the following crimes reported to law enforcement authorities: murder and nonnegligent manslaughter, rape, robbery, aggravated assault, burglary, larceny-theft, motor vehicle theft, and arson. Law enforcement agencies also report arrest data for 21 additional crime categories.

The UCR Program compiles data from monthly law enforcement reports and from individual crime incident records transmitted directly to the FBI or to centralized state agencies that report to the FBI. The program thoroughly examines each report it receives for reasonableness, accuracy, and deviations that may indicate errors. Large variations in crime levels may indicate modified records procedures, incomplete reporting, or changes in a jurisdiction's boundaries. To identify any unusual fluctuations in an agency's crime counts, the program compares monthly reports to previous submissions of the agency and to those for similar agencies.

The FBI annually publishes its findings in a preliminary release in the spring of the following calendar year, followed by a detailed annual report, *Crime in the United States*, issued in the fall. (The printed copy of *Crime in the United States* is published by Bernan Press.) In addition to crime counts and trends, this report includes data on crimes cleared, persons arrested (age, sex, and race), law enforcement personnel (including the number of sworn officers killed or assaulted), and the characteristics of homicides (including age, sex, and race of victims and offenders; victim-offender relationships; weapons used; and circumstances surrounding the homicides). Other periodic reports are also available from the UCR Program. Any deviations from UCR standard data are noted in the table.

Note for Users

Since crime is a sociological phenomenon influenced by a variety of factors, the FBI discourages data users from ranking agencies and using the data as a measurement of the effectiveness of law enforcement. Until data users examine all the variables that affect crime in a town, city, county, state, region, or college or university, they can make no meaningful comparisons.

Violent crime is composed of four offenses: murder and nonnegligent manslaughter, rape, robbery, and aggravated assault. According to the UCR Program's definition, violent crimes involve force or threat of force.

Murder and nonnegligent manslaughter is the willful (nonnegligent) killing of one human being by another. Deaths caused by negligence, attempts to kill, assaults to kill, suicides, and accidental deaths are excluded. The program classifies justifiable homicides separately and limits the definition to (1) the killing of a felon by a law enforcement officer in the line of duty; or (2) the killing of a felon, during the commission of a felony, by a private citizen.

Rape is defined as: penetration, no matter how slight, of the vagina or anus with any body part or object, or oral penetration by a sex organ of another person, without the consent of the victim. The FBI UCR Program's definition of rape, formerly "forcible rape," was revised in 2013. Attempts or assaults to commit rape are also included; however, statutory rape (no force used—victim is under the age of consent) and incest are excluded. Due to the revised definition, figures for rape in 2013 and later are not comparable to data from previous years.

Robbery is the taking or attempted taking of anything of value from the care, custody, or control of a person or persons by force or threat of force or violence and/or by putting the victim in fear.

Aggravated assault is an unlawful attack by one person upon another for the purpose of inflicting severe or aggravated bodily injury. This type of assault usually is accompanied by the use of a weapon or by means likely to produce death or great bodily harm. Attempted aggravated assaults that involve the display of—or threat to use—a gun, knife, or other weapon is included in this crime category because serious personal injury would likely result if the assault were completed. When aggravated assault and larceny-theft occur together, the offense falls under the category of robbery. Simple assaults are excluded.

Property crime includes the offenses of burglary, larceny-theft, motor vehicle theft, and arson. The object of the theft-type offenses is the taking of money or property, but there is no force or threat of force against the victims. The property crime category includes arson because the offense involves the destruction of property; however, arson victims may be subjected to force.

Burglary (breaking or entering) is the unlawful entry of a structure to commit a felony or a theft. The use of force to gain entry need not have occurred. The Program has three subclassifications for burglary: forcible entry, unlawful entry where no force is used, and attempted forcible entry. The UCR definition of "structure" includes, for example, apartment, barn, house trailer or houseboat when used as a permanent dwelling, office, railroad car (but not automobile), stable, and vessel (i.e., ship).

Larceny-theft (except motor vehicle theft) is the unlawful taking, carrying, leading, or riding away of property from the possession or constructive possession of another. Examples are thefts of bicycles or automobile accessories, shoplifting, pocket-picking, or the stealing of any property or article that is not taken by force and violence or by fraud. Attempted larcenies are included. Embezzlement, confidence games, forgery, worthless checks, and the like, are excluded.

Motor vehicle theft is the theft or attempted theft of a motor vehicle. It includes the stealing of automobiles, trucks, buses, motorcycles, snowmobiles, and the like. The taking of a motor vehicle for temporary use by persons having lawful access is excluded from this definition. A motor vehicle is self-propelled and runs on land surface and not on rails. Motorboats, construction equipment, airplanes, and farming equipment are specifically excluded from this category.

Table 15.
Source: U.S. Department of Commerce. U.S Census Bureau.
<http://www.census.gov/govs/index.html>.

The Census Bureau conducts an annual survey covering a range of government finance activities carried out by all state and local governments in the United States, including revenue, expenditures, debt, and assets. The data in this volume relate to state revenues and expenditures only, with the exception of the District of Columbia, for which local government data was used. Data generally reference state government fiscal year 2015, but data for the District of Columbia is for fiscal year 2014. General revenue comprises all revenue except utilities, liquor store, and insurance trust revenue. Intergovernmental revenue is funds from other governments (mainly the federal government), including general support, grants, shared taxes, and loans or advances. Other data on government finance by state, not shown in this volume, include federal government expenditures, obligations, contract awards, and insurance programs.

Table 16.
Source: U.S. Department of Commerce. U.S Census Bureau.
<http://www.census.gov/govs/statetax/>.

State tax data include all required taxes taken by government for public purposes, except for employer and employee assessments for Social Security and unemployment compensation. The data are shown in this volume are for each state's fiscal year 2016. The data in last year's volume was for FY2014, because the data were released too late to be included in the 8th edition, but they can be found at the URL listed above. New in this year's edition are government tax collection data for the District of Columbia (Table DC-16). The Census Bureau did not previously provide detailed data for the District of Columbia.

INDEX

HIGH SCHOOL GRADUATES

HISPANIC OR LATINO ORIGIN, POPULATION BY

HOMEOWNERSHIP RATES

HOUSEHOLDS AND HOUSING CHARACTERISTICS

I

IDAHO

ILLINOIS

INCOME

W
WAGES BY INDUSTRY

WASHINGTON